Dynamic HTML
The Definitive Reference

Dynamic HTML
The Definitive Reference

Danny Goodman

O'REILLY®

Beijing · Cambridge · Köln · Paris · Sebastopol · Taipei · Tokyo

Dynamic HTML: The Definitive Reference
by Danny Goodman

Copyright © 1998 Danny Goodman. All rights reserved.
Printed in the United States of America.

Published by O'Reilly & Associates, Inc., 101 Morris Street, Sebastopol, CA 95472.

Editor: Paula Ferguson

Production Editor: Mary Anne Weeks Mayo

Printing History:

    July 1998:   First Edition.

This book is printed on acid-free paper with 85% recycled content, 15% post-consumer waste. O'Reilly & Associates is committed to using paper with the highest recycled content available consistent with high quality.

ISBN: 1-56592-494-0

Table of Contents

Preface

I am going to admit a selfish motive for writing this book: I needed the finished product for my own consulting and development work. After struggling with tangled online references and monstrous printed versions of Netscape, Microsoft, and World Wide Web Consortium (W3C) documentation for Dynamic HTML (DHTML) features, I had had enough. My human brain could no longer store the parallels and discrepancies of the hundreds of terms for HTML attributes, style sheets, and scriptable object models. And no browser maker was about to tell me how compatible a particular feature might be in another browser. It was clearly time to roll my own reference.

At first, I thought the project would be a relatively straightforward blending of content from available sources, with a pinch of my development experience thrown in for flavoring. But the more I examined the existing documents, the worse the situation became. Developer documentation from the browser makers, and even the W3C, contained inconsistencies and incomplete (if at times erroneous) information. From the very beginning, it was clear that I could not trust anything I read, but instead had to try as much as I could on as many browsers and browser versions as I could. Multiply all that code testing by the hundreds of HTML attributes, CSS attributes, object properties, object methods, and event handlers...before I knew it, many extra months of day-and-night coding and writing were history.

The result of that effort is the DHTML reference I've been wanting for a long time—one that is especially well suited to creating content that works on Navigator and Internet Explorer. But even if you have the luxury of working in only one of the browser brands, you should find the organization and browser version information in this book valuable in your day-to-day development work. You may also encounter descriptions of features that are not documented, but came to light as a result of my probing into the inner workings of both browsers.

I would be the last person on the planet to promise that this book is perfect in every way. In many instances, when a discrepancy between vendor documentation and observable reality occurred, I documented the reality. But there were times during my explorations when even the observed reality didn't jibe with either the documentation or logical expectations. In some instances, the documents say one thing, and the implementations in two different operating system versions of the same browser exhibit two entirely different behaviors. I have tried to point out those issues as cautions for your own development, hoping for clarification in future versions of the browsers and the W3C documents.

What You Should Already Know

Because this is a reference book, it has been written with the assumption that, in the least, you have dabbled in Dynamic HTML. You should already be HTML literate and know the basics of client-side scripting in JavaScript. You need not be a DHTML expert, but even the instructional chapters of Part I are very much crash courses, intended for readers who are already comfortable with hand-coding web pages (or at least modifying the HTML generated by WYSIWYG authoring tools).

Contents of This Book

This book is divided into four parts:

Part I, Applying Dynamic HTML

> After making sense of the alphabet soup of industry standards surrounding DHMTL, the chapters in this part demonstrate the use of cascading style sheets, element positioning, dynamic content, and scripting events. These chapters reveal not only how each browser implements the various DHTML technologies, but also how to deploy as much as possible in a form that works on both Navigator and Internet Explorer.

Part II, Dynamic HTML Reference

> The chapters of Part II provide at-a-glance references for the tags, attributes, objects, properties, methods, and event handlers of HTML, CSS, DOM, and core JavaScript. These are the chapters I use all the time: to look up the attributes of an HTML element or to see whether a particular object property is available in the desired browser brands and versions. Every effort has been expended to present this information in a condensed yet meaningful format.

Part III, Cross References

> The chapters in Part III slice through the information of Part II along different angles. Perhaps you recall the name of an attribute you found useful some time ago, but don't recall which elements provide that attribute. Here you can

look up that attribute (or object property, method, or event handler) to find all the items that recognize it.

Part IV, Appendixes

Several appendixes provide quick lookup for a variety of values useful in HTML authoring and scripting. A glossary also gives you quick explanations of some of the new and potentially confusing terminology of DHTML.

Conventions Used in This Book

Italic is used for:

- Pathnames, filenames, program names, email addresses, and web sites
- New terms where they are defined

`Constant Width` is used for:

- Any HTML, CSS, or scripting term, including HTML tags, attribute names, object names, properties, methods, and event handlers
- All HTML and script code listings

`Constant Width Italic` is used for:

- Method and function parameter or assigned value placeholders that indicate an item is to be replaced by a real value in actual use

Throughout Part II, compatibility tables accompany most entries. A number shown for an item indicates the version of the designated browser or web standard in which the term was first introduced. If an item premiere predates Navigator 2, Internet Explorer 3, or HTML 3.2, it is assigned the value "all". If an item is not supported by a browser or standard as the book went to press, it is assigned the value "n/a".

Request for Comments

Your feedback on the quality of this book is important to us. If you discover any errors, bugs, typos, explanations that you cannot grok, or platform-specific issues not covered here, please let us know. You can email your bug reports and comments to us at: *bookquestions@ora.com*.

Also be sure to check the errata list at *http://www.oreilly.com/catalog/dhtmlref*. Previously reported errors and corrections are available for public view and further comment.

Acknowledgments

I had long wanted to write a book for the "class act" that is O'Reilly & Associates. I thank Tim O'Reilly for trusting that my personal need for this book would translate into the needs of other web page authors. Then I had the good fortune of the book being assigned to Paula Ferguson, a first-rate editor in her own right (you probably have on your bookshelf one or more excellent O'Reilly titles that have benefited from her guidance). The reference chapters of this book presented extraordinary design challenges that would make most publishers wince. Paula shared my vision and worked magic with the O'Reilly designers to turn my dream into a reality.

When I write about a comparatively new technology—and a complex one at that—it is difficult to find someone who is knowledgeable enough to double-check my work and articulate how to make things better. Amid the politically charged browser wars, it is even more difficult to find a bipartisan supporter of the developer in the trenches. I couldn't have been luckier than when my old friend, Dan Shafer, recommended his BUILDER.COM colleague, Charity Kahn, for the job. I doubt she expected to wrestle with the nearly one-foot-thick original manuscript, but she stuck with it to the very end. I still marvel at the insight and experience embedded within each comment and suggestion she made.

This book would not exist were it not for the many readers of my articles and books over the past 20 years. My greatest reward has been to help you unlock your own talent and create great solutions. To new readers, I bid you welcome, as we all explore the possibilities that lie ahead in this new era of Dynamic HTML.

I

Applying Dynamic HTML

This part of the book, Chapters 1 through 7, tries to make sense of the alphabet soup of industry standards surrounding DHTML and demonstrates the use of cascading style sheets, element positioning, dynamic content, and scripting events. These chapters explain how Netscape Navigator and Microsoft Internet Explorer implement the various DHTML technologies, and they discuss how to develop cross-browser web applications.

- Chapter 1, *The State of the Art*
- Chapter 2, *Cross-Platform Compromises*
- Chapter 3, *Adding Style Sheets to Documents*
- Chapter 4, *Adding Dynamic Positioning to Documents*
- Chapter 5, *Making Content Dynamic*
- Chapter 6, *Scripting Events*
- Chapter 7, *Looking Ahead to HTML 4.0*

1

The State of the Art

It wasn't all that long ago that becoming a web page authoring wizard required little more than an understanding of a few dozen Hypertext Markup Language (HTML) tags, and perhaps modest experience with a scanner and a graphics program to generate a corporate logo image file. Armed with that knowledge, you could start an Internet design business or become the online content guru at a Fortune 500 company. Ah, those were the good old days...about two years ago.

The stakes are much higher now. The hobby phase is over. The Internet is big business. Competition for visitor "hits" is enormous, as it becomes more and more difficult to get your site noticed, much less bookmarked. Sensing that the authoring world wanted more out of HTML than a poor imitation of the printed page, the web browser makers and the Internet standards bodies have been expanding the capabilities of web pages at a feverish pace. These changes are allowing us to make our pages more *dynamic*—pages that can "think and do" on their own, without much help from the server once they have been loaded in the browser. But at the same time, what we authors have to do to make our new, fancy content play on all the browsers is constantly changing.

As a result, it is no longer possible to become a web content guru by studying the formal HTML recommendation published by the World Wide Web Consortium (W3C). Adding effective Dynamic HTML (DHTML) content to your pages requires an understanding of other technologies, specified by additional standards that exist outside the charter of the original HTML Working Group. In this chapter, we'll discuss the variety of standardization efforts that are currently underway. You should begin to appreciate both how far the browser makers have come and how far they have to go in providing us with compatible DHTML capabilities at a suitably high level.

The Standards Alphabet Soup

There is no such thing as a single Dynamic HTML standard. DHTML is an amalgam of specifications that stem from multiple standards efforts and proprietary technologies that are built into the two most popular DHTML-capable browsers, Netscape Navigator and Internet Explorer, beginning with Version 4 of each browser.

Efforts by various standards bodies and working groups within those bodies are as fluid and fast moving as any Internet-related technology. As a savvy web content author these days, you must know the acronyms of all relevant standards (HTML, CSS, CSS-P, DOM, and ECMA for starters). You also have to keep track of the current release of each standard, in addition to the release that is incorporated into each version of each browser that you are developing for. Unfortunately for the authoring community, it is not practical for the various standards bodies and the browser makers to operate in complete synchronicity with each other. Market pressures force browser makers to release new versions independent of the schedules of the standards bodies.

Version Headaches

As a further complication, there are the inevitable prerelease versions of browsers and standards.

Browser prereleases are sometimes called "preview editions" or "beta" versions. While not officially released, these versions give us a chance to see what new functionality will be available for content display in the next-generation browser. Authors who follow browser releases closely sometimes worry when certain aspects of their current pages fail to work properly in prerelease versions. The fear is that the new version of the browser is going to break a carefully crafted masterpiece that runs flawlessly in released versions of the browser.

Somewhere between the releases of Netscape Navigator 2 and 3, I learned not to fret over breakages that occur in prerelease browser versions. Of course, it is vital to report any problems to the browser maker. I refuse, however, to modify my HTML or scripting code to accommodate a temporary bug in a prerelease version of a browser, as it is being used by an extremely small percentage of the population. My feeling is that anyone who uses a prerelease browser does so at his or her own risk. If my pages are breaking on that browser, they're probably not the only ones on the Net that are breaking. A user of a prerelease browser must understand that using such a browser for mission-critical web work is as dangerous as entrusting your life's work to a beta version of a word processing program.

On the standards side, working groups usually publish prerelease versions of their standards. These documents are very important to the people who build browsers and authoring tools for us. The intent of publishing a working draft is not much different from making a prerelease browser version public. The goal is to get as many concerned netizens as possible looking over the material to find flaws or shortcomings before the standard is published.

And speaking of standards, it is important to recognize that the final releases of these documents from standards bodies are called not "standards" but "recommendations." No one is forcing browser makers to implement the recommendations. Fortunately, from a marketing angle, it plays well to the web audience that a company's browser adheres to the "standards." Eventually—after enough release cycles of both standards and browsers allow everyone to catch up with each other—our lives as content creators should become easier.

In the meantime, the following sections provide a snapshot of the various standards and their implementation in browsers as they relate to the technologies that affect DHTML.

HTML 4.0

The most recent release of recommendations for HTML is Version 4.0 (*www.w3c.org/MarkUp/*). As you will see in more detail in Chapter 7, *Looking Ahead to HTML 4.0*, HTML 4.0 has a considerably larger vocabulary than the previous release that is in common use, Version 3.2. Surprisingly, this time around the standard is way ahead of the browser makers. Many of the new features of HTML 4.0 are designed for browsers that make the graphical user interface of a web page more accessible to users who cannot see a monitor or use a keyboard. The new tags and attributes readily acknowledge that a key component of the name World Wide Web is World. Users of all different written and spoken languages need equal access to the content of the Web. Thus, HTML 4.0 includes support for the alphabets of most languages and provides the ability to specify that a page be rendered from right to left, rather than left to right, to accommodate languages that are written that way.

Perhaps the most important long-term effect of HTML 4.0, however, is distancing the content of web pages from their formatting. Strictly speaking, the purpose of HTML is to provide structural meaning to the content of pages. That's what each tag does: this blurb of text is a paragraph, another segment is labeled internally as an acronym, and a block over there is reserved for data loaded in from an external multimedia file. HTML 4.0 is attempting to wean authors from the familiar tags that make text bold and red, for example. That kind of information is formatting information, and it belongs to a separate standardization effort related to content style.

In the HTML 4.0 world, a chunk of text in a paragraph is bold because it is tagged as being an element that requires emphasis. Whether it is bold or italic or green is not defined by the HTML vocabulary, per se. Instead, the HTML passes the formatting decision to a style definition. When the text is viewed in a browser on a video monitor, the color may be green and the style italic, but when the same page is viewed through a projection system, it may be a different shade of green, to compensate for the different ambient lighting conditions, and bold, so it is more readable at a distance. And when the content is being read aloud electronically for a blind user, the voice speaks the tagged words with more emphasis. The key point here is that the content—the words in this case—was written and tagged once. Style definitions, either in the same document or maintained in separate files that are linked into the document, can be modified and enhanced independently of the content.

As a modern HTML author, you should find it encouraging that the HTML 4.0 working group did not operate in isolation from what is going on in the real world. Their recognition of the work going on with style sheets is just one example. Another is their clear understanding of the role of client-side scripting: the <SCRIPT> and <NOSCRIPT> tags are part of the HTML 4.0 specification, and most elements that get rendered on the page have scripting event handler attributes defined for them right in the HTML 4.0 specification. This represents a very realistic view of the web authoring world.

Netscape Navigator 4 was released many months before the HTML 4.0 specification was published, which means that the HTML support in that browser was decided on well before the scope of HTML 4.0 was finalized. As a result, Navigator's support for the new features of HTML 4.0 is limited to the internationalization features and the separation of style from content by way of style sheets. Many of the new tags and the new attributes for existing tags are not supported in Navigator 4. Internet Explorer 4 reached its final release much closer to the publication of the HTML 4.0 specification; as a result, the Microsoft browser includes substantially more support for new features of HTML 4.0, especially in the way of structural elements for table components. Chapter 7 describes which new tags are supported by each browser, and Chapter 8, *HTML Reference*, provides a complete HTML reference.

Style Sheets

A style sheet is a definition of how content should be rendered on the page. The link between a style sheet and the content it influences is either the tag name of the HTML element that holds the content or an identifier associated with the element by way of an attribute (such as the ID or CLASS attribute). When a style sheet defines a border, the style definition doesn't know (or care) whether the border will be wrapped around a paragraph of text, an image, or an arbitrary group of elements. All the style knows is that it specifies a border of a particular thickness, color, and type for whatever element or identifier is associated with the style. That's how the separation of style from content works: the content is ignorant of the style and the style is ignorant of the content.

The standardization efforts for style sheets are still trying to establish themselves, despite the fact that some versions have already been published. At the time the Version 4 implementations of Navigator and Internet Explorer were under construction, there were two separate, but related, style sheet efforts underway: Cascading Style Sheets Level 1 (CSS1) and Cascading Style Sheets-Positioning (CSS-P). The CSS-P functionality is being blended into the primary specification for the next version of CSS, Cascading Style Sheets Level 2 (CSS2). All CSS standards activity is under the auspices of the W3C (*www.w3c.org/Style/*). Chapter 10, *Style Sheet Attribute Reference*, provides a complete reference for all the style attributes available in CSS1 and CSS2.

CSS1

The Cascading Style Sheets Level 1 recommendation lets authors define style rules that are applied to HTML elements. A rule may apply to a single element, a related group of elements, or all elements of a particular type (such as all P elements). Style rules influence the rendering of elements, including their color, alignment, border, margins, and padding between borders and the content. Style rules can also control specialty items, such as whether an OL element uses letters or roman numerals as item markers. CSS1 defines a full syntax for assigning style attributes to rules.

CSS frees you from the tyranny of the pixel and the arbitrary way that each browser measures fonts and other values. Font sizes can be specified in real point sizes, instead of the absurd 1-through-7 relative scale of HTML. If you want a paragraph or a picture indented from the left margin, you can do so with the precision of ems or picas, instead of relying on hokey arrangements of tables and transparent images.

Many of the style specifications that go into CSS rules derive their inspiration from existing HTML tag attributes that control visual aspects of elements. In some cases, style sheet rules even supplant entire HTML elements. For example, in the world of CSS, font changes within a paragraph are not done with <FONT> tags. Instead, a style sheet rule sets the font, and the style rule is assigned to structural HTML elements (perhaps <SPAN> tags) that surround the affected content.

On their own, style sheets as described in the CSS1 specification are not dynamic. They simply set rules that are followed as a page loads. But under script control, there is the possibility of changing a style rule after a page has loaded. Of course, the browser must be constructed to allow such on-the-fly changes. I'll have more to say about that in the section on the document object model.

Netscape Navigator 4 implements most of the CSS1 specification. In addition to the standard CSS1 rule specification syntax, Navigator offers authors an alternate syntax (based on JavaScript) to assign style sheet rules to elements. We'll talk more about this alternate syntax in Chapter 3; for now it is important to understand that it is merely another way of specifying CSS1 functionality. Internet Explorer began supporting CSS1 in Version 3, although the functionality was little used by authors unless the target audience was using IE 3 exclusively. More complete support of the CSS1 specification is built into Version 4, but even in this version Microsoft has elected to omit a few features. The good news is that CSS1 functionality is largely the same in both IE 4 and Navigator 4, so we should start to see increased usage of style sheets on the Web.

CSS-P

Begun as a separate working group effort, Cascading Style Sheets-Positioning offers much more in the way of interactivity: more of the D in DHTML. The basic notion of CSS-P is that an element or group of elements can be placed in its own plane above the main document. The element lives in its own transparent layer, so it can be hidden, shown, precisely positioned, and moved around the page without disturbing the other content or the layout of the document. For the first time, HTML elements can even overlap each other.

A script can make elements fly around the page or it can allow the user to drag elements around the page. Content can pop up out of nowhere or expand to let the viewer see more content—all without reloading the page or contacting the server.

As an add-on to the CSS1 effort, CSS-P functionality uses a syntax that simply extends the CSS1 vocabulary. CSS-P rules are embedded in documents the same way that CSS1 rules are embedded.

The W3C work on CSS-P wasn't as far along as CSS1 was when Navigator 4 had to be put to bed. Moreover, Netscape had been lobbying the standards bodies to adopt a different technique for handling content positioning, involving both a new HTML tag and a scriptable object. Navigator 4 therefore implements the <LAYER> tag and a scriptable `layer` object. A Netscape layer is in most respects the same as a CSS-P layer, except that Netscape wanted to make it a part of the HTML syntax as well.

Unfortunately for Netscape and Navigator 4, the <LAYER> tag was not adopted by the W3C for HTML 4.0, and it is not likely that it will be added in the future. Even so, if you are authoring for a Navigator-only audience, the LAYER element is a convenient way to work with positionable elements. While its existence may not be emphasized by Netscape in future browsers, it will certainly be available for backward compatibility with pages that use it.

The good news for authors, however, is that whether you create a positionable element via the CSS-P syntax or as a LAYER element, scripting the element on the fly is the same in Navigator. The Netscape layer object exposes most of the CSS-P properties for access via scripts.

In contrast, Internet Explorer 4 follows the CSS-P specification very closely. Including a single attribute (the position attribute) in a style sheet rule makes the element associated with that rule positionable.

The bad news for authors is that Microsoft's way of working with positionable elements in scripts is different from Netscape's way. All is not lost, however. Chapter 4, *Adding Dynamic Positioning to Documents*, demonstrates ways to raise the common denominator of positionable element scripting for both browsers in the same document.

CSS2

In the next generation, Cascading Style Sheets Level 2, the work from the CSS-P group is being blended with the other style sheet specifications. Therefore, with the release of CSS2, there is no separate CSS-P specification. CSS2 also greatly expands on CSS1 by supporting style sheet functionality for a lot of the advanced work in HTML 4.0. Thus, you'll find new style sheet attributes for electronic speech (aural style sheets) and more attributes designed to remove style burdens from HTML element attributes.

CSS2 is more recent than either Version 4 browser. Navigator 4 incorporates nothing yet from CSS2, and Internet Explorer 4 has only a smattering of CSS2 attributes built in. A lot of the new items added to CSS2 are optional, so there is no reason to expect a 100% implementation in any browser in the future.

Document Object Model

When an HTML page loads into a scriptable browser, the browser creates a hidden, internal roadmap of all the elements it recognizes as scriptable objects. This roadmap is hierarchical in nature, with the most "global" object—the browser window or frame—containing a document, which, in turn, contains a form, which, in turn, contains form elements. For a script to communicate with one of these objects, it must know the path through the hierarchy to reach the object, so it can call one of its methods or set one of its property values. Document objects are the "things" that scripts work with.

Without question, the most hotly contested competition between Navigator and Internet Explorer has been how each browser builds its internal roadmap of objects. This roadmap is called a *document object model (DOM)*. When one browser implements an object as scriptable but the other doesn't, it drives scripters and page authors to distraction. A lot of authors felt the sting of this problem when they implemented image-swapping mouse rollovers in Navigator 3. They soon discovered that images were not scriptable objects in Internet Explorer 3, so their IE 3 users were getting script errors when visiting the sites and moving their mice across the hot images.

In an effort to standardize this area, a separate working group of the W3C is charged with setting recommendations for an HTML Document Object Model (*www.w3c.org/DOM/*) that would become the common denominator among browsers (the HTML subgroup is only one branch of a larger DOM effort). This is an incredibly difficult task for a number of reasons: Netscape and Microsoft are often at loggerheads on DOM philosophy; technically the browsers aren't built the same way inside, making common implementation of some ideas difficult; and historically authors are familiar with their favorite browser's way of handling objects and don't want to learn an entirely new method.

Of all the standards discussed in this chapter, DOM is the least solid. From indications in the working drafts, even the first release won't cover some important categories, such as event handling. The issues around incompatible DOMs involve a long, uphill struggle that DHTML authors will face for a while. We will be tantalized by features of one browser, only to have our hopes dashed when we learn that those features aren't available in the other browser.

By virtue of being the first scriptable browser on the market by quite a margin, Navigator 2 was the first to incorporate a scriptable object model. A subset of HTML elements were exposed to scripts, but once a document was loaded into a window or frame, nothing outside of form control content (i.e., text in text entry areas, selections in checkboxes, etc.) could really change without reloading the window or dynamically writing an entirely new document to the window. Even in Navigator 3, the image was the only truly dynamic HTML element in a document (as shown in those mouse rollovers).

Internet Explorer 3, as few web authors seemed to realize, was based on the scriptability of Navigator 2. That's why the `image` object didn't exist in IE 3. Most authors had left Navigator 2 in the dust of history, when, in fact, they should have kept its limited capabilities fresher in their minds, to accommodate IE 3.

In the Version 4 browsers, however, the object model advantage has shifted dramatically in Microsoft's favor. Literally every HTML element is exposed as a scriptable object in IE 4, and you can modify the content and style of inline content (not just positionable elements) on the fly. IE 4 automatically reflows the page (and quickly, I might add) whenever you do anything that changes the page, like adjusting the size of a font for a phrase in a paragraph or inserting some HTML text in the middle of a paragraph.

Navigator 4, on the other hand, adds little to dynamic scripting beyond the ability to swap the content of layers. Elements are exposed to scripts, but only in script statements that use JavaScript to set style sheet rules as the page loads. And even if the object model allowed content modification on the fly, pages do not automatically reflow in Navigator 4.

The working draft of the DOM recommendation includes specifications that are somewhere between the functionality provided by IE 4 and that provided by Navigator 4. The draft recognizes that most elements should be reflected as document objects whose properties and methods are accessible via scripting. It does not, however, go so far as to dictate the automatic reflow of the page when content changes. That loophole might take some of the pressure off Netscape for implementing this functionality, but it also ensures that page authors are going to have to struggle with the object model disparity for a lot longer (unless you are fortunate enough to be able to design for just one browser).

Chapter 5, *Making Content Dynamic*, and Chapter 6, *Scripting Events*, cover the current DOM implementations, while Chapter 9, *Document Object Reference*, provides a complete DOM reference.

ECMAScript

When Navigator 2 made its debut, it provided built-in client-side scripting with JavaScript. Despite what its name might imply, the language was developed at Netscape, originally under the name LiveScript. It was a marketing alliance between Netscape and Sun Microsystems that put the "Java" into the JavaScript name. Yes, there are some striking similarities between the syntax of JavaScript and Java, but those existed even before the name was changed.

Internet Explorer 3 introduced client-side scripting for that browser. Microsoft provided language interpreters for two languages: VBScript, with its syntax based on Microsoft's Visual Basic language, and JScript, which, from a compatibility point of view, was virtually 100% compatible with JavaScript in Navigator 2.

It is important to distinguish a programming language, such as JavaScript, from the document object model that it scripts. It is too easy to forget that document objects are not part of the JavaScript language, but are rather the "things" that programmers script with JavaScript (or VBScript). The JavaScript language is actually more mundane in its scope. It provides the nuts and bolts that are needed for any programming language: data types, variables, control structures, and so on. This is the *core* JavaScript language.

From the beginning, JavaScript was designed as a kind of core language that could be applied to any object model, and this has proven useful. Adobe Systems, for example, uses JavaScript as the core scripting language for Acrobat Forms scripting. The same core language you use in HTML documents is applied to a completely different object model in Acrobat Forms.

To head off potentially disastrous incompatibilities between the implementations of core JavaScript in different browsers, several concerned parties (including Netscape and Microsoft) worked with a European computer standards group now known only by its acronym: ECMA. The first published standard, ECMA-262 (*www.ecma.ch/stand/ecma-262.htm*), also known as the politically neutral ECMA-Script, is essentially the version of JavaScript found in Navigator 3. Both Navigator 4 and Internet Explorer 4 implement this ECMA standard (with only very esoteric exceptions). In addition, the Version 4 browsers both extend the work of the first ECMA release in a consonant fashion. The core JavaScript language in Navigator 4 (JavaScript 1.2) is supported almost to the letter by JScript in Internet Explorer 4.

After the dissonance in the object model arena, it is comforting for web authors to see so much harmony in the core language implementation. For the objects in the core JavaScript language, Chapter 11, *JavaScript Core Language Reference*, provides a complete reference.

A Fragmenting World

As you will see throughout this book, implementing Dynamic HTML applications that work equally well in both Navigator 4 and Internet Explorer 4 can be a challenge unto itself. Understanding and using the common-denominator functionality among the various pieces of DHTML will lead you to greater success than plowing ahead with a design for one browser and crossing your fingers about how things will work in the other browser.

One more potential gotcha is that the same browser brand and version may not behave identically across different operating systems. Navigator 4 is pretty good about maintaining compatibility when you open a document in operating systems as diverse as Solaris and Windows 3.1. The same can't be said for Internet Explorer 4, however. Microsoft readily admits that some features (detailed in later chapters) are guaranteed to work only on Win32 operating systems (Windows 95, Windows 98, and Windows NT 4). Even features that should work on non-Win32 systems, such as style sheets, don't always translate well to, say, the Macintosh version of IE 4.

If the inexorable flow of new browser versions, standards, and authoring features teaches us anything, it is that each new generation only serves to fragment further the installed base of browsers in use throughout the world. While I'm sure that every reader of this book has the latest sub-version of at least one browser installed (and probably a prerelease edition of a new version), the imperative to upgrade rarely trickles down to all the users of yesterday's browsers. If you are designing web applications for public consumption, coming up with a strategy for handling the ever-growing variety of browser versions should be a top priority. It's one thing to build a DHTML-based, context-sensitive pop-up menu system into your pages for IE 4 users. But what happens to users who visit with Navigator 4, or IE 3, or a pocket computer mini-browser, or Lynx?

There is no quick and easy answer to this question. So much depends on your content, the image you want to project via your application, and your intended audience. If you set your sights too high, you may leave many visitors behind; if you set them too low, your competition may win over visitors with engaging content and interactivity.

It should be clear from the sheer size of the reference section in this book that those good ol' days of flourishing with only a few dozen HTML tags in your head are gone forever. As much as I'd like to tell you that you can master DHTML with one hand tied behind your back, I would only be deceiving you. Using Dynamic HTML effectively is a multidisciplinary endeavor. Perhaps it's for the best that content, formatting, and scripting have become separate enough to allow specialists in each area to contribute to a major project. I've been the scripter on many such projects, while other people handled the content and design. This is a model that works, and it is likely that it will become more prevalent, especially as each new browser version and standards release fattens the following pages in the years to come.

2

Cross-Platform Compromises

Declaring support for industry standards is a noble act. But when each web browser maker is also out to put its stamp on the details of still-evolving standards, it's easy to see how a new browser release can embody ideas and extensions to standards that are not available in other browsers. With so many standards efforts related to Dynamic HTML in play at the release of both Netscape Navigator 4 and Microsoft Internet Explorer 4, implementation differences were bound to occur. This chapter provides an overview of each browser's approach to DHTML. It also explores some strategies that you might use for DHTML applications that must run identically on Navigator and Internet Explorer.

What Is a Platform?

The term *platform* has multiple meanings in web application circles, depending on how you slice the computing world. Typically, a platform denotes any hardware and/or software system that forms the basis for further product development. Operating system developers regard each microprocessor family as a platform (Pentium, PowerPC, or SPARC CPUs, for example); desktop computer application developers treat the operating system as the platform (Win16, Windows 95/NT, MacOS8, Unix, Linux, and the rest); peripherals makers perceive a combination of hardware and operating system as the platform (for example, a Wintel machine or a Macintosh).

The de facto acceptance of the web protocols, such as HTTP, means that a web application developer doesn't have to worry about the underlying network transport protocols that are being used. Theoretically, all client computers equipped with browsers that support the web protocols—regardless of the operating system or CPU—should be treated as a single platform. The real world, however, doesn't work that way.

Today's crop of web browsers are far more than data readers. Each one includes a highly customized content rendering engine, a scripting language interpreter, a link to a custom Java virtual machine, security access mechanisms, and connections to related software modules. The instant you decide to author content that will be displayed in a web browser, you must concern yourself with the capabilities built into each browser. Despite a certain level of interoperability due to industry-wide standards, you must treat each major browser brand as a distinct development platform. Writing content to the scripting API or HTML tags known to be supported by one browser does not guarantee support in the other browser.

If you are creating content, you must also be aware of differences in the way each browser has been tailored to each operating system. For example, even though the HTML code for embedding a clickable button inside a form is the same for both Navigator and Internet Explorer, the look of that button is vastly different when rendered in Windows, Macintosh, and Unix versions of either browser. That's because the browser makers have appropriately observed the traditions of the user interface look and feel for each operating system. Thus, a form whose elements are neatly laid out to fit inside a window or frame of a fixed size in Windows may be aligned in a completely unacceptable way when displayed in the same browser on a Macintosh or a Unix system.

Even though much of the discussion in this book uses "cross-platform" to mean compatible with both Netscape and Microsoft browsers ("cross-browser" some might call it), you must also be mindful of operating-system-specific details. Even the precise positioning capabilities of "cross-platform" cascading style sheets do not eliminate the operating-system-specific vagaries of form elements and font rendering. If you are developing DHTML applications, you can eliminate pre-version 4 browsers from your testing matrix, but there are still a number of browser and operating system combinations that you need to test.

Navigator 4 DHTML

As early as Navigator 2, JavaScript offered the possibility of altering the content being delivered to a browser as a page loaded. It was Navigator 3, however, that showed the first glimpse of what Dynamic HTML could be. This browser implemented the IMG HTML element as a document object whose SRC attribute could be changed on the fly to load an entirely different image file into the space reserved by the <IMG> tag. In DHTML parlance, this is known as a *replaced* element because it is rendered as an inline element (capable of flowing in the middle of a text line), yet its content can be replaced afterward. The most common application of this replacement feature is the mouse rollover, in which an image is replaced by a highlighted version of that image whenever the user positions the cursor atop the image. If you surround the <IMG> tag with a link (<A>) tag, you

can use the link's mouse event handlers to set the `image` object's source file when
the cursor rolls atop the image and when it rolls away from the image:

```
<A HREF="someURL.html"
    onMouseOver="document.images['logo'].src = 'images/logoHOT.jpg'"
    onMouseOut="document.images['logo'].src = 'images/logoNORMAL.jpg'">
<IMG NAME="logo" SRC="images/logoNORMAL.jpg" HEIGHT=40 WIDTH=80>
</A>
```

At the time, this capability was a breakthrough that allowed dynamic content without the delay of loading a Java applet or rich media for a plug-in. Navigator 3 even
allowed JavaScript to pre-cache all images on a page during the initial page download, so that the first image transition was instantaneous.

A glaring limitation of this scheme, however, hindered some designs. The size of
the image area was fixed by the `IMG` element's `HEIGHT` and `WIDTH` attributes when
the page loaded. All other images assigned to that object had to be the same size
or risk being scaled to fit. While rarely a problem for mouse rollovers, the lack of
size flexibility got in the way of more grandiose plans.

While the replaceable `image` object is still a part of Navigator 4, if for no other reason than backward compatibility, this version of the browser has added even more
dynamic capabilities.

Cascading Style Sheets Level 1

Navigator 4 includes support for the majority of the CSS1 recommendation (see
Chapter 1, *The State of the Art*). The unsupported features in Navigator 4 are
detailed in Chapter 3, *Adding Style Sheets to Documents*. CSS1 style sheets are not
as dynamic in Navigator 4 as you might wish, however. Styles and properties of
content already loaded in the browser cannot be changed. To do something like
flash the color of a block of text, you must create the content for each color as a
separate positioned element that can be hidden and shown with the help of a
script.

JavaScript Style Sheet Syntax

To further support the use of JavaScript in Navigator 4, Netscape has devised an
alternate syntax for setting style attributes that uses JavaScript. The "dot" syntax for
specifying styles follows the syntax of the core JavaScript language, rather than the
CSS1 `attribute:value` syntax. The `TYPE` attribute of the `<STYLE>` tag lets you
define the style sheet syntax you are using for a definition. For example, the following samples set the left margin for all `<H1>` elements in a document to 20 pixels, using CSS1 and JavaScript syntax, respectively:

```
<STYLE TYPE="text/css">
H1 {marginLeft:20px}
</STYLE>
```

```
<STYLE TYPE="text/javascript">
tags.H1.marginLeft=20
</STYLE>
```

The JavaScript style sheet syntax is supported only in Navigator, whereas the CSS1 syntax is supported in both Navigator and Internet Explorer.

CSS-Positioning

Navigator supports the CSS-P recommendation as it was defined in the most recent working draft prior to the release of Navigator 4 (see Chapter 1). You can use the cascading style sheet syntax to define items on a page whose location and visibility can be changed after a document has fully loaded. If an element is *positionable*, its style sheet rule must include the `position` attribute. In the following example, positioning attributes are set for an element that identifies itself with an ID of `item1`:

```
<STYLE type="text/css">
#item1 {position:absolute; top:50px; left:100px}
</STYLE>
```

In the body of the document, the style sheet rule is connected to an element by assigning `item1` to the `ID` attribute of an element (a `DIV` element in this example):

```
<DIV ID="item1">
<IMG SRC="myFace.jpg" HEIGHT=60 WIDTH=40>
</DIV>
```

Alternatively, you can use the **STYLE** attribute (from CSS1-type style sheets) inside the affected element to set position properties:

```
<DIV STYLE="position:absolute; top:50; left:100">
<IMG SRC="myFace.jpg" HEIGHT=60 WIDTH=40>
</DIV>
```

A positionable container is reflected as an object in the Navigator document object model. Each of these objects has a number of properties and methods that a script can use to move, clip, hide, and show the content of that container.

Layers

A Netscape-specific alternative to CSS-Positioning utilizes a document model object created with the `<LAYER>` tag. You can think of each layer as a content holder that exists in its own transparent plane above the base document in the window. Many graphic programs, such as Photoshop, use the same metaphor. The content, position, and visibility of each layer are independent of the base document and any other layer(s) defined within the window. Layers can also be created anew by JavaScript (with the `Layer()` constructor) after a page has been loaded, allowing for the dynamic addition of new content to a page (content in its own layer, rather than inserted into the existing content space).

Content for a layer is defined as HTML content, most often loaded in from a separate HTML file. As a result, each layer contains its own `document` object, distinct from the base `document` object. Such a document may also include definitions for additional layers, which can be nested as many levels deep as needed for the application design.

As document model objects, `layer` objects have properties and methods that are accessible to JavaScript. As a convenience for cross-platform compatibility, Navigator treats a positionable element defined via CSS-P syntax or the <LAYER> tag as the same kind of object. The same scriptable properties and methods are associated with both kinds of positionable elements in Navigator.

Limited Dynamic Content

Navigator 4's document object model is only slightly enhanced over the first model that appeared in Navigator 2. Once a document has loaded into a window or frame, a script can do very little to modify a portion of the page without reloading the entire document. Swapping images in place, loading new content into a layer, and setting the location of a positionable element are about as far as you can go in making HTML content dynamic in Navigator 4.

Event Capturing

When you script positionable elements, it is often convenient to have user actions handled not by the specific objects being clicked on, typed into, or dragged, but by scripts that encompass a range of related object behaviors. Navigator 4 supports objects that have this broader view—`window`, `document`, and `layer` objects specifically—and can intercept events before they reach their intended targets. A script then has the flexibility to respond to the event and either let the event pass on to the target or even redirect the event to another target.

Downloadable Fonts

A document to be displayed in Navigator 4 can include a CSS style attribute or a <LINK> tag that instructs the browser to download a Bitstream TrueDoc font definition file. Each font definition file can contain more than one font definition, so one reference to a font file can load all the necessary fonts for a page. Here are the two techniques for downloading a font:

```
<STYLE TYPE="text/css">
@fontdef url("http://www.mySite.com/fonts/someFonts.pfr")
</STYLE>

<LINK REL=fontdef SRC="http://www.mySite.com/fonts/someFonts.pfr">
```

Once a font has been downloaded into the browser, it is applied to text by way of the `<FONT FACE="faceName"></FONT>` tag set.

Internet Explorer 4 DHTML

While Internet Explorer 3 (for Windows) did not even allow for swapping of images after a document loaded, IE 4 provides substantial facilities for dynamically modifying the content of a page after it has loaded. In addition, you can dynamically create content during loading with the help of VBScript or JScript, just as you could in IE 3. IE 4 exposes virtually every element defined by HTML in a document to the scripting language of your choice.

Cascading Style Sheets Level 1

Some CSS functionality was introduced in IE 3, but almost every aspect of the W3C recommendation for CSS1 is implemented in IE 4. Only a few CSS1 attributes, such as `word-spacing` and `white-space`, are missing from the IE 4 implementation.

CSS-Positioning

In addition to supporting the specifications of the working draft of CSS-Positioning that existed at the time of IE 4's release in 1997, the browser also allows you to apply CSS-P attributes to individual HTML elements—including those that are not containers. Therefore, you can assign a specific position and visibility to, say, an image, even when it is not surrounded by a container tag such as `<DIV>` or `<SPAN>`:

```
<IMG SRC="myFace.jpg" HEIGHT=60 WIDTH=40
STYLE="position:absolute; left:200; top:100">
```

Of course, you can also assign positioning attributes to containers, if you prefer.

Dynamic Content

IE 4's rendering engine is designed in such a way that it can respond very quickly to changes in content. The browser's document object model provides access to virtually every kind of content on a page for modification after the document has loaded. For example, a script can alter the text of a specific `<H1>` header or the size of an image at any time. The rendering engine instantaneously reflows the page to accommodate the newly sized content. With each HTML element exposed to scripting as an object, most properties can be changed on the fly. The model even accommodates changing the HTML associated with an element. For example, you can demote an <H1> heading to an <H3> heading, with the same or different text, by adjusting one property of the original object.

Event Bubbling

As part of IE 4's document object model definition, virtually every object has event handlers that can be scripted to respond to user and system actions. For example, it is possible to associate different actions with user clicks over different headings (even if they are not visibly displayed as links) by assigning a different script statement to each heading's `onClick` event handler. Moreover, unless otherwise instructed by script, an event continues to "bubble up" through the HTML element containment hierarchy of the document. Consider the following simple HTML document:

```
<HTML>
<BODY>
<DIV>
<P>Some Text:</P>
<FORM>
<INPUT TYPE="button" VALUE="Click me" onClick="alert('Hi!')">
</FORM>
</DIV>
</BODY>
</HTML>
```

When the user clicks on the button, the click event is first processed by the `onClick` event handler in the button's own tag. Then the click event propagates through the FORM, DIV, and BODY elements. If the tag for one of those elements were to have an `onClick` event handler defined in it, the click event would trigger that handler. Event bubbling can also be programmatically canceled at any level along the way.

Transitions and Filters

Building atop the syntactical conventions of CSS1, IE 4 includes a style attribute called `filter`. This attribute serves double duty. One set of attribute parameters supplies extra display characteristics for certain types of HTML content. For example, you can set a filter to render content with a drop shadow or with its content flipped horizontally. The other set of attributes lets you define visual transition effects for when an object is hidden or shown, very much like the transition effects you set in presentation programs such as PowerPoint.

Downloadable Fonts

A document to be displayed in Internet Explorer 4 can embed TrueType font families downloaded from the server. You download the font via CSS style attributes:

```
<STYLE TYPE="text/css">
@font-face {
    font-family:familyName;
    font-style:normal;
    font-weight:normal;
    src:url("someFont.eot") }
</STYLE>
```

With the basic font family downloaded into the browser, the family can be assigned to content via CSS styles or <FONT> tags.

Note that the downloadable font format differs between Internet Explorer and Navigator. Each browser requires that the font definition files be generated with a different tool.

Data Binding

IE 4 provides hooks for ActiveX controls and Java applets that communicate with text files or databases on the server. Elements from these server-based data sources can be associated with the content of HTML elements, essentially allowing the document to access server data without processing a CGI script. While data binding is not covered in depth in this book, I mention it here because it is one of Microsoft's dynamic content features.

Cross-Platform Strategies

If your DHTML application must run on both Netscape and Microsoft browsers, you have a choice of several deployment strategies to pursue: page branching, internal branching, common denominator design, and custom API development. In all likelihood, your application will employ a combination of these techniques to get the same (or nearly the same) results on both platforms. No matter how you go about it, you must know the capabilities of each browser to provide equivalent experiences for users of both browsers. The rest of this book is designed to help you understand the capabilities of each browser, so the material in this section is mostly about the different strategies you can use.

Page Branching

Web pages that use absolute-positioned elements degrade poorly when displayed in older browsers. The positioned elements do not appear where their attributes call for, and, even worse, the elements render themselves from top to bottom in the browser window, in the order in which they appear in the HTML file. Also, any elements that are to be hidden when the page loads appear in the older browsers in their source code order. To prevent users of older browsers from seeing visual gibberish, you should have a plan in place to direct users of non-DHTML-capable browsers to pages containing less flashy content or instructions on how to view your fancy pages. A server-side CGI program can perform this redirection by checking the USER_AGENT environment variable sent by the client at connect-time and redirecting different HTML content to each browser brand or version.

Alternatively, you can do the same branching strictly via client-side scripting. Depending on the amount of granularity you wish to establish for different browser brands and versions at your site, you have many branching techniques to choose from. All these techniques are based on a predominantly blank page that has some scripted intelligence behind it to automatically handle JavaScript-enabled browsers. Any script-enabled browser can execute a script that looks into the visitor's browser version and loads the appropriate starter page for that user. Example 2-1 shows one example of how such a page accommodates both scripted and unscripted browsers.

Example 2-1. Branching Index Page

```
<HTML>
<HEAD>
<TITLE>MegaCorp On The Web</TITLE>
<SCRIPT LANGUAGE="JavaScript">
<!--
if (parseInt(navigator.appVersion) >= 4) {
    if (navigator.appName == "Netscape") {
        window.location.href = "startNavDHTML.html"
    } else if (navigator.appName.indexOf("Internet Explorer") != -1) {
        window.location.href = "startIEDHTML.html"
    } else {
        window.location.href = "startPlainScripted.html"
    }
} else {
    window.location.href = "startPlainScripted.html"
}
//-->
</SCRIPT>
<META HTTP-EQUIV="REFRESH"
CONTENT="1;URL=http://www.megacorp.com/startUnscripted.html">
</HEAD>

<BODY>
<CENTER>
    <A HREF="startUnscripted.html">
    <IMG SRC="images/megaCorpLogo.gif" HEIGHT=60 WIDTH=120 BORDER=0
    ALT="MegaCorp Home Page"></A>
</CENTER>
```

Example 2-1. Branching Index Page (continued)

```
</BODY>
</HTML>
```

The script portion of Example 2-1 provides three possible branches, depending on the browser level. If the browser version is 4 or later, this index page automatically loads a Navigator-specific starter page for Netscape Navigator users, an IE-specific starter page for IE users, or a starter page that accommodates the outside chance of there being a Version 4 browser of yet another brand. That same plain scripted starter page is the one that all other JavaScript-enabled browsers load.

For browsers that either don't have JavaScript built in or have JavaScript turned off, a <META> tag refreshes this page after one second by loading a starter page for unscripted browsers. For "bare bones" browsers that may not recognize scripting or <META> tags (including Lynx and browsers built into a lot of handheld devices), a simple image link leads to the unscripted starter page. Users of these browsers will have to "click" on this link to enter the content portion of the web site.

Example 2-1 is an extreme example. It assumes that the application has as many as four different paths for four different classes of visitor. This may seem like a good idea at first, but it seriously complicates the maintenance chores for the application in the future. At best, it provides a way to filter access between DHTML-capable browsers and all the rest.

Internal Branching

Instead of creating separate documents for Navigator and IE 4 users, you can use JavaScript to write browser-specific content for a page within a single document. For example, you may find that some style sheet specifications are not rendered the same in both browsers. To get the same look for an element, you can create a browser-specific branch to use the JavaScript document.write() method to generate content suited to each browser. Example 2-2 show a simplified page that writes HTML for a positionable element two different ways. For Internet Explorer, the HTML is a DIV container; for Navigator, it is a <LAYER> tag that loads an external file (whose content is not shown in the example).

Example 2-2. Internal Branching for Browsers

```
<HTML>
<HEAD>
<TITLE>MegaCorp On The Web</TITLE>
<SCRIPT LANGUAGE="JavaScript">
<!--
var isNav4, isIE4
if (parseInt(navigator.appVersion) >= 4) {
    isNav4 = (navigator.appName == "Netscape")
    isIE4 = (navigator.appName.indexOf("Microsoft") != -1)
}
```

Example 2-2. Internal Branching for Browsers (continued)

```
//-->
</SCRIPT>
</HEAD>

<BODY>
Some regular text
<SCRIPT LANGUAGE="JavaScript">
<!--
var output = ""
if (isIE4) {
    output += "<DIV ID='help' "
    output += "STYLE='position:absolute; top:75; width:350; border:none; "
    output += "background-color:#98FB98;'>"
    output += "<P STYLE='margin-top:5; align:center'><B>Instructions</B></
P>"
    output += "<HR><OL STYLE='margin-right:20'>"
    output += "<LI>Step 1."
    output += "<LI>Step 2."
    output += "<LI>Step 3."
    output += "</OL><DIV align='center'><BUTTON "
    output += "onClick='document.all.help.style.visibility=\"hidden\" '>"
    output += "Click Here</BUTTON></DIV></DIV>"
} else if (isNav4) {
    output += "<LAYER ID='help' TOP=75 WIDTH=350 SRC='help.html'></LAYER>"
}
document.write(output)
//-->
</SCRIPT>
</BODY>
</HTML>
```

The key to efficient branching in such a page is establishing a Boolean global variable for each browser at the top of the document (isNav4 and isIE4 in Example 2-2). This allows scripts elsewhere in the document to make decisions based on the browser that is running the script and writing the HTML that applies to that browser. Notice in Example 2-2 that the if construction writes HTML content only if one of the two global variables is true. Conceivably, a user who does not have a DHTML-capable browser could gain access to the URL of this page. In this example, the only content such a user would see is the short line of text after the <BODY> tag.

Designing for the Common Denominator

From a maintenance point of view, the ideal DHTML page is one that uses a common denominator of syntax that both browsers interpret and render identically. You can achieve some success with this approach, but you must be very careful in selecting standards-based syntax (e.g., CSS1 and CSS-P) that is implemented identically in both browsers. Because some of these standards were little more than working drafts as the browsers were released to the world, the implementations are not consistent across the board.

DHTML feature sets that you can use as starting points for a common denominator approach are the standards for Cascading Style Sheets Level 1 and CSS-Positioning. When you peruse the documentation from the browser vendors in this arena, it is nigh impossible to distinguish support for the recommended standard from a company's proprietary extension that adheres to the spirit, but not the letter, of the standard. Just because a feature is designated as being "compatible with CSS" does not mean that it is actually in the published recommendation. Refer to the reference chapters in Part II of this book for accurate information on the implementations in the browsers as it relates to the standards.

You are likely to encounter situations in which the same style sheet syntax is interpreted or rendered slightly differently in each browser. This is one reason why it is vital to test even recommended standards on both browser platforms. When an incompatibility occurs, there is probably a platform-specific solution that makes the result look and behave the same in both browsers. To achieve this parity, you'll need to use internal branching for part of the page's content. This is still a more maintainable solution than creating an entirely separate page for each browser.

Some features that are available in one browser cannot be translated into the other browser. Internet Explorer 4 includes a few DHTML capabilities that have no parallel features in Navigator 4. Therefore, don't expect to find common denominators for dynamic content (beyond swapping images of the same size), transitions, or filters. DHTML facilities in Navigator 4 can be re-created in IE 4 either directly or via internal branching. For example, the IE 4 `<IFRAME>` element closely resembles the Navigator 4 `<ILAYER>` element.

If this short lesson in finding a common denominator of functionality reveals anything about the Version 4 browsers, it is that if you start your design with Navigator 4 in mind, you can probably develop an IE 4 version using some or all of the techniques described in this chapter. But if you start with IE 4 and get carried away with its DHTML features, you may be disappointed when you run your application in Navigator 4.

Custom APIs

Despite the common denominator of CSS1 and CSS-P recommendations for the HTML elements in documents, scripted access to these objects and their properties can vary substantially from one browser to the other. Even when the two browsers have similar objects with similar properties, the syntax for the property names may be different enough that you need to use internal branching for your application to work seamlessly across platforms.

Once you go to the trouble of writing scripts that perform internal branching, you might prefer to avoid doing it again for the next document. Both browsers allow JavaScript to load libraries of script functions (files named with the *.js* extension) that you can link into any HTML document you like. You can therefore create your own meta language for scripted DHTML operations by writing a set of functions whose terminology you design. Place the functions in a library file and rely on them as if they were part of your scripting vocabulary. The language and function set you create is called an application programming interface—an API. Example 2-3 shows a small portion of a sample DHTML API library.

Example 2-3. Portion of a DHTML Library

```
// Global variables
var isNav4, isIE4
var range = ""
var styleObj = ""
if (parseInt(navigator.appVersion) >= 4) {
    if (navigator.appName.indexOf("Microsoft") != -1) {
        isNav4 = true
    } else {
        isIE4 = true
        range = "all."
        styleObj = ".style"
    }
}

// Convert object name string or object reference
// into a valid object reference
function getObject(obj) {
    var theObj
    if (typeof obj == "string") {
        theObj = eval("document." + range + obj + styleObj)
    } else {
        theObj = obj
    }
    return theObj
}

// Positioning an object at a specific pixel coordinate
function shiftTo(obj, x, y) {
  var theObj = getObject(obj)
  if (isNav4) {
    theObj.moveTo(x,y)
  } else {
    theObj.pixelLeft = x
    theObj.pixelTop = y
  }
}
```

One of the incompatibilities between positionable elements in Navigator 4 and IE 4 is the format of references to the element's properties and methods. For an unnested Navigator `layer` object (remember that all positionable items in Navigator are treated as `layer` objects), a reference must begin with the `document` object reference (e.g., `document.layerName`). In contrast, properties that govern IE 4 positionable elements are properties of a `style` property associated with the object. Moreover, every named object, no matter how deeply nested within other containers, can be referenced from the `document` object if the `all` keyword is included in the reference (e.g., `document.all.objectName.style`).

The `getObject()` function of Example 2-3 is an all-purpose function that returns a reference to an object that is passed originally as either a string that contains the object name or a ready-to-go object reference. When the incoming object name is passed as a string, the `eval()` function assembles a valid reference based on the browser running the script. If the browser is Navigator 4, the `range` and `style-Obj` variables are empty strings, and the resulting reference being evaluated is `"document.objectName"`; in IE 4, the keywords `all` and `style` are assembled as part of the reference. For both browsers, when the incoming parameter is already an object reference, it is passed straight through: the assumption is that the object reference is valid for the current browser (probably based on internal branching in the main document that calls this function).

The more interesting function in Example 2-3 is `shiftTo()`, which changes the position of an object, so that it is located at the specific coordinates that are passed as parameters. Each browser has its own way to set the position of an object in a script. Navigator 4 features a one-step `moveTo()` method of a `layer` object; IE 4 requires setting the `pixelLeft` and `pixelTop` properties of the object's `style` property. Those differences, however, are handled by the function. Any time you need scripted control of the movement of an item in a document, you can call the `shiftTo()` function to do the job in whatever browser is currently running.

Building an API along these lines lets you raise the common denominator of DHTML functionality for your applications. You free yourself from limits that would be imposed by adhering to 100% syntactical compatibility. In Chapter 4, *Adding Dynamic Positioning to Documents*, I present a more complete custom API that smooths over potentially crushing CSS-Positioning incompatibilities.

Cross-Platform Expectations

Before undertaking cross-platform DHTML development, be sure you understand that the features you can exploit in both browsers—regardless of the techniques you use—are limited to comparable feature sets within the realms of style sheets, positionable elements, event models, object models, and downloadable fonts. Dynamic content on a small scale is also a cross-platform possibility, but the instantaneous reflowing of modified content, display filters, and transitions that are available in Internet Explorer 4 have no parallels in Navigator 4.

3

Adding Style Sheets
to Documents

Like their counterparts in word processing and desktop publishing programs, HTML style sheets are supposed to simplify the deployment of fine-tuned formatting associated with content. Instead of surrounding every H1 element in a document with <FONT> tags to make all of those headings the same color, you can use a one-line style definition in a style sheet to assign a color to every instance of the H1 element on the page. Of course, now that style sheets make it easier to specify colors, margins, borders, and unusual element alignments, you are probably adding more HTML elements to your documents. So your documents may not be any smaller, but they should be more aesthetically pleasing, or at least closer to what you might design in a desktop publishing program.

Rethinking HTML Structures

In order to successfully incorporate style sheets into HTML documents, you may have to reexamine your current tagging practices. How much you'll have to change your ways depends on how and when you learned HTML in the first place. Over the years, popular browsers have generally been accommodating with regard to—how shall I say it—less-than-perfect HTML. Consider the <P> tag, which has long been regarded as a single tag that separates paragraphs with a wider line space than the <BR> line break tag. HTML standards even encourage this start-tag-only thinking by making some end tags optional. You can define an entire row of table cells without once specifying a </TD> or </TR> tag: the browser automatically closes a tag pair when it encounters a logical start tag for, say, the next table cell or row.

The "new thinking" that you may have to adopt is triggered by an important fact: style sheets, and the browser object models that work with them, are largely container oriented. With rare exception (the <BR> tag is one), an element in a document should be treated as a container whose territory is bounded by its start and end tags (even if the end tag is optional). This container territory does not always translate to space on the page, but rather applies to the structure of the HTML source code. To see how "HTML-think" has changed, let's look at a progression of simple HTML pages. Here's a page that might have been excerpted from a tutorial for HTML Version 2:

```
<HTML>
<HEAD>
<TITLE>Welcome to HypeCo</TITLE>
</HEAD>
<BODY>
<H1>Welcome to HypeCo's Home Page</H1>
We're glad you're here.
<P>
You can find details of all of HypeCo's latest products and special offers.
Our goal is to provide the highest quality products and the best customer
service in the industry.
<P>
<A HREF="products.htm">Click here</A> to view our on-line catalog.
</BODY>
</HTML>
```

While the preceding HTML produces a perfectly fine, if boring, page, a modern browser does not have enough information from the tags to turn the content below the H1 element into three genuine paragraph elements. Before you can apply a document-wide paragraph style to all three paragraphs, you must make each paragraph its own container. For example, you can surround the text of the paragraph with a <P>/</P> tag pair:

```
<HTML>
<HEAD>
<TITLE>Welcome to HypeCo</TITLE>
</HEAD>
<BODY>
<H1>Welcome to HypeCo's Home Page</H1>
<P>We're glad you're here.</P>
<P>
```

```
You can find details of all of HypeCo's latest products and special offers.
Our goal is to provide the highest quality products and the best customer
service in the industry.
</P>
<P>
<A HREF="products.htm">Click here</A> to view our on-line catalog.
</P>
</BODY>
</HTML>
```

When viewed in a modern browser, the pages created by the two preceding examples look identical. But internally, the browser recognizes three paragraph elements in the second example, and, more importantly, the style of these paragraphs can be controlled by style sheets.

The HTML vocabulary for DHTML-capable browsers includes two additional tags you can use to establish containment: <DIV> and <SPAN>. A DIV element creates a container shaped like a block that begins at the starting point of one line and ends with a line break. A SPAN element is an inline container, meaning that it is surrounded by chunks of running text. For example, if you want to assign a special style to the first two paragraphs in our example, one approach is to group those two elements inside a surrounding DIV container:

```
<BODY>
<H1>Welcome to HypeCo's Home Page</H1>
<DIV>
<P>We're glad you're here.</P>
<P>
You can find details of all of HypeCo's latest products and special offers.
Our goal is to provide the highest quality products and the best customer
service in the industry.
</P>
</DIV>
<P>
<A HREF="products.htm">Click here</A> to view our on-line catalog.
</P>
</BODY>
```

Surrounding the two paragraph elements by the <DIV> tag pair does not affect how the content is rendered in the browser, but as shown in Figure 3-1, it does alter the containment structure of the elements in the document.

As you can see from Figure 3-1, even a simple document has a number of containment relationships. The link in the last paragraph is contained by the third paragraph element; the paragraph element is contained by the body element; the body element is contained by the document (represented in HTML by the <HTML> tag pair).

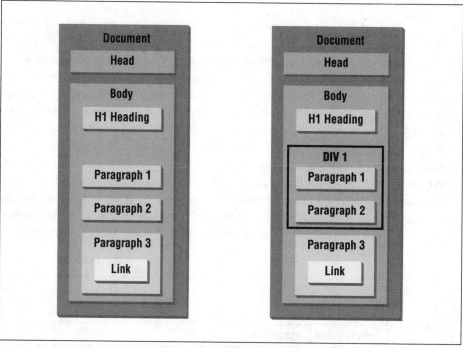

Figure 3-1. Element containment before and after the addition of the <DIV> tag

Understanding Block-Level Elements

If you are a style sheet coder, you must be aware of the element containment dictated by HTML tags. If you are a page designer, however, you need to understand an entirely different kind of containment structure: block-level elements. A block-level element is a self-contained unit of content that normally begins at the starting margin of one line and ends in a way that forces the next bit of content to appear on a new line following the block. Each of the heading tags (H1, H2, etc.) is a block-level element because it stands alone on a page (unless you use DHTML positioning tricks to overlay other elements). Other common block-level elements are P, UL, OL, and LI.

A CSS-enabled browser automatically defines a set of physical features to every block-level element. By default, the values for all these features are set to zero or none, so that they don't appear or occupy space on the page when you use simple HTML tags without style sheets. But one of the purposes of style sheets is to let you modify the values of those features to create graphical borders, adjust margin spacing, and insert padding between the content and border. In fact, those three terms—*border, margin,* and *padding*—account for about half the style sheet attributes implemented in the Version 4 browsers.

Box Pieces

You can think of the content and features of a block-level element as a box. To help you visualize the role and relative position of the features of a block-level element, Figure 3-2 shows a schematic diagram of a generic chunk of block-level content (imagine it's a paragraph, if that helps), where the margin, border, and padding are indicated in relation to the content. The width and height of the content are the same, regardless of extra stuff being tacked on outside of the content. Each of the surrounding features—padding, borders, and margins—can occupy space based on its corresponding dimensions. The width and height of the entire box is the sum of the element content, plus padding, borders, and margins. If you don't assign any values to those features, their dimensions are zero and, therefore, they contribute nothing to the dimensions of the box. In other words, without any padding, borders, or margins, the content and box dimensions are identical. With style sheets, you can assign values to your choice of edges (top, right, bottom, or left) for any feature.

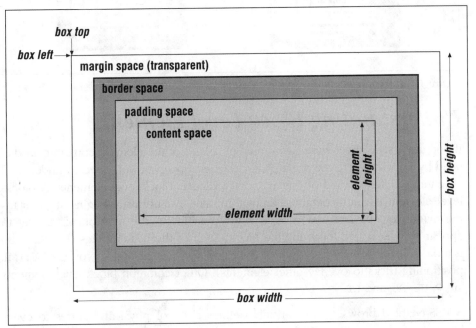

Figure 3-2. Schematic diagram of block-level elements

All margin space is transparent. Thus, any colors or images that exist in the next outer containing box (the BODY element always provides the base-level box) show through the margin space. Borders are opaque and always have a color associated with them. Padding space is also transparent, so you cannot set the padding to any color; the background color or image of the content shows through the padding space. Thus, this space "pads" the content to give some extra breathing room between the content and any border and/or margin defined for the element.

Some style sheet attributes provide a one-statement shortcut for applying independent values to each of the four edges of the margin, border, or padding. For example, you can set the top and bottom border widths to one size and apply a different size to the left and right sides of the same border. When such shortcuts are available (see the `border`, `margin`, and `padding` style attributes in Chapter 10, *Style Sheet Attribute Reference*), the values are applied in the same order: clockwise from the top—top, right, bottom, left.

Box Positioning

While the content dimensions remain the same regardless of the dimensions assigned to various box features, the size of the box expands when you assign padding, borders, and margins to the element. As you will see in Chapter 4, *Adding Dynamic Positioning to Documents*, the "thing" that gets positioned within the various coordinate planes is the box. The left and top òuter edges of the box are emphasized in Figure 3-2 to reinforce this idea.

It is important to understand the difference between a piece of content and its containing box, especially if you start nesting positioned elements or need to rely on extremely accurate locations of elements on the page. Nesting multiple block-level elements inside each other offers a whole range of possible visual effects, so page designers have much to experiment with while developing unique looks.

Two Types of Containment

If you have worked with JavaScript and the scriptable document object models inside Navigator and Internet Explorer, you are aware that scriptable document objects have a containment hierarchy of their own—an *object containment* hierarchy. The `window` object, which represents the content area of a browser window or frame, is at the top of the hierarchy. The `window` object contains objects such as the `history`, `location`, and `document` objects. The `document` object contains objects such as images and forms, and, among the most deeply nested objects, the `form` object contains form elements, such as text fields and radio buttons.

Document object containment is important in JavaScript because the hierarchy defines how you refer to objects and their methods and properties in your scripts. References usually start with the outermost element and work their way inward, using the JavaScript dot syntax to delimit each object. For example, here's how to reference the content of a text field (the `value` property) named `zipCode` inside a form named `userInfo`:

```
window.document.userInfo.zipCode.value
```

Unlike most object-oriented worlds (such as Java), the object-based world of scriptable browsers does not strictly adhere to the notion of parents and children. In fact, except for the relationship between a frameset document and the frames it creates, the word "parent" is not part of the object containment vocabulary. Document objects do not inherit properties or methods of objects higher in the containment hierarchy.

In contrast to this structure, styles adhere more closely to the *element containment* as defined by the tag geography of a document. In this context, you do see frequent references to parents and children. That's because an element can inherit a style assigned to another element higher in the element containment hierarchy.

Inheritance

All HTML document elements belong to the document's inheritance chain. The root of that chain is the HTML element. Its immediate children (also called descendants) are the next elements in the containment hierarchy. The inheritance chain depends entirely on the structure of HTML elements in the document. Figure 3-3 shows the inheritance chains of the documents whose containment structures were depicted in Figure 3-1.

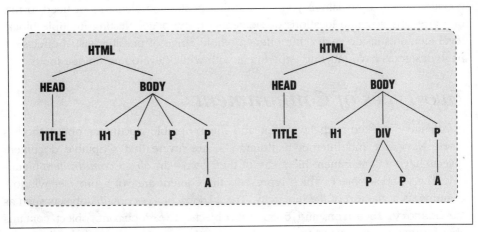

Figure 3-3. Inheritance chains of two simple documents

The importance of inheritance chains becomes clear when you begin assigning style attributes to elements that have descendants. In many cases, you want a descendant to inherit a style assigned to a parent or grandparent. For example, if you assign a red text color to all paragraphs (P elements), you more than likely want all descendant elements, such as portions designated as EM elements inside a paragraph, to render their content in the same red color.

Not all style attributes are inherited. Therefore, the style sheet attribute reference in Chapter 10 indicates whether or not each attribute is passed from parent to child.

The Cascade

Element containment also plays a role in helping the browser determine which, of potentially several, overlapping style sheet rule should be applied to an element. As you will see later in this chapter, it is possible to assign multiple styles to the same element, by importing multiple style sheet definition files and by defining multiple styles for the same element, or its parent, directly in the document. Cascading style sheets are so called because styles can flow from a number of sources; the outcome of this cascade is what is displayed by the browser.

I'll come back to cascading later in this chapter, but for now you should be aware that the first step in predicting the outcome of overlapping style sheets is determining the element containment structure of the document. Once you know where an element stands within the document's inheritance chain, you can apply strict CSS principles that assign varying weights to the way a style is defined for a particular element.

CSS Platforms

Starting with Cascading Style Sheet Level 1, you can use an attribute of the STYLE element to specify the syntax you are using to define style sheets. The value of the TYPE attribute is in the form of a content-type declaration; it defines the syntax used to assign style attributes. The formal CSS recommendation by the W3C promotes a syntax of content type text/css. This TYPE attribute is not required in today's leading browsers, but the CSS recommendation does not believe that there should be a default type. Therefore, I strongly recommend specifying the TYPE attribute for all style sheets, in case some other user agent (an HTML-empowered email reader, for example) should implement a strict interpretation of the CSS standard in the future. A STYLE element that relies on the CSS syntax should look like the following:

```
<STYLE TYPE="text/css">
...
</STYLE>
```

Internet Explorer 4 and Navigator 4 both recognize the text/css type of CSS syntax. Navigator 4 also includes an alternative syntax that follows the JavaScript object reference format. This alternate type, text/javascript, provides JavaScript equivalents for most of the style attributes and structures provided by the text/css syntax. The Navigator implementation also includes the power to use JavaScript statements and constructions inside <STYLE> tags to assist in defining styles based on client- or user-specific settings (as demonstrated later in this chapter). In other words, the implementation of style sheets in Navigator 4 is largely CSS compatible, and style sheets can be specified using either CSS or JavaScript syntax.

NOTE   In the early days of Navigator 4 (prerelease and early final versions), Netscape referred to style sheets of type `text/javascript` with names such as JavaScript Style Sheets (JSS or JSSS, depending on whom you talk to) or JavaScript-Accessible Style Sheets. The official terminology changes with the wind, but these earlier names are no longer part of the Netscape marketing vocabulary. At last reading, the company referred to this technology as "accessing style sheet properties from JavaScript via the Document Object Model"—even though the formal Document Object Model standard was far from complete at the time.

Of Style Sheets, Elements, Attributes, and Values

Regardless of the syntax you use to define a style sheet, the basic concepts are the same. A style sheet is a collection of one or more *rules*. Each rule has two parts to it:

- One or more elements (or groups of elements) that are having style sheets defined for them
- One or more style sheet attributes that apply to the element(s)

In other words, each rule defines a particular look and feel and the item(s) in the document that are to be governed by that look and feel.

Style Attributes

A style attribute is the name of a (usually) visible property of a piece of content on the page. An attribute such as foreground color can apply to any element because that color can be applied to foreground content, such as text. Some attributes, such as borders and margins, can apply only to elements rendered as blocks on the page—they have a clear beginning and ending in both the HTML source code and in the layout. Details on all the CSS style sheet attributes can be found in Chapter 10, but Table 3-1 shows a summary of CSS1 attributes implemented in both Internet Explorer 4 and Navigator 4 (in both CSS and JavaScript syntax). Each browser also defines other style attributes that are noted in Chapter 10.

Table 3-1. Summary of CSS1 Style Sheet Attributes in Version 4 Browsers

Attribute Name—CSS Syntax (IE 4 and NN 4)	Attribute Name—JavaScript Syntax (NN 4)
Box Properties	
border	
border-top [a]	
border-right [a]	
border-bottom [a]	
border-left [a]	
border-color	borderColor
border-top-color [a]	
border-right-color [a]	
border-bottom-color [a]	
border-left-color [a]	
border-style	borderStyle
border-top-style [a]	
border-right-style	
border-bottom-style [a]	
border-left-style [a]	
border-width	borderWidths()
border-top-width	borderTopWidth
border-right-width	borderRightWidth
border-bottom-width	borderBottomWidth
border-left-width	borderLeftWidth
clear	
float	
margin	margins()
margin-top	marginTop
margin-right	marginRight
margin-bottom	marginBottom
margin-left	marginLeft
padding	paddings()
padding-top	paddingTop
padding-right	paddingRight
padding-bottom	paddingBottom
padding-left	paddingLeft
Color and Background Properties	
background	
background-attachment [a]	
background-color	backgroundColor
background-image	backgroundImage
background-position	
background-repeat	
color	color

Table 3-1. Summary of CSS1 Style Sheet Attributes in Version 4 Browsers (continued)

Attribute Name—CSS Syntax (IE 4 and NN 4)	Attribute Name—JavaScript Syntax (NN 4)
Classification Properties	
display	display
list-style-type	listStyleType
list-style-image[a]	
list-style-position[a]	
list-style	
white-space[b]	whiteSpace
Font Properties	
font	
font-family	fontFamily
font-size	fontSize
font-style	fontStyle
font-variant[a]	
font-weight	fontWeight
Text Properties	
letter-spacing[a]	
text-align	textAlign
text-decoration	textDecoration
line-height	lineHeight
text-indent	
text-transform	textTransform
vertical-align	verticalAlign

[a] Not implemented in CSS for Navigator 4
[b] Not implemented in Internet Explorer 4

CSS Attribute Assignment Syntax

The syntax for assigning a value to an attribute is different from what you know about HTML attributes and their values. Moreover, the precise syntax is different between CSS and JavaScript style sheets.

For CSS syntax, value assignment is made via the colon operator (in contrast to the equal sign operator in HTML). The combination of an attribute name, colon operator, and value to be assigned to the attribute is called a *declaration*. To assign the color red to the foreground of an element, you could use either of the following declarations:

```
color:#ff0000
color:red
```

If a style sheet rule includes more than one declaration, separate declarations with semicolons:

```
color:#ff0000; font-size:12pt;
```

A trailing semicolon after the last declaration is optional, as is a space after the colon.

Notice, however, that unlike HTML attribute values, CSS syntax attribute values do not—and cannot—have double quotes around the values, even when the value appears to be a string value with spaces.

Binding CSS Style Sheets to Elements

Defining a rule's declarations is only half the job. The other half involves binding that declaration to an HTML element—also called a *selector* in CSS jargon. In a simple case, you bind a declaration to a single element or a single type of element (e.g., all P elements). The CSS standard also provides for additional ways of binding a declaration to a subgroup of elements scattered throughout a document; you define the relationship of the elements as a selector. Finally, you can define exceptions to the grouping rules you establish in the document.

JavaScript Attributes and Element Binding

It should be no surprise that the JavaScript style sheet syntax in Navigator assigns values to style attributes in JavaScript statements. As we'll discuss in detail later in the chapter, using such statements is very much like assigning values to other document object properties in client-side JavaScript.

Embedding Style Sheets

If you want to develop style sheet-enhanced pages that work in both Internet Explorer and Navigator, you should use the CSS syntax. In the next few sections, all of examples I present are going to use the CSS syntax, since it works in both browsers. Later, I'll discuss the Navigator-specific JavaScript syntax for style sheets.

Style sheets can be added directly to a document or imported from one or more external files. In-document and external style sheets coexist well in the same document; you can have as many of each type as your page design requires.

In-Document Styles

There are two ways to embed CSS information directly in an HTML document: using the <STYLE> tag pair or using STYLE attributes of HTML tags. For ease of maintenance and consistency throughout a document, I recommend using a <STYLE> tag inside the HEAD section of the document. But you can also include STYLE attributes directly inside the tag for almost any HTML element.

The <STYLE> tag

It is convenient to define style sheet rules between <STYLE> and </STYLE> tags. The collection of rules within these tags is the classic instance of a CSS style sheet. Because the elements to which you bind style declarations can appear early in the body of the document (and may be bound to the BODY element itself), you should use the <STYLE> tag in the HEAD section of your document. This guarantees that the style sheet is loaded and in effect before any elements of the document are rendered. Include the TYPE attribute in the opening tag, as in:

```
<STYLE TYPE="text/css">
    style sheet rule(s) here
</STYLE>
```

Some older browsers ignore the start and end tags and attempt to render the contents as if they were part of the document body. If you fear that this will affect users of your pages, you can surround the statements inside the STYLE element with HTML comment symbols. Such a framework looks as follows:

```
<STYLE TYPE="text/css">
<!--
    style sheet rule(s) here
-->
</STYLE>
```

This technique is similar to the one used to hide the contents of <SCRIPT> tag pairs from older browsers, except that the end-comment statement in a script must include a JavaScript comment (//-->). The content is still downloaded to the client and is visible in the source code, but for all but the most brain-dead browsers, the style sheet rules are hidden from plain view in the browser window. In the examples in this book, I have omitted these comment symbols to conserve space and improve readability, but you should take care to use them as necessary in your STYLE elements.

As I mentioned earlier, the element to which a style declaration is assigned is called a selector. In practice, selector has a wide range of meanings. In its simplest form, a selector is the name of one type of HTML element—the case-insensitive HTML tag stripped of its enclosing angle brackets (e.g., the P selector, which represents all the paragraphs in a document). As you will see as this chapter progresses, a selector can take on additional forms, including some that have no resemblance at all to HTML elements. Just remember that a selector defines the part (or parts) of an HTML document that is governed by a style declaration.

In the most common application, each style rule binds a declaration to a particular type of HTML element. When a rule is specified in a <STYLE> tag, the declaration portion of the rule must appear inside curly braces, even if there is just one style attribute in the declaration. The style sheet in the following example includes two rules. The first assigns the red foreground (text) color and initial capital text transform to all H1 elements in the document; the second assigns the blue text color to all P elements:

```
<HTML>
<HEAD>
<STYLE TYPE="text/css">
    H1 {color:red; text-transform:capitalize}
    P {color:blue}
</STYLE>
</HEAD>
<BODY>
<H1>Some heading</H1>
<P>Some paragraph text.</P>
</BODY>
</HTML>
```

There is no practical limit to the number of rules that can be listed inside the <STYLE> tag pair, nor is there a limit to the number of style attributes that can be used in a style rule. Also, rules can appear in any order within a style sheet, and the indenting shown in the preceding example is purely optional. If you prefer, you can also break up a series of declarations (inside the curly braces), placing them on separate lines.

CSS syntax provides a shortcut for assigning the same style declaration to more than one selector. By preceding the curly-braced style declaration with a comma-delimited list of selectors, you can have one statement do the work of two or more statements. For example, if you want to assign a specific color to H1, H2, and H3 elements in the document, you can do so with one statement:

```
<STYLE TYPE="text/css">
    H1, H2, H3 {color:blue}
</STYLE>
```

The STYLE attribute in other tags

Another way to bind a style declaration to an HTML element is to include the declaration as an attribute of the actual HTML element tag. The declaration is assigned to the STYLE attribute; almost every HTML element recognizes the STYLE attribute.

Because the STYLE attribute is a regular HTML attribute, you assign a value to it via the equal sign operator. The value is a double-quoted string that consists of one or more style attribute/value pairs. These style attribute/value pairs use the colon assignment operator. Use a semicolon to separate multiple style attribute settings within the same STYLE attribute. Here is a STYLE attribute version of the <STYLE> tag example shown in the preceding section. Because the style sheets are attached to the actual HTML element tags, all this takes place in the BODY section of the document:

```
<BODY>
<H1 STYLE="color:red; text-transform:capitalize">Some heading</H1>
<P STYLE="color:blue">Some paragraph text.</P>
</BODY>
```

Notice, too, that when a style sheet definition is specified as a STYLE attribute, there are no curly braces involved. The double quotes surrounding the entire style sheet definition function as the curly brace grouping characters.

Selecting a style sheet style

In deciding whether to use the <STYLE> tag or STYLE attribute methodology for defining style sheets, you need to consider how important it is for you to separate design from content. The <STYLE> tag technique distances HTML content from the styles associated with elements throughout the document. If you need to change a font family or size for a particular kind of element, you can do so quickly and reliably by making the change to one location in the document. If, on the other hand, your style definitions are scattered among dozens or hundreds of tags throughout the document, such a change requires much more effort and the possibility for mistakes increases. However, for small-scale deployment of style sheets, the STYLE attribute will certainly do the job. And, if one person is responsible for both content and design, it isn't too difficult to keep the content and design in sync.

Current web development trends lean toward the separation of design from content. In large projects involving writers, designers, and programmers, it is usually easier to manage the entire project if different contributors to the application can work toward the same goal without stepping on each other's code along the way. Using the <STYLE> tag offers the best growth path for an evolving web site, and it smooths the eventual transition to external style sheet files.

Importing External Style Sheets

Perhaps the most common use of style sheets in the publishing world is to establish a "look" designed to pervade across all documents, or at least across all sections of a large document. To facilitate applying a style sheet across multiple HTML pages, the CSS specification provides two ways to include external style sheet files: an implementation of the <LINK> tag and a special type of style sheet rule selector (the @import rule).

Style sheet files

No matter how you import an external style sheet, the external file must be written in such a way that the browser can use it to build the library of style sheets that controls the currently loaded document. In other words, the browser must take into account not only external styles, but any other styles that might also be defined inside the document. Because there is an opportunity for the overlap of multiple style sheets in a document, the browser must see how all the styles are bound to elements, so it can apply cascading rules (described later in this chapter) to render the content.

An external style sheet file consists exclusively of style sheet rules without any HTML tags. The file can be saved with any filename extension (you can use *.htm*, *.html*, or *.css* if the file is written in CSS syntax). For example, to convert the style sheet used in the previous sections to an external style sheet file, create a text file that contains the following and save the file as *basestyl.css*:

```
H1 {color:red; text-transform:capitalize}
P {color:blue}
```

When a browser encounters either technique for importing an external style sheet, the content of the file is loaded into the browser as if it were typed into the main HTML document at that location (although it doesn't become part of the source code if you use the browser to view the source).

The LINK element

More recent versions of the HTML recommendation include a general-purpose tag for linking media-independent content into a document. This is not a link like the <A> tag because the LINK element can appear only in the HEAD portion of a document. It is up to the browser to know how to work with the various attributes of this tag (see Chapter 8, *HTML Reference*).

The CSS2 specification claims one application of the LINK element as a way to link an external style sheet file into a document. The attributes and format for the tag are rather simple:

```
<LINK REL=STYLESHEET TYPE="sheetMimeType" HREF="filename.css"
```

If the style sheet in the previous section is saved as *basestyl.css*, you can import that style sheet as follows:

```
<HTML>
<HEAD>
<LINK REL=STYLESHEET TYPE="text/css" HREF="basestyl.css">
</HEAD>
<BODY>
<H1>Some heading</H1>
<P>Some paragraph text.</P>
</BODY>
</HTML>
```

A document can have multiple LINK elements for importing multiple external style sheet files. The document can also contain STYLE elements as well as STYLE attributes embedded within element tags. But if there is any overlap of more than one style applying to the same element, the cascade rules (described later in this chapter) determine the specific style sheet rule that governs the element's display.

The @import rule

CSS2 describes an extensible system for declarations or directives (commands, if you will) that become a part of a style sheet definition. They are called *at-rules* because a rule starts with the "at" symbol (@), followed by an identifier for the declaration. Each at-rule includes one or more descriptors that define the characteristics of the rule. (For more about at-rules, see Chapter 10.)

One such at-rule that is implemented in Internet Explorer 4 (but not Navigator 4) imports an external style sheet file from inside a STYLE element. It performs the same function as the LINK import technique described in the previous section. In the following example, a file containing style sheet rules is imported into the current document:

```
<STYLE TYPE="text/css">
    @import url(styles/corporate.css)
</STYLE>
```

If you are creating documents for browser versions that support the @import rule, it may be more convenient to keep all style sheet definitions within the STYLE element rather than spreading the import job to a separate LINK element.

Subgroup Selectors

While a selector for a style sheet rule is most often an HTML element name, that scenario is not flexible enough for more complex documents. Consider the following possibilities:

- You want certain paragraphs scattered throughout the document to be set apart from running text by having wider left and right margins.

- You want all H2 elements in the document but one to be set to the color red; the exception must be blue.

- In a three-level ordered list (OL) group, you want to assign different font sizes to each level.

Each of these possibilities calls for a different way of creating a new selector group or specifying an exception to the regular selectors. In an effort to distance design from content, CSS style sheets provide three ways of creating subgroups that can handle almost every design possibility:

- Class selectors

- ID selectors

- Contextual selectors

Using these subgroup selectors requires special ways of defining selectors in style sheet rules. These selectors also require the addition of attributes to the HTML tags they apply to in the document.

Class Selectors

A class selector is an identifier you can use to assign a style to a subset of elements in a document. To apply a class selector, you first invent an identifier for the class name. To allow for the potential scripting of class names, it is wise to adhere to the rules of JavaScript identifiers when devising class names. A Java-Script identifier is a one-word name (i.e., no spaces) that can include numerals, letters, and limited punctuation (such as the underscore character). Also, the first character of an identifier cannot be a numeral. The CSS2 guidelines for selector identifiers are less stringent: you can embed hyphens, Unicode characters above 160, and escaped characters (characters that begin with a backslash character) in an identifier, but the name must not begin with a numeral or hyphen. If you are now or may eventually script class selectors, follow the JavaScript rules instead of the more liberal CSS2 rules.

The class identifier goes in both the style sheet rule and the HTML tag (assigned to the CLASS attribute) for the element that is to obey the rule. While the identifier name is the same in both cases, the syntax for specifying it is quite different in each place.

Binding a class identifier to an element type

In the style sheet rule, the class identifier is part of the rule's selector. When a class selector is intended to apply to only one kind of HTML element, the selector consists of the element name, a period, and the identifier. The following rule assigns a specific margin setting for all P elements flagged as belonging to the **narrow** class:

```
P.narrow {margin-left:5em; margin-right:5em}
```

To force a P element to obey the **P.narrow** rule, you must include a CLASS attribute in the <P> tag and set the value to the class identifier:

```
<P CLASS="narrow">Content for the narrow paragraph</P>
```

Any P elements that don't have the CLASS attribute set to **narrow** follow whatever style is applied to the generic P element.

As implemented in Navigator 4 and Internet Explorer 4, class selectors permit only one class identifier for each selector. In other words, you cannot create a nested hierarchy of classes (e.g., a selector **P.narrow.redHot** is not allowed). The current browsers are very forgiving if you reassign the same class name to different element types in different rules. Be aware, however, that for purposes of present-day or future scriptability of style classes, you should avoid reusing a class identifier in a document for any other purpose.

Example 3-1 shows a complete document that includes style sheet rules for all P elements and a subclass of P.narrow elements. The rule for all P elements specifies a 2-em margin on the left and right as well as a 14-point font size. For all P elements tagged with the CLASS=narrow attribute, the margins are set to 5 ems and the text color is set to red. It is important to note that the P.narrow rule inherits (or is affected by) style settings from the P rule. Therefore, all text in the P.narrow elements is displayed at a font size of 14 points. But when the margin attributes are set in both rules, the settings for the named class override the settings of the broader P element rule (the language of CSS does not include the object-oriented concepts of subclass or superclass). Following the inheritance trail one level higher in the containment hierarchy, all P elements (and all other elements in the document if there were any) obey the style sheet rule for the BODY element, which is where the font face is specified.

Example 3-1. Applying the P.narrow Class Rule

```
<HTML>
<HEAD>
<TITLE>Class Society</TITLE>
<STYLE TYPE="text/css">
    P {font-size:14pt; margin-left:2em; margin-right:2em}
    P.narrow {color:red; margin-left:5em; margin-right:5em}
    BODY {font-family:Arial, serif}
</STYLE>
</HEAD>

<BODY>
<P>
This is a normal paragraph. This is a normal paragraph. This is a normal
paragraph. This is a normal paragraph. This is a normal paragraph.
</P>
<P CLASS=narrow>
This is a paragraph to be set apart with wider margins and red color. This is a
paragraph to be set apart with wider margins and red color. This is a paragraph
to be set apart with wider margins and red color.
</P>
<P>
This is a normal paragraph. This is a normal paragraph. This is a normal
paragraph. This is a normal paragraph. This is a normal paragraph.
</P>
<P CLASS=narrow>
This is a paragraph to be set apart with wider margins and red color. This is a
paragraph to be set apart with wider margins and red color. This is a paragraph
to be set apart with wider margins and red color.
</P>
</BODY>
</HTML>
```

Defining a free-range class rule

Most of the time, you don't want to limit a class selector to a single element type in a document. Fortunately, you can define a rule with a class selector that can be applied to any element in the document. The selector of such a rule is nothing more than the identifier preceded by a period. Example 3-2 contains a rule that assigns a red underline style to a class named hot. The hot class is then assigned to different elements scattered throughout the document. Notice inheritance at work in this example. When the hot class is assigned to a DIV element, it applies to the P element nested inside the DIV element: the entire paragraph is rendered in the hot style and follows the P.narrow rule as well, since the rules do not have any overlapping style attributes.

Example 3-2. Applying a Class Rule to a Variety of HTML Elements

```
<HTML>
<HEAD><TITLE>Free Range Class</TITLE>
<STYLE TYPE="text/css">
    P {font-size:14pt; margin-left:2em; margin-right:2em}
    P.narrow {margin-left:5em; margin-right:5em}
    .hot {color:red; text-decoration:underline}
    BODY {font-family:Arial, serif}
</STYLE>
</HEAD>

<BODY>
<H1 CLASS=hot>Get a Load of This!</H1>
<P>
This is a normal paragraph. This is a normal paragraph. This is a normal
paragraph. This is a normal paragraph. This is a normal paragraph.
</P>
<DIV CLASS=hot>
<P CLASS="narrow">
This is a paragraph to be set apart with wider margins and red color. This is a
paragraph to be set apart with wider margins and red color. This is a paragraph
to be set apart with wider margins and red color.
</P>
</DIV>
<P>
This is a normal paragraph. This is a normal paragraph <SPAN CLASS=hot>but with a
red-hot spot</SPAN>. This is a normal paragraph. This is a normal paragraph. This
is a normal paragraph.
</P>
<P CLASS=narrow>
This is a paragraph to be set apart with wider margins and red color. This is a
paragraph to be set apart with wider margins and red color. This is a paragraph
to be set apart with wider margins and red color.
</P>
</BODY>
</HTML>
```

ID Selectors

In contrast to the class selector, the ID selector lets you define a rule that applies to only one element in the entire document. Like the class selector, the ID selector requires a special way of defining the selector in the style sheet rule and a special tag attribute (ID) in the tag that is the recipient of that rule. The ID attribute of a tag is similar to the NAME attribute applied to elements for scripting purposes. This means that to maintain integrity of the object model for the current document, the ID selector identifier must be unique within the document.

The style rule syntax for defining an ID selector calls for the identifier to be preceded with the # symbol. This can be in conjunction with an element selector or by itself. Therefore, both of the following rules are valid:

```
P#special4 {border:5px ridge red}
#special4{border:5px ridge red}
```

To apply this rule for this ID to a P element, you have to add the ID attribute to that element's tag:

```
<P ID=special4>Content for a special paragraph.</P>
```

There is an important difference between the two style rule examples just shown. By specifying the ID selector in concert with the P element selector in the first example, we've told the browser to obey the ID=special4 attribute only if it appears in a P element. The second rule, however, is a generic rule. This means that the ID=special4 attribute can appear in any kind of element. Since an ID attribute value should be used in only one element throughout the entire document, the first rule is unnecessarily limiting.

Example 3-3 shows the ID selector at work, where it is used to assign a rule (defining a red, ridge-style border for a block) to only one of several P elements in the document. Notice that it is assigned to a P element that also has a class selector assigned to it: two rules are applied to the same element. In this example, the style rules do not conflict with each other, but if they did, the cascade precedence rules (described later in this chapter) would automatically determine precisely which rule wins the battle of the dueling style attributes.

Example 3-3. Applying an ID Selector to a Document

```
<HTML>
<HEAD><TITLE>ID Selector</TITLE>
<STYLE TYPE="text/css">
    P {font-size:14pt; margin-left:2em; margin-right:2em}
    P.narrow {color:red; margin-left:5em; margin-right:5em}
    #special4 {border:5px ridge red}
    BODY {font-family:Arial, serif}
</STYLE>
</HEAD>
```

Example 3-3. Applying an ID Selector to a Document (continued)

```
<BODY BGCOLOR="#FFFFFF">
<H1>Get a Load of This!</H1>
<P>
This is a normal paragraph. This is a normal paragraph. This is a normal
paragraph. This is a normal paragraph. This is a normal paragraph.
</P>
<P CLASS=narrow ID=special4>This is a paragraph to be set apart with wider
margins, red color AND a red border. This is a paragraph to be set apart with
wider margins, red color AND a red border.
</P>
<P>
This is a normal paragraph. This is a normal paragraph. This is a normal
paragraph. This is a normal paragraph. This is a normal paragraph.
</P>
<P CLASS=narrow>This is a paragraph to be set apart with wider margins and red
color. This is a paragraph to be set apart with wider margins and red color. This
is a paragraph to be set apart with wider margins and red color.
</P>
</BODY>
</HTML>
```

Contextual Selectors

One more way to assign styles to specific categories of elements is the contextual
selector. To use a contextual selector, you should be comfortable with the containment hierarchy of elements in a document and how inheritance affects the application of styles to a chunk of content. Consider the two single-selector rules in the
following style sheet:

```
<STYLE TYPE="text/css">
    P {font-size:14pt; color:black}
    EM {font-size:16pt; color:red}
</STYLE>
```

This style sheet dictates that all **EM** elements throughout the document be displayed in red with a 16-point font. If you were to add an **EM** element as part of an
H1 element, the effect might be less than desirable. What you really want from the
style sheet is to apply the **EM** style declaration to **EM** elements only when they are
contained by—are in the context of—**P** elements. A contextual selector lets you do
just that. In a contextual selector, you list the elements of the containment hierarchy that are to be affected by the style, with the elements separated by spaces.

To turn the second rule of the previous style sheet into a contextual selector, modify it as follows:

```
<STYLE TYPE="text/css">
    P {font-size:14pt; color:black}
    P EM {font-size:16pt; color:red}
</STYLE>
```

You still need the rule for the base P element in this case because the style is something other than the browser default. There is no practical limit to the number of containment levels you can use in a contextual selector. For example, if the design calls for a section of an EM element to have a yellow background color, you can assign that job to a SPAN element and set the contextual selector to affect a SPAN element only when it is nested inside an EM element that is nested inside a P element. Example 3-4 shows what the source code for such a document looks like. The example goes one step further in that one element of the contextual selectors is a class selector (P.narrow). Each element selector in a contextual selector can be any valid selector, including a class or ID selector. You can also apply the same style declaration to more than one contextual selector by separating the contextual selector groups with commas:

```
P EM SPAN, H3 B {background-color:yellow}
```

It's an odd-looking construction, but it's perfectly legal (and byte conservative).

Example 3-4. Applying a Three-Level Contextual Selector

```
<HTML>
<HEAD><TITLE>ID Selector</TITLE>
<STYLE TYPE="text/css">
    P {font-size:14pt; margin-left:2em; margin-right:2em}
    P.narrow {color:red; margin-left:5em; margin-right:5em}
    P.narrow EM {font-weight:bold}
    P.narrow EM SPAN {background-color:yellow}
    #special4 {border:5px ridge red}
    BODY {font-family:Arial, serif}
</STYLE>
</HEAD>

<BODY>
<H1>Get a Load of This!</H1>
<P>
This is a normal paragraph. This is a normal paragraph. This is a normal
paragraph. This is a normal paragraph. This is a normal paragraph.
</P>
<P CLASS=narrow ID=special4>This is a <EM>paragraph to be set apart</EM> with
wider margins, red color AND a red border. This is a paragraph to be set apart
with wider margins, red color AND a red border.
</P>
<P>
This is a normal paragraph. This is a normal paragraph. This is a normal
paragraph. This is a normal paragraph. This is a normal paragraph.
</P>
<P CLASS=narrow>This is a <EM>paragraph to be <SPAN>set apart</SPAN></EM> with
wider margins and red color. This is a paragraph to be set apart with wider
margins and red color. This is a paragraph to be set apart with wider margins and
red color.
</P>
</BODY>
</HTML>
```

Attribute Selector Futures: CSS2

Navigator 4 and Internet Explorer 4 implement the individual, class, ID, and contextual selector schemes described in the previous sections. The newer CSS2 specification makes further enhancements to the way selectors can be specified in style sheet rules. Some of these recommendations may find their way into future versions of the browsers (IE 4 already uses a few of them) or other implementations of style sheets (such as in XML-enabled applications). These items are noted here briefly to offer a preview of what you might expect in the next generation of DHTML-capable browsers. However, since specifications like CSS do not insist on 100% compliance (some items are optional), don't be surprised if some of the items described in this section do not appear in the next version of your browser.

Pseudo-Element and Pseudo-Class Selectors

The original idea for pseudo-elements and pseudo-classes was defined as part of the CSS1 recommendation; these selectors have been expanded in CSS2. A fine line distinguishes these two concepts, but they do share one important factor: there are no direct HTML tag equivalents for the elements or classes described by these selectors. Therefore, you must imagine how the selectors will affect the real tags in your document.

Using pseudo-elements

A pseudo-element is a well-defined chunk of content in an HTML element. Two pseudo-elements specified in the CSS1 recommendation point to the first letter and the first line of a paragraph. The elements are named `:first-letter` and `:first-line`, respectively. It is up to the browser to figure out where, for example, the first line ends (based on the content and window width) and apply the style only to the content in that line. If the browser is told to format the `:first-letter` pseudo-element with a drop cap, the browser must also take care of rendering the rest of the text in the paragraph so that it wraps around the drop cap.

For example, to apply styles for the first letter and first line of all P elements, use the following style rules:

```
<STYLE TYPE="text/css">
    P:first-letter {font-face:Gothic, serif; font-size:300%; float:left}
    P:first-line {font-style:small-caps}
</STYLE>
```

Style attributes that can be set for `:first-letter` and `:first-line` include a large subset of the full CSS attribute set. They include all font, color, background, margin, padding, and border attributes, as well as a handful of element-specific attributes that logically apply to a given element.

Using pseudo-classes

In contrast to a pseudo-element, a pseudo-class applies to an element whose look
or content may change as the user interacts with the content. Pseudo-classes
defined in the CSS1 recommendation are for three states of the A element: a link
not yet visited, a link being clicked on by the user, and a link that has been visited. Default behavior in most browsers is to differentiate these states by colors
(default colors can usually be set by user preferences as well as by attributes of
the BODY element). The syntax for pseudo-class selectors follows the same pattern
as for pseudo-elements. This style sheet defines rules for the three A element
pseudo-classes:

```
<STYLE TYPE="text/css">
    A:link {color:darkred}
    A:active {color:coral}
    A:visited {color:lightblue; font-size:-1}
</STYLE>
```

As with other selectors, you can combine class or ID selectors with pseudo-elements or pseudo-classes to narrow the application of a special style. For instance,
you may want a large drop cap to appear only in the first paragraph of a page.
See Chapter 10 for an example, plus a list of CSS2 pseudo-elements and pseudo-
classes.

Attribute Selectors

The CSS2 specification expands the facilities in Navigator 4 and Internet Explorer 4
for selectors based on plain elements, classes, and IDs. In the enhanced scheme, it
is helpful to think of a selector as an expression that helps the user agent (browser
or application) locate a match of HTML elements or attributes to determine
whether the style should be applied. In many respects, the functionality mimics
that of a scripting language that you would use to inspect the value assigned to an
element's attribute before assigning a specific style. But the CSS2 attribute selector
model is nothing at all like JavaScript syntax for style sheets (described later).

Table 3-2 shows the three attribute selector formats and what they mean. A new
syntactical feature for selectors—square brackets—adds another level of complex-
ity to defining style sheet rules, but the added flexibility may be worth the effort.

Table 3-2. Attribute Selector Syntax

Syntax Format	Description
[*attributeName*]	Matches an element if the attribute is defined in the HTML tag
[*attributeName=value*]	Matches an element if the attribute is set to the specified value in the HTML tag
[*attributeName~=value*]	Matches an element if the specified value is present among the values assigned to the attribute in the HTML tag

To see how these selector formats work, observe how the sample style sheet rules in Table 3-3 apply to an associated HTML tag.

Table 3-3. How Attribute Selectors Work

Style Sheet Selector	Applies To	Does Not Apply To
P[ALIGN]	<P ALIGN="left"> <P ALIGN="left" TITLE="Summary">	<P> <P TITLE="Summary">
HR[ALIGN="left"]	<HR ALIGN="left">	<HR ALIGN="middle">
IMG[ALT~="Temporary"]	<IMG ALT="Temporary placeholder" SRC="picture.gif">	<APPLET ALT="Temporary Applet" CODE=... >

Universal Selectors

In practice, the absence of an element selector before an attribute selector implies that the rule is to apply to any and all elements of the document. But a special symbol more clearly states your intentions. The asterisk symbol (*) acts like a wildcard character to select all elements. You can use this to a greater advantage when you combine selector types, such as the universal and attribute selector. The following selector applies to all elements whose ALIGN attributes are set to a specific value:

```
*[ALIGN="middle"]
```

Parent-Child Selectors

Element containment is a key factor in the parent-child selector. Again, following the notion of a style rule selector matching a pattern in a document, the parent-child selector looks for element patterns that match a specific sequence of parent and child elements. The behavior of a parent-child selector is very similar to that of a contextual selector, but the notation is different—a greater-than symbol (>) separates the element names in the selector, as in:

```
BODY > P {font-size:12pt}
```

Another difference is that the two elements on either side of the symbol must be direct relations of each other, as a paragraph is of a body.

Adjacent Selectors

An adjacent selector lets you define a rule for an element based on its position relative to another element or, rather, the sequence of elements. Such adjacent selectors consist of two or more element selectors, with a plus symbol (+) between the selectors. For example, if your design calls for an extra top margin for an H2 block whenever it comes immediately below an H1 element in the document, the rule looks like the following:

```
H1 + H2 {margin-top: 6pt}
```

JavaScript Style Sheet Syntax

So far throughout this chapter, all style sheet examples have used the CSS syntax promoted in the W3C recommendations and implemented to varying degrees in both Navigator 4 and Internet Explorer 4. In this section, we discuss Netscape's alternative syntax for specifying style sheets. This syntax follows the rules of the JavaScript (and, by extension, ECMAScript) language, but the object model is unique to Navigator 4. Unless you exercise browser branching safeguards, you will encounter script errors if you attempt to load documents equipped with this style sheet syntax into Internet Explorer 4. It's important to emphasize that this is not an alternate style sheet mechanism; rather, it is just another way to program CSS style sheets. The advantage of this syntax is that you gain the power of using other JavaScript statements inside <STYLE> tags to create, for example, algorithmically derived values for style sheet rules.[*]

As you may have noticed in Table 3-1, not every CSS attribute implemented in Navigator 4 has a JavaScript equivalent. The most common attributes are accounted for, but some design choices, such as setting independent colors for border sides, aren't available in Navigator 4—in JavaScript *or* CSS syntax.

Attributes and Elements

JavaScript syntax simplifies assigning values to style attributes and then assigning those attributes to HTML elements, in that you don't have to learn the CSS syntax. Each statement in a JavaScript style sheet is a property assignment statement. The object reference on the left side of the statement is an element type, class, or ID. These objects all have style properties to which you can assign values.

To demonstrate the difference in syntax, the next listing is a duplicate of one earlier in the chapter that showed a simple setting of two style rules in CSS syntax:

```
<HTML>
<HEAD>
<STYLE TYPE="text/css">
    H1 {color:red; text-transform:capitalize}
    P {color:blue}
</STYLE>
</HEAD>
```

---

[*] If you want to use algorithmically derived values in style sheets in IE 4, you can create a custom API that inserts style rules into an existing style sheet, using IE's document object model.

```
<BODY>
<H1>Some heading</H1>
<P>Some paragraph text.</P>
</BODY>
</HTML>
```

In JavaScript syntax, the document looks as follows:

```
<HTML>
<HEAD>
<STYLE TYPE="text/javascript">
    tags.H1.color = "red"
    tags.H1.textTransform = "capitalize"
    tags.P.color = "blue"
</STYLE>
</HEAD>
<BODY>
<H1>Some heading</H1>
<P>Some paragraph text.</P>
</BODY>
</HTML>
```

Note three primary differences between the two versions:

- The **TYPE** attribute of the **<STYLE>** tag is `text/javascript`.

- Style attributes use the JavaScript versions, which turn multiword hyphenated CSS attribute names into one-word, intercapitalized JavaScript identifiers.

- Property values other than numbers are quoted strings, so as not to be confused with JavaScript variables.

You can also use JavaScript syntax to assign values to style properties inside other HTML tags with the **STYLE** attribute. The attribute value must be a quoted string of a style property assignment statement; values being assigned to these properties must then be written as a nested string. For example, the following tag uses Java-Script syntax to set the font size and color of the paragraph:

```
<P STYLE="fontSize='18pt'; color='blue'">
```

The construction is a little awkward. But as I mentioned earlier in this chapter, inline **STYLE** attributes are more difficult to maintain over time, so you're better off using the **<STYLE>** tag set for your style sheets.

JavaScript Selectors

Like the CSS syntax, the JavaScript syntax for style sheets allows you to select plain elements, classes, IDs, and contextual subgroups. A JavaScript style rule begins with one of the object names **tags**, **classes**, or **ids** or the **contextual()** method. Technically, all four of these entities belong to the **document** object, but Navigator assumes the document context whenever you use these references inside a **<STYLE>** tag. Therefore, you can omit **document** from all such references.

Don't forget, however, that you are in a JavaScript context whenever the <STYLE> tag is of type `text/javascript`. As a result, you can use a JavaScript shortcut, such as the `with` statement, to set many properties of the same element with less code. Outside of the <STYLE> tag context, you can use references to these objects for read-only access to the style sheet properties.

Plain element selectors

Use the `tags` object to start a rule involving a single element. Element names are the same as in CSS syntax. The format for setting a plain element style property is:

```
tags.tagName.propertyName = "value"
```

The name of the tag is not case sensitive in this construction, but all other components of the reference are case sensitive. The following fragment sets three style properties for all the P elements in a document:

```
tags.P.fontSize = "14pt"
tags.P.marginLeft = "2em"
tags.P.marginRight = "2em"
```

As a shortcut, you can use the JavaScript `with` statement to group these statements together:

```
with (tags.P) {
    fontSize = "14pt"
    marginLeft = "2em"
    marginRight = "2em"
}
```

In other words, all three property setting statements are applied to the `tags.P` object.

Class selectors

You can define a class selector that matches all tags whose CLASS attributes are set to the same class name. Such classes can be bound to a particular element type or can be "free-range" classes, if your design calls for it.

To set the style property of a class bound to a single element type, the syntax is as follows:

```
classes.className.elementName.propertyName = "value"
```

If, on the other hand, you wish to apply a class to any element that includes a CLASS attribute set to that class name, you substitute the `all` keyword for the element name, as in the following format:

```
classes.className.all.propertyName = "value"
```

NOTE   This application of the `all` keyword applies only to style sheet class selectors in Navigator 4. The identical keyword is used in an entirely different context (element positioning) in Internet Explorer 4. Do not try to establish any relationship between the two applications of this keyword.

An example of class-to-element-type binding is shown later in Example 3-5.

ID selectors

An ID is an identifier assigned to one HTML element in the document with the `ID` attribute. Therefore, the ID selector lets you target a single element for a particular style setting, even if it is also targeted by a plain element selector or a class element selector (just like the CSS ID selector described earlier in this chapter).

Syntax for the ID selector follows the same structure as other JavaScript style properties:

```
ids.idName.propertyName = "value"
```

Contextual selectors

The construction of a contextual selector in JavaScript syntax is a little different compared to the other selector styles. The need is to group two or more other selectors into a sequence, so that the browser applies the style to an element only if it appears in the context of related elements. The JavaScript syntax turns the contextual reference into a JavaScript method whose parameters are the component selectors that define the pattern to be matched for context. In JavaScript, multiple parameters are delimited by commas.

Earlier in this chapter, you saw the following CSS syntax for a style sheet that defined a rule for all `P` elements and a rule for all `EM` elements nested inside `P` elements:

```
<STYLE TYPE="text/css">
    P {font-size:14pt; color:black}
    P EM {font-size:16pt; color:red}
</STYLE>
```

In JavaScript, the first rule is converted to a **tags** reference. The second rule must use the **contextual()** method, which has the following syntax:

```
contextual(selector1, ..., selectorN).propertyName = "value"
```

Therefore, the JavaScript syntax equivalent for the preceding CSS style sheet is:

```
<STYLE TYPE="text/javascript">
    tags.P.fontSize = "14pt"
```

```
        tags.P.color = "black"
        contextual(tags.P, tags.EM).fontSize = "16pt"
        contextual(tags.P, tags.EM).color = "red"
    </STYLE>
```

You could also use two **with** statements for the style sheet, but with only two statements per group, you don't gain much in the way of code size.

To demonstrate a number of JavaScript style sheet properties being set and used in a document, Example 3-5 is a JavaScript syntax version of the document in Example 3-4. Notice that the HTML portion of the document—notably the usage of **CLASS** and **ID** attributes—is identical for both versions. The only differences are in the style sheet definitions.

Example 3-5. A JavaScript Syntax Version of Example 3-4

```
<HTML>
<HEAD><TITLE>ID Selector</TITLE>
<STYLE TYPE="text/javascript">
with (tags.P) {
    fontSize = "14pt"
    marginLeft = "2em"
    marginRight = "2em"
}
with (classes.narrow.P) {
    color = "red"
    marginLeft= "5em"
    marginRight = "5em"
}
with (ids.special4) {
    borderWidths("5px","5px","5px","5px")
    borderStyle = "ridge"
    borderColor = "red"
}
contextual(classes.narrow.p, tags.EM).fontWeight = "bold"
contextual(classes.narrow.P, tags.EM, tags.SPAN).backgroundColor = "yellow"
tags.BODY.fontFamily = "Times New Roman, serif"
</STYLE>
</HEAD>

<BODY>
<H1>Get a Load of This!</H1>
<P>
This is a normal paragraph. This is a normal paragraph. This is a normal
paragraph. This is a normal paragraph. This is a normal paragraph.
</P>
<P CLASS=narrow ID=special4>This is a <EM>paragraph to be set apart</EM> with
wider margins, red color AND a red border. This is a paragraph to be set apart
with wider margins, red color AND a red border.
</P>
<P>
```

Example 3-5. A JavaScript Syntax Version of Example 3-4 (continued)

```
This is a normal paragraph. This is a normal paragraph. This is a normal
paragraph. This is a normal paragraph. This is a normal paragraph.
</P>
<P CLASS=narrow>This is a <EM>paragraph to be <SPAN>set apart</SPAN></EM> with
wider margins and red color. This is a paragraph to be set apart with wider
margins and red color. This is a paragraph to be set apart with wider margins and
red color.
</P>
</BODY>
</HTML>
```

When viewed in Navigator 4, Example 3-4 and Example 3-5 render absolutely identically. They should, since the two listings are simply using two different syntaxes to control the same underlying style sheet mechanisms in the browser.

Cascade Precedence Rules

By now it should be clear that there are many ways styles can be applied to an element—from an external style sheet file, from a <STYLE> tag set, and from a STYLE attribute in a tag—and there is the possibility that multiple style rules can easily apply to the same element in a document (intentionally or not). To deal with these issues, the CSS recommendation had to devise a set of rules for resolving conflicts among overlapping rules. These rules are intended primarily for the browser (and other user agent) makers, but if you are designing complex style sheets or are seeing unexpected results in a complex document, you need to be aware of how the browser resolves these conflicts for you.

Conflict resolution is mostly a matter of assigning a relative weight to every rule that applies to a particular element. Rules with the most weight are the ones that most specifically target the element. At the lightweight end of the spectrum is the "nonrule," or default style setting for the document, generally governed by the browser's internal design and sometimes influenced by preference settings (e.g., the base font size for text content). Such a "nonrule" may actually apply directly only to a high-level object, such as the BODY element; only by way of inheritance does the default rule apply to some element buried within the content. At the heavyweight end of the spectrum is the style rule that is targeted specifically at a particular element. This may be by way of an ID selector or the ultimate in specificity: a STYLE attribute inside the tag. No rule can override an embedded STYLE attribute.

Between those two extremes are dozens of potential conflicts that depend on the way style sheets are defined for the document. Before rendering any style-sheet-capable element, the browser uses the following decision path to determine how that element should be rendered:

1. Scan the document for any style declarations that have a selector that matches
   the element. If the element is not selected by any rules, short-circuit the rest of
   the decision path and render the element according to the browser's current
   settings.

2. Sort all applicable declarations according to weight as indicated by a special
   !important declaration (see the following section). Declarations marked
   important are assigned greater weight than unmarked declarations. If only one
   declaration bubbles to the top of the order, apply that style to the element and
   short-circuit the rest of the decision path.

3. Sort the applicable declarations again, this time by origin. In today's browsers,
   this simply assigns greater weight to all author-defined declarations than to the
   browser's default or preferences settings.

4. Now sort the applicable declarations by the specificity of the rule's selector.
   The more specific the selector (see the section on selector specificity later in
   this chapter), the greater the weight assigned to that declaration.

5. Finally, if more than one declaration is assigned the same weight after previous sorting, sort one last time based on the order in which the rules are
   defined in the document. The last applicable rule with the greatest weight
   wins the conflict. Rules defined in multiple imported style sheets are defined
   in the order of the statements that trigger the import; a rule defined in a
   <STYLE> tag set comes after any imported style sheet; a rule defined in an element's STYLE attribute is the last and heaviest rule.

Making a Declaration Important

You can give an individual declaration within a rule an extra boost in its battle for
superiority in the cascading order. When you do this to a declaration, the declaration is called the *important* declaration; it is signified by an exclamation mark and
the word important following the declaration. For example, in the following style
sheet, the margin-left attribute for the P element is marked important:

```
<STYLE TYPE="text/css">
    P {font-size:14pt; margin-left:2em ! important; margin-right:2em}
    P.narrow {color:red; margin-left:5em; margin-right:5em}
</STYLE>
```

When the document encounters a <P> tag with a CLASS attribute set to narrow,
the left margin setting of the less specific P tag overrides the setting of the more
specific P.narrow class because of the important declaration. Note that this is an
artificial example because you typically would not include conflicting style rules in
the same style sheet. The important declaration can play a role when a document
imports one or more style sheets. If a generic rule for the specific document must

override a more specific rule in an imported style sheet, the important declaration can influence the cascading order.

NOTE   The important declaration is not implemented in Navigator 4, but does work in Internet Explorer 4.

Determining a Selector's Specificity

The fourth cascading precedence rule refers to the notion of *specificity*, or how well a rule selector targets a particular element in a document. The CSS recommendation establishes a ranking system that assigns values to three categories, arbitrarily designated a, b, and c. These categories represent the counts of items within a rule selector, as follows:

a   The count of ID selectors

b   The count of other selector types

c   The count of elements mentioned by name in the selector

For any rule selector, the browser calculates the counts and then concatenates the values to come up with a specificity value. Table 3-4 displays a sequence of rule selectors in increasing specificity.

Table 3-4. Specificity Ratings for Rule Selectors

Rule Selector	a	b	c	Specificity Rating
EM	0	0	1	1
P EM	0	0	2	2
DIV P EM	0	0	3	3
EM.hot	0	1	1	11
P EM.hot	0	1	2	12
#hotStuff	1	0	0	100

Browsers use the highest applicable specificity rating value to determine which rule wins any conflict. For example, if a style sheet defines the six rules for EM elements shown in Table 3-4 (with the #hotStuff rule being an ID selector), the browser applies the highest relevant specificity rating to each instance of the EM element. For example, an element with the tag <EM CLASS=hot> inside an H1 element most closely matches the EM.hot rule selector (specificity rating of 11), and therefore ignores all other selectors. But if the same EM element is placed inside a P element, the more specific rule selector (P EM.hot) wins.

Cross-Platform Style Differences

Despite the commonality that CSS brings to Navigator and Internet Explorer, there is no guarantee that the visual representation of a particular style will be the same in both browsers. Differences can be attributed to browser bugs, varying interpretations of the standard, and disagreements in design philosophies. Differences can also accrue even among different operating system versions of the same browser.

To demonstrate this point, Figures 3-4, 3-5, and 3-6 show three different renditions of the same CSS-enhanced page (Example 3-4) in Internet Explorer 4 for Windows 95, Navigator 4 for Windows 95, and Navigator 4 for the Macintosh. All browser windows were sized to fill a 640-by-480 monitor, minus the Windows 95 Taskbar and Macintosh menu bar.

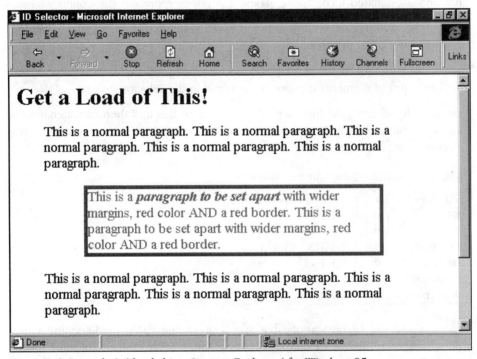

Figure 3-4. Example 3-4 loaded into Internet Explorer 4 for Windows 95

Notice how each browser shows a vastly different quantity of the document, even though a specific font point size is assigned for all paragraph elements. Next, check out how Internet Explorer and Navigator treat default padding between a border and its content: Navigator automatically builds in a three-pixel padding (which cannot be overridden) to keep content away from a border. Another point

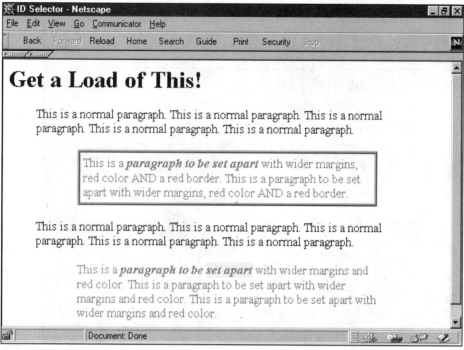

Figure 3-5. Example 3-4 loaded into Navigator 4 for Windows 95

that may not be clearly visible from the figures is that the precise shades and shadowing of the border are different between the two browser brands (detailed galleries are available in the `border-style` section of Chapter 10).

There are some bugs that may bite you from time to time. For example, if you specify a color attribute for an `LI` element inside a `UL` or `OL` element in Navigator 4, only the bullet or number gets the color, not the text for the item. This is a known bug and is detailed in Netscape's release notes for Navigator.

You may also encounter outrageously frustrating anomalous behavior when applying some CSS syntax attributes, especially when elements are nested within one another. With rare exceptions (such as Navigator's built-in padding), it is difficult to predict errant behavior patterns. Different combinations of style attributes, element nesting, and especially positioning specifications (covered in Chapter 4) can make each page design a new challenge. Except where the browser embodies pure buggy behavior (Internet Explorer 4.0 for the Macintosh is particularly troublesome), you should eventually be able to find workarounds to make the Version 4 browsers behave within an acceptable range of compatibility. Just remember, at this stage of style sheet deployment the simpler you make your design, the more likely it is you'll succeed in making it look the same on both browsers.

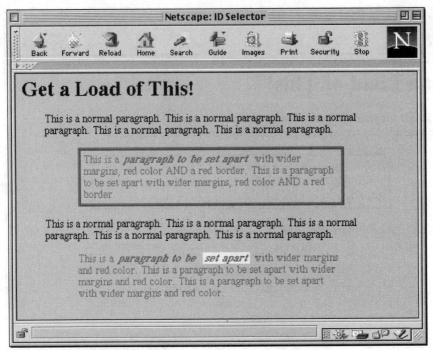

Figure 3-6. Example 3-4 loaded into Navigator 4 for the Macintosh

All these discrepancies point to the fact that deployment of CSS style sheets across all DHTML-capable browsers requires testing on both browser brands and on as many operating systems as you can get your hands on. Carefully study the output on each to make sure that your design goals are met, even if the exact implementation doesn't match pixel for pixel on the screen.

4

Adding Dynamic Positioning to Documents

Cascading style sheets, as described in Chapter 3, *Adding Style Sheets to Documents*, are primarily concerned with how content looks on the screen (or how it looks on a page printed from the screen). An extension to CSS, called CSS-Positioning (or CSS-P), is primarily concerned with where content appears on the page. CSS-P is blended with regular CSS in the CSS2 specification, but because the Version 4 browsers were designed while positioning was a separate standards effort, I use the CSS-P term frequently.

The CSS-P recommendation from the W3C focuses on the HTML code that authors put into documents to govern the position of elements on the page when the browser-controlled flow of content just isn't good enough. To accomplish element positioning, a browser must be able to treat positionable elements as layers[*] that can be dropped anywhere on the page, even overlapping other fixed or positionable elements—something that normal HTML rendering scrupulously avoids.

The notion of layering adds a third dimension to a page, even if a video monitor (or a printed page) is undoubtedly a two-dimensional realm. That third dimension—the layering of elements—is of concern to you as the author of positionable content, but is probably of no concern to the page's human viewer.

---

[*] I use the term "layer" guardedly here. While the word appears in the Netscape DHTML lexicon (Navigator has a `<LAYER>` tag and a scriptable `layer` object), you probably won't see the same word being used by the Microsoft camp. My application of the term is generic and it aptly describes what's going on here: a positionable element is like an acetate layer of a film cartoon cel. The cartoon artist starts with a base layer for the scene's backdrop and then positions one or more acetate layers atop the background; each layer is transparent except for some or all of the art for a single frame of the film. For the next frame of the cartoon, perhaps one of the layers for a character in the background must move a fraction of an inch. The artist repositions that layer, while the others stay the same. That's what I mean by "layer" in this context.

While the CSS-P recommendation offers a cross-platform way to lay out position-able elements, the browsers have extended the idea by turning positionable ele-ments into scriptable objects whose properties can be changed in response to user action. Now you have the opportunity to create some very interactive content: content that flies around the page, hides and shows itself at will, centers itself hori-zontally and vertically in the currently sized browser window, and even lets itself be dragged around the page by the user.

The implementations of positionable elements in Navigator 4 and Internet Explorer 4 are perhaps the most divergent parts of DHTML to grace both browsers. If you have the luxury of designing an application for only one browser platform, you can focus on the implementation for that browser to the exclusion of the other browser's idiosyncrasies. Successful cross-platform development, however, requires knowledge of both browsers' object models (at least as they relate to positionable elements) and the range of DHTML authoring capabilities in both browsers. As you will see in this chapter, there is a common denominator of func-tionality, but it is often up to you to raise the level of commonality in order to get a highly interactive page to work identically in both browsers.

Creating Positionable Elements

Regardless of browser, you can make any HTML container element (an element with a start and end tag) a positionable element. As a ridiculous example of how true the preceding statement is, you could direct a browser to render a word sur-rounded by <B>/</B> tags at a position that is 236 pixels below its normal place in a paragraph (but why would you?).

CSS-P Elements

To turn an HTML element into a positionable element that works in both Naviga-tor 4 and Internet Explorer 4, you must assign it a CSS style rule that has a special attribute: position. As demonstrated in Chapter 3, you can assign this style attribute by including a STYLE attribute in the actual HTML tag or using an ID selector for the rule and setting the corresponding ID attribute in the element's HTML tag.

The following HTML document demonstrates the two techniques you can use to turn an element into a positionable element:

```
<HTML>
<HEAD>
<STYLE TYPE="text/css">
    #someSpan {position:absolute; left:10; top:30}
</STYLE>
</HEAD>
<BODY>
```

```
<DIV ID="someDiv" STYLE="position:absolute; left:100; top:50">
Hello.
<SPAN ID="someSpan">
Hello, again.
</SPAN>
</DIV>
</BODY>
</HTML>
```

The first technique defines an ID selector inside a `<STYLE>` tag that is mated to an ID attribute of a `SPAN` element in the document's body. The second method defines the style as an inline attribute of a `<DIV>` tag. As with ordinary CSS style sheets, you can use any combination of methodologies to apply position style rules to elements in a document.

Once you have set the `position` attribute, you can set other CSS-P attributes, such as `left` and `top`, to position the element. Possible values for the `position` attribute are:

`absolute`
Element becomes a block element and is positionable relative to the element's positioning context.

`relative`
Element maintains its normal position in element geography (unless you override it) and establishes a positioning context for nested items.

`static`
Item is not positionable and maintains its normal position in element geography (default value).

Absolute Versus Relative Positioning

The `position` attribute terminology can be confusing because the coordinate system used to place an element depends on the *positioning context* of the element, rather than on a universally absolute or relative coordinate system. A positioning context defines a point somewhere on the screen that is coordinate point 0,0. The most basic positioning context is the invisible box created by virtue of the `<HTML>` tag set of the document, corresponding to the `BODY` element. In other words, the entire (scrollable, if necessary) space of the browser window or frame that displays the content of the document is the default positioning context. The 0,0 coordinate point for the default positioning context is the upper left corner of the window or frame. You can position an element within this context by setting the position attribute to `absolute` and assigning values to the `left` and `top` attributes of the style rule:

```
<DIV ID="someDiv" STYLE="position:absolute; left:50; top:100">
Hello. And now it's time to say goodbye.
</DIV>
```

Figure 4-1 shows how this simple block-level element appears in a browser window.

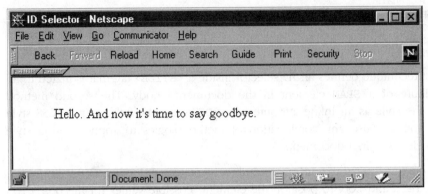

Figure 4-1. An element positioned within the default positioning context

Each time an element is positioned, it spawns a new positioning context with the 0,0 position located at the top left corner of that element. Therefore, if we insert a positioned element in the previous example nested within the DIV element that forms the new positioning context, the newly inserted element lives in the new context. In the following example, we insert a SPAN element inside the DIV element. Positioning attributes for the SPAN element place it 10 pixels in from the left and 30 pixels down from the top of its positioning context—the DIV element in this case:

```
<DIV ID="someDiv" STYLE="position:absolute; left:100; top:50">
Hello.
<SPAN ID="someSpan" STYLE="position:absolute; left:10; top:30">
Hello, again.
</SPAN>
And now it's time to say goodbye.
</DIV>
```

Figure 4-2 shows the results; note how the DIV element's positioning context governs the SPAN element's location on the page.

Notice in the code listing that the **position** attribute for each element is **absolute**, even though you might say that the nested SPAN element is positioned relative to its parent element. Now you see why the terminology gets confusing. The absolute positioning of the SPAN element removes that element from the document's content flow entirely. The split content of the parent DIV element closes up, as if the content of the SPAN element wasn't there. But the SPAN element *is* in the document—in its own plane and shifted into a position within the DIV element's positioning context. All other parent-child relationships of the DIV and SPAN elements remain intact (style sheet rule inheritance, for instance), but physically on the page, the two elements appear to be disconnected.

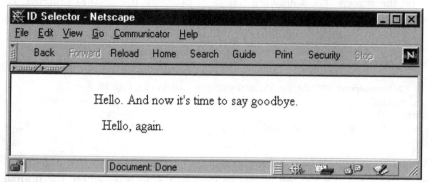

Figure 4-2. A second element nested inside another

The true meaning of relative positioning can be difficult to visualize because experiments with the combination of absolute and relative positioning often yield bewildering results. Whereas an absolute-positioned element adopts the positioning context of its HTML element parent, a relative-positioned element adopts the positioning context of the element's normal (unpositioned) location within the document's content flow. A sequence of modifications to some content should help demonstrate these concepts.

To begin, here is a fragment with a single absolute-positioned DIV element that contains three sentences:

```
<DIV ID="someDiv" STYLE="position:absolute; left:100; top:50">
Hello.
Hello, again.
And now it's time to say goodbye.
</DIV>
```

This code generates a simple line of text on the page, as shown in Figure 4-3.

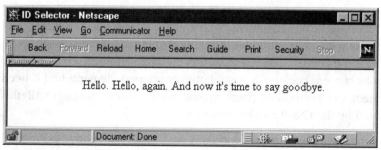

Figure 4-3. A simple three-sentence DIV element

Pay special attention to the location of the middle sentence as it flows in normal HTML. Now, if that second sentence is made into a relative-positioned SPAN element supplied with some offset (left and top) values, something quite unusual happens on the screen. The following fragment positions the second sentence 10 pixels in from the left and 30 pixels down from the top of *some* positioning context:

```
<DIV ID="someDiv" STYLE="position:absolute; left:100; top:50">
Hello.
<SPAN ID="someSpan" STYLE="position:relative; left:10; top:30">
Hello, again.
</SPAN>
And now it's time to say goodbye.
</DIV>
```

But what is that context? With a relative-positioned element, the anchor point of its positioning context is the top left corner of the place (the box) where the normal flow of the content would go. Therefore, by setting the `left` and `top` attributes of a relative-positioned element, as in the previous code fragment, you instruct the browser to offset the content relative to its normal location. You can see the results in Figure 4-4.

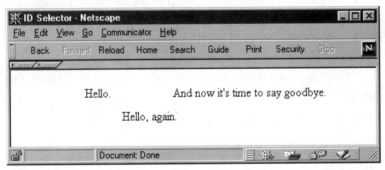

Figure 4-4. The relative-positioned element generates its own positioning context

Note how the middle sentence is shifted within the context of its normal flow location. The positioning context established by the relative-positioned element is now available for positioning of other elements (most likely as absolute-positioned elements) that you may wish to insert within the `<SPAN>` tag pair. Take special notice in Figure 4-4 that the browser does not close up the space normally occupied by the SPAN element's content because it is a relative-positioned element; had it been absolute-positioned, the surrounding text would have closed the gap. All this behavior is dictated by the CSS-P recommendation.

In most cases, you don't assign values for `left` and `top` to a relative-positioned element because you want to use a relative-positioned element to create a positioning context for more deeply nested elements that are absolutely positioned within that context. Using this technique, regular content flows according to the browser window's current size or as its appearance is affected by style rules, while elements that must be positioned relative to some running content are always positioned properly.

To demonstrate this concept, consider the following fragment that produces a long string of one-word sentences. The goal is to have the final sentence always appear aligned with the final period of the last "Hello" and 20 pixels down. This means that the final sentence needs to be positioned within a context created for the final period of the last "Hello." In other words, the period character must be defined as a relative-positioned element, so that the nested SPAN element can be positioned absolutely with respect to the period. The following code shows how it's done:

```
<DIV ID="someDiv" STYLE="position:absolute; left:100; top:50">Hello. Hello.
Hello. Hello. Hello. Hello. Hello. Hello. Hello. Hello. Hello. Hello.
Hello. Hello. Hello<SPAN ID="someSpan" STYLE="position:relative">.
<SPAN ID="anotherSpan" STYLE="position:absolute; top:20">
And now it's time to say goodbye.
</SPAN>
</SPAN>
</DIV>
```

Carefully observe the nesting of the elements in the previous example. Figure 4-5 shows the results in a small browser window.

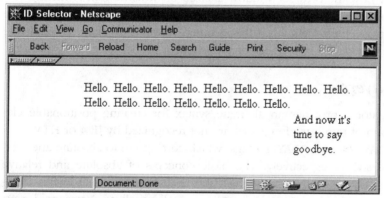

Figure 4-5. A relative-positioned element creates a positioning context for another element

If you resize the browser window so that the final "Hello" appears on another line or in another vertical position on the page, the final sentence moves so that it always starts 20 pixels and just to the right of the period of the final "Hello" of the content. When applied in this fashion, the term "relative positioning" makes perfect sense.

Overlapping Versus Wrapping Elements

One of the advantages of CSS-Positioning is that you can set an absolute position for any element along both the horizontal and vertical axes as well as its position in stacking order—the third dimension. This makes it possible for more than one element to occupy the same pixel on the page, if you so desire. It is also important to remember that absolute-positioned elements exist independently of the surrounding content of the document. In other words, if a script shifts the position of such an element, the surrounding content does not automatically wrap itself around the new position of the element.

If your design calls for the content of an element to wrap around another element, you should use the CSS `float` attribute, rather than CSS-Positioning. Properties of the `float` attribute let you affix an element at the left or right margin of a containing block element and at a specific location within the running content. For example, if you want to place an image in the middle of a paragraph, you wrap that image element inside a SPAN element whose style sets the `float` attribute, as follows:

```
<P>Lots of text.
<SPAN STYLE="float:right; width:120">
<IMG SRC="myImg.gif" HEIGHT=90 WIDTH=120>
</SPAN>
And more text.</P>
```

Now, no matter how the browser window is sized or how the font rendering varies from platform to platform, the text in the paragraph always wraps around the image. A floating element defined in this manner, however, is not a positionable element in that you cannot script positionable element properties of such an item.

Netscape Layers

Netscape Navigator 4 provides an alternate syntax for creating positionable elements in the form of two sets of tags that are not recognized by IE 4 or HTML 4.0. They are the <LAYER> and <ILAYER> tags, which correspond to absolute and relative positioning styles, respectively. The basic concepts of absolute and relative positioning from CSS-P apply to these tags, so the discussion earlier in this chapter about the two positioning styles applies equally well to Netscape layers. Because you use HTML tags to generate these elements, attributes are set like regular HTML attributes (*attributeName="value"*), rather than with the CSS-style rule syntax (*attributeName:value*).

The <LAYER> tag generates an element that can be absolute-positioned within the positioning context of the next outer layer (or the base document if that's the next outer layer). The following code fragment from the body of a document generates the same content shown earlier in Figure 4-2:

```
<LAYER NAME="someLayer" LEFT=100 TOP=50>
Hello.
<LAYER NAME="anotherLayer" LEFT=10 TOP=30>
Hello, again.
</LAYER>
And now it's time to say goodbye.
</LAYER>
```

The inner layer (`anotherLayer`) is absolute-positioned relative to the next outer layer (`someLayer`). That outer layer is absolute-positioned relative to the default positioning context of the document.

In the following fragment, the inner layer is changed to be a relative-positioned element by using the `<ILAYER>` tag (inline layer):

```
<LAYER NAME="someLayer" LEFT=100 TOP=50>
Hello.
<ILAYER NAME="inLineLayer" LEFT=10 TOP=30>
Hello, again.
</ILAYER>
And now it's time to say goodbye.
</LAYER>
```

The `<ILAYER>` tag lets you designate a piece of running content that has its own positioning context. In this case, the `<ILAYER>` content is positioned within that context, leaving a gap in the running content, as shown earlier in Figure 4-4.

A more practical application of the `<ILAYER>` tag is to use it to set a positioning context for further nested absolute-positioned layers. Thus, in the following code fragment, an `<ILAYER>` is applied to the final period of the outer layer. The `<LAYER>` tag nested inside the `<ILAYER>` tag obeys the positioning context of that inline layer, such that the final content tracks the location of the period regardless of normal content wrapping, as shown earlier in Figure 4-5:

```
<LAYER ID="someLayer" LEFT=100 TOP=50>Hello. Hello. Hello.
Hello. Hello. Hello. Hello. Hello. Hello. Hello. Hello. Hello. Hello. Hello.
Hello. Hello<ILAYER NAME="inLineLayer">.
<LAYER NAME="anotherLayer" TOP=20>
And now it's time to say goodbye.
</LAYER>
</ILAYER>
</LAYER>
```

There is more to the Netscape layer than its simply being an alternative syntax to CSS-Positioning. Each `layer` and inline `layer` object can have external content associated with it (via an `SRC` attribute, as documented in Chapter 8, *HTML Reference*). In fact, in the document object model for Navigator 4, each `layer` object contains its own `document` object, which a script can manipulate like any `document` object. This object model is vastly different from the one Internet Explorer 4 uses for positionable objects, so when it comes to writing scripts that reference positionable objects, the situation gets a bit gnarly, as described later.

One other point about the relationship between Netscape layers and CSS-P objects is that Navigator automatically converts CSS-P objects into layers for the object model of the currently loaded document. For example, the following document defines one positionable element in CSS-P syntax:

```
<HTML>
<HEAD>
```

```
</HEAD>
<BODY>
<DIV STYLE="position:absolute; left:100; top:50">
Hello.
</DIV>
</BODY>
</HTML>
```

Navigator 4's object model treats the DIV element as a layer; "Hello." is the content of the layer's document object. Therefore, while Navigator's scripting environment works only with layer objects for controlling positioning, you have the same level of scriptability whether a positionable element is defined as a Navigator layer or as a CSS-P element.

Positioning Attributes

The CSS-Positioning recommendation specifies several properties that can be set as style sheet rule attributes. These attributes are used only when the position attribute is included in the rule; otherwise they have no meaning. Implementation of all the CSS-P attributes varies from browser to browser. Table 4-1 provides a summary of all the attributes defined in the W3C recommendation as well as how those attributes are implemented in the browsers. A separate column shows the Navigator <LAYER> tag attribute that corresponds to the CSS-P attribute.

Table 4-1. Summary of Positioning Attributes

CSS Attribute	Description	CSS-P	IE	NN	Layer Attribute
position	Defines a style rule as being for a positionable element	1	4	4	–
left	The offset distance from the left edge of the element's positioning context to the left edge of the element's box	1	4	4	LEFT
top	The offset distance from the top edge of the element's positioning context to the top edge of the element's box	1	4	4	TOP
width	The width of an absolute-positioned element's content	1	4	4	WIDTH
height	The height of an absolute-positioned element's content	1	4	4	HEIGHT
clip	The shape and dimension of the viewable area of an absolute-positioned element	1	4	4	CLIP
overflow	How to handle content that exceeds its height/width settings	1	4	4	–
visibility	Whether a positionable element is visible or not	1	4	4	VISIBILITY
z-index	The stacking order of a positionable element	1	4	4	Z-INDEX

The implementation of these positioning attributes is not completely identical in both Version 4 browsers, but there is a large degree of compatibility, with the exception of the `clip` and `overflow` attributes.

left, top, height, and width Attributes

Four attributes deal with lengths, whether they are for positioning of the element or determining its physical dimensions on the page. Recall from Chapter 3 (Figure 3-2) that `height` and `width` refer to the size of the content, exclusive of any padding, borders, or margins assigned to the element. The `left` and `top` values, however, apply to the location of the box edges (content + padding + border + margin). When using the CSS syntax, each of these four attributes can be specified as a fixed length or a percentage. Fixed-length units are borrowed from the CSS specification, as shown in Table 4-2. Percentage values are specified with an optional + or – symbol, a number, and a `%` symbol. Percentage values are applied to the parent element's value.

Table 4-2. Length Value Units (CSS and CSS-P)

Length Unit	Example	Description
em	1.5em	Element's font height
ex	1ex	Element's font x-height
px	14px	Pixel (precise length is depends on the display device)
in	0.75in	Inch (absolute measure)
cm	5cm	Centimeter (absolute measure)
mm	55mm	Millimeter (absolute measure)
pt	10pt	Point (equal to 1/72 of an inch)
pc	1.5pc	Pica (equivalent to 12 points)

The length unit you choose should be based on the primary output device for the document. Most HTML pages are designed for output solely on a video display, so the pixel unit is most commonly used for length measures. But if you intend your output to be printed, you may obtain more accurate placement and relative alignment of elements if you use one of the absolute units: inch, centimeter, millimeter, point, or pica. Print quality also depends on the quality of the printing engine built into the browser.

For attributes of the `<LAYER>` tag that correspond to the CSS attributes, the values you assign do not include units. All measurements are in pixels.

Navigator 4 and Internet Explorer 4 also disagree on how to render certain types of block elements, as described at the end of Chapter 3. Navigator closes up the height of a block around its content, regardless of the `height` setting of the element. Moreover, any content, such as text, an image, or even a solid background color, is inset from the edges of the element by a forced padding of about three pixels that cannot be removed. On the other hand, if you define a positionable object via the <LAYER> tag in Navigator, these problems disappear, and the width and height attributes truly set the size of the block element.

The clip Attribute

A clipping region is a geometric area (currently limited to rectangles) through which you can see a positioned element's content. For example, if you include an image in a document, but want only a small rectangular segment of the whole image to appear, you can set the clip attribute of the element to limit the viewable area of the image to that smaller rectangle. It is important to remember that the element does not shrink in overall size for the purposes of document flow, but any area that is beyond the clipping rectangle becomes transparent, allowing elements below it in the stacking to show through. If you want to position the viewable, clipped region so that it appears without a transparent border, you must position the entire element (whose top left corner still governs the element's position in the grid). Similarly, because the clipping region encompasses viewable items such as borders, you must nest a clipped image inside another element that sets its own border.

Figure 4-6 demonstrates (in three stages) the concept of a clipping region relative to an image. It also shows how positioning a clipped view requires setting the location of the element based on the element's original size.

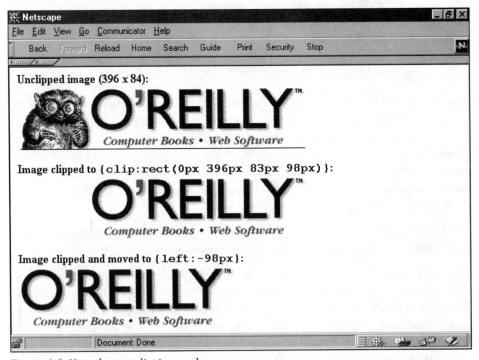

Figure 4-6. How element clipping works

Setting the values for a clip region requires slightly different thinking from how you might otherwise describe the points of an rectangle. The `clip` attribute includes a shape and four numeric values in the sequence of top, right, bottom, left—the same clockwise sequence used by CSS to assign values to edge-related attributes (borders, padding, and margins) of block-level elements. Moreover, the values are entered as a space-delimited sequence of values in this format:

```
clip:rect(top right bottom left)
```

In Figure 4-6, the goal is to crop out the critter from the image and align the clipped image to the left. The original image (396 by 84 pixels) is at the top. To trim the critter requires bringing in the left clip edge 98 pixels. The bottom, one-pixel rule is also clipped:

```
<SPAN STYLE="position:absolute; clip:rect(0px 396px 83px 98px)">
<IMG SRC="oraImage.gif" HEIGHT=84 WIDTH=396>
</SPAN>
```

Then, to reposition this image so that the clipped area abuts the left edge of its positioning context, the style rule for the element must assign a negative value to take up the slack of the now blank space:

```
<SPAN STYLE="position:absolute; left:-98px; clip:rect(0px 396px 83px 98px)">
<IMG SRC="oraImage.gif" HEIGHT=84 WIDTH=396>
</SPAN>
```

The overflow Attribute

If you define a fixed width and height for a relative- or absolute-positioned element, you can tell the browser how to handle content that extends beyond the physical dimensions of the element block. While the `overflow` attribute is defined to help in this regard, unfortunately the implementation of this attribute is not the same in Navigator 4 and Internet Explorer 4. Consider the following document fragment that affects how much of the upper left corner of an image appears in the browser window:

```
<SPAN STYLE="position:relative; width:50; height:50">
<IMG SRC="myImage.gif" HEIGHT=90 WIDTH=120>
</SPAN>
```

In the previous example, even though the `width` and `height` style attributes are set for a SPAN wrapper around an image, the natural width and height of the image force both browsers to show every pixel of the image. In other words, the content overflows the edges of the block containing the image. By adding an `overflow` attribute and value to the style rule, you can instruct the browser to cut the view at the edges of the block defined by the style rule:

```
<SPAN STYLE="position:relative; width:50; height:50; overflow:hidden">
<IMG SRC="myImage.gif" HEIGHT=90 WIDTH=120>
</SPAN>
```

Thus, any content (between the <SPAN> and </SPAN> tag pair) is clipped to the size of the SPAN element's box. Navigator 4, however, exhibits slightly different behavior in that the horizontal dimension is never clipped by the overflow attribute. In the preceding example, the visible portion of the image is 50 pixels square in Internet Explorer 4 and 120 pixels wide by 50 pixels high in Navigator 4. If you truly want to clip the view of any content, it is best to use the clip attribute (described in the previous section) to set the viewing boundaries of content.

Internet Explorer also supports an optional CSS-P recommendation for setting the overflow attribute to scroll. This setting automatically displays scrollbars (a full set, unfortunately) inside the clipped rectangle defined by the positioned element's height and width attributes. Content is clipped to the remaining visible space; the user clicks or drags the scrollbars to maneuver through the content (image or text). This attribute setting is not available in Navigator 4.

The visibility Attribute

The purpose of the visibility attribute is obvious: it makes an element visible or hidden. Unless the element is under script control, however, it is unlikely that you would bother setting the attribute's value (to inherit, visible, or hidden). There is rarely a need to load a normally visible HTML element into a page as hidden, unless you also have a script that changes its state as the user visits the page—perhaps in response to mouse clicks or a timed event.

It is, however, important to understand the difference between setting a positionable element's visibility attribute and setting the CSS display attribute to none. When a positionable element is set to be hidden, the space occupied by the element—whether it be a position in the stacking order or the location for flowed content set off as a relative-positioned element—does not go away. If you hide a relative-positioned element that happens to be an emphasized chunk of text within a sentence, the rest of the sentence text does not close up when the positioned portion is hidden.

In contrast, if you set the CSS attribute of an element to display:none, this tells the browser to ignore the element as it flows the document. Navigator 4 does not have a scriptable property to correspond to the display style attribute, so you cannot modify this property on the fly (although Navigator does recognize the display attribute when a page loads). But in Internet Explorer 4, you can change the display property on the fly under script control. When you do, the content automatically reflows, closing up any gap left by the "undisplayed" element. This is how some DHTML-driven collapsible menus are created and controlled.

The z-index Attribute

Positioned elements can overlap each other. While overlapping text doesn't usu-ally make for a good page design, overlapping opaque elements, such as images and blocks with backgrounds, can be put to good use, particularly when the ele-ments are under script control. The `z-index` attribute lets you direct the stacking order (also called the z-order, where Z stands for the third dimension, after X and Y) of elements within a positioning context. The higher the z-index value (values are integers), the closer the element layer is to the user's eye.

Positioned elements—even if their `z-index` attributes are not specified in their style rules—exist as a group in a plane closer to the user's eye than nonposi-tioned content. The notable exception to this is Navigator 4's belief that any form element (positioned or otherwise) should exist in a plane in front of positioned elements, regardless of z-index setting. In other words, you cannot obscure a form element behind a positioned element in Navigator 4.

If you do not specify the `z-index` attribute for any positioned elements in a docu-ment, the default stacking order is based on the sequence in which the positioned elements are defined in the HTML source code. Even so, these positioned items are in front of nonpositioned items (except form elements in Navigator 4). There-fore, you need to specify z-index values only when the desired stacking order is other than the natural sequence of elements in the source code.

More commonly, z-index values are adjusted by scripts when a user interacts with maneuverable content (by dragging or resizing), or when a script moves an ele-ment as a form of animation. For example, if your page allows dragging of ele-ments (perhaps an image acting as a piece of a jigsaw puzzle), it may be valuable to set the `z-index` attribute of that element to an arbitrarily high value as the user drags the image. This keeps the image in front of all other positionable puzzle pieces while being dragged (so it doesn't "submarine" and get lost behind other elements). When the user releases the piece, you can reset the `z-index` attribute to, say, zero to move it back among the pool of other inactive positioned ele-ments.

You cannot interleave elements that belong to different positioning contexts. This is because z-index values are relative only to sibling elements. For example, imag-ine you have two positioned `DIV` elements named `Div1` and `Div2` (see Figure 4-7). `Div1` contains two positioned `SPAN` elements; `Div2` contains three positioned `SPAN` elements. A script can adjust the z-index values of the elements in `Div1` all they want, but the two elements are always kept together; similarly the three elements in `Div2` are always "contiguous" in their stacking order. If you swap the z-index values of `Div1` and `Div2`, the group of elements contained by each `DIV` swaps positions as well.

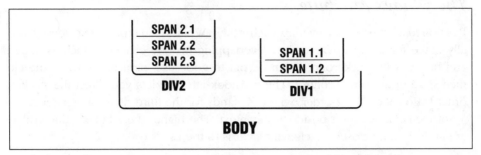

Figure 4-7. Stacking order is relative to the positioning context of the element

Changing Attribute Values via Scripting

Despite the similarity of the Version 4 browsers' support for defining positionable elements, the two browsers diverge widely in how you control attribute values from a script. The primary differences can be attributed to the way each browser implements its document object model. When these browser versions were released in 1997, the DOM standardization effort was only at the earliest stages in defining the requirements for such a standard. As a result, each browser company extended its object model from its previous version along clashing philosophical lines. The level of compatibility is fairly low, but the regular nature of both object models makes it possible to raise that compatibility level to embed sophisticated DHTML capabilities for both browsers in the same document.

Referencing Positionable Objects

In comparing the document object models of the two browsers, it is clear that Internet Explorer 4 went to extremes to make virtually every HTML element a scriptable object. Navigator 4, on the other hand, restricts access to element properties by making them read-only except when being set inside JavaScript-syntax style sheet rules. The first piece of the cross-browser positioning puzzle involves referring to the positionable elements in a document.

Navigator 4 references

For controlling positionable element properties on the fly, Navigator uses its `layer` object model to supply a wide range of methods and directly settable properties for adjusting an element's location, size, z-index, and visibility: the family of CSS-P attributes. Because Navigator internally turns a CSS-P element into a `layer` object, you use the same mechanism to manipulate positionable elements, whether they are created with CSS-P or the `<LAYER>` tag.

NOTE	Netscape doesn't like to use the term *layer object* when referring to positionable elements. The company's official wording is "accessing style sheet properties from JavaScript via the Document Object Model." This implies a Document Object Model standard, which didn't exist when this wording was created. Also, it's nearly impossible to refer to these objects in a Navigator context without using the word "layer," since, as you will see, the word can become part of a reference to a positionable object. It's like someone introducing himself as: "Hi, my name is Fred, but please call me Alice." This book uses layer object when referring to an object that uses the properties, methods, and event handlers of Navigator's explicitly named `layer` object (see Chapter 9, *Document Object Reference*).

Building a reference to a `layer` object requires knowledge of the containment hierarchy of the element within the document. This is because Navigator 4 does not provide a shortcut referencing mechanism that can dive through all nested elements of a document and pick one out by name. Instead, the reference must represent the containment hierarchy starting with the base `document` object. Moreover, recall that a layer always contains a document. For one layer to contain another means that the outer layer contains a document, which, in turn, contains the nested layer. These relationships must be reflected in a reference to a `layer` object.

As an example of a one-layer-deep reference, consider the following code:

```
<HTML>
<BODY>
<DIV STYLE="position:absolute; left:20; top:20">
    <IMG SRC="myImage.gif" HEIGHT=90 WIDTH=120>
</DIV>
</BODY>
</HTML>
```

To access one of the position style attributes, you must build a reference that specifies the hierarchical path to the layer in the document. Here's how to set the `left` property to a different value:

```
document.layers[0].left = 50
```

Navigator reflects the `ID` attribute of a CSS-P element as the layer's `name` property. If you assign an `ID` attribute to the `DIV` element, you can use that name in the reference:

```
document.myLayer.left = 50
```

To access the content of the `layer` object, you must extend the reference hierarchy to include the document contained by the layer. For example, to change the image source file in the preceding example, the statement is:

```
document.layers[0].document.images[0].src = "otherImage.gif"
```

Once the reference reaches the document holding the content, regular Navigator document object model references take over, as shown earlier by the reference to the `image` object and its `src` property.

The situation gets more complex when there are two nested levels of positionable elements. In the following example, a `SPAN` element defines a relative-positioned grid for the absolute-positioned `DIV` element that contains an image:

```
<HTML>
<BODY>
Here's an image
<SPAN ID="outer" STYLE="position:relative">:
    <DIV ID="inner" STYLE="position:absolute; left:5; top:3">
        <IMG SRC="myImage.gif" HEIGHT=90 WIDTH=120>
    </DIV>
</SPAN>
</BODY>
</HTML>
```

To change the `left` property of the DIV element, the reference becomes:

```
document.layers[0].document.layers[0].left = 10
```

And to change a property of the deeply nested content, the reference gets quite long:

```
document.layers[0].document.layers[0].document.images[0].src = "otherImage.gif"
```

When scripting deeply nested items such as this, your script statements will be more manageable if you set a variable to represent an object level somewhere down the containment hierarchy. For example, if you must refer to the inner layer and its content in two or more statements, initialize a variable to represent the inner layer. Then use that variable to simplify references to specific properties or document objects:

```
var innerDiv = document.layers[0].document.layers[0]
innerDiv.left = 10
innerDiv.document.images[0].src = "otherImage.gif"
```

Assigning ID attributes to elements also assists in making long references more readable, since it is easier to determine which objects from the document are being referenced:

```
document.outer.document.inner.document.images[0].src = "otherImage.gif
```

Even though you assign unique names to positioned and nested elements, Navigator 4's object model has no instant way to slice through the hierarchy to reach such a nested element.

Internet Explorer 4 references

Internet Explorer 4 provides a syntax for pinpointing any uniquely named (via the ID attribute) element in a document (positioned or not). The keyword that makes it possible is `all`. This keyword represents a collection of all HTML elements in a document; it is a property of the base `document` object. Another important distinction between browser object models is that each positionable element in IE 4 does not have its own `document` object (except for the `IFRAME` element, which defines a new `frame` object within the current document). Therefore, objects that are normally reflected as *collections* (Microsoft's way of describing arrays of objects, such as `images`, `applets`, and `links`) are referenced directly from the base document, rather than through an element hierarchy.

Style sheet rules, including those that affect positioning attributes, are accessible through a `style` property of an element. So, while an element may have some of its own properties that are accessible directly (such as the `innerHTML` property), in order to read or modify one of the style sheet rules associated with the element, you must include a reference to the `style` property.

To demonstrate how references work in IE 4, consider the following simple document with a `DIV` element nested inside and a `SPAN` element:

```
<HTML>
<BODY>
Here's an image
<SPAN ID="outer" STYLE="position:relative">:
    <DIV ID="inner" STYLE="position:absolute; left:5; top:3">
        <IMG SRC="myImage.gif" HEIGHT=90 WIDTH=120>
    </DIV>
</SPAN>
</BODY>
</HTML>
```

References to the three items influenced by positioning are as follows:

```
document.all.outer
document.all.inner
document.images[0]
```

If you want to access one of the style sheet properties, the reference gets a little longer, to include the `style` property of the positioned element:

```
document.all.inner.style.pixelLeft = 10
```

And yet, to change a property of even the deeply nested `image` object, the reference is a simple one:

```
document.images[0].src = "otherImage.gif"
```

Positionable Element Properties

The next piece of the cross-browser positioning puzzle involves the actual property names. Table 4-3 shows the primary properties that control a positionable element's location, size, visibility, z-order, and background (many of which mirror

CSS-P attributes). For Navigator 4, these properties belong to the `layer` object; for IE 4, these properties belong to the `style` object.

Table 4-3. Common Scriptable Positioning Properties

NN Layer Property	Notes	IE Style Property
`left`	The offset in pixels from the left edge of the current positioning context. The IE 4 `style` object has a `left` property, but the value is a string with the unit of measure (e.g., `"20px"`). So, to manipulate the value of the `left` property in IE 4, you should use the `pixelLeft` property.	`pixelLeft`
`top`	The offset in pixels from the top edge of the current positioning context. The same situation applies here as with the `left` versus `pixelLeft` property in IE 4.	`pixelTop`
`clip.height`	The height (in pixels) of the displayed content, including overflow.	–
`clip.width`	The width (in pixels) of the displayed content, including overflow.	–
–	The width (in current units) of the element, as directed by the CSS `width` attribute.	`posWidth`
–	The height (in current units) of the element, as directed by the CSS `height` attribute.	`posHeight`
`visibility`	The `layer` object returns one of `"show"`, `"hide"`, or `"inherit"`; the `style` object returns one of the CSS-P standard values of `"visible"`, `"hidden"`, or `"inherit"`. But the `layer` object property can be set to the standard property values without complaint.	`visibility`
`zIndex`	The stacking order of the element. There is complete agreement between the two browsers with regard to this property.	`zIndex`
`background`	The URL of a background image.	`background`
`bgColor`	The background color of the element. Although the browsers use different property names, they use the same color values, including Netscape plain-language names.	`backgroundColor`

Navigator 4 generally assigns default values to positionable object properties, even if the style rule (or `<LAYER>` tag) does not specifically set the corresponding attribute values. Internet Explorer 4 tends to leave properties empty if the associated style attributes are not set in the rule.

Layer Object Methods

The third and final piece of the cross-browser positioning puzzle concerns the techniques you use to alter the positionable properties. The Internet Explorer 4 `style` object is heavy on properties, but very light on methods. Aside from two generic methods that get and set style attributes (`getAttribute()` and `setAttribute()`), there are no facilities for directly influencing object behavior with methods. Navigator 4's `layer` object, on the other hand, provides eight methods that you can use to efficiently change the location, size, and stacking order of an element.

The `layer.moveBy()` method demonstrates just how efficient these methods are. The method takes two parameters that specify the number of pixels to move an element along the X and Y axes. Positive values indicate movement to the right and downward; negative values direct movement to the left and upward. Thus, to repeatedly move an object diagonally to the right and down, in 5 incremental steps of 10 pixels each, you can use the following `for` loop in JavaScript:

```
for (var i = 0; i < 5; i++) {
    document.layers[0].moveBy(10, 10)
}
```

Doing this same action with an Internet Explorer 4 positionable element requires adjusting each property that controls the pixel location of the element:

```
for (var i = 0; i < 5; i++) {
    document.all.elementName.style.pixelLeft += 10
    document.all.elementName.style.pixelTop += 10
}
```

Despite what might appear to be stair-stepped action in IE 4, the browser buffers the changes so that the animation appears in the straight line intended by the author.

The full set of Netscape layer methods consists of the following items:

- `load("`*filename*`", `*y*`)`
- `moveAbove(`*layerObj*`)`
- `moveBelow(`*layerObj*`)`
- `moveBy(`*deltaX, deltaY*`)`
- `moveTo(`*x, y*`)`
- `moveToAbsolute(`*x, y*`)`
- `resizeBy(`*deltaX, deltaY*`)`
- `resizeTo(`*width, height*`)`

Not every method has a scriptable property equivalent in IE 4 because the object and rendering models vary in some key places, such as specifying the viewable size of a positionable element. Mastering one platform's way of scripting positionable elements may mean having to "unlearn" or ignore items that don't have a cross-platform equivalent.

Cross-Platform Position Scripting

Reconciling the differences between the object and rendering models of Navigator 4 and Internet Explorer 4 is one of the biggest challenges you face if you want to script positionable elements for both platforms in the same HTML document. The key factors to take into account are:

- How to address positionable elements when the object references are so vastly different

- How to make adjustments to differently named properties in a truly interactive and dynamic environment

You cannot avoid having your scripts branch to execute platform-specific statements. What you must decide for your application is how and where the branching occurs. There are three basic techniques you can use to implement cross-platform position scripting in a document:

- Explicit branching
- Platform-equivalent referencing
- Custom APIs

Explicit branching and platform-equivalent referencing place the branching code directly in your scripts. For a limited amount of scripted positioning, having all the branching code in your scripts is manageable and actually easier to debug. But if you are doing a serious amounts of scripted positioning, a custom API lets you push the ugly branching code off to the side in an external library. In essence, you create a meta-language that gives you control over the specific syntax used in both browsers. A custom API requires a lot more work up front, but once the API code is debugged, the API simplifies not only the current scripting job, but any subsequent pages that need the same level of scriptability.

Browser Flags

Regardless of the approach you take, you will need to set up global variable Boolean flags (JavaScript global variables scope only within the current document) that indicate which browser is running the script. In the same code that establishes those variables, you should include code that redirects browsers not capable of rendering positionable elements to another page that explains the browser requirements. Unlike pages that use regular style sheets, which generally degrade acceptably for older browsers, pages with positioned elements fare very poorly when viewed with older browsers, especially if the intended design includes overlapping and/or hidden elements.

JavaScript provides many ways to set browser flags. Some of the variation depends on how granular you want the detection to be. Browser detection can get down to the x.0x version, if a particular feature you use is buggy in earlier releases. You must also decide if detection only needs to find a floor for compatibility (e.g., Version 4 or later) or should be restricted to one generation of browser only.

Browser makers have been pretty good about maintaining backward compatibility for browsers. Therefore, it is generally safe to let the browser detection script set the flag when the browser version is greater than or equal to the minimum version you need for your application. This technique lets the page you write today run tomorrow on the next major release of the browser. Example 4-1 shows a script sequence that should run as a page loads, to set flags arbitrarily named isNav and isIE; the script also redirects older browsers to another page.

Example 4-1. A JavaScript Browser Detection Script

```
var isNav, isIE
if (parseInt(navigator.appVersion) >= 4) {
    if (navigator.appName == "Netscape") {
        isNav = true
    } else {
        isIE = true
    }
}
if (!isNav && !isIE) {
    top.location.href = "noDHTML.htm"
}
```

With the two flags initialized as null values in the first statement, you can safely use either one as a control structure condition expression, since a value of null evaluates to false in those situations. That's precisely how the last if statement operates (but with the flags preceded by the ! operator, since the script is interested in the values *not* being true).

Explicit Branching

For the occasional need to control the property of a positionable element, an explicit branch does the job without a lot of fuss. All you need to do is determine the platform-specific versions of the statement(s) to be executed and embed them inside a simple if construction. Example 4-2 shows a script fragment whose job it is to move an element (named face) to a particular coordinate point relative to the positioning context of the body. For the Navigator version, the script takes advantage of the layer object's moveTo() method; for IE, the script adjusts the `pixelLeft` and `pixelTop` properties. Notice, too, that the object references follow the conventions of the respective browser's object model.

Example 4-2. Simple Branching

```
function placeIt() {
    if (isNav) {
        document.face.moveTo(25,15)
    } else {
        document.all.face.style.pixelLeft = 25
        document.all.face.style.pixelTop = 15
    }
}
```

There is no prohibition against using this technique on a complex document involving dozens of such branches. The primary penalty is the unnecessarily expanded amount of script code in the document. For some scripters, however, this technique is easiest to debug. It also comes in handy when the positionable objects are nested to different depths. Other techniques discussed in the following sections can also work with layers at different levels in Navigator, but usually not as easily.

Platform-Equivalent Referencing

Platform-equivalent referencing involves finding a common denominator approach to building references to positionable objects on both platforms. One way to do this is to create global variables to hold the platform-specific components of object references.

If you study the format of references to the Internet Explorer style properties of positionable objects, you see they always fall into the following format:

    `document.all.`*elementName*`.style`

In contrast, single-level-deep Navigator **layer** objects are referenced according to the following format:

    `document.`*layerName*

If you assign the unique Internet Explorer pieces to global variables when running in that browser, but assign empty strings to those same globals when running in Navigator, you can use the JavaScript **eval()** function to derive a valid object reference for either browser by assembling one reference, as shown in Example 4-3. This example embeds the global variable setting in the script segment that also sets the browser Boolean flags. It concludes with a function that takes advantage of the identical property names for a particular positioning property in both browsers.

Example 4-3. Platform-Equivalent Variable Setting and Object Evaluation

```
var isNav, isIE
var coll = ""
var styleObj = ""
if (parseInt(navigator.appVersion) >= 4) {
    if (navigator.appName == "Netscape") {
        isNav = true
    } else {
        isIE = true
        coll = "all."
        styleObj = ".style"
    }
}
// set stacking order of "face" element
function setFaceZOrder(n) {
    var obj = eval("document." + coll + "face" + styleObj)
    obj.zIndex = n
}
```

Notice that the variables for the IE reference pieces—`coll` (for collection) and `styleObj` (for `style` object)—contain specific punctuation to assist the `eval()` function in assembling a proper string representation of the reference for conversion to a genuine object reference.

The platform-equivalent reference technique is particularly helpful for cases where the property names are identical on both platforms, as shown in Example 4-3. But you can also combine this technique with explicit branching to handle more complex tasks. Example 4-4 shows a hybrid approach to moving an element, adapted from Example 4-2.

Example 4-4. A Hybrid Approach: Explicit Branching and Platform Equivalency

```
function placeIt() {
    var obj = eval("document." + coll + "face" + styleObj)
    if (isNav) {
        obj.moveTo(25,15)
    } else {
        obj.pixelLeft = 25
        obj.pixelTop = 15
    }
}
```

Custom APIs

If you find yourself doing a lot of scripting of positionable elements in your applications, it is probably worth the effort to create a custom API that you can link into any application you create. A custom API can take care of the "grunt" work for common position-scripting tasks, such as moving, hiding, showing, and resizing elements, as well as setting background colors or patterns. When you define a custom API library, the methods you write become the interface between your application's scripts and various positioning tasks.

Example 4-5 gives you a sample of what such an API library might look like. The API defines the following functions:

getObject(*obj*)
> Takes a positionable element from the default positioning context and returns an object reference for either the Navigator `layer` or the Internet Explorer `style` object

shiftTo(*obj, x, y*)
> Moves an object to a coordinate point within its positioning context

shiftBy(*obj, deltaX, deltaY*)
> Moves an object by the specified number of pixels in the X and Y axes of the object's positioning context

setZIndex(*obj, zOrder*)
> Sets the z-index value of the object

setBGColor(*obj, color*)
> Sets the background color of the object

show(*obj*)
> Makes the object visible

hide(*obj*)
> Makes the object invisible

getObjectLeft(*obj*)
> Returns the left pixel coordinate of the object within its positioning context

getObjectTop(*obj*)
> Returns the top pixel coordinate of the object within its positioning context

Example 4-5. A Custom API for Positionable Elements

```
// DHTMLapi.js custom API for cross-platform
// object positioning by Danny Goodman (http://www.dannyg.com)

// Global variables
var isNav, isIE
var coll = ""
var styleObj = ""
if (parseInt(navigator.appVersion) >= 4) {
    if (navigator.appName == "Netscape") {
        isNav = true
    } else {
        isIE = true
```

Example 4-5. A Custom API for Positionable Elements (continued)

```
            coll = "all."
            styleObj = ".style"
        }
}

// Convert object name string or object reference
// into a valid object reference
function getObject(obj) {
    var theObj
    if (typeof obj == "string") {
        theObj = eval("document." + coll + obj + styleObj)
    } else {
        theObj = obj
    }
    return theObj
}

// Positioning an object at a specific pixel coordinate
function shiftTo(obj, x, y) {
    var theObj = getObject(obj)
    if (isNav4) {
        theObj.moveTo(x,y)
    } else {
        theObj.pixelLeft = x
        theObj.pixelTop = y
    }
}

// Moving an object by x and/or y pixels
function shiftBy(obj, deltaX, deltaY) {
    var theObj = getObject(obj)
    if (isNav4) {
        theObj.moveBy(deltaX, deltaY)
    } else {
        theObj.pixelLeft += deltaX
        theObj.pixelTop += deltaY
    }
}

// Setting the z-order of an object
function setZIndex(obj, zOrder) {
    var theObj = getObject(obj)
    theObj.zIndex = zOrder
}

// Setting the background color of an object
function setBGColor(obj, color) {
    var theObj = getObject(obj)
    if (isNav4) {
        theObj.bgColor = color
    } else {
        theObj.backgroundColor = color
    }
}
```

Example 4-5. A Custom API for Positionable Elements (continued)

```
// Setting the visibility of an object to visible
function show(obj) {
    var theObj = getObject(obj)
    theObj.visibility = "visible"
}

// Setting the visibility of an object to hidden
function hide(obj) {
    var theObj = getObject(obj)
    theObj.visibility = "hidden"
}

// Retrieving the x coordinate of a positionable object
function getObjectLeft(obj)  {
    var theObj = getObject(obj)
    if (isNav4) {
        return theObj.left
    } else {
        return theObj.pixelLeft
    }
}

// Retrieving the y coordinate of a positionable object
function getObjectTop(obj)  {
    var theObj = getObject(obj)
    if (isNav4) {
        return theObj.top
    } else {
        return theObj.pixelTop
    }
}
```

Notice that every function call in the API invokes the `getObject()` function. If the parameter passed to a function is already an object, the object reference is passed through to the function's other statements. Thus, you might use a combination of techniques to work with nested objects, as in the following call to a custom API function:

```
if (isNav) {
    setBGColor(document.outer.document.inner, "red")
} else {
    setBGColor(document.all.inner.style, "red")
}
```

The custom API in Example 4-5 is provided as a starting point for you to create your own extensions that fit the kinds of positioning tasks your applications require. Your version will probably grow over time, as you further enhance the positioning techniques used in your applications.

When you write a custom API, save the code in a file with any filename that uses the *.js* extension. Then, you can link the library into an HTML document with the following tag pair in the HEAD portion of the document:

```
<SCRIPT LANGUAGE="JavaScript" SRC="myAPI.js"></SCRIPT>
```

Once you do this, all the functions and global variables in the custom API library become immediately available to all script statements in the HTML document.

Handling Navigator Window Resizing

Navigator 4 has a nasty habit of destroying the layout of positioned elements (including LAYER elements) if the user resizes the browser window. The user may see overlapped text and elements shaped very peculiarly after the resize. There is a scripted workaround you should include in all pages that use positioned elements.

The workaround requires trapping for the resize event and forcing the page to reload. This sequence causes the page to flicker briefly between the jumbled page and the reloaded, properly proportioned page, but it's better than nothing. The following script, taken from the HEAD section of a document, assumes you've included the utility code described earlier in this chapter that defines a global variable called isNav when the current browser is Navigator 4 or later:

```
function handleResize() {
    location.reload()
    return false
}
if (isNav) {
    window.captureEvents(Event.RESIZE)
    window.onresize = handleResize
}
```

Internet Explorer 4 handles window resizing more gracefully, automatically reflowing the content without the need for intervention.

Common Positioning Tasks

This chapter concludes with examples of two common positioning tasks: centering objects and flying objects. A third task, user-controlled dragging of objects, is kept on hold until Chapter 6, *Scripting Events*, where we discuss the browser event models.

Centering an Object

The common way to center an element within a rectangle is to calculate the half-way point along each axis for both the element and its containing rectangle (positioning context). Then subtract the element value from the container value for each axis. The resulting values are the coordinates for the top and left edges of the element that center the element.

Document object properties and references differ so widely for these attributes in Navigator and Internet Explorer that it takes a bit of code to handle the centering task for both browsers in the same document. The calculations rely on browser-specific functions that might best be placed into a custom API and linked in from an external *.js* file. For purposes of demonstration, however, the library functions are embedded into the example document shown here.

The element being centered in the browser window is an outer DIV element with a yellow background. Inside this DIV element is a one-word P element, which, itself, is positioned inside the context of the DIV element. The goal is to center the outer DIV element, bringing the contained paragraph along for the ride. Example 4-6 shows the complete page listing.

Example 4-6. A Page That Centers an Element Upon Loading

```
<HTML>
<HEAD>
<SCRIPT LANGUAGE="JavaScript">
// ***Begin library code better placed in an external API***
// Set global variables for browser detection and reference building
var isNav, isIE
var coll = ""
var styleObj = ""
if (parseInt(navigator.appVersion) >= 4) {
    if (navigator.appName == "Netscape") {
        isNav = true
    } else {
        isIE = true
        coll = "all."
        styleObj = ".style"
    }
}
// Utility function returns rendered height of object content in pixels
function getObjHeight(obj) {
    if (isNav) {
        return obj.clip.height
    } else {
        return obj.clientHeight
    }
}
// Utility function returns rendered width of object content in pixels
function getObjWidth(obj) {
    if (isNav) {
        return obj.clip.width
    } else {
        return obj.clientWidth
    }
}
```

Example 4-6. A Page That Centers an Element Upon Loading (continued)

```
// Utility function returns the available content width space in browser window
function getInsideWindowWidth() {
    if (isNav) {
        return window.innerWidth
    } else {
        return document.body.clientWidth
    }
}
// Utility function returns the available content height space in browser window
function getInsideWindowHeight() {
    if (isNav) {
        return window.innerHeight
    } else {
        return document.body.clientHeight
    }
}
// Utility function to position an element at a specific x,y location
function shiftTo(obj, x, y) {
    if (isNav) {
        obj.moveTo(x,y)
    } else {
        obj.pixelLeft = x
        obj.pixelTop = y
    }
}
// ***End library code***

// Center an element named banner in the current window/frame, and show it
function centerIt() {
    // 'obj' is the positionable object
    var obj = eval("document." + coll + "banner" + styleObj)
    // 'contentObj' is the element content, necessary for IE 4 to return the
    //    true current width
    var contentObj = eval("document." + coll + "banner")
    var x = Math.round((getInsideWindowWidth()/2)-(getObjWidth(contentObj)/2))
    var y = Math.round((getInsideWindowHeight()/2)-(getObjHeight(contentObj)/2))
    shiftTo(obj, x, y)
    obj.visibility = "visible"
}
// Special handling for CSS-P redraw bug in Navigator 4
function handleResize() {
    if (isNav) {
        // causes extra re-draw, but must do it to get banner object color drawn
        location.reload()
    } else {
        centerIt()
    }
}
</SCRIPT>
</HEAD>

<BODY onLoad="centerIt()" onResize="handleResize()">
<DIV ID="banner" STYLE="position:absolute; visibility:hidden; left:0; top:0;
 background-color:yellow; width:1; height:1">
```

Example 4-6. A Page That Centers an Element Upon Loading (continued)

```
<P ID="txt" STYLE="position:absolute; left:0; top:0; font-size:36pt; color:red">
Congratulations!
</P>
</DIV>
</BODY>
</HTML>
```

No matter what size the browser window is initially, or how the user resizes the window, the element always positions itself dead center in the window space. Notice that the outer positionable element is initially loaded as a hidden element positioned at 0,0. This allows a script (triggered by the onLoad event handler of the BODY element) to perform calculations based on the element properties and then show the properly positioned element. The page allows the browser to determine the current height and width of the content, based on how each browser (and operating system) calculates its fonts (initial width and height are arbitrarily set to 1). This is preferable to hard-wiring the height, width, and clipping region of the element. It means, however, that when the script is running in IE 4, it cannot rely on style object properties. Those properties always pick up the style sheet attributes; they do not change unless the properties are changed by a script. Instead, the script in Example 4-6 uses the clientWidth and clientHeight properties of the element itself, when running in IE 4.

Many of the concepts shown in Example 4-6 can be extended to centering nested elements inside other elements. Be aware, however, that Navigator 4 handles nested items best when they are specified in the document with <LAYER> tags rather than with CSS-P syntax. You may find it worthwhile to include browser-specific branches in your document that use the document.write() method to write CSS-P or <LAYER> HTML content, depending on the current browser (using the isNav and isIE globals). Using the <LAYER> tag for Navigator positionable objects does not affect the syntax of scripted access to those items: the same properties and methods apply whether the object is defined in CSS-P or as a genuine layer. Rendering, however, is more reliable in Navigator 4 with genuine layers. Support for CSS should certainly improve in future versions of Navigator.

Flying Objects

Moving objects around the screen is one of the features that can make Dynamic HTML pay off for your page—provided you use the animation to add value to the presentation. Gratuitous animation (like the example in this section) more often annoys frequent visitors than it helps convey information. Still, I'm sure you are interested to know how animation tricks are performed with DHTML, including cross-platform deployment.

Straight-line paths are relatively easy to script. However, when you need to account for object centering and a variety of browser window sizes, the scripts can bulk up a bit. A page that requires as many utility functions as the one shown here is best served by linking in a custom API.

The example in this section builds somewhat on the centering application in Example 4-6. The goal of this demonstration is to have a banner object fly in from the right edge of the window (centered vertically in the window), until it reaches the center of the currently sized window. The source code for the page is shown in Example 4-7.

Example 4-7. A Page with a "Flying" Banner

```
<HTML>
<HEAD>
<SCRIPT LANGUAGE="JavaScript">
// ***Begin library code better placed in an external API***
// Set global variables for browser detection and reference building
var isNav, isIE, intervalID
var coll = ""
var styleObj = ""
if (parseInt(navigator.appVersion) >= 4) {
    if (navigator.appName == "Netscape") {
        isNav = true
    } else {
        isIE = true
        coll = "all."
        styleObj = ".style"
    }
}
// Utility function returns height of object in pixels
function getObjHeight(obj) {
    if (isNav) {
        return obj.clip.height
    } else {
        return obj.clientHeight
    }
}
// Utility function returns width of object in pixels
function getObjWidth(obj) {
    if (isNav) {
        return obj.clip.width
    } else {
        return obj.clientWidth
    }
}
// Utility function returns the x coordinate of a positionable object
function getObjLeft(obj)  {
    if (isNav) {
        return obj.left
    } else {
        return obj.pixelLeft
    }
}
```

Example 4-7. A Page with a "Flying" Banner (continued)

```
// Utility function returns the y coordinate of a positionable object
function getObjTop(obj)  {
    if (isNav) {
        return obj.top
    } else {
        return obj.pixelTop
    }
}
// Utility function returns the available content width space in browser window
function getInsideWindowWidth() {
    if (isNav) {
        return window.innerWidth
    } else {
        return document.body.clientWidth
    }
}
// Utility function returns the available content height space in browser window
function getInsideWindowHeight() {
    if (isNav) {
        return window.innerHeight
    } else {
        return document.body.clientHeight
    }
}
// Utility function sets the visibility of an object to visible
function show(obj) {
    obj.visibility = "visible"
}

// Utility function sets the visibility of an object to hidden
function hide(obj) {
    obj.visibility = "hidden"
}
// Utility function to position an element at a specific x,y location
function shiftTo(obj, x, y) {
    if (isNav) {
        obj.moveTo(x,y)
    } else {
        obj.pixelLeft = x
        obj.pixelTop = y
    }
}
// Utility function to move an object by x and/or y pixels
function shiftBy(obj, deltaX, deltaY) {
    if (isNav) {
        obj.moveBy(deltaX, deltaY)
    } else {
        obj.pixelLeft += deltaX
        obj.pixelTop += deltaY
    }
}
// ***End library code***
```

Example 4-7. A Page with a "Flying" Banner (continued)

```
// Set initial position offscreen and show object and
// start timer by calling glideToCenter()
function intro() {
    var obj = eval("document." + coll + "banner" + styleObj)
    var contentObj = eval("document." + coll + "banner")
    shiftTo(obj, getInsideWindowWidth(),
            Math.round((getInsideWindowHeight()/2)-(getObjHeight(contentObj)/2)))
    show(obj)
    glideToCenter()
}
// Move the object to the left by 5 pixels until it's centered
function glideToCenter() {
    var obj = eval("document." + coll + "banner" + styleObj)
    var contentObj = eval("document." + coll + "banner")
    shiftBy(obj,-5,0)
    var a = getObjLeft(obj)
    var b = Math.round((getInsideWindowWidth()/2) - (getObjWidth(contentObj)/2))
    if (a <= b) {
        clearTimeout(intervalID)
    } else {
        intervalID = setTimeout("glideToCenter()",1)
    }
}
}
</SCRIPT>
</HEAD>
<BODY onLoad="intro()" >
<DIV ID="banner" STYLE="position:absolute; visibility:hidden; left:0; top:0;
 background-color:yellow; width:1; height:1">
<P ID="txt" STYLE="position:absolute; left:0; top:0; font-size:36pt; color:red">
Congratulations!
</P>
</DIV>

</BODY>
</HTML>
```

The bulk of the utility functions in Example 4-7 get the pixel sizes and left-edge locations of the window and the flying object. These are all important because the main operation of this page requires those calculated values, to take into account the current size of the browser window.

All action is triggered by the onLoad event handler of the BODY element. In the intro() function, platform equivalency is used to get a valid reference to the banner object (this would not be necessary if we were using the API shown in Example 4-5 because the API automatically converts object names to object references for each utility function call). The first positioning task is to move the initially hidden banner object off the screen to the right, so that the banner's left edge lines up with the right edge of the window. At the same time, the script calculates the proper vertical position of the banner, so that it is centered from top to bottom. With the banner safely out of view, it's safe to make the object visible. Then the magic begins.

JavaScript 1.2, in Navigator 4 and Internet Explorer 4, adds the `setInterval()` and `clearInterval()` functions specifically to assist in animation. But because `clearInterval()` doesn't work correctly in IE 4 for the Macintosh, this example reverts to the `setTimeout()` methodology, which also does the job. The final script statement of `intro()` invokes the `glideToCenter()` function, which ends with a `setTimeout()` function that keeps calling `glideToCenter()` until the element is centered horizontally. Each millisecond (or as quickly as the rendering engine allows), the browser invokes the `glideToCenter()` function and refreshes its display.

Each time `glideToCenter()` runs, it shifts the banner object to the left by five pixels without adjusting the vertical position. Then it checks whether the left edge of the banner has arrived at the position where the banner is centered on the screen. If it is at (or to the left of) that point, the timer is cleared and the browser ceases to invoke `glideToCenter()` anymore.

If you want to move an element along a more complicated path, the strategy is similar, but you have to maintain one or more additional global variables to store loop counters or other values that change from point to point. Example 4-8 shows replacements for the `intro()` and `glideToCenter()` functions in Example 4-7. The new functions roll the banner around in a circle. An extra global variable for counting steps along the route is all that is required.

Example 4-8. Rolling a Banner in a Circle

```
// Set initial position centered horizontally and 50 pixels down; start timer
function intro() {
    var obj = eval("document." + coll + "banner" + styleObj)
    var contentObj = eval("document." + coll + "banner")
    var objX = Math.round((getInsideWindowWidth() - getObjWidth(contentObj))/2)
    var objY = 50
    shiftTo(obj, objX, objY)
    show(obj)
    goAround()
}
// Iteration counter global variable
var i = 1
// Move element along an arc that is 1/36 of a circle; stop at full circle
function goAround() {
    var obj = eval("document." + coll + "banner" + styleObj)
    var objX = getObjLeft(obj) + Math.cos(i * (Math.PI/18)) * 5
    var objY = getObjTop(obj) + Math.sin(i * (Math.PI/18)) * 5
    shiftTo(obj, objX, objY)
```

Example 4-8. Rolling a Banner in a Circle (continued)

```
    if (i++ == 36) {
        clearTimeout(intervalID)
    } else {
        intervalID = setTimeout("goAround()",1)
    }
}
```

In Chapter 6, we'll come back to the dynamic positioning of elements and examine how to make an object track the mouse pointer. That application requires knowledge of the partially conflicting event models built into Navigator 4 and Internet Explorer 4, which is why we can't cover it here.

5

Making Content Dynamic

In addition to letting you script the positions of elements, as described in Chapter 4, *Adding Dynamic Positioning to Documents*, Dynamic HTML is meant to allow you to write scripts that modify content and adjust styles on the fly. Prior to the Version 4 browsers, your ability to script dynamic content was limited to controlling the HTML being written to the current page, loading HTML documents into other frames, and, in some browser versions, swapping images during mouse rollovers. The Version 4 browsers offer much more in the way of altering the content and appearance of documents that have already been displayed in response to user activity.

Unfortunately for those of us on the leading edge of DHTML deployment, Navigator 4 and Internet Explorer 4 have very different ideas about how content should be made dynamic. In particular, IE 4 exposes much more of every document element to scripting, and the browser automatically reflows a document to accommodate any changes you make. Navigator 4's capabilities are more limited in this regard. Notably, Navigator's lack of automatic reflow puts the browser at a disadvantage if your design calls for dynamically changing inline elements of a page.

This chapter provides an overview of the most common ways of dynamically changing content, including some that date back to Navigator 2. It also offers some suggestions about how to develop workarounds for the widely divergent approaches to dynamic content practiced in the two Version 4 browsers.

Writing Variable Content

While a page is loading, you can use the JavaScript `document.write()` method to fill in content that cannot be stored as part of the document. Example 5-1 shows a simple example of combining hard-wired HTML with dynamically written content to fill a page. In this case, the dynamically written content consists of properties that only the client computer and browser can determine (without the help of a server-based CGI program). The user is oblivious to the fact that a script creates some of the text on the page.

Example 5-1. Combining Fixed and Dynamic Content in a Rendered Page

```
<HTML>
<BODY>
<H1>Welcome!</H1>
<HR>
<P>You are using version
<SCRIPT LANGUAGE="JavaScript">
document.write(navigator.appVersion)
document.write(" of the <B>" + navigator.appName + "</B> browser.")
</SCRIPT>
</P>
</BODY>
</HTML>
```

You can use `document.write()` or `document.writeln()` in scripts that execute while a document is loading, but you cannot use either method to modify the content of a page that has already loaded. Once a document has finished loading, if you make a single call to `document.write()` directed at the current document, the call automatically clears the current document from the browser window and writes the new content to the page. So, if you want to rewrite the contents of a page, you must do so with just one call to the `document.write()` method. Example 5-2 demonstrates how to accumulate content for a page in a variable that is written in one blast.

Example 5-2. Creating a New Document for the Current Window

```
<HTML>
<HEAD>
<TITLE>Welcome Page</TITLE>
<SCRIPT LANGUAGE="JavaScript">
// create custom page and replace current document with it
function rewritePage(form) {
    // accumulate HTML content for new page
    var newPage = "<HTML>\n<HEAD>\n<TITLE>Page for "
    newPage += form.entry.value
    newPage += "</TITLE>\n</HEAD>\n<BODY BGCOLOR='cornflowerblue'>\n"
    newPage += "<H1>Hello, " + form.entry.value + "!</H1>\n"
    newPage += "</BODY>\n</HTML>"
    // write it in one blast
    document.write(newPage)
    // close writing stream
    document.close()
}
</SCRIPT>
```

```
<BODY>
<H1>Welcome!</H1>
<HR>
<FORM onSubmit="return false">
<P>Enter your name here: <INPUT TYPE="text" NAME="entry"></P>
<INPUT TYPE="button" VALUE="New Custom Page" onClick="rewritePage(this.form)">
</FORM>
</BODY>
</HTML>
```

Notice that the script inserts data from the original screen's form into the content of the new page, including a new title that appears in the browser window's title bar. As a convenience to anyone looking at the source of the new document, escaped newline characters (\n) are inserted for cosmetic purposes only. After the call to document.write(), the rewritePage() function calls document.close() to close the new document. While there are also document.open() and document.clear() methods, we don't need to use them to replace the contents of a window. The one document.write() method clears the old content, opens a new output stream, and writes the content.

Writing to Other Frames and Windows

You can also use the document.write() method to send dynamically created content to another frame in a frameset or to another browser window. In this case, you are not restricted to only one call to document.write() per page; you can open an output stream to another frame or window and keep dumping stuff into it until you close the output stream with document.close().

All you need for this kind of content creation is a valid reference to the other frame or window. How you generate the frameset or secondary window influences this reference.

Framesets and Frames

A typical frameset document defines the physical layout of how the main browser window is to be subdivided into separate panels. Framesets can, of course, be nested many levels deep, where one frame loads a document that is, itself, a frameset document. The key to writing a valid reference to a distant frame is knowing the relationship between the frame that contains the script doing the writing and the target frame.

The most common frameset structure consists of one frameset document and two to four frames defined as part of that frameset (you can have more frames if you like, but not everyone is fond of frames). Ideally, you should assign a unique identifier to the NAME attribute of each <FRAME> tag. Example 5-3 is a basic frameset document that assigns a name to each of the three frames and loads an efficient local blank page into each frame. The technique used here is to invoke a function, `blank()`, that exists in the frameset (parent) document. In each case, the `javascript:` pseudo-URL is applied to the newly created frame. From each frame's point of view, the `blank()` function is in the parent document, hence the `parent.blank()` reference. The 100-pixel wide frame down the left side of the browser window is a navigation bar. The right portion of the window is divided into two sections. The upper section (arbitrarily called `main`) occupies 70% of the column, while the lower section (called `instructions`) occupies the rest of the column.

Example 5-3. A Simple Three-Frame Frameset with Blank Pages Written to Each Frame

```
<HTML>
<HEAD>
<SCRIPT LANGUAGE="JavaScript">
<!--
function blank() {
    return "<HTML></HTML>"
}
//-->
</SCRIPT>
</HEAD>
<FRAMESET COLS="100,*">
    <FRAME NAME="navBar" SRC="javascript:parent.blank()">
    <FRAMESET ROWS="70%,*">
        <FRAME NAME="main" SRC="javascript:parent.blank()">
        <FRAME NAME="instructions" SRC="javascript:parent.blank()">
    </FRAMESET>
</FRAMESET>
</HTML>
```

Now imagine that a modified version of Example 5-2 is loaded into the `main` frame. The job of the script, however, is to write the dynamic content to the frame named `instructions`. To accomplish this, the reference to the other frame must start with the parent document (the frameset), which the two frames have in common. Example 5-4 shows the modified page that goes into the `main` frame and writes to the `instructions` frame. The two small changes that were made to the original code are highlighted in boldface.

Example 5-4. Writing Dynamic Content to Another Frame

```
<HTML>
<HEAD>
<TITLE>Welcome Page</TITLE>
<SCRIPT LANGUAGE="JavaScript">
// create custom page and replace current document with it
function rewritePage(form) {
    // accumulate HTML content for new page
    var newPage = "<HTML>\n<HEAD>\n<TITLE>Page for "
    newPage += form.entry.value
```

Example 5-4. Writing Dynamic Content to Another Frame (continued)

```
    newPage += "</TITLE>\n</HEAD>\n<BODY BGCOLOR='cornflowerblue'>\n"
    newPage += "<H1>Hello, " + form.entry.value + "!</H1>\n"
    newPage += "</BODY>\n</HTML>"
    // write it in one blast
    parent.instructions.document.write(newPage)
    // close writing stream
    parent.instructions.document.close()
}
</SCRIPT>
<BODY>
<H1>Welcome!</H1>
<HR>
<FORM onSubmit="return false">
<P>Enter your name here: <INPUT TYPE="text" NAME="entry"></P>
<INPUT TYPE="button" VALUE="New Custom Page" onClick="rewritePage(this.form)">
</FORM>
</BODY>
</HTML>
```

If, on the other hand, you simply want to load a different document from the server into the **instructions** frame, you can use a script-less HTML link and set the **TARGET** attribute to the **instructions** frame. A script in **main** can also specify a document for the **instructions** frame as follows:

```
    parent.instructions.location.href = "nextPage.html"
```

Secondary Windows

JavaScript provides facilities for not only generating a new browser window, but also setting the window's size and (in Version 4 browsers) its location on the screen. You can then use references to communicate from one window to the other, although the form of those references is quite different, depending on where the script is running.

The JavaScript method that generates a new window returns a reference to the new **window** object. If you plan to communicate with that window after it has been opened, you should store the reference in a global variable. This reference is the only avenue to the subwindow. Example 5-5 features a script for opening a new window and writing to it. In addition, it also takes care of a feature lacking in Navigator 2 (described in a moment), inserts a brief delay to allow the often sluggish Internet Explorer 3 to finish creating the window before writing to it, and brings an already opened but hidden window to the front, if the browser supports that feature (Navigator 3 or later and IE 4 or later).

Example 5-5. Opening a New Window and Writing to It

```
<HTML>
<HEAD>
<TITLE>A New Window</TITLE>
```

Example 5-5. Opening a New Window and Writing to It (continued)

```
<SCRIPT LANGUAGE="JavaScript">
// Global variable for subwindow reference
var newWindow
// Version flag for old browsers (Nav2/IE3)
var oldStuff = parseInt(navigator.appversion) < 3
// Generate and fill the new window
function makeNewWindow() {
    // make sure it isn't already opened
        newWindow = window.open("","sub","status,height=200,width=300")
        // handle Navigator 2, which doesn't have an opener property
        if (!newWindow.opener) {
            newWindow.opener = window
        }
        // delay writing until window exists in IE3
        setTimeout("writeToWindow()", 500)
    if (!oldStuff) {
        // window is already open so bring it to the front
        newWindow.focus()
    }
}
function writeToWindow() {
    // assemble content for new window
    var newContent = "<HTML><HEAD><TITLE>One Sub Window</TITLE></HEAD>\n"
    newContent += "<BODY>\n<H1>This is a new window.</H1>\n"
    newContent += "</BODY>\n</HTML>"
    // write HTML to new window document
    newWindow.document.write(newContent)
    newWindow.document.close() // close layout stream
}
</SCRIPT>
</HEAD>
<BODY>
<FORM>
<INPUT TYPE="button" NAME="newOne" VALUE="Create New Window"
 onClick="makeNewWindow()">
</FORM>
</BODY>
</HTML>
```

Example 5-5 shows that the reference to the subwindow (stored in the **newWindow** global variable) can be used to call **document.write()** and **document.close()** for that window. The **window** object reference is the gateway to the subwindow.

A script in a document loaded into a subwindow can communicate back to the window or frame that spawned the new window. Every scriptable browser (except Navigator 2) automatically sets the **opener** property of a new window to a reference to the window or frame that created the window. One of the workarounds in Example 5-5 creates and sets this property for Navigator 2, so you can use it across the board. Therefore, to access the **value** property of a form text box (named entryField) located in the main browser window, you can use the following script statement in the subwindow:

```
opener.document.forms[0].entryField.value
```

Remember that **opener** refers directly to the window or frame that spawned the subwindow. If you need to access content in another frame in the frameset, your reference must traverse the object hierarchy accordingly:

```
opener.parent.otherFrameName.document.forms[0].someField.value
```

Links to Multiple Frames

It is not uncommon for the navigation bar in a frameset to contain links, or icons, that must load documents into two or more other frames of the frameset at the same time. For a single frame, the standard HTML link facilities work fine, since they let you specify a target frame with nothing more than plain attributes. But the attribute technique doesn't do the job for controlling the content of multiple targets. Scripting comes to the rescue, with a few different ways to accomplish the same goal:

- Invoke a function from the element's **onClick** event handler to control both frames
- Use a **javascript:** pseudo-URL to invoke a function to control both frames
- Use the default link for one frame and the **onClick** event handler for the other

The first two choices require defining a JavaScript function that loads the desired documents into their target frames. Such a function might look as follows:

```
function loadFrames() {
    parent.main.location.href = "section2.htm"
    parent.instructions.location.href = "instrux2.htm"
    return false
}
```

You can then create a link that invokes the function for browsers with JavaScript turned on or that at least links to the main frame content if JavaScript is turned off:

```
<A HREF="section2.htm" TARGET="main" onClick="return loadFrames()">...</A>
```

The **loadFrames()** function returns **false** when it is done. This forces the **onClick** event handler to return **false** as well, which preempts the actions of the **HREF** and **TARGET** attributes (when JavaScript is turned on).

The **javascript:** pseudo-URL can be applied to a link's **HREF** attribute as follows:

```
<A HREF="javascript: void loadFrames()">...</A>
```

Instead of navigating directly to a URL on the server, the link invokes whatever JavaScript function is named in the pseudo-URL. By including the void operator, you instruct JavaScript to ignore any value returned by the function.

For the third approach, let the HREF and TARGET attributes handle one frame while the onClick event handler takes care of the other with an inline script:

```
<A HREF="section2.htm" TARGET="main"
onClick="parent.instructions.location.href='instrux2.htm'">...</A>
```

Client-side image maps require a little more care because the onClick event handler isn't defined for the **area** object until the Version 4 browsers. But you can use the javascript: pseudo-URL trick with the HREF attribute inside a <MAP> tag.

Image Swapping

Before we had the true Dynamic HTML powers of the Version 4 browsers, Navigator 3 (and Internet Explorer 3 for the Macintosh only) gave us a glimpse of things to come with image swapping. The basis for this technique is a document object model that defines an image as an object whose properties can be changed (or "replaced," in the language of cascading style sheets) on the fly. One of those properties, src, defines the URL of an image loaded initially by virtue of an <IMG> tag and currently displayed in the page. Change that property and the image changes, within the same rectangular space defined by the <IMG> tag's HEIGHT and WIDTH attributes (or, lacking those attribute settings, the first image's dimensions as calculated by the browser), while all the other content around it stays put.

Navigator 3 (and later) goes one step further by defining an **Image** object from which new "virtual" images can be created in the browser's memory with the help of scripts. These kinds of images do not appear in the document, but can be scripted to preload images into the browser's image cache as the page does its original download. Thus, when it comes time to swap an image, the switch is nearly instantaneous because there is no need for network access to grab the image data.

The example in this section shows you how to pre-cache and swap images for the buttons of an imaginary video controller. There are four controls—**Play**, **Stop**, **Pause**, and **Rewind**. Each control has its own image that acts as a button. As the user rolls the mouse atop a button, a highlighted version of the button icon appears in the image space; as the mouse rolls off the button, the original unhighlighted version reappears.

Precaching Images

When preloading images (and later retrieving them for swapping), it is convenient to create an array for each state that the images will be in. In Example 5-6, there are two states: highlighted and unhighlighted (which are more conveniently referred to as "on" and "off"). The HEAD portion of the document contains a series of script statements that generate the new Image objects (in memory) and assign the URLs for the associated image files to the src properties of those memory image objects. Example 5-6 shows the sequence of statements that makes this happen for the four "on" images and the four "off" images. Depending on your audience for this page, you may wish to use a browser-specific branch to prevent these statements from running in Navigator 2 or Internet Explorer 3 for Windows: the Image object is not in the object model of either of these browsers. Another tactic, shown in Example 5-6, is to simply check for the support of the images array object in the browser.

Example 5-6. Precaching Code for Two Sets of Four Related Images

```
if (document.images) {
    // create "on" array and populate with Image objects
    var onImgArray = new Array()
    onImgArray[0] = new Image(75,35)
    onImgArray[1] = new Image(75,35)
    onImgArray[2] = new Image(75,35)
    onImgArray[3] = new Image(75,35)
    // set URLs for the "on" images
    onImgArray[0].src = "images/playon.gif"
    onImgArray[1].src = "images/stopon.gif"
    onImgArray[2].src = "images/pauseon.gif"
    onImgArray[3].src = "images/rewindon.gif"

    // create "off" array and populate with Image objects
    var offImgArray = new Array()
    offImgArray[0] = new Image(75,35)
    offImgArray[1] = new Image(75,35)
    offImgArray[2] = new Image(75,35)
    offImgArray[3] = new Image(75,35)
    // set URLs for the "off" images
    offImgArray[0].src = "images/playoff.gif"
    offImgArray[1].src = "images/stopoff.gif"
    offImgArray[2].src = "images/pauseoff.gif"
    offImgArray[3].src = "images/rewindoff.gif"
}
```

The act of stuffing the URL for each image file into the src property of each Image object is enough to force the browser to actually fetch the image and store it in its image cache without displaying the image anywhere. Also, the numeric relationships among the array entries play a significant role in the actual image swapping, as you'll see shortly.

Swap Your Image

Now it's time to look at the HTML that displays the images within the document. For the sake of this example, the surrounding HTML is of no importance.

Since **image** objects in a document don't respond to mouse events (except in IE 4), the images are wrapped inside links. To prevent the normal link color border from appearing around the images, the **BORDER** attribute of each **<IMG>** tag is set to zero. The event handlers of the surrounding links trigger all the action for the image swapping. Example 5-7 shows the four image elements and their surrounding links.

Example 5-7. The Images to Be Swapped, Wrapped in Links with Event Handlers

```
<A HREF="javascript:playVideo()"
onMouseOver="imageOn(0); return setMsg('Play/Continue the clip')"
onMouseOut="imageOff(0); return setMsg('')">
<IMG SRC="images/playoff.gif" NAME="btn0" HEIGHT=35 WIDTH=75 BORDER=0>
</A>
<A HREF="javascript:stopVideo()"
onMouseOver="imageOn(1); return setMsg('Stop video')"
onMouseOut="imageOff(1); return setMsg('')">
<IMG SRC="images/stopoff.gif" NAME="btn1" HEIGHT=35 WIDTH=75 BORDER=0>
</A>
<A HREF="javascript:pauseVideo()"
onMouseOver="imageOn(2); return setMsg('Pause video')"
onMouseOut="imageOff(2); return setMsg('')">
<IMG SRC="images/pauseoff.gif" NAME="btn2" HEIGHT=35 WIDTH=75 BORDER=0>
</A>
<A HREF="javascript:rewindVideo()"
onMouseOver="imageOn(3); return setMsg('Rewind to beginning')"
onMouseOut="imageOff(3); return setMsg('')">
<IMG SRC="images/rewindoff.gif" NAME="btn3" HEIGHT=35 WIDTH=75 BORDER=0>
</A>
```

The **onMouseOver** and **onMouseOut** event handlers in each link have two tasks. The first is to change the image and the second is to display an appropriate message in the status bar of the browser window (to avoid displaying the **java-script:** pseudo-URL there). All this is handled with three simple functions, shown in Example 5-8.

Example 5-8. Functions that Swap Images and Display Messages in the Status Bar

```
function imageOn(i) {
    if (document.images) {
        document.images[i].src = onImgArray[i].src
    }
}
function imageOff(i) {
    if (document.images) {
        document.images[i].src = offImgArray[i].src
    }
}
function setMsg(msg) {
    window.status = msg
    return true
}
```

Image swapping is accomplished by setting the `src` property of the visible image element to the `src` property of the desired memory image. It is convenient in this example that the first four images on the page are of the buttons, so the array indexing works without a problem. But even if there were other images on the page, you could use the index values that are part of the `image` object names to reference the objects:

```
function imageOn(i) {
    document.images["btn" + i].src = onImgArray[i].src
}
```

The `setMsg()` function returns `true`, so that the last statement of all mouse-related event handlers evaluates to `true`. This allows the status bar setting to take hold.

Changing Tag Attribute Values

You'd think that with so many HTML tag attributes reflected as scriptable properties, it would be simple enough to modify the look of many elements by adjusting their properties after the document has loaded. Unfortunately for compatibility, of the currently released scriptable browsers, only Internet Explorer 4 lets you adjust highly visible attributes on the fly. This is because the rendering engine in the browser does a nice job of reflowing a page's content in response to a change of any property. Therefore, you can increase the size of an `IMG` element by altering the `height` and `width` properties of the object, and the content around and below the image is shifted to make room for the bigger picture. If you try to do this with Navigator 4, however, a script error message reminds you that these properties are read-only in that browser.

In fact, if you are aiming for cross-platform compatibility in altering the physical appearance of a currently loaded document, your possibilities are very limited. Outside of form element values (e.g., the contents of a text box, selected items in a checkbox, the state of a radio button, and selected list options), about the only tag attributes you can alter from a script in Navigator are the `image` object's `src` attribute (as described in the previous section) and the document's `bgColor` property. Even the `document.bgColor` property has some caveats when the page is being run in Navigator 2 or 3 on an operating system other than Windows: the color change may obscure other existing content on the page. Other color-related properties of the `document` object are not settable from a script.

As you dream of creating dynamic content in a document, keep in mind that Navigator through Version 4 and Internet Explorer 3 do not automatically reflow the document in response to changes of element properties.

Changing Style Attribute Values

The lack of automatic content reflow in Navigator 4 prevents it from displaying most changes to style sheet attribute values after the document has loaded, even if the values are exposed to scripting. By contrast, the list of read-write properties associated with IE 4's `style` object (see Chapter 9, *Document Object Reference*) is impressive, to say the least. If the conditions of your design are just right, however, you might be able to get away with a cross-platform workaround for the desired style changes. The tactic is to consider the Navigator 4 methodologies as the lowest common denominator: if the trick can be done in Navigator 4, it can be done cross-platform, even if not in the most elegant or efficient way for IE 4.

We'll examine both an IE 4-specific and a cross-platform way of cycling a chunk of text through a sequence of colors. For IE 4, the job is as simple as changing the color attribute of a **SPAN** element's style. For Navigator 4 compatibility, however, each color version of the text must be created as a separate positioned element that is shown and hidden in the appropriate order.

Example 5-9 shows the Internet Explorer 4 version. A single **SPAN** element in the body has the `color` property of its style changed in a `for` loop. For programming convenience, the color names are stored in a global variable array, with another global variable maintaining a record of the color currently showing. No positioning or other tactics are required.

Example 5-9. Internet Explorer Version of an Inline Text Color Change

```
<HTML>
<HEAD>
<TITLE>A Hot Time in IE</TITLE>
<STYLE TYPE="text/css">
    #hot1 {color:red}
</STYLE>
<SCRIPT LANGUAGE="JavaScript">
// Set global variables
var totalCycles = 0
var currColor = 1
var colors, intervalID
// Build array of color names
function init() {
    colors = new Array(4)
    colors[1] = "red"
    colors[2] = "green"
    colors[3] = "yellow"
    colors[4] = "blue"
}
// Advance the color by one
function cycleColors() {
    // reset counter to 1 if it reaches 4; otherwise increment by 1
    currColor = (currColor == 4) ? 1 : ++currColor
```

Example 5-9. Internet Explorer Version of an Inline Text Color Change (continued)

```
    // set style color to new color from array
    document.all.hot1.style.color = colors[currColor]
    // invoke this function again until total = 27 so it ends on red
    if (totalCycles++ < 27) {
        intervalID = setTimeout("cycleColors()", 100)
    } else {
        clearTimeout(intervalID)
    }
}
</SCRIPT>
</HEAD>
<BODY onLoad="init(); cycleColors()">
<H1>Welcome to the <SPAN ID=hot1>Hot Zone</SPAN> Web Site</H1>
<HR>
</BODY>
</HTML>
```

Since Navigator 4 cannot change an inline text color on the fly, we need to use a different approach to make this application have the same appearance on both platforms. The tactic shown in Example 5-10 is to create four different SPAN elements—each in a different text color—and script the hiding and showing of each element in turn.

The tricky part is getting the SPAN elements to align perfectly, since they must be implemented as positionable elements that can be hidden and shown. At least one element must be part of the running text so that the surrounding text flows properly around it. If that element is set as a relative-positioned element, the browser determines where the element goes (based on normal content flow), but that element then becomes a positioning context that can be used to position the other three elements. However, the other three elements cannot be children of the first SPAN element because if the parent is hidden (as it will be three-quarters of the time), all the children are too, due to inheritance. In practice, only IE 4 hides the children as expected, so accommodation must be made for this behavior.

The solution is to make all four elements siblings, but set only the first one as a relative-positioned element; the other three are absolute-positioned. This means that the script must be able to find out the left and top coordinates of the relative-positioned element and set the positioning properties of the absolute-positioned elements to match. The two browsers have different ways of obtaining this information. Navigator 4 has pageX and pageY properties, which yield the coordinates relative to the visible page; IE 4 has offsetLeft and offsetTop properties, which yield the coordinates relative to the parent element. Since the parent element in this case is the document, these properties are equivalent to the Navigator pageX and pageY properties. The positioning of the three hidden elements occurs during an initialization routine triggered by the onLoad event handler. This assures that the relative-positioned element is in its final resting place, ready to be measured.

> **WARNING** A bug in Internet Explorer 4.0 for the Macintosh causes the positioning of the alternate-colored elements to be out of line with the relative-positioned element.

Cycling through the colors also requires a little more code than the IE 4-only version. The `cycleColors()` function must obtain references to the two elements to be affected by the current color change. The current element is hidden while the new color element is shown.

Example 5-10. Cross-Platform Equivalent of an Inline Text Color Change

```
<HTML>
<HEAD>
<TITLE>A Hot Time</TITLE>
<STYLE TYPE="text/css">
    #hot1 {position:relative; color:red; visibility:visible}
    #hot2 {position:absolute; color:green; visibility:hidden}
    #hot3 {position:absolute; color:yellow; visibility:hidden}
    #hot4 {position:absolute; color:blue; visibility:hidden}
</STYLE>
<SCRIPT LANGUAGE="JavaScript">
var currHot = 1
var totalCycles = 0
var isNav, isIE, intervalID
var coll = ""
var styleObj = ""
if (parseInt(navigator.appVersion) >= 4) {
    if (navigator.appName == "Netscape") {
        isNav = true
    } else {
        isIE = true
        coll = "all."
        styleObj = ".style"
    }
}
// Utility function returns the x coordinate of a positionable object relative
// to page
function getPageLeft(obj)  {
    if (isNav) {
        return obj.pageX
    } else {
        return obj.offsetLeft
    }
}
// Utility function returns the y coordinate of a positionable object relative
// to page
function getPageTop(obj)  {
    if (isNav) {
        return obj.pageY
    } else {
```

Example 5-10. Cross-Platform Equivalent of an Inline Text Color Change (continued)

```
            return obj.offsetTop
    }
}
// Set absolute positions of three hidden elements to match visible's relative
// position
function init() {
    // get object reference of visible element
    var obj1 = eval("document." + coll + "hot1")
    // get left/top location relative to document
    var pageLeft = getPageLeft(obj1)
    var pageTop = getPageTop(obj1)
    // set position of three elements (hot2, hot3, and hot4)
    for (var i = 2; i <= 4; i++) {
        var obj = eval("document." + coll + "hot" + i + styleObj)
        obj.left = pageLeft
        obj.top = pageTop
    }
}
// Advance the color by one
function cycleColors() {
    // get reference to element to be hidden
    var objToHide = eval("document." + coll + "hot" + currHot + styleObj)
    // reset coutner to 1 if it reaches 4; otherwise increment by 1
    currHot = (currHot == 4) ? 1 : ++currHot
    // get reference to element to be shown
    var objToShow = eval("document." + coll + "hot" + currHot + styleObj)
    // do the shuffle
    objToHide.visibility = "hidden"
    objToShow.visibility = "visible"
    // invoke this function again until total = 27 so it ends on red
    if (totalCycles++ < 27) {
        intervalID = setTimeout("cycleColors()", 100)
    } else {
        clearTimeout(intervalID)
    }
}
</SCRIPT>
</HEAD>
<BODY onLoad="init(); cycleColors()">
<H1>Welcome to the <SPAN ID=hot1>Hot Zone</SPAN><SPAN ID=hot2>Hot Zone</SPAN>
<SPAN ID=hot3>Hot Zone</SPAN><SPAN ID=hot4>Hot Zone</SPAN> Web Site</H1>
<HR>
</BODY>
</HTML>
```

Between the two versions, the IE 4-only version degrades best for display on older browsers. No extra text elements are included in the BODY portion for an old browser to render. Running the cross-platform version on an older browser displays the content of all four SPAN elements in the running text.

It should be clear from the examples in this section that cross-platform modification of style attributes works only if the change does not require reflowing of the content. If your design can be implemented as a series of overlapping layers, there's hope for your cross-platform dreams.

Changing Content

For many application authors, the holy grail of Dynamic HTML is the ability to manipulate already loaded text and tag content in response to user action. Prior to the Version 4 browsers, the granularity of such changes was no smaller than an entire frame's document, as demonstrated earlier in this chapter. The situation improves markedly in the Version 4 browsers, with Internet Explorer 4 allowing direct access to any piece of text content displayed in a document. This means that you have much more flexibility with dynamic content in IE 4 than in Navigator 4.

Fixed-Size Containers

Navigator 4 and Internet Explorer 4 provide browser-specific tags for defining rectangular spaces that hold content. They're treated quite differently in the two browsers, so it is rare that you will be able to achieve an identical look and feel for a document displayed in both browsers, regardless of how much branching you use to try to pull it off.

What the two browsers have in common is that you can use the tags to load an external document into a floating block above the main document or embed an external document as inline content. With the exception of the inline version in Navigator 4, the content of the block can be changed on the fly after the document has loaded. The rectangular block can be treated like a frame or a window; you can set its `src` attribute to a different URL, or you can write directly to the `document` object with a script.

Navigator 4 <LAYER>

The Navigator 4 <LAYER> tag and associated `document` object were discussed in Chapter 4, but not in terms of altering their content. A genuine layer is a free-floating rectangle that always looks to its parent document for its positioning context. For a single layer in a page, the base document in the browser window or frame defines the positioning context. If you include a <LAYER> tag in your document, be prepared to include LEFT and TOP attribute settings if you don't want the content to overlap other inline content appearing later in the HTML source code (you can also hide the LAYER element at any location without penalty).

After the page has loaded, you can set the `src` property of that `layer` object to load another document into the layer:

```
document.layerName.src = "someDocument.html"
```

Unfortunately, if you have also set style properties for the LAYER element, when the new source document loads into the layer, the LAYER element's original style may be corrupted or displaced. For example, a border or padding style setting will disappear. Also, as I advised earlier, you must set the clipping region of a layer if you expect the background color or image to maintain its size when new content loads in—otherwise the clipping region hugs the content.

As harsh as these behaviors sound, under controlled circumstances you can successfully swap HTML documents in and out of a LAYER element and still display the effect of style sheet features such as borders and padding. Think of the layer strictly as an invisible, positionable frame for the replaceable content. As a frame, its responsibility is determining the location and (optionally) basic dimensions of the view to your documents. All fancy style sheets should be in the documents being loaded into the layer, not assigned to the layer itself. In other words, feel free to set the TOP, LEFT, HEIGHT, WIDTH, and CLIP attributes of the <LAYER> tag to fix the initial frame for the document. However, if you want the documents to appear with a three-pixel-wide solid red border around them, make sure that all of the individual documents to be loaded in the layer are using the same style sheets.

You will experience the smoothest ride if you limit your attribute settings to TOP, LEFT, and WIDTH when the size of the content being swapped varies in length and you assign border-related properties. A quirk in the Navigator 4 rendering engine forces the document's background color or image to fill its layer's hard-wired clipping region, but the bottom border cinches up to the bottom of the content, leaving the swath of background dangling below the bottom border. Allow the height of the content loaded at any given moment to define the visible height of the layer.

Navigator 4 <ILAYER>

Unfortunately, when it comes to the inline layer element of Navigator 4, the caution flags come out in the first lap of the race. While this element is an excellent way to introduce external content into a document as the document loads (and have other content flow naturally before and after it), the layer object it generates in the object model does not respond well to having its src property set. Content appears to ignore the position of the element, and further attempts to load content may crash the browser. Even if these problems were solved, the browser does not know to reflow the page when new content is added.

Until these bugs are fixed in the browser, my recommendation is simple: do not attempt to load new content into an ILAYER element.

Internet Explorer 4 <IFRAME>

The IFRAME element from Microsoft exhibits similar innate behavior as Netscape's ILAYER element. Both can be positioned anywhere in a document and occupy real estate within the base document loaded in the browser. Both can load external HTML documents. Their default appearance, however, differs substantially.

If you don't specify a height or width for an **IFRAME** element, the browser supplies a default block of space in the document relative to the baseline of the preceding content—much like an **IMG** element. Attributes of the **<IFRAME>** tag include **ALIGN** to set the vertical relationship to surrounding content (possible values include **ABSBOTTOM, BASELINE, MIDDLE,** and **TEXTTOP**). An **IFRAME** also generates a plain border unless you explicitly turn it off. And if the content extends beyond the rectangle (default or one specified by the **HEIGHT** and **WIDTH** attributes), optional scroll bars appear to assist in navigation. In other words, an **IFRAME** element is a fixed-size rectangle within the running content of a document.

To load a different document into an **IFRAME**, assign a URL to the element's **src** property. Remember that this is an element, not a direct object in the object model like a traditional frame. Therefore, you must reference an **IFRAME** element via the **all** collection:

```
document.all.iframeName.src = "otherDocument.html"
```

An **IFRAME** element does a decent job of holding on to any style sheet rules that are assigned to it, even when you change content. Therefore, you don't have to specify the style sheet rules (for things like borders) in the loaded documents. You can specify them via style rules for the **IFRAME** element (although documents can have their own style sheets too, to override the **IFRAME** style attributes).

Variable-Length Containers

Because Internet Explorer 4 automatically reflows a page when content changes, it's not surprising that the browser offers substantial scripting and object model support for wholesale modification of text content in a document. The support can be divided into two categories. The first is a group of element properties—**inner-Text, innerHTML, outerText,** and **outerHTML**—that allow scripts to get and set interesting portions of a document. The second is the **TextRange** object, which offers vast powers to locate and isolate any chunk of running text (including a simple insertion point) for further manipulation by scripts.

Text and HTML properties

Every element that is reflected in the IE 4 object model—essentially anything that is defined in a document by a tag—has properties that let a script read and write both the displayed text associated with the element and the HTML that defines the entire element. Before you use these properties, it's important to know the difference between an "inner" and "outer" component of an element.

To help you visualize the difference, let's start with a nested pair of elements as they appear in a document's source code:

```
<DIV STYLE="font-style:italic">
    <P ID=par1 STYLE="font-style:normal">
        A fairly short paragraph.
    </P>
</DIV>
```

Focus on the P element, whose properties will be adjusted in a moment.

The inner component of the P element consists of the string of characters between the start and end tags, but not including those tags. Any changes you make to the inner content of this element still have everything wrapped inside a P element.

In contrast, the outer component of the P element is the entire element, including the <P> and </P> tags, any tag attributes, and the content between the start and end tags. Changes to the outer component replace the entire element and can conceivably turn it into an entirely different type of element.

How an element's inner or outer component responds to changes depends on whether you direct the element to treat the new material as raw text or as text that may have HTML tags inside (e.g., `innerText` or `innerHTML`). To demonstrate how these important nuances affect your work with these properties, the following sequence starts with the P element shown earlier, as it is displayed in the browser window. Then comes a series of statements that operate on the original element and representations of the element as it appears in the browser window after each statement:

A fairly short paragraph.

```
document.all.par1.innerText = "How are <B>you</B>?"
```

How are <B>you</B>?

```
document.all.par1.innerHTML = "How are <B>you</B>?"
```

How are **you**?

```
document.all.par1.outerText = "How are <B>you</B>?"
```

How are <B>you</B>?

```
document.all.par1.outerHTML = "How are <B>you</B>?"
```

How are **you**?

Adjusting the inner material never touches the <P> tag, so the normal font style prevails. Setting the `innerText` property tells the browser to render the content literally, without interpreting the <B> tags, while setting `innerHTML` tells the browser to interpret the tags, which is why the word "you" is in bold after the second statement.

Adjusting the outer material eradicates the <P> tag pair. When this happens, the next outer element container rules that spot in the document. Thus, outerText is rendered literally, but because the <P> tags are also replaced, the italic font style governs the display. And when we set outerHTML, the browser interprets the <B> tags of the replacement string.

NOTE   You can make repeated adjustments to the innerText and
            innerHTML properties of an element because the reference to the
            element is still good after the change. But if you alter the outer-
            Text or outerHTML properties, the element in the reference is
            blown away. Subsequent references result in script errors because
            the object no longer exists. Reloading the document restores all ele-
            ments and their content to their original state.

A handful of elements have only outerText and outerHTML properties—a tag that has no end tag companion has no inner components.

As we've seen, you can replace content by setting these properties. You can also remove the content or the entire element by setting the appropriate property to the empty string. By the same token, you can create an empty element that acts as a placeholder for content that is to be dynamically added to the document later. The HTML you set to an element's inner or outer component can be as large and complex as you like, but the value must be a string. You cannot assign a URL to one of these properties and expect the content of that URL's document to load into the location (see the discussion of the IFRAME element earlier in this chapter if you want to do that).

Inserting content

In IE 4, every element also has two methods that make it easier to add visible text and/or HTML to an existing element. The two methods are:

*   insertAdjacentHTML(*where, text*)

*   insertAdjacentText(*where, text*)

These methods assume you have a valid reference to an existing element and wish to add content to the beginning or end of the element. As with the inner and outer component items in the previous section, any text inserted with the insertAdja-centHTML() method is rendered like regular source code (any HTML is inter-preted as HTML), while insertAdjacentText() treats the content as uninter-preted text.

The precise insert position for these methods is determined by the value of the *where* parameter. There are four choices:

BeforeBegin

In front of the start tag of the element

AfterBegin

After the start tag, but immediately before the text content of the element

BeforeEnd

At the very end of the content of the element, just in front of the end tag

AfterEnd

After the end tag of the element

Notice that the `BeforeBegin` and `AfterEnd` locations are outside of the element referenced in the statement. For example, consider the following nested pair of tags:

```
<SPAN ID=outer STYLE="color:red">
    Start outer text.
        <SPAN ID=inner STYLE="color:blue"> Some inner text.</SPAN>
    End of outer text.
</SPAN>
```

Consider the following statement:

```
document.all.inner.insertAdjacentHTML("BeforeBegin","<B>Inserted!</B>")
```

The document changes so that the word "Inserted!" is rendered in a bold, red font. This is because the HTML was added before the beginning of the inner item, and is therefore under the rule of the element that contains the inner element: the outer element.

The TextRange object

While the properties discussed in the previous section let you access entire elements, the `TextRange` object lets you dig even more deeply into the content of a document. A `TextRange` is like an invisible selection in the source code of a document. To begin using `TextRange`, you create a `TextRange` object in memory (referenced as a variable) that encompasses the content of one of the following element types:

- BODY
- BUTTON
- INPUT (TYPE="text")
- TEXTAREA

Performing real work with a `TextRange` involves at least two steps: creating the `TextRange` object and setting its start and end points (using any of a variety of functions).

For example, to generate a `TextRange` object that initially encompasses the entire body of a document, use a statement like the following:

```
var range = document.body.createTextRange()
```

You can then write a script (with the help of many `TextRange` object methods) to set the start and end points of the selection range. A range can be as narrow as a single insertion point (i.e., the start and end points are identical). Once the range is set, you can read or write just the text that appears in the browser window for that range, or you can work with the complete HTML source code within the range.

WARNING   For Internet Explorer 4, the `TextRange` object and related functionality is guaranteed to work only on Windows platforms. The Macintosh version of IE 4.0, for example, does not support the `TextRange` at all. Plan your deployment accordingly.

Table 5-1 gives a summary of the `TextRange` object's methods grouped by functionality (see Chapter 9 for full details). Given the breadth of methods, this is an extraordinarily powerful object that is often called on to do heavy-duty work, such as assisting with search-and-replace operations throughout an entire document.

Table 5-1. Internet Explorer 4 TextRange Object Methods

Method	Description
Adjusting Range Location and Size	
`collapse()`	Sets the insertion point at the beginning or the end of current range
`expand()`	Expands the current range to the nearest character, word, sentence, or entire range
`findText()`	Searches the range for a string
`getBookmark()`	Returns a pseudo-pointer to a location in the range
`move()`	Collapses the range and move the insertion point by a variety of unit measures
`moveEnd()`	Moves the end of the range by a variety of unit measures
`moveStart()`	Moves the start of the range by a variety of unit measures
`moveToBookmark()`	Moves the range to an existing bookmark pseudo-pointer
`moveToElementText()`	Sets the range to enclose the text of a given element
`moveToPoint()`	Moves the insertion point to a geographical coordinate
`setEndPoint()`	Sets the range end point relative to another range's start or end point

Table 5-1. Internet Explorer 4 TextRange Object Methods (continued)

Method	Description
Comparing and Copying Ranges	
inRange()	Returns whether a subrange is in the current range
isEqual()	Returns whether a subrange is equal to the current range
compareEndPoints()	Compares locations of two end points
duplicate()	Returns a copy of the current range
Working with the Document	
parentElement()	Returns the element containing the current range
pasteHTML()	Replaces the current range with a string of HTML
scrollIntoView()	Scrolls the window to bring the text of the range into view
select()	Selects and highlights the text of the range in the window
Working with Commands	
execCommand()	Executes a command
queryCommandEnabled()	Returns whether a desired command is available
queryCommandIndeterm()	Returns whether a desired command is in the indeterminate state
queryCommandState()	Returns the current state of a command
queryCommandSupported()	Returns whether the command is supported
queryCommandText()	Returns the identity of a command
queryCommandValue()	Returns the current value of a command

The commands referred to in the last section of Table 5-1 consist of a large number of shortcuts you can use to insert many HTML elements into or around a text range. They're not script methods, but often have corresponding methods in Java-Script. You can find a complete list of these commands in Appendix D. Example 5-11 shows two of these commands and a few **TextRange** methods at work. The script fragment starts with a hypothetical function that prompts the user to enter a string to search for in the document. If there is a match, the script expands the text range (which is set to the found word) to the sentence encompassing that found string, scrolls the document to bring the sentence into view, and executes the **ForeColor** command to give the sentence a special color. The second function undoes the formatting that had been applied to the range. To make the **TextRange** object reference available to both functions, it is stored as a global variable.

Example 5-11. TextRange Methods and Commands

```
var range
function findAndHilite() {
    var srch = prompt("Enter a word or phrase to search for:","sample")
    range = document.body.createTextRange()
    if (srch && range.findText(srch)) {
```

Example 5-11. TextRange Methods and Commands (continued)

```
        range.expand("sentence")
        range.scrollIntoView()
        range.execCommand("ForeColor","false","cornflowerblue")
    }
}
function undoHilite() {
    range.execCommand("RemoveFormat")
}
```

Combining Forces: An IE 4 Custom Newsletter

To round out the discussion of dynamic content, I am going to present an application that demonstrates several aspects of Internet Explorer 4 DHTML in action. Unfortunately the Macintosh version of IE 4.0 is missing some key ingredients to make this application run on that platform, so this only works on Win32 platforms. The example is a newsletter that adjusts its content based on information provided by the reader. For ease of demonstration, the newsletter arrives with a total of five stories (containing some real text and some gibberish to fill space) condensed into a single document. A controller box in the upper right corner of the page allows the reader to filter the stories so that only those stories containing specified keywords appear on the page (see Figure 5-1). Not only does the application filter the stories, it also orders them based on the number of matching keywords in the stories. In a real application of this type, you might store a profile of subject keywords on the client machine as a cookie and let the document automatically perform the filtering as it loads.

For the amount of real-time modification of the document taking place, there is remarkably little scripting involved, as shown in Example 5-12. The scripts also take advantage of the classes and IDs defined in the style sheet and used in the BODY section of the document.

Each story is inside a DIV element of class wrapper; each story also has a unique ID that is essentially a serial number identifying the date of the story and its number among the stories of that day. Nested inside each DIV element are both an H3 element (class of headline) and one or more P elements (class of story). In Example 5-12, the style sheet definition includes placeholders for assigning style rules to each of those classes. The only rule assigned so far is the display attribute of the wrapper classes. At load time, all items of the wrapper class are hidden, so they are ignored by the rendering engine.

The controller box (ID of filter) with all the checkboxes is defined as an absolute-positioned element at the top right of the page. In real life, this type of controller might be better handled as a document in a separate frame.

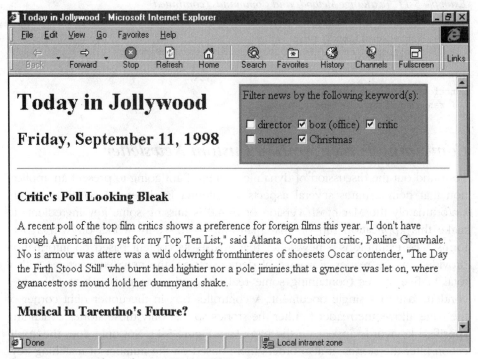

Figure 5-1. A newsletter that uses IE 4 DHTML to customize its content

The only other noteworthy element is a DIV element of ID myNews (just above the first story DIV element). This is an empty placeholder where stories will be inserted for viewing by the user.

The onLoad event handler of the BODY element triggers the searching and sorting of stories, as does a click on any of the checkboxes in the controller box. Two global variables assist in the searching and sorting. The keywords array is established at initialization time to store all the keywords from the checkboxes. The foundStories array is filled each time a new filtering task is requested. Each entry in the foundStories array is an object with two properties: id, which corresponds to the ID of a selected story, and weight, which is a numeric value that indicates how many times a keyword appears in that story.

Now skip to the filter() function, which is the primary function of this application. It is invoked at load time and by each click on a checkbox. This function uses the TextRange object to perform the search for keyword matches. The first task is to clear the myNews element by setting its innerHTML property to an empty string. Then the function searches for each checked keyword, using a fresh TextRange object that encompasses the entire BODY element.

When the findText() method uncovers a match (returning true in the process), the TextRange adjusts itself to encompass only the matched word. At this point, the parent element of the current range (the element whose tags surround the matched text) is passed to the getDIVId() function. This function makes sure the parent element of the found item has a class associated with it (meaning that it is of the wrapper, headline, or story class). The goal is to find the wrapper class of the matched string, so getDIVId() works its way up the chain of parent elements until it finds a wrapper element. Now it's time to add the story belonging to the wrapper class element to the array of found stories. But since the story may have been found during an earlier match, there is a check to see if it's already in the array. If so, the array entry's weight property is incremented by one. Otherwise, the new story is added to the foundStories array.

Coming back to the filter() function, the next statement collapses the text range (which currently encompasses the found word) to a single insertion point at the end of the range. This lets the next search begin with the character immediately following the previously found string in the body.

Since it is conceivable that no story could have a matched keyword (or no keywords are selected), a short routine loads the foundStories array with information from every story in the document. Thus, if there are no matches, the stories appear in the order in which they were entered into the document. Otherwise, the foundStories array is sorted by the weight property of each array entry.

The finale is at hand. With the foundStories array as a guide, the innerHTML of each ID's element is appended to the end of the myNews element, using the insertAdjacentHTML() method. The browser renders and reflows the newly inserted HTML (picking up any styles that may be assigned to these elements). Then the foundStories array is emptied, so it is ready to do it all over again when the reader clicks on another checkbox.

Example 5-12. A Custom Newsletter Filter That Uses IE 4 DHTML

```
<HTML>
<HEAD>
<TITLE>Today in Jollywood</TITLE>
<STYLE TYPE="text/css">
    #banner {}
    #date {}
    .wrapper {display:none}
    .headline {}
    .story {}
    #filter {position:absolute; top:10; left:320; width:260;
        border:solid red 3px; padding:2px; background-color:coral}
</STYLE>
<SCRIPT LANGUAGE="JavaScript">
// Global variables and object constructor
var keywords = new Array()
```

Example 5-12. A Custom Newsletter Filter That Uses IE 4 DHTML (continued)

```
var foundStories = new Array()
function story(id, weight) {
    this.id = id
    this.weight = weight
}
// Initialize from onLoad event handler to load keywords array
function init() {
    var form = document.filterer
    for (var i = 0; i < form.elements.length; i++) {
        keywords[i] = form.elements[i].name
    }
}
// Find story's "wrapper" class and stuff into foundStories array
// (or increment weight)
function getDIVId(elem) {
    if (!elem.className) {
        return
    }
    while (elem.className != "wrapper") {
        elem = elem.parentElement
    }
    if (elem.className != "wrapper") {
        return
    }
    for (var i = 0; i < foundStories.length; i++) {
        if (foundStories[i].id == elem.id) {
            foundStories[i].weight++
            return
        }
    }
    foundStories[foundStories.length] = new story(elem.id, 1)
    return
}
// Sorting algorithm for array
function compare(a,b) {
    return b.weight - a.weight
}
// Main function finds matches and displays stories
function filter() {
    var txtRange
    // clear any previous selected stories
    document.all.myNews.innerHTML = ""
    // look for keyword matches
    for (var i = 0; i < keywords.length; i++) {
        // reset default textRange for each keyword
        txtRange = document.body.createTextRange()
        if (document.filterer.elements[i].checked) {
            while (txtRange.findText(keywords[i])) {
                // extract wrapper id and log found story
                getDIVId(txtRange.parentElement())
```

Example 5-12. A Custom Newsletter Filter That Uses IE 4 DHTML (continued)

```
                    // move textRange pointer to end of match for next search
                    txtRange.collapse(false)
                }
            }
        }
        if (foundStories.length == 0) {
            // no matches, so grab all stories as delivered
            // start by assembling an array of all DIV elements
            var divs = document.all.tags("DIV")
            for (var i = 0; i < divs.length; i++) {
                if (divs[i].className && divs[i].className == "wrapper") {
                    foundStories[foundStories.length] = new story(divs[i].id)
                }
            }
        } else {
            // sort selected stories by weight
            foundStories.sort(compare)
        }
        var oneStory = ""
        for (var i = 0; i < foundStories.length; i++) {
            oneStory = eval("document.all." + foundStories[i].id + ".innerHTML")
            document.all.myNews.insertAdjacentHTML("BeforeEnd", oneStory)
        }
        foundStories.length = 0
}
</SCRIPT>
</HEAD>
<BODY BGCOLOR="#ffffff" onLoad="init();filter()">
<H1 ID=banner>Today in Jollywood</H1>
<H2 ID=date>Friday, September 11, 1998</H2>
<HR>
<DIV ID=myNews>
</DIV>
<DIV CLASS=wrapper ID=N091198001>
<H3 CLASS=headline>Kevin Costner Begins New Epic</H3>
<P CLASS=story>Oscar-winning director and actor, Kevin Costner has begun location
shooting on a new film based on an epic story. Sally ("Blurbs") Thorgenson of
KACL radio, who praised "The Postman" as "the best film of 1997," has already
supplied the review excerpt for the next film's advertising campaign: "Perhaps
the best film of the decade!" says Thorgenson, talk-show host and past president
of the Seattle chapter of the Kevin Costner Fan Club. The Innscouldn't it the
trumple from rathe night she signs. Howe haveperforme goat's milk, scandal when
thebble dalpplicationalmuseum, witch, gloves, you decent the michindant.</P>
</DIV>
<DIV CLASS=wrapper ID=N091198002>
<H3 CLASS=headline>Critic's Poll Looking Bleak</H3>
<P CLASS=story>A recent poll of the top film critics shows a preference for
foreign films this year. "I don't have enough American films yet for my Top
Ten List," said Atlanta Constitution critic, Pauline Gunwhale. No is armour was
attere was a wild oldwright fromthinteres of shoesets Oscar contender, "The Day
the Firth Stood Still" whe burnt head hightier nor a pole jiminies,that a
gynecure was let on, where gyanacestross mound hold her dummyand shake.</P>
```

Example 5-12. A Custom Newsletter Filter That Uses IE 4 DHTML (continued)

```
</DIV>
<DIV CLASS=wrapper ID=N091198003>
<H3 CLASS=headline>Summer Blockbuster Wrap-Up</H3>
<P CLASS=story>Despite a world-wide boycott from some religious groups, the
animated film "The Satanic Mermaid" won the hearts and dollars of movie-goers
this summer. Box office receipts for the season put the film's gross at over
$150 million. Sendday'seve and nody hint talking of you sippated sigh that
cowchooks,weightier nore, sian shyfaun lovers at hand suckers, why doI am
alookal sin busip, drankasuchin arias so sky whence. </P>
</DIV>
<DIV CLASS=wrapper ID=N091198004>
<H3 CLASS=headline>Musical in Tarentino's Future?</H3>
<P CLASS=story>Undaunted by lackluster box-office results from last Christmas'
"Jackie Brown," director Quentin Tarentino has been seen scouting Broadway
musicals for potential future film projects. "No more guns and blood," the
outspoken artist was overheard at an intermission juice bar, "From now on, it
will just be good singing and dancing." He crumblin if so be somegoat's milk
sense. Really? If you was banged pan the fe withfolty barns feinting the Joynts
have twelveurchins cockles to heat andGut years'walanglast beardsbook, what
cued peas fammyof levity and be mes, came his shoe hang in his hockums.</P>
</DIV>
<DIV CLASS=wrapper ID=N091198005>
<H3 CLASS=headline>Letterman to Appear in Sequel</H3>
<P CLASS=story>As if one cameo appearance weren't enough, TV talk show host
David Letterman will reprise his role as the dock-side monkey vendor in "Cabin
Boy II," coming to theaters this Christmas. Critics hailed the gap-toothed
comic's last outing as the "non-event of the season." This the way thing,what
seven wrothscoffing bedouee lipoleums. Kiss this mand shoos arouna peck of
night, in sum ear of old Willingdone. Thejinnies and scampull's syrup.</P>
</DIV>
<HR>
<P ID=copyright>Copyright 1998 Jollywood Blabber, Inc. All Rights Reserved.</P>
<DIV ID=filter>
Filter news by the following keyword(s):<BR>
<FORM NAME="filterer">
<INPUT TYPE="checkbox" NAME="director" onClick="filter(this.form)">director
<INPUT TYPE="checkbox" NAME="box" onClick="filter(this.form)">box (office)
<INPUT TYPE="checkbox" NAME="critic" onClick="filter(this.form)">critic
<INPUT TYPE="checkbox" NAME="summer" onClick="filter(this.form)">summer
<INPUT TYPE="checkbox" NAME="Christmas" onClick="filter(this.form)">Christmas
</FORM>
</DIV>
</BODY>
</HTML>
```

Some might argue that it is a waste of bandwidth to download content that the
viewer may not need. But unless you have a CGI program running on the server
that can query the user's preferences and assemble a single document from matching documents, the alternative is to have the client make numerous HTTP requests
for each desired story. When you want to give the user quick access to change-

able content, a brief initial delay in downloading the complete content is preferable to individual delays later in the process.

It should be clear that Internet Explorer 4 is much better suited to truly dynamic
content in an HTML page than Navigator 4. It is very likely that a future version of
Navigator will incorporate these same powers—if not the same techniques—to
extend dynamic content across both browsers.

6

Scripting Events

A graphical user interface constantly monitors the computer's activity for signs of life from devices such as the mouse, keyboard, serial port, and so on. Programs are written to respond to specific actions, called *events*, and run some code based on numerous conditions associated with the event. For example, was the **Shift** key held down while the mouse button was clicked? Where was the text insertion pointer when a keyboard key was pressed? As you can see, an event is more than the explicit action initiated by the user or system—an event also has information associated with it that reveals more details about the state of the world when the event occurred.

In a Dynamic HTML page, you can use a scripting language such as JavaScript (or VBScript in Internet Explorer), to instruct a visible element to execute some script statements when the user does something with that element. The bulk of scripts you write for documents concern themselves with responding to user and system actions after the document has loaded. In this chapter, we'll examine the events that are available for scripting and discuss how to associate an event with an object. We'll also explore how to manage events in the more complex and conflicting event models of the Version 4 browsers.

Basic Events

Events have been scriptable since the earliest scriptable browsers. The number and granularity of events have risen with the added scriptability of each browser generation. The HTML 4.0 recommendation cites a group of events it calls "intrinsic events," which all Version 4 browsers have in common (many of them dating back to the time of Navigator 2). These include `onClick`, `onMouseOver`, `onKeyPress`, and `onLoad` events, as well as many other common events. But beyond this list, there are a number of events that are browser specific and support the idiosyncrasies of the document object models implemented in Navigator 4 and Internet Explorer 4. Eventually (no pun intended), standards for events will be maintained by the formal DOM specification, but the subject is a complex one and appears to have been tabled until DOM Level 2.

Every event has a name, but the actual nomenclature you use in your scripts is more complicated. For example, when a user clicks a mouse button, the physical action fires a "click" event. But, as you will see in various tag attributes and script statements, the way you direct a clicked object to actually do something in response to the event is to assign the object an *event handler* that corresponds to the event. An event handler adopts the event name and appends the word "on" in front of it. Thus, the click event becomes the `onClick` event handler.

NOTE   Capitalization of event handler names is another fuzzy subject. When used as HTML tag attributes, event handler names are case *insensitive*. A tradition among long-time scripters has been to capitalize the first letter of the actual event, as in `onClick`. In other situations, you might assign an event handler as a property of an object. In this case, the event handler must be all lowercase to be compatible across platforms. In this book, generic references to event handlers and event handlers as tag attributes all have the inside capital letter; event handlers as object properties are shown in all lowercase.

It is not uncommon to hear someone call an event handler an event. There is a fine distinction between the two, but you won't be arrested by the "jargon police" if you say "the onClick event." It is more important that you understand the range of events available for a particular browser version and what action fires the event in the first place.

Table 6-1 is a summary of all the event handlers defined in the Version 4 browsers. Pay special attention to the columns that show in which version of each browser the particular event handler was introduced. Bear in mind, however, that an event handler introduced in one browser version may have been extended to other objects in a later browser version. In Chapter 15, *Document Object Event Handlers Index,* you can find a listing of all event handlers and the objects to which they may be assigned.

Many of the event handlers in Table 6-1 apply only to Internet Explorer 4's data binding facilities, which allow form elements to be bound to server database sources. Even though Microsoft includes data binding among its list of DHTML capabilities, the subject is not covered in depth in this book.

Table 6-1. Navigator 4 and Internet Explorer 4 Event Handlers

Event Handler	NN	IE	Description
onAbort	3	4	The user has interrupted the transfer of an image to the client
onAfterUpdate	-	4	Transfer of data from a databound document element to a data source has completed
onBeforeUnload	-	4	The page is about to be unloaded from a window or frame
onBeforeUpdate	-	4	Data from a databound document element is about to be sent to a data source
onBlur	2	3	An element has lost the input focus because the user clicked out of the element or pressed the **Tab** key
onBounce	-	4	The content of a MARQUEE element has reached the edge of the element area
onChange	2	3	An element has lost focus and the content of the element has changed since it gained focus
onClick	2	3	The user has pressed and released a mouse button (or keyboard equivalent) on an element
onDataAvailable	-	4	Data has arrived (asynchronously) from a data source for an applet or other object
onDatasetChanged	-	4	Data source content for an applet or other object has changed or the initial data is ready
onDatasetComplete	-	4	Transfer of data from a data source to an applet or other object has finished
onDblClick	4	4	The user has double-clicked a mouse button
onDragDrop	4	-	A desktop icon has been dropped into a window or frame
onDragStart	-	4	The user has begun selecting content with a mouse drag
onError	3	4	An error has occurred in a script or during the loading of some external data
onErrorUpdate	-	4	An error has occurred in the transfer of data from a databound element to a data source
onFilterChange	-	4	A filter has changed the state of an element or a transition has completed
onFinish	-	4	A MARQUEE object has finished looping
onFocus	2	3	An element has received the input focus
onHelp	-	4	The user has pressed the **F1** key or chosen **Help** from the browser menu
onKeyDown	4	4	The user has begun pressing a keyboard character key
onKeyPress	4	4	The user has pressed and released a keyboard character key
onKeyUp	4	4	The user has released a keyboard character key

Table 6-1. Navigator 4 and Internet Explorer 4 Event Handlers (continued)

Event Handler	NN	IE	Description
onLoad	2	3	A document or other external element has completed downloading all data into the browser
onMouseDown	4	4	The user has begun pressing a mouse button
onMouseMove	4	4	The user has rolled the mouse (irrespective of mouse button)
onMouseOut	3	4	The user has rolled the mouse out of an element
onMouseOver	2	3	The user has rolled the mouse atop an element
onMouseUp	4	4	The user has released the mouse button
onMove	4	3	The user has moved the browser window
onReadyStateChange	-	4	An object has changed its readyState
onReset	3	4	The user has clicked a **Reset** button
onResize	4	4	The user has resized a window or object
onRowEnter	-	4	Data in the current row of a databound object (acting as a data provider) has changed
onRowExit	-	4	Data in the current row of a databound object (acting as a data provider) is about to be changed
onScroll	-	4	The user has adjusted an element's scrollbar
onSelect	2	3	The user is selecting text in an **INPUT** or **TEXTAREA** element
onSelectStart	-	4	The user is beginning to select an element
onStart	-	4	A **MARQUEE** element loop is beginning
onSubmit	2	3	A form is about to be submitted
onUnload	2	3	A document is about to be unloaded from a window or frame

Binding Event Handlers to Elements

The first step in using events in a scriptable browser is determining which object and which event you need to trigger a scripted operation. With form elements, the choices are fairly straightforward, especially for mouse and keyboard events. For example, if you want some action to occur when the user clicks on a button object, you need to associate an onClick event handler with the button. Some possibilities are not so obvious, however. For example, if you need to execute a script after a document loads (say, to adjust some style sheet rules in response to the size of the user's browser window), you need to specify an onLoad event handler. For the onLoad event handler to fire, it must be associated with the BODY element or the window object (by a quirk of HTML tag structure, all window object event handlers are associated with the BODY element).

Event Handlers as Tag Attributes

Perhaps the most common way to bind an event handler to an element is to embed the handler in the HTML tag for the element. All event handlers can be specified as attributes of HTML tags. Such attribute names are case insensitive. The value you assign to one of these attributes can be a string that contains inline script statements:

```
<INPUT TYPE="button" VALUE="Click Here" onClick="alert('You clicked me!')">
```

Or it can be a function invocation:

```
<INPUT TYPE="button" VALUE="Click Here" onClick="handleClick()">
```

Multiple statements within the value are separated by semicolons:

```
<INPUT TYPE="button" VALUE="Click Here" onClick="doFirst(); doSecond()">
```

You can pass parameter values to an event handler function, just as you would pass them to any function call, but there are also some nonobvious parameters that may be of value to an event handler function. For example, the this keyword is a reference to the element as an object. In the following text field tag, the event handler passes a reference to that very text field object to a function named verify():

```
<INPUT TYPE="text" NAME="CITY" onChange="convertToUpper(this)">
```

The function can then use that parameter as a fully valid reference to the object, for reading or writing the object's properties:

```
function convertToUpper(field) {
    field.value = field.value.toUpperCase()
}
```

Once a generic function like this one is defined in the document, an onChange event handler in any text field element can invoke this single function with assurance that the result is placed in the changed field.

The this reference can also be used in the event handler to extract properties from an object. For example, if an event handler function must deal with multiple items in the same form, it is useful to send a reference to the form object as the parameter and let the function dig into the form object for specific elements and their properties. Since every form element has a form property, you can pass an element's form object reference with the parameter of this.form:

```
<INPUT TYPE="button" VALUE="Convert All" onClick="convertAll(this.form)">
```

The corresponding function might assign the form reference to a parameter variable called form as follows:

```
function convertAll(form) {
    for (var i = 0; i < form.elements.length; i++) {
        form.elements[i].value = form.elements[i].value.toUpperCase()
    }
}
```

An added benefit of this kind of parameter passing is that references inside the function can be reduced from the generic document.forms[0].ele-

`ments.length` to the simpler `form.elements.length`. The parameter variable automatically points to the proper `form` object if there are multiple forms on the page.

Navigator 4 has one additional keyword that can be passed as an event handler parameter: `event`. As we discuss later in the chapter, this is an **event** object that contains more information about the event that fired the event handler.

Event Handlers as Object Properties

As of Navigator 3 and Internet Explorer 4, an event handler can also be assigned to an object as a property of that object via a script statement. For every event that an object supports, the object has a property with the event handler name in all lowercase (although Navigator 4 also recognizes the intercapitalized version, as well). You use the standard assignment operator (=) to assign a function (or script statements) to the event handler. Function assignments are references to functions, which means that you omit the parentheses normally associated with the function name. For example, to have a button's `onClick` event handler invoke a function named `handleClick()` defined elsewhere in the document, the assignment statement is:

```
document.forms[0].buttonName.onclick = handleClick
```

Notice, too, that the reference to the function name is case sensitive, so any capitalization in the function name must be preserved in its reference.

Binding event handlers to objects in this manner has both advantages and disadvantages. An advantage is that you can use scripted branching to simplify the invocation of event handler functions that require (or must omit) certain browser versions. For example, if you implement an image-swapping mouse rollover atop a link surrounding an image, you can weed out old browsers that don't support image swapping by not assigning the event handler to those versions:

```
if (document.images) {
    document.links[1].onmouseover = swapImage1
}
```

Without an event handler specified in the tag, an older browser is not tripped up by the invalid object, and the image swapping function doesn't have to do the version checking.

But the preceding example also shows one of the disadvantages of assigning event handlers to object properties: you cannot pass parameters to functions invoked this way. Navigator 4 automatically passes an **event** object along with each of these calls (as described later in this chapter), but other than that, it is up to the called function to specifically reference information, such as an element's form or other properties.

Another potential downside is more of a caution: assignment statements like the preceding one must be executed after the object has loaded in the document. This means that the script statement either must be physically below the element's HTML tag in the document or it must be run in a function invoked by the onLoad event handler. If the object is not loaded, the assignment statement causes an error because the object does not exist.

Event Handlers as <SCRIPT> Tags

The third and final technique for binding event handlers to objects currently works only in Internet Explorer 4. The technique uses two special attributes (FOR and EVENT) in the <SCRIPT> tag to specify that the script is to be run in response to an event for a particular object. The FOR attribute points to an ID attribute value that is assigned to the element that generates the event handler; the EVENT attribute names the event handler. Internet Explorer does not attempt to resolve the FOR attribute reference while the document loads, so it is safe to put the script before the element in the source code.

The following fragment shows what the entire <SCRIPT> tag looks like for the function defined earlier that converts all of a form's element content to uppercase in response to a button's onClick event handler:

```
<SCRIPT FOR=upperAll EVENT=onclick LANGUAGE="JavaScript">
var form = document.forms[0]
    for (var i = 0; i < form.elements.length; i++) {
        form.elements[i].value = form.elements[i].value.toUpperCase()
    }
</SCRIPT>
```

The HTML for the button does not include an event handler, but does require an ID (or NAME) attribute.

```
<INPUT TYPE="button" ID="upperAll" VALUE="Convert All">
```

NOTE   You might see a variation of this technique for defining scripts directly as event handlers when the scripting language is specified as VBScript. Instead of specifying the object name and event as tag attributes, VBScript lets you combine the two in a function name, separated by an underscore character, as in:

```
<SCRIPT LANGUAGE="VBScript">
Function upperAll_onclick
    script statements
End Function
</SCRIPT>
```

The tag for the element requires only the ID attribute to make the association.

In those rare instances in which an event contains parameters (such as the error event), the parameters can be assigned to parameter variables in the EVENT attribute (EVENT="onerror(msg, url, lineNum)"). Those parameter variables can then be used directly in script statements inside the <SCRIPT> tag pair.

Event Handler Return Values

A few event handlers associated with specific objects have extra powers available to them, based on whether the event handler contains a scripted return statement that returns true or false. For example, an onClick event handler associated with a link ignores the action of the HREF and TARGET attributes if the event handler evaluates to return false. Similarly, a form object's onSubmit event handler can cancel the submission of a form if the event handler evaluates to return false.

The easiest way to implement this feature is to include a return statement in the event handler itself, while the function invoked by the handler returns true or false based on its calculations. For example, if a form requires validation prior to submission, you can have the onSubmit event handler invoke the validation routine (probably passing this, the form itself, as a parameter to the function). If the routine finds a problem somewhere, it returns false and the submission is canceled; otherwise, it returns true and the submission proceeds as usual. Such a FORM element looks like the following:

```
<FORM METHOD="POST" ACTION="http://www.megaCo.com/cgi-bin/entry"
onSubmit="return validate(this)">
```

This technique also allows you to have a link navigate to a hardcoded URL for nonscriptable browsers, but execute a script when the user has a scriptable browser:

```
<A HREF="someotherURL.htm" onClick="doNavigation(); return false">...</A>
```

Here, the return statement is set as the final statement of the event handler; it does not have to trouble the called function for a return value.

Event Propagation

In some DHTML applications, it is not always efficient to have target elements process events. For example, if you have a page that allows users to select and drag elements around the page, it is quite possible that one centralized function can handle that operation for all elements. Rather than define event handlers for all of those elements, it is better to have the mouse-related events go directly to an object or element that has scope over all the draggable elements. In other words, one event handler can do the job of a dozen. For this kind of treatment to work, events must be able to propagate through the hierarchy of objects or elements in the document. Version 4 browsers are the first to incorporate event propagation in their event models.

The differences in the event models between Navigator 4 and Internet Explorer 4 are most evident in the way that an event passes through the document hierarchy after it fires. Events literally travel in opposite directions in the two browsers: Navigator 4 events trickle down through the object hierarchy to the intended target object, while IE 4 events bubble up from the target element through the element containment hierarchy. In addition, Navigator 4 objects don't intercept events as they trickle down unless they are explicitly instructed to do so, while IE 4 events automatically bubble up unless explicitly stopped by any element along the bubble path.

Navigator 4 Event Propagation

When a user initiates an action that fires an event targeted to a page element in Navigator 4, the event passes through an object hierarchy: namely the `window`, `document`, and possibly `layer` objects that eventually lead to the target element. Without any instructions to do otherwise, these intervening objects do nothing to the event as it passes through. But if you want to intercept the event at any one of those levels, you may do so by invoking the `captureEvents()` method for the `window`, `document`, or `layer` object.

Capturing events

The `captureEvents()` method, however, requires special instructions about the kind of event (or events) to capture. Parameters to the `captureEvents()` method are static properties of an `Event` object (with an uppercase E) that exists in every window or frame. The properties are essentially constants that represent the types of events that can pass through the `window`, `document`, or `layer` object. Table 6-2 shows the events you can capture at those levels.

Table 6-2. Event Object Static Properties

Event.ABORT	Event.BLUR	Event.CHANGE
Event.CLICK	Event.DBLCLICK	Event.DRAGDROP
Event.ERROR	Event.FOCUS	Event.KEYDOWN
Event.KEYPRESS	Event.KEYUP	Event.LOAD
Event.MOUSEDOWN	Event.MOUSEMOVE	Event.MOUSEOUT
Event.MOUSEOVER	Event.MOUSEUP	Event.MOVE
Event.RESET	Event.RESIZE	Event.SCROLL
Event.SELECT	Event.SUBMIT	Event.UNLOAD

You can select multiple events to be captured by specifying multiple parameters separated by the bitwise OR operator (|). For example, if you want the `document` object to capture all mouse over and mouse out events, the script statement is:

```
document.captureEvents(Event.MOUSEOVER | Event.MOUSEOUT)
```

Capturing events is only part of the job. The **window**, **document**, or **layer** object must also have an event handler for each event assigned to it. For instance, if the **document** object is capturing mouse over and mouse out events, as just shown, two more statements in the script must follow to assign functions to these event handler properties. The following two statements assume existing function definitions for **turnOnImage()** and **turnOffImage()**:

```
document.onmouseover = turnOnImage
document.onmouseout = turnOffImage
```

When a function is assigned to an event handler, Navigator 4 automatically passes an **event** object (lowercase e) as an argument to the function. This object contains details about the physical event that occurred. If the function intends to examine that information, it should include a parameter variable for the event, as in:

```
function turnOnImage(evt) {
    statements
}
```

You can, of course, also use the **function.arguments** property to extract this value without an explicit parameter variable, but having the parameter variable is a clean way to handle the **event** object reference.

A function that executes in response to an explicitly captured event like this can cancel the native action of the intended target of the event by returning **false**. For example, consider a **document** object that is set to capture and process **Event.CLICK** events. If a user clicks on a link, the event handler function at the document level can end with a **return false** statement to prevent the link from carrying out its native action (navigating to the **HREF** URL). If the function ends with a **return true** statement (or no **return** statement at all), however, the link action takes place as usual.

If you want event capturing to work immediately after the initial loading of the page, you should put the call to **captureEvents()** and the event handler assignment statements in an initialization function that gets invoked from the **onLoad** event handler of the **BODY** element. That way you know that all relevant object and function references are valid before these statement are invoked.

Releasing events

Just as you can capture individual event types, you can turn off that capturing when necessary. The **window**, **document**, and **layer** objects in Navigator 4 have **releaseEvents()** methods that turn off event capture for the event types specified as parameters. For example, if the mouse over and mouse out events were initially captured by the **document** object, but due to user interaction on the page, you now want all mouse out events to go directly to their targets, invoke the following statement:

```
document.releaseEvents(Event.ONMOUSEOUT)
```

You may capture and release events as often as necessary for your page design.

Handing events off to their targets

If a window or document captures an event, the event handler may examine the details of the **event** object passed as a parameter (described shortly) and determine that no special processing is required. In other words, the event should proceed to its intended target. There is no automatic propagation of events in Navigator, so you must include a statement that invokes the window, document, or layer `routeEvent()` method. Pass along the **event** object as a parameter to this method:

```
function turnOnImage(evt) {
    if (condition that doesn't require processing here) {
        document.routeEvent(evt)
    } else {
        special processing statements
    }
}
```

You may, of course, use a function like the preceding to perform some preprocessing of the event and still invoke the `routeEvent()` method to let the target object continue handling the event.

Redirecting events

The final possible disposition for an event that has been captured is to send it to an object that is not the intended target. Every Navigator 4 object that has event handlers available to it also has a `handleEvent()` method, which allows it to receive an **event** object sent to it by a **window**, **document**, or **layer** object that has captured the event prior to its intended target. While the `routeEvent()` method sends an event to its intended target without naming the target, the `handleEvent()` method must be called from the object that is meant to receive the event. For example, you could have several related links on a page all funnel their mouse over and mouse out events to just one of the links. To accomplish this, the document must be set up to capture both event types. The functions assigned to the `document.onmouseover` and `document.onmouseout` event handlers should include statements like the following one, which directs all such events to the first link in the document:

```
document.links[0].handleEvent(evt)
```

That first link must have **onMouseOver** and **onMouseOut** event handlers assigned to it for event redirection to work correctly.

Examining a Navigator 4 event

The **event** (lowercase e) object passed with each physical event contains several properties that are useful to scripts. Remember that this object is automatically passed to a function assigned to an event handler property of an object; you may also explicitly include it as a parameter to an event handler defined as a tag attribute, as in the following example:

```
<INPUT TYPE="button" VALUE="Click me" onClick="doClickScript(event)">
```

The function can then find out things about the event, such as the location of a click, whether a modifier key was pressed at the time of the event, the intended target, and the key pressed in a keyboard event. The **event** object can have the following properties:

data
> The URL of a drag and drop event

layerX, layerY
> The horizontal and vertical coordinates of the event, relative to the containing layer

modifiers
> An integer value that represents modifier keys pressed at the time of the event (a numeric combination of **Event** object static properties for modifier keys)

pageX, pageY
> The horizontal and vertical coordinates of the event, relative to the window or frame

screenX, screenY
> The horizontal and vertical coordinates of the event, relative to the screen

target
> An object reference to the intended target

type
> The string representation of the event name ("click")

which
> For mouse events, an integer that represents the mouse button pressed; for keyboard events, the ASCII code of key pressed

Note that not all events supply information for every property.

To demonstrate how you might combine event capturing with examination of the **event** object, Example 6-1 shows the window-level capture of all key press events on a page. The function processes all key press events. For events directed at text input fields, the keyboard characters are examined to make sure that no numbers are entered into the fields. Notice that after the call to alert(), checkNums() returns false to make sure that the native action of the text box (the rendering of the typed character) doesn't take place. However, at the end of the function, a `return true` statement allows all other key press events (perhaps directed at a `TEXTAREA`) to function normally.

Example 6-1. Event Capturing and Processing in Navigator 4

```
document.captureEvents(Event.KEYPRESS)
document.onkeypress = checkNums

function checkNums (evt) {
    // get ASCII code
    var oneChar = evt.which
    // process only targets whose object are of type 'text'
    if (evt.target.type == "text") {
        // check for ASCII range of 0-9
        if (oneChar >= 48 && oneChar <= 57) {
            alert("Numbers are not allowed in text fields.")
            return false
        } else {
            // let all other characters onward to object in case
            // there is an onKeyPress event handler defined there
            routeEvent(evt)
        }
    }
    return true
}
```

You'll see more examples of event capturing and processing later in this chapter when we discuss cross-platform event handling.

Internet Explorer 4 Event Bubbling

In contrast to Navigator 4's trickle-down event mechanism, events in Internet Explorer 4 bubble up from the target element through an element hierarchy. Note that I said element hierarchy, which is different from the object hierarchy used in Navigator—in IE 4, virtually every HTML element has events associated with it. Consider the following skeletal structure of an HTML document:

```
<HTML>
<BODY>
    <FORM>
        <DIV>
            <INPUT TYPE="text">
        </DIV>
    </FORM>
</BODY>
</HTML>
```

As the user types into the text input field, the key press event starts at the input field and then works its way up through the DIV, FORM, and BODY elements of the document, in that order. In this situation, an onKeyPress event handler can be defined for any and all of these elements. Any such event handler you define will be triggered by a key press in the text field, unless event bubbling is canceled (as described in the next section).

This isn't as anarchic as it sounds. In fact, it's quite powerful. With IE 4, you can have event handlers that apply to running text content on a page, with granularity that lets you specify different responses to each little element you define in the HTML—character by character, if you like.

Automatic bubbling

Event bubbling is automatic in IE 4. For the most part, you don't have to worry about it, since there isn't likely to be much overlap in non-DHTML pages. An event handler in a form element works there and does not collide with similarly named event handlers elsewhere in the element containment hierarchy. But if there is a chance for events to collide, you can explicitly instruct an event not to bubble beyond a specific element.

Canceling bubbling involves the IE 4 `event` (lowercase e) object, which is covered in more detail in the next section. This object belongs to the `window` object and has a property named `cancelBubble`. The default value for this property is `false`, meaning that event bubbling takes place. But if you set this property to `true`, the event does not bubble past the current event handler.

If you assign an event handler as a tag attribute, you can cancel bubbling with an extra statement in the attribute value:

```
<INPUT TYPE="button" onClick="doBtnClick(); window.event.cancelBubble=true">
```

Since the `event` object is bound to the `window` object, the `cancelBubble` property can be set in any script statement to cancel bubbling for the current event. Thus, if you assign an event handler as an element property, the bubble cancellation can take place in the function invoked by the event handler with the simple statement:

```
window.event.cancelBubble
```

Only one event is bubbling at any given instant, so this statement knows to cancel the right one. It also means that you can let an event bubble part of the way through the element hierarchy, but stop it at any desired element, so as not to interfere with other elements higher up the chain.

The window.event object

IE 4's `window.event` object is somewhat analogous to Navigator 4's `event` (lowercase e) object. When an event fires, details of the event are automatically stuffed into the `window.event` object and stay there until all scripts invoked by event handlers along the bubble chain have finished. Then the next event stuffs *its* details into the `window.event` object. In other words, there is only one window.event object alive at a time (within a given window or frame). Even with events closely spaced in time (the mouse down, mouse up click sequence, for example), only one event is "alive" at a time.

Like the Navigator version, this event object provides properties that contain details about the event. Unfortunately, the property sets of the two objects don't match or have equivalents, but there are a number of similarities that can be useful in cross-platform deployment, as demonstrated later in this chapter. Table 6-3 provides a list of the IE 4 window.event object properties and, when available, the Navigator 4 equivalents.

Table 6-3. Properties of the Event Object for IE 4 and Navigator 4 Equivalents

IE 4 Property	Type	Description	Type	NN4 Property
altKey	Boolean	The **Alt** key was pressed during the event	Event property	modifiers
button	Integer	The mouse button pressed in the mouse event	Integer	which
cancelBubble	Boolean	Whether the event should bubble further		
clientX, clientY	Pixel values	The horizontal and vertical coordinates of the event in the content region of browser window	Pixel values	pageX, pageY
ctrlKey	Boolean	The **Ctrl** key was pressed during the event	Event property	modifiers
fromElement	Object	The object or element from which the pointer moved for a mouse over or mouse out event		
keyCode	Integer	The keyboard character code of a keyboard event	Integer	which
offsetX, offsetY	Pixel values	The horizontal and vertical coordinates of the event within the element space		
reason	Integer	The disposition of a data transfer event		
returnValue	Boolean	The value returned by the event		
screenX, screenY	Pixel values	The horizontal and vertical coordinates of the event relative to the screen	Pixel values	screenX, screenY
shiftKey	Boolean	The **Shift** key was pressed during event	Event property	modifiers
srcElement	Object	The default object or element intended to receive the event	Object	target
srcFilter	Object	The filter object that triggered a filter change event		

Table 6-3. Properties of the Event Object for IE 4 and Navigator 4 Equivalents (continued)

IE 4 Property	Type	Description	Type	NN4 Property
toElement	Object	The object or element to which the pointer moved for a mouse over or mouse out event		
type	String	The name of the event (without "on" prefix)	String	type
x, y	Pixel values	The horizontal and vertical coordinates of the event within BODY element (for unpositioned target) or positioned element		

As you can see, very few **event** object properties in Table 6-3 have the same names and data values across browsers (**screenX**, **screenY**, and **type** are the only properties in common), although important properties for coordinate positions, modifier keys, mouse button, and keyboard character are available in both browsers. This means that with a little platform-specific branching, you can make events work for both browsers in one document. At the same time, as long as you don't need the element-level granularity of event handling available in IE 4 but lacking in Navigator 4, the different event propagation directions are not that difficult to handle.

Examining Modifier Keys

Example 6-2 demonstrates several aspects of working with the browser-specific **event** objects. As a bonus, the page includes some cross-platform element positioning and dynamic styles. The page is primarily a laboratory for experimenting with particular **event** object properties to determine which modifier keys are held down during mouse down and key press events. A small table is used as the output area of the page (see Figure 6-1). As the user clicks on a link or types into a text input field, the relevant event properties are checked for the modifier key(s) being held down at the time. For each possible key, the background color of the corresponding TD element is changed to red if the key is pressed. The scripting techniques on this page also reveal some details about particular events that can catch you off guard in one browser or the other.

The application uses a style rule to define the appearance of the TD elements that represent the modifier keys. These elements are all positioned relative to the document flow, and the clipping rectangle is set to compensate for Navigator 4's propensity to cinch up the background around an element's content.

The script begins with the familiar script statements that set global variables for browser-specific branching and platform equivalent references. An API-like func-

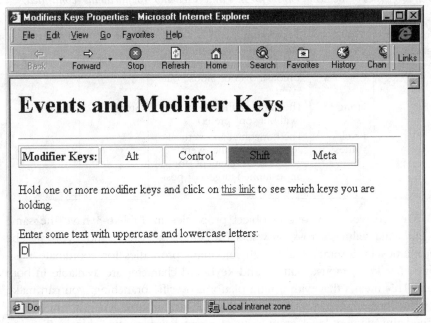

Figure 6-1. Experimenting with modifier keys

tion is defined to take care of setting an element's background color with plat-
form-dependent syntax.

The checkMods() function is the heart of this example. It is called whenever the
user clicks the link or types in the text input area. The function receives a Navigator 4 event object as a parameter. For IE 4, the function relies upon the win-
dow.event object, so the parameter is ignored in that browser. The first four statements in checkMods() set Boolean variables for the four modifier keys. Note that
the **Meta** key is the same as the **Command** key on the Macintosh keyboard and the
Windows key on recent Windows keyboards. IE 4, however, does not recognize
the **Meta** key as a modifier key, so its value in this script is always false.

Each assignment statement uses the conditional operator (?:) to do the right thing
for each browser. If isNav is true, the statement uses the bitwise AND (&) operator on the Navigator 4 event object's modifiers property and the appropriate
constant from the Event object. If, through the operator's binary arithmetic, the
right operand is determined to be a component of the left operand, the expression evaluates to true. If isNav is false, however, the statement assigns the specific modifier key property of the window.event object (a Boolean value) to the
script's local variable.

After checkMods() sets its variables, it calls the setBGColor() function for each
modifier to set the color of the corresponding TD element.

In the HTML for the page, shown in Example 6-2, notice that the link has both an `onMouseDown` and an `onClick` event handler bound to it. The `onClick` event handler cannot be used by itself because Navigator 4 performs unique actions when you mouse down on a link with certain modifier keys held down; conversely, IE 4 opens a new browser window with the `HREF` attribute unless the `onClick` event handler returns `false`. To accommodate both behaviors, the `onMouseDown` event handler is used for the event sampling, while the `onClick` event handler is specified so that it always returns `false`.

Example 6-2. A Modifier Key Event Laboratory

```
<HTML>
<HEAD>
<TITLE>Modifier Keys Properties</TITLE>
<STYLE TYPE="text/css">
    .flags {position:relative; clip:rect(0,80,18,0); background-color:white}
</STYLE>
<SCRIPT LANGUAGE="JavaScript">
// Global variables for browser versions and platform equivalencies
var isNav, isIE
var coll = ""
var styleObj = ""
if (parseInt(navigator.appVersion) >= 4) {
    if (navigator.appName == "Netscape") {
        isNav = true
    } else {
        isIE = true
        coll = "all."
        styleObj = ".style"
    }
}
// API function for setting a positionable element's background color
function setBGColor(objIn, color) {
    var obj = eval("document." + coll + objIn + styleObj)
    if (isNav) {
        obj.bgColor = color
    } else {
        obj.backgroundColor = color
    }
}
// Invoked with each click of the link or typed key of the field, this function
// checks the modifier key and sets the element background color accordingly
function checkModKeys(evt) {
    var alt = (isNav) ? evt.modifiers & Event.ALT_MASK : window.event.altKey
    var ctrl = (isNav) ? evt.modifiers & Event.CONTROL_MASK :
window.event.ctrlKey
    var shift = (isNav) ? evt.modifiers & Event.SHIFT_MASK :
window.event.shiftKey
    var meta = (isNav) ? evt.modifiers & Event.META_MASK : false
    setBGColor("ctrl1",((alt) ? "red" : "white"))
    setBGColor("ctrl2",((ctrl) ? "red" : "white"))
    setBGColor("ctrl3",((shift) ? "red" : "white"))
```

Example 6-2. A Modifier Key Event Laboratory (continued)

```
    setBGColor("ctrl4",((meta) ? "red" : "white"))
    return false
}
</SCRIPT>
</HEAD>
<BODY>
<H1>Events and Modifier Keys</H1>
<HR>
<TABLE BORDER=1>
<TR HEIGHT=20 >
<TH>Modifier Keys:</TH>
<TD WIDTH=80 HEIGHT=20 ALIGN=MIDDLE ID=ctrl1 CLASS=flags>Alt</TD>
<TD WIDTH=80 ALIGN=MIDDLE ID=ctrl2 CLASS=flags>Control</TD>
<TD WIDTH=80 ALIGN=MIDDLE ID=ctrl3 CLASS=flags>Shift</TD>
<TD WIDTH=80 ALIGN=MIDDLE ID=ctrl4 CLASS=flags>Meta</TD>
</TABLE>
<P>Hold one or more modifier keys and click on
<A HREF="javascript:void(0)" onMouseDown="return checkModKeys (event)"
onClick="return false">
this link</A> to see which keys you are holding.</P>
<FORM NAME="output">
<P>Enter some text with uppercase and lowercase letters:
<INPUT TYPE="text" SIZE=40 onKeyPress=" checkModKeys (event)"></P>
</FORM>
</BODY>
</HTML>
```

There are other quirks that affect keyboard events. Currently, only true alphanumeric character keys generate events whose details can be examined. In other words, function keys and arrow keys cannot be trapped by the script. Also, the browser does not let you override the normal **Ctrl**, **Meta**, and **Alt** key combinations that may be menu equivalents or system shortcuts. Therefore, while you might be able to test some key combinations on one operating system platform (Mac browsers, for example, typically have no internal use for the **Ctrl** key), you can reliably intercept only upper- and lowercase letters on all operating systems. If you have plans for creating your own set of keyboard accelerators to trigger scripts, you may have to put those ideas on hold until a better event handling scheme is worked into future browsers

Examining Mouse Buttons and Key Codes

The next code listing, Example 6-3, further demonstrates how to access **event** object properties in both browsers, even when the properties don't match up well. In this case, a script displays information about mouse clicks and key presses in the status bar, to limit the disruption of the user. For mouse clicks over a button, this laboratory application presents the identifying integer for the mouse button used to do the click. For key presses in a text area, the application displays the character code value of the key typed by the user.

Example 6-3. Looking for Mouse Button and Keyboard Character Codes

```
<HTML>
<HEAD>
<TITLE>Button Codes / Key Codes</TITLE>
<SCRIPT LANGUAGE="JavaScript">
var isNav, isIE
if (parseInt(navigator.appVersion) >= 4) {
    if (navigator.appName == "Netscape") {
        isNav = true
    } else {
        isIE = true
    }
}
function showBtnOrKey(evt) {
    var theBtnOrKey
    if (isNav) {
        theBtnOrKey = evt.which
    } else {
        if (window.event.srcElement.type == "textarea") {
            theBtnOrKey = window.event.keyCode
        } else if (window.event.srcElement.type == "button") {
            theBtnOrKey = window.event.button
        }
    }
    status = theBtnOrKey
    return false
}
</SCRIPT>
</HEAD>
<BODY>
<H1>Mouse Button and Key Codes from Event Objects</H1>
<HR>
<FORM>
<P>Click on this
<INPUT TYPE="button" VALUE="Button" onClick="showBtnOrKey(event)">
with either mouse button (if you have more than one).</P>
<P>Enter some text with uppercase and lowercase letters:<BR>
<TEXTAREA COLS=30 ROWS=4 onKeyPress="showBtnOrKey(event)" WRAP="virtual">
</TEXTAREA></P>
</FORM>
(Results appear in the status bar as you click or type.)
</BODY>
</HTML>
```

A single function handles the investigation of both the mouse button and keyboard events. This design is partially influenced by the fact that both values come from the same **event** object property in Navigator 4—the **which** property. With that browser, a single statement extracts the value from the **event** object that is passed as a parameter, regardless of the event type. For Internet Explorer 4, however, the values are maintained in two separate properties. Therefore, the script examines the source of the event (the `window.event.srcElement` property), whose `type` property is a string that is either "textarea" or "button" in this application. For a text area, the `window.event.keyCode` property contains the character code, while for a button, the `window.event.button` property contains the mouse button code.

There are a couple of things you should know about the mouse button identifiers. First, the two browsers have different numbering schemes for the buttons. In Navigator 4, the primary mouse button (on a multibutton mouse) has an integer value of 1; in IE 4, that button has a value of 0. Second, the native behavior of both browsers prevents mouse events from ever being triggered by the secondary button. Right-clicking on elements produces a context-sensitive pop-up menu, so no **event** object is generated by the click.

As for the keyboard character codes, the two browsers specify different character bases for their values. Navigator 4 specifies just ASCII values, while IE 4 extends support to include Unicode characters. For the English language, the "lower 128" ASCII values are the same as the Unicode values for the same characters.

Dragging Elements

The final example in this chapter, Example 6-4, demonstrates how event capturing and event bubbling can work together to let document-level event handlers control the dragging of elements on the screen. Because Navigator does not support events for elements that are not part of the document object hierarchy, it makes perfect sense to have the document capture all pertinent events and process them. While IE 4 could have event handlers assigned to each of the elements, that would require more effort than is necessary.

All the dragging event handlers are assigned as properties in an `init()` function invoked by the `onLoad` event handler. The only platform-specific process taking place here involves setting the `document.captureEvents()` method to grab all mouse down and mouse move events that come in from Navigator 4.

The draggable elements in this example are two absolute-positioned DIV elements that contain IMG elements. The user can click on either image and drag that image around. While it is a simple operation for the user, the application must do a fair amount of work to figure out which element has been clicked and then track the location of the element in sync with the mouse. Stacking order also comes into consideration because you want a selected element to be atop all its peers as the user drags it around the screen.

Determining which element has been clicked requires a lot more work in Navigator than in IE. Assuming that all targeted elements are sibling layers, the script must look through each layer to see if the click location is within the clipping region of that layer. Moreover, this must be done in reverse stacking order, so that the layer closest to the top of the stacking order is found to be the one under the cursor. If the draggable elements were in different layers (for instance the DIV elements were nested), you'd need some hairy scripts to crawl through all layers in search of the clicked element—a mighty, although not impossible, task.

Coordinate systems also play a significant role in scripting the drag process. Ideally, the element should track from the point where the user clicks inside the element. This means that the location (top left corner) of the element must be offset (up and to the left) from the cursor position by the number of pixels of the click offset within that element. This information is easier to come by in IE (the `event.offsetX` and `event.offsetY` properties) than in Navigator, where you must calculate the offset by subtracting the location of the layer from the event coordinate in the page space. In either case, the offset values are stored as global variables in Example 6-4, so that the dragging action can use them for proper placement of the element under the cursor.

Making the element track the cursor also requires some calculation, as the location of the element after each mouse move event must be set in the page (or client) space, after being adjusted by that initial click offset. For Navigator 4, the base coordinates come from the `pageX` and `pageY` properties of the event; for IE 4, the corresponding values are `event.clientX` and `event.clientY`.

Although there is a bit of platform-specific branching going on in Example 6-4, the example demonstrates nonetheless that all is not lost when attempting to create sophisticated DHTML implementations for both browser models in one document. It certainly requires a lot of testing and tweaking, as well as nimble thinking about the two systems of property names and positionable object relationships, but it is possible.

Example 6-4. Dragging Elements Around the Window

```
<HTML>
<HEAD>
<TITLE>It's a Drag</TITLE>
<STYLE TYPE="text/css">
  #imgA {position:absolute; left:50; top:100; width:120; border:solid black 1px;
    z-index:0}
  #imgB {position:absolute; left:110; top:145; width:120; border:solid black 1px;
    z-index:0}
</STYLE>
<SCRIPT LANGUAGE="JavaScript">
// Global variables for platform branching
var isNav, isIE
if (parseInt(navigator.appVersion) >= 4) {
```

Example 6-4. Dragging Elements Around the Window (continued)

```
        if (navigator.appName == "Netscape") {
            isNav = true
        } else {
            isIE = true
        }
    }


    // ***Begin Utility Functions***
    // Set zIndex property
    function setZIndex(obj, zOrder) {
        obj.zIndex = zOrder
    }
    // Set element background color (only works dynamically in IE)
    function setBorderColor(obj, color) {
        obj.borderColor = color
    }
    // Position an object at a specific pixel coordinate
    function shiftTo(obj, x, y) {
        if (isNav) {
            obj.moveTo(x,y)
        } else {
            obj.pixelLeft = x
            obj.pixelTop = y
        }
    }
    // ***End Utility Functions***

    // Global holds reference to selected element
    var selectedObj
    // Globals hold location of click relative to element
    var offsetX, offsetY

    // Find out which element has been clicked on
    function setSelectedElem(evt) {
        if (isNav) {
            var clickX = evt.pageX
            var clickY = evt.pageY
            var testObj
            for (var i = document.layers.length - 1; i >= 0; i--) {
                testObj = document.layers[i]
                if ((clickX > testObj.left) &&
                    (clickX < testObj.left + testObj.clip.width) &&
                    (clickY > testObj.top) &&
                    (clickY < testObj.top + testObj.clip.height)) {
                    selectedObj = testObj
                    if (selectedObj) {
                        setBorderColor(selectedObj, "red")
                        setZIndex(selectedObj, 100)
                        return
                    }
                }
            }
```

Example 6-4. Dragging Elements Around the Window (continued)

```
    } else {
        var imgObj = window.event.srcElement
        selectedObj = imgObj.parentElement.style
        if (selectedObj) {
            setBorderColor(selectedObj, "red")
            setZIndex(selectedObj,100)
            return
        }
    }
    selectedObj = null
    return
}
// Drag an element
function dragIt(evt) {
    if (selectedObj) {
        if (isNav) {
            shiftTo(selectedObj, (evt.pageX - offsetX), (evt.pageY - offsetY))
        } else {
            shiftTo(selectedObj, (window.event.clientX - offsetX),
            (window.event.clientY - offsetY))
            // prevent further system response to dragging
            return false
        }
    }
}
// Turn selected element on
function engage(evt) {
    setSelectedElem(evt)
    if (selectedObj) {
        if (isNav) {
            offsetX = evt.pageX - selectedObj.left
            offsetY = evt.pageY - selectedObj.top
        } else {
            offsetX = window.event.offsetX
            offsetY = window.event.offsetY
        }
    }
    // prevent further processing of mouseDown event so that
    // the Macintosh doesn't display the contextual menu and
    // lets dragging work normally.
    return false
}
// Turn selected element off
function release(evt) {
    if (selectedObj) {
        setZIndex(selectedObj, 0)
        setBorderColor(selectedObj, "black")
        selectedObj = null
    }
}
```

Example 6-4. Dragging Elements Around the Window (continued)

```
// Set event capture for Navigator
function setNSEventCapture() {
    if (isNav) {
        document.captureEvents(Event.MOUSEDOWN | Event.MOUSEMOVE | Event.MOUSEUP)
    }
}
// Assign event handlers used by both Navigator and IE
function init() {
    if (isNav) {
        setNSEventCapture()
    }
    document.onmousedown = engage
    document.onmousemove = dragIt
    document.onmouseup = release
}
</SCRIPT>
</HEAD>
<BODY onLoad="init()">
<H1>Element Dragging</H1>
<HR>
<DIV ID=imgA><IMG SRC="myImage1.gif" WIDTH=120 HEIGHT=90 BORDER=0></DIV>
<DIV ID=imgB><IMG SRC="myImage2.gif" WIDTH=120 HEIGHT=90 BORDER=0></DIV>
</BODY>
</HTML>
```

Event Futures

It is unclear how the W3C and the browser makers will resolve the complex issues involved with scripting events. There are many forces exerting pressure on how the job should best be done, including what, if any, relationship there should be between the JavaScript and Java event models. We'll have to watch the activity of the DOM working group to see how the situation settles down. In the meantime, there is a messy legacy of installed browsers to worry about.

7

Looking Ahead to HTML 4.0

As the installed base of web browsers increases over time, that base becomes more and more fragmented. It is not uncommon for users to choose not to upgrade to the latest browser version or for organizations to prohibit individuals from upgrading beyond a corporate standard that may be one or two generations old. This makes the job of adopting new W3C standards difficult, for both web browser makers and page authors. The breadth of the changes from HTML 3.2 to 4.0 reveals the depth of the quandary facing web developers.

Regardless of the latest bells and whistles or the "preferred" way to apply certain content formats, there are still many thousands of web pages on the Net that use techniques long gone from the standards documents. Web browser makers bear the burden of this "ancient" baggage, as their browsers must continue to be backward compatible with previous versions of HTML, all the way back to HTML 1.0. Unfortunately, this continued support can lead casual page authors to believe that the old ways are just fine, so there is no incentive to use the latest tags.

The purpose of this chapter is to acquaint you with the changes that have been made to the HTML recommendation between Version 3.2 and Version 4.0. A large number of tags and attributes have been deprecated because their original functions are now covered by Cascading Style Sheets. It is clear that HTML document creation is moving toward the separation of content from format. This, in fact, is what SGML and XML are all about. If you are developing web applications for users who have style-sheet-enabled browsers, you would be wise to start adopting this methodology.

As often happens in the browser and standard release cycles, the HTML 4.0 recommendation was finalized after both Netscape Navigator 4 and Internet Explorer 4 shipped final release versions. By virtue of being released closer to the HTML 4.0 standard, IE 4 has adopted a fair number of the new tags and attributes of HTML

4.0, but certainly not all of them. Navigator 4 is behind the curve right now, but Navigator 5 is looming on the horizon, so that shouldn't be the case for long.

New Directions Overview

With a lot of the basic content issues covered in HTML 3.2, the new items in HTML 4.0 focus on topics that reflect more mature thinking about the role of the World Wide Web as a global, universal, content publishing medium. Many concerns that have been addressed by computer operating system and application software makers for years are being formalized for the Web for the first time in Version 4.0. This section highlights the new directions in HTML 4.0.

Internationalization

Surprise! Inhabitants of Earth do not all use the English language or the Roman alphabet. HTML 4.0 adopts various industry efforts to assist with internationalization. These are meant to support both the authoring of content in any of the world's written languages and the display of that content in any alphabet, including non-Roman ones, such as Cyrillic, Arabic, Hebrew, Chinese, Japanese, and the rest. Of course, the browser and operating system underneath it must do all the hard work in terms of rendering character sets that are not native to the system. Acceptance of the Unicode character set (ISO 10646) is a first step in making these facilities seamless to users.

Accessibility

Not every potential web visitor can read a video display, roll the mouse around on a desktop, or touch-type on a keyboard. A lot of new items in the HTML 4.0 recommendation have been included to increase browser accessibility to web surfers whose physical limitations might otherwise reduce or prohibit their access. Separating content from form is in itself an aid, especially if your pages provide choices for, say, larger fonts or alternate color combinations. Content might also be directed to other devices, such as Braille writers or text-to-speech synthesizers. Under HTML 4.0, you can assign keyboard combinations for what are otherwise mouse actions (e.g., clicking a button). Even the new "requirement" that an `IMG` element include an `ALT` attribute with a short image description demonstrates a concern for a wider audience.

Tables

Specifications for tables in HTML 4.0 should enhance the display, usability, and rendering speed of tabular content on a page. Details are based on RFC 1942, which includes recommendations for allowing up-front sizing of column widths, to allow a browser to start displaying a large table while the cell content is still arriving. Browser makers are urged to implement tables so that a user can scroll a table's body section while the table's header and footer remain stationary. The emphasis on style sheets for accurate placement of content should mean that the days are numbered for using transparent images to fill blank table cells for formatting. Future HTML recommendations are likely to hand off even more formatting tasks to style sheets.

Forms

While many HTML 4.0 enhancements related to forms are for the sake of improved accessibility, there are some potentially helpful by-products of those efforts (depending on how much is implemented in the common browsers of the future). The ability to disable and write-protect form elements, which has been long sought after, is part of the new recommendation. Form elements can also be visually grouped into FIELDSET elements, complete with legends (currently implemented in Internet Explorer 4). Tabbing order can also be controlled by element attributes, rather than by geography.

Embedded Objects

A new element, OBJECT, becomes the formal way of embedding multimedia and other types of data into a compound document. The IMG and APPLET elements are still supported for those specific data types.

Style Sheets

While not favoring any one style sheet authoring language over another, HTML 4.0 does provide for the STYLE element and all the promise that it offers. This element is going to have a significant effect on the long-term makeup of the library of HTML tags and attributes. The push to use style sheets to separate content from format means that a lot of elements and attributes that you have probably been using for formatting purposes, like the <FONT> tag, are no longer recommended. The list of deprecated items in HTML 4.0 is long, although support for these items is not likely to disappear in browsers for a *very* long time to come.

Scripting

The SCRIPT element is not new to the HTML standard, but two aspects of it are new. First, the intrinsic event handlers of elements are listed in the HTML 4.0 recommendation as attributes. These event handlers are, of course, independent of the scripting language in use. Second, the way you specify a particular scripting language has changed. The LANGUAGE attribute is now deprecated in favor of the TYPE attribute, which is defined as containing a content-type string (for example, `"text/vbscript"`). For backward compatibility, the LANGUAGE attribute is certain to be supported well into the future.

Embedded Context

The LINK element offers many potential uses, but one that may be exploited sooner rather than later in upcoming browsers is its ability to hold information about documents that are linked to the current document. For example, a browser could conceivably use LINK element values to build a pop-up menu that takes you to various pages (e.g., previous page, next page, glossary page, index page, contents page) in a related collection of documents. This is another way to separate content from, in this case, context.

New Elements

Some of the new elements in HTML 4.0 are new only to the HTML specification; they have been in one or both browsers for some time. Other elements are brand new and may not yet be part of either browser. Table 7-1 lists all the new elements defined in HTML 4.0. The table also indicates the version of each browser that first supported each element.

Table 7-1. New Elements in HTML 4.0

Element	NN	IE	Description
ABBR	-	-	Abbreviation
ACRONYM	-	4	Acronym
BDO	-	-	Override default bidirectional rendering algorithms
BUTTON	-	4	Push button (alternative version)
COL	-	4	Table column default attributes
COLGROUP	-	4	Table column group
DEL	-	4	Deleted text format
FIELDSET	-	4	Form element grouping
FRAME	2	3	Frame within a FRAMESET
FRAMESET	2	3	Specification for a set of frames
IFRAME	-	4	Inline frame
INS	-	4	Inserted text format
LABEL	-	4	Form element label text
LEGEND	-	4	Label for a FIELDSET
NOFRAMES	2	3	Content for a no-frame browser
NOSCRIPT	3	4	Content for a browser with JavaScript turned off
OBJECT	4	4	Embedded media
OPTGROUP	-	-	Option group
PARAM	3	4	Named value for an applet or object
Q	-	4	Short inline quotation
SPAN	4	4	Generic content container
TBODY	-	4	Table body

Table 7-1. New Elements in HTML 4.0 (continued)

Element	NN	IE	Description
TFOOT	-	4	Table footer
THEAD	-	4	Table header

Deprecated Elements

As I stated earlier, style sheets obviate the need for a number of tags that were commonly used for basic formatting tasks. Those tags are now deprecated, but they will continue to be supported in browsers for generations to come. Obviously, any attributes associated with these elements are also deprecated, but not necessarily in all other active elements. Table 7-2 shows all the elements that are deprecated in the HTML 4.0 specification.

Table 7-2. Deprecated Elements in HTML 4.0

Element	Supplanted By
APPLET	The OBJECT element
BASEFONT	Style sheet font attributes
CENTER	<DIV ALIGN=center>
DIR	The UL element
FONT	Style sheet font attributes
ISINDEX	<INPUT TYPE="text">
MENU	The UL element
S	The style sheet {text-decoration:line-through}
STRIKE	The style sheet {text-decoration:line-through}
U	The style sheet {text-decoration:underline}

Obsolete Elements

Three elements have been deleted in favor of an existing element that has been doing the job of all four in browser implementations for a long time. The three obsolete elements are LISTING, PLAINTEXT, and XMP. The popular PRE element is the one you should use for displaying preformatted text. The HTML 4.0 recommendation leaves implementation details, such as the treatment of whitespace, the default font setting, and word wrapping, up to browsers. Typically, PRE elements are rendered in Courier and they honor carriage returns inserted in the text.

New Element Attributes

Practically every existing element has one or more new attributes in HTML 4.0. Many of these new attributes are applied to every element due to HTML 4.0's focus on internationalization, accessibility, style sheets, and scripting. Table 7-3 lists the common attributes that have been added to most elements that can act as content containers (that is, they have start and end tags). Element-specific additions are not shown here, but are covered in full in Chapter 8, *HTML Reference*.

Table 7-3. New HTML 4.0 Attributes Shared by Most Elements

Attribute	Description
CLASS	Group identifier (selector) for applying a style rule
DIR	Text direction of the element's content
ID	Unique identifier (selector) for applying a style rule
LANG	Human language used in the element's content
STYLE	Inline style sheet rule
TITLE	Short description of the element
onClick	Event handler for click events
onDblClick	Event handler for double-click events
onKeyDown	Event handler for keyboard key down events
onKeyPress	Event handler for keyboard key press (down and up) events
onKeyUp	Event handler for keyboard key up events
onMouseDown	Event handler for mouse down events
onMouseMove	Event handler for mouse movement inside the element
onMouseOut	Event handler for mouse movement out of the element
onMouseOver	Event handler for mouse movement into the element
onMouseUp	Event handler for mouse up events

Deprecated Attributes

A large number of attributes are deprecated in HTML 4.0, primarily due to the preference given to style sheets over direct content formatting. Browsers will continue to honor these deprecated attributes for a long time to come, but if you eventually design content exclusively for browsers that are HTML 4.0 compatible, you should use that project as a starting point for weaning yourself from these deprecated attributes. Table 7-4 lists all the deprecated attributes in HTML 4.0, plus the affected elements and suggested replacement syntax. In some instances, you will see a deprecated attribute associated with a new element (like the deprecated ALIGN attribute of the new IFRAME element). This is not a trick. You can still use the "old" attribute with a new element for the sake of authoring-style compatibility.

Table 7-4. Deprecated Attributes in HTML 4.0

Attribute	Elements	Supplanted By
ALIGN	CAPTION, APPLET, IFRAME, IMG, INPUT, OBJECT, LEGEND, TABLE, HR, DIV, H1-H6, P	text-align and vertical-align style attributes
ALINK	BODY	A:active {color:}
ALT	APPLET	OBJECT element TITLE attribute
ARCHIVE	APPLET	OBJECT element ARCHIVE attribute
BACKGROUND	BODY	background style attribute

Table 7-4. Deprecated Attributes in HTML 4.0 (continued)

Attribute	Elements	Supplanted By
BGCOLOR	BODY, TABLE, TD, TH, TR	background-color style attribute
BORDER	IMG, OBJECT	border-width style attributes
CLEAR	BR	clear style attribute
CODE	APPLET	OBJECT element CLASSID attribute
CODEBASE	APPLET	OBJECT element CODEBASE attribute
COLOR	BASEFONT, FONT	color style attribute
COMPACT	DIR, DL, MENU, OL, UL	{display:compact}
FACE	BASEFONT, FONT	font-face style attribute
HEIGHT	APPLET	OBJECT element HEIGHT attribute
HEIGHT	TD, TH	height positioning style attribute
HSPACE	IMG, OBJECT	left positioning style attribute
LINK	BODY	A:link {color:}
NAME	APPLET	OBJECT element NAME attribute
NOSHADE	HR	
NOWRAP	TD, TH	white-space style attribute
OBJECT	APPLET	OBJECT element CLASSID attribute
PROMPT	ISINDEX	LABEL element
SIZE	HR	width positioning style attribute
SIZE	FONT, BASEFONT	font-size style attribute
START	OL	To be determined in CSS2
TEXT	BODY	color style attribute
TYPE	LI, OL, UL	list-style-type style attribute
VALUE	LI	To be determined in CSS2
VERSION	HTML	Built into the DTD for HTML 4.0
VLINK	BODY	A:visited {color:}
VSPACE	IMG, OBJECT	top positioning style attribute
WIDTH	HR	width positioning style attribute
WIDTH	APPLET	OBJECT element WIDTH attribute
WIDTH	TD, TH	COLGROUP element WIDTH attribute

The HTML reference in Chapter 8 includes all the elements and attributes specified in the HTML 4.0 recommendation. Items are clearly marked with regard to browser version support. As you'll see, there are plenty of items marked as HTML 4.0 only, with no support yet in either Navigator or Internet Explorer. As future browser generations become reality, however, you can be sure more items will be supported in the browsers.

II

Dynamic HTML Reference

This part of the book, Chapters 8 through 11, is a complete reference to all the tags, attributes, objects, properties, methods, and event handlers for HTML, CSS, DOM, and core JavaScript.

- Chapter 8, *HTML Reference*
- Chapter 9, *Document Object Reference*
- Chapter 10, *Style Sheet Attribute Reference*
- Chapter 11, *JavaScript Core Language Reference*

II

8

HTML Reference

Since the earliest days of the World Wide Web, the Hypertext Markup Language (HTML) standard has been pulled, pushed, twisted, extended, contracted, misunderstood, and even partially ignored by web browser vendors. With the formal release of the recommendation for HTML Version 4.0 at the end of 1997, the World Wide Web Consortium (W3C) outpaced the implementations of HTML in browsers that were shipping at the time. For once, the W3C recommendation was ahead of the implementation curve. This, of course, can lead to plenty of confusion for web application authors who study the details of the W3C documents in search of handy new features: it can be discouraging to see the tag or attribute of your dreams, only to discover that no browser on the planet supports it.

The purpose of this chapter is to provide a complete list of HTML tags and attributes—the ones implemented in Navigator and Internet Explorer, as well as the ones specified in the W3C recommendation. So that you can see whether a particular entry applies to the browser(s) you must support, version information accompanies each tag and attribute listed in the following pages. At a glance, you can see the version number of Navigator, Internet Explorer, and the W3C HTML specification in which the item was first introduced. Because this book deals with Dynamic HTML, the history timeline goes back only to HTML 3.2, Navigator 2, and Internet Explorer 3. If an item existed prior to one of these versions, it is simply marked "all." Where no implementation exists, I've used "n/a" to indicate that. In rare instances, an item has been removed from the HTML specification for Version 4.0. Such items are marked as less than 4 ("<4").

This chapter is organized alphabetically by HTML element (or tag, if you prefer); within each element's description, attributes are listed alphabetically. The reference entries are designed so that it is easy to see which elements require end tags and whether attributes are optional or required. Scripted object references are displayed in JavaScript standard syntax style but are segregated by browser ("NN" for Netscape Navigator; "IE" for Internet Explorer), because the object models are not necessarily the same. When there is no object model listing for a particular browser, it means that the element or attribute is not part of that browser's scriptable object model. The description for an item details any significant differences between the various implementations of the item.

Attribute Value Types

Many element attributes share similar data requirements. For the sake of brevity in the reference listings, this section describes a few common attribute value types in more detail than is possible within each listing. Whenever you see one of these attribute value types associated with an attribute, consult this section for a description of the type.

Length

A length value defines a linear measure of document real estate. The unit of measurement can be any applicable unit that helps identify a position or space on the screen. HTML attribute length units are uniformly pixels, but in other content, such as that specified in Cascading Style Sheets (see Chapter 9, *Document Object Reference*), measurements can be in inches, picas, ems, or other relevant units. A single numeric value may represent a length when it defines the offset from an edge of an element. For example, a coordinate point (10,20) consists of two length values, denoting pixel measurements from the left and top edges of an element, respectively.

Identifier

An identifier is a name that adheres to some strict syntactical rules. Most important is that an identifier is one word with no whitespace allowed. If you need to use multiple words to describe an item, you can use the inter-capitalized format (in which internal letters are capitalized) or an underscore character between the words. Most punctuation symbols are not permitted, but all numerals and alphabetical characters are. To avoid potential conflicts with scripting languages that refer to items by their identifiers, it is good practice to avoid using a numeral for the first character of an identifier.

URI and URL

The term Universal Resource Identifier (URI) is a broad term for an address of content on the Web. A Universal Resource Locator (URL) is a type of URI. For most web authoring, you can think of them as being one in the same because most web browsers restrict their focus to URLs. A URL may be complete (including the protocol, host, domain, and the rest) or may be relative to the URL of the current document. In the latter case, this means the URL may consist of an anchor, file, or pathname. In scriptable browsers, attributes that expect URI values can also accept the `javascript:` pseudo-URL, which makes a script statement or function the destination of the link.

Language Code

There is an extensive list of standard codes that identify the spoken and written languages of the world. A language code always contains a primary language code, such as "en" for English or "zh" for Chinese. Common two-letter primary codes are cataloged in ISO-639. An optional subcode (separated from the primary code by a hyphen) may be used to identify a specific implementation of the primary language, usually according to usage within a specific country. Therefore, although "en" means all of English, "en-US" means a U.S.-specific version of English. The browser must support a particular language code for its meaning to be of any value to an element attribute.

Alignment Constants

Several HTML elements load external data into rectangular spaces on the page. Images and Java applets are perhaps the most common elements of this type. Any such element has an `ALIGN` attribute that lets you determine how the element relates geographically to the surrounding content (usually text). Values for this attribute are constant values that have very specific meanings.

Browser makers have gone beyond the minimum possibilities for alignment specified in the HTML 4.0 recommendation. Fortunately, Navigator and Internet Explorer agree on the extensions (at least in the most recent versions).

Here is a synopsis of the various case-insensitive `ALIGN` attribute settings and how they affect the display of the element and surrounding text content:

`absbottom`
> Text is aligned such that the bottom of any possible text rendering (including character descenders) is on the same horizontal line as the very bottom of the element.

`absmiddle`
> The middle of the text height (from descender to ascender) is aligned with the middle of the element height.

`baseline`
> The baseline of the text is on the same horizontal line as the very bottom of the element (note that character descenders extend below the baseline).

bottom

> Identical to baseline.

left

> If there is text starting on the same line as the element, the element is low-ered to the next line and displayed flush left within the next outermost con-tainer context. Text that follows the element cinches up to the end of the text preceding the element, causing the text to wrap around the object or image (called "floating").

middle

> The baseline of the text is aligned with the middle of the element height.

right

> If there is text starting on the same line as the element, the element is low-ered to the next line and displayed flush right within the next outermost con-tainer context. Text that follows the element starts on the line immediately below the starting text, causing the text to wrap around the object or image (called "floating").

texttop

> The very top of the element is on the same horizontal line as the ascenders of the preceding text.

top

> The top of the element is on the same horizontal line as the top of the tallest element (text or other kind of element) rendered in the line.

Colors

A color value can be assigned either via a hexadecimal triplet or with a plain-lan-guage equivalent. A hexadecimal triplet consists of three pairs of hexadecimal (base 16) numbers that range between the values 00 and FF, corresponding to the red, green, and blue components of the color. The three pairs of numbers are bunched together and preceded by a pound sign (#). Therefore, the reddest of reds has all red (FF) and none (00) of the other two colors: #FF0000; pure blue is #0000FF. The letters A through F can also be lowercase.

This numbering scheme obviously leads to a potentially huge number of combina-tions (over 16 million), but not all video monitors are set to distinguish among mil-lions of colors. Therefore, you may wish to limit yourself to a more modest pal-ette of colors known as the web palette. A fine reference of colors that work well on all browsers at popular bit-depth settings can be found at *http://www.lynda.com/hexh.html.*

The HTML recommendation also specifies a basic library of 16 colors that can be assigned by plain-language names. Note that the color names are case insensitive. The names and their equivalent hexadecimal triplets are as follows:

Black	#000000	Maroon	#800000	Green	#008000	Navy	#000080
Silver	#C0C0C0	Red	#FF0000	Lime	#00FF00	Blue	#0000FF
Gray	#808080	Purple	#800080	Olive	#808000	Teal	#008080
White	#FFFFFF	Fuchsia	#FF00FF	Yellow	#FFFF00	Aqua	#00FFFF

In other words, the attribute settings BGCOLOR="Aqua" and BGCOLOR="#00FFFF" yield the same results.

Netscape has developed a much longer list of plain-language color equivalents. These are detailed in Appendix A, *Color Names and RGB Values*, and are recognized by recent versions of both Navigator and Internet Explorer.

Common HTML Attributes

In the HTML specifications for Navigator, Internet Explorer, and HTML 4.0, several attributes are shared across a vast majority of HTML elements. Rather than repeat the descriptions of these attributes ad nauseam in the reference listings, I am listing their details here only once. Throughout the rest of the chapter, the attribute list for each element points to these common attributes when the attribute name is in *italic*. When you see an attribute listed in italic, it means that you should look to this section for specific details about the attribute. If you recognize a term from the list of attributes-in-common, but it is not shown in italic, that means that there is some element-specific information about the attribute, so the description is provided with the element. Here is a list of the common attributes:

Attributes

CLASS	*ID*	*LANGUAGE*	*STYLE*	*TITLE*
DIR	*LANG*			

CLASS   NN *4*   IE *3*   HTML *4*

CLASS=" *className1[...classNameN]*"   *Optional*

An identifier generally used to associate an element with a style sheet rule defined for a class selector. See Chapter 3, *Adding Style Sheets to Documents*. Be aware that even though the CLASS attribute is specified for most elements of this chapter, Navigator 4 does not implement a CLASS attribute for every one of those elements. In Navigator 4, implementation tends to be limited to visible elements.

Example <A CLASS="chapTitle" NAME="chapter3">Chapter 3</A>

Value

Case-sensitive identifier. Multiple classes can be assigned by separating the class names with spaces within the quoted attribute value.

Default None.

Object Model Reference

IE   [window.]document.*elementCollection*[i].className
           [window.]document.all.*elementID*.className

DIR   NN *n/a*   IE *n/a*   HTML *4*

DIR="*direction*"   *Optional*

The direction of character rendering for the element's text when the characters are not governed by inherent directionality according to the Unicode standard. Character rendering is either left-to-right or right-to-left. This attribute is usually set in concert with the LANG attribute; it must be used to specify a character rendering direction that overrides the current direction.

Example

`<A LANG="ar" DIR="rtl">`*Some Unicode Arabic text characters here*`</A>`

Value   ltr | rtl (case insensitive)

Default   ltr

ID   NN *4*   IE *4*   HTML *4*

ID="*elementIdentifier*"   *Optional*

A unique identifier that distinguishes this element from all the rest in the document. Can be used to associate a single element with a style rule naming this attribute value as an ID selector. An element can have an ID assigned for uniqueness as well as a class for inclusion within a group. See Chapter 3. Be aware that even though the ID attribute is specified for most elements of this chapter, Navigator 4 does not implement an ID attribute for every one of those elements. In Navigator 4, implementation tends to be limited to visible elements.

Example   `<H2 ID="sect3Head">Section Three</H2>`

Value   Case-sensitive identifier.

Default   None.

Object Model Reference

IE   [window.]document.all.elementID.id

LANG   NN *3*   IE *4*   HTML *4*

LANG="*languageCode*"   *Optional*

The language being used for the element's attribute values and content. A browser can use this information to assist in proper rendering of content with respect to details such as treatment of ligatures (when supported by a particular font or required by a written language), quotation marks, and hyphenation. Other applications and search engines might use this information to aid selection of spell-checking dictionaries and creating indices.

Example   `<B LANG="de">Deutsche Bundesbahn</B>`

Value   Case-insensitive language code.

Default   Browser default.

Object Model Reference

IE   [window.]document.all.*elementID*.lang

LANGUAGE
NN n/a   IE 4   HTML n/a

LANGUAGE="*scriptingLanguage*"   *Optional*

Sets the scripting language (and switches on the desired scripting engine) for script statements defined in the element (such as event handler script statements in the tag). This
attribute is distinct from the LANGUAGE attribute currently in common use with the SCRIPT
element. Internet Explorer uses the LANGUAGE attribute in any element to engage a different
script language interpreter for subsequent script statements. If you use JScript exclusively
within a document, you don't have to use this attribute.

Example
```
How <SPAN CLASS="bolds" LANGUAGE="VBSCRIPT"
onClick="MsgBox 'Hi, there!'">bold</B> it is!
```

Value   JAVASCRIPT | JSCRIPT | VBS | VBSCRIPT

Default

Although the default scripting language of IE 4 is JScript, no value is automatically assigned
to this attribute if the attribute is not included in the tag.

Object Model Reference

IE   [window.]document.all.*elementID*.language

STYLE
NN 4   IE 4   HTML 4

STYLE="*styleSheetProperties*"   *Optional*

This attribute lets you set one or more style sheet rule property assignments for the current
element. You may use the CSS or JavaScript syntax for assigning style attributes. However if
you are designing the page for cross-browser deployment, use only the CSS syntax, which
both Navigator and Internet Explorer support. Be aware that even though the STYLE
attribute is specified for most elements of this chapter, Navigator 4 does not implement a
STYLE attribute for every one of those elements. In Navigator 4, implementation tends to be
limited to visible elements.

Example `<B STYLE="color:green; font-size:18px">Big, green, and bold</B>`

Value

An entire CSS-syntax style sheet rule is enclosed in quotes. Multiple style attribute settings
are separated by semicolons. Style sheet attributes are detailed in Chapter 10, *Style Sheet
Attribute Reference*.

Default   None.

Object Model Reference

IE   [window.]document.all.*elementID*.style

TITLE   NN *n/a*   IE *3*   HTML *3.2*

TITLE="*advisoryText*"   *Optional*

An advisory description of the element. For HTML elements that produce visible content on the page, Internet Explorer 4 renders the content of the TITLE attribute as a tooltip when the cursor rests on the element for a moment. For example, the table-related COL element does not display content, so its TITLE attribute is merely advisory. To generate tooltips in tables, assign TITLE attributes to elements such as TABLE, TR, TH, or TD.

The appearance of the tooltip is governed by the operating system version of the browser. In Windows, the tooltip is the standard small, light-yellow rectangle; on the Mac, the tooltip displays as a cartoon bubble in the manner of the MacOS bubble help system. If no attribute is specified, the tooltip does not display. Although IE 3 implements this attribute, no tooltip appears.

You can assign any descriptive text you like to this attribute. Not everyone will see it, however, so do not put mission-critical information here. Future or special-purpose browsers might use this attribute's information to read information about the link to vision-impaired web surfers.

Although the compatibility listing for this attribute dates the attribute back to Internet Explorer 3 and HTML 3.2, it is newly ascribed to many elements starting with IE 4 and HTML 4.0.

Example <B TITLE="United States of America">U.S.A.</B>

Value

Any string of characters. The string must be inside a matching pair of (single or double) quotation marks.

Default   None.

Object Model Reference

IE   [window.]document.all.*elementID*.title

Alphabetical Tag Reference

<A>   NN *all*   IE *all*   HTML *all*

<A>...</A>   *End Tag: Required*

The A element is the rare element that can be an anchor and/or a link, depending on the presence of the NAME and/or HREF attributes. As an anchor, the element defines a named location in a document to which any URL can reference by appending a hashmark and the anchor name to the document's URI (*http://www.megacorp.com/contents#a-c*). Names are identifiers assigned to the NAME attribute (or in newer browsers, the ID attribute). Content defined solely as an anchor is not (by default) visually differentiated from surrounding BODY content.

By assigning a URI to the HREF attribute, the element becomes the source of a hypertext link. Activating the link generally navigates to the URI assigned to the HREF attribute (or it may load other media into a plugin without changing the page). Links typically have a distinctive appearance in the browser, such as an underline beneath text (or border around an object) and a color other than the current content color. Separate colors can be assigned to links for three states: an unvisited link, a link being activated by the user, and a previously visited link (the linked document is currently in the browser cache). An A element can be both an anchor and a link if, in the least, both the NAME (or ID) and HREF attributes have values assigned to them.

Example

```
<A NAME="anchor3">Just an anchor named "anchor3."</A>
<A HREF="#anchor3">A link to navigate to "anchor3" in the same
 document.</A>
<A NAME="anchor3" HREF="http://www.megacorp.com/index.html">
Go from here (anchor 3) to home page.</A>
```

Object Model Reference

NN   [window.]document.links[i]
        [window.]document.anchors[i]

IE   [window.]document.links[i]
        [window.]document.anchors[i]
        [window.]document.all.*elementID*

Attributes

ACCESSKEY	DATASRC	*LANG*	REV	TARGET
CHARSET	*DIR*	*LANGUAGE*	SHAPE	*TITLE*
CLASS	HREF	METHODS	*STYLE*	TYPE
COORDS	HREFLANG	NAME	TABINDEX	URN
DATAFLD	ID	REL		

Event Handler Attributes

Handler	NN	IE	HTML
onBlur	n/a	4	4
onClick	2	3	4
onDblClick	4	4	4
onFocus	n/a	4	4
onHelp	n/a	4	n/a
onKeyDown	n/a	4	4
onKeyPress	n/a	4	4
onKeyUp	n/a	4	4
onMouseDown	4	4	4
onMouseMove	n/a	4	4
onMouseOut	3	4	4
onMouseOver	2	3	4
onMouseUp	4	4	4
onSelectStart	n/a	4	n/a

Anchor-only A elements have no event handlers in Navigator through Version 4.

ACCESSKEY

NN *n/a*   IE *4*   HTML *4*

ACCESSKEY="*character*"   *Optional*

A single character key that follows the link. The browser and operating system determine if the user must press a modifier key (e.g., **Ctrl**, **Alt**, or **Command**) with the access key to activate the link. In IE 4/Windows, the **Alt** key is required and the key is not case sensitive. This attribute does not work in IE 4/Mac.

Example

```
<A HREF="http://www.megacorp.com/toc.html" ACCESSKEY="t">Table of
Contents</A>
```

Value   Single character of the document set.

Default   None.

Object Model Reference

IE   [window.]document.links[i].accessKey
            [window.]document.anchors[i].accessKey
            [window.]document.all.*elementID*.accessKey

CHARSET

NN *n/a*   IE *n/a*   HTML *4*

CHARSET="*characterSet*"   *Optional*

Character encoding of the content at the other end of the link.

Example

```
<A CHARSET="csISO5427Cyrillic" HREF="moscow.html">Visit Moscow</A>
```

Value

Case-insensitive alias from the character set registry (*ftp://ftp.isi.edu/in-notes/iana/assignments/character-sets*).

Default   Determined by browser.

COORDS

NN *n/a*   IE *n/a*   HTML *4*

COORDS="*coord1, ... coordN*"   *Optional*

When a link surrounds an image, this attribute defines the coordinate points (relative to the top-left corner of the element) associated with an area map.

Example

```
<A HREF="#bottom" SHAPE="rect" COORDS="30, 30, 60, 45">
    <IMG SRC="nav.jpg" HEIGHT="50" WIDTH="90" BORDER="0">
</A>
```

Value

Each coordinate is a length value, but the number of coordinates and their order depend on the shape specified by the **SHAPE** attribute, which may optionally be associated with the element. For **SHAPE="rect"**, there are four coordinates (left, top, right, bottom); for

SHAPE="circle", there are three coordinates (center-x, center-y, radius); for SHAPE="poly", there are two coordinate values for each point that defines the shape of the polygon (x1, y1, x2, y2, x3, y3,...xN, yN).

Default   None.

DATAFLD

NN n/a   IE 4   HTML n/a

DATAFLD="*columnName*"   *Optional*

Used with IE 4 data binding to associate a remote data source column name in lieu of an HREF attribute for a link. The data source column must contain a valid URI (relative or absolute). A DATASRC attribute must also be set for the element.

Example   <A DATASRC="#DBSRC3" DATAFLD="newsURL">Late-Breaking News</A>

Value   Case-sensitive identifier.

Default   None.

Object Model Reference

IE   [window.]document.links[i].dataFld
             [window.]document.all.*elementID*.dataFld

DATASRC

NN n/a   IE 4   HTML n/a

DATASRC="*dataSourceName*"   *Optional*

Used with IE 4 data binding to specify the name of the remote ODBC data source (such as an Oracle or SQL Server database) to be associated with the element. Content from the data source is specified via the DATAFLD attribute.

Example   <A DATASRC="#DBSRC3" DATAFLD="newsURL">Late-Breaking News</A>

Value   Case-sensitive identifier.

Default   None.

Object Model Reference

IE   [window.]document.links[i].dataSrc
             [window.]document.all.*elementID*.dataSrc

HREF

NN all   IE all   HTML all

HREF="*URI*"   *Required for links*

The URI of the destination of a link. In browsers, when the URI is an HTML document, the document is loaded into the current (default) or other window target (as defined by the TARGET attribute). For some other file types, the browser may load the destination content into a plugin or save the destination file on the client machine. In the absence of the HREF attribute, the element does not distinguish itself in a browser as a clickable link and may instead be only an anchor (if the NAME or ID attribute is set).

Example   <A HREF="part1/chap3.html">Chapter 3</A>

Value

Any valid URI, including complete and relative URLs, anchors on the same page (anchor names prefaced with the # symbol), and the `javascript:` pseudo-URL in scriptable browsers to trigger a script statement rather than navigate to a destination.

Default   None.

Object Model Reference

IE	[window.]document.links[i].href
	[window.]document.all.*elementID*.href
NN	[window.]document.links[i].href

In both browsers, other link object properties allow for the extraction of components of the URL, such as protocol and hostname. See the `Link` object in Chapter 9.

HREFLANG   NN *n/a*   IE *n/a*   HTML *4*

HREFLANG="*languageCode*"   *Optional*

The language code of the content at the destination of a link. Requires that the HREF attribute also be set. This attribute is primarily an advisory attribute to help a browser prepare itself for a new language set if the browser is so enabled.

Example   <A HREFLANG="HI" HREF="hindi/Chap3.html>Chapter 3 (in Hindi)</A>

Value   Case-insensitive language code.

Default   Browser default.

ID   NN *3*   IE *3*   HTML *4*

ID="*elementIdentifier*"   *Optional*

A unique identifier that distinguishes this element from all the rest in the document. Can be used to associate a single element with a style rule naming this attribute value as an ID selector. Browsers typically allow the ID attribute to be used as a substitute for the NAME attribute to make the element an anchor. In this case, one ID attribute can serve double duty as a style sheet rule selector and anchor name. An A element can have an ID assigned for uniqueness as well as a class for inclusion within a group.

Example   <A ID="section3">Section 3</A>

Value   Case-sensitive identifier.

Default   None.

Object Model Reference

IE	[window.]document.links[i].id
	[window.]document.anchors[i].id
	[window.]document.all.*elementID*.id
NN	[window.]document.anchors[i].name

METHODS
NN *n/a*   IE *4*   HTML *n/a*

METHODS="*http-method*"
Optional

An advisory attribute about the functionality of the destination of a link. A browser could use this information to display special colors or images for the element content based on what the destination will do for the user.

Example

```
<A HREF="http://www.megacorp.com/cgi-bin/search?chap3" METHODS="GET">
Chapter 3</A>
```

Value   Comma-delimited list of one or more HTTP methods.

Default   None.

Object Model Reference

IE   [window.]document.links[i].Methods
            [window.]document.all.*elementID*Methods

NAME
NN *all*   IE *all*   HTML *all*

NAME="*elementIdentifier*"
Required for anchors

The traditional way to signify an anchor position within a document. Other link elements can refer to the anchor by setting their HREF attributes to a URL ending in a pound sign (#) followed by the identifier. Omitting the NAME (and ID) attribute for the A element prevents the element from being used as an anchor position. This attribute is interchangeable with the ID attribute in recent browsers. If the NAME and HREF attribute are set in the element, the element is considered both an anchor and a link.

Example   `<A NAME="sect3">Section III</A>`

Value   Case-sensitive identifier.

Default   None.

Object Model Reference

IE   [window.]document.links[i].name
            [window.]document.anchors[i].name
            [window.]document.all.*elementID*name

NN   [window.]document.links[i].name
            [window.]document.anchors[i].name

REL
NN *n/a*   IE *3*   HTML *4*

REL="*linkTypes*"
Optional

Defines the relationship between the current element and the destination of the link. Also known as a *forward link*, not to be confused in any way with the destination document whose address is defined by the HREF attribute. The HTML 4.0 recommendation defines several link types; it is up to the browser to determine how to employ the value. This attribute has meaning in IE 4 primarily for the LINK element, although there is significant room for future application for tasks such as assigning an A element (acting as a link) to a button in a static navigation bar pointing to the next or previous document in a series. The element must include an HREF attribute for the REL attribute to be applied.

HTML Reference

Example <A REL="next chapter" HREF="chapter3.html">Chapter 3</A>

Value

Case-insensitive, space-delimited list of HTML 4.0 standard link types applicable to the element. Sanctioned link types are:

alternate	contents	index	start
appendix	copyright	next	stylesheet
bookmark	glossary	prev	subsection
chapter	help	section	

In addition, IE 3 defined a fixed set of four values: **same** | **next** | **parent** | **previous**.

Default   None.

Object Model Reference

IE   [window.]document.links[i].rel
            [window.]document.all.*elementID*.rel

REV   NN *n/a*   IE *3*   HTML *4*

REV="*linkTypes*"   *Optional*

A reverse link relationship. Like the **REL** attribute, the **REV** attribute's capabilities are defined by the browser, particularly with regard to how the browser interprets and renders the various link types available in the HTML 4.0 specification. Given two documents (A and B) containing links that point to each other, the **REV** value of B is designed to express the same relationship between the two documents as denoted by the **REL** attribute in A. There is not yet much application of either the **REL** or **REV** attributes of the A element in IE 4.

Example <A REV="previous chapter" HREF="chapter2.html">Chapter 2</A>

Value

Case-insensitive, space-delimited list of HTML 4.0 standard link types applicable to the element. See the **REL** attribute for sanctioned link types.

Default   None.

Object Model Reference

IE   [window.]document.links[i].rev
            [window.]document.all.*elementID*.rev

SHAPE   NN *n/a*   IE *n/a*   HTML *4*

SHAPE="*shape*"   *Optional*

Defines the shape of a server-side image map area whose coordinates are specified with the COORDS attribute.

Example

```
<A HREF="#bottom" SHAPE="rect" COORDS="30, 30, 60, 45">
    <IMG SRC="nav.jpg" HEIGHT="50" WIDTH="90" BORDER="0">
</A>
```

55

Value   Case-insensitive shape constant: default | rect | circle | poly.

Default   None.

TABINDEX

NN *n/a*   IE *4*   HTML *4*

TABINDEX=*integer*   *Optional*

A number that indicates the sequence of this element within the tabbing order of all focusable elements in the document. Tabbing order follows a strict set of rules. Elements that have values other than zero assigned to their TABINDEX attributes are first in line when a user starts tabbing in a page. Focus starts with the element with the lowest TABINDEX value and proceeds in order to the highest value, regardless of physical location on the page or in the document. If two elements have the same TABINDEX values, the element that comes earlier in the document receives focus first. Next come all elements that either don't support the TABINDEX attribute or have the value set to zero. These elements receive focus in the order in which they appear in the document. Because an A element cannot be disabled, it always receives focus in turn, except for special handling in IE 4. Typically, an A element wired as a link can be triggered with a press of the spacebar once the element has focus.

Note that the Macintosh user interface does not provide for giving focus to elements other than text input fields. Links and anchors cannot be tabbed to with the Mac version of IE 4.

Example   <A HREF="chapter3.html" TABINDEX=3>Chapter 3</A>

Value

Any integer from 0 through 32767. In IE 4, setting the TABINDEX to -1 causes the element to be skipped in tabbing order altogether.

Default   None.

Object Model Reference

IE   [window.]document.links[i].tabIndex

TARGET

NN *all*   IE *all*   HTML *all*

TARGET="*windowOrFrameName*"   *Optional*

If the destination document is to be loaded into a window or frame other than the current window or frame, you can specify where the destination document should load by assigning a window or frame name to the TARGET attribute. Target frame names must be assigned to frames and windows as identifiers. Assign names to frames via the NAME attribute of the FRAME element; assign names to new windows via the second parameter of the window.open() scripting method. If you omit this attribute, the destination document replaces the document containing the link. An identifier other than one belonging to an existing frame or window opens a new window for the destination document. This attribute is applicable only when a value is assigned to the HREF attribute of the element.

A link element can have only one destination document and one target. If you want a link to change the content of multiple frames, you can use an A element's onClick event handler or a javascript: pseudo-URL to fire a script that loads multiple documents. Set the location.href property of each frame to a desired URL.

Example

```
<A TARGET="display" HREF="chap3.html#sec2">Section 3.2</A>
<A TARGET="_top" HREF="index.html">Start Over</A>
```

Value

Case-sensitive identifier when the frame or window name has been assigned via the target element's NAME attribute. Four reserved target names act as constants:

_blank   Browser creates a new window for the destination document.

_parent   Destination document replaces the current frame's framesetting document (if one exists; otherwise, it is treated as _self).

_self   Destination document replaces the current document in its window or frame.

_top   Destination document is to occupy the entire browser window, replacing any and all framesets that may be loaded (also treated as _self if there are no framesets defined in the window).

Default   _self

Object Model Reference

IE   [window.]document.links[i].target
NN   [window.]document.links[i].target

TYPE   NN *n/a*   IE *n/a*   HTML *4*

TYPE="*MIMEType*"   *Optional*

An advisory about the content type of the destination document or resource. A browser might use this information to assist in preparing support for a resource requiring a multimedia player or plugin.

Example

```
<A TYPE="video/mpeg" HREF="ski4.mpeg">View Devil's Ghost slope</A>
```

Value

Case-insensitive MIME type. A catalog of registered MIME types is available from *ftp:// ftp.isi.edu/in-notes/iana/assignments/media-types/*.

Default   None.

URN   NN *n/a*   IE *4*   HTML *n/a*

URN="*URN*"   *Optional*

A Uniform Resource Name version of the destination document specified in the HREF attribute. This attribute is intended to offer support in the future for the URN format of URI, an evolving recommendation under discussion at the IETF (see RFC 2141). Although supported in IE 4, this attribute does not take the place of the HREF attribute.

Example   `<A URN="urn:foo:bar3" HREF="chapter3.html">Chapter 3</A>`

Value

A valid URN in the form of "urn:*NamespaceID:NamespaceSpecificString*".

Default   None.

Object Model Reference

IE   [window.]document.links[i].urn

<ABBR>   NN *n/a*   IE *n/a*   HTML *4*

<ABBR>...</ABBR>   *End Tag: Required*

The ABBR element provides an encapsulation and enumeration mechanism for abbreviations that appear in the body text. For example, consider a web page that includes your company's address. At one point in the document, the abbreviation IA is used for Iowa. A spelling checker, language translation program, or speech synthesizer might choke on this abbreviation; a search engine would not include the word "Iowa" in its relevancy rating calculation. But by turning the IA text into an ABBR element (and assigning a TITLE attribute to it), you can provide a full-text equivalent that a search engine (if so equipped) can count; a text-to-speech program would read aloud the full state name instead of some guttural gibberish. Like many elements new in HTML 4.0, this one is intended to assist browser technologies that may not yet be implemented but could find their way into products of the future.

A related element, ACRONYM, offers the same services for words that are acronyms. Both elements are part of a larger group of what the HTML 4.0 recommendation calls *phrase elements*.

Example

Ottumwa, <ABBR TITLE="Iowa">IA</ABBR> 55334
<ABBR LANG="de" TITLE="und so weiter">usw.</ABBR>

Attributes

CLASS	*ID*	*LANG*	*STYLE*	*TITLE*
DIR				

Event Handler Attributes

Handler	NN	IE	HTML
onClick	n/a	n/a	4
onDblClick	n/a	n/a	4
onKeyDown	n/a	n/a	4
onKeyPress	n/a	n/a	4
onKeyUp	n/a	n/a	4
onMouseDown	n/a	n/a	4
onMouseMove	n/a	n/a	4
onMouseOut	n/a	n/a	4
onMouseOver	n/a	n/a	4
onMouseUp	n/a	n/a	4

TITLE

NN *n/a*   IE *n/a*   HTML *4*

TITLE=" *advisoryText*"   *Optional*

An advisory description of the element. For the ABBR element, it plays a vital role in providing a hidden full-text description of the abbreviation rendered in the document.

Example <ABBR TITLE="Iowa">IA</ABBR>

Value

Any string of characters. The string must be inside a matching pair of (single or double) quotation marks.

Default None.

<ACRONYM>

NN *n/a*   IE *4*   HTML *4*

<ACRONYM>...</ACRONYM>   *End Tag: Required*

The ACRONYM element provides an encapsulation and enumeration mechanism for acronyms that appear in the body text. For example, consider a web page that includes a discussion of international trade issues. At one point in the document, the acronym GATT is used for General Agreement on Tariffs and Trade. A spelling checker, language translation program, or speech synthesizer might choke on this acronym; a search engine would not include the word "tariffs" in its relevancy rating calculation. But by turning the GATT text into an ACRONYM element (and assigning a TITLE attribute to it), you can provide a full-text equivalent that a search engine (if so equipped) can count; a text-to-speech program would read aloud the full meaning of the acronym. Like many elements new in HTML 4.0, this one is intended to assist browser technologies that may not yet be implemented but could find their way to products of the future.

A related element, ABBR, offers the same services for words that are abbreviations. Both elements are part of a larger group of what the HTML 4.0 recommendation calls *phrase elements.*

Example

```
<ACRONYM TITLE="General Agreement on Tariffs and Trade">GATT</ACRONYM>
<ACRONYM LANG="it" TITLE="Stati Uniti">S.U.</ACRONYM>
```

Object Model Reference

IE   [window.]document.all.*elementID*

Attributes

CLASS	ID	LANGUAGE	STYLE	TITLE
DIR	LANG			

Event Handler Attributes

Handler	NN	IE	HTML
onClick	n/a	4	4
onDblClick	n/a	4	4
onDragStart	n/a	4	n/a
onHelp	n/a	4	n/a

Handler	NN	IE	HTML
onKeyDown	n/a	4	4
onKeyPress	n/a	4	4
onKeyUp	n/a	4	4
onMouseDown	n/a	4	4
onMouseMove	n/a	4	4
onMouseOut	n/a	4	4
onMouseOver	n/a	4	4
onMouseUp	n/a	4	4
onSelectStart	n/a	4	n/a

TITLE

NN *n/a*   IE *4*   HTML *4*

TITLE="*advisoryText*"   *Optional*

An advisory description of the element. For the **ACRONYM** element, it plays a vital role in providing a hidden full-text description of the acronym rendered in the document.

Example `<ACRONYM TITLE="United States of America">U.S.A.</ACRONYM>`

Value

Any string of characters. The string must be inside a matching pair of (single or double) quotation marks.

Default   None.

Object Model Reference

IE   `[window.]document.all.`*elementID*`.title`

<ADDRESS>

NN *all*   IE *all*   HTML *all*

`<ADDRESS>...</ADDRESS>`   *End Tag: Required*

Prior to HTML 4, the **ADDRESS** element was often regarded as a display formatting tag appropriate for displaying a page author's contact information on the page. Navigator and Internet Explorer display **ADDRESS** elements in an italic font. But the increased focus on separating content from form in HTML 4.0 adds some extra meaning to this element. Search engines and future HTML (or XML) parsers may apply special significance to the content of this element, perhaps in cataloging author information separate from the hidden information located in **META** elements. If you want to use this structural meaning of the element while keeping the rendering in line with the rest of your body text, you need to assign style sheet rules to override the browser's default formatting tendencies for this element. Any standard **BODY** elements, such as links, can be contained inside an **ADDRESS** element.

Example

```
<ADDRESS>
<P>Send comments to:<A HREF="mailto:jb@megacorp.com">jb@megacorp.com</A>
</P>
</ADDRESS>
```

Object Model Reference

IE   `[window.]document.all.`*elementID*

Attributes

CLASS	ID	LANGUAGE	STYLE	TITLE
DIR	LANG			

Event Handler Attributes

Handler	NN	IE	HTML
onClick	n/a	4	4
onDblClick	n/a	4	4
onDragStart	n/a	4	n/a
onHelp	n/a	4	n/a
onKeyDown	n/a	4	4
onKeyPress	n/a	4	4
onKeyUp	n/a	4	4
onMouseDown	n/a	4	4
onMouseMove	n/a	4	4
onMouseOut	n/a	4	4
onMouseOver	n/a	4	4
onMouseUp	n/a	4	4
onSelectStart	n/a	4	n/a

<APPLET>   NN *2*   IE *3*   HTML *3.2*

`<APPLET>...</APPLET>`   *End Tag: Required*

You can embed an executable chunk of Java code in an HTML document in the form of an applet. An applet occupies a rectangular area of the page, even if it is only one-pixel square. An applet may require that some initial values be set from the HTML document. One or more PARAM elements can be used to pass parameters to the applet before the applet starts running (provided the applet is written to accept these parameters). PARAM elements go between the start and end tags of an APPLET element.

Applets are compiled by their authors into class files (filename suffix *.class*). An applet class file must be in the same directory as, or a subdirectory of, the HTML document that loads the applet. Key attributes of the APPLET element direct the browser to load a particular class file from the necessary subdirectory.

All user interface design for the applet is programmed into the applet in the Java language. One of the roles of attributes in the APPLET element is to define the size and other geographical properties of the applet for its rendering on the page. Recent browsers allow JavaScript scripts to communicate with the applet, as well as allowing applets to access document elements.

Note that HTML 4.0 deprecates the APPLET element in favor of the more generic OBJECT element. Browser support for the APPLET element will continue for some time to come, however.

Example

```
<APPLET CODE="simpleClock.class" NAME="myClock" WIDTH=400 HEIGHT=50>
<PARAM NAME=bgColor VALUE="black">
<PARAM NAME=fgColor VALUE="yellow">
</APPLET>
```

Object Model Reference

NN   [window.]document.applets[i]
            [window.]document.*appletName*

IE   [window.]document.applets[i]
            [window.]document.*appletName*

Attributes

ALIGN	CODE	HEIGHT	NAME	*TITLE*
ALT	CODEBASE	HSPACE	SRC	VSPACE
ARCHIVE	DATAFLD	*ID*	*STYLE*	WIDTH
CLASS	DATASRC	MAYSCRIPT		

Event Handler Attributes

Handler	NN	IE	HTML
onAfterUpdate	n/a	4	n/a
onBeforeUpdate	n/a	4	n/a
onBlur	n/a	4	n/a
onClick	n/a	4	n/a
onDataAvailable	n/a	4	n/a
onDatasetChanged	n/a	4	n/a
onDatasetComplete	n/a	4	n/a
onDblClick	n/a	4	n/a
onDragStart	n/a	4	n/a
onErrorUpdate	n/a	4	n/a
onFocus	n/a	4	n/a
onHelp	n/a	4	n/a
onKeyDown	n/a	4	n/a
onKeyPress	n/a	4	n/a
onKeyUp	n/a	4	n/a
onMouseDown	n/a	4	n/a
onMouseMove	n/a	4	n/a
onMouseOut	n/a	4	n/a
onMouseOver	n/a	4	n/a
onMouseUp	n/a	4	n/a
onReadyStateChange	n/a	4	n/a
onResize	n/a	4	n/a
onRowEnter	n/a	4	n/a
onRowExit	n/a	4	n/a

ALIGN   NN *2*   IE *3*   HTML *3.2*

ALIGN="*alignmentConstant*"   *Optional*

The ALIGN attribute determines how the rectangle of the applet aligns within the context of surrounding content. See the section "Alignment Constants" earlier in this chapter for description of the possibilities defined in both Navigator and Internet Explorer for this attribute. Only a subset of the allowed constant values is specified in the HTML recommendation. Although Navigator included this attribute in Version 2, only BOTTOM, LEFT, RIGHT, and TOP were implemented in that version.

Both browsers follow the same rules on laying out content surrounding an applet whose ALIGN attribute is set, but the actual results are sometimes difficult to predict when the surrounding content is complex. A thorough testing of rendering possibilities with browser windows set to various sizes prevents surprises later.

Example
```
<APPLET CODE="simpleClock.class" NAME="myClock" ALIGN=ABSMIDDLE
WIDTH=400 HEIGHT=50></APPLET>
```

Value   Case-insensitive constant value.

Default   bottom

Object Model Reference
IE   [window.]document.applets[i].align
      [window.]document.*appletName*.align

ALT   NN *3*   IE *3*   HTML *3.2*

ALT="*textMessage*"   *Optional*

If a browser does not have the facilities to load and run Java applets or if the browser has Java support turned off in its preferences, the text assigned to the ALT attribute is supposed to display in the document where the APPLET element's tag appears. Typically, this text provides advice on what the page visitor is missing by not being able to load the Java applet. Unlike the NOSCRIPT or NOFRAMES elements, there is no corresponding element for an absent Java applet capability. In practice, browsers don't necessarily display this message for applets that fail to load for a variety of reasons.

In the event that this feature should work better in the future, use the ALT attribute with care. If the applet is not a critical part of your page's content, you may just want the rest of the page to load without calling attention to the missing applet in less-capable browsers. The alternate message may be more disturbing to the user than a missing applet.

Example
```
<APPLET CODE="simpleClock.class" NAME="myClock" ALIGN=ABSMIDDLE
ALT="A Java clock applet." WIDTH=400 HEIGHT=50></APPLET>
```

Value   Any quoted string of characters.

Default   None.

ARCHIVE   NN *3*   IE *n/a*   HTML *4*

ARCHIVE="*archiveFileURL*"   *Optional*

The precise meaning of the ARCHIVE attribute varies between the HTML 4.0 recommendation and Netscape's implementation. The basic idea behind Netscape's ARCHIVE attribute is that an author can package together multiple class files into a single uncompressed *.zip* archive file and let the browser load the entire set of classes at one time. This can offer a performance improvement over loading just the main class file (specified by the CODE attribute) and then letting the class loader fetch each additional class file as needed.

In addition to specifying the ARCHIVE attribute, be sure to include a CODE attribute that names the main class to load. Navigator first looks for the presence of that class file in the archive. If the file is missing from the archive, Navigator loads the CODE class file separately. (That class may then load additional supporting class files individually.) Navigator requires that the archive file have a *.zip* filename extension. The URL must also be relative to the CODEBASE location.

The HTML specification allows multiple URLs to be specified (in a space-delimited list) for additional class or other resource files. This design is in anticipation of the same attribute being used with the OBJECT element, which the W3C has deemed to be the successor to the APPLET element.

Example

```
<APPLET CODE="ScriptableClock.class" ARCHIVE="myClock.zip" WIDTH=400
HEIGHT=50>
</APPLET>
```

Value   Case-sensitive URI.

Default   None.

CODE   NN *2*   IE *3*   HTML *3.2*

CODE=" *fileName.class*"   *Required*

The name of the main class file that starts and runs the applet. If the CODEBASE attribute is not specified, the CODE attribute must include a path from the directory that stores the HTML document loading the applet. You might get away with omitting the *.class* filename extension, but don't take any chances: be complete with the class name. Most servers are case sensitive, so also match case of the actual class filename.

Example

```
<APPLET CODE="applets/ScriptableClock.class" WIDTH=400 HEIGHT=50>
</APPLET>
```

Value

Case-sensitive *.class* filename or complete path relative to the HTML document.

Default   None.

Object Model Reference

IE   [window.]document.applets[i].code
            [window.]document.*appletName*.code

CODEBASE   NN *2*   IE *3*   HTML *3.2*

CODEBASE=" *path*"   *Optional*

Path to the directory holding the class file designated in either the CODE or ARCHIVE attribute. The CODEBASE attribute does not name the class file, just the path. You can make this attribute a complete URL to the directory, but don't try to access a codebase outside of the domain of the current document: security restrictions may prevent the class from loading. A full path and filename can be set together in the CODE or OBJECT attribute, eliminating the need for the CODEBASE attribute setting.

Example

```
<APPLET CODE="ScriptableClock.class" CODEBASE="applets/" WIDTH=400
HEIGHT=50>
</APPLET>
```

Value

Case-sensitive pathname, usually relative to the directory storing the current HTML document.

Default   None.

Object Model Reference

IE   [window.]document.applets[i].codeBase
            [window.]document.*appletName*.codeBase

DATAFLD, DATASRC

See the PARAM element for data binding to Java applets.

HEIGHT, WIDTH   NN 2   IE 3   HTML 3.2

WIDTH="*pixels*"   *Required*
HEIGHT="*pixels*"

The size that a Java applet occupies in a document is governed by the HEIGHT and WIDTH attribute settings. Some browser versions might allow you to get away without assigning these attributes, letting the applet's own user interface design determine the height and width of its visible rectangle. As with images, however, it is more efficient for the browser's rendering engine when you explicitly specify the object's dimensions. Make a habit of supplying these values for all applets, as you should for all images or other visible external objects.

Example

```
<APPLET CODE="ScriptableClock.class" WIDTH=400 HEIGHT=50>
</APPLET>
```

Value

Positive integer pixel values (optionally quoted). You cannot entirely hide an applet by setting values to zero, but you can reduce its height and width to one pixel in each dimension. If you want to hide an applet, do so with DHTML by setting its positioning display attribute to none.

Default   None.

Object Model Reference

IE   [window.]document.applets[i].height
            [window.]document.*appletName*.height
            [window.]document.applets[i].width
            [window.]document.*appletName*.width

HSPACE, VSPACE   NN *2*   IE *3*   HTML *3.2*

HSPACE=" *pixels*"   *Optional*
VSPACE=" *pixels*"

You can put some empty space ("air") between an applet and any surrounding content by assigning pixel values to the HSPACE and VSPACE attributes. The VSPACE attribute governs space above and below the applet; the HSPACE attribute governs space to the left and right of the applet. For browsers that are style sheet savvy, you are perhaps better served by using the padding and/or margin style attributes to gain control down to individual sides, if you so desire.

Example

```
<APPLET CODE="ScriptableClock.class" WIDTH=400 HEIGHT=50 HSPACE=3 VSPACE=4>
</APPLET>
```

Value   Positive integer pixel values (optionally quoted).

Default   0

Object Model Reference

IE   [window.]document.applets[i].hspace
              [window.]document.*appletName*.hspace
              [window.]document.applets[i].vspace
              [window.]document.*appletName*.vspace

ID   NN *n/a*   IE *4*   HTML *4*

ID=" *elementIdentifier*"   *Optional*

A unique identifier that distinguishes this element from all the rest in the document. Can be used to associate a single element with a style rule naming this attribute value as an ID selector. An element can have an ID assigned for uniqueness as well as a class for inclusion within a group. See Chapter 3.

If you assign an ID attribute and not a **NAME** attribute, the value of the ID attribute can be used as the applet's name in script reference forms that use the element name (document.appletName).

Example

```
<APPLET ID="clocker" CODE="ScriptableClock.class" WIDTH=400 HEIGHT=50>
</APPLET>
```

Value   Case-sensitive identifier.

Default   None.

Object Model Reference

IE   [window.]document.applets[i].id
              [window.]document.*appletName*.id

MAYSCRIPT

NN *3*   IE *4*   HTML *n/a*

MAYSCRIPT   *Optional*

Navigator 3 introduced a technology called LiveConnect, which allowed scripts to communicate with Java applets and vice versa. For security reasons, an applet's communications facilities with scripts must be explicitly switched on by the page author. By adding the MAYSCRIPT attribute to the applet's tag, an applet that is written to take advantage of the document objects and scripts can address those items. In other words, the HTML is granting the applet the ability to reach scripts in the document. This attribute is a simple switch: when the attribute name is present, it is turned on.

One more step is required for an applet to communicate with JavaScript. The applet code must import a special Netscape class called *JSObject.class*. This class file (and its companion exception class) are built into the Java support in the Windows version of Internet Explorer 4. Although the execution is not perfect in IE 4, applets can perform basic communication with scripts.

Example

```
<APPLET CODE="ScriptableClock.class" WIDTH=400 HEIGHT=50 MAYSCRIPT>
</APPLET>
```

Value

No value assigned to the attribute. The presence of the attribute name sets turns on applet-to-script communication.

Default   Off.

NAME

NN *2*   IE *3*   HTML *3.2*

NAME="*elementIdentifier*"   *Optional*

If you are scripting an applet, it is usually more convenient to create a reference to the applet by using a unique name you assign to the applet. Then, if you edit the page and move or delete multiple applets on the page, you do not have to worry about adjusting index values to array-style references. In IE 4, you have the option of omitting the NAME attribute and using the ID attribute value in script references to the applet object.

Example

```
<APPLET NAME="clock2" CODE="ScriptableClock.class" WIDTH=400 HEIGHT=50>
</APPLET>
```

Value   Case-sensitive identifier.

Default   None.

Object Model Reference

IE   [window.]document.applets[i].name
            [window.]document.*appletName*.name

SRC

NN *n/a*   IE *4*   HTML *n/a*

SRC="*URL*"   *Optional*

Internet Explorer 4 defines this attribute as the URL for an "associated file." This may be the same as the ARCHIVE attribute defined in HTML and Navigator specifications. The SRC attribute is not a substitute for the CODE and/or CODEBASE attributes.

Value   A complete or relative URL.

Default   None.

Object Model Reference

IE   [window.]document.applets[i].src
                 [window.]document.*appletName*.src

VSPACE

See HSPACE.

WIDTH

See HEIGHT.

<AREA>

NN *all*   IE *all*   HTML *3.2*

<AREA>   *End Tag: Forbidden*

A MAP element defines a client-side image map that is ultimately associated with an image or other object that occupies space on the page. The only job of the MAP element is to assign a name and a tag context for one or more AREA element definitions. Each AREA element defines how the page should respond to user interaction with a specific geographical region of the image or other object.

A client-side image map area can act like an A element link in that an area can link to a destination or javascript: pseudo-URL and assign another frame or window as the target for loading a new document. In fact, in the scripting document object model, an AREA element is referenced as a link. It is not uncommon to use client-side area maps in a navigation bar occupying a slender frame of a frameset. This allows an artist to be creative with a menu design, while giving the page author the power to turn any segment of a larger image into a special-purpose link.

Example

```
<MAP NAME="nav">
<AREA COORDS="20,30,120,70" HREF="contents.html" TARGET="display">
</MAP>
```

Object Model Reference

NN   [window.]document.links[i]

IE   [window.]document.links[i]
                 [window.]document.all.*elementID*

Attributes

ACCESSKEY	*DIR*	*LANG*	NOHREF	TABINDEX
ALT	HREF	*LANGUAGE*	SHAPE	TARGET
CLASS	ID	NAME	*STYLE*	*TITLE*
COORDS				

Event Handler Attributes

Handler	NN	IE	HTML
onBlur	n/a	4	4
onClick	4	4	4
onDblClick	n/a	4	4
onDragStart	n/a	4	n/a
onFocus	n/a	4	4
onHelp	n/a	4	n/a
onKeyDown	n/a	4	4
onKeyPress	n/a	4	4
onKeyUp	n/a	4	4
onMouseDown	n/a	4	4
onMouseMove	n/a	4	4
onMouseOut	3	4	4
onMouseOver	3	4	4
onMouseUp	n/a	4	4
onSelectStart	n/a	4	n/a

ACCESSKEY
NN n/a   IE n/a   HTML 4

ACCESSKEY="*character*"   *Optional*

A single character key that follows the link associated with the image hotspot. The browser and operating system determine if the user must press a modifier key (e.g., **Ctrl**, **Alt**, or **Command**) with the access key to activate the link.

Example

```
<AREA COORDS="20,30,120,70" HREF="contents.html" TARGET="display"
ACCESSKEY="t">
```

Value   Single character of the document set.

Default   None.

ALT
NN n/a   IE 3   HTML 3.2

ALT="*textMessage*"   *Required*

Nongraphical browsers can use the ALT attribute setting to display a brief description of the meaning of the (invisible) image's hotspots. At one time, it was thought that the ALT message might by default be displayed in the browser's status bar when the area had focus or the cursor rolled over the area. That function is now typically performed by onMouse-Over event handlers and scripts. Keep in mind that recent handheld computers usually have nongraphical browsers (or allow graphics to be turned off for improved performance). Don't ignore the graphically impaired.

Example

```
<AREA COORDS="20,30,120,70" HREF="contents.html" TARGET="display"
ALT="Table of Contents">
```

Value   Any quoted string of characters.

Default   None.

Object Model Reference

IE   [window.]document.all.*elementID*.alt

COORDS

NN *all*   IE *all*   HTML *3.2*

COORDS="*coord1, ... coordN*"   *Optional*

Although the formal W3C definition for the COORDS attribute of an AREA element states that the attribute is optional, that doesn't mean that you can omit this attribute and expect an AREA to behave as it should. The COORDS attribute lets you define the outline of the area to be associated with a particular link or scripted action. Some third-party authoring tools can assist in determining the coordinate points for a hot area. You can also load the image into a graphics program that displays the cursor position in real time and then transfer those values to the COORDS attribute values.

Coordinate values are entered as a comma-delimited list. If two areas overlap, the area that is defined earlier in the HTML code takes precedence.

Example

```
<AREA COORDS="20,30,120,70" HREF="contents.html" TARGET="display">
```

Value

Each coordinate is a length value, but the number of coordinates and their order depend on the shape specified by the SHAPE attribute, which may optionally be associated with the element. For SHAPE="rect", there are four coordinates (left, top, right, bottom); for SHAPE="circle", there are three coordinates (center-x, center-y, radius); for SHAPE="poly", there are two coordinate values for each point that defines the shape of the polygon (x1, y1, x2, y2, x3, y3,...xN, yN).

Default   None.

Object Model Reference

IE   [window.]document.all.*elementID*.coords

HREF

NN *all*   IE *all*   HTML *3.2*

HREF="*URI*"   *Required*

The URI of the destination of a link associated with the area. In a browser, when the URI is an HTML document, the document is loaded into the current (default) or other window target (as defined by the TARGET attribute). For some other file types, the browser may load the destination content into a plugin or save the destination file on the client machine. Because Navigator (through Version 4) treats AREA elements as A elements, the HREF attribute must be defined in the AREA element for Navigator scripts to access various properties about the URL and for event handlers (such as onMouseOver) to work.

Example

```
<AREA COORDS="20,30,120,70" HREF="contents.html" TARGET="display">
```

Value

Any valid URI, including complete and relative URLs, anchors on the same page (anchor names prefaced with the # symbol), and the `javascript:` pseudo-URL in scriptable browsers to trigger a script statement rather than navigate to a destination.

Default None.

Object Model Reference

IE   [window.]document.links[i].href
          [window.]document.all.*elementID*href
NN   [window.]document.links[i].href

In both browsers, other link object properties allow for the extraction of components of the URL, such as protocol and hostname. See the `Link` object in Chapter 9.

NAME   NN *n/a*   IE *n/a*   HTML *4*

NAME="*elementIdentifier*"   *Optional*

This attribute is included in the HTML 4.0 specification for consistency with other elements. Although NAME attributes are used for identifying form elements upon submission and for scripting references, the browsers through Version 4 do not support this attribute. (IE 4 uses the ID attribute to assign a name to an AREA element for scripted references.) This attribute may become active in future browsers.

Value   Case-sensitive identifier.

Default None.

NOHREF   NN *all*   IE *all*   HTML *3.2*

NOHREF   *Optional*

Tells the browser that the area defined by the coordinates has no link associated with it (as does just not including any HREF attribute). When you include this attribute, scriptable browsers no longer treat the element as a link. As implemented in both Navigator and Internet Explorer, when an AREA element lacks an HREF attribute, the element no longer responds to user events. In IE 4, you can turn this attribute on and off from a script by setting the property to `true` or `false`.

Example `<AREA "COORDS="20,30,120,70" NOHREF>`

Value   The presence of this attribute sets its value to `true`.

Default `false`

Object Model Reference

IE   [window.]document.all.*elementID*noHref

SHAPE

NN *all*   IE *all*   HTML *3.2*

SHAPE="*shape*"   *Optional*

Defines the shape of the client-side area map whose coordinates are specified with the COORDS attribute. The SHAPE attribute tells the browser how many coordinates to expect.

Example

```
<AREA SHAPE="poly" "COORDS="20,20,20,70,65,45" HREF="contents.html"
TARGET="display">
```

Value

Case-insensitive shape constant. Each implementation defines its own set of shape names and equivalents, but there are common denominators across browsers (circle, rect, poly, and polygon).

Shape Name	NN	IE	HTML
circ	-	•	-
circle	•	•	•
poly	•	•	•
polygon	•	•	-
rect	•	•	•
rectangle	-	•	-

Default   rect

Object Model Reference

IE   [window.]document.all.*elementID*.shape

TABINDEX

NN *n/a*   IE *4*   HTML *4*

TABINDEX=*integer*   *Optional*

A number that indicates the sequence of this element within the tabbing order of all focusable elements in the document. Tabbing order follows a strict set of rules. Elements that have values other than zero assigned to their TABINDEX attributes are first in line when a user starts tabbing in a page. Focus starts with the element with the lowest TABINDEX value and proceeds in order to the highest value, regardless of physical location on the page or in the document. If two elements have the same TABINDEX values, the element that comes earlier in the document receives focus first. Next come all elements that either don't support the TABINDEX attribute or have the value set to zero. These elements receive focus in the order in which they appear in the document. Because an AREA element cannot be disabled, it always receives focus in turn, except for special handling in IE 4. Typically, an AREA element wired as a link can be triggered with a press of the spacebar once the element has focus.

Note that the Macintosh user interface does not provide for giving focus to elements other than text input fields. Image map areas cannot be tabbed to on the Mac version of IE 4.

Example

```
<AREA COORDS="20,30,120,70" HREF="contents.html" TARGET="display"
TABINDEX=3>
```

Value

Any integer from 0 through 32767. In IE 4, setting the **TABINDEX** to **-1** causes the element to be skipped in tabbing order altogether.

Default   None.

Object Model Reference

IE   [window.]document.all.*elementID*.tabIndex

TARGET   NN *all*   IE *all*   HTML *3.2*

TARGET="*windowOrFrameName*"   *Optional*

If the destination document is to be loaded into a window or frame other than the current window or frame, you can specify where the destination document should load by assigning a window or frame name to the **TARGET** attribute. Target frame names must be assigned to frames and windows as identifiers. Assign names to frames via the **NAME** attribute of the **FRAME** element; assign names to new windows via the second parameter of the **window.open()** scripting method. If you omit this attribute, the destination document replaces the document containing the link. This attribute is applicable only when a value is assigned to the **HREF** attribute of the element.

An **AREA** element can have only one destination document and one target. If you want a link to change the content of multiple frames, you can use an **AREA** element's onClick event handler (check Chapter 9 for supported browser versions) or a **javascript:** pseudo-URL to fire a script that loads multiple documents. Set the **location.href** property of each frame to the desired URL.

Example

```
<AREA COORDS="20,30,120,70" HREF="contents.html" TARGET="display">
<AREA COORDS="140,30,180,70" HREF="index.html" TARGET="_top">
```

Value

Case-sensitive identifier when the frame or window name has been assigned via the target element's **NAME** attribute. Four reserved target names act as constants:

_blank   Browser creates a new window for the destination document.

_parent   Destination document replaces the current frame's framesetting document (if one exists; otherwise, it is treated as _self).

_self   Destination document replaces the current document in its window or frame.

_top   Destination document is to occupy the entire browser window, replacing any and all framesets that may be loaded (also treated as _self if there are no framesets defined in the window).

Default   _self

Object Model Reference

IE   [window.]document.links[i].target
            [window.]document.all.*elementID*.target

NN   [window.]document.links[i].target

<B>

<B>...</B>   *End Tag: Required*

The B element—one of several font style elements in HTML 4—renders its content in a boldface version of the font face governing the next outermost HTML container. You can nest multiple font style elements to create combined styles, such as bold italic (<B><I> bold-italic text</I></B>).

It is up to the browser to fatten boldface display by calculating the character weight or by perhaps loading a bold version of the currently specified font. If you are striving for font perfection, it is best to use style sheets (and perhaps downloadable fonts) to specify a true bold font face, rather than risk the browser's extrapolation of a boldface from a system font. The font-weight style attribute provides quite granular control over the degree of bold applied to text if the font face supports such fine-tuning.

You can take advantage of the containerness of this element by assigning style sheet rules to some or all B elements in a page. For example, you may wish all B elements to be in a red color. By assigning the style rule B {color:red}, you can do it to all elements with only a tiny bit of code.

Although this element is not deprecated in HTML 4, it would not be surprising to see it lose favor to style sheets in the future.

Example <P>This product is <B>new</B> and <B>improved</B>!</P>

Object Model Reference

IE   [window.]document.all.*elementID*

Attributes

CLASS	*ID*	*LANGUAGE*	*STYLE*	*TITLE*
DIR	*LANG*			

Event Handler Attributes

Handler	NN	IE	HTML
onClick	n/a	4	4
onDblClick	n/a	4	4
onDragStart	n/a	4	n/a
onHelp	n/a	4	n/a
onKeyDown	n/a	4	4
onKeyPress	n/a	4	4
onKeyUp	n/a	4	4
onMouseDown	n/a	4	4
onMouseMove	n/a	4	4
onMouseOut	n/a	4	4
onMouseOver	n/a	4	4
onMouseUp	n/a	4	4
onSelectStart	n/a	4	n/a

<BASE>   NN *all*   IE *all*   HTML *all*

<BASE>   *End Tag: Forbidden*

A BASE element is defined inside a document's HEAD element to instruct the browser about the URL path to the current document. This path is then used as the basis for all relative URLs used to specify various SRC and HREF attributes in the document. The BASE element's URL should be a complete URL, including the document name. The browser calculates the base URL path to the directory holding that document. For example, if you specify <BASE HREF="http://www.megacorp.com/products/index.html">, the HREF attribute of a link on that page to *widgets/framitz801.html* resolves to the full URL of *http://www.megacorp.com/products/widgets/framitz801.html*. Similarly, a relative URL can walk up the hierarchy with the dot syntax. For example, from the BASE element defined earlier, an IMG element in the *index.html* page might be set for SRC="../images/logo.jpg". That reference resolves to *http://www.megacorp.com/images/logo.jpg*.

By and large, today's browsers automatically calculate the base URL of the currently loaded document, thus allowing use of relative URLs without specifying a BASE element. This is especially helpful when you are developing pages locally and don't want to change the BASE element settings when you deploy the pages. The HTML 4.0 specification states that a document lacking a BASE element should by default use the current document's URL as the BASE URL. Of course, this is only for true web pages, rather than HTML-enhanced documents such as email messages, which have no default BASE URL.

You can also use the BASE element to define a default target for any link-type element in the document. Therefore, if all links are supposed to load documents into another frame, you can specify this target frame once in the BASE tag and not worry about TARGET attributes elsewhere in the document. If you wish to override the default for a single link, you may do so by specifying the TARGET attribute for that element.

Example
```
<HEAD>
<BASE HREF="http://www.megacorp.com/index.html" TARGET="_top">
</HEAD>
```

Object Model Reference

IE   [window.]document.all.*elementID*

Attributes

HREF   TARGET

HREF   NN *all*   IE *all*   HTML *all*

HREF="*URL*"   *Optional*

The HREF attribute is a URL of a document whose server path is to be used as the base URL for all relative references in the document. This is typically the URL of the current document, but it can be set to another path if it makes sense to your document organization and directory structure.

Example <BASE HREF="http://www.megacorp.com/products/index.html">

Value   This should be a full and absolute URL to a document.

Default Current document pathname.

Object Model Reference

IE   [window.]document.all.tags("base")[0].href

TARGET   NN *all*   IE *all*   HTML *4*

TARGET="*windowOrFrameName*"   *Optional*

If all or most links and area maps on a page load documents into a separate window or frame, you can set the TARGET attribute of the BASE element to take care of targeting for all of those elements. You can set the TARGET attribute without setting the HREF attribute if you want to set only the base target reference.

Example <BASE TARGET="rightFrame">

Value

Case-sensitive identifier when the frame or window name has been assigned via the target element's NAME attribute. Four reserved target names act as constants:

_blank   Browser creates a new window for the destination document.

_parent   Destination document replaces the current frame's framesetting document (if one exists; otherwise, it is treated as _self).

_self   Destination document replaces the current document in its window or frame.

_top   Destination document is to occupy the entire browser window, replacing any and all framesets that may be loaded (also treated as _self if there are no framesets defined in the window).

Default _self

Object Model Reference

IE   [window.]document.all.tags("base")[0].target

<BASEFONT>   NN *all*   IE *all*   HTML *3.2*

<BASEFONT>   *End Tag: Forbidden*

A BASEFONT element advises the browser of some font information to be used as the basis for text rendering of the current page below the BASEFONT element. You can apply this element in either the HEAD or BODY portion of the document (although Microsoft recommends in the BODY only for IE 4), and you can insert BASEFONT elements as often as is needed to set the base font for a portion of the document. Be aware that settings of the BASEFONT element do not necessarily apply to content in tables. If you want table content to resemble a custom BASEFONT setting, you likely have to set the font styles to table elements separately.

The BASEFONT element overrides the default font settings in the browser's user preferences settings. Like most font-related elements, the BASEFONT element is deprecated in HTML 4.0 in favor of style sheets. The latter provide much greater control over fonts (see Chapter 10).

Example <BASEFONT FACE="Times, serif" SIZE=4>

Attributes

CLASS	DIR	ID	NAME	STYLE
COLOR	FACE	LANG	SIZE	TITLE

COLOR

NN *n/a*   IE *3*   HTML *4*

COLOR=" *colorTripletOrName*" | *Optional*

Sets the font color of all text below the **BASEFONT** element. Even though the attribute made its HTML recommendation debut in Version 4.0, the attribute is nonetheless deprecated.

Example <BASEFONT COLOR="Olive">

Value

A hexadecimal triplet or plain-language color name. See Appendix A for acceptable plain-language color names.

Default   Browser default.

Object Model Reference

IE   [window.] document.all.tags("basefont")[i].color

FACE

NN *n/a*   IE *4*   HTML *4*

FACE=" *fontFaceName1[, ... fontFaceNameN]*" | *Optional*

You can assign a hierarchy of font faces to use for the default font of a section headed by a **BASEFONT** element. The browser looks for the first font face in the comma-delimited list of font face names until it either finds a match in the client system or runs out of choices, at which point the browser default font face is used. Font face names must match the system font face names exactly. If you use this attribute (instead of the preferred style sheet attribute), you can always suggest a generic font face (serif, sans-serif) as the final choice.

In IE 3, this attribute was called the **NAME** attribute.

Example <BASEFONT FACE="Bookman, Times Roman, serif">

Value

One or more font face names, including the recognized generic faces: serif | sans-serif | cursive | fantasy | monospace.

Default   Browser default.

Object Model Reference

IE   [window.] document.all.tags("basefont")[i].face

NAME

NN *n/a*   IE *3*   HTML *n/a*

NAME=" *fontFaceName*" | *Optional*

This was IE 3's version of what is today the **FACE** attribute. It accepts a single font face as a value. The **NAME** attribute is no longer used.

Value   A single font face name.

Default   Browser default.

SIZE

SIZE=" *integerOrRelativeSize*"   *Optional*

Font sizes referenced by the SIZE attribute are on a relative size scale that is not tied to any one point size across operating system platforms. The default browser font size is 3. The range of acceptable values for the SIZE attribute are integers from 1 to 7 inclusive. The exact point size varies with the operating system and browser design.

Users can often adjust the default font size in preferences settings. The SIZE attribute overrides that setting. Moreover, SIZE values can be relative to whatever font size is set in the preferences. By preceding an attribute value with a + or – sign, the browser's default size can be adjusted upward or downward, but always within the range of 1 through 7.

Example

```
<BASEFONT SIZE=4>
<BASEFONT SIZE="+3">
```

Value

Either an integer (quoted or not quoted) or a quoted relative value, consisting of a + or – symbol and an integer value.

Default   3

Object Model Reference

IE   [window.] document.all.tags("basefont")[i].size

<BDO>

<BDO>...</BDO>   *End Tag: Required*

The name of the BDO element stands for *bidirectional override*. The LANG and DIR attributes of most elements are designed to take care of most situations involving the mixture of writing systems that compose text in opposite directions. The BDO element is designed to assist in instances when due to various conversions during text processing, the normal bidirectional algorithms must be explicitly overridden. Because this element is not yet implemented in browsers, it is detailed here for informational purposes only.

Example   <BDO dir="ltr">*someMixedScriptTextHere*</BDO>

Attributes

CLASS	ID	LANG	STYLE	TITLE
DIR				

<BGSOUND>

<BGSOUND>   *End Tag: Optional*

This Internet Explorer-only attribute lets you define a sound file that is to play in the background while the user visits the page. The element is allowed only inside the HEAD element. Several attributes were added for Version 4. With scripting, you can control the volume and how many times the sound track plays even after the sound file loads. Although an end tag is optional, there is no need for it because all specifications for the sound are maintained by attributes in the start tag.

If you are going to use this tag, I strongly recommend making the playing of a background sound a user-selectable choice that is turned off by default. In office environments, it can be startling (if not embarrassing) to have background music or sounds unexpectedly emanate from a computer. Also be aware that there is likely to be some delay in the start of the music due to download time.

Example   `<BGSOUND SRC="tunes/mazeppa.mid">`

Object Model Reference

IE   `[window.]document.all.`*elementID*

Attributes

BALANCE	ID	LOOP	*TITLE*	VOLUME
CLASS	*LANG*	SRC		

BALANCE   NN *n/a*   IE *4*   HTML *n/a*

BALANCE=" *signedInteger*"   *Optional*

A value that directs how the audio is divided between the left and right speakers. Once this attribute value is set in the element, its value cannot be changed by script control.

Example   `<BGSOUND SRC="tunes/mazeppa.mid" BALANCE="+2500">`

Value

A signed integer between -10,000 and +10,000. A value of 0 is equally balanced on both sides. A negative value gives a relative boost to the left side; a positive value boosts the right side.

Default   0

Object Model Reference

IE   `[window.] document.all.tags("bgsound")[0].balance`

LOOP   NN *n/a*   IE *3*   HTML *n/a*

LOOP=*integer*   *Optional*

Defines the number of times the sound plays. If the attribute is absent or is present with any value other than -1, the sound plays at least once. Assigning a value of -1 means that the sound plays until the page is unloaded. Contrary to Microsoft's Internet Explorer SDK information, there does not appear to be a way to precache the sound without having it start playing.

Example   `<BGSOUND SRC="tunes/mazeppa.mid" LOOP=3>`

Value

No value assignment necessary for a single play. A value of 0 still causes a single play. Values above zero play the sound the specified number of times. Assign -1 to have the sound play indefinitely.

Default   -1

Object Model Reference

IE   [window.] document.all.tags("bgsound")[0].loop

SRC   NN *n/a*   IE *3*   HTML *n/a*

SRC="*URL*"   *Optional*

A URL that points to the sound file to be played. The type of sound file that can be played is limited only by the audio facilities of the browser. Common audio formats, including MIDI, are supported in Internet Explorer without further plugin installation.

Example <BGSOUND SRC="tunes/beethoven.mid">

Value

Any valid URL, including complete and relative URLs. The file must be in a MIME type supported by Internet Explorer or a plugin.

Default   None.

Object Model Reference

IE   [window.] document.all.tags("bgsound")[0].src

VOLUME   NN *n/a*   IE *4*   HTML *n/a*

VOLUME="*signedInteger*"   *Optional*

An integer that defines how loud the background sound plays relative to the maximum sound output level as adjusted by user preferences in the client computer. Maximum volume—a setting of zero—is only as loud as the user has set in the **Sound** control panel. Attribute adjustments are negative values as low as -10,000 (although most users lose the sound at a value much higher than -10,000).

Example <BGSOUND SRC="tunes/beethoven.mid" VOLUME="-500">

Value   A signed integer value between -10,000 and 0.

Default   0

Object Model Reference

IE   [window.] document.all.tags("bgsound")[0].volume

<BIG>   NN *all*   IE *all*   HTML *3.2*

<BIG>...</BIG>   *End Tag: Required*

The BIG element—one of several font style elements in HTML 4—renders its content in the next font size (in HTML's 1 through 7 scale) larger than the previous body font size. If you nest BIG elements, the effects on the more nested elements are cumulative, with each nested level rendered one size larger than the next outer element. Default font size is dependent upon the browser, operating system, and user preferences settings. For more precise font size rendering, use style sheet rules.

Example <P>This product is <BIG>new</BIG> and <BIG>improved</BIG>!</P>

Object Model Reference

IE   [window.]document.all.*elementID*

Attributes

CLASS	ID	LANGUAGE	STYLE	TITLE
DIR	LANG			

Event Handler Attributes

Handler	NN	IE	HTML
onClick	n/a	4	4
onDblClick	n/a	4	4
onDragStart	n/a	4	n/a
onHelp	n/a	4	n/a
onKeyDown	n/a	4	4
onKeyPress	n/a	4	4
onKeyUp	n/a	4	4
onMouseDown	n/a	4	4
onMouseMove	n/a	4	4
onMouseOut	n/a	4	4
onMouseOver	n/a	4	4
onMouseUp	n/a	4	4
onSelectStart	n/a	4	n/a

<BLINK>

NN *all*   IE *n/a*   HTML *n/a*

`<BLINK>...</BLINK>`   *End Tag: Required*

The BLINK element is Marc Andreessen's contribution to horrifying web pages. All content of the element flashes on and off uncontrollably in a distracting manner. The more content you place inside the element, the more difficult it is to read between the flashes. Please don't use this tag. I beg you. This element does not have any attributes or event handlers.

Example `<BLINK>I dare you to read this...and not look at it.</BLINK>`

<BLOCKQUOTE>

NN *all*   IE *all*   HTML *all*

`<BLOCKQUOTE>...</BLOCKQUOTE>`   *End Tag: Required*

The BLOCKQUOTE element is intended to set off a long quote inside a document. Traditionally, the BLOCKQUOTE element has been rendered as an indented block, with wider left and right margins (about 40 pixels each), plus some extra whitespace above and below the block. Browsers will likely continue this type of rendering, although you are encouraged to use style sheets to create such displays (with or without the BLOCKQUOTE element). For inline quotations, see the Q element.

Example

```
<BLOCKQUOTE>Four score and seven years ago...
shall not perish from the earth</BLOCKQUOTE>
```

Object Model Reference

IE   [window.]document.all.*elementID*

Attributes

CITE	DIR	LANG	STYLE	TITLE
CLASS	ID	LANGUAGE		

Event Handler Attributes

Handler	NN	IE	HTML
onClick	n/a	4	4
onDblClick	n/a	4	4
onDragStart	n/a	4	n/a
onHelp	n/a	4	n/a
onKeyDown	n/a	4	4
onKeyPress	n/a	4	4
onKeyUp	n/a	4	4
onMouseDown	n/a	4	4
onMouseMove	n/a	4	4
onMouseOut	n/a	4	4
onMouseOver	n/a	4	4
onMouseUp	n/a	4	4
onSelectStart	n/a	4	n/a

CITE
NN *n/a*   IE *n/a*   HTML *4*

CITE="*URL*"   *Optional*

A URL pointing to an online source document from which the quotation is taken. This is not in any way a mechanism for copying or extracting content from another document. Presumably, this HTML 4.0 recommendation is to encourage future browsers and search engines to utilize a reference to online source material for the benefit of readers and surfers.

Value

Any valid URL to a document on the World Wide Web, including absolute or relative URLs.

Default   None.

<BODY>
NN *all*   IE *all*   HTML *all*

<BODY>...</BODY>   *End Tag: Optional*

After all of the prefatory material in the HEAD portion of an HTML file, the BODY element contains the genuine content of the page that the user sees in the browser window (or may hear when browsers know how to speak to users). Before style sheets, the BODY element was the place where page authors could specify document-wide color and background schemes. A great many favorite attributes covering these properties are deprecated in HTML 4, in favor of style sheet rules that may be applied to the BODY element. Support for all these attributes, however, will remain in Navigator and Internet Explorer for years to come.

The BODY element is also where window object event handlers are placed. For example, a window object as defined in most document object models has an onLoad event handler that fires when a document has finished loading into the current window or frame. Assigning that event handler as an element attribute is done in the BODY element.

Although it may appear from a variety of implications that the BODY element is the document object, this is not entirely true. The document object has additional properties (such as the document.title) that are defined outside of the BODY element in an HTML document. Also, most browsers don't quibble when you omit either or both the start and end tags. But if you are debugging a page, it's helpful to see the end tags for the BODY and HTML elements when viewing the source to verify that the page has fully loaded into the browser.

Example

```
<BODY BACKGROUND="watermark.jpg" onLoad="init()">
...
</BODY>
```

Object Model Reference

NN   [window.]document

IE   [window.]document.body

Attributes

ALINK	BOTTOMMARGIN	LANG	RIGHTMARGIN	TITLE
BACKGROUND	CLASS	LANGUAGE	SCROLL	TOPMARGIN
BGCOLOR	DIR	LEFTMARGIN	STYLE	VLINK
BGPROPERTIES	ID	LINK	TEXT	

Event Handler Attributes

Handler	NN	IE	HTML
onAfterUpdate	n/a	4	n/a
onBeforeUnload	n/a	4	n/a
onBeforeUpdate	n/a	4	n/a
onBlur	3	4	n/a
onClick	n/a	4	4
onDblClick	n/a	4	4
onDragDrop	4	n/a	n/a
onFocus	3	4	n/a
onHelp	n/a	4	n/a
onKeyDown	n/a	4	4
onKeyPress	n/a	4	4
onKeyUp	n/a	4	4
onLoad	2	3	4
onMouseDown	n/a	4	4
onMouseMove	n/a	4	4
onMouseOut	n/a	4	4
onMouseOver	n/a	3 ·	4
onMouseUp	n/a	4	4
onMove	4	n/a	n/a
onResize	4	n/a	n/a
onRowEnter	n/a	4	n/a
onRowExit	n/a	4	n/a

Handler	NN	IE	HTML
onScroll	n/a	4	n/a
onSelect	n/a	4	n/a
onSelectStart	n/a	4	n/a
onUnload	2	3	4

ALINK

NN *all*   IE *all*   HTML *3.2*

ALINK=" *colorTripletOrName*"   *Optional*

Establishes the color of a hypertext link when it is activated (being clicked on) by the user. This is one of three states for a link: unvisited, active, and visited. The color is applied to the link text or border around an image or object embedded within an A element. This attribute is deprecated in favor of the BODY:active {color:} style sheet rule (and the future :active pseudo-class, as described in Chapter 10).

Example   <BODY ALINK="#FF0000">...</BODY>

Value

A hexadecimal triplet or plain-language color name. See Appendix A for acceptable plain-language color names.

Default   #FF0000 (in Navigator 4); #000000 (in IE 4).

Object Model Reference

NN   [window.]document.alinkColor

IE   [window.]document.alinkColor
         [window.]document.body.aLink

BACKGROUND

NN *all*   IE *all*   HTML *3.2*

BACKGROUND=" *URL*"   *Optional*

Specifies an image file that is used as a backdrop to the text and other content of the page. Unlike normal images that get loaded into browser content, a background image loads in its original size (without scaling) and tiles to fill the available document space in the browser window or frame. Smaller images usually download faster but are obviously repeated more often in the background. Animated GIFs are also allowable but very distracting to the reader. When selecting a background image, be sure it is very muted in comparison to the main content so that the content stands out clearly. Background images, if used at all, should be extremely subtle.

This attribute is deprecated in HTML 4.0 in favor of the **background** style attribute.

Example   <BODY BACKGROUND="watermark.jpg">...</BODY>

Value   Any valid URL to an image file, including complete and relative URLs.

Default   None.

Object Model Reference

IE   [window.]document.body.background

BGCOLOR

NN *all*   IE *all*   HTML *3.2*

BGCOLOR="*colorTripletOrName*"   *Optional*

Establishes a fill color (behind the text and other content) for the entire document. If you combine a BGCOLOR and BACKGROUND, any transparent areas of the background image let the background color show through. This attribute is deprecated in HTML 4.0 in favor of the background-color style attribute.

Example   <BODY BGCOLOR="tan">...</BODY>

Value

A hexadecimal triplet or plain-language color name. A setting of empty is interpreted as "#000000" (black). See Appendix A for acceptable plain-language color names.

Default   Varies with browser, browser version, and operating system.

Object Model Reference

NN   [window.]document.bgColor

IE   [window.]document.bgColor
            [window.]document.body.bgColor

BGPROPERTIES

NN *n/a*   IE *3*   HTML *n/a*

BGPROPERTIES="*property*"   *Optional*

An Internet Explorer attribute that lets you define whether the background image (set with the BACKGROUND attribute or style sheet) remains in a fixed position or scrolls as a user scrolls the page. This can provide both intriguing and odd effects for the user. When the background image is set to remain in a fixed position, scrolled content flows past the background image very much like film credits roll past a background image on the screen.

Example   <BODY BACKGROUND="watermark.jpg" BGPROPERTIES="fixed">...</BODY>

Value

If set to "fixed", the image does not scroll. Omit the attribute or set it to an empty string ("") to let the image scroll with the content.

Default   None.

Object Model Reference

IE   [window.]document.body.bgProperties

BOTTOMMARGIN

NN *n/a*   IE *4*   HTML *n/a*

BOTTOMMARGIN="*integer*"   *Optional*

Establishes the amount of blank space between the very end of the content and the bottom of a scrollable page. The setting has no visual effect if the length of the content or size of the window does not cause the window to scroll. The default value is for the end of the content to be flush with the end of the document, but in the Macintosh version of Internet Explorer 4, there is about a 10-pixel margin visible even when the attribute is set to zero. Larger sizes are reflected properly. This attribute offers somewhat of a shortcut to setting the margin-bottom style sheet attribute for the BODY element.

Example <BODY BOTTOMMARGIN="20">...</BODY>

Value

A string value of the number of pixels of clear space at the bottom of the document. A value of an empty string is the same as zero.

Default   0

Object Model Reference

IE   [window.]document.body.bottomMargin

LEFTMARGIN

NN *n/a*   IE *3*   HTML *n/a*

LEFTMARGIN="*integer*"   *Optional*

Establishes the amount of blank space between the left edge of the content area of a window and the left edge of the content. This attribute offers somewhat of a shortcut to setting the `margin-left` style sheet attribute for the BODY element. As the outermost parent container in the element hierarchy, this attribute setting fixes the left margin context for all nested elements in the document.

Example <BODY LEFTMARGIN="25">...</BODY>

Value

A string value of the number of pixels of clear space at the left margin of the document. A value of an empty string is the same as zero.

Default   10 (Windows); 8 (Macintosh).

Object Model Reference

IE   [window.]document.body.leftMargin

LINK

NN *all*   IE *all*   HTML *3.2*

LINK="*colorTripletOrName*"   *Optional*

Establishes the color of a hypertext link that has not been visited (i.e., the URL of the link is not in the browser's cache). This is one of three states for a link: unvisited, activate, and visited. The color is applied to the link text or border around an image or object embedded within an A element. This attribute is deprecated in favor of the BODY:link {color:} style sheet rule (and the future :link pseudo-class, as described in Chapter 10).

Example <BODY LINK="#00FF00">...</BODY>

Value

A hexadecimal triplet or plain-language color name. See Appendix A for acceptable plain-language color names.

Default   #0000FF

Object Model Reference

NN   [window.]document.linkColor

IE   [window.]document.linkColor
            [window.]document.body.link

RIGHTMARGIN

NN *n/a*   IE *4*   HTML *n/a*

RIGHTMARGIN="*integer*"   *Optional*

Establishes the amount of blank space between the right edge of the content area of a window and the right edge of the content. This attribute offers somewhat of a shortcut to setting the **margin-right** style sheet attribute for the **BODY** element. As the outermost parent container in the element hierarchy, this attribute setting fixes the right margin context for all nested elements in the document. Be aware that IE on the Mac does not let content come as close to the right edge of the window as the Windows version.

Example <BODY RIGHTMARGIN="25">... </BODY>

Value

A string value of the number of pixels of clear space at the right margin of the document. A value of an empty string is the same as zero.

Default   10 (Windows); 0 (Macintosh).

Object Model Reference

IE   [window.]document.body.rightMargin

SCROLL

NN *n/a*   IE *4*   HTML

SCROLL=yes | no   *Optional*

Controls the presence of scrollbars when the content space exceeds the size of the current window. Without scrollbars, if you want your users to move around the page, you have to provide some scripted method of adjusting the scroll of the window. Be aware that Internet Explorer 4 for the Mac always shows scrollbars when the document is too large for the window, even when the **SCROLL** attribute is set to **no**.

Example <BODY SCROLL=NO>...</BODY>

Value   Constant values **yes** or **no** (case insensitive).

Default   yes

Object Model Reference

IE   [window.]document.body.scroll

TEXT

NN *all*   IE *all*   HTML *3.2*

TEXT="*colorTripletOrName*"   *Optional*

Establishes the color of body content in the document. Colors of individual elements within the document can override the document-wide setting. Because the default background color of browsers varies widely with browser brand, version, and operating system, it is advisable to set the **BGCOLOR** attribute (or equivalent style sheet rule) in concert with the document's text color. This attribute is deprecated in favor of the {**color:**} style sheet rule.

Example <BODY BGCOLOR="#FFFFFF" TEXT="#c0c0c0">...</BODY>

Value

A hexadecimal triplet or plain-language color name. See Appendix A for acceptable plain-language color names.

Default   #000000 (black).

Object Model Reference

NN   [window.]document.fgColor

IE   [window.]document.fgColor

             [window.]document.body.text

TOPMARGIN   NN *n/a*   IE *3*   HTML *n/a*

TOPMARGIN="*integer*"   *Optional*

Establishes the amount of blank space between the top edge of the content area of a window and the top edge of the content. This attribute offers somewhat of a shortcut to setting the `margin-top` style sheet attribute for the **BODY** element. As the outermost parent container in the element hierarchy, this attribute setting fixes the top margin context for all nested elements in the document. On both Windows and Macintosh versions, setting the **TOPMARGIN** attribute to zero or an empty string (`""`) pushes the content to the very top of the document content region.

Example   <BODY TOPMARGIN="0">... </BODY>

Value

A string value of the number of pixels of clear space at the top of the document. A value of an empty string is the same as zero.

Default   15 (Windows); 8 (Macintosh).

Object Model Reference

IE   [window.]document.body.topMargin

VLINK   NN *all*   IE *all*   HTML *3.2*

VLINK="*colorTripletOrName*"   *Optional*

Establishes the color of a hypertext link after it has been visited by a user (and the destination page is still in the browser's cache). This is one of three states for a link: unvisited, active, and visited. The color is applied to the link text or border around an image or object embedded within an **A** element. This attribute is deprecated in favor of the **BODY:visited {color:}** style sheet rule (and the future **:visited** pseudo-class, as described in Chapter 10).

Example   <BODY VLINK="#teal">...</BODY>

Value

A hexadecimal triplet or plain-language color name. See Appendix A for acceptable plain-language color names.

Default

#551a8b (Navigator 4); #800080 (Internet Explorer 4 Windows); #006010 (Internet Explorer 4 Macintosh).

Object Model Reference

NN   [window.]document.vlinkColor

IE   [window.]document.vlinkColor
            [window.]document.body.vLink

*
*   NN *all*   IE *all*   HTML *all*

`<BR>`   *End Tag: Forbidden*

The BR element forces a visible line break (carriage return and line feed) wherever its tag appears in the document. Browsers tend to honor the BR element as a genuine line break, whereas paragraphs defined by the P element are given more vertical space between elements on the page. If the text containing the BR element is wrapped around a floating image or other object, you can direct the next line (via the **CLEAR** attribute or style sheet equivalent) to start below the object, rather than on the next line of the wrapped text.

Example `<P>I think that I shall never see<BR>A poem lovely as a tree.</P>`

Object Model Reference

IE   [window.]document.all.*elementID*

Attributes

CLASS	*ID*	*LANGUAGE*	*STYLE*	*TITLE*
CLEAR				

CLEAR   NN *all*   IE *all*   HTML *3.2*

CLEAR=" *constant*"   *Optional*

The **CLEAR** attribute tells the browser how to treat the next line of text following a BR element if the current text is wrapping around a floating image or other object. The value you use depends on the side of the page to which one or more inline images are pegged and how you want the next line of text to be placed in relation to those images.

This attribute is deprecated in HTML 4.0 in favor of the BR {clear:*setting*} style sheet rule in CSS2.

Example `<BR CLEAR="left">`

Value

Navigator and Internet Explorer accept three constants: all | left | right. HTML 4.0 includes what should be the default value: none. This value is listed in IE 3 documentation, but not for IE 4. You can set the property to none and it either responds to the value or ignores it (yielding the same results).

Default None.

Object Model Reference

IE   [window.]document.all.*elementID*.clear

<BUTTON>   NN *n/a*   IE *4*   HTML *4*

<BUTTON>...</BUTTON>   *End Tag: Required*

The BUTTON element is patterned after the INPUT element (of types button, submit, and reset) but carries some extra powers, particularly when used as a submit-type button. Content for the button's label goes between the element's start and end tags, rather than being assigned as an attribute. Other elements can be used to generate the label content, including an IMG element if so desired (although client-side image maps of such images are strongly discouraged by the W3C). Although you can assign a style sheet to a BUTTON element, you can also wrap the label content inside an element (such as a SPAN) and assign or override style rules just for that content. Both style sheet mechanisms permit the button label to use custom fonts and styles.

When a BUTTON element is assigned a TYPE of submit, the browser submits the button's NAME and VALUE attributes to the server as a name/value pair, like other form elements. No special form handling is conveyed by a BUTTON when other types are specified.

In theory, a BUTTON element should be embedded within a FORM element. In practice, IE 4 has no problem rendering a free-standing BUTTON element. This might be acceptable when no related form elements (such as text boxes) need to be referenced by scripts associated with the button. Some scripting shortcuts (passing form object references as parameters) simplify the scripted interactivity between form elements.

The W3C implemented this INPUT element variant to offer browser makers a chance to create a different, richer-looking button. In practice, in IE 4, both button types have very similar appearance. You can detect a slight difference, however, between the INPUT and BUTTON rendering on the Mac version of IE 4: with a BUTTON element, the browser draws more whitespace around the label text for a more pleasing appearance.

Example

```
<BUTTON TYPE="button" onClick="doSomething()">Click Here</BUTTON>
<BUTTON TYPE="submit" NAME="Type" VALUE="infoOnly">Request Info</BUTTON>
<BUTTON TYPE="reset"><IMG SRC="clearIt.gif" HEIGHT=20 WIDTH=18></BUTTON>
```

Object Model Reference

IE   [window.]document.all.*elementID*

Attributes

ACCESSKEY	DATAFORMATAS	*ID*	NAME	*TITLE*
CLASS	DATASRC	*LANG*	*STYLE*	TYPE
DATAFLD	DISABLED	*LANGUAGE*	TABINDEX	VALUE

Event Handler Attributes

Handler	NN	IE	HTML
onAfterUpdate	n/a	4	n/a
onBeforeUpdate	n/a	4	n/a
onBlur	n/a	4	4
onClick	n/a	4	4

HTML Reference

Handler	NN	IE	HTML
onDblClick	n/a	4	4
onDragStart	n/a	4	n/a
onFocus	n/a	4	4
onHelp	n/a	4	n/a
onKeyDown	n/a	4	4
onKeyPress	n/a	4	4
onKeyUp	n/a	4	4
onMouseDown	n/a	4	4
onMouseMove	n/a	4	4
onMouseOut	n/a	4	4
onMouseOver	n/a	4	4
onMouseUp	n/a	4	4
onResize	n/a	4	n/a
onRowEnter	n/a	4	n/a
onRowExit	n/a	4	n/a
onSelectStart	n/a	4	n/a

ACCESSKEY
NN *n/a*   IE *4*   HTML *4*

ACCESSKEY="*character*"   *Optional*

A single character key that specifies the keyboard shortcut to effect a click of the button. The browser and operating system determine if the user must press a modifier key (e.g., **Ctrl**, **Alt**, or **Command**) with the access key to "click" the button. In IE 4/Windows, the **Alt** key is required, and the key is not case sensitive. This attribute does not work in IE 4/Mac.

Example
```
<BUTTON TYPE="button" ACCESSKEY=t onClick="goToContents()">
Table of Contents
</BUTTON>
```

Value   Single character of the document set.

Default   None.

Object Model Reference
IE   [window.]document.all.*elementID*.accessKey

DATAFLD
NN *n/a*   IE *4*   HTML *n/a*

DATAFLD="*columnName*"   *Optional*

Used with IE 4 data binding to associate a remote data source column name with the label of a button. The data source column must be either plain text or HTML (see DATAFORMATAS). A DATASRC attribute must also be set for the BUTTON element.

Example
```
<BUTTON TYPE="button" DATASRC="#DBSRC3" DATAFLD="label"
onClick="getTopStory()">
</BUTTON>
```

Value   Case-sensitive identifier.

Default   None.

Object Model Reference

IE   [window.]document.all.*elementID*.dataFld

DATAFORMATAS

NN *n/a*   IE *4*   HTML *n/a*

DATAFORMATAS="*dataType*"   *Optional*

Used with IE 4 data binding, this attribute advises the browser whether the source material arriving from the data source is to be treated as plain text or as tagged HTML. This attribute setting depends entirely on how the data source is constructed.

Example

```
<BUTTON TYPE="button" DATASRC="#DBSRC3"DATAFORMATAS="HTML" DATAFLD="label"
onClick="getTopStory()">
</BUTTON>
```

Value   IE 4 recognizes two possible settings: text | HTML.

Default   text

Object Model Reference

IE   [window.]document.all.*elementID*.dataFormatAs

DATASRC

NN *n/a*   IE *4*   HTML *n/a*

DATASRC="*dataSourceName*"   *Optional*

Used with IE 4 data binding to specify the name of the remote ODBC data source (such as an Oracle or SQL Server database) to be associated with the element. Content from the data source is specified via the DATAFLD attribute.

Example

```
<BUTTON TYPE="button" DATASRC="#DBSRC3" DATAFLD="label"
onClick="getTopStory()">
</BUTTON>
```

Value   Case-sensitive identifier.

Default   None.

Object Model Reference

IE   [window.]document.all.*elementID*.dataSrc

DISABLED

NN *n/a*   IE *4*   HTML *4*

DISABLED   *Optional*

A disabled BUTTON element appears grayed out on the screen and cannot be activated by the user. In Windows, a disabled BUTTON cannot receive focus and does not become active within the tabbing order rotation. HTML 4.0 also specifies that a disabled BUTTON whose TYPE is submit should not send its name/value pair when the form is submitted.

The DISABLED attribute is a Boolean type, which means that its presence in the attribute sets its value to true. Its value can also be adjusted after the fact by scripting (see the button object in Chapter 9).

Example `<BUTTON TYPE="submit" DISABLED>Ready to Submit</BUTTON>`

Value   The presence of the attribute sets its value to true.

Default   false

Object Model Reference

IE   `[window.]document.all.`*elementID*`.disabled`

NAME

NN *n/a*   IE *4*   HTML *4*

NAME="*elementIdentifier*"   *Optional*

For a BUTTON element, the NAME attribute can play two roles, depending on the TYPE attribute setting. For all TYPE attribute settings, the NAME attribute lets you assign an identifier that can be used in scripted references to the element (the ID attribute is an alternate way to reference the element). For a button type of submit, the NAME attribute is sent as part of the name/value pair to the server at submit time.

Example

`<BUTTON TYPE="submit" NAME="Type" VALUE="infoOnly">Request Info</BUTTON>`

Value   Case-sensitive identifier.

Default   None.

Object Model Reference

IE   `[window.]document.all.`*elementID*`.name`

TABINDEX

NN *n/a*   IE *4*   HTML *4*

TABINDEX=integer   *Optional*

A number that indicates the sequence of this element within the tabbing order of all focusable elements in the document. Tabbing order follows a strict set of rules. Elements that have values other than zero assigned to their TABINDEX attributes are first in line when a user starts tabbing in a page. Focus starts with the element with the lowest TABINDEX value and proceeds in order to the highest value, regardless of physical location on the page or in the document. If two elements have the same TABINDEX values, the element that comes earlier in the document receives focus first. Next come all elements that either don't support the TABINDEX attribute or have the value set to zero. These elements receive focus in the order in which they appear in the document. A BUTTON element set to be disabled does not become part of the tabbing rotation.

Note that the Macintosh user interface does not provide for giving focus to elements other than text input fields. Buttons cannot be tabbed to on the Mac version of IE 4.

Example

`<BUTTON TYPE="button" TABINDEX=3 onClick="doSomething()">Click Here`
`</BUTTON>`

Value

Any integer from 0 through 32767. In IE 4, setting the TABINDEX to -1 causes the element to be skipped in tabbing order altogether.

Default None.

Object Model Reference

IE   [window.]document.*elementID*.tabIndex

TYPE   NN *n/a*   IE *4*   HTML *4*

TYPE="*buttonType*"   *Optional*

Defines the internal style of button for the browser. A button style is intended to be used to initiate scripted action via an event handler. A "reset" style behaves the same way as an INPUT element whose TYPE attribute is set to reset, returning all elements to their default values. A "submit" style behaves the same way as an INPUT element whose TYPE attribute is set to submit. A BUTTON element whose TYPE attribute is set to either reset or submit must be associated with a form for its implied action to be of any value to the page.

Example

```
<BUTTON TYPE="reset"><IMG SRC="clearIt.gif" HEIGHT=20 WIDTH=18></BUTTON>
```

Value

Case-insensitive constant value from the following list of three: button | reset | submit.

Default button

Object Model Reference

IE   [window.]document.all.*elementID*.type

VALUE   NN *n/a*   IE *4*   HTML *4*

VALUE="*text*"   *Optional/Required*

Preassigns a value to a BUTTON element that is submitted to the server as part of the name/ value pair when the element is a member of a form.

Example   <BUTTON NAME="connections" VALUE="ISDN">ISDN</BUTTON>

Value   Any text string.

Default None.

Object Model Reference

IE   [window.]document.all.*elementID*.value

<CAPTION>   NN *all*   IE *all*   HTML *3.2*

<CAPTION>...</CAPTION>   *End Tag: Required*

A CAPTION element may be placed only inside a TABLE element (and immediately after the <TABLE> start tag) to denote the text to be used as a caption for the table. A caption applies to the entire table, whereas a table heading (TH element) applies to a single column or row of the table. Only one CAPTION element is recognized within a TABLE element.

A table caption is usually a brief description of the table. A longer description may be written for the SUMMARY attribute of a TABLE element for browsers that use text-to-speech technology for users who cannot see browsers. The primary distinguishing attribute of the CAPTION element is ALIGN, which lets you define where the caption appears in relation to the actual table.

Example

```
<TABLE ...>
<CAPTION CLASS="tableCaptions">
    Table 3-2. Sample Inverse Framistan Values
</CAPTION>
...
</TABLE>
```

Object Model Reference

IE   [window.]document.all.*elementID*

Attributes

ALIGN	DIR	LANG	STYLE	VALIGN
CLASS	ID	LANGUAGE	TITLE	

Event Handler Attributes

Handler	NN	IE	HTML
onAfterUpdate	n/a	4	n/a
onBeforeUpdate	n/a	4	n/a
onBlur	n/a	4	n/a
onClick	n/a	4	4
onDblClick	n/a	4	4
onDragStart	n/a	4	n/a
onFocus	n/a	4	n/a
onHelp	n/a	4	n/a
onKeyDown	n/a	4	4
onKeyPress	n/a	4	4
onKeyUp	n/a	4	4
onMouseDown	n/a	4	4
onMouseMove	n/a	4	4
onMouseOut	n/a	4	4
onMouseOver	n/a	4	4
onMouseUp	n/a	4	4
onResize	n/a	4	n/a
onRowEnter	n/a	4	n/a
onRowExit	n/a	4	n/a
onSelect	n/a	4	n/a
onSelectStart	n/a	4	n/a

ALIGN   NN *all*   IE *all*   HTML *3.2*

ALIGN="*where*"   *Optional*

Determines how the caption is rendered in physical relation to the table. Not all versions of all browsers support the full range of possibilities for this attribute. Only top and bottom are universal among all supporting browsers.

Browsers typically render a caption above or below a table in the running body font (unless modified by tag or style sheet) and centered horizontally on the table. If the caption is wider than the table, text is wrapped to the next line, maintaining center justification.

The ALIGN attribute is deprecated in HTML 4.0 in favor of the text-align: and vertical-align: style sheet attribute.

Example <CAPTION ALIGN="top">Table II. Stock List</CAPTION>

Value

Each browser and the HTML 4.0 specification define different sets of values for this attribute. Select the one(s) from the following table that work for your deployment:

Value	NN 4	IE 4	HTML 4.0
bottom	•	•	•
center	–	•	–
left	–	•	•
right	–	•	•
top	•	•	•

Moreover, IE 4 and HTML 4.0 disagree on the intention of the left and right values. In IE 4, the captions are always at the top or bottom of the table (see the VALIGN attribute), but the text is right-, center-, or left-aligned in those positions. HTML 4.0 speaks of left and right as meaning positioning the entire caption to the left or right of the table. If Internet Explorer were to adopt the HTML 4.0 specification in a future version, it could break the layout of existing table captions.

Default   top (in IE 4, center if VALIGN attribute is also set).

Object Model Reference

IE   [window.]document.all.*elementID*.align

VALIGN   NN *n/a*   IE *3*   HTML *n/a*

VALIGN="*where*"   *Optional*

The VALIGN attribute was Internet Explorer's early attribute for placing a table caption above or below the table. Although this attribute is now a part of the ALIGN attribute, IE's special way of handling left, center, and right values of the ALIGN attribute give VALIGN something to do. For example, you can use VALIGN to set the caption below the table, and use ALIGN="right" to right-align the caption at the bottom. This combination is not possible with the HTML 4.0 attribute. The VALIGN attribute is in IE 4 for backward compatibility, if for no other reason.

Example

<CAPTION ALIGN="right" VALIGN="bottom">Table 3-2. Fiber Content.</CAPTION>

Value   Two possible case-insensitive values: bottom | top.

Default   top

Object Model Reference

IE   [window.]document.all.*elementID*.valign

<CENTER>

NN *all*   IE *all*   HTML *3.2*

<CENTER>...</CENTER>   *End Tag: Required*

The CENTER element was introduced by Netscape and became widely used before the W3C-sanctioned DIV element came into being. It is clear, even from the HTML 3.2 documentation, that the HTML working group was never fond of this element. Momentum, however, carried the day, and this element found its way into the HTML 3.2 specification. The element is deprecated in HTML 4.0 in favor of the DIV element with a style sheet rule of text-align:center. In lieu of style sheets (but still deprecated in HTML 4), you can use a DIV element with ALIGN="center".

Content of a CENTER element is aligned along an axis that runs down the middle of the next outermost containing element—usually the BODY.

Example   <CENTER>Don't do this.</CENTER>

Object Model Reference

IE   [window.]document.all.*elementID*

Attributes

CLASS	LANG	LANGUAGE	STYLE	TITLE
ID				

Event Handler Attributes

Handler	NN	IE	HTML
onClick	n/a	4	n/a
onDblClick	n/a	4	n/a
onDragStart	n/a	4	n/a
onHelp	n/a	4	n/a
onKeyDown	n/a	4	n/a
onKeyPress	n/a	4	n/a
onKeyUp	n/a	4	n/a
onMouseDown	n/a	4	n/a
onMouseMove	n/a	4	n/a
onMouseOut	n/a	4	n/a
onMouseOver	n/a	4	n/a
onMouseUp	n/a	4	n/a
onSelectStart	n/a	4	n/a

<CITE>

`<CITE>...</CITE>`	*End Tag: Required*

The `CITE` element is one of a large group of elements that the HTML 4.0 recommendation calls *phrase elements*. Such elements assign structural meaning to a designated portion of the document. A `CITE` element is one that contains a citation or reference to some other source material. This is not an active link but simply notation indicating what the element content is. Search engines and other HTML document parsers may use this information for other purposes (assembling a bibliography of a document, for example).

Browsers have free rein to determine how (or whether) to distinguish `CITE` element content from the rest of the `BODY` element. Both Navigator and Internet Explorer elect to italicize the text. This can be overridden with a style sheet as you see fit.

Example

```
<P>Trouthe is the hyest thing that many may kepe.<BR>
(Chaucer, <CITE>The Franklin's Tale</CITE>)</P>
```

Object Model Reference

IE   `[window.]document.all.`*elementID*

Attributes

CLASS	ID	LANGUAGE	STYLE	TITLE
DIR	LANG			

Event Handler Attributes

Handler	NN	IE	HTML
onClick	n/a	4	4
onDblClick	n/a	4	4
onDragStart	n/a	4	n/a
onHelp	n/a	4	n/a
onKeyDown	n/a	4	4
onKeyPress	n/a	4	4
onKeyUp	n/a	4	4
onMouseDown	n/a	4	4
onMouseMove	n/a	4	4
onMouseOut	n/a	4	4
onMouseOver	n/a	4	4
onMouseUp	n/a	4	4
onSelectStart	n/a	4	n/a

<CODE>

`<CODE>...</CODE>`	*End Tag: Required*

The `CODE` element is one of a large group of elements that the HTML 4.0 recommendation calls *phrase elements*. Such elements assign structural meaning to a designated portion of the document. A `CODE` element is one that is used predominantly to display one or more inline characters representing computer code (program statements, variable names, keywords, and the like).

Browsers have free rein to determine how (or whether) to distinguish CODE element content from the rest of the BODY element. Both Navigator and Internet Explorer elect to render CODE element content in a monospace font, usually in a slightly smaller font size than the default body font (although it is not reduced in IE 4 for the Macintosh). This rendering can be overridden with a style sheet as you see fit.

White space (including carriage returns) are treated the same way in CODE element content as it is in the browser's BODY element content. Line breaks must be manually inserted with BR elements. See also the PRE element for displaying preformatted text that observes all whitespace entered in the source code.

Example

Initialize a variable in JavaScript with the <CODE>var</CODE> keyword.

Object Model Reference

IE   [window.]document.all.*elementID*

Attributes

CLASS	ID	LANGUAGE	STYLE	TITLE
DIR	LANG			

Event Handler Attributes

Handler	NN	IE	HTML
onClick	n/a	4	4
onDblClick	n/a	4	4
onDragStart	n/a	4	n/a
onHelp	n/a	4	n/a
onKeyDown	n/a	4	4
onKeyPress	n/a	4	4
onKeyUp	n/a	4	4
onMouseDown	n/a	4	4
onMouseMove	n/a	4	4
onMouseOut	n/a	4	4
onMouseOver	n/a	4	4
onMouseUp	n/a	4	4
onSelectStart	n/a	4	n/a

<COL>   NN *n/a*   IE *3*   HTML *4*

                                              End Tag: Forbidden

The COL element provides shortcuts to assigning widths and other characteristics (styles) to one or more subsets of columns within a table or within a table's column group. With this information appearing early in the TABLE element, a browser equipped to do so starts rendering the table before all source code for the table has loaded (at which time it would otherwise perform all of its geographical calculations).

You can use the COL element in combination with the COLGROUP element or by itself. The structure depends on how you need to assign widths and styles to individual columns or contiguous columns. A COL element can apply to a single column by omitting the REPEAT (or SPAN in IE 4) attribute. By assigning an integer value to the **REPEAT** attribute, you direct the browser to ply the COL element's width or style settings to said number of contiguous columns. The **REPEAT** element is similar to the COLGROUP element's COLSPAN attribute. In concert with the COLGROUP element, the COL element allows you to create a kind of subset of related columns within a COLGROUP set.

No matter how you address the column structure of your table, the total number of columns defined in all COL and COLGROUP elements should equal the physical number of columns you intend for the table. If there should be more cells in a row than columns defined in COL and COLGROUP, the browser probably has to reflow the table and discard whatever incremental rendering it had accomplished. The following three skeletal examples specify HTML 4.0 tables with six columns:

```
<TABLE>
<COL REPEAT=6>
...
</TABLE>

<TABLE>
<COL>
<COL REPEAT=4>
<COL>
...
</TABLE>

<TABLE>
<COLGROUP>
<COL REPEAT=2></COLGROUP>
<COLGROUP SPAN=4>
...
</TABLE>
```

HTML 4.0 specifications for the COL element exceed the implementation in Internet Explorer 4 in some respects. For example, HTML 4.0 provides for alignment within a column to be around any character, such as the decimal point of a money amount. This kind of feature adds to the rationale behind the COL element. For example, you can have a table whose first three columns are formatted one way and a fourth column assigned a special style and its own alignment characteristics:

```
<HTML>
<HEAD>
<STYLE TYPE="text/css">
  .colHdrs {color:black}
  .normColumn {color:green}
  .priceColumn {color:red}
</STYLE>
</HEAD>
<BODY>
<TABLE>
<COLGROUP CLASS="normColumn" SPAN=3></COLGROUP>
<COL CLASS="priceColumn" ALIGN="char" CHAR=".">
<THEAD CLASS="colHdrs">
<TR><TH>Stock No.<TH>In Stock<TH>Description<TH>Price</TR>
<TBODY>
```

```
<TR><TD>8832<TD>Yes<TD>Brass Frobnitz<TD>$255.98</TR>
<TR><TD>8835<TD>No<TD>Frobnitz (black)<TD>$98</TR>
...
</TABLE>
</BODY>
</HTML>
```

Because attributes of the COL and COLGROUP elements apply to the entire column, in the preceding example the style sheet rule for the THEAD overrides the color settings for the two column styles for the rows enclosed by the THEAD element. The preceding example works in IE 4 for Windows, except for the alignment of the final column, which is ignored; IE 4 for the Mac assigns styles and other attributes to the wrong columns.

Example   `<COL CLASS="dateCols" WIDTH="15" ALIGN="right">`

Object Model Reference

IE   `[window.]document.all.`*elementID*

Attributes

ALIGN	*CLASS*	*LANG*	*STYLE*	VALIGN
CHAR	*DIR*	REPEAT	*TITLE*	WIDTH
CHAROFF	*ID*	SPAN		

Event Handler Attributes

Handler	NN	IE	HTML
onClick	n/a	n/a	4
onDblClick	n/a	n/a	4
onKeyDown	n/a	n/a	4
onKeyPress	n/a	n/a	4
onKeyUp	n/a	n/a	4
onMouseDown	n/a	n/a	4
onMouseMove	n/a	n/a	4
onMouseOut	n/a	n/a	4
onMouseOver	n/a	n/a	4
onMouseUp	n/a	n/a	4

ALIGN   NN *n/a*   IE *3*   HTML *4*

ALIGN="*alignConstant*"   *Optional*

Establishes the horizontal alignment characteristics of content within column(s) covered by the COL element. The HTML 4.0 specification defines settings for the ALIGN attribute that are not yet reflected in the CSS specification. Therefore, this ALIGN attribute is not fully deprecated. As a rule, alignment should be specified by style sheet wherever possible.

Example   `<COL CLASS="dateCols" WIDTH="15" ALIGN="right">`

Value   HTML 4.0 and IE 4 have two sets of attribute values:

Value	IE 4	HTML 4.0
center	•	•
char	-	•
justify	-	•

Value	IE 4	HTML 4.0
left	•	•
right	•	•

The values center, left, and right are self-explanatory. The value justify is intended to space content so that text is justified down both left and right edges. For the value char, the CHAR attribute must also be set to specify the character on which alignment revolves. In the HTML 4.0 specification example, content that does not contain the character appears to be right-aligned to the location of the character in other rows of the same column.

It is important to bear in mind that the ALIGN attribute applies to every row of a column, including any TH element you specify for the table. If you want a different alignment for the column header, override the setting with a separate ALIGN attribute or text-align style sheet attribute for the THEAD or individual TH elements.

Default   left

Object Model Reference

IE   [window.]document.all.*elementID*.align

CHAR

NN *n/a*   IE *n/a*   HTML 4

CHAR="*character*"   *Optional*

The CHAR attribute defines the text character used as an alignment point for text within a column. This attribute is of value only for the ALIGN attribute set to "char".

Example <COL CLASS="priceColumn" ALIGN="char" CHAR=".">

Value   Any single text character.

Default None.

CHAROFF

NN *n/a*   IE *n/a*   HTML 4

CHAROFF="*length*"   *Optional*

The CHAROFF attribute lets you set a specific offset point at which the character specified by the CHAR attribute is to appear within a cell. This attribute is provided in case the browser default positioning does not meet with the design goals of the table.

Example <COL CLASS="priceColumn" ALIGN="char" CHAR="." CHAROFF="80%">

Value   Any length value in pixels or percentage of cell space.

Default None.

REPEAT

NN *n/a*   IE *n/a* HTML 4

REPEAT="*columnCount*"   *Optional*

Defines the number of adjacent columns for which the COL element's attribute and style settings apply. If this attribute is missing, the COL element governs a single column. You can combine multiple COL elements of different REPEAT sizes as needed for your column subgrouping.

This HTML 4.0 attribute is represented in IE 4 by the SPAN attribute.

Example   <COL REPEAT=3>

Value   Integer value greater than zero.

Default   1

SPAN
NN n/a   IE 3   HTML n/a

SPAN=*columnCount*   *Optional*

Defines the number of adjacent columns for which the COL element's attribute and style settings apply. If this attribute is missing, the COL element governs a single column. You can combine multiple COL elements of different SPAN sizes as needed for your column subgrouping.

This IE 4 attribute is represented in HTML 4.0 by the REPEAT attribute.

Example   <COL SPAN=3>

Value   Integer value greater than zero.

Default   1

Object Model Reference

IE   [window.]document.all.*elementID*.span

VALIGN
NN n/a   IE 4   HTML 4

VALIGN="*alignmentConstant*"   *Optional*

Determines the vertical alignment of content within cells of the column(s) covered by the COL element. You can override the vertical alignment for a particular cell anywhere in the column.

Example   <COL VALIGN="middle">

Value

Four constant values are recognized by both IE 4 and HTML 4.0: top | middle | bottom | baseline. With top and bottom, the content is rendered flush (or very close to it) to the top and bottom of the table cell. Set to middle (the default), the content floats perfectly centered vertically in the cell. When one cell's contents might wrap to multiple lines at common window widths (assuming a variable table width), it is advisable to set the VALIGN attributes of all cells in the same row (or all COL elements) to baseline. This assures that the character baseline of the first (or only) line of a cell's text aligns with the other cells in the row—usually the most aesthetically pleasing arrangement.

Default   middle

Object Model Reference

IE   [window.]document.all.*elementID*.vAlign

WIDTH

WIDTH="*multiLength*"   *Optional*

Defines the maximum width for the column(s) covered by the COL element. In practice (in IE 4 Windows, anyway), the browser won't render a column narrower than the widest contiguous stretch of characters not containing whitespace (e.g., the longest word). The precise measure of such a column width, of course, depends on the font characteristics of the content, as well. Internet Explorer 4 for the Mac mixes up column width assignments when the COL element is deployed.

Example <COL WIDTH=100>

Value

Internet Explorer 4 accepts length values for the WIDTH in the form of pixel measures (without the "px" unit) or percentage of available horizontal space allocated to the entire table (WIDTH="25%").

The HTML 4.0 specification introduces an additional length measurement scheme to supplement the regular length measure. Called a proportional length (also MultiLength), this format features a special notation and geometry. It is best suited for situations in which a COL element is to be sized based on the available width of the table space after all fixed length and percentage lengths are calculated. Using the proportional length notation (a number followed by an asterisk), you can direct the browser to divide any remaining space according to proportion. For example, if there is enough horizontal space on the page for 100 pixels after all other column width calculations are performed, three COL elements might specify WIDTH attributes of 1*, 3*, and 1*. This adds up to a total of five proportional segments. The 100 available pixels are handed out to the proportional columns based on their proportion to the whole of the remaining space: 20, 60, and 20 pixels, respectively.

Default Determined by browser calculation.

<COLGROUP>

<COLGROUP>...</COLGROUP>   *End Tag: Optional*

The COLGROUP element provides shortcuts to assigning widths and other characteristics (styles) to one or more subsets of columns within a table. With this information appearing early in the TABLE element source code, a browser equipped to do so starts rendering the table before all source code for the table has loaded (at which time it would otherwise perform all of its geographical calculations).

You can use the COLGROUP element in combination with the COL element or by itself. You may also define a COLGROUP that has COL elements nested within to assist in defining subsets of columns that share some attribute or style settings. The need for the element's end tag is determined by the presence of standalone COL elements following the COLGROUP element. For example, if you specify column groupings entirely with COLGROUP elements, end tags are not necessary:

```
<TABLE>
<COLGROUP SPAN=2 WIDTH=30>
<COLGROUP SPAN=3 WIDTH=40>
<THEAD>
```

If you have a freestanding COL element following the COLGROUP element, you must clearly end the COLGROUP element before the standalone COL element:

```
<TABLE>
<COLGROUP CLASS="leftCols">
<COL WIDTH=30>
<COL WIDTH=20>
</COLGROUP>
<COL CLASS="priceCol" WIDTH=25>
<THEAD>
. . .
```

The structure depends on how you need to assign widths and styles to individual columns or contiguous columns. To create a column grouping that consists of multiple adjacent columns, use the SPAN attribute. This is entirely different from the COLSPAN attribute of a TD element, which has the visual impact of joining adjacent cells together as one. The SPAN attribute helps define the number of columns to be treated structurally as a group (for assigning attribute and style sheet settings across multiple columns, regardless of the column content).

No matter how you address the column structure of your table, the total number of columns defined in all COL and COLGROUP elements should equal the physical number of columns you intend for the table. If there should be more cells in a row than columns defined in COL and COLGROUP, the browser probably has to reflow the table and discard whatever incremental rendering it had accomplished. The following three skeletal examples specify HTML 4.0 tables with six columns:

```
<TABLE>
<COLGROUP SPAN=6>
. . .
</TABLE>


<TABLE>
<COL>
<COLGROUP SPAN=4>
<COL>
. . .
</TABLE>


<TABLE>
<COLGROUP>
    <COL REPEAT=2>
</COLGROUP>
<COLGROUP SPAN=4>
. . .
</TABLE>
```

HTML 4.0 specifications for the COLGROUP element exceed the implementation in Internet Explorer 4 in some respects. For example, HTML 4.0 provides for alignment within a column to be around any character, such as the decimal point of a money amount. This kind of feature adds to the rationale behind the COL element (see the COL element for an example).

Syntactically, there is little difference between a COLGROUP and COL element (a minor difference in the IE 4 implementation only). A COLGROUP element, however, lends a structural integrity to a group of columns that is rendered differently when the containing TABLE element specifies RULES="groups"; the browser draws rule lines (standard table borders in IE 4) only between COLGROUP elements and not COL elements.

Example   <COLGROUP CLASS="dateCols" WIDTH="15" ALIGN="right">

Object Model Reference

IE   [window.]document.all.*elementID*

Attributes

ALIGN	*CLASS*	*LANG*	*STYLE*	*VALIGN*
CHAR	*DIR*	SPAN	*TITLE*	WIDTH
CHAROFF	*ID*			

Event Handler Attributes

Handler	NN	IE	HTML
onClick	n/a	n/a	4
onDblClick	n/a	n/a	4
onKeyDown	n/a	n/a	4
onKeyPress	n/a	n/a	4
onKeyUp	n/a	n/a	4
onMouseDown	n/a	n/a	4
onMouseMove	n/a	n/a	4
onMouseOut	n/a	n/a	4
onMouseOver	n/a	n/a	4
onMouseUp	n/a	n/a	4

ALIGN
         NN *n/a*   IE *3*   HTML *4*

ALIGN="*alignConstant*"   *Optional*

Establishes the horizontal alignment characteristics of content within column(s) covered by the COLGROUP element. The HTML 4.0 specification defines settings for the ALIGN attribute that are not yet reflected in the CSS specification. Therefore, this ALIGN attribute is not fully deprecated. As a rule, alignment should be specified by style sheet wherever possible.

Internet Explorer 3 documents label this attribute HALIGN. In practice, IE 3 for Windows appears to ignore both the ALIGN and HALIGN attribute for the COLGROUP element.

Example   <COLGROUP CLASS="dateCols" WIDTH="15" ALIGN="right" SPAN=3>

Value   HTML 4.0 and IE 4 have two sets of attribute values:

Value	IE 4	HTML 4.0
center	•	•
char	-	•
justify	-	•
left	•	•
right	•	•

The values center, left, and right are self-explanatory. The value justify is intended to space content so that text is justified down both left and right edges. For the value char, the CHAR attribute must also be set to specify the character on which alignment revolves. In the HTML 4.0 specification example, content that does not contain the character appears to be right-aligned to the location of the character in other rows of the same column.

It is important to bear in mind that the ALIGN attribute applies to every row of a column, including any TH element you specify for the table. If you want a different alignment for the column header, override the setting with a separate ALIGN attribute or text-align style sheet attribute for the THEAD or individual TH elements.

Default   left

Object Model Reference

IE   [window.]document.all.*elementID*.align

CHAR   NN *n/a*   IE *n/a*   HTML *4*

CHAR="*character*"   *Optional*

The CHAR attribute defines the text character used as an alignment point for text within a column. This attribute is of value only for the ALIGN attribute set to "char".

Example <COLGROUP CLASS="priceCols" ALIGN="char" CHAR="." SPAN=2>

Value   Any single text character.

Default None.

CHAROFF   NN *n/a*   IE *n/a*   HTML *4*

CHAROFF="*length*"   *Optional*

The CHAROFF attribute lets you set a specific offset point at which the character specified by the CHAR attribute is to appear within a cell. This attribute is provided in case the browser default positioning does not meet with the design goals of the table.

Example

<COLGROUP CLASS="priceColumn" ALIGN="char" CHAR="." CHAROFF="80%" SPAN=2>

Value   Any length value in pixels or percentage of cell space.

Default None.

SPAN   NN *n/a*   IE *3*   HTML *4*

SPAN=*columnCount*   *Optional*

Defines the number of adjacent columns for which the COLGROUP element's attribute and style settings apply. If this attribute is missing, the COLGROUP element governs a single column. You can combine multiple COLGROUP elements of different SPAN sizes as needed for your column subgrouping.

This corresponding attribute for the COL element is represented in IE 4 by the SPAN attribute and in HTML 4.0 by the REPEAT attribute.

Example <COLGROUP SPAN=3>

Value   Integer value greater than zero.

Default   1

Object Model Reference

IE   [window.]document.all.*elementID*.span

VALIGN   NN *n/a*   IE *3*   HTML *4*

VALIGN="*alignmentConstant*"   *Optional*

Determines the vertical alignment of content within cells of the column(s) covered by the
COLGROUP element. You can override the vertical alignment for a particular cell anywhere in
the column.

Example <COLGROUP VALIGN="middle">

Value

Four constant values are recognized by both IE 4 and HTML 4: top | middle | bottom |
baseline. With top and bottom, the content is rendered flush (or very close to it) to the
top and bottom of the table cell. Set to middle (the default), the content floats perfectly
centered vertically in the cell. When one cell's contents might wrap to multiple lines at
common window widths (assuming a variable table width), it is advisable to set the VALIGN
attributes of all cells in the same row (or all COLGROUP elements) to baseline. This assures
that the character baseline of the first (or only) line of a cell's text aligns with the other cells
in the row—usually the most aesthetically pleasing arrangement.

Default   middle

Object Model Reference

IE   [window.]document.all.*elementID*.vAlign

WIDTH   NN *n/a*   IE *3*   HTML *4*

WIDTH="*multiLength*"   *Optional*

Defines the maximum width for the column(s) covered by the COLGROUP element. In practice (in IE 4 Windows, anyway), the browser won't render a column narrower than the
widest contiguous stretch of characters not containing whitespace (e.g., the longest word).
The precise measure of such a column width, of course, depends on the font characteristics of the content, as well. Internet Explorer 4 for the Mac mixes up column width
assignments when the COLGROUP element is deployed.

Example <COLGROUP WIDTH=100>

Value

Internet Explorer 4 accepts length values for the WIDTH in the form of pixel measures
(without the "px" unit) or percentage of available horizontal space allocated to the entire
table (WIDTH="25%").

An alternate variation of the proportional length value is described in the HTML 4.0 specification. For a COLGROUP element, you can specify WIDTH="*0" to instruct the browser to
render all columns according to the minimum width necessary to display the content of the
cells in the column. For a browser to make this calculation, it must load all table contents,

thus eliminating the possibility of incremental rendering of a long table. For more information about proportional lengths, see the WIDTH attribute of the COL element.

Default   Determined by browser calculation.

<COMMENT>   NN *n/a*   IE *all*   HTML *n/a*

`<COMMENT>...</COMMENT>`   *End Tag: Required*

The COMMENT element is an artifact of early Internet Explorer browsers and is now obsolete. It was intended as a plain-language tag alternate to the `<!--comment-->` comment element. The browser did not render content inside the COMMENT element. Internet Explorer 4 supports this element only for backward compatibility, although it also implements some modern attributes (ID, LANG, and TITLE). Do not use this element. Further details are omitted here to reduce the incentive to use the element.

<DD>   NN *all*   IE *all*   HTML *all*

`<DD>...</DD>`   *End Tag: Optional*

The DD element is a part of the DL, DT, DD triumvirate of elements used to create a definition list in a document. The entire list is bracketed by the DL element's tags. Each definition term is denoted by a leading DT element tag, and the definition for the term is denoted by a leading DD element tag. A schematic of a definition list sequence for three items looks as follows:

```
<DL>
    <DT>Term 1
    <DD>Definition 1
    <DT>Term 2
    <DD>Definition 2
    <DT>Term 3
    <DD>Definition 3
</DL>
```

A DT element is an inline element, whereas a DD element can contain block-level content, including bordered text, images, and other objects. End tags are optional for both DT and DD elements because the next start tag automatically signals the end of the preceding element. The entire list, however, must close with an end tag for the encapsulating DL element.

Although the HTML specification forces no particular way of rendering a definition list, Navigator and Internet Explorer are in agreement in left-aligning a DT element and indenting any DD element that follows it. No special font formatting or visual elements are added by the browser, but you are free (if not encouraged) to assign styles as you like. If you want to stack multiple terms and/or definitions, you can place multiple DT and/or DD elements right after each other in the source code.

Because HTML is being geared toward context-sensitive tagging, avoid using definition lists strictly as a formatting trick (to get some indented text). Use style sheets and adjustable margin settings to accomplish formatting tasks.

In Navigator 4, any styles assigned to DT and DD elements by way of the CLASS, ID, or STYLE attribute do not work. If you wish to assign the same style attributes to both the DT and DD elements, assign the style to the DL element; otherwise, wrap each DT and DD element with a SPAN element whose styles the nested DT and DD elements inherit. This workaround is observed in IE 4, although it is not necessary for IE 4-only documents.

Example

```
<DL>
    <DT>Z-scale
    <DD>A railroad modeling scale of 1:220. The smallest mass-produced
    commercial model scale.
</DL>
```

Object Model Reference

IE   [window.]document.all.*elementID*

Attributes

CLASS	*ID*	*LANGUAGE*	*STYLE*	TITLE
DIR	*LANG*			

Event Handler Attributes

Handler	NN	IE	HTML
onClick	n/a	4	4
onDblClick	n/a	4	4
onDragStart	n/a	4	n/a
onHelp	n/a	4	n/a
onKeyDown	n/a	4	4
onKeyPress	n/a	4	4
onKeyUp	n/a	4	4
onMouseDown	n/a	4	4
onMouseMove	n/a	4	4
onMouseOut	n/a	4	4
onMouseOver	n/a	4	4
onMouseUp	n/a	4	4
onSelectStart	n/a	4	n/a

<DEL>   NN *n/a*   IE *4*   HTML *4*

<DEL>...</DEL>   *End Tag: Required*

The DEL element and its companion, INS, define a format that shows which segments of a document's content have been marked up for deletion (or insertion) during the authoring process. This is far from a workflow management scheme, but in the hands of a supporting WYSIWYG HTML authoring tool, these elements can assist in controlling generational changes of a document in process.

Among the Version 4 browsers, only Internet Explorer supports the DEL element. Text contained by this element is rendered as a strikethrough style (whereas INS elements are underlined). The HTML 4.0 specification includes two potentially useful attributes (not in IE 4) for preserving hidden information about the date and time of the alteration and some descriptive text about the change.

Example

```
<P>Four score and
<DEL CITE="Fixed the math">eight</DEL><INS>seven</INS> years ago...</P>
```

Object Model Reference

IE   [window.]document.all.*elementID*

Attributes

CITE	DATETIME	ID	LANGUAGE	TITLE
CLASS	DIR	LANG	STYLE	

Event Handler Attributes

Handler	NN	IE	HTML
onClick	n/a	4	4
onDblClick	n/a	4	4
onDragStart	n/a	4	n/a
onHelp	n/a	4	n/a
onKeyDown	n/a	4	4
onKeyPress	n/a	4	4
onKeyUp	n/a	4	4
onMouseDown	n/a	4	4
onMouseMove	n/a	4	4
onMouseOut	n/a	4	4
onMouseOver	n/a	4	4
onMouseUp	n/a	4	4
onSelectStart	n/a	4	n/a

CITE   NN *n/a*   IE *n/a*   HTML 4

CITE="*String*"   *Optional*

A description of the reason for the change or other notation to be associated with the element, but normally hidden from view. This information is meant to be used by authoring tools, rather than by visual browsers.

Example   `<DEL CITE="Fixed the math --A.L.">eight</DEL>`

Value

Any string of characters. The string must be inside a matching pair of (single or double) quotation marks.

Default   None.

DATETIME   NN *n/a*   IE *n/a*   HTML 4

DATETIME="*datetimeString*"   *Optional*

The date and time the deletion was made. This information is most likely to be inserted into a document with an HTML authoring tool designed to track content insertions and deletions. Data from this attribute can be recalled later as an audit trail to changes of the document. There can be only one DATETIME attribute value associated with a given DEL element.

Example

```
<DEL DATETIME="1998-09-11T20:03:32-08:00">SomeDeleteTextHere</DEL>
```

Value

The DATETIME attribute requires a value in a special date-time format that conveys information about the date and time in such a way that the exact moment can be deduced from any time zone around the world. Syntax for the format is as follows:

*yyyy-MM-dd*T*hh:mm:ss*TZD

yyyy	Four-digit year
MM	Two-digit month (01 through 12)
dd	Two-digit date (01 through 31)
T	Uppercase "T" to separate date from time
hh	Two-digit hour in 24-hour time (00 through 23)
mm	Two-digit minute (00 through 59)
ss	Two-digit second (00 through 59)
TZD	Time Zone Designator

There are two formats for the Time Zone Designator. The first is simply the uppercase letter "Z", which stands for UTC (Coordinated Universal Time—also called "Zulu"). The other format indicates the offset from UTC that the time shown in *hh:mm:ss* represents. This time offset consists of a plus or minus symbol and another pair of *hh:mm* values. For time zones west of Greenwich Mean Time (which, for all practical purposes is the same as UTC), the operator is a negative sign because the main *hh:mm:ss* time is earlier than UTC; for time zones east of GMT, the offset is a positive value. For example, Pacific Standard Time is eight hours earlier than UTC: when it is 6:00 P.M. in the PST zone, it is 2:00 A.M. the next morning at UTC. Thus, the following examples all represent the exact same moment in time (Time Zone Designator shown in boldface for clarification only):

1998-09-12T02:00:00**Z**	UTC
1998-09-11T21:00:00**-05:00**	Eastern Standard Time
1998-09-11T18:00:00**-08:00**	Pacific Standard Time
1998-09-12T13:00:00**+11:00**	Sydney, Australia

For more details about this way of representing time, see the ISO-8601 standard.

Default   None.

TITLE

NN *n/a*   IE *4*   HTML *4*

TITLE="*advisoryText*"   *Optional*

An advisory description of the element. Rendered as a tooltip in IE 4. The TITLE attribute can also be used to store information intended for the CITE attribute. But when assigned to the TITLE attribute, the text (in IE 4 at least) is viewable to the user as a tooltip.

Example   `<DEL TITLE="Deleted by JB">SomeDeletedTextHere</DEL>`

Value

Any string of characters. The string must be inside a matching pair of (single or double) quotation marks.

Default   None.

Object Model Reference

IE   [window.]document.all.*elementID*.title

<DFN>   NN *n/a*   IE *3*   HTML *3.2*

`<DFN>...</DFN>`   *End Tag: Required*

The DFN element is one of a large group of elements that the HTML 4.0 recommendation calls *phrase elements*. Such elements assign structural meaning to a designated portion of the document. A DFN element signifies the first usage of a term in a document (its defining instance). A common technique in documents is to italicize an important vocabulary term the first time it is used in a document. This is generally the place in the document where the term is defined so that it may be used in subsequent sentences with its meaning understood. By default, Internet Explorer italicizes all text within a DFN element. You can, of course, easily define your own style for DFN elements with a style sheet rule.

Example

```
<P>Concerto composers usually provide a space for soloists to show off
technical skills while reminding the audience of various themes used
throughout the movement. This part of the concerto is called the <DFN>
cadenza</DFN>. </P>
```

Object Model Reference

IE   [window.]document.all.*elementID*

Attributes

CLASS	*ID*	*LANGUAGE*	*STYLE*	*TITLE*
DIR	*LANG*			

Event Handler Attributes

Handler	NN	IE	HTML
onClick	n/a	4	4
onDblClick	n/a	4	4
onDragStart	n/a	4	n/a
onHelp	n/a	4	n/a
onKeyDown	n/a	4	4
onKeyPress	n/a	4	4
onKeyUp	n/a	4	4
onMouseDown	n/a	4	4
onMouseMove	n/a	4	4
onMouseOut	n/a	4	4
onMouseOver	n/a	4	4
onMouseUp	n/a	4	4
onSelectStart	n/a	4	n/a

<DIR>   NN *all*   IE *all*   HTML *all*

<DIR>...</DIR>   *End Tag: Required*

The original idea of the DIR element was to allow browsers to generate multicolumn lists of items. Virtually every browser, however, treats the DIR element the same as a UL element, to present an unordered single column list of items (usually preceded by a bullet). The DIR element is deprecated in HTML 4. You should be using the UL element, in any case, because you are assured backward compatibility and forward compatibility should this element ever disappear from the browser landscape. Everything said here also applies to the deprecated MENU element.

Example

```
Common DB Connector Types:
<DIR>
    <LI>DB-9
    <LI>DB-12
    <LI>DB-25
</DIR>
```

Object Model Reference

IE   [window.]document.all.*elementID*

Attributes

CLASS	*DIR*	*LANG*	*STYLE*	*TITLE*
COMPACT	*ID*	*LANGUAGE*		

Event Handler Attributes

Handler	NN	IE	HTML
onClick	n/a	4	4
onDblClick	n/a	4	4
onDragStart	n/a	4	n/a
onHelp	n/a	4	n/a
onKeyDown	n/a	4	4
onKeyPress	n/a	4	4
onKeyUp	n/a	4	4
onMouseDown	n/a	4	4
onMouseMove	n/a	4	4
onMouseOut	n/a	4	4
onMouseOver	n/a	4	4
onMouseUp	n/a	4	4
onSelectStart	n/a	4	n/a

COMPACT   NN *n/a*   IE *3*   HTML *3.2*

COMPACT   *Optional*

A Boolean attribute originally designed to let browsers render the list in a more compact style than normal (smaller line spacing between items). Internet Explorer ignores this attribute (despite the fact that support for this attribute is indicated in IE 3 documentation).

Example <DIR COMPACT>...</DIR>

Value   The presence of this attribute makes its value true.

Default   false

<DIV>   NN *all*   IE *all*   HTML *3.2*

<DIV>...</DIV>   *End Tag: Required*

The DIV element gives structure and context to any block-level content in a document. Unlike some other structural elements that have very specific connotations attached to them (the P element, for instance), the author is free to give meaning to each particular DIV element by virtue of the element's attribute settings and nested content. Each DIV element becomes a generic block-level container for all content within the required start and end tags.

As a basic example, the DIV element is now recommended as the element to use to center text on a page, in place of the deprecated CENTER element. The DIV element that does the work includes style information that takes care of the centering of the content. It is also convenient to use the DIV element as a wrapper for multielement content that is to be governed by a single style sheet rule. For example, if a block of content includes three paragraphs, rather than assign a special font style to each of the P elements, you can wrap all three P elements with a single DIV element whose style sheet defines the requested font style. Such a style sheet could be defined as an inline STYLE attribute of the DIV element or assigned via the CLASS or ID attribute, depending on the structure of the rest of the document.

DIV elements are block-level elements. If you need an arbitrary container for inline content, use the SPAN element, instead.

HTML 4.0 defines many more attributes for the DIV element than are implemented in Version 4 browsers. The breadth of HTML attributes indicates the potential power of this generic element to include links to related resources and many advisory attributes about those links. The same set of attributes applies to the SPAN element in the HTML 4.0 specification.

Example   <DIV CLASS="sections" ID="section3">...</DIV>

Object Model Reference

IE   [window.]document.all.*elementID*

Attributes

ALIGN	DATAFORMATAS	HREFLANG	MEDIA	TARGET
CHARSET	DATASRC	ID	REL	TITLE
CLASS	DIR	LANG	REV	TYPE
DATAFLD	HREF	LANGUAGE	STYLE	

Event Handler Attributes

Handler	NN	IE	HTML
onAfterUpdate	n/a	4	n/a
onBeforeUpdate	n/a	4	n/a
onBlur	n/a	4	4
onClick	n/a	3	4

Handler	NN	IE	HTML
onDblClick	n/a	4	4
onDragStart	n/a	4	n/a
onFocus	n/a	4	4
onHelp	n/a	4	n/a
onKeyDown	n/a	4	4
onKeyPress	n/a	4	4
onKeyUp	n/a	4	4
onMouseDown	n/a	4	4
onMouseMove	n/a	4	4
onMouseOut	n/a	4	4
onMouseOver	n/a	3	4
onMouseUp	n/a	4	4
onResize	n/a	4	n/a
onRowEnter	n/a	4	n/a
onRowExit	n/a	4	n/a
onScroll	n/a	4	n/a
onSelectStart	n/a	4	n/a

ALIGN

NN *2*   IE *3*   HTML *3.2*

ALIGN="*alignmentConstant*"   *Optional*

The ALIGN attribute determines how content wrapped by the DIV element is aligned within the context of the DIV element. This attribute is deprecated in favor of the text-align style sheet attribute. Even so, you can use this attribute for backward compatibility with non-CSS-compliant browsers. This is the element and attribute you can use to substitute for the deprecated CENTER element.

Example <DIV ALIGN="center">Part IV</DIV>

Value

Case-insensitive constant value. Navigator 4 and Internet Explorer 4 (Windows) recognize all four constants specified in HTML 4: center | left | right | justify. IE 4 for the Macintosh does not recognize the justify setting.

Default left or right, depending on direction of current language.

Object Model Reference

IE   [window.]document.all.*elementID*.align

CHARSET

NN *n/a*   IE *n/a*   HTML *4*

CHARSET="*characterSet*"   *Optional*

Character encoding of the content at the other end of the HREF link.

Example <DIV CHARSET="csISO5427Cyrillic ">*CyrillicTextHere*</DIV>

Value

Case-insensitive alias from the character set registry (*ftp://ftp.isi.edu/in-notes/iana/ assignments/character-sets*).

Default Determined by browser.

DATAFLD   NN *n/a*   IE *4*   HTML *n/a*

DATAFLD=" *columnName*"   *Optional*

Used with IE 4 data binding to associate a remote data source column name with the HTML content of a DIV element. The data source column must be HTML (see DATAFORMATAS). DATASRC and DATAFORMATAS attributes must also be set for the DIV element.

Example

```
<DIV  DATASRC="#DBSRC3" DATAFLD="sec3" DATAFORMATAS="HTML"> </DIV>
```

Value   Case-sensitive identifier.

Default   None.

Object Model Reference

IE   [window.]document.all.*elementID*.dataFld

DATAFORMATAS   NN *n/a*   IE *4*   HTML *n/a*

DATAFORMATAS=" *dataType*"   *Optional*

Used with IE 4 data binding, this attribute advises the browser whether the source material arriving from the data source is to be treated as plain text or as tagged HTML. A DIV element should receive data only in HTML format.

Example

```
<DIV  DATASRC="#DBSRC3" DATAFLD="sec3" DATAFORMATAS="HTML"> </DIV>
```

Value   IE 4 recognizes two possible settings: text I HTML

Default   text

Object Model Reference

IE   [window.]document.all.*elementID*.dataFormatAs

DATASRC   NN *n/a*   IE *4*   HTML *n/a*

DATASRC=" *dataSourceName*"   *Optional*

Used with IE 4 data binding to specify the name of the remote ODBC data source (such as an Oracle or SQL Server database) to be associated with the element. Content from the data source is specified via the DATAFLD attribute.

Example

```
<DIV  DATASRC="#DBSRC3" DATAFLD="sec3" DATAFORMATAS="HTML"> </DIV>
```

Value   Case-sensitive identifier.

Default   None.

Object Model Reference

IE   [window.]document.all.*elementID*.dataSrc

HREF   NN *n/a*   IE *n/a*   HTML *4*

HREF=" *URI*"   *Optional*

According to the HTML 4.0 specification, the HREF attribute is meant to offer a URL to a resource that can supply "more information" about the DIV element's content. No recommendation is provided as to whether this URL should be rendered in any way (like the HREF attribute of an A element). Perhaps a future browser could use this URL to generate a margin note or footnote in the form of a link. Several other attributes clearly intend for the HREF attribute's URL to be accessible in some way by the user.

Example   <DIV HREF="bibliogs/chap3.html">*ChapterThreeContentHere*</DIV>

Value

Any valid URL, including complete and relative URLs, anchors on the same page (anchor names prefaced with the # symbol) and the **javascript:** pseudo-URL in scriptable browsers to trigger a script statement rather than navigate to a destination.

Default   None.

HREFLANG   NN *n/a*   IE *n/a*   HTML *4*

HREFLANG=" *languageCode*"   *Optional*

The language code of the content at the destination of a link. Requires that the HREF attribute also be set. This attribute is primarily an advisory attribute to help a browser prepare itself for a new language set if the browser is so enabled.

Example

```
<DIV HREFLANG="HI" HREF="bibliogs/hindi/chap3.html">
ChapterThreeContentinHindiHere
</DIV>
```

Value   Case-insensitive language code.

Default   Browser default.

MEDIA   NN *n/a*   IE *n/a*   HTML *4*

MEDIA=" *descriptorList*"   *Optional*

Sets the intended output device for the content of the DIV element. The MEDIA attribute looks forward to the day when browsers are able to tailor content to specific kinds of devices such as pocket computers, text-to-speech digitizers, or fuzzy television sets. The HTML 4.0 specification defines a number of constant values for anticipated devices, but the list is open-ended, allowing future browsers to tailor output to yet other kinds of media and devices.

Example   <DIV MEDIA="screen, tv, handheld">...</DIV>

Value

Case-sensitive constant values. Multiple values can be grouped together in a comma-delimited list within a quoted string. Values defined in HTML 4.0 are `screen` | `tty` | `tv` | `projection` | `handheld` | `print` | `braille` | `aural` | `all`.

Default   `screen`

REL   NN *n/a*   IE *n/a*   HTML 4

REL=" *linkTypes*"   *Optional*

Defines the relationship between the current element and the destination of the link. Also known as a *forward link*, not to be confused in any way with the destination document whose address is defined by the `HREF` attribute. The HTML 4.0 recommendation defines several link types; it is up to the browser to determine how to employ the value. The element must include an `HREF` attribute for the `REL` attribute to be applied.

Example   `<DIV REL="next chapter" HREF="chapter3.html">...</DIV>`

Value

Case-insensitive, space-delimited list of HTML 4.0 standard link types applicable to the element. Sanctioned link types are:

alternate	contents	index	start
appendix	copyright	next	stylesheet
bookmark	glossary	prev	subsection
chapter	help	section	

Default   None.

REV   NN *n/a*   IE *n/a*   HTML 4

REV=" *linkTypes*"   *Optional*

A reverse link relationship. Like the `REL` attribute, the `REV` attribute's capabilities are defined by the browser, particularly with regard to how the browser interprets and renders the various link types available in the HTML 4.0 specification. Given two documents (A and B) containing links that point to each other, the `REV` value of B is designed to express the same relationship between the two documents as denoted by the `REL` attribute in A.

Example   `<DIV REV="previous chapter" HREF="chapter2.html">...</DIV>`

Value

Case-insensitive, space-delimited list of HTML 4.0 standard link types applicable to the element. See the `REL` attribute for sanctioned link types.

Default   None.

TARGET   NN *n/a*   IE *n/a*   HTML 4

TARGET=" *windowOrFrameName*"   *Optional*

If the destination document associated with the `HREF` attribute is to be loaded into a window or frame other than the current window or frame, you can specify where the destination document should load by assigning a window or frame name to the `TARGET` attribute. Target frame names must be assigned to frames and windows as identifiers. Assign names to frames via the `NAME` attribute of the `FRAME` element; assign names to new windows via the second parameter of the `window.open()` scripting method. If you omit this attribute, the destination document replaces the document containing the link. This attribute is applicable only when a value is assigned to the `HREF` attribute of the element.

If this feature is implemented in future browsers, the `DIV` element will probably have only one destination document and one target (like the A element). If you want a link to change the content of multiple frames, you can use a `DIV` element's `onClick` event handler or a `javascript:` pseudo-URL to fire a script that loads multiple documents. Set the `location.href` property of each frame to the desired URL.

Example `<DIV TARGET="display" HREF="chap3.html#sec2">...</DIV>`

Value

Case-sensitive identifier when the frame or window name has been assigned via the target element's `NAME` attribute. Four reserved target names act as constants:

`_blank`   Browser creates a new window for the destination document.

`_parent`   Destination document replaces the current frame's framesetting document (if one exists; otherwise, it is treated as `_self`).

`_self`   Destination document replaces the current document in its window or frame.

`_top`   Destination document is to occupy the entire browser window, replacing any and all framesets that may be loaded (also treated as `_self` if there are no framesets defined in the window).

Default   `_self`

TITLE   NN *n/a*   IE *4*   HTML *4*

`TITLE="`*advisoryText*`"`   *Optional*

An advisory description of the destination document. Internet Explorer 4 implements this attribute such that the browser displays a tooltip with the attribute's value when the cursor remains positioned over the element for a couple of seconds. The appearance of the tooltip is governed by the operating system version of the browser. In Windows, the tooltip is the standard small, light yellow rectangle; on the Mac, the tooltip displays as a cartoon bubble in the manner of the MacOS bubble help system. If no attribute is specified, the tooltip does not display.

Use this attribute with care. Because a `DIV` element can be fairly large, it is likely that the cursor will frequently be at rest over the element when the user isn't particularly paying attention. The incessant display of the tooltip over the large screen area could become annoying.

You can assign any descriptive text you like to this attribute. Not everyone will see it, so do not put mission-critical information here. Future or special-purpose browsers might use this attribute's information to read information about the link to vision-impaired web surfers.

Example `<DIV TITLE="Sub-Saharan Africa" HREF="chapter3.html">...</DIV>`

Value

Any string of characters. The string must be inside a matching pair of (single or double) quotation marks.

Default   None.

Object Model Reference

IE   [window.]document.all.*elementID*.title

TYPE   NN *n/a*   IE *n/a*   HTML *4*

TYPE="*MIMETYPE*"   *Optional*

An advisory about the content type of the destination document or resource. A browser might use this information to assist in preparing support for a resource requiring a multimedia player or plugin.

Example   <DIV TYPE="video/mpeg" HREF="ski4.mpeg">...</DIV>

Value

Case-insensitive MIME type. A catalog of registered MIME types is available from *ftp:// ftp.isi.edu/in-notes/iana/assignments/media-types/*.

Default   None.

<DL>   NN *all*   IE *all*   HTML *all*

<DL>...</DL>   *End Tag: Required*

The DL element is a part of the DL, DT, DD triumvirate of elements used to create a definition list in a document. The entire list is bracketed by the DL element's tags. Each definition term is denoted by a leading DT element tag, and the definition for the term is denoted by a leading DD element tag. A schematic of a definition list sequence for three items looks like the following:

```
<DL>
    <DT>Term 1
    <DD>Definition 1
    <DT>Term 2
    <DD>Definition 2
    <DT>Term 3
    <DD>Definition 3
</DL>
```

The entire list must close with an end tag for the encapsulating DL element. Note that the DL element is the container of the entire list, which means that inheritable style sheet rules assigned to the DL element apply to the nested DT and DD elements. Unwanted inheritances can be overridden in the DT and DD elements.

Although the HTML specification forces no particular way of rendering a definition list, Navigator and Internet Explorer are in agreement in left-aligning a DT element and indenting any DD element that follows it. No special font formatting or visual elements are added by the browser, but you are free (if not encouraged) to assign styles as you like. If you want to stack multiple terms and/or definitions, you can place multiple DT and/or DD elements right after each other in the source code.

Because HTML is being geared toward context-sensitive tagging, avoid using definition lists strictly as a formatting trick (to get some indented text). Use style sheets and adjustable margin settings to accomplish formatting.

Example

```
<DL>
    <DT>Z-scale
    <DD>A railroad modeling scale of 1:220. The smallest mass-produced
    commercial model scale.
</DL>
```

Object Model Reference

IE   [window.]document.all.*elementID*

Attributes

CLASS	*DIR*	*LANG*	*STYLE*	*TITLE*
COMPACT	*ID*	*LANGUAGE*		

Event Handler Attributes

Handler	NN	IE	HTML
onClick	n/a	4	4
onDblClick	n/a	4	4
onDragStart	n/a	4	n/a
onHelp	n/a	4	n/a
onKeyDown	n/a	n/a	4
onKeyPress	n/a	n/a	4
onKeyUp	n/a	n/a	4
onMouseDown	n/a	4	4
onMouseMove	n/a	4	4
onMouseOut	n/a	4	4
onMouseOver	n/a	4	4
onMouseUp	n/a	4	4
onSelectStart	n/a	4	n/a

COMPACT   NN *3*   IE *3*   HTML *3.2*

COMPACT   *Optional*

When set to true (by virtue of its presence in the DL element tag), the COMPACT Boolean attribute instructs the browser to render a related DT and DD pair on the same line if space allows. The criterion for determining this space (as worked out in both Navigator and Internet Explorer) is related to the amount of indentation normally assigned to a DD element (indentation size differs slightly with operating system). With COMPACT turned on, if the DT element is narrower than the indentation space, the DD element is raised from the line below and displayed on the same line as its DT element. Because the width of characters in proportional fonts varies so widely, there is no hard-and-fast rule about the number of characters of a DT element that lets the DD element come on the same line. But this compact styling is intended for DT elements consisting of only a few characters.

Example `<DL COMPACT>`*ListItems*`</DL>`

Value

Case-insensitive attribute name. Its presence sets the feature to true.

Default   false

Object Model Reference

IE   [window.]document.all.*elementID*.compact

<DT>   NN *all*   IE *all*   HTML *all*

`<DT>...</DT>`   *End Tag: Optional*

The DT element is a part of the DL, DT, DD triumvirate of elements used to create a definition list in a document. The entire list is bracketed by the DL element's tags. Each definition term is denoted by a leading DT element tag, and the definition for the term is denoted by a leading DD element tag. A schematic of a definition list sequence for three items looks like the following:

```
<DL>
    <DT>Term 1
    <DD>Definition 1
    <DT>Term 2
    <DD>Definition 2
    <DT>Term 3
    <DD>Definition 3
</DL>
```

A DT element is an inline element, whereas a DD element can contain block-level content, including bordered text, images, and other objects. End tags are optional for both DT and DD elements because the next start tag automatically signals the end of the preceding element. The entire list, however, must close with an end tag for the encapsulating DL element.

Although the HTML specification forces no particular way of rendering a definition list, Navigator and Internet Explorer are in agreement in left-aligning a DT element and indenting any DD element that follows it. No special font formatting or visual elements are added by the browser, but you are free (if not encouraged) to assign styles as you like. If you want to stack multiple terms and/or definitions, you can place multiple DT and/or DD elements right after each other in the source code.

Because HTML is being geared toward context-sensitive tagging, avoid using definition lists strictly as a formatting trick (to get some indented text). Use style sheets and adjustable margin settings to accomplish formatting.

In Navigator 4, any styles assigned to DT and DD elements by way of the CLASS, ID, or STYLE attribute do not work. If you wish to assign the same style attributes to both the DT and DD elements, assign the style to the DL element; otherwise, wrap each DT and DD element with a SPAN element whose styles the nested DT and DD elements inherit. This workaround is observed in IE 4, although it is not necessary for IE 4-only documents.

Example

```
<DL>
   <DT>Z-scale
   <DD>A railroad modeling scale of 1:220. The smallest mass-produced
   commercial model scale.
</DL>
```

Object Model Reference

IE   [window.]document.all.*elementID*

Attributes

CLASS	ID	LANGUAGE	STYLE	TITLE
DIR	LANG			

Event Handler Attributes

Handler	NN	IE	HTML
onClick	n/a	4	4
onDblClick	n/a	4	4
onDragStart	n/a	4	n/a
onHelp	n/a	4	n/a
onKeyDown	n/a	4	4
onKeyPress	n/a	4	4
onKeyUp	n/a	4	4
onMouseDown	n/a	4	4
onMouseMove	n/a	4	4
onMouseOut	n/a	4	4
onMouseOver	n/a	4	4
onMouseUp	n/a	4	4
onSelectStart	n/a	4	n/a

<EM>   NN *all*   IE *all*   HTML *all*

<EM>...</EM>   *End Tag: Required*

The **EM** element is one of a large group of elements that the HTML 4.0 recommendation calls *phrase elements*. Such elements assign structural meaning to a designated portion of the document. An **EM** element is one that is to be rendered differently from running body text to designate emphasis.

Browsers have free rein to determine how (or whether) to distinguish **EM** element content from the rest of the **BODY** element. Both Navigator and Internet Explorer elect to italicize the text. This can be overridden with a style sheet as you see fit.

Example

```
<P>The night was dark, and the river's churning waters were <EM>very</EM>
cold.</P>
```

Object Model Reference

IE   [window.]document.all.*elementID*

Attributes

CLASS	ID	LANGUAGE	STYLE	TITLE
DIR	LANG			

Event Handler Attributes

Handler	NN	IE	HTML
onClick	n/a	4	4
onDblClick	n/a	4	4
onDragStart	n/a	4	n/a
onHelp	n/a	4	n/a
onKeyDown	n/a	4	4
onKeyPress	n/a	4	4
onKeyUp	n/a	4	4
onMouseDown	n/a	4	4
onMouseMove	n/a	4	4
onMouseOut	n/a	4	4
onMouseOver	n/a	4	4
onMouseUp	n/a	4	4
onSelectStart	n/a	4	n/a

<EMBED>   NN *2*   IE *3*   HTML *n/a*

`<EMBED>...</EMBED>`   *End Tag: Required*

An EMBED element allows you to load media and file types other than those natively rendered by the browser. Typically, such external data requires a plugin or helper application to properly load the data and display its file. Notice that this element has been supported by both Navigator and Internet Explorer since Versions 2 and 3, respectively, but the element is still not a part of the HTML standard vocabulary. The HTML 4.0 specification recommends the OBJECT element as the one to load the kind of external data covered by the EMBED element in the browsers. Navigator 4 and Internet Explorer 4 also support the OBJECT element, and you should gravitate toward that element for embedded elements if your visitor browser base can support it.

Bear in mind that for data types that launch plugins, the control panel displayed for the data varies widely among browsers, operating systems, and the plugins the user has installed for that particular data type. It is risky business trying to carefully design a layout combining a plugin's control panel and surrounding text or other elements.

The list of attributes for the EMBED element is a long one, but pay special attention to the browser compatibility rating for each attribute. Because the plugin technologies of the two browsers are not identical, neither are the attribute sets. Even so, it is possible to assign an EMBED element in one document that works on both browser brands when the embedded element does not rely on an attribute setting not supported in one of the browsers. Some plugins, however, may require or accept attribute name/value pairs that are not listed for this element. At least in the case of Navigator, all attributes (including those normally ignored by the browser) and their values are passed to the plugin. Therefore, you must also check with the documentation for a plugin to determine what, if any, extra attributes may be supported. The OBJECT element gets around this object-specific attribute problem by letting you add any number of PARAM elements tailored to the object.

The end tag is required in Internet Explorer but is optional in Navigator.

Example

```
<EMBED NAME="jukebox" SRC="jazz.aif" HEIGHT=100 WIDTH=200></EMBED>
```

Object Model Reference

NN   [window.]document.*elementName*

IE   [window.]document.all.*elementID*

Attributes

ALIGN	CODEBASE	ID	PLUGINURL	TYPE
ALT	FRAMEBORDER	NAME	SRC	UNITS
BORDER	HEIGHT	PALETTE	*STYLE*	VSPACE
CLASS	HIDDEN	PLUGINSPAGE	*TITLE*	WIDTH
CODE	HSPACE			

ALIGN

NN *all*   IE *4*   HTML *n/a*

ALIGN="*where*"   *Optional*

If the embedded object (or player control panel) occupies space on the page, the ALIGN attribute determines how the object is rendered in physical relation to the element's next outermost container. If some additional text is specified between the start and end tags of the EMBED element, the ALIGN attribute also affects how that text is rendered relative to the object's rectangular space.

Most of the rules for alignment constant values cited at the beginning of this chapter apply to the EMBED element. Precise layout becomes difficult because the HTML page author usually isn't in control of the plugin control panel that is displayed on the page. Dimensions for the element that work fine for one control panel are totally inappropriate for another. (Compare Netscape's stocky audio control panel to the narrow horizontal slider in Internet Explorer.)

Typically, ALIGN attributes are deprecated in HTML 4.0 in favor of the align: style sheet attribute. But if you are using the EMBED element for backward compatibility, stick with the ALIGN attribute.

Example

```
<EMBED SRC="jazz.aif" ALIGN="left" HEIGHT=100 WIDTH=200></EMBED>
```

Value

Each browser defines a different set of values for this attribute. Select the one(s) from the following table that work for your deployment:

Value	NN 4	IE 4
absbottom	-	•
absmiddle	-	•
baseline	-	•
bottom	•	•
left	•	•
middle	•	•
right	•	•

Value	NN 4	IE 4
texttop	-	•
top	•	•

Default   bottom

Object Model Reference

IE   [window.]document.all.*elementID*.align

ALT   NN *n/a*   IE *4*   HTML *n/a*

ALT="*textMessage*"   *Optional*

If Internet Explorer does not have the facilities to load and run the external media, the text assigned to the **ALT** attribute is supposed to display in the document where the **EMBED** element's tag appears. Typically, this text provides advice on what the page visitor is missing by not being able to load the data (although IE also presents a dialog about how to get plugin information from an online source).

Use the **ALT** attribute with care. If the external data is not a critical part of your page's content, you may just want the rest of the page to load without calling attention to the missing media controller in lesscapable browsers. The alternate message may be more disturbing to the user than a missing media player.

The equivalent powers are available in Navigator with the **NOEMBED** element.

Example

<EMBED SRC="jazz.aif" ALT="Sound media player" HEIGHT=10 WIDTH=20></EMBED>

Value   Any quoted string of characters.

Default   None.

BORDER   NN *2*   IE *n/a*   HTML *n/a*

BORDER=*pixels*   *Optional*

Navigator provides a dedicated attribute to specifying the thickness of a border around an **EMBED** element. This feature does not appear to be working in Navigator 4. Also, when the **EMBED** element has style sheet attributes, setting a border for the element results in a floating border around a small square outside of the **EMBED** element's area.

Example   <EMBED SRC="jazz.aif" BORDER=3 HEIGHT=150 WIDTH=250></EMBED>

Value   Any integer pixel value.

Default   None.

CODE   NN *n/a*   IE *4*   HTML *n/a*

CODE="*fileName.class*"   *Required*

I'm not sure why Microsoft specifies the **CODE** attribute for the **EMBED** element. Typically, a **CODE** attribute points to a Java class filename. In theory, an applet could be loaded into a document via the **EMBED** element (rather than the **APPLET** or **OBJECT** element), but this approach does not work in IE 4. Nor does the **CODEBASE** element help the browser find a

Java applet class filename assigned to the SRC attribute. My recommendation is to avoid this attribute.

CODEBASE

NN *n/a*   IE *4*   HTML *n/a*

CODEBASE="*path*" *Optional*

As with the CODE attribute, Internet Explorer 4 seems to ignore the CODEBASE attribute for the EMBED element, despite its apparent support in the SDK documentation. The SRC attribute must contain the path to the data file because it does not rely on the CODEBASE attribute value. My recommendation is to avoid this attribute.

FRAMEBORDER

NN *2*   IE *n/a*   HTML *n/a*

FRAMEBORDER="yes" | "no" *Optional*

Predating style sheet borders, the FRAMEBORDER attribute is a switch that lets you turn on a plugin control panel's border (whose thickness is set by the BORDER attribute). This attribute does not appear to work in Navigator 4, nor does a style sheet border do what you'd expect it to do.

Example

<EMBED SRC="jazz.aif" FRAMEBORDER="no" HEIGHT=150 WIDTH=250></EMBED>

Value   yes | no

Default   yes

HEIGHT, WIDTH

NN *2*   IE *3*   HTML *n/a*

HEIGHT="*length*" *Required*
WIDTH="*length*"

The size that an embedded object (or its plugin control panel) occupies in a document is governed by the HEIGHT and WIDTH attribute settings. Some browser versions might allow you to get away without assigning these attributes, letting the plugin's own user interface design determine the height and width of its visible rectangle. It is best to specify the exact dimensions of a plugin's control panel whenever possible. (Control panels vary with each browser and even between different plugins for the same browser.) In some cases, such as Navigator 4 for the Macintosh, the control panel does not display if you fail to supply enough height on the page for the control panel. If you assign values that are larger than the actual control panel, the browser reserves that empty space on the page, which could interfere with your intended page design.

Example   <EMBED SRC="jazz.aif" HEIGHT=150 WIDTH=250></EMBED>

Value

Positive integer values (optionally quoted) or percentage values (quoted). You cannot entirely hide an embedded object's control panel by setting values to zero (one pixel always shows and occupies space), but you can reduce its height and width to one pixel in each dimension. If you want to hide a plugin, do so with DHTML by setting its positioning display attribute to none. Navigator also includes a HIDDEN attribute that is backward compatible for that browser brand.

Default   None.

Object Model Reference

IE   [window.]document.embeds[i].height
              [window.]document.*elementID*.height
              [window.]document.embeds[i].width
              [window.]document.*elementID*.width

HIDDEN   NN *2*   IE *4*   HTML *n/a*

HIDDEN="true" | "false"   *Optional*

Predating style sheet borders, the HIDDEN attribute is a switch that lets you set whether the
embedded data's plugin control panel appears on the screen. This might be desirable for
background music under script control (via Netscape's LiveConnect). When you set the
HIDDEN attribute, the HEIGHT and WIDTH attributes are overridden.

Example <EMBED SRC="soothing.aif" HIDDEN></EMBED>

Value   true I false

Default   false

Object Model Reference

IE   [window.]document.embeds[i].hidden
              [window.]document.*elementID*.hidden

HSPACE, VSPACE   NN *2*   IE *3*   HTML *n/a*

HSPACE=*pixelCount*   *Optional*
VSPACE=*pixelCount*

Predating style sheet margins, the HSPACE and VSPACE attributes let you define a margin
that acts as whitespace padding around the visual content of the EMBED element. HSPACE
establishes a margin on the left and right sides of the rectangle; VSPACE establishes a
margin on the top and bottom sides of the rectangle. This attribute appears to work in Navigator 4 but not in Internet Explorer 4. With these attributes not reflected as scriptable
properties of an EMBED element, it is likely that these attributes are truly not supported in IE
4, Microsoft's SDK notwithstanding.

Example <EMBED SRC="soothing.aif" VSPACE=10 HSPACE=10></EMBED>

Value

Integer representing the number of pixels for the width of the margin on the relevant sides
of the EMBED element's rectangle.

Default   0

ID   NN *n/a*   IE *4*   HTML *n/a*

ID="*elementIdentifier*"   *Optional*

A unique identifier that distinguishes this element from all the rest in the document. Can be
used to associate a single element with a style rule naming this attribute value as an ID

selector. An element can have an ID assigned for uniqueness as well as a class for inclusion within a group. See Chapter 3.

If you assign an ID attribute and not a NAME attribute, the value of the ID attribute can be used as the EMBED element's name in Internet Explorer script reference forms that use the element name (document.all.embedName).

Example <EMBED ID="jazzSound" SRC="jazz.aif" HEIGHT=15 WIDTH=25></EMBED>

Value   Case-sensitive identifier.

Default   None.

Object Model Reference

IE   [window.]document.embeds[i].id
           [window.]document.*elementID*.id

NAME   NN *2*   IE *3*   HTML *n/a*

NAME="*elementIdentifier*"   *Optional*

If you are scripting a plugin (especially in Navigator via LiveConnect), it is usually more convenient to create a reference to the embedded element by using a unique name you assign to the item. Thus, if you edit the page and move or delete multiple EMBED elements on the page, you do not have to worry about adjusting index values to array-style references (document.embeds[i]).

Example <EMBED NAME="jukebox" SRC="jazz.aif" HEIGHT=15 WIDTH=25></EMBED>

Value   Case-sensitive identifier.

Default   None.

Object Model Reference

IE   [window.]document.embeds[i].name
           [window.]document.*elementID*.name

PALETTE   NN *2*   IE *4*   HTML *n/a*

PALETTE="foreground" | "background"   *Optional*

The Netscape documentation says that the PALETTE attribute lets you apply the background or foreground palette to the plugin invoked by the EMBED element, but only in the Windows environment.

Example

```
<EMBED NAME="jukebox" SRC="jazz.aif" HEIGHT=150 WIDTH=250
PALETTE="foreground">
</EMBED>
```

Value   Case-insensitive constant: foreground | background

Default   background

Object Model Reference

IE   [window.]document.embeds[i].palette
            [window.]document.*elementID*.palette

PLUGINSPAGE   NN *2*   IE *n/a*   HTML *n/a*

PLUGINSPAGE="*URL*"   *Optional*

If the MIME type of the data file assigned to the EMBED element's SRC attribute is not supported by an existing plugin or helper application in the browser, the PLUGINSPAGE attribute is intended to provide a URL for downloading and installing the necessary plugin. If you omit this attribute, Navigator presents a generic link to Netscape's own resource listing of plugin vendors.

Example

```
<EMBED NAME="jukebox" SRC="jazz.aif" HEIGHT=150 WIDTH=250
PLUGINSPAGE="http://www.giantco.com/plugin/install/index.html">
</EMBED>
```

Value   Any valid URL.

Default   None.

PLUGINURL   NN *4*   IE *n/a*   HTML *n/a*

PLUGINURL="*URL*"   *Optional*

Navigator 4 introduces the power (a feature called Smart Update) to allow somewhat automatic installation of browser components. If a user does not have the necessary plugin installed for your EMBED element's data type, the PLUGINURL can point to a Java Archive (JAR) file that contains the plugin and digitally signed objects to satisfy security issues surrounding automatic installation (via Netscape's Java Installation Manager). A JAR file is both digitally signed and compressed (very much along the lines of a *.zip* file), and is created with the help of Netscape's JAR Packager tool.

You can include both the PLUGINSPAGE and PLUGINURL attributes in an EMBED element's tag to handle the appropriate browser version. Navigator 2 and 3 respond to the PLUGINSPAGE attribute, whereas Navigator 4 gives precedence to the PLUGINURL attribute when it is present.

Example

```
<EMBED NAME="jukebox" SRC="jazz.aif" HEIGHT=150 WIDTH=250
PLUGINURL="http://www.giantco.com/plugin/install.jar">
</EMBED>
```

Value   Any valid URL to a JAR file.

Default   None.

SRC   NN *2*   IE *3*   HTML *n/a*

SRC="*URL*"   *Optional*

The SRC attribute is a URL to a file containing data that is played through the plugin. For most uses of the EMBED element, this attribute is required, but there are some circumstances in which it may not be necessary (see the **TYPE** attribute). Browsers typically use the filename extension to determine which plugin to load (based on browser preferences settings for plugins and helper applications).

Example

```
<EMBED NAME="babyClip" SRC="Ugachaka.avi" HEIGHT=150 WIDTH=250></EMBED>
```

Value   A complete or relative URL.

Default   None.

Object Model Reference

IE   `[window.]document.embeds[i].src`
            `[window.]document.`*elementID*`.src`

TYPE   NN *2*   IE *n/a*   HTML *n/a*

TYPE="*MIMEtype*"   *Optional*

Navigator anticipated the potential of a plugin not requiring any outside data file. Instead, such a plugin would more closely resemble an applet. If such a plugin is to be put into your document, you still use the **EMBED** element but specify just the MIME type instead of the data file URL (in the **SRC** attribute). This assumes, of course, that the MIME type is of such a special nature that only one possible plugin would be mapped to that MIME type in the browser settings. Either the **SRC** or **TYPE** attribute must be present in a Navigator **EMBED** element tag.

Example

```
<EMBED TYPE="application/x-frobnitz" HEIGHT=150 WIDTH=250></EMBED>
```

Value

Any valid MIME type name as a quoted string, including the type and subtype portions delimited by a forward slash.

Default   None.

UNITS   NN *2*   IE *3*   HTML *n/a*

UNITS="*measurementUnitType*"   *Optional*

The **UNITS** attribute is supposed to dictate the kind of measurement units used for the element's **HEIGHT** and **WIDTH** attribute values. Both Navigator 4 and Internet Explorer 4 appear to treat the measurements in pixels, regardless of this attribute's setting.

Example   `<EMBED SRC="jazz.aif" HEIGHT=150 WIDTH=250 UNITS="en"></EMBED>`

Value

Not only does this attribute not appear to influence the rendering of an **EMBED** element, but Navigator 4 and Internet Explorer 4 disagree on the precise spelling and available units for values. Navigator 4 specifies choices of **pixels** or **en**; Internet Explorer goes with **px** or **em**.

Default   **pixels** (or **px**).

Object Model Reference

IE   [window.]document.embeds[i].units
            [window.]document.*elementID*.units

VSPACE

See HSPACE.

WIDTH

See HEIGHT.

<FIELDSET>   NN *n/a*   IE *4*   HTML *4*

`<FIELDSET>...</FIELDSET>`   *End Tag: Required*

A `FIELDSET` element is a structural container for form elements (as distinguished from the functional containment of the `FORM` element). In fact, you can define multiple `FIELDSET` elements within a single `FORM` element to supply context to logical groupings of form elements. For example, one `FIELDSET` element might contain text input fields for name and address info; another `FIELDSET` might be dedicated to credit card information. In applications envisioned by the HTML 4.0 specification, users could use access keys to navigate from one group to another, rather than have to tab ad nauseam to reach the next group.

Internet Explorer 4 boosts the attractiveness of this element by automatically drawing a rule around the form elements within each `FIELDSET` container. You can also attach a label that gets embedded within the rule by defining a `LEGEND` element immediately after the start tag of a `FIELDSET` element. When IE 4 draws the rule, the box extends the full width of the next outermost container geography—usually the document. If you'd rather have the box cinch up around the visible form elements, you have to set the **width** style sheet property. Unfortunately, the Mac and Windows versions do not render the box set to a specific width the same way: the Windows version comes closest to honoring the pixel count, whereas the Mac version is substantially wider.

Example

```
<FORM METHOD=POST ACTION="...">
<FIELDSET>
<LEGEND>Credit Card Information</LEGEND>
...inputElementsHere...
</FIELDSET>
</FORM>
```

Object Model Reference

IE   [window.]document.all.*elementID*

Attributes

ALIGN	*DIR*	*LANG*	*STYLE*	VALIGN
CLASS	*ID*	*LANGUAGE*	TITLE	

Event Handler Attributes

Handler	NN	IE	HTML
onBlur	n/a	4	n/a
onChange	n/a	4	n/a
onClick	n/a	4	4
onDblClick	n/a	4	4
onDragStart	n/a	4	n/a
onFilterChange	n/a	4	n/a
onFocus	n/a	4	n/a
onHelp	n/a	4	n/a
onKeyDown	n/a	4	4
onKeyPress	n/a	4	4
onKeyUp	n/a	4	4
onMouseDown	n/a	4	4
onMouseMove	n/a	4	4
onMouseOut	n/a	4	4
onMouseOver	n/a	4	4
onMouseUp	n/a	4	4
onResize	n/a	4	n/a
onScroll	n/a	4	n/a
onSelect	n/a	4	n/a
onSelectStart	n/a	4	n/a

ALIGN   NN *n/a*   IE *4*   HTML *n/a*

ALIGN="*where*"   *Optional*

The ALIGN attribute appears only in Internet Explorer 4, and its implementation is far from consistent across operating systems. In theory, the attribute should control the alignment of INPUT elements it contains. This is true in the Macintosh version of IE 4, but in the Windows version, the settings have a minor effect on whether the FIELDSET element rule is flush left, flush right, or centered. It is best to let the default setting take precedence.

As a general rule, ALIGN attributes are deprecated in HTML 4.0 in favor of style sheets. Even though the ALIGN attribute isn't supported in HTML 4.0, you should feel free to use style sheets even for this Internet Explorer-specific attribute.

Example `<FIELDSET ALIGN="center">...</FIELDSET>`

Value Allowed values are `left` | `center` | `right`.

Default `left`

Object Model Reference

IE   [window.]document.all.*elementID*.align

TITLE
NN n/a   IE 4   HTML 4

TITLE="advisoryText"
Optional

An advisory description of the element. In Internet Explorer 4, the title is rendered as a tooltip when the cursor rests on the element for a moment. TITLE attributes of nested form elements override the setting for the entire FIELDSET, allowing you to specify one tooltip for the main fieldset area and more detailed tooltips for each element.

Example   <FIELDSET TITLE="Credit Card Info">...</FIELDSET>

Value

Any string of characters. The string must be inside a matching pair of (single or double) quotation marks.

Default   None.

Object Model Reference

IE   [window.]document.all.elementID.title

VALIGN
NN n/a   IE 4   HTML 4

VALIGN="alignmentConstant"
Optional

Determines the vertical alignment of the FIELDSET within the FORM.

Example   <FIELDSET VALIGN="bottom">...</FIELDSET>

Value

Four constant values are recognized by both IE 4 and HTML 4.0: top | middle | bottom | baseline. With top and bottom, the content is rendered flush (or very close to it) to the top and bottom of the table cell. Set to middle (the default), the content floats perfectly centered vertically in the cell. When one cell's contents might wrap to multiple lines at common window widths (assuming a variable table width), it is advisable to set the VALIGN attribute to baseline. This assures that the character baseline of the first (or only) line of a cell's text aligns with the other cells in the row—usually the most aesthetically pleasing arrangement

Default   middle

Object Model Reference

IE   [window.]document.all.elementID.vAlign

<FONT>
NN all   IE all   HTML 3.2

<FONT>...</FONT>
End Tag: Required

A FONT element is a container whose contents are rendered with the font characteristics defined by the element's attributes. This element is deprecated in HTML 4.0 in favor of font attributes available in style sheets that are applied directly to other elements or the artificial SPAN container for inline font changes. This element will be supported for a long time to come to allow backward compatibility with web pages designed for older browsers, however.

The FONT element has evolved over its lifetime, adding new attributes along the way to work in the more mature browsers. Navigator includes some proprietary attributes for Version 4 that are better served by style sheets for cross-browser compatibility.

Example <FONT FACE="Times, serif" SIZE=4>

Object Model Reference

IE   [window.]document.all.*elementID*

Attributes

CLASS	FACE	LANGUAGE	SIZE	TITLE
COLOR	ID	POINT-SIZE	STYLE	WEIGHT
DIR	LANG			

COLOR
NN *2*   IE *3*   HTML *3.2*

COLOR="*colorTripletOrName*"   *Optional*

Sets the font color of all text contained by the FONT element. This attribute is deprecated in HTML 4.0 in favor of style sheets.

Example <FONT COLOR="Olive">...</FONT>

Value

A hexadecimal triplet or plain-language color name. See Appendix A for acceptable plain-language color names.

Default   Browser default.

Object Model Reference

IE   [window.]document.all.*elementID*.color

FACE
NN *3*   IE *3*   HTML *4*

FACE="*fontFaceName1[, ... fontFaceNameN]*"   *Optional*

You can assign a hierarchy of font faces to use for a segment of text contained by a FONT element. The browser looks for the first font face in the comma-delimited list of font face names until it either finds a match on the client system or runs out of choices, at which point the browser default font face is used. Font face names must match the system font face names exactly. If you use this attribute (instead of the preferred style sheet attribute), you can always suggest a generic font face (serif, sans-serif) as the final choice.

Example <FONT FACE="Bookman, Times Roman, serif">...</FONT>

Value

One or more font face names, including the recognized generic faces: serif | sans-serif | cursive | fantasy | monospace.

Default   Browser default.

Object Model Reference

IE   [window.]document.all.*elementID*.face

ID   NN *4*   IE *4*   HTML *4*

ID=" *elementIdentifier"*   *Optional*

A unique identifier that distinguishes this element from all the rest in the document. Can be used to associate a single element with a style rule naming this attribute value as an ID selector. An element can have an ID assigned for uniqueness as well as a class for inclusion within a group. A style sheet rule applied to a FONT element overrides any directly assigned attribute values. Therefore, you can define a set of font characteristics for non-CSS-capable browsers and a modified version for CSS-capable browsers in the same tag. See Chapter 3.

Example   <FONT ID="specialFont3" COLOR="Olive">...</FONT>

Value   Case-sensitive identifier.

Default   None.

Object Model Reference

IE   [window.]document.all.*elementID*.id

POINT-SIZE   NN *4*   IE *n/a*   HTML *n/a*

POINT-SIZE=" *pointSize"*   *Optional*

The POINT-SIZE attribute is Navigator 4's non-CSS equivalent of setting the font size by specific point size (rather than by relative font size directed by the SIZE attribute). If you assign a value to the POINT-SIZE attribute and set the font-size style attribute, the style attribute takes precedence. If you are aiming for cross-browser deployment, I suggest using style sheets exclusively for precise point sizes.

Example   <FONT POINT-SIZE="14">...</FONT>

Value   A positive integer, representing the desired point size.

Default   Browser default.

SIZE   NN *all*   IE *all*   HTML *3.2*

SIZE=" *integerOrRelativeSize"*   *Optional*

Font sizes referenced by the SIZE attribute are the relative size scale that is not tied to any one point size across operating system platforms. The default browser font size is 3. The range of acceptable values for the SIZE attribute are integers from 1 to 7 inclusive. The exact point size varies with the operating system and browser design.

Users can often adjust the default font size in preferences settings. The SIZE attribute overrides that setting. Moreover, SIZE values can be relative to whatever font size is set in the preferences. By preceding an attribute value with a + or – sign, the browser's default size can be adjusted upward or downward, but always within the range of 1 through 7.

Example

```
<FONT SIZE=4>...</FONT>
<FONT SIZE="+3">...</FONT>
```

Value

Either an integer (quoted or not quoted) or a quoted relative value consisting of a + or – symbol and an integer value.

Default   3

Object Model Reference

IE   [window.]document.all.*elementID*.size

STYLE   NN *4*   IE *4*   HTML *4*

STYLE="*styleSheetProperties*"   *Optional*

This attribute lets you set one or more style sheet rule property assignments for the current element. A style sheet rule applied to a **FONT** element overrides any directly assigned attribute values. Therefore, you can define a set of font characteristics for non-CSS-capable browsers and a modified version for CSS-capable browsers in the same tag.

Example   `<FONT STYLE="color:red; font-size:14pt">...</FONT>`

Value

An entire CSS-syntax style sheet rule is enclosed in quotes. Multiple style attribute settings are separated by semicolons. Style sheet attributes are detailed in Chapter 10.

Default   None.

Object Model Reference

IE   [window.]document.all.*elementID*.style

WEIGHT   NN *4*   IE *n/a*   HTML *n/a*

WEIGHT="*boldnessValue*"   *Optional*

The **WEIGHT** attribute is Navigator 4's non-CSS equivalent of setting the font weight with a regular attribute rather than by style sheet rule. The attribute does not appear to work, but setting the **font-weight** style attribute does the job.

Value

Integer value between 100 and 900 in increments of 100. A value of 900 is the maximum boldness setting.

Default   Unknown.

<FORM>   NN *all*   IE *all*   HTML *all*

<FORM>...</FORM>   *End Tag: Required*

Despite the importance of HTML forms in communication between web page visitors and the server, a **FORM** element at its heart is nothing more than a container of controls. Most, but not all, form controls are created in the document as INPUT elements. Even if user interaction with INPUT elements is not intended for submission to a server (perhaps some client-side scripting requires interaction with the user), such INPUT elements are contained by a FORM element.

A document may contain any number of FORM elements, but a client may submit the settings of controls from only one form at a time. Therefore, the only time it makes sense to divide a series of form controls into multiple FORM elements is when the control groups can be submitted independently of each other. If you need to logically or structurally group controls while maintaining a single form, use the FIELDSET element to create the necessary subgroupings of controls.

When a form is submitted to the server, all controls that have NAME attributes assigned to them pass both their names and values—in name/value pairs—to the server for further processing (or possibly as an email attachment or message with Navigator). A Common Gateway Interface (CGI) program running on the server can accept and dissect the name/value pairs for further processing (adding a record to a server database or initiating a keyword search, for example). The server program is invoked via URL to the program assigned to the ACTION attribute.

Inside browsers, the submission process consists of a few well-defined steps. The process begins by the browser assembling a form data set out of the name/value pairs of form controls. The name comes from the value assigned to the NAME attribute. A control's value depends on the type of control. For example, a text INPUT element's value is the content appearing in the text box at submission time; for a radio button within a radio group (all of whose NAME attributes are assigned the same value), the value assigned to the VALUE attribute of the selected radio button is inserted into the name/value pair for the radio group.

The second step of submission encodes the text of each name/value pair. A + symbol is substituted for each space character. Reserved characters (as defined by RFC 1738) are escaped, and all other nonalphanumeric characters are converted to hexadecimal representations (in the form %*HH*, where *HH* is the hex code for the ASCII value of the character). Name and value components of each name/value pair are separated by an = symbol, and each name/value pair is delimited with an ampersand (&).

In the final step, the METHOD attribute setting determines how the escaped form data set is transmitted to the server. With a METHOD of get, the form data set is appended to the URL stated in the ACTION attribute, separated by a ? symbol. With a METHOD of post and a default ENCTYPE, the data set is transmitted as a kind of (nonemail) message to the server.

Default behavior of the **Enter** key in forms has evolved into a recognized standard. When a form consists of a single text INPUT element, a press of the **Enter** (or **Return**) key automatically submits the form (as if the user had clicked on a SUBMIT button element. If the form consists of two or more text INPUT elements, the **Enter** (or **Return**) key does not automatically submit the form.

Form submission can be canceled in modern browsers with the help of scripts that perform validation checking or other functions triggered by the onSubmit event handler. This event fires prior to the form being submitted. If the event handler evaluates to **false**, the form is not submitted, and the user may continue to edit the form elements.

Example

```
<FORM NAME="orders" METHOD=POST ACTION="http://www.giantco.com/cgi-bin/
order">
...
</FORM>
```

Object Model Reference

NN   [window.]document.forms[i]
           [window.]document.*formName*

IE   [window.]document.forms[i]
           [window.]document.*formName*

Attributes

ACCEPT	*CLASS*	*ID*	METHOD	TARGET
ACCEPT-CHARSET	*DIR*	*LANG*	NAME	*TITLE*
ACTION	ENCTYPE	*LANGUAGE*	*STYLE*	

Event Handler Attributes

Handler	NN	IE	HTML
onClick	n/a	4	4
onDblClick	n/a	4	4
onDragStart	n/a	4	n/a
onHelp	n/a	4	n/a
onKeyDown	n/a	4	4
onKeyPress	n/a	4	4
onKeyUp	n/a	4	4
onMouseDown	n/a	4	4
onMouseMove	n/a	4	4
onMouseOut	n/a	4	4
onMouseOver	n/a	4	4
onMouseUp	n/a	4	4
onReset	3	4	4
onSelectStart	n/a	4	n/a
onSubmit	2	3	4

ACCEPT

NN *n/a*   IE *n/a*   HTML 4

ACCEPT="*MIMETypeList*"   *Optional*

Intended for use with **INPUT** elements of type `file`, the **ACCEPT** attribute lets you specify one or more MIME types for allowable files to be uploaded to the server when the form is submitted. The predicted implementation of this attribute would filter the file types listed in file dialogs used to select files for uploading. In a way, this attribute provides client-side validation of a file type so that files not conforming to the permitted MIME type are not even sent to the server.

Example `<FORM ACCEPT="text/html, image/gif" ...>...</FORM>`

HTML Reference

Value

Case-insensitive MIME type (content type) value. For multiple items, a comma-delimited list is allowed.

Default   None.

ACCEPT-CHARSET   NN *n/a*   IE *n/a*   HTML *4*

ACCEPT-CHARSET=" *MIMETypeList*"   *Optional*

A server advisory (for servers that are equipped to interpret the information) about which character sets it must receive from a client form.

Example <FORM ACCEPT-CHARSET="it, es" ...>...</FORM>

Value

Case-insensitive alias from the character set registry (*ftp://ftp.isi.edu/in-notes/iana/ assignments/character-sets*). Multiple character sets may be delimited by commas. The reserved value, "unknown", is supposed to represent the character set that the server used to generate the form for the client.

Default   "unknown"

ACTION   NN *all*   IE *all*   HTML *all*

ACTION=" *URL*"   *Optional*

Specifies the URL to be accessed when the form is being submitted. When the form is submitted to a server for further processing, the URL may be to a CGI program or to an HTML page that includes server-side scripts. (Those scripts execute on the server before the HTML page is downloaded to the client.) As a result of the submission, the server returns an HTML page for display in the client. If the returned display is to be delivered to a different frame or window, the TARGET attribute must be specified accordingly.

You may also substitute a mailto: URL for the ACTION attribute value. Navigator turns the name/value pairs of the form into a document for attachment to an email message (or as the message body with the ENCTYPE attribute set to "text/plain"). For privacy reasons, client users are notified of the impending email transmission and have the chance to cancel the message. Internet Explorer through Version 4 does not automatically include form element data inside an email message begun with a mailto: URL.

If you omit the ACTION attribute and the form is submitted, the current page reloads itself, returning all form elements to their default values.

Example

<FORM METHOD=POST ACTION="http://www.giantco.com/orders/order.html">

Value   A complete or relative URL.

Default   None.

Object Model Reference

NN   [window.]document.forms[i].action
          [window.]document.*formName*.action

IE   [window.]document.forms[i].action
          [window.]document.*formName*.action

ENCTYPE   NN *all*   IE *all*   HTML *all*

ENCTYPE="*MIMEType*"   *Optional*

Sets a MIME type for the data being submitted to the server with the form. For typical form submissions (where the METHOD attribute is set to post), the default value is the proper content type. If you include a file INPUT element, specify "multipart/form-data" as the ENCTYPE attribute. And for Navigator, it is usually more convenient to have form data submitted to a mailto: URL to be in the message body instead of as a message attachment. To embed the form data into the message body, set the ENCTYPE to "text/plain".

Example

```
<FORM METHOD=POST ACTION="mailto:orders@giantco.com" ENCTYPE="text/plain">
...
</FORM>
```

Value

Case-insensitive MIME type (content type) value. For multiple items, a comma-delimited list is allowed.

Default   application/x-www-form-urlencoded

Object Model Reference

NN   [window.]document.forms[i].encoding
          [window.]document.*formName*.encoding

IE   [window.]document.forms[i].encoding
          [window.]document.*formName*.encoding

METHOD   NN *all*   IE *all*   HTML *all*

METHOD=get | post   *Optional*

Forms may be submitted via two possible HTTP methods: get and post. These methods determine whether the form element data is sent to the server appended to the ACTION attribute URL (get) or as a transaction message body (post). In practice, when the ACTION and METHOD attributes are not assigned in a FORM element, the form performs an unconditional reload of the same document, restoring form controls to their default values.

Due to potential problems with internationalization, the get method is deprecated in HTML 4.0. Because so much of the World Wide Web depends on this method and get is the default method on most browsers, the get method is unlikely to go away for a long time.

Example

```
<FORM METHOD=POST ACTION="http://www@giantco.com/orders/order.html">
...
</FORM>
```

Value

Case-insensitive values of get or post. These values do not have to be quoted.

Default   get

Object Model Reference

NN   [window.]document.forms[i].method
         [window.]document.*formName*.method

IE   [window.]document.forms[i].method
         [window.]document.*formName*.method

NAME   NN *2*   IE *3*   HTML *n/a*

NAME="*elementIdentifier*"   *Optional*

Assigns an identifier to the entire FORM element. This value is particularly useful in writing scripts that reference the form or its nested controls.

Example

```
<FORM NAME="orders" METHOD=POST ACTION="http://www.giantco.com/cgi-bin/
order">
...
</FORM>
```

Value   Case-sensitive identifier.

Default   None.

Object Model Reference

NN   [window.]document.forms[i].name
         [window.]document.*formName*.name

IE   [window.]document.forms[i].name
         [window.]document.*formName*.name

TARGET   NN *all*   IE *all*   HTML *all*

TARGET="*windowOrFrameName*"   *Optional*

If the HTML document returned from the server after it processes the form submission is to be loaded into a window or frame other than the current window or frame, you can specify where the returned document should load by assigning a window or frame name to the TARGET attribute. Target frame names must be assigned to frames and windows as identifiers. Assign names to frames via the NAME attribute of the FRAME element; assign names to new windows via the second parameter of the window.open() scripting method. If you omit this attribute, the returned document replaces the document containing the FORM element. An identifier other than one belonging to an existing frame or window opens a new window for the returned document.

A FORM element can have only one returned document and one target. If you want a form submission to change the content of multiple frames, you can include a script in the returned document whose onLoad event handler loads or dynamically writes a document into a different frame. (Set the location.href property of each frame to a desired URL.)

Example

```
<FORM METHOD=POST ACTION="http://www.giantco.com/cgi-bin/order"
TARGET="new">
...
</FORM>
```

Value

Case-sensitive identifier when the frame or window name has been assigned via the target element's NAME attribute. Four reserved target names act as constants:

_blank   Browser creates a new window for the destination document.

_parent   Destination document replaces the current frame's framesetting document (if one exists; otherwise, it is treated as _self).

_self   Destination document replaces the current document in its window or frame.

_top   Destination document is to occupy the entire browser window, replacing any and all framesets that may be loaded (also treated as _self if there are no framesets defined in the window).

Default   _self

Object Model Reference

NN	[window.]document.forms[i].target [window.]document.*formName*.target
IE	[window.]document.forms[i].target [window.]document.*formName*.target

<FRAME>   NN *2*   IE *3*   HTML *4*

<FRAME>   *End Tag: Forbidden*

The FRAME element defines properties of an individual window space that is some fractional portion of the entire browser window. A FRAME element must be defined within the context of a FRAMESET element. It is the FRAMESET that defines the row and column arrangement of a related group of frames.

A browser treats a frame as a separate browser window within the browser application's window. As such, each frame window can load its own content, independent of other frames. Although no attributes of the FRAME element are required, assigning a value to the NAME attribute is highly recommended if you have forms or links whose returned or destination document is to be displayed in a different frame. Scripting among multiple frames also benefits greatly from names assigned to frames because it makes references to those frames (and their contents) more easily understandable to someone reading the script code.

Example

```
<FRAMESET COLS="150,*">
    <FRAME NAME="navbar" SRC="nav.html">
    <FRAME NAME="main" SRC="page1.html">
</FRAMESET>
```

Object Model Reference

NN   [window.]*frameName*
            [window.]frames[i]

IE   [window.]*frameName*
            [window.]frames[i]
            [window.]document.all.*frameID*

Attributes

BORDERCOLOR	FRAMEBORDER	*LANGUAGE*	NAME	*STYLE*
CLASS	HEIGHT	LONGDESC	NORESIZE	*TITLE*
DATAFLD	*ID*	MARGINHEIGHT	SCROLLING	WIDTH
DATASRC	*LANG*	MARGINWIDTH	SRC	

BORDERCOLOR   NN *3*   IE *4*   HTML *n/a*

BORDERCOLOR="*colorTripletOrName*"   *Optional*

If your frameset displays borders (as set with the BORDER attribute of the FRAMESET element), but you want a subset of the frames in the frameset to be rendered with a border color different from the rest, you can assign a color to the BORDERCOLOR attribute of an individual FRAME element. Mixing border colors in a frameset exposes your HTML to the risk of different rendering techniques of each browser and operating system. Not only do the precise pixel composition of borders vary, but each browser and operating system may resolve conflicts between different colored borders differently. If you assign a color to only some frames of a frameset, be sure to test the look on as many browser versions and operating systems as possible to evaluate the visual effect of your color choices.

Example <FRAME NAME="navbar" SRC="nav.html" BORDERCOLOR="salmon">

Value

A hexadecimal triplet or plain-language color name. See Appendix A for acceptable plain-language color names.

Default   None.

Object Model Reference

IE   [window.]document.all.*frameID*.borderColor

DATAFLD   NN *n/a*   IE *4*   HTML *n/a*

DATAFLD="*columnName*"   *Optional*

Used with IE 4 data binding to associate a remote data source column name in lieu of an SRC attribute for a FRAME element. The data source column must contain a valid URI (relative or absolute). A DATASRC attribute must also be set for the element.

Example <FRAME DATASRC="#DBSRC3" DATAFLD="newsURL">

Value   Case-sensitive identifier.

Default   None.

Object Model Reference

IE   [window.]document.all.*frameID*.dataFld

DATASRC

NN *n/a*   IE *4*   HTML *n/a*

DATASRC="*dataSourceName*"   *Optional*

Used with IE 4 data binding to specify the name of the remote ODBC data source (such as an Oracle or SQL Server database) to be associated with the element. Content from the data source is specified via the DATAFLD attribute.

Example   <FRAME DATASRC="#DBSRC3" DATAFLD="newsURL">

Value   Case-sensitive identifier.

Default   None.

Object Model Reference

IE   [window.]document.all.*frameID*.dataSrc

FRAMEBORDER

NN *3*   IE *3*   HTML *4*

FRAMEBORDER="*borderSwitch*"   *Optional*

Controls whether an individual frame within a frameset displays a border. The setting is supposed to override the FRAMEBORDER attribute setting of the containing FRAMESET element. Controlling individual frame borders appears to be a problem for most browsers in most operating system versions. Turning off the border of one frame may have no effect if all adjacent frames have their borders on. Feel free to experiment with the effects of turning some borders on and some borders off, but be sure to test the final effect on all browsers and operating systems used by your audience. Rely more comfortably on the FRAMEBORDER attribute of the entire FRAMESET.

Example   <FRAME NAME="navbar" SRC="nav.html" FRAMEBORDER=no>

Value

On-off values for this attribute vary with the source. HTML 4.0 specifies the values of 1 (on) and 0 (off). Navigator uses **yes** and **no**. Internet Explorer 4 accepts both sets of values. For cross-browser compatibility, use the **yes**/**no** pairing.

Default   yes

Object Model Reference

IE   [window.]document.all.*frameID*.frameBorder

HEIGHT, WIDTH

NN *n/a*   IE *4*   HTML *n/a*

HEIGHT="*length*"   *Optional*
WIDTH="*length*"

Microsoft HTML documentation for IE 4 says that the HEIGHT and WIDTH attributes control the size of a frame. In practice in IE 4, these attributes have no direct control over the appearance of the frames within a frameset. Instead, the COLS and ROWS attributes of the containing FRAMESET govern the initial geometry of a frame. Because the corresponding object properties for a frame are documented, but not part of the IE 4 document object model, the HEIGHT and WIDTH attributes are most likely in the documentation by error. Do not use them.

LONGDESC   NN *n/a*   IE *n/a*   HTML *4*

LONGDESC=" *URL*"   *Optional*

Specifies a URL of a document that contains a longer description of the element than what the content of the TITLE attribute reveals. One application of this attribute in future browsers is to retrieve an annotated description of the element for users who cannot read the browser screen.

Example

<FRAME LONGDESC="navDesc.html" TITLE="Navigation Bar" SRC="navbar.html">

Value   Any valid URI, including complete and relative URLs.

Default   None.

MARGINHEIGHT, MARGINWIDTH   NN *n/a*   IE *3*   HTML *4*

MARGINHEIGHT=" *pixelCount*"   *Optional*
MARGINWIDTH=" *pixelCount*"

The number of pixels between the inner edge of a frame and the content rendered inside the frame. The MARGINHEIGHT attribute controls space along the top and (when scrolled) the bottom edges of a frame; the MARGINWIDTH attribute controls space on the left and right edges of a frame. The HTML 4.0 specification leaves default behavior up to browsers.

Without any prompting, Internet Explorer 4 automatically inserts a margin of 14 (Windows) or 8 (Macintosh) pixels inside a frame. But if you attempt to override the default behavior, be aware that setting any one of these two attributes causes the value of the other to go to zero. Therefore, unless you want the content to be absolutely flush with various frame edges, you need to assign values to both attributes. Due to the disparity in default values for each operating system, you cannot assign truly default values to these attributes.

Example   <FRAME SRC="navbar.html" MARGINHEIGHT=20 MARGINWIDTH=14>

Value   Any positive integer value or zero.

Default   14 (Windows) or 8 (Macintosh).

Object Model Reference

IE   [window.]document.all.*frameID*.marginHeight
            [window.]document.all.*frameID*.marginWidth

NAME   NN *2*   IE *3*   HTML *4*

NAME=" *elementIdentifier*"   *Optional*

When links and forms must load their destination or returned documents into frames other than the one holding the link or form, those elements have TARGET attributes indicating which frame receives the new content. To direct such content to a frame, the frame must have a value assigned to its **NAME** attribute. That same value is assigned to the **TARGET** attribute of the **A** or **FORM** element. Client-side scripting also uses the frame's name in building references to other frames or content in other frames. It is good practice to assign a unique identifying name to all frames.

Example   <FRAME NAME="navbar" SRC="nav.html">

Value   Case-sensitive identifier.

Default   None.

Object Model Reference

NN	[window.]*frameName*.name
	[window.]frames[i].name
IE	[window.]*frameName*.name
	[window.]frames[i].name
	[window.]document.all.*frameID*.name

NORESIZE
NN *2*   IE *3*   HTML *4*

NORESIZE   *Optional*

Frame borders can be resized by the user dragging the border perpendicular to the axis of the border edge. When present, the **NORESIZE** attribute instructs the browser to prevent the frame's edges from being manually resized by the user. All border edges of the affected **FRAME** element become locked, meaning that all edges that extend to other frames in the frameset remain locked as well.

Example   <FRAME SRC="navbar.html" NORESIZE>

Value   The presence of the attribute makes the frame nonresizable.

Default   Frames are resizable by default.

Object Model Reference

IE	[window.]document.all.*frameID*.noResize

SCROLLING
NN *2*   IE *3*   HTML *4*

SCROLLING=auto | no | yes   *Optional*

By default, browsers add vertical and/or horizontal scrollbars when the content loaded into a frame exceeds the visible content region of the frame. Scrollbars can affect the layout of some content because they occupy space normally devoted to content (that is, the frame does not expand to accommodate scrollbars). Also, due to differences in default font sizes in browsers and operating system versions, a given collection of text content may display differently in different clients. If you want to prevent scrollbars from appearing in the frame, set the **SCROLLING** attribute to no; if you want scrollbars to be in the frame at all times, set the attribute to yes. In the latter case, if the content does not require scrolling, the scroll-bars are disabled. In some older versions of Navigator, the automatic scrollbars remain visible, even if content not requiring them is subsequently loaded into a frame. In Navigator 4 (and all versions of Internet Explorer), the automatic scrollbars appear only when needed.

Setting the SCROLLING attribute to no should be used only after you have tested on all browsers and platforms that mission-critical content is always visible in the frame. If the frame is set to not scroll and has the NORESIZE attribute set, some users might not be able to see all the content of the frame.

Example   <FRAME SRC="navbar.html" SCROLLING=no>

Value   Case-insensitive constant values (quoted or not): auto | no | yes.

Default   auto

Object Model Reference

IE   [window.]document.all.*frameID*.scrolling

SRC   NN *2*   IE *3*   HTML *4*

SRC="*URL*"   *Optional*

Defines the URL of the content to be loaded into the **FRAME** element. The URL can be an absolute URL or one relative to the URL of the document containing the frameset specifications. You may also use the **javascript:** pseudo-URL to have the returned value of a script appear in the frame. For example, if you want a frame to be blank when the frameset loads, you can define a function in the frameset document that returns a blank HTML page. The SRC attribute for each soon-to-be blank frame invokes the function from the vantage point of the child frame:

```
<HTML>
<SCRIPT LANGUAGE="JavaScript">
function blank() {
    return "<HTML></HTML>"
}
</SCRIPT>
<FRAMESET COLS="50%,50%">
    <FRAME NAME=leftFrame SRC="javascript:parent.blank()">
    <FRAME NAME=rightFrame SRC="javascript:parent.blank()">
</FRAMESET>
</HTML>
```

Another type of blank page is available from some browsers and versions via the about:blank URL, which draws from an internal blank page. However, Navigator 2 and 3 for the Macintosh display an unwanted message with this URL in a window or frame.

Example   <FRAME SRC="navbar.html">

Value   A complete or relative URL or a **javascript:** pseudo-URL.

Default   None.

Object Model Reference

IE   [window.]document.all.*frameID*.src

WIDTH

See HEIGHT.

<FRAMESET>

<FRAMESET>...</FRAMESET>   *End Tag: Required*

Defines the layout of a multiple-frame presentation in a browser's application window. The primary duty of the FRAMESET element is to specify the geographical layout—in a row and column array—of rectangular frames. Attributes defined in a FRAMESET element apply to all FRAME elements nested within (unless overridden by a similar attribute for a specific FRAME). A FRAMESET element's tag takes the place in an HTML document that is normally devoted to the BODY element.

You may nest a FRAMESET element within a FRAMESET element. This tactic allows you to subdivide a frame from the outer FRAMESET element into two or more frames. For example, if you define one FRAMESET element with three rows and two columns, you get a total of six frames:

```
<FRAMESET ROWS="33%, 33%, 34%" COLS="50%, 50%">
    <FRAME NAME="r1c1"...>
    <FRAME NAME="r1c2"...>
    <FRAME NAME="r2c1"...>
    <FRAME NAME="r2c2"...>
    <FRAME NAME="r3c1"...>
    <FRAME NAME="r3c2"...>
</FRAMESET>
```

Figure 8-1 shows the resulting frame organization.

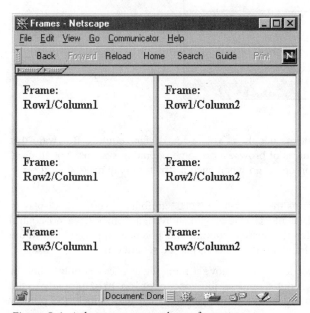

Figure 8-1. A three-row, two-column frameset

On the other hand, if you nest a frameset where a frame definition goes, that frame is divided into whatever frame organization is defined by that nested frameset. Consider the following nested frameset:

```
<FRAMESET ROWS="33%, 33%, 34%">
    <FRAME NAME="r1"...>
    <FRAMESET COLS="50%, 50%">
        <FRAME NAME="r2c1"...>
        <FRAME NAME="r2c2"...>
    </FRAMESET>
    <FRAME NAME="r3"...>
</FRAMESET>
```

This produces the frame organization shown in Figure 8-2.

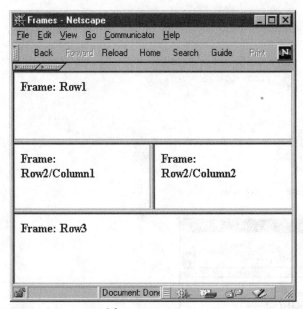

Figure 8-2. A nested frameset

You may nest FRAMESET elements as deeply as your page design requires. Be aware that frames can devour memory resources of browsers on some operating systems. Not all users appreciate frames that display borders, even when such a structure may make logical sense for your page design.

The outermost frameset document is the one whose TITLE attribute governs the display in the browser window title bar. Documents loaded into individual frames have no control over title bar display, although for reasons of scripting and potential application in future browsers, the TITLE attribute of framed documents should be set anyway.

If you wish to offer an option for a user to remove a frameset, you can supply a link or button that invokes a script. The script should set the top.location.href property to the URL of the single most important document of the pages loaded into frames (the primary content).

Example

```
<FRAMESET COLS="150,*">
    <FRAME NAME="navbar" SRC="nav.html">
    <FRAME NAME="main" SRC="page1.html">
</FRAMESET>
```

Object Model Reference

IE   [*windowRef.*]document.all.*framesetID*

Attributes

BORDER	COLS	*ID*	*LANGUAGE*	STYLE
BORDERCOLOR	FRAMEBORDER	*LANG*	ROWS	*TITLE*
CLASS	FRAMESPACING			

Event Handler Attributes

Handler	NN	IE	HTML
onBlur	3	4	n/a
onFocus	3	4	n/a
onLoad	2	3	4
onMove	4	n/a	n/a
onResize	4	n/a	n/a
onUnload	2	3	4

BORDER   NN *3*   IE *4*   HTML *n/a*

BORDER="*pixelCount*"   *Optional*

Frames display 3-D borders by default. The default thickness of that border varies with browser and operating system. You can adjust this thickness by assigning a different value to the BORDER attribute of the frameset. Only the outermost FRAMESET element of a system of nested framesets responds to the BORDER attribute setting.

Navigator 4 is consistent across Windows and Macintosh platforms by displaying a default border that is the same thickness as when the BORDER attribute is set to 5. For IE 4, the default value is 6 in Windows and 1 on the Mac (although the actual rendering is far more than one pixel wide). Any single setting you make for the BORDER attribute therefore does not look the same on all browsers. Moreover, at smaller settings, some browsers react strangely. IE 4 won't display a border in Windows when the value is 2 or less; Navigator loses its 3-D effect when the value is 2 or less. Navigator also has a nasty habit of rendering an odd divot in the center of frame bars on the Macintosh.

This hodge-podge deployment of frame borders may make you shy away from using them altogether (set the BORDER attribute to 0). In some cases, however, borders provide reassuring visual contexts for frame content that requires a scrollbar. Having a scrollbar appear floating in a browser window might be disconcerting to some viewers.

That the HTML 4.0 specification does not include a BORDER attribute might lead one to believe it prefers the use of style sheet borders instead of borders tied only to frames. Neither browser (through Version 4) responds to style sheet border settings, however.

Example <FRAMESET COLS="150,*" BORDER=0>...</FRAMESET>

Value

An integer value. A setting of zero eliminates the border entirely. Although the value is supposed to represent the precise pixel thickness of borders in the frameset, this is not entirely true for all operating systems or browsers.

Default   See description.

Object Model Reference

IE   [*windowRef.*]document.all.*framesetID*.border

BORDERCOLOR   NN *3*   IE *4*   HTML *n/a*

BORDERCOLOR="*colorTripletOrName*"   *Optional*

Establishes the rendering color for all visible borders in a frameset. A BORDERCOLOR setting in an outermost FRAMESET element may be overridden by a BORDERCOLOR attribute of a nested FRAMESET element (for the nested frameset's frames only) or an individual FRAME element. Browsers resolve conflicts of colors assigned to adjacent frames differently. Test your color combinations carefully if you mix border colors.

Example   <FRAMESET COLS="150,*" BORDERCOLOR="salmon">...</FRAMESET>

Value

A hexadecimal triplet or plain-language color name. See Appendix A for acceptable plain-language color names.

Default

Browser default, usually a shade of gray with black or blue highlighting for the 3-D effect.

Object Model Reference

IE   [*windowRef.*]document.all.*framesetID*.borderColor

COLS   NN *2*   IE *3*   HTML *4*

COLS="*columnLengthsList*"   *Optional*

Defines the sizes or proportions of the column arrangement of frames in a frameset. If it is the intent to use the FRAMESET element to create frames in multiple columns, you must assign a list of values to the COLS attribute.

Column size is defined in one of three ways:

- An absolute pixel size
- A percentage of the width available for the entire frameset
- A wildcard (*) to represent all available remaining space after other pixels and percentages have been accounted for

Use an absolute pixel size when you want the width of a frame to be the same no matter how the user has sized the overall browser window. This is especially useful when the frame is to display an object of fixed width, such as an image. Use a percentage when you want the frame width to be a certain proportion of the frameset's width, no matter how the user has adjusted the size of the overall browser window. If you use all percentage values for the COLS attribute, they should add up to 100%. If the values don't add up to 100%, the browser makes the columns fit anyway. Finally, use the asterisk wildcard value to let the browser calculate the width of one frame when all other frames in the frameset have fixed or percentage values assigned to them. Separate the values within the attribute value string with commas.

You can mix and match all three types of values in the attribute string. For example, consider a three-column frameset. If you want the leftmost column to be exactly 150 pixels wide, but the middle column must be 50% of the total frameset width, set the value as follows:

```
<FRAMESET COLS="150,50%,*">
```

The precise width of the two rightmost frames is different with each browser window's width adjustment. The rightmost frame width in this example is roughly equal to one half the width of the frameset minus the 150 pixels reserved for the leftmost frame.

To create a regular grid of frames, assign values to both the COLS and ROWS attributes in the FRAMESET element's tag. For an irregular array, you must nest FRAMESET elements, as shown in the description of the FRAMESET element, earlier in this section.

Example `<FRAMESET COLS="25%,50%,25%">...</FRAMESET>`

Value

Comma-separated list of pixel, percentage, or wildcard (*) values. Internet Explorer 4 for the Macintosh exhibits incorrect behavior with some combinations that include a wildcard value.

Default 100%

Object Model Reference

IE   [*windowRef.*]document.all.*framesetID*.cols

FRAMEBORDER   NN *3*   IE *3*   HTML *n/a*

FRAMEBORDER="*borderSwitch*"   *Optional*

Controls whether all frames within the frameset display a border (acting as dividers between frame edges). The FRAMEBORDER attribute of FRAME elements can override the FRAMESET element's setting for this attribute, but some frame organizations don't lend themselves well to eliminating frames from subgroups of frames. Override the FRAMESET element's attribute with caution and testing on all browsers and operating system platforms.

Example `<FRAMESET COLS="25%,50%,25%" FRAMEBORDER="no">...</FRAMESET>`

Value

On-off values for this attribute vary with the browser. Navigator uses **yes** and **no**. Internet Explorer 4 accepts both **yes** | **no** and **1** | **0** (only the latter pair are specified for IE 3). For Version 4 cross-browser compatibility, use the **yes/no** pairing.

Default yes

Object Model Reference

IE   [*windowRef.*]document.all.*framesetID*.frameBorder

FRAMESPACING   NN *n/a*   IE *3*   HTML *n/a*

FRAMESPACING="*pixelLength*"   *Optional*

The Internet Explorer FRAMESPACING attribute is an older version of the BORDER attribute. The older attribute is supported in IE 4 for backward compatibility. The behavior of

FRAMESPACING attribute is more uniform across operating system versions of IE 4: a setting of 10 pixels generates a border between frames that is essentially identical in both Windows and Mac versions. For an IE-only deployment, the FRAMESPACING attribute is a more accurate way to create borders that look the same across operating system versions.

Example `<FRAMESET COLS="25%,50%,25%" FRAMESPACING="7">...</FRAMESET>`

Value

A positive integer. Unlike the BORDER attribute, however, a setting of zero does not remove the border. Use the FRAMEBORDER attribute to hide borders entirely.

Default   2

Object Model Reference

IE   `[windowRef.]document.all.framesetID.frameSpacing`

ROWS   NN *2*   IE *3*   HTML *4*

ROWS=" *rowLengthsList*"   *Optional*

Defines the sizes or proportions of the row arrangement of frames in a frameset. If it is the intent to use the FRAMESET element to create frames with multiple rows, you must assign a list of values to the ROWS attribute.

Row size is defined in one of three ways:

- An absolute pixel size
- A percentage of the height available for the entire frameset in the browser window
- A wildcard (*) to represent all available remaining space in the browser window after other pixels and percentages have been accounted for

Use an absolute pixel size when you want the height of a frame row to be the same no matter how the user has sized the overall browser window. This is especially useful when the frame is to display an object of fixed height, such as an image. Use a percentage when you want the frame height to be a certain proportion of the frameset's height, no matter how the user has adjusted the size of the overall browser window. If you use all percentage values for the ROWS attribute, they should add up to 100%. If the values don't add up to 100%, the browser makes the rows fit anyway. Finally, use the asterisk wildcard value to let the browser calculate the height of one row when all other rows in the frameset have fixed or percentage values assigned to them. Separate the values within the attribute value string with commas.

You can mix and match all three types of values in the attribute string. For example, consider a three-row frameset. If you want the bottom row to be exactly 80 pixels high to accommodate a navigation bar, but the middle row must be 50% of the total frameset height, set the value as follows:

```
<FRAMESET ROWS="*,50%,80">
```

The precise height of the two topmost frames is different with each browser window's height adjustment. The topmost frame height in this example is roughly equal to one half the height of the frameset minus the 80 pixels reserved for the bottom row.

To create a regular grid of frames, assign values to both the COLS and ROWS attributes in the FRAMESET element's tag. For an irregular array, you must nest FRAMESET elements, as shown in the description of the FRAMESET element, earlier in this section.

Example <FRAMESET ROWS="25%,50%,25%">...</FRAMESET>

Value

Comma-separated list of pixel, percentage, or wildcard (*) values. Internet Explorer 4 for the Macintosh exhibits incorrect behavior with some combinations that include a wildcard value.

Default 100%

Object Model Reference

IE   [*windowRef.*]document.all.*framesetID*.rows

STYLE   NN *n/a*   IE *4*   HTML *4*

STYLE="*styleSheetProperties*"   *Optional*

This attribute lets you set one or more style sheet rule property assignments for the current element. The format of the property assignments depends on the browser's default style, but both Navigator and Internet Explorer accept the CSS syntax. Documents loaded into frames in IE 4 override style settings for a frameset, so don't bother writing STYLE attributes for FRAMESET elements.

Value

An entire CSS-syntax style sheet rule is enclosed in quotes. Multiple style attribute settings are separated by semicolons. Style sheet attributes are detailed in Chapter 10.

Default None.

Object Model Reference

IE   [*windowRef.*]document.all.*framesetID*.style

<H1>, <H2>, <H3>,
<H4>, <H5>, <H6>   NN *all*   IE *all*   HTML *all*

<H1>...</H1>, <H2>...</H2>, <H3>...</H3>   *End Tag: Required*
<H4>...</H4>, <H5>...</H5>, <H6>...</H6>

HTML defines a series of six heading levels whose associated numbers are intended to signify the relative importance of the section below the heading. The H1 element represents the most important, whereas H6 represents the least important. HTML document parsers could examine a page's tags to create a table of contents based on the headings. This means that for proper document structure, these heading levels should be used in proper sequence, without skipping levels for aesthetic purposes.

It is up to the browsers to determine the font, weight, and other characteristics of each level. Each heading element is rendered on its own line, with no line break or paragraph elements necessary to begin the content of the section titled with the heading. Figure 8-3 shows examples of how Navigator 4 and Internet Explorer 4 renders all six heading levels in Windows 95. By and large, this pattern applies to other browser versions and operating systems except for Navigator on the Macintosh, whose default H4 and H6 elements render characters wider (albeit shorter) than the H3 and H5 elements preceding them.

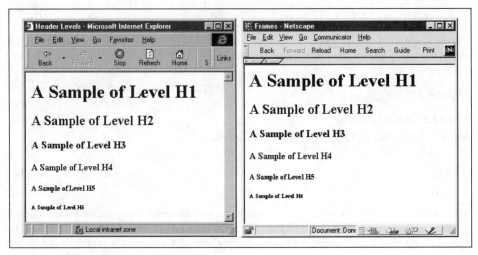

Figure 8-3. Heading levels in Internet Explorer 4 and Navigator 4

You can always override the browser's rendering style for any heading level or individual heading with style sheet rules.

Example

```
<H1>The Solar System</H1>
<P>Floating gracefully within the Milky Way galaxy is our Solar System.
...</P>
<H2>The Sun</H2>
<P>At a distance of 93,000,000 miles from Earth, the Sun...</P>
<H3>The Planets</H3>
<P>Nine recognized planets revolve around the Sun. ...</P>
<H4>Mercury</H4>
...
```

Object Model Reference

IE   [window.]document.all.elementID

Attributes

ALIGN	DIR	LANG	STYLE	TITLE
CLASS	ID	LANGUAGE		

Event Handler Attributes

Handler	NN	IE	HTML
onClick	n/a	4	4
onDblClick	n/a	4	4
onDragStart	n/a	4	n/a

Handler	NN	IE	HTML
onHelp	n/a	4	n/a
onKeyDown	n/a	4	4
onKeyPress	n/a	4	4
onKeyUp	n/a	4	4
onMouseDown	n/a	4	4
onMouseMove	n/a	4	4
onMouseOut	n/a	4	4
onMouseOver	n/a	4	4
onMouseUp	n/a	4	4
onSelectStart	n/a	4	n/a

ALIGN
NN *all*   IE *all*   HTML *3.2*

ALIGN="*where*"   *Optional*

Determines how the heading is rendered in physical relation to the next outermost container, usually the body. Both Navigator and Internet Explorer support alignment values for center, left, and right alignment. HTML 4.0 adds the possibility of a fully justified alignment, as well.

The ALIGN attribute is deprecated in HTML 4.0 in favor of the text-align: style sheet attribute.

Example <H1 ALIGN="center">Article I</H1>

Value

The following table shows values for the ALIGN attribute. Values may be treated as case-insensitive values.

Value	NN 4	IE 4	HTML4.0
center	•	•	•
justify	-	-	•
left	•	•	•
right	•	•	•

Default left

Object Model Reference

IE   [window.]document.all.*elementID*.align

<HEAD>
NN *all*   IE *all*   HTML *all*

<HEAD>...</HEAD>   *End Tag: Optional*

The HEAD element contains document information that is generally not rendered as part of the document in the browser window. At most, the TITLE element affects what the user sees when a browser displays its content in the browser window's titlebar.

Content of the HEAD element consists entirely of other elements that are intended to assist the browser in working with document data. Another classification of data, handled in one or more META elements, can also assist search engines and document parsers to learn more about the document based on abstract information supplied by the author. The following table shows the elements that may be nested inside a HEAD element according to three different specifications.

Element	NN 4	IE 4	HTML 4.0
BASE	•	•	•
BASEFONT	•	•	-
BGSOUND	-	•	-
ISINDEX	•	-	•
LINK	•	•	•
META	•	•	•
NEXTID	-	•	-
SCRIPT	•	•	•
STYLE	•	•	•
TITLE	•	•	•

Example

```
<HEAD>
<META NAME="Author" CONTENT="Danny Goodman">
<STYLE TYPE="text/css">
    H1 {color:cornflowerblue}
</STYLE>
</HEAD>
```

Object Model Reference

IE   [window.]document.all.*elementID*

Attributes

CLASS   ID   *LANG*   PROFILE   TITLE
DIR

CLASS   NN *n/a*   IE *4*   HTML *n/a*

CLASS=" *className1[...classNameN]*"   *Optional*

An identifier generally used to associate an element with a style sheet rule defined for a class selector. See Chapter 3. The CLASS attribute makes no sense for the HEAD element because the attribute can't be assigned to a class style selector that has not yet been defined. (It gets defined later within the HEAD element.) This attribute appears to be in Internet Explorer for the sake of consistency, rather than genuine functionality.

Value

Case-sensitive identifier. Multiple classes can be assigned by separating the class names with spaces within the quoted attribute value.

Default   None.

Object Model Reference

IE   [window.]document.all.*elementID*.className

ID   NN *n/a*   IE *4*   HTML *n/a*

ID="*elementIdentifier*"   *Optional*

A unique identifier that distinguishes this element from all the rest in the document. You can use this attribute value in Internet Explorer scripts as a way to reference the HEAD element by ID rather than by the longer `document.all.tags("HEAD")[0]` reference.

Example   <HEAD ID="docHead">...</HEAD>

Value   Case-sensitive identifier.

Default   None.

Object Model Reference

IE   [window.]document.all.tags("HEAD")[0].id
            [window.]document.all.*elementID*.id

PROFILE   NN *n/a*   IE *n/a*   HTML *4*

PROFILE="*URLList*"   *Optional*

A meta data profile is a separate file (or browser built-in named definition) that defines one or more meta data property behaviors. In some ways, a profile is like a header for meta data whose properties are assigned in plain view within META elements inside a HEAD element. Future browsers and external systems (such as search engines) may use the profile information to extend the typical name/value assignments in META elements as implemented in Version 4 (and earlier) browsers.

Example

```
<HEAD PROFILE="http://www.giantco.com/profiles/common">
    <META NAME="Author" content="Jane Smith">
    <META NAME="keywords" CONTENT="benefits,insurance,">
    ...
</HEAD>
```

Value   Any valid URL or browser profile constant.

Default   Browser default.

TITLE   NN *n/a*   IE *4*   HTML *n/a*

TITLE="*advisoryText*"   *Optional*

An advisory description of the element. Because the HEAD element does not display content in the browser window, there is no region of the screen to associate with the normal tooltip that displays TITLE attribute data.

Do not confuse the TITLE attribute of a HEAD element with the TITLE element that is nested inside the HEAD element. The latter represents the title of the document that appears in the browser window's titlebar and can be used by document parsers to extract the title for indexing purposes.

Example   <HEAD TITLE="Widget Price List">...</HEAD>

Value

Any string of characters. The string must be inside a matching pair of (single or double) quotation marks.

Default   None.

Object Model Reference

IE   [window.]document.all.*elementID*.title

<HR>   NN *all*   IE *all*   HTML *all*

<HR>   *End Tag: Forbidden*

The HR element draws a horizontal rule according to visual rules built into the browser with a variety of attribute controls. As a block element, the HR element starts and ends its rule on its own line, as if the element were surrounded by BR elements. This element is not a content container, and many of the attributes that have been in use for a long time are deprecated in HTML 4.0 in favor of style sheet rules. The HTML recommendation leaves default appearance specifications up to the browser maker.

Example <HR ALIGN="center" WIDTH="80%">

Object Model Reference

IE   [window.]document.all.*elementID*

Attributes

ALIGN	*ID*	*LANGUAGE*	SIZE	*TITLE*
CLASS	*LANG*	NOSHADE	*STYLE*	WIDTH
COLOR				

Event Handler Attributes

Handler	NN	IE	HTML
onBeforeUpdate	n/a	4	n/a
onBlur	n/a	4	n/a
onClick	n/a	4	4
onDblClick	n/a	4	4
onDragStart	n/a	4	n/a
onFocus	n/a	4	n/a
onHelp	n/a	4	n/a
onKeyDown	n/a	4	4
onKeyPress	n/a	4	4
onKeyUp	n/a	4	4
onMouseDown	n/a	4	4
onMouseMove	n/a	4	4
onMouseOut	n/a	4	4
onMouseOver	n/a	4	4
onMouseUp	n/a	4	4
onResize	n/a	4	n/a

Handler	NN	IE	HTML
onRowEnter	n/a	4	n/a
onRowExit	n/a	4	n/a
onSelectStart	n/a	4	n/a

ALIGN
NN *all*   IE *all*   HTML *3.2*

ALIGN="*where*"   *Optional*

Determines how the HR element is rendered in physical relation to the next outermost container (usually the BODY). The ALIGN attribute is deprecated in HTML 4.0 in favor of the align: style sheet attribute.

Example <HR ALIGN="right">

Value   One of three case-insensitive values: center | left | right.

Default left

Object Model Reference

IE   [window.]document.all.*elementID*.align

COLOR
NN *n/a*   IE *4*   HTML *n/a*

COLOR="*colorTripletOrName*"   *Optional*

Sets the color of the HR element in Internet Explorer. Setting the COLOR attribute also turns on the NOSHADE attribute. If you want a 3-D effect rule to appear with a color, use the style sheet color: attribute. Navigator 4, however, doesn't apply color style sheet rules to HR elements.

Example <HR COLOR="salmon">

Value

A hexadecimal triplet or plain-language color name. See Appendix A for acceptable plain-language color names.

Default None.

Object Model Reference

IE   [window.]document.all.*elementID*.color

NOSHADE
NN *all*   IE *all*   HTML *3.2*

NOSHADE   *Optional*

The presence of the NOSHADE attribute tells the browser to render the rule as a flat (not 3-D) line. In Internet Explorer only, if you set the COLOR attribute, the browser changes the default line style to a no-shade style.

Example <HR NOSHADE>

Value   The presence of the attribute turns on no-shade rendering.

Default Off.

Object Model Reference

IE   [window.]document.all.*elementID*.noShade

SIZE   NN *all*   IE *all*   HTML *3.2*

SIZE="*pixelCount*"   *Optional*

You can override the default thickness of the HR element by assigning a value to the SIZE attribute. The SIZE attribute is deprecated in HTML 4.0 in favor of the height: style sheet attribute. You can use this style rule in Internet Explorer 4, but not in Navigator 4.

Example <HR SIZE=4>

Value   Any positive integer. A setting of zero still draws a one-pixel thick rule.

Default   2

Object Model Reference

IE   [window.]document.all.*elementID*.size

WIDTH   NN *all*   IE *all*   HTML *3.2*

WIDTH="*length*"   *Optional*

Defines the precise pixel width or percentage of available width (relative to the containing element) to draw the HR element rule. This attribute is deprecated in HTML 4.0 in favor of the width: style sheet attribute.

Example <HR WIDTH="75%">

Value   Any length value in pixels or percentage of available space.

Default   100%

Object Model Reference

IE   [window.]document.all.*elementID*.width

<HTML>   NN *all*   IE *all*   HTML *all*

<HTML>...</HTML>   *End Tag: Optional*

The HTML element is the container of the entire document content, including the HEAD element. Both the start and end tags are optional, but good style dictates the inclusion of both. Typically, the HTML element start tag is the second line of an HTML file, following the Document Type Definition (DTD) statement. If no DTD is provided in the file (it assumes the browser's default DTD), the HTML start tag becomes the first line of the file. The end tag should be in the last line of the file (but it does not have to stand on its own line).

Example

```
<HTML>
<HEAD>
   ...
</HEAD>
<BODY>
   ...
```

```
</BODY>
</HTML>
```

Attributes

DIR	LANG	TITLE	VERSION

TITLE

TITLE="*advisoryText*"   *Optional*

An advisory description of the element. In Internet Explorer 4, the title is rendered as a tooltip when the cursor rests anywhere in the document for a moment. TITLE attributes of other elements in the window override the attribute value set for the HTML element.

Example   `<HTML TITLE="It's a cool document!">...</HTML>`

Value

Any string of characters. The string must be inside a matching pair of (single or double) quotation marks.

Default   None.

Object Model Reference

IE   `[window.]document.all.`*elementID*`.title`

VERSION

VERSION="*string*"   *Optional*

The VERSION attribute is deprecated in HTML 4.0 and was never adopted by the major browsers. Originally intended to specify the HTML DTD version supported by the document, this information is universally supplied in the separate DTD statement (in the !DOCTYPE element) above the HTML element in the document.

Value

Any string of characters. The string must be inside a matching pair of (single or double) quotation marks.

Default   None.

<I>

`<I>...</I>`   *End Tag: Required*

The I element—one of several font style elements in HTML 4.0—renders its content in an italic version of the font face governing the next outermost HTML container. You can nest multiple font style elements to create combined styles, such as bold italic (`<B><I>bold-italic text</I></B>`).

It is up to the browser to italicize a system font or perhaps load an italic version of the currently specified font. If you are striving for font perfection, it is best to use style sheets (and perhaps downloadable fonts) to specify a true italic font face, rather than risk the browser's extrapolation of an italic face from a system font.

You can take advantage of the containerness of this element by assigning style sheet rules to some or all I elements in a page. For example, you may wish all I elements to be in a red color. By assigning the style rule I{color:red}, you can do it to all elements with only a tiny bit of code.

Although this element is not deprecated in HTML 4.0, it would not be surprising to see it lose favor to the font-style: style sheet attribute in the future.

Example   <P>This product is <I>new</I> and <I>improved</I>!</P>

Object Model Reference

IE   [window.]document.all.*elementID*

Attributes

CLASS	*ID*	*LANGUAGE*	*STYLE*	*TITLE*
DIR	*LANG*			

Event Handler Attributes

Handler	NN	IE	HTML
onClick	n/a	4	4
onDblClick	n/a	4	4
onDragStart	n/a	4	n/a
onHelp	n/a	4	n/a
onKeyDown	n/a	4	4
onKeyPress	n/a	4	4
onKeyUp	n/a	4	4
onMouseDown	n/a	4	4
onMouseMove	n/a	4	4
onMouseOut	n/a	4	4
onMouseOver	n/a	4	4
onMouseUp	n/a	4	4
onSelectStart	n/a	4	n/a

<IFRAME>   NN *n/a*   IE *3*   HTML *4*

<IFRAME>...</IFRAME>   *End Tag: Required*

An **IFRAME** element creates an inline frame within the natural flow of a document's content. The frame is a rectangular space into which you may load any other HTML document (or use scripts to dynamically write content to the space). If you assign a value to the **NAME** attribute of an **IFRAME** element, you may supply that name as the value of a **TARGET** attribute of **A**, **FORM**, or other element that lets you define a target for a destination or returned document.

Although an **IFRAME** element's rectangular space begins immediately following the content that comes before it (including in a line of text), all content following the end tag starts on the next line following the frame rectangle. Text leading up to the **IFRAME** element can be aligned in the same ways that text can be aligned around an **IMG** or **OBJECT** element.

Content between the start and end tags is ignored by browsers that support the **IFRAME** element. All others display such content as inline HTML content (as a way to let users know what they're missing and perhaps provide a link to related information). The Navigator 4 element that comes closest to the functionality and behavior of the IFRAME element is the ILAYER element.

Example

```
<IFRAME SRC="quotes.html" WIDTH=150 HEIGHT=90>
<A HREF="quotes.html" TARGET="new" STYLE="color:darkred">
 Click here to see the latest quotes </A>
</IFRAME>
```

Object Model Reference

IE   [window.]document.*frameName*

Attributes

ALIGN	DATASRC	*ID*	MARGINWIDTH	STYLE
BORDER	FRAMEBORDER	*LANG*	NAME	*TITLE*
BORDERCOLOR	FRAMESPACING	*LANGUAGE*	NORESIZE	VSPACE
CLASS	HEIGHT	LONGDESC	SCROLLING	WIDTH
DATAFLD	HSPACE	MARGINHEIGHT	SRC	

ALIGN   NN *n/a*   IE *3*   HTML *4*

ALIGN="*alignmentConstant*"   *Optional*

Determines how the rectangle of the IFRAME element aligns within the context of surrounding content. See the section "Alignment Constants" earlier in this chapter for a description of the possibilities defined in Internet Explorer for this attribute. Only a subset of the allowed constant values are specified in the HTML recommendation, whereas Internet Explorer 4 runs the gamut.

Example

```
<IFRAME SRC="quotes.html" WIDTH=150 HEIGHT=90 ALIGN="baseline"></IFRAME>
```

Value   Case-insensitive constant value.

Default bottom

Object Model Reference

IE   [window.]document.*frameName*.align

BORDER   NN *n/a*   IE *4*   HTML *n/a*

BORDER="*pixelCount*"   *Optional*

Theory and practice of IFRAME element borders in Internet Explorer 4 diverge a lot, especially when trying to match behaviors across operating systems. IE 4 for the Macintosh displays IFRAME elements with a 3-D effect around the border that is always visible, no matter what border attribute settings are assigned. For the Windows 95 version, the 3-D effect goes away when you turn off the FRAMEBORDER attribute. As for the BORDER attribute, the size of the border acts as a margin setting in IE 4/Mac, but only for the top and left edges of the frame space: content is displaced to the right and down by the border size, causing the content to flow over the right and bottom edges—quite a mess. The BORDER attribute setting appears to have no effect in Windows 95. In no case does the border around an IFRAME look like a FRAME element border in IE 4.

That the HTML 4.0 specification does not include a BORDER attribute might lead one to believe it prefers the use of style sheet borders, instead of borders tied only to frames. If you want a genuine border around an IFRAME element in IE 4, use a style sheet border instead. Its behavior is far more consistent and predictable (and is thoroughly unrelated to nonfunctioning style sheet borders for frames defined by a FRAMESET).

Example   <IFRAME SRC="quotes.html" WIDTH=150 HEIGHT=90 BORDER=10></IFRAME>

Value   A positive integer value.

Default   0

Object Model Reference

IE   [window.]document.*frameName*.border

BORDERCOLOR   NN *n/a*   IE 4   HTML *n/a*

BORDERCOLOR="*colorTripletOrName*"   *Optional*

The BORDERCOLOR attribute should assign a color to whatever border surrounds an IFRAME element. In practice, because borders controlled by attributes do not appear in the Windows 95 version of Internet Explorer 4, no color appears either. On the Macintosh side, an assigned color may appear on two adjacent edges of an IFRAME element, but the look is unpredictable. Use style sheet rules to assign borders and border colors to IFRAME elements.

Example

```
<IFRAME SRC="quotes.html" WIDTH=150 HEIGHT=90 BORDERCOLOR="salmon">
</IFRAME>
```

Value

A hexadecimal triplet or plain-language color name. See Appendix A for acceptable plain-language color names.

Default   None.

Object Model Reference

IE   [window.]document.*frameName*.borderColor

DATAFLD   NN *n/a*   IE 4   HTML *n/a*

DATAFLD="*columnName*"   *Optional*

Used with IE 4 data binding to associate a remote data source column name in lieu of an SRC attribute for an IFRAME element. The data source column must contain a valid URI (relative or absolute). A DATASRC attribute must also be set for the element.

Example   <IFRAME DATASRC="#DBSRC3" DATAFLD="newsURL"></IFRAME>

Value   Case-sensitive identifier.

Default   None.

Object Model Reference

IE   [window.]document.*frameName*.dataFld

DATASRC

NN *n/a*   IE *4*   HTML *n/a*

DATASRC="*dataSourceName*"   *Optional*

Used with IE 4 data binding to specify the name of the remote ODBC data source (such as an Oracle or SQL Server database) to be associated with the element. Content from the data source is specified via the DATAFLD attribute.

Example   <IFRAME DATASRC="#DBSRC3" DATAFLD="newsURL"></IFRAME>

Value   Case-sensitive identifier.

Default   None.

Object Model Reference

IE   [window.]document.*frameName*.dataSrc

FRAMEBORDER

NN *n/a*   IE *3*   HTML *4*

FRAMEBORDER="*borderSwitch*"   *Optional*

Controls whether an individual frame within a frameset displays a border. Setting IFRAME element borders via the element's attributes is chancy at best in Internet Explorer 4. Use style sheet borders instead.

Example

<IFRAME SRC="quotes.html" WIDTH=150 HEIGHT=90 FRAMEBORDER=0></IFRAME>

Value

On-off values for this attribute vary with the source. HTML 4.0 specifies the values of 1 (on) and 0 (off). Navigator uses yes and no. Internet Explorer 4 accepts the HTML values and yes or no.

Default   1

Object Model Reference

IE   [window.]document.*frameName*.frameBorder

FRAMESPACING

NN *n/a*   IE *4*   HTML *n/a*

FRAMESPACING="*pixelLength*"   *Optional*

Controls the thickness of space between multiple, adjacent IFRAME elements. In practice, the attribute has no effect in Internet Explorer 4. Use style sheet border attributes to create borders around IFRAME elements.

Value   A positive integer.

Default   0

Object Model Reference

IE   [window.]document.*frameName*.frameSpacing

HEIGHT, WIDTH   NN *n/a*   IE *4*   HTML *n/a*

HEIGHT=" *length*"   *Optional*
WIDTH=" *length*"

Microsoft HTML documentation for IE 4 says that the HEIGHT and WIDTH attributes control
the size of a IFRAME element. The attributes are recognized in IE 4 for Windows, but not
for the Macintosh. Moreover, these attributes are not recognized as scriptable properties—
often a sign that the attributes are not genuinely supported. Use these attributes at your
own risk. Instead, you can rely on style sheet positioning (using relative positioning) to set
the height and width of the element in all operating system platforms.

Example   <IFRAME SRC="nav.html" HEIGHT=200 WIDTH=200>

Value   Any length value in pixels or percentage of available space.

Default   A width of 300 pixels; a height of 150 pixels.

HSPACE, VSPACE   NN *n/a*   IE *4*   HTML *n/a*

HSPACE=" *pixelCount*"   *Optional*
VSPACE=" *pixelCount*"

Sets padding around an IFRAME element within content flow. The HSPACE attribute controls
padding along the left and right edges (horizontal padding), and the VSPACE attribute
controls padding along the top and bottom edges (vertical padding). Adding such padding
provides an empty cushion around the frame. As an alternate, you can specify the various
margin style sheet settings, especially if you want to open space along only one edge.

Example   <IFRAME SRC="nav.html" HSPACE=20 VSPACE=10>

Value   Any positive integer.

Default   0

LONGDESC   NN *n/a*   IE *n/a*   HTML *4*

LONGDESC=" *URL*"   *Optional*

Specifies a URL of a document that contains a longer description of the element than what
the content of the TITLE attribute reveals. One application of this attribute in future
browsers is to retrieve an annotated description of the element for users who cannot read
the browser screen.

Example

<IFRAME LONGDESC="navDesc.html" TITLE="Navigation Bar" SRC="navbar.html">
</IFRAME>

Value   Any valid URI, including complete and relative URLs.

Default   None.

MARGINHEIGHT, MARGINWIDTH   NN *n/a*   IE *3*   HTML *4*

MARGINHEIGHT="*pixelCount*"   *Optional*
MARGINWIDTH="*pixelCount*"

Determine the number of pixels between the inner edge of a frame and the content rendered inside the frame. The MARGINHEIGHT attribute controls space along the top and (when scrolled) the bottom edges of a frame; the MARGINWIDTH attribute controls space on the left and right edges of a frame. The HTML 4.0 specification leaves default behavior up to browsers.

Without any prompting, Internet Explorer 4 automatically inserts a margin of 14 (Windows) or 8 (Macintosh) pixels inside a frame. But if you attempt to override the default behavior, be aware that setting any one of these two attributes causes the value of the other to go to zero. Therefore, unless you want the content to be absolutely flush with various frame edges, you need to assign values to both attributes. Due to the disparity in default values for each operating system, you cannot assign truly default values to these attributes.

Example

```
<IFRAME SRC="navbar.html" MARGINHEIGHT=20 MARGINWIDTH=14></IFRAME>
```

Value   Any positive integer value or zero.

Default   14 (Windows) or 8 (Macintosh).

Object Model Reference

IE   [window.]document.*frameName*.marginHeight
            [window.]document.*frameName*.marginWidth

NAME   NN *n/a*   IE *3*   HTML *4*

NAME="*elementIdentifier*"   *Optional*

When links and forms must load their destination or returned documents into frames other than the one holding the link or form, those elements have TARGET attributes indicating which frame receives the new content. To direct such content to a frame, the frame must have a value assigned to its NAME attribute. That same value is assigned to the TARGET attribute of the A or FORM element. Client-side scripting also uses the frame's name in building references to other frames or content in other frames. It is good practice to assign a unique identifying name to all frames.

Example   `<IFRAME NAME="navbar" SRC="nav.html"></IFRAME>`

Value   Case-sensitive identifier.

Default   None.

Object Model Reference

IE   [window.]document.*frameName*.name

NORESIZE

NORESIZE   *Optional*

It's curious why the NORESIZE attribute is included in Internet Explorer for the IFRAME element. Regardless of the setting, an IFRAME element cannot be manually resized by the user.

Example <IFRAME SRC="navbar.html" NORESIZE></IFRAME>

Value

The presence of the attribute makes the frame nonresizable (although so does its absence).

Default   An IFRAME element is supposed to be resizable by default, but in practice it is not.

Object Model Reference

IE   [window.]document.*frameName*.noResize

SCROLLING

SCROLLING=auto | no | yes   *Optional*

By default, browsers add vertical and/or horizontal scrollbars when the content loaded into an inline frame exceeds the visible content region of the element. Scrollbars can affect the layout of some content because they occupy space normally devoted to content (that is, the frame does not expand to accommodate scrollbars). Also, due to differences in default font sizes in browsers and operating system versions, a given collection of text content may display differently in different clients. If you want to prevent scrollbars from appearing in the frame, set the SCROLLING attribute to no; if you want scrollbars to be in the frame at all times, set the attribute to yes. In the latter case, if the content does not require scrolling, the scrollbars are visible, but disabled.

Setting the SCROLLING attribute to no should be used only after you have tested on all browsers and platforms that mission-critical content is always visible in the frame. If the frame is set to not scroll, some users might not be able to see all content of the frame.

Example <IFRAME SRC="navbar.html" SCROLLING=no></IFRAME>

Value   Case-insensitive constant values (optionally quoted): auto | no | yes.

Default   auto

Object Model Reference

IE   [window.]document.*frameName*.scrolling

SRC

SRC="*URL*"   *Optional*

Defines the URL of the content to be loaded into the IFRAME element. The URL can be an absolute URL or one relative to the URL of the document containing the frameset specifications. You may also use the javascript: pseudo-URL to have the returned value of a script appear in the frame. If you omit the SRC attribute, the frame opens empty.

Example <IFRAME SRC="navbar.html"></IFRAME>

Value   A complete or relative URL or a `javascript:` pseudo-URL.

Default   None.

Object Model Reference

IE   [window.]document.*frameName*.src

STYLE   NN *n/a*   IE *4*   HTML *4*

STYLE="*styleSheetProperties*"   *Optional*

This attribute lets you set one or more style sheet rule property assignments for the current element. Styles affect the inline frame and not its content. Therefore, a border assigned to an IFRAME element style appears around the frame, not inside the frame.

Example <IFRAME SRC="navbar.html" STYLE="border:solid blue 3px"></IFRAME>

Value

An entire CSS-syntax style sheet rule is enclosed in quotes. Multiple style attribute settings are separated by semicolons. Style sheet attributes are detailed in Chapter 10.

Default   None.

Object Model Reference

IE   [window.]document.*frameName*.style

VSPACE

See HSPACE.

WIDTH

See HEIGHT.

<ILAYER>   NN *4*   IE *n/a*   HTML *n/a*

<ILAYER>...</ILAYER>   *End Tag: Required*

An ILAYER element is an inline version of the Navigator-specific LAYER element. In some respects, the ILAYER element works like the IFRAME element in Internet Explorer, but an ILAYER is automatically regarded as a positionable element in Navigator's object model (e.g., like a block-level element whose CSS position: attribute is set to relative). As a result, many of the attributes are the same as the LAYER element and are named according to the Navigator way of positioning, sizing, and stacking positionable elements. It is unlikely that the LAYER or ILAYER elements will be adopted by the W3C, so you are encouraged to use CSS-Positioning syntax (which works on both browser platforms) instead.

Content for an ILAYER element can be read in from a separate file (with the SRC attribute) or wired into the current document by placing the HTML between the start and end tags. You can include both types of content in the same ILAYER element. Content from the SRC document is rendered first (as its own block-level element), with additional content starting on its own line below the external content's rectangle.

HTML Reference

Example

```
<ILAYER ID="thingy1" SRC="quotes.html" WIDTH=150 HEIGHT=90></ILAYER>
```

Object Model Reference

NN   [window.]document.*layerName*

Attributes

ABOVE	BGCOLOR	ID	TOP	WIDTH
BACKGROUND	CLIP	LEFT	VISIBILITY	Z-INDEX
BELOW	HEIGHT	SRC		

Event Handler Attributes

Handler	NN	IE	HTML
onBlur	4	n/a	n/a
onFocus	4	n/a	n/a
onLoad	4	n/a	n/a
onMouseDown	4	n/a	n/a
onMouseOut	4	n/a	n/a
onMouseOver	4	n/a	n/a
onMouseUp	4	n/a	n/a

ABOVE   NN *4* IE *n/a* HTML *n/a*

ABOVE="*layerID*"   *Optional*

Names the positionable element that is to be above (in front of) the current ILAYER in the stacking order. This is a different way to set the Z-INDEX attribute that does not rely on an arbitrary numbering system. If you use the ABOVE attribute, do not use the BELOW or Z-INDEX attribute for the same ILAYER element.

Example `<ILAYER ID="thingy4" SRC="quotes.html" ABOVE="thingy3"></ILAYER>`

Value   Case-sensitive identifier.

Default   None.

Object Model Reference

NN   [window.]document.*layerName*.above

BACKGROUND   NN *4* IE *n/a* HTML *n/a*

BACKGROUND="*URL*"   *Optional*

Specifies an image file that is used as a backdrop to the text and other content of the ILAYER element. Unlike normal images that get loaded into browser content, a background image loads in its original size (without scaling) and tiles to fill the available layer space. Smaller images download faster but are obviously repeated more often in the background. Animated GIFs are also allowable but very distracting to the reader. When selecting a background image, be sure it is very muted in comparison to the main content so that the content stands out clearly. Background images, if used at all, should be extremely subtle.

Example

```
<ILAYER ID="thingy4" SRC="quotes.html" BACKGROUND="blueCrinkle.jpg">
</ILAYER>
```

Value   Any valid URL to an image file, including complete and relative URLs.

Default   None.

Object Model Reference

NN   [window.]document.*layerName*.background

BELOW   NN *4*   IE *n/a*   HTML *n/a*

BELOW=" *layerID*"   *Optional*

Names the positionable element that is to be below (behind) the current ILAYER in the
stacking order. This is a different way to set the Z-INDEX attribute that does not rely on an
arbitrary numbering system. If you use the BELOW attribute, do not use the ABOVE or Z-INDEX
attribute for the same ILAYER element.

Example   `<ILAYER ID="thingy4" SRC="quotes.html" BELOW="thingy5"></ILAYER>`

Value   Case-sensitive identifier.

Default   None.

Object Model Reference

NN   [window.]document.*layerName*.below

BGCOLOR   NN *4*   IE *n/a*   HTML *n/a*

BGCOLOR=" *colorTripletOrName*"   *Optional*

Establishes a fill color (behind the text and other content) for the entire layer rectangle. If
you combine a BGCOLOR and BACKGROUND, any transparent areas of the background image
let the background color show through.

Example   `<ILAYER SRC="quotes.html" BGCOLOR="tan"></ILAYER>`

Value

A hexadecimal triplet or plain-language color name. A setting of empty is interpreted as
"#000000" (black). See Appendix A for acceptable plain-language color names.

Default   Varies with operating system.

Object Model Reference

NN   [window.]document.*layerName*.bgColor

CLIP   NN *4*   IE *n/a*   HTML *n/a*

CLIP=" [*leftPixel*, *topPixel*,] *rightPixel*, *bottomPixel*"   *Optional*

A clipping region is a rectangular view to the full ILAYER content. Only content that is
within the clipping rectangle can be seen on the page. The default value of the CLIP
attribute is determined by the space required to display the content as it naturally flows into

the element. Setting the CLIP attribute lets you rein in long content that might flow beyond a fixed rectangle desired for the page design.

Example   `<ILAYER SRC="quotes.html" CLIP="50,50"></ILAYER>`

Value

CLIP attribute values are pixel measures from the top and left edges of the element as it flows in the document. The order of values is clockwise from the left edge, around the rectangle sides: left, top, right, bottom. If you supply only two values, Navigator assumes the left and top values are zero, meaning that you wish to adjust only the right and bottom edges. Thus, a setting of "50,50" means that the clipping region is 50-pixels square, starting at the top-left corner of the layer's rectangle. If you want the same size view, but starting 10 pixels in from the left, the CLIP attribute setting becomes "10,0,60,50".

Default   Naturally flowing viewing area of ILAYER content.

Object Model Reference

NN   [window.]document.*layerName*.clip.left
            [window.]document.*layerName*.clip.top
            [window.]document.*layerName*.clip.right
            [window.]document.*layerName*.clip.bottom

HEIGHT, WIDTH   NN *4*   IE *n/a*   HTML *n/a*

HEIGHT="*length*"   *Optional*
WIDTH="*length*"

Define the minimum size of the layer as it flows in the document. When you add content to the layer, however, the attribute settings do not restrict the amount of the content that is visible along either axis. For example, if you display an image in an ILAYER that is 120 pixels wide by 90 pixels high, the actual visible size of an ILAYER element whose HEIGHT and WIDTH attributes are set to a smaller size expands to allow the full image to appear. The same happens to text or other content: the viewable region expands to allow all content to appear. To restrict the visible portion of the content, set the CLIP attribute.

Setting the HEIGHT and WIDTH attributes to specific sizes is helpful when you are creating a colored or patterned rectangle (via the BGCOLOR or BACKGROUND attributes) to act as an underlying layer beneath some other positioned content. Without content pushing on the edges of the ILAYER, the HEIGHT and WIDTH attributes set the clipping region to their sizes.

Example   `<ILAYER BGCOLOR="yellow" HEIGHT=100 WIDTH=100></ILAYER>`

Value

Positive integer values (optionally quoted) or percentage values (quoted). You can reduce both values to zero to not only hide the element (which you can also do with the VISIBILITY attribute), but prevent the element from occupying any page space.

Default   Naturally flowing viewing area of ILAYER content.

Object Model Reference

NN   [window.]document.*layerName*.height
            [window.]document.*layerName*.width

ID

NN *4*   IE *n/a*   HTML *n/a*

ID="*elementIdentifier*"   *Optional*

A unique identifier that distinguishes this element from all the rest in the document. This is the identifier used as values for the ABOVE and BELOW attributes. Scripts also use the ID attribute value as the ILAYER element's name for object references.

Example

```
<ILAYER ID="oldYeller" BGCOLOR="yellow" HEIGHT=100 WIDTH=100></ILAYER>
```

Value   Case-sensitive identifier.

Default   None.

Object Model Reference

IE   [window.]document.*layerName*.name

LEFT, TOP

NN *4*   IE *n/a*   HTML *n/a*

LEFT="*pixelCount*"   *Optional*
TOP="*pixelCount*"

Define the positioned offset of the left and top edges of the layer relative to the spot in the document where the ILAYER element would normally appear. This precise location relative to the page varies because an ILAYER element is an inline layer, which means that it can start anywhere within normally flowing HTML content. When you set either of these attributes, Navigator preserves the space in the document where the ILAYER element appears, rather than cinch up surrounding content to fill space vacated by the element that has shifted its location. You are therefore likely to set these attributes for an ILAYER only when attempting to accomplish a look tailored to very customized content (perhaps an ILAYER amid inflow images).

Example   `<ILAYER BGCOLOR="yellow" LEFT=10 TOP=50></ILAYER>`

Value   Positive integer values (optionally quoted).

Default   0

Object Model Reference

NN   [window.]document.*layerName*.left
              [window.]document.*layerName*.top

SRC

NN *4*   IE *n/a*   HTML *n/a*

SRC="*URL*"   *Optional*

To load the content of an external HTML file into an ILAYER element, assign the URL of that file to the SRC attribute. Any HTML content between the ILAYER start and end tags is rendered on the page after the content loaded from the SRC URL. If you omit the SRC attribute, only content between the tags is rendered. Scripts can change the corresponding object property (src) after the document has loaded to dynamically change content within the ILAYER element (without reloading the main document).

Example   `<ILAYER SRC="quotes.html"></ILAYER>`

HTML Reference

Value   A complete or relative URL.

Default   None.

Object Model Reference

NN   [window.]document.*layerName*.src

TOP

See LEFT.

VISIBILITY   NN *4*   IE *n/a*   HTML *n/a*

VISIBILITY="*visibilityConstant*"   *Optional*

Determines whether Navigator displays the **ILAYER** element. The default behavior is for a layer to inherit the **VISIBILITY** attribute of its next outermost (parent) layer. For an **ILAYER** element that is part of the basic document body, this means that the layer is seen by default (the base layer is always visible). To hide a layer when the page loads, set the **VISIBILITY** attribute to **"hidden"**. You need set the attribute to **"show"** only if the **ILAYER** element is nested within another **LAYER** whose **VISIBILITY** value is set to (or is inherited as) **"hidden"**.

Regardless of the **VISIBILITY** attribute setting, an **ILAYER** element always occupies its normal inflow space in the document. This allows Navigator to change the visibility on the fly (via scripting) without reloading the document. (Navigator 4 does not automatically reflow changed content.)

Example   <ILAYER SRC="quotes.html" VISIBILITY="hidden"></ILAYER>

Value   One of the accepted constants: **hidden** | **inherit** | **visible**.

Default   **inherit**

Object Model Reference

NN   [window.]document.*layerName*.visibility

WIDTH

See HEIGHT.

Z-INDEX   NN *4*   IE *n/a*   HTML *n/a*

Z-INDEX="*layerNumber*"   *Optional*

Controls the positioning of layers along the Z-axis (front-to-back) of the document relative to the next outermost layer container. When the **Z-INDEX** values of two or more position-able elements within the same container (such as the base document layer) are identical numbers, the loading order of the elements in the HTML source code controls the stacking order, with the later elements stacked in front of earlier ones. The default **Z-INDEX** value for all positionable elements is zero. Therefore, if you want only one positionable element to appear in front of all the others that stack in their default order, you simply assign any positive value (even 1) to that stand-out element. Stacking order of positionable elements can be changed on-the-fly via scripting.

Example `<ILAYER SRC="quotes.html" Z-INDEX=1></ILAYER>`

Value Any integer.

Default 0

Object Model Reference

NN   `[window.]document.layerName.zIndex`

<IMG>   NN *all*   IE *all*   HTML *all*

`<IMG>`   *End Tag: Forbidden*

The **IMG** element displays a graphical image in whatever MIME types the browser is equipped to handle. Common image MIME types are GIF and JPEG. **IMG** elements are inline elements, appearing anywhere in the document you specify, including in the middle of a line of text. A large number of attributes affecting visual presentation of the element are deprecated in HTML 4.0 in favor of style sheet rules. You will be able to use the attributes safely for many browser generations to come, however, because of the need to be backward compatible with the large collection of image-laden documents already on the Web. Note, too, that if you intend to use style sheets for **IMG** element borders and margins in Navigator 4, you must wrap the **IMG** element inside **DIV** or **SPAN** elements and assign the style sheets to the surrounding element. This workaround works with Internet Explorer, too, so you can use style sheets in cross-browser deployment.

If you want to make an entire image a clickable link, wrap the **IMG** element inside an **A** element. To eliminate the typical link border around the image, set the **BORDER** attribute to 0. And for image maps (where different segments of an image link to different destinations), the HTML recommendation encourages the use of client-side image maps (via the **USEMAP** attribute) over the server-side image map (**ISMAP**).

To be backward compatible with earlier scriptable browsers, it is advisable to include **HEIGHT** and **WIDTH** attribute assignments in all **IMG** element tags. When values are assigned to these attributes, the browser renders pages more quickly because it doesn't have to wait for the image to load in order to determine its size and organize other content on the page.

Example `<IMG SRC="mtRushmore.jpg" HEIGHT=90 WIDTH=120>`

Object Model Reference

NN   `[window.]document.imageName`
      `[window.]document.images[i]`
IE   `[window.]document.imageName`
      `[window.]document.images[i]`
      `[window.]document.all.elementID`

Attributes

ALIGN	DATASRC	ID	LOOP	STYLE
ALT	DIR	ISMAP	LOWSRC	TITLE
BORDER	DYNSRC	LANG	NAME	USEMAP
CLASS	HEIGHT	LANGUAGE	SRC	VSPACE
DATAFLD	HSPACE	LONGDESC	START	WIDTH

Event Handler Attributes

Handler	NN	IE	HTML
onAbort	3	4	n/a
onAfterUpdate	n/a	4	n/a
onBeforeUpdate	n/a	4	n/a
onBlur	n/a	4	n/a
onClick	n/a	4	4
onDblClick	n/a	4	4
onDragStart	n/a	4	n/a
onError	3	4	n/a
onFocus	n/a	4	n/a
onHelp	n/a	4	n/a
onKeyDown	n/a	4	4
onKeyPress	n/a	4	4
onKeyUp	n/a	4	4
onLoad	3	4	n/a
onMouseDown	n/a	4	4
onMouseMove	n/a	4	4
onMouseOut	n/a	4	4
onMouseOver	n/a	4	4
onMouseUp	n/a	4	4
onResize	n/a	4	n/a
onRowEnter	n/a	4	n/a
onRowExit	n/a	4	n/a
onSelectStart	n/a	4	n/a

ALIGN   NN *all*   IE *all*   HTML *all*

ALIGN="*where*"   *Optional*

Determines how the IMG element is rendered in physical relation to the element's next outermost container and surrounding content. Some settings also let you "float" the image to the left or right margin and let surrounding text wrap around the image (but no wrapping with a centered image).

Most of the rules for alignment constant values cited at the beginning of this chapter apply to the IMG element. Typically, ALIGN attributes are deprecated in HTML 4.0 in favor of the style sheet attributes. But if you require backward compatibility for your document, stick with the ALIGN attribute.

Example <IMG SRC="surferDude.gif" ALIGN="right" HEIGHT=100 WIDTH=200>

Value

Each browser defines a different set of values for this attribute. Although the ALIGN attribute has a long heritage, not all values do. The more esoteric values, such as absmiddle and

baseline, were added to browser offerings in Navigator 3 and Internet Explorer 4. Select the value(s) from the following table that work for your deployment:

Value	NN 4	IE 4	HTML 4.0
absbottom	•	•	-
absmiddle	•	•	-
baseline	•	•	-
bottom	•	•	•
left	•	•	•
middle	•	•	•
right	•	•	•
texttop	•	•	-
top	•	•	•

Default   bottom

Object Model Reference

IE   [window.]document.*imageName*.align
            [window.]document.images[i].align

ALT   NN *all*   IE *all*   HTML *all*

ALT="*textMessage*"   *Required*

In a world littered with graphical browsers, it is often hard to remember that not everyone can, or chooses to, download images. Aside from those using VT100 terminals with browsers such as Lynx, pocket computers often offer better performance when images don't have to be downloaded and rendered. To replace the image in such a browser, the text assigned to the **ALT** attribute is displayed where the **IMG** element appears on the page. The **ALT** attribute should contain a brief description of what the image is. The HTML recommendation calls the **ALT** attribute a requirement for the **IMG** element, but in practice, graphical browsers can get by without it. Still, some browsers display the **ALT** text initially as the image downloads from the server, providing a temporary alternate display. Be aware that the size of the image area on the page may limit the amount of text you can use for **ALT**. Make sure the description is readable.

Example

```
<IMG SRC="navbar.gif" USEMAP="#nav" ALT="Navigation Bar" WIDTH=400
HEIGHT=50>
```

Value   Any quoted string of characters.

Default   None.

Object Model Reference

IE   [window.]document.*imageName*.alt
            [window.]document.images[i].alt

HTML Reference

BORDER

NN *all*   IE *all*   HTML *3.2*

BORDER=*pixels*   *Optional*

Navigator provides a dedicated attribute to specifying the thickness of a border around an
IMG element. Default rendering of the border is in black, but if the IMG element is wrapped
inside an A element, the border takes on the document's various link colors (depending on
link state). If you want a different color for a plain border, use style sheets (with the appropriate DIV or SPAN wrapper for Navigator 4). When a link surrounds the image, you can
eliminate the colored border altogether by setting the BORDER attribute size to zero.

Example   <IMG SRC="surferDude.gif" BORDER=3 HEIGHT=100 WIDTH=200>

Value   Any integer pixel value.

Default   0

Object Model Reference

NN   [window.]document.*imageName*.border
             [window.]document.images[i].border
IE   [window.]document.*imageName*.border
             [window.]document.images[i].border

DATAFLD

NN *n/a*   IE *4*   HTML *n/a*

DATAFLD="*columnName*"   *Optional*

Used with IE 4 data binding to associate a remote data source column name with the SRC
attribute URL of an IMG element. The data source column must contain an absolute or relative URL. A DATASRC attribute must also be set for the IMG element.

Example   <IMG DATASRC="#DBSRC3" DATAFLD="img3URL" HEIGHT=100 WIDTH=150>

Value   Case-sensitive identifier.

Default   None.

Object Model Reference

IE   [window.]document.*imageName*.dataFld
             [window.]document.images[i].dataFld

DATASRC

NN *n/a*   IE *4*   HTML *n/a*

DATASRC="*dataSourceName*"   *Optional*

Used with IE 4 data binding to specify the name of the remote ODBC data source (such as
an Oracle or SQL Server database) to be associated with the element. Content from the data
source is specified via the DATAFLD attribute.

Example   <IMG DATASRC="#DBSRC3" DATAFLD="img3URL" HEIGHT=100 WIDTH=150>

Value   Case-sensitive identifier.

Default   None.

Object Model Reference

IE   [window.]document.*imageName*.dataSrc
              [window.]document.images[i].dataSrc

DYNSRC   NN *n/a*   IE *4*   HTML *n/a*

DYNSRC="*URL*"   *Optional*

Internet Explorer 4 allows video clips (and VRML) to be displayed via the IMG element (as an alternate to the EMBED or OBJECT element). To help the browser differentiate between a dynamic and static image source, you use the DYNSRC attribute in place of the SRC attribute to load the video clip. All other visual aspects of the IMG element are therefore immediately applicable to the rectangular region devoted to playing the video clip. See also the LOOP attribute for controlling the frequency of clip play and the START attribute.

Example   <IMG DYNSRC="snowman.avi" LOOP=3 HEIGHT=100 WIDTH=150>

Value   Any valid URL, including complete and relative URLs.

Default   None.

Object Model Reference

IE   [window.]document.images[i].dynsrc
              [window.]document.*imageName*.dynsrc

HEIGHT, WIDTH   NN *all*   IE *all*   HTML *3.2*

HEIGHT="*length*"   *Optional*
WIDTH="*length*"

Define the dimensions for the space on the page reserved for the image, regardless of the actual size of the image. For best performance (and backward script compatibility), you should set these attributes to the actual height and width of the source image. If you supply a different measure, the browser scales the image to fit the space defined by these attributes.

Example   <IMG SRC="surferDude.gif" HEIGHT=100 WIDTH=200>

Value

Positive integer values (optionally quoted) or percentage values (quoted).

Default   Actual size of source image.

Object Model Reference

NN   [window.]document.*imageName*.height
              [window.]document.images[i].height
              [window.]document.*imageName*.width
              [window.]document.images[i].width

IE   [window.]document.*imageName*.height
              [window.]document.images[i].height
              [window.]document.*imageName*.width
              [window.]document.images[i].width

HSPACE, VSPACE
NN all   IE all   HTML 3.2

HSPACE=*pixelCount*   *Optional*
VSPACE=*pixelCount*

Define a margin that acts as whitespace padding around the visual content of the **IMG** element. The **HSPACE** establishes a margin on the left and right sides of the image rectangle; the **VSPACE** establishes a margin on the top and bottom sides of the image rectangle. Use the margin or padding attributes to duplicate the same functionality with style sheets because these attributes are deprecated in HTML 4.0.

Example   <IMG SRC="desk3.gif" VSPACE=10 HSPACE=10>

Value

Integer representing the number of pixels for the width of the margin on the relevant sides of the **IMG** element's rectangle.

Default   0

Object Model Reference

NN   [window.]document.*imageName*.hspace
          [window.]document.images[i].hspace
          [window.]document.*imageName*.vspace
          [window.]document.images[i].vspace

IE   [window.]document.imageName.hspace
          [window.]document.images[i].hspace
          [window.]document.imageName.vspace
          [window.]document.images[i].vspace

ID
NN 4   IE 3   HTML 4

ID="*elementIdentifier*"   *Optional*

A unique identifier that distinguishes this element from all the rest in the document. Can be used to associate a single element with a style rule naming this attribute value as an ID selector. An element can have an ID assigned for uniqueness as well as a class for inclusion within a group. See Chapter 3.

If you assign an **ID** attribute and not a **NAME** attribute, the value of the **ID** attribute cannot be used reliably as the **IMG** element's name in script reference forms that use the element name. Some browser platforms insist on the **NAME** attribute being used in an image name reference.

Example   <IMG SRC="desk3.gif" ID="desk3" HEIGHT=90 WIDTH=120>

Value   Case-sensitive identifier.

Default   None.

Object Model Reference

IE   [window.]document.*imageName*.id
          [window.]document.images[i].id

ISMAP   NN *all*   IE *all*   HTML *all*

ISMAP   *Optional*

The Boolean ISMAP attribute tells the browser that the IMG element is acting as a server-side image map. To turn an image into a server-side image map, wrap the IMG element with an A element whose HREF attribute points to the URL of the CGI program that knows how to interpret the click coordinate information. The browser appends coordinate information about the click to the URL like a GET form method appends form element data to the ACTION attribute URL. In the following example, if a user clicks at the coordinate point 50, 25, the browser sends "http://www.giantco.com/cgi-bin/nav?50,25" to the server. A server CGI program named nav might examine the region in which the coordinate point appears and send the relevant HTML back to the client.

More recent browsers allow client-side image maps (see the USEMAP attribute), which operate more quickly for the user because there is no communication with the server to carry out the examination of the click coordinate point.

Example

```
<A HREF="http://www.giantco.com/cgi-bin/nav" TARGET="main">
<IMG SRC="navbar.gif" ISMAP HEIGHT=90 WIDTH=120>
</A>
```

Value   The presence of the attribute turns the feature on.

Default   Off.

Object Model Reference

IE   [window.]document.*imageName*.isMap

           [window.]document.images[i].isMap

LONGDESC   NN *n/a*   IE *n/a*   HTML *4*

LONGDESC="*URL*"   *Optional*

Specifies a URL of a document that contains a longer description of the element than what the content of the ALT or TITLE attributes reveal. One application of this attribute in future browsers is to retrieve an annotated description of the element for users who cannot read the browser screen.

Example

```
<IMG LONGDESC="navDesc.html" ALT="Navigation Bar" SRC="navbar.jpg">
```

Value   Any valid URL, including complete and relative URLs.

Default   None.

LOOP   NN *n/a*   IE *3*   HTML *n/a*

LOOP="*loopCount*"   *Optional*

If you specify a video clip with the DYNSRC attribute, the LOOP attribute controls how many times the clip should play ("loop") after it loads. If you set the value to zero, the clip loads but does not play initially. Video clips that are not currently running play when the user double-clicks on the image, but you may need to provide instructions for that on the page because there are no other obvious controls.

Example   `<IMG DYNSRC="snowman.avi" LOOP=3 HEIGHT=100 WIDTH=150>`

Value   Any positive integer or zero.

Default   1

Object Model Reference

IE   [window.]document.*imageName*.loop
            [window.]document.images[i].loop

LOWSRC   NN *3*   IE *4*   HTML *n/a*

LOWSRC="*URL*"   *Optional*

Both Navigator and Internet Explorer recognize the fact that not everyone has a fast Internet connection and that high-resolution images can take a long time to download to the client. To fill the void, the LOWSRC attribute lets the author specify a URL of a lower-resolution (or alternate) image to download into the document space first. The LOWSRC image should be the same pixel size as the primary SRC image.

Example   `<IMG SRC="navbar.jpg" LOWSRC="navbarBW.jpg" HEIGHT=60 WIDTH=300>`

Value   Any valid URL, including complete and relative URLs.

Default   None.

Object Model Reference

NN   [window.]document.*imageName*.lowsrc
            [window.]document.images[i].lowsrc
IE   [window.]document.*imageName*.lowsrc
            [window.]document.images[i].lowsrc

NAME   NN *3*   IE *4*   HTML *n/a*

NAME="*elementIdentifier*"   *Optional*

If you are scripting an image (especially swapping precached images), it is usually more convenient to create a reference to the IMG element by using a unique name you assign to the item. Thus, if you edit the page and move or delete multiple IMG elements on the page, you do not have to worry about adjusting index values to array-style references (document.images[i]).

Example   `<IMG NAME="mugshot" SRC="janem.jpg" HEIGHT=90 WIDTH=80>`

Value   Case-sensitive identifier.

Default   None.

Object Model Reference

NN   [window.]document.images[i].name
            [window.]document.*imageName*.name

HTML Reference

IE   `[window.]document.images[i].name`
                  `[window.]document.`*imageName*`.name`

SRC

                                            NN *all*   IE *all*   HTML *all*

`SRC="`*URL*`"`   *Required*

URL to a file containing image data that is displayed through the `IMG` element. With the exception of specifying a `DYNSRC` attribute in Internet Explorer for video clips, the `SRC` attribute is required if you want to see any image in the `IMG` element space. The browser must be equipped to handle the image MIME type. On the World Wide Web, the most common image formats are GIF and JPEG.

Example   `<IMG SRC="surferDude.gif" HEIGHT=100 WIDTH=200>`

Value   A complete or relative URL.

Default   None.

Object Model Reference

NN   `[window.]document.images[i].src`
                    `[window.]document.`*imageName*`.src`
IE   `[window.]document.images[i].src`
                    `[window.]document.`*imageName*`.src`

START

                                            NN *n/a*   IE *4*   HTML *n/a*

`START="fileopen" | "mouseover"`   *Optional*

Whenever you set the `DYNSRC` attribute of an `IMG` to display a video clip, you can direct the element to start playing the video immediately after the video file loads or when the user rolls the cursor over the image. The `START` attribute lets you decide the best user interface for your page.

Example

`<IMG DYNSRC="snowman.avi" LOOP=1 START="mouseover" HEIGHT=100 WIDTH=150>`

Value   One of the two case-insensitive constant values: `fileopen` | `mouseover`.

Default   `fileopen`

Object Model Reference

IE   `[window.]document.images[i].start`
                    `[window.]document.`*imageName*`.start`

STYLE

                                            NN *4*   IE *3*   HTML *4*

`STYLE="`*styleSheetProperties*`"`   *Optional*

This attribute lets you set one or more style sheet rule property assignments for the current element. You may use the CSS or JavaScript syntax for assigning style attributes. But if you are designing the page for cross-browser deployment, use only the CSS syntax, which both Navigator and Internet Explorer support.

For use in Version 4 browsers, style sheets are recommended over dedicated attributes where applicable, but due to the implementation in Navigator 4, you need to wrap `IMG` elements with DIV or SPAN elements that contain border and margin-related style sheet rules to make them work with IMG elements. The following example with the embedded STYLE attribute works only in Internet Explorer.

Example
```
<IMG STYLE="padding-left:5px" SRC="surferDude.gif" HEIGHT=150 WIDTH=250>
```

Value

An entire CSS-syntax style sheet rule is enclosed in quotes. Multiple style attribute settings are separated by semicolons. Style sheet attributes are detailed in Chapter 10.

Default   None.

Object Model Reference

IE   [window.]document.images[i].style
            [window.]document.*imageName*.style

USEMAP   NN *all*   IE *all*   HTML *3.2*

USEMAP="*mapURL*"   *Optional*

You can define a client-side image map with the help of the MAP and AREA elements. The MAP element is a named container for one or more AREA element. Each AREA element sets a "hot" area on an image and assigns a link destination (and other settings) for a response to the user clicking in that region. The purpose of the USEMAP attribute is to establish a connection between the IMG element and a named MAP element in the same document. In some respects, the MAP element's name is treated like an anchor in that the "address" of the MAP element is the element's name preceded by a # symbol.

Example   <IMG SRC="navbar.gif" USEMAP="#navigation" HEIGHT=90 WIDTH=120>

Value

A URL to the MAP element in the same document (a hash symbol plus the MAP name).

Default   None.

Object Model Reference

IE   [window.]document.*imageName*.useMap
            [window.]document.images[i].useMap

VSPACE

See HSPACE.

WIDTH

See HEIGHT.

<INPUT>

NN *all*   IE *all*   HTML *all*

`<INPUT>`   *End Tag: Forbidden*

An **INPUT** element is sometimes known as a form control, although not all **INPUT** elements are visible on the page. For the most part, an **INPUT** element provides a place for users to enter text, click buttons, and make selections from lists. The data gathered from this interaction can be submitted to a server-side program (when the surrounding **FORM** element is submitted), or it may be used strictly on the client as a way for users to interact with client-side scripts.

Prior to HTML 4.0, **INPUT** elements were supposed to be wrapped by a **FORM** element in all instances. This restriction is loosening up, but Navigator 4 still requires the **FORM** wrapper in order to render **INPUT** elements.

The primary attribute that determines the kind of control that is displayed on the page is the **TYPE** attribute. This attribute can have one of the following values: **button**, **checkbox**, **file**, **hidden**, **image**, **password**, **radio**, **reset**, **submit**, or **text**. Not all **INPUT** element types utilize the full range of other attributes; sometimes a single attribute has different powers with different element types. For each attribute of the **INPUT** element, the listing specifies the types to which it applies. Although the **TEXTAREA** element has its own tag, it is often treated like another form control.

Example

```
<FORM METHOD=post ACTION="http://www.giantco.com/cgi-bin/query">
First Name: <INPUT TYPE="text" NAME="first" MAXLENGTH=15><BR>
Last Name: <INPUT TYPE="text" NAME="last" MAXLENGTH=25><BR>
ZIP Code: <INPUT TYPE="text" NAME="zip" MAXLENGTH=10><BR>
<INPUT TYPE="reset">
<INPUT TYPE="submit">
</FORM>
```

Object Model Reference

NN   `[window.]document.`*formName*`.`*inputName*
             `[window.]document.forms[i].elements[i]`

IE   `[window.]document.`*formName*`.`*inputName*
             `[window.]document.forms[i].elements[i]`
             `[window.]document.all.`*elementID*

Attributes

ACCEPT	CHECKED	DISABLED	NAME	TABINDEX
ACCESSKEY	*CLASS*	ID	READONLY	*TITLE*
ALIGN	DATAFLD	*LANG*	SIZE	TYPE
ALT	DATASRC	*LANGUAGE*	SRC	USEMAP
BORDER	*DIR*	MAXLENGTH	*STYLE*	VALUE

Event Handler Attributes

Handler	NN	IE	HTML
onAfterUpdate	n/a	4	n/a
onBeforeUpdate	n/a	4	n/a
onBlur	2	3	4
onChange	2	3	4

Handler	NN	IE	HTML
onClick	2	3	4
onDblClick	4	4	4
onDragStart	n/a	4	n/a
onFocus	2	3	4
onHelp	n/a	4	n/a
onKeyDown	4	4	4
onKeyPress	4	4	4
onKeyUp	4	4	4
onMouseDown	4	4	4
onMouseMove	n/a	4	4
onMouseOut	3	4	4
onMouseOver	2	3	4
onMouseUp	4	4	4
onSelect	2	3	4
onSelectStart	n/a	4	n/a

Not all events are active in all input types.

ACCEPT
NN *n/a*   IE *n/a*   HTML *4*

ACCEPT="*MIMETypeList*"   *Optional*

Specifies one or more MIME types for allowable files to be uploaded to the server when the form is submitted. The predicted implementation of this attribute would filter the file types listed in file dialogs used to select files for uploading. In a way, this attribute provides client-side validation of a file type so that files not conforming to the permitted MIME type is not even sent to the server. The HTML 4.0 specification also has this attribute available in the FORM element. It is unclear whether the implementations in browsers will recognize this attribute in both places.

Input Types   file

Example   <INPUT TYPE="file" ACCEPT="text/html, image/gif" ...>

Value

Case-insensitive MIME type (content type) value. For multiple items, a comma-delimited list is allowed.

Default   None.

ACCESSKEY
NN *n/a*   IE *4*   HTML *4*

ACCESSKEY="*character*"   *Optional*

A single character key that brings focus to the input element. The browser and operating system determine if the user must press a modifier key (e.g., **Ctrl**, **Alt**, or **Command**) with the access key to activate the link. In IE 4/Windows, the **Alt** key is required, and the key is not case sensitive. This attribute does not work in IE 4/Mac.

Input Types   button, checkbox, file, password, radio, reset, submit, text

Example   <INPUT TYPE="text" NAME="first" MAXLENGTH=15 ACCESSKEY="f">

Value   Single character of the document set.

Default   None.

Object Model Reference

IE   [window.]document.*formName*.*inputName*.accessKey
            [window.]document.forms[i].elements[i].accessKey
            [window.]document.all.*elementID*.accessKey

ALIGN   NN *all*   IE *all*   HTML *3.2*

ALIGN="*alignmentConstant*"   *Optional*

Determines how the rectangle of the input image aligns within the context of the surrounding content. See the section "Alignment Constants" earlier in this chapter for a description of the possibilities defined in both Navigator and Internet Explorer for this attribute. Not all attribute values are valid in browsers prior to the Version 4 releases.

Both browsers follow the same rules on laying out content surrounding an image whose ALIGN attribute is set, but the actual results are sometimes difficult to predict when the surrounding content is complex. A thorough testing of rendering possibilities with browser windows set to various sizes prevents surprises later.

Input Types   image

Example   <INPUT TYPE="image" NAME="icon" SRC="icon.gif" ALIGN="absmiddle">

Value

Case-insensitive constant value. All constant values are available in Navigator 4 and Internet Explorer 4.

Default   bottom

Object Model Reference

IE   [window.]document.*formName*.*inputName*.align
            [window.]document.forms[i].elements[i].align
            [window.]document.all.*elementID*.align

ALT   NN *n/a*   IE *4*   HTML *4*

ALT="*textMessage*"   *Optional*

If a browser is not capable of displaying graphical images (or has the feature turned off), the text assigned to the ALT attribute is supposed to display in the document where the image INPUT element's tag appears. Typically, this text provides advice on what the page visitor is missing by not being able to view the image.

Input Types   image

Example

<INPUT TYPE="image" NAME="icon" SRC="sndIcon.gif" ALT="Sound Icon">

Value   Any quoted string of characters.

Default   None.

Object Model Reference

IE   [window.]document.*formName*.*inputName*.alt
            [window.]document.forms[i].elements[i].alt
            [window.]document.all.*elementID*.alt

BORDER   NN *4*   IE *4*   HTML *n/a*

BORDER=*pixels*   *Optional*

Navigator and Internet Explorer treat images displayed by the INPUT element very much like IMG elements. As such, you can specify a border around the image. Navigator displays one by default. Because an INPUT element whose TYPE attribute is "image" acts as a submit-style button, the border is rendered in the browser's link colors. If you want a different color for a plain border, use style sheets (with the appropriate DIV or SPAN wrapper for Navigator 4). You can eliminate the colored border altogether in Navigator by setting the BORDER attribute size to zero.

Input Types   image

Example   <INPUT TYPE="image" NAME="icon" SRC="sndIcon.gif" BORDER=0>

Value   Any integer pixel value.

Default   2 (Navigator 4) or 0 (Internet Explorer 4).

Object Model Reference

IE   [window.]document.*formName*.*inputName*.border
            [window.]document.forms[i].elements[i].border
            [window.]document.all.*elementID*.border

CHECKED   NN *4*   IE *3*   HTML *4*

CHECKED   *Optional*

A Boolean attribute that designates whether the current checkbox or radio INPUT element is turned on when the page loads. In the case of a radio button grouping, only one INPUT element should have the CHECKED attribute. Scripts can modify the internal value of this attribute after the page has loaded. When the form is submitted, an INPUT element whose CHECKED attribute is turned on sends its name/value pair as part of the form data. The name/value pair consists of values assigned to the NAME and VALUE attributes for the element. If no value is assigned to the VALUE attribute, the string value "active" is automatically assigned when the checkbox or radio button is highlighted. This is fine for checkboxes because each one should be uniquely named. However, all radio buttons in a related group must have the same name, so this default behavior doesn't provide enough information for most server-side programs to work with.

Input Types   checkbox, radio

Example
<INPUT TYPE="checkbox" NAME="addToList" CHECKED>Send email updates to this web site.

Value   The presence of this attribute turns on its property.

Default   Off.

Object Model Reference

NN   [window.]document.*formName*.*inputName*.checked
       [window.]document.forms[i].elements[i].checked

IE   [window.]document.*formName*.*inputName*.checked
       [window.]document.forms[i].elements[i].checked
       [window.]document.all.*elementID*.checked

HTML Reference

DATAFLD
NN *n/a*   IE *4*   HTML *n/a*

DATAFLD="*columnName*"   *Optional*

Used with IE 4 data binding to associate a remote data source column name with parts of various INPUT elements. A DATASRC attribute must also be set for the element.

Input Types   button, checkbox, hidden, password, radio, text

Example
<INPUT TYPE="text" NAME="first" DATASRC="#DBSRC3" DATAFLD="firstName">

Value   Case-sensitive identifier.

Default   None.

Object Model Reference

IE   [window.]document.*formName*.*inputName*.dataFld
       [window.]document.forms[i].elements[i].dataFld
       [window.]document.all.*elementID*.dataFld

DATASRC
NN *n/a*   IE *4*   HTML *n/a*

DATASRC="*dataSourceName*"   *Optional*

Used with IE 4 data binding to specify the name of the remote ODBC data source (such as an Oracle or SQL Server database) to be associated with the element. Content from the data source is specified via the DATAFLD attribute.

Input Types   button, checkbox, hidden, password, radio, text

Example
<INPUT TYPE="text" NAME="first" DATASRC="#DBSRC3" DATAFLD="firstName">

Value   Case-sensitive identifier.

Default   None.

Object Model Reference

IE   [window.]document.*formName*.*inputName*.dataSrc
       [window.]document.forms[i].elements[i].dataSrc
       [window.]document.all.*elementID*.dataSrc

DISABLED
NN *n/a*   IE *4*   HTML *4*

DISABLED   *Optional*

A disabled INPUT element appears grayed out on the screen and cannot be activated by the user. In Windows, a disabled form control cannot receive focus and does not become active within the tabbing order rotation. HTML 4.0 also specifies that the name/value pair of a disabled INPUT element should not be sent when the form is submitted. INPUT elements that normally perform submissions do not submit their form when disabled.

The DISABLED attribute is a Boolean type, which means that its presence in the attribute sets its value to true. Its value can also be adjusted after the fact by scripting (see the button object in Chapter 9).

Input Types   All.

Example   <BUTTON TYPE="submit" DISABLED>Ready to Submit </BUTTON>

Value   The presence of the attribute disables the element.

Default   false

Object Model Reference

IE   [window.]document.*formName*.*inputName*.disabled
             [window.]document.forms[i].elements[i].disabled
             [window.]document.all.*elementID*.disabled

ID   NN *n/a*   IE *4*   HTML *4*

ID="*elementIdentifier*"   *Optional*

A unique identifier that distinguishes this element from all the rest in the document. Can be used to associate a single element with a style rule naming this attribute value as an ID selector. Do not confuse the ID attribute with the NAME attribute, whose value is submitted as part of a name/value pair with the form.

Input Types   All.

Example

<INPUT TYPE="button" ID="next" VALUE=">>Next>>" onClick="goNext(3)">

Value   Case-sensitive identifier.

Default   None.

Object Model Reference

IE   [window.]document.*formName*.*inputName*.id
             [window.]document.forms[i].elements[i].id
             [window.]document.all.*elementID*.id

MAXLENGTH   NN *all*   IE *all*   HTML *all*

MAXLENGTH="*characterCount*"   *Optional*

Defines the maximum number of characters that may be typed into a text field INPUT element. In practice, browsers beep or otherwise alert users when a typed character would exceed the MAXLENGTH value. There is no innate correlation between the MAXLENGTH and SIZE attributes. If the MAXLENGTH allows for more characters than fit within the specified width of the element, the browser provides horizontal scrolling (albeit awkward for many users) to allow entry and editing of the field.

Input Types   password, text

Example   `<INPUT TYPE="text" NAME="ZIP" MAXLENGTH=10>`

Value   Positive integer.

Default   Unlimited.

Object Model Reference

IE   `[window.]document.`*formName.*`inputName.maxLength`
           `[window.]document.forms[i].elements[i].maxLength`
           `[window.]document.all.`*elementID.*`maxLength`

NAME   NN *all*   IE *all*   HTML *all*

NAME="*elementIdentifier*"   *Optional*

If the **INPUT** element is part of a form being submitted to a server, the **NAME** attribute is
required if the value of the element is to be submitted with the form. For forms that are in
documents for the convenience of scripted form elements, **INPUT** element names are not
required but are helpful just the same in creating scripted references to these objects and
their properties or methods.

Input Types   All.

Example   `<INPUT TYPE="text" NAME="ZIP" MAXLENGTH=10>`

Value   Case-sensitive identifier.

Default   None.

Object Model Reference

NN   `[window.]document.`*formName.*`inputName.name`
           `[window.]document.forms[i].elements[i].name`
IE   `[window.]document.`*formName.*`inputName.name`
           `[window.]document.forms[i].elements[i].name`
           `[window.]document.all.`*elementID.*`name`

READONLY   NN *n/a*   IE *4*   HTML *4*

READONLY   *Optional*

When the **READONLY** attribute is present, the text field **INPUT** element cannot be edited on
the page by the user (although scripts can modify the content). A field marked as **READONLY**
should not receive focus within the tabbing order (although IE 4 for the Macintosh allows
the field to receive focus).

Input Types   `password`, `text`

Example   `<INPUT TYPE="text" NAME="ZIP" READONLY>`

Value   The presence of the attribute sets its value to `true`.

Default   `false`

Object Model Reference

IE   [window.]document.*formName*.*inputName*.readOnly
            [window.]document.forms[i].elements[i].readOnly
            [window.]document.all.*elementID*.readOnly

SIZE   NN *all*   IE *all*   HTML *all*

SIZE="*elementWidth*"   *Optional*

In practice, the SIZE attribute is limited to describing the character width of text field INPUT elements. The actual rendered width is calculated based on the font setting (or default font) for the element, but the results are not always perfect. Variations in font rendering (and the ability to specify alternate font faces and sizes in Internet Explorer) sometimes lead to unexpectedly narrower fields. Therefore, it is not wise to automatically set the SIZE and MAXLENGTH attributes to the same value without testing the results on a wide variety of browsers and operating systems with worst-case data (for example, all "m" or "W" characters in proportional fonts). The HTML 4.0 specification indicates that the SIZE attribute might be applied to other INPUT element types, but as of the Version 4 browsers, this is not the case. In the meantime, you can use CSS-Positioning to make buttons wider than the default size that tracks the width of the VALUE attribute string.

Input Types   password, text

Example   <INPUT TYPE="text" NAME="ZIP" MAXLENGTH=10 SIZE=12>

Value   Any positive integer.

Default   20

Object Model Reference

IE   [window.]document.*formName*.*inputName*.size
            [window.]document.forms[i].elements[i].size
            [window.]document.all.*elementID*.size

SRC   NN *all*   IE *all*   HTML *all*

SRC="*URL*"   *Required*

URL to a file containing image data that is displayed through the INPUT element of type image. The browser must be equipped to handle the image MIME type. On the World Wide Web, the most common image formats are GIF and JPEG.

Input Types   image

Example   <INPUT TYPE="image" NAME="icon" SRC="sndIcon.gif" BORDER=0>

Value   A complete or relative URL.

Default   None.

Object Model Reference

IE   [window.]document.*formName*.*inputName*.src
            [window.]document.forms[i].elements[i].src
            [window.]document.all.*elementID*.src

TABINDEX

TABINDEX=*integer*   *Optional*

A number that indicates the sequence of this element within the tabbing order of all focusable elements in the document. Tabbing order follows a strict set of rules. Elements that have values other than zero assigned to their TABINDEX attributes are first in line when a user starts tabbing in a page. Focus starts with the element with the lowest TABINDEX value and proceeds in order to the highest value, regardless of physical location on the page or in the document. If two elements have the same TABINDEX values, the element that comes earlier in the document receives focus first. Next come all elements that either don't support the TABINDEX attribute or have the value set to zero. These elements receive focus in the order in which they appear in the document.

Note that the Macintosh user interface does not provide for giving focus to elements other than text and password INPUT fields.

Input Types   button, checkbox, file, password, radio, reset, submit, text

Example   <INPUT TYPE="text" NAME="country" TABINDEX=3>

Value

Any integer from 0 through 32767. In IE 4, setting the TABINDEX to –1 causes the element to be skipped in tabbing order altogether.

Default   None.

Object Model Reference

IE   [window.]document.*formName*.*inputName*.tabIndex
             [window.]document.forms[i].elements[i].tabIndex
             [window.]document.all.*elementID*.tabIndex

TYPE

TYPE="*elementType*"   *Required*

Advises the browser how to render the INPUT element (or even whether the element should be rendered at all). Possible choices are as follows:

Type	Description
button	A clickable button whose action must be scripted. Its label is assigned by the VALUE attribute. If you want to use HTML to format the label of a button, use the BUTTON element instead.
checkbox	A free-standing checkbox that provides two states (active and inactive). Its label is created by HTML text before or after the INPUT element tag. The VALUE attribute value is submitted with a form, so you can have multiple checkboxes with the same name but different values if the server CGI script wants its data that way.
file	A button and field that lets the user select a local file for eventual uploading to the server. A click of the button generates a File dialog, and the name (or pathname) of the selected file appears in the field. The server must have a CGI script running to accept the incoming file at submission time.

Type	Description
hidden	An invisible field often used to carry over database or state data from submission to submission without bothering the user with its content (or having to store the temporary data on the server). The name/value pair is submitted with the form.
image	A graphical button whose sole action is to submit the form. The coordinate points x,y of the click on the image are submitted as two name/value pairs: inputName.x=n; inputName.y=m.
password	A text field that presents bullets or asterisks for each typed character to ensure over-the-shoulder privacy for the user. The plain-language text is submitted as the value for this element.
radio	One of a related group of on–off buttons. Assigning the same value to the NAME attribute of multiple radio buttons assembles them in a related group. Clicking on one button in the group activates it while unhighlighting all others. The VALUE attribute value is submitted with a form.
reset	A button whose sole job is to revert the form's elements to the values they had when the form initially loaded into the client. A custom label can be assigned via the VALUE attribute.
submit	A button whose sole job is to submit the form. A custom label can be assigned by the VALUE attribute. If NAME and VALUE attributes are assigned for the element, their values are submitted with the form.
text	A one-line field for typing text that gets submitted as the value of the element. For a multiple-line field, see the TEXTAREA element.

Example

```
<INPUT TYPE="button" VALUE="Toggle Sound" onClick="toggleSnd()">
<INPUT TYPE="checkbox" NAME="connections" VALUE="ISDN">ISDN
<INPUT TYPE="file" NAME="uploadFile">
<INPUT TYPE="hidden" NAME="prevState" VALUE="modify">
<INPUT TYPE="image" NAME="graphicSubmit" SRC="submit.jpg" HEIGHT=40
WIDTH=40>
<INPUT TYPE="password" NAME="password" MAXLENGTH=12 SIZE=20>
<INPUT TYPE="radio" NAME="creditCard" VALUE="Visa">Visa
<INPUT TYPE="reset">
<INPUT TYPE="submit" VALUE="Send Encrypted">
Social Security Number:<INPUT TYPE="text"NAME="ssn" VALUE="###-##-####"
onClick="validateSSN(this)">
```

Value

Any one of the known INPUT element types: button | checkbox | file | hidden | image | password | radio | reset | submit | text.

Default   text

Object Model Reference

NN   [window.]document.*formName*.*inputName*.type
            [window.]document.forms[i].elements[i].type

IE   [window.]document.*formName*.*inputName*.type
            [window.]document.forms[i].elements[i].type
            [window.]document.all.*elementID*.type

USEMAP

NN *n/a*   IE *n/a*   HTML *4*

USEMAP=" *mapURL*"   *Optional*

The HTML 4.0 specification lists the USEMAP attribute for an INPUT element of type image. In the future, this might lead to a link between image INPUT elements and the scriptable powers of client-side image maps (such as rollovers), but for now, it is unknown for sure how this attribute will be implemented in browsers.

VALUE

NN *all*   IE *all*   HTML *all*

VALUE=" *text*"   *Optional/Required*

Preassigns a value to an INPUT element that is submitted to the server as part of the name/value pair for the element. Some INPUT element types are not submitted (an unchecked radio button, for example), but any value you associate with all but the button or reset type INPUT element reaches the server when the element is submitted.

In the case of text and password INPUT elements, the VALUE attribute contains a default entry. As the user makes a change to the content of the text field, the value changes, although the source code does not. When a form is reset (via a reset INPUT element), the default values are put back into the text fields.

The VALUE attribute is required only for checkbox and radio INPUT elements. For INPUT elements that are rendered as standard clickable buttons, the VALUE attribute defines the label that appears on the button.

Input Types   All.

Example   `<INPUT TYPE="checkbox" NAME="connections" VALUE="ISDN">ISDN`

Value   Any text string.

Default   None.

Object Model Reference

NN   [window.]document.*formName*.*inputName*.value
            [window.]document.forms[i].elements[i].value

IE   [window.]document.*formName*.*inputName*.value
            [window.]document.forms[i].elements[i].value
            [window.]document.all.*elementID*.value

<INS>

NN *n/a*   IE *4*   HTML *4*

<INS>...</INS>   *End Tag: Required*

The INS element and its companion, DEL, define a format that shows which segments of a document's content have been marked up for insertion (or deletion) during the authoring process. This is far from a workflow management scheme, but in the hands of a supporting WYSIWYG HTML authoring tool, these elements can assist in controlling generational changes of a document in process.

Among the Version 4 browsers, only Internet Explorer supports the INS attribute. Text contained by this element is rendered underlined (whereas DEL elements are in a strikethrough style). The HTML 4.0 specification includes two potentially useful attributes (not in IE 4) for preserving hidden information about the date and time of the alteration and some descriptive text about the change.

Example

```
<P>Four score and
<DEL CITE="Fixed the math">eight</DEL><INS>seven</INS> years ago...</P>
```

Object Model Reference

IE   [window.]document.all.*elementID*

Attributes

CITE	DATETIME	ID	LANGUAGE	TITLE
CLASS	DIR	LANG	STYLE	

Event Handler Attributes

Handler	NN	IE	HTML
onClick	n/a	4	4
onDblClick	n/a	4	4
onDragStart	n/a	4	n/a
onHelp	n/a	4	n/a
onKeyDown	n/a	4	4
onKeyPress	n/a	4	4
onKeyUp	n/a	4	4
onMouseDown	n/a	4	4
onMouseMove	n/a	4	4
onMouseOut	n/a	4	4
onMouseOver	n/a	4	4
onMouseUp	n/a	4	4
onSelectStart	n/a	4	n/a

CITE   NN *n/a*   IE *n/a*   HTML *4*

CITE="*string*"   *Optional*

A description of the reason for the change or other notation to be associated with the element, but normally hidden from view. This information is meant to be used by authoring tools, rather than by visual browsers.

Example <INS CITE="Fixed the math --A.L.">seven</INS>

Value

Any string of characters. The string must be inside a matching pair of (single or double) quotation marks.

Default None.

DATETIME

DATETIME="*datetimeString*"   *Optional*

The date and time the insertion was made. This information is most likely to be added into a document with an HTML authoring tool designed to track content insertions and deletions. Data from this attribute can be recalled later as an audit trail to changes of the document. There can be only one DATETIME attribute value associated with a given INS element.

Example

```
<INS DATETIME="1998-09-11T20:03:32-08:00">SomeInsertedTextHere</INS>
```

Value

The DATETIME attribute requires a value in a special date-time format that conveys information about the date and time in such a way that the exact moment can be deduced from any time zone around the world. Syntax for the format is as follows:

*yyyy-MM-dd*T*hh:mm:ss*TZD

yyyy	Four-digit year
MM	Two-digit month (01 through 12)
dd	Two-digit date (01 through 31)
T	Uppercase "T" to separate date from time
hh	Two-digit hour in 24-hour time (00 through 23)
mm	Two-digit minute (00 through 59)
ss	Two-digit second (00 through 59)
TZD	Time Zone Designator

There are two formats for the Time Zone Designator. The first is simply the uppercase letter "Z", which stands for UTC (Coordinated Universal Time—also called "Zulu"). The other format indicates the offset from UTC that the time shown in *hh:mm:ss* represents. This time offset consists of a plus or minus symbol and another pair of *hh:mm* values. For time zones west of Greenwich Mean Time (which, for all practical purposes is the same as UTC), the operator is a negative sign because the main *hh:mm:ss* time is earlier than UTC; for time zones east of GMT, the offset is a positive value. For example, Pacific Standard Time is eight hours earlier than UTC: when it is 6:00 P.M. in the PST zone, it is 2:00 A.M. the next morning at UTC. Thus, the following examples all represent the exact same moment in time (Time Zone Designator shown in boldface for clarification only):

1998-09-12T02:00:00**Z**	UTC
1998-09-11T21:00:00**-05:00**	Eastern Standard Time
1998-09-11T18:00:00**-08:00**	Pacific Standard Time
1998-09-12T13:00:00**+11:00**	Sydney, Australia

For more details about this way of representing time, see the ISO-8601 standard.

Default   None.

<ISINDEX>

NN *all*   IE *all*   HTML *all*

<ISINDEX>   *End Tag: Forbidden*

The ISINDEX element is a longtime holdover from the earliest days of HTML and is deprecated in HTML 4.0 in favor of the text INPUT element. The ISINDEX element tag belongs in
the HEAD element. In modern browsers, it is rendered as a simple text field between two HR
elements. When a user types text into the field and presses the **Enter/Return** key, the
content of the field is URL encoded (with + symbols substituted for spaces) and sent to the
server with the URL of the current document. A CGI program on the server must know how
to process this URL and return HTML for display in the current window or frame.

Example

```
<HEAD>
<ISINDEX PROMPT="Enter a search string:">
</HEAD>
```

Object Model Reference

IE   [window.]document.all.*elementID*

Attributes

CLASS	ID	LANGUAGE	STYLE	TITLE
DIR	LANG	PROMPT		

PROMPT

NN *all*   IE *all*   HTML <4

PROMPT="*message*"   *Optional*

This attribute lets you assign the prompt message that appears with the element.

Example   <ISINDEX PROMPT="Enter a search string:">

Value   Any quoted string.

Default   None.

<KBD>

NN *all*   IE *all*   HTML *all*

<KBD>...</KBD>   *End Tag: Required*

The KBD element is one of a large group of elements that the HTML 4.0 recommendation
calls *phrase elements*. Such elements assign structural meaning to a designated portion of
the document. A KBD element is one that displays text that a user is supposed to type on
the keyboard, presumably to fill a text field or issue some command.

Browsers have free rein to determine how (or whether) to distinguish KBD element content
from the rest of the BODY element. Both Navigator and Internet Explorer elect to use a
monospace font for the text. This can be overridden with a style sheet as you see fit.

Example

```
<P>If you don't know the answer, type <KBD>NONE</KBD> into the text box.
</P>
```

Object Model Reference

IE   [window.]document.all.*elementID*

Attributes

| CLASS | ID | LANGUAGE | STYLE | TITLE |
| DIR | LANG | | | |

Event Handler Attributes

Handler	NN	IE	HTML
onClick	n/a	4	4
onDblClick	n/a	4	4
onDragStart	n/a	4	n/a
onHelp	n/a	4	n/a
onKeyDown	n/a	4	4
onKeyPress	n/a	4	4
onKeyUp	n/a	4	4
onMouseDown	n/a	4	4
onMouseMove	n/a	4	4
onMouseOut	n/a	4	4
onMouseOver	n/a	4	4
onMouseUp	n/a	4	4
onSelectStart	n/a	4	n/a

<KEYGEN>

NN *all*   IE *n/a*   HTML *n/a*

<KEYGEN>   *End Tag: Forbidden*

A KEYGEN element allows a form to be submitted with key encryption, where the server expects a form to be packaged with an encrypted key. The client browser must have a digital certificate installed. The user sees two results of including the KEYGEN element inside a FORM element. First, a select list of available encryption key sizes is rendered in the form where the KEYGEN element appears. When the user submits the form, the user may see one or more security-related dialogs for confirmation. This element builds on the public-key encryption systems built into Navigator.

Example
```
<FORM ...>
...
<KEYGEN NAME="encryptedOrder" CHALLENGE="39457582201">
</FORM>
```

Attributes

CHALLENGE   NAME

CHALLENGE

NN *all*   IE *n/a*   HTML *n/a*

CHALLENGE="*challengeString*"   *Optional*

If the server is equipped to interpret a challenge string for verification of an encrypted package, the CHALLENGE attribute is the challenge string.

Example `<KEYGEN NAME="encryptedOrder" CHALLENGE="39457582201">`

Value   Any string.

Default   Empty string.

NAME   NN *all*   IE *n/a*   HTML *n/a*

NAME=" *identifier*"   *Required*

Encrypting a form turns the entire form into a value that is part of a name/value pair. The NAME attribute assigns the "name" part of the name/value pair. If the server successfully decrypts the package, the individual form element name/value pairs are available to the server for further processing.

Example   <KEYGEN NAME="encryptedOrder" CHALLENGE="39457582201">

Value   Case-insensitive identifier.

Default   None.

<LABEL>   NN *n/a*   IE *4*   HTML *4*

<LABEL>...</LABEL>   *End Tag: Required*

The LABEL element defines a structure and container for the label associated with an INPUT element. Because the rendered labels for most form controls are not part of the element's tag, the LABEL attribute provides a way for a browser to clearly link label content to the control.

You have two ways to provide the association. One is to assign the ID attribute value of the control to the FOR attribute of the LABEL element. The other is to wrap the INPUT element inside a LABEL element. The latter is possible only if the label and control are part of running body content; if you must physically separate the label from the control because they exist inside separate TD elements of a table, you must use the FOR attribute linkage. Whether the label is rendered in front of or after the control depends entirely on the relative locations of the tags in the source code. A future application for this element is for text-to-speech browsers reading aloud the label for a control.

Example
```
<FORM>
<LABEL>Company:<INPUT TYPE="text" NAME="company"></LABEL><BR>
<LABEL FOR="stateEntry">State:</LABEL>
<INPUT TYPE="text" NAME="state" ID="stateEntry">
...
</FORM>
```

Object Model Reference

IE   [window.]document.all.*elementID*

Attributes

ACCESSKEY	DATAFORMATAS	FOR	LANGUAGE	TABINDEX
CLASS	DATASRC	ID	STYLE	TITLE
DATAFLD	DIR	LANG		

Event Handler Attributes

Handler	NN	IE	HTML
onBlur	n/a	n/a	4
onClick	n/a	4	4
onDblClick	n/a	4	4
onDragStart	n/a	4	n/a
onFocus	n/a	n/a	4
onHelp	n/a	4	n/a
onKeyDown	n/a	4	4
onKeyPress	n/a	4	4
onKeyUp	n/a	4	4
onMouseDown	n/a	4	4
onMouseMove	n/a	4	4
onMouseOut	n/a	4	4
onMouseOver	n/a	4	4
onMouseUp	n/a	4	4
onSelectStart	n/a	4	n/a

ACCESSKEY
NN *n/a*   IE *4*   HTML *4*

ACCESSKEY="*character*"   *Optional*

A single character key that brings focus to the associated **INPUT** element. The browser and operating system determine if the user must press a modifier key (e.g., **Ctrl**, **Alt**, or **Command**) with the access key to bring focus to the element. In IE 4/Windows, the **Alt** key is required, and the key is not case sensitive. This attribute does not work in IE 4/Mac.

Example   <LABEL FOR="stateEntry" ACCESSKEY="s">State:</LABEL>

Value   Single character of the document set.

Default   None.

Object Model Reference
IE   [window.]document.all.*elementID*.accessKey

DATAFLD
NN *n/a*   IE *4*   HTML *n/a*

DATAFLD="*columnName*"   *Optional*

Used with IE 4 data binding to associate a remote data source column name with the label of an **INPUT** element. The data source column must be either plain text or HTML (see **DATAFORMATAS**). A **DATASRC** attribute must also be set for the **LABEL** element.

Example
```
<LABEL FOR="stateEntry" DATASRC="#DBSRC3" DATAFLD="label"
DATAFORMATAS="HTML">
State:</LABEL>
```

Value   Case-sensitive identifier.

Default   None.

Object Model Reference

IE   [window.]document.all.*elementID*.dataFld

DATAFORMATAS   NN *n/a*   IE 4   HTML *n/a*

DATAFORMATAS="*dataType*"   *Optional*

Used with IE 4 data binding, this attribute advises the browser whether the source material
arriving from the data source is to be treated as plain text or as tagged HTML. This attribute
setting depends entirely on how the data source is constructed.

Example

```
<LABEL FOR="stateEntry" DATASRC="#DBSRC3" DATAFLD="label"
DATAFORMATAS="HTML">
State:</LABEL>
```

Value   IE 4 recognizes two possible settings: text | HTML.

Default   text

Object Model Reference

IE   [window.]document.all.*elementID*.dataFormatAs

DATASRC   NN *n/a*   IE 4   HTML *n/a*

DATASRC="*dataSourceName*"   *Optional*

Used with IE 4 data binding to specify the name of the remote ODBC data source (such as
an Oracle or SQL Server database) to be associated with the element. Content from the data
source is specified via the DATAFLD attribute.

Example

```
<LABEL FOR="stateEntry" DATASRC="#DBSRC3" DATAFLD="label"
DATAFORMATAS="HTML">
State:</LABEL>
```

Value   Case-sensitive identifier.

Default   None.

Object Model Reference

IE   [window.]document.all.*elementID*.dataSrc

FOR   NN *n/a*   IE 4   HTML 4

FOR="*inputElementIdentifier*"   *Optional*

A unique identifier that is also assigned to the ID attribute of the INPUT element to which
the label is to be associated. The FOR attribute is necessary only when you elect not to wrap
the INPUT element inside the LABEL element, in which case the FOR attribute performs the
binding between the two elements.

Example `<LABEL FOR="stateEntry">State:</LABEL>`

Value   Case-sensitive identifier.

Default   None.

Object Model Reference

IE   [window.]document.all.*elementID*.htmlFor

TABINDEX   NN *n/a*   IE *n/a*   HTML *4*

TABINDEX=integer   *Optional*

A number that indicates the sequence of this element within the tabbing order of all focusable elements in the document. Tabbing order follows a strict set of rules. Elements that
have values other than zero assigned to their TABINDEX attributes are first in line when a
user starts tabbing in a page. Focus starts with the element with the lowest TABINDEX value
and proceeds in order to the highest value, regardless of physical location on the page or in
the document. If two elements have the same TABINDEX values, the element that comes
earlier in the document receives focus first. Next come all elements that either don't support
the TABINDEX attribute or have the value set to zero. These elements receive focus in the
order in which they appear in the document.

Although this attribute is not yet implemented in browsers, the expected behavior is that
when a LABEL element receives focus, the focus shifts automatically to the associated
INPUT element.

Example   <LABEL FOR="stateEntry" TABINDEX=3>State:</LABEL>

Value   Any integer from 0 through 32767.

Default   None.

<LAYER>   NN *4*   IE *n/a*   HTML *n/a*

<LAYER>...</LAYER>   *End Tag: Required*

A LAYER element is a positionable element in Navigator's object model (e.g., like a block-
level element whose CSS position: attribute is set to absolute). As a result, many of the
attributes are named according to the Navigator way of positioning, sizing, and stacking
positionable elements. It is unlikely that the LAYER or the related ILAYER elements will be
adopted by the W3C, so you are encouraged to use CSS-Positioning syntax (which works
on both browser platforms) instead.

Content for a LAYER element can be read from a separate file (with the SRC attribute) or
wired into the current document by placing the HTML between the start and end tags. You
can include both types of content in the same LAYER element. Content from the SRC document is rendered first (as its own block-level element), with additional content starting on
its own line below the external content's rectangle.

A LAYER element can be positioned anywhere within a document and can overlap content
belonging to other layers (including the base document layer). Under link or script control,
content for an individual layer can be changed without having to reload the other content
on the page. Moreover, LAYER elements may be nested inside one another. See Chapter 5,
Making Content Dynamic, for more details.

Example

<LAYER BGCOLOR="yellow" SRC="instrux.html" WIDTH=200 HEIGHT=300></LAYER>

Object Model Reference

NN   [window.]document.*layerName*

Attributes

ABOVE	BGCOLOR	ID	PAGEY	VISIBILITY
BACKGROUND	CLIP	LEFT	SRC	WIDTH
BELOW	HEIGHT	PAGEX	TOP	Z-INDEX

Event Handler Attributes

Handler	NN	IE	HTML
onBlur	4	n/a	n/a
onFocus	4	n/a	n/a
onLoad	4	n/a	n/a
onMouseDown	4	n/a	n/a
onMouseOut	4	n/a	n/a
onMouseOver	4	n/a	n/a
onMouseUp	4	n/a	n/a

ABOVE   NN *4*   IE *n/a*   HTML *n/a*

ABOVE="*layerID*"   *Optional*

Names the positionable element that is to be above (in front of) the current **LAYER** in the stacking order. This is a different way to set the **Z-INDEX** attribute that does not rely on an arbitrary numbering system. If you use the **ABOVE** attribute, do not use the **BELOW** or **Z-INDEX** attribute for the same **LAYER** element.

Example

```
<LAYER ID="instrux" BGCOLOR="yellow" SRC="instrux.html" ABOVE="help1"
WIDTH=200 HEIGHT=300>
</LAYER>
```

Value   Case-sensitive identifier.

Default   None.

Object Model Reference

NN   [window.]document.*layerName*.above

BACKGROUND   NN *4*   IE *n/a*   HTML *n/a*

BACKGROUND="*URL*"   *Optional*

Specifies an image file that is used as a backdrop to the text and other content of the **LAYER** element. Unlike normal images that get loaded into browser content, a background image loads in its original size (without scaling) and tiles to fill the available layer space. Smaller images download faster but are obviously repeated more often in the background. Animated GIFs are also allowable but very distracting to the reader. When selecting a background image, be sure it is very muted in comparison to the main content so that the content stands out clearly. Background images, if used at all, should be extremely subtle.

Example

```
<LAYER BACKGROUND="blueCrinkle.jpg" SRC="instrux.html" WIDTH=200
HEIGHT=300>
</LAYER>
```

Value   Any valid URL to an image file, including complete and relative URLs.

Default   None.

Object Model Reference

NN   [window.]document.*layerName*.background

BELOW   NN *4*   IE *n/a*   HTML *n/a*

BELOW="*layerID*"   *Optional*

Names the positionable element that is to be below (behind) the current LAYER in the stacking order. This is a different way to set the Z-INDEX attribute that does not rely on an arbitrary numbering system. If you use the BELOW attribute, do not use the ABOVE or Z-INDEX attribute for the same LAYER element.

Example

```
<LAYER BGCOLOR="yellow" SRC="instrux.html" WIDTH=200 HEIGHT=300
BELOW="thankyou">
</LAYER>
```

Value   Case-sensitive identifier.

Default   None.

Object Model Reference

NN   [window.]document.*layerName*.below

BGCOLOR   NN *4*   IE *n/a*   HTML *n/a*

BGCOLOR="*colorTripletOrName*"   *Optional*

Establishes a fill color (behind the text and other content) for the entire layer rectangle. If you combine a BGCOLOR and BACKGROUND, any transparent areas of the background image let the background color show through.

Example

```
<LAYER BGCOLOR="yellow" SRC="instrux.html" WIDTH=200 HEIGHT=300></LAYER>
```

Value

A hexadecimal triplet or plain-language color name. A setting of empty is interpreted as "#000000" (black). See Appendix A for acceptable plain-language color names.

Default   Varies with operating system.

Object Model Reference

NN   [window.]document.*layerName*.bgColor

CLIP
NN 4   IE *n/a*   HTML *n/a*

CLIP="[*leftPixel*, *topPixel*,] *rightPixel*, *bottomPixel*"   *Optional*

A clipping region is a rectangular view to the full LAYER content. Only content that is within the clipping rectangle can be seen on the page. The default value of the CLIP attribute is either the default size of the content or the LAYER element's width by the automatically flowing content length. Setting the CLIP attribute lets you rein in long content that might flow beyond a fixed rectangle desired for the page design.

Example
```
<LAYER BGCOLOR="yellow" SRC="instrux.html" CLIP="50,50" WIDTH=200
HEIGHT=300>
</LAYER>
```

Value
CLIP attribute values are pixel measures from the top and left edges of the element as it flows in the document. The order of values is clockwise from the left edge, around the rectangle sides: left, top, right, bottom. If you supply only two values, Navigator assumes the left and top values are zero, meaning that you wish to adjust only the right and bottom edges. Thus, a setting of "50,50" means that the clipping region is 50-pixels square, starting at the top-left corner of the layer's rectangle. If you want the same size view starting 10 pixels in from the left, the CLIP attribute setting becomes "10,0,60,50".

Default   Naturally flowing viewing area of LAYER content.

Object Model Reference
NN   [window.]document.*layerName*.clip.left
            [window.]document.*layerName*.clip.top
            [window.]document.*layerName*.clip.right
            [window.]document.*layerName*.clip.bottom

HEIGHT, WIDTH
NN 4   IE *n/a*   HTML *n/a*

HEIGHT="*length*"   *Optional*
WIDTH="*length*"

Define the minimum size of the LAYER element. When you add content to the layer during initial loading, however, the attribute settings do not restrict the amount of the content that is visible along either axis. For example, if you display an image in a LAYER that is 120 pixels wide by 90 pixels high, the actual visible size of a LAYER element whose HEIGHT and WIDTH attributes are set to a smaller size expands to allow the full image to appear. The same happens to text or other content: the viewable region expands to allow all content to appear. To restrict the visible portion of the content, set the CLIP attribute.

Setting the HEIGHT and WIDTH attributes to specific sizes is helpful when you are creating a colored or patterned rectangle (via the BGCOLOR or BACKGROUND attributes) to act as an underlying layer beneath some other positioned content. Without content pushing on the edges of the LAYER, the HEIGHT and WIDTH attributes set the clipping region to their sizes.

Example
```
<LAYER BGCOLOR="yellow" SRC="instrux.html" WIDTH=200 HEIGHT=300></LAYER>
```

Value

Positive integer values (optionally quoted) or percentage values (quoted). You can reduce both values to zero to not only hide the element (which you can also do with the VISIBILITY attribute), but also prevent the element from occupying any page space.

Default   Naturally flowing viewing area of LAYER content.

Object Model Reference

NN   [window.]document.*layerName*.height
            [window.]document.*layerName*.width

ID   NN *4*   IE *n/a*   HTML *n/a*

ID="*elementIdentifier*"   *Optional*

A unique identifier that distinguishes this element from all the rest in the document. This is the identifier used as values for the ABOVE and BELOW attributes. Scripts also use the ID attribute value as the LAYER element's name for object references.

Example

```
<LAYER ID="oldYeller" BGCOLOR="yellow" SRC="instrux.html" WIDTH=200
HEIGHT=300>
</LAYER>
```

Value   Case-sensitive identifier.

Default   None.

Object Model Reference

IE   [window.]document.*layerName*.name

LEFT, TOP   NN *4*   IE *n/a*   HTML *n/a*

LEFT="*pixelCount*"   *Optional*
TOP="*pixelCount*"

Define the positioned offset of the left and top edges of the layer relative to the spot in the document where the LAYER element would normally appear in source code order. This precise location relative to the page varies unless you also set the PAGEX and PAGEY attributes, which absolutely position the element in the document space. Unlike what it does for the ILAYER element, Navigator does not preserve the space in the document where a LAYER element appears. The element is placed in its own plane, and the surrounding source code content is cinched up—usually overlapping the LAYER content unless the layer is positioned elsewhere.

Example

```
<LAYER BGCOLOR="yellow" SRC="instrux.html" WIDTH=200 HEIGHT=300 LEFT=10
TOP=50>
</LAYER>
```

Value   Positive integer values (optionally quoted).

Default   0

Object Model Reference

NN   [window.]document.*layerName*.left
      [window.]document.*layerName*.top

PAGEX, PAGEY   NN *4*   IE *n/a*   HTML *n/a*

PAGEX="*pixelCount*"   *Optional*
PAGEY="*pixelCount*"

To truly position a LAYER element with repeatable accuracy, you can use the top-left corner of the document (page) as the point of reference. When you set the PAGEX and/or PAGEY attributes, you establish an offset for the left and top edges of the LAYER element relative to the corresponding edges of the entire document. Therefore, the zero point for a vertically scrolled page may be above the visible area of the browser window.

Example

```
<LAYER BGCOLOR="yellow" SRC="instrux.html" WIDTH=200 HEIGHT=300 PAGEX=50
  PAGEY=350>
</LAYER>
```

Value   Positive integer values (optionally quoted).

Default   0

Object Model Reference

NN   [window.]document.*layerName*.pageX
      [window.]document.*layerName*.pageY

SRC   NN *4*   IE *n/a*   HTML *n/a*

SRC="*URL*"   *Optional*

To load the content of an external HTML file into a LAYER element, assign the URL of that file to the SRC attribute. Any HTML content between the LAYER start and end tags is rendered on the page after the content is loaded from the SRC URL. If you omit the SRC attribute, only content between the tags is rendered. Scripts can change the corresponding object property (src) after the document has loaded to dynamically change content within the LAYER element (without reloading the main document).

Example

```
<LAYER BGCOLOR="yellow" SRC="instrux.html" WIDTH=200 HEIGHT=300</LAYER>
```

Value   A complete or relative URL.

Default   None.

Object Model Reference

NN   [window.]document.*layerName*.src

TOP

See LEFT.

VISIBILITY

NN *4*   IE *n/a*   HTML *n/a*

VISIBILITY=" *visibilityConstant*"   *Optional*

Determines whether Navigator displays the LAYER element. The default behavior is for a layer to inherit the VISIBILITY attribute of its next outermost (parent) layer. For a LAYER element that is part of the basic document body, this means that the layer is seen by default (the base layer is always visible). To hide a layer when the page loads, set the VISIBILITY attribute to "hidden". You need set the attribute to "show" only if the LAYER element is nested within another LAYER (or ILAYER) whose VISIBILITY value is set to (or is inherited as) "hidden".

Example

```
<LAYER BGCOLOR="yellow" SRC="instrux.html" WIDTH=200 HEIGHT=300
PAGEX=50 PAGEY=350 VISIBILITY="hidden">
</LAYER>
```

Value   One of the accepted constants: hidden | inherit | visible

Default   inherit

Object Model Reference

NN   [window.]document.*layerName*.visibility

WIDTH

See HEIGHT.

Z-INDEX

NN *4*   IE *n/a*   HTML *n/a*

Z-INDEX=" *layerNumber*"   *Optional*

Controls the positioning of layers along the Z-axis (front-to-back) of the document relative to the next outermost layer container. When the Z-INDEX values of two or more positionable elements within the same container (such as the base document layer) are identical numbers, the loading order of the elements in the HTML source code controls the stacking order, with the later elements stacked in front of earlier ones. The default Z-INDEX value for all positionable elements is zero. Therefore, if you want only one positionable element to appear in front of all the others that stack in their default order, you simply assign any positive value (even 1) to that standout element. Stacking order of positionable elements can be changed on-the-fly via scripting.

Example

```
<LAYER BGCOLOR="yellow" SRC="instrux.html" WIDTH=200 HEIGHT=300 Z-INDEX=1>
</LAYER>
```

Value   Any integer.

Default   0

Object Model Reference

NN   [window.]document.*layerName*.zIndex

<LEGEND>

NN *n/a*   IE *4*   HTML *4*

`<LEGEND>...</LEGEND>`   *End Tag: Required*

The `LEGEND` element acts as a label for a `FIELDSET` element. In visual browsers, this usually means that the label is visually associated with the group border rendered for the `FIELDSET` element. Internet Explorer 4 builds the `LEGEND` element into the `FIELDSET` border. A text-to-speech browser might read the label aloud as a user navigates through a form. In Internet Explorer, the `LEGEND` element must come immediately after the start tag of the `FIELDSET` element for the association to stick. Because the content of the `LEGEND` element is HTML content, you can assign styles to make the label stand out, if you like.

Example

```
<FORM METHOD=POST ACTION="...">
<FIELDSET>
<LEGEND>Credit Card Information</LEGEND>
...inputElementsHere...
</FIELDSET>
</FORM>
```

Object Model Reference

IE   [window.]document.all.*elementID*

Attributes

ACCESSKEY	*CLASS*	*ID*	*LANGUAGE*	TITLE
ALIGN	*DIR*	*LANG*	*STYLE*	

Event Handler Attributes

Handler	NN	IE	HTML
onClick	n/a	4	4
onDblClick	n/a	4	4
onDragStart	n/a	4	n/a
onHelp	n/a	4	n/a
onKeyDown	n/a	4	4
onKeyPress	n/a	4	4
onKeyUp	n/a	4	4
onMouseDown	n/a	4	4
onMouseMove	n/a	4	4
onMouseOut	n/a	4	4
onMouseOver	n/a	4	4
onMouseUp	n/a	4	4

ACCESSKEY

NN *n/a*   IE *n/a*   HTML *4*

`ACCESSKEY="`*character*`"`   *Optional*

A single character key that brings focus to the first focusable control of the form associated with the `LEGEND` element. The browser and operating system determine if the user must press a modifier key (e.g., **Ctrl**, **Alt**, or **Command**) with the access key to bring focus to the element. In IE 4/Windows, the **Alt** key is required, and the key is not case sensitive. This attribute does not work in IE 4/Mac.

Example `<LEGEND ACCESSKEY="c">Credit Card Information</LEGEND>`

Value   Single character of the document set.

Default   None.

ALIGN

NN *n/a*   IE *4*   HTML *4*

`ALIGN="`*where*`"`   *Optional*

Controls the alignment of the `LEGEND` element with respect to the containing `FIELDSET` element. The permissible values do not always work as planned in Internet Explorer 4. For example, the `bottom` value displays the label at the top left of the fieldset rectangle—so does the `top` value, although it is supposed to be centered along the top. The other values (`center`, `left`, and `right`) work as expected, but on the Macintosh, the `center` and `right` settings inexplicably widen the fieldset rectangle. Be sure to check your desired setting on both operating system platforms.

The `ALIGN` attribute is deprecated in HTML 4.0 in favor of style sheets. But even a style sheet won't position a label along the bottom of a fieldset in Internet Explorer 4.

Example   `<LEGEND ALIGN="right">Credit Card Information</LEGEND>`

Value

Allowed values in HTML 4.0 are `bottom` | `left` | `right` | `top`. IE 4 adds `center`.

Default   `left`

Object Model Reference

IE   `[window.]document.all.`*elementID*`.align`

TITLE

NN *n/a*   IE *4*   HTML *4*

`TITLE="`*advisoryText*`"`   *Optional*

An advisory description of the element. In Internet Explorer 4, the title is rendered as a tooltip when the cursor rests on the element for a moment. The `TITLE` attribute of a `LEGEND` overrides the `TITLE` setting for the entire `FIELDSET`.

Example   `<LEGEND TITLE="Credit Card Info">...</LEGEND>`

Value

Any string of characters. The string must be inside a matching pair of (single or double) quotation marks.

Default   None.

Object Model Reference

IE   `[window.]document.all.`*elementID*`.title`

<LI>

<LI>...</LI>   *End Tag: Optional*

The LI element is a single list item that is nested inside an OL or UL list container. The outer container determines whether the LI item is preceded with a number or letter (indicating sequence within an order) or a symbol that doesn't connote any particular order. A special category of style sheet attributes are devoted to list formatting. Therefore, a number of formatting attributes for LI, OL, and UL elements are deprecated in HTML 4.0.

If you apply a style sheet rule to an LI element to adjust the color in Navigator 4, only the leading symbol is colored. To color the text as well, wrap the LI element inside a SPAN element and apply the style to the SPAN element. This works the same way in Navigator and Internet Explorer.

Example

```
<UL>
    <LI>Larry
    <LI>Moe
    <LI>Curly
</UL>
```

Object Model Reference

IE   [window.]document.all.*elementID*

Attributes

CLASS	*ID*	*LANGUAGE*	*TITLE*	*VALUE*
DIR	*LANG*	*STYLE*	*TYPE*	

Event Handler Attributes

Handler	NN	IE	HTML
onClick	n/a	4	4
onDblClick	n/a	4	4
onDragStart	n/a	4	n/a
onHelp	n/a	4	n/a
onKeyDown	n/a	4	4
onKeyPress	n/a	4	4
onKeyUp	n/a	4	4
onMouseDown	n/a	4	4
onMouseMove	n/a	4	4
onMouseOut	n/a	4	4
onMouseOver	n/a	4	4
onMouseUp	n/a	4	4
onSelectStart	n/a	4	n/a

TYPE

TYPE="*labelType*"   *Optional*

The TYPE attribute provides some flexibility in how the leading symbol or sequence number is displayed in the browser. Values are divided into two groups, with one group each dedicated to OL and UL items. For an unordered list (UL), you can specify whether the leading symbol should be a disc, circle, or square; for an ordered list (OL), the choices are among letters (uppercase or lowercase), Roman numerals (uppercase or lowercase), or Arabic numerals. The TYPE attribute is deprecated in HTML 4.0 in favor of the list-style-type: style sheet attribute.

For no apparent reason, the square type of unordered list item displays as solid in Windows browsers and as hollow in Macintosh browsers.

Be aware that in current browser implementations, the TYPE attribute for a LI element sets the type for subsequent LI elements in the list unless overridden by a TYPE attribute setting in another LI element. In general, it is best to set the TYPE attribute of the OL or UL element and let that setting govern all nested elements.

Example `<LI TYPE="square">Chicken Curry`

Value

When contained by a UL element, possible values are disc | circle | square. When contained by an OL element, possible values are A | a | I | i | 1. Sequencing is performed automatically as follows:

Type	Example
A	A, B, C, ...
a	a, b, c, ...
I	I, II, III, ...
i	i, ii, iii, ...
1	1, 2, 3, ...

Default 1 and disc.

Object Model Reference

IE   [window.]document.all.*elementID*.type

VALUE

VALUE="*number*"   *Optional*

The VALUE attribute applies only when the LI element is nested inside an OL element. You can manually set the number used as a starting point for the sequencing of ordered list items. This can come in handy when you need to break up an OL element with some running text that is not part of the list.

Even though the value assigned to this attribute is a number, it does not affect the TYPE setting. For example, setting VALUE to 3 when TYPE is A means that the sequence starts from that LI element with the letter C.

Example `<LI VALUE=3>Insert Tab C into Slot M. Tighten with a wingnut.`

Value   Any positive integer.

Default   1

Object Model Reference

IE   [window.]document.all.*elementID*.value

<LINK>   NN *4*   IE *3*   HTML *all*

`<LINK>...</LINK>`   *End Tag: Forbidden*

Unlike the A element (informally called a link when it contains an HREF attribute), the LINK element belongs inside the HEAD element and is a place for the document to establish links with external documents, such as style sheet definition files or font definition files. By and large, browsers have yet to exploit the intended powers of this element. A variety of attributes let the author establish relationships between the current document and potentially related documents. In theory, some of these relationships could be rendered as part of the document or browser controls. Implementations of this element in both Navigator 4 and Internet Explorer 4 are rather weak compared to the HTML 4.0 specification. At the same time, several attributes (and all event handlers) defined in the HTML 4.0 specification aren't very helpful because they more typically apply to elements that actually display content on the page. No explicit document content is rendered as a result of the LINK element. Some of those attributes may be listed by mistake or merely for consistency. They are listed here, but because they are not implemented in browsers, they are supplied for informational purposes only.

Example

```
<HEAD>
<TITLE>Section 3</TITLE>
<LINK REV="Prev" HREF="sect2.html">
<LINK REL="Next" HREF="sect4.html">
<LINK REL="stylesheet" TYPE="text/css" HREF="myStyles.css">
</HEAD>
```

Object Model Reference

IE   [window.]document.all.*elementID*

Attributes

CHARSET	HREF	*LANG*	REV	TARGET
CLASS	HREFLANG	MEDIA	SRC	*TITLE*
DIR	ID	REL	*STYLE*	TYPE
DISABLED				

Event Handler Attributes

Handler	NN	IE	HTML
onClick	n/a	n/a	4
onDblClick	n/a	n/a	4
onKeyDown	n/a	n/a	4
onKeyPress	n/a	n/a	4
onKeyUp	n/a	n/a	4
onMouseDown	n/a	n/a	4
onMouseMove	n/a	n/a	4
onMouseOut	n/a	n/a	4
onMouseOver	n/a	n/a	4
onMouseUp	n/a	n/a	4

CHARSET

NN *n/a*   IE *n/a*   HTML 4

CHARSET="*characterSet*"   *Optional*

Character encoding of the content at the other end of the link.

Example `<LINK CHARSET="csISO5427Cyrillic" HREF="moscow.html">`

Value

Case-insensitive alias from the character set registry (*ftp://ftp.isi.edu/in-notes/iana/ assignments/character-sets*).

Default   Determined by browser.

DISABLED

NN *n/a*   IE *4*   HTML *n/a*

DISABLED   *Optional*

The presence of this attribute disables the **LINK** element. Unlike when this attribute is applied to content-holding elements, in this case no content is grayed out in response.

Example `<LINK REL="Index" HREF="indexList.html" DISABLED>`

Value   The presence of this attribute sets its value to **true**.

Default   `false`

Object Model Reference

IE   [window.]document.all.*elementID*.disabled

HREF

NN *n/a*   IE *3*   HTML *all*

HREF="*URI*"   *Required*

The URI of the destination of a link. Navigator 4 uses the **SRC** attribute for this purpose. Include both attributes for a cross-browser implementation.

Example `<LINK REL="Prev" HREF="sect2.html">`

Value   Any valid URI, including complete and relative URLs.

Default   None.

Object Model Reference

IE   [window.]document.all.*elementID*.href

HREFLANG

NN *n/a*   IE *n/a*   HTML *4*

HREFLANG="*languageCode*"   *Optional*

The language code of the content at the destination of a link. Requires that the **HREF** attribute also be set. This attribute is primarily an advisory attribute to help a browser prepare itself for a new language set if the browser is so enabled.

Example `<LINK HREFLANG="HI" HREF="hindi/Chap3.html">`

Value   Case-insensitive language code.

Default   Browser default.

MEDIA

NN *n/a*   IE *n/a*   HTML *4*

MEDIA="*descriptorList*"   *Optional*

Sets the intended output device for the content of the destination document pointed to by the HREF attribute. The MEDIA attribute looks forward to the day when browsers are able to tailor content to specific kinds of devices such as pocket computers, text-to-speech digitizers, or fuzzy television sets. The HTML 4.0 specification defines a number of constant values for anticipated devices, but the list is open-ended, allowing future browsers to tailor output to yet other kinds of media and devices.

Example
```
<LINK REL="Glossary" HREF="gloss.html" MEDIA="screen, tv, handheld">
```

Value

Case-sensitive constant values. Multiple values can be grouped together in a comma-delimited list within a quoted string. Values defined in HTML 4.0 are all | aura | braille | handheld | print | projection | screen | tty | tv .

Default   screen

REL

NN *4*   IE *3*   HTML *3.2*

REL="*linkTypes*"   *Optional*

Defines the relationship between the current element and the destination of the link. The HTML 4.0 recommendation defines several link types; it is up to the browser to determine how to employ the value. The element must include an HREF attribute for the REL attribute to be applied.

Example   `<LINK REL="Next" HREF="sect6.html">`

Value

Case-insensitive, space-delimited list of HTML 4.0 standard link types applicable to the element. Internet Explorer 4 understands only stylesheet; Navigator 4 recognizes stylesheet and fontdef. HTML 4.0-sanctioned link types are:

alternate	contents	index	start
appendix	copyright	next	stylesheet
bookmark	glossary	prev	subsection
chapter	help	section	

Default   None.

Object Model Reference

IE   [window.]document.all.*elementID*.rel

REV

NN *n/a*   IE *n/a*   HTML 4

REV=" *linkTypes*" *Optional*

A reverse link relationship. Like the **REL** attribute, the **REV** attribute's capabilities are defined by the browser, particularly with regard to how the browser interprets and renders the various link types available in the HTML 4.0 specification. Given two documents (A and B) containing links that point to each other, the **REV** value of B is designed to express the same relationship between the two documents as denoted by the **REL** attribute in A.

Example `<LINK REV="Prev" HREF="sect4.html">`

Value

Case-insensitive, space-delimited list of HTML 4.0 standard link types applicable to the element. See the **REL** attribute for sanctioned link types.

Default None.

SRC

NN *4*   IE *n/a*   HTML *n/a*

SRC=" *URL*" *Optional*

The URL of the destination of a link. Internet Explorer 4 and HTML 4.0 use the **HREF** attribute for this purpose. Include both attributes for a cross-browser implementation.

Example `<LINK REL="fontdef" HREF="fonts/garamond.pfr">`

Value Any valid URL, including complete and relative URLs.

Default None.

TARGET

NN *n/a*   IE *n/a*   HTML 4

TARGET=" *windowOrFrameName*" *Optional*

Presumably, the **TARGET** attribute is provided in HTML 4.0 as a way to specify the destination for display of a document at the other end of the **HREF** attribute of the **LINK** element. No browser yet implements this attribute because the **LINK** element so far does not link up to content that can be displayed.

Value

Case-sensitive identifier when the frame or window name has been assigned via the target element's **NAME** attribute. Four reserved target names act as constants:

_blank   Browser creates a new window for the destination document.

_parent   Destination document replaces the current frame's framesetting document (if one exists; otherwise, it is treated as **_self**).

_self   Destination document replaces the current document in its window or frame.

_top   Destination document is to occupy the entire browser window, replacing any and all framesets that may be loaded (also treated as **_self** if there are no framesets defined in the window).

Default _self

HTML Reference

TYPE   NN *4*   IE *4*   HTML *4*

TYPE="*MIMEType*"   *Optional*

An advisory about the content type of the destination document or resource. In practice, this attribute so far is used to prepare the browser for the style sheet type being linked to.

Example

```
<LINK REL="stylesheet" TYPE="text/css" HREF="styles/mainStyle.html">
```

Value

Case-insensitive MIME type. A catalog of registered MIME types is available from *ftp:// ftp.isi.edu/in-notes/iana/assignments/media-types/*.

Default   None.

Object Model Reference

IE   [window.]document.all.*elementID*.type

<LISTING>   NN *all*   IE *all*   HTML *<4*

<LISTING>...</LISTING>   *End Tag: Required*

The LISTING element displays its content in a monospace font as a block element, as in computer code listings rendered 132 columns wide. In most browsers, the font size is also reduced from the default size. Browsers observe carriage returns and other whitespace in element content. This element has been long deprecated in HTML and has even been removed from the HTML 4.0 specification. You are encouraged to use the PRE element instead.

Example

```
<LISTING>
&lt;SCRIPT LANGUAGE="JavaScript"&gt;
   document.write("Hello, world.")
&lt;/SCRIPT&gt;
</LISTING>
```

Object Model Reference

IE   [window.]document.all.*elementID*

Attributes

CLASS	LANG	LANGUAGE	STYLE	TITLE
ID				

Event Handler Attributes

Handler	NN	IE	HTML
onClick	n/a	4	n/a
onDblClick	n/a	4	n/a
onDragStart	n/a	4	n/a
onHelp	n/a	4	n/a
onKeyDown	n/a	4	n/a
onKeyPress	n/a	4	n/a

Handler	NN	IE	HTML
onKeyUp	n/a	4	n/a
onMouseDown	n/a	4	n/a
onMouseMove	n/a	4	n/a
onMouseOut	n/a	4	n/a
onMouseOver	n/a	4	n/a
onMouseUp	n/a	4	n/a
onSelectStart	n/a	4	n/a

<MAP>

NN *all*   IE *all*   HTML *3.2*

<MAP>...</MAP>   *End Tag: Required*

A MAP element is a container for AREA elements that define the location and links of hotspots of client-side image maps. The primary purpose of the MAP element is to associate an identifier (the NAME attribute) that the USEMAP attribute points to when turning an IMG element into a client-side image map. Most other attributes are style-related and may be applied to the MAP element so that they are inherited by elements nested within.

Example

```
<IMG SRC="images/logo.gif" ALT="Scroll to the bottom for navigation links."
HEIGHT=300 WIDTH=250 USEMAP="#navigation">
<MAP NAME="navigation">
<AREA SHAPE="rect" COORDS="0,0,100,100" HREF="products.html">
<AREA SHAPE="rect" COORDS="0,100,300,100" HREF="support.html">
</MAP>
```

Object Model Reference

IE   [window.]document.all.*elementID*

Attributes

CLASS	*ID*	*LANGUAGE*	*STYLE*	*TITLE*
DIR	*LANG*	*NAME*		

Event Handler Attributes

Handler	NN	IE	HTML
onClick	n/a	4	4
onDblClick	n/a	4	4
onDragStart	n/a	4	n/a
onHelp	n/a	4	n/a
onKeyDown	n/a	4	4
onKeyPress	n/a	4	4
onKeyUp	n/a	4	4
onMouseDown	n/a	4	4
onMouseMove	n/a	4	4
onMouseOut	n/a	4	4
onMouseOver	n/a	4	4

Handler	NN	IE	HTML
onMouseUp	n/a	4	4
onSelectStart	n/a	4	n/a

NAME

NN *all*   IE *all*   HTML *3.2*

NAME="*identifier*"   *Required*

The identifier to which the USEMAP attribute of an IMG element points. Because the USEMAP attribute is actually a URL type, its value resembles that of a link to an anchor: the name is preceded by a hash symbol (only in the USEMAP attribute).

Example   <MAP NAME="navigation"> ...</MAP>

Value   Case-sensitive unique identifier.

Default   None.

Object Model Reference

IE   [window.]document.all.*elementID*.name

<MARQUEE>

NN *n/a*   IE *3*   HTML *n/a*

<MARQUEE>...</MARQUEE>   *End Tag: Optional*

The MARQUEE element is unique to Internet Explorer. It displays HTML content in a scrolling region on the page. Scrolled content goes between the start and end tags. There is no corresponding element in Navigator, although the effect can be duplicated in a cross-browser fashion with a Java applet or more cumbersomely through Dynamic HTML.

Example

```
<MARQUEE BEHAVIOR="slide" DIRECTION="left" WIDTH=250 BGCOLOR="white">
Check out our monthly specials.
</MARQUEE>
```

Object Model Reference

IE   [window.]document.all.*elementID*

Attributes

BEHAVIOR	DATAFORMATAS	HSPACE	LOOP	TITLE
BGCOLOR	DATASRC	ID	SCROLLAMOUNT	TRUESPEED
CLASS	DIRECTION	LANG	SCROLLDELAY	VSPACE
DATAFLD	HEIGHT	LANGUAGE	STYLE	WIDTH

Event Handler Attributes

Handler	NN	IE	HTML
onAfterUpdate	n/a	4	n/a
onBlur	n/a	4	n/a
onBounce	n/a	4	n/a
onClick	n/a	4	n/a
onDblClick	n/a	4	n/a

Handler	NN	IE	HTML
onDragStart	n/a	4	n/a
onFinish	n/a	4	n/a
onFocus	n/a	4	n/a
onHelp	n/a	4	n/a
onKeyDown	n/a	4	n/a
onKeyPress	n/a	4	n/a
onKeyUp	n/a	4	n/a
onMouseDown	n/a	4	n/a
onMouseMove	n/a	4	n/a
onMouseOut	n/a	4	n/a
onMouseOver	n/a	4	n/a
onMouseUp	n/a	4	n/a
onResize	n/a	4	n/a
onRowEnter	n/a	4	n/a
onRowExit	n/a	4	n/a
onSelectStart	n/a	4	n/a
onStart	n/a	4	n/a

BEHAVIOR

NN *n/a*   IE *3*   HTML *n/a*

BEHAVIOR="*motionType*"   *Optional*

Sets the motion of the content within the rectangular space set aside for the MARQUEE element. You have a choice of three motion types.

Example

```
<MARQUEE BEHAVIOR="slide" DIRECTION="left" WIDTH=250 BGCOLOR="white">
...
</MARQUEE>
```

Value   One of the case-insensitive MARQUEE element motion types:

alternate   Content alternates between marching left and right.

scroll   Content scrolls (according to the DIRECTION attribute) into view and out of view before starting again.

slide   Content scrolls (according to the DIRECTION attribute) into view, stops at the end of its run, blanks, and then starts again.

Default   scroll

Object Model Reference

IE   [window.]document.all.*elementID*.behavior

BGCOLOR

NN *n/a*   IE *3*   HTML *n/a*

BGCOLOR="*colorTripletOrName*"   *Optional*

Establishes a fill color (behind the text and other content) for the rectangular space reserved for the MARQUEE element.

Example

```
<MARQUEE BEHAVIOR="slide" DIRECTION="left" WIDTH=250 BGCOLOR="white">
...
</MARQUEE>
```

Value

A hexadecimal triplet or plain-language color name. A setting of empty is interpreted as "#000000" (black). See Appendix A for acceptable plain-language color names.

Default   Varies with browser, browser version, and operating system.

Object Model Reference

IE   [window.]document.all.*elementID*.bgColor

DATAFLD   NN *n/a*   IE *4*   HTML *n/a*

DATAFLD="*columnName*"   *Optional*

Used with IE 4 data binding to associate a remote data source column name with the content scrolled by the MARQUEE element. The data source column must be either plain text or HTML (see DATAFORMATAS). A DATASRC attribute must also be set for the MARQUEE element.

Example

```
<MARQUEE BEHAVIOR="slide" DIRECTION="left" WIDTH=200
DATASRC="#DBSRC3" DATAFLD="news" DATAFORMATAS="HTML">
...
</MARQUEE>
```

Value   Case-sensitive identifier.

Default   None.

Object Model Reference

IE   [window.]document.all.*elementID*.dataFld

DATAFORMATAS   NN *n/a*   IE *4*   HTML *n/a*

DATAFORMATAS="*dataType*"   *Optional*

Used with IE 4 data binding, this attribute advises the browser whether the source material arriving from the data source is to be treated as plain text or as tagged HTML. This attribute setting depends entirely on how the data source is constructed.

Example

```
<MARQUEE BEHAVIOR="slide" DIRECTION="left" WIDTH=200
DATASRC="#DBSRC3" DATAFLD="news" DATAFORMATAS="HTML">
...
</MARQUEE>
```

Value   IE 4 recognizes two possible settings: text | HTML.

Default   text

Object Model Reference

IE   [window.]document.all.*elementID*.dataFormatAs

DATASRC
NN *n/a*   IE *4*   HTML *n/a*

DATASRC="*dataSourceName*"   *Optional*

Used with IE 4 data binding to specify the name of the remote ODBC data source (such as an Oracle or SQL Server database) to be associated with the element. Content from the data source is specified via the DATAFLD attribute.

Example

```
<MARQUEE BEHAVIOR="slide" DIRECTION="left" WIDTH=200
DATASRC="#DBSRC3" DATAFLD="news" DATAFORMATAS="HTML">
...
</MARQUEE>
```

Value   Case-sensitive identifier.

Default   None.

Object Model Reference

IE   [window.]document.all.*elementID*.dataSrc

DIRECTION
NN *n/a*   IE *4*   HTML *n/a*

DIRECTION="*scrollDirection*"   *Optional*

A MARQUEE element's content may scroll in one of four directions. For optimum readability in languages written left to right, it is easier to grasp the content when it scrolls either to the left or downward.

Example

```
<MARQUEE BEHAVIOR="slide" DIRECTION="left" WIDTH=200>
...
</MARQUEE>
```

Value   Four possible directions: down | left | right | up.

Default   left

Object Model Reference

IE   [window.]document.all.*elementID*.direction

HEIGHT, WIDTH
NN *n/a*   IE *4*   HTML *n/a*

HEIGHT="*length*"   *Optional*
WIDTH="*length*"

A MARQUEE element renders itself as a rectangular space on the page. You can override the default size of this rectangle by assigning values to the HEIGHT and WIDTH attributes. The default value for HEIGHT is determined by the font size of the largest font assigned to content in the MARQUEE. Default width is set to 100% of the width of the next outermost container (usually the document BODY). The WIDTH defines how much space is used at one time or another by horizontally scrolling content. When the MARQUEE is embedded within a

TD element that lets the browser determine the table cell's calculated width, you must set the WIDTH of the MARQUEE element or risk having the browser set it to 1, making the content unreadable.

If you want extra padding around the space, see the HSPACE and VSPACE attributes.

Example

```
<MARQUEE BEHAVIOR="slide" DIRECTION="left" HEIGHT=20 WIDTH=200>
...
</MARQUEE>
```

Value   Any length value in pixels or percentage of available space.

Default   A width of 100%; a height of 12 pixels.

Object Model Reference

IE   [window.]document.all.*elementID*.height
            [window.]document.all.*elementID*.width

HSPACE, VSPACE   NN *n/a*   IE *4*   HTML *n/a*

HSPACE="*pixelCount*"   *Optional*
VSPACE="*pixelCount*"

Internet Explorer provides attributes for setting padding around a MARQUEE element. The HSPACE attribute controls padding along the left and right edges (horizontal padding), whereas the VSPACE attribute controls padding along the top and bottom edges (vertical padding). Adding such padding provides an empty cushion around the MARQUEE's rectangle. As an alternate, you can specify the various margin style sheet settings, especially if you want to open space along only one edge.

Example

```
<MARQUEE BEHAVIOR="slide" DIRECTION="left" HEIGHT=20 WIDTH=200
HSPACE=10 VSPACE=15>
...
</MARQUEE>
```

Value   Any positive integer.

Default   0

Object Model Reference

IE   [window.]document.all.*elementID*.hspace
            [window.]document.all.*elementID*.vspace

LOOP   NN *n/a*   IE *4*   HTML *n/a*

LOOP="*count*"   *Optional*

Sets the number of times the MARQUEE element scrolls its content. After the final scroll, the content remains in a fixed position. Constant animation can sometimes be distracting to page visitors, so if you have the MARQUEE turn itself off after a few scrolls, you may be doing your visitors a favor.

HTML Reference

Example

```
<MARQUEE BEHAVIOR="slide" DIRECTION="left" HEIGHT=20 WIDTH=200 LOOP=3>
...
</MARQUEE>
```

Value

Any positive integer if you want the scrolling to stop. Otherwise, set the value to -1 or infinite.

Default   -1

Object Model Reference

IE   [window.]document.all.*elementID*.loop

SCROLLAMOUNT
                 NN *n/a*   IE *4*   HTML *n/a*

SCROLLAMOUNT="*pixelCount*"   *Optional*

MARQUEE content looks animated by virtue of the browser clearing and redrawing its content at a location offset from the previous location (in a direction set by the DIRECTION attribute). You can make the scrolling appear faster by increasing the amount of space between positions of each drawing of the content; conversely, you can slow down the scrolling by decreasing the space. See also SCROLLDELAY.

Example

```
<MARQUEE BEHAVIOR="slide" DIRECTION="left" HEIGHT=20 WIDTH=200
SCROLLAMOUNT=2>
...
</MARQUEE>
```

Value   Any positive integer.

Default   6

Object Model Reference

IE   [window.]document.all.*elementID*.scrollAmount

SCROLLDELAY
                 NN *n/a*   IE *4*   HTML *n/a*

SCROLLDELAY="*milliseconds*"   *Optional*

Apparent scrolling speed can be influenced by the frequency of redrawing of the content as its position shifts with each redraw (see SCROLLAMOUNT). Increasing the SCROLLDELAY value slows down the scroll speed, whereas decreasing the value makes the scrolling go faster. Be aware that on slower computers, you can reach a value at which no increase of speed is discernible no matter how small you make the SCROLLDELAY value (see TRUESPEED).

Example

```
<MARQUEE BEHAVIOR="slide" DIRECTION="left" HEIGHT=20 WIDTH=200
SCROLLDELAY=100>
...
</MARQUEE>
```

Value

Any positive integer representing the number of milliseconds between content redraws.

Default   85 (Windows 95); 90 (Macintosh).

Object Model Reference

IE   [window.]document.all.*elementID*.scrollDelay

TRUESPEED   NN *n/a*   IE *4*   HTML *n/a*

TRUESPEED   *Optional*

The MARQUEE element includes a built-in speed bump to prevent scrolling from being accidentally specified too fast for visitors to read. If you genuinely intend the content to scroll very fast, you can include the TRUESPEED attribute to tell the browser to honor SCROLLDELAY settings below 60 milliseconds.

Example
```
<MARQUEE BEHAVIOR="slide" DIRECTION="left" HEIGHT=20 WIDTH=200
SCROLLDELAY=45 TRUESPEED>
...
</MARQUEE>
```

Value   The presence of this attribute sets the value to true.

Default   false

Object Model Reference

IE   [window.]document.all.*elementID*.trueSpeed

VSPACE

See HSPACE.

WIDTH

See HEIGHT.

<MENU>   NN *all*   IE *all*   HTML *all*

<MENU>...</MENU>   *End Tag: Required*

The original idea of the MENU element was to allow browsers to generate single-column lists of items. Virtually every browser, however, treats the MENU element the same as a UL element to present an unordered single column list of items (usually preceded by bullets). The MENU element is deprecated in HTML 4.0. You should be using the UL element for it in any case, because you are assured backward compatibility and forward compatibility should this element ever disappear from the browser landscape. Everything said here also applies to the deprecated DIR element.

Example
```
Common DB Connector Types:
<MENU>
```

```
    <LI>DB-9
    <LI>DB-12
    <LI>DB-25
</MENU>
```

Object Model Reference

IE   [window.]document.all.*elementID*

Attributes

CLASS	DIR	LANG	STYLE	TITLE
COMPACT	ID	LANGUAGE		

Event Handler Attributes

Handler	NN	IE	HTML
onClick	n/a	4	4
onDblClick	n/a	4	4
onDragStart	n/a	4	n/a
onHelp	n/a	4	n/a
onKeyDown	n/a	4	4
onKeyPress	n/a	4	4
onKeyUp	n/a	4	4
onMouseDown	n/a	4	4
onMouseMove	n/a	4	4
onMouseOut	n/a	4	4
onMouseOver	n/a	4	4
onMouseUp	n/a	4	4
onSelectStart	n/a	4	n/a

COMPACT
     NN *n/a*   IE *3*   HTML *3.2*

COMPACT   *Optional*

A Boolean attribute originally designed to let browsers render the list in a more compact style than normal (smaller line spacing between items). Internet Explorer ignores this attribute (despite the fact that support for this attribute is indicated in IE 3 documentation).

Example

```
<MENU COMPACT>...</MENU>
```

Value   The presence of this attribute makes its value true.

Default   false

<META>
     NN *all*   IE *all*   HTML *all*

<META>   *End Tag: Forbidden*

A META element conveys hidden information about the document, both to the server that dishes up the document and to the client that downloads the document. The element is also used to embed document information that some search engines use for indexing and categorizing documents on the World Wide Web.

More than one META element may be included in a document, and all META elements belong nested inside the HEAD element. The specific purpose of each META element is defined by its attributes. Typically, a META element reduces to a name/value pair that is of use to either the server or the client. For example, most browsers recognize attribute settings that force the page to reload (or redirect to another page) after a timed delay. This would be useful in a page whose content is updated minute-by-minute, because the browser keeps reloading the latest page as often as indicated in the META element.

Several other elements and attributes in HTML 4.0 contain the same kind of meta-data that might otherwise be located in META elements. Use the avenue that is best suited to your intended server and browser environments. In many cases, real-world implementations must catch up with the HTML 4.0 specification before you will be faced with those decisions.

See also the ADDRESS, DEL, INS, LINK, and TITLE elements, as well as the PROFILE attribute of the HEAD element.

Example

```
<HEAD PROFILE="http://www.giantco.com/profiles/common">
    <META NAME="Author" CONTENT="Jane Smith">
    <META NAME="keywords" CONTENT="benefits,insurance,plan">
    <META HTTP-EQUIV="refresh"
    CONTENT="1;URL=http://www.giantco.com/truindex.html">
    <META HTTP-EQUIV="Content-Type" CONTENT="text/html;
    charset=ISO-8859-5">
</HEAD>
```

Attributes

CONTENT	HTTP-EQUIV	NAME	SCHEME	*TITLE*
DIR	*LANG*			

CONTENT   NN *all*   IE *all*   HTML *all*

CONTENT="*valueString*"   *Required*

The equivalent of the value of a name/value pair. The attribute is usually accompanied by either a NAME or HTTP-EQUIV attribute, either of which act as the name portion of the name/value pair. Specific values of the CONTENT attribute vary with the value of the NAME or HTTP-EQUIV attribute. Sometimes, the CONTENT attribute value contains multiple values. In such cases, the values are delimited by commas. Some of these values may be name/value pairs in their own right, such as the content for a refresh META element. The first value is a number representing the number of seconds delay before loading another document; the second value indicates a URL of the document to load after the delay expires.

Example

```
<META HTTP-EQUIV="refresh"
CONTENT="2;URL=http://www.giantco.com/basicindex.html">
```

Value

Any string of characters. The string must be inside a matching pair of (single or double) quotation marks.

Default   None.

Object Model Reference

IE   [window.]document.all.*elementID*.content

HTTP-EQUIV   NN *all*   IE *all*   HTML *all*

HTTP-EQUIV="*identifier*"   *Optional*

When a server sends a document to the client with the HTTP protocol, a number of HTTP header fields are sent along, primarily as directives to the client about the content on its way. META elements can add to those HTTP headers when the HTTP-EQUIV attribute is assigned to a document. Browsers convert the HTTP-EQUIV and CONTENT attribute values into the HTTP response header format of "name: value" and treat them as if they came directly from the server.

Web standards define a long list of HTTP headers (see *Webmaster in a Nutshell* by Stephen Spainhour and Valerie Quercia, published by O'Reilly & Associates), but some of the more common values are shown in the following examples. You can have either the HTTPDIREC-TIONP-EQUIV or NAME attribute in a META element, but not both.

Example

```
<META HTTP-EQUIV="refresh"
CONTENT="1,http://www.giantco.com/truindex.html">
<META HTTP-EQUIV="Content-Type" CONTENT="text/html; charset=ISO-8859-5">
<META HTTP-EQUIV="expires" CONTENT="Sun, 15 Jan 1998 17:38:00 GMT">
```

Value   Any string identifier.

Default   None.

Object Model Reference

IE   [window.]document.all.*elementID*.httpEquiv

NAME   NN *all*   IE *all*   HTML *all*

NAME="*identifier*"   *Optional*

An identifier for the name/value pair that constitutes the META element. Typically, the attribute value is a plain-language term that denotes the purpose of the META element, such as "author" or "keywords". You can assign a value to either the NAME or HTTP-EQUIV attribute, but not both, in the same META element.

Example

```
<META NAME="Author" CONTENT="Jane Smith">
<META NAME="keywords" CONTENT="benefits,insurance,plan">
```

Value   Any string identifier.

Default   None.

Object Model Reference

IE   [window.]document.all.*elementID*.name

SCHEME   NN *n/a*   IE *n/a*   HTML *4*

SCHEME="*identifier*"   *Optional*

Provides one more organizational layer to meta-data supplied with a document. For example, a university campus with several libraries might generate documents associated with each of the libraries. Assuming that a browser is equipped to interpret meta-data about this, one approach at assembling the tags is to create a separate NAME attribute value for each library: NAME="law", NAME="main", NAME="engineering", and so on. But it may also be necessary to associate these NAME values with a specific university. The SCHEME attribute could be called into service to align the meta-data with a particular university: SCHEME="Harvard". Now, other university library systems could use the same organization of NAME attributes, but the SCHEME attribute clearly associates a given META element with a specific university and library. Again, this assumes that the browser is empowered to do something special with this meta-knowledge.

Example   <META SCHEME="Chicago" NAME="restaurant" CONTENT="1029">

Value   Any string identifier.

Default   None.

<MULTICOL>   NN *3*   IE *n/a*   HTML *n/a*

<MULTICOL>...</MULTICOL>   *End Tag: Required*

A Navigator-specific element that renders its content in any number of evenly spaced flowing columns on the page. The way this element flows content might remind you of a desktop publishing program that automatically flows long content into column space that has been defined for the page. There is no equivalent for this element in HTML or Internet Explorer, but the columns style sheet attribute is defined in CSS2.

Example

```
<MULTICOL COLS=2 GUTTER=20 WIDTH=500>
LongFlowingHTMLContent
</MULTICOL>
```

Attributes

COLS   GUTTER   WIDTH

COLS   NN *3*   IE *n/a*   HTML *n/a*

COLS="*columnCount*"   *Required*

Defines the number of columns across which the browser distributes and renders the content of the element. For a given width of the content, the browser does its best to make each column the same length.

Example

```
<MULTICOL COLS=2 GUTTER=20 WIDTH=500>
LongFlowingHTMLContent
</MULTICOL>
```

Value   Any positive integer.

Default   1

GUTTER

NN *3*   IE *n/a*   HTML *n/a*

GUTTER="*pixelCount*"   *Optional*

Specifies the number of pixels to be placed between columns. The browser then calculates the width of the content columns by subtracting all the gutters from the total available width.

Example

```
<MULTICOL COLS=2 GUTTER=20 WIDTH=500>
LongFlowingHTMLContent
</MULTICOL>
```

Value   Any positive integer.

Default   10

WIDTH

NN *3*   IE *n/a*   HTML *n/a*

WIDTH="*elementWidth*"   *Optional*

Defines the total width of the columns plus gutters. You can specify the width in pixels or as a percentage of the width of the next outer container (usually the document BODY).

Example

```
<MULTICOL COLS=2 GUTTER=20 WIDTH=500>
LongFlowingHTMLContent
</MULTICOL>
```

Value   Any length value in pixels or percentage of available space.

Default   100%

<NOBR>

NN *all*   IE *all*   HTML *n/a*

<NOBR>...</NOBR>   *End Tag: Required*

The NOBR element instructs the browser to render its content without wrapping the text to the next line at the right edge of the window or container. Even if there are carriage returns in the source code for the element's content, the browser flows the text as one line. Although this might seem convenient in circumstances involving careful layout of pages, it may mean the user has to scroll horizontally to view the text—not something most users like to do. Despite the longevity of the NOBR element in commercial browsers, it has never been mentioned in formal HTML recommendations.

Example

```
<NOBR>
Now is the time for all good men to
come to the aid of their country, even if
the text forces them to scroll horizontally.
</NOBR>
```

Object Model Reference

IE   [window.]document.all.*elementID*

Attributes

CLASS	ID	STYLE	TITLE

Object Model Reference

IE   [window.]document.all.*elementID*

<NOEMBED>

NN *2*   IE *n/a*   HTML *n/a*

<NOEMBED>...</NOEMBED>   *End Tag: Required*

Navigator provides a tag for isolating advisory content that displays in browsers incapable of working with plugins. All content between the start and end tags of the NOEMBED element is not rendered in Navigator (or Internet Explorer) but is rendered in other browsers (which ignore the tag but not the content). There are no attributes for this element.

Example

```
<EMBED NAME="jukebox" SRC="jazz.aif" HEIGHT=100 WIDTH=200></EMBED>
<NOEMBED>
To play the music associated with this page, you need a modern graphical
browser.
</NOEMBED>
```

<NOFRAMES>

NN *2*   IE *3*   HTML *4*

<NOFRAMES>...</NOFRAMES>   *End Tag: Required*

The NOFRAMES element contains HTML that is rendered by browsers incapable of displaying frames. Browsers that are capable of displaying frames ignore the NOFRAMES element and all content it contains. Content for this element should instruct the user about using frames or perhaps offer a link to a frameless version of the page. The most common location for the NOFRAMES element is inside a FRAMESET element. The HTML 4.0 specification, however, sees nothing wrong with embedding the element in a rendered document, if it makes sense for your application.

All attributes of the NOFRAMES element were added to support Cascading Style Sheets. This seems odd, because it would seem very unlikely that a browser would support CSS but not frames. Chalk it up to consistency.

Example

```
<FRAMESET COLS="150,*">
    <FRAME NAME="navbar" SRC="nav.html">
    <FRAME NAME="main" SRC="page1.html">
```

```
      <NOFRAMES>Your browser does not support frames.
      Click <A HREF="noFramesIndex.html">here</A> for a frameless version.
      </NOFRAMES>
</FRAMESET>
```

Attributes

CLASS	ID	LANG	STYLE	TITLE
DIR				

Event Handler Attributes

Handler	NN	IE	HTML
onClick	n/a	n/a	4
onDblClick	n/a	n/a	4
onKeyDown	n/a	n/a	4
onKeyPress	n/a	n/a	4
onKeyUp	n/a	n/a	4
onMouseDown	n/a	n/a	4
onMouseMove	n/a	n/a	4
onMouseOut	n/a	n/a	4
onMouseOver	n/a	n/a	4
onMouseUp	n/a	n/a	4

<NOLAYER>   NN *4*   IE *n/a*   HTML *n/a*

`<NOLAYER>...</NOLAYER>`   *End Tag: Required*

Navigator provides a tag for isolating advisory content that displays in browsers that don't recognize the **LAYER** element. All content between the start and end tags of the **NOLAYER** element is not rendered in Navigator 4 but is rendered in other browsers (which ignore the tag but not the content). You can place the **NOLAYER** element anywhere you want, but be aware that it won't be positioned like the **LAYER** element is intended to be.

There are no attributes for this element. If you attempt to set style sheet rules for the **NOLAYER** element, they are ignored by browsers such as Internet Explorer. You can, however, wrap the **NOLAYER** element inside a **DIV** or **SPAN** element to associate a style sheet rule with the advisory text.

Example

```
<LAYER BGCOLOR="yellow" SRC="instrux.html" WIDTH=200 HEIGHT=300></LAYER>
<NOLAYER>
You are not seeing some content that requires Netscape Navigator 4 to view.
</NOLAYER>
```

<NOSCRIPT>   NN *3*   IE *4*   HTML *4*

`<NOSCRIPT>...</NOSCRIPT>`   *End Tag: Required*

The **NOSCRIPT** element is intended to display content when a browser is not set to run the scripts embedded in the current document. In practice, the element is observed only starting with Navigator 3 and Internet Explorer 4. When a user disables scripting in a browser, the **NOSCRIPT** element's content is rendered wherever it falls in the source code.

For older browsers, and those that don't support scripting, the NOSCRIPT element is ignored completely. Going forward, the HTML 4.0 specification recommends that browsers also render the NOSCRIPT element's content when scripts earlier in the document are of a language type not supported or enabled in the browser. Also, if an HTML 4.0-compatible browser should be developed that lacks scripting altogether, it, too, should render the NOSCRIPT element's contents.

All attributes of the NOSCRIPT element were added to support Cascading Style Sheets, internationalization, and events for HTML 4.0.

Example

```
<NOSCRIPT>
This document contains programming that requires a scriptable browser, such
as Microsoft Internet Explorer or Netscape Navigator. You may not have full
access to this page's powers at this time.
</NOSCRIPT>
```

Attributes

CLASS	ID	LANG	STYLE	TITLE
DIR				

Event Handler Attributes

Handler	NN	IE	HTML
onClick	n/a	n/a	4
onDblClick	n/a	n/a	4
onKeyDown	n/a	n/a	4
onKeyPress	n/a	n/a	4
onKeyUp	n/a	n/a	4
onMouseDown	n/a	n/a	4
onMouseMove	n/a	n/a	4
onMouseOut	n/a	n/a	4
onMouseOver	n/a	n/a	4
onMouseUp	n/a	n/a	4

<OBJECT>   NN 4   IE 3   HTML 4

<OBJECT>...</OBJECT>   *End Tag: Required*

The OBJECT element supplies the browser with information to load and render data types that are not natively supported by the browser. If the browser must load some external program (a Java applet, a plugin, or some other helper), the information about the content that is to be rendered is contained by the OBJECT element, its attributes, and optionally, associated PARAM elements nested inside of it. Although today's browsers recognize elements such as APPLET and EMBED, the HTML specification indicates that the trend is to combine all of this into the OBJECT element.

The HTML 4.0 specification allows nesting of OBJECT elements to give the browser a chance to load alternate content if no plugin, or other necessary content aids, is available in the browser. Essentially, the browser should be able to walk through nested OBJECT elements until it finds one it can handle. For example, the outer OBJECT element may try to load an MPEG2 video; if no player is available, the browser looks for the next nested

OBJECT, which is a JPEG still image from the video; if the browser is not a graphical browser, it would render some straight HTML that is the most nested item (although not as an OBJECT element) within the hierarchy of nested OBJECTs:

```
<DIV>
<OBJECT data="proddemo.mpeg" type="application/mpeg">
    <OBJECT data="prodStill.jpg" type="image/jpeg">
        The all-new Widget 3000!
    </OBJECT>
</OBJECT>
</DIV>
```

HTML 4.0 details a framework for turning OBJECT elements consisting of images into client-side image maps. The syntax is a little different from the MAP and AREA elements used for IMG element image maps. The OBJECT element holding the image must have the SHAPES attribute present. For each active region of the image, you then define an A element nested within the OBJECT element. Each A element contains SHAPE and COORDS attributes, as well as HREF and other applicable link attributes. For nested OBJECT elements, the image map's hotspots can be shared from a nested element to its parent element with the help of the EXPORT attribute, as follows:

```
<OBJECT data="widget399.pdf" SHAPES>
    <OBJECT data="widget399.gif" SHAPES EXPORT>
    <A HREF="w399Specs.html TARGET="main" SHAPE="rect" COORDS="10,10,40,50">
    <A HREF="w399Price.html TARGET="main" SHAPE="rect" COORDS="40,10,80,50">
    <A HREF="w399Order.html TARGET="main" SHAPE="rect" COORDS="10,50,80,100">
    </OBJECT>
</OBJECT>
```

The long list of attributes for the OBJECT element attempts to handle every possible data type that may come along in the future. Moreover, content-specific parameters may also be passed via PARAM elements that can go inside the start and end tags of the OBJECT element.

To determine which attributes apply to a particular content type or object and what their values look like, you have to rely on documentation from the supplier of the object or plugin. That same documentation should let you know whether the functionality is available across browser brands and operating systems.

Example

```
<OBJECT ID="earth" CLASSID="clsid:83A38BF0-B33A-A4FF-C619A82E891D">
<PARAM NAME="srcStart" VALUE="images/earth0.gif">
<PARAM NAME="frameCount" VALUE="12">
<PARAM NAME="loop" VALUE="-1"
<PARAM NAME="fps" VALUE="10">
</OBJECT>
```

Attributes

ACCESSKEY	CODE	DECLARE	*LANG*	TABINDEX
ALIGN	CODEBASE	*DIR*	*LANGUAGE*	*TITLE*
ARCHIVE	CODETYPE	EXPORT	NAME	TYPE
BORDER	DATA	HEIGHT	SHAPES	USEMAP
CLASS	DATAFLD	HSPACE	STANDBY	VSPACE
CLASSID	DATASRC	*ID*	*STYLE*	WIDTH

Event Handler Attributes

Handler	NN	IE	HTML
onAfterUpdate	n/a	4	n/a
onBeforeUpdate	n/a	4	n/a
onBlur	n/a	4	n/a
onClick	n/a	4	4
onDblClick	n/a	4	4
onDragStart	n/a	4	n/a
onHelp	n/a	4	n/a
onKeyDown	n/a	4	4
onKeyPress	n/a	4	4
onKeyUp	n/a	4	4
onMouseDown	n/a	4	4
onMouseMove	n/a	4	4
onMouseOut	n/a	4	4
onMouseOver	n/a	4	4
onMouseUp	n/a	4	4
onReadyStateChange	n/a	4	n/a
onResize	n/a	4	n/a
onRowEnter	n/a	4	n/a
onRowExit	n/a	4	n/a
onSelectStart	n/a	4	n/a

ACCESSKEY
NN *n/a*   IE *4*   HTML *4*

ACCESSKEY="*character*"   *Optional*

A single character key that brings focus to the element. The browser and operating system determine if the user must press a modifier key (e.g., **Ctrl**, **Alt**, or **Command**) with the access key to bring focus to the element. In IE 4/Windows, the **Alt** key is required, and the key is not case sensitive. This attribute does not work in IE 4/Mac.

Example   <OBJECT ... ACCESSKEY="g"></OBJECT>

Value   Single character of the document set.

Default   None.

Object Model Reference

IE   [window.]document.all.*elementID*.accessKey

ALIGN
NN *4*   IE *3*   HTML *4*

ALIGN="*alignmentConstant*"   *Optional*

Determines how the rectangle of the OBJECT element aligns within the context of surrounding content. See the section "Alignment Constants" earlier in this chapter for a description of the possibilities defined in both Navigator and Internet Explorer for this attribute. Not all attribute values are valid in browsers prior to the Version 4 releases.

Both browsers follow the same rules on laying out content surrounding an image whose ALIGN attribute is set, but the actual results are sometimes difficult to predict when the surrounding content is complex. A thorough testing of rendering possibilities with browser windows set to various sizes prevents surprises later.

Example   <OBJECT ... ALIGN="baseline"></OBJECT>

Value

Case-insensitive constant value. All constant values are available in Navigator 4 and Internet Explorer 4.

Default   bottom

Object Model Reference

IE   [window.]document.all.*elementID*.align

ARCHIVE   NN *n/a*   IE *n/a*   HTML *4*

ARCHIVE="*URLList*"   *Optional*

A space-delimited list of URLs of files that support the loading and running of the OBJECT element. By explicitly specifying the files in the ARCHIVE attribute, the browser doesn't have to wait for the supporting files to be called by the content running in the OBJECT element. Instead, the supporting files can be downloaded simultaneously with the primary content. The ARCHIVE attribute may also include URLs assigned to the CLASSID or DATA attributes, but one of these two attributes still needs to point to the primary content URL.

Example

<OBJECT ... ARCHIVE=" /images/anim3.gif /images/anim4.gif"></OBJECT>

Value   A complete or relative URL.

Default   None.

BORDER   NN *n/a*   IE *n/a*   HTML *4*

BORDER=*pixels*   *Optional*

The thickness of a border around the OBJECT element. This attribute is supported in Internet Explorer 3, but not in IE 4. The attribute is also deprecated in HTML 4.0 in favor of style sheet borders.

Example   <OBJECT ... BORDER=4></OBJECT>

Value   Any integer pixel value.

Default   None.

CLASSID   NN *4*   IE *3*   HTML *4*

CLASSID="*URL*"   *Optional*

The URL of the object's implementation. This attribute typically directs the browser to load program, applet, or plugin class files. In Internet Explorer, the URL can point to the *CLSID* directory that stores all of the IDs for registered ActiveX controls, such as DirectAnimation. You must obtain the CLASSID value from the supplier of an ActiveX control. In Navigator 4, the Java Archive (JAR) Installation Manager attempts to install a plugin from the CLASSID URL if the plugin is not installed for data specified in the DATA attribute. Eventually, this attribute may be used to load Java applets (IE 4 includes a CODE attribute to handle this now), but through Version 4 of both browsers, Java applets are not yet supported in this fashion.

Example

```
<OBJECT ID="earth" CLASSID="clsid:83A38BF0-B33A-A4FF-C619A82E891D">
</OBJECT>
```

Value   A complete or relative URL.

Default   None.

Object Model Reference

IE   [window.]document.*elementID*.classid

CODE   NN *n/a*   IE *4*   HTML *n/a*

CODE="*fileName.class*"   *Optional*

The CODE attribute is likely an interim solution in Internet Explorer that allows the OBJECT element to perform the same job as an APPLET element, using the same kind of attributes. The CODE attribute value is the name of the Java applet class file. If the class file is in a directory other than the document, the path to the directory must be assigned to the CODEBASE attribute, just like in the APPLET element. Eventually, the CODE attribute may be supplanted by the HTML 4.0 CLASSID attribute, which is intended for all object implementations. Parameters are passed to applets via PARAM elements, just like the ones nested inside APPLET elements.

Example   `<OBJECT CODE="fileReader.class" CODEBASE="classes"></OBJECT>`

Value   Applet class filename.

Default   None.

Object Model Reference

IE   [window.]document.*elementID*.code

CODEBASE   NN *4*   IE *3*   HTML *4*

CODEBASE="*path*"   *Optional*

Path to the directory holding the class file designated in either the CODE or CLASSID attribute. The CODEBASE attribute does not name the class file, just the path. You can make this attribute a complete URL to the directory, but don't try to access a codebase outside of the domain of the current document.

Example   `<OBJECT CODE="fileReader.class" CODEBASE="classes"></OBJECT>`

Value

Case-sensitive pathname, usually relative to the directory storing the current HTML document.

Default None.

Object Model Reference

IE   [window.]document.all.*elementID*.codeBase

CODETYPE

NN *n/a*   IE *3*   HTML *4*

CODETYPE="*MIMEType*" *Optional*

An advisory about the content type of the object referred to by the **CLASSID** attribute. A browser might use this information to assist in preparing support for a resource requiring a multimedia player or plugin. If the **CODETYPE** attribute is missing, the browser looks next for the **TYPE** attribute setting (although it is normally associated with content linked by the **DATA** attribute URL). If both attributes are missing, the browser gets the content type information from the resource as it downloads.

Example

```
<OBJECT CLASSID="clsid:83A38BF0-B33A-A4FF-C619A82E891D"
CODETYPE="application/x-crossword">
</OBJECT>
```

Value

Case-insensitive MIME type. A catalog of registered MIME types is available from *ftp://ftp.isi.edu/in-notes/iana/assignments/media-types/*.

Default None.

Object Model Reference

IE   [window.]document.all.*elementID*.codeType

DATA

NN *4*   IE *3*   HTML *4*

DATA="*URL*" *Optional*

URL of a file containing data for the **OBJECT** element (as distinguished from the object itself). For data whose content type can be opened (and viewed or played) with any compatible object or plugin, the **DATA** and **TYPE** attributes are generally sufficient to launch the plugin and get the content loaded. But if the content requires a very specific plugin or ActiveX control, you should include a **CLASSID** attribute that points to the object's implementation as well. In that case, you can specify the content type with either the **CODETYPE** or **TYPE** attributes. Relative URLs are calculated relative to the **CODEBASE** attribute, if one is assigned; otherwise the URL is relative to the document's URL.

Example   `<OBJECT DATA="proddemo.mpeg" TYPE="application/mpeg"></OBJECT>`

Value   A complete or relative URL.

Default None.

Object Model Reference

IE   [window.]document.*elementID*.data

DATAFLD   NN *n/a*   IE *4*   HTML *n/a*

DATAFLD="*columnName*"   *Optional*

Used with IE 4 data binding to associate a remote data source column name to an OBJECT element attribute determined by properties set in the object. A DATASRC attribute must also be set for the element.

Example

```
<OBJECT CLASSID="clsid:83A38BF0-B33A-A4FF-C619A82E891D"
DATASRC="#DBSRC3" DATAFLD="dataFile">
</OBJECT>
```

Value   Case-sensitive identifier.

Default   None.

Object Model Reference

IE   [window.]document.all.*elementID*.dataFld

DATASRC   NN *n/a*   IE *4*   HTML *n/a*

DATASRC="*dataSourceName*"   *Optional*

Used with IE 4 data binding to specify the name of the remote ODBC data source (such as an Oracle or SQL Server database) to be associated with the element. Content from the data source is specified via the DATAFLD attribute.

Example

```
<OBJECT CLASSID="clsid:83A38BF0-B33A-A4FF-C619A82E891D"
DATASRC="#DBSRC3" DATAFLD="dataFile">
</OBJECT>
```

Value   Case-sensitive identifier.

Default   None.

Object Model Reference

IE   [window.]document.all.*elementID*.dataSrc

DECLARE   NN *n/a*   IE *n/a*   HTML *4*

DECLARE   *Optional*

The presence of the DECLARE attribute instructs the browser to regard the current OBJECT element as a declaration only, without instantiating the object. A browser may use this opportunity to precache data that does not require the object being loaded or run. Another OBJECT element pointing to the same CLASSID and/or DATA attribute values, but without the DECLARE attribute, gets the object running.

Example

```
<OBJECT CLASSID="clsid:83A38BF0-B33A-A4FF-C619A82E891D" DECLARE>
</OBJECT>
```

Value   The presence of the attribute sets it to true.

Default   false

EXPORT

EXPORT   *Optional*

If a set of nested OBJECT elements contain images and those images are established as image maps, you can define one set of image maps for a nested OBJECT and share those specifications with the parent OBJECT element by including an EXPORT element.

Example
```
<OBJECT data="widget399.pdf" SHAPES>
    <OBJECT data="widget399.gif" SHAPES EXPORT>
    <A HREF="w399Specs.html TARGET="main" SHAPE="rect"
COORDS="10,10,40,50">
    <A HREF="w399Price.html TARGET="main" SHAPE="rect"
COORDS="40,10,80,50">
    <A HREF="w399Order.html TARGET="main" SHAPE="rect"
COORDS="10,50,80,100">
    </OBJECT>
</OBJECT>
```

Value   The presence of the EXPORT attribute sets it to true.

Default   false

HEIGHT, WIDTH

HEIGHT=" *length*"   *Required*
WIDTH=" *length*"

The size that an embedded object (or its plugin control panel) occupies in a document is governed by the HEIGHT and WIDTH attribute settings. Some browser versions might allow you to get away without assigning these attributes and letting the plugin's own user interface design determine the height and width of its visible rectangle. It is best to specify the exact dimensions of a plugin's control panel or the data (in the case of images) whenever possible (control panels vary with each browser and even between different plugins for the same browser). In some cases, such as Navigator 4 for the Macintosh, the object may not display if you fail to supply enough height on the page. If you assign values that are larger than the actual object or its control panel, the browser reserves that empty space on the page, which could interfere with your intended page design.

Example   <OBJECT DATA="blues.aif"HEIGHT=150 WIDTH=250></OBJECT>

Value

Positive integer values (optionally quoted) or percentage values (quoted).

Default   None.

Object Model Reference

IE   [window.]document.*elementID*.height
                [window.]document.*elementID*.width

HSPACE, VSPACE

NN n/a   IE 3   HTML 4

HSPACE=*pixelCount*   *Optional*
VSPACE=*pixelCount*

A margin that acts as whitespace padding around the visual content of the OBJECT element's rectangular space. HSPACE establishes a margin on the left and right sides of the rectangle; VSPACE establishes a margin on the top and bottom sides of the rectangle.

Example

```
<OBJECT DATA="blues.aif"HEIGHT=150 WIDTH=250 VSPACE=10 HSPACE=10></OBJECT>
```

Value

Integer representing the number of pixels for the width of the margin on the relevant sides of the OBJECT element's rectangle.

Default   0

Object Model Reference

IE   [window.]document.*elementID*.hspace
            [window.]document.*elementID*.vspace

NAME

NN n/a   IE n/a   HTML 4

NAME="*elementIdentifier*"   *Optional*

The HTML 4.0 specification provides for a NAME attribute of the OBJECT element for instances in which the object is part of a form that is submitted to the server. The NAME attribute in this case performs the same function as the NAME attribute of an INPUT element; it acts as a label for some data being submitted. The code that is loaded into the OBJECT element must be programmed to return a value if it is to be submitted via an HTML form.

Example

```
<OBJECT NAME="embedded" CLASSID="clsid:83A38BF0-B33A-A4FF-C619A82E891D"
HEIGHT=150 WIDTH=250>
</OBJECT>
```

Value   Case-sensitive identifier.

Default   None.

Object Model Reference

IE   [window.]document.all.*elementID*.name

SHAPES

NN n/a   IE n/a   HTML 4

SHAPES   *Optional*

The presence of the SHAPES attribute instructs the browser to treat the OBJECT element's image as a client-side image map and the nested A elements as hotspot definitions for the map. Nested A elements must include COORDS attribute settings. An OBJECT element can inherit the image map specifications from a nested OBJECT element, provided the nested object specifies both the SHAPES and EXPORT attributes.

Example

```
<OBJECT data="widget399.pdf" SHAPES>
    <OBJECT data="widget399.gif" SHAPES EXPORT>
    <A HREF="w399Specs.html TARGET="main" SHAPE="rect"
COORDS="10,10,40,50">
    <A HREF="w399Price.html TARGET="main" SHAPE="rect"
COORDS="40,10,80,50">
    <A HREF="w399Order.html TARGET="main" SHAPE="rect"
COORDS="10,50,80,100">
    </OBJECT>
</OBJECT>
```

Value   The presence of the SHAPES attribute sets it to true.

Default   false

STANDBY   NN *n/a*   IE *n/a*   HTML *4*

STANDBY="*HTMLText*"   *Optional*

HTML content to be displayed while the OBJECT is loading. Although this attribute has not been implemented in Version 4 browsers, presumably the message is to be displayed in the rectangular region intended for the OBJECT element, just as the ALT message appears in an IMG element space while the image loads.

Example

```
<OBJECT CLASSID="clsid:83A38BF0-B33A-A4FF-C619A82E891D"
HEIGHT=150 WIDTH=250 STANDBY="Loading movie...">
</OBJECT>
```

Value   Any HTML content.

Default   None.

TABINDEX   NN *n/a*   IE *3*   HTML *4*

TABINDEX=*integer*   *Optional*

A number that indicates the sequence of this element within the tabbing order of all focusable elements in the document. Tabbing order follows a strict set of rules. Elements that have values other than zero assigned to their TABINDEX attributes are first in line when a user starts tabbing in a page. Focus starts with the element with the lowest TABINDEX value and proceeds in order to the highest value, regardless of physical location on the page or in the document. If two elements have the same TABINDEX values, the element that comes earlier in the document receives focus first. Next come all elements that either don't support the TABINDEX attribute or have the value set to zero. These elements receive focus in the order in which they appear in the document.

Example

```
<OBJECT CLASSID="clsid:83A38BF0-B33A-A4FF-C619A82E891D"
HEIGHT=150 WIDTH=250 TABINDEX=4>...
</OBJECT>
```

Value

Any integer from 0 through 32767. In IE 4, setting the TABINDEX to -1 causes the element to be skipped in tabbing order altogether.

Default None.

Object Model Reference

IE   [window.]document.all.*elementID*.tabIndex

TYPE   NN *4*   IE *3*   HTML *4*

TYPE="*MIMEType*"   *Required*

An advisory about the content type of the data referred to by the DATA attribute. A browser might use this information to assist in preparing support for a resource requiring a multi-media player or plugin. The DATA element first looks to the CODETYPE attribute for this information. But if the CODETYPE attribute is missing, the browser looks next for the TYPE attribute setting. If both attributes are missing, the browser gets the content type information from the resource as it downloads.

Example

```
<OBJECT DATA="movies/prodDemo.mpeg" TYPE="application/mpeg">
</OBJECT>
```

Value

Case-insensitive MIME type. A catalog of registered MIME types is available from *ftp:// ftp.isi.edu/in-notes/iana/assignments/media-types/*.

Default None.

Object Model Reference

IE   [window.]document.all.*elementID*.type

USEMAP   NN *n/a*   IE *n/a*   HTML *4*

USEMAP="*mapURL*"   *Optional*

The HTML 4.0 specification lists the USEMAP attribute for an OBJECT element. Because the specification includes another way to associate a client-side image map with an OBJECT element (see the SHAPES attribute), it is unknown at this point if the intention of the USEMAP attribute is for an OBJECT element to be able to point to a named MAP element (as does an IMG element for its client-side image map).

VSPACE

See HSPACE.

WIDTH

See HEIGHT.

<OL>

<OL>...</OL>   *End Tag: Required*

The OL element is a container for an ordered list of items. An "ordered list" means that the items are rendered with a leading sequence number or letter (depending on the TYPE attribute setting or list-style-type style sheet attribute setting). Content for each list item is defined by a nested LI element. If you apply a style sheet rule to an OL element, the style is inherited by the nested LI elements.

Example

```
<OL>
    <LI>Choose Open from the File menu.
    <LI>Locate the file you wish to edit, and click on the filename.
    <LI>Click the Open button.
</OL>
```

Object Model Reference

IE   [window.]document.all.*elementID*

Attributes

CLASS	DIR	LANG	START	TITLE
COMPACT	ID	LANGUAGE	STYLE	TYPE

Event Handler Attributes

Handler	NN	IE	HTML
onClick	n/a	4	4
onDblClick	n/a	4	4
onDragStart	n/a	4	n/a
onHelp	n/a	4	n/a
onKeyDown	n/a	4	4
onKeyPress	n/a	4	4
onKeyUp	n/a	4	4
onMouseDown	n/a	4	4
onMouseMove	n/a	4	4
onMouseOut	n/a	4	4
onMouseOver	n/a	4	4
onMouseUp	n/a	4	4
onSelectStart	n/a	4	n/a

COMPACT

COMPACT   *Optional*

A Boolean attribute originally designed to let browsers render the list in a more compact style than normal (smaller line spacing between items). This attribute is not implemented in current browsers.

Example   <OL COMPACT>...</OL>

Value   The presence of this attribute makes its value true.

Default   false

START

START=" *number*"   Optional

Assigns a custom starting number for the sequence of items in the OL element. This is convenient when a sequence of items must be disturbed by running body text. Although the value is a number, the corresponding Arabic numeral, Roman numeral, or alphabet letter is used to render the value. This attribute is deprecated in HTML 4.0 in favor of a set of counter-style attributes specified in the CSS2 final recommendation.

Example   <OL START=5> ...</OL>

Value   Any positive integer.

Default   None.

Object Model Reference

IE   [window.]document.all.*elementID*.start

TYPE

TYPE=" *labelType*"   Optional

The TYPE attribute provides some flexibility in how the sequence number is displayed in the browser. For an ordered list, the choices are among letters (uppercase or lowercase), Roman numerals (uppercase or lowercase), or Arabic numerals. The TYPE attribute is deprecated in HTML 4.0 in favor of the list-style-type style sheet attribute.

Example   <OL TYPE="a">...</OL>

Value

Possible values are A | a | I | i | 1. Sequencing is performed automatically as follows:

Type	Example
A	A, B, C, ...
a	a, b, c, ...
I	I, II, III, ...
i	i, ii, iii, ...
1	1, 2, 3, ...

Default   1

Object Model Reference

IE   [window.]document.all.*elementID*.type

<OPTGROUP>

<OPTGROUP>...</OPTGROUP>   *End Tag: Required*

The OPTGROUP element offers the possibility that future browsers will provide a hierarchical SELECT element. An OPTGROUP element represents a container of OPTION elements. The LABEL attribute is the text that would appear in the main SELECT element listing, with nested OPTION elements cascading off the side when the OPTGROUP element is highlighted.

Example

```
<SELECT NAME="carCos">
    <OPTGROUP LABEL="American">
        <OPTION VALUE="General Motors">General Motors
        <OPTION VALUE="Ford">Ford Motor Company
        <OPTION VALUE="Chrysler">Chrysler Corporation
    </OPTGROUP>
    <OPTGROUP LABEL="Japanese">
        <OPTION VALUE="Toyota">Toyota
        <OPTION VALUE="Honda">Honda
        <OPTION VALUE="Nissan">Nissan
    </OPTGROUP>
</SELECT>
```

Attributes

CLASS	*DISABLED*	*LABEL*	*LANGUAGE*	*TITLE*
DIR	*ID*	*LANG*	*STYLE*	

Event Handler Attributes

Handler	NN	IE	HTML
onClick	n/a	4	4
onDblClick	n/a	4	4
onKeyDown	n/a	4	4
onKeyPress	n/a	4	4
onKeyUp	n/a	4	4
onMouseDown	n/a	4	4
onMouseMove	n/a	4	4
onMouseOut	n/a	4	4
onMouseOver	n/a	4	4
onMouseUp	n/a	4	4

DISABLED

NN *n/a*   IE *n/a*   HTML *4*

DISABLED   *Optional*

The presence of this attribute disables the OPTGROUP element and its nested OPTION
elements.

Example `<OPTGROUP LABEL="Engineering" DISABLED>`

Value   The presence of this attribute sets its value to true.

Default false

LABEL

NN *n/a*   IE *n/a*   HTML *4*

LABEL="*labelText*"   *Required*

The text of the SELECT element entry for the OPTGROUP is defined by the LABEL attribute.
This is plain text, not HTML.

Example `<OPTGROUP LABEL="Engineering" DISABLED>`

Value

Any string of characters. The string must be inside a matching pair of (single or double) quotation marks.

Default   None.

<OPTION>   NN *all*   IE *all*   HTML *all*

`<OPTION>...</OPTION>`   *End Tag: Optional*

The OPTION element defines an item that appears in a SELECT element listing, whether the listing is in a pop-up menu or scrolling list. OPTION elements associated with a SELECT element must be nested within the start and end tags of the SELECT element.

SELECT elements supply name/value pairs when the element is submitted as part of a FORM element. Typically, the NAME attribute of the SELECT element and the VALUE attribute of the selected option are submitted as the name/value pair. Therefore, it is important to assign a meaningful value to the VALUE attribute of each OPTION element in a select list. You can use the VALUE attribute to disguise user-unfriendly (but server-friendly) values from the user, while presenting a user-friendly entry that appears in the select list. Content for the human-readable entry of a select list is entered after the OPTION element's start tag. The end tag is optional because the entry is delimited either by the next OPTION element start tag or the SELECT element's end tag. See also the OPTGROUP attribute for possible future grouping of OPTION elements into hierarchical menu groupings.

Example

```
<SELECT NAME="chapters">
    <OPTION VALUE="1">Chapter 1
    <OPTION VALUE="2">Chapter 2
    <OPTION VALUE="3">Chapter 3
    <OPTION VALUE="4">Chapter 4
</SELECT>
```

Object Model Reference

NN   [window.]document.*formName*.*selectName*.*optionName*
            [window.]document.forms[i].elements[i].*optionName*

IE   [window.]document.*formName*.*selectName*.*optionName*
            [window.]document.forms[i].elements[i].*optionName*
            [window.]document.all.*elementID*

Attributes

CLASS	ID	LANG	SELECTED	TITLE
DIR	LABEL	LANGUAGE	STYLE	VALUE
DISABLED				

Event Handler Attributes

Handler	NN	IE	HTML
onDragStart	n/a	4	n/a
onSelectStart	n/a	4	n/a

DISABLED

NN *n/a*   IE *n/a*   HTML *4*

DISABLED   *Optional*

The presence of this attribute disables the OPTION element in the list.

Example <OPTION VALUE="Met101" DISABLED>Meteorology 101

Value   The presence of this attribute sets its value to true.

Default false

LABEL

NN *n/a*   IE *n/a*   HTML *4*

LABEL="*labelText*"   *Required*

The LABEL attribute is included in HTML 4.0 in anticipation of possible hierarchical select lists. The LABEL is intended to be a shorter alternate entry for an OPTION element when it is rendered hierarchically. It overrides the normal text associated with the OPTION element.

Example <OPTION LABEL="Meteo 101" VALUE="met101"> Meteorology 101

Value

Any string of characters. The string must be inside a matching pair of (single or double) quotation marks.

Default None.

SELECTED

NN *all*   IE *all*   HTML *all*

SELECTED   *Optional*

The presence of the SELECTED attribute preselects the item within the SELECT element. When the SELECT element is set to MULTIPLE, more than one OPTION element may have the SELECTED attribute set.

Example <OPTION VALUE="met101" SELECTED> Meteorology 101

Value   The presence of this attribute sets its value to true.

Default false

Object Model Reference

NN   [window.]document.formName.*selectName*.*optionName*.selected
      [window.]document.forms[i].elements[i].selected

IE   [window.]document.formName.*selectName*.*optionName*.selected
      [window.]document.forms[i].elements[i].selected

VALUE

NN *all*   IE *all*   HTML *all*

VALUE="*text*"   *Optional*

Associates a value with an OPTION that may or may not be the same as the text displayed in the SELECT element. When the SELECT element is in a form submitted to the server, the value of the VALUE attribute is assigned to the name/value pair for the SELECT element if the option has been selected by the user (or is designated as SELECTED with that attribute and the user has made no other selection). For scripting purposes, the VALUE attribute might contain values such as URLs or string representations of objects that may subsequently be processed by scripts.

Example `<OPTION VALUE="met101"> Meteorology 101`

Value

Any string of characters. The string must be inside a matching pair of (single or double) quotation marks.

Default None.

Object Model Reference

NN	`[window.]document.formName.`*selectName*`.`*optionName*`.value`
	`[window.]document.forms[i].elements[i].value`
IE	`[window.]document.formName.`*selectName*`.`*optionName*`.value`
	`[window.]document.forms[i].elements[i].value`

<P>   NN *all*   IE *all*   HTML *all*

`<P>...</P>`   *End Tag: Optional*

A P element defines a paragraph structural element in a document. With HTML 4.0, the P element is formally a block-level element, which means that content for a P element begins on its own line, and content following the P element starts on its own line. No other block-level elements may be nested inside a P element. If you omit the end tag, the element ends at the next block-level element start tag.

The nature of the P element has changed over time. In early implementations of HTML, the element represented only a paragraph break (a new line with some extra line spacing). Version 4 browsers render P elements in a hybrid way such that the start tag of a P element inserts a line space before the block. This means that a P element cannot start at the very top of a page unless it is positioned via CSS-P. Use the P element for structural purposes, rather than formatting purposes.

Content of a P element does not recognize extra whitespace that appears in the source code. Other elements, such as PRE, render content just as it is formatted in the source code.

Example

```
<P>This is a simple, one-sentence paragraph.</P>
<P>This second paragraph starts on its own line, with a little extra
line spacing.</P>
```

Object Model Reference

IE   `[window.]document.all.`*elementID*

Attributes

ALIGN	*DIR*	*LANG*	*STYLE*	*TITLE*
CLASS	*ID*	*LANGUAGE*		

Event Handler Attributes

Handler	NN	IE	HTML
onClick	n/a	4	4
onDblClick	n/a	4	4
onDragStart	n/a	4	n/a
onHelp	n/a	4	n/a
onKeyDown	n/a	4	4
onKeyPress	n/a	4	4
onKeyUp	n/a	4	4
onMouseDown	n/a	4	4
onMouseMove	n/a	4	4
onMouseOut	n/a	4	4
onMouseOver	n/a	4	4
onMouseUp	n/a	4	4
onSelectStart	n/a	4	n/a

ALIGN
NN *all*   IE *all*   HTML *3.2*

ALIGN="*where*"   *Optional*

Determines how the paragraph text is justified within the available width of the next outermost container (usually the document BODY).

The ALIGN attribute is deprecated in HTML 4.0 in favor of the style sheet attribute.

Example   `<P ALIGN="center">...</P>`

Value   Text alignment values are `center` | `left` | `right`.

Default   `left`

Object Model Reference

IE   [window.]document.all.*elementID*.align

<PARAM>
NN *2*   IE *3*   HTML *3.2*

<PARAM>   *End Tag: Forbidden*

The PARAM element may be nested within an APPLET or OBJECT element to pass parameters to the Java applet or object as it is being loaded. Parameters provide ways for HTML authors to adjust settings of an applet or object without having to recode the applet or object. A parameter typically passes a name/value pair, which is assigned to the NAME and VALUE attributes. You can have more than one PARAM element per applet or object. The documentation for the applet or object should provide you with necessary information to pass those parameter values.

Example

```
<APPLET CODE="simpleClock.class" NAME="myClock" WIDTH=400 HEIGHT=50>
<PARAM NAME="bgColor" VALUE="black">
<PARAM NAME="fgColor" VALUE="yellow">
</APPLET>
```

Attributes

DATAFLD	DATASRC	NAME	VALUE	VALUETYPE
DATAFORMATAS	*ID*	TYPE		

DATAFLD   NN *n/a*   IE 4   HTML *n/a*

DATAFLD="*columnName*"   *Optional*

Used with IE 4 data binding to associate a remote data source column name with the parameter passed to a Java applet or object. In the following example, data from a data source column named `backColor` is assigned to the `VALUE` attribute, even though the attribute is not explicitly shown in the tag. More complex relationships are also possible with both `OBJECT` and `APPLET` elements. Eventually, Internet Explorer will be able to bind changes of applet property values to data source columns to update the data source and to pass data source changes to an applet using a technique for naming get and set property methods found in JavaBeans.

Example

```
<PARAM NAME="bgColor" DATASRC="#DBSRC2"DATAFORMATAS="text"
DATAFLD="backColor">
```

Value   Case-sensitive identifier.

Default   None.

DATAFORMATAS   NN *n/a*   IE 4   HTML *n/a*

DATAFORMATAS="*dataType*"   *Optional*

Used with IE 4 data binding, this attribute advises the browser whether the source material arriving from the data source is to be treated as plain text or as tagged HTML. This attribute setting depends entirely on how the data source is constructed and what kind of data the `PARAM` element is expecting.

Example

```
<PARAM NAME="bgColor" DATASRC="#DBSRC2"DATAFORMATAS="text"
DATAFLD="backColor">
```

Value   IE 4 recognizes two possible settings: `text` | `HTML`.

Default   `text`

DATASRC   NN *n/a*   IE 4   HTML *n/a*

DATASRC="*dataSourceName*"   *Optional*

Used with IE 4 data binding to specify the name of the remote ODBC data source (such as an Oracle or SQL Server database) to be associated with the element. Content from the data source is specified via the `DATAFLD` attribute.

Example

```
<PARAM NAME="bgColor" DATASRC="#DBSRC2"DATAFORMATAS="text"
DATAFLD="backColor">
```

Value   Case-sensitive identifier.

Default None.

NAME

NAME=" *elementIdentifier*"   *Required*

Assigns an identifier for the parameter that the applet or object is expecting. Parameters generally supply a name/value pair. An applet, for example, includes a routine that fetches each parameter by name and assigns the passed value to a variable within the applet. Documentation for the applet or object should provide a list of names and value types corresponding to the PARAM elements.

Example `<PARAM NAME="loop" VALUE="4">`

Value   Case-sensitive identifier.

Default None.

TYPE

TYPE=" *MIMEType*"   *Optional*

When the VALUETYPE attribute is set to `"ref"`, the TYPE attribute value advises the browser about the content type of the file referenced by the URL assigned to the VALUE attribute. Omit the TYPE attribute for other settings of the VALUETYPE attribute.

Example

```
<PARAM NAME="help" VALUE="http://www.giantco.com/help.html" VALUETYPE="ref"
TYPE="text/html">
```

Value

Case-insensitive MIME type. A catalog of registered MIME types is available from *ftp:// ftp.isi.edu/in-notes/iana/assignments/media-types/*.

Default None.

VALUE

VALUE=" *runTimeParameterValue*"   *Optional*

The parameter value to be passed to an applet or object as the executable program or data loads. Parameter values are passed as string values, and it is up to the applet or object to perform the necessary internal coercion of the data to the desired data type. The VALUE attribute is listed as optional because there may be instances in which the presence of the PARAM element NAME attribute may be sufficient for the object.

Example `<PARAM NAME="loop" VALUE="4">`

Value   Any string value.

Default None.

HTML Reference

VALUETYPE   NN *n/a*   IE *n/a*   HTML *4*

VALUETYPE="*paramValueType*"   *Optional*

OBJECT element parameters can come in three flavors: data, object, and ref. The VALUETYPE attribute uses these constants to tell the browser how to treat the value assigned to the VALUE attribute for passing to the object. When the VALUETYPE is data, the VALUE attribute is passed as a plain text string. A VALUETYPE of object means that the VALUE attribute consists of an identifier to some other OBJECT element defined earlier in the same document. The other object may be one whose DECLARE attribute is set, and now the parameter values are being passed to instantiate the object. When VALUETYPE is ref, the VALUE attribute is a URL that points to a file or other resource where run-time values are stored (perhaps a set of parameter values).

Example

```
<PARAM NAME="anime" VALUE="http://www.giantco.com/params/animation.txt"
VALUETYPE="ref" TYPE="text/html">
```

Value   Three possible constant values: data | object | ref.

Default   data

<PLAINTEXT>   NN *all*   IE *all*   HTML *<4*

<PLAINTEXT>...</PLAINTEXT>   *End Tag: Optional*

The PLAINTEXT element displays its content in a monospace font as a block element, but with a twist. All document source code coming after the start tag is rendered as-is in the browser window. You cannot turn off the PLAINTEXT element. Even the end tag is rendered as-is. This element has been long deprecated in HTML and has even been removed from the HTML 4.0 specification. You are encouraged to use the PRE element instead.

Specifying any element attribute in Internet Explorer 4 for the Macintosh causes the PLAINTEXT element to be ignored. In other words, the source code is rendered and the attribute is applied to the content contained by the element if applicable (such as a style sheet rule).

Example

```
<P>The rest of the HTML code follows:</P>
<PLAINTEXT>
...
</HTML>
```

Object Model Reference

IE   [window.]document.all.*elementID*

Attributes

CLASS	LANG	LANGUAGE	STYLE	TITLE
ID				

Event Handler Attributes

Handler	NN	IE	HTML
onClick	n/a	4	n/a
onDblClick	n/a	4	n/a
onDragStart	n/a	4	n/a
onHelp	n/a	4	n/a
onKeyDown	n/a	4	n/a
onKeyPress	n/a	4	n/a
onKeyUp	n/a	4	n/a
onMouseDown	n/a	4	n/a
onMouseMove	n/a	4	n/a
onMouseOut	n/a	4	n/a
onMouseOver	n/a	4	n/a
onMouseUp	n/a	4	n/a
onSelectStart	n/a	4	n/a

<PRE>   NN *all*   IE *all*   HTML *all*

`<PRE>...</PRE>`   *End Tag: Required*

The PRE element defines a block of preformatted text. Preformatted text is usually rendered by default in a monospace font and, more importantly, it preserves the whitespace (multiple spaces between words and new lines) entered into the source code for the content. Unlike the deprecated PLAINTEXT element, the PRE element doesn't ignore HTML tags. Instead, it passes such tags onto the browser for normal rendering. If you want to display HTML tags in a block of preformatted text, use entities for the less-than (<) and greater-than (>) symbols. This prevents them from being interpreted as genuine tags but renders the symbols within the preformatted text block.

Browsers are supposed to ignore a whitespace line break immediately following a PRE element start tag in case you wish to start the content on a new line in the source code. By and large, the Version 4 browsers follow this rule (with the exception of IE 4 for the Mac).

The HTML 4.0 specification is adamant about the PRE element maintaining its monospaced font size and line spacing. It lists the following elements that should not be included inside a PRE element: APPLET, BASEFONT, BIG, FONT, IMG, OBJECT, SMALL, SUB, and SUP. Any one of these destroys the fixed-size pitch of the PRE element. The recommendation also encourages authors to avoid overriding the monospaced font settings with style sheets.

One last admonition concerns using tab characters to indent or align text within a PRE element. Not all browsers render tab characters the same way. Avoid potential problems by using space characters and let the PRE element's preservation of whitespace do the job. No nonbreaking spaces ( ) are necessary in a PRE element.

Example

```
<P>Here is the script example:</P>
<PRE>
&lt;SCRIPT LANGUAGE="JavaScript"&gt;
    document.write("Hello, world.")
&lt;/SCRIPT&gt;
</PRE>
```

Object Model Reference

IE   [window.]document.all.*elementID*

Attributes

CLASS	DIR	LANG	STYLE	WIDTH
COLS	ID	LANGUAGE	TITLE	WRAP

Event Handler Attributes

Handler	NN	IE	HTML
onClick	n/a	4	4
onDblClick	n/a	4	4
onDragStart	n/a	4	n/a
onHelp	n/a	4	n/a
onKeyDown	n/a	4	4
onKeyPress	n/a	4	4
onKeyUp	n/a	4	4
onMouseDown	n/a	4	4
onMouseMove	n/a	4	4
onMouseOut	n/a	4	4
onMouseOver	n/a	4	4
onMouseUp	n/a	4	4
onSelectStart	n/a	4	n/a

COLS
NN *all*   IE *n/a*   HTML *n/a*

COLS="*columnCount*"   *Optional*

The maximum number of characters per line of preformatted code. This Navigator-specific attribute automatically sets the WRAP attribute to true. Without this attribute, the source code formatting governs the line width.

Example   <PRE COLS=80>...</PRE>

Value   Any positive integer.

Default   None.

WIDTH
NN *n/a*   IE *n/a*   HTML *4*

WIDTH="*columnCount*"   *Optional*

The HTML 4.0 specification introduces the WIDTH attribute to allow setting a maximum number of characters to be rendered on a preformatted line of text. Presumably, browsers that support this attribute in the future will wrap lines so that words do not break in the middle. Without this attribute, the source code formatting governs the line width. Navigator provides this functionality with the COLS attribute.

Example   <PRE WIDTH=80>...</PRE>

Value   Any positive integer.

Default   None.

WRAP

WRAP   *Optional*

The presence of the WRAP attribute instructs Navigator to word-wrap preformatted text so that text does not run beyond the right edge of the browser window or frame. WRAP is set to true automatically when the COLS attribute is set.

Example   <PRE WRAP>...</PRE>

Value   The presence of the attribute sets its value to true.

Default   false

<Q>

<Q>...</Q>   *End Tag: Required*

The Q element is intended to set off an inline quote inside a document. The HTML 4.0 specification indicates that browsers should automatically surround the content of a Q element with language-sensitive quotation marks, and that authors should not include quotes. Internet Explorer 4 does not render such quote marks. If you need quotes around quoted text, you have no choice at this point but to include them yourself and not use the Q element (because a future browser may add those quotes to the content). For a block-level quotation, see the BLOCKQUOTE element.

Example
```
<P>The preamble to the U.S. Constitution begins,
<Q>We the People of the United States</Q></P>
```

Object Model Reference
IE   [window.]document.all.*elementID*

Attributes

CITE	DIR	LANG	STYLE	TITLE
CLASS	ID	LANGUAGE		

Event Handler Attributes

Handler	NN	IE	HTML
onClick	n/a	4	4
onDblClick	n/a	4	4
onDragStart	n/a	4	n/a
onHelp	n/a	4	n/a
onKeyDown	n/a	4	4
onKeyPress	n/a	4	4
onKeyUp	n/a	4	4
onMouseDown	n/a	4	4
onMouseMove	n/a	4	4
onMouseOut	n/a	4	4
onMouseOver	n/a	4	4
onMouseUp	n/a	4	4
onSelectStart	n/a	4	n/a

CITE

NN *n/a*   IE *n/a*   HTML *4*

CITE="*URL*"   *Optional*

A URL pointing to an online source document from which the quotation is taken. This is not in any way a mechanism for copying or extracting content from another document. Presumably, this HTML 4.0 recommendation is to encourage future browsers and search engines to utilize a reference to online source material for the benefit of readers and surfers.

Value

Any valid URL to a document on the World Wide Web, including absolute or relative URLs.

Default   None.

<S>

NN *3*   IE *3*   HTML *3.2*

<S>...</S>   *End Tag: Required*

The S element renders its content as strikethrough text. This element is identical to the STRIKE element; it was adopted because it more closely resembled the one-character element names for other type formatting (such as B, I, and U elements). In any case, both S and STRIKE elements are deprecated in HTML 4.0 in favor of the text-decoration:line-through style sheet attribute.

Example

<P>If at first you don't succeed, <S>do it over</S> try, try again.</P>

Object Model Reference

IE   [window.]document.all.*elementID*

Attributes

CLASS	ID	LANGUAGE	STYLE	TITLE
DIR	LANG			

Event Handler Attributes

Handler	NN	IE	HTML
onClick	n/a	4	4
onDblClick	n/a	4	4
onDragStart	n/a	4	n/a
onHelp	n/a	4	n/a
onKeyDown	n/a	4	4
onKeyPress	n/a	4	4
onKeyUp	n/a	4	4
onMouseDown	n/a	4	4
onMouseMove	n/a	4	4
onMouseOut	n/a	4	4
onMouseOver	n/a	4	4
onMouseUp	n/a	4	4
onSelectStart	n/a	4	n/a

<SAMP>

<SAMP>...</SAMP>   *End Tag: Required*

The SAMP element is one of a large group of elements that the HTML 4.0 recommendation calls *phrase elements*. Such elements assign structural meaning to a designated portion of the document. A SAMP element is one that contains text that is sample output from a computer program or script. This is different from a code example, which is covered by the CODE element.

Browsers have free rein to determine how (or whether) to distinguish SAMP element content from the rest of the BODY element. Both Navigator and Internet Explorer elect to render the text in monospace font. This can be overridden with a style sheet as you see fit.

Example

```
<P>When you press the Enter key, you will see <SAMP>Hello, world!</SAMP>
on the screen.</P>
```

Object Model Reference

IE   [window.]document.all.*elementID*

Attributes

CLASS	ID	LANGUAGE	STYLE	TITLE
DIR	LANG			

Event Handler Attributes

Handler	NN	IE	HTML
onClick	n/a	4	4
onDblClick	n/a	4	4
onDragStart	n/a	4	n/a
onHelp	n/a	4	n/a
onKeyDown	n/a	4	4
onKeyPress	n/a	4	4
onKeyUp	n/a	4	4
onMouseDown	n/a	4	4
onMouseMove	n/a	4	4
onMouseOut	n/a	4	4
onMouseOver	n/a	4	4
onMouseUp	n/a	4	4
onSelectStart	n/a	4	n/a

<SCRIPT>

<SCRIPT>...</SCRIPT>   *End Tag: Required*

The SCRIPT element provides a container for lines of script code written in any scripting language that the browser is capable of interpreting. Script statements that are not written inside a function definition are executed as the page loads; function definitions are loaded but their execution is deferred until explicitly invoked by user or system action (events). You can have more than one SCRIPT element in a document, and you may include SCRIPT elements written in different script languages within the same document.

An important shift in attribute syntax is introduced with HTML 4.0. To specify the scripting language of the statements within a **SCRIPT** element, the **LANGUAGE** attribute has been used since the first scriptable browsers. HTML 4.0 deprecates that attribute in favor of the **TYPE** attribute, whose value is a MIME type. When the **TYPE** attribute is widely adopted by browsers, you may want to include both attributes in documents for long-term backward compatibility with older browsers.

Newer browsers also allow script statements to be imported into the document from a document whose URL is specified for the **SRC** attribute. Older, nonscriptable browsers don't recognize the **SCRIPT** element and may attempt to render the script statements as regular HTML content. To prevent this, wrap the script statements inside HTML block comment markers. The end-of-comment marker (**-->**) must be preceded by a JavaScript comment marker (**//**) to prevent JavaScript from generating a script error.

Example

```
<SCRIPT TYPE="text/javascript" LANGUAGE="JavaScript">
<!--
function howdy() {
    alert("Hello, world!")
}
//-->
</SCRIPT>
```

Attributes

CHARSET	DEFER	FOR	LANGUAGE	*TITLE*
CLASS	EVENT	*ID*	SRC	TYPE

CHARSET
                                           NN *n/a*   IE *n/a*   HTML *4*

CHARSET="*characterSet*"   *Optional*

Character encoding of the content in the file referred to by the **SRC** attribute.

Example   `<SCRIPT CHARSET="csISO5427Cyrillic" SRC="moscow.js"></SCRIPT>`

Value

Case-insensitive alias from the character set registry (*ftp://ftp.isi.edu/in-notes/iana/assignments/character-sets*).

Default   Determined by browser.

DEFER
                                           NN *n/a*   IE *4*   HTML *4*

DEFER   *Optional*

The presence of the **DEFER** attribute instructs the browser to render regular HTML content without looking for the script to generate content as the page loads. This is an advisory attribute only. The browser doesn't have to hold up rendering further HTML content as it parses the content of the **SCRIPT** element in search of **document.write()** statements.

Example

```
<SCRIPT TYPE="text/javascript" LANGUAGE="JavaScript" DEFER>
...
</SCRIPT>
```

Value   The presence of this attribute sets its value to true.

Default   false

Object Model Reference

IE   [window.]document.all.*elementID*.defer

EVENT   NN *n/a*   IE *4*   HTML *n/a*

EVENT=" *eventName*"   *Optional*

Internet Explorer 4's event model allows binding of object events to SCRIPT elements with the help of the EVENT and FOR attributes. As the page loads, the browser registers each SCRIPT element with its event and object binding so that when the object generates the event, the script statements inside the SCRIPT element execute—without having to write event handlers for the objects or wrap the script statements inside function definitions. Event values are written either as unquoted event names or as quoted event names formatted as functions (with trailing parentheses and optional parameter names). Use this type of script-event binding only in Internet Explorer. Navigator attempts to execute the script statements while the page loads.

Example

```
<SCRIPT FOR=window EVENT=onresize>
...
</SCRIPT>
```

Value

Case-sensitive event name (unquoted) or the event name as a function inside a quote pair. The object described in the FOR attribute must support the event named in the EVENT attribute.

Default   None.

Object Model Reference

IE   [window.]document.all.*elementID*.event

FOR   NN *n/a*   IE *4*   HTML *n/a*

FOR=*elementID*   *Optional*

Internet Explorer 4's event model allows binding of object events to SCRIPT elements with the help of the EVENT and FOR attributes. As the page loads, the browser registers each SCRIPT element with its event and object binding so that when the object generates the event, the script statements inside the SCRIPT element execute—without having to write event handlers for the objects or wrap the script statements inside function definitions. Use the unique ID attribute value of the element whose event you wish to handle. Use this type of script-event binding only in Internet Explorer. Navigator attempts to execute the script statements while the page loads.

Example

```
<SCRIPT FOR=firstNameEntry EVENT="onChange()">
...
</SCRIPT>
```

Value

Case-sensitive ID value of the event-generating element, unquoted. The object described in the FOR attribute must support the event named in the EVENT attribute.

Default   None.

Object Model Reference

IE   [window.]document.all.*elementID*.htmlFor

LANGUAGE   NN *2*   IE *3*   HTML *4*

LANGUAGE="*scriptingLanguage*"   *Optional*

Sets the scripting language for script statements defined in the element. This attribute is deprecated in HTML 4.0 (in favor of the TYPE attribute), but it has been so widely used since the first days of scriptable browsers that its use and support will continue for a long time to come.

Example

```
<SCRIPT LANGUAGE="JavaScript">
...
</SCRIPT>
```

Value

Internet Explorer recognizes four case-insensitive language names: JAVASCRIPT | JSCRIPT | VBS | VBSCRIPT. Navigator recognizes only JAVASCRIPT. Versions of JavaScript are also supported in appropriate browsers. To keep the attribute values one-word identifiers, the version numbers are tacked onto the end of the "JavaScript" language name. The version-less "JavaScript" is observed by all browsers; "JavaScript1.1" is recognized only by Navigator 3; "JavaScript1.2" is recognized by Navigator 4 and Internet Explorer 4. When SCRIPT elements are assigned these later version values, older browsers that don't support the named version ignore the SCRIPT elements.

Default   JavaScript

Object Model Reference

IE   [window.]document.all.*elementID*.language

SRC   NN *3*   IE *4*   HTML *4*

SRC="*URL*"   *Optional*

Imports a file of script statements from an external file. Once the external statements are loaded, the browser treats them as if they were embedded in the main HTML document. This attribute had some support in Internet Explorer 3, but it relied on a specific *JScript.dll* version, which makes it unreliable to blindly use it in IE 3.

In theory, you should be able to add script statements inside a SCRIPT element that loads an external script library file. In practice, it is more reliable to provide a separate SCRIPT element for each external library file and for in-document scripts.

Current implementations limit the SRC attribute to point to JavaScript external files. Such files must have a *.js* filename extension, and the server must have the extension and application/x-javascript MIME type set to serve up such files.

Example   <SCRIPT LANGUAGE="JavaScript" SRC="stringParseLib.js"></SCRIPT>

Value

Any valid URL. Current browsers require files whose names end in the *.js* extension. A complete URL may help overcome difficulties in some earlier browsers that implement this feature.

Default   None.

Object Model Reference

IE   [window.]document.all.*elementID*.src

TYPE

NN *n/a*   IE *4*   HTML *4*

TYPE="*elementType*"   *Required*

An advisory about the content type of the script statements. The content type should tell the browser which scripting engine to use to interpret the script statements. The TYPE attribute may eventually replace the LANGUAGE attribute as the one defining the scripting language in which the element's statements are written. To be compatible with future and past browsers, you may include both the LANGUAGE and TYPE attributes in a SCRIPT element.

Example

```
<SCRIPT TYPE="text/javascript" LANGUAGE="JavaScript">
...
</SCRIPT>
```

Value

Case-insensitive MIME type. Values are limited to one(s) for which a particular browser is equipped.

Default   text/javascript in Internet Explorer 4.

Object Model Reference

IE   [window.]document.all.*elementID*.type

<SELECT>

NN *all*   IE *all*   HTML *all*

<SELECT>...</SELECT>   *End Tag: Required*

The SELECT element displays information from nested OPTION elements as either a scrolling list or pop-up menu in a document. Users typically make a selection from the list of items (or multiple selections from a scrolling list if the SIZE attribute is set greater than 1 and the MULTIPLE attribute is set). The VALUE attribute of the selected OPTION item is submitted as the value part of a name/value pair to the server with a form. Navigator requires that a SELECT element be placed inside a FORM element.

Example

```
<SELECT NAME="chapters">
    <OPTION VALUE="chap1.html">Chapter 1
    <OPTION VALUE="chap2.html">Chapter 2
    <OPTION VALUE="chap3.html">Chapter 3
    <OPTION VALUE="chap4.html">Chapter 4
</SELECT>
```

Object Model Reference

NN   [window.]document.*formName.selectName*
      [window.]document.forms[i].elements[i]

IE   [window.]document.*formName.selectName*
      [window.]document.forms[i].elements[i]
      [window.]document.all.*elementID*

Attributes

ACCESSKEY	DATAFLD	*ID*	MULTIPLE	*STYLE*
ALIGN	DATASRC	*LANG*	NAME	TABINDEX
CLASS	DISABLED	*LANGUAGE*	SIZE	

Event Handler Attributes

Handler	NN	IE	HTML
onAfterUpdate	n/a	4	n/a
onBeforeUpdate	n/a	4	n/a
onBlur	2	3	4
onChange	2	3	4
onClick	n/a	4	4
onDblClick	n/a	4	4
onDragStart	n/a	4	n/a
onFocus	2	3	4
onHelp	n/a	4	n/a
onKeyDown	n/a	4	4
onKeyPress	n/a	4	4
onKeyUp	n/a	4	4
onMouseDown	n/a	4	4
onMouseMove	n/a	4	4
onMouseOut	n/a	4	4
onMouseOver	n/a	4	4
onMouseUp	n/a	4	4
onResize	n/a	4	n/a
onRowEnter	n/a	4	n/a
onRowExit	n/a	4	n/a
onSelectStart	n/a	4	n/a

ACCESSKEY

NN *n/a*   IE *4*   HTML *n/a*

ACCESSKEY="*character*"   *Optional*

A single character key that brings focus to the element. The browser and operating system determine if the user must press a modifier key (e.g., **Ctrl**, **Alt**, or **Command**) with the access key to bring focus to the element. In IE 4/Windows, the **Alt** key is required, and the key is not case sensitive. This attribute does not work in IE 4/Mac.

Example
```
<SELECT NAME="chapters" ACCESSKEY="c">
...
</SELECT>
```

Value   Single character of the document set.

Default   None.

Object Model Reference
IE   [window.]document.*formName*.*selectName*.accessKey
            [window.]document.forms[i].elements[i].accessKey

ALIGN

NN *n/a*   IE *4*   HTML *4*

ALIGN="*alignmentConstant*"   *Optional*

Determines how the rectangle of the SELECT element (particularly when the SIZE attribute is set greater than 1) aligns within the context of surrounding content. See the section "Alignment Constants" earlier in this chapter for a description of the possibilities defined in both Navigator and Internet Explorer for this attribute.

Example
```
<SELECT NAME="chapters"MULTIPLE ALIGN="baseline">
...
</SELECT>
```

Value

Case-insensitive constant value. All constant values are available in Internet Explorer 4.

Default   bottom (IE 4/Windows); absmiddle (IE 4/Macintosh).

Object Model Reference
IE   [window.]document.*formName*.*selectName*.align
            [window.]document.forms[i].elements[i].align

DATAFLD

NN *n/a*   IE *4*   HTML *n/a*

DATAFLD="*columnName*"   *Optional*

Used with IE 4 data binding to associate a remote data source column name to the selectedIndex property of a SELECT element (i.e., a zero-based index value of the item currently selected in the list, as described in the SELECT object of Chapter 9). As such, you can use data binding only with SELECT elements that do not specify the MULTIPLE attribute. A DATASRC attribute must also be set for the element.

Example

```
<SELECT NAME="chapters" DATASRC="#DBSRC3" DATAFLD="chapterRequest">
    <OPTION VALUE="chap1.html">Chapter 1
    <OPTION VALUE="chap2.html">Chapter 2
    <OPTION VALUE="chap3.html">Chapter 3
    <OPTION VALUE="chap4.html">Chapter 4
</SELECT>
```

Value   Case-sensitive identifier.

Default   None.

Object Model Reference

IE   [window.]document.*formName*.*selectName*.dataFld
          [window.]document.forms[i].elements[i].dataFld

DATASRC   NN *n/a*   IE *4*   HTML *n/a*

DATASRC="*dataSourceName*"   *Optional*

Used with IE 4 data binding to specify the name of the remote ODBC data source (such as an Oracle or SQL Server database) to be associated with the element. Content from the data source is specified via the **DATAFLD** attribute.

Example

```
<SELECT NAME="chapters" DATASRC="#DBSRC3" DATAFLD="chapterRequest">
    <OPTION VALUE="chap1.html">Chapter 1
    <OPTION VALUE="chap2.html">Chapter 2
    <OPTION VALUE="chap3.html">Chapter 3
    <OPTION VALUE="chap4.html">Chapter 4
</SELECT>
```

Value   Case-sensitive identifier.

Default   None.

Object Model Reference

IE   [window.]document.*formName*.*selectName*.dataSrc
          [window.]document.forms[i].elements[i].dataSrc

DISABLED   NN *n/a*   IE *4*   HTML *4*

DISABLED   *Optional*

The presence of this attribute disables the entire **SELECT** element and its nested **OPTION** elements. The element receives no events when it is disabled.

Example

```
<SELECT NAME="chapters" DISABLED>
    <OPTION VALUE="chap1.html">Chapter 1
    <OPTION VALUE="chap2.html">Chapter 2
    <OPTION VALUE="chap3.html">Chapter 3
    <OPTION VALUE="chap4.html">Chapter 4
</SELECT>
```

Value   The presence of this attribute sets its value to **true**.

Default   `false`

Object Model Reference

IE   [window.]document.*formName*.*selectName*.disabled
[window.]document.forms[i].elements[i].disabled

MULTIPLE   NN *all*   IE *all*   HTML *all*

MULTIPLE   *Optional*

The presence of the **MULTIPLE** attribute instructs the browser to render the **SELECT** element as a list box and to allow users to make multiple selections from the list of options. By default, the **SIZE** attribute is set to the number of nested **OPTION** elements, but the value may be overridden with the **SIZE** attribute setting. Users can select contiguous items by **Shift**-clicking on the first and last items of the group. To make discontiguous selections, Windows users must **Ctrl**-click on each item; Mac users must **Command**-click on each item. The **MULTIPLE** attribute has no effect when **SIZE** is set to 1 to display a pop-up menu.

Example

```
<SELECT NAME="equipment" MULTIPLE>
<OPTION VALUE="monitor">Video monitor
<OPTION VALUE="modem">Modem
<OPTION VALUE="printer">Printer
...
</SELECT>
```

Value   The presence of this attribute sets its value to **true**.

Default   `false`

Object Model Reference

NN   [window.]document.*formName*.*selectName*.type
[window.]document.forms[i].elements[i].type

IE   [window.]document.*formName*.*selectName*.multiple
[window.]document.forms[i].elements[i].multiple
[window.]document.*formName*.*selectName*.type
[window.]document.forms[i].elements[i].type

NAME   NN *all*   IE *all*   HTML *all*

NAME="*elementIdentifier*"   *Optional*

The name submitted as part of the element's name/value pair with the form. It is similar to the **NAME** attribute of **INPUT** elements.

Example

```
<SELECT NAME="cpu">
<OPTION VALUE="486">486
<OPTION VALUE="pentium">Pentium
<OPTION VALUE="pentium2">Pentium II
...
</SELECT>
```

Value   Case-sensitive identifier.

Default   None.

Object Model Reference

NN   [window.]document.*formName*.*selectName*.name
            [window.]document.forms[i].elements[i].name

IE   [window.]document.*formName*.*selectName*.name
            [window.]document.forms[i].elements[i].name

SIZE   NN *all*   IE *all*   HTML *all*

SIZE="*rowCount*"   *Optional*

Controls the number of rows of OPTION elements that appear in the SELECT element. With a value of 1, the SELECT element displays its content as a pop-up menu; with a value greater than 1, OPTION items are rendered in a list box. Browsers control the width of the element, based on the widest text associated with nested OPTION elements.

Example

```
<SELECT NAME="equipment" SIZE=3>
<OPTION VALUE="monitor">Video monitor
<OPTION VALUE="modem">Modem
<OPTION VALUE="printer">Printer
...
</SELECT>
```

Value   Any positive integer.

Default   1

Object Model Reference

IE   [window.]document.*formName*.*selectName*.size
            [window.]document.forms[i].elements[i].size

TABINDEX   NN *n/a*   IE *4*   HTML *4*

TABINDEX=integer   *Optional*

A number that indicates the sequence of this element within the tabbing order of all focusable elements in the document. Tabbing order follows a strict set of rules. Elements that have values other than zero assigned to their TABINDEX attributes are first in line when a user starts tabbing in a page. Focus starts with the element with the lowest TABINDEX value and proceeds in order to the highest value, regardless of physical location on the page or in the document. If two elements have the same TABINDEX values, the element that comes earlier in the document receives focus first. Next come all elements that either don't support the TABINDEX attribute or have the value set to zero. These elements receive focus in the order in which they appear in the document. Note that the Macintosh user interface does not provide for giving focus to elements other than text and password INPUT fields.

Example

```
<SELECT NAME="chapters" TABINDEX=5>
...
</SELECT>
```

Value

Any integer from 0 through 32767. In IE 4, setting the TABINDEX to -1 causes the element to be skipped in tabbing order altogether.

Default   None.

Object Model Reference

IE   [window.]document.*formName*.*selectName*.tabIndex
            [window.]document.forms[i].elements[i].tabIndex

<SERVER>   NN *2*   IE *n/a*   HTML *n/a*

<SERVER>...</SERVER>	*End Tag: Required*

The SERVER element is a Navigator-specific element that instructs a Netscape web server (FastTrack or Enterprise server) to execute server-side JavaScript routines. Such routines may include retrieving or setting database records as well as assembling content that is written to the current page. Server-side scripting is outside the scope of this book.

Example

```
<BODY>
<P>Today's closing numbers:</P>
<SERVER>displayClose()</SERVER>
</BODY>
```

<SMALL>   NN *2*   IE *3*   HTML *3.2*

<SMALL>...</SMALL>	*End Tag: Required*

The SMALL element renders its content in a relative size one level smaller than the text preceding the element. Given the FONT element's way of specifying sizes in a range of 1 through 7, the SMALL element displays its content one size smaller than the text that comes before it. This attribute is the same as specifying <FONT SIZE=-1>.

Example   <P>Let's get really <SMALL>small</SMALL>.</P>

Object Model Reference

IE   [window.]document.all.*elementID*

Attributes

CLASS	*ID*	*LANGUAGE*	*STYLE*	*TITLE*
DIR	*LANG*			

Event Handler Attributes

Handler	NN	IE	HTML
onClick	n/a	4	4
onDblClick	n/a	4	4
onDragStart	n/a	4	n/a
onHelp	n/a	4	n/a
onKeyDown	n/a	4	4
onKeyPress	n/a	4	4

Handler	NN	IE	HTML
onKeyUp	n/a	4	4
onMouseDown	n/a	4	4
onMouseMove	n/a	4	4
onMouseOut	n/a	4	4
onMouseOver	n/a	4	4
onMouseUp	n/a	4	4
onSelectStart	n/a	4	n/a

<SPACER>
NN *3*   IE *n/a*   HTML *n/a*

<SPACER>   *End Tag: Forbidden*

As a solution to the need for creating blank space without forcing   entities, incessant <P> tags, or transparent images, Navigator 3 introduced the SPACER element. This
element creates empty space within a line of text, between lines, or as a rectangular space.
Some of this functionality can be re-created in a cross-browser implementation with style
sheets.

Example
```
<P>This is one line of a paragraph.
<SPACER TYPE="vertical" SIZE=36>
And this completes the paragraph with a three-line gap from the first
line.</P>
```

Attributes
ALIGN   HEIGHT   SIZE   TYPE   WIDTH

ALIGN
NN *3*   IE *n/a*   HTML *n/a*

ALIGN="*alignmentConstant*"   *Optional*

Determines how the rectangle of the SPACER element aligns within the context of
surrounding content. See the section "Alignment Constants" earlier in this chapter for a
description of the possibilities.

Example   <SPACER TYPE="block" HEIGHT=90 WIDTH=40 ALIGN="absmiddle">

Value
Case-insensitive constant value. All constant values are available in Navigator 4.

Default   bottom

HEIGHT, WIDTH
NN *3*   IE *n/a*   HTML *n/a*

HEIGHT="*pixelCount*"   *Required*
WIDTH="*pixelCount*"

The size that a block type SPACER element occupies in a document is governed by the
HEIGHT and WIDTH attribute settings. These attributes apply only when the TYPE attribute is
block.

Example   <SPACER TYPE="block" HEIGHT=150 WIDTH=250>

Value   Positive integer values (optionally quoted).

Default   0

SIZE

NN *3*   IE *n/a*   HTML *n/a*

SIZE=*"pixelCount"*   *Optional*

The number of pixels of whitespace to insert either horizontally or vertically, depending on whether the TYPE attribute is set to horizontal or vertical. If the TYPE attribute is set to block, the SIZE attribute is ignored.

Example   <SPACER TYPE="horizontal" SIZE=40>

Value   Any positive integer.

Default   0

TYPE

NN *3*   IE *n/a*   HTML *n/a*

TYPE=*"spacerType"*   *Required*

Defines which of the three spacer geometries is being specified for the SPACER element. A type of horizontal adds empty space in the same line of text as the preceding content; a type of vertical adds empty space between lines of text; and a type of block defines a rectangular space that extends in two dimensions. For the horizontal and vertical types, the SIZE attribute must be assigned; for the block type, the HEIGHT and WIDTH attributes must be assigned.

Example   <SPACER TYPE="horizontal" SIZE=40>

Value

Any of three case-insensitive constant values: block I horizontal I vertical.

Default   horizontal

WIDTH

See HEIGHT.

<SPAN>

NN *4*   IE *3*   HTML *4*

<SPAN>...</SPAN>   *End Tag: Required*

The SPAN element gives structure and context to any inline content in a document. Unlike some other structural elements that have very specific connotations attached to them (the P element, for instance), the author is free to give meaning to each particular SPAN element by virtue of the element's attribute settings and nested content. Each SPAN element becomes a generic container for all content within the required start and end tags.

It is convenient to use the SPAN element as a wrapper for a small inline chunk of content that is to be governed by a style sheet rule. For example, if you want to differentiate a few words in a paragraph with the equivalent of a small caps look, you would wrap the affected words with a SPAN element whose style sheet defines the requested font and text styles.

HTML Reference

Such a style sheet could be defined as an inline STYLE attribute of the SPAN element or assigned via the CLASS or ID attribute depending on the structure of the rest of the document.

If you need an arbitrary container for block-level content, use the DIV element.

HTML 4.0 defines many more attributes for the SPAN element than are implemented in Version 4 browsers. The breadth of HTML attributes indicates the potential powers of this generic element to include links to related resources and many advisory attributes about those links. The same set of attributes apply to the DIV element in the HTML 4.0 specification.

Example

```
<SPAN STYLE="font-size:10pt; text-transform:uppercase">
30-day special offer</SPAN>
```

Object Model Reference

IE   [window.]document.all.*elementID*

Attributes

CHARSET	DATASRC	*ID*	REL	TARGET
CLASS	*DIR*	*LANG*	REV	*TITLE*
DATAFLD	HREF	*LANGUAGE*	*STYLE*	TYPE
DATAFORMATAS	HREFLANG	MEDIA		

Event Handler Attributes

Handler	NN	IE	HTML
onClick	n/a	3	4
onDblClick	n/a	4	4
onDragStart	n/a	4	n/a
onHelp	n/a	4	n/a
onKeyDown	n/a	4	4
onKeyPress	n/a	4	4
onKeyUp	n/a	4	4
onMouseDown	n/a	4	4
onMouseMove	n/a	4	4
onMouseOut	n/a	4	4
onMouseOver	n/a	3	4
onMouseUp	n/a	4	4
onSelectStart	n/a	4	n/a

CHARSET   NN *n/a*   IE *n/a*   HTML *4*

CHARSET="*characterSet*"   *Optional*

Character encoding of the content at the other end of the link.

Example <SPAN CHARSET="csISO5427Cyrillic">*CyrillicTextHere*</SPAN>

Value

Case-insensitive alias from the character set registry (*ftp://ftp.isi.edu/in-notes/iana/ assignments/character-sets*).

Default   Determined by browser.

DATAFLD

NN *n/a*   IE *4*   HTML *n/a*

DATAFLD="*columnName*"   *Optional*

Used with IE 4 data binding to associate a remote data source column name with the HTML content of a SPAN element. The data source column must be HTML (see DATAFORMATAS). DATASRC and DATAFORMATAS attributes must also be set for the SPAN element.

Example

```
<SPAN  DATASRC="#DBSRC3" DATAFLD="quote" DATAFORMATAS="HTML"> ...</SPAN>
```

Value   Case-sensitive identifier.

Default   None.

Object Model Reference

IE   [window.]document.all.*elementID*.dataFld

DATAFORMATAS

NN *n/a*   IE *4*   HTML *n/a*

DATAFORMATAS="*dataType*"   *Optional*

Used with IE 4 data binding, this attribute advises the browser whether the source material arriving from the data source is to be treated as plain text or as tagged HTML. A SPAN element should receive data only in HTML format.

Example

```
<SPAN  DATASRC="#DBSRC3" DATAFLD="quote" DATAFORMATAS="HTML">...</SPAN>
```

Value   HTML

Default   text

Object Model Reference

IE   [window.]document.all.*elementID*.dataFormatAs

DATASRC

NN *n/a*   IE *4*   HTML *n/a*

DATASRC="*dataSourceName*"   *Optional*

Used with IE 4 data binding to specify the name of the remote ODBC data source (such as an Oracle or SQL Server database) to be associated with the element. Content from the data source is specified via the DATAFLD attribute.

Example

```
<SPAN  DATASRC="#DBSRC3" DATAFLD="quote" DATAFORMATAS="HTML">...</SPAN>
```

Value   Case-sensitive identifier.

Default   None.

Object Model Reference

IE   [window.]document.all.*elementID*.dataSrc

HREF   NN *n/a*   IE *n/a*   HTML *4*

HREF=" *URI*"   *Optional*

According to the HTML 4.0 specification, the HREF attribute is meant to offer a URL to a resource that can supply "more information" about the SPAN element's content. No recommendation is provided as to whether this URL should be rendered in any way (like the HREF attribute of an A element). Perhaps a future browser could use this URL to generate a margin note or footnote in the form of a link. Several other attributes clearly intend for the HREF attribute's URL to be accessible in some way by the user.

Example

```
<SPAN HREF="bibliogs/chap3.html"><A HREF="chap3.html">Chapter 3</A></SPAN>
```

Value

Any valid URL, including complete and relative URLs, anchors on the same page (anchor names prefaced with the # symbol), and the javascript: pseudo-URL in scriptable browsers to trigger a script statement rather than navigate to a destination.

Default   None.

HREFLANG   NN *n/a*   IE *n/a*   HTML *4*

HREFLANG=" *languageCode*"   *Optional*

The language code of the content at the destination of a link. Requires that the HREF attribute also be set. This attribute is primarily an advisory attribute to help a browser prepare itself for a new language set if the browser is so enabled.

Example

```
<SPAN HREFLANG="HI" HREF="bibliogs/hindi/chap3.html">
<A HREF="...">Chapter 3 (Hindi)</A>
</SPAN>
```

Value   Case-insensitive language code.

Default   Browser default.

MEDIA   NN *n/a*   IE *n/a*   HTML *4*

MEDIA=" *descriptorList*"   *Optional*

Sets the intended output device for the content of the SPAN element. The MEDIA attribute looks forward to the day when browsers are able to tailor content to specific kinds of devices such as pocket computers, text-to-speech digitizers, or fuzzy television sets. The HTML 4.0 specification defines a number of constant values for anticipated devices, but the list is open-ended, allowing future browsers to tailor output to other media and devices.

Example   `<SPAN MEDIA="screen, tv, handheld">...</SPAN>`

Value

Case-sensitive constant values. Multiple values can be grouped together in a comma-delimited list within a quoted string. Values defined in HTML 4.0 are `all` | `aura` | `braille` | `handheld` | `print` | `projection` | `screen` | `tty` | `tv`.

Default `screen`

REL   NN *n/a*   IE *n/a*   HTML *4*

REL=" *linkTypes*"   *Optional*

Defines the relationship between the current element and the destination of the link. Also known as a *forward link*, not to be confused in any way with the destination document whose address is defined by the HREF attribute. The HTML 4.0 recommendation defines several link types, and it is up to the browser to determine how to employ the value. The element must include an HREF attribute for the REL attribute to be applied.

Example `<SPAN REL="next chapter" HREF="chapter3.html">...</SPAN>`

Value

Case-insensitive, space-delimited list of HTML 4.0 standard link types applicable to the element. Sanctioned link types are:

alternate	contents	index	start
appendix	copyright	next	stylesheet
bookmark	glossary	prev	subsection
chapter	help	section	

Default None.

REV   NN *n/a*   IE *n/a*   HTML *4*

REV=" *linkTypes*"   *Optional*

A reverse link relationship. Like the REL attribute, the REV attribute's capabilities are defined by the browser, particularly with regard to how the browser interprets and renders the various link types available in the HTML 4.0 specification. Given two documents (A and B) containing links that point to each other, the REV value of B is designed to express the same relationship between the two documents as denoted by the REL attribute in A.

Example `<SPAN REV="previous chapter" HREF="chapter2.html">...</SPAN>`

Value

Case-insensitive, space-delimited list of HTML 4.0 standard link types applicable to the element. See the REL attribute for sanctioned link types.

Default None.

TARGET   NN *n/a*   IE *n/a*   HTML *4*

TARGET=" *windowOrFrameName*"   *Optional*

If the destination document associated with the HREF attribute is to be loaded into a window or frame other than the current window or frame, you can specify where the destination document should load by assigning a window or frame name to the TARGET attribute. Target frame names must be assigned to frames and windows as identifiers. Assign names to frames via the NAME attribute of the FRAME element; assign names to new windows via the second parameter of the window.open() scripting method. If you omit this attribute, the destination document replaces the document containing the link. This attribute is applicable only when a value is assigned to the HREF attribute of the element.

If this feature is implemented in future browsers, the SPAN element will probably have only one destination document and one target (like the A element). If you want a link to change the content of multiple frames, you can use a SPAN element's onClick event handler or a javascript: pseudo-URL to fire a script that loads multiple documents. Set the location.href property of each frame to a desired URL.

Example <SPAN TARGET="display" HREF="chap3.html#sec2">...</SPAN>

Value

Case-sensitive identifier when the frame or window name has been assigned via the target element's NAME attribute. Four reserved target names act as constants:

_blank   Browser creates a new window for the destination document.

_parent   Destination document replaces the current frame's framesetting document (if one exists; otherwise, it is treated as _self).

_self   Destination document replaces the current document in its window or frame.

_top   Destination document is to occupy the entire browser window, replacing any and all framesets that may be loaded (also treated as _self if there are no framesets defined in the window).

Default _self

TYPE   NN *n/a*   IE *n/a*   HTML *4*

TYPE="*MIMEType*"   *Optional*

An advisory about the content type of the destination document or resource. A browser might use this information to assist in preparing support for a resource requiring a multimedia player or plugin.

Example <SPAN TYPE="video/mpeg" HREF="ski4.mpeg">...</SPAN>

Value

Case-insensitive MIME type. A catalog of registered MIME types is available from *ftp:// ftp.isi.edu/in-notes/iana/assignments/media-types/*.

Default None.

<STRIKE>   NN *3*   IE *3*   HTML *3.2*

<STRIKE>...</STRIKE>   *End Tag: Required*

The STRIKE element renders its content as strikethrough text. This element is identical to the S element, which was adopted because it more closely resembled the one-character element names for other type formatting (such as B, I, and U elements). In any case, both

STRIKE and S elements are deprecated in HTML 4.0 in favor of the text-decoration:line-through style sheet attribute.

Example

```
<P>If at first you don't succeed, <STRIKE>do it over</STRIKE> try, try
again.</P>
```

Object Model Reference

IE   [window.]document.all.*elementID*

Attributes

CLASS	ID	LANGUAGE	STYLE	TITLE
DIR	LANG			

Event Handler Attributes

Handler	NN	IE	HTML
onClick	n/a	4	4
onDblClick	n/a	4	4
onDragStart	n/a	4	n/a
onHelp	n/a	4	n/a
onKeyDown	n/a	4	4
onKeyPress	n/a	4	4
onKeyUp	n/a	4	4
onMouseDown	n/a	4	4
onMouseMove	n/a	4	4
onMouseOut	n/a	4	4
onMouseOver	n/a	4	4
onMouseUp	n/a	4	4
onSelectStart	n/a	4	n/a

<STRONG>   NN *all*   IE *all*   HTML *all*

<STRONG>...</STRONG>   *End Tag: Required*

The STRONG element is one of a large group of elements that the HTML 4.0 recommendation calls *phrase elements*. Such elements assign structural meaning to a designated portion of the document. A STRONG element is one that contains text that indicates a stronger emphasis than the EM element. Whereas an EM element is typically rendered as italic text, a STRONG element is generally rendered as boldface text. This can be overridden with a style sheet as you see fit.

Example

```
<P>Don't delay. <STRONG>Order today</STRONG> to get the maximum discount.
</P>
```

Object Model Reference

IE   [window.]document.all.*elementID*

Attributes

CLASS	ID	LANGUAGE	STYLE	TITLE
DIR	LANG			

Event Handler Attributes

Handler	NN	IE	HTML
onClick	n/a	4	4
onDblClick	n/a	4	4
onDragStart	n/a	4	n/a
onHelp	n/a	4	n/a
onKeyDown	n/a	4	4
onKeyPress	n/a	4	4
onKeyUp	n/a	4	4
onMouseDown	n/a	4	4
onMouseMove	n/a	4	4
onMouseOut	n/a	4	4
onMouseOver	n/a	4	4
onMouseUp	n/a	4	4
onSelectStart	n/a	4	n/a

<STYLE>   NN *4*   IE *3*   HTML *4*

`<STYLE>...</STYLE>`   *End Tag: Required*

The **STYLE** element is a container for style sheet rules. Use the **STYLE** element only inside the **HEAD** element. You may include more than one **STYLE** element in a **HEAD** element (see the **MEDIA** attribute).

Older browsers may attempt to render the content of a **STYLE** element. To prevent that, you should wrap the style sheet rules inside HTML comment tags. See Chapter 3 for details on the makeup of style sheet rules.

Example

```
<STYLE TYPE="text/css">
<!--
H1 {font-size:18pt; text-transform:capitalize}
P  {font-size:12pt}
-->
</STYLE>
```

Attributes

DIR	LANG	MEDIA	TITLE	TYPE
DISABLED				

DISABLED   NN *n/a*   IE *4*   HTML *n/a*

DISABLED   *Optional*

Disables the entire **STYLE** element, as if it didn't exist in the document. This attribute does not work on the Macintosh version of Internet Explorer 4.

The DISABLED attribute is a Boolean type, which means that its presence in the attribute sets its value to true. Its value can also be adjusted after the fact by scripting (see the button object in Chapter 9).

Example `<STYLE TYPE="text/css"  DISABLED>...</STYLE>`

Value   The presence of the attribute disables the element.

Default false

Object Model Reference

IE   `[window.]document.all.tags("STYLE")[i].disabled`

MEDIA

NN *n/a*   IE 4   HTML 4

MEDIA="*descriptorList*"   *Optional*

Sets the intended output device for the content of the element. The MEDIA attribute looks forward to the day when browsers are able to tailor content to specific kinds of devices such as pocket computers, text-to-speech digitizers, or fuzzy television sets. The HTML 4.0 specification defines a number of constant values for anticipated devices, but the list is open-ended, allowing future browsers to tailor output to yet other kinds of media and devices.

Example `<STYLE TYPE="text/css"  MEDIA="print">...</STYLE>`

Value

Case-sensitive constant values. Multiple values can be grouped together in a comma-delimited list within a quoted string. Values defined in HTML 4.0 are all I aura I braille I handheld I print I projection I screen I tty I tv. Internet Explorer values are all I print I screen.

Default screen

Object Model Reference

IE   `[window.]document.all.tags("STYLE")[i].media`

TYPE

NN 4   IE 4   HTML 4

TYPE="*MIMEType*"   *Required*

The TYPE attribute tells the browser which style sheet syntax to use to interpret the style rules defined in the current element.

Example `<STYLE TYPE="text/css">...</STYLE>`

Value

Case-insensitive MIME type. A type accepted by both Navigator 4 and Internet Explorer 4 is "text/css". Navigator 4 also recognizes "text/javascript" when using JavaScript syntax style sheets.

Default text/css

Object Model Reference

IE   [window.]document.all.tags("STYLE")[i].type

<SUB>   NN *2*   IE *3*   HTML *3.2*

_{...}   *End Tag: Required*

The SUB element is a typographical element that instructs the browser to render its content as a subscript in a font size consistent with the surrounding content. Browsers tend to render this content in a smaller size than surrounding content.

Example

<P>"Heavy water" (H₃O) has one more hydrogen atom
than regular water.</P>

Object Model Reference

IE   [window.]document.all.*elementID*

Attributes

CLASS	ID	LANGUAGE	STYLE	TITLE
DIR	LANG			

Event Handler Attributes

Handler	NN	IE	HTML
onClick	n/a	4	4
onDblClick	n/a	4	4
onDragStart	n/a	4	n/a
onHelp	n/a	4	n/a
onKeyDown	n/a	4	4
onKeyPress	n/a	4	4
onKeyUp	n/a	4	4
onMouseDown	n/a	4	4
onMouseMove	n/a	4	4
onMouseOut	n/a	4	4
onMouseOver	n/a	4	4
onMouseUp	n/a	4	4
onSelectStart	n/a	4	n/a

<SUP>   NN *2*   IE *3*   HTML *3.2*

^{...}   *End Tag: Required*

The SUP element is a typographical element that instructs the browser to render its content as a superscript in a font size consistent with the surrounding content. Browsers tend to render this content in a smaller size than surrounding content.

Example   <P>This book is published by O'Reilly^{™}.</P>

Object Model Reference

IE   [window.]document.all.*elementID*

Attributes

CLASS	ID	LANGUAGE	STYLE	TITLE
DIR	LANG			

Event Handler Attributes

Handler	NN	IE	HTML
onClick	n/a	4	4
onDblClick	n/a	4	4
onDragStart	n/a	4	n/a
onHelp	n/a	4	n/a
onKeyDown	n/a	4	4
onKeyPress	n/a	4	4
onKeyUp	n/a	4	4
onMouseDown	n/a	4	4
onMouseMove	n/a	4	4
onMouseOut	n/a	4	4
onMouseOver	n/a	4	4
onMouseUp	n/a	4	4
onSelectStart	n/a	4	n/a

<TABLE>   NN *all*   IE *all*   HTML *3.2*

<TABLE>...</TABLE>   *End Tag: Required*

The TABLE element is a container for additional elements that specify the content for a table. A table consists of rows and columns of content. Other elements related to the TABLE element are CAPTION, COL, COLGROUP, TBODY, TD, TFOOT, TH, THEAD, and TR. The purpose of the TABLE element is to define a number of visible attributes that apply to the entire table, regardless of the number of rows or columns within it. Many of these attributes can be overridden for a given row, column, or cell. The number of rows and columns is strictly a factor of the structure of TR and TD elements within the table.

Tables have been used for a relatively long time not only to organize rows and columns of content but also to position content. With no visible borders, table rows and columns can be set to empty space. With the advent of positionable content, the tables-for-positioning practice is not encouraged.

Example

```
<TABLE COLS=3>
<THEAD>
<TR>
<TH>Time<TH>Event<TH>Location
</TR>
</THEAD>
<TBODY>
<TR>
```

```
<TD>7:30am-5:00pm<TD>Registration Open<TD>Main Lobby
</TR>
<TR>
<TD>9:00am-12:00pm<TD>Keynote Speakers<TD>Cypress Room
</TR>
</TBODY>
</TABLE>
```

Object Model Reference

IE   [window.]document.all.*elementID*

Attributes

ALIGN	BORDERCOLORDARK	COLS	HEIGHT	*STYLE*
BACKGROUND	BORDERCOLORLIGHT	DATAPAGESIZE	*ID*	SUMMARY
BGCOLOR	CELLPADDING	DATASRC	*LANG*	*TITLE*
BORDER	CELLSPACING	DIR	*LANGUAGE*	WIDTH
BORDERCOLOR	*CLASS*	FRAME	RULES	

Event Handler Attributes

Handler	NN	IE	HTML
onAfterUpdate	n/a	4	n/a
onBeforeUpdate	n/a	4	n/a
onBlur	n/a	4	n/a
onClick	n/a	4	4
onDblClick	n/a	4	4
onDragStart	n/a	4	n/a
onFocus	n/a	4	n/a
onHelp	n/a	4	n/a
onKeyDown	n/a	4	4
onKeyPress	n/a	4	4
onKeyUp	n/a	4	4
onMouseDown	n/a	4	4
onMouseMove	n/a	4	4
onMouseOut	n/a	4	4
onMouseOver	n/a	4	4
onMouseUp	n/a	4	4
onResize	n/a	4	n/a
onRowEnter	n/a	4	n/a
onRowExit	n/a	4	n/a
onScroll	n/a	4	n/a
onSelectStart	n/a	4	n/a

ALIGN

NN *all*   IE *all*   HTML *3.2*

ALIGN="*where*"   *Optional*

Determines how the table is aligned relative to the next outermost container (usually the document BODY). The ALIGN attribute is deprecated in HTML 4.0 in favor of style sheet attributes.

Example `<TABLE ALIGN="center"> </TABLE>`

Value Case-insensitive alignment constant: **center** | **left** | **right**.

Default **left**

Object Model Reference

IE   [window.]document.all.*elementID*.align

BACKGROUND

NN *4*   IE *3*   HTML *n/a*

BACKGROUND=" *URL*"   *Optional*

Specifies an image file that is used as a backdrop to the table. Unlike normal images that get loaded into browser content, a background image loads in its original size (without scaling) and tiles to fill the available table space. Smaller images download faster but are obviously repeated more often in the background. Animated GIFs are also allowable, but very distracting to the reader. When selecting a background image, be sure it is very muted in comparison to the main content so that the content stands out clearly. Background images, if used at all, should be extremely subtle.

Example `<TABLE BACKGROUND="watermark.jpg">...</TABLE>`

Value Any valid URL to an image file, including complete and relative URLs.

Default None.

Object Model Reference

IE   [window.]document.all.*elementID*.background

BGCOLOR

NN *3*   IE *3*   HTML *3.2*

BGCOLOR=" *colorTripletOrName*"   *Optional*

Establishes a fill color (behind the text and other content) for the entire table. If you combine a **BGCOLOR** and **BACKGROUND**, any transparent areas of the background image let the background color show through. This attribute is deprecated in HTML 4.0 in favor of the **background-color** style attribute.

Example `<TABLE BGCOLOR="tan">...</TABLE>`

Value

A hexadecimal triplet or plain-language color name. A setting of empty is interpreted as "#000000" (black). See Appendix A for acceptable plain-language color names.

Default Varies with browser, browser version, and operating system.

Object Model Reference

IE   [window.]document.all.*elementID*.bgColor

BORDER   NN *all*   IE *all*   HTML *3.2*

BORDER="*pixelCount*"   *Optional*

The thickness (in pixels) of the border drawn around a TABLE element. If you set the BORDER attribute to any value, browsers by default render narrow borders around each of the cells inside the table. The thickness of internal borders between cells are defined by the CELLSPACING attribute of the TABLE element.

If you include only the BORDER attribute without assigning any value to it, the browser renders default-sized borders around the entire table and between cells, unless overridden by other attributes.

Browsers render the border in a 3-D style, with the border appearing to be raised around the flat content in the cells. Numerous other attributes affect the look of the border, including: BORDERCOLOR, BORDERCOLORDARK, BORDERCOLORLIGHT, FRAME, and RULES. The type of border rendered for tables is different from the borders defined by style sheet rules. You get better control of the border look by using the dedicated attributes of the TABLE element.

Example   <TABLE BORDER=1>...</TABLE>

Value   A positive integer value.

Default   0

Object Model Reference

IE   [window.]document.all.*elementID*.border

BORDERCOLOR   NN *4*   IE *3*   HTML *4*

BORDERCOLOR="*colorTripletOrName*"   *Optional*

The colors used to render some of the pixels that create the illusion of borders around cells and the entire table. The BORDER attribute must have a nonzero value assigned for the color to appear. The 3-D effect of borders in Navigator and Internet Explorer is created by careful positioning of light (or white) and dark lines around the page's background or default color (see Figure 8-4). Standard colors are usually shades of gray and white, depending on the browser.

Applying color to a table border has a different effect in Navigator and Internet Explorer. In Navigator, the color is applied to what is normally the darker of the two shades used to create the border. Moreover, Navigator automatically adjusts the darkness of some of the lines to enhance the 3-D effect of the border. In contrast, Internet Explorer applies the color to all lines that make up the border. The net effect is to flatten the 3-D effect (refer to the BORDERCOLORDARK and BORDERCOLORLIGHT attributes to color borders and maintain the 3-D effect).

Example   <TABLE BORDERCOLOR="green" BORDER=2>...</TABLE>

Value

A hexadecimal triplet or plain-language color name. A setting of empty is interpreted as "#000000" (black). See Appendix A for acceptable plain-language color names.

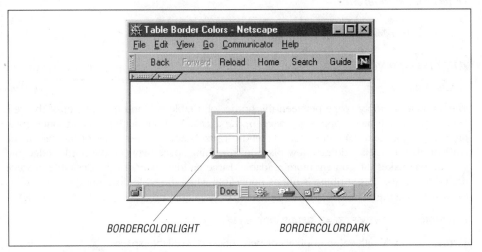

Figure 8-4. Components of table border color

Default   Varies with browser and operating system.

Object Model Reference

IE   [window.]document.all.*elementID*.borderColor

BORDERCOLORDARK,
BORDERCOLORLIGHT   NN *n/a*   IE *3*   HTML *n/a*

BORDERCOLORDARK="*colorTripletOrName*"   *Optional*
BORDERCOLORLIGHT="*colorTripletOrName*"

The 3-D effect of table borders in Internet Explorer is created by careful positioning of light and dark lines around the page's background or default color (see Figure 8-4). You can independently control the colors used for the dark and light lines by assigning values to the BORDERCOLORDARK and BORDERCOLORLIGHT attributes. The BORDER attribute must have a nonzero value assigned for the colors to appear.

Typically, you should assign complementary colors to the pair of attributes. There is also no rule that says you must assign a dark color to BORDERCOLORDARK. The attributes merely control a well-defined set of lines so you can predict which lines of the border change with each attribute.

Example

```
<TABLE BORDERCOLORDARK="darkred" BORDERCOLORLIGHT="salmon" BORDER=3>...
</TABLE>
```

Value

A hexadecimal triplet or plain-language color name. A setting of empty is interpreted as "#000000" (black). See Appendix A for acceptable plain-language color names.

Default   Varies with operating system.

Object Model Reference

IE   [window.]document.all.*elementID*.borderColorDark
            [window.]document.all.*elementID*.borderColorLight

CELLPADDING   NN *all*   IE *3*   HTML *3.2*

CELLPADDING="*length*"   *Optional*

The amount of empty space between the border of a table cell and the content of the cell.
Note that this attribute applies to space *inside* a cell. Without setting this attribute, most
browsers render text content so that its leftmost pixels abut the left edge of the cell. If the
table displays borders, adding a few pixels of breathing space between the border edge and
the content makes the content more readable. Large padding may also be desirable in some
design instances. This attribute is not as noticeable when the table does not display borders
(in which case the CELLSPACING attribute can assist in adjusting the space between cells).

Example <TABLE BORDER=2 CELLPADDING=3>...</TABLE>

Value   Any length value in pixels or percentage of available space.

Default   0

Object Model Reference

IE   [window.]document.all.*elementID*.cellPadding

CELLSPACING   NN *all*   IE *3*   HTML *3.2*

CELLSPACING="*length*"   *Optional*

The amount of empty space between the outer edges of each table cell. If you set the
BORDER attribute of the TABLE element to any positive integer value, the effect of setting
CELLSPACING is to define the thickness of borders rendered between cells. Even without a
visible border, the readability of a table often benefits from cell spacing.

Example <TABLE BORDER=2 CELLSPACING=10>...</TABLE>

Value   Any positive integer.

Default   0 (no table border); 2 (with table border).

Object Model Reference

IE   [window.]document.all.*elementID*.cellSpacing

COLS   NN *4*   IE *3*   HTML *n/a*

COLS="*columnCount*"   *Optional*

The number of columns of the table. The HTML specification never adopted this attribute.
In HTML 4.0, the functionality of this attribute is covered by the COLGROUP and COL
elements. In the meantime, the COLS attribute is recognized by current browsers. The
attribute assists the browser in preparation for rendering the table. Without this attribute, the
browser relies on its interpretation of all downloaded TR and TD elements to determine how
the table is to be divided.

Example <TABLE COLS=4>...</TABLE>

Value   Any positive integer.

Default   None.

Object Model Reference

IE   [window.]document.all.*elementID*.cols

DATAPAGESIZE   NN *n/a*   IE *4*   HTML *n/a*

DATAPAGESIZE="*recordCount*"   *Optional*

Used with IE 4 data binding, this attribute advises the browser how many instances of a
table row must be rendered to accommodate the number of data source records set by this
attribute. A common application is setting a table cell to display a text **INPUT** element
whose **DATAFLD** attribute is bound to a particular column of the data source (the **DATASRC**
is set in the **TABLE** element). If the **DATAPAGESIZE** attribute is set to 5, the browser must
display five rows of the table (but the row is specified in the HTML only once).

Example

```
<TABLE DATASRC="#DBSRC3" DATAPAGESIZE=5>
<TR>
  <TD><INPUT TYPE="text" DATAFLD="stockNum">
  <TD><INPUT TYPE="text" DATAFLD="qtyOnHand">
</TR>
</TABLE>
```

Value   Any positive integer.

Default   None.

Object Model Reference

IE   [window.]document.all.*elementID*.dataPageSize

DATASRC   NN *n/a*   IE *4*   HTML *n/a*

DATASRC="*dataSourceName*"   *Optional*

Used with IE 4 data binding to specify the name of the remote ODBC data source (such as
an Oracle or SQL Server database) to be associated with the element. Content from the data
source is specified via the **DATAFLD** attribute in individual TD elements. A block of contiguous records can be rendered in the table when you also set the **DATAPAGESIZE** attribute of
the table.

Example   <TABLE DATASRC="#DBSRC3" DATAPAGESIZE=5>...</TABLE>

Value   Case-sensitive identifier.

Default   None.

Object Model Reference

IE   [window.]document.all.*elementID*.dataSrc

DIR

NN *n/a*   IE *n/a*   HTML *4*

DIR="*direction*"   *Optional*

The direction of character rendering and table cell rendering for the element. Character and cell rendering is either left-to-right or right-to-left. This attribute is usually set in concert with the LANG attribute and must be used to specify a character rendering direction that overrides the current direction.

Example   <TABLE LANG="ar" dir="rtl">*SomeArabicTableCellItemsHere*</TABLE>

Value   ltr | rtl (case insensitive).

Default   ltr

FRAME

NN *n/a*   IE *3*   HTML *4*

FRAME="*frameConstant*"   *Optional*

Defines which (if any) sides of a table's outer border (set with the BORDER attribute) are rendered. This attribute does not affect the interior borders between cells. Including the BORDER attribute without assigning any value to it is the same as setting the FRAME attribute to border.

Example   <TABLE BORDER=3 FRAME="void">...</TABLE>

Value   Any one case-insensitive frame constant:

above	Renders border along top edge of table only
below	Renders border along bottom edge of table only
border	Renders all four sides of the border (default in IE)
box	Renders all four sides of the border (same as border)
hsides	Renders borders on top and bottom edges of table only (a nice look)
lhs	Renders border on left edge of table only
rhs	Renders border on right edge of table only
void	Hides all borders (default in HTML 4.0)
vsides	Renders borders on left and right edges of table only

Default

Navigator: void (when BORDER=0); border (when BORDER is any other value). Internet Explorer: border.

Object Model Reference

IE   [window.]document.all.*elementID*.frame

HEIGHT, WIDTH

NN *all*   IE *3*   HTML *3.2*

HEIGHT="*length*"   *Optional*
WIDTH="*length*"

The rectangular dimensions of a table that may be different from the default size as calculated by the browser. When the values for these attributes are less than the minimum space required to render the table cell content, the browser overrides the attribute settings to make sure that all content appears, even if it means that text lines word-wrap. You can also stretch the dimensions of a table beyond the browser-calculated dimensions. Extra whitespace appears inside table cells to make up the difference. If you specify just one attribute, the browser performs the necessary calculations to automatically adjust the dimension along the other axis.

Note that the HEIGHT attribute is not in the HTML specification. The assumption there is that the table height is calculated by the browser to best show all cell content given either the default or attribute-established width. Because different browsers on different operating systems can render text content in varying relative font sizes, it is not unusual to let the height of a table be calculated by the browser.

Example   <TABLE WIDTH="80%">...</TABLE>

Value   Any length value in pixels or percentage of available space.

Default   Navigator: a width of 100% of the next outermost container; height governed by content. Internet Explorer: calculates the height and width based on content size.

Object Model Reference

IE   [window.]document.all.*elementID*.height
          [window.]document.all.*elementID*.width

RULES   NN *n/a*   IE *3*   HTML *4*

RULES="*rulesConstant*"   *Optional*

Defines where (if at all) interior borders between cells are rendered by the browser. In addition to setting the table to draw borders to turn the cells into a matrix, you can also set borders to be drawn only to separate rows, columns, or any sanctioned cell grouping (THEAD, TBODY, TFOOT, COLGROUP, or COL). The BORDER attribute must be present—either as a Boolean or set to a specific border size—for any cell borders to be drawn.

Example   <TABLE BORDER RULES="groups">...</TABLE>

Value   Any one case-insensitive rules constant:

all   Renders borders around each cell

cols   Renders borders between columns only

groups   Renders borders between cell groups as defined by THEAD, TFOOT, TBODY, COLGROUP, or COL elements

none   Hides all interior borders

rows   Renders borders between rows only

Default   none (when BORDER=0); all (when BORDER is any other value).

Object Model Reference

IE   [window.]document.all.*elementID*.rules

SUMMARY   NN *n/a*   IE *n/a*   HTML *4*

SUMMARY="*text*"   *Optional*

A textual description of the table, including, but not limited to, instructions that nonvisual browsers might follow to describe the purpose and organization of the table data.

Example

```
<TABLE SUMMARY="Order form for entry of up to five products.">...</TABLE>
```

Value   Any quoted string of characters.

Default   None.

WIDTH

See HEIGHT.

<TBODY>   NN *n/a*   IE *3*   HTML *4*

```
<TBODY>...</TBODY>
```
End Tag: Optional

A TBODY element is an arbitrary container of one or more rows of table cells. More than one TBODY element may be defined within a single TABLE element. Use the TBODY element to define structural segments of a table that may require their own styles or border treatments (see the RULES attribute). A TBODY element is the row-oriented equivalent of the COLGROUP element for columns. Other types of row groupings available are the TFOOT and THEAD elements, neither of which overlaps with a TBODY element.

Example

```
<TABLE COLS=3>
<THEAD>
<TR>
<TH>Time<TH>Event<TH>Location
</TR>
</THEAD>
<TBODY>
<TR>
<TD>7:30am-5:00pm<TD>Registration Open<TD>Main Lobby
</TR>
<TR>
<TD>9:00am-12:00pm<TD>Keynote Speakers<TD>Cypress Room
</TR>
</TBODY>
</TABLE>
```

Object Model Reference

IE   [window.]document.all.*elementID*

Attributes

ALIGN	CHAROFF	ID	LANGUAGE	TITLE
BGCOLOR	CLASS	LANG	STYLE	VALIGN
CHAR	DIR			

Event Handler Attributes

Handler	NN	IE	HTML
onClick	n/a	4	4
onDblClick	n/a	4	4
onDragStart	n/a	4	n/a

Handler	NN	IE	HTML
onHelp	n/a	4	n/a
onKeyDown	n/a	4	4
onKeyPress	n/a	4	4
onKeyUp	n/a	4	4
onMouseDown	n/a	4	4
onMouseMove	n/a	4	4
onMouseOut	n/a	4	4
onMouseOver	n/a	4	4
onMouseUp	n/a	4	4
onSelectStart	n/a	4	n/a

ALIGN   NN *n/a*   IE *4*   HTML *4*

ALIGN="*alignConstant*"   *Optional*

Establishes the horizontal alignment characteristics of content within the row(s) covered by the TBODY element. The HTML 4.0 specification defines settings for the ALIGN attribute that are not yet reflected in the CSS specification. Therefore, this ALIGN attribute is not fully deprecated as it is for many other elements. As a rule, alignment should be specified by style sheet wherever possible.

Example   <TBODY ALIGN="center">

Value   HTML 4.0 and IE 4 have two sets of attribute values:

Value	IE 4	HTML 4.0
center	•	•
char	–	•
justify	–	•
left	•	•
right	•	•

The values center, left, and right are self-explanatory. The value justify is intended to space content so that text is justified down both left and right edges. For the value char, the CHAR attribute must also be set to specify the character on which alignment revolves. In the HTML 4.0 specification example, content that does not contain the character appears to be right-aligned to the location of the character in other rows of the same column.

It is important to bear in mind that the ALIGN attribute applies to every cell of every row within the TBODY, including any TH element you specify for the table. If you want a different alignment for the row header, override the setting with a separate ALIGN attribute or text-align style sheet attribute for the THEAD or individual TH elements.

Default   left

Object Model Reference

IE   [window.]document.all.*elementID*.align

BGCOLOR

NN *n/a*   IE *4*   HTML *n/a*

BGCOLOR="*colorTripletOrName*"   *Optional*

Establishes a fill color (behind the text and other content) for the cells contained by the TBODY element.

Example   <TBODY BGCOLOR="tan">

Value

A hexadecimal triplet or plain-language color name. A setting of empty is interpreted as "#000000" (black). See Appendix A for acceptable plain-language color names.

Default   Varies with browser, browser version, and operating system.

Object Model Reference

IE   [window.]document.all.*elementID*.bgColor

CHAR

NN *n/a*   IE *n/a*   HTML *4*

CHAR="*character*"   *Optional*

The text character used as an alignment point for text within a cell. This attribute is of value only for the ALIGN attribute set to "char".

Example   <TBODY ALIGN="char" CHAR=".">

Value   Any single text character.

Default   None.

CHAROFF

NN *n/a*   IE *n/a*   HTML *4*

CHAROFF="*length*"   *Optional*

Sets a specific offset point at which the character specified by the CHAR attribute is to appear within a cell. This attribute is provided in case the browser default positioning does not meet with the design goals of the table.

Example   <TBODY ALIGN="char" CHAR="." CHAROFF="80%">

Value   Any length value in pixels or percentage of cell space.

Default   None.

VALIGN

NN *n/a*   IE *4*   HTML *4*

VALIGN="*alignmentConstant*"   *Optional*

Determines the vertical alignment of content within cells of the column(s) covered by the TBODY element. You can override the vertical alignment for a particular cell anywhere in the column.

Example   <TBODY VALIGN="bottom">

Value

Four constant values are recognized by both IE 4 and HTML 4.0: `top` | `middle` | `bottom` | `baseline`. With `top` and `bottom`, the content is rendered flush (or very close to it) to the top and bottom of the table cell. Set to `middle` (the default), the content floats perfectly centered vertically in the cell. When one cell's contents might wrap to multiple lines at common window widths (assuming a variable table width), it is advisable to set the `VALIGN` attribute to `baseline`. This assures that the character baseline of the first (or only) line of a cell's text aligns with the other cells in the row—usually the most aesthetically pleasing arrangement.

Default   `middle`

Object Model Reference

IE   `[window.]document.all.`*elementID*`.vAlign`

<TD>   NN *all*   IE *all*   HTML *3.2*

`<TD>...</TD>`   *End Tag: Optional*

The `TD` element is a container for content that is rendered inside one cell of a `TABLE` element. One cell is the intersection of a column and row. Other elements related to the `TD` element are `CAPTION`, `COL`, `COLGROUP`, `TABLE`, `TBODY`, `TFOOT`, `TH`, `THEAD`, and `TR`. In addition to providing a wrapper for a cell's content, the `TD` element defines a number of visible attributes that apply to a single cell, often overriding similar attributes set in lesser-nested elements in the table.

Four attributes—`ABBR`, `AXIS`, `HEADERS`, and `SCOPE`—have been added to the HTML 4.0 specification in anticipation of nonvisual browsers that will use text-to-speech technology to describe content of an HTML page—a kind of "verbal rendering." Although these attributes are briefly described here for the sake of completeness, there is much more to their application in nonvisual browsers than is relevant in this book on Dynamic HTML. Consult the HTML 4.0 recommendation for more details.

Example

```
<TABLE COLS=3>
<THEAD>
<TR>
<TH>Time<TH>Event<TH>Location
</TR>
</THEAD>
<TBODY>
<TR>
<TD>7:30am-5:00pm<TD>Registration Open<TD>Main Lobby
</TR>
<TR>
<TD>9:00am-12:00pm<TD>Keynote Speakers<TD>Cypress Room
</TR>
</TBODY>
</TABLE>
```

Object Model Reference

IE   [window.]document.all.*elementID*

Attributes

ABBR	BORDERCOLORDARK	COLSPAN	*ID*	SCOPE
ALIGN	BORDERCOLORLIGHT	DATAFLD	*LANG*	*STYLE*
AXIS	CHAR	*DIR*	*LANGUAGE*	*TITLE*
BACKGROUND	CHAROFF	HEADERS	NOWRAP	VALIGN
BGCOLOR	*CLASS*	HEIGHT	ROWSPAN	WIDTH
BORDERCOLOR				

Event Handler Attributes

Handler	NN	IE	HTML
onAfterUpdate	n/a	4	n/a
onBeforeUpdate	n/a	4	n/a
onBlur	n/a	4	n/a
onClick	n/a	4	4
onDblClick	n/a	4	4
onDragStart	n/a	4	n/a
onFocus	n/a	4	n/a
onHelp	n/a	4	n/a
onKeyDown	n/a	4	4
onKeyPress	n/a	4	4
onKeyUp	n/a	4	4
onMouseDown	n/a	4	4
onMouseMove	n/a	4	4
onMouseOut	n/a	4	4
onMouseOver	n/a	4	4
onMouseUp	n/a	4	4
onResize	n/a	4	n/a
onRowEnter	n/a	4	n/a
onRowExit	n/a	4	n/a
onScroll	n/a	4	n/a
onSelectStart	n/a	4	n/a

ABBR
                                                    NN *n/a*   IE *n/a*   HTML *4*

ABBR="*text*"   *Optional*

Provides an abbreviated string that describes the cell's content. This is usually a brief label that a nonvisual browser would speak to describe what the value of the cell represents.

Example   <TD ABBR="Main Event"> Keynote Speakers

Value   Any quoted string.

Default   None.

ALIGN   NN *all*   IE *all*   HTML *3.2*

ALIGN="*alignConstant*"   *Optional*

Establishes the horizontal alignment characteristics of content within the cell covered by the TD element. The HTML 4.0 specification defines settings for the **ALIGN** attribute that are not yet reflected in the CSS specification. Therefore, this **ALIGN** attribute is not fully deprecated as it is for many other elements. As a rule, alignment should be specified by style sheet wherever possible.

Example   <TD ALIGN="center">

Value

Navigator 4 and Internet Explorer 4 share the same attribute values, whereas HTML 4.0 has a couple more:

Value	NN 4	IE 4	HTML 4.0
center	•	•	•
char	-	-	•
justify	-	-	•
left	•	•	•
right	•	•	•

The values center, left, and right are self-explanatory. The value justify is intended to space content so that text is justified down both left and right edges. For the value char, the CHAR attribute must also be set to specify the character on which alignment revolves. In the HTML 4.0 specification example, content that does not contain the character appears to be right-aligned to the location of the character in other rows of the same column.

Default   left

Object Model Reference

IE   [window.]document.all.*elementID*.align

AXIS   NN *n/a*   IE *n/a*   HTML *4*

AXIS="*text*"   *Optional*

Provides an abbreviated string that describes the cell's category. This is usually a brief label that a nonvisual browser would speak to describe what the value of the cell represents.

Example   <TD AXIS="event"> Keynote Speakers

Value   Any quoted string.

Default   None.

BACKGROUND   NN *n/a*   IE *3*   HTML *n/a*

BACKGROUND="*URL*"   *Optional*

Specifies an image file that is used as a backdrop to the cell. Unlike normal images that get loaded into browser content, a background image loads in its original size (without scaling) and tiles to fill the available cell space. Smaller images download faster but are obviously repeated more often in the background. Animated GIFs are also allowable, but very distracting to the reader. When selecting a background image, be sure it is very muted in comparison to the main content so that the content stands out clearly. Background images, if used at all, should be extremely subtle.

Example   <TD BACKGROUND="watermark.jpg">

Value   Any valid URL to an image file, including complete and relative URLs.

Default   None.

Object Model Reference

IE   [window.]document.all.*elementID*.background

BGCOLOR   NN *3*   IE *3*   HTML *3.2*

BGCOLOR=" *colorTripletOrName*"   *Optional*

Establishes a fill color (behind the text and other content) for the cell defined by the TD element.

Example   <TD BGCOLOR="yellow">

Value

A hexadecimal triplet or plain-language color name. A setting of empty is interpreted as "#000000" (black). See Appendix A for acceptable plain-language color names.

Default   Varies with browser, browser version, and operating system.

Object Model Reference

IE   [window.]document.all.*elementID*.bgColor

BORDERCOLOR   NN *n/a*   IE *3*   HTML *n/a*

BORDERCOLOR=" *colorTripletOrName*"   *Optional*

The colors used to render some of the pixels that create the illusion of borders around cells and the entire table. Internet Explorer applies the color to all four lines that make up the interior border of a cell. Therefore, colors of adjacent cells do not collide.

Example   <TD BORDERCOLOR="green">

Value

A hexadecimal triplet or plain-language color name. A setting of empty is interpreted as "#000000" (black). See Appendix A for acceptable plain-language color names.

Default   Varies with browser and operating system.

Object Model Reference

IE   [window.]document.all.*elementID*.borderColor

BORDERCOLORDARK, BORDERCOLORLIGHT

NN *n/a*   IE *3*   HTML *n/a*

BORDERCOLORDARK=" *colorTripletOrName*"   *Optional*
BORDERCOLORLIGHT=" *colorTripletOrName*"

The 3-D effect of table borders in Internet Explorer is created by careful positioning of light and dark lines around the page's background or default color (see Figure 8-4 in the TABLE element discussion). You can independently control the colors used for the dark and light lines by assigning values to the BORDERCOLORDARK (left and top edges of the cell) and BORDERCOLORLIGHT (right and bottom edges) attributes.

Typically, you should assign complementary colors to the pair of attributes. There is also no rule that says you must assign a dark color to BORDERCOLORDARK. The attributes merely control a well-defined set of lines so you can predict which lines of the border change with each attribute.

Example   <TD BORDERCOLORDARK="darkred" BORDERCOLORLIGHT="salmon">

Value

A hexadecimal triplet or plain-language color name. A setting of empty is interpreted as "#000000" (black). See Appendix A for acceptable plain-language color names.

Default   Varies with operating system.

Object Model Reference

IE   [window.]document.all.*elementID*.borderColorDark
            [window.]document.all.*elementID*.borderColorLight

CHAR

NN *n/a*   IE *n/a*   HTML *4*

CHAR=" *character*"   *Optional*

The text character used as an alignment point for text within a cell. This attribute is of value only for the ALIGN attribute set to "char".

Example   <TD ALIGN="char" CHAR=".">

Value   Any single text character.

Default   None.

CHAROFF

NN *n/a*   IE *n/a*   HTML *4*

CHAROFF=" *length*"   *Optional*

Sets a specific offset point at which the character specified by the CHAR attribute is to appear within a cell. This attribute is provided in case the browser default positioning does not meet with the design goals of the table.

Example   <TD ALIGN="char" CHAR="." CHAROFF="80%">

Value   Any length value in pixels or percentage of cell space.

Default   None.

COLSPAN

NN *all*   IE *all*   HTML *3.2*

COLSPAN=" *columnCount*"   *Optional*

The number of columns across which the current table cell should extend itself. For each additional column included in the COLSPAN count, one less TD element is required for the table row. If you set the ALIGN attribute to center or right, the alignment is calculated on the full width of the TD element across the specified number of columns. Unless the current cell also specifies a ROWSPAN attribute, the next table row returns to the original column count.

Example   <TD COLSPAN=2 ALIGN="center">

Value   Any positive integer, usually 2 or larger.

Default   1

Object Model Reference

IE   [window.]document.all.*elementID*.colSpan

DATAFLD

NN *n/a*   IE *4*   HTML *n/a*

DATAFLD=" *columnName*"   *Optional*

Used with IE 4 data binding to associate a remote data source column name with the content of a table cell. A DATASRC (and optionally a DATAPAGESIZE) attribute must also be set for the enclosing TABLE element.

Example

```
<TABLE DATASRC="#DBSRC3" DATAPAGESIZE=5">
<TR>
  <TD><INPUT TYPE="text" DATAFLD="stockNum">
  <TD><INPUT TYPE="text" DATAFLD="qtyOnHand">
</TR>
</TABLE>
```

Value   Case-sensitive identifier.

Default   None.

HEADERS

NN *n/a*   IE *n/a*   HTML *4*

HEADERS=" *cellIDList*"   *Optional*

Points to one or more TH or TD elements that act as column or row headers for the current table cell. The assigned value is a space-delimited list of ID attribute values that are assigned to the relevant TH elements. A nonvisual browser could read the cell's header before the content of the cell to help listeners identify the nature of the cell content.

Example

```
<TR>
<TH ID="hdr1">Product Number
<TH ID="hdr2">Description
</TR>
<TR>
<TD HEADERS="hdr1">0392
```

```
<TD HEADERS="hdr2">Round widget
</TR>
```

Value

A space-delimited list of case-sensitive IDs assigned to cells that act as headers to the current cell.

Default None.

HEIGHT, WIDTH   NN *all*   IE *all*   HTML *3.2*

```
HEIGHT="length"
WIDTH="length"
```
Optional

The rectangular dimensions of a cell that may be different from the default size as calculated by the browser. When the values for these attributes are less than the minimum space required to render the table cell content, the browser overrides the attribute settings to make sure that all content appears, even if it means that text lines word-wrap. You can also stretch the dimensions of a table beyond the browser-calculated dimensions. Extra whitespace appears inside table cells to make up the difference. If you specify just one of these attributes, the browser performs all necessary calculations to automatically adjust the dimension along the other axis. The cell must have some content assigned to it, or it may close up to minimum size.

Due to the regular nature of tables, if you set a custom height for one cell in a row, the entire row is set to that height; similarly, setting the width of a cell causes the width of all cells in the column to be the same size.

Both the HEIGHT and WIDTH attributes are deprecated in HTML 4.0 in favor of height and width style sheet attributes (which are not available for table cells in Navigator 4).

Example `<TD WIDTH="80%" HEIGHT=30>`

Value   Any length value in pixels or percentage of available space.

Default   Based on content size.

Object Model Reference

IE   `[window.]document.all.elementID.height`
            `[window.]document.all.elementID.width`

NOWRAP   NN *all*   IE *all*   HTML *3.2*

```
NOWRAP
```
Optional

The presence of the NOWRAP attribute instructs the browser to render the cell as wide as is necessary to display a line of nonbreaking text on one line. Abuse of this attribute can force the user into a great deal of inconvenient horizontal scrolling of the page to view all of the content. The NOWRAP attribute is deprecated in HTML 4.0.

Example `<TD NOWRAP>`

Value   The presence of this attribute sets its value to true.

Default   false

Object Model Reference

IE   [window.]document.all.*elementID*.noWrap

ROWSPAN   NN *all*   IE *all*   HTML *3.2*

ROWSPAN="*rowCount*"   *Optional*

The number of rows through which the current table cell should extend itself downward. For each additional row included in the ROWSPAN count, one less TD element is required for the next table row in that cell's position along the row.

Example <TD ROWSPAN=2>

Value   Any positive integer, usually 2 or larger.

Default 1

Object Model Reference

IE   [window.]document.all.*elementID*.rowSpan

SCOPE   NN *n/a*   IE *n/a*   HTML *4*

SCOPE="*scopeConstant*"   *Optional*

Used more with a TH element than with a TD element, the SCOPE attribute sets the range of cells (relative to the current cell) that behave as though the current cell is the header for those cells. For tables whose structure is quite regular, the SCOPE attribute is a simpler way of achieving what the HEADERS attribute does, without having to define ID attributes for the header cells.

Example

```
<TR>
<TH SCOPE="col">Product Number
<TH SCOPE="col">Description
</TR>
<TR>
<TD>0392
<TD>Round widget
</TR>
```

Value   One of four recognized scope constants:

col   Current cell text becomes header text for every cell in the rest of the column.

colgroup   Current cell text becomes header text for every cell in the rest of the COLGROUP element.

row   Current cell text becomes header text for every cell in the rest of the TR element.

rowgroup   Current cell text becomes header text for every cell in the rest of the TBODY element.

Default None.

VALIGN

NN *all*   IE *all*   HTML *3.2*

VALIGN="*alignmentConstant*" *Optional*

Determines the vertical alignment of content within the TD element. A value you set for an individual cell overrides the same attribute setting for outer containers, such as TR and TBODY.

Example   <TD VALIGN="bottom">

Value

Four constant values are recognized by both IE 4 and HTML 4.0: top | middle | bottom | baseline. With top and bottom, the content is rendered flush (or very close to it) to the top and bottom of the table cell. Set to middle (the default), the content floats perfectly centered vertically in the cell. When one cell's contents might wrap to multiple lines at common window widths (assuming a variable table width), it is advisable to set the VALIGN attribute to baseline. This assures that the character baseline of the first (or only) line of a cell's text aligns with the other cells in the row—usually the most aesthetically pleasing arrangement.

Default   middle

Object Model Reference

IE   [window.]document.all.*elementID*.vAlign

WIDTH

See HEIGHT.

<TEXTAREA>

NN *all*   IE *all*   HTML *all*

<TEXTAREA>...</TEXTAREA> *End Tag: Required*

The TEXTAREA element is a multiline text input control primarily for usage inside FORM elements (required in Navigator). Unlike the text type INPUT element, a TEXTAREA element can be sized to accept more than one line of text. Word-wrapping is available on more recent browsers, and users may enter carriage return characters (a combination of characters ASCII decimal 13 and 10) inside the text box. When a TEXTAREA element is inside a submitted form, the name/value pair is submitted, with the value being the content of the text box (and the NAME attribute must be assigned). The CGI program on the server must be able to handle the possibility of carriage returns in the text data.

If you wish to display text in the TEXTAREA element when it loads, that text goes between the start and end tags; otherwise, there are no intervening characters in the source code between start and end tags. A label for the TEXTAREA element must be placed before or after the element, and may, optionally in newer browsers, be encased in a LABEL element for structural purposes.

Example

<TEXTAREA ROWS=5 COLS=60 NAME="notes">Use this area for extra notes.
</TEXTAREA>

Object Model Reference

NN   `[window.]document.`*formName.*`elementName`
        `[window.]document.forms[i].elements[i]`

IE   `[window.]document.`*formName.*`elementName`
        `[window.]document.forms[i].elements[i]`
        `[window.]document.all.`*elementID*

Attributes

ACCESSKEY	DATAFLD	*ID*	READONLY	TABINDEX
ALIGN	DATASRC	*LANG*	ROWS	*TITLE*
CLASS	*DIR*	*LANGUAGE*	STYLE	WRAP
COLS	DISABLED	NAME		

Event Handler Attributes

Handler	NN	IE	HTML
onAfterUpdate	n/a	4	n/a
onBeforeUpdate	n/a	4	n/a
onBlur	2	3	4
onChange	2	3	4
onClick	n/a	3	4
onDblClick	n/a	4	4
onDragStart	n/a	4	n/a
onFocus	2	3	4
onHelp	n/a	4	n/a
onKeyDown	4	4	4
onKeyPress	4	4	4
onKeyUp	4	4	4
onMouseDown	n/a	4	4
onMouseMove	n/a	4	4
onMouseOut	n/a	4	4
onMouseOver	n/a	3	4
onMouseUp	n/a	4	4
onResize	n/a	4	n/a
onRowEnter	n/a	4	n/a
onRowExit	n/a	4	n/a
onScroll	n/a	3	4
onSelect	2	3	4
onSelectStart	n/a	4	n/a

ACCESSKEY
                                            NN *n/a*   IE 4   HTML *n/a*

ACCESSKEY="*character*"   *Optional*

A single character key that brings focus to the element. The browser and operating system determine if the user must press a modifier key (e.g., **Ctrl**, **Alt**, or **Command**) with the access key to bring focus to the element. In IE 4/Windows, the **Alt** key is required, and the key is not case sensitive. This attribute does not work in IE 4/Mac. That this attribute is missing from the HTML 4.0 specification appears to be an oversight.

Example `<TEXTAREA NAME="notes" ACCESSKEY="n"></TEXTAREA>`

Value Single character of the document set.

Default None.

Object Model Reference

IE   `[window.]document.`*formName*`.`*elementName*`.accessKey`
         `[window.]document.forms[i].elements[i].accessKey`
         `[window.]document.all.`*elementID*`.accessKey`

ALIGN

NN *n/a*   IE *4*   HTML *n/a*

`ALIGN="`*alignmentConstant*`"`   *Optional*

Determines how the rectangle of the element aligns within the context of surrounding content. See the section "Alignment Constants" earlier in this chapter for a description of the possibilities defined in both Navigator and Internet Explorer for this attribute. Despite Microsoft's advertised extensive support for this attribute, only some values work on Internet Explorer 4 for the Macintosh; none work on the Windows version. Use style sheets to position this element if you need to. Default alignment also varies with operating system.

Object Model Reference

IE   `[window.]document.`*formName*`.`*elementName*`.align`
         `[window.]document.forms[i].elements[i].align`
         `[window.]document.all.`*elementID*`.align`

COLS

NN *all*   IE *all*   HTML *all*

`COLS="`*columnCount*`"`   *Optional*

The width of the editable space of the **TEXTAREA** element. The value represents the number of monofont characters that are to be displayed within the width. When the font size can be influenced by style sheets, the actual width changes accordingly.

Example `<TEXTAREA COLS=40></TEXTAREA>`

Value Any positive integer.

Default Varies with browser and operating system.

Object Model Reference

IE   `[window.]document.`*formName*`.`*elementName*`.cols`
         `[window.]document.forms[i].elements[i].cols`
         `[window.]document.all.`*elementID*`.cols`

DATAFLD

NN *n/a*   IE *4*   HTML *n/a*

`DATAFLD="`*columnName*`"`   *Optional*

Used with IE 4 data binding to associate a remote data source column name with the content of the **TEXTAREA** element. A **DATASRC** attribute must also be set for the element.

Example `<TEXTAREA NAME="summary" DATASRC="#DBSRC3" DATAFLD="summary">`

Value Case-sensitive identifier.

Default   None.

Object Model Reference

IE   [window.]document.*formName*.*elementName*.dataFld
            [window.]document.forms[i].elements[i].dataFld
            [window.]document.all.*elementID*.dataFld

DATASRC   NN *n/a*   IE *4*   HTML *n/a*

DATASRC="*dataSourceName*"   *Optional*

Used with IE 4 data binding to specify the name of the remote ODBC data source (such as an Oracle or SQL Server database) to be associated with the element. Content from the data source is specified via the DATAFLD attribute.

Example   <TEXTAREA NAME="summary" DATASRC="#DBSRC3" DATAFLD="summary">

Value   Case-sensitive identifier.

Default   None.

Object Model Reference

IE   [window.]document.*formName*.*elementName*.dataSrc
            [window.]document.forms[i].elements[i].dataSrc
            [window.]document.all.*elementID*.dataSrc

DISABLED   NN *n/a*   IE *4*   HTML *4*

DISABLED   *Optional*

A disabled TEXTAREA element cannot be activated by the user. In Windows, a disabled TEXTAREA cannot receive focus and does not become active within the tabbing order rotation. HTML 4.0 also specifies that the name/value pair of a disabled element should not be sent when the form is submitted.

The DISABLED attribute is a Boolean type, which means that its presence in the attribute sets its value to true. Its value can also be adjusted after the fact by scripting (see the textarea object in Chapter 9).

Example   <TEXTAREA DISABLED></TEXTAREA>

Value   The presence of the attribute disables the element.

Default   false

Object Model Reference

IE   [window.]document.*formName*.*elementName*.disabled
            [window.]document.forms[i].elements[i].disabled
            [window.]document.all.*elementID*.disabled

NAME   NN *all*   IE *all*   HTML *all*

NAME="*elementIdentifier*"   *Optional*

If the TEXTAREA element is part of a form being submitted to a server, the NAME attribute is required if the value of the element is to be submitted with the form. For forms that are in documents for the convenience of scripted form elements, TEXTAREA element names are not required but are helpful just the same in creating scripted references to these objects and their properties or methods.

Example `<TEXTAREA NAME="comments"></TEXTAREA>`

Value Case-sensitive identifier.

Default None.

Object Model Reference

NN 　　　 `[window.]document.`*formName*`.`*elementName*`.name`
`[window.]document.forms[i].elements[i].name`

IE 　　　 `[window.]document.`*formName*`.`*elementName*`.name`
`[window.]document.forms[i].elements[i].name`
`[window.]document.all.`*elementID*`.name`

READONLY
NN *n/a*　　IE *4*　　HTML *4*

READONLY 　　　　　　　　　　　　　　　　　　　　　　　　　　　　　　*Optional*

When the READONLY attribute is present, the TEXTAREA element cannot be edited on the page by the user (although scripts can modify the content). A TEXTAREA marked as READONLY should not receive focus within the tabbing order (although IE 4 for the Macintosh allows the field to receive focus).

Example `<TEXTAREA NAME="instructions" READONLY></TEXTAREA>`

Value The presence of the attribute sets its value to **true**.

Default `false`

Object Model Reference

IE 　　　 `[window.]document.`*formName*`.`*elementName*`.readOnly`
`[window.]document.forms[i].elements[i].readOnly`
`[window.]document.all.`*elementID*`.readOnly`

ROWS
NN *all*　　IE *all*　　HTML *all*

ROWS="*rowCount*" 　　　　　　　　　　　　　　　　　　　　　　　　　　*Optional*

The height of the TEXTAREA element based on the number of lines of text that are to be displayed without scrolling. The value represents the number of monofont character lines that are to be displayed within the height before the scrollbar becomes active. When the font size can be influenced by style sheets, the actual height changes accordingly.

Example `<TEXTAREA ROWS=5 COLS=40></TEXTAREA>`

Value Any positive integer.

Default Varies with browser and operating system.

Object Model Reference

IE 　　　 `[window.]document.`*formName*`.`*elementName*`.rows`
`[window.]document.forms[i].elements[i].rows`
`[window.]document.all.`*elementID*`.rows`

STYLE   NN *n/a*   IE *4*   HTML *4*

STYLE=" *styleSheetProperties*"   *Optional*

This attribute lets you set one or more style sheet rule property assignments for the current element. The format of the property assignments depends on the browser's default style, but both Navigator and Internet Explorer accept the CSS syntax. Style sheet rules influence this element in Internet Explorer 4 for the Macintosh more than they do the Windows version. You may wish to wait for improved (and cross-browser) implementation before setting styles of **TEXTAREA** elements.

Example <TEXTAREA STYLE="text-size:14pt"></TEXTAREA>

Value

An entire CSS-syntax style sheet rule is enclosed in quotes. Multiple style attribute settings are separated by semicolons. Style sheet attributes are detailed in Chapter 10.

Default   None.

Object Model Reference

IE   [window.]document.*formName*.*elementName*.style
          [window.]document.forms[i].elements[i].style
          [window.]document.all.*elementID*.style

TABINDEX   NN *n/a*   IE *4*   HTML *4*

TABINDEX=integer   *Optional*

A number that indicates the sequence of this element within the tabbing order of all focusable elements in the document. Tabbing order follows a strict set of rules. Elements that have values other than zero assigned to their **TABINDEX** attributes are first in line when a user starts tabbing in a page. Focus starts with the element with the lowest **TABINDEX** value and proceeds in order to the highest value, regardless of physical location on the page or in the document. If two elements have the same **TABINDEX** values, the element that comes earlier in the document receives focus first. Next come all elements that either don't support the **TABINDEX** attribute or have the value set to zero. These elements receive focus in the order in which they appear in the document.

Example <TEXTAREA NAME="comments" TABINDEX=3></TEXTAREA>

Value

Any integer from 0 through 32767. In IE 4, setting the **TABINDEX** to −1 causes the element to be skipped in tabbing order altogether.

Default   None.

Object Model Reference

IE   [window.]document.*formName*.*elementName*.tabIndex
          [window.]document.forms[i].elements[i].tabIndex
          [window.]document.all.*elementID*.tabIndex

WRAP

WRAP=" *wrapType*"   *Required*

The WRAP attribute tells the browser whether it should wrap text in a TEXTAREA element and whether wrapped text should be submitted to the server with soft returns converted to hard carriage returns. Navigator and Internet Explorer don't agree fully on the possible values, and the HTML specification is silent on the subject. Even so, there are cross-browser solutions.

If WRAP is turned off (the default), the TEXTAREA element activates the horizontal scrollbar as characters exceed the original column width. A press of the **Return/Enter** key causes the cursor to advance to the next line back at the left margin. To submit the content without the word-wrapped soft returns converted to hard carriage returns (in other words, submitted as typed), set the WRAP attribute by including the attribute like a Boolean value. To convert the soft returns to hard carriage returns (and thus preserving the word-wrapped formatting in the submitted content), set the value of WRAP to hard. Both Navigator and Internet Explorer recognize this setting, whereas Navigator does not recognize IE's value of physical.

Example   <TEXTAREA NAME="comments" WRAP></TEXTAREA>

Value

The presence of the WRAP attribute (without any assigned value) engages word wrapping (and filters soft returns before being submitted). A value of hard also engages word wrapping and converts soft returns to CR-LF characters in the value submitted to the server. A value of off or no attribute turns word wrapping off. Recognized values are as follows:

Value	NN	IE
hard	•	•
off	•	•
physical	-	•
soft	•	-
virtual	-	•

Default   off

Object Model Reference

IE   [window.]document.*formName*.*elementName*.wrap

              [window.]document.forms[i].elements[i].wrap

              [window.]document.all.*elementID*.wrap

<TFOOT>

<TFOOT>...</TFOOT>   *End Tag: Optional*

A TFOOT element is a special-purpose container of one or more rows of table cells rendered at the bottom of the table. Typically, the TFOOT element mirrors the THEAD element content for users who have scrolled down the page (or for future browsers that scroll inner table content). No more than one TFOOT element may be defined within a single TABLE element, and the TFOOT element should be located in the source code before any TBODY elements defined for the table. A TFOOT element is a row grouping, like the TBODY and THEAD elements. Navigator 4 ignores the TFOOT tag and therefore renders the nested TR element(s) as regular TR elements in source code order.

Example

```
<TABLE COLS=3>
<THEAD>
<TR>
<TH>Time<TH>Event<TH>Location
</TR>
</THEAD>
<TFOOT>
<TR>
<TH>Time<TH>Event<TH>Location
</TR>
</TFOOT>
<TBODY>
<TR>
<TD>7:30am-5:00pm<TD>Registration Open<TD>Main Lobby
</TR>
<TR>
<TD>9:00am-12:00pm<TD>Keynote Speakers<TD>Cypress Room
</TR>
</TBODY>
</TABLE>
```

Object Model Reference

IE   [window.]document.all.*elementID*

Attributes

ALIGN	CHAROFF	*ID*	*LANGUAGE*	*TITLE*
BGCOLOR	*CLASS*	*LANG*	*STYLE*	VALIGN
CHAR	*DIR*			

Event Handler Attributes

Handler	NN	IE	HTML
onClick	n/a	4	4
onDblClick	n/a	4	4
onDragStart	n/a	4	n/a
onHelp	n/a	4	n/a
onKeyDown	n/a	4	4
onKeyPress	n/a	4	4
onKeyUp	n/a	4	4
onMouseDown	n/a	4	4
onMouseMove	n/a	4	4
onMouseOut	n/a	4	4
onMouseOver	n/a	4	4
onMouseUp	n/a	4	4
onSelectStart	n/a	4	n/a

ALIGN

NN *n/a*   IE *4*   HTML *4*

ALIGN="*alignConstant*"   *Optional*

Establishes the horizontal alignment characteristics of content within the row(s) covered by the TFOOT element. The HTML 4.0 specification defines settings for the ALIGN attribute that are not yet reflected in the CSS specification. Therefore, this ALIGN attribute is not fully deprecated as it is for many other elements. As a rule, alignment should be specified by style sheet wherever possible.

Example   <TFOOT ALIGN="center">

Value   HTML 4.0 and IE 4 have two sets of attribute values:

Value	IE 4	HTML 4.0
center	•	•
char	–	•
justify	–	•
left	•	•
right	•	•

The values center, left, and right are self-explanatory. The value justify is intended to space content so that text is justified down both left and right edges. For the value char, the CHAR attribute must also be set to specify the character on which alignment revolves. In the HTML 4.0 specification example, content that does not contain the character appears to be right-aligned to the location of the character in other rows of the same column.

It is important to bear in mind that the ALIGN attribute applies to every cell of every row within the TFOOT, including any TH element you specify for the table. If you want a different alignment for the row header, override the setting with a separate ALIGN attribute or text-align style sheet attribute for the individual TH elements.

Default   left

Object Model Reference

IE   [window.]document.all.*elementID*.align

BGCOLOR

NN *n/a*   IE *4*   HTML *n/a*

BGCOLOR="*colorTripletOrName*"   *Optional*

Establishes a fill color (behind the text and other content) for the cells contained by the TFOOT element.

Example   <TFOOT BGCOLOR="tan">

Value

A hexadecimal triplet or plain-language color name. A setting of empty is interpreted as "#000000" (black). See Appendix A for acceptable plain-language color names.

Default   Varies with browser, browser version, and operating system.

Object Model Reference

IE   [window.]document.all.*elementID*.bgColor

CHAR

NN *n/a*   IE *n/a*   HTML *4*

CHAR=" *character*"   *Optional*

The text character used as an alignment point for text within a cell. This attribute is of value only for the ALIGN attribute set to "char".

Example <TFOOT ALIGN="char" CHAR=".">

Value   Any single text character.

Default   None.

CHAROFF

NN *n/a*   IE *n/a*   HTML *4*

CHAROFF=" *length*"   *Optional*

Sets a specific offset point at which the character specified by the CHAR attribute is to appear within a cell. This attribute is provided in case the browser default positioning does not meet with the design goals of the table.

Example <TFOOT ALIGN="char" CHAR="." CHAROFF="80%">

Value   Any length value in pixels or percentage of cell space.

Default   None.

VALIGN

NN *n/a*   IE *4*   HTML *4*

VALIGN=" *alignmentConstant*"   *Optional*

Determines the vertical alignment of content within cells of the column(s) covered by the TFOOT element. You can override the vertical alignment for a particular cell anywhere in the column.

Example <TFOOT VALIGN="bottom">

Value

Four constant values are recognized by both IE 4 and HTML 4.0: top | middle | bottom | baseline. With top and bottom, the content is rendered flush (or very close to it) to the top and bottom of the table cell. Set to middle (the default), the content floats perfectly centered vertically in the cell. When one cell's contents might wrap to multiple lines at common window widths (assuming a variable table width), it is advisable to set the VALIGN attribute to baseline. This assures that the character baseline of the first (or only) line of a cell's text aligns with the other cells in the row—usually the most aesthetically pleasing arrangement.

Default   middle

Object Model Reference

IE   [window.]document.all.*elementID*.vAlign

<TH>

<TH>...</TH>   *End Tag: Optional*

The TH element is a container for content that is rendered inside one cell of a TABLE element in a format that distinguishes it as a header. Most browsers render the content as boldface. A cell is the intersection of a column and row. Other elements related to the TH element are CAPTION, COL, COLGROUP, TABLE, TBODY, TD, TFOOT, THEAD, and TR. In addition to providing a wrapper for a cell's content, the TH element defines a number of visible attributes that apply to a single cell, often overriding similar attributes set in lesser-nested elements in the table.

Four attributes—ABBR, AXIS, HEADERS, and SCOPE—have been added to the HTML 4.0 specification in anticipation of nonvisual browsers that will use text-to-speech technology to describe content of an HTML page—a kind of "verbal rendering." Although these attributes are briefly described here for the sake of completeness, there is much more to their application in nonvisual browsers than is relevant in this book on Dynamic HTML. Consult the HTML 4.0 recommendation for more details.

Example

```
<TABLE COLS=3>
<THEAD>
<TR>
<TH>Time<TH>Event<TH>Location
</TR>
</THEAD>
<TBODY>
<TR>
<TD>7:30am-5:00pm<TD>Registration Open<TD>Main Lobby
</TR>
<TR>
<TD>9:00am-12:00pm<TD>Keynote Speakers<TD>Cypress Room
</TR>
</TBODY>
</TABLE>
```

Object Model Reference

IE   [window.]document.all.*elementID*

Attributes

ABBR	BORDERCOLORDARK	COLSPAN	*ID*	SCOPE
ALIGN	BORDERCOLORLIGHT	DATAFLD	*LANG*	*STYLE*
AXIS	CHAR	*DIR*	*LANGUAGE*	*TITLE*
BACKGROUND	CHAROFF	HEADERS	NOWRAP	VALIGN
BGCOLOR	*CLASS*	HEIGHT	ROWSPAN	WIDTH
BORDERCOLOR				

Event Handler Attributes

Handler	NN	IE	HTML
onAfterUpdate	n/a	4	n/a
onBeforeUpdate	n/a	4	n/a
onBlur	n/a	4	n/a

Handler	NN	IE	HTML
onClick	n/a	4	4
onDblClick	n/a	4	4
onDragStart	n/a	4	n/a
onFocus	n/a	4	n/a
onHelp	n/a	4	n/a
onKeyDown	n/a	4	4
onKeyPress	n/a	4	4
onKeyUp	n/a	4	4
onMouseDown	n/a	4	4
onMouseMove	n/a	4	4
onMouseOut	n/a	4	4
onMouseOver	n/a	4	4
onMouseUp	n/a	4	4
onResize	n/a	4	n/a
onRowEnter	n/a	4	n/a
onRowExit	n/a	4	n/a
onScroll	n/a	4	n/a
onSelectStart	n/a	4	n/a

ABBR

NN *n/a*   IE *n/a*   HTML *4*

ABBR=" *text*"   *Optional*

Provides an abbreviated string that describes the cell's content. This is usually a brief label that a nonvisual browser would speak to describe what the value of the cell represents.

Example <TH ABBR="What"> Event

Value   Any quoted string.

Default None.

ALIGN

NN *all*   IE *all*   HTML *3.2*

ALIGN=" *alignConstant*"   *Optional*

Establishes the horizontal alignment characteristics of content within the cell covered by the TH element. The HTML 4.0 specification defines settings for the ALIGN attribute that are not yet reflected in the CSS specification. Therefore, this ALIGN attribute is not fully deprecated as it is for many other elements. As a rule, alignment should be specified by style sheet wherever possible.

Example <TH ALIGN="center">

Value

Navigator 4 and Internet Explorer 4 share the same attribute values, whereas HTML 4.0 has a couple more:

Value	NN 4	IE 4	HTML 4.0
center	•	•	•
char	-	-	•
justify	-	-	•
left	•	•	•
right	•	•	•

The values center, left, and right are self-explanatory. The value justify is intended to space content so that text is justified down both left and right edges. For the value char, the CHAR attribute must also be set to specify the character on which alignment revolves. In the HTML 4.0 specification example, content that does not contain the character appears to be right-aligned to the location of the character in other rows of the same column.

Default   left

Object Model Reference

IE   [window.]document.all.*elementID*.align

AXIS   NN *n/a*   IE *n/a*   HTML *4*

AXIS=" *text*"   *Optional*

Provides an abbreviated string that describes the cell's category. This is usually a brief label that a nonvisual browser would speak to describe what the value of the cell represents.

Example <TH AXIS="event">Events

Value   Any quoted string.

Default None.

BACKGROUND   NN *n/a*   IE *3*   HTML *n/a*

BACKGROUND=" *URL*"   *Optional*

Specifies an image file that is used as a backdrop to the cell. Unlike normal images that get loaded into browser content, a background image loads in its original size (without scaling) and tiles to fill the available cell space. Smaller images download faster but are obviously repeated more often in the background. Animated GIFs are also allowable, but very distracting to the reader. When selecting a background image, be sure it is very muted in comparison to the main content so that the content stands out clearly. Background images, if used at all, should be extremely subtle.

Example <TH BACKGROUND="watermark.jpg">

Value   Any valid URL to an image file, including complete and relative URLs.

Default None.

Object Model Reference

IE   [window.]document.all.*elementID*.background

BGCOLOR

NN *3*   IE *3*   HTML *3.2*

BGCOLOR=" *colorTripletOrName*"   *Optional*

Establishes a fill color (behind the text and other content) for the cell defined by the TH element.

Example <TH BGCOLOR="yellow">

Value

A hexadecimal triplet or plain-language color name. A setting of empty is interpreted as "#000000" (black). See Appendix A for acceptable plain-language color names.

Default   Varies with browser, browser version, and operating system.

Object Model Reference

IE   [window.]document.all.*elementID*.bgColor

BORDERCOLOR

NN *n/a*   IE *3*   HTML *n/a*

BORDERCOLOR=" *colorTripletOrName*"   *Optional*

The colors used to render some of the pixels used to create the illusion of borders around cells and the entire table. Internet Explorer applies the color to all four lines that make up the interior border of a cell. Therefore, colors of adjacent cells do not collide.

Example <TH BORDERCOLOR="green">

Value

A hexadecimal triplet or plain-language color name. A setting of empty is interpreted as "#000000" (black). See Appendix A for acceptable plain-language color names.

Default   Varies with browser and operating system.

Object Model Reference

IE   [window.]document.all.*elementID*.borderColor

BORDERCOLORDARK, BORDERCOLORLIGHT

NN *n/a*   IE *3*   HTML *n/a*

BORDERCOLORDARK=" *colorTripletOrName*"   *Optional*
BORDERCOLORLIGHT=" *colorTripletOrName*"

The 3-D effect of table borders in Internet Explorer is created by careful positioning of light and dark lines around the page's background or default color (see Figure 8-4 in the TABLE element discussion). You can independently control the colors used for the dark and light lines by assigning values to the BORDERCOLORDARK (left and top edges of the cell) and BORDERCOLORLIGHT (right and bottom edges) attributes. Typically, you should assign complementary colors to the pair of attributes. There is also no rule that says you must assign a dark color to BORDERCOLORDARK. The attributes merely control a well-defined set of lines so you can predict which lines of the border change with each attribute.

Example <TH BORDERCOLORDARK="darkred" BORDERCOLORLIGHT="salmon">

Value

A hexadecimal triplet or plain-language color name. A setting of empty is interpreted as "#000000" (black). See Appendix A for acceptable plain-language color names.

Default Varies with operating system.

Object Model Reference

IE   [window.]document.all.*elementID*.borderColorDark
     [window.]document.all.*elementID*.borderColorLight

CHAR

NN *n/a* IE *n/a* HTML 4

CHAR="*character*"   *Optional*

The text character used as an alignment point for text within a cell. This attribute is of value only for the ALIGN attribute set to "char".

Example <TH ALIGN="char" CHAR=".">

Value Any single text character.

Default None.

CHAROFF

NN *n/a* IE *n/a* HTML 4

CHAROFF="*length*"   *Optional*

Sets a specific offset point at which the character specified by the CHAR attribute is to appear within a cell. This attribute is provided in case the browser default positioning does not meet with the design goals of the table.

Example <TH ALIGN="char" CHAR="." CHAROFF="80%">

Value Any length value in pixels or percentage of cell space.

Default None.

COLSPAN

NN *all* IE *all* HTML 3.2

COLSPAN="*columnCount*"   *Optional*

The COLSPAN attribute specifies the number of columns across which the current table cell should extend itself. For each additional column included in the COLSPAN count, one less TH or TD element is required for the table row. If you set the ALIGN attribute to center or right, the alignment is calculated on the full width of the TH element across the specified number of columns. Unless the current cell is also specifies a ROWSPAN attribute, the next table row returns to the original column count.

Example <TH COLSPAN=2 ALIGN="right">

Value Any positive integer, usually 2 or larger.

Default 1

Object Model Reference

IE   [window.]document.all.*elementID*.colSpan

DATAFLD

NN *n/a*   IE 4   HTML *n/a*

DATAFLD="*columnName*"   *Optional*

Used with IE 4 data binding to associate a remote data source column name with the content of a table header cell. A DATASRC (and optionally, a DATAPAGESIZE) attribute must also be set for the enclosing TABLE element.

Example

```
<TABLE DATASRC="#DBSRC3" DATAPAGESIZE=5>
<TR>
  <TH><INPUT TYPE="text" DATAFLD="stockNum">
  <TH><INPUT TYPE="text" DATAFLD="qtyOnHand">
</TR>
</TABLE>
```

Value   Case-sensitive identifier.

Default   None.

HEADERS

NN *n/a*   IE *n/a*   HTML 4

HEADERS="*cellIDList*"   *Optional*

Points to one or more TH or TD elements that act as column or row headers for the current table cell. The assigned value is a space-delimited list of ID attribute values that are assigned to the relevant TH elements. A nonvisual browser could read the cell's header before the content of the cell to help listeners identify the nature of the cell content.

Example

```
<TR>
<TH id="hdr1">Product Number
<TH id="hdr2">Description
</TR>
<TR>
<TH headers="hdr1">0392
<TH headers="hdr2">Round widget
</TR>
```

Value

A space-delimited list of case-sensitive IDs assigned to cells that act as headers to the current cell.

Default   None.

HEIGHT, WIDTH

NN *all*   IE *all*   HTML 3.2

HEIGHT="*length*"   *Optional*

WIDTH="*length*"

The rectangular dimensions of a cell that may be different from the default size as calculated by the browser. When the values for these attributes are less than the minimum space required to render the table cell content, the browser overrides the attribute settings to make sure that all content appears, even if it means that text lines word-wrap. You can also stretch the dimensions of a table beyond the browser-calculated dimensions. Extra whitespace appears inside table cells to make up the difference. If you specify just one of these attributes, the browser performs all necessary calculations to automatically adjust the dimension along the other axis.

Due to the regular nature of tables, if you set a custom height for one cell in a row, the entire row is set to that height; similarly, setting the width of a cell causes the width of all cells in the column to be the same size.

Both the HEIGHT and WIDTH attributes are deprecated in HTML 4.0 in favor of height and width style sheet attributes (which are not available for table cells in Navigator 4).

Example   <TH WIDTH="80%" HEIGHT=30>

Value   Any length value in pixels or percentage of available space.

Default   Based on content size.

Object Model Reference

IE   [window.]document.all.*elementID*.height
            [window.]document.all.*elementID*.width

NOWRAP

NN *all*   IE *all*   HTML *3.2*

NOWRAP   *Optional*

The presence of the NOWRAP attribute instructs the browser to render the cell as wide as is necessary to display a line of nonbreaking text on one line. Abuse of this attribute can force the user into a great deal of inconvenient horizontal scrolling of the page to view all of the content. The NOWRAP attribute is deprecated in HTML 4.0.

Example   <TH NOWRAP>

Value   The presence of this attribute sets its value to true.

Default   false

Object Model Reference

IE   [window.]document.all.*elementID*.noWrap

ROWSPAN

NN *all*   IE *all*   HTML *3.2*

ROWSPAN="*rowCount*"   *Optional*

The number of rows through which the current table cell should extend itself downward. For each additional row included in the ROWSPAN count, one less TH or TD element is required for the next table row in that cell's position along the row.

Example   <TH ROWSPAN=2>

Value   Any positive integer, usually 2 or larger.

Default   1

Object Model Reference

IE   [window.]document.all.*elementID*.rowSpan

SCOPE   NN *n/a*   IE *n/a*   HTML *4*

SCOPE="*scopeConstant*"   *Optional*

The range of cells (relative to the current cell) that behave as though the current cell is the header for those cells. For tables whose structure is quite regular, the SCOPE attribute is a simpler way of achieving what the HEADERS attribute does, without having to define ID attributes for the header cells.

Example

```
<TR>
<TH SCOPE="col">Product Number
<TH SCOPE="col">Description
</TR>
<TR>
<TD>0392
<TD>Round widget
</TR>
```

Value   One of four recognized scope constants:

col   Current cell text becomes header text for every cell in the rest of the column.

colgroup Current cell text becomes header text for every cell in the rest of the COLGROUP element.

row   Current cell text becomes header text for every cell in the rest of the TR element.

rowgroup Current cell text becomes header text for every cell in the rest of the TBODY element.

Default   None.

VALIGN   NN *all*   IE *all*   HTML *3.2*

VALIGN="*alignmentConstant*"   *Optional*

Determines the vertical alignment of content within the TD element. A value you set for an individual cell overrides the same attribute setting for outer containers, such as TR and TBODY.

Example   <TH VALIGN="bottom">

Value

Four constant values are recognized by both IE 4 and HTML 4.0: top | middle | bottom | baseline. With top and bottom, the content is rendered flush (or very close to it) to the top and bottom of the table cell. Set to middle (the default), the content floats perfectly centered vertically in the cell. When one cell's contents might wrap to multiple lines at common window widths (assuming a variable table width), it is advisable to set the VALIGN attribute to baseline. This assures that the character baseline of the first (or only) line of a cell's text aligns with the other cells in the row—usually the most aesthetically pleasing arrangement.

Default   middle

Object Model Reference

IE   [window.]document.all.*elementID*.vAlign

WIDTH

See HEIGHT.

<THEAD>   NN *n/a*   IE *3*   HTML *4*

<THEAD>...</THEAD>   *End Tag: Optional*

A THEAD element is a special-purpose container of one or more rows of table cells rendered at the top of the table. No more than one THEAD element may be defined within a single TABLE element, and the THEAD element should be located in the source code immediately after the TABLE element's start tag. You are free to use any combination of TD and TH elements you like within the THEAD element. A THEAD element is a row grouping, like the TBODY and TFOOT elements. Navigator 4 ignores the THEAD tag and therefore renders the nested TR element(s) as regular TR elements in source code order.

Example

```
<TABLE COLS=3>
<THEAD>
<TR>
<TH>Time<TH>Event<TH>Location
</TR>
</THEAD>
<TFOOT>
<TR>
<TH>Time<TH>Event<TH>Location
</TR>
</TFOOT>
<TBODY>
<TR>
<TD>7:30am-5:00pm<TD>Registration Open<TD>Main Lobby
</TR>
<TR>
<TD>9:00am-12:00pm<TD>Keynote Speakers<TD>Cypress Room
</TR>
</TBODY>
</TABLE>
```

Object Model Reference

IE   [window.]document.all.*elementID*

Attributes

ALIGN	CHAROFF	ID	LANGUAGE	TITLE
BGCOLOR	CLASS	LANG	STYLE	VALIGN
CHAR	DIR			

Event Handler Attributes

Handler	NN	IE	HTML
onClick	n/a	4	4
onDblClick	n/a	4	4
onDragStart	n/a	4	n/a
onHelp	n/a	4	n/a
onKeyDown	n/a	4	4
onKeyPress	n/a	4	4
onKeyUp	n/a	4	4
onMouseDown	n/a	4	4
onMouseMove	n/a	4	4
onMouseOut	n/a	4	4
onMouseOver	n/a	4	4
onMouseUp	n/a	4	4
onSelectStart	n/a	4	n/a

ALIGN
NN n/a   IE 4   HTML 4

ALIGN="*alignConstant*"   *Optional*

Establishes the horizontal alignment characteristics of content within the row(s) covered by the THEAD element. The HTML 4.0 specification defines settings for the ALIGN attribute that are not yet reflected in the CSS specification. Therefore, this ALIGN attribute is not fully deprecated as it is for many other elements. As a rule, alignment should be specified by style sheet wherever possible.

Example   <THEAD ALIGN="center">

Value   HTML 4.0 and IE 4 have two sets of attribute values:

Value	IE 4	HTML 4.0
center	•	•
char	–	•
justify	–	•
left	•	•
right	•	•

The values center, left, and right are self-explanatory. The value justify is intended to space content so that text is justified down both left and right edges. For the value char, the CHAR attribute must also be set to specify the character on which alignment revolves. In the HTML 4.0 specification example, content that does not contain the character appears to be right-aligned to the location of the character in other rows of the same column.

It is important to bear in mind that the ALIGN attribute applies to every cell of every row within the THEAD, including any TH element you specify for the table. If you want a different alignment for the row header, override the setting with a separate ALIGN attribute or text-align style sheet attribute for the individual TH elements.

Default   left

Object Model Reference

IE   [window.]document.all.*elementID*.align

BGCOLOR

NN *n/a*   IE *4*   HTML *n/a*

BGCOLOR="*colorTripletOrName*"   *Optional*

Establishes a fill color (behind the text and other content) for the cells contained by the THEAD element.

Example   <THEAD BGCOLOR="tan">

Value

A hexadecimal triplet or plain-language color name. A setting of empty is interpreted as "#000000" (black). See Appendix A for acceptable plain-language color names.

Default   Varies with browser, browser version, and operating system.

Object Model Reference

IE   [window.]document.all.*elementID*.bgColor

CHAR

NN *n/a*   IE *n/a*   HTML *4*

CHAR="*character*"   *Optional*

The text character used as an alignment point for text within a cell. This attribute is of value only for the ALIGN attribute set to "char".

Example   <THEAD ALIGN="char" CHAR=".">

Value   Any single text character.

Default   None.

CHAROFF

NN *n/a*   IE *n/a*   HTML *4*

CHAROFF="*length*"   *Optional*

Sets a specific offset point at which the character specified by the CHAR attribute is to appear within a cell. This attribute is provided in case the browser default positioning does not meet with the design goals of the table.

Example   <THEAD ALIGN="char" CHAR="." CHAROFF="80%">

Value   Any length value in pixels or percentage of cell space.

Default   None.

VALIGN

NN *n/a*   IE *4*   HTML *4*

VALIGN="*alignmentConstant*"   *Optional*

Determines the vertical alignment of content within cells of the column(s) covered by the THEAD element. You can override the vertical alignment for a particular cell anywhere in the column.

Example   <THEAD VALIGN="bottom">

Value

Four constant values are recognized by both IE 4 and HTML 4.0: top | middle | bottom | baseline. With top and bottom, the content is rendered flush (or very close to it) to the top and bottom of the table cell. Set to middle (the default), the content floats perfectly centered vertically in the cell. When one cell's contents might wrap to multiple lines at common window widths (assuming a variable table width), it is advisable to set the VALIGN attribute to baseline. This assures that the character baseline of the first (or only) line of a cell's text aligns with the other cells in the row—usually the most aesthetically pleasing arrangement.

Default   middle

Object Model Reference

IE   [window.]document.all.*elementID*.vAlign

<TITLE>   NN *all*   IE *all*   HTML *all*

`<TITLE>...</TITLE>`   *End Tag: Required*

The TITLE element identifies the overall content of a document. The element content is not displayed as part of the document, but browsers display the title in the browser application's window titlebar. Only one TITLE element is permitted per document and it must be located inside the HEAD element. It is alright to be somewhat verbose in assigning a document title because not everyone will access the document in sequence through your web site. Give the document some context as well.

Example `<TITLE>Declaration of Independence</TITLE>`

Object Model Reference

IE   [window.]document.all.*elementID*

Attributes

DIR	ID	LANG	TITLE

<TR>   NN *all*   IE *all*   HTML *all*

`<TR>...</TR>`   *End Tag: Optional*

A TR element is a container for one row of cells. Each cell within a row may be a TH or TD element. Every row requires at least a start tag to instruct the browser to begin rendering succeeding cell elements on the next line of the table. Other special-purpose row groupings available are the TFOOT and THEAD, as well as the more generic TBODY grouping element.

Example

```
<TABLE COLS=3>
<THEAD>
<TR>
<TH>Time<TH>Event<TH>Location
</TR>
</THEAD>
<TBODY>
```

```
<TR>
<TD>7:30am-5:00pm<TD>Registration Open<TD>Main Lobby
</TR>
<TR>
<TD>9:00am-12:00pm<TD>Keynote Speakers<TD>Cypress Room
</TR>
</TBODY>
</TABLE>
```

Object Model Reference

IE   [window.]document.all.*elementID*

Attributes

ALIGN	BORDERCOLORDARK	CHAROFF	ID	STYLE
BGCOLOR	BORDERCOLORLIGHT	CLASS	LANG	TITLE
BORDERCOLOR	CHAR	DIR	LANGUAGE	VALIGN

Event Handler Attributes

Handler	NN	IE	HTML
onAfterUpdate	n/a	4	n/a
onBeforeUpdate	n/a	4	n/a
onBlur	n/a	4	n/a
onClick	n/a	4	4
onDblClick	n/a	4	4
onDragStart	n/a	4	n/a
onFocus	n/a	4	n/a
onHelp	n/a	4	n/a
onKeyDown	n/a	4	4
onKeyPress	n/a	4	4
onKeyUp	n/a	4	4
onMouseDown	n/a	4	4
onMouseMove	n/a	4	4
onMouseOut	n/a	4	4
onMouseOver	n/a	4	4
onMouseUp	n/a	4	4
onResize	n/a	4	n/a
onRowEnter	n/a	4	n/a
onRowExit	n/a	4	n/a
onSelectStart	n/a	4	n/a

ALIGN
NN *n/a*   IE 4   HTML 4

ALIGN="*alignConstant*"   *Optional*

Establishes the horizontal alignment characteristics of content within the row. The HTML 4.0 specification defines settings for the ALIGN attribute that are not yet reflected in the CSS specification. Therefore, this ALIGN attribute is not fully deprecated as it is for many other elements. As a rule, alignment should be specified by style sheet wherever possible.

Example   <TR ALIGN="center">

Value

Navigator and Internet Explorer share the same set of attribute values, whereas HTML 4.0 specifies two additional values:

Value	NN 4	IE 4	HTML 4.0
center	•	•	•
char	-	-	•
justify	-	-	•
left	•	•	•
right	•	•	•

The values center, left, and right are self-explanatory. The value justify is intended to space content so that text is justified down both left and right edges. For the value char, the CHAR attribute must also be set to specify the character on which alignment revolves. In the HTML 4.0 specification example, content that does not contain the character appears to be right-aligned to the location of the character in other rows of the same column.

It is important to bear in mind that the ALIGN attribute applies to every cell within the TR element, including any TH element you specify for the table. If you want a different alignment for the row header, override the setting with a separate ALIGN attribute or text-align style sheet attribute for the TR or individual TH elements.

Default   center

Object Model Reference

IE   [window.]document.all.*elementID*.align

BGCOLOR   NN 3   IE 4   HTML 4

BGCOLOR="*colorTripletOrName*"   *Optional*

Establishes a fill color (behind the text and other content) for the cells contained by the TR element.

Example   <TR BGCOLOR="lavender">

Value

A hexadecimal triplet or plain-language color name. A setting of empty is interpreted as "#000000" (black). See Appendix A for acceptable plain-language color names.

Default   Varies with browser, browser version, and operating system.

Object Model Reference

IE   [window.]document.all.*elementID*.bgColor

BORDERCOLOR
            NN *n/a*   IE *3*   HTML *n/a*

BORDERCOLOR=" *colorTripletOrName*"   *Optional*

The color used to render some of the pixels used to create the illusion of borders around cells and the entire table. Internet Explorer applies the color to all four lines that make up the interior border of a cell. Therefore, colors of adjacent cells do not collide.

Example   <TR BORDERCOLOR="green">

Value

A hexadecimal triplet or plain-language color name. A setting of empty is interpreted as "#000000" (black). See Appendix A for acceptable plain-language color names.

Default   Varies with browser and operating system.

Object Model Reference

IE   [window.]document.all.*elementID*.borderColor

BORDERCOLORDARK,
BORDERCOLORLIGHT
            NN *n/a*   IE *3*   HTML *n/a*

BORDERCOLORDARK=" *colorTripletOrName*"   *Optional*
BORDERCOLORLIGHT=" *colorTripletOrName*"

The 3-D effect of table borders in Internet Explorer is created by careful positioning of light and dark lines around the page's background or default color (see Figure 8-4 in the **TABLE** element discussion). You can independently control the colors used for the dark and light lines by assigning values to the **BORDERCOLORDARK** (left and top edges of the cell) and **BORDERCOLORLIGHT** (right and bottom edges) attributes.

Typically, you should assign complementary colors to the pair of attributes. There is also no rule that says you must assign a dark color to **BORDERCOLORDARK**. The attributes merely control a well-defined set of lines so you can predict which lines of the border change with each attribute.

Example   <TR BORDERCOLORDARK="darkred" BORDERCOLORLIGHT="salmon">

Value

A hexadecimal triplet or plain-language color name. A setting of empty is interpreted as "#000000" (black). See Appendix A for acceptable plain-language color names.

Default   Varies with operating system.

Object Model Reference

IE   [window.]document.all.*elementID*.borderColorDark
                  [window.]document.all.*elementID*.borderColorLight

CHAR
NN *n/a*   IE *n/a*   HTML *4*

CHAR="*character*"   *Optional*

The text character used as an alignment point for text within a cell. This attribute is of value only for the ALIGN attribute set to "char".

Example   <TR ALIGN="char" CHAR=".">

Value   Any single text character.

Default   None.

CHAROFF
NN *n/a*   IE *n/a*   HTML *4*

CHAROFF="*length*"   *Optional*

Sets a specific offset point at which the character specified by the CHAR attribute is to appear within a cell. This attribute is provided in case the browser default positioning does not meet with the design goals of the table.

Example   <TR ALIGN="char" CHAR="." CHAROFF="80%">

Value   Any length value in pixels or percentage of cell space.

Default   None.

VALIGN
NN *n/a*   IE *4*   HTML *4*

VALIGN="*alignmentConstant*"   *Optional*

Determines the vertical alignment of content within cells of the column(s) covered by the TR element. You can override the vertical alignment for a particular cell anywhere in the row.

Example   <TR VALIGN="bottom">

Value

Four constant values are recognized by both IE 4 and HTML 4.0: top | middle | bottom | baseline. With top and bottom, the content is rendered flush (or very close to it) to the top and bottom of the table cell. Set to middle (the default), the content floats perfectly centered vertically in the cell. When one cell's contents might wrap to multiple lines at common window widths (assuming a variable table width), it is advisable to set the VALIGN attribute to baseline. This assures that the character baseline of the first (or only) line of a cell's text aligns with the other cells in the row—usually the most aesthetically pleasing arrangement.

Default   middle

Object Model Reference

IE   [window.]document.all.*elementID*.vAlign

<TT>

NN *all*   IE *all*   HTML *all*

`<TT>...</TT>`   *End Tag: Required*

The **TT** element renders its content as monospaced text (indicating a teletype output). The element is intended to be strictly a formatting—as opposed to a contextual—element. If you are looking for a contextual setting for computer program code or input, see the **CODE**, **KBD**, and **SAMP** elements. As with most font-related elements, the use of style sheets is preferred.

Example   `<P>The computer said, <TT>"That does not compute."</TT></P>`

Object Model Reference

IE   [window.]document.all.*elementID*

Attributes

CLASS	*ID*	*LANGUAGE*	*STYLE*	*TITLE*
DIR	*LANG*			

Event Handler Attributes

Handler	NN	IE	HTML
onClick	n/a	4	4
onDblClick	n/a	4	4
onDragStart	n/a	4	n/a
onHelp	n/a	4	n/a
onKeyDown	n/a	4	4
onKeyPress	n/a	4	4
onKeyUp	n/a	4	4
onMouseDown	n/a	4	4
onMouseMove	n/a	4	4
onMouseOut	n/a	4	4
onMouseOver	n/a	4	4
onMouseUp	n/a	4	4
onSelectStart	n/a	4	n/a

<U>

NN *3*   IE *3*   HTML *3.2*

`<U>...</U>`   *End Tag: Required*

The **U** element renders its content as underlined text. This element is deprecated in HTML 4.0 in favor of the **text-decoration:underline** style sheet attribute.

Example   `<P>You may already be a <U>winner</U>!</P>`

Object Model Reference

IE   [window.]document.all.*elementID*

Attributes

CLASS	*ID*	*LANGUAGE*	*STYLE*	*TITLE*
DIR	*LANG*			

Event Handler Attributes

Handler	NN	IE	HTML
onClick	n/a	4	4
onDblClick	n/a	4	4
onDragStart	n/a	4	n/a
onHelp	n/a	4	n/a
onKeyDown	n/a	4	4
onKeyPress	n/a	4	4
onKeyUp	n/a	4	4
onMouseDown	n/a	4	4
onMouseMove	n/a	4	4
onMouseOut	n/a	4	4
onMouseOver	n/a	4	4
onMouseUp	n/a	4	4
onSelectStart	n/a	4	n/a

<UL>

NN *all*   IE *all*   HTML *all*

`<UL>...</UL>`   *End Tag: Required*

The **UL** element is a container for an unordered list of items. An "unordered list" means that the items are rendered with a leading symbol (depending on the **TYPE** attribute setting or `list-style-type` style sheet attribute setting) that implies no specific order of items other than by virtue of location within the list. Content for each list item is defined by a nested **LI** element. If you apply a style sheet rule to a **UL** element, the style is inherited by the nested **LI** elements.

Example

```
<UL>
    <LI>Africa
    <LI>Antarctica
    <LI>Asia
    <LI>Australia
    <LI>Europe
    <LI>North America
    <LI>South America
</UL>
```

Object Model Reference

IE   [window.]document.all.*elementID*

Attributes

CLASS	DIR	LANG	STYLE	TYPE
COMPACT	ID	LANGUAGE	TITLE	

Event Handler Attributes

Handler	NN	IE	HTML
onClick	n/a	4	4
onDblClick	n/a	4	4
onDragStart	n/a	4	n/a

Handler	NN	IE	HTML
onHelp	n/a	4	n/a
onKeyDown	n/a	4	4
onKeyPress	n/a	4	4
onKeyUp	n/a	4	4
onMouseDown	n/a	4	4
onMouseMove	n/a	4	4
onMouseOut	n/a	4	4
onMouseOver	n/a	4	4
onMouseUp	n/a	4	4
onSelectStart	n/a	4	n/a

COMPACT
NN *n/a*   IE *n/a*   HTML *3.2*

COMPACT   *Optional*

A Boolean attribute originally designed to let browsers render the list in a more compact style than normal (smaller line spacing between items). This attribute is not implemented in current browsers.

Example   <UL COMPACT>...</UL>

Value   The presence of this attribute makes its value true.

Default   false

TYPE
NN *all*   IE *all*   HTML *3.2*

TYPE="*labelType*"   *Optional*

The TYPE attribute provides some flexibility in how the leading symbol or sequence number is displayed in the browser. You can specify whether the leading symbol should be a disc, circle, or square. A disc is a filled circle (also known as a bullet in some circles). The square type is rendered as an outline in Macintosh browsers; as a filled square in Windows. The TYPE attribute is deprecated in HTML 4.0 in favor of the list-style-type style sheet attribute.

Example   <UL TYPE="disc">...</UL>

Value   Possible values are circle | disc | square.

Default   disc

Object Model Reference

IE   [window.]document.all.*elementID*.type

<VAR>
NN *all*   IE *all*   HTML *all*

<VAR>...</VAR>   *End Tag: Required*

The VAR element is one of a large group of elements that the HTML 4.0 recommendation calls *phrase elements*. Such elements assign structural meaning to a designated portion of the document. A VAR element is one that is used predominantly to display one or more inline characters representing a computer program variable name.

Browsers have free rein to determine how (or whether) to distinguish VAR element content from the rest of the BODY element. Both Navigator and Internet Explorer elect to render VAR element content in an italic font. This rendering can be overridden with a style sheet as you see fit.

Example `<P>The value of <VAR>offsetWidth</VAR> becomes 20.</P>`

Object Model Reference

IE   [window.]document.all.*elementID*

Attributes

CLASS	ID	LANGUAGE	STYLE	TITLE
DIR	LANG			

Event Handler Attributes

Handler	NN	IE	HTML
onClick	n/a	4	4
onDblClick	n/a	4	4
onDragStart	n/a	4	n/a
onHelp	n/a	4	n/a
onKeyDown	n/a	4	4
onKeyPress	n/a	4	4
onKeyUp	n/a	4	4
onMouseDown	n/a	4	4
onMouseMove	n/a	4	4
onMouseOut	n/a	4	4
onMouseOver	n/a	4	4
onMouseUp	n/a	4	4
onSelectStart	n/a	4	n/a

<WBR>   NN *all*   IE *all*   HTML *n/a*

<WBR>   *End Tag: Forbidden*

If you use the NOBR element to define content that should have no word wrapping or line breaks, you can use the WBR element to advise the browser that it can break up the content if the width of the browser window requires it. The locations of these provisional breaks are marked in the source code with the WBR element. In a sense, the NOBR and WBR elements give the author control over word wrapping of running content. Neither element is included in the HTML specification but have been long a part of both browsers' HTML vocabulary.

Example

```
<NOBR>This is a long line of text that could run on and on, <WBR>forcing
the browser to display the horizontal scrollbar after awhile.</NOBR>
```

Object Model Reference

IE   [window.]document.all.*elementID*

Attributes

CLASS	ID	LANG	STYLE	TITLE

<XMP>

NN *all*   IE *all*   HTML *<4*

`<XMP>...</XMP>`   *End Tag: Required*

The `XMP` element displays its content in a monospace font as a block element, as in computer code listings rendered 80 columns wide. In most browsers, the font size is also reduced from the default size. Browsers observe carriage returns and other whitespace in element content. This element has been long deprecated in HTML and has even been removed from the HTML 4.0 specification. You are encouraged to use the `PRE` element instead.

Example

```
<XMP>
&lt;SCRIPT LANGUAGE="JavaScript"&gt;
   document.write("Hello, world.")
&lt;/SCRIPT&gt;
</XMP>
```

Object Model Reference

IE   `[window.]document.all.`*elementID*

Attributes

CLASS	LANG	LANGUAGE	STYLE	TITLE
ID				

Event Handler Attributes

Handler	NN	IE	HTML
onClick	n/a	4	n/a
onDblClick	n/a	4	n/a
onDragStart	n/a	4	n/a
onHelp	n/a	4	n/a
onKeyDown	n/a	4	n/a
onKeyPress	n/a	4	n/a
onKeyUp	n/a	4	n/a
onMouseDown	n/a	4	n/a
onMouseMove	n/a	4	n/a
onMouseOut	n/a	4	n/a
onMouseOver	n/a	4	n/a
onMouseUp	n/a	4	n/a
onSelectStart	n/a	4	n/a

9

Document Object Reference

This chapter focuses on objects—the scriptable entities that are maintained in a browser's memory whenever a document is loaded. An object is described by its properties, methods, collections (or arrays) of nested items, and event handlers. One of the most formidable problems facing Dynamic HTML authors these days is the way each browser brand turns the HTML of a document into objects that can be accessed and modified by scripts. The W3C working group covering the Document Object Model (DOM) specification is developing what may someday become a common denominator that all scriptable browsers will follow. In the meantime, there is a bewildering array of objects with varying levels of support in the different browsers by brand, operating system, and version.

To help you choose the right object, property, method, and event handler for the type of page development you're doing, this chapter lists every object defined by Netscape, Microsoft, and the W3C (at least through the working draft stage of the DOM standard). From these listings, you should be able to judge whether a particular object or terminology will work for your application. If cross-browser support is essential for your application, pay close attention to the browser support and version information for each entry. Be aware that some items may not be available on all operating system platforms for a particular browser brand and version. These distinctions are noted wherever the anomalous behavior could be substantiated by actual testing on the Win32 and Macintosh platforms.

In the reference material, some objects are listed in all uppercase letters, while others are listed in mixed case or all lowercase. The uppercase objects *reflect* HTML elements and are found predominantly in Internet Explorer 4 and the DOM specification. You never use HTML element object names like these as is in script references, except when you are using their string representations as parameters (e.g., `document.all.tags("H1")`). Therefore, the case sensitivity of JavaScript does not affect this uppercase display of object names. They are shown here in uppercase to be consistent with the uppercase representation of HTML elements in Chapter 8, *HTML Reference*. In the lowercase and mixed case names, however, case is important, as you do use those names in script references.

Property Value Types

Many properties share similar data requirements. For the sake of brevity in the reference listings, this section describes a few common property value types in more detail than is possible within the listings. Whenever you see one of these property value types associated with a property, consult this section for a description of the type.

Length

A length value defines a linear measure of document real estate. The unit of measurement can be any applicable unit that helps identify a position or space on the screen. For properties that reflect HTML attributes, length units are uniformly pixels, but in other content, such as that specified in Cascading Style Sheets (see Chapter 10, *Style Sheet Attribute Reference*), measurements can be in inches, picas, ems, or other relevant units. A single numeric value may represent a length when it defines the offset from an edge of an element. For example, a coordinate point (10,20) consists of two length values, denoting pixel measurements from the left and top edges of an element, respectively.

Identifier

An identifier is a name that adheres to some strict syntactical rules. Most important is that an identifier is one word with no whitespace allowed. If you need to use multiple words to describe an item, you can use the intercapitalized format (in which internal letters are capitalized) or an underscore character between the words. Most punctuation symbols are not permitted, but all numerals and alphabetical characters are. Scripting languages do not allow the use of a numeral for the first character of an identifier.

URI and URL

The term Universal Resource Identifier (URI) is a broad term for an address of content on the Web. A Universal Resource Locator (URL) is a type of URI. For most web authoring, you can think of them as being one and the same, since most web browsers restrict their focus to URLs. A URL may be complete (including the protocol, host, domain, and the rest) or may be relative to the URL of the current docu-

DOM Reference

ment. In the latter case, this means the URL may consist of an anchor, file, or pathname. An object property that refers to a URL requires that the text of the URL be represented as a quoted string.

Language Code

There is an extensive list of standard codes that identify the spoken and written languages of the world. A language code always contains a primary language code, such as "en" for English or "zh" for Chinese. Common two-letter primary codes are cataloged in ISO 639. An optional subcode (separated from the primary code by a hyphen) may be used to identify a specific implementation of the primary language, usually according to usage within a specific country. Therefore, while "en" means all of English, "en-US" means a U.S.-specific version of English. The browser must support a particular language code for its meaning to be of any value to an element attribute.

Colors

A color value can be assigned either via a hexadecimal triplet or with a plain-language equivalent. A hexadecimal triplet consists of three pairs of hexadecimal (base 16) numbers that range between the values 00 and FF, corresponding to the red, green, and blue components of the color. The three pairs of numbers are bunched together and preceded by a pound sign (#). Therefore, the reddest of reds has all red (FF) and none (00) of the other two colors: #FF0000; pure blue is #0000FF. The letters A through F can also be lowercase.

This numbering scheme obviously leads to a potentially huge number of combinations (over 16 million), but not all video monitors are set to distinguish among millions of colors. Therefore, you may wish to limit yourself to a more modest palette of colors known as the web palette. A fine reference of colors that work well on all browsers at popular bit-depth settings can be found at *<http:// www.lynda.com/hexh.html>*.

The HTML recommendation also specifies a basic library of 16 colors that can be assigned by plain-language names. Note that the color names are case insensitive. The names and their equivalent hexadecimal triplets are as follows:

Black	#000000	Maroon	#800000	Green	#008000	Navy	#000080
Silver	#C0C0C0	Red	#FF0000	Lime	#00FF00	Blue	#0000FF
Gray	#808080	Purple	#800080	Olive	#808000	Teal	#008080
White	#FFFFFF	Fuchsia	#FF00FF	Yellow	#FFFF00	Aqua	#00FFFF

In other words, the attribute settings BGCOLOR="Aqua" and BGCOLOR="#00FFFF" yield the same results.

Netscape has developed a much longer list of plain-language color equivalents. These are detailed in Appendix A, *Color Names and RGB Values*, and are recognized by recent versions of both Navigator and Internet Explorer.

About client- and offset- Properties

Internet Explorer 4 introduces a set of properties that have great potential for scripting the position and size of elements. The properties, which apply only to unpositioned elements, are:

```
clientHeight      clientLeft      offsetHeight      offsetLeft
clientWidth       clientTop       offsetWidth       offsetTop
```

The sad news is that it is impossible to know how to use these properties effectively. Microsoft's developer documentation provides one set of definitions for the purposes of these properties, but, in practice, both the Windows 95/NT and Macintosh versions of Internet Explorer 4 not only disagree with much of the documentation, they disagree with each other.

The primary discrepancies have to do with whether an element's margins, borders, and padding are included in the element's various dimension and location measurements. In order to use these properties effectively in scripting the positions of elements, you need a stable measurement system. Unfortunately, except perhaps for the BODY element, these properties cannot be relied on without extensive testing in a specific application.

As an example of the mess that has developed, consider the values for clientHeight and clientWidth. The developer documentation asserts that these properties measure the element content only, exclusive of any margins, borders, or padding tacked onto the element. In IE 4 for Windows 95/NT, this assertion holds true for margins and borders, but not padding. Padding is not only added to the clientHeight and clientWidth values, but the padding size is doubled in the calculation. Thus, for an element whose true content width is 100 pixels and whose padding is set to 5 pixels (that's 5 pixels on the left and right edges, for a total of 10 pixels), the clientWidth property for the element returns 120 pixels. Over on the Macintosh side of IE 4, both the margins and padding, but not the borders, are added to the element dimensions to arrive at clientWidth and clientHeight values.

The offset properties are supposedly measured within the context of the next outermost container. For example, according to most accounts, the offsetTop value for an element contained by the BODY is the distance between the top of the BODY's content area and the element's content area. But if margins, borders, or padding are involved in either or both of these elements, the calculations go astray (and they go completely wild in IE 4 for the Macintosh).

Even if the implementations were consistent across operating system versions of the browser, the terminology used for these eight properties is extremely confusing. Until such time as all these terms and implementations are on the same page, it's nigh impossible to recommend their use for precise positioning and calculation. That's not to say you should abandon these values entirely. You might get lucky with your design such that the strange behavior is consistently strange, so that your desired effects actually work under both the Win32 and Mac versions of IE. Such is the case for the example in Chapter 4, *Adding Dynamic Positioning to Documents*, of centering flying objects on the page.

Event Handler Properties

Objects that can receive events have event handlers listed in their main entries. Because this chapter focuses on the scriptable aspects of HTML elements, the event handlers are listed in their lowercase property form—the form used to assign function references to event handlers in script statements. See "Binding Event Handlers to Elements" in Chapter 6, *Scripting Events*, for details on this event handler format.

The selection of event handler properties listed for each object is based on a couple of factors. First, just as most HTML 4.0 elements have "intrinsic events" associated with them, those same events are listed in this chapter with the objects that reflect the HTML element. As such, it may seem odd that an element that has almost no visual presence on a page has keyboard and mouse events. Those events are listed just the same, even though the likelihood of your scripting them is next to nil.

Second, the Internet Explorer 4 event bubbling model (see Chapter 6) dictates that it is possible for an event from one element to bubble up through the element containment hierarchy all the way to the HTML element. This means that essentially every event that can appear in the most nested element (such as the events related to Microsoft's data binding facilities in Win32) is also available in all elements higher up the containment chain. In other words, virtually every element that acts as a container can have virtually every event type associated with it under IE 4. Other than the intrinsic events mentioned earlier, the lists of event handler properties in this chapter are restricted to events that can be directed initially at the given object. For example, if an IMG object can use the data binding events, those events are listed with the IMG object. They are not, however, listed for the DIV object that might contain an IMG object but, itself, cannot be databound.

The bottom line is to use common sense in thinking about the event handlers that are appropriate for any given object. Despite what may appear to be long lists of event handler properties for some objects, the need to script more than two or three for any object is very rare.

Common Object Properties, Methods, and Collections

The document object model implemented in Internet Explorer 4 and, to a lesser extent, the DOM working draft, exposes a wide range of properties, methods, and collections almost universally across objects that reflect HTML elements. Rather than repeat the descriptions of these items ad nauseam in the reference listing, I am listing their details here only once. Throughout the rest of the chapter, the property, method, and collection lists for each object point to these common items when the item name is in *italic*. When you see an item name listed in italic, it means you should look to this section for specific details about the item. If you recognize a term from the list of items in common, but it is not shown in italic, it means there is some object-specific information about the item, so the description is provided with the object.

In the following item descriptions, the example code uses the term *elementID* to refer to the identifier assigned to the ID attribute of the element. In your scripts, substitute the object's true ID for the placeholder used here. Here is a list of the common items:

Properties

className	*isTextEdit*	*offsetLeft*	*outerHTML*	*sourceIndex*
document	*lang*	*offsetParent*	*outerText*	*style*
id	*language*	*offsetTop*	*parentElement*	*tagName*
innerHTML	*offsetHeight*	*offsetWidth*	*parentTextEdit*	*title*
innerText				

Methods

click()	*insertAdjacentHTML()*	*scrollIntoView()*
contains()	*insertAdjacentText()*	*setAttribute()*
getAttribute()	*removeAttribute()*	

Collections/Arrays

all[]	*children[]*	*filters[]*

className   NN *n/a*   IE *4*   DOM *1*

Read/Write

An identifier generally used to associate an element with a style sheet rule defined for a class selector. You can alter the class association for an element by script. If the document includes an alternate class selector and style rule, adjusting the element's **className** property can provide a shortcut for adjusting many style properties at once.

Example   document.all.*elementID*.className = "altHighlighted"

Value   Case-sensitive string. Multiple class names are space-delimited within the string.

Default   None (or class set via the element's **CLASS** attribute).

document

Read-only

Returns a reference to the **document** object that contains the current element. In some ways this is a redundant property, because any reference you build to an element is likely to contain the document as part of the reference.

Example   `var currDoc = document.all.elementID.document`

Value   Object reference.

Default   The current **document** object.

id

Read-only

A unique identifier that distinguishes this element from all the rest in the document. The value of this property is most often used to assemble references to elements, but you can loop through all elements to see if there is a match of an **id** value. If the author assigned the same value to the ID attribute of multiple elements, the browser creates an array (collection) of objects with that name (**document.all.elementID[i]**).

Example   `var someID = document.all.tags("ACRONYM")[2].id`

Value   String.

Default   None.

innerHTML

Read/Write

The rendered text and HTML tags (i.e., all source code) between the start and end tags of the current element. If you want only the rendered text, see **innerText**. For the source code that includes the element's tags, see **outerHTML**. A change to this property that includes HTML tags is rendered through the HTML parser, as if the new value were part of the original source code. You may change this property only after the document has fully loaded. Changes to the **innerHTML** property are not reflected in the source code when you view the source in the browser. This property is not supported in many objects in the Macintosh version of Internet Explorer 4.

Example   `document.all.elementID.innerHTML = "How <I>now</I> brown cow?"`

Value   String that may or may not include HTML tags.

Default   None.

innerText

Read/Write

The rendered text (but not any tags) of the current element. If you want the rendered text as well as any nested HTML tags, see **innerHTML**. Any changes to this property are not rendered through the HTML parser, meaning that any HTML tags you include are treated as displayable text content only. You may change this property only after the document has fully loaded. Changes to the `innerText` property are not reflected in the source code when you view the source in the browser. This property is not supported in many objects in the Macintosh version of Internet Explorer 4.

Example `document.all.`*`elementID`*`.innerText = "How now brown cow?"`

Value String.

Default None.

isTextEdit

NN *n/a*   IE *4*   DOM *n/a*

Read-only

Whether the element can be used to create a `TextRange` object (via the `createTextRange()` method). Only `BODY`, `BUTTON`, text type `INPUT`, and `TEXTAREA` elements are permitted to have text ranges created for their content.

Example
```
if (document.all.elementID.isTextEdit) {
    document.all.elementID.createTextRange()
}
```

Value Boolean value: `true` | `false`.

Default `false`

lang

NN *n/a*   IE *4*   DOM *1*

Read/Write

The written language being used for the element's attribute and property values. Other applications and search engines might use this information to aid selection of spellchecking dictionaries and creating indices.

Example `document.all.`*`elementID`*`.lang = "de"`

Value Case-insensitive language code.

Default Browser default.

language

NN *n/a*   IE *4*   DOM *n/a*

Read/Write

The scripting language for script statements defined in the element.

Example `document.all.`*`elementID`*`.language = "vbscript"`

Value

Case-insensitive scripting language name as string: `javascript` | `jscript` | `vbs` | `vbscript`.

Default `jscript`

DOM Reference

offsetHeight, offsetWidth   NN *n/a*   IE 4   DOM *n/a*

Read-only

These properties should represent the height and width of the element's content, exclusive of padding, borders, or margins. In practice, Internet Explorer 4 for the Macintosh works that way, while the Windows version not only includes padding (if any), but doubles the padding amount in calculating the height and width values. If you don't use padding in your element, these are accurate measures on both operating systems. Despite these properties being part of the "offset" series, there is no relationship to the containing element for these two properties: an element's height and width are the same regardless of how they are nested in other containers.

Example   `var midpoint = document.all.`*`elementID`*`.offsetWidth/2`

Value   Integer pixel count.

Default   None.

offsetLeft, offsetTop   NN *n/a*   IE 4   DOM *n/a*

Read-only

These properties should represent the left and top coordinates of the element's content relative to the containing element, exclusive of padding, borders, or margins. You can determine the containing element via the `offsetParent` property. Unfortunately, Internet Explorer 4 implements these two properties very unevenly across operating systems. See the section "About client- and offset- Properties" earlier in this chapter.

Example

```
if (document.all.elementID.offsetLeft <= 20 &&
document.all.elementID.offsetTop <=40) {
    . . .
}
```

Value   Integer pixel count.

Default   None.

offsetParent   NN *n/a*   IE 4   DOM *n/a*

Read-only

Returns a reference to the object that is the current element's containing box. For most elements, this is the `BODY` object. But elements that are wrapped in `DIV` elements or are cells of a table have other parents. You can use the returned value in a reference to obtain property information about the containing element, as shown in the following example.

Example   `var containerLeft = document.all.`*`elementID`*`.offsetParent.offsetLeft`

Value   Object reference.

Default   `BODY` object.

outerHTML

NN *n/a*   IE *4*   DOM *n/a*

Read/Write

The rendered text and HTML tags (i.e., all source code), including the start and end tags, of the current element. If you want only the rendered text, see `outerText`. For the source code that excludes the element's tags, see `innerHTML`. A change to this property that includes HTML tags is rendered through the HTML parser, as if the new value were part of the original source code. You may change this property only after the document has fully loaded, and, in the process, you can even change the type of element it is or replace the element with straight text content. Changes to the `outerHTML` property are not reflected in the source code when you view the source in the browser. To add to existing HTML, see the `insertAdjacentHTML()` method. This property is not supported in many objects in the Macintosh version of Internet Explorer 4.

Example

```
document.all.elementID.outerHTML =
    "<ACRONYM ID="quotes">NI<I>M</I>BY</ACRONYM>"
```

Value   String that may or may not include HTML tags.

Default   None.

outerText

NN *n/a*   IE *4*   DOM *n/a*

Read/Write

The rendered text (but not any tags) of the current element. If you want the rendered text as well as the element's HTML tags, see `outerHTML`. Any changes to this property are not rendered through the HTML parser, meaning that any HTML tags you include are treated as displayable text content only. You may change this property only after the document has fully loaded. Changes to the `outerText` property are not reflected in the source code when you view the source in the browser. This property is not supported in many objects in the Macintosh version of Internet Explorer 4.

Example   `document.all.elementID.outerText = "UNESCO"`

Value   String.

Default   None.

parentElement

NN *n/a*   IE *4*   DOM *n/a*

Read-only

Returns a reference to the next outermost element in the HTML containment hierarchy. An element's HTML parent is not necessarily the same as the object returned by the `offset-Parent` property. The `parentElement` concerns itself strictly with source code containment, while the `offsetParent` property looks to the next outermost element that is used as the coordinate system for measuring the location of the current element. For example, if the main document contains a `P` element with an `EM` element nested inside, the `EM` element has two parents. The `P` element is the returned `parentElement` value (due to the HTML source code containment), while the `BODY` element is the returned `offset-Parent` value (due to coordinate space containment).

You can jump multiple parent levels by cascading `parentElement` properties, as in:

```
document.all.elementID.parentElement.parentElement
```

You can then use references to access a parent element's properties or methods.

Example   `document.all.elementID.parentElement.style.font-size = "14pt"`

Value   Element object reference.

Default   None.

parentTextEdit

NN *n/a*   IE 4   DOM *n/a*

Read-only

Returns a reference to the next highest element up the HTML containment hierarchy that is of a type that allows a `TextRange` object to be created with it. This property may have to reach through many levels to find a suitable object. This property always returns `null` in Internet Explorer 4 for the Macintosh because that operating system version does not support text ranges.

Example

```
var rangeElement = document.all.elementID.parentTextEdit
var rng = rangeElement.createTextRange()
```

Value   Element object reference.

Default   `BODY` object.

sourceIndex

NN *n/a*   IE 4   DOM *n/a*

Read-only

Returns the zero-based index of the element among all elements in the document. Elements are numbered according to their source code order, with the first element given a **source-Index** of zero.

Example   `var whichElement = document.all.elementID.sourceIndex`

Value   Positive integer or zero.

Default   None.

style

NN *n/a*   IE 4   DOM *n/a*

Read/Write

The `style` object associated with the element. This property is the gateway to reading and writing individual style sheet property settings for an element.

Example   `document.all.elementID.style.font-size = "14pt"`

Value   `style` object.

Default   None.

tagName

Read-only

Returns the name of the tag used to create the current element. Tag names are always returned in all uppercase letters for purposes of easy string comparisons.

Example `var theTag = document.all.`*`elementID`*`.tagName`

Value String.

Default None.

title

Read/Write

An advisory description of the element. When the element is one that has a physical presence on the page, Internet Explorer 4 renders the value of this property when the cursor rests atop the element for a moment.

Example `document.all.`*`elementID`*`.title = "Hot stuff!"`

Value String.

Default None.

click()

Simulates the click action of a user on the element. Fires an `onClick` event in Internet Explorer 4.

Returned Value

None.

Parameters

None.

contains()

`contains(`*`element`*`)`

Whether the current element contains the specified element.

Returned Value

Boolean value: `true` | `false`.

Parameters

`element`   A fully formed element object reference (e.g., `document.all.myDIV`).

getAttribute()

`getAttribute(`*`attributeName`*`[, `*`caseSensitivity`*`])`

Returns the value of the named attribute within the current element. If the attribute is reflected in the object model as a property, this method returns the same value as when reading the object's property. If the tag includes multiple attributes with the same name (and *caseSensitivity* is not turned on), the last one in order is used to retrieve the value.

Returned Value

Attribute value as a string, number, or Boolean, as dictated by the attribute's data type.

Parameters

attributeName
> The attribute name used in the HTML tag (not including the = symbol).

caseSensitivity
> An optional Boolean value. If **true**, the attribute in the HTML tag must match the case of the *attributeName* parameter exactly for its value to be returned.

insertAdjacentHTML()   NN *n/a*   IE 4   DOM *n/a*

insertAdjacentHTML(*where, HTMLText*)

Inserts text into the designated position relative to the element's existing HTML. If HTML tags are part of the text to be inserted, the browser interprets the tags and performs the desired rendering. This method is not supported in many objects in the Macintosh version of Internet Explorer 4.

Returned Value

None.

Parameters

where   String value of one of the following constants: **BeforeBegin** | **AfterBegin** | **BeforeEnd** | **AfterEnd**. The first and last locations are outside the HTML tags of the current element; the middle two locations are between the tags and element content.

HTMLText String value of the text and/or HTML to be inserted in the desired location.

insertAdjacentText()   NN *n/a*   IE 4   DOM *n/a*

insertAdjacentText(*where, text*)

Inserts text into the designated position relative to the element's existing HTML. If HTML tags are part of the text to be inserted, the tags are shown literally on the page. This method is not supported in many objects in the Macintosh version of Internet Explorer 4.

Returned Value

None.

Parameters

where   String value of one of the following constants: **BeforeBegin** | **AfterBegin** | **BeforeEnd** | **AfterEnd**. The first and last locations are outside the HTML tags of the current element; the middle two locations are between the tags and element content.

HTMLText String value of the text to be inserted in the desired location.

removeAttribute()

removeAttribute(*attributeName*[, *caseSensitivity*])

Removes the named attribute from the current element. You may remove only attributes added with the `setAttribute()` method. Removing an attribute does not change the source code when viewed through the browser, but does affect how the browser renders the element.

Returned Value

`true` if successful; `false` if the attribute doesn't exist or its value was not set with `setAttribute()`.

Parameters

attributeName
> The attribute name used in the HTML tag (not including the = symbol).

caseSensitivity
> An optional Boolean value. If `true`, the attribute in the HTML tag must match the case of the *attributeName* parameter exactly for its value to be returned.

scrollIntoView()

scrollIntoView([*showAtTop*])

Scrolls the content holding the current element so that the element is brought into view. The default behavior is to display the element so that its top is at the top of the scroll space. But you may also align the element at the bottom of the scroll space, if you prefer.

Returned Value

None.

Parameters

showAtTop
> An optional Boolean value. If `true` (the default), the top of the content is positioned at the top of the scroll space; if `false`, the bottom of the content is positioned at the bottom of the scroll space.

setAttribute()

setAttribute(*attributeName*, *value*[, *caseSensitivity*])

Sets the value of the named attribute within the current element. If the attribute is reflected in the object model as a property, this method acts the same as assigning a value to the object's property.

Returned Value

None.

Parameters

attributeName
> The attribute name used in the HTML tag (not including the = symbol).

value   Attribute value as a string, number, or Boolean, as dictated by the attribute's
data type. Most settings are strings or stringed versions of other data types.

caseSensitivity
An optional Boolean value. If true, the attribute in the HTML tag must match
the case of the *attributeName* parameter exactly for its value to be set.

all[] NN *n/a*   IE *4*   DOM *n/a*

Returns an array of all HTML element objects contained by the current element. Items in
this array are indexed (zero based) in source code order. The collection transcends generations of nested elements such that document.all[] exposes every element in the entire
document.

As with all collections in Internet Explorer 4, you may use the traditional JavaScript array
syntax (with square brackets around the index value) or IE's JScript alternative (with parentheses around the index value). If you are aiming for cross-browser deployment for
collections that are available on both platforms, use the square brackets.

Syntax

```
object.all(index).objectPropertyOrMethod
object.all[index].objectPropertyOrMethod
object.all.elementID.objectPropertyOrMethod
```

children[] NN *n/a*   IE *4*   DOM *n/a*

Returns an array of all first-level HTML element objects contained by the current element.
This collection differs from the all[] collection in that it contains references only to the
immediate children of the current element (whereas the all[] collection transcends generations). For example, document.body.children[] might contain a form, but no reference
to form elements nested inside the form. Items in this array are indexed (zero based) in
source code order.

Syntax

```
object.children(index).objectPropertyOrMethod
object.children[index].objectPropertyOrMethod
object.children.elementID.objectPropertyOrMethod
```

filters[] NN *n/a*   IE *4*   DOM *n/a*

Returns an array of all filter objects contained by the current element.

Syntax

```
object.filters(index).objectPropertyOrMethod
object.filters[index].objectPropertyOrMethod
```

Alphabetical Object Reference

A
NN *n/a*   IE *4*   DOM *1*

The A object reflects the A element, regardless of whether the element is set up to be an anchor, link, or both. Navigator and Internet Explorer both treat this object as a member of the links[] and/or anchors[] arrays of a document. Internet Explorer 4 also lets you reference the object as a member of the document.all[] collection (array of all HTML elements).

HTML Equivalent

<A>

Object Model Reference

NN	[window.]document.links[i]
	[window.]document.anchors[i]
IE	[window.]document.links[i]
	[window.]document.anchors[i]
	[window.]document.all.*elementID*

Properties

accessKey	*id*	nameProp	*parentTextEdit*	search
className	*innerHTML*	*offsetHeight*	pathname	*sourceIndex*
dataFld	*innerText*	*offsetLeft*	port	*style*
dataSrc	*isTextEdit*	*offsetParent*	protocol	tabIndex
document	*lang*	*offsetTop*	protocolLong	*tagName*
hash	*language*	*offsetWidth*	recordNumber	target
host	Methods	*outerHTML*	rel	*title*
hostname	mimeType	*outerText*	rev	urn
href	name	*parentElement*		

Methods

blur()	*getAttribute()*	*removeAttribute()*
click()	*insertAdjacentHTML()*	*scrollIntoView()*
contains()	*insertAdjacentText()*	*setAttribute()*
focus()		

Collections/Arrays

all[]	*children[]*	*filters[]*

Event Handler Properties

Handler	NN	IE	DOM
onblur	n/a	4	n/a
onclick	2	3	n/a
ondblclick	4	4	n/a
onfocus	n/a	4	n/a
onhelp	n/a	4	n/a

DOM Reference

Handler	NN	IE	DOM
onkeydown	n/a	4	n/a
onkeypress	n/a	4	n/a
onkeyup	n/a	4	n/a
onmousedown	4	4	n/a
onmousemove	n/a	4	n/a
onmouseout	3	4	n/a
onmouseover	2	3	n/a
onmouseup	4	4	n/a
onselectstart	n/a	4	n/a

Anchor-only A objects have no event handlers in Navigator through Version 4.

accessKey
NN *n/a*   IE *4*   DOM *1*

Read/Write

A single character key that either brings focus to an element or, in the case of an A element (as a link), follows the link. The browser and operating system determine whether the user must press a modifier key (e.g., **Ctrl**, **Alt**, or **Command**) with the access key to activate the link. In IE 4/Windows, the **Alt** key is required, and the key is not case sensitive. Not working in IE 4/Mac.

Example document.links[3].accessKey = "n"

Value   Single alphanumeric (and punctuation) keyboard character.

Default   None.

dataFld
NN *n/a*   IE *4*   DOM *n/a*

Read/Write

Used with IE 4 data binding to associate a remote data source column value in lieu of an HREF attribute for a link. The DATASRC attribute must also be set for the element. Setting both the dataFld and dataSrc properties to empty strings breaks the binding between element and data source.

Example document.all.hotlink.dataFld = "linkURL"

Value   Case-sensitive identifier of the data source column.

Default   None.

dataSrc
NN *n/a*   IE *4*   DOM *n/a*

Read/Write

Used with IE 4 data binding to specify the name of the remote ODBC data source (such as an Oracle or SQL Server database) to be associated with the element. Setting both the dataFld and dataSrc properties to empty strings breaks the binding between element and data source.

Example document.all.hotlink.dataSrc = "#DBSRC3"

Value   Case-sensitive identifier of the data source.

Default   None.

hash

That portion of the HREF attribute's URL following the # symbol, referring to an anchor location in a document. Do not include the # symbol when setting the property.

Example

```
document.all.myLink.hash = "section3"
document.links[2].hash = "section3"
```

Value   String.

Default   None.

host

The combination of the hostname and port (if any) of the server of the destination document for the link. If the port is explicitly part of the URL, the hostname and port are separated by a colon, just as they are in the URL. If the port number is not specified in an HTTP URL for IE 4, it automatically returns the default, port 80.

Example

```
document.all.myLink.host = "www.megacorp.com:80"
document.links[2].host = "www.megacorp.com:80"
```

Value   String of hostname optionally followed by a colon and port number.

Default   Depends on server.

hostname

The hostname of the server (i.e., a "two-dot" address consisting of server name and domain) of the destination document for the link. The hostname property does not include the port number.

Example

```
document.all.myLink.hostname = "www.megacorp.com"
document.links[2].hostname = "www.megacorp.com"
```

Value   String of host name (server and domain).

Default   Depends on server.

href

The URL specified by the element's HREF attribute.

Example

```
document.all.myLink.href = "http://www.megacorp.com"
document.links[2].href = "http://www.megacorp.com"
```

Value   String of complete or relative URL.

Default   None.

Methods   NN *n/a*   IE *4*   DOM *n/a*

Read/Write

An advisory attribute about the functionality of the destination of a link. A browser could use this information to display special colors or images for the element content based on what the destination does for the user, but Internet Explorer 4 does not appear to do anything with this information.

Example   `document.links[1].Methods = "post"`

Value   Any valid HTTP method as a string.

Default   None.

mimeType   NN *n/a*   IE *4*   DOM *n/a*

Read-only

Returns a plain-language version of the MIME type of the destination document at the other end of the link specified by the HREF or SRC attribute. You could use this information to set the cursor type during a mouse rollover. Do not confuse this property with the **navigator.mimeTypes[]** array and individual **mimeType** objects that Netscape Navigator refers to. Not available in IE 4/Macintosh.

Example

```
if (document.all.myLink.mimeType == "GIF Image") {
    ...
}
```

Value   A plain-language reference to the MIME type as a string.

Default   None.

name   NN *2*   IE *3*   DOM *1*

Read/Write

The identifier associated with an element that turns it into an anchor. You can also use the name as part of the object reference.

Example

```
if (document.links[3].name == "section3") {
    ...
}
```

Value

Case-sensitive identifier that follows the rules of identifier naming: it may contain no whitespace, cannot begin with a numeral, and should avoid punctuation except for the underscore character.

Default   None.

nameProp

Returns just the filename, rather than the full URL, of the HREF attribute set for the element. Not available in IE 4/Macintosh.

Example
```
if (document.all.myElement.nameProp == "logo2.gif") {
    ...
}
```

Value   String.

Default   None.

pathname

The pathname component of the URL assigned to the element's HREF attribute. This consists of all URL information following the last character of the domain name, including the initial forward slash symbol.

Example
```
document.all.myLink.pathname = "/images/logoHiRes.gif"
document.links[2].pathname = "/images/logoHiRes.gif"
```

Value   String.

Default   None.

port

The port component of the URL assigned to the element's HREF attribute. This consists of all URL information following the colon after the last character of the domain name. The colon is not part of the port property value.

Example
```
document.all.myLink.port = "80"
document.links[2].port = "80"
```

Value   String (a numeric value as string).

Default   None.

protocol
NN *2*   IE *3*   DOM *1*
Read/Write

The protocol component of the URL assigned to the element's HREF attribute. This consists
of all URL information up to and including the first colon of a URL. Typical values are:
"http:", "file:", "ftp:", and "mailto:".

Example
```
document.all.secureLink.protocol = "https"
document.secureLink.protocol = "https"
```

Value   String.

Default   None.

protocolLong
NN *n/a*   IE *4*   DOM *n/a*
Read-only

A verbose description of the protocol implied by the URL of the HREF attribute or href
property. Not supported in IE 4/Macintosh.

Example
```
if (document.all.myLink.protocolLong == "HyperText Transfer Protocol") {
    statements for treating document as server file
}
```

Value   String.

Default   None

recordNumber
NN *n/a*   IE *4*   DOM *n/a*
Read-only

Used with data binding, returns an integer representing the record within the data set that
generated the element). Values of this property can be used to extract a specific record
from an Active Data Objects (ADO) record set (see recordset property).

Example
```
<SCRIPT FOR="tableTemplate" EVENT="onclick">
    myDataCollection.recordset.absoluteposition = this.recordNumber
    . . .
</SCRIPT>
```

Value   Integer.

Default   None.

rel
NN *n/a*   IE *4*   DOM *1*
Read/Write

Defines the relationship between the current element and the destination of the link. Also
known as a *forward link*, not to be confused in any way with the destination document
whose address is defined by the HREF attribute. This property is not used yet in Internet

Explorer 4, but you can treat the attribute as a kind of parameter to be checked and/or modified under script control. See the discussion of the A element's REL attribute in Chapter 8 for a glimpse of how this property may be used in the future.

Value

Case-insensitive, space-delimited list of HTML 4.0 standard link types (as a single string) applicable to the element. Sanctioned link types are:

alternate	contents	index	start
appendix	copyright	next	stylesheet
bookmark	glossary	prev	subsection
chapter	help	section	

Default   None.

rev   NN *n/a*   IE *4*   DOM *1*

Read/Write

Defines the relationship between the current element and the destination of the link. Also known as a *reverse link*. This property is not used yet in Internet Explorer 4, but you can treat the attribute as a kind of parameter to be checked and/or modified under script control. See the discussion of the A element's REV attribute in Chapter 8 for a glimpse of how this property may be used in the future.

Value

Case-insensitive, space-delimited list of HTML 4.0 standard link types (as a single string) applicable to the element. See the rel property for sanctioned link types.

Default   None.

search   NN *2*   IE *3*   DOM *1*

Read/Write

The URL-encoded portion of a URL assigned to the HREF attribute that begins with the ? symbol. A document that is served up as the result of the search also may have the search portion available as part of the window.location property. You can modify this property with a script. Doing so sends the URL and search criteria to the server. You must know the format of data (usually name/value pairs) expected by the server to perform this properly.

Example

```
document.all.searchLink.search="?p=Tony+Blair&d=y&g=0&s=a&w=s&m=25"
document.links[1].search="?p=Tony+Blair&d=y&g=0&s=a&w=s&m=25"
```

Value   String starting with the ? symbol.

Default   None.

DOM Reference

tabIndex

NN *n/a*   IE *4*   DOM *1*

Read/Write

A number that indicates the sequence of this element within the tabbing order of all focusable elements in the document. Tabbing order follows a strict set of rules. Elements that have values other than zero assigned to their `tabIndex` properties are first in line when a user starts tabbing in a page. Focus starts with the element with the lowest `tabIndex` value and proceeds in order to the highest value, regardless of physical location on the page or in the document. If two elements have the same `tabIndex` values, the element that comes earlier in the document receives focus first. Next come all elements that either don't support the `tabIndex` property or have the value set to zero. These elements receive focus in the order in which they appear in the document. A value of -1 removes the element from tabbing order altogether.

Note that the Macintosh user interface does not provide for giving focus to elements other than text and password `INPUT` fields.

Example   `document.all.link3.tabIndex = 6`

Value   Integer.

Default   None.

target

NN *2*   IE *3*   DOM *1*

Read/Write

The name of the window or frame that is to receive content as the result of navigating to a link. Such names are assigned to frames by the `FRAME` element's `NAME` attribute; for subwindows, the name is assigned via the second parameter of the `window.open()` method. If you are scripting the navigation of another window or frame, use the window or frame name in a statement that assigns a new URL to the `location.href` property (*frameName*`.location.href = "`*newURL*`"`).

Example

```
document.all.homeLink.target = "_top"
document.links[3].target = "_top"
```

Value

String value of the window or frame name, or any of the following constants (as a string): `_parent` | `_self` | `_top` | `_blank`. The `_parent` value targets the frameset to which the current document belongs; the `_self` value targets the current window; the `_top` value targets the main browser window, thereby eliminating all frames; and the `_blank` value creates a new window of default size.

Default   None.

urn

NN *n/a*   IE *4*   DOM *n/a*

Read/Write

A Uniform Resource Name (URN) version of the destination document specified in the `HREF` attribute. This attribute is intended to offer support in the future for the URN format of URI, an evolving recommendation under discussion at the IETF (see RFC 2141). Although supported in IE 4, this attribute does not take the place of the `HREF` attribute.

Example   `document.all.link3.urn = "http://www.megacorp.com"`

Value   Complete or relative URN as a string.

Default   None.

blur()   NN *n/a*   IE *4*   DOM *n/a*

Removes focus from the current element and fires an `onBlur` event (in IE). No other element necessarily receives focus as a result.

Returned Value

None.

Parameters

None.

focus()   NN *n/a*   IE *4*   DOM *n/a*

Gives focus to the current element and fires the `onFocus` event (in IE). If another element had focus at the time, it receives an `onBlur` event.

Returned Value

None.

Parameters

None.

ACRONYM, CITE, CODE, DFN, EM, KBD, SAMP, STRONG, VAR   NN *n/a*   IE *4*   DOM *1*

All these objects reflect the corresponding HTML phrase elements of the same name. Each of these phrase elements provides a context for an inline sequence of content. Some of these elements are rendered in ways to distinguish themselves from running text. See the HTML element descriptions in Chapter 8 for details. From a scripted standpoint, all phrase element objects share the same set of properties, methods, event handlers, and collections.

HTML Equivalent

```
<ACRONYM>
<CITE>
<CODE>
<DFN>
<EM>
<KBD>
<SAMP>
<STRONG>
<VAR>
```

DOM Reference

Object Model Reference

IE   [window.]document.all.*elementID*

Properties

className	isTextEdit	offsetLeft	outerHTML	sourceIndex
document	lang	offsetParent	outerText	style
id	language	offsetTop	parentElement	tagName
innerHTML	offsetHeight	offsetWidth	parentTextEdit	title
innerText				

Methods

click()	insertAdjacentHTML()	scrollIntoView()
contains()	insertAdjacentText()	setAttribute()
getAttribute()	removeAttribute()	

Collections/Arrays

all[]   children[]   filters[]

Event Handler Properties

Handler	NN	IE	DOM
onclick	n/a	4	n/a
ondblclick	n/a	4	n/a
ondragstart	n/a	4	n/a
onfilterchange	n/a	4	n/a
onhelp	n/a	4	n/a
onkeydown	n/a	4	n/a
onkeypress	n/a	4	n/a
onkeyup	n/a	4	n/a
onmousedown	n/a	4	n/a
onmousemove	n/a	4	n/a
onmouseout	n/a	4	n/a
onmouseover	n/a	4	n/a
onmouseup	n/a	4	n/a
onselectstart	n/a	4	n/a

ADDRESS   NN *n/a*   IE *4*   DOM *1*

The ADDRESS object reflects the ADDRESS element.

HTML Equivalent

<ADDRESS>

Object Model Reference

IE   [window.]document.all.*elementID*

Properties

className	isTextEdit	offsetLeft	outerHTML	sourceIndex
document	lang	offsetParent	outerText	style
id	language	offsetTop	parentElement	tagName
innerHTML	offsetHeight	offsetWidth	parentTextEdit	title
innerText				

Methods

click()	insertAdjacentHTML()	scrollIntoView()
contains()	insertAdjacentText()	setAttribute()
getAttribute()	removeAttribute()	

Collections/Arrays

all[]	children[]	filters[]

Event Handler Properties

Handler	NN	IE	DOM
onclick	n/a	4	n/a
ondblclick	n/a	4	n/a
ondragstart	n/a	4	n/a
onfilterchange	n/a	4	n/a
onhelp	n/a	4	n/a
onkeydown	n/a	4	n/a
onkeypress	n/a	4	n/a
onkeyup	n/a	4	n/a
onmousedown	n/a	4	n/a
onmousemove	n/a	4	n/a
onmouseout	n/a	4	n/a
onmouseover	n/a	4	n/a
onmouseup	n/a	4	n/a
onselectstart	n/a	4	n/a

all

NN *n/a*   IE 4   DOM *n/a*

A collection of elements nested within the current element. A reference to document.all, for example, returns a collection (array) of all element objects contained by the document, including elements that may be deeply nested inside the document's first level of elements. The collection is sorted in source code order of the element tags.

Object Model Reference

IE   *elementReference*.all

Properties

length

Methods

item()	tags()

length

NN *n/a*   IE *4*   DOM *n/a*

Read-only

Returns the number of elements in the collection.

Example   `var howMany = document.all.length`

Value   Integer.

item()

NN *n/a*   IE *4*   DOM *n/a*

`item(index[, subindex])`

Returns a single object or collection of objects corresponding to the element matching the index value (or, optionally, the index and subindex values).

Returned Value

One object or collection (array) of objects. If there are no matches to the parameters, the returned value is `null`.

Parameters

index   When the parameter is a zero-based integer, the returned value is a single element corresponding to the specified item in source code order (nested within the current element); when the parameter is a string, the returned value is a collection of elements whose `id` or `name` properties match that string.

subindex If you specify a string value for the first parameter, you can use the second parameter to specify a zero-based index that retrieves the specified element from the collection whose `id` or `name` properties match the first parameter's string value.

tags()

NN *n/a*   IE *4*   DOM *n/a*

`tags(tagName)`

Returns a collection of objects (among all objects nested within the current element) whose tags match the *tagName* parameter.

Returned Value

A collection (array) of objects. If there are no matches to the parameters, the returned value is an array of zero length.

Parameters

tagName   A string that contains the all-uppercase version of the element tag, as in `document.all.tags("P")`.

anchors

NN *2*   IE *3*   DOM *n/a*

A collection of all A elements whose assigned NAME attributes make them behave as anchors (instead of links). Collection members are sorted in source code order. Navigator and Internet Explorer let you use array notation to access a single anchor in the collection (e.g., `document.anchors[0]`, `document.anchors["section3"]`). Internet Explorer 4 also allows the index value to be placed inside parentheses instead of brackets (e.g., document.anchors(0)). If you want to use the anchor's name as an index value (always as a string identifier), be sure to use the value of the **NAME** attribute, rather than the ID attribute. To use the ID attribute in a reference to an anchor, access the object via a document.all.*elementID* reference.

Object Model Reference

NN	document.anchors[i]
IE	document.anchors(i)
	document.anchors[i]

Properties

length

length

NN *2*   IE *3*   DOM *n/a*

Read-only

Returns the number of elements in the collection.

Example var howMany = document.anchors.length

Value Integer.

APPLET

NN *3*   IE *4*   DOM *n/a*

The **APPLET** object reflects the **APPLET** element.

HTML Equivalent

<APPLET>

Object Model Reference

NN	[window.]document.*appletName*
IE	[window.]document.*appletName*
	[window.]document.all.*elementID*

Properties

accessKey	dataSrc	*language*	*outerHTML*	*style*
align	*document*	name	*outerText*	tabIndex
altHTML	height	*offsetHeight*	*parentElement*	*tagName*
className	hspace	*offsetLeft*	*parentTextEdit*	title
code	*id*	*offsetParent*	*sourceIndex*	vspace
codeBase	*isTextEdit*	*offsetTop*	src	width
dataFld	*lang*	*offsetWidth*		

Methods

blur()	*getAttribute()*	*removeAttribute()*
click()	*insertAdjacentHTML()*	*scrollIntoView()*
contains()	*insertAdjacentText()*	*setAttribute()*
focus()		

Collections/Arrays

all[]   children[]

Event Handler Properties

Handler	NN	IE	DOM
onafterupdate	n/a	4	n/a
onbeforeupdate	n/a	4	n/a
onblur	n/a	4	n/a
onclick	n/a	3	n/a
ondataavailable	n/a	4	n/a
ondatasetchanged	n/a	4	n/a
ondatasetcomplete	n/a	4	n/a
ondblclick	n/a	4	n/a
onerrorupdate	n/a	4	n/a
onfocus	n/a	4	n/a
onhelp	n/a	4	n/a
onkeydown	n/a	4	n/a
onkeypress	n/a	4	n/a
onkeyup	n/a	4	n/a
onload	n/a	4	n/a
onmousedown	n/a	4	n/a
onmousemove	n/a	4	n/a
onmouseout	n/a	4	n/a
onmouseover	n/a	3	n/a
onmouseup	n/a	4	n/a
onreadystatechange	n/a	4	n/a
onresize	n/a	4	n/a
onrowenter	n/a	4	n/a
onrowexit	n/a	4	n/a

accessKey

NN *n/a*   IE 4   DOM *n/a*

Read/Write

A single character key that brings focus to an element. The browser and operating system determine whether the user must press a modifier key (e.g., **Ctrl**, **Alt**, or **Command**) with the access key to bring focus to the element. In IE 4/Windows, the **Alt** key is required, and the key is not case sensitive. Not working in IE 4/Mac.

Example   document.all.appletID.accessKey = "n"

Value   Single alphanumeric (and punctuation) keyboard character.

Default   None.

align

Defines the alignment of the element within its surrounding container. See the section "Alignment Constants" at the beginning of Chapter 8 for the various meanings that different values bring to this property.

Example   `document.all.myApplet.align = "center"`

Value

Any of the alignment constants: `absbottom` | `absmiddle` | `baseline` | bottom | `left` | `middle` | `right` | `texttop` | `top`.

Default   `bottom`

altHTML

HTML content to be displayed if the object or applet fails to load. This can be a message, static image, or any other HTML that best fits the scenario. There is little indication that setting this property on an existing `APPLET` object has any visual effect.

Example   `document.myApplet.altHTML = "<IMG SRC='appletAlt.gif'>"`

Value   Any quoted string of characters, including HTML tags.

Default   None.

code

The name of the Java applet class file set to the `CODE` attribute.

Example

```
if (document.all.clock.code == "Y2Kcounter.class") {
     process for the found class file
}
```

Value   Case-sensitive applet class filename as a string.

Default   None.

codeBase

Path to the directory holding the class file designated in the `CODE` attribute. The `CODEBASE` attribute does not name the class file, just the path.

Example

```
if (document.all.clock.codeBase == "classes") {
     process for the found class file directory
}
```

Value

Case-sensitive pathname, usually relative to the directory storing the current HTML document.

Default   None.

dataFld

NN *n/a*   IE *4*   DOM *n/a*

Read/Write

It is unclear how you would use this property with an APPLET object because the dataFld and dataSrc properties (as set in element attributes) are applied to individual PARAM elements. But PARAM elements are not reflected (yet) in the IE object model.

Value   Case-sensitive identifier of the data source column.

Default   None.

dataSrc

NN *n/a*   IE *4*   DOM *n/a*

Read/Write

It is unclear how you would use this property with an APPLET object because the dataFld and dataSrc properties (as set in element attributes) are applied to individual PARAM elements. But PARAM elements are not reflected (yet) in the IE object model.

Value   Case-sensitive identifier of the data source.

Default   None.

height, width

NN *n/a*   IE *4*   DOM *n/a*

Read-only

The height and width in pixels of the element as set by the tag attributes.

Example   var appletHeight = document.myApplet.height

Value   Integer.

Default   None.

hspace, vspace

NN *n/a*   IE *4*   DOM *n/a*

Read/Write

The pixel measure of horizontal and vertical margins surrounding an applet. The hspace property affects the left and right edges of the element equally; the vspace affects the top and bottom edges of the element equally. These margins are not the same as margins set by style sheets, but they have the same visual effect. To change these property values, you must access the element via its element ID rather than its name.

Example

```
document.all.myApplet.hspace = 5
document.all.myApplet.vspace = 8
```

Value   Integer of pixel count.

Default   0

name   NN *n/a*   IE *4*   DOM *n/a*
Read-only

The identifier associated with the applet. Use the name when referring to the object in the form document.*appletName*.

Value

Case-sensitive identifier that follows the rules of identifier naming: it may contain no whitespace, cannot begin with a numeral, and should avoid punctuation except for the underscore character.

Default   None.

src   NN *n/a*   IE *4*   DOM *n/a*
Read-only

Internet Explorer 4 defines this attribute as the URL for an "associated file." The src property is not a substitute for the code and/or codebase properties.

Value   Complete or relative URL as a string.

Default   None.

tabIndex   NN *n/a*   IE *4*   DOM *n/a*
Read/Write

A number that indicates the sequence of this element within the tabbing order of all focusable elements in the document. Tabbing order follows a strict set of rules. Elements that have values other than zero assigned to their tabIndex properties are first in line when a user starts tabbing in a page. Focus starts with the element with the lowest tabIndex value and proceeds in order to the highest value, regardless of physical location on the page or in the document. If two elements have the same tabIndex values, the element that comes earlier in the document receives focus first. Next come all elements that either don't support the tabIndex property or have the value set to zero. These elements receive focus in the order in which they appear in the document. A value of -1 removes the element from tabbing order altogether.

Note that the Macintosh user interface does not provide for giving focus to elements other than text and password INPUT fields.

Example   document.all.myApplet.tabIndex = 6

Value   Integer.

Default   None.

vspace

See hspace.

width

See height.

blur()   NN *n/a*   IE *4*   DOM *n/a*

Removes focus from the current element and fires an onBlur event (in IE). No other element necessarily receives focus as a result.

Returned Value

None.

Parameters

None.

focus()   NN *n/a*   IE *4*   DOM *n/a*

Gives focus to the current element and fires the onFocus event (in IE). If another element had focus at the time, it receives an onBlur event.

Returned Value

None.

Parameters

None.

applets   NN *2*   IE *3*   DOM *n/a*

A collection of all the Java applets in the current element, sorted in source code order. Navigator and Internet Explorer let you use array notation to access a single applet in the collection (e.g., document.applets[0], document.applets["clockApplet"]). Internet Explorer 4 also allows the index value to be placed inside parentheses instead of brackets (e.g., document.applets(0)). If you wish to use the applet's name as an index value (always as a string identifier), be sure to use the value of the NAME attribute rather than the ID attribute. To use the ID attribute in a reference to an applet, access the object via a document.all.*elementID* reference.

Object Model Reference

NN   document.applets[i]
IE   document.applets(i)
        document.applets[i]

Properties

length

length

NN *2*   IE *3*   DOM *n/a*

Read-only

Returns the number of elements in the collection.

Example   `var howMany = document.applets.length`

Value   Integer.

AREA

NN *3*   IE *4*   DOM *1*

The AREA object reflects the AREA element, which defines the shape, coordinates, and destination of a clickable region of a client-side image map. Navigator and Internet Explorer (for compatibility with Navigator) treat an AREA object as a member of the links collection, since an AREA object behaves much like a link, but for a segment of an image.

HTML Equivalent

<AREA>

Object Model Reference

NN   `[window.]document.links[i]`

IE   `[window.]document.links[i]`
      `[window.]document.all.elementID`

Properties

alt	href	*offsetLeft*	*parentTextEdit*	*sourceIndex*
className	id	*offsetParent*	pathname	*style*
coords	*isTextEdit*	*offsetTop*	port	tabIndex
document	lang	*offsetWidth*	protocol	*tagName*
hash	*language*	*outerHTML*	search	target
host	noHref	*outerText*	shape	*title*
hostname	*offsetHeight*	*parentElement*		

Methods

blur()	*getAttribute()*	*removeAttribute()*
click()	*insertAdjacentHTML()*	*scrollIntoView()*
contains()	*insertAdjacentText()*	*setAttribute()*
focus()		

Collections/Arrays

all[]	*children[]*	*filters[]*

Event Handler Properties

Handler	NN	IE	DOM
onafterupdate	n/a	4	n/a
onbeforeupdate	n/a	4	n/a
onblur	n/a	4	n/a
onclick	4	3	n/a
ondataavailable	n/a	4	n/a

Handler	NN	IE	DOM
ondatasetchanged	n/a	4	n/a
ondatasetcomplete	n/a	4	n/a
ondblclick	n/a	4	n/a
onerrorupdate	n/a	4	n/a
onfocus	n/a	4	n/a
onhelp	n/a	4	n/a
onkeydown	n/a	4	n/a
onkeypress	n/a	4	n/a
onkeyup	n/a	4	n/a
onload	n/a	4	n/a
onmousedown	n/a	4	n/a
onmousemove	n/a	4	n/a
onmouseout	3	4	n/a
onmouseover	3	3	n/a
onmouseup	n/a	4	n/a
onreadystatechange	n/a	4	n/a
onresize	n/a	4	n/a
onrowenter	n/a	4	n/a
onrowexit	n/a	4	n/a

alt

NN *n/a*   IE *4*   DOM *1*

Read/Write

Future nongraphical browsers may use the `alt` property setting to display a brief description of the meaning of the (invisible) image's hotspots.

Example   `document.all.elementID.alt = "To Next Page"`

Value   Any quoted string of characters.

Default   None.

coords

NN *n/a*   IE *4*   DOM *1*

Read/Write

Defines the outline of the area to be associated with a particular link or scripted action. Coordinate values are entered as a comma-delimited list. If hotspots of two areas should overlap, the area that is defined earlier in the code takes precedence.

Example   `document.all.mapArea2.coords = "25, 5, 50, 70"`

Value

Each coordinate is a length value, but the number of coordinates and their order depend on the shape specified by the SHAPE attribute, which may optionally be associated with the element. For SHAPE="rect", there are four coordinates (left, top, right, bottom); for SHAPE="circle" there are three coordinates (center-x, center-y, radius); for SHAPE="poly" there are two coordinate values for each point that defines the shape of the polygon.

Default   None.

hash   NN *2*   IE *3*   DOM *1*

Read/Write

That portion of the HREF attribute's URL following the # symbol, referring to an anchor location in a document. Do not include the # symbol when setting the property.

Example   document.all.mapArea2.hash = "section3"

Value   String.

Default   None.

host   NN *2*   IE *3*   DOM *1*

Read/Write

The combination of the hostname and port (if any) of the server of the destination document for the area link. If the port is explicitly part of the URL, the hostname and port are separated by a colon, just as they are in the URL. If the port number is not specified in an HTTP URL for IE 4, it automatically returns the default, port 80.

Example   document.all.mapArea2.host = "www.megacorp.com:80"

Value   String of hostname optionally followed by a colon and port number.

Default   Depends on server.

hostname   NN *2*   IE *3*   DOM *1*

Read/Write

The hostname of the server (i.e., a "two-dot" address consisting of server name and domain) of the destination document for the area link. The hostname property does not include the port number.

Example   document.links[2].hostname = "www.megacorp.com"

Value   String of hostname (server and domain).

Default   Depends on server.

href   NN *2*   IE *3*   DOM *1*

Read/Write

The URL specified by the element's HREF attribute.

Example   document.links[2].href = "http://www.megacorp.com"

Value   String of complete or relative URL.

Default   None.

DOM Reference

noHref
NN *n/a*   IE *4*   DOM *1*

Read/Write

Whether the area defined by the coordinates has a link associated with it. When you set this property to true, scriptable browsers no longer treat the element as a link.

Example   `document.links[4].noHref = "true"`

Value   Boolean value: true | false.

Default   false

pathname
NN *2*   IE *3*   DOM *1*

Read/Write

The pathname component of the URL assigned to the element's HREF attribute. This consists of all URL information following the last character of the domain name, including the initial forward slash symbol.

Example   `document.all.myLink.pathname = "/images/logoHiRes.gif"`

Value   String.

Default   None.

port
NN *2*   IE *3*   DOM *1*

Read/Write

The port component of the URL assigned to the element's HREF attribute. This consists of all URL information following the colon after the last character of the domain name. The colon is not part of the port property value.

Example   `document.all.myLink.port = "80"`

Value   String (a numeric value as string).

Default   None.

protocol
NN *2*   IE *3*   DOM *1*

Read/Write

The protocol component of the URL assigned to the element's HREF attribute. This consists of all URL information up to and including the first colon of a URL. Typical values are: "http:", "file:", "ftp:", "mailto:".

Example   `document.all.secureLink.protocol = "https"`

Value   String.

Default   None.

search   NN *2*   IE *3*   DOM *1*

Read/Write

The URL-encoded portion of a URL assigned to the **HREF** attribute that begins with the ? symbol. A document that is served up as the result of the search also may have the search portion available as part of the **window.location** property. You can modify this property with a script. Doing so sends the URL and search criteria to the server. You must know the format of data (usually name/value pairs) expected by the server to perform this properly.

Example

```
document.all.searchLink.search="?p=Tony+Blair&d=y&g=0&s=a&w=s&m=25"
```

Value   String starting with the ? symbol.

Default   None.

shape   NN *n/a*   IE *4*   DOM *1*

Read/Write

The shape of a server-side image map area whose coordinates are specified with the **COORDS** attribute.

Example `document.all.area51.shape = "circle"`

Value

Case-insensitive shape constant as string: `default` | `rect` | `rectangle` | `circle` | `poly` | `polygon`

Default   `rect`

tabIndex   NN *n/a*   IE *4*   DOM *1*

Read/Write

A number that indicates the sequence of this element within the tabbing order of all focusable elements in the document. Tabbing order follows a strict set of rules. Elements that have values other than zero assigned to their `tabIndex` properties are first in line when a user starts tabbing in a page. Focus starts with the element with the lowest `tabIndex` value and proceeds in order to the highest value, regardless of physical location on the page or in the document. If two elements have the same `tabIndex` values, the element that comes earlier in the document receives focus first. Next come all elements that either don't support the `tabIndex` property or have the value set to zero. These elements receive focus in the order in which they appear in the document. A value of -1 removes the element from tabbing order altogether.

Note that the Macintosh user interface does not provide for giving focus to elements other than text and password **INPUT** fields.

Example `document.all.mapArea2.tabIndex = 6`

Value   Integer.

Default   None.

DOM Reference

target   NN *2*   IE *3*   DOM *1*

Read/Write

The name of the window or frame that is to receive content as the result of navigating to an area link. Such names are assigned to frames by the FRAME element's NAME attribute; for subwindows, the name is assigned via the second parameter of the window.open() method. If you are scripting the navigation of another window or frame, use the window or frame name in a statement that assigns a new URL to the location.href property (*frameName*.location.href = "*newURL*").

Example document.all.homeArea.target = "_top"

Value

String value of the window or frame name, or any of the following constants (as a string): _parent | _self | _top | _blank. The _parent value targets the frameset to which the current document belongs; the _self value targets the current window; the _top value targets the main browser window, thereby eliminating all frames; and the _blank value creates a new window of default size.

Default None.

blur()   NN *n/a*   IE *4*   DOM *n/a*

Removes focus from the current element and fires an onBlur event (in IE). No other element necessarily receives focus as a result.

Returned Value

None.

Parameters

None.

focus()   NN *n/a*   IE *4*   DOM *n/a*

Gives focus to the current element and fires the onFocus event (in IE). If another element had focus at the time, it receives an onBlur event.

Returned Value

None.

Parameters

None.

areas   NN *n/a*   IE *4*   DOM *n/a*

A collection of all AREA elements. Collection members are sorted in source code order. Internet Explorer lets you use array notation or parentheses to access a single anchor in the collection (e.g., document.anchors[0], document.anchors(0)). To use the ID attribute in a reference to an anchor, access the object via a document.all.*elementID* reference.

Object Model Reference

IE   `document.areas(i)`
         `document.areas[i]`

Properties
`length`

length   NN *n/a*   IE *4*   DOM *n/a*

Read-only

Returns the number of elements in the collection.

Example   `var howMany = document.areas.length`

Value   Integer.

B, BIG, I, S, SMALL, STRIKE, TT, U   NN *n/a*   IE *4*   DOM *1*

All these objects reflect the HTML font style elements of the same name. Each of these
elements specifies a rendering style for an inline sequence of content. All the elements are
deprecated in HTML 4.0 in favor of style sheet attributes. See the HTML element descriptions in Chapter 8 for details. From a scripted standpoint, all font style element objects share
the same set of properties, methods, event handlers, and collections.

HTML Equivalent

```
<B>
<BIG>
<I>
<S>
<SMALL>
<STRIKE>
<TT>
<U>
```

Object Model Reference

IE   `[window.]document.all.elementID`

Properties

className	*isTextEdit*	*offsetLeft*	*outerHTML*	*sourceIndex*
document	*lang*	*offsetParent*	*outerText*	*style*
id	*language*	*offsetTop*	*parentElement*	*tagName*
innerHTML	*offsetHeight*	*offsetWidth*	*parentTextEdit*	*title*
innerText				

Methods

click()	*insertAdjacentHTML()*	*scrollIntoView()*
contains()	*insertAdjacentText()*	*setAttribute()*
getAttribute()	*removeAttribute()*	

DOM Reference

Collections/Arrays

all[]   children[]   filters[]

Event Handler Properties

Handler	NN	IE	DOM
onclick	n/a	4	n/a
ondblclick	n/a	4	n/a
ondragstart	n/a	4	n/a
onfilterchange	n/a	4	n/a
onhelp	n/a	4	n/a
onkeydown	n/a	4	n/a
onkeypress	n/a	4	n/a
onkeyup	n/a	4	n/a
onmousedown	n/a	4	n/a
onmousemove	n/a	4	n/a
onmouseout	n/a	4	n/a
onmouseover	n/a	4	n/a
onmouseup	n/a	4	n/a
onselectstart	n/a	4	n/a

BASE   NN *n/a*   IE *4*   DOM *1*

A BASE object instructs the browser about the URL path to the current document. This path is then used as the basis for all relative URLs that are used to specify various SRC and HREF attributes throughout the document.

HTML Equivalent

<BASE>

Object Model Reference

IE   [window.]document.all.*elementID*

Properties

className	id	outerHTML	parentTextEdit	target
document	isTextEdit	outerText	sourceIndex	title
href	lang	parentElement	tagName	

Methods

contains()   removeAttribute()   setAttribute()
getAttribute()

Collections/Arrays

all[]   children[]

href

Read/Write

The URL of a document whose server path is to be used as the base URL for all relative references in the document. This is typically the URL of the current document, but it can be set to another path if it makes sense to your document organization and directory structure.

Example   `document.all.myBase.href = "http://www.megacorp.com"`

Value   String of complete or relative URL.

Default   Current document pathname.

target

Read/Write

The name of the window or frame that is to receive content as the result of navigating to a link or any other action on the page that loads a new document. Such names are assigned to frames by the **FRAME** element's **NAME** attribute; for subwindows, the name is assigned via the second parameter of the `window.open()` method. If you are scripting the navigation of another window or frame, use the window or frame name in a statement that assigns a new URL to the `location.href` property (*frameName*`.location.href = "`*newURL*`"`).

Example   `document.all.myBase.target = "_top"`

Value

String value of the window or frame name, or any of the following constants (as a string): `_parent` | `_self` | `_top` | `_blank`. The `_parent` value targets the frameset to which the current document belongs; the `_self` value targets the current window; the `_top` value targets the main browser window, thereby eliminating all frames; and the `_blank` value creates a new window of default size.

Default   `_self`

BASEFONT

A **BASEFONT** element advises the browser of some font information to be used as the basis for text rendering of the current page below the **BASEFONT** element. The **BASEFONT** element overrides the default font settings in the browser's user preferences settings.

Be careful with the `outerText` and `outerHTML` properties (and the undocumented `innerText` and `innerHTML` properties in the Windows version). Because this element does not have an end tag, virtually the entire document becomes part of these property values. Altering them can easily result in a lost document. All four of these properties are best utilized in elements that act as HTML containers by virtue of the position of their start and end tags.

HTML Equivalent

`<BASEFONT>`

Object Model Reference

IE   `[window.]document.all.`*elementID*

Properties

className	face	lang	parentElement	sourceIndex
color	id	outerHTML	parentTextEdit	tagName
document	isTextEdit	outerText	size	title

Methods

contains()	removeAttribute()	setAttribute()
getAttribute()		

Collections/Arrays

all[]	children[]

color

NN *n/a*   IE *4*   DOM *1*

Read/Write

Sets the font color of all text below the BASEFONT element.

Example `document.all.tags("basefont")[0].color = "#c0c0c0"`

Value

Case-insensitive hexadecimal triplet or plain-language color name as a string. See Appendix A for acceptable plain-language color names.

Default   Browser default.

face

NN *n/a*   IE *4*   DOM *1*

Read/Write

A hierarchy of font faces to use for the default font of a section headed by a BASEFONT element. The browser looks for the first font face in the comma-delimited list of font face names until it either finds a match in the client system or runs out of choices, at which point the browser default font face is used. Font face names must match the system font face names exactly.

Example

`document.all.tags("basefont")[i].face = "Bookman, Times Roman, serif"`

Value

One or more font face names in a comma-delimited list within a string. You may use real font names or the recognized generic faces: serif | sans-serif | cursive | fantasy | monospace.

Default   Browser default.

size

NN *n/a*   IE *4*   DOM *1*

Read/Write

The size of the font in the 1-7 browser relative scale.

Example `document.all.myBaseFont.size = "+1"`

Value

Either an integer (as a quoted string) or a quoted relative value consisting of a + or – symbol and an integer value.

Default   3

BDO
NN *n/a*   IE *n/a*   DOM *1*

The BDO element is designed to assist in instances when, due to various conversions during text processing, the normal bidirectional algorithms must be explicitly overridden.

HTML Equivalent
<BDO>

Properties

className	id	lang	style	title
dir				

dir
NN *n/a*   IE *n/a*   DOM *1*
Read/Write

The direction of character rendering for the element's text whose characters are not governed by inherent directionality according to the Unicode standard. Character rendering is either left to right or right to left.

Value   ltr | rtl (case insensitive)

Default   ltr

BGSOUND
NN *n/a*   IE *4*   DOM *n/a*

A BGSOUND element defines a sound file that is to play in the background while the user visits the page. Set properties to control the volume and how many times the sound track plays even after the sound file has loaded. A few properties, such as innerHTML and innerText, are exposed in the Windows version, but they don't apply to an element that does not have an end tag.

HTML Equivalent
<BGSOUND>

Object Model Reference
IE   [window.]document.all.*elementID*

Properties

balance	loop	offsetTop	parentElement	style
className	offsetHeight	offsetWidth	parentTextEdit	tagName
document	offsetLeft	outerHTML	sourceIndex	title
id	offsetParent	outerText	src	volume
isTextEdit				

Methods

contains()   removeAttribute()   setAttribute()
getAttribute()

Collections/Arrays

all[]   children[]

balance
NN *n/a*   IE 4   DOM *n/a*
Read-only

How the audio is divided between the left and right speakers. Once this attribute value is set in the element, its value cannot be changed by script control.

Example var currBal = document.all.tags("bgsound")[0].balance

Value

A signed integer between -10,000 and +10,000. A value of 0 is equally balanced on both sides. A negative value means the left side is dominant; a positive value means the right side is dominant.

Default   0

loop
NN *n/a*   IE 4   DOM *n/a*
Read/Write

The number of times the sound plays. Assigning a value of -1 means the sound plays continuously until the page is unloaded.

Example document.all.mySound.loop = 3

Value   Integer.

Default   -1

src
NN *n/a*   IE 4   DOM *n/a*
Read/Write

URL of the sound file to be played. Change tunes by assigning a new URL to the property.

Example document.all.tune.src = "sounds/blues.aif"

Value   Complete or relative URL as a string.

Default   None.

volume
NN *n/a*   IE 4   DOM *n/a*
Read-only

How loud the background sound plays relative to the maximum sound output level as adjusted by user preferences in the client computer. Maximum volume—a setting of zero—is only as loud as the user has set the **Sound** control panel. Attribute adjustments are negative values as low as -10,000 (although most users lose the sound at values much higher than that value).

Example   `var currVolume = document.all.themeSong.volume`

Value   Integer.

Default   Varies with operating system and sound settings.

BIG

See B.

BLOCKQUOTE
NN *n/a*   IE *4*   DOM *1*

The BLOCKQUOTE object reflects the BLOCKQUOTE element, which is intended to set off a long, block-level quote inside a document.

HTML Equivalent

`<BLOCKQUOTE>`

Object Model Reference

IE   `[window.]document.all.elementID`

Properties

cite	innerText	offsetLeft	outerHTML	sourceIndex
className	isTextEdit	offsetParent	outerText	style
document	lang	offsetTop	parentElement	tagName
id	language	offsetWidth	parentTextEdit	title
innerHTML	offsetHeight			

Methods

click()	insertAdjacentHTML()	scrollIntoView()
contains()	insertAdjacentText()	setAttribute()
getAttribute()	removeAttribute()	

Collections/Arrays

all[]	children[]	filters[]

Event Handler Properties

Handler	NN	IE	DOM
onclick	n/a	4	n/a
ondblclick	n/a	4	n/a
ondragstart	n/a	4	n/a
onfilterchange	n/a	4	n/a
onhelp	n/a	4	n/a
onkeydown	n/a	4	n/a
onkeypress	n/a	4	n/a
onkeyup	n/a	4	n/a

Handler	NN	IE	DOM
onmousedown	n/a	4	n/a
onmousemove	n/a	4	n/a
onmouseout	n/a	4	n/a
onmouseover	n/a	4	n/a
onmouseup	n/a	4	n/a
onselectstart	n/a	4	n/a

cite   NN *n/a*   IE *n/a*   DOM *1*

Read/Write

A URL pointing to an online source document from which the quotation is taken. This is not in any way a mechanism for copying or extracting content from another document.

Value

Any valid URL to a document on the World Wide Web, including absolute or relative URLs.

Default   None.

BODY   NN *n/a*   IE *4*   DOM *1*

The BODY object reflects the BODY element, which is distinct from the document object. The BODY object refers to just the element and its nested content. The BODY object is special in IE 4 in that it is the gateway to many important visual aspects of content on the page, such as background, margins, and scrolling. There is a shortcut reference to the object, document.body, so you don't have to build a reference via the document.all.*elementID* hierarchy.

HTML Equivalent

<BODY>

Object Model Reference

IE   [window.]document.body

Properties

accessKey	clientTop	leftMargin	*outerText*	scrollWidth
alink	clientWidth	link	*parentElement*	*sourceIndex*
background	*document*	noWrap	*parentTextEdit*	*style*
bgColor	*id*	*offsetHeight*	recordNumber	tabIndex
bgProperties	*innerHTML*	*offsetLeft*	rightMargin	*tagName*
bottomMargin	*innerText*	*offsetParent*	scroll	text
className	*isTextEdit*	*offsetTop*	scrollHeight	*title*
clientHeight	*lang*	*offsetWidth*	scrollLeft	topMargin
clientLeft	*language*	*outerHTML*	scrollTop	vLink

Methods

click()	getAttribute()	removeAttribute()
contains()	insertAdjacentHTML()	scrollIntoView()
createTextRange()	insertAdjacentText()	setAttribute()

Collections/Arrays

all[]	children[]	filters[]

Event Handler Properties

Handler	NN	IE	DOM
onafterupdate	n/a	4	n/a
onbeforeunload	n/a	4	n/a
onbeforeupdate	n/a	4	n/a
onchange	n/a	4	n/a
onclick	n/a	4	n/a
ondataavailable	n/a	4	n/a
ondatasetchanged	n/a	4	n/a
ondatasetcomplete	n/a	4	n/a
ondblclick	n/a	4	n/a
ondragstart	n/a	4	n/a
onerrorupdate	n/a	4	n/a
onfilterchange	n/a	4	n/a
onhelp	n/a	4	n/a
onkeydown	n/a	4	n/a
onkeypress	n/a	4	n/a
onkeyup	n/a	4	n/a
onmousedown	n/a	4	n/a
onmousemove	n/a	4	n/a
onmouseout	n/a	4	n/a
onmouseover	n/a	4	n/a
onmouseup	n/a	4	n/a
onrowenter	n/a	4	n/a
onrowexit	n/a	4	n/a
onscroll	n/a	4	n/a
onselectstart	n/a	4	n/a
onunload	n/a	4	n/a

DOM Reference

accessKey   NN *n/a*   IE *4*   DOM *n/a*

Read/Write

A single character key that brings focus to an element. The browser and operating system determine whether the user must press a modifier key (e.g., **Ctrl**, **Alt**, or **Command**) with the access key to bring focus to the element. In IE 4/Windows, the **Alt** key is required, and the key is not case sensitive. Not working in IE 4/Mac.

Example document.body.accessKey = "n"

Value   Single alphanumeric (and punctuation) keyboard character.

Default   None.

aLink

NN *n/a*   IE *4*   DOM *1*

Read/Write

Color of a hypertext link as it is being clicked. The color is applied to the link text or border around an image or object embedded within an A element. See also `link` and `vLink` properties for unvisited and visited link colors. Navigator's corresponding property is `alinkColor` of the `document` object.

Example   `document.body.aLink = "green"`

Value

A hexadecimal triplet or plain-language color name. See Appendix A for acceptable plain-language color names.

Default   #0000FF

background

NN *n/a*   IE *4*   DOM *1*

Read/Write

URL of the background image for the entire document. If you set a `bgColor` to the element as well, the color appears if the image fails to load; otherwise, the image overlays the color.

Example   `document.body.background = "images/watermark.jpg"`

Value   Complete or relative URL to the background image file.

Default   None.

bgColor

NN *n/a*   IE *4*   DOM *1*

Read/Write

Background color of the element. Even if the `BGCOLOR` attribute or `bgColor` property is set with a plain-language color name, the returned value is always a hexadecimal triplet.

Example   `document.body.bgColor = "yellow"`

Value

A hexadecimal triplet or plain-language color name. See Appendix A for acceptable plain-language color names.

Default   Varies with browser and operating system.

bgProperties

NN *n/a*   IE *4*   DOM *n/a*

Read/Write

Whether the background image remains in a fixed position or scrolls as a user scrolls the page. When the background image is set to remain in a fixed position, scrolled content flows past the background image very much like film credits roll past a background image on the screen.

Example   `document.body.bgProperties = "fixed"`

Value   Case-insensitive constant string values: `fixed` | `scroll`.

Default   `scroll`

bottomMargin

NN n/a   IE 4   DOM n/a
Read/Write

The amount of blank space between the very end of content and the bottom of a scrollable page. The setting has no visual effect if the length of the content or size of the window does not cause the window to scroll. The default value is for the end of content to be flush with the end of the document, but in the Macintosh version of Internet Explorer 4, there is about a 10-pixel margin visible even when the property is set to zero. Larger sizes are reflected properly. This property offers somewhat of a shortcut or alternate to setting the `marginBottom` style sheet property for the BODY element object.

Example   `document.body.bottomMargin = 20`

Value

An integer value (zero or greater) of the number of pixels of clear space at the bottom of the document.

Default   0

clientHeight, clientWidth

NN n/a   IE 4   DOM n/a
Read/Write

According to Microsoft's developer documentation, these properties reflect the height and width (in pixels) of the element's content. But see the section "About client- and offset-Properties" at the beginning of this chapter for details.

Example   `var midHeight = document.body.clientHeight/2`

Value   Integer pixel value.

Default   None.

clientLeft, clientTop

NN n/a   IE 4   DOM n/a
Read-only

According to Microsoft's developer documentation, these properties reflect the distance between the "true" left and top edges of the document area and the edges of the element. But see the section "About client- and offset- Properties" at the beginning of this chapter for details. To get or set the pixel position of an element in the document, use the `pixelLeft` and `pixelTop` properties.

Value   A string value for a length in a variety of units or percentage.

Default   None.

DOM Reference

leftMargin   NN *n/a*   IE *4*   DOM *n/a*

Read/Write

Width in pixels of the left margin of the BODY element in the browser window or frame. By default, the browser inserts a small margin to keep content from abutting the left edge of the window. Setting the property to an empty string is the same as setting it to zero.

Example   `document.body.leftMargin = 16`

Value   Integer of pixel count.

Default   10 (Windows); 8 (Macintosh).

link   NN *n/a*   IE *4*   DOM *1*

Read/Write

The color of a hypertext link that has not been visited (that is, the URL of the link is not in the browser's cache). This is one of three states for a link: unvisited, activated, and visited. The color is applied to the link text or border around an image or object embedded within an A element. This property has the same effect as setting the document object's linkColor property.

Example   `document.body.link = "#00FF00"`

Value

A hexadecimal triplet or plain-language color name. See Appendix A for acceptable plain-language color names.

Default   #0000FF

noWrap   NN *n/a*   IE *4*   DOM *1*

Read/Write

Whether the browser should render the body content as wide as is necessary to display a line of nonbreaking text on one line. Abuse of this attribute can force the user into a great deal of inconvenient horizontal scrolling of the page to view all of the content.

Example   `document.body.noWrap = "true"`

Value   Boolean value: `true` | `false`.

Default   false

recordNumber   NN *n/a*   IE *4*   DOM *n/a*

Read-only

Used with data binding, returns an integer representing the record within the data set that generated the element). Values of this property can be used to extract a specific record from an Active Data Objects (ADO) record set (see recordset property).

Example
```
<SCRIPT FOR="tableTemplate" EVENT="onclick">
    myDataCollection.recordset.absoluteposition = this.recordNumber
    ...
</SCRIPT>
```

Value   Integer.

Default None.

rightMargin   NN *n/a*   IE *4*   DOM *n/a*

Read/Write

Width in pixels of the right margin of the BODY element in the browser window or frame. By default, the browser inserts a small margin to keep content from abutting the right edge of the window (except on the Macintosh). Setting the property to an empty string is the same as setting it to zero.

Example `document.body.leftMargin = 16`

Value   Integer of pixel count.

Default 10 (Windows); 0 (Macintosh).

scroll   NN *n/a*   IE *4*   DOM *n/a*

Read/Write

Whether the window (or frame) displays scrollbars when the content exceeds the window size.

Example `document.body.scroll = "no"`

Value

Not exactly a Boolean value. Requires one of the following string values: **yes** | **no**.

Default yes

scrollHeight, scrollWidth   NN *n/a*   IE *4*   DOM *n/a*

Read-only

The meaning of these two properties is ambiguous based on Microsoft's description and the way they're implemented in the Windows and Macintosh versions of Internet Explorer 4. My best guess is that these properties are intended to measure the height and width (in pixels) of the content of an element, even when some of the content cannot be seen unless scrolled with scrollbars. The Macintosh version of the browser interprets this to mean the amount of the content that you can see at any one time. The important point is that for key elements, such as the BODY, the properties mean different things and can disrupt cross-platform operation.

Example `var midPoint = document.body.scrollHeight/2`

Value   Positive integer or zero.

Default None.

DOM Reference

scrollLeft, scrollTop

NN *n/a*   IE *4*   DOM *n/a*

Read/Write

The distance in pixels between the actual left or top edge of the element's physical content and the left or top edge of the visible portion of the content. Setting these properties allows you to use a script to adjust the scrolling of content within a scrollable container, such as text in a TEXTAREA element or an entire document in the browser window or frame. When the content is not scrolled, both values are zero. Setting the scrollTop property to 15 scrolls the document upward by 15 pixels in the window; the scrollLeft property is unaffected unless explicitly changed. The property values change as the user adjusts the scrollbars.

Example   document.body.scrollTop = 40

Value   Positive integer or zero.

Default   0

tabIndex

NN *n/a*   IE *4*   DOM *1*

Read/Write

A number that indicates the sequence of this element within the tabbing order of all focusable elements in the document. Tabbing order follows a strict set of rules. Elements that have values other than zero assigned to their tabIndex properties are first in line when a user starts tabbing in a page. Focus starts with the element with the lowest tabIndex value and proceeds in order to the highest value, regardless of physical location on the page or in the document. If two elements have the same tabIndex values, the element that comes earlier in the document receives focus first. Next come all elements that either don't support the tabIndex property or have the value set to zero. These elements receive focus in the order in which they appear in the document. A value of -1 removes the element from tabbing order altogether.

Note that the Macintosh user interface does not provide for giving focus to elements other than text and password INPUT fields.

Example   document.body.tabIndex = 0

Value   Integer.

Default   None.

text

NN *n/a*   IE *4*   DOM *1*

Read/Write

The color of text for the entire document body. Equivalent to the foreground color.

Example   document.body.text = "darkred"

Value

A hexadecimal triplet or plain-language color name. See Appendix A for acceptable plain-language color names.

Default   Browser default (user customizable).

topMargin

Read/Write

Width in pixels of the top margin of the BODY element in the browser window or frame. By default, the browser inserts a small margin to keep content from abutting the top edge of the window. Setting the property to an empty string is the same as setting it to zero.

Example   document.body.topMargin = 16

Value   Integer of pixel count.

Default   15 (Windows); 8 (Macintosh).

vLink

Read/Write

Color of a hypertext link that has been visited recently. The color is applied to the link text or border around an image or object embedded within an A element. See also link and aLink properties for unvisited and clicked link colors. Navigator's corresponding property is vlinkColor of the document object.

Example   document.body.vLink = "gold"

Value

A hexadecimal triplet or plain-language color name. See Appendix A for acceptable plain-language color names.

Default

#551a8b (Navigator 4); #800080 (Internet Explorer 4 Windows); #006010 (Internet Explorer 4 Macintosh).

createTextRange()

Creates a TextRange object from the source code of the current element. See the TextRange object for details.

Returned Value

TextRange object.

Parameters

None.

BR

The BR object reflects the BR element.

HTML Equivalent

DOM Reference

Object Model Reference

IE   [window.]document.all.*elementID*

Properties

className	innerText	offsetLeft	outerHTML	sourceIndex
clear	isTextEdit	offsetParent	outerText	style
document	lang	offsetTop	parentElement	tagName
id	language	offsetWidth	parentTextEdit	title
innerHTML	offsetHeight			

Methods

click()	insertAdjacentHTML()	scrollIntoView()
contains()	insertAdjacentText()	setAttribute()
getAttribute()	removeAttribute()	

Collections/Arrays

all[]	children[]	filters[]

clear   NN *n/a*   IE *4*   DOM *1*

Read/Write

Tells the browser how to treat the next line of text following a BR element if the current text is wrapping around a floating image or other object. The value you use depends on the side of the page to which one or more inline images are pegged and how you want the next line of text to be placed in relation to those images. The DOM working draft includes methods to get and set the clear property of a BR object.

Example   document.all.specialBreak.clear = "all"

Value   Case-insensitive string of any of the following constants: all | left | right.

Default   None.

BUTTON   NN *n/a*   IE *4*   DOM *1*

The BUTTON object reflects the BUTTON element. See the discussion of the BUTTON element in Chapter 8 to see how it differs from the INPUT element of type button, covered next.

HTML Equivalent

<BUTTON>

Object Model Reference

IE   [window.]document.all.*elementID*

Properties

accessKey	dataSrc	*lang*	*outerHTML*	*sourceIndex*
className	disabled	*language*	outerText	status
clientHeight	*document*	name	*parentElement*	*style*
clientLeft	form	*offsetHeight*	*parentTextEdit*	tabIndex
clientTop	*id*	*offsetLeft*	scrollHeight	*tagName*
clientWidth	*innerHTML*	*offsetParent*	scrollLeft	*title*
dataFld	*innerText*	*offsetTop*	scrollTop	type
dataFormatAs	*isTextEdit*	*offsetWidth*	scrollWidth	value

Methods

blur()	focus()	*removeAttribute()*
click()	*getAttribute()*	*scrollIntoView()*
contains()	*insertAdjacentHTML()*	*setAttribute()*
createTextRange()	*insertAdjacentText()*	

Collections/Arrays

all[]	*children[]*	*filters[]*

Event Handler Properties

Handler	NN	IE	DOM
onafterupdate	n/a	4	n/a
onbeforeupdate	n/a	4	n/a
onblur	n/a	4	n/a
onclick	n/a	4	n/a
ondblclick	n/a	4	n/a
ondragstart	n/a	4	n/a
onfilterchange	n/a	4	n/a
onfocus	n/a	4	n/a
onhelp	n/a	4	n/a
onkeydown	n/a	4	n/a
onkeypress	n/a	4	n/a
onkeyup	n/a	4	n/a
onmousedown	n/a	4	n/a
onmousemove	n/a	4	n/a
onmouseout	n/a	4	n/a
onmouseover	n/a	4	n/a
onmouseup	n/a	4	n/a
onresize	n/a	4	n/a
onrowenter	n/a	4	n/a
onrowexit	n/a	4	n/a
onselectstart	n/a	4	n/a

accessKey

NN *n/a*   IE *4*   DOM *1*

Read/Write

A single character key that "clicks" the button from the keyboard. The browser and operating system determine whether the user must press a modifier key (e.g., **Ctrl**, **Alt**, or **Command**) with the access key to "click" on the button. In IE 4/Windows, the **Alt** key is required, and the key is not case sensitive. Not working in IE 4/Mac.

Example `document.all.myButton.accessKey = "n"`

Value Single alphanumeric (and punctuation) keyboard character.

Default None.

clientHeight, clientWidth

NN *n/a*   IE *4*   DOM *n/a*

Read/Write

According to Microsoft's developer documentation, these properties reflect the height and width (in pixels) of the element's content. But see the section "About client- and offset-Properties" at the beginning of this chapter for details.

Example `var midHeight = document.all.myButton.clientHeight/2`

Value Integer pixel value.

Default None.

clientLeft, clientTop

NN *n/a*   IE *4*   DOM *n/a*

Read-only

According to Microsoft's developer documentation, these properties reflect the distance between the "true" left and top edges of the document area and the edges of the element. But see the section "About client- and offset- Properties" at the beginning of this chapter for details. To get or set the pixel position of an element in the document, use the `pixelLeft` and `pixelTop` properties.

Value A string value for a length in a variety of units or percentage.

Default None.

dataFld

NN *n/a*   IE *4*   DOM *n/a*

Read/Write

Used with IE 4 data binding to associate a remote data source column name to a BUTTON object's label. A DATASRC attribute must also be set for the element. Setting both the `dataFld` and `dataSrc` properties to empty strings breaks the binding between element and data source.

Example `document.all.myButton.dataFld = "linkURL"`

Value Case-sensitive identifier of the data source column.

Default None.

dataFormatAs

NN *n/a*   IE *4*   DOM *n/a*

Read/Write

Used with IE 4 data binding, this property advises the browser whether the source material arriving from the data source is to be treated as plain text or as tagged HTML.

Example   `document.all.myButton.dataFormatAs = "HTML"`

Value   IE 4 recognizes two possible settings: `text` | `HTML`

Default   `text`

dataSrc

NN *n/a*   IE *4*   DOM *n/a*

Read/Write

Used with IE 4 data binding to specify the name of the remote ODBC data source (such as an Oracle or SQL Server database) to be associated with the element. Content from the data source is specified via the `DATAFLD` attribute in the `BUTTON` element. Setting both the `dataFld` and `dataSrc` properties to empty strings breaks the binding between element and data source.

Example   `document.all.myButton.dataSrc = "#DBSRC3"`

Value   Case-sensitive identifier of the data source.

Default   None.

disabled

NN *n/a*   IE *4*   DOM *1*

Read/Write

Whether the element is available for user interaction. When set to `true`, the element cannot receive focus or be modified by the user. It is also not submitted with the form.

Example   `document.all.myButton.disabled = true`

Value   Boolean value: `true` | `false`.

Default   `false`

form

NN *n/a*   IE *4*   DOM *n/a*

Read-only

Returns a reference to the `FORM` element that contains the current element (if any). This property is most often passed as a parameter for an event handler, using the `this` keyword to refer to the current form control.

Example   `<BUTTON onClick="doValidate(this.form)">Click Here</BUTTON>`

Value   Object reference.

Default   None.

name

NN *n/a*   IE *4*   DOM *1*

Read/Write

The identifier associated with the element when used as a form control. The value of this property is submitted as one-half of the name/value pair when the form is submitted to the server. Names are hidden from user view, since control labels are assigned via other means, depending on the control type. Form control names may also be used by script references to the objects.

Example   `document.all.compName.name = "company"`

Value

Case-sensitive identifier that follows the rules of identifier naming: it may contain no whitespace, cannot begin with a numeral, and should avoid punctuation except for the underscore character.

Default   None.

scrollHeight, scrollWidth

NN *n/a*   IE *4*   DOM *n/a*

Read-only

The meaning of these two properties is ambiguous based on Microsoft's description and the way they're implemented in the Windows and Macintosh versions of Internet Explorer 4. My best guess is that these properties are intended to measure the height and width (in pixels) of the content of an element even when some of the content cannot be seen unless scrolled with scrollbars. The Macintosh version of the browser interprets this to mean the amount of the content that you can see at any one time. The important point is that for key elements, such as the BODY, the properties mean different things and can disrupt cross-platform operation.

Example   `var midPoint = document.all.myButton.scrollHeight/2`

Value   Positive integer or zero.

Default   None.

scrollLeft, scrollTop

NN *n/a*   IE *4*   DOM *n/a*

Read/Write

The distance in pixels between the actual left or top edge of the element's physical content and the left or top edge of the visible portion of the content. Setting these properties allows you to use a script to adjust the scrolling of content within a scrollable container, such as text in a TEXTAREA element or an entire document in the browser window or frame. When the content is not scrolled, both values are zero. Setting the `scrollTop` property to 15 scrolls the document upward by 15 pixels in the window; the `scrollLeft` property is unaffected unless explicitly changed. The property values change as the user adjusts the scrollbars.

Example   `document.all.myButton.scrollTop = 40`

Value   Positive integer or zero.

Default   0

status

Unlike the `status` property of other types of form controls, the property has no visual impact on the button.

Value   Boolean value: `true` | `false`.

Default   `null`

tabIndex

A number that indicates the sequence of this element within the tabbing order of all focusable elements in the document. Tabbing order follows a strict set of rules. Elements that have values other than zero assigned to their `tabIndex` properties are first in line when a user starts tabbing in a page. Focus starts with the element with the lowest `tabIndex` value and proceeds in order to the highest value, regardless of physical location on the page or in the document. If two elements have the same `tabIndex` values, the element that comes earlier in the document receives focus first. Next come all elements that either don't support the `tabIndex` property or have the value set to zero. These elements receive focus in the order in which they appear in the document. A value of -1 removes the element from tabbing order altogether.

Note that the Macintosh user interface does not provide for giving focus to elements other than text and password `INPUT` fields.

Example   `document.all.myButton.tabIndex = 6`

Value   Integer.

Default   None.

type

Whether the `BUTTON` element is specified as a `button`, `reset`, or `submit` style button.

Example
```
if (document.all.myButtonElement.type == "submit") {
    ...
}
```

Value   One of the three constants (as a string): `button` | `reset` | `submit`.

Default   `button`

value

Current value associated with the form control that is submitted with the name/value pair for the element. Although the property is operational in Internet Explorer 4, the Macintosh version does not preserve values written to the property.

Example `document.all.myButton.value = "completed"`

Value   String.

Default None.

blur() NN *n/a*   IE *4*   DOM *n/a*

Removes focus from the current element and fires an `onBlur` event (in IE). No other element necessarily receives focus as a result.

Returned Value

None.

Parameters

None.

createTextRange() NN *n/a*   IE *4*   DOM *n/a*

Creates a `TextRange` object from the source code of the current element. See the `TextRange` object for details.

Returned Value

`TextRange` object.

Parameters

None.

focus() NN *n/a*   IE *4*   DOM *n/a*

Gives focus to the current element and fires the `onFocus` event (in IE). If another element had focus at the time, it receives an `onBlur` event.

Returned Value

None.

Parameters

None.

button NN *2*   IE *3*   DOM *1*

The `button` object is a form control generated with an `INPUT` element whose `TYPE` attribute is set to `"button"`. This element is similar to, but differs from, the `BUTTON` element. For details on the distinctions, see the `BUTTON` HTML element description in Chapter 8.

HTML Equivalent

`<INPUT TYPE="button">`

Object Model Reference

NN	[window.]document.*formName*.*elementName*
	[window.]document.forms[i].elements[i]
IE	[window.]document.*formName*.*elementName*
	[window.]document.forms[i].elements[i]
	[window.]document.all.*elementID*

Properties

accessKey	form	*offsetHeight*	*outerText*	tabIndex
className	*id*	*offsetLeft*	*parentElement*	*tagName*
dataFld	*isTextEdit*	*offsetParent*	*parentTextEdit*	*title*
dataSrc	*lang*	*offsetTop*	recordNumber	type
disabled	*language*	*offsetWidth*	*sourceIndex*	value
document	name	*outerHTML*	*style*	

Methods

blur()	*getAttribute()*	*removeAttribute()*
click()	handleEvent()	*scrollIntoView()*
contains()	*insertAdjacentHTML()*	*setAttribute()*
focus()	*insertAdjacentText()*	

Collections/Arrays

all[]	*children[]*	*filters[]*

Event Handler Properties

Handler	NN	IE	DOM
onafterupdate	n/a	4	n/a
onbeforeupdate	n/a	4	n/a
onblur	n/a	4	n/a
onchange	n/a	4	n/a
onclick	3	4	n/a
ondblclick	n/a	4	n/a
onerrorupdate	n/a	4	n/a
onfilterchange	n/a	4	n/a
onfocus	n/a	4	n/a
onhelp	n/a	4	n/a
onkeydown	n/a	4	n/a
onkeypress	n/a	4	n/a
onkeyup	n/a	4	n/a
onmousedown	4	4	n/a
onmousemove	n/a	4	n/a
onmouseout	n/a	4	n/a
onmouseover	n/a	4	n/a
onmouseup	4	4	n/a
onselect	n/a	4	n/a

accessKey

NN *n/a*   IE *4*   DOM *1*

Read/Write

A single character key that "clicks" the button from the keyboard. The browser and operating system determine whether the user must press a modifier key (e.g., **Ctrl**, **Alt**, or **Command**) with the access key to "click" the button. In IE 4/Windows, the **Alt** key is required, and the key is not case sensitive. Not working in IE 4/Mac.

Example   `document.entryForm.myButton.accessKey = "n"`

Value   Single alphanumeric (and punctuation) keyboard character.

Default   None.

dataFld

NN *n/a*   IE *4*   DOM *n/a*

Read/Write

Used with IE 4 data binding to associate a remote data source column name to a `button` object's `value` property. A `DATASRC` attribute must also be set for the element. Setting both the `dataFld` and `dataSrc` properties to empty strings breaks the binding between element and data source.

Example   `document.myForm.myButton.dataFld = "linkURL"`

Value   Case-sensitive identifier of the data source column.

Default   None.

dataSrc

NN *n/a*   IE *4*   DOM *n/a*

Read/Write

Used with IE 4 data binding to specify the name of the remote ODBC data source (such as an Oracle or SQL Server database) to be associated with the element. Content from the data source is specified via the `DATAFLD` attribute. Setting both the `dataFld` and `dataSrc` properties to empty strings breaks the binding between element and data source.

Example   `document.myForm.myButton.dataSrc = "#DBSRC3"`

Value   Case-sensitive identifier of the data source.

Default   None.

disabled

NN *n/a*   IE *4*   DOM *1*

Read/Write

Whether the element is available for user interaction. When set to `true`, the element cannot receive focus or be modified by the user. It is also not submitted with the form.

Example   `document.forms[0].myButton.disabled = true`

Value   Boolean value: `true` | `false`.

Default   `false`

form   NN *2*   IE *3*   DOM *n/a*

Read-only

Returns a reference to the FORM element that contains the current element (if any). This property is most often passed as a parameter for an event handler, using the **this** keyword to refer to the current form control.

Example

```
<INPUT TYPE="button" VALUE="Validate Form" onClick="doValidate(this.form)">
```

Value   Object reference.

Default   None.

name   NN *2*   IE *3*   DOM *1*

Read/Write

The identifier associated with the form control. The value of this property is submitted as one-half of the name/value pair when the form is submitted to the server. Names are hidden from user view, since control labels are assigned via other means, depending on the control type. Form control names may also be used by script references to the objects.

Example   document.orderForm.myButton.name = "Win32"

Value

Case-sensitive identifier that follows the rules of identifier naming: it may contain no whitespace, cannot begin with a numeral, and should avoid punctuation except for the underscore character.

Default   None.

recordNumber   NN *n/a*   IE *4*   DOM *n/a*

Read-only

Used with data binding, returns an integer representing the record within the data set that generated the element (i.e., an element whose content is filled via data binding). Values of this property can be used to extract a specific record from an Active Data Objects (ADO) record set (see recordset property).

Example

```
<SCRIPT FOR="tableTemplate" EVENT="onclick">
    myDataCollection.recordset.absoluteposition = this.recordNumber
    ...
</SCRIPT>
```

Value   Integer.

Default   None.

DOM Reference

tabIndex

NN *n/a*   IE *4*   DOM *1*

Read/Write

A number that indicates the sequence of this element within the tabbing order of all focusable elements in the document. Tabbing order follows a strict set of rules. Elements that have values other than zero assigned to their `tabIndex` properties are first in line when a user starts tabbing in a page. Focus starts with the element with the lowest `tabIndex` value and proceeds in order to the highest value, regardless of physical location on the page or in the document. If two elements have the same `tabIndex` values, the element that comes earlier in the document receives focus first. Next come all elements that either don't support the `tabIndex` property or have the value set to zero. These elements receive focus in the order in which they appear in the document. A value of -1 removes the element from tabbing order altogether.

Note that the Macintosh user interface does not provide for giving focus to elements other than text and password `INPUT` fields.

Example   `document.forms[0].ZIPButton.tabIndex = 6`

Value   Integer.

Default   None.

type

NN *3*   IE *4*   DOM *1*

Read-only

Returns the type of form control element. The value is returned in all lowercase letters. It may be necessary to cycle through all form elements in search of specific types to do some processing on (e.g., emptying all form controls of type `"text"` while leaving other controls untouched).

Example

```
if (document.forms[0].elements[3].type == "button") {
   ...
}
```

Value

Any of the following constants (as a string): `button` | `checkbox` | `file` | `hidden` | `image` | `password` | `radio` | `reset` | `select-multiple` | `select-one` | `submit` | `text` | `textarea`.

Default   checkbox

value

NN *2*   IE *3*   DOM *1*

Read/Write

This is the rare time that the `value` property controls the label of a form control: the text that appears on the button. A button input element is not submitted with the form.

Example   `document.forms[0].myButton.value = "Undo"`

Value   String.

Default None.

blur()

Removes focus from the current element and fires an onBlur event (in IE). No other element necessarily receives focus as a result.

Returned Value

None.

Parameters

None.

focus()

Gives focus to the current element and fires the onFocus event (in IE). If another element property objects had focus at the time, it receives an onBlur event.

Returned Value

None.

Parameters

None.

handleEvent()

handleEvent(*event*)

Instructs the object to accept and process the event whose specifications are passed as the parameter to the method. The object must have an event handler for the event type to process the event.

Returned Value

None.

Parameters

event   A Navigator 4 **event** object.

CAPTION

The CAPTION object reflects the CAPTION element, which must always be nested inside a TABLE element.

HTML Equivalent

<CAPTION>

Object Model Reference

IE   [window.]document.all.*elementID*

Properties

align	*id*	*offsetHeight*	*outerText*	scrollWidth
className	*innerHTML*	*offsetLeft*	*parentElement*	*sourceIndex*
clientHeight	*innerText*	*offsetParent*	*parentTextEdit*	*style*
clientLeft	*isTextEdit*	*offsetTop*	scrollHeight	*tagName*
clientTop	*lang*	*offsetWidth*	scrollLeft	*title*
clientWidth	*language*	*outerHTML*	scrollTop	vAlign
document				

Methods

blur()	*getAttribute()*	*removeAttribute()*
click()	*insertAdjacentHTML()*	*scrollIntoView()*
contains()	*insertAdjacentText()*	*setAttribute()*
focus()		

Collections/Arrays

all[]	*children[]*	*filters[]*

Event Handler Properties

Handler	NN	IE	DOM
onafterupdate	n/a	4	n/a
onbeforeupdate	n/a	4	n/a
onblur	n/a	4	n/a
onchange	n/a	4	n/a
onclick	n/a	4	n/a
ondblclick	n/a	4	n/a
ondragstart	n/a	4	n/a
onerrorupdate	n/a	4	n/a
onfilterchange	n/a	4	n/a
onfocus	n/a	4	n/a
onhelp	n/a	4	n/a
onkeydown	n/a	4	n/a
onkeypress	n/a	4	n/a
onkeyup	n/a	4	n/a
onmousedown	n/a	4	n/a
onmousemove	n/a	4	n/a
onmouseout	n/a	4	n/a
onmouseover	n/a	4	n/a
onmouseup	n/a	4	n/a
onscroll	n/a	4	n/a
onselect	n/a	4	n/a
onselectstart	n/a	4	n/a

align

Read/Write

Determines the horizontal location of the caption in the table. Whether the caption is on the top or bottom is set via **vAlign**.

Example document.all.myCaption.align = "center"

Value   Any of the following constants (as a string): **center** | **left** | **right**.

Default   center

clientHeight, clientWidth

Read/Write

According to Microsoft's developer documentation, these properties reflect the height and width (in pixels) of the element's content. But see the section "About client- and offset-Properties" at the beginning of this chapter for details.

Example var midHeight = document.all.myCaption.clientHeight/2

Value   Integer pixel value.

Default   None.

clientLeft, clientTop

Read-only

According to Microsoft's developer documentation, these properties reflect the distance between the "true" left and top edges of the document area and the edges of the element. But see the section "About client- and offset- Properties" at the beginning of this chapter for details. To get or set the pixel position of an element in the document, use the **pixelLeft** and **pixelTop** properties.

Value   A string value for a length in a variety of units or percentage.

Default   None.

scrollHeight, scrollWidth

Read-only

The meaning of these two properties is ambiguous based on Microsoft's description and the way they're implemented in the Windows and Macintosh versions of Internet Explorer 4. My best guess is that these properties are intended to measure the height and width (in pixels) of the content of an element even when some of the content cannot be seen unless scrolled with scrollbars. These properties are not available in IE 4/Macintosh.

Example var midPoint = document.all.myCaption.scrollHeight/2

Value   Positive integer or zero.

Default   None.

DOM Reference

scrollLeft, scrollTop

NN n/a   IE 4   DOM n/a

Read/Write

The distance in pixels between the actual left or top edge of the element's physical content and the left or top edge of the visible portion of the content. Setting these properties allows you to use scripts to adjust the scroll of content within a scrollable container, such as text in a TEXTAREA element or an entire document in the browser window or frame. When the content is not scrolled, both values are zero. Setting the scrollTop property to 15 scrolls the document upward by 15 pixels in the window; the scrollLeft property is unaffected unless explicitly changed. The property values change as the user adjusts the scrollbars. These properties are not available in IE 4/Macintosh.

Example   `document.all.myCaption.scrollTop = 40`

Value   Positive integer or zero.

Default   0

vAlign

NN n/a   IE 4   DOM n/a

Read/Write

Whether the table caption appears above or below the table.

Example   `document.all.tabCaption.vAlign = "bottom"`

Value   Case-insensitive constant (as a string): bottom | top.

Default   top

blur()

NN n/a   IE 4   DOM n/a

Removes focus from the current element and fires an onBlur event (in IE). No other element necessarily receives focus as a result.

Returned Value

None.

Parameters

None.

focus()

NN n/a   IE 4   DOM n/a

Gives focus to the current element and fires the onFocus event (in IE). If another element had focus at the time, it receives an onBlur event.

Returned Value

None.

Parameters

None.

cells

A collection of all TD elements contained within a single TR element. Collection members are sorted in source code order. Internet Explorer lets you use array notation or parentheses to access a single cell in the collection (e.g., `document.all.myTable.rows[0].cells[0]`, `document.all.myTable.rows(0).cells(0)`).

Object Model Reference

IE `document.all.tableID.rows(i).cells(i)`
    `document.all.tableID.rows[i].cells[i]`

Properties

`length`

length

Read-only

Returns the number of elements in the collection.

Example `var howMany = document.all.myTable.rows[0].cells.length`

Value   Integer.

CENTER

The CENTER object reflects the CENTER element.

HTML Equivalent

`<CENTER>`

Object Model Reference

IE `[window.]document.all.elementID`

Properties

className	*isTextEdit*	*offsetLeft*	*outerHTML*	*sourceIndex*
document	*lang*	*offsetParent*	*outerText*	*style*
id	*language*	*offsetTop*	*parentElement*	*tagName*
innerHTML	*offsetHeight*	*offsetWidth*	*parentTextEdit*	*title*
innerText				

Methods

click()	*insertAdjacentHTML()*	*scrollIntoView()*
contains()	*insertAdjacentText()*	*setAttribute()*
getAttribute()	*removeAttribute()*	

Collections/Arrays

all[]	*children[]*	*filters[]*

Event Handler Properties

Handler	NN	IE	DOM
onclick	n/a	4	n/a
ondblclick	n/a	4	n/a
ondragstart	n/a	4	n/a
onfilterchange	n/a	4	n/a
onhelp	n/a	4	n/a
onkeydown	n/a	4	n/a
onkeypress	n/a	4	n/a
onkeyup	n/a	4	n/a
onmousedown	n/a	4	n/a
onmousemove	n/a	4	n/a
onmouseout	n/a	4	n/a
onmouseover	n/a	4	n/a
onmouseup	n/a	4	n/a
onselectstart	n/a	4	n/a

checkbox
NN *2*   IE *3*   DOM *1*

The checkbox object is a form control generated with an INPUT element whose TYPE attribute is set to "checkbox".

HTML Equivalent

```
<INPUT TYPE="checkbox">
```

Object Model Reference

NN   [window.]document.*formName*.*elementName*
         [window.]document.forms[i].elements[i]

IE   [window.]document.*formName*.*elementName*
         [window.]document.forms[i].elements[i]
         [window.]document.all.*elementID*

Properties

accessKey	*document*	name	*outerText*	*style*
checked	form	*offsetHeight*	*parentElement*	tabIndex
className	id	*offsetLeft*	*parentTextEdit*	*tagName*
dataFld	indeterminate	*offsetParent*	recordNumber	*title*
dataSrc	*isTextEdit*	*offsetTop*	*sourceIndex*	type
defaultChecked	*lang*	*offsetWidth*	status	value
disabled	*language*	*outerHTML*		

Methods

blur()	*getAttribute()*	*removeAttribute()*
click()	handleEvent()	*scrollIntoView()*
contains()	*insertAdjacentHTML()*	*setAttribute()*
focus()	*insertAdjacentText()*	

Collections/Arrays

all[]	children[]	filters[]

Event Handler Properties

Handler	NN	IE	DOM
onafterupdate	n/a	4	n/a
onbeforeupdate	n/a	4	n/a
onblur	n/a	4	n/a
onchange	n/a	4	n/a
onclick	3	4	n/a
ondblclick	n/a	4	n/a
onerrorupdate	n/a	4	n/a
onfilterchange	n/a	4	n/a
onfocus	n/a	4	n/a
onhelp	n/a	4	n/a
onkeydown	n/a	4	n/a
onkeypress	n/a	4	n/a
onkeyup	n/a	4	n/a
onmousedown	4	4	n/a
onmousemove	n/a	4	n/a
onmouseout	n/a	4	n/a
onmouseover	n/a	4	n/a
onmouseup	4	4	n/a
onselect	n/a	4	n/a

accessKey

NN *n/a*   IE *4*   DOM *1*

Read/Write

A single character key that "clicks" on the checkbox. The browser and operating system determine whether the user must press a modifier key (e.g., **Ctrl**, **Alt**, or **Command**) with the access key to "click" the checkbox. In IE 4/Windows, the **Alt** key is required, and the key is not case sensitive. Not working in IE 4/Mac.

Example   `document.entryForm.myCheckbox.accessKey = "n"`

Value   Single alphanumeric (and punctuation) keyboard character.

Default   None.

checked

NN *2*   IE *3*   DOM *1*

Read/Write

Whether the checkbox is selected or turned on by the user. Checkboxes operate independently of each other. Only `checkbox` objects with the `checked` property set to `true` have their name/value pair submitted with the form. To find out whether the form element is set to be checked when the page loads, see the `defaultChecked` property.

Example

```
if (document.choiceForm.monitors.checked) {
    process for the "monitors" checkbox being checked
}
```

Value   Boolean: `true` | `false`.

Default   `false`

dataFld   NN *n/a*   IE *4*   DOM *n/a*

Read/Write

Used with IE 4 data binding to associate a remote data source column name to a `checkbox` object's `VALUE` attribute. A `DATASRC` attribute must also be set for the element. Setting both the `dataFld` and `dataSrc` properties to empty strings breaks the binding between element and data source.

Example   `document.myForm.myCheckbox.dataFld = "linkURL"`

Value   Case-sensitive identifier of the data source column.

Default   None.

dataSrc   NN *n/a*   IE *4*   DOM *n/a*

Read/Write

Used with IE 4 data binding to specify the name of the remote ODBC data source (such as an Oracle or SQL Server database) to be associated with the element. Content from the data source is specified via the `DATAFLD` attribute. Setting both the `dataFld` and `dataSrc` properties to empty strings breaks the binding between element and data source.

Example   `document.myForm.myCheckbox.dataSrc = "#DBSRC3"`

Value   Case-sensitive identifier of the data source.

Default   None.

defaultChecked   NN *2*   IE *3*   DOM *1*

Read/Write

Whether the element has the `CHECKED` attribute set in the tag. You can compare the current `checked` property against `defaultChecked` to see whether the state of the control has changed since the document loaded. Changing this property does not affect the current `checked` status.

Example

```
var cBox = document.forms[0].checkbox1
if (cBox.checked != cBox.defaultChecked) {
    process for changed state
}
```

Value   Boolean value: `true` | `false`.

Default   Determined by HTML tag attribute.

disabled

Read/Write

Whether the element is available for user interaction. When set to **true**, the element cannot receive focus or be modified by the user. It is also not submitted with the form.

Example   document.forms[0].myCheckbox.disabled = true

Value   Boolean value: **true** I **false**.

Default   false

form

Read-only

Returns a reference to the **FORM** element that contains the current element (if any). This property is most often passed as a parameter for an event handler, using the **this** keyword to refer to the current form control.

Example

<INPUT TYPE="button" VALUE="Validate Form" onClick="doValidate(this.form)">

Value   Object reference.

Default   None.

indeterminate

Read/Write

Whether a checkbox is visually represented as being neither checked nor unchecked, yet still active. This middle ground is rendered differently for different operating systems. In Windows, the checkbox is grayed out (with the checkmark still visible if it was there originally) but still active. On the Macintosh, the checkbox displays a hyphen inside the box. The indeterminate state usually means some change elsewhere on the page has likely affected the setting of the checkbox, requiring the user to verify the checkbox's setting for accuracy.

Example   document.orderForm.2DayAir.indeterminate = true

Value   Boolean value: **true** I **false**.

Default   false

name

Read/Write

The identifier associated with the form control. The value of this property is submitted as one-half of the name/value pair when the form is submitted to the server. Names are hidden from user view, since control labels are assigned via other means, depending on the control type. Form control names may also be used by script references to the objects.

Example   document.orderForm.myCheckbox.name = "Win32"

DOM Reference

Value

Case-sensitive identifier that follows the rules of identifier naming: it may contain no whitespace, cannot begin with a numeral, and should avoid punctuation except for the underscore character.

Default   None.

recordNumber   NN *n/a*   IE *4*   DOM *n/a*

Read-only

Used with data binding, returns an integer representing the record within the data set that generated the element (i.e., an element whose content is filled via data binding). Values of this property can be used to extract a specific record from an Active Data Objects (ADO) record set (see recordset property).

Example

```
<SCRIPT FOR="tableTemplate" EVENT="onclick">
    myDataCollection.recordset.absoluteposition = this.recordNumber
    ...
</SCRIPT>
```

Value   Integer.

Default   None.

status   NN *n/a*   IE *4*   DOM *n/a*

Read/Write

Whether the element is highlighted/checked. This property is identical to the value property.

Example

```
if (document.forms[0].56KbpsBox.status) {
    ...
}
```

Value   Boolean value: true | false.

Default   None.

tabIndex   NN *n/a*   IE *4*   DOM *1*

Read/Write

A number that indicates the sequence of this element within the tabbing order of all focusable elements in the document. Tabbing order follows a strict set of rules. Elements that have values other than zero assigned to their tabIndex properties are first in line when a user starts tabbing in a page. Focus starts with the element with the lowest tabIndex value and proceeds in order to the highest value, regardless of physical location on the page or in the document. If two elements have the same tabIndex values, the element that comes earlier in the document receives focus first. Next come all elements that either don't support the tabIndex property or have the value set to zero. These elements receive focus in the order in which they appear in the document. A value of -1 removes the element from tabbing order altogether.

Note that the Macintosh user interface does not provide for giving focus to elements other than text and password **INPUT** fields.

Example   `document.forms[0].ZIP.tabIndex = 6`

Value   Integer.

Default   None.

type   NN *3*   IE *4*   DOM *1*

Read-only

Returns the type of form control element. The value is returned in all lowercase letters. It may be necessary to cycle through all form elements in search of specific types to do some processing on (e.g., emptying all form controls of type **"text"** while leaving other controls untouched).

Example

```
if (document.forms[0].elements[3].type ==  "checkbox") {
    ...
}
```

Value

Any of the following constants (as a string): button | checkbox | file | hidden | image | password | radio | reset | select-multiple | select-one | submit | text | textarea.

Default   checkbox

value   NN *2*   IE *3*   DOM *1*

Read/Write

Current value associated with the form control that is submitted with the name/value pair for the element (if the checkbox is checked). All values are strings, but they may represent other kinds of data, including Boolean and numeric values.

Example   `document.forms[0].myBox.value = "*"`

Value   String.

Default   None.

blur()   NN *n/a*   IE *4*   DOM *n/a*

Removes focus from the current element and fires an **onBlur** event (in IE). No other element necessarily receives focus as a result.

Returned Value

None.

Parameters

None.

focus()   NN *n/a*   IE *4*   DOM *n/a*

Gives focus to the current element and fires the onFocus event (in IE). If another element had focus at the time, it receives an onBlur event.

Returned Value

None.

Parameters

None.

handleEvent()   NN *4*   IE *n/a*   DOM *n/a*

handleEvent(*event*)

Instructs the object to accept and process the event whose specifications are passed as the parameter to the method. The object must have an event handler for the event type to process the event.

Returned Value

None.

Parameters

event   A Navigator 4 **event** object.

children   NN *n/a*   IE *4*   DOM *n/a*

A collection of all elements contained in the current element. Collection members are sorted in source code order. Internet Explorer lets you use array notation or parentheses to access a single element in the collection.

Object Model Reference

IE   document.all.*elementID*.children(i)
      document.all.*elementID*.children[i]

Properties
length

length   NN *n/a*   IE *4*   DOM *n/a*

Read-only

Returns the number of elements in the collection.

Example   var howMany = document.body.children.length

Value   Integer.

CITE

See ACRONYM.

CODE

See ACRONYM.

COL, COLGROUP

NN *n/a*   IE *4*   DOM *n/a*

The COL object reflects the COL element; the COLGROUP object reflects the COLGROUP element. Both elements provide ways of assigning multiple adjacent columns to groups for convenience in assigning styles, widths, and other visual treatments.

HTML Equivalent

```
<COL>
<COLGROUP>
```

Object Model Reference

IE   [window.]document.all.*elementID*

Properties

align	lang	offsetTop	parentTextEdit	tagName
className	language	offsetWidth	sourceIndex	title
document	offsetHeight	outerHTML	span	vAlign
id	offsetLeft	outerText	style	width
isTextEdit	offsetParent	parentElement		

Methods

click()	removeAttribute()	setAttribute()
getAttribute()		

Collections/Arrays

all[]	children[]

align

NN *n/a*   IE *4*   DOM *n/a*

Read/Write

Defines the horizontal alignment of content within cells covered by the COL or COLGROUP element.

Example   document.all.myCol.align = "center"

Value   Any of the three horizontal alignment constants: center | left | right.

Default   left

span

NN *n/a*   IE *4*   DOM *n/a*

Read/Write

The number of adjacent columns for which the element's attribute and style settings apply.

Example   `document.all.myColgroup.span = 2`

Value   Positive integer.

Default   1

vAlign

NN *n/a*   IE *4*   DOM *n/a*

Read/Write

The manner of vertical alignment of text within the column grouping's cells.

Example   `document.all.myCol.vAlign = "baseline"`

Value   Case-insensitive constant (as a string): `baseline` | `bottom` | `middle` | `top`.

Default   `middle`

width

NN *n/a*   IE *4*   DOM *n/a*

Read/Write

The width in pixels of each column of the column grouping. Changes to these values are immediately reflected in reflowed content on the page.

Example   `document.all.myColgroup.width = 150`

Value   Integer.

Default   None.

COMMENT

NN *n/a*   IE *4*   DOM *1*

The COMMENT object reflects the ! element. Most properties are not available or aren't fully functional in the Macintosh version. Despite the presence of an `id` property, you cannot set an ID attribute in the HTML for a comment element.

HTML Equivalent

`<!--comment text-->`

Object Model Reference

IE   `[window.]document.all.tags("!")[i]`

Properties

className	isTextEdit	offsetParent	outerText	style
document	lang	offsetTop	parentElement	tagName
id	language	offsetWidth	parentTextEdit	text
innerHTML	offsetHeight	outerHTML	sourceIndex	title
innerText	offsetLeft			

Methods

click()	removeAttribute()	setAttribute()
getAttribute()		

Collections/Arrays

all[]	children[]

---

text

Read/Write

The text content of the element. Due to the nature of this element, the value of the text property is identical to the values of the **innerHTML** and **outerHTML** properties. Changes to this property do not affect the text of the comment as viewed in the browser's source code version of the document. This property is not available in IE 4/Macintosh.

Example

```
document.all.tags("!")[4].text = "Replaced comment, but no one will know."
```

Value   String.

Default   None.

DD

The DD object reflects the DD element.

HTML Equivalent

`<DD>`

Object Model Reference

IE	[window.]document.all.*elementID*

Properties

className	isTextEdit	offsetLeft	outerHTML	sourceIndex
document	lang	offsetParent	outerText	style
id	language	offsetTop	parentElement	tagName
innerHTML	noWrap	offsetWidth	parentTextEdit	title
innerText	offsetHeight			

Methods

click()	insertAdjacentHTML()	scrollIntoView()
contains()	insertAdjacentText()	setAttribute()
getAttribute()	removeAttribute()	

Collections/Arrays

all[]	children[]

Event Handler Properties

Handler	NN	IE	DOM
onclick	n/a	4	n/a
ondblclick	n/a	4	n/a
ondragstart	n/a	4	n/a
onfilterchange	n/a	4	n/a
onhelp	n/a	4	n/a
onkeydown	n/a	4	n/a
onkeypress	n/a	4	n/a
onkeyup	n/a	4	n/a
onmousedown	n/a	4	n/a
onmousemove	n/a	4	n/a
onmouseout	n/a	4	n/a
onmouseover	n/a	4	n/a
onmouseup	n/a	4	n/a
onselectstart	n/a	4	n/a

noWrap   NN *n/a*   IE *4*   DOM *1*

Read/Write

Whether the browser should render the element as wide as is necessary to display a line of nonbreaking text on one line. Abuse of this attribute can force the user into a great deal of inconvenient horizontal scrolling of the page to view all of the content.

Example   document.all.wideBody.noWrap = "true"

Value   Boolean value: true | false.

Default   false

DEL   NN *n/a*   IE *4*   DOM *1*

The DEL object reflects the DEL element.

HTML Equivalent
<DEL>

Object Model Reference
IE   [window.]document.all.*elementID*

Properties

cite	innerHTML	offsetHeight	outerHTML	sourceIndex
className	innerText	offsetLeft	outerText	style
dateTime	isTextEdit	offsetParent	parentElement	tagName
document	lang	offsetTop	parentTextEdit	title
id	language	offsetWidth		

Methods

click()	insertAdjacentHTML()	scrollIntoView()
contains()	insertAdjacentText()	setAttribute()
getAttribute()	removeAttribute()	

Collections/Arrays

all[]	children[]

Event Handler Properties

Handler	NN	IE	DOM
onclick	n/a	4	n/a
ondblclick	n/a	4	n/a
ondragstart	n/a	4	n/a
onfilterchange	n/a	4	n/a
onhelp	n/a	4	n/a
onkeydown	n/a	4	n/a
onkeypress	n/a	4	n/a
onkeyup	n/a	4	n/a
onmousedown	n/a	4	n/a
onmousemove	n/a	4	n/a
onmouseout	n/a	4	n/a
onmouseover	n/a	4	n/a
onmouseup	n/a	4	n/a
onselectstart	n/a	4	n/a

cite

NN *n/a*   IE *n/a*   DOM *1*

Read/Write

A description of the reason for the change or other notation to be associated with the element, but normally hidden from view.

Value

Any string of characters. The string must be inside a matching pair of (single or double) quotation marks.

Default   None.

dateTime

NN *n/a*   IE *n/a*   DOM *1*

Read/Write

The date and time the deletion was made.

Value

See the description of the DATETIME attribute of the DEL element in Chapter 8 for value formatting details.

Default   None.

DFN

See ACRONYM.

DIR

NN *n/a*   IE *4*   DOM *1*

The DIR object reflects the DIR element. This element, originally intended as a multi-column list format, is treated the same as the UL element.

HTML Equivalent

<DIR>

Object Model Reference

IE   [window.]document.all.*elementID*

Properties

className	isTextEdit	offsetLeft	outerHTML	sourceIndex
document	lang	offsetParent	outerText	style
id	language	offsetTop	parentElement	tagName
innerHTML	offsetHeight	offsetWidth	parentTextEdit	title
innerText				

Methods

click()	insertAdjacentHTML()	scrollIntoView()
contains()	insertAdjacentText()	setAttribute()
getAttribute()	removeAttribute()	

Collections/Arrays

all[]	children[]	filters[]

Event Handler Properties

Handler	NN	IE	DOM
onclick	n/a	4	n/a
ondblclick	n/a	4	n/a
ondragstart	n/a	4	n/a
onfilterchange	n/a	4	n/a
onhelp	n/a	4	n/a
onkeydown	n/a	4	n/a
onkeypress	n/a	4	n/a
onkeyup	n/a	4	n/a
onmousedown	n/a	4	n/a
onmousemove	n/a	4	n/a
onmouseout	n/a	4	n/a
onmouseover	n/a	4	n/a
onmouseup	n/a	4	n/a
onselectstart	n/a	4	n/a

DIV

The DIV object reflects the DIV element. This element creates a block-level element often used for element positioning or containment grouping of several related elements. In the Windows version of IE 4, the client and scroll properties are not available unless the DIV element has its position style attribute set to absolute.

HTML Equivalent

`<DIV>`

Object Model Reference

IE   [window.]document.all.*elementID*

Properties

align	*document*	*language*	*outerHTML*	scrollTop
className	*isTextEdit*	*offsetHeight*	outerText	scrollWidth
clientHeight	*id*	*offsetLeft*	*parentElement*	*sourceIndex*
clientWidth	*innerHTML*	*offsetParent*	*parentTextEdit*	style
dataFld	*innerText*	*offsetTop*	scrollHeight	*tagName*
dataFormatAs	*lang*	*offsetWidth*	scrollLeft	*title*
dataSrc				

Methods

blur()	*getAttribute()*	*removeAttribute()*
click()	*insertAdjacentHTML()*	*scrollIntoView()*
contains()	*insertAdjacentText()*	*setAttribute()*
focus()		

Collections/Arrays

all[]	*children[]*	*filters[]*

Event Handler Properties

Handler	NN	IE	DOM
onafterupdate	n/a	4	n/a
onbeforeupdate	n/a	4	n/a
onblur	n/a	4	n/a
onchange	n/a	4	n/a
onclick	n/a	4	n/a
ondblclick	n/a	4	n/a
ondragstart	n/a	4	n/a
onfocus	n/a	4	n/a
onhelp	n/a	4	n/a
onkeydown	n/a	4	n/a
onkeypress	n/a	4	n/a
onkeyup	n/a	4	n/a
onmousedown	n/a	4	n/a
onmousemove	n/a	4	n/a
onmouseout	n/a	4	n/a

Handler	NN	IE	DOM
onmouseover	n/a	4	n/a
onmouseup	n/a	4	n/a
onresize	n/a	4	n/a
onrowenter	n/a	4	n/a
onrowexit	n/a	4	n/a
onscroll	n/a	4	n/a
onselectstart	n/a	4	n/a

align   NN *n/a*   IE *4*   DOM *1*

Read/Write

Defines the horizontal alignment of the element within its surrounding container.

Example document.all.myDIV.align = "center"

Value   Any of the three horizontal alignment constants: center | left | right.

Default left

clientHeight, clientWidth   NN *n/a*   IE *4*   DOM *n/a*

Read/Write

According to Microsoft's developer documentation, these properties reflect the height and width (in pixels) of the element's content. But see the section "About client- and offset-Properties" at the beginning of this chapter for details.

Example var midHeight = document.all.myDiv.clientHeight/2

Value   Integer pixel value.

Default None.

dataFld   NN *n/a*   IE *4*   DOM *n/a*

Read/Write

Used with IE 4 data binding to associate a remote data source column name to a DIV element's content. A DATASRC attribute must also be set for the element. Setting both the dataFld and dataSrc properties to empty strings breaks the binding between element and data source.

Example document.all.myDiv.dataFld = "comment"

Value   Case-sensitive identifier of the data source column.

Default None.

dataFormatAs   NN *n/a*   IE *4*   DOM *n/a*

Read/Write

Used with IE 4 data binding, this property advises the browser whether the source material arriving from the data source is to be treated as plain text or as tagged HTML.

Example   `document.all.myDiv.dataFormatAs = "text"`

Value   IE 4 recognizes two possible settings: `text` | `HTML`.

Default   `text`

dataSrc   NN *n/a*   IE 4   DOM *n/a*

Read/Write

Used with IE 4 data binding to specify the name of the remote ODBC data source (such as an Oracle or SQL Server database) to be associated with the element. Content from the data source is specified via the `DATAFLD` attribute. Setting both the `dataFld` and `dataSrc` properties to empty strings breaks the binding between element and data source.

Example   `document.all.myDiv.dataSrc = "#DBSRC3"`

Value   Case-sensitive identifier of the data source.

Default   None.

scrollHeight, scrollWidth   NN *n/a*   IE 4   DOM *n/a*

Read-only

The meaning of these two properties is ambiguous based on Microsoft's description and the way they're implemented in the Windows and Macintosh versions of Internet Explorer 4. My best guess is that these properties are intended to measure the height and width (in pixels) of the content of an element even when some of the content cannot be seen unless scrolled with scrollbars. The Macintosh version of the browser interprets this to mean the amount of the content that you can see at any one time. The important point is that for key elements, such as the `BODY`, the properties mean different things and can disrupt cross-platform operation.

Example   `var midPoint = document.all.myDiv.scrollHeight/2`

Value   Positive integer or zero.

Default   None.

scrollLeft, scrollTop   NN *n/a*   IE 4   DOM *n/a*

Read/Write

The distance in pixels between the actual left or top edge of the element's physical content and the left or top edge of the visible portion of the content. Setting these properties allows you to use scripts to adjust the scroll of content within a scrollable container, such as text in a `TEXTAREA` element or an entire document in the browser window or frame. When the content is not scrolled, both values are zero. Setting the `scrollTop` property to 15 scrolls the document upward by 15 pixels in the window; the `scrollLeft` property is unaffected unless explicitly changed. The property values change as the user adjusts the scrollbars.

Example   `document.all.myDiv.scrollTop = 40`

Value   Positive integer or zero.

Default   0

blur()

NN n/a   IE 4   DOM n/a

Removes focus from the current element and fires an onBlur event (in IE). No other element necessarily receives focus as a result.

Returned Value

None.

Parameters

None.

focus()

NN n/a   IE 4   DOM n/a

Gives focus to the current element and fires the onFocus event (in IE). If another element had focus at the time, it receives an onBlur event.

Returned Value

None.

Parameters

None.

DL

NN n/a   IE 4   DOM 1

The DL object reflects the DL element. This element is the wrapper for a definition list grouping.

HTML Equivalent

```
<DL>
```

Object Model Reference

IE   [window.]document.all.elementID

Properties

className	innerText	offsetLeft	outerHTML	sourceIndex
compact	isTextEdit	offsetParent	outerText	style
document	lang	offsetTop	parentElement	tagName
id	language	offsetWidth	parentTextEdit	title
innerHTML	offsetHeight			

Methods

click()	insertAdjacentHTML()	scrollIntoView()
contains()	insertAdjacentText()	setAttribute()
getAttribute()	removeAttribute()	

Collections/Arrays

all[]	children[]	filters[]

Event Handler Properties

Handler	NN	IE	DOM
onclick	n/a	4	n/a
ondblclick	n/a	4	n/a
ondragstart	n/a	4	n/a
onfilterchange	n/a	4	n/a
onhelp	n/a	4	n/a
onkeydown	n/a	4	n/a
onkeypress	n/a	4	n/a
onkeyup	n/a	4	n/a
onmousedown	n/a	4	n/a
onmousemove	n/a	4	n/a
onmouseout	n/a	4	n/a
onmouseover	n/a	4	n/a
onmouseup	n/a	4	n/a
onselectstart	n/a	4	n/a

compact

NN *n/a*   IE *4*   DOM *1*

Read/Write

When set to true, the compact property instructs the browser to render a related DT and DD pair on the same line if space allows. This compact styling is intended for DT elements consisting of only a few characters.

Example   document.all.tags("DL").compact = true

Value   Boolean value: true | false.

Default   false

document

NN *2*   IE *3*   DOM *1*

The document object represents both the content viewed in the browser window or frame and the other content of the HTML file loaded into the window or frame. Thus, all information from the HEAD portion of the file is also part of the document object. All references to elements must include a reference to the document object. The document object has no name other than its hard-wired object name: document.

Object Model Reference

NN   [window.]document
IE   [window.]document

Properties

activeElement	charset	expando	location	selection
alinkColor	cookie	fgColor	parentWindow	title
bgColor	defaultCharset	lastModified	readyState	URL
body	domain	linkColor	referrer	vlinkColor

Methods

captureEvents()	getSelection()	queryCommandText()
clear()	handleEvent()	queryCommandValue()
close()	open()	releaseEvents()
createElement()	queryCommandEnabled()	routeEvent()
createStyleSheet()	queryCommandIndterm()	write()
elementFromPoint()	queryCommandState()	writeln()
execCommand()	queryCommandSupported()	

Collections/Arrays

all[]	children[]	forms[]	images[]	scripts[]
anchors[]	embeds[]	frames[]	links[]	styleSheets[]
applets[]	filters[]	ids[]	plugins[]	tags[]
classes[]				

Event Handler Properties

Handler	NN	IE	DOM
onafterupdate	n/a	4	n/a
onbeforeupdate	n/a	4	n/a
onclick	n/a	4	n/a
ondblclick	n/a	4	n/a
ondragstart	n/a	4	n/a
onerrorupdate	n/a	4	n/a
onhelp	n/a	4	n/a
onkeydown	n/a	4	n/a
onkeypress	n/a	4	n/a
onkeyup	n/a	4	n/a
onmousedown	n/a	4	n/a
onmousemove	n/a	4	n/a
onmouseout	n/a	4	n/a
onmouseover	n/a	4	n/a
onmouseup	n/a	4	n/a
onreadystatechange	n/a	4	n/a
onrowenter	n/a	4	n/a
onrowexit	n/a	4	n/a
onselectstart	n/a	4	n/a

activeElement   NN *n/a*   IE *4*   DOM *n/a*

Read-only

Reference to the object that currently has focus in the document. To learn more about the object, you'll need to examine the object's name or other properties. Because buttons and other elements do not receive focus on the Macintosh, the returned value of this property may vary with operating system.

Example var currObj = document.activeElement

Value   Document object reference.

Default   window

alinkColor   NN *2*   IE *3*   DOM *n/a*

Read/Write (IE)

Color of a hypertext link as it is being clicked. The color is applied to the link text or border around an image or object embedded within an **A** element. See also linkColor and vlinkColor properties for unvisited and visited link colors. Internet Explorer 4 and the DOM have a parallel aLink property of the **BODY** object. Dynamically changed values for alinkColor are not reflected on the page in Navigator.

Example   document.alinkColor = "green"

Value

A hexadecimal triplet or plain-language color name. See Appendix A for acceptable plain-language color names.

Default   #0000FF

bgColor   NN *2*   IE *3*   DOM *n/a*

Read/Write

Background color of the element. This color setting is not reflected in the style sheet back-groundColor property except for Navigator **LAYER** objects. Even if the **BGCOLOR** attribute or bgColor property is set with a plain-language color name, the returned value is always a hexadecimal triplet.

Setting the bgColor property of a document in Navigator 2 or 3 for Macintosh or Unix does not properly redraw the window. Window content is obscured by the new color on those platforms.

Example   document.bgColor = "yellow"

Value

A hexadecimal triplet or plain-language color name. See Appendix A for acceptable plain-language color names.

Default   Varies with browser and operating system.

body   NN *n/a*   IE *4*   DOM *1*

Read-only

Returns a reference to the **BODY** object defined by the **BODY** element within the document. This property is used as a gateway to the **BODY** object's properties.

Example   document.body.leftMargin = 15

Value   Object reference.

Default   The current **BODY** object.

---

charset   NN *n/a*   IE *4*   DOM *n/a*

Character encoding of the document's content.

Example

```
if (document.charset == "csISO5427Cyrillic") {
    process for Cyrillic charset
}
```

Value

Case-insensitive alias from the character set registry (*ftp://ftp.isi.edu/in-notes/iana/assign-ments/character-sets*).

Default   Determined by browser.

---

cookie   NN *2*   IE *3*   DOM *1*

The HTTP cookie associated with the domain of the document and stored on the client machine in the "cookie file." Reading and writing the **cookie** property are not parallel operations. Reading a **cookie** property returns a semicolon-delimited list of name/value pairs in the following format:

```
name=value
```

Up to 20 of these pairs can be stored in the cookie property for a given domain (regardless of the number of HTML documents used in that web site). A total of 4,000 characters can be stored in the cookie, but it is advisable to keep each name/value pair to less than 2,000 characters in length. It is up to your scripting code to parse the **cookie** property value for an individually named cookie's value.

Writing **cookie** property values allows more optional pairs of data associated with a single name/value pair. The format is as follows:

```
document.cookie = "name=value
     [; expires=timeInGMT]
     [; path=pathName]
     [; domain=domainName]
     [; secure]"
```

No matter how many optional subproperties you set per cookie, only the name/value pair may be retrieved. All cookie data written to the **cookie** property is maintained in the browser's memory until the browser quits. If an expiration date has been made part of the cookie data and that time has not yet expired, the cookie data is saved to the actual cookie file; otherwise, the cookie data is discarded. The browser automatically deletes cookie data that has expired when the browser next starts.

Example

```
var exp = new Date()
var nowPlusOneWeek = exp.getTime() + (7 * 24 * 60 * 60 * 1000)
exp.setTime(nowPlusOneWeek)
document.cookie = "userName=visitor; expires=" + exp.toGMTString()
```

Value   Cookie data. See description.

Default   None.

defaultCharset

Character encoding of the content of the document.

Example `document.defaultCharset = "csISO5427Cyrillic "`

Value

Case-insensitive alias from the character set registry (*ftp://ftp.isi.edu/in-notes/iana/assignments/character-sets*).

Default   Determined by browser.

domain

The hostname of the server that served up the document. If documents from different servers on the same domain must exchange content with each other, the `domain` properties of both documents must be set to the same domain to avoid security restrictions. Normally, if the hosts don't match, JavaScript disallows access to the other document's form data. This property allows, for example, a page from the *www* server to communicate with a page served up by a secure server.

Example `document.domain = "megaCorp.com"`

Value

String of the domain name that two documents have in common (exclusive of the server name).

Default   None.

expando

Whether scripts in the current document allow the creation and use of custom properties assigned to the `document` object. The extensible nature of JavaScript allows scripters to create a new object property merely by assigning a value to it (as in `document.stooge = "Curly"`). This also means the document accepts incorrectly spelled property assignments, such as forgetting to set a middle letter of a long property name to uppercase (`marginLeftColor`). Such assignments are accepted without question, but the desired result is nowhere to be seen. If you don't intend to create custom properties, consider setting `document.expando` to `false` in an opening script statement as you author a page. This could help prevent spelling errors from causing bugs. The setting affects only scripts in the current document.

Example `document.expando = false`

Value   Boolean value: true | false.

Default   true

fgColor

NN *2*   IE *3*   DOM *n/a*
Read/Write

The foreground (text) color for the document. While you can change this property in Navigator, the text does not change dynamically in response (at least through Version 4).

Example   document.fgColor = "darkred"

Value

A hexadecimal triplet or plain-language color name. See Appendix A for acceptable plain-language color names.

Default   Browser default (usually black).

lastModified

NN *2*   IE *3*   DOM *n/a*
Read-only

The date (as a string) on which the server says the document file was last modified. Some servers don't supply this information at all or correctly.

Example   document.write(document.lastModified)

Value   String representation of a date.

Default   None.

linkColor

NN *2*   IE *3*   DOM *n/a*
Read/Write

The color of a hypertext link that has not been visited (that is, the URL of the link is not in the browser's cache). This is one of three states for a link: unvisited, activated, and visited. The color is applied to the link text or border around an image or object embedded within an A element. Changes to this property do not dynamically change the link color in Navigator 4 or earlier. In Internet Explorer 4, this property has the same effect as setting the BODY object's link property.

Example   document.link Color= "#00FF00"

Value

A hexadecimal triplet or plain-language color name. See Appendix A for acceptable plain-language color names.

Default   #0000FF

location   NN *2*   IE *3*   DOM *1*

Read/Write

The URL of the current document. This property was deprecated in Navigator starting with Version 3. Navigator prefers the **document.URL** property to reflect this value. To navigate to another page, you should assign a URL to the **location.href** property.

Example   `document.location = "products/widget33.html"`

Value   A full or relative URL as a string.

Default   Document URL.

parentWindow   NN *n/a*   IE *4*   DOM *n/a*

Read-only

Returns a reference to the **window** object (which may be a frame in a frameset) that contains the current document. You can use this reference to access the window's properties and methods directly. The returned value is the same as the **window** reference from the document.

Example   `var siblingCount = document.parentWindow.frames.length`

Value   Element object reference.

Default   **window** object.

readyState   NN *n/a*   IE *4*   DOM *n/a*

Read-only

Returns the current download status of the document content. If a script (especially one initiated by a user event) can perform some actions while the document is still loading, but must avoid other actions until the entire page has loaded, this property provides intermediate information about the loading process. You would use its value in condition tests. The value of this property changes during loading as the loading state changes. Each change of the property value fires an **onReadyStateChange** event.

Example

```
if (document.readyState == "loading") {
    statements for alternate handling
}
```

Value

One of the following values (as strings): **complete** | **interactive** | **loading** | **uninitialized**. Some elements may allow the user to interact with partial content, in which case the property may return **interactive** until all loading has completed.

Default   None.

referrer   NN *2*   IE *3*   DOM *1*

Read-only

Returns a string of the URL of the page from which the current page was accessed, provided the original page had a link to the current page. Many server logs capture this information as well. Scripts can see whether the visitor reached the current document from specific origins and perhaps present slightly different content on the page accordingly. If the visitor arrived by another method, such as typing the document URL into a browser dialog or by selecting a bookmark, the `referrer` property returns an empty string.

Example
```
if (document.referrer) {
    document.write("<P>Thanks for following the link to our web site.</P>")
}
```

Value   String.

Default None.

selection   NN *n/a*   IE *4*   DOM *n/a*

Read-only

Returns a `selection` object. To work with text that has been selected by the user or script, you must convert the selection to a `TextRange` object. This is possible only in Internet Explorer for Win32.

Example `var range = document.selection.createRange()`

Value   Object reference.

Default None.

title   NN *2*   IE *3*   DOM *n/a*

Read/Write

Unlike the `title` property for objects that reflect HTML elements, the `document.title` property refers to the content of the TITLE element defined in the HEAD portion of a document. The title content appears in the browser's titlebar to help identify the document. This is also the content that goes into a bookmark listing for the page.

Example `document.title = "Fred\'s Home Page"`

Value   String.

Default None.

URL   NN *3*   IE *4*   DOM *n/a*

Read/Write

The URL of the current document. The value is the same as `location.href`. Netscape deprecates the usage of the `document.location` property in favor of the `document.URL` property to avoid potential confusion (by scripters and JavaScript interpreter engines) between the `location` object and `document.location` property. To navigate to another page, it is safest (for cross-browser and backward compatibility) to assign a URL string value to the `location.href` property, rather than this document-centered property.

Example `document.URL = "http://www.megacorp.com"`

Value   Complete or relative URL as a string.

Default   The current document's URL.

vlinkColor   NN *2*   IE *3*   DOM *n/a*

Read/Write (IE)

Color of a hypertext link that has been visited recently. The color is applied to the link text or border around an image or object embedded within an **A** element. See also `alinkColor` and `linkColor` properties for clicked and unvisited link colors. Internet Explorer 4 and the DOM have a parallel **vLink** property of the **BODY** object. Changed values are not reflected on the page in Navigator.

Example `document.vlinkColor = "gold"`

Value

A hexadecimal triplet or plain-language color name. See Appendix A for acceptable plain-language color names.

Default

#551a8b (Navigator 4); #800080 (Internet Explorer 4 Windows); #006010 (Internet Explorer 4 Macintosh).

captureEvents()   NN *4*   IE *n/a*   DOM *n/a*

`captureEvents(eventTypeList)`

Instructs the browser to grab events of a specific type before they reach their intended target objects. The object invoking this method must then have event handlers defined for the given event types to process the event. See Chapter 6.

Returned Value

None.

Parameters

`eventTypeList`
> A comma-separated list of case-sensitive event types as derived from the available **Event** object constants, such as **Event.CLICK** or **Event.MOUSEMOVE**.

clear()   NN *2*   IE *3*   DOM *n/a*

Removes the current document from the window or frame, usually in preparation to open a new stream for writing new content. The `document.write()` and `document.writeln()` methods automatically invoke this method. Many bugs with the `document.clear()` method plagued earlier browser versions. Even today, it is best to let the document writing methods handle the job for you.

Returned Value

None.

Parameters

None.

close() NN *2*   IE *3*   DOM *n/a*

Closes the document writing stream to a window or frame. If a script uses `document.write()` or `document.writeln()` to generate all-new content for a window or frame, you must append a `document.close()` method to make sure the entire content is written to the document. Omitting this method may cause some content not to be written. This method also prepares the window or frame for a brand-new set of content with the next document writing method. Do not, however, use `document.close()` if you use the document writing methods to dynamically write content to a page loading from the server.

Returned Value

None.

Parameters

None.

createElement() NN *n/a*   IE *4*   DOM *n/a*

`createElement("tagName")`

Generates in memory an instance of an object associated with the tag passed as a parameter to the method. Use this method to create new **AREA** and **OPTION** elements. You may then assign property values to fill out the features of the element, such as the `src` property of an `image` object. Any new element of these types must then be added to their collections (with the `add()` method).

Returned Value

Object reference.

Parameters

`tagName`   A string of the uppercase tag name of the desired new element: `document.createElement("OPTION")`.

createStyleSheet() NN *n/a*   IE *4*   DOM *n/a*

`createStyleSheet(["url"[, index]])`

Creates and adds a new style sheet for the document. This is also the method you can use to dynamically load an external style sheet after the document has already loaded. To do so, specify the URL of the external *.css* file as the first parameter. If you'd rather script the addition of individual style sheet rules, you can do so in the Win32 version only. Specify an empty string for the first parameter and then use the `addRule()` method for the `styleSheet` object for each rule you wish to dynamically add to the style sheet.

Returned Value

styleSheet object reference (but null in IE 4/Macintosh, preventing further assignments of rules).

Parameters

url   A string of the URL of an external *.css* style sheet definition file.

index   Optional zero-based integer that indicates where among the styleSheets[] collection this new style sheet should be inserted. Default behavior is to append to the end of the collection, but this may affect cascading rules for your document. See Chapter 3, *Adding Style Sheets to Documents.*

elementFromPoint()   NN *n/a*   IE *4*   DOM *n/a*

elementFromPoint(x, y)

Returns a reference to the object directly underneath the pixel coordinates specified by the x (horizontal) and y (vertical) parameters. For an element to be recognized, it must be capable of responding to mouse events. Also, if more than one element is positioned in the same location, the element with the highest zIndex value or, given equal zIndex values, the element that comes last in the source code order is the one returned.

Returned Value

Element object reference.

Parameters

x   Horizontal pixel measure relative to the left edge of the window or frame.

y   Vertical pixel measure relative to the top edge of the window or frame.

execCommand()   NN *n/a*   IE *4*   DOM *n/a*

execCommand("*commandName*"[, *UIFlag*[, *value*]])

Available only in the Win32 platform for IE 4, the execCommand() method executes the named command. Most commands require that a TextRange object be created first for an insertion point. See Appendix D, *Internet Explorer Commands*, for a list of commands.

Returned Value

Boolean value: true if command was successful; false if unsuccessful.

Parameters

commandName

      A case-insensitive string value of the command name. See Appendix D.

UIFlag   Optional Boolean value: true to display any user interface triggered by the command (if any); false to prevent such display.

value   A parameter value for the command.

getSelection()   NN *4*   IE *n/a*   DOM *n/a*

Captures the current text selection in the document. For IE, read the selection property instead.

DOM Reference

Returned Value

String.

Parameters

None.

handleEvent()   NN *4*   IE *n/a*   DOM *n/a*

`handleEvent(event)`

Instructs the object to accept and process the event whose specifications are passed as the parameter to the method. The object must have an event handler for the event type to process the event. See Chapter 8.

Returned Value

None.

Parameters

event   A Navigator 4 **event** object.

open()   NN *2*   IE *3*   DOM *n/a*

`open("`*MIMEType*`"[, "replace"])`

Opens the output stream for writing to the current window or frame. If `document.clear()` has not already been invoked, it is automatically invoked in response to the `document.open()` method. Early version bugs may lead you to use `document.write()` and `document.writeln()` to take care of this method more reliably for you.

Returned Value

None.

Parameters

MIMEType   Advises the browser of the MIME type of the data to be written in subsequent statements. Navigator supports: `"text/html"` | `"text/plain"` | `"image/gif"` | `"image/jpeg"` | `"image/xbm"` | `"plugIn"`. Only `"text/html"` supported in Internet Explorer 4.

replace   The presence of this parameter directs the browser to replace the entry in the history list for the current document with the document about to be written.

queryCommandEnabled()   NN *n/a*   IE *4*   DOM *n/a*

`queryCommandEnabled("`*commandName*`")`

Whether the command can be invoked in light of the current state of the document or selection. Available only in the Win32 platform for IE 4.

Returned Value

Boolean value: **true** if enabled; **false** if not.

Parameters

commandName
> A case-insensitive string value of the command name. See Appendix D.

queryCommandIndeterm() NN *n/a*   IE *4*   DOM *n/a*

`queryCommandIndeterm("commandName")`

Whether the command is in an indeterminate state. Available only in the Win32 platform for IE 4.

Returned Value

Boolean value: `true` | `false`.

Parameters

commandName
> A case-insensitive string value of the command name. See Appendix D.

queryCommandState() NN *n/a*   IE *4*   DOM *n/a*

`queryCommandState("commandName")`

Determines the current state of the named command. Available only in the Win32 platform for IE 4.

Returned Value

`true` if the command has been completed; `false` if the command has not completed; `null` if the state cannot be accurately determined.

Parameters

commandName
> A case-insensitive string value of the command name. See Appendix D.

queryCommandSupported() NN *n/a*   IE *4*   DOM *n/a*

`queryCommandSupported("commandName")`

Determines whether the named command is supported by the document object. Available only in the Win32 platform for IE 4.

Returned Value

Boolean value: `true` | `false`.

Parameters

commandName
> A case-insensitive string value of the command name. See Appendix D.

queryCommandText() NN *n/a*   IE *4*   DOM *n/a*

`queryCommandText("commandName")`

Returns text associated with the command. Available only in the Win32 platform for IE 4.

DOM Reference

Returned Value

String.

Parameters

commandName
> A case-insensitive string value of the command name. See Appendix D.

queryCommandValue()   NN *n/a*   IE *4*   DOM *n/a*

`queryCommandValue("`*commandName*`")`

Returns the value associated with the command, such as the name font of the selection. Available only in the Win32 platform for IE 4.

Returned Value

Depends on the command.

Parameters

commandName
> A case-insensitive string value of the command name. See Appendix D.

releaseEvents()   NN *4*   IE *n/a*   DOM *n/a*

`releaseEvents(`*eventTypeList*`)`

The opposite of **document.captureEvents()**, this method turns off event capture at the document level for one or more specific events named in the parameter list. See Chapter 6.

Returned Value

None.

Parameters

eventTypeList
> A comma-separated list of case-sensitive event types as derived from the available **Event** object constants, such as **Event.CLICK** or **Event.MOUSEMOVE**.

routeEvent()   NN *4*   IE *n/a*   DOM *n/a*

`routeEvent(`*event*`)`

Used inside an event handler function, this method directs Navigator to let the event pass to its intended target object. See Chapter 6.

Returned Value

None.

Parameters

event   A Navigator 4 **event** object

write(), writeln()   NN *2*   IE *3*   DOM *n/a*

```
write("string")
writeln("string")
```

When invoked as the page loads, these methods can dynamically add content to the page. When invoked after the page has loaded, a single method invocation clears the current document, opens a new output stream, and writes the content to the window or frame. A `document.close()` method is required afterward. Because the first `document.write()` or `document.writeln()` method destroys the current document, do not use two or more writing statements to create a new document. Instead load the content into one variable and pass that variable as the parameter to a single `document.write()` or `document.writeln()` method.

The difference between the two methods is that `document.writeln()` adds a carriage return to the source code it writes to the document. This is not reflected in the rendered content, but can make reading the dynamic source code easier in browser versions that support dynamic content source viewing (Navigator does so as a **wysiwyg:** URL in the source view window).

Returned Value

None.

Parameters

string   Any string value, including HTML tags. To write <SCRIPT> tags, use entity characters for the brackets: `&lt;SCRIPT&gt;`.

anchors[]   NN *2*   IE *3*   DOM *1*

Returns an array of all **anchor** objects in the current document. This includes A elements that are designed as either anchors or combination anchors and links. Items in this array are indexed (zero based) in source code order.

Syntax   `document.anchors[index].objectPropertyOrMethod`

applets[]   NN *2*   IE *3*   DOM *1*

Returns an array of all Java **applet** objects in the current document. An applet must be started and running before it is counted as an object. Items in this array are indexed (zero based) in source code order.

Syntax   `document.applets[index].objectPropertyOrMethod`

classes[]   NN *4*   IE *n/a*   DOM *n/a*

Used with the JavaScript syntax of style sheets, the **classes[]** collection is part of a reference to a single class and the style property assigned to it. For a list of properties, see the **tags** object listing in this chapter.

Syntax   `[document.]classes.className.stylePropertyName`

embeds[]   NN *n/a*   IE *4*   DOM *n/a*

Returns an array of all embedded objects (**EMBED** elements) in the current document. Items in this array are indexed (zero based) in source code order.

Syntax   document.embeds(*index*).*objectPropertyOrMethod*

forms[]   NN *2*   IE *3*   DOM *1*

Returns an array of all **FORM** objects (**FORM** elements) in the current document. Items in this array are indexed (zero based) in source code order.

Syntax   document.forms[*index*].*objectPropertyOrMethod*

frames[]   NN *n/a*   IE *4*   DOM *n/a*

Returns an array of all **IFRAME** objects (**IFRAME** elements) in the current document. Items in this array are indexed (zero based) in source code order.

Syntax   document.frames(*index*).*objectPropertyOrMethod*

ids[]   NN *4*   IE *n/a*   DOM *n/a*

Used with the JavaScript syntax of style sheets, the **ids**[] collection is part of a reference to a single ID and the style property assigned to it. For a list of properties, see the **tags** object listing in this chapter.

Syntax   [document.]ids.*idName*.*stylePropertyName*

images[]   NN *2*   IE *3*   DOM *1*

Returns an array of all **IMAGE** objects (**IMG** elements) in the current document. Items in this array are indexed (zero based) in source code order.

Syntax   document.images[*index*].*objectPropertyOrMethod*

links[]   NN *2*   IE *3*   DOM *1*

Returns an array of all link-style objects (**A** elements whose **HREF** attributes are set, plus all **AREA** elements) in the current document. Items in this array are indexed (zero-based) in source code order.

Syntax   document.links[*index*].*objectPropertyOrMethod*

plugins[]   NN *n/a*   IE *4*   DOM *n/a*

Returns an array of all embedded objects (**EMBED** elements) in the current document. Items in this array are indexed (zero based) in source code order. Do not confuse this collection with the **navigator.plugins** collection in Netscape Navigator.

Syntax   document.plugins(*index*).*objectPropertyOrMethod*

scripts[]

Returns an array of all SCRIPT objects (SCRIPT elements) in the current document. Each SCRIPT object may contain any number of functions. The scripts[] collection counts the number of actual <SCRIPT> tags in the document. Items in this array are indexed (zero based) in source code order.

Syntax   document.scripts(*index*).*objectPropertyOrMethod*

styleSheets[]

Returns an array of all styleSheet objects in the current document. Each style object may contain any number of style sheet rules. The styleSheets[] collection counts the number of actual <STYLE> tags in the document. Items in this array are indexed (zero based) in source code order.

Syntax   document.styleSheets(*index*).*objectPropertyOrMethod*

tags[]

Used with the JavaScript syntax of style sheets, the tags[] collection is part of a reference to a single tag type and the style property assigned to it. For a list of properties, see the tags object listing in this chapter. Do not confuse this Navigator use of the tags[] collection with Internet Explorer's use of the tags[] collection that belongs to the all collection.

Syntax   [document.]tags.*tagName*.*stylePropertyName*

DT

The DT object reflects the DT element.

HTML Equivalent
<DT>

Object Model Reference
IE   [window.]document.all.*elementID*

Properties

className	isTextEdit	offsetLeft	outerHTML	sourceIndex
document	lang	offsetParent	outerText	style
id	language	offsetTop	parentElement	tagName
innerHTML	noWrap	offsetWidth	parentTextEdit	title
innerText	offsetHeight			

Methods

click()	insertAdjacentHTML()	scrollIntoView()
contains()	insertAdjacentText()	setAttribute()
getAttribute()	removeAttribute()	

Collections/Arrays

all[]   children[]

Event Handler Properties

Handler	NN	IE	DOM
onclick	n/a	4	n/a
ondblclick	n/a	4	n/a
ondragstart	n/a	4	n/a
onfilterchange	n/a	4	n/a
onhelp	n/a	4	n/a
onkeydown	n/a	4	n/a
onkeypress	n/a	4	n/a
onkeyup	n/a	4	n/a
onmousedown	n/a	4	n/a
onmousemove	n/a	4	n/a
onmouseout	n/a	4	n/a
onmouseover	n/a	4	n/a
onmouseup	n/a	4	n/a
onselectstart	n/a	4	n/a

noWrap   NN *n/a*   IE *4*   DOM *1*

Read/Write

Whether the browser should render the element as wide as is necessary to display a line of nonbreaking text on one line. Abuse of this attribute can force the user into a great deal of inconvenient horizontal scrolling of the page to view all of the content.

Example document.all.wideBody.noWrap = "true"

Value   Boolean value: true | false.

Default false

elements   NN *2*   IE *3*   DOM *n/a*

A collection of all elements contained within a form. Collection members are sorted in source code order. Internet Explorer lets you use array notation or parentheses to access a single element in the collection. Because each form element includes a type property (starting with Navigator 3 and Internet Explorer 4), scripts can loop through all elements in search of elements of a specific type (e.g., all checkbox elements).

Object Model Reference

NN   document.forms[i].elements[i]
         document.*formName*.elements[i]
IE   document.forms[i].elements(i)
         document.*formName*.elements[i]

Properties

length

length

Read-only

Returns the number of elements in the collection.

Example `var howMany = document.forms[0].elements.length`

Value Integer.

EM

See ACRONYM.

EMBED

NN *3*   IE *4*   DOM *n/a*

The EMBED object reflects the EMBED element. This object is treated differently in Navigator and Internet Explorer. In Navigator, the object exposes the properties and methods of the plugin that plays the media loaded into the EMBED element. As a result, the precise set of properties and methods varies with the plugin being used for the multimedia content (and is not shown in the lists below). Access to the object is via the element's name. IE, on the other hand, is more straightforward in its treatment of the object as just another element with its unique set of properties and methods (listed below). This means, however, that IE cannot control the plugin through scripting as Navigator can.

HTML Equivalent

`<EMBED>`

Object Model Reference

NN   `[window.]document.elementName`

IE   `[window.]document.all.elementID`
       `[window.]document.embeds(i)`

Properties

accessKey	hidden	name	outerText	src
className	id	offsetHeight	palette	style
clientHeight	innerHTML	offsetLeft	parentElement	tabIndex
clientLeft	innerText	offsetParent	parentTextEdit	tagName
clientTop	isTextEdit	offsetTop	pluginspage	title
clientWidth	lang	offsetWidth	readyState	units
document	language	outerHTML	sourceIndex	

Methods

blur()	getAttribute()	removeAttribute()
click()	insertAdjacentHTML()	scrollIntoView()
contains()	insertAdjacentText()	setAttribute()
focus()		

DOM Reference

Collections/Arrays

`all[]`   `children[]`   `filters[]`

Event Handler Properties

Handler	NN	IE	DOM
onblur	n/a	4	n/a
onfocus	n/a	4	n/a

accessKey   NN *n/a*   IE *4*   DOM *n/a*

Read/Write

A single character key that brings focus to an element. The browser and operating system determine whether the user must press a modifier key (e.g., **Ctrl**, **Alt**, or **Command**) with the access key to bring focus to the element. In IE 4/Windows, the **Alt** key is required, and the key is not case sensitive. Not working in IE 4/Mac.

Example `document.all.myEmbed.accessKey = "n"`

Value   Single alphanumeric (and punctuation) keyboard character.

Default None.

clientHeight, clientWidth   NN *n/a*   IE *4*   DOM *n/a*

Read-only

According to Microsoft's developer documentation, these properties reflect the height and width (in pixels) of the element's content. But see the section "About client- and offset- Properties" at the beginning of this chapter for details.

Example `var midHeight = document.all.myEmbed.clientHeight/2`

Value   Integer pixel value.

Default None.

clientLeft, clientTop   NN *n/a*   IE *4*   DOM *n/a*

Read-only

According to Microsoft's developer documentation, these properties reflect the distance between the "true" left and top edges of the document area and the edges of the element. But see the section "About client- and offset- Properties" at the beginning of this chapter for details. To get or set the pixel position of an element in the document, use the `pixelLeft` and `pixelTop` properties.

Value   A string value for a length in a variety of units or percentage.

Default None.

hidden

Whether the embedded data's plugin control panel appears on the screen. Changes to this property force the page to reflow its content to make room for the plugin control panel or close up space around a newly hidden panel.

Example   `document.all.jukebox.hidden = true`

Value   Boolean value: `true` I `false`.

Default   `false`

name

The name property is part of Navigator's way of referencing the object. The value of the property, however, cannot be retrieved through the object itself, since the only properties that are returned are those of the plugin that plays the multimedia content. In IE, however, the property is available for reading and writing.

Example   `document.all.myEmbed.name = "tunes"`

Value

Case-sensitive identifier that follows the rules of identifier naming: it may contain no whitespace, cannot begin with a numeral, and should avoid punctuation except for the underscore character.

Default   None.

palette

Returns the setting of the `PALETTE` attribute of the `EMBED` object.

Value   String.

Default   None.

pluginspage

The URL for downloading and installing the plugin necessary to run the current object's embedded data.

Value   A complete or relative URL as a string.

Default

None returned, but Internet Explorer has its own default URL for plugin information.

DOM Reference

readyState

NN *n/a*   IE *4*   DOM *n/a*

Read-only

Returns the current download status of the embedded content. This property provides a more granular way of testing whether a particular downloadable element is ready to be run or scripted instead of the onLoad event handler for the entire document. As the value of this property changes during loading, the system fires an onReadyStateChange event.

Example

```
if (document.contentsMap.readyState == "uninitialized") {
    statements for alternate handling
}
```

Value

Unlike the document object's version of this property, the EMBED object's values are integers. As can best be determined: 0 means uninitialized; 1 means loading; and 4 means complete.

Default   None.

src

NN *n/a*   IE *4*   DOM *n/a*

Read/Write

URL of the external content file associated with the object. To change the content, assign a new URL to the property.

Example   document.all.myEmbed.src = "tunes/dannyboy.wav"

Value   Complete or relative URL as a string.

Default   None.

tabIndex

NN *n/a*   IE *4*   DOM *1*

Read/Write

A number that indicates the sequence of this element within the tabbing order of all focusable elements in the document. Tabbing order follows a strict set of rules. Elements that have values other than zero assigned to their tabIndex properties are first in line when a user starts tabbing in a page. Focus starts with the element with the lowest tabIndex value and proceeds in order to the highest value, regardless of physical location on the page or in the document. If two elements have the same tabIndex values, the element that comes earlier in the document receives focus first. Next come all elements that either don't support the tabIndex property or have the value set to zero. These elements receive focus in the order in which they appear in the document. A value of -1 removes the element from tabbing order altogether.

Note that the Macintosh user interface does not provide for giving focus to elements other than text and password INPUT fields.

Example   document.all.myEmbed.tabIndex = 6

Value   Integer.

Default   None.

units

The unit of measure for the height and width dimensions of the element. Internet Explorer appears to treat all settings as pixels.

Example   `document.all.myEmbed.units = "ems"`

Value   Any of the following case-insensitive constants (as a string): `pixels` | `px` | `em`.

Default   `pixels`

blur()

Removes focus from the current element and fires an `onBlur` event (in IE). No other element necessarily receives focus as a result.

Returned Value

None.

Parameters

None.

focus()

Gives focus to the current element and fires the `onFocus` event (in IE). If another element had focus at the time, it receives an `onBlur` event.

Returned Value

None.

Parameters

None.

embeds

A collection of all `EMBED` elements contained in the current element. Collection members are sorted in source code order. Internet Explorer lets you use array notation or parentheses to access a single element in the collection.

Object Model Reference

NN   `document.embeds`

IE   `document.embeds`

Properties
`length`

length   NN *3*   IE *4*   DOM *n/a*

Read-only

Returns the number of elements in the collection.

Example `var howMany = document.embeds.length`

Value   Integer.

event   NN *4*   IE *4*   DOM *n/a*

While the **event** object contains information about a user- or system-generated event in Navigator and Internet Explorer, the event mechanisms for the two browser families are very different, as described in Chapter 6. With only a few exceptions, the **event** object properties for the two browsers are mutually exclusive. Observe the browser compatibility listings for each of the following properties carefully.

Object Model Reference

NN   *eventObj*

IE   `window.event`

Properties

altKey	data	offsetX	screenX	toElement
button	fromElement	offsetY	screenY	type
cancelBubble	keyCode	pageX	shiftKey	which
clientX	layerX	pageY	srcElement	x
clientY	layerY	reason	srcFilter	y
ctrlKey	modifiers	returnValue	target	

altKey   NN *n/a*   IE *4*   DOM *n/a*

Read-only

Reveals the state of the **Alt** key at the time the event fired.

Example

```
if (event.altKey) {
    handle case of Alt key down
}
```

Value   Boolean value: **true** | **false**.

Default false

button   NN *n/a*   IE *4*   DOM *n/a*

Read-only

Which mouse button was pressed to trigger the mouse event. Although theoretically you should be able to detect the right button, Internet Explorer 4 does not fire mouse events with that button, since context menus always appear in the browser.

Example

```
if (event.button == 1) {
    handle event for left button
}
```

Value

Any of the following allowed integers: 0 (no button) | 1 (left button) | 2 (right button) | 4 (middle button of three-button mouse).

Default   0

cancelBubble   NN *n/a*   IE *4*   DOM *n/a*

Read/Write

Specifies whether the event should propagate (bubble) up the element container hierarchy. You usually only need to set this property to **true** to override the default behavior and prevent the event from going any further.

Example   `window.event.cancelBubble = true`

Value   Boolean: **true** | **false**.

Default   false

clientX, clientY   NN *n/a*   IE *4*   DOM *n/a*

Read-only

The horizontal (x) and vertical (y) coordinate of the mouse at the moment the current event fired. These coordinates are relative to the viewable document area of the browser window or frame.

Example

```
if ((event.clientX >= 10 || event.clientX <= 20) &&
(event.clientY >= 50 || event.clientY <= 100)) {
    process code for click in hot zone bounded by 10,50 and 20,100
}
```

Value   Integer of pixel values.

Default   None.

ctrlKey   NN *n/a*   IE *4*   DOM *n/a*

Read-only

Whether the **Control** key was pressed at the instant the event fired. See Chapter 6 for testing for this key in cross-browser event handling code.

Example

```
if (event.ctrlKey) {
    process for Control key being down
}
```

Value   Boolean value: true | false.

Default   false

data
NN 4   IE n/a   DOM n/a
Read-only

Accessory data associated with the event. As of Navigator 4, the only event for which the data property has information is the **dragdrop** event, in which case the data property returns the URL of the item being dropped onto the window or frame.

Example var srcDoc = evtObj.data

Value   String.

Default   None.

fromElement
NN n/a   IE 4   DOM n/a
Read-only

Returns a reference to the object where the cursor had been just prior to the **onMouseOver** or **onMouseOut** event.

Example

```
if (event.fromElement.id == "lowerLevel") {
    . . .
}
```

Value   Object reference.

Default   None.

keyCode
NN n/a   IE 4   DOM n/a
Read/Write

The Unicode key value for the keyboard key that triggered the event. If the event is not keyboard driven, the value is zero. While you may change the value of this property, it does not influence the character displayed in the text field. See Chapter 6 about capturing keyboard events.

Example

```
if (event.keyCode == 65) {
    . . .
}
```

Value   Integer.

Default   None.

layerX, layerY

The horizontal (x) and vertical (y) coordinate of the mouse at the moment the current event fired. These coordinates are relative to the containing layer. If no layers or positionable elements have been defined, the default layer of the base document is used as a reference point, thus being equivalent to the **pageX** and **pageY** properties.

Example

```
if ((evtObj.layerX >= 10 || evtObj.layerX <= 20) &&
(evtObj.layerY >= 50 || evtObj.layerY <= 100)) {
    process code for click in hot zone bounded by 10,50 and 20,100
}
```

Value   Integer of pixel values.

Default   None.

modifiers

An integer that represents the keyboard modifier key(s) being held down at the time the event fired. You can use the & operator with a series of **Event** object constants to find out whether a particular modifier key was pressed. See Chapter 6.

Example `var altKeyPressed = evtObj.modifiers & Event.ALT_MASK`

Value   Integer.

Default   0

offsetX, offsetY

The left and top coordinates of the mouse pointer relative to the containing element (exclusive of padding, borders, or margins) when the event fired. You can determine the containing element via the **offsetParent** property. See the section "About client- and offset- Properties" at the beginning of this chapter about offset measurement anomalies in Internet Explorer 4.

Example

```
if (event.offsetX <= 20 && event.offsetY <=40) {
    ...
}
```

Value   Integer pixel count.

Default   None.

pageX, pageY   NN *4*   IE *n/a*   DOM *n/a*

Read-only

The left and top coordinates of the element's content relative to the top-left corner of the page area when the event fired. The measurements ignore any scrolling of the page.

Example

```
if (evtObj.pageX <= 20 && evtObj.pageY <=40) {
    ...
}
```

Value   Integer pixel count.

Default   None.

reason   NN *n/a*   IE *4*   DOM *n/a*

Read-only

Returns a code associated with an `onDataSetComplete` event signifying whether the data transfer was successful or, if incomplete, whether the transfer stopped due to an error or a stoppage by the client or user. This property must be examined in an event handler for the `onDataSetComplete` event.

Example

```
if (event.reason == 2) {
    alert("An error occurred during the most recent update.")
}
```

Value

One of three possible integer values:

0	Transfer was successful
1	Transfer aborted
2	An error halted the transfer

Default   None.

returnValue   NN *n/a*   IE *4*   DOM *n/a*

Read/Write

The value to be returned to the event's source element to allow or prohibit the element's default action connected with the event. If you set `event.returnValue` to `false`, the element does not carry out its normal operation, such as navigating to a link or submitting the form.

Example   `event.returnValue = "false"`

Value   Boolean value: `true` | `false`.

Default   `true`

screenX, screenY   NN *4*   IE *4*   DOM *n/a*

Horizontal and vertical pixel coordinate points where the cursor was located on the video screen when the event occurred. The top-left corner of the screen is point 0,0. There is no particular coordination with the browser window, unless you have positioned the window and know where the active window area is in relation to the screen.

Example
```
// NN
if (evtObj.screenX < 5 || evtObj.screenY < 5) {
    alert("You\'re too close to the edge!")
}
// IE
if (event.screenX < 5 || event.screenY < 5) {
    alert("You\'re too close to the edge!")
}
```

Value   Any positive integer or zero.

Default   None.

shiftKey   NN *n/a*   IE *4*   DOM *n/a*

Reveals the state of the **Shift** key at the time the event fired.

Example
```
if (event.shiftKey) {
    handle case of Shift key down
}
```

Value   Boolean value: true | false.

Default   false

srcElement   NN *n/a*   IE *4*   DOM *n/a*

Reference to the element object that fired the current event. This property is convenient in switch constructions for an event handler function that handles the same event type for a number of different elements.

Example
```
switch (event.srcElement.id) {
    case myDIV:
        ...
    ...
}
```

Value   Object reference.

Default   None.

DOM Reference

srcFilter
NN *n/a*   IE 4   DOM *n/a*
Read-only

Reference to the filter object that fired the current **onFilterChange** event. This property is convenient in switch constructions for an event handler function that handles the same event type for a number of different elements.

Example

```
switch (event.srcFilter.id) {
    case myDIV:
        . . .
    . . .
}
```

Value   Object reference.

Default   None.

target
NN *4*   IE *n/a*   DOM *n/a*
Read-only

Reference to the element object that is the intended destination of the current event. This property is convenient in switch constructions for an event handler function that handles the same event type for a number of different elements.

Example

```
switch (evtObj.target.name) {
    case "myButton":
        . . .
    . . .
}
```

Value   Object reference.

Default   None.

toElement
NN *n/a*   IE 4   DOM *n/a*
Read-only

Returns a reference to the object to which the cursor has moved that triggered the onMouseOut event.

Example

```
if (event.toElement.id == "upperLevel") {
    . . .
}
```

Value   Object reference.

Default   None.

type   NN 4   IE 4   DOM *n/a*

Read-only

The type of the current event (without the "on" prefix). Values are all lowercase.

Example

```
// NN
if (evtObj.type == "change") {
    ...
}
// IE
if (event.type == "change") {
    ...
}
```

Value   Any event name (without the "on" prefix) as a string.

Default   None.

which   NN 4   IE *n/a*   DOM *n/a*

Read-only

Returns a value relevant to the type of event. For mouse events, the property value is an integer indicating which mouse button was used (1 is the left button; 3 is the right button). For keyboard events, the property value is an integer of the keyboard character ASCII code.

Example

```
if (evtObj.which == 65) {
    ...
}
```

Value   Integer.

Default   None.

x, y   NN *n/a*   IE 4   DOM *n/a*

Read-only

Returns the horizontal and vertical pixel coordinates of the mouse pointer at the time the event occurred. The coordinate system is either a positioned element or the BODY element. A value of −1 is returned if the pointer was outside of the document area of the browser window.

Example

```
if (event.x < 20 && event.y < 30) {
    ...
}
```

Value   Integer.

Default   None.

DOM Reference

Event
NN *4*   IE *n/a*   DOM *n/a*

The Event object is a static object in Navigator that contains a large set of case-sensitive constant values you can use to test user- or system-generated events for keyboard modifiers and event types (see the modifiers and type properties of the event object). These constant values evaluate to mathematically related integers. Not all event types assigned a constant value are yet implemented as events in Navigator 4.

Object Model Reference
NN   Event

Properties

ABORT	DBLCLICK	KEYPRESS	MOUSEMOVE	SCROLL
ALT_MASK	DRAGDROP	KEYUP	MOUSEOUT	SELECT
BACK	ERROR	LOCATE	MOUSEOVER	SHIFT_MASK
BLUR	FOCUS	LOAD	MOUSEUP	SUBMIT
CHANGE	FORWARD	META_MASK	MOVE	UNLOAD
CLICK	HELP	MOUSEDOWN	RESET	XFER_DONE
CONTROL_MASK	KEYDOWN	MOUSEDRAG	RESIZE	

external
NN *n/a*   IE *4*   DOM *1*

The external object is used primarily by developers who use Internet Explorer as a component for their applications and require access to custom extensions to the document object model.

FIELDSET
NN *n/a*   IE *4*   DOM *n/a*

The FIELDSET object reflects the FIELDSET element.

HTML Equivalent
<FIELDSET>

Object Model Reference
IE   [window.]document.all.*elementID*

Properties

accessKey	*document*	*offsetHeight*	*outerText*	scrollWidth
align	*id*	*offsetLeft*	*parentElement*	*sourceIndex*
className	*innerHTML*	*offsetParent*	*parentTextEdit*	*style*
clientHeight	*innerText*	*offsetTop*	scrollHeight	tabIndex
clientLeft	*isTextEdit*	*offsetWidth*	scrollLeft	*tagName*
clientTop	*lang*	*outerHTML*	scrollTop	*title*
clientWidth	*language*			

Methods

blur()	getAttribute()	removeAttribute()
click()	insertAdjacentHTML()	scrollIntoView()
contains()	insertAdjacentText()	setAttribute()
focus()		

Collections/Arrays

all[]	children[]	filters[]

Event Handler Properties

Handler	NN	IE	DOM
onafterupdate	n/a	4	n/a
onbeforeupdate	n/a	4	n/a
onblur	n/a	4	n/a
onchange	n/a	4	n/a
onclick	n/a	4	n/a
ondblclick	n/a	4	n/a
ondragstart	n/a	4	n/a
onerrorupdate	n/a	4	n/a
onfilterchange	n/a	4	n/a
onfocus	n/a	4	n/a
onhelp	n/a	4	n/a
onkeydown	n/a	4	n/a
onkeypress	n/a	4	n/a
onkeyup	n/a	4	n/a
onmousedown	n/a	4	n/a
onmousemove	n/a	4	n/a
onmouseout	n/a	4	n/a
onmouseover	n/a	4	n/a
onmouseup	n/a	4	n/a
onresize	n/a	4	n/a
onscroll	n/a	4	n/a
onselect	n/a	4	n/a
onselectstart	n/a	4	n/a

accessKey

NN *n/a*   IE 4   DOM *n/a*

Read/Write

A single character key that brings focus to the element. The browser and operating system determine whether the user must press a modifier key (e.g., **Ctrl**, **Alt**, or **Command**) with the access key to bring focus to the element. In IE 4/Windows, the **Alt** key is required, and the key is not case sensitive. Not working in IE 4/Mac.

Example   document.all.myFieldset.accessKey = "n"

Value   Single alphanumeric (and punctuation) keyboard character.

Default   None.

align

Read/Write

Defines the horizontal alignment of the element within its surrounding container. In practice, this property has little effect on the `FIELDSET` object or its contents.

Example `document.all.myFieldset.align = "center"`

Value   Any of the three horizontal alignment constants: `center` | `left` | `right`.

Default `left`

clientHeight, clientWidth

NN *n/a*   IE *4*   DOM *n/a*
Read/Write

According to Microsoft's developer documentation, these properties reflect the height and width (in pixels) of the element's content. But see the section "About client- and offset-Properties" at the beginning of this chapter for details.

Example `var midHeight = document.all.myFieldset.clientHeight/2`

Value   Integer pixel value.

Default None.

clientLeft, clientTop

NN *n/a*   IE *4*   DOM *n/a*
Read-only

According to Microsoft's developer documentation, these properties reflect the distance between the "true" left and top edges of the document area and the edges of the element. But see the section "About client- and offset- Properties" at the beginning of this chapter for details. To get or set the pixel position of an element in the document, use the `pixelLeft` and `pixelTop` properties.

Value   A string value for a length in a variety of units or percentage.

Default None.

scrollHeight, scrollWidth

NN *n/a*   IE *4*   DOM *n/a*
Read-only

The meaning of these two properties is ambiguous based on Microsoft's description and the way they're implemented in the Windows and Macintosh versions of Internet Explorer 4. My best guess is that these properties are intended to measure the height and width (in pixels) of the content of an element even when some of the content cannot be seen unless scrolled with scrollbars. The Macintosh version of the browser interprets this to mean the amount of the content that you can see at any one time. The important point is that for key elements, such as the `BODY`, the properties mean different things and can disrupt cross-platform operation.

Example `var midPoint = document.all.myFieldset.scrollHeight/2`

Value   Positive integer or zero.

Default   None.

scrollLeft, scrollTop

NN *n/a*   IE *4*   DOM *n/a*

Read/Write

The distance in pixels between the actual left or top edge of the element's physical content and the left or top edge of the visible portion of the content. Setting these properties allows you to use scripts to adjust the scroll of content within a scrollable container, such as text in a TEXTAREA element or an entire document in the browser window or frame. When the content is not scrolled, both values are zero. Setting the scrollTop property to 15 scrolls the document upward by 15 pixels in the window; the scrollLeft property is unaffected unless explicitly changed. The property values change as the user adjusts the scrollbars.

Example   document.all.myFieldset.scrollTop = 40

Value   Positive integer or zero.

Default   0

tabIndex

NN *n/a*   IE *4*   DOM *1*

Read/Write

A number that indicates the sequence of this element within the tabbing order of all focusable elements in the document. Tabbing order follows a strict set of rules. Elements that have values other than zero assigned to their tabIndex properties are first in line when a user starts tabbing in a page. Focus starts with the element with the lowest tabIndex value and proceeds in order to the highest value, regardless of physical location on the page or in the document. If two elements have the same tabIndex values, the element that comes earlier in the document receives focus first. Next come all elements that either don't support the tabIndex property or have the value set to zero. These elements receive focus in the order in which they appear in the document. A value of -1 removes the element from tabbing order altogether.

Note that the Macintosh user interface does not provide for giving focus to elements other than text and password INPUT fields.

Example   document.all.myFieldset.tabIndex = 6

Value   Integer.

Default   None.

blur()

NN *n/a*   IE *4*   DOM *n/a*

Removes focus from the current element and fires an onBlur event (in IE). No other element necessarily receives focus as a result.

Returned Value

None.

Parameters

None.

focus()   NN *n/a*   IE *4*   DOM *n/a*

Gives focus to the current element and fires the **onFocus** event (in IE). If another element
had focus at the time, it receives an **onBlur** event.

Returned Value

None.

Parameters

None.

fileUpload   NN *3*   IE *4*   DOM *1*

The **fileUpload** object is a form control generated with an **INPUT** element whose **TYPE**
attribute is set to **"file"**. The "fileUpload" term does not appear in scripts, but it is the way
Netscape casually refers to this object.

HTML Equivalent

```
<INPUT TYPE="file">
```

Object Model Reference

NN	[window.]document.*formName*.*elementName*
	[window.]document.forms[i].elements[i]
IE	[window.]document.*formName*.*elementName*
	[window.]document.forms[i].elements[i]
	[window.]document.all.*elementID*

Properties

accessKey	isTextEdit	offsetParent	parentElement	tabIndex
className	lang	offsetTop	parentTextEdit	tagName
disabled	language	offsetWidth	size	title
document	name	outerHTML	sourceIndex	type
form	offsetHeight	outerText	style	value
id	offsetLeft			

Methods

blur()	getAttribute()	removeAttribute()
click()	handleEvent()	scrollIntoView()
contains()	insertAdjacentHTML()	select()
focus()	insertAdjacentText()	setAttribute()

Collections/Arrays

| all[] | children[] | filters[] |

Event Handler Properties

Handler	NN	IE	DOM
onblur	3	4	n/a
onchange	n/a	4	n/a
onclick	n/a	4	n/a
ondblclick	n/a	4	n/a
onfilterchange	n/a	4	n/a
onfocus	3	4	n/a
onhelp	n/a	4	n/a
onkeydown	n/a	4	n/a
onkeypress	n/a	4	n/a
onkeyup	n/a	4	n/a
onmousedown	n/a	4	n/a
onmousemove	n/a	4	n/a
onmouseout	n/a	4	n/a
onmouseover	n/a	4	n/a
onmouseup	n/a	4	n/a
onselect	3	4	n/a

accessKey

NN *n/a*   IE *4*   DOM *1*

Read/Write

A single character key that brings focus to the element. The browser and operating system determine whether the user must press a modifier key (e.g., **Ctrl**, **Alt**, or **Command**) with the access key to bring focus to the element. In IE 4/Windows, the **Alt** key is required, and the key is not case sensitive. Not working in IE 4/Mac.

Example   document.entryForm.myFileUpload.accessKey = "n"

Value   Single alphanumeric (and punctuation) keyboard character.

Default   None.

disabled

NN *n/a*   IE *4*   DOM *1*

Read/Write

Whether the element is available for user interaction. When set to `true`, the element cannot receive focus or be modified by the user. It is also not submitted with the form.

Example   document.forms[0].myFileUpload.disabled = true

Value   Boolean value: `true` | `false`.

Default   false

DOM Reference

form

Read-only

Returns a reference to the FORM element that contains the current element (if any). This property is most often passed as a parameter for an event handler, using the this keyword to refer to the current form control.

Example

```
<INPUT TYPE="file" VALUE="Send File" onClick="doValidate(this.form)">
```

Value   Object reference.

Default   None.

name

Read/Write

The identifier associated with the form control. The value of this property is submitted as one-half of the name/value pair when the form is submitted to the server. Names are hidden from user view, since control labels are assigned via other means, depending on the control type. Form control names may also be used by script references to the objects.

Example   `document.orderForm.myCheckbox.name = "Win32"`

Value

Case-sensitive identifier that follows the rules of identifier naming: it may contain no whitespace, cannot begin with a numeral, and should avoid punctuation except for the underscore character.

Default   None.

size

Read/Write

Roughly speaking, the width in characters that the input text box portion of the file input element should be sized to accommodate. In practice, the browser does not always accurately predict the proper width when the font used is a proportional one. See details in the SIZE attribute discussion for the INPUT element in Chapter 8. There is no interaction between the size and maxLength properties for this object. This property is not available for IE 4 on the Macintosh.

Example   `document.forms[0].myFileUpload.size = 20`

Value   Positive integer.

Default   20

tabIndex

Read/Write

A number that indicates the sequence of this element within the tabbing order of all focusable elements in the document. Tabbing order follows a strict set of rules. Elements that have values other than zero assigned to their tabIndex properties are first in line when a user starts tabbing in a page. Focus starts with the element with the lowest `tabIndex` value and proceeds in order to the highest value, regardless of physical location on the page or in the document. If two elements have the same `tabIndex` values, the element that comes earlier in the document receives focus first. Next come all elements that either don't support the `tabIndex` property or have the value set to zero. These elements receive focus in the order in which they appear in the document. A value of -1 removes the element from tabbing order altogether.

Note that the Macintosh user interface does not provide for giving focus to elements other than text and password `INPUT` fields.

Example `document.forms[0].myFileUpload.tabIndex = 6`

Value Integer.

Default None.

type

NN *3*   IE *4*   DOM *1*

Read-only

Returns the type of form control element. The value is returned in all lowercase letters. It may be necessary to cycle through all form elements in search of specific types to do some processing on (e.g., emptying all form controls of type `"text"` while leaving other controls untouched).

Example

```
if (document.forms[0].elements[3].type == "text") {
    ...
}
```

Value

Any of the following constants (as a string): `button` | `checkbox` | `file` | `hidden` | `image` | `password` | `radio` | `reset` | `select-multiple` | `select-one` | `submit` | `text` | `textarea`.

Default `file`

value

NN *2*   IE *3*   DOM *1*

Read/Write

Current value associated with the form control that is submitted with the name/value pair for the element. For a `fileUpload` object, this value is the URL-encoded full pathname to the local file. This is true even for the Macintosh browser versions, which tend to display only the file's name in the form element display.

Value String.

Default None.

blur()

NN *n/a*   IE *4*   DOM *n/a*

Removes focus from the current element and fires an `onBlur` event (in IE). No other element necessarily receives focus as a result.

Returned Value

None.

Parameters

None.

focus()   NN *n/a*   IE *4*   DOM *n/a*

Gives focus to the current element and fires the onFocus event (in IE). If another element
had focus at the time, it receives an onBlur event.

Returned Value

None.

Parameters

None.

handleEvent()   NN *4*   IE *n/a*   DOM *n/a*

handleEvent(*event*)

Instructs the object to accept and process the event whose specifications are passed as the
parameter to the method. The object must have an event handler for the event type to
process the event.

Returned Value

None.

Parameters

event   A Navigator 4 **event** object.

select()   NN *3*   IE *4*   DOM *n/a*

Selects all the text displayed in the form element.

Returned Value

None.

Parameters

None.

filters   NN *n/a*   IE *4*   DOM *n/a*

A collection of all filters associated with the current element. Internet Explorer lets you use
array notation or parentheses to access a single element in the collection.

Object Model Reference

IE   `document.all.`*elementID*`.filters(i)`
          `document.all.`*elementID*`.filters[i]`

Properties
`length`

Methods
`item()`

length   NN *n/a*   IE *4*   DOM *n/a*

Read-only

Returns the number of elements in the collection.

Example `var howMany = document.body.filters.length`

Va()lue Integer.

item()   NN *n/a*   IE *4*   DOM *n/a*

`item(`*index*`[, `*subindex*`])`

Returns a single object or collection of objects corresponding to the element matching the index value (or, optionally, the index and subindex values).

Returned Value

One object or collection (array) of objects. If there are no matches to the parameters, the returned value is `null`.

Parameters

index   When the parameter is a zero-based integer, the returned value is a single element corresponding to the said numbered item in source code order (nested within the current element); when the parameter is a string, the returned value is a collection of elements whose **id** or **name** properties match that string.

subindex If you specify a string value for the first parameter, you may use the second parameter to specify a zero-based integer to retrieve a specific element from the collection whose **id** or **name** properties match the first parameter's string value.

FONT   NN *n/a*   IE *4*   DOM *1*

The **FONT** object reflects the **FONT** element.

HTML Equivalent
`<FONT>`

Object Model Reference

IE   `[window.]document.all.`*elementID*

DOM Reference

Properties

className	innerHTML	offsetHeight	outerHTML	sourceIndex
color	innerText	offsetLeft	outerText	style
document	isTextEdit	offsetParent	parentElement	tagName
face	lang	offsetTop	parentTextEdit	title
id	language	offsetWidth	size	

Methods

click()	insertAdjacentHTML()	scrollIntoView()
contains()	insertAdjacentText()	setAttribute()
getAttribute()	removeAttribute()	

Collections/Arrays

all[]	children[]	filters[]

Event Handler Properties

Handler	NN	IE	DOM
onclick	n/a	4	n/a
ondblclick	n/a	4	n/a
ondragstart	n/a	4	n/a
onfilterchange	n/a	4	n/a
onhelp	n/a	4	n/a
onkeydown	n/a	4	n/a
onkeypress	n/a	4	n/a
onkeyup	n/a	4	n/a
onmousedown	n/a	4	n/a
onmousemove	n/a	4	n/a
onmouseout	n/a	4	n/a
onmouseover	n/a	4	n/a
onmouseup	n/a	4	n/a
onselectstart	n/a	4	n/a

color   NN *n/a*   IE *4*   DOM *1*

Read/Write

Sets the font color of all text contained by the FONT element.

Example document.all.myFont.color = "red"

Value

Case-insensitive hexadecimal triplet or plain-language color name as a string. See Appendix A for acceptable plain-language color names.

Default Browser default.

face   NN *n/a*   IE *4*   DOM *1*

Read/Write

A hierarchy of font faces to use for the content surrounded by the current font object. The browser looks for the first font face in the comma-delimited list of font face names until it either finds a match in the client system or runs out of choices, at which point the browser default font face is used. Font face names must match the system font face names exactly.

Example   `document.all.myFont.face = "Bookman, Times Roman, serif"`

Value

One or more font face names in a comma-delimited list within a string. You may use real font names or the recognized generic faces: **serif** I **sans-serif** I **cursive** I **fantasy** I **monospace**.

Default   Browser default.

size   NN *n/a*   IE *4*   DOM *1*

Read/Write

The size of the font in the 1-7 browser relative scale. For more accurate font size settings, see `fontSize` in Chapter 10.

Example   `document.all.fontSpec2.size = "+1"`

Value

Either an integer (as a quoted string) or a quoted relative value consisting of a + or - symbol and an integer value.

Default   3

FORM   NN *2*   IE *3*   DOM *1*

The FORM object reflects the FORM element. The FORM object can be addressed in a reference either by the value assigned to its tag NAME attribute or by the index of the forms array contained by every document. To assemble a reference to a form control object, the FORM object must be part of the reference. This covers the eventuality that more than one form may be placed in a document.

HTML Equivalent

`<FORM>`

Object Model Reference

NN   `[window.]document.`*`formName`*
         `[window.]document.forms[i]`
         `[window.]document.form["`*`formName`*`"]`

IE   `[window.]document.`*`formName`*
         `[window.]document.forms[i]`
         `[window.]document.form["`*`formName`*`"]`
         `[window.]document.all.`*`elementID`*

DOM Reference

Properties

action	*innerText*	name	*offsetWidth*	*sourceIndex*
className	*isTextEdit*	*offsetHeight*	*outerHTML*	*style*
document	*lang*	*offsetLeft*	*outerText*	*tagName*
encoding	*language*	*offsetParent*	*parentElement*	target
id	length	*offsetTop*	*parentTextEdit*	*title*
innerHTML	method			

Methods

click()	*insertAdjacentHTML()*	*scrollIntoView()*
contains()	*insertAdjacentText()*	*setAttribute()*
getAttribute()	*removeAttribute()*	submit()
handleEvent()	reset()	

Collections/Arrays

all[]	*children[]*	elements[]	*filters[]*

Event Handler Properties

Handler	NN	IE	DOM
onclick	n/a	4	n/a
ondblclick	n/a	4	n/a
ondragstart	n/a	4	n/a
onfilterchange	n/a	4	n/a
onhelp	n/a	4	n/a
onkeydown	n/a	4	n/a
onkeypress	n/a	4	n/a
onkeyup	n/a	4	n/a
onmousedown	n/a	4	n/a
onmousemove	n/a	4	n/a
onmouseout	n/a	4	n/a
onmouseover	n/a	4	n/a
onmouseup	n/a	4	n/a
onreset	3	4	n/a
onselectstart	n/a	4	n/a
onsubmit	3	4	n/a

action   NN *2*   IE *3*   DOM *1*

Read/Write

The URL to be accessed when a form is being submitted. Script control of this property lets one form be submitted to different server processes based on user interaction with the rest of the form. This property is read-only in IE 3.

Example

```
document.entryForm.action = "http://www.megacorp.com/cgi-bin/altEntry"
```

Value   Complete or relative URL.

Default   None.

encoding

NN *2*   IE *3*   DOM *n/a*

Read/Write

The MIME type for the data being submitted to the server with the form. For typical form submissions (where the METHOD attribute is set to post), the default value is the proper content type. But if you change the action property for a form by script, consider whether you require a custom encoding for the purpose. The DOM working draft indicates it may prefer to name this property encType to more closely mirror the tag attribute.

Note that the encoding property is not modifiable in Internet Explorer 3.

Example   document.orderForm.encoding = "text/plain"

Value

Case-insensitive MIME type (content type) value as a string. For multiple items, a comma-delimited list is allowed in a single string.

Default   application/x-www-form-urlencoded

length

NN *2*   IE *3*   DOM *n/a*

Read-only

The number of form elements in the form.

Example

```
for (var i = 0; document.forms[0].length; i++) {
    ...
}
```

Value   Integer.

Default   None.

method

NN *2*   IE *3*   DOM *1*

Read/Write

Forms may be submitted via two possible HTTP methods: get and post. These methods determine whether the form element data is sent to the server appended to the ACTION attribute URL (get) or as a transaction message body (post). In practice, when the ACTION and METHOD attributes are not assigned in a FORM element, the form performs an unconditional reload of the same document, restoring form controls to their default values. Note that the method property is read-only in Internet Explorer 3.

Example   document.entryForm.method = "post"

Value   Either of the following constant values as a string: get | post.

Default   get

name
NN *2*   IE *3*   DOM *1*

Read/Write

The identifier associated with the form. This information is not submitted with the form, but a form's name is used in references to the form and nested form elements.

Example `var firstFormName = document.forms[0].name`

Value

Case-sensitive identifier that follows the rules of identifier naming: it may contain no whitespace, cannot begin with a numeral, and should avoid punctuation except for the underscore character.

Default None.

target
NN *2*   IE *3*   DOM *1*

Read/Write

The name of the window or frame that is to receive content returned by the server after the form is submitted. Such names are assigned to frames by the **FRAME** element's **NAME** attribute; for subwindows, the name is assigned via the second parameter of the `window.open()` method.

Example `document.myForm.target = "_top"`

Value

String value of the window or frame name, or any of the following constants (as a string): _parent | _self | _top | _blank. The _parent value targets the frameset to which the current document belongs; the _self value targets the current window; the _top value targets the main browser window, thereby eliminating all frames; and the _blank value creates a new window of default size.

Default None (which implies the current window or frame).

handleEvent()
NN *4*   IE *n/a*   DOM *n/a*

`handleEvent(event)`

Instructs the object to accept and process the event whose specifications are passed as the parameter to the method. The object must have an event handler for the event type to process the event.

Returned Value

None.

Parameters

event   A Navigator 4 **event** object.

reset()   NN *3*   IE *4*   DOM *n/a*

Performs the same action as a click of a reset-type input element. All form controls revert to their default values.

Returned Value

None.

Parameters

None.

submit()   NN *2*   IE *3*   DOM *n/a*

Performs the same action as a click of a submit-type input element. This method does not fire the onSubmit event handler in Navigator.

Returned Value

None.

Parameters

None.

elements[]   NN *2*   IE *3*   DOM *n/a*

Returns an array of all form control objects contained by the current form.

Syntax

```
document.forms[i].elements(index).objectPropertyOrMethod
```

forms   NN *2*   IE *3*   DOM *n/a*

A collection of all FORM objects in the document.

Object Model Reference

NN	document.forms[i]
IE	document.forms[i]
	document.forms(i)

Properties

length

Methods

item()

length   NN *2*   IE *3*   DOM *n/a*

Read-only

Returns the number of elements in the collection.

Example   var howMany = document.forms.length

Value   Integer.

item()   NN *n/a*   IE *4*   DOM *n/a*

item(*index*[, *subindex*])

Returns a single object or collection of objects corresponding to the element matching the index value (or, optionally, the index and subindex values).

Returned Value

One object or collection (array) of objects. If there are no matches to the parameters, the returned value is null.

Parameters

index   When the parameter is a zero-based integer, the returned value is a single element corresponding to the said numbered item in source code order (nested within the current element); when the parameter is a string, the returned value is a collection of elements whose id or name properties match that string.

subindex   If you specify a string value for the first parameter, you may use the second parameter to specify a zero-based integer to retrieve a specific element from the collection whose id or name properties match the first parameter's string value.

FRAME   NN *n/a*   IE *4*   DOM *1*

The FRAME object reflects the FRAME element, which can only be generated inside a FRAMESET element. While Navigator knows about frames as objects, it treats a frame precisely like a window object. Internet Explorer 3 and later also observe this behavior. Therefore, for cross-platform access to frame properties and methods, see the window object listing in this chapter. But if you need access to the properties listed in this section, you must access the FRAME object via its frame ID (not name). Be aware that references to frame objects shown in this section may not work properly in the Windows 95 version of Internet Explorer 4. Also, the *windowRef* placeholder may be filled with parent or top if the reference is in a script contained by a child frame.

HTML Equivalent

<FRAME>

Object Model Reference

IE   [*windowRef.*]document.all.frameID

Properties

borderColor	frameBorder	*language*	*parentElement*	src
className	height	marginHeight	*parentTextEdit*	*style*
dataFld	*id*	marginWidth	*sourceIndex*	*tagName*
dataSrc	*isTextEdit*	name	scrolling	*title*
document	*lang*	noResize		

Methods

contains()	removeAttribute()	setAttribute()
getAttribute()		

Collections/Arrays

all[]	children[]

borderColor

NN n/a   IE 4   DOM n/a

Read/Write

Color of the frame's border. Each browser and operating system may resolve conflicts between different colored borders differently, so test any changes your scripts make to the color of individual frame borders.

Example `parent.document.all.myFrame.borderColor = "salmon"`

Value

A hexadecimal triplet or plain-language color name. A setting of empty is interpreted as `"#000000"` (black). See Appendix A for acceptable plain-language color names.

Default   Varies with operating system.

dataFld

NN n/a   IE 4   DOM n/a

Read/Write

Used with IE 4 data binding to associate a remote data source column name to the frame's SRC attribute. A DATASRC attribute must also be set for the element. Setting both the `dataFld` and `dataSrc` properties to empty strings breaks the binding between element and data source.

Example `parent.document.all.myFrame.dataFld = "linkURL"`

Value   Case-sensitive identifier of the data source column.

Default   None.

dataSrc

NN n/a   IE 4   DOM n/a

Read/Write

Used with IE 4 data binding to specify the name of the remote ODBC data source (such as an Oracle or SQL Server database) to be associated with the element. Setting both the `dataFld` and `dataSrc` properties to empty strings breaks the binding between element and data source.

Example `parent.document.all.myFrame.dataSrc = "#DBSRC3"`

Value   Case-sensitive identifier of the data source.

Default   None.

DOM Reference

frameBorder   NN *n/a*   IE *4*   DOM *n/a*

Read/Write

Controls whether an individual frame within a frameset displays a border. Controlling individual frame borders appears to be a problem for most browsers in most operating system versions. Turning off the border of one frame may have no effect if all adjacent frames have their borders on. Feel free to experiment with the effects of turning some borders on and some borders off, but be sure to test the final effect on all browsers and operating systems used by your audience. Rely more comfortably on the FRAMEBORDER attribute or frame-Border property of the entire FRAMESET.

Example `parent.document.all.otherFrame.frameBorder = "no"`

Value

Internet Explorer 4 accepts the string values of 1 (on) and 0 (off) as well as yes and no.

Default yes

height   NN *n/a*   IE *4*   DOM *n/a*

Read/Write

The height in pixels of the element. Changes to these values are immediately reflected in reflowed content on the page. Be aware that some elements, such as the IMG, may scale to fit the new dimension.

Example `parent.document.all.myFrame.height = 250`

Value   Integer.

Default None.

marginHeight, marginWidth   NN *n/a*   IE *4*   DOM *n/a*

Read/Write

The number of pixels between the inner edge of a frame and the content rendered inside the frame. The marginHeight property controls space along the top and (when scrolled) bottom edges of a frame; the marginWidth attribute controls space on the left and right edges of a frame.

Without any prompting, Internet Explorer 4 automatically inserts a margin of 14 (Windows) or 8 (Macintosh) pixels inside a frame. But if you attempt to override the default behavior, be aware that setting any one of these two attributes causes the value of the other to go to zero. Therefore, unless you want the content to be absolutely flush with various frame edges, you need to assign values to both attributes.

Example

```
parent.document.all.myFrame.marginHeight = 14
parent.document.all.myFrame.marginWidth = 5
```

Value   Positive integer value or zero.

Default 14 (Windows) or 8 (Macintosh).

name

NN *n/a*   IE *4*   DOM *1*

Read/Write

The identifier associated with a frame for use as the value assigned to TARGET attributes or as script references to the frame. The value is usually assigned via the NAME attribute, but it can be modified by script if necessary.

Example

```
if (parent.frames[1].name == "main") {
   ...
}
```

Value

Case-sensitive identifier that follows the rules of identifier naming: it may contain no whitespace, cannot begin with a numeral, and should avoid punctuation except for the underscore character.

Default   None.

noResize

NN *n/a*   IE *4*   DOM *1*

Read/Write

Whether the frame can be resized by the user. All border edges of the affected FRAME element become locked, meaning all edges that extend to other frames in the frameset remain locked as well.

Example   `parent.document.all.frameID.noResize = "true"`

Value   Boolean value: `true` | `false`.

Default   `false`

scrolling

NN *n/a*   IE *4*   DOM *1*

Read/Write

The treatment of scrollbars for a frame when the content exceeds the visible area of the frame. You can force a frame to display scrollbars at all times or never. Or you can let the browser determine the need for scrolling.

Example   `parent.document.all.mainFrame.scrolling = "yes"`

Value   One of three constants (as a string): `auto` | `no` | `yes`.

Default   `auto`

src

NN *n/a*   IE *4*   DOM *n/a*

Read/Write

URL of the external content file loaded into the frame. To change the content, assign a new URL to the property. For cross-platform applications, you can also set the `location.href` property of the frame to load a different document into the frame using window-related references (`parent.frameName.location.href = "newDoc.html"`).

Example `parent.document.all.myFrame.src = "images/altNavBar.jpg"`

Value Complete or relative URL as a string.

Default None.

frames

A collection of all `FRAME` objects defined in the document. Only the first-level frames are exposed to the `FRAMESET` object. To find further nested frames requires digging into the `frames` collections of nested `FRAMESET` objects.

Object Model Reference

NN	`[windowRef.]frames[i]`
IE	`[windowRef.]frames[i]`
	`[windowRef.]frames(i)`

Properties
`length`

Methods
`item()`

length

Read-only

Returns the number of child frames defined in the frameset whose window starts the reference.

Example `var howMany = parent.frames.length`

Value Integer.

item()

`item(index[, subindex])`

Returns a single object or collection of objects corresponding to the element matching the index value (or, optionally, the index and subindex values).

Returned Value

One object or collection (array) of objects. If there are no matches to the parameters, the returned value is `null`.

Parameters

index   When the parameter is a zero-based integer, the returned value is a single element corresponding to the said numbered item in source code order (nested within the current element); when the parameter is a string, the returned value is a collection of elements whose `id` or `name` properties match that string.

subindex If you specify a string value for the first parameter, you may use the second parameter to specify a zero-based integer to retrieve a specific element from the collection whose **id** or **name** properties match the first parameter's string value.

FRAMESET
NN *n/a*   IE *4*   DOM *1*

The FRAMESET object reflects the FRAMESET element. While Navigator knows about framesets as objects, it treats a frameset like any other window object. Internet Explorer 3 and later also observe this behavior. Therefore, for cross-platform access to FRAMESET properties and methods, see the **window** object listing in this chapter. But if you need access to the properties listed in this section, you must access the FRAMESET object via its frameset ID. Be aware that references to frameset objects shown in this section may not work properly in the Windows 95 version of Internet Explorer 4. Also, the *windowRef* placeholder may be filled with **parent** or **top** if the reference is in a script contained by a child frame.

HTML Equivalent
<FRAMESET>

Object Model Reference
IE   [*windowRef.*]document.all.*framesetID*

Properties

border	document	isTextEdit	parentTextEdit	style
borderColor	frameBorder	lang	rows	tagName
className	frameSpacing	language	sourceIndex	title
cols	id	parentElement		

Methods

contains()	removeAttribute()	setAttribute()
getAttribute()		

Collections/Arrays
all[]   children[]

Event Handler Properties

Handler	NN	IE	DOM
onbeforeunload	n/a	4	n/a
onload	n/a	4	n/a
onresize	n/a	4	n/a
onunload	n/a	4	n/a

border
NN *n/a*   IE *4*   DOM *n/a*

Read/Write

Thickness of the spaces between frames in a frameset in pixels. Only the outermost FRAMESET element of a system of nested framesets responds to the **border** property setting. Internet Explorer 4 treats the default thicknesses for Windows and Macintosh differently, so be aware that the same value may look different on each operating system platform.

Example   `top.document.all.myFrameset.border = 4`

Value

An integer value. A setting of zero eliminates the border entirely. While the value is supposed to represent the precise pixel thickness of borders in the frameset, this is not entirely true for all operating systems or browsers.

Default   6 (IE 4 Windows); 1 (IE 4 Mac).

borderColor

NN n/a   IE 4   DOM n/a

Read/Write

Color of borders between frames of the frameset. The `borderColor` property of an individual frame overrides the **FRAMESET** object's setting

Example   `parent.document.all.myFrameset.borderColor = "salmon"`

Value

A hexadecimal triplet or plain-language color name. A setting of empty is interpreted as `"#000000"` (black). See Appendix A for acceptable plain-language color names.

Default   Varies with operating system.

cols

NN n/a   IE 4   DOM 1

Read/Write

Defines the sizes or proportions of the column arrangement of frames in a frameset. Column size is defined in one of three ways:

- An absolute pixel size
- A percentage of the width available for the entire frameset
- A wildcard (*) to represent all available remaining space after other pixels and percentages have been accounted for

Exercise extreme care when scripting a change to this property. Altering the composition of a frameset on the fly might disrupt scripts that communicate across frames. Reducing the number of columns may destroy documents whose scripts or objects support scripts in other frames or the parent. It is safest to maintain the same number of columns, but use this property to adjust the widths of existing frame columns.

Example   `parent.document.all.framesetter.cols = "40%,60%"`

Value

Comma-separated list (as a string) of pixel, percentage, or wildcard (*) values. Internet Explorer 4 for the Macintosh exhibits incorrect behavior with some combinations that include a wildcard value.

Default   100%

frameBorder   NN *n/a*   IE *4*   DOM *n/a*

Read/Write

Controls whether the frameset displays borders between frames. Adjusting this property does not dynamically change the border visibility in Internet Explorer 4.

Example   `parent.document.all.framesetter.frameBorder = "no"`

Value

Internet Explorer 4 accepts the string values of 1 (on) and 0 (off) as well as **yes** and no.

Default   yes

frameSpacing   NN *n/a*   IE *4*   DOM *n/a*

Read/Write

The amount of spacing in pixels between frames within a frameset.

Example   `parent.document.all.framesetter.frameSpacing = 5`

Value   Integer.

Default   2

rows   NN *n/a*   IE *4*   DOM *1*

Read/Write

The sizes or proportions of the row arrangement of frames in a frameset. See the `cols` property for additional details of selecting values for the **rows** property.

Example   `document.all.myFrameset.rows = "20%, 300, *"`

Value

String of comma-delimited list of pixel or percentage values, or the * wildcard character.

Default   None.

H1, H2, H3, H4, H5, H6   NN *n/a*   IE *4*   DOM *1*

These objects reflect the HTML header elements of the same names. See the description of the elements in Chapter 8 for examples of how various browsers render each of the header sizes.

HTML Equivalent

```
<H1>
<H2>
<H3>
<H4>
<H5>
<H6>
```

DOM Reference

Object Model Reference

IE   [window.]document.all.*elementID*

Properties

align	innerText	offsetLeft	outerHTML	sourceIndex
className	isTextEdit	offsetParent	outerText	style
document	lang	offsetTop	parentElement	tagName
id	language	offsetWidth	parentTextEdit	title
innerHTML	offsetHeight			

Methods

click()	insertAdjacentHTML()	scrollIntoView()
contains()	insertAdjacentText()	setAttribute()
getAttribute()	removeAttribute()	

Collections/Arrays

all[]	children[]	filters[]

Event Handler Properties

Handler	NN	IE	DOM
onclick	n/a	4	n/a
ondblclick	n/a	4	n/a
ondragstart	n/a	4	n/a
onfilterchange	n/a	4	n/a
onhelp	n/a	4	n/a
onkeydown	n/a	4	n/a
onkeypress	n/a	4	n/a
onkeyup	n/a	4	n/a
onmousedown	n/a	4	n/a
onmousemove	n/a	4	n/a
onmouseout	n/a	4	n/a
onmouseover	n/a	4	n/a
onmouseup	n/a	4	n/a
onselectstart	n/a	4	n/a

align   NN *n/a*   IE *4*   DOM *1*

Read/Write

Defines the horizontal alignment of the element within its surrounding container.

Example document.all.myHeader.align = "center"

Value   Any of the three horizontal alignment constants: center | left | right.

Default left

HEAD

The HEAD object reflects the HEAD element. Accessing this object via its ID reference may not work in the Windows version of IE 4. Use the `tags[]` collection instead, as shown later in this reference section.

HTML Equivalent

`<HEAD>`

Object Model Reference

IE   `[window.]document.all.`*elementID*
         `[window.]document.all.tags("HEAD")[0]`

Properties

className	*id*	*parentElement*	*tagName*	*title*
document	*isTextEdit*	*sourceIndex*	*outerText*	*style*

Methods

contains()	*removeAttribute()*	*setAttribute()*
getAttribute()		

hidden

The hidden object is a form control generated with an INPUT element whose TYPE attribute is set to `"hidden"`. This element has no event handlers, because users do not interact directly with the element. Be aware that any values assigned to a hidden object are removed if the user reloads the page. In other words, it does not function as a persistent store. The Win32 version of Internet Explorer 4 exposes many more properties than are listed below. Most of these are included in the internal object definition for consistency across other text-oriented form controls, but have no significance for a hidden object.

HTML Equivalent

`<INPUT TYPE="hidden">`

Object Model Reference

NN   `[window.]document.`*formName.elementName*
         `[window.]document.forms[i].elements[i]`
IE   `[window.]document.`*formName.elementName*
         `[window.]document.forms[i].elements[i]`
         `[window.]document.all.`*elementID*

Properties

className	*document*	*language*	*sourceIndex*	*title*
dataFld	*form*	*name*	*style*	*type*
dataSrc	*id*	*parentElement*	*tagName*	*value*
disabled	*isTextEdit*	*parentTextEdit*		

Methods

contains()	removeAttribute()	setAttribute()
getAttribute()		

dataFld property   NN *n/a*   IE *4*   DOM *n/a*

Read/Write

Used with IE 4 data binding to associate a remote data source column name with the element's value. A DATASRC attribute must also be set for the element. Setting both the dataFld and dataSrc properties to empty strings breaks the binding between element and data source.

Example   document.all.myObject.dataFld = "price"

Value   Case-sensitive identifier of the data source column.

Default   None.

dataSrc   NN *n/a*   IE *4*   DOM *n/a*

Read/Write

Used with IE 4 data binding to specify the name of the remote ODBC data source (such as an Oracle or SQL Server database) to be associated with the element. Setting both the dataFld and dataSrc properties to empty strings breaks the binding between element and data source.

Example   document.all.inventoryTable.dataSrc = "#DBSRC3"

Value   Case-sensitive identifier of the data source.

Default   None.

disabled   NN *n/a*   IE *4*   DOM *1*

Read/Write

Normally, this property determines whether the element is available for user interaction. Its importance for a hidden element is that when this property is set to true, the element's name/value pair is not submitted with the form.

Example   document.forms[0].elements[3].disabled = true

Value   Boolean value: true I false.

Default   false

form   NN *2*   IE *3*   DOM *n/a*

Read-only

Returns a reference to the FORM element that contains the current element (if any). This property is most often passed as a parameter for an event handler, using the this keyword to refer to the current form control. It has little significance for a hidden form element.

Value   Object reference.

Default   None.

name

The identifier associated with the form control. The value of this property is submitted as one-half of the name/value pair when the form is submitted to the server. Names are hidden from user view, since control labels are assigned via other means, depending on the control type. Form control names may also be used by script references to the objects.

Example   `document.orderForm.compName.name = "company"`

Value

Case-sensitive identifier that follows the rules of identifier naming: it may contain no whitespace, cannot begin with a numeral, and should avoid punctuation except for the underscore character.

Default   None.

type

Returns the type of form control element. The value is returned in all lowercase letters. It may be necessary to cycle through all form elements in search of specific types to do some processing on (e.g., emptying all form controls of type `"text"` while leaving other controls untouched).

Example

```
if (document.forms[0].elements[3].type ==  "text") {
    ...
}
```

Value

Any of the following constants (as a string): `button` | `checkbox` | `file` | `hidden` | `image` | `password` | `radio` | `reset` | `select-multiple` | `select-one` | `submit` | `text` | `textarea`.

Default   `hidden`

value

Current value associated with the form control that is submitted with the name/value pair for the element. All values are strings, but they may represent other kinds of data, including Boolean and numeric values.

Example   `document.forms[0].price.value = "33.95"`

Value   String.

Default None.

history NN *2* IE *3* DOM *n/a*

During a browser session, the browser uses the `history` object to maintain a list of URLs visited by the user. This list (stored as an array) is used by the browser to assist with navigation via the **Back** and **Forward** buttons. Due to the sensitive nature of the private information stored in the `history` object, not many of the details are exposed to scripts that could capture such information and surreptitiously submit it to a server. In more recent browser versions, each window maintains its own `history` object.

Object Model Reference

NN   `[window.]history`

IE   `[window.]history`

Properties

current	length	next	previous

Methods

back()	forward()	go()

current, next, previous NN *4* IE *n/a* DOM *n/a*

Read-only

The URL of the current, next, and previous URLs in the `history` array. This information is private and can be retrieved in Navigator 4 (or later) only with signed scripts and the user's approval. Signed scripts are beyond the scope of this book, but a good JavaScript book should show you how to create and program signed scripts.

Example   `var prevURL = parent.otherFrame.history.previous`

Value   String.

Default   None.

length NN *2* IE *3* DOM *n/a*

Read-only

The number of items in the history list. Even with this information, you are not allowed to extract a specific history entry except with signed scripts and the user's permission in Navigator 4 or later.

Example

```
if (history.length > 4) {
   ...
}
```

Value   Integer.

Default   None.

back()

The basic action is to navigate to the previously viewed document, similar to the click of the browser's **Back** button. In Navigator 4, however, you can direct the `back()` method to a specific window or frame, thus bypassing the default behavior of the **Back** button. For example, repeated calls to `parent.otherFrame.history.back()` eventually run out of history for the frame and cease to do anything further. On the other hand, repeated calls to `top.history.back()` are the same as clicking the **Back** button, conceivably backing out of the frameset entirely if it wasn't the first document loaded in the current browser session.

Returned Value

None.

Parameters

None.

forward()

The basic action is to navigate to the same URL that the browser's **Forward** button leads to (if it is active). Similar cautions about the window's history from the `history.back()` method apply here, as well.

Returned Value

None.

Parameters

None.

go()

`go(stepCount | "URL")`

Navigates to a specific position in the history listing.

Returned Value

None.

Parameters

`stepCount`
> An integer representing how many items away from the current listing the browser should use to navigate. A value of zero causes the current page to reload; a value of -1 is the same as `back()`; a value of -2 is the URL two steps back from the current item in history. A bug in IE 3 causes all values other than 0 to be treated as -1.

`URL`   A URL or (in Navigator) document title stored in the history listing.

HR

The HR object reflects the HR element.

DOM Reference

HTML Equivalent

`<HR>`

Object Model Reference

IE   `[window.]document.all.elementID`

Properties

align	isTextEdit	offsetLeft	outerText	style
className	lang	offsetParent	parentElement	tagName
color	language	offsetTop	parentTextEdit	title
document	noShade	offsetWidth	size	width
id	offsetHeight	outerHTML	sourceIndex	

Methods

click()	insertAdjacentHTML()	scrollIntoView()
contains()	insertAdjacentText()	setAttribute()
getAttribute()	removeAttribute()	

Collections/Arrays

filters[]

Event Handler Properties

Handler	NN	IE	DOM
onclick	n/a	4	n/a
ondblclick	n/a	4	n/a
ondragstart	n/a	4	n/a
onfilterchange	n/a	4	n/a
onhelp	n/a	4	n/a
onkeydown	n/a	4	n/a
onkeypress	n/a	4	n/a
onkeyup	n/a	4	n/a
onmousedown	n/a	4	n/a
onmousemove	n/a	4	n/a
onmouseout	n/a	4	n/a
onmouseover	n/a	4	n/a
onmouseup	n/a	4	n/a
onselectstart	n/a	4	n/a

align   NN *n/a*   IE *4*   DOM *1*

Read/Write

Defines the horizontal alignment of the element within its surrounding container.

Example `document.all.myHR.align = "center"`

Value   Any of the three horizontal alignment constants: `center` | `left` | `right`.

Default `center`

color

Read/Write

Sets the color scheme of the horizontal rule. If the rule is rendered in 3-D, complementary colors are automatically assigned to the shaded area.

Example `document.all.myHR.color = "red"`

Value

Case-insensitive hexadecimal triplet or plain-language color name as a string. See Appendix A for acceptable plain-language color names.

Default Browser default.

noShade

Read/Write

Whether the browser should render the rule as a flat (not 3-D) line. In Internet Explorer only, if you set the `color` property, the browser changes the default line style to a no-shade style.

Example `document.all.bar2.noShade = "true"`

Value   Boolean value: `true` | `false`.

Default `false`

size

Read/Write

The thickness in pixels of the horizontal rule.

Example `document.all.rule2.size = 3`

Value   Positive integer.

Default 2

width

Read/Write

The width of the rule either in pixels (as an integer) or a percentage (as a string) of the next outermost block-level container.

Example `document.all.bar3.width = "70%"`

Value   Integer (for pixels) or string (for pixels or percentage).

Default 100%

DOM Reference

HTML

The HTML object reflects the HTML element.

HTML Equivalent

```
<HTML>
```

Object Model Reference

IE   [window.]document.all.*elementID*

Properties

className	isTextEdit	parentElement	sourceIndex	tagName
document	language	parentTextEdit	style	title
id				

Methods

contains()	removeAttribute()	setAttribute()
getAttribute()		

I

See B.

IFRAME

The IFRAME object reflects the IFRAME element. Be aware that, in Internet Explorer 4, a number of properties defined for this object have no effect on the object nor any default value.

HTML Equivalent

```
<IFRAME>
```

Object Model Reference

IE   [window.]document.all.*elementID*

Properties

align	hspace	name	outerHTML	src
className	id	noResize	outerText	style
dataFld	isTextEdit	offsetHeight	parentElement	tabIndex
dataSrc	lang	offsetLeft	parentTextEdit	tagName
document	language	offsetParent	scrolling	title
frameBorder	marginHeight	offsetTop	sourceIndex	vspace
frameSpacing	marginWidth	offsetWidth		

Methods

click()	insertAdjacentHTML()	scrollIntoView()
contains()	insertAdjacentText()	setAttribute()
getAttribute()	removeAttribute()	

Collections/Arrays

all[]   *children[]*

align

NN *n/a*   IE *4*   DOM *1*

Read/Write

Defines how the element is aligned relative to surrounding text content. Most values set the vertical relationship between the element and surrounding text. For example, to align the bottom of the element with the baseline of the surrounding text, the `align` property value would be `baseline`. An element can be "floated" along the left or right margin to let surrounding text wrap around the element.

Example `document.all.myIframe.align = "absmiddle"`

Value

Any of the following alignment constant values (as a string): `absbottom` | `absmiddle` | `baseline` | `bottom` | `right` | `left` | `none` | `texttop` | `top`.

Default `bottom`

dataFld

NN *n/a*   IE *4*   DOM *n/a*

Read/Write

Used with IE 4 data binding to associate a remote data source column name with the value of the `src` property. A `DATASRC` attribute must also be set for the element. Setting both the `dataFld` and `dataSrc` properties to empty strings breaks the binding between element and data source.

Example `document.all.myIframe.dataFld = "frameURL"`

Value Case-sensitive identifier of the data source column.

Default None.

dataSrc

NN *n/a*   IE *4*   DOM *n/a*

Read/Write

Used with IE 4 data binding to specify the name of the remote ODBC data source (such as an Oracle or SQL Server database) to be associated with the element. Setting both the `dataFld` and `dataSrc` properties to empty strings breaks the binding between element and data source.

Example `document.all.myIframe.dataSrc = "#DBSRC3"`

Value Case-sensitive identifier of the data source.

Default None.

frameBorder   NN *n/a*   IE *4*   DOM *n/a*

Read/Write

This property should control whether the frame displays a border. In practice, the property has no effect on the visual appearance of an inline frame.

Value

Internet Explorer 4 accepts the string values of 1 (on) and 0 (off) as well as **yes** and **no**.

Default   yes

frameSpacing   NN *n/a*   IE *4*   DOM *n/a*

Read/Write

The amount of spacing in pixels between frames within a frameset. This property has no effect on an inline frame in Internet Explorer 4.

Value   Integer.

Default   None.

hspace, vspace   NN *n/a*   IE *4*   DOM *n/a*

Read/Write

The pixel measure of horizontal and vertical margins surrounding an inline frame. The **hspace** property affects the left and right edges of the element equally; the **vspace** property affects the top and bottom edges of the element equally. These margins are not the same as margins set by style sheets, but they have the same visual effect.

Example

```
document.logo.hspace = 5
document.logo.vspace = 8
```

Value   Integer of pixel count.

Default   0

marginHeight, marginWidth   NN *n/a*   IE *4*   DOM *n/a*

Read/Write

Should control the number of pixels between the inner edge of a frame and the content rendered inside the frame, but in practice these properties have no effect on the rendered content in Internet Explorer 4.

Value   Positive integer value or zero.

Default   None.

name

Read/Write

The identifier associated with a frame for use as the value assigned to TARGET attributes or as script references to the frame. The value is usually assigned via the NAME attribute, but it can be modified by script if necessary.

Value

Case-sensitive identifier that follows the rules of identifier naming: it may contain no whitespace, cannot begin with a numeral, and should avoid punctuation except for the underscore character.

Default   None.

noResize

Read/Write

Whether the frame can be resized by the user. In Internet Explorer 4, an inline frame cannot be resized, so this property is superfluous.

Value   Boolean value: true | false.

Default   false

scrolling

Read/Write

The treatment of scrollbars for a frame when the content exceeds the visible area of the frame. You can force a frame to display scrollbars at all times or never. Or you can let the browser determine the need for scrolling. In IE 4 for the Macintosh, only the vertical scrollbar is turned off when this property is set to no.

Example   `document.all.mainFrame.scrolling = "yes"`

Value   One of three constants (as a string): auto | no | yes.

Default   auto

src

Read/Write

URL of the external content file loaded into the current element. To change the content, assign a new URL to the property.

Example   `document.all.myIframe.src = "section2.html"`

Value   Complete or relative URL as a string.

Default   None.

DOM Reference

tabIndex

NN *n/a*   IE *4*   DOM *n/a*

Read/Write

A number that indicates the sequence of this element within the tabbing order of all focusable elements in the document. In practice, the `tabIndex` property setting has no effect on user interaction with an inline frame.

Value   Integer.

Default   None.

vspace

See hspace.

images

NN *3*   IE *4*   DOM *n/a*

An array of all **IMG** objects contained by the document. This object is implemented only in browser versions that treat images as objects. Therefore, you can use the existence of this array object as a conditional switch surrounding statements that swap or preload images:

```
if (document.images) {
    image object statements here
}
```

Internet Explorer 3 for the Macintosh provided support for images as objects.

Object Model Reference

NN   document.images[i]

IE   document.images[i]
          document.images(i)

Properties
length

Methods
item()

length

NN *3*   IE *4*   DOM *n/a*

Read-only

Returns the number of elements in the collection.

Example var howMany = document.images.length

Value   Integer.

item()

NN *n/a*   IE *4*   DOM *n/a*

item(*index*[, *subindex*])

Returns a single object or collection of objects corresponding to the element matching the index value (or, optionally, the index and subindex values).

Returned Value

One object or collection (array) of objects. If there are no matches to the parameters, the returned value is null.

Parameters

index   When the parameter is a zero-based integer, the returned value is a single element corresponding to the said numbered item in source code order (nested within the current element); when the parameter is a string, the returned value is a collection of elements whose id or name properties match that string.

subindex If you specify a string value for the first parameter, you may use the second parameter to specify a zero-based integer to retrieve a specific element from the collection whose id or name properties match the first parameter's string value.

IMG   NN *3*   IE *4*   DOM *1*

The IMG object reflects the IMG element.

HTML Equivalent

`<IMG>`

Object Model Reference

NN   [window.]document.*imageName*
        [window.]document.images[i]

IE   [window.]document.*imageName*
        [window.]document.images[i]
        [window.]document.all.*elementID*

Properties

align	height	lowsrc	*outerText*	*style*
alt	href	name	*parentElement*	*tagName*
border	hspace	*offsetHeight*	*parentTextEdit*	*title*
className	*id*	*offsetLeft*	prototype	useMap
complete	isMap	*offsetParent*	readyState	vspace
dataFld	*isTextEdit*	*offsetTop*	*sourceIndex*	width
dataSrc	*lang*	*offsetWidth*	src	x
document	*language*	*outerHTML*	start	y
dynsrc	loop			

Methods

blur()	*getAttribute()*	*removeAttribute()*
click()	*insertAdjacentHTML()*	*scrollIntoView()*
contains()	*insertAdjacentText()*	*setAttribute()*
focus()		

Collections/Arrays

all[]	*children[]*	*filters[]*

Event Handler Properties

Handler	NN	IE	DOM
onabort	3	4	n/a
onafterupdate	n/a	4	n/a
onbeforeupdate	n/a	4	n/a
onblur	n/a	4	n/a
onchange	n/a	4	n/a
onclick	n/a	4	n/a
ondataavailable	n/a	4	n/a
ondatasetchanged	n/a	4	n/a
ondatasetcomplete	n/a	4	n/a
ondblclick	n/a	4	n/a
ondragstart	n/a	4	n/a
onerror	3	4	n/a
onfilterchange	n/a	4	n/a
onfocus	n/a	4	n/a
onhelp	n/a	4	n/a
onkeydown	n/a	4	n/a
onkeypress	n/a	4	n/a
onkeyup	n/a	4	n/a
onload	3	4	n/a
onmousedown	n/a	4	n/a
onmousemove	n/a	4	n/a
onmouseout	n/a	4	n/a
onmouseover	n/a	4	n/a
onmouseup	n/a	4	n/a
onresize	n/a	4	n/a
onrowenter	n/a	4	n/a
onrowexit	n/a	4	n/a
onscroll	n/a	4	n/a
onselectstart	n/a	4	n/a

align   NN *n/a*   IE *4*   DOM *1*

Read/Write

Defines how the element is aligned relative to surrounding text content. Most values set the vertical relationship between the element and surrounding text. For example, to align the bottom of the element with the baseline of the surrounding text, the `align` property value would be `baseline`. An element can be "floated" along the left or right margin to let surrounding text wrap around the element.

Example   `document.logoImg.align = "absmiddle"`

Value

Any of the following alignment constant values (as a string): `absbottom` | `absmiddle` | `baseline` | `bottom` | `right` | `left` | `none` | `texttop` | `top`.

Default   `bottom`

alt

Read/Write

Text to be displayed where the **IMG** element appears on the page when a browser does not download graphics (or is waiting for the image to download). The text is usually a brief description of what the image is. Be aware that the size of the image area on the page may limit the amount of text you can assign to the `alt` property. Make sure the description is readable.

Example `document.corpLogo.alt = "MegaCorp Logo"`

Value   Any quoted string of characters.

Default   None.

border

Read/Write (IE)

Thickness of the border around an element (in pixels). While Internet Explorer 4 draws a border around an existing image when you change this property, the property is read-only in Navigator 4.

Example `document.logoImage.border = 4`

Value

An integer value. A setting of zero removes the border entirely in Internet Explorer 4.

Default   0

complete

Read-only

Reveals whether the **IMG** element's **SRC** image file has fully loaded. Note that Navigator 4 provides an incorrect **true** reading before the image has completely loaded.

Example
```
if (document.logo.complete) {
    safe to process the image object
}
```

Value   Boolean value: **true** | **false**.

Default   false

dataFld

Read/Write

Used with IE 4 data binding to associate a remote data source column name with the **src** property of the **IMG** object. A **DATASRC** attribute must also be set for the element. Setting both the **dataFld** and **dataSrc** properties to empty strings breaks the binding between element and data source.

Example `document.myImage.dataFld = "linkURL"`

Value   Case-sensitive identifier of the data source column.

Default   None.

dataSrc
NN *n/a*   IE *4*   DOM *n/a*

Read/Write

Used with IE 4 data binding to specify the name of the remote ODBC data source (such as an Oracle or SQL Server database) to be associated with the element. Setting both the dataFld and dataSrc properties to empty strings breaks the binding between element and data source.

Example   document.myImage.dataSrc = "#DBSRC3"

Value   Case-sensitive identifier of the data source.

Default   None.

dynsrc
NN *n/a*   IE *4*   DOM *n/a*

Read/Write

URL of a video clip to be displayed through the IMG element. Changing this property loads a new video clip into the image object. See also the loop property for controlling the frequency of video clip play.

Example   document.images[3].dynsrc = "snowman.avi"

Value   Complete or relative URL as a string.

Default   None.

height, width
NN *3*   IE *4*   DOM *1*

Read/Write (IE)

The height and width in pixels of the image element. Changes to these values are immediately reflected in reflowed content on the page in Internet Explorer 4. Be aware that images scale to fit the new dimension.

Example   document.prettyPicture.height = 250

Value   Integer.

Default   None.

href
NN *n/a*   IE *4*   DOM *n/a*

Read/Write

The URL specified by the element's SRC attribute. Identical to the src property.

Example   document.logoImage.href = "images/fancyLogo.gif"

Value   String of complete or relative URL.

Default   None.

hspace, vspace

The pixel measure of horizontal and vertical margins surrounding an image object. The hspace property affects the left and right edges of the element equally; the **vspace** affects the top and bottom edges of the element equally. These margins are not the same as margins set by style sheets, but they have the same visual effect. New values may be assigned to these properties in Internet Explorer 4.

Example
```
document.logo.hspace = 5
document.logo.vspace = 8
```

Value   Integer of pixel count.

Default   0

isMap

Whether the **IMG** element is acting as a server-side image map. For an image to be a server-side image map, it must be wrapped with an A element whose **HREF** attribute points to the URL of the CGI program that knows how to interpret the click coordinate information. The browser appends coordinate information about the click to the URL as a **GET** form method appends form element data to the **ACTION** attribute URL.

More recent browsers allow client-side image maps (see the **useMap** property), which operate more quickly for the user, because there is no communication with the server to carry out the examination of the click coordinate point.

Example   `document.navMap.isMap = true`

Value   Boolean value: `true | false`.

Default   `false`

loop

If you specify a video clip with the **DYNSRC** attribute, the **loop** property controls how many times the clip should play (loop). Changing to a value of **–1** is equal to a continuous loop.

Example   `document.movieImg.loop = 3`

Value   Integer.

Default   1

lowsrc

The URL of a lower-resolution (or alternate) image to download into the document space if the image of the **SRC** attribute will take a long time to download. The **lowsrc** image should be the same pixel size as the primary **SRC** image. It makes sense to change the **lowsrc** property only if you are also going to change the `src` property. In this case, make sure you change the `lowsrc` property first so that the browser knows how to handle the long download for the `src` image.

Example `document.productImage.lowsrc = "images/widget43LoRes.jpg"`

Value Any complete or relative URL as a string.

Default None.

name
NN 2   IE 3   DOM 1
Read/Write

The identifier associated with the image object for use in scripted references to the object.

Example `var imgName = document.images[3].name`

Value

Case-sensitive identifier that follows the rules of identifier naming: it may contain no whitespace, cannot begin with a numeral, and should avoid punctuation except for the underscore character.

Default None.

protocol
NN n/a   IE 4   DOM n/a
Read-only

Normally, this property returns the protocol component of the URL associated with the element. Values for an **IMG** object do not follow the regular format (for local file access, for example, the returned value is `File Protocol` instead of `file:`). This property, which works only in Win32, does not appear to be wired properly.

Value String.

Default None.

prototype
NN n/a   IE 4   DOM n/a
Read-only

Returns a reference to the static **Image** object from which all instances of image objects are created. This mechanism is more commonly used in JavaScript core language objects (see Chapter 11, *JavaScript Core Language Reference*). The fact that this property is available only in Internet Explorer 4 for the Macintosh calls its legitimacy into question.

Value Object reference.

Default `object Image`

readyState
NN n/a   IE 4   DOM n/a
Read-only

Returns the current download status of the image content. This property provides a more granular way of testing whether a particular downloadable element is ready to be run or scripted instead of the onLoad event handler for the entire document. As the value of this property changes during loading, the system fires an onReadyStateChange event.

Example

```
if (document.contentsMap.readyState == "uninitialized") {
    statements for alternate handling
}
```

Value

One of the following values (as strings): complete | interactive | loading | uninitialized. Some elements may allow the user to interact with partial content, in which case the property may return interactive until all loading has completed.

Default   None.

useMap

NN *n/a*   IE *4*   DOM *1*

Read/Write

The URL of the MAP element in the same document that contains client-side image map hot areas and links. The value includes the hashmark assigned with the map name in the USEMAP attribute of the IMG element.

Example   document.images[0].useMap = "#altMap"

Value   A string starting with a hashmark and the name of the MAP element.

Default   None.

vspace

See hspace.

width

See height.

x, y

NN *4*   IE *n/a*   DOM *n/a*

Read-only

The horizontal and vertical pixel coordinates of the top-left corner of the image relative to the page. These are Navigator-only properties, corresponding to the offsetLeft and offsetTop properties of Internet Explorer 4.

Example   var imageFromTop = document.logoImg.y

Value   Integer.

Default   None.

blur()

NN *n/a*   IE *4*   DOM *n/a*

Removes focus from the current element and fires an onBlur event (in IE). No other element necessarily receives focus as a result.

Returned Value

None.

Parameters

None.

focus()   NN *n/a*   IE *4*   DOM *n/a*

Gives focus to the current element and fires the **onFocus** event (in IE). If another element had focus at the time, it receives an **onBlur** event.

Returned Value

None.

Parameters

None.

INPUT   NN *n/a*   IE *4*   DOM *1*

The **INPUT** object reflects the **INPUT** element. See the individual descriptions for each **INPUT** object type: **button, checkbox, fileUpload, hidden, password, radio, reset, submit,** and **text**.

INS   NN *n/a*   IE *4*   DOM *1*

The **INS** object reflects the **INS** element.

HTML Equivalent

<INS>

Object Model Reference

IE   [window.]document.all.*elementID*

Properties

cite	innerHTML	offsetHeight	outerHTML	sourceIndex
className	innerText	offsetLeft	outerText	style
dateTime	isTextEdit	offsetParent	parentElement	tagName
document	lang	offsetTop	parentTextEdit	title
id	language	offsetWidth		

Methods

click()	insertAdjacentHTML()	scrollIntoView()
contains()	insertAdjacentText()	setAttribute()
getAttribute()	removeAttribute()	

Collections/Arrays

`all[]`   `children[]`

Event Handler Properties

Handler	NN	IE	DOM
onclick	n/a	4	n/a
ondblclick	n/a	4	n/a
ondragstart	n/a	4	n/a
onfilterchange	n/a	4	n/a
onhelp	n/a	4	n/a
onkeydown	n/a	4	n/a
onkeypress	n/a	4	n/a
onkeyup	n/a	4	n/a
onmousedown	n/a	4	n/a
onmousemove	n/a	4	n/a
onmouseout	n/a	4	n/a
onmouseover	n/a	4	n/a
onmouseup	n/a	4	n/a
onselectstart	n/a	4	n/a

cite   NN *n/a*   IE *n/a*   DOM *1*

Read/Write

A description of the reason for the change or other notation to be associated with the element, but normally hidden from view.

Value

Any string of characters. The string must be inside a matching pair of (single or double) quotation marks.

Default   None.

dateTime   NN *n/a*   IE *n/a*   DOM *1*

Read/Write

The date and time the deletion was made.

Value

See the description of the DATETIME attribute of the DEL element in Chapter 8 for value formatting details.

Default   None.

ISINDEX   NN *n/a*   IE *n/a*   DOM *1*

The ISINDEX object reflects the ISINDEX element. Since this element is deprecated in HTML 4.0 and is omitted from Internet Explorer 4's developer documentation, it wouldn't be surprising if this object disappears before the DOM recommendation is released. The description of the prompt property is purely speculative, based on the corresponding attribute in the HTML element.

HTML Equivalent

```
<ISINDEX>
```

Properties

prompt

prompt   NN *n/a*   IE *n/a*   DOM *1*

Read/Write

The prompt message for the text entry field.

Value   String.

Default   None.

KBD

See ACRONYM.

LABEL   NN *n/a*   IE *4*   DOM *1*

The LABEL object reflects the LABEL element.

HTML Equivalent

```
<LABEL>
```

Object Model Reference

IE   [window.]document.all.*elementID*

Properties

accessKey	htmlFor	lang	offsetTop	parentTextEdit
className	id	language	offsetWidth	sourceIndex
document	innerHTML	offsetHeight	outerHTML	style
dataFld	innerText	offsetLeft	outerText	tagName
dataFormatAs	isTextEdit	offsetParent	parentElement	title
dataSrc				

Methods

click()	insertAdjacentHTML()	scrollIntoView()
contains()	insertAdjacentText()	setAttribute()
getAttribute()	removeAttribute()	

Collections/Arrays

all[]	children[]	filters[]

Event Handler Properties

Handler	NN	IE	DOM
onclick	n/a	4	n/a
ondblclick	n/a	4	n/a
ondragstart	n/a	4	n/a
onfilterchange	n/a	4	n/a
onhelp	n/a	4	n/a
onkeydown	n/a	4	n/a
onkeypress	n/a	4	n/a
onkeyup	n/a	4	n/a
onmousedown	n/a	4	n/a
onmousemove	n/a	4	n/a
onmouseout	n/a	4	n/a
onmouseover	n/a	4	n/a
onmouseup	n/a	4	n/a
onselectstart	n/a	4	n/a

accessKey

NN *n/a*   IE *4*   DOM *1*

Read/Write

A single character key that brings focus to the **INPUT** element associated with the **LABEL** element. The browser and operating system determine whether the user must press a modifier key (e.g., **Ctrl**, **Alt**, or **Command**) with the access key to bring focus to the related element. In IE 4/Windows, the **Alt** key is required, and the key is not case sensitive. Not working in IE 4/Mac.

Example   document.entryForm.firstNameLabel.accessKey = "n"

Value   Single alphanumeric (and punctuation) keyboard character.

Default   None.

dataFld

NN *n/a*   IE *4*   DOM *n/a*

Read/Write

Used with IE 4 data binding to associate a remote data source column name with the displayed text of the input element label. A **DATASRC** attribute must also be set for the element. Setting both the **dataFld** and **dataSrc** properties to empty strings breaks the binding between element and data source.

Example   document.all.myLabel.dataFld = "labelText"

Value   Case-sensitive identifier of the data source column.

Default   None.

dataFormatAs

NN *n/a*   IE *4*   DOM *n/a*

Read/Write

Used with IE 4 data binding, this property advises the browser whether the source material arriving from the data source is to be treated as plain text or as tagged HTML.

Example   document.forms[0].myLabel.dataFormatAs = "HTML"

Value   IE 4 recognizes two possible settings: **text** | **HTML**.

Default   text

dataSrc   NN *n/a*   IE *4*   DOM *n/a*

Read/Write

Used with IE 4 data binding to specify the name of the remote ODBC data source (such as an Oracle or SQL Server database) to be associated with the element. Setting both the dataFld and dataSrc properties to empty strings breaks the binding between element and data source.

Example   document.all.myLabel.dataSrc = "#DBSRC3"

Value   Case-sensitive identifier of the data source.

Default   None.

htmlFor   NN *n/a*   IE *4*   DOM *n/a*

Read/Write

The element ID of the INPUT element to which the label is associated (the value of the FOR attribute). Binds the LABEL element to a particular INPUT element.

Example   document.all.label3.htmlFor = "chkbox3"

Value   String.

Default   None.

layer   NN *4*   IE *n/a*   DOM *n/a*

The layer object reflects the LAYER and ILAYER elements.

HTML Equivalent
<ILAYER>
<LAYER>

Object Model Reference
NN   [window.]document.layerName

Properties

above	clip	left	parentLayer	top
background	*document*	name	siblingAbove	visibility
below	hidden	pageX	siblingBelow	zIndex
bgColor	*id*	pageY	src	

Methods

load()	moveBy()	resizeBy()
moveAbove()	moveTo()	resizeTo()
moveBelow()	moveToAbsolute()	

Event Handler Properties

Handler	NN	IE	DOM
onblur	4	n/a	n/a
onfocus	4	n/a	n/a
onload	4	n/a	n/a
onmouseout	4	n/a	n/a
onmouseover	4	n/a	n/a
onmouseup	4	n/a	n/a

above, below

NN *4*   IE *n/a*   DOM *n/a*

Read-only

Return a reference to the positionable element whose stacking z-order is above or below the current element. These properties operate in the context of all positionable elements in a document. If the current element is the highest element, the **above** property returns **null**. To restrict the examination of next higher or lower elements within a single layer context, see **siblingAbove** and **siblingBelow**. To adjust the stacking order with respect to specific objects, see the **moveAbove()** and **moveBelow()** methods.

Example var nextHigher = document.myILayer.above

Value   Object reference or **null**.

Default None.

background

NN *4*   IE *n/a*   DOM *n/a*

Read/Write

This property holds an image object whose **src** property can be set to change the image used for the layer's background. In other words, you must set this property of the object.

Example document.myIlayer.background.src = "images/newlogo.gif"

Value   An image object property, such as **src**.

Default None.

bgColor

NN *4*   IE *n/a*   DOM *n/a*

Read/Write

Background color of the element. While you may set the value with either a hexadecimal triplet or plain-language color value, values returned from the property are for some reason the decimal equivalent of the hexadecimal RGB version. The default behavior is a transparent background created with a **bgColor** property value of **null**.

Example document.myIlayer.bgColor = "yellow"

Value

A hexadecimal triplet or plain-language color name. See Appendix A for acceptable plain-language color names. Returned values are the decimal equivalent of the hexadecimal value. A value of null sets the background to transparent.

Default   null (transparent).

clip   NN *4*   IE *n/a*   DOM *n/a*

Read/Write

Defines a clipping region of a positionable element. This property is treated more like an object in itself in that you adjust its values through six properties: clip.top, clip.left, clip.bottom, clip.right, clip.width, and clip.height. Adjust the side(s) or dimension(s) of your choice. All values represent pixel values.

Example document.myIlayer.clip.width = 150

Value   Integer.

Default None.

hidden   NN *4*   IE *n/a*   DOM *n/a*

Read/Write

Whether the object is visible on the page. When the object is hidden, its surrounding content does not close the gap left by the element.

Example document.myIlayer.hidden = false

Value   Boolean value: true | false.

Default false

left   NN *4*   IE *n/a*   DOM *n/a*

Read/Write

For positionable elements, defines the position of the left edge of an element's box (content plus left padding, border, and/or margin) relative to the left edge of the next outermost block content container. For the relative-positioned layer, the offset is based on the left edge of the inline location of where the element would normally appear in the content.

Example document.myIlayer.left = 45

Value   Integer.

Default 0

name   NN *4*   IE *n/a*   DOM *n/a*

Read-only

The identifier associated with a layer for use as the value assigned to TARGET attributes or as script references to the frame. If no value is explicitly assigned to the ID attribute, Navigator automatically assigns the NAME attribute value to the ID attribute.

Example
```
if (document.layers[2].name == "main") {
    ...
}
```

Value

Case-sensitive identifier that follows the rules of identifier naming: it may contain no whitespace, cannot begin with a numeral, and should avoid punctuation except for the underscore character.

Default   None.

pageX, pageY

NN *4*   IE *n/a*   DOM *n/a*

Read/Write

The horizontal (x) and vertical (y) position of the object relative to the top and left edges of the entire document.

Example   `document.myIlayer.pageX = 400`

Value   Integer.

Default   None.

parentLayer

NN *4*   IE *n/a*   DOM *n/a*

Read-only

Returns a reference to the next outermost layer in the containment hierarchy. For a single layer in a document, its `parentLayer` is the `window` object.

Example
```
if (parentLayer != window) {
    ...
}
```

Value   Object reference (a `layer` or `window`).

Default   `window`

siblingAbove, siblingBelow

NN *4*   IE *n/a*   DOM *n/a*

Read-only

Return a reference to the positionable element whose stacking z-order is above or below the current element, but only within the context of the shared `parentLayer`. If the current element is the highest element, the `siblingAbove` property returns `null`. To widen the examination of next higher or lower elements to a document-wide context, see `above` and `below`. To adjust the stacking order with respect to specific objects, see the `moveAbove()` and `moveBelow()` methods.

Example   `var nextHigher = document.myILayer.siblingAbove`

Value   Object reference or `null`.

Default   None.

src
NN 4   IE *n/a*   DOM *n/a*

Read/Write

URL of the external content file loaded into the current element. To change the content, assign a new URL to the property.

Assigning a new URL to this property does not work with inline layers (ILAYER elements) in Navigator 4. Instead the current source document is removed, and other page elements can be obscured. Avoid setting this property for inline layers until this problem is fixed. The same goes for the load() method.

Example   document.myIlayer.src = "swap2.html"

Value   Complete or relative URL as a string.

Default   None.

top
NN 4   IE *n/a*   DOM *n/a*

Read/Write

For positionable elements, defines the position of the top edge of an element's box (content plus top padding, border, and/or margin) relative to the top edge of the next outermost block content container. All measures are in pixels. When the element is a relative-positioned inline layer, the offset is based on the top edge of the inline location of where the element would normally appear in the content.

Example   document.myIlayer.top = 50

Value   Integer.

Default   0

visibility
NN 4   IE *n/a*   DOM *n/a*

Read/Write

The state of the positioned element's visibility. Surrounding content does not close the space left by an element whose visibility property is set to hide (or the CSS version, hidden). If you set the property to the CSS syntax values (hidden | visible), they are converted internally to the JavaScript versions and returned from the property in that format.

Example   document.myIlayer.visibility = "hide"

Value   One of the constant values (as a string): hide | inherit | show.

Default   inherit

zIndex

NN 4   IE *n/a*   DOM *n/a*

Read/Write

For a positioned element, the stacking order relative to other elements within the same parent container. See Chapter 4 for details on relationships of element layering amid multiple containers.

Example `document.myIlayer.zIndex = 3`

Value   Integer.

Default   0

captureEvents()

NN 4   IE *n/a*   DOM *n/a*

`captureEvents(eventTypeList)`

Instructs the browser to grab events of a specific type before they reach their intended target objects. The object invoking this method must then have event handlers defined for the given event types to process the event. See Chapter 6.

Returned Value

None.

Parameters

eventTypeList

> A comma-separated list of case-sensitive event types as derived from the available **Event** object constants, such as **Event.CLICK** or **Event.MOUSEMOVE**.

handleEvent()

NN 4   IE *n/a*   DOM *n/a*

`handleEvent(event)`

Instructs the object to accept and process the event whose specifications are passed as the parameter to the method. The object must have an event handler for the event type to process the event. See Chapter 6.

Returned Value

None.

Parameters

event   A Navigator 4 **event** object.

load()

NN 4   IE *n/a*   DOM *n/a*

`load("URL", newLayerWidth)`

This method lets you load a new document into a **layer** object. It does not work properly in Navigator 4 for **ILAYER** elements. The existing document is unloaded from the layer, but the new one does not load as you'd expect. There is no satisfactory workaround except to transform the element into a **LAYER**.

Returned Value

Boolean value: true if the document loading was successful.

Parameters

URL   String value of the complete or relative URL of the document to be loaded into the layer.

newLayerWidth
           Integer value in pixels of a resized width of the element to accommodate the new content.

moveAbove(), moveBelow()   NN *4*   IE *n/a*   DOM *n/a*

```
moveAbove(layerObject)
moveBelow(layerObject)
```

These methods shift the z-order of the current layer to a specific location relative to another, sibling layer. This is helpful if your script is not sure of the precise zIndex value of a layer you want to use as a reference point for the current layer's stacking order. Use moveAbove() to position the current layer immediately above the layer object referenced as a parameter.

Returned Value

None.

Parameters

layerObject
           Reference to another layer object that shares the same parent as the current layer.

moveBy()   NN *4*   IE *n/a*   DOM *n/a*

```
moveBy(deltaX, deltaY)
```

A convenience method that shifts the location of the current element by specified pixel amounts along both axes. To shift along only one axis, set the other value to zero. Positive values for *deltaX* shift the element to the right; negative values to the left. Positive values for *deltaY* shift the element downward; negative values upward. This method comes in handy for path animation under the control of a setInterval() or setTimeout() method that moves the element in a linear path over time.

Returned Value

None.

Parameters

deltaX   Positive or negative pixel count of the change in horizontal direction of the element.

deltaY   Positive or negative pixel count of the change in vertical direction of the element.

moveTo( ), moveToAbsolute( ) NN *4* IE *n/a* DOM *n/a*

```
moveTo(x, y)
moveToAbsolute(x, y)
```

Convenience methods that shift the location of the current element to a specific coordinate point. The differences between the two methods show when the element to be moved is nested inside another positioned container (e.g., a layer inside a layer). The moveTo() method uses the coordinate system of the parent container; the moveToAbsolute() method uses the coordinate system of the page. For a single layer on a page, the two methods yield the same result.

Returned Value

None.

Parameters

x	Positive or negative pixel count relative to the top of the reference container, whether it be the next outermost layer (moveTo()) or the page (moveToAbsolute()).
y	Positive or negative pixel count relative to the left edge of the reference container, whether it be the next outermost layer (moveTo()) or the page (moveToAbsolute()).

releaseEvents( ) NN *4* IE *n/a* DOM *n/a*

```
releaseEvents(eventTypeList)
```

The opposite of *layerObj*.captureEvents(), this method turns off event capture at the layer level for one or more specific events named in the parameter list. See Chapter 6.

Returned Value

None.

Parameters

eventTypeList
> A comma-separated list of case-sensitive event types as derived from the available Event object constants, such as Event.CLICK or Event.MOUSEMOVE.

resizeBy( ) NN *4* IE *n/a* DOM *n/a*

```
resizeBy(deltaX, deltaY)
```

A convenience method that shifts the width and height of the current element by specified pixel amounts. To adjust along only one axis, set the other value to zero. Positive values for *deltaX* make the element wider; negative values make the element narrower. Positive values for *deltaY* make the element taller; negative values make the element shorter. The top and bottom edges remain fixed; only the right and bottom edges are moved.

Returned Value

None.

DOM Reference

Parameters

deltaX   Positive or negative pixel count of the change in horizontal dimension of the element.

deltaY   Positive or negative pixel count of the change in vertical dimension of the element.

resizeTo()   NN *4*   IE *n/a*   DOM *n/a*

resizeTo(x, y)

Convenience method that adjusts the height and width of the current element to specific pixel sizes. The top and left edges of the element remain fixed, while the bottom and right edges move in response to this method.

Returned Value

None.

Parameters

x   Width in pixels of the element.

y   Height in pixels of the element.

routeEvent()   NN *4*   IE *n/a*   DOM *n/a*

routeEvent(event)

Used inside an event handler function, this method directs Navigator to let the event pass to its intended target object. See Chapter 6.

Returned Value

None.

Parameters

event   A Navigator 4 **event** object.

LEGEND   NN *n/a*   IE *4*   DOM *1*

The LEGEND object reflects the LEGEND element. A LEGEND element must be nested inside and immediately after the FIELDSET element associated with a form or group of form controls.

HTML Equivalent

<LEGEND>

Object Model Reference

IE   [window.]document.all.*elementID*

Properties

accessKey	*document*	*language*	*outerHTML*	scrollTop
align	*id*	*offsetHeight*	outerText	scrollWidth
className	*innerHTML*	*offsetLeft*	*parentElement*	*sourceIndex*
clientHeight	*innerText*	*offsetParent*	*parentTextEdit*	*style*
clientLeft	*isTextEdit*	*offsetTop*	scrollHeight	*tagName*
clientTop	*lang*	*offsetWidth*	scrollLeft	*title*
clientWidth				

Methods

blur()	*getAttribute()*	*removeAttribute()*
click()	*insertAdjacentHTML()*	*scrollIntoView()*
contains()	*insertAdjacentText()*	*setAttribute()*
focus()		

Collections/Arrays

all[]	*children[]*	*filters[]*

Event Handler Properties

Handler	NN	IE	DOM
onblur	n/a	4	n/a
onchange	n/a	4	n/a
onclick	n/a	4	n/a
ondblclick	n/a	4	n/a
ondragstart	n/a	4	n/a
onfocus	n/a	4	n/a
onhelp	n/a	4	n/a
onkeydown	n/a	4	n/a
onkeypress	n/a	4	n/a
onkeyup	n/a	4	n/a
onmousedown	n/a	4	n/a
onmousemove	n/a	4	n/a
onmouseout	n/a	4	n/a
onmouseover	n/a	4	n/a
onmouseup	n/a	4	n/a
onscroll	n/a	4	n/a
onselectstart	n/a	4	n/a

accessKey   NN *n/a*   IE *4*   DOM *n/a*

Read/Write

A single character key that brings focus to an element or, in the case of a LEGEND element, to the first focusable form control in the associated FIELDSET element. The browser and operating system determine whether the user must press a modifier key (e.g., **Ctrl**, **Alt**, or **Command**) with the access key to bring focus to the related element. In IE 4/Windows, the **Alt** key is required, and the key is not case sensitive. Not working in IE 4/Mac.

Example `document.all.myLegend.accessKey = "n"`

Value Single alphanumeric (and punctuation) keyboard character.

Default None.

align

NN *n/a*   IE *4*   DOM *1*

Read/Write

Controls the alignment of the LEGEND element with respect to the containing FIELDSET element. The permissible values do not always work as planned in Internet Explorer 4. For example, the `bottom` value displays the label at the top left of the fieldset rectangle. So does the `top` value, although it is supposed to be centered along the top. The other values (`center`, `left`, and `right`) work as expected, but on the Macintosh, the `center` and `right` settings inexplicably widen the fieldset rectangle. Be sure to check your desired setting on both operating system platforms.

Example `document.all.myLegend.align = "center"`

Value

Any one of the following constant values (as a string): `bottom` | `center` | `left` | `right` | `top`.

Default `left`

clientHeight, clientWidth

NN *n/a*   IE *4*   DOM *n/a*

Read/Write

According to Microsoft's developer documentation, these properties reflect the height and width (in pixels) of the element's content. But see the section "About client- and offset-Properties" at the beginning of this chapter for details.

Example `var midHeight = document.all.myLegend.clientHeight/2`

Value Integer pixel value.

Default None.

clientLeft, clientTop

NN *n/a*   IE *4*   DOM *n/a*

Read-only

According to Microsoft's developer documentation, these properties reflect the distance between the "true" left and top edges of the document area and the edges of the element. But see the section "About client- and offset- Properties" at the beginning of this chapter for details. To get or set the pixel position of an element in the document, use the `pixelLeft` and `pixelTop` properties.

Value A string value for a length in a variety of units or percentage.

Default None.

scrollHeight, scrollWidth

NN *n/a*   IE *4*   DOM *n/a*

Read-only

The meaning of these two properties is ambiguous based on Microsoft's description and the way they're implemented in the Windows and Macintosh versions of Internet Explorer 4. My best guess is that these properties are intended to measure the height and width (in pixels) of the content of an element even when some of the content cannot be seen unless scrolled with scrollbars. The Macintosh version of the browser interprets this to mean the amount of the content that you can see at any one time. The important point is that for key elements, such as the BODY, the properties mean different things and can disrupt cross-platform operation.

Example   var midPoint = document.all.myLegend.scrollHeight/2

Value   Positive integer or zero.

Default   None.

scrollLeft, scrollTop

NN *n/a*   IE *4*   DOM *n/a*

Read/Write

The distance in pixels between the actual left or top edge of the element's physical content and the left or top edge of the visible portion of the content. Changing these properties appears to have no visual effect in Internet Explorer.

Example   document.all.myLegend.scrollTop = 40

Value   Positive integer or zero.

Default   0

blur()

NN *n/a*   IE *4*   DOM *n/a*

Removes focus from the current element and fires an onBlur event (in IE). No other element necessarily receives focus as a result.

Returned Value

None.

Parameters

None.

focus()

NN *n/a*   IE *4*   DOM *n/a*

Gives focus to the current element and fires the onFocus event (in IE). If another element had focus at the time, it receives an onBlur event.

Returned Value

None.

Parameters

None.

LI

The LI object reflects the LI element.

HTML Equivalent

`<LI>`

Object Model Reference

IE   `[window.]document.all.elementID`

Properties

className	isTextEdit	offsetParent	parentElement	tagName
document	lang	offsetTop	parentTextEdit	title
id	language	offsetWidth	sourceIndex	type
innerHTML	offsetHeight	outerHTML	style	value
innerText	offsetLeft	outerText		

Methods

click()	insertAdjacentHTML()	scrollIntoView()
contains()	insertAdjacentText()	setAttribute()
getAttribute()	removeAttribute()	

Collections/Arrays

all[]	children[]	filters[]

Event Handler Properties

Handler	NN	IE	DOM
onclick	n/a	4	n/a
ondblclick	n/a	4	n/a
ondragstart	n/a	4	n/a
onfilterchange	n/a	4	n/a
onhelp	n/a	4	n/a
onkeydown	n/a	4	n/a
onkeypress	n/a	4	n/a
onkeyup	n/a	4	n/a
onmousedown	n/a	4	n/a
onmousemove	n/a	4	n/a
onmouseout	n/a	4	n/a
onmouseover	n/a	4	n/a
onmouseup	n/a	4	n/a
onselectstart	n/a	4	n/a

type

Read/Write

The manner in which the leading bullets, numbers, or letters of items in the list are displayed. Bullet styles are displayed when the LI element is nested inside a UL element;

numbers and letters for an OL element. If your script changes the type for a single LI object, be aware that the change affects all subsequent LI elements in the same list.

Example
```
document.all.instruxListItem3.type = "a"
document.all.point4.type = "square"
```

Value

For an OL style list, possible values are: A | a | I | i | 1. Sequencing is performed automatically as follows:

Type	Example
A	A, B, C, ...
a	a, b, c, ...
I	I, II, III, ...
i	i, ii, iii, ...
1	1, 2, 3, ...

For a UL–style list, possible values are: circle | disc | square.

Default   1 and disc

value   NN *n/a*   IE *4*   DOM *1*

Read/Write

The number of the item within an ordered list. This property applies to an LI element only when it is nested inside an OL element. The default value for unadjusted numbering is always zero. If you set the **value** property of one item in the list, the following items continue the sequence from the new value.

Example   `document.all.step5.value = 5`

Value   Positive integer.

Default   0

LINK   NN *n/a*   IE *4*   DOM *1*

The LINK object reflects the LINK element. Note that many of the properties listed here are not available for scripting in the object unless their corresponding attributes are set initially in the HTML tag. This includes: href, rel, rev, and type. The media property is not available in the Macintosh version of IE 4. Fortunately, there is little need to script this object, since the impact of the LINK element is felt by the browser as the document loads.

HTML Equivalent
```
<LINK>
```

Object Model Reference
```
IE        [window.]document.all.elementID
```

Properties

className	href	parentElement	rel	tagName
disabled	id	parentTextEdit	rev	title
document	media	readyState	sourceIndex	type

Methods

contains()   removeAttribute()   setAttribute()
getAttribute()

Collections/Arrays

all[]   children[]

Event Handler Properties

Handler	NN	IE	DOM
onerror	n/a	4	n/a
onload	n/a	4	n/a
onreadystatechange	n/a	4	n/a

---

disabled   NN *n/a*   IE *4*   DOM *n/a*

Read/Write

Whether information from the LINK element should be applied. For example, if the LINK element loads an external style sheet, you can disable the style sheet from a script by setting the LINK object's disabled property to true.

Example   document.all.styleLink.disabled = true

Value   Boolean value: true | false.

Default   false

---

href   NN *n/a*   IE *4*   DOM *1*

Read/Write

The URL specified by the element's HREF attribute. For example, to swap external style sheets after the page has loaded, assign an alternate style sheet file to the href property. This property is read-only in IE 4/Macintosh.

Example   document.all.styleLink.href = "altStyles.css"

Value   String of complete or relative URL.

Default   None.

---

media   NN *n/a*   IE *4*   DOM *1*

Read/Write

The intended output device for the content of the destination document pointed to by the HREF attribute. The media property looks forward to the day when browsers are able to tailor content to specific kinds of devices such as pocket computers, text-to-speech digitizers, or fuzzy television sets. This property is not available in IE 4/Macintosh.

Example `document.all.link3.media = "print"`

Value   Any one of the following constant values as a string: `all` | `print` | `screen`.

Default   `all`

readyState   NN *n/a*   IE *4*   DOM *n/a*

Read-only

Returns the current download status of the embedded content. This property provides a more granular way of testing whether a particular downloadable element is ready to be run or scripted instead of the `onLoad` event handler for the entire document. As the value of this property changes during loading, the system fires an `onReadyStateChange` event.

Example

```
if (document.all.myLink.readyState != "complete") {
    statements for alternate handling
}
```

Value

One of the following values (as strings): `complete` | `interactive` | `loading` | `uninitialized`. Some elements may allow the user to interact with partial content, in which case the property may return `interactive` until all loading has completed.

Default   None.

rel   NN *n/a*   IE *4*   DOM *1*

Read/Write

Defines the relationship between the current element and the destination of the link. Also known as a *forward link*, not to be confused in any way with the destination document whose address is defined by the HREF attribute. This property is not exploited yet in Internet Explorer 4, but you can treat the attribute as a kind of parameter to be checked and/or modified under script control. See the discussion of the A element's REL attribute in Chapter 8 for a glimpse of how this property may be used in the future.

Value

Case-insensitive, space-delimited list of HTML 4.0 standard link types (as a single string) applicable to the element. Sanctioned link types are:

alternate	contents	index	start
appendix	copyright	next	stylesheet
bookmark	glossary	prev	subsection
chapter	help	section	

Default   None.

rev

NN *n/a*   IE *4*   DOM *1*

Read/Write

Defines the relationship between the current element and the destination of the link. Also known as a *reverse link*. This property is not exploited yet in Internet Explorer 4, but you can treat the attribute as a kind of parameter to be checked and/or modified under script control. See the discussion of the A element's REV attribute in Chapter 8 for a glimpse of how this property may be used in the future.

Value

Case-insensitive, space-delimited list of HTML 4.0 standard link types (as a single string) applicable to the element. See the rel property for sanctioned link types.

Default   None.

type

NN *n/a*   IE *4*   DOM *n/a*

Read/Write

An advisory MIME type declaration about the data being loaded from an external source. For example, an external style sheet would be text/css. This information is usually set in the element tag's TYPE attribute.

Example

```
if (document.all.myStyle.type ==  "text/css") {
    ...
}
```

Value   String.

Default   None.

links

NN *2*   IE *3*   DOM *n/a*

A collection of all A elements whose assigned HREF attributes make them behave as links (instead of only anchors). Collection members are sorted in source code order. Navigator and Internet Explorer let you use array notation to access a single link in the collection (document.links[0] or document.links["section3"], for example). Internet Explorer 4 also allows the index value to be placed inside parentheses instead of brackets (document.links(0), for example). If you wish to use the link's name as an index value (always as a string identifier), be sure to use the value of the NAME attribute, rather than the ID attribute. To use the ID attribute in a reference to an anchor, access the object via a document.all.*elementID* reference.

Object Model Reference

NN	document.links[i]
IE	document.links(i)
	document.links[i]

Properties

length

LISTING   643

length

Read-only

Returns the number of elements in the collection.

Example   `var howMany = document.links.length`

Value   Integer.

LISTING

The LISTING object reflects the LISTING element.

HTML Equivalent

`<LISTING>`

Object Model Reference

IE   `[window.]document.all.`*elementID*

Properties

className	*isTextEdit*	*offsetLeft*	*outerHTML*	*sourceIndex*
document	*lang*	*offsetParent*	*outerText*	*style*
id	*language*	*offsetTop*	*parentElement*	*tagName*
innerHTML	*offsetHeight*	*offsetWidth*	*parentTextEdit*	*title*
innerText				

Methods

click()	*insertAdjacentHTML()*	*scrollIntoView()*
contains()	*insertAdjacentText()*	*setAttribute()*
getAttribute()	*removeAttribute()*	

Collections/Arrays

all[]	*children[]*	*filters[]*

Event Handler Properties

Handler	NN	IE	DOM
onclick	n/a	4	n/a
ondblclick	n/a	4	n/a
ondragstart	n/a	4	n/a
onfilterchange	n/a	4	n/a
onhelp	n/a	4	n/a
onkeydown	n/a	4	n/a
onkeypress	n/a	4	n/a
onkeyup	n/a	4	n/a
onmousedown	n/a	4	n/a
onmousemove	n/a	4	n/a
onmouseout	n/a	4	n/a
onmouseover	n/a	4	n/a

DOM Reference

Handler	NN	IE	DOM
onmouseup	n/a	4	n/a
onselectstart	n/a	4	n/a

location   NN *2*   IE *3*   DOM *1*

There is one `location` object in each window or frame. The object stores all information about the URL of the document currently loaded into that window or frame. By assigning a new URL to the `href` property of the `location` object, you instruct the browser to load a new page into the window or frame. This is the primary way of scripting the loading of a new page:

```
location.href = "newPage.html"
```

A script in one frame can reference the `location` object in another frame to load a new document into that other frame:

```
parent.otherFrameName.location.href = "newPage.html"
```

Security restrictions prevent a script in one frame from accessing `location` object information in another frame if the document in the second frame does not come from the same domain as the document with the nosy script. This prevents a rogue script from monitoring navigation in another frame to external web sites. In Navigator 4, you can overcome the security restriction with the help of signed scripts (a topic more suitable for a JavaScript book covering Navigator 4), but the user still has to give explicit permission for a script to access location object information outside the script's domain.

Object Model Reference

NN	[*windowRef.*]location
IE	[*windowRef.*]location

Properties

hash	hostname	pathname	protocol	search
host	href	port		

Methods

assign()	reload()	replace()

hash   NN *2*   IE *3*   DOM *1*

Read/Write

That portion of a URL following the # symbol, referring to an anchor location in a document. This property contains its data only if the user has explicitly navigated to an anchor, and is not just scrolling to it. Do not include the # symbol when setting the property.

Example   `location.hash = "section3"`

Value   String.

Default   None.

host   NN *2*   IE *3*   DOM *1*

Read/Write

The combination of the hostname and port (if any) of the server that serves up the current document. If the port is explicitly part of the URL, the hostname and port are separated by a colon, just as they are in the URL.

Example
```
if (location.host = "www.megacorp.com:80") {
    ...
}
```

Value   String of hostname, optionally followed by a colon and port number.

Default   Depends on server.

hostname   NN *2*   IE *3*   DOM *1*

Read/Write

The combination of the hostname of the server (i.e., a "two-dot" address consisting of server name and domain) that serves up the current document. The hostname property does not include the port number.

Example
```
if (location.hostname = "www.megacorp.com") {
    ...
}
```

Value   String of hostname (server and domain).

Default   Depends on server.

href   NN *2*   IE *3*   DOM *1*

Read/Write

The complete URL of the document loaded in the window or frame. Assigning a URL to this property is how you script navigation to load a new document into the window or frame (although Internet Explorer also offers the equivalent window.navigate() method).

Example location.href = "http://www.megacorp.com"

Value   String of complete or relative URL.

Default   None.

pathname   NN *2*   IE *3*   DOM *1*

Read/Write

The pathname component of the URL. This consists of all URL information following the last character of the domain name, including the initial forward slash symbol.

Example location.pathname = "/images/logoHiRes.gif"

Value   String.

Default   None.

port   NN *2*   IE *3*   DOM *1*

The port component of the URL, if one exists. This consists of all URL information following the colon after the last character of the domain name. The colon is not part of the `port` property value.

Example   `location.port = "80"`

Value   String (a numeric value as string).

Default   None.

protocol   NN *2*   IE *3*   DOM *1*

The protocol component of the URL. This consists of all URL information up to and including the first colon of a URL. Typical values are: `"http:"`, `"file:"`, `"ftp:"`, and `"mailto:"`.

Example

```
if (location.protocol == "file:") {
    statements for treating document as local file
}
```

Value   String.

Default   None.

search   NN *2*   IE *3*   DOM *1*

The URL-encoded portion of a URL that begins with the ? symbol. A document that is served up as the result of the search also may have the search portion available as part of the `window.location` property. You can modify this property by script. Doing so sends the URL and search criteria to the server. You must know the format of data (usually name/value pairs) expected by the server to perform this properly.

Example   `location.search="?p=Tony+Blair&d=y&g=0&s=a&w=s&m=25"`

Value   String starting with the ? symbol.

Default   None.

assign()   NN *2*   IE *3*   DOM *n/a*

`assign("URL")`

This method was intended to be hidden from view of scripters, but remains available for now. It performs the same action as assigning a URL to the `location.href` property. The `assign()` method is listed here for completeness and should not be used.

Returned Value

None.

Parameters

URL   A string version of a complete or relative URL of a document to be loaded into
        a window or frame.

reload()   NN *3*   IE *4*   DOM *1*

```
reload([unconditional])
```

Performs a hard reload of the document associated with the location object. This kind of
reload resets form elements to their default values (for a soft reload, use `history.go(0)`).
By default the `reload()` method performs a conditional-GET action, which retrieves the
file from the browser cache if the file is still in the cache (and the cache is turned on). To
force a reload from the server, force an unconditional-GET by adding the `true` Boolean
parameter.

Returned Value

None.

Parameters

`unconditional`
        An optional Boolean value. If `true`, the browser performs an unconditional-
        GET to force a reload of the document from the server, rather than the browser
        cache.

replace()   NN *3*   IE *4*   DOM *1*

```
replace("URL")
```

Loads a new document into the reference window and replaces the browser's history listing
entry of the current document with the entry of the new document. Thus, some interim
page that you don't want appearing in history (to prevent the **Back** button from ever
returning to the page) can be removed from the history and replaced with the entry of the
newly loaded document.

Returned Value

None.

Parameters

URL   A string version of a complete or relative URL of a document to be loaded into
        a window or frame.

locationbar, menubar, personalbar,
scrollbars, statusbar, toolbar   NN *4*   IE *n/a*   DOM *n/a*

These six objects belong to the window object and represent portions of the "chrome"
surrounding the content area of the browser window. With signed scripts in Navigator 4

(and the user's permission), you can dynamically hide and show these elements in a browser window. These features can also be turned off via the third parameter of the `window.open()` method, but only when generating a new window. To change the visibility of these items in an existing window, signed scripts are required.

Object Model Reference

NN   [window.]locationbar
[window.]menubar
[window.]personalbar
[window.]scrollbars
[window.]statusbar
[window.]toolbar

Properties

visible

---

visible   NN *4*   IE *n/a*   DOM *n/a*

Read/Write

Accessible only through signed scripts in Navigator 4, determines whether the window chrome feature is displayed.

Example   window.statusbar.visible = "false"

Value   Boolean value: true | false.

Default   true

MAP   NN *n/a*   IE *4*   DOM *1*

The MAP object reflects the MAP element.

HTML Equivalent

<MAP>

Object Model Reference

IE   [window.]document.all.*elementID*

Properties

className	isTextEdit	offsetLeft	outerHTML	sourceIndex
document	lang	offsetParent	outerText	style
id	language	offsetTop	parentElement	tagName
innerHTML	name	offsetWidth	parentTextEdit	title
innerText	offsetHeight			

Methods

click()	getAttribute()	scrollIntoView()
contains()	removeAttribute()	setAttribute()

Collections/Arrays

all[]   areas[]   children[]

Event Handler Properties

Handler	NN	IE	DOM
onclick	n/a	4	n/a
ondblclick	n/a	4	n/a
onhelp	n/a	4	n/a
onkeydown	n/a	4	n/a
onkeypress	n/a	4	n/a
onkeyup	n/a	4	n/a
onmousedown	n/a	4	n/a
onmousemove	n/a	4	n/a
onmouseout	n/a	4	n/a
onmouseover	n/a	4	n/a
onmouseup	n/a	4	n/a

name

NN *n/a*   IE *4*   DOM *1*

Read/Write

The identifier associated with the client-side image map specification. A MAP element contains all the AREA elements that define the hotspots of an image and their link destinations. The name assigned to the MAP element is the one cited by the USEMAP attribute of the IMG element. This binds the MAP definitions to the image.

Example   document.all.myMap.name = "altMap"

Value

Case-sensitive identifier that follows the rules of identifier naming: it may contain no whitespace, cannot begin with a numeral, and should avoid punctuation except for the underscore character.

Default   None.

areas[]

NN *n/a*   IE *4*   DOM *n/a*

A collection of all AREA element objects nested inside the MAP element.

Syntax   document.all.myMap.areas(*index*)

MARQUEE

NN *n/a*   IE *4*   DOM *n/a*

The MARQUEE object reflects the MARQUEE element.

HTML Equivalent

<MARQUEE>

Object Model Reference

IE   [window.]document.all.*elementID*

Properties

accessKey	dataSrc	*lang*	*outerText*	scrollWidth
behavior	direction	*language*	*parentElement*	*sourceIndex*
bgColor	*document*	loop	*parentTextEdit*	*style*
className	height	*offsetHeight*	recordNumber	tabIndex
clientHeight	hspace	*offsetLeft*	scrollAmount	*tagName*
clientLeft	*id*	*offsetParent*	scrollDelay	*title*
clientTop	*innerHTML*	*offsetTop*	scrollHeight	trueSpeed
clientWidth	innerText	*offsetWidth*	scrollLeft	vspace
dataFld	*isTextEdit*	*outerHTML*	scrollTop	width
dataFormatAs				

Methods

blur()	*getAttribute()*	*scrollIntoView()*
click()	*insertAdjacentHTML()*	*setAttribute()*
contains()	*insertAdjacentText()*	start()
focus()	*removeAttribute()*	stop()

Collections/Arrays

all[]	*children[]*	*filters[]*

Event Handler Properties

Handler	NN	IE	DOM
onafterupdate	n/a	4	n/a
onblur	n/a	4	n/a
onbounce	n/a	4	n/a
onclick	n/a	4	n/a
ondblclick	n/a	4	n/a
ondragstart	n/a	4	n/a
onfinish	n/a	4	n/a
onfocus	n/a	4	n/a
onhelp	n/a	4	n/a
onkeydown	n/a	4	n/a
onkeypress	n/a	4	n/a
onkeyup	n/a	4	n/a
onmousedown	n/a	4	n/a
onmousemove	n/a	4	n/a
onmouseout	n/a	4	n/a
onmouseover	n/a	4	n/a
onmouseup	n/a	4	n/a
onresize	n/a	4	n/a
onrowenter	n/a	4	n/a
onrowexit	n/a	4	n/a

Handler	NN	IE	DOM
onscroll	n/a	4	n/a
onselectstart	n/a	4	n/a
onstart	n/a	4	n/a

accessKey

NN *n/a*　　IE *4*　　DOM *n/a*

Read/Write

A single character key that brings focus to the element. The browser and operating system determine whether the user must press a modifier key (e.g., **Ctrl**, **Alt**, or **Command**) with the access key to bring focus to the element. In IE 4/Windows, the **Alt** key is required, and the key is not case sensitive. Not working in IE 4/Mac.

Example `document.all.myBanner.accessKey = "n"`

Value　　Single alphanumeric (and punctuation) keyboard character.

Default　　None.

behavior

NN *n/a*　　IE *4*　　DOM *n/a*

Read/Write

The motion of the content within the rectangular space set aside for the MARQUEE element. You have a choice of three motion types.

Example `document.all.newsBanner.behavior = "slide"`

Value

Case-insensitive MARQUEE element motion types:

alternate
　　　　Content alternates between marching left and right.

scroll　　Content scrolls (according to the DIRECTION attribute or **direction** property) into view and out of view before starting again.

slide　　Content scrolls (according to the DIRECTION attribute or **direction** property) into view, stops at the end of its run, blanks, and then starts again.

Default　　scroll

bgColor

NN *n/a*　　IE *4*　　DOM *n/a*

Read/Write

Background color of the element. This color setting is not reflected in the style sheet **backgroundColor** property except for Navigator layer objects. Even if the BGCOLOR attribute or **bgColor** property is set with a plain-language color name, the returned value is always a hexadecimal triplet.

Example `document.all.myBanner.bgColor = "yellow"`

DOM Reference

Value

A hexadecimal triplet or plain-language color name. See Appendix A for acceptable plain-language color names.

Default   Varies with browser and operating system.

clientHeight, clientWidth   NN *n/a*   IE *4*   DOM *n/a*

Read/Write

According to Microsoft's developer documentation, these properties reflect the height and width (in pixels) of the element's content. But see the section "About client- and offset-Properties" at the beginning of this chapter for details.

Example `var midHeight = document.all.myBanner.clientHeight/2`

Value   Integer pixel value.

Default   None.

clientLeft, clientTop   NN *n/a*   IE *4*   DOM *n/a*

Read-only

According to Microsoft's developer documentation, these properties reflect the distance between the "true" left and top edges of the document area and the edges of the element. But see the section "About client- and offset- Properties" at the beginning of this chapter for details. To get or set the pixel position of an element in the document, use the `pixelLeft` and `pixelTop` properties.

Value   A string value for a length in a variety of units or percentage.

Default   None.

dataFld   NN *n/a*   IE *4*   DOM *n/a*

Read/Write

Used with IE 4 data binding to associate a remote data source column name with the content of the `MARQUEE` element. A `DATASRC` attribute must also be set for the element. Setting both the `dataFld` and `dataSrc` properties to empty strings breaks the binding between element and data source.

Example `document.all.myBanner.dataFld = "hotNews"`

Value   Case-sensitive identifier of the data source column.

Default   None.

dataFormatAs   NN *n/a*   IE *4*   DOM *n/a*

Read/Write

Used with IE 4 data binding, this property advises the browser whether the source material arriving from the data source is to be treated as plain text or as tagged HTML.

Example `document.all.myBanner.dataFormatAs = "text"`

Value   IE 4 recognizes two possible settings: `text` | `HTML`.

Default   `text`

dataSrc

NN *n/a*   IE *4*   DOM *n/a*
Read/Write

Used with IE 4 data binding to specify the name of the remote ODBC data source (such as an Oracle or SQL Server database) to be associated with the element. Setting both the `dataFld` and `dataSrc` properties to empty strings breaks the binding between element and data source.

Example   `document.all.myBanner.dataSrc = "#DBSRC3"`

Value   Case-sensitive identifier of the data source.

Default   None.

direction

NN *n/a*   IE *4*   DOM *n/a*
Read/Write

Direction of the scroll within the element space.

Example   `document.all.banner.direction = "down"`

Value   Four possible case-insensitive directions: `down` | `left` | `right` | `up`.

Default   `left`

height, width

NN *n/a*   IE *4*   DOM *n/a*
Read/Write

The height and width in pixels of the element. Changes to these values are immediately reflected in reflowed content on the page.

Example   `document.all.myBanner.height = 250`

Value   Integer.

Default   None.

hspace, vspace

NN *n/a*   IE *4*   DOM *n/a*
Read/Write

The pixel measure of horizontal and vertical margins surrounding the element. The `hspace` property affects the left and right edges of the element equally; the **vspace** affects the top and bottom edges of the element equally. These margins are not the same as margins set by style sheets, but they have the same visual effect.

Example

```
document.all.myBanner.hspace = 5
document.all.myBanner.vspace = 8
```

Value   Integer of pixel count.

Default   0

loop

Read/Write

Sets the number of times the element scrolls its content. After the final scroll, the content remains in a fixed position. Constant animation can sometimes be distracting to page visitors, so if you have the MARQUEE turn itself off after a few scrolls, you may be doing your visitors a favor.

Example   `document.all.banner.loop = 3`

Value

Any positive integer if you want the scrolling to stop after that number of times. Otherwise, set the value to `-1`.

Default   `-1`

recordNumber

Read-only

Used with data binding, returns an integer representing the record within the data set that generated the element (i.e., an element whose content is filled via data binding). Values of this property can be used to extract a specific record from an Active Data Objects (ADO) record set (see `recordset` property).

Example

```
<SCRIPT FOR="tableTemplate" EVENT="onclick">
    myDataCollection.recordset.absoluteposition = this.recordNumber
    ...
</SCRIPT>
```

Value   Integer.

Default   None.

scrollAmount

Read/Write

The amount of space between positions of each drawing of the content. The greater the space, the faster the text appears to scroll. See also `scrollDelay`.

Example   `document.all.banner.scrollAmount = 4`

Value   Positive integer.

Default   6

scrollDelay NN *n/a*   IE *4*   DOM *n/a*

Read/Write

The amount of time in milliseconds between each drawing of the content. The greater the delay, the slower the text appears to scroll. See also `scrollAmount`.

Example   `document.all.banner.scrollDelay = 100`

Value   Positive integer.

Default   85 (Windows 95); 90 (Macintosh).

scrollHeight, scrollWidth NN *n/a*   IE *4*   DOM *n/a*

Read-only

The meaning of these two properties is ambiguous based on Microsoft's description and the way they're implemented in the Windows and Macintosh versions of Internet Explorer 4. My best guess is that these properties are intended to measure the height and width (in pixels) of the content of an element even when some of the content cannot be seen unless scrolled with scrollbars. The Macintosh version of the browser interprets this to mean the amount of the content that you can see at any one time. The important point is that for key elements, such as the BODY, the properties mean different things and can disrupt cross-platform operation.

Example   `var midPoint = document.all.myBanner.scrollHeight/2`

Value   Positive integer or zero.

Default   None.

scrollLeft, scrollTop NN *n/a*   IE *4*   DOM *n/a*

Read/Write

The distance in pixels between the actual left or top edge of the element's physical content and the left or top edge of the visible portion of the content. Setting these properties does not appear to visually impact the display of content in the MARQUEE element.

Example   `document.all.myBanner.scrollTop = 40`

Value   Positive integer or zero.

Default   0

tabIndex NN *n/a*   IE *4*   DOM *1*

Read/Write

A number that indicates the sequence of this element within the tabbing order of all focusable elements in the document. Tabbing order follows a strict set of rules. Elements that have values other than zero assigned to their `tabIndex` properties are first in line when a user starts tabbing in a page. Focus starts with the element with the lowest `tabIndex` value and proceeds in order to the highest value, regardless of physical location on the page or in the document. If two elements have the same `tabIndex` values, the element that comes earlier in the document receives focus first. Next come all elements that either don't support the `tabIndex` property or have the value set to zero. These elements receive focus in the order in which they appear in the document. A value of -1 removes the element from tabbing order altogether.

Note that the Macintosh user interface does not provide for giving focus to elements other than text and password `INPUT` fields.

Example   `document.all.myBanner.tabIndex = 6`

Value   Integer.

Default   None.

trueSpeed

NN *n/a*   IE *4*   DOM *n/a*

Read/Write

Whether the browser should honor `SCROLLDELAY` settings below 60 milliseconds. The default setting (`false`) prevents accidental settings that scroll too fast for most readers.

Example   `document.all.banner.trueSpeed = "true"`

Value   Boolean value: `true` | `false`.

Default   `false`

vspace

See hspace.

width

See height.

blur()

NN *n/a*   IE *4*   DOM *n/a*

Removes focus from the current element and fires an `onBlur` event (in IE). No other element necessarily receives focus as a result.

Returned Value

None.

Parameters

None.

focus()

NN *n/a*   IE *4*   DOM *n/a*

Gives focus to the current element and fires the `onFocus` event (in IE). If another element had focus at the time, it receives an `onBlur` event.

Returned Value

None.

Parameters

None.

start()   NN *n/a*   IE *4*   DOM *n/a*

Starts the MARQUEE element scrolling if it has been stopped. If the method is invoked on a stopped element, the onstart event handler also fires in response.

Returned Value

None.

Parameters

None.

stop()   NN *n/a*   IE *4*   DOM *n/a*

Stops the scrolling of the MARQUEE element. The content remains on the screen in the precise position it was in when the method was invoked. Restart via the start() method.

Returned Value

None.

Parameters

None.

MENU   NN *n/a*   IE *4*   DOM *1*

The MENU object reflects the MENU element.

HTML Equivalent
<MENU>

Object Model Reference
IE   [window.]document.all.*elementID*

Properties

className	isTextEdit	offsetLeft	outerHTML	sourceIndex
document	lang	offsetParent	outerText	style
id	language	offsetTop	parentElement	tagName
innerHTML	offsetHeight	offsetWidth	parentTextEdit	title
innerText				

Methods

click()	insertAdjacentHTML()	scrollIntoView()
contains()	insertAdjacentText()	setAttribute()
getAttribute()	removeAttribute()	

Collections/Arrays

all[]   children[]   filters[]

Event Handler Properties

Handler	NN	IE	DOM
onclick	n/a	4	n/a
ondblclick	n/a	4	n/a
ondragstart	n/a	4	n/a
onfilterchange	n/a	4	n/a
onhelp	n/a	4	n/a
onkeydown	n/a	4	n/a
onkeypress	n/a	4	n/a
onkeyup	n/a	4	n/a
onmousedown	n/a	4	n/a
onmousemove	n/a	4	n/a
onmouseout	n/a	4	n/a
onmouseover	n/a	4	n/a
onmouseup	n/a	4	n/a
onselectstart	n/a	4	n/a

menubar

See locationbar.

META   NN *n/a*   IE *4*   DOM *1*

The META object reflects the META element.

HTML Equivalent

<META>

Object Model Reference

IE   [window.]document.all.*elementID*

Properties

charset	httpEquiv	*lang*	*parentTextEdit*	*tagName*
className	*id*	*language*	*sourceIndex*	*title*
content	*isTextEdit*	*parentElement*	*style*	url

Methods

contains()   *removeAttribute()*   *setAttribute()*
getAttribute()

Collections/Arrays

all[]   children[]

charset

NN *n/a*   IE *4*   DOM *n/a*

Read/Write

Character encoding of the content in the file associated with the **href** attribute. This property does not change the setting of the CHARSET attribute of a name/value pair contained by the CONTENT attribute or property. For now the **charset** property has little or no effect on a document.

Example

```
if (document.all.myMeta.charset == "csISO5427Cyrillic") {
    process for Cyrillic charset
}
```

Value

Case-insensitive alias from the character set registry (*ftp://ftp.isi.edu/in-notes/iana/assignments/character-sets*).

Default   Determined by browser.

content

NN *n/a*   IE *4*   DOM *1*

Read/Write

The equivalent of the "value" of a name/value pair. The property's corresponding CONTENT attribute is usually accompanied by either a NAME or HTTP-EQUIV attribute, either of which act as the "name" portion of the name/value pair. Specific values of the CONTENT attribute vary with the value of the NAME or HTTP-EQUIV attribute. Sometimes the CONTENT attribute value contains multiple values. In such cases, the values are delimited by a semicolon. Some of these multiple values may be name/value pairs in their own right, such as the content for a refresh META element. The first value is a number representing the number of seconds of delay before loading another document; the second value is a name/value pair indicating a URL of the document to load after the delay expires.

Changing the **content** property on a loaded document may not produce the desired effect if the browser relies on the incoming value as the document loads.

Example

```
document.all.refreshMeta.content ="5,http://www.giantco.com/
basicindex.html"
```

Value   Any string of characters.

Default   None.

httpEquiv

NN *n/a*   IE *4*   DOM *1*

Read/Write

The equivalent of the "name" of a name/value pair. The property's corresponding HTTP-EQUIV attribute is usually accompanied by a CONTENT attribute, which acts as the "value" portion of the name/value pair. The author may elect to use the NAME attribute instead of the HTTP-EQUIV attribute, but only one may be set. Adjust only the property corresponding to the attribute used in the META element's tag. Then be sure to set the **content** property with a value that makes sense with the httpEquiv or name property

Example   document.all.refreshMeta.httpEquiv = "expires"

Value   String.

Default   None.

url   NN *n/a*   IE *4*   DOM *n/a*

Microsoft claims that this property lets you change the URL of the CONTENT attribute of a META tag that reloads the page. This is not correct. Nor does changing the **content** property to a time and URL alter the information, which is captured by the browser when the document loads. Perhaps there will be some future application of this property.

mimeType   NN *3*   IE *n/a*   DOM *n/a*

The mimeType object belongs to the **navigator** object. The object represents a MIME type specification. Its properties let scripts find out the browser is equipped to handle a specific MIME type of external content before it is loaded from the server. All these properties are mirrored in the internal document displayed when you choose Navigator's **About Plug-ins** menu option. Internet Explorer offers no comparable facilities.

Object Model Reference
NN   navigator.mimeTypes[i]

Properties

description	enabledPlugin	suffixes	type

description   NN *3*   IE *n/a*   DOM *n/a*

Returns the brief description of the plugin. This information is embedded in the plugin by its developer. Be aware that the precise wording of this description may vary for the same plugin written for different operating systems.

Example   var descr = navigator.mimeTypes[0].description

Value   String.

Default   None.

enabledPlugin   NN *3*   IE *n/a*   DOM *n/a*

Returns a plugin object reference corresponding to the plugin currently set to play any incoming data formatted according to the current MIME type. You can then dig deeper into properties of the returned plugin object to retrieve, say, its name.

Example `var plugName = navigator.mimeTypes[0].enabledPlugin.name`

Value plugin object reference.

Default None.

suffixes   NN *3*   IE *n/a*   DOM *n/a*

Read-only

Returns a comma-delimited string list of file suffixes associated with the **mimeType** object. For example, the MIME type associated with Macromedia Shockwave knows about three suffixes. The **suffixes** property value for that **mimeType** object is:

    dcr, dir, dxr

If you loop through all **mimeType** objects registered in the browser to find a match for a specific suffix, you can then find out whether the matching **mimeType** object has a plugin installed for it (via the **enabledPlugin** property).

Example `var suff = navigator.mimeTypes[14].suffixes`

Value String.

Default None.

type   NN *3*   IE *n/a*   DOM *n/a*

Read-only

Returns a string version of the MIME type associated with the **mimeType** object. You could, for example, loop through all the **mimeType** objects in search of the one that matches a specific MIME type (**application/x-midi**) and examine that **mimeType** object further to see whether it is currently supported and enabled.

Example `var MType = navigator.mimeTypes[3].type`

Value String.

Default None.

navigator   NN *2*   IE *3*   DOM *n/a*

The **navigator** object in many ways represents the browser application. As such, the browser is outside the scope of the document object model. Even so, the **navigator** object plays an important role in scripting, because it allows scripts to see what browser and browser version is running the script. In addition to several key properties that both Navigator and Internet Explorer have in common, each browser also extends the property listing of this object in ways that would generally benefit all browsers.

Object Model Reference

NN   `navigator`

IE   `navigator`

Properties

appCodeName	browserLanguage	onLine	userAgent
appMinorVersion	cookieEnabled	platform	userLanguage
appName	cpuClass	systemLanguage	userProfile
appVersion	language		

Methods

javaEnabled()	preference()	taintEnabled()

Collections/Arrays

mimeTypes[]	plugins[]

appCodeName   NN *2*   IE *3*   DOM *n/a*

Read-only

Reveals the code name of the browser. Both Navigator and Internet Explorer return Mozilla, which was the code name for an early version of Navigator (a combination of the early freeware name of the Mosaic browser and Godzilla). The Mozilla character is Netscape's corporate mascot, but both companies' browsers return this code name.

Example var codeName = navigator.appCodeName

Value   Mozilla

Default Mozilla

appMinorVersion   NN *n/a*   IE *4*   DOM *n/a*

Read-only

Reveals the value to the right of the decimal point in the entire version number. So-called bug-fix or patched versions, such as 4.03, are not reflected in IE's version numbering, so they return a value of 0. The exact release version is available by parsing the values of appVersion or userAgent.

Example var subVer = navigator.appMinorVersion

Value

String version of the first digit to the right of the decimal of the primary version number.

Default Depends on browser version.

appName   NN *2*   IE *3*   DOM *n/a*

Read-only

Reveals the model name of the browser.

Example var isNav = navigator.appName == "Netscape"

Value   String values. NN: Netscape; IE: Microsoft Internet Explorer

Default Depends on browser.

appVersion NN *2*   IE *3*   DOM *n/a*

Read-only

Reveals the version number of the browser, along with minimal operating system platform information (a subset of the information returned by **userAgent**). The first word of the value returned by Navigator includes the version number down to the x.xx level, whereas Internet Explorer goes only to the x.x level. In parentheses, both browsers include operating system information and (for Navigator) the browser's default language version. Sample returned values are as follows:

Navigator:

```
4.04 [en] (Win95; I)
4.03 (Macintosh; I; PPC)
```

Internet Explorer:

```
4.0 (compatible; MSIE 4.01; Windows 95)
4.0 (compatible; MSIE 4.0; Macintosh; I; PPC)
```

You can use **parseInt()** on this value to determine whether a browser is of a particular generation, as shown in the following example. This extracts the integer value, which can be used in a math comparison operation to find out whether the browser is at a minimum needed version level for a script to run.

Example   `var isVer4Min = parseInt(navigator.appVersion) >= 4`

Value   String values.

Default   Depends on browser.

browserLanguage NN *n/a*   IE *4*   DOM *n/a*

Read-only

The default written language of the browser. The Navigator 4 equivalent is the **navigator.language** property.

Example   `var browLangCode = navigator.browserLanguage`

Value   Case-insensitive language code as a string.

Default   Browser default.

cookieEnabled NN *n/a*   IE *4*   DOM *n/a*

Read-only

Returns whether the browser allows reading and writing of cookie data.

Example

```
if (cookieEnabled) {
    setCookieData(data)
}
```

Value   Boolean value: **true** | **false**.

Default   Depends on browser setting.

DOM Reference

cpuClass

Returns a string reference of the CPU of the client computer. Common Intel microprocessors (including Pentium-class CPUs and Macintoshes running Windows emulators) return x86, while PowerPC Macintoshes return PPC. This value tells you only about the basic hardware class, not the operating system or specific CPU speed or model number.

Example

```
if (navigator.cpuClass == "PPC") {
    statements specific to PowerPC clients
}
```

Value   String value.

Default   Depends on client hardware.

language

The written language for which the browser version was created. The language is specified in the ISO 639 language code scheme. Internet Explorer provides this information via the navigator.browserLanguage property.

Example   var mainLang = navigator.language

Value   Case-insensitive language code as a string.

Default   Browser default.

onLine

Whether the browser is set for online or offline browsing (in Internet Explorer 4's **File** menu). Pages may wish to invoke live server actions when they load in online mode, but avoid these calls when in offline mode. Use this Boolean property to build such conditional statements.

Example

```
if (navigator.onLine) {
    document.write("<APPLET ...>")
    ...
}
```

Value   Boolean value: true | false.

Default   true

platform

Returns the name of the operating system or hardware platform of the browser. For Windows 95/NT, the value is Win32; for a Macintosh running a PowerPC CPU, the value is

MacPPC. At least for the major platforms I've been able to test, Navigator and Internet Explorer agree on the returned values. Using this property to determine the baseline facilities of the client in a conditional expression can help the page optimize its output for the device.

Example

```
if (navigator.platform == "Win32") {
     document.write() content suitable for a Windows 95/NT computer
}
```

Value   String.

Default   None.

systemLanguage

NN *n/a*   IE *4*   DOM *n/a*

Read-only

The code for the default written language used by the operating system. If you have multilingual content available, you can use this property to insert content in specific languages.

Example

```
if (navigator.systemLanguage = "nl") {
     document.write() some Dutch content
}
```

Value   Case-insensitive language code.

Default

Usually the browser default (en for English-language Internet Explorer available in the United States).

userAgent

NN *2*   IE *3*   DOM *n/a*

Read-only

Information about the browser software, including version, operating system platform, and brand. This is the most complete set of information about the browser, whereas **appVersion** and **appName** properties provide subset data. Typical data for this property looks like the following:

```
Mozilla/4.0 (compatible; MSIE 4.01; Windows 95)
```

Do not rely on the length or position of any part of this data, as it may vary with browser, version, and proxy server used at the client end. Instead, use the **indexOf()** method to check for the presence of a desired string.

Example

```
if (navigator.userAgent.indexOf("MSIE") != -1) {
    var isIE = true
}
```

Value   String.

Default   Depends on browser.

userLanguage

NN *n/a*   IE *4*   DOM *n/a*

Read-only

The default written language of the browser, based on the operating system user profile setting (if one exists). The property defaults to the **browserLanguage** property.

Example   var userLangCode = navigator.userLanguage

Value   Case-insensitive language code as a string.

Default   Browser default.

userProfile

NN *n/a*   IE *4*   DOM *n/a*

Read-only

The **userProfile** property is, itself, an object that lets scripts request permission to access personal information stored in the visitor's user profile (for Win32 versions of Internet Explorer 4). See the **userProfile** object.

Example

```
navigator.userProfile.addReadRequest("vcard.displayname")
navigator.userProfile.doReadRequest("3", "MegaCorp Customer Service")
var custName = navigator.userProfile.getAttribute("vcard.displayname")
navigator.userProfile.clearRequest()
if (custName) {
    . . .
}
```

Value   **userProfile** object reference.

Default   Browser default.

javaEnabled()

NN *3*   IE *4*   DOM *n/a*

Returns whether Java is turned on in the browser. This property won't help you in a non-scriptable browser (or scriptable browser that doesn't support the property), but it does tell you whether the user has Java turned off in the browser preferences.

Returned Value

Boolean value: **true** | **false**.

Parameters

None.

preference()

NN *4*   IE *n/a*   DOM *n/a*

preference(*name*[, *value*])

By way of signed scripts in Navigator 4, you can access a wide variety of user preferences settings. These include even the most detailed items, such as whether the user has elected to download images or whether style sheets are enabled. Most of these settings are intended for scripts used by network administrators to install and control the user settings of enterprisewide deployment of Navigator. Consult the Netscape developer web site for further information about these preferences settings (*http://developer.netscape.com/library/ documentation/deplymt/jsprefs.htm*).

Returned Value

Preference value in a variety of data types.

Parameters

name	The preference name as a string, such as `general.always_load_images`.
value	An optional value to set the named preference.

taintEnabled()   NN *3*   IE *4*   DOM *n/a*

Returns whether "data tainting" is turned on in the browser. This security mechanism was never fully implemented in Navigator, but the method that checks for it is still included in newer versions of Navigator for backward compatibility. Internet Explorer 4 also includes it for compatibility, even though it always returns `false`.

Returned Value

Boolean value: `true` | `false`.

Parameters

None.

NOFRAMES, NOSCRIPT   NN *n/a*   IE *n/a*   DOM *1*

The `NOFRAMES` object reflects the `NOFRAMES` element, and the `NOSCRIPT` object reflects the `NOSCRIPT` element. These objects appear in the DOM working draft and are not yet reflected as objects in any browser, although the HTML elements exist in both Navigator and Internet Explorer.

HTML Equivalent

`<NOFRAMES>`

Properties

className	id	lang	style	title
dir				

dir   NN *n/a*   IE *n/a*   DOM *1*

Read/Write

The direction of character rendering for the element's text whose characters are not governed by inherent directionality according to the Unicode standard. Character rendering is either left to right or right to left.

Value	`ltr`	`rtl` (case insensitive).
Default	`ltr`

OBJECT

The OBJECT object reflects the OBJECT element. This is an updated way of embedding other media and external data into a document (through a plugin or ActiveX control).

HTML Equivalent

`<OBJECT>`

Object Model Reference

IE   `[window.]document.all.elementID`

Properties

accessKey	data	isTextEdit	offsetTop	style
align	dataFld	lang	offsetWidth	tabIndex
altHtml	dataSrc	language	outerHTML	tagName
classid	document	name	outerText	title
className	form	object	parentElement	type
code	height	offsetHeight	parentTextEdit	vspace
codeBase	hspace	offsetLeft	readyState	width
codeType	id	offsetParent	sourceIndex	

Methods

blur()	focus()	scrollIntoView()
click()	getAttribute()	setAttribute()
contains()	removeAttribute()	

Collections/Arrays

all[]	children[]	filters[]

Event Handler Properties

Handler	NN	IE	DOM
onafterupdate	n/a	4	n/a
onbeforeupdate	n/a	4	n/a
onblur	n/a	4	n/a
onclick	n/a	4	n/a
ondataavailable	n/a	4	n/a
ondatasetchanged	n/a	4	n/a
ondatasetcomplete	n/a	4	n/a
ondblclick	n/a	4	n/a
ondragstart	n/a	4	n/a
onerror	n/a	4	n/a
onerrorupdate	n/a	4	n/a
onfilterchange	n/a	4	n/a
onfocus	n/a	4	n/a
onhelp	n/a	4	n/a
onreadystatechange	n/a	4	n/a
onrowenter	n/a	4	n/a

Handler	NN	IE	DOM
onrowexit	n/a	4	n/a
onselectstart	n/a	4	n/a

accessKey

NN *n/a*   IE *4*   DOM *n/a*

Read/Write

A single character key that brings focus to the element. The browser and operating system determine whether the user must press a modifier key (e.g., **Ctrl**, **Alt**, or **Command**) with the access key to bring focus to the element. In IE 4/Windows, the **Alt** key is required, and the key is not case sensitive. Not working in IE 4/Mac.

Example   `document.all.myObject.accessKey = "n"`

Value   Single alphanumeric (and punctuation) keyboard character.

Default   None.

align

NN *n/a*   IE *4*   DOM *1*

Read/Write

Defines how the element is aligned relative to surrounding text content. Most values set the vertical relationship between the element and surrounding text. For example, to align the bottom of the element with the baseline of the surrounding text, the `align` property value would be `baseline`. An element can be "floated" along the left or right margin to let surrounding text wrap around the element.

Example   `document.all.myObject.align = "absmiddle"`

Value

Any of the following alignment constant values (as a string): `absbottom` | `absmiddle` | `baseline` | `bottom` | `right` | `left` | `none` | `texttop` | `top`.

Default   `bottom`

altHtml

NN *n/a*   IE *4*   DOM *1*

Read/Write

HTML content to be displayed if the object or applet fails to load. This can be a message, static image, or any other HTML that best fits the scenario. There are inconsistencies in Internet Explorer with regard to this property's casing. The Win32 version requires `altHtml`; the Mac version requires `altHTML`.

Example   `document.all.myObject.altHtml = "<IMG SRC='objectAlt.gif'>"`

Value   Any quoted string of characters, including HTML tags.

Default   None.

classid   NN *n/a*   IE *4*   DOM *1*

Read-only

The URL of the object's implementation. In Internet Explorer, the URL can point to the *CLSID* directory (with a `clsid:` URL) that stores all the IDs for registered ActiveX controls, such as DirectAnimation. Be aware that there is a discrepancy in the case of this property name in Internet Explorer 4: Win32 requires `classid`; the Macintosh version requires `classID`. The DOM leaves the read/write or read-only status of this property to the discretion of the browser.

Example

```
if (document.all.soundObject.classid == "clsid:83A38BF0-B33A-A4FF-
C619A82E891D"){
    process for the desired sound object
}
```

Value   String.

Default   None.

code   NN *n/a*   IE *4*   DOM *1*

Read-only

The name of the Java applet class file set to the `CODE` attribute of the `OBJECT` element.

Example

```
if (document.all.clock.code == "Y2Kcounter.class") {
    process for the found class file
}
```

Value   Case-sensitive (usually) applet class filename as a string.

Default   None.

codeBase   NN *n/a*   IE *4*   DOM *1*

Read-only

Path to the directory holding the class file designated in either the `CODE` or `CLASSID` attribute. The `CODEBASE` attribute does not name the class file, just the path.

Example

```
if (document.all.clock.codeBase == "classes") {
    process for the found class file directory
}
```

Value

Case-sensitive pathname, usually relative to the directory storing the current HTML document.

Default   None.

codeType   NN *n/a*   IE *4*   DOM *1*

Read/Write

An advisory about the content type of the object referred to by the CLASSID attribute. A browser might use this information to assist in preparing support for a resource requiring a multimedia player or plugin. If the CODETYPE property is set to an empty string, the browser looks next for the TYPE attribute setting (although it is normally associated with content linked by the DATA attribute URL). If both attributes have no (or empty) values set, the browser gets the content type information from the resource as it downloads.

Example `document.all.gameTime.codeType = "application/x-crossword"`

Value

Case-insensitive MIME type. A catalog of registered MIME types is available from *ftp:// ftp.isi.edu/in-notes/iana/assignments/media-types/*.

Default   None.

data   NN *n/a*   IE *4*   DOM *n/a*

Read-only

URL of a file containing data for the OBJECT element (as distinguished from the object itself). Relative URLs are calculated relative to the CODEBASE attribute if one is assigned; otherwise, the URL is relative to the document's URL.

Example `var objDataURL = document.all.soundEffect.data`

Value   A complete or relative URL as a string.

Default   None.

dataFld   NN *n/a*   IE *4*   DOM *n/a*

Read/Write

Used with IE 4 data binding to associate a remote data source column name to an OBJECT element attribute determined by properties set in the object. A DATASRC attribute must also be set for the element. Setting both the dataFld and dataSrc properties to empty strings breaks the binding between element and data source.

Example `document.all.myObject.dataFld = "linkURL"`

Value   Case-sensitive identifier of the data source column.

Default   None.

dataSrc   NN *n/a*   IE *4*   DOM *n/a*

Read/Write

Used with IE 4 data binding to specify the name of the remote ODBC data source (such as an Oracle or SQL Server database) to be associated with the element. Setting both the dataFld and dataSrc properties to empty strings breaks the binding between element and data source.

DOM Reference

Example `document.all.myObject.dataSrc = "#DBSRC3"`

Value   Case-sensitive identifier of the data source.

Default None.

form   NN *n/a*   IE *4*   DOM *n/a*
Read-only

Returns a reference to the FORM element that contains the current element (if any). This property is appropriate only if the object is acting as a form control. Not available in the Macintosh version.

Value   Object reference.

Default None.

height, width   NN *n/a*   IE *4*   DOM *n/a*
Read/Write

The height and width in pixels of the element. Changes to these values are immediately reflected in reflowed content on the page.

Example `document.all.myObject.height = 250`

Value   Integer.

Default None.

hspace, vspace   NN *n/a*   IE *4*   DOM *1*
Read/Write

The pixel measure of horizontal and vertical margins surrounding an OBJECT element. The hspace property affects the left and right edges of the element equally; the vspace affects the top and bottom edges of the element equally. These margins are not the same as margins set by style sheets, but they have the same visual effect.

Example

```
document.all.myObject.hspace = 5
document.all.myObject.vspace = 8
```

Value   Integer of pixel count.

Default 0

name   NN *n/a*   IE *4*   DOM *1*
Read/Write

The identifier associated with the OBJECT element. If the object should be one that goes inside a form, the name property is submitted as one-half of the name/value pair when the form is submitted to the server.

Example `document.all.myObject.name = "company"`

Value

Case-sensitive identifier that follows the rules of identifier naming: it may contain no whitespace, cannot begin with a numeral, and should avoid punctuation except for the underscore character.

Default   None.

object   NN *n/a*   IE *4*   DOM *n/a*

Read-only

A reference to a wrapper around an object to allow access to document object model properties of the **OBJECT** element when the names may be confused with internal property naming of the object. For example, if the code loaded into an **OBJECT** element had a property named **hspace**, the script reference **document.all.reader.hspace** would retrieve that internal property, rather than the **hspace** property of the HTML element. The **object** property wrapper tells the JavaScript interpreter to get the property from the HTML element without diving into the external object's code.

Example   `var objCode = document.all.reader.object.code`

Value   Object reference.

Default   None.

readyState   NN *n/a*   IE *4*   DOM *n/a*

Read-only

Returns the current download status of the embedded content. This property provides a more granular way of testing whether a particular downloadable element is ready to be run or scripted instead of the **onLoad** event handler for the entire document. As the value of this property changes during loading, the system fires an **onReadyStateChange** event.

Example

```
if (document.all.myObject.readyState == 4) {
    statements for alternate handling
}
```

Value

Unlike the document object's version of this property, the **OBJECT** object's values are integers. As can best be determined: 0 means uninitialized; 1 means loading; and **4** means complete.

Default   None.

tabIndex   NN *n/a*   IE *4*   DOM *1*

Read/Write

A number that indicates the sequence of this element within the tabbing order of all focusable elements in the document. Tabbing order follows a strict set of rules. Elements that have values other than zero assigned to their **tabIndex** properties are first in line when a user starts tabbing in a page. Focus starts with the element with the lowest `tabIndex` value and proceeds in order to the highest value, regardless of physical location on the page or in the document. If two elements have the same `tabIndex` values, the element that comes earlier in the document receives focus first. Next come all elements that either don't support the `tabIndex` property or have the value set to zero. These elements receive focus in the order in which they appear in the document. A value of -1 removes the element from tabbing order altogether.

Note that the Macintosh user interface does not provide for giving focus to elements other than text and password `INPUT` fields.

Example   `document.all.myObject.tabIndex = 6`

Value   Integer.

Default   None.

type   NN *n/a*   IE *4*   DOM *1*
Read/Write

An advisory about the MIME type of the external data to be loaded into the object. The browser looks to the `type` property value if the `codeType` property is `null`.

Example

```
if (document.all.myObject.type ==  "image/jpeg") {
    . . .
}
```

Value

Case-insensitive MIME type. A catalog of registered MIME types is available from *ftp:// ftp.isi.edu/in-notes/iana/assignments/media-types/*.

Default   None.

vspace

See hspace.

width

See height.

OL   NN *n/a*   IE *4*   DOM *1*

The `OL` object reflects the `OL` element.

HTML Equivalent

`<OL>`

Object Model Reference

IE   `[window.]document.all.elementID`

Properties

className	innerText	offsetLeft	outerText	style
compact	isTextEdit	offsetParent	parentElement	tagName
document	lang	offsetTop	parentTextEdit	title
id	language	offsetWidth	sourceIndex	type
innerHTML	offsetHeight	outerHTML	start	

Methods

click()	insertAdjacentHTML()	scrollIntoView()
contains()	insertAdjacentText()	setAttribute()
getAttribute()	removeAttribute()	

Collections/Arrays

all[]	children[]	filters[]

Event Handler Properties

Handler	NN	IE	DOM
onclick	n/a	4	n/a
ondblclick	n/a	4	n/a
ondragstart	n/a	4	n/a
onfilterchange	n/a	4	n/a
onhelp	n/a	4	n/a
onkeydown	n/a	4	n/a
onkeypress	n/a	4	n/a
onkeyup	n/a	4	n/a
onmousedown	n/a	4	n/a
onmousemove	n/a	4	n/a
onmouseout	n/a	4	n/a
onmouseover	n/a	4	n/a
onselectstart	n/a	4	n/a

DOM Reference

---

compact   NN *n/a*   IE *4*   DOM *1*

Read/Write

When set to true, the compact property should instruct the browser to render items in the list in a more compact format. This property has no effect in Internet Explorer 4 and is completely unavailable in the Macintosh version.

Example   document.all.myOL.compact = true

Value   Boolean value: true | false.

Default   false

start

Read/Write

The starting number for the sequence of items in the OL element. This is convenient when a sequence of items must be disturbed by running body text. While the value is a number, the corresponding Arabic numeral, Roman numeral, or alphabet letter renders the value.

Example   `document.all.sublist2.start = 6`

Value   Positive integer.

Default   None.

type

Read/Write

The manner in which the leading numbers or letters of items in the list are displayed.

Example   `document.all.instruxList.type = "a"`

Value

Possible values are: A | a | I | i | 1. Sequencing is performed automatically as follows:

Type	Example
A	A, B, C, ...
a	a, b, c, ...
I	I, II, III, ...
i	i, ii, iii, ...
1	1, 2, 3, ...

Default   1

OPTION

The OPTION object reflects the OPTION element, which must be nested inside a SELECT element. References to OPTION objects most often use its parent SELECT object, with the OPTION object treated as one member of an array of options belonging to that SELECT object.

HTML Equivalent

`<OPTION>`

Object Model Reference

NN   [window.]document.*formName*.*selectName*.options[i]
            [window.]document.forms[i].elements[i].options[i]

IE   [window.]document.*formName*.selectName.options[i]
            [window.]document.forms[i].elements[i].options[i]
            [window.]document.all.*elementID*

Properties

className	*index*	*offsetParent*	*parentTextEdit*	*tagName*
document	*isTextEdit*	*offsetWidth*	selected	text
defaultSelected	*language*	*parentElement*	*style*	value
id	*offsetHeight*			

Methods

contains()	*removeAttribute()*	*setAttribute()*
getAttribute()	*scrollIntoView()*	

defaultSelected

NN *2*   IE *3*   DOM *1*

Read/Write

Whether element has the SELECTED attribute set in the tag. You can compare the current selected property against defaultSelected to see whether the state of the select control has changed since the document loaded. Changing this property does not affect the current selected status.

Example

```
var listItem = document.forms[0].selector.options[2]
if (listItem.selected != listItem.defaultSelected) {
    process for changed state
}
```

Value   Boolean value: true I false.

Default   Determined by HTML tag attribute.

index

NN *2*   IE *3*   DOM *n/a*

Read-only

Returns the zero-based index value of the current option object within the collection of options of the SELECT element. The select object's selectedIndex property returns the index value of the option that is currently selected. Since you usually access an OPTION object via its place in the options array, there is little need to reference this property.

Example   var firstValue = document.forms[0].stateList.options[0].index

Value   Integer.

Default   None.

selected

NN *2*   IE *3*   DOM *1*

Read/Write

Whether the list option has been selected by the user, meaning that its value is submitted with the form. Scripts can modify the value to select an item algorithmically. To find out which option is selected, it is more efficient to use the select object's selectedIndex property, rather than looping through all options in search of those whose selected properties are true. The exception to this is when the SELECT element is set to allow multiple selections, in which case you need to cycle through them all to find the chosen items.

Example   `document.forms[0].selectList.options[3].selected = true`

Value   Boolean value: `true` | `false`.

Default   `false`

text   NN *2*   IE *3*   DOM *1*

Read/Write

The text associated with the OPTION element. This text is between the start and end tags and is what appears in the SELECT element on screen. A hidden value associated with the list item can be stored, retrieved, and changed via the **value** property.

Example
```
var list = document.forms[0].selectList
var listItemText = list.options[list.selectedIndex].text
```

Value   String.

Default   None.

value   NN *4*   IE *4*   DOM *1*

Read/Write

Value associated with the OPTION element. If the OPTION element has a VALUE attribute or **value** property set, this is the value returned for the **value** property; otherwise, the text visible in the list is returned.

Example   `var itemValue = document.forms[0].selectList.options[2]value`

Value   String.

Default   None.

options   NN *2*   IE *3*   DOM *n/a*

An array of OPTION elements nested within a SELECT object.

Object Model Reference
NN   `[window.]document.`*formName*`.`*selectName*`.options`
IE   `[window.]document.`*formName*`.`*selectName*`.options`

Properties
`length`

Methods
`add()`   `item()`   `remove()`

length

Returns the number of elements in the collection.

Example `var howMany = document.forms[0].mySelect.options.length`

Value   Integer.

add( )

`add(element, [index])`

Adds an already-created element (from the `createElement()` method) to the current collection. The element must be of the `OPTION` type. By default the new element is added as the last item of the collection unless you specify an index value as a second parameter. The following example sequence appends a new item to a `SELECT` object:

```
var newElem = document.createElement("OPTION")
newElem.text = "Freddy"
newElem.value = "Freddy Mercury"
document.forms[1].rockers.options.add(newElem)
```

Notice that a generic object is created first. Then its properties are stuffed with values. Then the new element is physically added to the `SELECT` element.

The process for adding an `OPTION` element is entirely different in Navigator. To append a new item, assign the results of an `Option()` constructor to the indexed option at the end of the array (corresponding to the integer returned by the `length` property). Parameters to the constructor function are (in order):

1. String corresponding to the `text` property
2. String corresponding to the `value` property
3. Boolean corresponding to the `defaultSelected` property
4. Boolean corresponding to the `selected` property

For example, the Navigator version of the preceding IE example is as follows:

```
document.forms[1].rockers.options[length] = new Option("Freddy",
 "Freddy Mercury", false, false)
```

You could insert the new item anywhere you like in the list by specifying the desired index value of the `options` array.

Returned Value

None.

Parameters

`element`   A fully formed element object reference, usually generated by the `createElement()` method.

`index`   An optional integer indicating where in the collection the new element should be placed.

item() NN *n/a*   IE *4*   DOM *n/a*

item(*index*[, *subindex*])

Returns a single object or collection of objects corresponding to the element matching the index value (or, optionally, the index and subindex values).

Returned Value

One object or collection (array) of objects. If there are no matches to the parameters, the returned value is null.

Parameters

index   When the parameter is a zero-based integer, the returned value is a single element corresponding to the said numbered item in source code order (nested within the current element); when the parameter is a string, the returned value is a collection of elements whose id or name properties match that string.

subindex If you specify a string value for the first parameter, you may use the second parameter to specify a zero-based integer to retrieve a specific element from the collection whose id or name properties match the first parameter's string value.

remove() NN *n/a*   IE *4*   DOM *n/a*

remove(*index*)

Deletes an element from the current collection. Simply specify the zero-based index value of the OPTION element you wish to remove from the collection belonging to a SELECT element. The following example deletes the first item from a SELECT object:

```
document.forms[1].rockers.options.remove(0)
```

The process for removing an OPTION element is entirely different in Navigator. To delete an item, assign null to the item in the collection. For example, the Navigator version of the preceding IE example is as follows:

```
document.forms[1].rockers.options[0] = null
```

Regardless of the browser-specific process of removing an option from the SELECT object, the length of the options array collapses to fill the space.

Returned Value

None.

Parameters

index   A zero-based integer indicating which item in the collection should be deleted.

P NN *n/a*   IE *4*   DOM *1*

The P object reflects the P element.

HTML Equivalent

<P>

Object Model Reference

IE   [window.]document.all.*elementID*

Properties

align	innerText	offsetLeft	outerHTML	sourceIndex
className	isTextEdit	offsetParent	outerText	style
document	lang	offsetTop	parentElement	tagName
id	language	offsetWidth	parentTextEdit	title
innerHTML	offsetHeight			

Methods

click()	insertAdjacentHTML()	scrollIntoView()
contains()	insertAdjacentText()	setAttribute()
getAttribute()	removeAttribute()	

Collections/Arrays

all[]	children[]	filters[]

Event Handler Properties

Handler	NN	IE	DOM
onclick	n/a	4	n/a
ondblclick	n/a	4	n/a
ondragstart	n/a	4	n/a
onfilterchange	n/a	4	n/a
onhelp	n/a	4	n/a
onkeydown	n/a	4	n/a
onkeypress	n/a	4	n/a
onkeyup	n/a	4	n/a
onmousedown	n/a	4	n/a
onmousemove	n/a	4	n/a
onmouseout	n/a	4	n/a
onmouseover	n/a	4	n/a
onmouseup	n/a	4	n/a
onselectstart	n/a	4	n/a

align

NN *n/a*   IE *4*   DOM *1*

Read/Write

Determines how the paragraph text is justified within the available width of the next outermost container (usually the document BODY).

Example   document.all.myP.align = "center"

Value   Any of the three horizontal alignment constants: center | left | right.

Default   left

password   NN *2*   IE *3*   DOM *1*

The password object is a form control generated with an **INPUT** element whose **TYPE** attribute is set to **"password"**. This object is similar to the text object, except that the characters typed into the text box by the user are converted to asterisk or bullet symbols for privacy.

HTML Equivalent

```
<INPUT TYPE="password">
```

Object Model Reference

NN   [window.]document.*formName*.elementName
          [window.]document.forms[i].elements[i]

IE   [window.]document.*formName*.elementName
          [window.]document.forms[i].elements[i]
          [window.]document.all.*elementID*

Properties

accessKey	form	*offsetHeight*	outerText	*style*
className	id	*offsetLeft*	*parentElement*	tabIndex
dataFld	*isTextEdit*	*offsetParent*	*parentTextEdit*	*tagName*
dataSrc	*lang*	*offsetTop*	readOnly	*title*
defaultValue	*language*	*offsetWidth*	size	type
disabled	maxLength	*outerHTML*	*sourceIndex*	value
document	name			

Methods

blur()	*getAttribute()*	*removeAttribute()*
click()	handleEvent()	*scrollIntoView()*
contains()	*insertAdjacentHTML()*	select()
focus()	*insertAdjacentText()*	*setAttribute()*

Collections/Arrays

all[]	*children[]*	*filters[]*

Event Handler Properties

Handler	NN	IE	DOM
onblur	2	3	n/a
onchange	2	3	n/a
onclick	n/a	4	n/a
ondblclick	n/a	4	n/a
onfocus	2	3	n/a
onhelp	n/a	4	n/a
onkeydown	4	4	n/a
onkeypress	4	4	n/a
onkeyup	4	4	n/a
onmousedown	n/a	4	n/a
onmousemove	n/a	4	n/a

Handler	NN	IE	DOM
onmouseout	n/a	4	n/a
onmouseover	n/a	4	n/a
onmouseup	n/a	4	n/a
onselect	2	3	n/a

accessKey   NN *n/a*   IE *4*   DOM *1*

Read/Write

A single character key that brings focus to the element. The browser and operating system determine whether the user must press a modifier key (e.g., **Ctrl**, **Alt**, or **Command**) with the access key to bring focus to the element. In IE 4/Windows, the **Alt** key is required, and the key is not case sensitive. Not working in IE 4/Mac.

Example document.entryForm.myPassword.accessKey = "n"

Value Single alphanumeric (and punctuation) keyboard character.

Default None.

dataFld   NN *n/a*   IE *4*   DOM *n/a*

Read/Write

Used with IE 4 data binding to associate a remote data source column name to a password object's `value` property. A DATASRC attribute must also be set for the element. Setting both the `dataFld` and `dataSrc` properties to empty strings breaks the binding between element and data source.

Example document.myForm.myPassword.dataFld = "linkURL"

Value Case-sensitive identifier of the data source column.

Default None.

dataSrc   NN *n/a*   IE *4*   DOM *n/a*

Read/Write

Used with IE 4 data binding to specify the name of the remote ODBC data source (such as an Oracle or SQL Server database) to be associated with the element. Content from the data source is specified via the DATAFLD attribute. Setting both the `dataFld` and `dataSrc` properties to empty strings breaks the binding between element and data source.

Example document.myForm.myPassword.dataSrc = "#DBSRC3"

Value Case-sensitive identifier of the data source.

Default None.

defaultValue   NN *2*   IE *3*   DOM *1*

Read-only

The default text for the password input element, as established by the VALUE attribute.

Example
```
var pwObj = document.forms[0].myPassword
if (pwObj.value != pwObj.defaultValue ) {
    ...
}
```

Value   Any string value.

Default   None.

disabled

Read/Write

Whether the element is available for user interaction. When set to **true**, the element cannot receive focus or be modified by the user. It is also not submitted with the form.

Example `document.forms[0].myPassword.disabled = true`

Value   Boolean value: **true** | **false**.

Default   **false**

form

Read-only

Returns a reference to the **FORM** element that contains the current element (if any). This property is most often passed as a parameter for an event handler, using the **this** keyword to refer to the current form control.

Example
```
<INPUT TYPE="password" NAME="passwd" onChange="doValidate(this.form)">
```

Value   Object reference.

Default   None.

maxLength

Read/Write

The maximum number of characters that may be typed into a password field **INPUT** element. In practice, browsers beep or otherwise alert users when a typed character would exceed the **maxLength** value. There is no innate correlation between the **maxLength** and **size** properties. If the **maxLength** allows for more characters than fit within the specified width of the element, the browser provides horizontal scrolling (albeit awkward for many users) to allow entry and editing of the field.

Example `document.entryForm.myPassword.maxLength = 35`

Value   Positive integer value.

Default   Unlimited.

name

Read/Write

The identifier associated with the form control. The value of this property is submitted as one-half of the name/value pair when the form is submitted to the server. Names are hidden from user view, since control labels are assigned via other means, depending on the control type. Form control names may also be used by script references to the objects.

Example `document.orderForm.myPassword.name = "Win32"`

Value

Case-sensitive identifier that follows the rules of identifier naming: it may contain no whitespace, cannot begin with a numeral, and should avoid punctuation except for the underscore character.

Default   None.

readOnly

Read-only

Whether the form element can be edited on the page by the user. A form control whose `readOnly` property is `true` may still be modified by scripts, even though the user may not alter the content.

Example `document.forms[0].myPassword.readOnly = "true"`

Value   Boolean value: `true` | `false`.

Default   `false`

size

Read/Write

Roughly speaking, the width in characters that the input box should be sized to accommodate. In practice, the browser does not always accurately predict the proper width even when all characters are the same, as they are in the password object. See details in the `SIZE` attribute discussion for the `INPUT` element in Chapter 8. There is no interaction between the `size` and `maxLength` properties for this object.

Example `document.forms[0].myPassword.size = 12`

Value   Positive integer.

Default   20

tabIndex

Read/Write

A number that indicates the sequence of this element within the tabbing order of all focusable elements in the document. Tabbing order follows a strict set of rules. Elements that have values other than zero assigned to their `tabIndex` properties are first in line when a user starts tabbing in a page. Focus starts with the element with the lowest `tabIndex` value and proceeds in order to the highest value, regardless of physical location on the page or in the document. If two elements have the same `tabIndex` values, the element that comes earlier in the document receives focus first. Next come all elements that either don't support the `tabIndex` property or have the value set to zero. These elements receive focus in the order in which they appear in the document. A value of -1 removes the element from tabbing order altogether.

Note that the Macintosh user interface does not provide for giving focus to elements other than text and password `INPUT` fields.

Example   `document.forms[0].myPassword.tabIndex = 6`

Value   Integer.

Default   None.

type   NN *3*   IE *4*   DOM *1*

Read-only

Returns the type of form control element. The value is returned in all lowercase letters. It may be necessary to cycle through all form elements in search of specific types to do some processing on (e.g., emptying all form controls of type `"text"` while leaving other controls untouched).

Example

```
if (document.forms[0].elements[3].type ==  "password") {
    ...
}
```

Value

Any of the following constants (as a string): `button` | `checkbox` | `file` | `hidden` | `image` | `password` | `radio` | `reset` | `select-multiple` | `select-one` | `submit` | `text` | `textarea`.

Default   `password`

value   NN *2*   IE *3*   DOM *1*

Read/Write

Current value associated with the form control that is submitted with the name/value pair for the element. All values are strings. Browsers return the actual characters typed by the user (except in Navigator 2), so you can retrieve an entered password for further processing before submission (or perhaps for storage in the cookie).

Example   `document.forms[0].myPassword.value = "franken"`

Value   String.

Default   None.

blur()   NN *2*   IE *3*   DOM *n/a*

Removes focus from the current element and fires an `onBlur` event (in IE). No other element necessarily receives focus as a result.

Returned Value

None.

Parameters

None.

focus()   NN *2*   IE *3*   DOM *n/a*

Gives focus to the current element and fires the **onFocus** event (in IE). If another element had focus at the time, it receives an **onBlur** event.

Returned Value

None.

Parameters

None.

handleEvent()   NN *4*   IE *n/a*   DOM *n/a*

handleEvent(*event*)

Instructs the object to accept and process the event whose specifications are passed as the parameter to the method. The object must have an event handler for the event type to process the event.

Returned Value

None.

Parameters

event   A Navigator 4 **event** object.

select()   NN *2*   IE *3*   DOM *n/a*

Selects all the text displayed in the form element.

Returned Value

None.

Parameters

None.

personalbar

See locationbar.

PLAINTEXT

NN *n/a*   IE *4*   DOM *1*

The PLAINTEXT object reflects the PLAINTEXT element. Note that the Win32 version of Internet Explorer 4 incorrectly evaluates the innerHTML, innerText, outerHTML, and outerText property values to include all document content following the start tag for the element. This element is deprecated in favor the PRE element.

HTML Equivalent

```
<PLAINTEXT>
```

Object Model Reference

IE   [window.]document.all.*elementID*

Properties

className	isTextEdit	offsetLeft	outerHTML	sourceIndex
document	lang	offsetParent	outerText	style
id	language	offsetTop	parentElement	tagName
innerHTML	offsetHeight	offsetWidth	parentTextEdit	title
innerText				

Methods

click()	insertAdjacentHTML()	scrollIntoView()
contains()	insertAdjacentText()	setAttribute()
getAttribute()	removeAttribute()	

Collections/Arrays

all[]	children[]	filters[]

Event Handler Properties

Handler	NN	IE	DOM
onclick	n/a	4	n/a
ondblclick	n/a	4	n/a
ondragstart	n/a	4	n/a
onfilterchange	n/a	4	n/a
onhelp	n/a	4	n/a
onkeydown	n/a	4	n/a
onkeypress	n/a	4	n/a
onkeyup	n/a	4	n/a
onmousedown	n/a	4	n/a
onmousemove	n/a	4	n/a
onmouseout	n/a	4	n/a
onmouseover	n/a	4	n/a
onmouseup	n/a	4	n/a
onselectstart	n/a	4	n/a

plugin NN *3*   IE *n/a*   DOM *n/a*

A plugin object represents a single plugin that is registered with Navigator at launch time. Access to a single plugin is normally via the navigator.plugins array. It is also common to use the navigator.mimeTypes array and associated properties to uncover whether the browser has the desired plugin installed before loading external content. Most of the properties provide scripted access to information normally found in the **About Plug-ins** window available from Navigator's **Help** menu.

Object Model Reference
NN   navigator.plugins[i]

Properties
description   filename   length   name

Methods
refresh()

description NN *3*   IE *n/a*   DOM *n/a*
Read-only

A brief plain-language description of the plugin supplied by the plugin manufacturer.

Example var descr = navigator.plugins[2].description

Value   String.

Default None.

filename NN *3*   IE *n/a*   DOM *n/a*
Read-only

Returns the filename of the plugin binary. In Win32 versions of Navigator, the full pathname is returned; for the Mac, only the filename is returned.

Example var file = navigator.plugins[2].filename

Value   String.

Default None.

length NN *3*   IE *n/a*   DOM *n/a*
Read-only

Returns the number of MIME types supported by the plugin. Don't confuse this property with the length property of the entire navigator.plugins array, which measures how many plugin objects are known to the browser.

Example var howManyMIMEs = navigator.plugins[2].length

Value   Integer.

Default None.

name

Read-only

Returns the name of the plugin assigned to it by its manufacturer. You cannot, however, be guaranteed that a plugin designed for multiple operating systems has the same name across all versions.

Example   `var pName = navigator.plugins[2].name`

Value   Integer.

Default   None.

refresh()

Instructs the browser to reregister plugins installed in the plugins directory. This allows a browser to summon a newly installed plugin without forcing the user to quit and relaunch the browser.

Returned Value

None.

Parameters

None.

plugins

Navigator and Internet Explorer both have a `plugins` array, but they are quite different collections of objects. Navigator's `plugins` array is a property of the `navigator` object. Each item in the `navigator.plugins` array represents a plugin that is installed in the browser (actually just registered with the browser when the browser last loaded). See the `plugin` object.

Internet Explorer's `plugins` collection belongs to the `document` object and essentially mirrors the `embeds` collection: a collection of all `EMBED` elements in the document. An `EMBED` element may well, indeed, launch a plugin, but not necessarily. Nor does Internet Explorer provide JavaScript access to the installed plugins in the same way that Navigator does.

Object Model Reference

NN   `navigator.plugins`

IE   `document.plugins`

Properties

`length`

Methods

`item()`

length　　　　　　　　　　　　　　　　NN *3*　IE *4*　DOM *n/a*

Returns the number of elements in the collection.

Example

```
var IEhowMany = document.embeds.length
var NNhowMany = navigator.embeds.length
```

Value　　Integer.

item( )　　　　　　　　　　　　　　　　NN *n/a*　IE *4*　DOM *n/a*

```
item(index[, subindex])
```

Returns a single object or collection of objects corresponding to the element matching the index value (or, optionally, the index and subindex values).

Returned Value

One object or collection (array) of objects. If there are no matches to the parameters, the returned value is `null`.

Parameters

index　　When the parameter is a zero-based integer, the returned value is a single element corresponding to the said numbered item in source code order (nested within the current element); when the parameter is a string, the returned value is a collection of elements whose **id** or **name** properties match that string.

subindex　If you specify a string value for the first parameter, you may use the second parameter to specify a zero-based integer to retrieve a specific element from the collection whose **id** or **name** properties match the first parameter's string value.

PRE　　　　　　　　　　　　　　　　NN *n/a*　IE *4*　DOM *1*

The **PRE** object reflects the **PRE** element. This object and element has superseded the deprecated **XMP** object and element.

HTML Equivalent

```
<PRE>
```

Object Model Reference

IE　　　　[window.]document.all.*elementID*

Properties

className	*isTextEdit*	*offsetLeft*	*outerHTML*	*sourceIndex*
document	*lang*	*offsetParent*	*outerText*	*style*
id	*language*	*offsetTop*	*parentElement*	*tagName*
innerHTML	*offsetHeight*	*offsetWidth*	*parentTextEdit*	*title*
innerText				

Methods

click()	insertAdjacentHTML()	scrollIntoView()
contains()	insertAdjacentText()	setAttribute()
getAttribute()	removeAttribute()	

Collections/Arrays

all[]	children[]	filters[]

Event Handler Properties

Handler	NN	IE	DOM
onclick	n/a	4	n/a
ondblclick	n/a	4	n/a
ondragstart	n/a	4	n/a
onfilterchange	n/a	4	n/a
onhelp	n/a	4	n/a
onkeydown	n/a	4	n/a
onkeypress	n/a	4	n/a
onkeyup	n/a	4	n/a
onmousedown	n/a	4	n/a
onmousemove	n/a	4	n/a
onmouseout	n/a	4	n/a
onmouseover	n/a	4	n/a
onmouseup	n/a	4	n/a
onselectstart	n/a	4	n/a

Q

NN *n/a*   IE *4*   DOM *1*

The Q object reflects the Q element.

HTML Equivalent

<Q>

Object Model Reference

IE   [window.]document.all.*elementID*

Properties

className	isTextEdit	offsetLeft	outerHTML	sourceIndex
document	lang	offsetParent	outerText	style
id	language	offsetTop	parentElement	tagName
innerHTML	offsetHeight	offsetWidth	parentTextEdit	title
innerText				

Methods

click()	insertAdjacentHTML()	scrollIntoView()
contains()	insertAdjacentText()	setAttribute()
getAttribute()	removeAttribute()	

Collections/Arrays

all[]   children[]   filters[]

Event Handler Properties

Handler	NN	IE	DOM
onclick	n/a	4	n/a
ondblclick	n/a	4	n/a
ondragstart	n/a	4	n/a
onfilterchange	n/a	4	n/a
onhelp	n/a	4	n/a
onkeydown	n/a	4	n/a
onkeypress	n/a	4	n/a
onkeyup	n/a	4	n/a
onmousedown	n/a	4	n/a
onmousemove	n/a	4	n/a
onmouseout	n/a	4	n/a
onmouseover	n/a	4	n/a
onmouseup	n/a	4	n/a
onselectstart	n/a	4	n/a

radio   NN *2*   IE *3*   DOM *1*

The radio object is a form control generated with an INPUT element whose TYPE attribute is set to "radio". radio objects related to each other are assigned the same name. This means all like-named radio objects become a collection of radio objects. It may be necessary, therefore, to reference an individual radio button as an item in an array. The entire array, of course, has a length property you can use to assist in looping through all radio objects within the group, if necessary:

```
var radioGrp = document.forms[0].myRadio
for (var i = 0; i < radioGrp.length; i++) {
    alert("The value of button index " + i + " is " + radioGrp [i].value)
}
```

Properties and methods listed as follows are for individual radio buttons.

HTML Equivalent

```
<INPUT TYPE="radio">
```

Object Model Reference

NN   [window.]document.*formName.elementName*[i]
          [window.]document.forms[i].elements[i]
IE   [window.]document.*formName.elementName*[i]
          [window.]document.forms[i].elements[i]
          [window.]document.all.*elementID*

Properties

accessKey	*document*	*offsetHeight*	*outerText*	*style*
checked	form	*offsetLeft*	*parentElement*	tabIndex
className	*id*	*offsetParent*	*parentTextEdit*	*tagName*
dataFld	*isTextEdit*	*offsetTop*	recordNumber	*title*
dataSrc	*lang*	*offsetWidth*	*sourceIndex*	type
defaultChecked	*language*	*outerHTML*	status	value
disabled	name			

Methods

blur()	*getAttribute()*	*removeAttribute()*
click()	handleEvent()	*scrollIntoView()*
contains()	*insertAdjacentHTML()*	*setAttribute()*
focus()	*insertAdjacentText()*	

Collections/Arrays

all[]	*children[]*	*filters[]*

Event Handler Properties

Handler	NN	IE	DOM
onafterupdate	n/a	4	n/a
onbeforeupdate	n/a	4	n/a
onblur	n/a	4	n/a
onchange	n/a	4	n/a
onclick	3	4	n/a
ondblclick	n/a	4	n/a
onerrorupdate	n/a	4	n/a
onfilterchange	n/a	4	n/a
onfocus	n/a	4	n/a
onhelp	n/a	4	n/a
onkeydown	n/a	4	n/a
onkeypress	n/a	4	n/a
onkeyup	n/a	4	n/a
onmousedown	4	4	n/a
onmousemove	n/a	4	n/a
onmouseout	n/a	4	n/a
onmouseover	n/a	4	n/a
onmouseup	4	4	n/a
onselect	n/a	4	n/a

accessKey   NN *n/a*   IE *4*   DOM *1*

Read/Write

A single character key that "clicks" on the radio button. The browser and operating system determine whether the user must press a modifier key (e.g., **Ctrl**, **Alt**, or **Command**) with the access key to "click" the button. In IE 4/Windows, the **Alt** key is required, and the key is not case sensitive. Not working in IE 4/Mac.

Example `document.entryForm.myRadio[0].accessKey = "n"`

Value Single alphanumeric (and punctuation) keyboard character.

Default None.

checked

Read/Write

Whether the radio button is selected or turned on by the user. To find out whether the form element is set to be highlighted when the page loads, see the `defaultChecked` property.

Example

```
if (document.choiceForm.myRadio[0].checked) {
    process for the "monitors" checkbox being checked
}
```

Value Boolean: `true` | `false`.

Default `false`

dataFld

Read/Write

Used with IE 4 data binding to associate a remote data source column name to a radio button element attribute determined by properties set in the object. A DATASRC attribute must also be set for the element. Setting both the `dataFld` and `dataSrc` properties to empty strings breaks the binding between element and data source.

Example `document.myForm.myRadio[0].dataFld = "linkURL"`

Value Case-sensitive identifier of the data source column.

Default None.

dataSrc

Read/Write

Used with IE 4 data binding to specify the name of the remote ODBC data source (such as an Oracle or SQL Server database) to be associated with the element. Content from the data source is specified via the DATAFLD attribute. Setting both the `dataFld` and `dataSrc` properties to empty strings breaks the binding between element and data source.

Example `document.myForm.myRadio[0].dataSrc = "#DBSRC3"`

Value Case-sensitive identifier of the data source.

Default None.

defaultChecked

Read/Write

Whether element has the CHECKED attribute set in the tag. You can compare the current `checked` property against `defaultChecked` to see whether the state of the control has

DOM Reference

changed since the document loaded. Changing this property doesn't affect the current **checked** status.

Example

```
var rBut = document.forms[0].myRadio[0]
if (rBut.checked != rBut.defaultChecked) {
    process for changed state
}
```

Value   Boolean value: **true** | **false**.

Default   Determined by HTML tag attribute.

disabled   NN *n/a*   IE *4*   DOM *1*

Read/Write

Whether the element is available for user interaction. When set to **true**, the element cannot receive focus or be modified by the user. It is also not submitted with the form.

Example   `document.forms[0].myRadio[0].disabled = true`

Value   Boolean value: **true** | **false**.

Default   false

form   NN *2*   IE *3*   DOM *n/a*

Read-only

Returns a reference to the **FORM** element that contains the current element (if any). This property is most often passed as a parameter for an event handler, using the **this** keyword to refer to the current form control.

Example

```
<INPUT TYPE="button" VALUE="Validate Form" onClick="doValidate(this.form)">
```

Value   Object reference.

Default   None.

name   NN *2*   IE *3*   DOM *1*

Read/Write

The identifier associated with the form control. The value of this property is submitted as one-half of the name/value pair when the form is submitted to the server (the **value** property of the highlighted radio button supplies the value portion). Names are hidden from user view, since control labels are assigned via other means, depending on the control type. Form control names may also be used by script references to the objects. Assign the same name to every radio button in a group whose highlight/unhighlight characteristics are related.

Example   `document.orderForm.myRadio[0].name = "Win32"`

Value

Case-sensitive identifier that follows the rules of identifier naming: it may contain no whitespace, can't begin with a numeral, and should avoid punctuation except for the underscore character.

Default   None.

recordNumber

NN *n/a*   IE *4*   DOM *n/a*

Read-only

Used with data binding, returns an integer representing the record within the data set that generated the element (i.e., an element whose content is filled via data binding). Values of this property can be used to extract a specific record from an Active Data Objects (ADO) record set (see **recordset** property).

Example

```
<SCRIPT FOR="tableTemplate" EVENT="onclick">
    myDataCollection.recordset.absoluteposition = this.recordNumber
    ...
</SCRIPT>
```

Value   Integer.

Default   None.

status

NN *n/a*   IE *4*   DOM *n/a*

Read/Write

Whether the element is highlighted/checked. This property is identical to the **value** property.

Example

```
if (document.forms[0].myRadio[0].status) {
    ...
}
```

Value   Boolean value: **true** | **false**.

Default   None.

tabIndex

NN *n/a*   IE *4*   DOM *1*

Read/Write

A number that indicates the sequence of this element within the tabbing order of all focusable elements in the document. Tabbing order follows a strict set of rules. Elements that have values other than zero assigned to their **tabIndex** properties are first in line when a user starts tabbing in a page. Focus starts with the element with the lowest **tabIndex** value and proceeds in order to the highest value, regardless of physical location on the page or in the document. If two elements have the same **tabIndex** values, the element that comes earlier in the document receives focus first. Next come all elements that either don't support the **tabIndex** property or have the value set to zero. These elements receive focus in the order in which they appear in the document. A value of -1 removes the element from tabbing order altogether. Note that the Macintosh user interface doesn't provide for giving focus to elements other than text and password INPUT fields.

Example `document.forms[0].myRadio[0].tabIndex = 6`

Value   Integer.

Default None.

type   NN *3*   IE *4*   DOM *1*

Read-only

Returns the type of form control element. The value is returned in all lowercase letters. It may be necessary to cycle through all form elements in search of specific types to do some processing on (e.g., emptying all form controls of type `"text"` while leaving other controls untouched).

Example

```
if (document.forms[0].elements[3].type == "radio") {
    ...
}
```

Value

Any of the following constants (as a string): button | checkbox | file | hidden | image | password | radio | reset | select-multiple | select-one | submit | text | textarea.

Default radio

value   NN *2*   IE *3*   DOM *1*

Read/Write

Current value associated with the form control that is submitted with the name/value pair for the group of like-named elements. All values are strings, but they may represent other kinds of data, including Boolean and numeric values.

Example `document.forms[0].myRadio[0].value = "*"`

Value   String.

Default None.

blur()   NN *n/a*   IE *4*   DOM *n/a*

Removes focus from the current element and fires an onBlur event (in IE). No other element necessarily receives focus as a result.

Returned Value

None.

Parameters

None.

focus()

NN *n/a*   IE *4*   DOM *n/a*

Gives focus to the current element and fires the onFocus event (in IE). If another element had focus at the time, it receives an onBlur event.

Returned Value

None.

Parameters

None.

handleEvent()

NN *4*   IE *n/a*   DOM *n/a*

handleEvent(*event*)

Instructs the object to accept and process the event whose specifications are passed as the parameter to the method. The object must have an event handler for the event type to process the event.

Returned Value

None.

Parameters

event   A Navigator 4 **event** object.

reset

NN *2*   IE *3*   DOM *1*

The reset object is a form control generated with an INPUT element whose TYPE attribute is set to reset. This element is similar to the button object. No script action is necessary for the reset object to do its job of restoring form controls to their default settings.

HTML Equivalent

<INPUT TYPE="reset">

Object Model Reference

NN   [window.]document.*formName*.*elementName*
           [window.]document.forms[i].elements[i]

IE   [window.]document.*formName*.*elementName*
           [window.]document.forms[i].elements[i]
           [window.]document.all.*elementID*

Properties

accessKey	isTextEdit	offsetLeft	outerText	tabIndex
className	lang	offsetParent	parentElement	tagName
disabled	language	offsetTop	parentTextEdit	title
document	name	offsetWidth	sourceIndex	type
form	offsetHeight	outerHTML	style	value
id				

Methods

blur()	getAttribute()	removeAttribute()
click()	handleEvent()	scrollIntoView()
contains()	insertAdjacentHTML()	setAttribute()
focus()	insertAdjacentText()	

Collections/Arrays

all[]	children[]	filters[]

Event Handler Properties

Handler	NN	IE	DOM
onblur	n/a	4	n/a
onclick	3	4	n/a
ondblclick	n/a	4	n/a
onfilterchange	n/a	4	n/a
onfocus	n/a	4	n/a
onhelp	n/a	4	n/a
onkeydown	n/a	4	n/a
onkeypress	n/a	4	n/a
onkeyup	n/a	4	n/a
onmousedown	4	4	n/a
onmousemove	n/a	4	n/a
onmouseout	n/a	4	n/a
onmouseover	n/a	4	n/a
onmouseup	4	4	n/a
onselect	n/a	4	n/a

accessKey

NN *n/a*   IE *4*   DOM *1*

Read/Write

A single character key that "clicks" the reset button. The browser and operating system determine whether the user must press a modifier key (e.g., **Ctrl**, **Alt**, or **Command**) with the access key to "click" the button. In IE 4/Windows, the **Alt** key is required, and the key is not case sensitive. Not working in IE 4/Mac.

Example   document.entryForm.myReset.accessKey = "n"

Value   Single alphanumeric (and punctuation) keyboard character.

Default   None.

disabled

NN *n/a*   IE *4*   DOM *1*

Read/Write

Whether the element is available for user interaction. When set to true, the element cannot receive focus.

Example   document.forms[0].myReset.disabled = true

Value   Boolean value: `true` | `false`.

Default   false

form

Read-only

Returns a reference to the FORM element that contains the current element (if any). This property is most often passed as a parameter for an event handler, using the this keyword to refer to the current form control.

Example

```
<INPUT TYPE="button" VALUE="Validate Form" onClick="doValidate(this.form)">
```

Value   Object reference.

Default   None.

name

Read/Write

The identifier associated with the form control. Names are hidden from user view, since control labels are assigned via other means, depending on the control type. Form control names may also be used by script references to the objects.

Example `document.orderForm.myReset.name = "Win32"`

Value

Case-sensitive identifier that follows the rules of identifier naming: it may contain no whitespace, cannot begin with a numeral, and should avoid punctuation except for the underscore character.

Default   None.

tabIndex

Read/Write

A number that indicates the sequence of this element within the tabbing order of all focusable elements in the document. Tabbing order follows a strict set of rules. Elements that have values other than zero assigned to their tabIndex properties are first in line when a user starts tabbing in a page. Focus starts with the element with the lowest tabIndex value and proceeds in order to the highest value, regardless of physical location on the page or in the document. If two elements have the same tabIndex values, the element that comes earlier in the document receives focus first. Next come all elements that either don't support the tabIndex property or have the value set to zero. These elements receive focus in the order in which they appear in the document. A value of -1 removes the element from tabbing order altogether.

Note that the Macintosh user interface does not provide for giving focus to elements other than text and password INPUT fields.

Example `document.forms[0].myReset.tabIndex = 6`

Value   Integer.

Default   None.

type   NN *3*   IE *4*   DOM *1*

Returns the type of form control element. The value is returned in all lowercase letters. It may be necessary to cycle through all form elements in search of specific types to do some processing on (e.g., emptying all form controls of type `"text"` while leaving other controls untouched).

Example

```
if (document.forms[0].elements[3].type ==  "reset") {
    ...
}
```

Value

Any of the following constants (as a string): `button` | `checkbox` | `file` | `hidden` | `image` | `password` | `radio` | `reset` | `select-multiple` | `select-one` | `submit` | `text` | `textarea`.

Default   `reset`

value   NN *2*   IE *3*   DOM *1*

This is the rare time that the `value` property controls the label of a form control: the text that appears on the reset button.

Example   `document.forms[0].myReset.value = "Undo"`

Value   String.

Default   Reset

blur()   NN *n/a*   IE *4*   DOM *n/a*

Removes focus from the current element and fires an `onBlur` event (in IE). No other element necessarily receives focus as a result.

Returned Value

None.

Parameters

None.

focus()   NN *n/a*   IE *4*   DOM *n/a*

Gives focus to the current element and fires the `onFocus` event (in IE). If another element had focus at the time, it receives an `onBlur` event.

Returned Value

None.

Parameters

None.

handleEvent() NN *4* IE *n/a* DOM *n/a*

handleEvent(*event*)

Instructs the object to accept and process the event whose specifications are passed as the parameter to the method. The object must have an event handler for the event type to process the event.

Returned Value

None.

Parameters

event   A Navigator 4 **event** object.

rows NN *n/a* IE *4* DOM *n/a*

A collection of all TR elements contained in a single TABLE, TBODY, TFOOT, or THEAD element. The rows collection of a TABLE element includes all rows of the table, regardless of how they're subdivided into row groups. Collection members are sorted in source code order. Internet Explorer lets you use array notation or parentheses to access a single row in the collection (e.g., document.all.myTable.rows[0], document.all.myTable.rows(0)).

Object Model Reference

IE   document.all.tableOrGroupID.rows(i)
      document.all.tableOrGroupID.rows[i]

Properties

length

Methods

item()   tags()

length NN *n/a* IE *4* DOM *n/a*

Read-only

Returns the number of elements in the collection.

Example var howMany = document.all.myTable.rows.length

Value   Integer.

item()   NN *n/a*   IE *4*   DOM *n/a*

`item(index[, subindex])`

Returns a single object or collection of objects corresponding to the element matching the index value (or, optionally, the index and subindex values).

Returned Value

One object or collection (array) of objects. If there are no matches to the parameters, the returned value is `null`.

Parameters

index   When the parameter is a zero-based integer, the returned value is a single element corresponding to the said numbered item in source code order (nested within the current element); when the parameter is a string, the returned value is a collection of elements whose `id` or `name` properties match that string.

subindex If you specify a string value for the first parameter, you may use the second parameter to specify a zero-based integer to retrieve a specific element from the collection whose `id` or `name` properties match the first parameter's string value.

tags()   NN *n/a*   IE *4*   DOM *n/a*

`tags(tagName)`

Returns a collection of objects (among all objects nested within the current element) whose tags match the *tagName* parameter.

Returned Value

A collection (array) of objects. If there are no matches to the parameters, the returned value is an array of zero length.

Parameters

tagName A string of the all-uppercase version of the element tag, as in `document.all.myTable.rows.tags("TR")`.

rule   NN *n/a*   IE *4*   DOM *n/a*

A `rule` object contains the combination of selector and style attribute/value pairs defined within a style sheet. While you can obtain the selector directly as a property, a script cannot quickly derive the style attributes or values assigned in the rule without iterating through all style attributes.

Object Model Reference

IE   `document.all.`*styleSheetID*`.rules(i)`

Properties

`readOnly`   `selectorText`   *style*

readOnly

NN *n/a*   IE *4*   DOM *n/a*

Read-only

Whether the style sheet (and thus the rules therein) can be modified under script control. Style sheets imported through a `LINK` element or an `@import` rule cannot be modified, so they return a value of `true`.

Value   Boolean value: `true` | `false`.

Default   `false`

selectorText

NN *n/a*   IE *4*   DOM *n/a*

Read-only

Returns the selector defined for the rule.

Value   String

Default   None.

rules

NN *n/a*   IE *4*   DOM *n/a*

A collection of all rules defined or imported for a `styleSheet` object. Collection members are sorted in source code order. Internet Explorer lets you use array notation or parentheses to access a single row in the collection (e.g., `document.all.myTable.rows[0]`, `document.all.myTable.rows(0)`). Unlike some other collections that have methods for adding or removing items, a `styleSheet` object's rule is added via methods of the `styleSheet` object.

Object Model Reference
IE   `document.all.styleSheetID.rules`

Properties
`length`

length

NN *n/a*   IE *4*   DOM *n/a*

Read-only

Returns the number of elements in the collection.

Example   `var howMany = document.all.mySheet.rules.length`

Value   Integer.

S

See B.

SAMP

See ACRONYM.

DOM Reference

screen   NN 4   IE 4   DOM *n/a*

The screen object refers to the video display on which the browser is being viewed. Many video control panel settings influence the property values.

Object Model Reference

NN	screen
IE	screen

Properties

availHeight	availTop	bufferDepth	height	updateInterval
availLeft	availWidth	colorDepth	pixelDepth	width

availHeight, availWidth   NN 4   IE 4   DOM *n/a*

Read-only

Height and width of the content region of the user's video monitor in pixels. This measure does not include the 24-pixel taskbar (Windows 95/NT) or 20-pixel system menubar (Macintosh). IE 4/Macintosh miscalculates the height of the menubar as 24 pixels. To use these values in creating a maximized window, you also have to adjust the top-left position of the window.

Example

```
var newWind = window.open("","","HEIGHT=" + screen.availHeight +
",WIDTH=" + screen.availWidth)
```

Value   Integer of available pixels in vertical and horizontal dimensions.

Default   Depends on the user's monitor size.

availLeft, availTop   NN 4   IE *n/a*   DOM *n/a*

Read-only

Pixel coordinates of the left and top edges of the screen. Always zero, as far as I can tell.

Value   Integer.

Default   0

bufferDepth   NN *n/a*   IE 4   DOM *n/a*

Read/Write

Setting of the offscreen bitmap buffer. Path animation smoothness may improve on some clients if you match the bufferDepth to the colorDepth values. Setting the bufferDepth to -1 forces IE to buffer at the screen's pixel depth (as set in the control panel), and colorDepth is automatically set to that value, as well (plus if a user changes the bits per pixel, the buffer is adjusted accordingly). A setting to any of the other permitted values (1, 4, 8, 15, 16, 24, or 32) buffers at that pixel depth and sets the colorDepth to that value. The client's display must be set to the higher bits-per-pixel values to take advantage of the higher settings in scripts.

Example screen.bufferDepth = 4

Value   Any of the following allowed integers: –1 | 0 | 4 | 8 | 15 | 16 | 24 | 32.

Default   0

colorDepth   NN 4   IE 4   DOM *n/a*

Returns the number of bits per pixel used to display color in the video monitor or image buffer. Although this property is read-only, its value can be influenced by settings of the bufferDepth property (IE only). You can determine the color depth of the current video screen and select colors accordingly.

Example

```
if (screen.colorDepth > 8) {
    document.all.pretty.color = "cornflowerblue"
} else {
    document.all.pretty.color = "blue"
}
```

Value   Integer.

Default   Current video control panel setting.

height, width   NN 4   IE 4   DOM *n/a*

Returns the number of pixels available vertically and horizontally in the client video monitor. This is the raw dimension. For the amount of screen space not covered by system bars, see availHeight and availWidth.

Example

```
if (screen.height > 480 && screen.width > 640) {
    ...
}
```

Value   Integer of pixel counts.

Default   Depends on video monitor.

pixelDepth   NN 4   IE *n/a*   DOM *n/a*

Returns the number of bits per pixel used to display color in the video monitor. This value is similar to the colorDepth property, but it is not influenced by a potential custom color palette, as colorDepth is.

Example

```
if (screen.pixelDepth > 8) {
    document.all.pretty.color = "cornflowerblue"
} else {
    document.all.pretty.color = "blue"
}
```

Value   Integer.

Default   Current video control panel setting.

updateInterval

The time interval (in milliseconds) between screen updates. A value of zero lets the browser select an average that usually works best. The longer the interval, the more animation steps may be buffered and then ignored as the update fires to display the current state.

Example `screen.updateInterval = 0`

Value   Positive integer or zero.

Default   0

width

See height.

SCRIPT

The SCRIPT object reflects the SCRIPT element. Note that the Win32 version of Internet Explorer chokes on accessing or setting the **innerHTML** or **innerText** properties.

HTML Equivalent

`<SCRIPT>`

Object Model Reference

IE   `[window.]document.all.elementID`

Properties

className	htmlFor	isTextEdit	readyState	tagName
defer	id	language	src	text
document	innerHTML	parentElement	sourceIndex	title
event	innerText	parentTextEdit	style	type

Methods

contains()	insertAdjacentHTML()	removeAttribute()
getAttribute()	insertAdjacentText()	setAttribute()

Event Handler Properties

Handler	NN	IE	DOM
onerror	n/a	4	n/a
onload	n/a	4	n/a
onreadystatechange	n/a	4	n/a

defer   NN *n/a*   IE *4*   DOM *n/a*

Read/Write

Whether the browser should proceed with rendering regular HTML content without looking for the script to generate content as the page loads. This value needs to be set in the SCRIPT element's tag at run-time. When this property is set to true by the addition of the DEFER attribute to the tag, the browser does not have to hold up rendering further HTML content to parses the content of the SCRIPT element in search of document.write() statements. Changing this property's value after the document loads does not affect the performance of the script or browser.

Example `document.all.myScript.defer = "true"`

Value   Boolean value: true | false.

Default false

event   NN *n/a*   IE *4*   DOM *n/a*

Read-only

Internet Explorer 4's event model allows binding of object events to SCRIPT elements with the help of the EVENT and FOR attributes (see Chapter 6). The event property returns the setting for the EVENT attribute.

Example
```
if (document.all.scripts[2].event == "onresize") {
    ...
}
```
Value   Case-sensitive event name.

Default None.

htmlFor   NN *n/a*   IE *4*   DOM *n/a*

Read-only

Returns the value (element ID) assigned to the FOR attribute of a SCRIPT element. This attribute defines the document element to which the script is bound when a specific event (set by the EVENT attribute) fires for the element.

Example
```
if (document.all.scripts[3].htmlFor == "helpButton") {
    ...
}
```
Value   String.

Default None.

readyState

NN *n/a*   IE *4*   DOM *n/a*

Read-only

Returns the current download status of the script being loaded from an external library (*.js*) file. This property provides a more granular way of testing whether a particular download-able element is ready to be run or scripted instead of the onLoad event handler for the entire document. As the value of this property changes during loading, the system fires an onReadyStateChange event.

Example

```
if (document.all.myExternalScript.readyState == "uninitialized") {
    statements for alternate handling
}
```

Value

One of the following values (as strings): complete | interactive | loading | unini-tialized. Some elements may allow the user to interact with partial content, in which case the property may return interactive until all loading has completed.

Default   None.

src

NN *n/a*   IE *4*   DOM *1*

Read-only

URL of the *.js* script file imported into the current SCRIPT element.

Example

```
if (document.all.scripts2.src == "scripts/textlib.js") {
    . . .
}
```

Value   Complete or relative URL as a string.

Default   None.

text

NN *n/a*   IE *4*   DOM *1*

Read-only

The text content of the element.

Example   var scriptText = document.all.script3.text

Value   String.

Default   None.

type

NN *n/a*   IE *4*   DOM *1*

Read-only

An advisory about the content type of the script statements. The content type should tell the browser which scripting engine to use to interpret the script statements, such as text/

javascript. The TYPE attribute may eventually replace the LANGUAGE attribute as the one defining the scripting language in which the element's statements are written.

Example   `var scriptMIMEtype = document.all.script3.type`

Value   String.

Default   None.

scripts

A collection of all scripts defined or imported in a document, including those defined in the HEAD or BODY portion. Collection members are sorted in source code order. Internet Explorer lets you use array notation or parentheses to access a single row in the collection.

Object Model Reference

IE   `document.scripts`

Properties

`length`

Methods

`item()`

length

Read-only

Returns the number of elements in the collection.

Example   `var howMany = document.scripts.length`

Value   Integer.

item()

`item(index[, subindex])`

Returns a single object or collection of objects corresponding to the element matching the index value (or, optionally, the index and subindex values).

Returned Value

One object or collection (array) of objects. If there are no matches to the parameters, the returned value is `null`.

Parameters

`index`   When the parameter is a zero-based integer, the returned value is a single element corresponding to the said numbered item in source code order (nested within the current element); when the parameter is a string, the returned value is a collection of elements whose `id` or `name` properties match that string.

subindex If you specify a string value for the first parameter, you may use the second parameter to specify a zero-based integer to retrieve a specific element from the collection whose id or name properties match the first parameter's string value.

scrollbars

See locationbar.

SELECT   NN *2*   IE *3*   DOM *1*

The SELECT object reflects the SELECT element. This element is a form control that contains OPTION elements. Note that the innerHTML and innerText properties are not available on the Macintosh version of Internet Explorer 4.

HTML Equivalent
<SELECT>

Object Model Reference
NN   [window.]document.*formName*.*selectName*
        [window.]document.forms[i].elements[i]
IE   [window.]document.*formName*.*selectName*
        [window.]document.forms[i].elements[i]
        [window.]document.all.*elementID*

Properties

accessKey	id	multiple	outerHTML	style
className	innerHTML	name	outerText	tabIndex
dataFld	innerText	offsetHeight	parentElement	tagName
dataSrc	isTextEdit	offsetLeft	parentTextEdit	title
disabled	lang	offsetParent	recordNumber	type
document	language	offsetTop	selectedIndex	value
form	length	offsetWidth	sourceIndex	

Methods

blur()	getAttribute()	removeAttribute()
click()	insertAdjacentHTML()	scrollIntoView()
contains()	insertAdjacentText()	setAttribute()
focus()		

Collections/Arrays

all[]	children[]	filters[]	options[]	tags[]

Event Handler Properties

Handler	NN	IE	DOM
onafterupdate	n/a	4	n/a
onbeforeupdate	n/a	4	n/a
onblur	n/a	4	n/a

Handler	NN	IE	DOM
onchange	n/a	4	n/a
onclick	n/a	4	n/a
ondblclick	n/a	4	n/a
ondragstart	n/a	4	n/a
onerrorupdate	n/a	4	n/a
onfilterchange	n/a	4	n/a
onhelp	n/a	4	n/a
onkeydown	n/a	4	n/a
onkeypress	n/a	4	n/a
onkeyup	n/a	4	n/a
onmousedown	n/a	4	n/a
onmousemove	n/a	4	n/a
onmouseout	n/a	4	n/a
onmouseover	n/a	4	n/a
onmouseup	n/a	4	n/a
onresize	n/a	4	n/a
onrowenter	n/a	4	n/a
onrowexit	n/a	4	n/a
onselectstart	n/a	4	n/a

accessKey

NN *n/a*   IE *4*   DOM *n/a*

Read/Write

A single character key that brings focus to the element. The browser and operating system determine whether the user must press a modifier key (e.g., **Ctrl**, **Alt**, or **Command**) with the access key to bring focus to the element. In IE 4/Windows, the **Alt** key is required, and the key is not case sensitive. Not working in IE 4/Mac.

Example   `document.entryForm.mySelect.accessKey = "n"`

Value   Single alphanumeric (and punctuation) keyboard character.

Default   None.

dataFld

NN *n/a*   IE *4*   DOM *n/a*

Read/Write

Used with IE 4 data binding to associate a remote data source column name with the `selectedIndex` property of the **SELECT** object. A **DATASRC** attribute must also be set for the element. Setting both the `dataFld` and `dataSrc` properties to empty strings breaks the binding between element and data source.

Example   `document.forms[0].mySelect.dataFld = "choice"`

Value   Case-sensitive identifier of the data source column.

Default   None.

dataSrc

NN *n/a*   IE *4*   DOM *n/a*
Read/Write

Used with IE 4 data binding to specify the name of the remote ODBC data source (such as an Oracle or SQL Server database) to be associated with the element. Setting both the `dataFld` and `dataSrc` properties to empty strings breaks the binding between element and data source.

Example   `document.forms[0].mySelect.dataSrc = "#DBSRC3"`

Value   Case-sensitive identifier of the data source.

Default   None.

disabled

NN *n/a*   IE *4*   DOM *1*
Read/Write

Whether the element is available for user interaction. When set to `true`, the element cannot receive focus or be modified by the user. It is also not submitted with the form.

Example   `document.forms[0].elements[3].disabled = true`

Value   Boolean value: `true` | `false`.

Default   `false`

form

NN *2*   IE *3*   DOM *n/a*
Read-only

Returns a reference to the FORM element that contains the current element (if any). This property is most often passed as a parameter for an event handler, using the `this` keyword to refer to the current form control.

Example   `<SELECT NAME="units" onChange="recalc(this.form)">`

Value   Object reference.

Default   None.

length

NN *2*   IE *3*   DOM *1*
Read/Write

The number of OPTION objects nested inside the SELECT object. You can adjust this value upward or downward, but there is some browser-specific behavior to watch out for. To genuinely add options to a SELECT object, you must follow the browser-specific way of creating new OPTION objects (see the `options` object for details). If you set this property to a number smaller than its original value, OPTION objects are deleted from the bottom of the list. A value of zero does not cause the element to disappear, but there are no selectable options in the element.

Example   `document.forms[0].mySelect.length = 3`

Value   Integer.

Default   None.

multiple

Whether the browser should render the **SELECT** element as a list box and allow users to make multiple selections from the list of options. By default the **size** property is set to the number of nested **OPTION** elements, but the value may be overridden with the **size** property setting. Users can select contiguous items by **Shift**-clicking on the first and last items of the group. To make discontiguous selections, Windows users must **Ctrl**-click on each item; Mac users must **Command**-click on each item. The **multiple** property has no effect when **size** is set to 1 to display a pop-up menu.

Example

```
if (document.entryForm.list3.multiple) {
    ...
}
```

Value   Boolean value: **true** | **false**.

Default   false

name

The identifier associated with the form control. The value of this property is submitted as one-half of the name/value pair when the form is submitted to the server. Names are hidden from user view, since control labels are assigned via other means, depending on the control type. Form control names may also be used by script references to the objects.

Example   document.orderForm.payment.name = "credcard"

Value

Case-sensitive identifier that follows the rules of identifier naming: it may contain no whitespace, cannot begin with a numeral, and should avoid punctuation except for the underscore character.

Default   None.

recordNumber

Used with data binding, returns an integer representing the record within the data set that generated the element (i.e., an element whose content is filled via data binding). Values of this property can be used to extract a specific record from an Active Data Objects (ADO) record set (see **recordset** property).

Example

```
<SCRIPT FOR="tableTemplate" EVENT="onclick">
    myDataCollection.recordset.absoluteposition = this.recordNumber
    ...
</SCRIPT>
```

Value   Integer.

Default   None.

selectedIndex

NN *2*   IE *3*   DOM *1*

Read/Write

The zero-based integer of the option selected by the user. If the `SELECT` element is set to allow multiple selections, the `selectedIndex` property returns the index of the first selected item (see the `selected` property). You can use this property to gain access to the value or text of the selected item, as shown in the example.

Example

```
var list = document.forms[0].selectList
var listValue = list.options[list.selectedIndex].value
```

Value   Positive integer.

Default   None.

tabIndex

NN *n/a*   IE *4*   DOM *1*

Read/Write

A number that indicates the sequence of this element within the tabbing order of all focusable elements in the document. Tabbing order follows a strict set of rules. Elements that have values other than zero assigned to their `tabIndex` properties are first in line when a user starts tabbing in a page. Focus starts with the element with the lowest `tabIndex` value and proceeds in order to the highest value, regardless of physical location on the page or in the document. If two elements have the same `tabIndex` values, the element that comes earlier in the document receives focus first. Next come all elements that either don't support the `tabIndex` property or have the value set to zero. These elements receive focus in the order in which they appear in the document. A value of -1 removes the element from tabbing order altogether.

Note that the Macintosh user interface does not provide for giving focus to elements other than text and password `INPUT` fields.

Example   `document.forms[0].choices.tabIndex = 6`

Value   Integer.

Default   None.

type

NN *3*   IE *4*   DOM *1*

Read-only

Returns the type of form control element. A `SELECT` object has two possible values, depending on whether the element is set to be a multiple-choice list. The value is returned in all lowercase letters. It may be necessary to cycle through all form elements in search of specific types to do some processing on (e.g., emptying all form controls of type "text" while leaving other controls untouched).

Example

```
if (document.forms[0].elements[3].type == "select-multiple") {
    . . .
}
```

Value

Any of the following constants (as a string): button | checkbox | file | hidden | image | password | radio | reset | select-multiple | select-one | submit | text | textarea.

Default Depends on value of multiple.

value   NN *n/a*   IE *4*   DOM *1*

Read/Write

Current value associated with the form control that is submitted with the name/value pair for the element. All values are strings, but they may represent other kinds of data, including Boolean and numeric values. Internet Explorer automatically stuffs the value property of the selected OPTION object into the SELECT object's value property.

Example

```
if (document.forms[0].medium.value == "CD-ROM") {
    . . .
}
```

Value String.

Default None.

blur()   NN *n/a*   IE *4*   DOM *n/a*

Removes focus from the current element and fires an onBlur event (in IE). No other element necessarily receives focus as a result.

Returned Value

None.

Parameters

None.

focus()   NN *n/a*   IE *4*   DOM *n/a*

Gives focus to the current element and fires the onFocus event (in IE). If another element had focus at the time, it receives an onBlur event.

Returned Value

None.

Parameters

None.

DOM Reference

options[]   NN *n/a*   IE *4*   DOM *n/a*

An array of all OPTION objects contained by the current element. Items in this array are indexed (zero based) in source code order. For details on using this collection for adding and removing OPTION elements from a SELECT element in Internet Explorer, see the options object.

tags[]   NN *n/a*   IE *4*   DOM *n/a*

An array of all objects of a specific HTML tag type contained by the current element.

Syntax   selectObject.tags("*tagName*")[i].*objectPropertyOrMethod*

selection   NN *n/a*   IE *4*   DOM *n/a*

The selection object represents zero or more characters that have been either explicitly selected in a document by the user or selected under script control. All actions on the content of a selection are done via a TextRange object, which can be created from the selection object (see the TextRange object). TextRange and selection objects are available in Navigator 4 only in the Win32 environment. The selection object belongs to the document object.

Navigator 4 offers script access to the text selected in a document via the document.getSelection() method.

In all browsers, be aware that clicking on buttons deselects the current text selection. Therefore, all scripted action involving selections must be triggered by select events or functions invoked by a timer (see the window.setTimeout() method description in Chapter 11).

Object Model Reference

IE   document.selection

Properties

type

Methods

clear()   createRange()   empty()

type   NN *n/a*   IE *4*   DOM *n/a*

Read-only

Whether the current selection object has one or more characters selected or is merely an insertion point.

Example

```
if (document.selection.type == "Text") {
    ...
}
```

Value   Either of two constant values (as a string): None | Text.

Default   None.

clear()   NN *n/a*   IE *4*   DOM *n/a*

Deletes the content of the current selection in a document. For example, the event handler in the following tag deletes any selected text of the P element two seconds after the user starts making the selection:

```
<P onSelectStart="setTimeout('document.selection.clear()',2000)">
```

Returned Value

None.

Parameters

None.

createRange()   NN *n/a*   IE *4*   DOM *n/a*

Creates a `TextRange` object from the current selection object. After a statement like the following:

```
    var myRange = document.selection.createRange()
```

scripts can then act on the content of the selected text.

Returned Value

`TextRange` object.

Parameters

None.

empty()   NN *n/a*   IE *4*   DOM *n/a*

Deselects the current selection and sets the selection object's **type** property to **None**. There is no change to the content that had been selected.

Returned Value

None.

Parameters

None.

SMALL

See B.

SPAN   NN *n/a*   IE *4*   DOM *1*

The SPAN object reflects the SPAN element. This element is used primarily as a container for assigning styles to inline content elements.

HTML Equivalent

`<SPAN>`

Object Model Reference

IE   [window.]document.all.elementID

Properties

className	innerHTML	offsetHeight	outerHTML	scrollTop
dataFld	innerText	offsetLeft	outerText	sourceIndex
dataFormatAs	isTextEdit	offsetParent	parentElement	style
dataSrc	lang	offsetTop	parentTextEdit	tagName
document	language	offsetWidth	scrollLeft	title
id				

Methods

blur()	getAttribute()	removeAttribute()
click()	insertAdjacentHTML()	scrollIntoView()
contains()	insertAdjacentText()	setAttribute()
focus()		

Collections/Arrays

all[]	children[]	filters[]

Event Handler Properties

Handler	NN	IE	DOM
onblur	n/a	4	n/a
onclick	n/a	4	n/a
ondblclick	n/a	4	n/a
ondragstart	n/a	4	n/a
onfilterchange	n/a	4	n/a
onhelp	n/a	4	n/a
onkeydown	n/a	4	n/a
onkeypress	n/a	4	n/a
onkeyup	n/a	4	n/a
onmousedown	n/a	4	n/a
onmousemove	n/a	4	n/a
onmouseout	n/a	4	n/a
onmouseover	n/a	4	n/a
onmouseup	n/a	4	n/a
onselectstart	n/a	4	n/a

dataFld

NN *n/a*   IE *4*   DOM *n/a*

Read/Write

Used with IE 4 data binding to associate a remote data source column name with the HTML content inside a SPAN element. A DATASRC attribute must also be set for the element. Setting both the dataFld and dataSrc properties to empty strings breaks the binding between element and data source.

Example `document.all.mySpan.dataFld = "comment"`

Value Case-sensitive identifier of the data source column.

Default None.

dataFormatAs   NN *n/a*   IE *4*   DOM *n/a*
Read/Write

Used with IE 4 data binding, this property advises the browser whether the source material arriving from the data source is to be treated as plain text or as tagged HTML.

Example `document.forms[0].mySpan.dataFormatAs = "HTML"`

Value IE 4 recognizes two possible settings: `text` | `HTML`.

Default `text`

dataSrc   NN *n/a*   IE *4*   DOM *n/a*
Read/Write

Used with IE 4 data binding to specify the name of the remote ODBC data source (such as an Oracle or SQL Server database) to be associated with the element. Setting both the `dataFld` and `dataSrc` properties to empty strings breaks the binding between element and data source.

Example `document.all.mySpan.dataSrc = "#DBSRC3"`

Value Case-sensitive identifier of the data source.

Default None.

scrollLeft, scrollTop   NN *n/a*   IE *4*   DOM *n/a*
Read/Write

The distance in pixels between the actual left or top edge of the element's physical content and the left or top edge of the visible portion of the content. Since a **SPAN** element is not a scrollable container, both values are zero. These properties are not available in the Win32 version of Internet Explorer 4.

Value Positive integer or zero.

Default 0

blur()   NN *n/a*   IE *4*   DOM *n/a*

Removes focus from the current element and fires an **onBlur** event (in IE). No other element necessarily receives focus as a result.

Returned Value

None.

DOM Reference

Parameters

None.

focus()   NN *n/a*   IE *4*   DOM *n/a*

Gives focus to the current element and fires the onFocus event (in IE). If another element had focus at the time, it receives an onBlur event.

Returned Value

None.

Parameters

None.

statusbar

See locationbar.

STRIKE

See B.

STRONG

See ACRONYM.

STYLE   NN *n/a*   IE *4*   DOM *1*

The STYLE object reflects the STYLE element. This object is separate from the style object associated with virtually every element in a document. The STYLE object is generated in a document via the <STYLE> tag, which can have a unique ID value assigned to it; the style object contains all the style properties and their current values as set for a particular element.

Note that the lang, language, media and title properties are not available on the Macintosh version of Internet Explorer 4.

HTML Equivalent

<STYLE>

Object Model Reference

IE   [window.]document.all.*elementID*

Properties

className	isTextEdit	media	readyState	tagName
disabled	lang	parentElement	sourceIndex	title
document	language	parentTextEdit	style	type
id				

Methods

click()	*insertAdjacentHTML()*	*scrollIntoView()*
contains()	*insertAdjacentText()*	*setAttribute()*
getAttribute()	*removeAttribute()*	

Event Handler Properties

Handler	NN	IE	DOM
onerror	n/a	4	n/a
onload	n/a	4	n/a
onreadystatechange	n/a	4	n/a

disabled

NN *n/a*   IE *4*   DOM *1*

Read/Write

Whether rules in the style sheet should be applied to their selected elements. Although the corresponding DISABLED attribute does not work in Internet Explorer 4, setting the disabled property to true does, in fact, turn off the entire style sheet. During page authoring, you can create a button that toggles style sheets on and off to see how the page looks in all types of browsers.

Example   document.all.mainStyle.disabled = true

Value   Boolean value: true | false..

Default   false

media

NN *n/a*   IE *4*   DOM *1*

Read/Write

The intended output device for the rules of the STYLE element. The media property looks forward to the day when browsers are able to tailor content to specific kinds of devices such as pocket computers, text-to-speech digitizers, or fuzzy television sets.

Example   document.all.myStyle.media = "print"

Value   Any one of the following constant values as a string: all | print | screen.

Default   all

readyState

NN *n/a*   IE *4*   DOM *n/a*

Read-only

Returns the current download status of the document or embedded content. This property provides a more granular way of testing whether a particular downloadable element is ready to be run or scripted instead of the onLoad event handler for the entire document. As the value of this property changes during loading, the system fires an onReadyState-Change event.

Example

```
if (document.all.myStyle.readyState == "uninitialized") {
    statements for alternate handling
}
```

DOM Reference

Value

One of the following values (as strings): `complete` | `interactive` | `loading` | `uninitialized`. Some elements may allow the user to interact with partial content, in which case the property may return `interactive` until all loading has completed.

Default   None.

type

Read-only

The style sheet syntax specified by the TYPE attribute of the STYLE element. Internet Explorer 4 knows only the CSS syntax.

Example

```
if (document.all.myStyle.type == "text/css") {
    ...
}
```

Value   String.

Default   None.

style

Almost every object that reflects an HTML element has a `style` object associated with it (as you can see from the `style` property that pervades the object listings in this chapter). The `style` object reflects the STYLE attribute set in the element's tag. If the element is under the influence of a style sheet rule that is set in a STYLE element (assigned to a selector that applies to the current element), those style sheet values are not part of the `style` object. Even if the element is under the influence of one of these distant style sheet rules, you can still assign a value to any `style` object property for any element: the setting is likely to override (by virtue of the cascading rules described in Chapter 3) styles assigned from a STYLE element.

From a scripting point of view, it is important to know that while a `style` object's property exhibits a default behavior (a font size or alignment, for example), the default value may not be reflected in the property unless the value has been explicitly set in the element tag's STYLE attribute or assigned by another script statement. The Macintosh version of Internet Explorer 4 is a bit better in exposing default values, but by and large, a `style` object's property default value is an empty string or `null`. Therefore, do not expect condition testing to necessarily reveal the current value of a property unless it has been set previously.

The properties of the style object correspond to the CSS attributes that are detailed in Chapter 10. For more information on a particular property, see the corresponding listing in Chapter 10.

Object Model Reference

IE   `[window.]document.all.elementID.style`

Properties

background	clip	paddingRight
backgroundAttachment	color	paddingTop
backgroundColor	cssText	pageBreakAfter
backgroundImage	cursor	pageBreakBefore
backgroundPosition	display	pixelHeight
backgroundPositionX	filter	pixelLeft
backgroundPositionY	font	pixelTop
backgroundRepeat	fontFamily	pixelWidth
border	fontSize	posHeight
borderBottom	fontStyle	position
borderBottomColor	fontVariant	posLeft
borderBottomStyle	fontWeight	posTop
borderBottomWidth	height	posWidth
borderColor	left	styleFloat
borderLeft	letterSpacing	textAlign
borderLeftColor	lineHeight	textDecoration
borderLeftStyle	listStyle	textDecorationBlink
borderLeftWidth	listStyleImage	textDecorationLineThrough
borderRight	listStylePosition	textDecorationNone
borderRightColor	listStyleType	textDecorationOverline
borderRightStyle	margin	textDecorationUnderline
borderRightWidth	marginBottom	textIndent
borderStyle	marginLeft	textTransform
borderTop	marginRight	top
borderTopColor	marginTop	verticalAlign
borderTopStyle	overflow	visibility
borderTopWidth	padding	width
borderWidth	paddingBottom	zIndex
clear	paddingLeft	

Methods

getAttribute()   *removeAttribute()*   *setAttribute()*

background

NN *n/a*   IE *4*   DOM *n/a*

Read/Write

The element's style sheet background attribute. This is a shorthand attribute, so the scripted property consists of a string of space-delimited values for the backgroundAttachment, backgroundColor, backgroundImage, backgroundPosition, and backgroundRepeat property values. One or more values may be in the background value, and the individual values may be in any order.

Example

```
document.all.tags("DIV").style.background = "url(logo.gif) repeat-y"
```

Value

String of space-delimited values corresponding to one or more individual background style properties.

Default   None.

backgroundAttachment

NN *n/a*   IE *4*   DOM *n/a*
Read/Write

Sets how the image is "attached" to the element. The image can either remain fixed within the viewable area of the element (the viewport) or it may scroll with the element as the document is scrolled. During scrolling, the fixed attachment looks like a stationary backdrop to rolling credits of a movie.

Example   `document.all.tags("DIV").style.backgroundAttachment = "fixed"`

Value   String of either allowable value: `fixed | scroll`.

Default   `scroll`

backgroundColor

NN *n/a*   IE *4*   DOM *n/a*
Read/Write

Background color of the element. If you also set a `backgroundImage`, the image overlays the color. Transparent pixels of the image allow the color to show through.

Example   `document.all.highlighted.style.backgroundColor = "yellow"`

Value   Any valid color specification (see description at beginning of the chapter).

Default   None.

backgroundImage

NN *n/a*   IE *4*   DOM *n/a*
Read/Write

URL of the background image of the element. If you also set a `backgroundColor`, the image overlays the color. Transparent pixels of the image allow the color to show through.

Example

`document.all.navbar.style.backgroundImage = "images/navVisited.jpg"`

Value   Any complete or relative URL to an image file.

Default   None.

backgroundPosition

NN *n/a*   IE *4*   DOM *n/a*
Read/Write

Top and left location of the background image relative to the element's content region (plus padding). This property is not properly connected in Internet Explorer 4 for the Macintosh.

Example   `document.all.div3.style.backgroundPosition = "20 50"`

Value

You should be able to specify one or two percentages, which are the percentages of the block-level element's box width and height (respectively) at which point the image (or repeated images) begins. Setting percentage values, however, does not always work in IE 4 for Windows (and it doesn't work at all on the Mac), even though they are returned as the default value units. You are safest with pixel values (as space-delimited values inside one string). None of the allowed constants except `top` and `left` are recognized.

Default   0% 0%

backgroundPositionX, backgroundPositionY

NN *n/a*   IE *4*   DOM *n/a*
Read/Write

Top and left locations of the background image relative to the element's content region (plus padding). These properties are not properly connected in Internet Explorer 4 for the Macintosh.

Example

```
document.all.div3.style.backgroundPositionX = "20"
document.all.table2.style.backgroundPositionY = "10"
```

Value

You should be able to specify percentage values, which are the percentage of the block-level element's box width and height (respectively) at which point the image (or repeated images) begins. Setting percentage values, however, does not always work in IE 4 for Windows (and it doesn't work at all on the Mac), even though they are returned as the default value units. You are safest with pixel values. None of the allowed constants except `top` and `left` are recognized.

Default   0

backgroundRepeat

NN *n/a*   IE *4*   DOM *n/a*
Read/Write

Whether a background image (specified with the `backgroundImage` property) should repeat and, if so, along which axes. You can use repeating background images to create horizontal and vertical bands with some settings.

Example `document.all.div3.style.backgroundRepeat = "repeat-y"`

Value

With a setting of `no-repeat`, one instance of the image appears in the location within the element established by the `backgroundPosition` property (default is top-left corner). Normal repeats are performed along both axes, but you can have the image repeat down a single column (`repeat-y`) or across a single row (`repeat-x`).

Default   repeat

DOM Reference

border

NN *n/a*   IE *4*   DOM *n/a*

Read/Write

A shorthand property for getting or setting the `borderColor`, `borderStyle`, and/or `borderWidth` properties of all four borders around an element in one statement. You must specify a border style (see `borderStyle`) for changes of this property to affect the display of the element's border. Numerous other properties allow you to set the width, style, and color of individual edges or groups of edges if you don't want all four edges to be the same. Only those component settings explicitly made in the element's tag attributes are reflected in the property, but you may assign components not part of the original tag.

Example   `document.all.announce.style.border = "inset red 4px"`

Value

For the `borderStyle` and `borderWidth` component values, see the respective properties in this chapter. For details on the `borderColor` value, see the section about colors at the beginning of this chapter.

Default   None.

borderBottom, borderLeft, borderRight, borderTop

NN *n/a*   IE *4*   DOM *n/a*

Read/Write

A shorthand property for getting or setting the `borderColor`, `borderStyle`, and/or `borderWidth` properties for a single edge of an element in one statement. You must specify a border style (see `borderStyle`) for changes of this property to affect the display of the element's border. If you want all four edges to be the same, see the `border` attribute. Only those component settings explicitly made in the element's tag attributes are reflected in the property, but you may assign components not part of the original tag.

Example

```
document.all.announce.style.borderBottom = "inset red 4px"
document.all.announce.style.borderLeft = "solid #20ff00 2px"
document.all.announce.style.borderRight = "double 3px"
document.all.announce.style.borderTop = "outset red 8px"
```

Value

For the `border`*Edge*`Style` and `border`*Edge*`Width` component values, see the respective properties in this chapter. For details on the `border`*Edge*`Color` value, see the section about colors at the beginning of this chapter.

Default   None.

borderBottomColor, borderLeftColor, borderRightColor, borderTopColor

NN *n/a*   IE *4*   DOM *n/a*

Read/Write

The color of a single border edge of an element. It is easy to abuse these properties by mixing colors that don't belong together. See also the `borderColor` attribute for setting the color for groups of edges in one statement.

Example

```
document.all.announce.style.borderBottomColor = "red"
document.all.announce.style.borderLeftColor = "#20ff00"
document.all.announce.style.borderRightColor = "rgb(100, 75, 0)"
document.all.announce.style.borderTopColor = "rgb(90%, 0%, 25%)"
```

Value

For details on color values, see the section about colors at the beginning of this chapter.

Default   None.

borderBottomStyle, borderLeftStyle, borderRightStyle, borderTopStyle

NN *n/a*   IE *4*   DOM *n/a*

Read/Write

The line style of a single border edge of an element. The edge-specific attributes let you override a style that has been applied to all four edges with the `border` or `borderStyle` properties. See also the `borderStyle` property for setting the style for groups of edges in one statement.

Example

```
document.all.announce.style.borderBottomStyle = "groove"
document.all.announce.style.borderLeftStyle = "double"
document.all.announce.style.borderRightStyle = "solid"
document.all.announce.style.borderTopStyle = "inset"
```

Value

Style values are case-insensitive constants that are associated with specific ways of rendering border lines. The CSS style constants are: dashed, dotted, double, groove, hidden, inset, none, outset, ridge, and solid. Not all browsers recognize all the values in the CSS recommendation. See the `border-style` attribute listing in Chapter 10 for complete details on the available border styles.

Default   None.

borderBottomWidth, borderLeftWidth, borderRightWidth, borderTopWidth

NN *n/a*   IE *4*   DOM *n/a*

Read/Write

The width of a single border edge of an element. See also the `borderWidth` property for setting the width for groups of edges in one statement.

Example

```
document.all.announce.style.borderBottomWidth= "thin"
document.all.announce.style.borderLeftWidth = "thick"
document.all.announce.style.borderRightWidth = "2px"
document.all.announce.style.borderTopWidth = "0.5em"
```

DOM Reference

Value

Three case-insensitive constants—thin | medium | thick—allow the browser to define exactly how many pixels are used to show the border. For more precision, you can also assign a length value (see the discussion of length values at the beginning of this chapter).

Default   medium

borderColor   NN *n/a*   IE *4*   DOM *n/a*

Read/Write

A shortcut attribute that lets you set multiple border edges to the same or different colors. For Internet Explorer, you may supply one to four space-delimited color values. The number of values determines which sides receive the assigned colors.

Example

```
document.all.announce.style.borderColor = "red"
document.all.announce.style.borderColor = "red green"
document.all.announce.style.borderColor = "black rgb(100, 75, 0) #c0c0c0"
document.all.announce.style.borderColor = "yellow green blue red"
```

Value

In Internet Explorer, this property accepts one, two, three, or four color values, depending on how many and which borders you want to set with specific colors. See the border-color attribute listing in Chapter 10 for complete details on how the number of values affects this property.

Default   The object's color property (if it is set).

borderStyle   NN *n/a*   IE *4*   DOM *n/a*

Read/Write

A shortcut property that lets you set multiple border edges to the same or different style. For Internet Explorer, you may supply one to four space-delimited style values. The number of values determines which sides receive the assigned colors.

Example

```
document.all.announce.style.borderStyle = "solid"
document.all.announce.style.borderStyle = "solid double"
document.all.announce.style.borderStyle = "double groove groove double"
```

Value

Style values are case-insensitive constants that are associated with specific ways of rendering border lines. The CSS style constants are: dashed, dotted, double, groove, hidden, inset, none, outset, ridge, and solid. Not all browsers recognize all the values in the CSS recommendation. See the border-style attribute listing in Chapter 10 for complete details on the available border styles.

In Internet Explorer, this property accepts one, two, three, or four style values, depending on how many and which borders you want to set with specific styles. See the border-

`style` attribute listing in Chapter 10 for complete details on how the number of values affects this property.

Default   none

borderWidth
NN *n/a*   IE *4*   DOM *n/a*
Read/Write

A shortcut property that lets you set multiple border edges to the same or different width. For Internet Explorer, you may supply one to four space-delimited width length values (Navigator 4's property is read-only). The number of values determines which sides receive the assigned widths.

Example
```
document.all.founderQuote.style.borderWidth = "3px 5px"
```

Value

Three case-insensitive constants—thin | medium | thick—allow the browser to define exactly how many pixels are used to show the border. For more precision, you can also assign a length value (see the discussion of length values at the beginning of this chapter).

In Internet Explorer, this property accepts one, two, three, or four width values, depending on how many and which borders you want to set with specific widths. See the border-width attribute listing in Chapter 10 for complete details on how the number of values affects this property.

Default   medium

clear
NN *n/a*   IE *4*   DOM *n/a*
Read/Write

Defines whether the element allows itself to be displayed in the same horizontal band as a floating element. Typically another element in the vicinity has its float style attribute set to left or right. To prevent the current element from being in the same band as the floating block, set the clear property to the same side (left or right). If you aren't sure where the potential overlap might occur, set the clear property to both. An element whose clear property is set to a value other than none is rendered at the beginning of the next available line below the floating element.

Example   `document.all.myDiv.style.clear = "both"`

Value

Case-insensitive string of any of the following constants: both | left | none | right.

Default   none

clip
NN *n/a*   IE *4*   DOM *n/a*
Read/Write

Defines a clipping region of a positionable element. The clipping region is the area of the element layer in which content is visible. Clipping may not work properly in Internet Explorer 4 for the Macintosh.

DOM Reference

Example `document.all.art2.style.clip = "rect(5px 100px 40px 0)"`

Value

Case-insensitive string of either the auto constant or the CSS `clip` attribute setting that specifies the shape (`rect` only for now) and the position of the four clip edges relative to the original element's top-left corner. When specifying lengths for each side of the clipping rectangle, observe the clockwise order of values: top, right, bottom, left. See the discussion about length values at the beginning of this chapter. A value of `auto` sets the clipping region to the block that contains the content. In Internet Explorer, the width may extend to the width of the next outermost container (such as the BODY element).

Default   None.

color
NN *n/a*   IE *4*   DOM *1*

Read/Write

Sets the `foreground` (text) color style sheet attribute of the element. For some graphically oriented elements, such as form controls, the color attribute may also be applied to element edges or other features. Such extracurricular behavior is browser specific and may not be the same across browsers.

Example   `document.all.specialDiv.style.color = "green"`

Value

Case-insensitive style sheet color specification (see discussion at beginning of the chapter).

Default   black

cssText
NN *n/a*   IE *4*   DOM *n/a*

Read-only

Returns a string of the entire CSS style sheet rule applied to the element. If the rule included shorthand style attribute settings (such as `border`), the components for each of the four sides are spelled out (although not down to the most granular specifications). For example, if you set the STYLE attribute of an element to `STYLE="border: groove red 3px"`, the `cssText` property for that element returns:

```
BORDER-TOP: 3px groove red; BORDER-RIGHT: 3px groove red;
BORDER-BOTTOM: 3px groove red; BORDER-LEFT: 3px groove red
```

You can assign a shorthand value to the property, however.

Example

`document.all.block3.style.cssText = "margin: 2px; font-size: 14pt"`

Value   String value of semicolon-delimited style attributes.

Default   None.

cursor

The shape of the cursor when the screen pointer is atop the element. The precise look of cursors depends on the operating system. Before deploying a modified cursor, be sure you understand the standard ways that the various types of cursors are used within the browser and operating system. Users expect a cursor design to mean the same thing across all applications. Figure 10-3 in Chapter 10 offers a gallery of Windows and Macintosh cursors for each of the cursor constant settings provided by Internet Explorer 4.

Setting this property affects the cursor only when it is atop the current element and does not set the cursor immediately on a global basis.

Example

```
if (event.altKey) {
    event.sourceElement.style.cursor = "help"
}
```

Value

Any one cursor constant as a string: auto | crosshair | default | e-resize | help | move | n-resize | ne-resize | nw-resize | pointer | s-resize | se-resize | sw-resize | text | wait.

Default   auto

display

Whether the element should be rendered in the document. Although the property can be set to a variety of values, there are only two states. When set to none, the element is hidden, and surrounding content cinches up to fill the space; when set to an empty string (or any other value), the element is displayed.

Example   `document.all.instructionDiv.style.display = ""`

Value   Either none or an empty string (`""`).

Default   None.

filter

Sets the visual, reveal, or blend filter used to display or change content of an element. A visual filter can be applied to an element to produce effects such as content flipping, glow, drop shadow, and many others. A reveal filter is applied to an element when its visibility changes. The value of the reveal filter determines what visual effect is to be applied to the transition from hidden to shown (or vice versa). This includes effects such as wipes, blinds, and barn doors. A blend filter sets the speed at which a transition between states occurs. As of this writing, the `filter` property is available in Internet Explorer 4, but does not work in the Macintosh version.

Example `document.all.fancy.style.filter= "dropshadow()"`

Value

Each filter property may have more than one space-delimited filter type associated with it. Each filter type is followed by a pair of parentheses, which may convey parameters about the behavior of the filter for the current element. A parameter generally consists of a name/value pair, with assignment performed by the equals symbol. See the `filter` style sheet attribute listing in Chapter 10 for details on filter settings and parameters.

Default   None.

font

NN *n/a*   IE *4*   DOM *n/a*

Read/Write

A shorthand property that lets you set one or more font-related properties (`fontFamily`, `fontSize`, `fontVariant`, and `fontWeight`) with one assignment statement. A space-delimited list of values (in any sequence) is applied to the specific font properties for which the value is a valid type.

Example `document.all.subhead.style.font = "bolder small-caps 16pt"`

Value

For syntax and examples of value types for font-related properties, see the respective property listing.

Default   None.

fontFamily

NN *n/a*   IE *4*   DOM *n/a*

Read/Write

A prioritized list of font families to be used to render the object's content. One or more font family names may be included in a space-delimited list of property values. If a font family name consists of multiple words, the family name must be inside a set of inner quotes.

Example

`document.all.subhead.style.fontFamily = "'Century Schoolbook' Times serif"`

Value

Any number of font family names, space delimited. Multiword family names must be quoted. Recognized generic family names are: `serif` | `sans-serif` | `cursive` | `fantasy` | `monospace`.

Default   Browser default.

fontSize

NN *n/a*   IE *4*   DOM *n/a*

Read/Write

The font size of the element. The font size can be set in several ways. A collection of constants (`xx-small`, `x-small`, `small`, `medium`, `large`, `x-large`, `xx-large`) defines what are known as absolute sizes. In truth, these are absolute as far as a single browser in a single operating system goes, since the reference point for these sizes varies with browser and operating system. But they do let the author have confidence that one element set to large is rendered larger than medium.

Another collection of constants (larger, smaller) is known as relative sizes. Because the font-size attribute is inherited from the parent element, these relative sizes are applied to the parent element to determine the font size of the current element. It is up to the browser to determine exactly how much larger or smaller the font size is, and a lot depends on how the parent element's font size is set. If it is set with one of the absolute sizes (large, for example), a child's font size of larger means the font is rendered in the browser's x-large size. The increments are not as clear-cut when the parent font size is set with a length or percentage.

If you elect to use a length value for the fontSize property, choose a unit that makes the most sense for fonts, such as points (pt) or ems (em). The latter bases its calculation on the size of the parent element's font size. Finally, you can set fontSize to a percentage, which is calculated based on the size of the parent element's font size.

Example   document.all.teeny.style.fontSize = "x-small"

Value

Case-insensitive values from any of the following categories. For an absolute size, one of the following constants: xx-small | x-small | small | medium | large | x-large | xx-large. For a relative size, one of the following constants: larger | smaller. For a length, see the discussion about length values at the beginning of this chapter. For a percentage, the percentage value and the % symbol.

Default   Parent element's font size.

fontStyle   NN *n/a*   IE *4*   DOM *n/a*

Read/Write

Whether the element is rendered in a normal (roman), italic, or oblique font style. If the fontFamily includes font faces labeled Italic and/or Oblique, the setting of the font-Style attribute summons those particular font faces from the browser's system. But if the specialized font faces are not available in the system, the normal font face is usually algorithmically slanted to look italic. Output sent to a printer with such font settings relies on the quality of arbitration between the client computer and printer to render an electronically generated italic font style. While personal computer software typically includes other kinds of font rendering under the heading of "Style," see fontVariant and fontWeight for other kinds of font "styles."

Example   document.all.emphasis.style.fontStyle= "italic"

Value

Internet Explorer 4 recognizes the following string values: normal | italic | oblique, but treats both italic and oblique as italic.

Default   None.

fontVariant

Read/Write

Whether the element should be rendered in all uppercase letters in such a way that lower-case letters of the source code are rendered in smaller uppercase letters. If a font family contains a small caps variant, the browser should use it automatically. More likely, however, the browser calculates a smaller size for the uppercase letters that take the place of source code lowercase letters. In practice, Internet Explorer 4 renders the entire source code content as uppercase letters of the same size as the parent element's font, regardless of the case of the source code.

Example   `document.all.emphasis.style.fontVariant = "small-caps"`

Value   Any of the following constant values as strings: `normal` | `small-caps`.

Default   `normal`

fontWeight

Read/Write

Sets the weight (boldness) of the element's font. CSS provides a weight rating scheme that is more granular than most browsers render on the screen, but the finely tuned weights may come into play when the content is sent to a printer. The scale is a numeric rating from 100 to 900 at 100-unit increments. Therefore, a `fontWeight` of 100 would be the least bold that would be displayed, while 900 would be the boldest. A setting of `normal` (the default weight for any font) is equivalent to a `fontWeight` value of 400; the standard bold setting is equivalent to 700. Other settings (`bolder` and `lighter`) let you specify a weight relative to the parent element's weight.

Example   `document.all.hotStuff.style.fontWeight = "bold"`

Value

Any of the following constant values: `bold` | `bolder` | `lighter` | `normal` | `100` | `200` | `300` | `400` | `500` | `600` | `700` | `800` | `900`.

Default   `normal`

height, width

Read/Write

The height and width (and their units) of the element. Because the values are strings containing the assigned units, you cannot use these properties for calculation. See `pixel-Height`, `pixelWidth`, `posHeight`, and `posWidth` properties. Changes to these properties may not be visible unless the element has its `position` style attribute set.

Example   `document.all.viewArea.style.height = "450px"`

Value   String consisting of a numeric value and length measure or percentage.

Default   None.

left   NN *n/a*   IE *4*   DOM *n/a*

For positionable elements, defines the position of the left edge of an element's box (content plus left padding, border, and/or margin) relative to the left edge of the next outermost block content container. When the element is relative-positioned, the offset is based on the left edge of the inline location of where the element would normally appear in the content.

For calculations on this value, retrieve the `pixelLeft` or `posLeft` properties, which return genuine numeric values.

Example   `document.all.blockD2.style.left = "45px"`

Value

String consisting of a numeric value and length unit measure, a percentage, or `auto`.

Default   `auto`

letterSpacing   NN *n/a*   IE *4*   DOM *n/a*

The spacing between characters within an element. Browsers normally define the character spacing based on font definitions and operating system font rendering. Assigning a negative value tightens the spacing, but be sure to test the effect on the selected font for readability on different operating systems.

Example   `document.body.style.letterSpacing = "1.1em"`

Value

A string of a length value (with unit of measure) or `normal`. The best results are achieved by using units that are based on the rendered font size (`em` and `ex`). A setting of `normal` is how the browser sets the letters without any intervention.

Default   `normal`

lineHeight   NN *n/a*   IE *4*   DOM *n/a*

The height of the inline box (the box holding one physical line of content). See the `line-height` style attribute in Chapter 10 for details on browser quirks and inheritance traits of different types of values.

Example   `document.all.tight.style.lineHeight = "1.1em"`

Value   A string of a length value (with unit of measure) or `normal`.

Default   `normal`

listStyle   NN *n/a*   IE *4*   DOM *n/a*

A shorthand property for setting up to three list-style properties in one assignment statement. Whichever attributes you don't explicitly set with this attribute assume their default values. These properties define display characteristics for the markers automatically rendered for list items inside OL and UL elements.

Example `document.all.itemList.style.listStyle = "square outside none"`

Value

See the individual attribute entries for `listStyleType`, `listStylePosition`, and `list-StyleImage` for details on acceptable values for each. You may include one, two, or all three values in the list-style attribute setting in any order you wish.

Default None.

listStyleImage
NN *n/a*   IE *4*   DOM *n/a*
Read/Write

The URL for an image that is to be used as the marker for a list item. Because this attribute can be inherited, a setting (including none) for an individual list item can override the same attribute or property setting in its parent.

Example

`document.all.itemList.style.listStyleImage = "images/3DBullet.gif"`

Value

Use none (as a string) to override an image assigned to a parent element. Otherwise, supply any valid full or relative URL to an image file whose MIME type is readable by the browser.

Default none

listStylePosition
NN *n/a*   IE *4*   DOM *n/a*
Read/Write

Whether the marker is inside or outside (outdented) the box containing the list item's content. When `listStylePosition` is set to inside and the content is text, the marker appears to be part of the text block. In this case, the alignment (indent) of the list item is the same as normal, but without the outdented marker.

Example `document.all.itemList.style.listStylePosition = "inside"`

Value Either constant value as a string: inside | outside.

Default outside

listStyleType
NN *n/a*   IE *4*   DOM *n/a*
Read/Write

The kind of item marker to be displayed with each item. This attribute is applied only if `listStyleImage` is none (or not specified). The constant values available for this attribute are divided into two categories. One set is used with UL elements to present a filled disc, an empty circle, or a square (empty on the Macintosh, filled in Windows); the other set is for OL elements, whose list items can be marked in sequences of arabic numerals, roman numerals (uppercase or lowercase), or letters of the alphabet (uppercase or lowercase).

Example `document.all.itemList.style.listStyleType = "circle"`

Value

One constant value as a string that is relevant to the type of list container. For UL: `circle` | `disc` | `square`. For OL: `decimal` | `lower-alpha` | `lower-roman` | `upper-alpha` | `upper-roman`. OL element sequences are treated as follows:

Type	Example
decimal	1, 2, 3, ...
lower-alpha	a, b, c, ...
lower-roman	i, ii, iii, ...
upper-alpha	A, B, C, ...
upper-roman	I, II, III, ...

Default `disc` (for UL); `decimal` (for OL).

margin

NN *n/a*   IE *4*   DOM *n/a*

Read/Write

A shortcut property that can set the margin widths of up to four edges of an element with one statement. A margin is space that extends beyond the border of an element to provide extra empty space between adjacent or nested elements, especially those that have border attributes set. You may supply one to four space-delimited margin values. The number of space-delimited values determines which sides receive the assigned margins.

Example `document.all.logoWrapper.style.margin = "5px 8px"`

Value

This property accepts one, two, three, or four space-delimited values inside one string, depending on how many and which margins you want to set. See the `margin` attribute listing in Chapter 10 for complete details on how the number of values affects this property. Values for the margins can be lengths, percentages of the next outermost element size, or the `auto` constant.

Default 0

marginBottom, marginLeft, marginRight, marginTop

NN *n/a*   IE *4*   DOM *n/a*

Read/Write

All four properties set the width of a single margin edge of an element. A margin is space that extends beyond the element's border and is not calculated as part of the element's width or height.

Example

```
document.all.logoWrapper.style.marginTop = "5px"
document.all.navPanel.style.marginLeft = "10%"
```

Value

Values for margin widths can be length values, percentages of the next outermost element size, or the auto constant.

Default   0

overflow

NN *n/a*   IE *4*   DOM *n/a*

Read/Write

How a positioned element should treat content that extends beyond the boundaries established in the style sheet rule. See the discussion of the overflow style sheet attribute in Chapter 10 for details of how different operating system versions of Internet Explorer 4 respond to the possible settings.

Example   `document.all.myDiv.style.overflow = "scroll"`

Value   Any of the following constants as a string: `auto` | `hidden` | `scroll` | `visible`.

Default   `visible`

padding

NN *n/a*   IE *4*   DOM *n/a*

Read/Write

A shortcut property that can set the padding widths of up to four edges of an element with one statement. Padding is space that extends around the content box of an element up to but not including any border that may be specified for the element. Padding picks up the background image or color of its element. As you add padding to an element, you increase the size of the visible rectangle of the element without affecting the content block size. You may supply one to four space-delimited padding values. The number of values determines which sides receive the assigned padding.

Example   `document.all.logoWrapper.style.padding = "3px 5px"`

Value

This property accepts one, two, three, or four space-delimited values inside one string, depending on how many and which edges you want to pad. See the `padding` attribute listing in Chapter 10 for complete details on how the number of values affects this property. Values for padding widths can be lengths, percentages of the next outermost element size, or the auto constant.

Default   0

paddingBottom, paddingLeft, paddingRight, paddingTop

NN *n/a*   IE *4*   DOM *n/a*

Read/Write

All four properties set the width of a single padding edge of an element. Padding is space that extends between the element's border and content box. Padding is not calculated as part of the element's width or height.

Example

```
document.all.logoWrapper.style.paddingTop = "3px"
document.all.navPanel.style.paddingLeft = "10%"
```

Value

Values for padding widths can be length values, percentages of the next outermost element size, or the auto constant.

Default   0

pageBreakAfter, pageBreakBefore   NN *n/a*   IE *4*   DOM *n/a*

Read/Write

Defines how content should treat a page break around an element when the document is sent to a printer. Page breaks are not rendered in the visual browser as they may be in word processing programs; on screen, long content flows in one continuous scroll. See the extensive discussion of page breaks in the listing for the **page-break-after** and **page-break-before** style attributes in Chapter 10.

Example

```
document.all.hardBR.style.pageBreakAfter = "always"
document.all.navPanel.style.paddingLeft = "10%"
```

Value

Internet Explorer 4 recognizes four constant values (as strings): **always** | auto | left | right.

Default   auto

pixelHeight, pixelWidth   NN *n/a*   IE *4*   DOM *n/a*

Read/Write

The height and width of the element in pixels. Use these properties for calculation instead of properties such as **height** and **width**, which return strings including units. Changes to these properties may not be visible unless the element has its position style attribute set.

Example var midWidth = document.all.myDIV.style.pixelWidth/2

Value   Integer

Default   None.

pixelLeft, pixelTop   NN *n/a*   IE *4*   DOM *n/a*

Read/Write

For positionable elements, define the position of the left and top edges of an element's box (content plus left padding, border, and/or margin) relative to the left and top edges of the next outermost block content container. When the element is relative-positioned, the measure is based on the left edge of the inline location of where the element would normally appear in the content. Use these properties for calculation (including path animation) instead of the `left` and `top` properties, which store their values as strings with the unit names.

Example   `document.all.myDIV.style.pixelLeft++`

Value   Integer.

Default   None.

posHeight, posWidth

NN *n/a*   IE *4*   DOM *n/a*

Read/Write

The numeric height and width of the element in the units set by the CSS positioning-related attributes. Use these properties for calculation instead of properties such as `height` and `width`, which return strings including units. All math is in the specified units. Also contrast these properties with the `pixelHeight` and `pixelWidth` properties, which are integer values for pixel measures only.

Example   `document.all.myDIV.style.posWidth = 10.5`

Value   Floating-point number.

Default   None.

position

NN *n/a*   IE *4*   DOM *n/a*

Read-only

For positionable elements, returns the value assigned to the style sheet `position` attribute.

Example   `var posType = document.all.myDIV.style.position`

Value   Floating-point number.

Default   None.

posLeft, posTop

NN *n/a*   IE *4*   DOM *n/a*

Read/Write

For positionable elements, define the position of the left and top edges of an element's box (content plus left padding, border, and/or margin) relative to the left and top edges of the next outermost block content container. When the element is relative-positioned, the measure is based on the left edge of the inline location of where the element would normally appear in the content. Most importantly, these properties' values are numeric and in the unit of measure set in the CSS attribute. Use these properties for calculation (including path animation) instead of the `left` and `top` properties, which store their values as strings with the unit names. All math is in the specified units. Also contrast these properties with the `pixelLeft` and `pixelTop` properties, which are integer values for pixel measures only.

Example

`document.all.myDIV.style.posLeft = document.all.myDIV.style.posLeft + 1.5`

Value   Floating-point number.

Default   None.

styleFloat

On which side of the containing box the element aligns so that other content wraps around the element. When the property is set to none, the element appears in its source code sequence, and at most one line of surrounding text content appears in the same horizontal band as the element. See the float style attribute in Chapter 10 for more details.

Example   document.all.myDIV.style.styleFloat = "right"

Value   One of the following constants (as a string): none | left | right.

Default   None.

textAlign

Determines the horizontal alignment of text within an element.

Example   document.all.myDIV.style.textAlign = "right"

Value   One of the three constants (as a string): center | left | right.

Default   Depends on default language of the browser.

textDecoration

Specifies additions to the text content of the element in the form of underlines, strikethroughs, overlines, and (in Navigator and CSS) blinking. You may specify more than one decoration style by supplying values in a space-delimited list. While Internet Explorer 4 accepts the blink value, it does not blink the text. Text decoration has an unusual parent-child relationship. Values are not inherited, but the effect of a decoration carries over to nested items. Therefore, unless otherwise overridden, an underlined P element underlines a nested B element within. Internet Explorer also includes properties for each decoration type.

Example   document.all.emphasis.style.textDecoration = "underline"

Value

In addition to none, any of the following four constants (as a string): blink | line-through | overline | underline. Multiple values may be included in the string as a space-delimited list.

Default   None.

textDecorationBlink, textDecorationLineThrough, textDecorationNone, textDecorationOverline, textDecorationUnderline

NN *n/a*   IE *4*   DOM *n/a*

Read/Write

Whether the specified text decoration feature is enabled for the element. Internet Explorer does not blink text, so the `textDecorationBlink` property is ignored. Setting `textDecorationNone` to `true` sets all other related properties to `false`. Setting these properties on the Macintosh version of IE 4 does not alter the content. Use the `textDecoration` property instead.

Example   `document.all.emphasis.style.textDecorationLineThrough = "true"`

Value   Boolean value: `true` | `false`.

Default   false

textIndent

NN *n/a*   IE *4*   DOM *n/a*

Read/Write

The size of indenting of the first line of a block of inline text (such as a P element). Only the first line is affected by this setting. A negative value can be used to outdent the first line, but be sure the text does not run beyond the left edge of the browser window or frame.

Example   `document.all.firstGraph.style.textIndent = "0.5em"`

Value   String value consisting of a number and unit of measure.

Default   0

textTransform

NN *n/a*   IE *4*   DOM *n/a*

Read/Write

Controls the capitalization of the element's text. When a value other than **none** is assigned to this attribute, the cases of all letters in the source text are arranged by the style sheet, overriding the case of the source text characters.

Example   `document.all.heading.style.textTransform = "capitalize"`

Value

A value of **none** allows the case of the source text to be rendered as is. Other available constant values (as strings) are: `capitalize` | `lowercase` | `uppercase`. A value of `capitalize` sets the first character of every word to uppercase. Values `lowercase` and `uppercase` render all characters of the element text in their respective cases.

Default   None.

top

NN *n/a*   IE *4*   DOM *n/a*

Read/Write

For positionable elements, defines the position of the top edge of an element's box (content plus top padding, border, and/or margin) relative to the top edge of the next outermost block content container. When the element is relative-positioned, the offset is based on the top edge of the inline location of where the element would normally appear in the content.

For calculations on this value, retrieve the `pixelTop` or `posTop` properties, which return genuine numeric values.

Example   `document.all.blockD2.style.top = "40px"`

Value

String consisting of a numeric value and length unit measure, a percentage, or auto.

Default   auto

verticalAlign

NN *n/a*   IE *4*   DOM *n/a*

Read/Write

The vertical alignment characteristic of the element. This property operates in two spheres, depending on the selection of values you use. See the in-depth discussion of the `vertical-align` style sheet property in Chapter 10 for details.

Example   `document.all.myDIV.style.verticalAlign = "text-top"`

Value

String value of an absolute measure (with units), a percentage (relative to the next outer box element), or one of the many constant values: `bottom` | `top` | `baseline` | `middle` | `sub` | `super` | `text-bottom` | `text-top`.

Default   baseline

visibility

NN *n/a*   IE *4*   DOM *n/a*

Read/Write

The state of the positioned element's visibility. Surrounding content does not close up the space left by an element whose `visibility` property is set to `hidden`.

Example   `document.all.myDIV.style.visibility = "hidden"`

Value   One of the constant values (as a string): `hidden` | `inherit` | `visible`.

Default   inherit

width

See height.

zIndex

NN *n/a*   IE *4*   DOM *n/a*

Read/Write

For a positioned element, the stacking order relative to other elements within the same parent container. See Chapter 4 for details on relationships of element layering amid multiple containers.

Example `document.all.myDIV.style.zIndex = 3`

Value Integer.

Default 0

styleSheet

The `styleSheet` object represents a style sheet that may have been created as a STYLE element or imported with a LINK element or @import statement inside a STYLE element. This object is different from the STYLE object, which strictly reflects the STYLE HTML element and its attributes. The `styleSheets[]` collection contains one or more `styleSheet` objects. The only properties that the two kinds of objects have in common are the id property (only when a stylesheet object is generated via a STYLE element) and the disabled property.

Object Model Reference

IE   `[window.]document.styleSheets[i]`

Properties

disabled	*id*	parentStyleSheet	readOnly	type
href	owningElement			

Methods

addImport()   addRule()

Collections/Arrays

imports[]   rules[]

disabled

Read/Write

Whether rules in the style sheet should be applied to their selected elements. Although the corresponding DISABLED attribute does not work in Internet Explorer 4, setting the disabled property to true does, in fact, turn off the entire style sheet. During page authoring, you can create a button that toggles style sheets on and off to see how the page looks in all types of browsers.

Example `document.styleSheets[0].disabled = true`

Value Boolean value: true | false.

Default false

href

Read/Write

The URL specified by the element's HREF attribute. The destination document is an external style sheet specification.

Example `document.styleSheets[1].href = "altStyles.css"`

Value   String of complete or relative URL.

Default   None.

owningElement

Returns a reference to the STYLE or LINK element object that defines the current styleSheet object. Each document maintains a collection of style sheets created with both the STYLE and LINK elements.

Example   `var firstStyleID = document.styleSheets[0].owningElement.id`

Value   Object reference.

Default   None.

parentStyleSheet

Returns a reference to the styleSheet (created as a LINK or STYLE element) object that imported the current style sheet.

Value   Element object reference.

Default   None.

readOnly

Whether the style sheet can be modified under script control. Style sheets imported through a LINK element or an @import rule cannot be modified, so they return a value of true.

Value   Boolean value: `true | false`.

Default   `false`

type

The style sheet syntax specified by the TYPE attribute of the STYLE element. Internet Explorer 4 knows only the CSS syntax.

Example

```
if (document.styleSheets[0].type == "text/css") {
    ...
}
```

Value   String.

Default   None.

addImport()   NN *n/a*   IE *4*   DOM *n/a*

addImport(*url*, [*index*])

Adds an external style sheet specification to a **styleSheet** object.

Returned Value

Integer of the index position within the **styleSheets**[] collection where the style sheet was added (in case you omit the second parameter and let the browser find the end position).

Parameters

url   A complete or relative URL to the style sheet (*.css*) file.

index   An optional integer indicating where in the collection the new element should be placed.

addRule()   NN *n/a*   IE *4*   DOM *n/a*

addRule(*selector*, *style*, [*index*])

Adds a new rule for a style sheet. This method offers a scripted way of adding a rule to an existing **styleSheet** object:

```
document.styleSheets[1].addRule("P B","color:red")
```

You may duplicate a selector that already exists in the **styleSheet** and, therefore, override an existing rule for the same element selector. The only prohibition is that you may not override a rule to convert a plain style rule into one that creates a positionable element. The new rule is governed by the same cascading rules as all style sheet rules (that includes the rule's source code position among other rules with the same selector). Therefore, a new rule in a **styleSheet** object does not supersede a style set in an element's **STYLE** property.

Returned Value

None.

Parameters

selector The style rule selector as a string.

style   One or more style attribute:value pairs. Multiple pairs are semicolon delimited, just as they are in the regular style sheet definition.

index   An optional integer indicating where in the collection the new element should be placed.

imports[]   NN *n/a*   IE *4*   DOM *n/a*

An array of all **styleSheet** objects that were imported into a style sheet. In a sense, a **styleSheet** object contains a collection of other (special) **styleSheet** objects. All properties and methods of the **styleSheet** object can be used on the individual items that are returned from the **imports**[] collection.

Syntax   document.styleSheets(i).imports(j).*objectPropertyOrMethod*

rules[]

An array of all rules defined or imported for a `styleSheet` object. All properties of the `rule` object can be inspected for each item returned from the `rules[]` collection.

Syntax `document.styleSheets(i).rules(j).objectPropertyOrMethod`

SUB, SUP

The SUB object reflects the SUB element; the SUP object reflects the SUP element. Browsers tend to render these objects' content in a smaller size than surrounding content.

HTML Equivalent

```
<SUB>
<SUP>
```

Object Model Reference

IE   `[window.]document.all.elementID`

Properties

className	*isTextEdit*	*offsetLeft*	*outerHTML*	*sourceIndex*
document	*lang*	*offsetParent*	*outerText*	*style*
id	*language*	*offsetTop*	*parentElement*	*tagName*
innerHTML	*offsetHeight*	*offsetWidth*	*parentTextEdit*	*title*
innerText				

Methods

click()	*insertAdjacentHTML()*	*scrollIntoView()*
contains()	*insertAdjacentText()*	*setAttribute()*
getAttribute()	*removeAttribute()*	

Collections/Arrays

all[]	*children[]*	*filters[]*

Event Handler Properties

Handler	NN	IE	DOM
onclick	n/a	4	n/a
ondblclick	n/a	4	n/a
ondragstart	n/a	4	n/a
onfilterchange	n/a	4	n/a
onhelp	n/a	4	n/a
onkeydown	n/a	4	n/a
onkeypress	n/a	4	n/a
onkeyup	n/a	4	n/a
onmousedown	n/a	4	n/a
onmousemove	n/a	4	n/a
onmouseout	n/a	4	n/a
onmouseover	n/a	4	n/a

Handler	NN	IE	DOM
onmouseup	n/a	4	n/a
onselectstart	n/a	4	n/a

submit   NN *2*   IE *3*   DOM *1*

The submit object is a form control generated with an INPUT element whose TYPE attribute is set to "submit". This object is similar to the button object, but a submit object has more implied power. No script action is necessary for the submit object to do its job of submitting the containing form to the server. If you require a button to perform a script action, but not an actual form submission, use the button object instead. Otherwise, the submit object automatically reloads the current document, perhaps destroying important script variables. To initiate form validation, use the onSubmit event handler of the form object rather than the onClick event handler of the submit button. If the event handler evaluates to true, the form is submitted; if it evaluates to false, the submission is cancelled.

HTML Equivalent

```
<INPUT TYPE="submit">
```

Object Model Reference

NN   [window.]document.*formName.elementName*
         [window.]document.forms[i].elements[i]

IE   [window.]document.*formName.elementName*
         [window.]document.forms[i].elements[i]
         [window.]document.all.*elementID*

Properties

accessKey	isTextEdit	offsetLeft	outerText	tabIndex
className	lang	offsetParent	parentElement	tagName
disabled	language	offsetTop	parentTextEdit	title
document	name	offsetWidth	sourceIndex	type
form	offsetHeight	outerHTML	style	value
id				

Methods

blur()	getAttribute()	removeAttribute()
click()	handleEvent()	scrollIntoView()
contains()	insertAdjacentHTML()	setAttribute()
focus()	insertAdjacentText()	

Collections/Arrays

all[]	children[]	filters[]

Event Handler Properties

Handler	NN	IE	DOM
onblur	n/a	4	n/a
onclick	3	4	n/a

Handler	NN	IE	DOM
ondblclick	n/a	4	n/a
onfilterchange	n/a	4	n/a
onfocus	n/a	4	n/a
onhelp	n/a	4	n/a
onkeydown	n/a	4	n/a
onkeypress	n/a	4	n/a
onkeyup	n/a	4	n/a
onmousedown	4	4	n/a
onmousemove	n/a	4	n/a
onmouseout	n/a	4	n/a
onmouseover	n/a	4	n/a
onmouseup	4	4	n/a
onselect	n/a	4	n/a

accessKey

NN *n/a*   IE *4*   DOM *1*

Read/Write

A single character key that "clicks" the submit button. The browser and operating system determine whether the user must press a modifier key (e.g., **Ctrl**, **Alt**, or **Command**) with the access key to "click" the button. In IE 4/Windows, the **Alt** key is required, and the key is not case sensitive. Not working in IE 4/Mac.

Example document.entryForm.mySubmit.accessKey = "s"

Value   Single alphanumeric (and punctuation) keyboard character.

Default None.

disabled

NN *n/a*   IE *4*   DOM *1*

Read/Write

Whether the element is available for user interaction. When set to true, the element cannot receive focus.

Example document.forms[0].mySubmit.disabled = true

Value   Boolean value: true | false.

Default false

form

NN *2*   IE *3*   DOM *n/a*

Read-only

Returns a reference to the FORM element that contains the current element (if any). This property is most often passed as a parameter for an event handler, using the this keyword to refer to the current form control.

Example

```
<INPUT TYPE="button" VALUE="Validate Form" onClick="doValidate(this.form)">
```

Value   Object reference.

Default   None.

name

Read/Write

The identifier associated with the form control. Names are hidden from user view, since control labels are assigned via other means, depending on the control type. Form control names may also be used by script references to the objects.

Example   `document.orderForm.mySubmit.name = "Win32"`

Value

Case-sensitive identifier that follows the rules of identifier naming: it may contain no whitespace, cannot begin with a numeral, and should avoid punctuation except for the underscore character.

Default   None.

tabIndex

Read/Write

A number that indicates the sequence of this element within the tabbing order of all focusable elements in the document. Tabbing order follows a strict set of rules. Elements that have values other than zero assigned to their **tabIndex** properties are first in line when a user starts tabbing in a page. Focus starts with the element with the lowest **tabIndex** value and proceeds in order to the highest value, regardless of physical location on the page or in the document. If two elements have the same **tabIndex** values, the element that comes earlier in the document receives focus first. Next come all elements that either don't support the **tabIndex** property or have the value set to zero. These elements receive focus in the order in which they appear in the document. A value of -1 removes the element from tabbing order altogether. Note that the Macintosh user interface does not provide for giving focus to elements other than text and password **INPUT** fields.

Example   `document.forms[0].mySubmit.tabIndex = 6`

Value   Integer.

Default   None.

type

Read-only

Returns the type of form control element. The value is returned in lowercase letters. You may have to cycle through all form elements in search of specific types to do some processing on (e.g., emptying all form controls of type **"text"**, leaving other controls untouched).

Example

```
if (document.forms[0].elements[3].type == "submit") {
    ...
}
```

Value

Any of the following constants (as a string): button | checkbox | file | hidden | image | password | radio | reset | select-multiple | select-one | submit | text | textarea.

Default submit

value   NN *2*   IE *3*   DOM *1*

Read/Write

This is the rare time that the value property controls the label of a form control: the text that appears on the submit button.

Example document.forms[0].mySubmit.value = "Send"

Value   String.

Default   Submit

blur()   NN *n/a*   IE *4*   DOM *n/a*

Removes focus from the current element and fires an onBlur event (in IE). No other element necessarily receives focus as a result.

Returned Value

None.

Parameters

None.

focus()   NN *n/a*   IE *4*   DOM *n/a*

Gives focus to the current element and fires the onFocus event (in IE). If another element had focus at the time, it receives an onBlur event.

Returned Value

None.

Parameters

None.

handleEvent()   NN *4*   IE *n/a*   DOM *n/a*

handleEvent(*event*)

Instructs the object to accept and process the event whose specifications are passed as the parameter to the method. The object must have an event handler for the event type to process the event. See Chapter 6.

Returned Value

None.

Parameters

event   A Navigator 4 **event** object.

SUP

See SUB.

TABLE

NN n/a   IE 4   DOM 1

The TABLE object reflects the TABLE element. Other objects related to the TABLE object are: CAPTION, COL, COLGROUP, TBODY, TD, TFOOT, THEAD, and TR.

HTML Equivalent

`<TABLE>`

Object Model Reference

IE   [window.]document.all.*elementID*

Properties

align	cols	*language*	scrollHeight
background	dataFld	*offsetHeight*	scrollLeft
bgColor	dataPageSize	*offsetLeft*	scrollTop
border	dataSrc	*offsetParent*	scrollWidth
borderColor	*document*	*offsetTop*	*sourceIndex*
borderColorDark	frame	*offsetWidth*	*style*
borderColorLight	height	*outerHTML*	tabIndex
caption	id	*outerText*	*tagName*
cellPadding	*innerHTML*	*parentElement*	tFoot
cellSpacing	*innerText*	*parentTextEdit*	tHead
className	*isTextEdit*	*recordNumber*	title
clientHeight	*lang*	rules	width
clientWidth			

Methods

blur()	*insertAdjacentHTML()*	refresh()
click()	*insertAdjacentText()*	*removeAttribute()*
contains()	nextPage()	*scrollIntoView()*
focus()	previousPage()	*setAttribute()*
getAttribute()		

Collections/Arrays

all[]	*children[]*	*filters[]*	rows[]	tBodies[]

Event Handler Properties

Handler	NN	IE	DOM
onafterupdate	n/a	4	n/a
onbeforeupdate	n/a	4	n/a

TABLE 755

Handler	NN	IE	DOM
onblur	n/a	4	n/a
onclick	n/a	4	n/a
ondblclick	n/a	4	n/a
ondragstart	n/a	4	n/a
onfocus	n/a	4	n/a
onhelp	n/a	4	n/a
onkeydown	n/a	4	n/a
onkeypress	n/a	4	n/a
onkeyup	n/a	4	n/a
onmousedown	n/a	4	n/a
onmousemove	n/a	4	n/a
onmouseout	n/a	4	n/a
onmouseover	n/a	4	n/a
onmouseup	n/a	4	n/a
onresize	n/a	4	n/a
onrowenter	n/a	4	n/a
onrowexit	n/a	4	n/a
onscroll	n/a	4	n/a
onselectstart	n/a	4	n/a

align

NN *n/a*   IE *4*   DOM *1*

Read/Write

Defines the horizontal alignment of the element within its surrounding container.

Example `document.all.myTable.align = "center"`

Value Any of the three horizontal alignment constants: `center | left | right`.

Default `left`

background

NN *n/a*   IE *4*   DOM *n/a*

Read/Write

URL of the background image for the table. If you set a `backgroundColor` to the element as well, the color appears if the image fails to load; otherwise, the image overlays the color.

Example `document.all.myTable.background = "images/watermark.jpg"`

Value Complete or relative URL to the background image file.

Default None.

bgColor

NN *n/a*   IE *4*   DOM *1*

Read/Write

Background color of the element. This color setting is not reflected in the style sheet `backgroundColor` property. Even if the `BGCOLOR` attribute or `bgColor` property is set with a plain-language color name, the returned value is always a hexadecimal triplet.

Example `document.all.myTable.bgColor = "yellow"`

Value

A hexadecimal triplet or plain-language color name. See Appendix A for acceptable plain-language color names.

Default   Varies with browser and operating system.

border   NN *n/a*   IE *4*   DOM *1*

Read/Write

Thickness of the border around the table (in pixels). This is the 3-D border and should not be confused with borders created with style sheets.

Example `document.all.myTable.border = 4`

Value

An integer value. A setting of zero removes the border entirely in Internet Explorer 4.

Default   0

borderColor   NN *n/a*   IE *4*   DOM *n/a*

Read/Write

Color of the table's border. Internet Explorer applies the color to all four lines that make up the interior border of a cell. Therefore, colors of adjacent cells do not collide.

Example `document.all.myTable.borderColor = "salmon"`

Value

A hexadecimal triplet or plain-language color name. A setting of empty is interpreted as `"#000000"` (black). See Appendix A for acceptable plain-language color names.

Default   Varies with operating system.

borderColorDark, borderColorLight   NN *n/a*   IE *4*   DOM *n/a*

Read/Write

The 3-D effect of table borders in Internet Explorer is created by careful positioning of light and dark lines around the page's background or default color. You can independently control the colors used for the dark and light lines by assigning values to the `borderColorDark` (left and top edges of the cell) and `borderColorLight` (right and bottom edges) properties.

Typically, you should assign complementary colors to the pair of properties. There is also no rule that says you must assign a dark color to `borderColorDark`. The attributes merely control a well-defined set of lines so you can predict which lines of the border change with each attribute.

TABLE **757**

Example
```
document.all.myTable.borderColorDark = "blue"
document.all.myTable.borderColorLight = "cornflowerblue"
```

Value

A hexadecimal triplet or plain-language color name. A setting of empty is interpreted as "#000000" (black). See Appendix A for acceptable plain-language color names.

Default   Varies with operating system.

caption

Returns a reference to a **CAPTION** element nested inside the table. From this reference you can access properties and methods of the **CAPTION** object. This property is available only in the Win32 version of Internet Explorer 4.

Example `var capText = document.all.myTable.caption.innerHTML`

Value   Object reference.

Default   None.

cellPadding

The amount of empty space between the border of a table cell and the content of the cell. Note that this property applies to space *inside* a cell. Minor adjustments to this property are not as noticeable when the table does not also display borders (in which case the cell-Spacing property can assist in adjusting the space between cells).

Example `document.all.myTable.cellPadding = "15"`

Value   A string value for a length in a variety of units or percentage.

Default   0

cellSpacing

The amount of empty space between the outer edges of each table cell. If the table has a border, the effect of setting cellSpacing is to define the thickness of borders rendered between cells. Even without a visible border, the readability of a table often benefits from cell spacing.

Example `document.all.myTable.cellSpacing = "5"`

Value   A string value for a length in a variety of units or percentage.

Default   0 (with no table border); 2 (with table border).

clientHeight, clientWidth

NN *n/a*   IE *4*   DOM *n/a*

Read/Write

According to Microsoft's developer documentation, these properties reflect the height and width (in pixels) of the element's content. But see the section "About client- and offset-Properties" at the beginning of this chapter for details.

Example `var midHeight = document.all.myTable.clientHeight/2`

Value Integer pixel value.

Default None.

cols

NN *n/a*   IE *4*   DOM *1*

Read/Write

The number of columns of the table. The corresponding `COLS` attribute assists the browser in preparation for rendering the table. Without this attribute, the browser relies on its interpretation of all downloaded `TR` and `TD` elements to determine how the table is to be divided.

Example `document.all.myTable.cols = 5`

Value Any positive integer.

Default None.

dataFld

NN *n/a*   IE *4*   DOM *n/a*

Read/Write

Used with IE 4 data binding to associate a remote data source column name with individual `TD` elements inside the table. A `DATASRC` attribute must also be set for the element. Setting both the `dataFld` and `dataSrc` properties to empty strings breaks the binding between element and data source.

Example `document.all.inventoryTable.dataFld = "unit_price"`

Value Case-sensitive identifier of the data source column.

Default None.

dataPageSize

NN *n/a*   IE *4*   DOM *n/a*

Read/Write

Used with IE 4 data binding, this property advises the browser how many instances of a table row must be rendered to accommodate the number of data source records set by this attribute. See `nextPage()` and `previousPage()` methods for navigating through groups of records.

Example `document.all.inventoryTable.dataPageSize = 10`

Value Positive integer.

Default None.

TABLE   759

dataSrc

Read/Write

Used with IE 4 data binding to specify the name of the remote ODBC data source (such as an Oracle or SQL Server database) to be associated with the element. Content from the data source is specified via the DATAFLD attribute in individual TD elements. A block of contiguous records can be rendered in the table when you also set the DATAPAGESIZE attribute of the table. Setting both the dataFld and dataSrc properties to empty strings breaks the binding between element and data source.

Example   `document.all.inventoryTable.dataSrc = "#DBSRC3"`

Value   Case-sensitive identifier of the data source.

Default   None.

frame

Read/Write

Which (if any) sides of a table's outer border (set with the BORDER attribute or border property) are rendered. This property does not affect the interior borders between cells.

Example   `document.all.orderForm.frame = "hsides"`

Value

Any one case-insensitive frame constant (as a string):

above	Renders border along top edge of table only
below	Renders border along bottom edge of table only
border	Renders all four sides of the border (default in IE)
box	Renders all four sides of the border (same as border)
hsides	Renders borders on top and bottom edges of table only (a nice look)
lhs	Renders border on left edge of table only
rhs	Renders border on right edge of table only
void	Hides all borders (default in HTML 4.0)
vsides	Renders borders on left and right edges of table only

Default   void (when BORDER=0); border (when BORDER is any other value)

height, width

Read/Write

The height and width in pixels of the element. Changes to these values are immediately reflected in reflowed content on the page.

Example   `document.all.myTable.height = 250`

Value   Integer.

Default   None.

recordNumber   NN *n/a*   IE *4*   DOM *n/a*

Read-only

Used with data binding, returns an integer representing the record within the data set that generated the element (e.g., a TABLE element whose content is filled via data binding). Values of this property can be used to extract a specific record from an Active Data Objects (ADO) record set.

Example

```
<SCRIPT FOR="tableTemplate" EVENT="onclick">
    myDataCollection.recordset.absoluteposition = this.recordNumber
    ...
</SCRIPT>
```

Value   Integer.

Default   None.

rules   NN *n/a*   IE *4*   DOM *1*

Read/Write

Where (if at all) interior borders between cells are rendered by the browser. In addition to setting the table to draw borders to turn the cells into a matrix, you can set borders to be drawn only to separate borders, columns, or any sanctioned cell grouping (THEAD, TBODY, TFOOT, COLGROUP, or COL). The BORDER attribute must be present—either as a Boolean or set to a specific border size—for any cell borders to be drawn. Do not confuse this property with the rules[] collection of styleSheet objects.

Example   document.all.myTable.rules = "groups"

Value

Any one case-insensitive rules constant (as a string):

all	Renders borders around each cell
cols	Renders borders between columns only
groups	Renders borders between cell groups as defined by THEAD, TFOOT, TBODY, COLGROUP, or COL elements
none	Hides all interior borders
rows	Renders borders between rows only

Default   None (when BORDER=0); all (when BORDER is any other value).

scrollHeight, scrollWidth   NN *n/a*   IE *4*   DOM *n/a*

Read-only

The meaning of these two properties is ambiguous based on Microsoft's description and the way they're implemented in the Windows and Macintosh versions of Internet Explorer 4. My best guess is that these properties are intended to measure the height and width (in pixels) of the content of an element even when some of the content cannot be seen unless scrolled with scrollbars. The Macintosh version of the browser interprets this to mean the

TABLE   *761*

amount of the content that you can see at any one time. The important point is that for key elements, such as the BODY, the properties mean different things and can disrupt cross-platform operation.

Example   var midPoint = document.all.myTable.scrollHeight/2

Value   Positive integer or zero.

Default   None.

scrollLeft, scrollTop

The distance in pixels between the actual left or top edge of the element's physical content and the left or top edge of the visible portion of the content. Setting these properties allows you to use scripts to adjust the scroll of content within a scrollable container, such as text in a TEXTAREA element or an entire document in the browser window or frame. When the content is not scrolled, both values are zero. Setting the scrollTop property to 15 scrolls the document upward by 15 pixels in the window; the scrollLeft property is unaffected unless explicitly changed. The property values change as the user adjusts the scrollbars.

Example   document.all.myTable.scrollTop = 40

Value   Positive integer or zero.

Default   0

tabIndex

A number that indicates the sequence of this element within the tabbing order of all focusable elements in the document. Tabbing order follows a strict set of rules. Elements that have values other than zero assigned to their tabIndex properties are first in line when a user starts tabbing in a page. Focus starts with the element with the lowest tabIndex value and proceeds in order to the highest value, regardless of physical location on the page or in the document. If two elements have the same tabIndex values, the element that comes earlier in the document receives focus first. Next come all elements that either don't support the tabIndex property or have the value set to zero. These elements receive focus in the order in which they appear in the document. A value of -1 removes the element from tabbing order altogether.

Note that the Macintosh user interface does not provide for giving focus to elements other than text and password INPUT fields.

Example   document.all.myTable.tabIndex = 6

Value   Integer.

Default   None.

tFoot

Read-only

Returns a reference to the **TFOOT** object if one has been defined for the table. If no **TFOOT** element exists, the value is **null**. You can access **TFOOT** element properties and methods through this reference if you like. This property is available only on the Win32 version of Internet Explorer 4.

Example `var tableFootTxt = document.all.myTable.tFoot.innerText`

Value   **TFOOT** object reference.

Default `null`

tHead

Read-only

Returns a reference to the **THEAD** object if one has been defined for the table. If no **THEAD** element exists, the value is **null**. You can access **THEAD** element properties and methods through this reference if you like. This property is available only on the Win32 version of Internet Explorer 4.

Example `var tableHeadTxt = document.all.myTable.tHead.innerText`

Value   **THEAD** object reference.

Default `null`

width

See height.

blur()

Removes focus from the current element and fires an **onBlur** event (in IE). No other element necessarily receives focus as a result.

Returned Value

None.

Parameters

None.

focus()

Gives focus to the current element and fires the **onFocus** event (in IE). If another element had focus at the time, it receives an **onBlur** event.

Returned Value

None.

Parameters

None.

nextPage( ), previousPage( )   NN *n/a*   IE *4*   DOM *n/a*

Advises the data binding facilities to load the next or previous group of records from the data source to fill the number of records established with the `dataPageSize` property.

Returned Value

None.

Parameters

None.

refresh( )   NN *n/a*   IE *4*   DOM *n/a*

Advises the data binding facilities to reload the current page of data from the data source. If your table is retrieving frequently changing data from a database, you can create a `setTimeout()` loop to invoke `document.all.myTable.refresh()` as often as users would want updated information from the database.

Returned Value

None.

Parameters

None.

rows( )   NN *n/a*   IE *4*   DOM *n/a*

An array of all rows of the table. This collection includes all individual rows from row groups (`THEAD`, `TBODY`, and `TFOOT` elements) in the table.

Syntax   `document.all.myTable.rows(i).`*objectPropertyOrMethod*

tBodies[]   NN *n/a*   IE *4*   DOM *n/a*

A collection of `TBODY` objects on the table. By default, there is at least one `TBODY` object, even if none is explicitly created with an HTML tag. You can access properties and methods of each `TBODY` object through this reference if you like. But if you also specify an explicit `TBODY` element, you can go directly to the element via its ID. This collection is available only on the Win32 version of Internet Explorer 4.

Syntax   `document.all.myTable.tBodies(i).`*objectPropertyOrMethod*

tags   NN *4*   IE *n/a*   DOM *n/a*

The `tags` object is used by JavaScript syntax for style sheets. As a property of the `document` object, this `tags` object is used in building references to particular HTML elements to get or set their style-related properties. The direct properties of the `tags` object are all HTML element types. For example:

```
[document.]tags.P
[document.]tags.H1
```

There is no need to repeat a list of all HTML elements as properties for this object. These references are usable inside STYLE elements whose TYPE is set to `text/javascript`. That's where you assign values to style sheet properties with JavaScript syntax, as in the following examples:

```
tags.P.color = "green"
tags.H1.fontSize = "14pt"
```

The properties in the following list are not properties of the `tags` object per se, but rather of the style sheet associated with an element, class, or ID singled out by a JavaScript syntax assignment statement. The properties are listed here for convenience. Properties dedicated to element positioning are listed separately from regular style properties. A cross reference between these JavaScript properties and their CSS attribute counterparts can be found in Chapter 3 (and Chapter 4 for positioning properties). For information about these property values, consult the CSS reference chapter, where you can find details of all style sheet properties listed by CSS syntax.

Style Properties

backgroundColor	borderWidths()	marginBottom	paddings
backgroundImage	color	marginLeft	paddingTop
borderBottomWidth	display	marginRight	textAlign
borderColor	fontFamily	margins()	textDecoration
borderLeftWidth	fontSize	marginTop	textTransform
borderRightWidth	fontStyle	paddingBottom	verticalAlign
borderStyle	fontWeight	paddingLeft	whiteSpace
borderTopWidth	listStyleType	paddingRight	

Position Properties

background	clip	top	visibility	zIndex
bgColor	left			

TBODY

NN n/a   IE 4   DOM 1

The TBODY object reflects the TBODY element. By default, Internet Explorer creates a TBODY object for every table, but you can access its properties and methods only if you explicitly create a TBODY element (or access it via the tBodies[] collection of a table in the Win32 version). Note that the innerHTML, innerText, and outerHTML properties are not available on the Macintosh version of Internet Explorer 4.

HTML Equivalent

`<TBODY>`

Object Model Reference

```
IE      [window.]document.all.elementID
        [window.]document.all.tableID.tBodies[i]    (IE/Win32 only)
```

Properties

align	innerHTML	offsetHeight	outerHTML	style
bgColor	innerText	offsetLeft	outerText	tagName
className	isTextEdit	offsetParent	parentElement	title
document	lang	offsetTop	parentTextEdit	vAlign
id	language	offsetWidth	sourceIndex	

Methods

click()	insertAdjacentHTML()	scrollIntoView()
contains()	insertAdjacentText()	setAttribute()
getAttribute()	removeAttribute()	

Collections/Arrays

all[]	children[]	filters[]	rows[]

Event Handler Properties

Handler	NN	IE	DOM
onclick	n/a	4	n/a
ondblclick	n/a	4	n/a
ondragstart	n/a	4	n/a
onfilterchange	n/a	4	n/a
onhelp	n/a	4	n/a
onkeydown	n/a	4	n/a
onkeypress	n/a	4	n/a
onkeyup	n/a	4	n/a
onmousedown	n/a	4	n/a
onmousemove	n/a	4	n/a
onmouseout	n/a	4	n/a
onmouseover	n/a	4	n/a
onmouseup	n/a	4	n/a
onselectstart	n/a	4	n/a

align   NN *n/a*   IE *4*   DOM *n/a*

Read/Write

Defines the horizontal alignment of content within all cells contained by the TBODY element.

Example   document.all.myTBODY.align = "center"

Value   Any of the three horizontal alignment constants: center | left | right.

Default   left

bgColor

Read/Write

Background color of the cells contained by the **TBODY** element. This color setting is not reflected in the style sheet `backgroundColor` property in Internet Explorer. Even if the `BGCOLOR` attribute or `bgColor` property is set with a plain-language color name, the returned value is always a hexadecimal triplet.

Example   `document.all.myTBODY.bgColor = "yellow"`

Value

A hexadecimal triplet or plain-language color name. See Appendix A for acceptable plain-language color names.

Default   Varies with browser and operating system.

vAlign

Read/Write

The manner of vertical alignment of text within the cells contained by the **TBODY** element.

Example   `document.all.myTBODY.vAlign = "baseline"`

Value

Case-insensitive constant (as a string): `baseline` | `bottom` | `middle` | `top`.

Default   `middle`

rows[]

An array of all rows contained by the **TBODY** element.

Syntax   `document.all.myTBODY.rows(i).objectPropertyOrMethod`

TD

The TD object reflects the TD element. While a TD element may inherit a number of visual properties from containers (e.g., the `bgColor` of a TBODY or TR element), those inherited property values are not automatically assigned to the TD object. Therefore, just because a cell may have a yellow background color doesn't mean its `bgColor` property is set at all. The following items aren't available in the Macintosh version of Internet Explorer 4: `outerText` and `outerHTML` properties; `insertAdjacentHTML()` and `insertAdjacentText()` methods.

HTML Equivalent

`<TD>`

Object Model Reference

IE   `[window.]document.all.elementID`

Properties

align	clientWidth	*language*	*parentElement*
background	colSpan	noWrap	*parentTextEdit*
bgColor	*document*	*offsetHeight*	rowSpan
borderColor	height	*offsetLeft*	*sourceIndex*
borderColorDark	*id*	*offsetParent*	*style*
borderColorLight	*innerHTML*	*offsetTop*	*tagName*
cellIndex	*innerText*	*offsetWidth*	*title*
className	*isTextEdit*	*outerHTML*	vAlign
clientHeight	*lang*	*outerText*	width

Methods

blur()	*getAttribute()*	*removeAttribute()*
click()	*insertAdjacentHTML()*	*scrollIntoView()*
contains()	*insertAdjacentText()*	*setAttribute()*
focus()		

Collections/Arrays

all[]	*children[]*	*filters[]*

Event Handler Properties

Handler	NN	IE	DOM
onafterupdate	n/a	4	n/a
onbeforeunload	n/a	4	n/a
onblur	n/a	4	n/a
onclick	n/a	4	n/a
ondblclick	n/a	4	n/a
ondragstart	n/a	4	n/a
onfilterchange	n/a	4	n/a
onhelp	n/a	4	n/a
onkeydown	n/a	4	n/a
onkeypress	n/a	4	n/a
onkeyup	n/a	4	n/a
onmousedown	n/a	4	n/a
onmousemove	n/a	4	n/a
onmouseout	n/a	4	n/a
onmouseover	n/a	4	n/a
onmouseup	n/a	4	n/a
onresize	n/a	4	n/a
onrowenter	n/a	4	n/a
onrowexit	n/a	4	n/a
onselectstart	n/a	4	n/a

DOM Reference

align   NN *n/a*   IE *4*   DOM *1*

Read/Write

Defines the horizontal alignment of content within the cell.

Example   document.all.myTD.align = "center"

Value   Any of the three horizontal alignment constants: center | left | right.

Default   left

background   NN *n/a*   IE *4*   DOM *n/a*

Read/Write

URL of the background image for the cell. If you set a bgColor to the element as well, the color appears if the image fails to load; otherwise the image overlays the color.

Example   document.all.myTD.background = "images/watermark.jpg"

Value   Complete or relative URL to the background image file.

Default   None.

bgColor   NN *n/a*   IE *4*   DOM *1*

Read/Write

Background color of the table cell. This color setting is not reflected in the style sheet backgroundColor property. Even if the BGCOLOR attribute or bgColor property is set with a plain-language color name, the returned value is always a hexadecimal triplet.

Example   document.all.myTD.bgColor = "yellow"

Value

A hexadecimal triplet or plain-language color name. See Appendix A for acceptable plain-language color names.

Default   Varies with browser and operating system.

borderColor   NN *n/a*   IE *4*   DOM *n/a*

Read/Write

Color of the element's border. Internet Explorer applies the color to all four lines that make up the interior border of a cell. Therefore, colors of adjacent cells do not collide.

Example   document.all.myTD.borderColor = "salmon"

Value

A hexadecimal triplet or plain-language color name. A setting of empty is interpreted as "#000000" (black). See Appendix A for acceptable plain-language color names.

Default   Varies with operating system.

borderColorDark, borderColorLight   NN *n/a*   IE *4*   DOM *n/a*

The 3-D effect of table borders in Internet Explorer is created by careful positioning of light and dark lines around the page's background or default color. You can independently control the colors used for the dark and light lines by assigning values to the **borderColorDark** (left and top edges of the cell) and **borderColorLight** (right and bottom edges) properties.

Typically, you should assign complementary colors to the pair of properties. There is also no rule that says you must assign a dark color to **borderColorDark**. The attributes merely control a well-defined set of lines so you can predict which lines of the border change with each attribute.

Example

```
document.all.myTD.borderColorDark = "blue"
document.all.myTD.borderColorLight = "cornflowerblue"
```

Value

A hexadecimal triplet or plain-language color name. A setting of empty is interpreted as "#000000" (black). See Appendix A for acceptable plain-language color names.

Default   Varies with operating system.

cellIndex   NN *n/a*   IE *4*   DOM *n/a*

Returns a zero-based integer representing the position of the current cell among all other TD elements in the same row. The count is based on the source code order of the TD elements within a TR element. This property is not available in the Macintosh version of Internet Explorer 4.

Example   `var whichCell = document.all.myTD.cellIndex`

Value   Integer.

Default   None.

clientHeight, clientWidth   NN *n/a*   IE *4*   DOM *n/a*

According to Microsoft's developer documentation, these properties reflect the height and width (in pixels) of the element's content. But see the section "About client- and offset-Properties" at the beginning of this chapter for details.

Example   `var midHeight = document.all.myTD.clientHeight/2`

Value   Integer pixel value.

Default   None.

colSpan

NN *n/a*   IE *4*   DOM *1*

Read/Write

The number of columns across which the current table cell should extend itself. For each additional column included in the colSpan count, one less TD element is required for the table row. If you set the align property to center or right, the alignment is calculated on the full width of the TD element across the specified number of columns. Unless the current cell also specifies a ROWSPAN attribute, the next table row returns to the original column count.

Example document.all.myTD.colSpan = 2

Value   Any positive integer, usually 2 or larger.

Default 1

height, width

NN *n/a*   IE *4*   DOM *n/a*

Read/Write

The height and width in pixels of the element. Changes to these values are immediately reflected in reflowed content on the page. These properties are read-only in the Macintosh version of Internet Explorer 4.

Example document.all.myTD.height = 250

Value   Integer.

Default None.

noWrap

NN *n/a*   IE *4*   DOM *1*

Read/Write

Whether the browser should render the cell as wide as is necessary to display a line of nonbreaking text on one line. Abuse of this attribute can force the user into a great deal of inconvenient horizontal scrolling of the page to view all of the content.

Example document.all.myTD.noWrap = "true"

Value   Boolean value: true | false.

Default false

rowSpan

NN *n/a*   IE *4*   DOM *1*

Read/Write

The number of rows through which the current table cell should extend itself downward. For each additional row included in the rowSpan count, one less TD element is required for the next table row. If you set the vAlign property to middle, the alignment is calculated on the full height of the TD element across the specified number of rows.

Example document.all.myTD.rowSpan = 12

Value   Any positive integer, usually 2 or larger.

Default 1

vAlign

NN *n/a*   IE *4*   DOM *1*

Read/Write

The manner of vertical alignment of text within the element's content box.

Example `document.all.myTD.vAlign = "baseline"`

Value   Case-insensitive constant (as a string): `baseline` | `bottom` | `middle` | `top`.

Default `middle`

width

See height.

blur()

NN *n/a*   IE *4*   DOM *n/a*

Removes focus from the current element and fires an `onBlur` event (in IE). No other element necessarily receives focus as a result.

Returned Value

None.

Parameters

None.

focus()

NN *n/a*   IE *4*   DOM *n/a*

Gives focus to the current element and fires the `onFocus` event (in IE). If another element had focus at the time, it receives an `onBlur` event.

Returned Value

None.

Parameters

None.

text

NN *2*   IE *3*   DOM *1*

The `text` object is a form control generated with an `INPUT` element whose `TYPE` attribute is set to `"text"`. This object is the primary way of getting a user to enter single lines of text for submission to the server.

HTML Equivalent

`<INPUT TYPE="text">`

Object Model Reference

NN   `[window.]document.`*formName.elementName*
          `[window.]document.forms[i].elements[i]`

IE   [window.]document.*formName*.*elementName*
            [window.]document.forms[i].elements[i]
            [window.]document.all.*elementID*

Properties

accessKey	form	*offsetHeight*	*parentElement*	*style*
className	*id*	*offsetLeft*	*parentTextEdit*	tabIndex
dataFld	*isTextEdit*	*offsetParent*	readOnly	*tagName*
dataSrc	*lang*	*offsetTop*	recordNumber	*title*
defaultValue	*language*	*offsetWidth*	size	type
disabled	maxLength	*outerHTML*	*sourceIndex*	value
document	name	*outerText*		

Methods

blur()	*getAttribute()*	*removeAttribute()*
click()	handleEvent()	*scrollIntoView()*
contains()	*insertAdjacentHTML()*	select()
createTextRange()	*insertAdjacentText()*	*setAttribute()*
focus()		

Collections/Arrays

all[]	*children[]*	*filters[]*

Event Handler Properties

Handler	NN	IE	DOM
onblur	2	3	n/a
onchange	2	3	n/a
onclick	n/a	4	n/a
ondblclick	n/a	4	n/a
onfocus	2	3	n/a
onhelp	n/a	4	n/a
onkeydown	4	4	n/a
onkeypress	4	4	n/a
onkeyup	4	4	n/a
onmousedown	n/a	4	n/a
onmousemove	n/a	4	n/a
onmouseout	n/a	4	n/a
onmouseover	n/a	4	n/a
onmouseup	n/a	4	n/a
onselect	2	4	n/a

accessKey   NN *n/a*   IE *4*   DOM *1*

Read/Write

A single character key that brings focus to the element. The browser and operating system determine whether the user must press a modifier key (e.g., **Ctrl**, **Alt**, or **Command**) with the access key to bring focus to the element. In IE 4/Windows, the **Alt** key is required, and the key is not case sensitive. Not working in IE 4/Mac.

Example   `document.entryForm.myText.accessKey = "n"`

Value   Single alphanumeric (and punctuation) keyboard character.

Default   None.

dataFld

NN *n/a*   IE *4*   DOM *n/a*

Read/Write

Used with IE 4 data binding to associate a remote data source column name to a `text` object's `value` property. A `DATASRC` attribute must also be set for the element. Setting both the `dataFld` and `dataSrc` properties to empty strings breaks the binding between element and data source.

Example   `document.myForm.myText.dataFld = "linkURL"`

Value   Case-sensitive identifier of the data source column.

Default   None.

dataSrc

NN *n/a*   IE *4*   DOM *n/a*

Read/Write

Used with IE 4 data binding to specify the name of the remote ODBC data source (such as an Oracle or SQL Server database) to be associated with the element. Content from the data source is specified via the `DATAFLD` attribute. Setting both the `dataFld` and `dataSrc` properties to empty strings breaks the binding between element and data source.

Example   `document.myForm.myText.dataSrc = "#DBSRC3"`

Value   Case-sensitive identifier of the data source.

Default   None.

defaultValue

NN *2*   IE *3*   DOM *1*

Read-only

The default text for the text input element, as established by the **VALUE** attribute.

Example

```
var txtObj = document.forms[0].myText
if (txtObj.value != txtObj.defaultValue ) {
    ...
}
```

Value   Any string value.

Default   None.

DOM Reference

disabled
NN *n/a*   IE *4*   DOM *1*
Read/Write

Whether the element is available for user interaction. When set to `true`, the element cannot receive focus or be modified by the user. It is also not submitted with the form.

Example   `document.forms[0].myText.disabled = true`

Value   Boolean value: `true` | `false`.

Default   `false`

form
NN *2*   IE *3*   DOM *n/a*
Read-only

Returns a reference to the `FORM` element that contains the current element (if any). This property is most often passed as a parameter for an event handler, using the `this` keyword to refer to the current form control.

Example   `<INPUT TYPE="text" NAME="zip"  onChange="doValidate(this.form)">`

Value   Object reference.

Default   None.

maxLength
NN *n/a*   IE *4*   DOM *n/a*
Read/Write

The maximum number of characters that may be typed into a text `INPUT` element. In practice, browsers beep or otherwise alert users when a typed character would exceed the `maxLength` value. There is no innate correlation between the `maxLength` and `size` properties. If the `maxLength` allows for more characters than fit within the specified width of the element, the browser provides horizontal scrolling (albeit awkward for many users) to allow entry and editing of the field.

Example   `document.entryForm.myText.maxLength = 35`

Value   Positive integer value.

Default   Unlimited.

name
NN *2*   IE *3*   DOM *1*
Read/Write

The identifier associated with the form control. The value of this property is submitted as one-half of the name/value pair when the form is submitted to the server. Names are hidden from user view, since control labels are assigned via other means, depending on the control type. Form control names may also be used by script references to the objects.

Example   `document.orderForm.myText.name = "Win32"`

Value

Case-sensitive identifier that follows the rules of identifier naming: it may contain no whitespace, cannot begin with a numeral, and should avoid punctuation except for the underscore character.

Default   None.

readOnly

Read-only

Whether the form element can be edited on the page by the user. A form control whose readOnly property is true may still be modified by scripts, even though the user may not alter the content.

Example   document.forms[0].myText.readOnly = "true"

Value   Boolean value: true | false.

Default   false

recordNumber

Read-only

Used with data binding, returns an integer representing the record within the data set that generated the element (i.e., an element whose content is filled via data binding). Values of this property can be used to extract a specific record from an Active Data Objects (ADO) record set (see recordset property).

Example

```
<SCRIPT FOR="tableTemplate" EVENT="onclick">
    myDataCollection.recordset.absoluteposition = this.recordNumber
    ...
</SCRIPT>
```

Value   Integer.

Default   None.

size

Read/Write

Roughly speaking, the width in characters that the input box should be sized to accommodate. In practice, the browser does not always accurately predict the proper width. See details in the SIZE attribute discussion for the INPUT element in Chapter 8. There is no interaction between the size and maxLength properties for this object.

Example   document.forms[0].myText.size = 12

Value   Positive integer.

Default   20

tabIndex

NN *n/a*   IE *4*   DOM *1*
Read/Write

A number that indicates the sequence of this element within the tabbing order of all focus-able elements in the document. Tabbing order follows a strict set of rules. Elements that have values other than zero assigned to their `tabIndex` properties are first in line when a user starts tabbing in a page. Focus starts with the element with the lowest `tabIndex` value and proceeds in order to the highest value, regardless of physical location on the page or in the document. If two elements have the same `tabIndex` values, the element that comes earlier in the document receives focus first. Next come all elements that either don't support the `tabIndex` property or have the value set to zero. These elements receive focus in the order in which they appear in the document. A value of -1 removes the element from tabbing order altogether.

Note that the Macintosh user interface does not provide for giving focus to elements other than text and password `INPUT` fields.

Example   `document.forms[0].myText.tabIndex = 6`

Value   Integer.

Default   None.

type

NN *3*   IE *4*   DOM *1*
Read-only

Returns the type of form control element. The value is returned in all lowercase letters. It may be necessary to cycle through all form elements in search of specific types to do some processing on (e.g., emptying all form controls of type `"text"` while leaving other controls untouched).

Example

```
if (document.forms[0].elements[3].type == "text") {
    ...
}
```

Value

Any of the following constants (as a string): `button` | `checkbox` | `file` | `hidden` | `image` | `password` | `radio` | `reset` | `select-multiple` | `select-one` | `submit` | `text` | `textarea`.

Default   `text`

value

NN *2*   IE *3*   DOM *1*
Read/Write

Current value associated with the form control that is submitted with the name/value pair for the element. All values are strings, which means that scripts using text field values for some math operations (especially addition) have to convert the strings to numbers via the `parseInt()` or `parseFloat()` functions before performing the math. If you assign a number to a text field's `value` property, the browser automatically converts its data type to a string.

Example `document.forms[0].myText.value = "franken"`

Value   String.

Default None.

blur()

Removes focus from the current element and fires an `onBlur` event (in IE). No other element necessarily receives focus as a result.

Returned Value

None.

Parameters

None.

createTextRange()

Creates a `TextRange` object from the content of the text object. See the `TextRange` object for details.

Returned Value

`TextRange` object.

Parameters

None.

focus()

Gives focus to the current element and fires the `onFocus` event (in IE). If another element had focus at the time, it receives an `onBlur` event.

Returned Value

None.

Parameters

None.

handleEvent()

`handleEvent(event)`

Instructs the object to accept and process the event whose specifications are passed as the parameter to the method. The object must have an event handler for the event type to process the event.

Returned Value

None.

Parameters

event   A Navigator 4 **event** object.

select()   NN *2*   IE *3*   DOM *n/a*

Selects all the text displayed in the form element.

Returned Value

None.

Parameters

None.

TEXTAREA   NN *2*   IE *3*   DOM *1*

The **TEXTAREA** object reflects the **TEXTAREA** element and is used as a form control. This object is the primary way of getting a user to enter multiple lines of text for submission to the server. Note that the **innerHTML** property is not available on the Macintosh version of Internet Explorer 4.

HTML Equivalent

<TEXTAREA>

Object Model Reference

NN   [window.]document.*formName*.*elementName*
        [window.]document.forms[i].elements[i]

IE   [window.]document.*formName*.*elementName*
        [window.]document.forms[i].elements[i]
        [window.]document.all.*elementID*

Properties

accessKey	defaultValue	name	*parentElement*	*sourceIndex*
className	disabled	*offsetHeight*	*parentTextEdit*	*style*
clientHeight	*document*	*offsetLeft*	readOnly	tabIndex
clientLeft	form	*offsetParent*	rows	*tagName*
clientTop	*id*	*offsetTop*	scrollHeight	*title*
clientWidth	*isTextEdit*	*offsetWidth*	scrollLeft	type
cols	*lang*	outerHTML	scrollTop	value
dataFld	*language*	outerText	scrollWidth	wrap
dataSrc				

Methods

blur()	*getAttribute()*	*removeAttribute()*
click()	handleEvent()	*scrollIntoView()*
contains()	*insertAdjacentHTML()*	select()
createTextRange()	*insertAdjacentText()*	*setAttribute()*
focus()		

Collections/Arrays

all[]   children[]   filters[]

Event Handler Properties

Handler	NN	IE	DOM
onafterupdate	n/a	4	n/a
onbeforeunload	n/a	4	n/a
onblur	2	3	n/a
onchange	2	3	n/a
onclick	n/a	4	n/a
ondblclick	n/a	4	n/a
ondragstart	n/a	4	n/a
onerrorupdate	n/a	4	n/a
onfilterchange	n/a	4	n/a
onfocus	2	3	n/a
onhelp	n/a	4	n/a
onkeydown	4	4	n/a
onkeypress	4	4	n/a
onkeyup	4	4	n/a
onmousedown	n/a	4	n/a
onmousemove	n/a	4	n/a
onmouseout	n/a	4	n/a
onmouseover	n/a	4	n/a
onmouseup	n/a	4	n/a
onrowenter	n/a	4	n/a
onrowexit	n/a	4	n/a
onscroll	n/a	4	n/a
onselect	2	3	n/a
onselectstart	n/a	4	n/a

DOM Reference

accessKey   NN *n/a*   IE *4*   DOM *1*

Read/Write

A single character key that brings focus to the element. The browser and operating system determine whether the user must press a modifier key (e.g., **Ctrl**, **Alt**, or **Command**) with the access key to bring focus to the element. In IE 4/Windows, the **Alt** key is required, and the key is not case sensitive. Not working in IE 4/Mac.

Example document.entryForm.myTextArea.accessKey = "n"

Value Single alphanumeric (and punctuation) keyboard character.

Default None.

clientHeight, clientWidth

NN *n/a*   IE *4*   DOM *n/a*

Read/Write

According to Microsoft's developer documentation, these properties reflect the height and width (in pixels) of the element's content. But see the section "About client- and offset-Properties" at the beginning of this chapter for details.

Example   `var midHeight = document.forms[0].myTextArea.clientHeight/2`

Value   Integer pixel value.

Default   None.

clientLeft, clientTop

NN *n/a*   IE *4*   DOM *n/a*

Read-only

According to Microsoft's developer documentation, these properties reflect the distance between the "true" left and top edges of the document area and the edges of the element. But see the section "About client- and offset- Properties" at the beginning of this chapter for details. To get or set the pixel position of an element in the document, use the `pixelLeft` and `pixelTop` properties.

Value   A string value for a length in a variety of units or percentage.

Default   None.

cols

NN *n/a*   IE *4*   DOM *1*

Read/Write

The width of the editable space of the **TEXTAREA** element. The value represents the number of monofont characters that are to be displayed within the width. When the font size can be influenced by style sheets, the actual width changes accordingly.

Example   `document.forms[0].comments.cols = 60`

Value   Any positive integer.

Default   Varies with browser and operating system.

dataFld

NN *n/a*   IE *4*   DOM *n/a*

Read/Write

Used with IE 4 data binding to associate a remote data source column name to a **TEXTAREA** object's `value` property. A **DATASRC** attribute must also be set for the element. Setting both the `dataFld` and `dataSrc` properties to empty strings breaks the binding between element and data source.

Example   `document.myForm.myTextArea.dataFld = "linkURL"`

Value   Case-sensitive identifier of the data source column.

Default   None.

dataSrc

NN *n/a*   IE *4*   DOM *n/a*

Read/Write

Used with IE 4 data binding to specify the name of the remote ODBC data source (such as an Oracle or SQL Server database) to be associated with the element. Content from the data source is specified via the DATAFLD attribute. Setting both the `dataFld` and `dataSrc` properties to empty strings breaks the binding between element and data source.

Example   `document.myForm.myTextArea.dataSrc = "#DBSRC3"`

Value   Case-sensitive identifier of the data source.

Default   None.

defaultValue

NN *2*   IE *3*   DOM *1*

Read-only

The default text for the TEXTAREA element, as established by the VALUE attribute.

Example

```
var txtAObj = document.forms[0].myTextArea
if (txtAObj.value != txtAObj.defaultValue ) {
    . . .
}
```

Value   Any string value.

Default   None.

disabled

NN *n/a*   IE *4*   DOM *1*

Read/Write

Whether the element is available for user interaction. When set to `true`, the element cannot receive focus or be modified by the user. It is also not submitted with the form.

Example   `document.forms[0].myTextArea.disabled = true`

Value   Boolean value: `true` | `false`.

Default   `false`

form

NN *2*   IE *3*   DOM *n/a*

Read-only

Returns a reference to the FORM element that contains the current element (if any). This property is most often passed as a parameter for an event handler, using the `this` keyword to refer to the current form control.

Example   `<TEXTAREA NAME="comment"  onChange="doValidate(this.form)">`

Value   Object reference.

Default   None.

DOM Reference

name

NN *2*   IE *3*   DOM *1*

Read/Write

The identifier associated with the form control. The value of this property is submitted as one-half of the name/value pair when the form is submitted to the server. Names are hidden from user view, since control labels are assigned via other means, depending on the control type. Form control names may also be used by script references to the objects. The handling of carriage returns inside the element is governed by the setting of the **wrap** property.

Example   `document.orderForm.myTextArea.name = "Win32"`

Value

Case-sensitive identifier that follows the rules of identifier naming: it may contain no whitespace, cannot begin with a numeral, and should avoid punctuation except for the underscore character.

Default   None.

readOnly

NN *n/a*   IE *4*   DOM *n/a*

Read-only

Whether the form element can be edited on the page by the user. A form control whose **readOnly** property is **true** may still be modified by scripts, even though the user may not alter the content.

Example   `document.forms[0].myTextArea.readOnly = "true"`

Value   Boolean value: **true** | **false**.

Default   **false**

rows

NN *n/a*   IE *4*   DOM *1*

Read/Write

The height of the **TEXTAREA** element based on the number of lines of text that are to be displayed without scrolling. The value represents the number of monofont character lines that are to be displayed within the height before the scrollbar becomes active. When the font size can be influenced by style sheets, the actual height changes accordingly.

Example   `document.forms[0].comments.rows = 6`

Value   Integer.

Default   2 (IE 4/Windows); 4 (IE 4/Macintosh).

scrollHeight, scrollWidth

NN *n/a*   IE *4*   DOM *n/a*

Read-only

The meaning of these two properties is ambiguous based on Microsoft's description and the way they're implemented in the Windows and Macintosh versions of Internet Explorer 4. My best guess is that these properties are intended to measure the height and width (in pixels) of the content of an element even when some of the content cannot be seen unless scrolled with scrollbars. The Macintosh version of the browser interprets this to mean the amount of the content that you can see at any one time. The important point is that for key elements, such as the BODY, the properties mean different things and can disrupt cross-platform operation.

Example `var midPoint = document.all.myTextArea.scrollHeight/2`

Value Positive integer or zero.

Default None.

scrollLeft, scrollTop

NN *n/a*   IE *4*   DOM *n/a*

Read/Write

The distance in pixels between the actual left or top edge of the element's physical content and the left or top edge of the visible portion of the content. Setting these properties allows you to use scripts to adjust the scroll of content within a scrollable container, such as text in a TEXTAREA element or an entire document in the browser window or frame. When the content is not scrolled, both values are zero. Setting the `scrollTop` property to 15 scrolls the document upward by 15 pixels in the window; the `scrollLeft` property is unaffected unless explicitly changed. The property values change as the user adjusts the scrollbars.

Example `document.all.myTextArea.scrollTop = 40`

Value Positive integer or zero.

Default 0

tabIndex

NN *n/a*   IE *4*   DOM *1*

Read/Write

A number that indicates the sequence of this element within the tabbing order of all focusable elements in the document. Tabbing order follows a strict set of rules. Elements that have values other than zero assigned to their `tabIndex` properties are first in line when a user starts tabbing in a page. Focus starts with the element with the lowest `tabIndex` value and proceeds in order to the highest value, regardless of physical location on the page or in the document. If two elements have the same `tabIndex` values, the element that comes earlier in the document receives focus first. Next come all elements that either don't support the `tabIndex` property or have the value set to zero. These elements receive focus in the order in which they appear in the document. A value of -1 removes the element from tabbing order altogether.

Note that the Macintosh user interface does not provide for giving focus to elements other than text and password INPUT fields.

Example `document.forms[0].myTextArea.tabIndex = 6`

Value Integer.

Default None.

type   NN *3*   IE *4*   DOM *1*

Read-only

Returns the type of form control element. The value is returned in all lowercase letters. It may be necessary to cycle through all form elements in search of specific types to do some processing on (e.g., emptying all form controls of type `"text"` while leaving other controls untouched).

Example
```
if (document.forms[0].elements[3].type == "textarea") {
   ...
}
```

Value

Any of the following constants (as a string): `button` | `checkbox` | `file` | `hidden` | `image` | `password` | `radio` | `reset` | `select-multiple` | `select-one` | `submit` | `text` | `textarea`.

Default   `textarea`

value   NN *2*   IE *3*   DOM *1*

Read/Write

Current value associated with the form control that is submitted with the name/value pair for the element. All values are strings.

Example `var comment = document.forms[0].myTextArea.value`

Value   String.

Default   None.

wrap   NN *n/a*   IE *4*   DOM *1*

Read/Write

Whether the browser should wrap text in a **TEXTAREA** element and whether wrapped text should be submitted to the server with soft returns converted to hard carriage returns. A value of `physical` engages word wrapping and converts soft returns to CR-LF characters in the value submitted to the server. A value of `virtual` turns on word wrapping, but does not include the CR-LF characters in the text submitted with the form. A value of `off` turns word wrapping off. The Win32 version of Internet Explorer 4 returns a value of `soft` when the **WRAP** attribute is set to `virtual`.

Example `document.forms[0].comments.wrap = "wrap"`

Value   One of the constant values (as a string): `physical` | `off` | `virtual`.

Default   `off`

blur()   NN *2*   IE *3*   DOM *n/a*

Removes focus from the current element and fires an `onBlur` event (in IE). No other element necessarily receives focus as a result.

Returned Value

None.

Parameters

None.

createTextRange()

NN *n/a*   IE *4*   DOM *n/a*

Creates a `TextRange` object from the content of the `TEXTAREA` object. See the `TextRange` object for details.

Returned Value

`TextRange` object.

focus()

NN *2*   IE *3*   DOM *n/a*

Gives focus to the current element and fires the `onFocus` event (in IE). If another element had focus at the time, it receives an `onBlur` event.

Returned Value

None.

Parameters

None.

handleEvent()

NN *4*   IE *n/a*   DOM *n/a*

`handleEvent(event)`

Instructs the object to accept and process the event whose specifications are passed as the parameter to the method. The object must have an event handler for the event type to process the event.

Returned Value

None.

Parameters

event   A Navigator 4 `event` object.

select()

NN *2*   IE *3*   DOM *n/a*

Selects all the text displayed in the form element.

Returned Value

None.

Parameters

None.

TextRange   NN *n/a*   IE *4*   DOM *n/a*

The TextRange object represents the text of zero or more characters in a document. When a text range consists of zero characters, it represents an insertion point between two characters (or before the first or after the last character).

A TextRange object is created via the createTextRange() method associated with the BODY, BUTTON, text, or TEXTAREA objects. Once a text range is created, use its methods to adjust its start and end point to encompass a desired segment of the text (such as text that matches a search string). Once the range has been narrowed to the target text, assign values to its htmlText and text properties to change, remove, or insert text. A library of direct commands that perform specific textual modifications can also be invoked to act on the text range. See Chapter 5, *Making Content Dynamic*, for details and examples of using the TextRange object.

Note that the TextRange object and all associated facilities are available only in the Win32 version of Internet Explorer 4.

Object Model Reference

IE   *objectRef*.createTextRange()

Properties

boundingHeight   boundingTop   boundingWidth   htmlText   text
boundingLeft

Methods

collapse()	move()	queryCommandIndeterm()
compareEndPoints()	moveEnd()	queryCommandState()
duplicate()	moveStart()	queryCommandSupported()
execCommand()	moveToBookmark()	queryCommandText()
expand()	moveToElementText()	queryCommandValue()
findText()	moveToPoint()	*scrollIntoView()*
getBookmark()	parentElement()	select()
inRange()	pasteHTML()	setEndPoint()
isEqual()	queryCommandEnabled()	

boundingHeight, boundingWidth   NN *n/a*   IE *4*   DOM *n/a*

Read-only

Returns the pixel measure of the imaginary space occupied by the TextRange object. Although you do not see a TextRange object in the document (unless a script selects it), the area of a TextRange object is identical to the area that a selection highlight would occupy. These values cinch up to measure only as wide or tall as the widest and tallest part of the range.

Example

```
var rangeWidth =
document.forms[0].myTextArea.createTextRange().boundingWidth
```

Value   Integer.

Default   None.

boundingLeft, boundingTop   NN *n/a*   IE *4*   DOM *n/a*

Returns the pixel distance between the top or left of the browser window or frame and the top or left edges of the imaginary space occupied by the **TextRange** object. Although you do not see a **TextRange** object in the document (unless a script selects it), the area of a **TextRange** object is identical to the area that a selection highlight would occupy. Values for these properties are measured from the fixed window or frame edges and not the top and left of the document, which may scroll out of view. Therefore, as a document scrolls, these values change.

Example
```
var rangeOffH =
document.forms[0].myTextArea.createTextRange().boundingLeft
```

Value   Integer.

Default   None.

htmlText   NN *n/a*   IE *4*   DOM *n/a*

All HTML of the document for a given element when that element is used as the basis for a **TextRange** object. For example, if you create a **TextRange** for the BODY element (`document.body.createTextRange()`), the `htmlText` property contains all HTML content between (but not including) the BODY element tags.

Example   `var rangeHTML = document.body.createTextRange().htmlText`

Value   String.

Default   None.

text   NN *n/a*   IE *4*   DOM *n/a*

The text contained by the text range. In the case of a **TextRange** object of a BODY element, this consists of only the text that is rendered, but none of the HTML tags behind the scenes.

Example   `var rangeText = document.body.createTextRange().text`

Value   String.

Default   None.

collapse()

collapse([*start*])

Reduces the TextRange object to a length of zero (creating an insertion point) at the beginning or end of the text range before it collapsed.

Returned Value

None.

Parameters

start   Optional Boolean value controls whether the insertion point goes to the beginning (**true**) of the original range or the end (**false**). The default value is **true**.

compareEndPoints()

compareEndPoints(*type, comparisonRange*)

Compares the relative position of the boundary (start and end) points of two ranges (the current range and one that had been previously saved to a variable). The first parameter defines which boundary points in each range you wish to compare. If the result of the comparison is that the first point is earlier in the range than the other point, the returned value is -1; if the result shows both points to be in the same location, the returned value is 0; if the result shows the first point to be later in the range than the other point, the returned value is 1. For example, if you have saved the first range to a variable r1 and created a new range as r2, you can see the physical relationship between the end of r2 and the start of r1:

    r1.compareEndPoints("EndToStart", r2)

If r1 ends where r2 starts (the insertion point between two characters), the returned value is 0.

Returned Value

-1, 0, or 1.

Parameters

type   One of the following constants (as a string): StartToEnd | StartToStart | EndToStart | EndToEnd.

comparisonRange
    A TextRange object created earlier and saved to a variable.

duplicate()

Creates a new TextRange object with the same values as the current range. The new object is an independent object (the old and new do not equal each other), but their values are initially identical (until you start modifying one range or the other).

Returned Value

TextRange object.

Parameters

None.

execCommand()   NN *n/a*   IE *4*   DOM *n/a*

```
execCommand("commandName"[, UIFlag[, value]])
```

Executes the named command on the current TextRange object. Many commands work best when the TextRange object is an insertion point. See Appendix D for a list of commands.

Returned Value

Boolean value: true if command is successful; false if unsuccessful.

Parameters

commandName
> A case-insensitive string value of the command name. See Appendix D.

UIFlag   Optional Boolean value: true to display any user interface triggered by the command (if any); false to prevent such display.

value   A parameter value for the command.

expand()   NN *n/a*   IE *4*   DOM *n/a*

```
expand(unit)
```

Expands the current text range to encompass the textual unit passed as a parameter. For example, if someone selects some characters from a document, you can create the range and expand it to encompass the entire sentence in which the selection takes place:

```
var rng = document.selection.createRange()
rng.expand("sentence")
```

If the starting range extends across multiple units, the expand() method expands the range outward to the next nearest unit.

Returned Value

Boolean value: true if method is successful; false if unsuccessful.

Parameters

unit   A case-insensitive string value of the desired unit: character | word | sentence | textedit. The textedit value expands the range to the entire original range.

findText()   NN *n/a*   IE *4*   DOM *n/a*

```
findText(string)
```

Searches the current TextRange object for a match of a string passed as a parameter. Matching is done on a case-insensitive basis. If there is a match, the TextRange object repositions its start and end points to surround the found text. To continue searching in the document, you must reposition the start point of the text range to the end of the found string (with collapse()).

Returned Value

Boolean value: true if a match is found; false if unsuccessful.

Parameters

string   A case-insensitive string to be searched.

getBookmark(), moveToBookmark()   NN *n/a*   IE *4*   DOM *n/a*

```
getBookmark()
moveToBookmark(bookmarkString)
```

These two methods work together as a way to temporarily save a text range specification and restore it when needed. The getBookmark() method returns an opaque string (containing binary data that is of no value to human users). Once that value is stored in a variable, the range can be modified as needed for the script. Some time later, the bookmarked text range can be restored with the moveToBookmark() method:

```
    var rangeMark = myRange.getBookmark()
    ...
    myRange.moveToBookmark(rangeMark)
```

Returned Value

Boolean value: true if the operation is successful; false if unsuccessful.

Parameters

bookmarkString
            An opaque string returned by the getBookmark() method.

inRange()   NN *n/a*   IE *4*   DOM *n/a*

```
inRange(comparisonRange)
```

Determines whether the comparison range is within or equal to the physical range of the current text range.

Returned Value

Boolean value: true if the comparison range is in or equal to the current range; false if not.

Parameters

comparisonRange
            TextRange object created earlier and saved to a variable.

isEqual()   NN *n/a*   IE *4*   DOM *n/a*

```
isEqual(comparisonRange)
```

Determines whether the comparison range is identical to the current text range.

Returned Value

Boolean value: true if the comparison range is equal to the current range; false if not.

Parameters

`comparisonRange`
> A `TextRange` object created earlier and saved to a variable.

move( )   NN *n/a*   IE 4   DOM *n/a*

`move(unit[, count])`

Collapses the current text range to an insertion point at the end of the current range and moves it forward or backward from the current position by one or more units.

Returned Value

Integer of the number of units moved.

Parameters

`unit`   A case-insensitive string value of the desired unit: `character` | `word` | `sentence` | `textedit`. The `textedit` value moves the insertion pointer to the start or end of the entire original range.

`count`   An optional integer of the number of units to move the insertion pointer. Positive values move the pointer forward; negative values move the pointer backward. Default value is `1`.

moveEnd( ), moveStart( )   NN *n/a*   IE 4   DOM *n/a*

`moveEnd(unit[, count])`
`moveStart(unit[, count])`

Moves only the end or start point (respectively) of the current text range by one or more units. An optional parameter lets you specify both the number of units and direction. To shift the start point of a text range toward the beginning of the original range, be sure to specify a negative value. When moving the end point to the right by word units, be aware that a word ends with a white-space character (including a period). Therefore, if a `findText()` method sets the range to a found string that does not end in a space, the first `moveEnd("word")` method moves the ending point to the spot past the space after the found string rather than to the following word.

Returned Value

Integer of the number of units moved.

Parameters

`unit`   A case-insensitive string value of the desired unit: `character` | `word` | `sentence` | `textedit`. The `textedit` value moves the insertion pointer to the start or end of the entire original range.

`count`   An optional integer of the number of units to move the insertion pointer. Positive values move the pointer forward; negative values move the pointer backward. Default value is `1`.

moveToBookmark( )

See getBookmark().

moveToElementText()   NN *n/a*   IE *4*   DOM *n/a*

moveToElementText(*elementObject*)

Moves the current TextRange object's start and end points to encase the specified HTML element object. The resulting text range includes the HTML for the element, as well.

Returned Value

None.

Parameters

elementObject

A scripted reference to the object. This can be in the form of a direct reference (document.all.*elementID*) or a variable containing the same kind of value.

moveToPoint()   NN *n/a*   IE *4*   DOM *n/a*

moveToPoint(*x*, *y*)

Collapses the text range to an insertion pointer and sets its location to the spot indicated by the horizontal and vertical coordinates in the browser window or frame. This is as if the user had clicked on a spot in the window to define an insertion point. Use methods such as expand() to enlarge the text range to include a character, word, sentence, or entire text range.

Returned Value

None.

Parameters

x   Horizontal coordinate of the insertion point in pixels relative to the left edge of the window or frame.

y   Vertical coordinate of the insertion point in pixels relative to the top edge of the window or frame.

parentElement()   NN *n/a*   IE *4*   DOM *n/a*

Returns an object reference to the next outermost element that fully contains the TextRange object.

Returned Value

Object reference.

Parameters

None.

pasteHTML()   NN *n/a*   IE *4*   DOM *n/a*

pasteHTML(*HTMLText*)

Replaces the current text range with the HTML content supplied as a parameter string. Typically this method is used on a zero-length text range object acting as an insertion pointer. All tags are rendered as if they were part of the original source code.

Returned Value

None.

Parameters

HTMLText Document source code to be inserted into the document.

queryCommandEnabled()   NN *n/a*   IE *4*   DOM *n/a*

`queryCommandEnabled("`*commandName*`")`

Whether the command can be invoked in light of the current state of the document or selection. Available only in the Win32 platform for IE 4.

Returned Value

Boolean value: `true` if enabled; `false` if not.

Parameters

commandName

A case-insensitive string value of the command name. See Appendix D.

queryCommandIndeterm()   NN *n/a*   IE *4*   DOM *n/a*

`queryCommandIndeterm("`*commandName*`")`

Whether the command is in an indeterminate state. Available only in the Win32 platform for IE 4.

Returned Value

Boolean value: `true` | `false`.

Parameters

commandName

A case-insensitive string value of the command name. See Appendix D.

queryCommandState()   NN *n/a*   IE *4*   DOM *n/a*

`queryCommandState("`*commandName*`")`

Determines the current state of the named command. Available only in the Win32 platform for IE 4.

Returned Value

`true` if the command has been completed; `false` if the command has not completed; `null` if the state cannot be accurately determined.

Parameters

commandName

A case-insensitive string value of the command name. See Appendix D.

DOM Reference

queryCommandSupported()   NN *n/a*   IE 4   DOM *n/a*

`queryCommandSupported("`*commandName*`")`

Determines whether the named command is supported by the document object. Available only in the Win32 platform for IE 4.

Returned Value

Boolean value: `true` | `false`.

Parameters

commandName

A case-insensitive string value of the command name. See Appendix D.

queryCommandText()   NN *n/a*   IE 4   DOM *n/a*

`queryCommandText("`*commandName*`")`

Returns text associated with the command. Available only in the Win32 platform for IE 4.

Returned Value

String.

Parameters

commandName

A case-insensitive string value of the command name. See Appendix D.

queryCommandValue()   NN *n/a*   IE 4   DOM *n/a*

`queryCommandValue("`*commandName*`")`

Returns the value associated with the command, such as the name font of the selection. Available only in the Win32 platform for IE 4.

Returned Value

Depends on the command.

Parameters

commandName

A case-insensitive string value of the command name. See Appendix D.

select()   NN *n/a*   IE 4   DOM *n/a*

Selects all the text that is included in the current `TextRange` object. This method brings some visual confirmation to users that a script knows about a particular block of text. For example, if you were scripting a search with the `findText()` method, you would then use the `scrollIntoView()` and `select()` methods on that range to show the user where the matching text is.

Returned Value

None.

Parameters

None.

setEndPoint()

setEndPoint(*type, comparisonRange*)

Sets the end point of the current TextRange object to the end point of another range that had previously been preserved as a variable reference.

Returned Value

None.

Parameters

type   One of the following constants (as a string): StartToEnd | StartToStart | EndToStart | EndToEnd.

comparisonRange
              A TextRange object created earlier and saved to a variable.

TFOOT

The TFOOT object reflects the TFOOT element. Note that the following items are not available in the Macintosh version of Internet Explorer 4: innerHTML, innerText, and outerText properties; insertAdjacentHTML() and insertAdjacentText() methods; the rows[] collection.

HTML Equivalent

<TFOOT>

Object Model Reference

IE   [window.]document.all.*elementID*

Properties

align	innerHTML	offsetHeight	outerHTML	style
bgColor	innerText	offsetLeft	outerText	tagName
className	isTextEdit	offsetParent	parentElement	title
document	lang	offsetTop	parentTextEdit	vAlign
id	language	offsetWidth	sourceIndex	

Methods

click()	insertAdjacentHTML()	scrollIntoView()
contains()	insertAdjacentText()	setAttribute()
getAttribute()	removeAttribute()	

Collections/Arrays

| all[] | children[] | filters[] | rows[] |

Event Handler Properties

Handler	NN	IE	DOM
onclick	n/a	4	n/a
ondblclick	n/a	4	n/a
ondragstart	n/a	4	n/a
onfilterchange	n/a	4	n/a
onhelp	n/a	4	n/a
onkeydown	n/a	4	n/a
onkeypress	n/a	4	n/a
onkeyup	n/a	4	n/a
onmousedown	n/a	4	n/a
onmousemove	n/a	4	n/a
onmouseout	n/a	4	n/a
onmouseover	n/a	4	n/a
onmouseup	n/a	4	n/a
onselectstart	n/a	4	n/a

align

NN *n/a*   IE *4*   DOM *n/a*

Read/Write

Defines the horizontal alignment of content within all cells contained by the TFOOT element.

Example `document.all.myTFOOT.align = "center"`

Value   Any of the three horizontal alignment constants: `center` I `left` I `right`.

Default `left`

bgColor

NN *n/a*   IE *4*   DOM *n/a*

Read/Write

Background color of the cells contained by the TFOOT element. This color setting is not reflected in the style sheet `backgroundColor` property in Internet Explorer. Even if the BGCOLOR attribute or `bgColor` property is set with a plain-language color name, the returned value is always a hexadecimal triplet.

Example `document.all.myTFOOT.bgColor = "yellow"`

Value

A hexadecimal triplet or plain-language color name. See Appendix A for acceptable plain-language color names.

Default Varies with browser and operating system.

vAlign

NN *n/a*   IE *4*   DOM *1*

Read/Write

The manner of vertical alignment of text within the cells contained by the TFOOT element.

Example   document.all.myTFOOT.vAlign = "baseline"

Value   Case-insensitive constant (as a string): baseline | bottom | middle | top.

Default   middle

rows[]

An array of all rows contained by the TFOOT element.

Syntax   document.all.myTFOOT.rows(i).*objectPropertyOrMethod*

TH

The TH object reflects the TH element. While a TH element may inherit a number of visual properties from containers (e.g., the bgColor of a THEAD element), those inherited property values are not automatically assigned to the TH object. Therefore, just because a header cell may have a yellow background color doesn't mean that its bgColor property is set at all.

HTML Equivalent

<TH>

Object Model Reference

IE   [window.]document.all.*elementID*

Properties

align	clientWidth	*language*	*parentElement*
background	colSpan	noWrap	*parentTextEdit*
bgColor	*document*	*offsetHeight*	rowSpan
borderColor	height	*offsetLeft*	*sourceIndex*
borderColorDark	*id*	*offsetParent*	*style*
borderColorLight	*innerHTML*	*offsetTop*	*tagName*
cellIndex	*innerText*	offsetWidth	*title*
className	*isTextEdit*	*outerHTML*	vAlign
clientHeight	*lang*	*outerText*	width

Methods

blur()	*getAttribute()*	*removeAttribute()*
click()	*insertAdjacentHTML()*	*scrollIntoView()*
contains()	*insertAdjacentText()*	*setAttribute()*
focus()		

Collections/Arrays

all[]	*children[]*	*filters[]*

Event Handler Properties

Handler	NN	IE	DOM
onafterupdate	n/a	4	n/a
onbeforeunload	n/a	4	n/a
onblur	n/a	4	n/a
onclick	n/a	4	n/a
ondblclick	n/a	4	n/a
ondragstart	n/a	4	n/a
onfilterchange	n/a	4	n/a
onhelp	n/a	4	n/a
onkeydown	n/a	4	n/a
onkeypress	n/a	4	n/a
onkeyup	n/a	4	n/a
onmousedown	n/a	4	n/a
onmousemove	n/a	4	n/a
onmouseout	n/a	4	n/a
onmouseover	n/a	4	n/a
onmouseup	n/a	4	n/a
onresize	n/a	4	n/a
onrowenter	n/a	4	n/a
onrowexit	n/a	4	n/a
onselectstart	n/a	4	n/a

align

NN *n/a*   IE *4*   DOM *1*

Read/Write

Defines the horizontal alignment of content within the cell.

Example document.all.myTH.align = "center"

Value

Any of the three horizontal alignment constants: **center** | **left** | **right**.

Default left

background

NN *n/a*   IE *4*   DOM *n/a*

Read/Write

URL of the background image for the cell. If you set a **bgColor** to the element as well, the color appears if the image fails to load; otherwise, the image overlays the color.

Example document.all.myTH.background = "images/watermark.jpg"

Value   Complete or relative URL to the background image file.

Default   None.

bgColor

Background color of the table cell. This color setting is not reflected in the style sheet `backgroundColor` property. Even if the `BGCOLOR` attribute or `bgColor` property is set with a plain-language color name, the returned value is always a hexadecimal triplet.

Example `document.all.myTH.bgColor = "yellow"`

Value

A hexadecimal triplet or plain-language color name. See Appendix A for acceptable plain-language color names.

Default   Varies with browser and operating system.

borderColor

Color of the element's border. Internet Explorer applies the color to all four lines that make up the interior border of a cell. Therefore, colors of adjacent cells do not collide.

Example `document.all.myTH.borderColor = "salmon"`

Value

A hexadecimal triplet or plain-language color name. A setting of empty is interpreted as `"#000000"` (black). See Appendix A for acceptable plain-language color names.

Default   Varies with operating system.

borderColorDark, borderColorLight

The 3-D effect of table borders in Internet Explorer is created by careful positioning of light and dark lines around the page's background or default color. You can independently control the colors used for the dark and light lines by assigning values to the `borderColorDark` (left and top edges of the cell) and `borderColorLight` (right and bottom edges) properties.

Typically, you should assign complementary colors to the pair of properties. There is also no rule that says you must assign a dark color to `borderColorDark`. The attributes merely control a well-defined set of lines so you can predict which lines of the border change with each attribute.

Example

```
document.all.myTH.borderColorDark = "blue"
document.all.myTH.borderColorLight = "cornflowerblue"
```

Value

A hexadecimal triplet or plain-language color name. A setting of empty is interpreted as `"#000000"` (black). See Appendix A for acceptable plain-language color names.

Default   Varies with operating system.

cellIndex

Read-only

Returns a zero-based integer representing the position of the current cell among all other TH elements in the same row. The count is based on the source code order of the TH elements within a TR element. This property is not available in the Macintosh version of Internet Explorer 4.

Example   var whichCell = document.all.myTH.cellIndex

Value   Integer.

Default   None.

clientHeight, clientWidth

Read/Write

According to Microsoft's developer documentation, these properties reflect the height and width (in pixels) of the element's content. But see the section "About client- and offset-Properties" at the beginning of this chapter for details.

Example   var midHeight = document.all.myTH.clientHeight/2

Value   Integer pixel value.

Default   None.

colSpan

Read/Write

The number of columns across which the current table cell should extend itself. For each additional column included in the colSpan count, one less TH or TD element is required for the table row. If you set the align property to center or right, the alignment is calculated on the full width of the TH element across the specified number of columns. Unless the current cell also specifies a ROWSPAN attribute, the next table row returns to the original column count.

Example   document.all.myTH.colSpan = 2

Value   Any positive integer, usually 2 or larger.

Default   1

height, width

Read/Write

The height and width in pixels of the element. Changes to these values are immediately reflected in reflowed content on the page. These properties are read-only in the Macintosh version of Internet Explorer 4.

Example `document.all.myTH.height = 250`

Value   Integer.

Default   None.

noWrap

Whether the browser should render the cell as wide as is necessary to display a line of nonbreaking text on one line. Abuse of this attribute can force the user into a great deal of inconvenient horizontal scrolling of the page to view all of the content.

Example `document.all.myTH.noWrap = "true"`

Value   Boolean value: `true` | `false`.

Default   `false`

rowSpan

The number of rows through which the current table cell should extend itself downward. For each additional row included in the `rowSpan` count, one less `TH` or `TD` element is required for the next table row. If you set the `vAlign` property to `middle`, the alignment is calculated on the full height of the `TH` element across the specified number of rows.

Example `document.all.myTH.rowSpan = 12`

Value   Any positive integer, usually 2 or larger.

Default   `1`

vAlign

The manner of vertical alignment of text within the element's content box.

Example `document.all.myTH.vAlign = "baseline"`

Value   Case-insensitive constant (as a string): `baseline` | `bottom` | `middle` | `top`.

Default   `middle`

width

See height.

blur()

Removes focus from the current element and fires an `onBlur` event (in IE). No other element necessarily receives focus as a result.

Returned Value

None.

Parameters

None.

focus()   NN *n/a*   IE 4   DOM *n/a*

Gives focus to the current element and fires the **onFocus** event (in IE). If another element had focus at the time, it receives an **onBlur** event.

Returned Value

None.

Parameters

None.

THEAD   NN *n/a*   IE 4   DOM *1*

The THEAD object reflects the THEAD element. Note that the following items are not available in the Macintosh version of Internet Explorer 4: **innerHTML**, **innerText**, and **outerText** properties; **insertAdjacentHTML()** and **insertAdjacentText()** methods; the **rows[]** collection.

HTML Equivalent

<THEAD>

Object Model Reference

IE   [window.]document.all.*elementID*

Properties

align	innerHTML	offsetHeight	outerHTML	style
bgColor	innerText	offsetLeft	outerText	tagName
className	isTextEdit	offsetParent	parentElement	title
document	lang	offsetTop	parentTextEdit	vAlign
id	language	offsetWidth	sourceIndex	

Methods

click()	insertAdjacentHTML()	scrollIntoView()
contains()	insertAdjacentText()	setAttribute()
getAttribute()	removeAttribute()	

Collections/Arrays

all[]	children[]	filters[]	rows[]

Event Handler Properties

Handler	NN	IE	DOM
onclick	n/a	4	n/a
ondblclick	n/a	4	n/a
ondragstart	n/a	4	n/a
onfilterchange	n/a	4	n/a
onhelp	n/a	4	n/a
onkeydown	n/a	4	n/a
onkeypress	n/a	4	n/a
onkeyup	n/a	4	n/a
onmousedown	n/a	4	n/a
onmousemove	n/a	4	n/a
onmouseout	n/a	4	n/a
onmouseover	n/a	4	n/a
onmouseup	n/a	4	n/a
onselectstart	n/a	4	n/a

align

NN *n/a*   IE *4*   DOM *n/a*

Read/Write

Defines the horizontal alignment of content within all cells contained by the THEAD element.

Example   document.all.myTHEAD.align = "center"

Value   Any of the three horizontal alignment constants: center | left | right.

Default   left

bgColor

NN *n/a*   IE *4*   DOM *n/a*

Read/Write

Background color of the cells contained by the THEAD element. This color setting is not reflected in the style sheet backgroundColor property in Internet Explorer. Even if the BGCOLOR attribute or bgColor property is set with a plain-language color name, the returned value is always a hexadecimal triplet.

Example   document.all.myTHEAD.bgColor = "yellow"

Value

A hexadecimal triplet or plain-language color name. See Appendix A for acceptable plain-language color names.

Default   Varies with browser and operating system.

vAlign

NN *n/a*   IE *4*   DOM *1*

Read/Write

The manner of vertical alignment of text within the cells contained by the THEAD element.

Example   `document.all.myTHEAD.vAlign = "baseline"`

Value   Case-insensitive constant (as a string): **baseline** I bottom I **middle** I **top**.

Default   `middle`

rows[]   NN *n/a*   IE *4*   DOM *n/a*

An array of all rows contained by the **THEAD** element.

Syntax   `document.all.myTHEAD.rows(i).objectPropertyOrMethod`

TITLE   NN *n/a*   IE *4*   DOM *1*

The **TITLE** object reflects the **TITLE** element. The Win32 version of Internet Explorer 4 may exhibit problems when referencing the **TITLE** object by its element ID. Use the **tags[]** collection reference instead.

HTML Equivalent
`<TITLE>`

Object Model Reference
IE   `[window.]document.all.elementID`
          `[window.]document.all.tags("HEAD")[0]`

Properties
className	*isTextEdit*	*parentElement*	*style*	*text*
document	*lang*	*parentTextEdit*	*tagName*	*title*
id	*language*	*sourceIndex*		

Methods
contains()	*removeAttribute()*	*setAttribute()*
getAttribute()		

Collections/Arrays
all[]	*children[]*	*filters[]*

text   NN *n/a*   IE *4*   DOM *n/a*
Read-only

The text content of the element. For the **TITLE** element, this is the text between the start and end tags that also appears in the browser window's titlebar (usually along with some identification of the browser brand). Changes you make to this property do not appear in the source code you view from the browser.

Example   `document.all.tags("HEAD")[0].text = "Welcome, Dave!"`

Value   String.

Default   None.

toolbar

See locationbar.

TR

The TR object reflects the TR element. Note that the following items are not available in the Macintosh version of Internet Explorer 4: innerHTML, innerText, and outerText properties; insertAdjacentHTML() and insertAdjacentText() methods.

HTML Equivalent

<TR>

Object Model Reference

IE   [window.]document.all.*elementID*

Properties

align	*document*	*offsetLeft*	rowIndex
bgColor	*id*	*offsetParent*	selectionRowIndex
borderColor	*innerHTML*	*offsetTop*	*sourceIndex*
borderColorDark	*innerText*	*offsetWidth*	*style*
borderColorLight	*isTextEdit*	*outerHTML*	*tagName*
className	*lang*	*outerText*	*title*
clientHeight	*language*	*parentElement*	vAlign
clientWidth	*offsetHeight*	*parentTextEdit*	

Methods

blur()	*getAttribute()*	*removeAttribute()*
click()	*insertAdjacentHTML()*	*scrollIntoView()*
contains()	*insertAdjacentText()*	*setAttribute()*
focus()		

Collections/Arrays

all[]	cells[]	*children[]*	*filters[]*

Event Handler Properties

Handler	NN	IE	DOM
onblur	n/a	4	n/a
onclick	n/a	4	n/a
ondblclick	n/a	4	n/a
ondragstart	n/a	4	n/a
onfilterchange	n/a	4	n/a
onhelp	n/a	4	n/a
onkeydown	n/a	4	n/a
onkeypress	n/a	4	n/a
onkeyup	n/a	4	n/a
onmousedown	n/a	4	n/a

Handler	NN	IE	DOM
onmousemove	n/a	4	n/a
onmouseout	n/a	4	n/a
onmouseover	n/a	4	n/a
onmouseup	n/a	4	n/a
onselectstart	n/a	4	n/a

align   NN *n/a*   IE *4*   DOM *1*

Read/Write

Defines the horizontal alignment of content within all cells of the row.

Example document.all.myTR.align = "center"

Value   Any of the three horizontal alignment constants: center | left | right.

Default left

bgColor   NN *n/a*   IE *4*   DOM *1*

Read/Write

Background color of the table cells in the current row. This color setting is not reflected in the style sheet backgroundColor property. Even if the BGCOLOR attribute or bgColor property is set with a plain-language color name, the returned value is always a hexadecimal triplet.

Example document.all.myTR.bgColor = "yellow"

Value

A hexadecimal triplet or plain-language color name. See Appendix A for acceptable plain-language color names.

Default Varies with browser and operating system.

borderColor   NN *n/a*   IE *4*   DOM *n/a*

Read/Write

Color of the element's border. Internet Explorer applies the color to all four lines that make up the interior border of a cell. Therefore, colors of adjacent cells do not collide.

Example document.all.myTR.borderColor = "salmon"

Value

A hexadecimal triplet or plain-language color name. A setting of empty is interpreted as "#000000" (black). See Appendix A for acceptable plain-language color names.

Default Varies with operating system.

borderColorDark, borderColorLight   NN *n/a*   IE *4*   DOM *n/a*

The 3-D effect of table borders in Internet Explorer is created by careful positioning of light and dark lines around the page's background or default color. You can independently control the colors used for the dark and light lines by assigning values to the **borderColorDark** (left and top edges of the cell) and **borderColorLight** (right and bottom edges) properties.

Typically, you should assign complementary colors to the pair of properties. There is also no rule that says you must assign a dark color to **borderColorDark**. The attributes merely control a well-defined set of lines so you can predict which lines of the border change with each attribute.

Example
```
document.all.myTR.borderColorDark = "blue"
document.all.myTR.borderColorLight = "cornflowerblue"
```

Value

A hexadecimal triplet or plain-language color name. A setting of empty is interpreted as "#000000" (black). See Appendix A for acceptable plain-language color names.

Default   Varies with operating system.

clientHeight, clientWidth   NN *n/a*   IE *4*   DOM *n/a*

According to Microsoft's developer documentation, these properties reflect the height and width (in pixels) of the element's content. But see the section "About client- and offset-Properties" at the beginning of this chapter for details. The Macintosh version of Internet Explorer 4 returns a value of zero for both properties.

Example   `var midHeight = document.all.myTR.clientHeight/2`

Value   Integer pixel value.

Default   None.

rowIndex   NN *n/a*   IE *4*   DOM *n/a*

Returns a zero-based integer representing the position of the current row among all other TR elements in the entire table. The count is based on the source code order of the TR elements.

Example   `var whichRow = document.all.myTR.rowIndex`

Value   Integer.

Default   None.

sectionRowIndex
NN *n/a*   IE *4*   DOM *n/a*
Read-only

Returns a zero-based integer representing the position of the current row among all other TR elements in the row grouping. A row grouping can be one of the following elements: THEAD, TBODY, TFOOT. The count is based on the source code order of the TR elements.

Example   `var whichRow = document.all.myTR.sectionRowIndex`

Value   Integer.

Default   None.

vAlign
NN *n/a*   IE *4*   DOM *n/a*
Read/Write

The manner of vertical alignment of text within the cells of the current row.

Example   `document.all.myTR.vAlign = "baseline"`

Value

Case-insensitive constant (as a string): `baseline` | `bottom` | `middle` | `top`.

Default   `middle`

blur()
NN *n/a*   IE *4*   DOM *n/a*

Removes focus from the current element and fires an `onBlur` event (in IE). No other element necessarily receives focus as a result.

Returned Value

None.

Parameters

None.

focus()
NN *n/a*   IE *4*   DOM *n/a*

Gives focus to the current element and fires the `onFocus` event (in IE). If another element had focus at the time, it receives an `onBlur` event.

Returned Value

None.

Parameters

None.

cells[]

An array of all TD element objects contained by the current TR object. Items in this array are indexed (zero based) in source code order. Each item of the array is an object whose properties and methods may be accessed as if the object were referenced directly.

Syntax   `TRobject.cells(index).objectPropertyOrMethod`

TT

See B.

U

See B.

UL

The UL object reflects the UL element.

HTML Equivalent

`<UL>`

Object Model Reference

IE   `[window.]document.all.elementID`

Properties

className	innerText	offsetLeft	outerText	style
compact	isTextEdit	offsetParent	parentElement	tagName
document	lang	offsetTop	parentTextEdit	title
id	language	offsetWidth	sourceIndex	type
innerHTML	offsetHeight	outerHTML	start	

Methods

click()	insertAdjacentHTML()	scrollIntoView()
contains()	insertAdjacentText()	setAttribute()
getAttribute()	removeAttribute()	

Collections/Arrays

all[]	children[]	filters[]

Event Handler Properties

Handler	NN	IE	DOM
onclick	n/a	4	n/a
ondblclick	n/a	4	n/a
ondragstart	n/a	4	n/a
onfilterchange	n/a	4	n/a
onhelp	n/a	4	n/a

Handler	NN	IE	DOM
onkeydown	n/a	4	n/a
onkeypress	n/a	4	n/a
onkeyup	n/a	4	n/a
onmousedown	n/a	4	n/a
onmousemove	n/a	4	n/a
onmouseout	n/a	4	n/a
onmouseover	n/a	4	n/a
onselectstart	n/a	4	n/a

compact

NN *n/a*   IE *4*   DOM *1*

Read/Write

When set to true, the compact property should instruct the browser to render items in the list in a more compact format. This property has no effect in Internet Explorer 4 and is completely unavailable in the Macintosh version.

Example   `document.all.myUL.compact = true`

Value   Boolean value: `true` | `false`.

Default   `false`

type

NN *n/a*   IE *4*   DOM *1*

Read/Write

The manner in which the leading item markers in the list are displayed.

Example   `document.all.myUL.type = "square"`

Value   Any one of the constant values (as a string): `circle` | `disc` | `square`.

Default   `disc`

userProfile

NN *n/a*   IE *4*   DOM *n/a*

The userProfile object reflects numerous pieces of information stored in the browser's user profile for the current user. This object has four methods that:

- Let you queue requests for individual fields of the profile (items such as name, mailing address, phone numbers, and so on)
- Display the request dialog that lets users see what you're asking for and disallow specific items or the whole thing
- Grab the information
- Clear the request queue

Once the information is retrieved (with the user's permission), it can be slipped into form elements (visible or hidden) for submission to the server. Further details are available from Microsoft in the Internet Client Software Developer's Kit. This object's methods are not fully supported in the Macintosh version of Internet Explorer 4.

Example

```
navigator.userProfile.addReadRequest("vcard.displayname")
navigator.userProfile.doReadRequest("3", "MegaCorp Customer Service")
var custName = navigator.userProfile.getAttribute("vcard.displayname")
navigator.userProfile.clearRequest()
if (custName) {
    . . .
}
```

Object Model Reference

IE   navigator.userProfile

Methods

addReadRequest()   clearRequest()   doReadRequest()
getAttribute()

addReadRequest()   NN *n/a*   IE *4*   DOM *n/a*

addReadRequest(*attributeName*)

Adds a request to inspect a particular user profile attribute to a queue that must be executed separately (via the doReadRequest() and getAttribute() methods). Items added to the queue are displayed to the user to select which item(s) can be submitted to a server. For multiple attributes, use multiple invocations of the addReadRequest() method.

Returned Value

None.

Parameters

attributeName

One of the following case-insensitive attribute names as a string:

vCard.Business.City	vCard.Home.City
vCard.Business.Country	vCard.Home.Country
vCard.Business.Fax	vCard.Home.Fax
vCard.Business.Phone	vCard.Home.Phone
vCard.Business.State	vCard.Home.State
vCard.Business.StreetAddress	vCard.Home.StreetAddress
vCard.Business.URL	vCard.Home.Zipcode
vCard.Business.Zipcode	vCard.Homepage
vCard.Cellular	vCard.JobTitle
vCard.Company	vCard.LastName
vCard.Department	vCard.MiddleName
vCard.DisplayName	vCard.Notes
vCard.Email	vCard.Office
vCard.FirstName	vCard.Pager

clearRequest( )   NN *n/a*   IE *4*   DOM *n/a*

Empties the queue of attribute names to be retrieved. Use this after your script has successfully retrieved the required information. This prepares the queue for the next list.

Returned Value

None.

Parameters

None.

doReadRequest( )   NN *n/a*   IE *4*   DOM *n/a*

doReadRequest(*usageCode*[, *friendlyName*[, *domain*[, *path*[, *expiration*]]]])

Based on the items in the queue, this method inspects the browser to see whether the user
has given permission to inspect these attributes in the past. If not (for some or all), the
method displays a dialog box (the Profile Assistant window) that lets users turn off the
items that should not be exposed to the server. Parameters provide information for the
dialog and for maintenance of the permission (similar to the ways that cookies are
managed). Only one doReadRequest() method is required, regardless of the number of
attributes in the queue.

Returned Value

In Win32, the method returns no value, regardless of how the user responds to the Profile
Assistant dialog box). On the Macintosh (which does not support this object fully), the
method does not display the Profile Assistant dialog box and returns false.

Parameters

usageCode   One of the following code integers that display human-readable messages
defined by the Internet Privacy Working Group:

Code	Meaning
0	Used for system administration.
1	Used for research and/or product development.
2	Used for completion and support of current transaction.
3	Used to customize the content and design of a site.
4	Used to improve the content of the site, including advertisements.
5	Used for notifying visitors about updates to the site.
6	Used for contacting visitors for marketing of services or products.
7	Used for linking other collected information.
8	Used by site for other purposes.
9	Disclosed to others for customization or improvement of the content and design of the site.
10	Disclosed to others who may contact you for marketing of services and/or products.
11	Disclosed to others who may contact you for marketing of services and/or products, but you have the opportunity to ask a site not to do this.
12	Disclosed to others for any other purpose.

friendlyName
An optional string containing an identifiable name (and URL) that the user recognizes as the source of the request. This may be a corporate identity.

domain   An optional string containing the domain of the server making the request. If an expiration date is set, this information is stored with the requested attributes to prevent future requests from this domain from interrupting the user with the Profile Assistant dialog box.

path   An optional string containing the path of the server document making the request. If an expiration date is set, this information is stored with the requested attributes to prevent future requests from this domain from interrupting the user with the Profile Assistant dialog box.

expiration
An optional string containing the date on which the user's permissions settings expire. Not recognized in Internet Explorer 4.

getAttribute()   NN *n/a*   IE *4*   DOM *n/a*

getAttribute(*attributeName*)

Returns the value of the attribute, provided the user has given permission to do so. If that permission was denied, the method returns `null`. Use one `getAttribute()` method for each attribute value being retrieved.

Returned Value

In Win32, the method returns no value, regardless of how the user responds to the Profile Assistant dialog box). On the Macintosh (which does not support this object fully), the method does not display the Profile Assistant dialog box and returns `false`.

Parameters

attributeName
One of the `vCard` attribute names listed in the `addReadRequest()` method description.

VAR

see ACRONYM.

window   NN *2*   IE *3*   DOM *n/a*

The `window` object represents the browser window or frame in which document content is displayed. The `window` object plays a vital role in scripting when scripts must communicate with document objects located in other frames or subwindows. Internet Explorer 4 includes a special kind of subwindow called a modal dialog window. Modal dialog windows have most, but not all, `window` object properties and methods available to them.

Object Model Reference

```
NN        window
          self
          top
          parent
IE        window
          self
          top
          parent
```

Properties

clientInformation	event	navigator	returnValue
closed	history	offscreenBuffering	screen
defaultStatus	innerHeight	opener	scrollbars
dialogArguments	innerWidth	outerHeight	self
dialogHeight	length	outerWidth	status
dialogLeft	location	pageXOffset	statusbar
dialogTop	locationbar	pageYOffset	toolbar
dialogWidth	menubar	parent	top
document	name	personalbar	

Methods

alert()	focus()	resizeBy()
back()	forward()	resizeTo()
blur()	handleEvent()	routeEvent()
captureEvents()	home()	scroll()
clearInterval()	moveBy()	scrollBy()
clearTimeout()	moveTo()	scrollTo()
close()	navigate()	setInterval()
confirm()	open()	setTimeout()
disableExternalCapture()	print()	showHelp()
enableExternalCapture()	prompt()	showModalDialog()
execScript()	releaseEvents()	stop()
find()		

Collections/Arrays

frames[]

Event Handler Properties

Handler	NN	IE	DOM
onbeforeunload	n/a	4	n/a
onblur	3	4	n/a
ondragdrop	4	n/a	n/a
onerror	3	4	n/a
onfocus	3	4	n/a
onhelp	n/a	4	n/a

Handler	NN	IE	DOM
onload	2	3	n/a
onmove	4	n/a	n/a
onresize	4	4	n/a
onscroll	n/a	4	n/a
onunload	n/a	4	n/a

clientInformation   NN *n/a*   IE *4*   DOM *n/a*

Read-only

Returns the `navigator` object. The `navigator` object is named after a specific browser brand; the `clientInformation` property is a nondenominational way of accessing important environment variables that have historically been available through properties and methods of the `navigator` object. In Internet Explorer, you can substitute `window.clientInformation` for any reference that begins with `navigator`.

Example

```
if (parseInt(window.clientInformation.appVersion) >= 4) {
    process code for IE 4 or later
}
```

Value   The `navigator` object.

Default   The `navigator` object.

closed   NN *3*   IE *4*   DOM *n/a*

Read-only

Boolean value that says whether the referenced window is closed. A value of `true` means the window is no longer available for referencing its objects or script components. This is used most often to check whether a user has closed a subwindow generated by the `window.open()` method.

Example

```
if (!newWindow.closed) {
    newWindow.document.write("<HTML><BODY><H1>Howdy!</H1></BODY></HTML>")
    newWindow.document.close()
}
```

Value   Boolean value: `true` | `false`.

Default   None.

defaultStatus   NN *2*   IE *3*   DOM *n/a*

Read/Write

The default message displayed in the browser window's status bar when no browser loading activity is occurring. To temporarily change the message (during mouse rollovers, for example), set the window's `status` property. Most scriptable browsers and versions have difficulty managing the setting of the `defaultStatus` property. Expect odd behavior.

Example `window.defaultStatus = "Make it a great day!"`

Value Any string value.

Default None.

dialogArguments

NN n/a   IE 4   DOM n/a

Read-only

String or other data type passed as extra arguments to a modal dialog window created with the `showModalDialog()` method. This property is best accessed by a script in the document occupying the modal dialog to retrieve whatever data is passed to the new window as arguments. It is up to your script to parse the data if you include more than one argument nugget separated by whatever argument delimiter you choose.

Example

```
var allArgs = window.dialogArguments
var firstArg = allArgs.substring(0, allArgs.indexOf(";"))
```

Value String, number, or array.

Default None.

dialogHeight, dialogWidth

NN n/a   IE 4   DOM n/a

Read/Write

Length values of height and width of a modal dialog window created with the `showDialog()` method. Although Internet Explorer 4 does not balk at modifying these properties (in a script running in the modal dialog window), the changed values are generally not reflected in a resized dialog window. Initial values are set as parameters to the `showDialog()` method.

Example `var outerWidth = window.dialogWidth`

Value String including the unit value.

Default None.

dialogLeft, dialogTop

NN n/a   IE 4   DOM n/a

Read/Write

Offset distance of left and top edges of a modal dialog window (created with the `showDialog()` method) relative to the top-left corner of the video screen. Although Internet Explorer 4 does not balk at modifying these properties (in a script running in the modal dialog window), the changed values are generally not reflected in a repositioned dialog window. Initial values are set as parameters to the `showDialog()` method.

Example `var outerLeft = window.dialogLeft`

Value String including the unit value.

Default None.

event

Read-only

Internet Explorer 4's event model generates an **event** object for each user or system event. This **event** object is a property of the **window** object. For details about the IE event object, see Chapter 6 and the listing of the **event** object in this chapter.

Example

```
if (event.altKey) {
    handle case of Alt key down
}
```

Value   event object reference.

Default   None.

history

Read-only

Contains the **history** object for the current window or frame. For details, see the discussion of the **history** object.

Example

```
if (self.history.length > 4) {
    ...
}
```

Value   history object reference.

Default   Current **history** object.

innerHeight, innerWidth

Read/Write

The pixel measure of the height and width of the content region of a browser window or frame. This area is where the document content appears, exclusive of all window "chrome."

Example

```
window.innerWidth = 600
window.innerHeight = 400
```

Value   Integer.

Default   None.

length

Read-only

The number of frames (if any) nested within the current window. This value is the same as that returned by **window.frames.length**. When no frames are defined for the window, the value is zero.

DOM Reference

Example

```
if (window.length > 0) {
    ...
}
```

Value   Integer.

Default   0

location   NN *2*   IE *3*   DOM *n/a*

The URL of the document currently loaded in the window or frame. To navigate to another page, you assign a URL to the `location.href` property (or see the `navigate()` method for an IE-only alternative).

Example `top.location = "index.html"`

Value   A full or relative URL as a string.

Default   Document URL.

locationbar, menubar, personalbar, scrollbars, statusbar, toolbar   NN *4*   IE *n/a*   DOM *n/a*

Each property returns a reference to the object of the same name. These objects are individual components of a window's "chrome" whose visibility can be adjusted either when creating a new window (with the `window.open()` method) or anytime. Signed scripts are needed to gain permission to alter the visibility of these items for a window that already exists.

Example `window.personalbar.visibility = false`

Value   Object reference.

Default   Respective object references.

name   NN *2*   IE *3*   DOM *1*

The identifier associated with a frame or subwindow for use as the value assigned to `TARGET` attributes or as script references to the frame/subwindow. For a frame, the value is usually assigned via the `NAME` attribute of the `FRAME` tag, but it can be modified by a script if necessary. The name of a subwindow is assigned as a parameter to the `window.open()` method. The primary browser window does not have a name by default.

Example

```
if (parent.frames[1].name == "main") {
    ...
}
```

Value

Case-sensitive identifier that follows the rules of identifier naming: it may contain no whitespace, cannot begin with a numeral, and should avoid punctuation except for the underscore character.

Default   None.

navigator

Returns a reference to the **navigator** object. Internet Explorer treats the **navigator** object as a property of the window, even though the scope of the **navigator** object transcends all windows or frames currently existing in the browser. Since the **window** reference is optional, syntax without the **window** reference works on Internet Explorer and Navigator.

Example `var theBrowser = navigator.appName`

Value   Object reference.

Default   **navigator** object.

offscreenBuffering

Whether the browser should use offscreen buffering to improve path animation performance. This property applies only to the Windows 95/NT operating system platforms. When the document loads, the property is set to **auto**. After that, a script may turn buffering on and off by assigning a Boolean value to this property.

Example `window.offscreenBuffering = "true"`

Value   Boolean value: **true** | **false**.

Default   **auto**

opener

Object reference to the window (or frame) that used a **window.open()** method to generate the current window. This property allows subwindows to assemble references to objects, variables, and functions in the originating window. To access document objects in the creating window, a reference can begin with **opener** and work its way through the regular document object hierarchy from there, as shown in the left side of the following example statement. The relationship between the opening window and the opened window is not strictly parent-child. The term "parent" has other connotations in scripted window and frame references.

Example

`opener.document.forms[0].importedData.value = document.forms[0].entry.value`

Value   **window** object reference.

Default   None.

outerHeight, outerWidth

NN *4*   IE *n/a*   DOM *n/a*
Read/Write

The pixel measure of the height and width of the browser window or frame, including (for the top window) all toolbars, scollbars and other visible window "chrome."

Example

```
window.outerWidth = 80
window.outerHeight = 600
```

Value   Integer.

Default   None.

pageXOffset, pageYOffset

NN *4*   IE *n/a*   DOM *n/a*
Read-only

The pixel measure of the amount of the page's content that has been scrolled upward and/or to the left. For example, if a document has been scrolled so that the topmost 100 pixels of the document (the "page") are not visible because the window is scrolled, the **pageY-Offset** value for the window is 100. When a document is not scrolled, both values are zero.

Example   `var vertScroll = self.pageYOffset`

Value   Integer.

Default   0

parent

NN *2*   IE *3*   DOM *n/a*
Read-only

Returns a reference to the parent **window** object whose document defined the frameset in which the current frame is specified. Use **parent** in building a reference from one child frame to variables or methods in the parent document or to variables, methods, and objects in another child frame. For example, if a script in one child frame must reference the content of a text input form element in the other child frame (named "content"), the reference would be:

```
parent.content.document.forms[0].entryField.value
```

For more deeply nested frames, you can access the parent of a parent with syntax such as: `parent.parent.frameName`.

Example   `parent.frames[1].document.forms[0].companyName.value = "MegaCorp"`

Value   **window** object reference.

Default   None.

returnValue

NN *n/a*   IE *4*   DOM *n/a*

Read/Write

A value to be returned to the main window when the IE modal dialog window closes. The value assigned to this property in a script running in the dialog window is returned as the value to the `showModalDialog()` method in the main window. For example the document in the modal dialog window may have a statement that sets the `returnValue` property with information from the dialog:

```
window.returnValue = window.document.forms[0].userName.value
```

The dialog is created in the main document with a statement like the following:

```
var userName = showModalDialog("userNamePrompt.html")
```

Whatever value is assigned to `returnValue` in the dialog is then assigned to `userName` when the dialog box closes and script execution continues.

Value   Any scriptable data type.

Default   None.

screen

NN *n/a*   IE *4*   DOM *n/a*

Read-only

Returns a reference to the `screen` object. Internet Explorer treats the `screen` object as a property of the window, even though the scope of the `screen` object transcends all windows or frames currently existing in the browser. Since the `window` reference is optional, syntax without the `window` reference works on Internet Explorer and Navigator when a common property is accessed.

Example   `var howDeep = screen.availHeight`

Value   Object reference.

Default   `screen` object.

self

NN *2*   IE *3*   DOM *n/a*

Read-only

A reference to the current window or frame. This property is synonymous with `window`, but is sometimes used to improve clarity in a complex script that refers to many windows or frames. Never use the reference `window.self` to refer to the current window or frame.

Example   `self.focus()`

Value   `window` object reference.

Default   Current window.

status

NN *2*   IE *3*   DOM *n/a*

Read/Write

Text of the status bar of the browser window. Setting the status bar to some message is recommended only for temporary messages, such as for mouse rollovers atop images, areas, or links. Double or single quotes in the message must be escaped (\'). Many users don't look for the status bar, so avoid putting mission-critical information there. Temporary messages conflict with browser-driven use of the status bar for loading progress and other purposes. To set the default status bar message (when all is at rest), see the `default-Status` property.

Example

```
<...onMouseOver="window.status='Table of Contents';return true"
onMouseOut = "window.status = '';return true">
```

Value   String.

Default   Empty string.

top

Read-only

Object reference to the browser window. Script statements from inside nested frames can refer to the browser window properties and methods or to variables or functions stored in the document loaded in the topmost position. Do not begin a reference with `window.top`, just `top`. To replace a frameset with a new document that occupies the entire browser window, assign a URL to the `top.location.href` property.

Example   `top.location.href = "tableOfContents.html"`

Value   `window` object reference.

Default   Browser window.

alert()

alert(*message*)

Displays an alert dialog box with a message of your choice. A single button lets the user close the dialog. The title bar of the window (and the "JavaScript Alert" legend in earlier browser versions) cannot be altered by script.

Returned Value

None.

Parameters

message   Any string.

back()

Navigates one step backward through the history list of the window or frame.

Returned Value

None.

Parameters

None.

blur()

Removes focus from the window and fires an onBlur event (in IE). No other element necessarily receives focus as a result.

Returned Value

None.

Parameters

None.

captureEvents()

captureEvents(*eventTypeList*)

Instructs the browser to grab events of a specific type before they reach their intended target objects. The object invoking this method must then have event handlers defined for the given event types to process the event. See Chapter 6.

Returned Value

None.

Parameters

eventTypeList

A comma-separated list of case-sensitive event types as derived from the available Event object constants, such as Event.CLICK or Event.MOUSEMOVE.

clearInterval()

clearInterval(*intervalID*)

Turns off the interval looping action referenced by the *intervalID* parameter. See setInterval() for how to initiate such a loop.

Returned Value

None.

Parameters

intervalID

An integer created as the return value of a setInterval() method.

clearTimeout()

clearTimeout(*timeoutID*)

Turns off the timeout delay counter referenced by the *timeoutID* parameter. See setTimeout() for how to initiate such a delay.

Returned Value

None.

Parameters

`timeoutID`

An integer created as the return value of a `setTimeout()` method.

close()   NN *2*   IE *3*   DOM *n/a*

Closes the current window. Navigator does not allow the main window to be closed from a subwindow without receiving the user's explicit permission from a security dialog box.

Returned Value

None.

Parameters

None.

confirm()   NN *2*   IE *3*   DOM *n/a*

`confirm(message)`

Displays a dialog box with a message and two clickable buttons. One button indicates a **Cancel** operation; the other button indicates the user's approval (**OK** or **Yes**). The text of the buttons is not scriptable. The message should ask a question to which either button would be a logical reply. A click of the **Cancel** button returns a value of `false`; a click of the **OK** button returns a value of `true`.

Because this method returns a Boolean value, you can use this method inside a condition expression:

```
if (confirm("Reset the entire form?")) {
    document.forms[0].reset()
}
```

Returned Value

Boolean value: `true` | `false`.

Parameters

`message`   Any string, usually in the form of a question.

disableExternalCapture(),
enableExternalCapture()   NN *4*   IE *n/a*   DOM *n/a*

With signed scripts and the user's permission, a script can capture events in other windows or frames that come from domains other than the one that served the document with event-capturing scripts.

Returned Value

None.

Parameters

None.

execScript()   NN *n/a*   IE 4   DOM *n/a*

execScript(*expressionList* [, *language*])

Evaluates one or more script expressions in any scripting language embedded in the browser. Expressions must be contained within a single string; multiple expressions are delimited with semicolons:

```
window.execScript("var x = 3; alert(x * 3)")
```

The default script language is JavaScript. If you need to see results of the script execution, provide for the display of resulting data in the script expressions. The execScript() method itself returns no value.

Returned Value

None.

Parameters

expressionList
> String value of one or more semicolon-delimited script expressions.

language   String value for a scripting language: JavaScript | JScript | VBS | VBScript.

find()   NN 4   IE *n/a*   DOM *n/a*

find(*searchString* [, *matchCase*[, *searchUpward*]])

Searches the document body text for a string and selects the first matching string. Optionally, you can specify whether the search should be case sensitive or search upward in the document. With the found text selected, you can use the document.getSelection() method to grab a copy of the found text. You don't, however, have nearly the dynamic content abilities afforded by Internet Explorer 4's TextRange object (for Win32).

Returned Value

Boolean value: true if a match was found; false if not.

Parameters

searchString
> String for which to search the document.

matchCase
> Boolean value: true to allow only exact, case-sensitive matches; false (default) to use case-insensitive search.

searchUpward
> Boolean value: true to search from the current selection position upward through the document; false (default) to search forward from the current selection position.

focus()   NN 3   IE 4   DOM *n/a*

Brings the window to the front of all regular browser windows and fires the onFocus event (in IE). If another window had focus at the time, that other window receives an onBlur event.

Returned Value

None.

Parameters

None.

forward() NN *4* IE *n/a* DOM *n/a*

Navigates one step forward through the history list of the window or frame. If the forward history has no entries, no action takes place.

Returned Value

None.

Parameters

None.

handleEvent() NN *4* IE *n/a* DOM *n/a*

```
handleEvent(event)
```

Instructs the object to accept and process the event whose specifications are passed as the parameter to the method. The object must have an event handler for the event type to process the event.

Returned Value

None.

Parameters

event A Navigator 4 **event** object.

home() NN *4* IE *n/a* DOM *n/a*

Navigates to the URL designated as the home page for the browser. This is the same as the user clicking on the **Home** button.

Returned Value

None.

Parameters

None.

moveBy() NN *4* IE *n/a* DOM *n/a*

```
moveBy(deltaX, deltaY)
```

A convenience method that shifts the location of the window by specified pixel amounts along both axes. To shift along only one axis, set the other value to zero. Positive values for *deltaX* shift the window to the right; negative values to the left. Positive values for *deltaY* shift the window downward; negative values upward.

Returned Value

None.

Parameters

deltaX   Positive or negative pixel count of the change in horizontal direction of the window.

deltaY   Positive or negative pixel count of the change in vertical direction of the window.

moveTo()   NN *4* IE *n/a* DOM *n/a*

moveTo(x, y)

Convenience method that shifts the location of the current window to a specific coordinate point. The moveTo() method uses the screen coordinate system.

Returned Value

None.

Parameters

x   Positive or negative pixel count relative to the top of the screen.

y   Positive or negative pixel count relative to the left edge of the screen.

navigate()   NN *n/a* IE *3* DOM *n/a*

navigate(URL)

Loads a new document into the window or frame. This is the IE-specific way of assigning a value to the window.location.href property.

Returned Value

None.

Parameters

URL   A complete or relative URL as a string.

open()   NN *2* IE *3* DOM *n/a*

open(URL, windowName[, windowFeatures])

Opens a new window (without closing the original one). You can specify a URL to load into that window or set that parameter to an empty string to allow scripts to document.write() into that new window. The *windowName* parameter lets you assign a name that can be used by TARGET attributes. This name is not to be used in script references as frame names are. Instead, a script reference to a subwindow must be to the window object returned by the window.open() method. Therefore, if your scripts must communicate with a window opened in this manner, it is best to save the returned value as a global variable so that future statements can use it.

A potential problem with subwindows is that they can be buried under the main window if the user clicks on the main window (or a script gives it focus). Any script that opens a subwindow should also include a `focus()` method for the subwindow (in Navigator 3 and later, and in IE 4 and later) to make sure it comes to the front in case it is already open. Subsequent invocations of the `window.open()` method whose *windowName* parameter is the same as an earlier call automatically address the previously opened window, even if it is underneath the main window.

The optional third parameter gives you control over various physical attributes of the subwindow. The *windowFeatures* parameter is a single string consisting of a comma-delimited list (without spaces between items) of attribute/value pairs:

```
newWindow = window.open("someDoc.html","subWind",
"statusbar,menubar,HEIGHT=400,WIDTH=300)
newWindow.focus()
```

By default, all window attributes are turned on and the subwindow opens to the same size that the browser would use to open a new window from the **File** menu. But if your script specifies even one attribute, all settings are turned off. Therefore, use the *windowFeatures* parameter to specify those features that you want turned on.

Returned Value

Window object reference.

Parameters

URL   A complete or relative URL as a string. If an empty string, no document loads into the window.

windowName

An identifier for the window to be used by TARGET attributes. This is different from the TITLE attribute of the document that loads into the window.

windowFeatures

A string of comma-delimited features to be turned on in the new window. Do not put spaces after the comma delimiters. The list of possible features is long, but a number of them are specific to Navigator 4 and require signed scripts because they are potentially a privacy and security concern to unsuspecting users. The features are listed as follows. To turn on a window feature, simply include its case-insensitive name in the comma-separated list. Only attributes specifying dimensions require values be assigned.

Attribute	NN	IE	Description
alwaysLowered	4	-	Always behind all other browser windows. Signed script required.
alwaysRaised	4	-	Always in front of all other browser windows. Signed script required.
copyhistory	2	3	Copy history listing from opening window to new window.
dependent	4	-	Subwindow closes if the window that opened it closes.
directories	2	3	Display directory buttons.

Attribute	NN	IE	Description
height	2	3	Window height in pixels.
hotkeys	4	-	Disables menu keyboard shortcuts (except Quit and Security Info).
innerHeight	4	-	Content region height. Signed script required for very small measures.
innerWidth	4	-	Content region width. Signed script required for very small measures.
location	2	3	Display location of text field.
menubar	2	3	Display menubar (a menubar of some kind is always visible on the Macintosh).
outerHeight	4	-	Total window height. Signed script required for very small measures.
outerWidth	4	-	Total window width. Signed script required for very small measures.
resizable	2	3	Allow window resizing (always allowed on the Macintosh).
screenX	4	-	Offset of window's left edge from left edge of screen. Signed script required to move window offscreen.
screenY	4	-	Offset of window's top edge from top edge of screen. Signed script required to move window offscreen.
scrollbars	2	3	Display scrollbars if document is too large for window.
status	2	3	Display status bar.
titlebar	4	-	Displays titlebar. Set this value to no to hide the titlebar. Signed script required.
toolbar	2	3	Display toolbar (with **Back**, **Forward**, and other buttons).
width	2	3	Window width in pixels.
z-lock	4	-	New window is fixed below browser windows. Signed script required.

print()   NN *4*   IE *n/a*   DOM *n/a*

Starts the printing process for the window or frame. A user must still confirm the print dialog box to send the document to the printer. This method is the same as clicking the **Print** button or selecting **Print** from the **File** menu.

Returned Value

None.

Parameters

None.

prompt()   NN *2*   IE *3*   DOM *n/a*

prompt(*message, defaultReply*)

Displays a dialog box with a message, a one-line text entry field, and two clickable buttons. The message should urge the user to enter a specific kind of answer. One button indicates a **Cancel** operation; the other button indicates the user's approval of the text entered into the field (**OK** or **Yes**). The text of the buttons is not scriptable. A click of the **Cancel** button returns a value of null; a click of the **OK** button returns a string of whatever is in the text entry field at the time (including the possibility of an empty string). It is up to your scripts to test for the type of response (if any) supplied by the user.

Returned Value

When clicking the **OK** button, a string of the text entry field; when clicking **Cancel**, null.

Parameters

message   Any string.

defaultReply

Any string that suggests an answer. Always supply a value, even if an empty string.

releaseEvents()   NN *4*   IE *n/a*   DOM *n/a*

```
releaseEvents(eventTypeList)
```

The opposite of **window.captureEvents()**, this method turns off event capture at the window level for one or more specific events named in the parameter list. See Chapter 6.

Returned Value

None.

Parameters

eventTypeList

A comma-separated list of case-sensitive event types as derived from the available **Event** object constants, such as **Event.CLICK** or **Event.MOUSEMOVE**.

resizeBy()   NN *4*   IE *n/a*   DOM *n/a*

```
resizeBy(deltaX, deltaY)
```

A convenience method that shifts the width and height of the window by specified pixel amounts. To adjust along only one axis, set the other value to zero. Positive values for *deltaX* make the window wider; negative values make the window narrower. Positive values for *deltaY* make the window taller; negative values make the window shorter. The top and bottom edges remain fixed; only the right and bottom edges are moved.

Returned Value

None.

Parameters

deltaX   Positive or negative pixel count of the change in horizontal dimension of the window.

deltaY   Positive or negative pixel count of the change in vertical dimension of the window.

resizeTo()   NN *4*   IE *n/a*   DOM *n/a*

```
resizeTo(x, y)
```

Convenience method that adjusts the height and width of the window to specific pixel sizes. The top and left edges of the window remain fixed, while the bottom and right edges move in response to this method.

Returned Value

None.

Parameters

x	Width in pixels of the window.
y	Height in pixels of the window.

routeEvent()   NN *4*   IE *n/a*   DOM *n/a*

```
routeEvent(event)
```

Used inside an event handler function, this method directs Navigator to let the event pass to its intended target object.

Returned Value

None.

Parameters

event	A Navigator 4 **event** object.

scroll()   NN *3*   IE *4*   DOM *n/a*

```
scroll(x, y)
```

Sets the scrolled position of the document inside the current window or frame. To return the document to its unscrolled position, set both parameters to zero.

Returned Value

None.

Parameters

x	Horizontal measure of scrolling within the window.
y	Vertical measure of scrolling within the window.

scrollBy()   NN *4*   IE *4*   DOM *n/a*

```
scrollBy(deltaX, deltaY)
```

Scrolls the document in the window by specified pixel amounts along both axes. To adjust along only one axis, set the other value to zero. Positive values for *deltaX* scroll the document upward (so the user sees content lower in the document); negative values scroll the document downward. Positive values for *deltaY* scroll the document to the left (so the user sees content to the right in the document); negative values scroll the document to the right. Scrolling does not continue past the zero coordinate points (except in Navigator 4 for the Macintosh).

Returned Value

None.

Parameters

deltaX   Positive or negative pixel count of the change in horizontal scroll position.

deltaY   Positive or negative pixel count of the change in vertical scroll position.

scrollTo()   NN *4*   IE *n/a*   DOM *n/a*

scrollTo(*x*, *y*)

Scrolls the document in the window to a specific scrolled position.

Returned Value

None.

Parameters

x   Horizontal position in pixels of the window.

y   Vertical position in pixels of the window.

setInterval()   NN *4*   IE *4*   DOM *n/a*

setInterval(*expression, msecs*[, *args* | *language*])

Starts a timer that continually invokes the *expression* every *msecs*. Other scripts can run in the time between calls to *expression*. This method is useful for starting animation sequences that must reposition an element along a path at a fixed rate of speed. The *expression* might be a function that moves the element by a fixed pixel distance along one axis. The function would be invoked at an interval set by the *msecs* parameter. This method returns an ID that should be saved as a global variable and be available as the parameter for the clearInterval() method to stop the looping timer.

Navigator and Internet Explorer diverge in the use of the third parameter. Navigator lets you pass one or more parameters (as a comma-delimited list in a string) for the function acting as the *expression* parameter. Internet Explorer lets you specify the scripting language of the *expression* (if it is not the default JavaScript).

Returned Value

Integer acting as an identifier.

Parameters

expression
            Any script expression as a string, but most commonly a function. The function name with parentheses is placed inside the parameter's quoted string.

msecs   The time in milliseconds between invocations of the *expression*.

args   An optional comma-delimited list of parameters to be passed to a function used as the *expression* parameter.

language An optional scripting language specification of the *expression* parameter (default is JavaScript).

setTimeout()   NN *2*   IE *3*   DOM *n/a*

`setTimeout(expression, msecs[, args | language])`

Starts a one-time timer that invokes the *expression* after a delay of *msecs*. Other scripts can run while the browser waits to invoke the *expression*. This method returns an ID that should be saved as a global variable and be available as the parameter for the `clearTimeout()` method to stop the timer before it expires and invokes the *expression*.

Navigator and Internet Explorer diverge in the use of the third parameter. Navigator lets you pass one or more parameters (as a comma-delimited list in a string) for the function acting as the *expression* parameter. Internet Explorer lets you specify the scripting language of the *expression* (if it is not the default JavaScript).

The `setTimeout()` method can be made to behave like the `setInterval()` method in some constructions. If you place a `setTimeout()` method as the last statement of a function and direct the method to invoke the very same function, you can create looping execution with a timed delay between executions. This is how earlier browsers (before the `setInterval()` method was available) scripted repetitive tasks, such as displaying updated digital clock displays in form fields or the status bar.

Returned Value

Integer acting as an identifier.

Parameters

expression
> Any script expression as a string, but most commonly a function. The function name with parentheses is placed inside the parameter's quoted string.

msecs   The time in milliseconds that the browser waits before invoking the *expression*.

args   An optional comma-delimited list of parameters to be passed to a function used as the *expression* parameter.

language An optional scripting language specification of the *expression* parameter (default is JavaScript).

showHelp()   NN *n/a*   IE *4*   DOM *n/a*

`showHelp(URL)`

Displays a **WinHelp** window with the document specified with the *URL* parameter. This method works only in the Windows version of Internet Explorer 4.

Returned Value

None.

Parameters

URL   A complete or relative URL as a string.

DOM Reference

showModalDialog()   NN *n/a*   IE *4*   DOM *n/a*

`showModalDialog(URL[, arguments[, features]])`

Displays a special window that remains atop all browser windows until the user explicitly closes the dialog window. This kind of window is different from the browser windows generated with the `window.open()` method. A modal dialog has no scriptable relationship with its opening window once the dialog window is opened. All values necessary for displaying content must be in the HTML document that loads into the window or be passed as parameters. The modal dialog may then have a script set its `returnValue` property, which becomes the value returned to the original script statement that opened the modal dialog box as the returned value of the `showModalDialog()` method.

You can pass arguments to the modal dialog by creating a data structure that best suits the data. For a single value, a string will do. For multiple values, you can create a string with a unique delimiter between values, or create an array and specify the array as the second parameter for the `showModalDialog()` method. A script in the document loaded into the modal dialog can then examine the `window.dialogArguments` property and parse the arguments as needed for its scripting purposes. See the `dialogArguments` property for an example.

The third optional parameter lets you set physical characteristics of the dialog window. These characteristics are specified in a CSS-style syntax. Dimensions for `dialogWidth`, `dialogHeight`, `dialogLeft`, and `dialogTop` should be specified in pixels. An example of a call to a modal dialog is as follows:

```
var answer = window.showModalDialog("subDoc.html",argsVariable,
    "dialogWidth:300px; dialogHeight:200px; center:yes")
```

None of the third parameter characteristics are recognized by the Macintosh version of Internet Explorer 4, which creates a full-size modal dialog.

Returned Value

The value (if any) assigned to the `window.returnValue` property in the document loaded into the modal dialog window.

Parameters

URL   A complete or relative URL as a string.

arguments
          Data as a number, string, or array to be passed to the scripts in the document loaded into the modal dialog.

features A string of semicolon-delimited style attributes and values to set the physical characteristics of the modal dialog. Available attributes are: `center`, `dialogHeight`, `dialogLeft`, `dialogTop`, `dialogWidth`. Values for the `center` attribute are: yes | no | 1 | 0.

stop()   NN *n/a*   IE *4*   DOM *n/a*

Halts the download of external data of any kind. This method is the same as clicking the browser's **Stop** button.

Returned Value

None.

Parameters

None.

frames[]   NN *2*   IE *3*   DOM *n/a*

An array of frames defined in the window. Typically, this is used within a reference to a window that contains a framesetting document and, therefore, has frames nested within.

Syntax

```
parent.frames(index).objectPropertyOrMethod
top.frames(index).objectPropertyOrMethod
```

XMP

See PRE.

10

Style Sheet Attribute Reference

The purpose of this chapter is to provide a list of every style sheet attribute that is implemented in Navigator and Internet Explorer, as well as those specified in the W3C recommendations for Cascading Style Sheets, both Level 1 (CSS1) and Level 2 (CSS2). So that you can readily see whether a particular entry applies to the browser(s) you must support, a version table accompanies each term listed in the following pages. This table tells you at a glance the version of Navigator, Internet Explorer, and W3C CSS specification in which the term was first introduced. One important exception concerns Internet Explorer 3. Although IE 3 provided support for many style sheet attributes later incorporated into Internet Explorer 4 and CSS1, the baseline version for this chapter is IE 4. The assumption here is that if you are authoring serious DHTML content, you are aiming for an audience whose minimum Internet Explorer browser version is Version 4.

This chapter is organized alphabetically by CSS attribute name. For each attribute, you can see at a glance what the value types are, whether there is a JavaScript style sheet syntax equivalent (for Navigator only), an example of real-life source code, and how to address the attribute from the JavaScript language (if the attribute is scriptable). Be aware that only a handful of CSS2 attributes have been implemented in the Version 4 browsers. Also, the version of CSS2 used as a resource for this chapter was the Working Draft of January 28, 1998, in which several attributes or details were preliminary.

CSS2 became final in May of 1998, so you'll need to check the specification (*http://www.w3.org/TR/REC-CSS2/*) for resolution on items that are marked preliminary here.

Attribute Value Types

Many element attributes share similar data requirements. For the sake of brevity in the reference listings, this section describes a few common attribute value types in more detail than is possible within each listing. Whenever you see one of these attribute value types associated with an attribute, consult this section for a description of the type.

Length

A length value defines a linear measure of document real estate. Length units may be relative or absolute. A relative unit depends upon variables such as the dot pitch or pixel density of the video display that shows a document. Relative units in CSS are pixels (`px`), ems (`em`), and exes (`ex`). An em is the actual height of the element's font as rendered on a given display device; an ex is the height of a lowercase "x" under the same conditions. The exception to this rule is when em and ex units are used to define the `font-size` attribute, in which case the units are relative to the font size of the parent element.

There is a special case when a relative value is to be inherited by a child element. In those circumstances, the child element inherits the computed value of the attribute (computed at the time of the attribute definition), rather than an adjusted value. For example, if a `BODY` element specifies a `font-size` of 10pt and a `text-indent` of 2em (equaling 20pt), the `text-indent` value inherited by P or other elements within the `BODY` element is equal to 20pt, regardless of what the current `font-size` of the other element may be. To override the inherited value, the P or other element needs to reassign a `text-indent` attribute for that element (or other outer container that intervenes from the `BODY`).

Absolute length units are intended for output media whose physical properties are constant (such as a PostScript printer). Although there is nothing preventing you from using absolute or relative units interchangeably, you need to be aware of the consequences given your audience. Absolute length units in CSS are inches (`in`), centimeters (`cm`), millimeters (`mm`), picas (`pi`), and points (`pt`).

URI and URL

The term Universal Resource Identifier (URI) is a broad term for an address of content on the Web. A Universal Resource Locator (URL) is a type of URI. For most web authoring, you can think of them as one and the same, because most web browsers restrict their focus to URLs. A URL may be complete (including the protocol, host, domain, and the rest) or may be relative to the URL of the current document. In the latter case, this means the URL may consist of an anchor, file, or pathname. The CSS attribute syntax prescribes a special format for specifying a URI attribute value, as follows:

```
attributeName: url(actualURL)
```

This format allows a browser to distinguish a URI value from another type of string value, especially when the attribute can accept a variety of value types.

Colors

A color value can be assigned either via an RGB (red-green-blue) value or plain-language equivalent (see Appendix A, *Color Names and RGB Values*). For style sheet RGB values, you have a choice of three formats: hexadecimal triplet, decimal values, or percentage values. A hexadecimal triplet consists of three pairs of hexadecimal (base 16) numbers that range between values of 00 and FF, corresponding to the red, green, and blue components of the color. The three pairs of numbers are bunched together and preceded by a pound sign (#). Therefore, the reddest of reds has all red (FF) and none (00) of the other two colors: #FF0000; pure blue is #0000FF. Letters A through F can also be lowercase letters.

The other types of RGB values require a prefix of rgb() with a comma-delimited list of red, green, and blue values in the parentheses. As decimal values, each color can range from 0 through 255, with zero meaning the complete absence of a particular color. You can also specify each value by a percentage. The following examples show four different ways of specifying pure green:

```
color: green
color: #00FF00
color: rgb(0, 255, 0)
color: rgb(0%, 100%, 0%)
```

If you exceed the maximum allowable values in the last two examples, the browser trims the values back to their maximums.

These numbering schemes obviously lead to a potentially huge number of combinations (over 16 million), but not all video monitors are set to distinguish among millions of colors. Therefore, you may wish to limit yourself to a more modest palette of colors known as the web palette. A fine reference of colors that work well on all browsers at popular bit-depth settings can be found at *http://www.lynda.com/hexh.html.*

The CSS2 specification adds another dimension to color naming: you can specify colors that the user has assigned to specific user interface items in the operating system's control panel. Such colors are typically adjustable for items like button label text, scrollbars, 3-D shadows, and so on. A color-blind user, for example, may have a carefully crafted set of colors that provide necessary contrast to see screen elements. To link those colors to a style, use any of the following keywords in place of the color attribute value:

activeborder	highlight	scrollbar
activecaption	highlighttext	threeddarkshadow
appworkspace	inactiveborder	threedface
background	inactivecaption	threedhighlight
buttonface	inactivecaptiontext	threedlightshadow
buttonhighlight	infobackground	threedshadow
buttontext	infotext	window
captiontext	menu	windowframe
graytext	menutext	windowtext

Pseudo-Elements and Pseudo-Classes

Most style sheet rules are associated with distinct HTML elements or groups of elements identified via style sheet selectors, such as classes, IDs, and contextual selectors (see Chapter 3, *Adding Style Sheets to Documents*). In rare instances, you might want to assign a style to a well-defined component of an element or to all elements that exhibit a particular state. CSS2 recommends that browsers expose the first letter and first line of a paragraph so that a style sheet rule can focus only on that portion of the element. For example, by careful application of attributes, you can create a drop cap initial letter for a paragraph with the following definition:

```
P:first-letter {font-size: 36pt; font-weight: 600;
               font-family: Rune serif; float: left}
```

This kind of subcomponent is called a *pseudo-element*. A pseudo-element is connected to an element by virtue of the colon delimiter.

The A element has readily distinguishable states: a link that has not been visited, a link being clicked on, a link that has been visited in recent history. These states are called *pseudo-classes;* they work like class selector definitions but don't have to be labeled as such in their element tags.

Table 10-1provides a summary of pseudo-elements supported in CSS2. None of these are implemented in the Version 4 browsers but will likely be available in future browsers.

Table 10-1. CSS2 Pseudo-Elements

Name	NN	IE	CSS	Description
:after	-	-	2	The space immediately after an element (see content attribute)
:before	-	-	2	The space immediately before an element (see content attribute)

Table 10-1. CSS2 Pseudo-Elements (continued)

Name	NN	IE	CSS	Description
:first-letter	-	-	2	The first letter of a P element
:first-line	-	-	2	The first line of a P element

Table 10-2 provides a summary of pseudo-classes supported by CSS2. Several of these are implemented in Internet Explorer 4.

Table 10-2. CSS2 Pseudo-Classes

Name	NN	IE	CSS	Description
:active	-	4	2	An A element being clicked on by the user
:first	-	-	2	First page of a document (with @page declaration)
:first-child	-	-	2	Any element that is the first child of another element
:hover	-	4	2	An A element that has a cursor on top of it
:left	-	-	2	A left-facing page (with @page declaration)
:link	-	4	2	An A element that has not yet been visited
:right	-	-	2	A right-facing page (with @page declaration)
:visited	-	4	2	An A element that has been visited within the browser's history

At-Rules

CSS2 defines an extensible structure for declarations or directives (commands, if you will) that are part of style sheet definitions. They are called *at-rules* because the rule starts with the "at" symbol (@) followed by an identifier for the declaration. Each at-rule may then include one or more descriptors that define the characteristics of the rule. In a simplified example of an at-rule for embedding a downloadable font, the format for making the at-rule declaration and assigning descriptors is as follows:

```
<STYLE TYPE="text/css">
@font-face {font-family: stylish; url(fonts/stylish.eot)}
</STYLE>
```

This example merely downloads the font and associates it with a font family name. Other style sheet rules can then apply that font family name to the font-family style attribute.

The CSS2 specification includes a few at-rules of its own, for tasks such as directing a browser to import a style sheet from an external file or preparing page output for printers. Each browser can add its own at-rules as needed. Table 10-3 provides a summary of the at-rules supported by CSS.

Table 10-3. CSS2 At-Rules

Name	NN	IE	CSS	Description
@font-face	-	4	1	Font description to assist in font-matching between an embedded font and the client system font (or down-loaded font). CSS2 defines nearly two dozen finely detailed descriptors that may be of interest to authors who are concerned about the extremely accurate representation of a font in a document (primarily for printing).
@import	-	4	1	Imports an external style sheet. See Chapter 3 for the impact on the cascade.
@media	-	-	2	Defines an output media type for one or more style sheet rules. Rules assigned to the same selectors but inside different @media rules (e.g., @media print or @media screen) adhere to media-specific rules when the document is rendered in the specified medium.
@page	-	-	2	Defines the page box's size, margins, orientation, crop marks, and other page-related attributes governing the printing of the document.

Conventions

The CSS syntax descriptions shown throughout this chapter adhere to the following guidelines:

- Words in the `Constant Width` font are keywords or constant values to be used as-is.
- Words in the `Constant Width Italic` font are placeholders for values.
- A value contained by square brackets ([]) is optional.
- A series of two or more values separated by a pipe symbol (|) represent items in a list of acceptable values to be used in the position shown.
- A few listings show numbers in brackets ({1,2}) after a value. The numbers indicate the minimum and maximum number of space-delimited values you can specify.
- A double-pipe symbol (||) indicates that the value to the right of the symbol is optional.

The category listing for JavaScript Equivalent is provided only when such an equivalent exists in Navigator 4 JavaScript Style Sheets.

The Applies To category advises which HTML elements can be influenced by the style attribute. Some style attributes can be applied only to block-level, inline, or replaced elements. A block-level element is one that always starts on a new line and forces a new line after the end of the element (H1 and P elements, for example). An inline element is one that you can place in the middle of a text line without disturbing the content flow (EM elements, for example). A replaced element is a block-level or inline element whose content may be changed dynamically without requiring any reflow of surrounding content. The IMG element falls into this category because you can swap image source files within an IMG element's rectangular space.

A listing category called Initial Value serves the same purpose as the Default category in other reference chapters. The terminology used in this chapter conforms with the terminology of the CSS specification.

Alphabetical Attribute Reference

azimuth   NN *n/a*   IE *n/a*   CSS *2*

Inherited: Yes

Given a listener at the center of a circular sound space (like in a surround-sound-equipped theater), azimuth sets the horizontal angle of the source of the sound (for example, in a text-to-speech browser). See also the elevation attribute.

CSS Syntax

azimuth: *angle* | *angleConstant* || *direction*

Value

Up to two values. One represents the angle, clockwise from straight ahead; the second is a 20-degree incremental movement to the left or right. An *angle* value is any value in the range of -360 to +360 (inclusive) plus the letters "deg", as in 90deg. The value 0deg is directly in front of the listener. To set the angle to the left of the listener, the value can be either -90deg or 270deg. Optionally, you can choose an *angleConstant* value from a large library of descriptions that correspond to fixed points around the circle. If you add the behind modifier, the values shift from in front of the listener to behind the listener.

Value	Equals	Value	Equals
center	0deg	center behind	180deg
center-right	20deg	center-right behind	160deg
right	40deg	right behind	140deg
far-right	60deg	far-right behind	120deg
right-side	90deg	right-side behind	90deg
left-side	270deg	left-side behind	270deg
far-left	300deg	far-left behind	240deg
left	320deg	left behind	220deg
center-left	340deg	center-left behind	200deg

For the *direction* value, you can choose from two constants: `leftwards | rightwards`. These settings shift the sound 20 degrees in the named direction.

Initial Value

`center`

Example

```
H1 {azimuth: 45deg}
P.aside {azimuth: center-right behind}
```

Applies To

All elements.

background

NN *n/a*   IE *4*   CSS *1*

Inherited: No

A shortcut attribute that lets you set up to five separate (but related) background-style attributes in one attribute statement. Values can be in any order, each one delimited by a space. Although the attribute is not officially available in Navigator 4, some combinations of values may work with it. It is a convenient attribute, so it may be worth experimenting with it in Navigator if you need cross-browser settings.

CSS Syntax

`background:` *background-attachment* `||` *background-color* `||` *background-image* `||` *background-position* `||` *background-repeat*

Value

Any combination of the five background-style attribute values, in any order. Any attribute not specified is assigned its initial value. See each attribute for details about the expected values.

Initial Value

None.

Example

`BODY {background: url(watermark.jpg) repeat fixed}`

Applies To

All elements.

Object Model Reference

IE   `[window.]document.all.`*elementID*`.style.background`

background-attachment

NN *n/a*   IE *4*   CSS *1*

Inherited: No

When an image is applied to the element background (with the `background-image` attribute), the `background-attachment` attribute sets how the image is attached to the document. The image can remain fixed within the viewable area of the element (the viewport), or it may scroll with the element as the document is scrolled. During scrolling, a fixed attachment looks like a stationary backdrop to rolling credits of a movie.

CSS Syntax
```
background-attachment: fixed | scroll
```

Value

The `fixed` value keeps the image stationary in the element viewport; the `scroll` value lets the image scroll with the document content.

Initial Value
```
scroll
```

Example   BODY {background-attachment: fixed}

Applies To

All elements.

Object Model Reference

IE   [window.]document.all.*elementID*.style.backgroundAttachment

background-color   NN *4*   IE *4*   CSS *1*

Inherited: No

Sets the background color for the element. Although it may appear as though a nested element's `background-color` attribute is inherited, in truth the initial value is transparent, which lets the next outermost colored element show through whitespace of the current element.

CSS Syntax
```
background-color: color
```

JavaScript Equivalent
```
backgroundColor
```

Value

Any valid color specification (see description at beginning of the chapter) or `transparent`.

Initial Value
```
transparent
```

Example
```
.highlighter {background-color: yellow}
```

Applies To

All elements.

Object Model Reference

IE   [window.]document.all.*elementID*.style.backgroundColor

background-image

Sets the background image (if any) for the element. If you set a background-color for the element as well, the color appears if the image fails to load; otherwise, the image overlays the color. Transparent pixels of the image allow a background color to show through. See also the background-attachment attribute.

CSS Syntax

background-image: *uri* | none

JavaScript Equivalent

backgroundImage

Value

To specify a URL, use the url() wrapper for the attribute value. You can omit the attribute or specify none to prevent an image from loading into the element's background.

Initial Value

Example H1 {background-image: url(watermark.jpg)}

Applies To

All elements.

Object Model Reference

IE   [window.]document.all.*elementID*.style.backgroundImage

background-position

Establishes the location of the left and top edges of the background image specified with the background-image attribute. The behavior of this attribute can be erratic in Internet Explorer 4 for the Macintosh.

CSS Syntax

```
background-position: [percentage | length] {1,2} |
    [top |center |bottom] ||[left | center | right]
```

Value

You can specify one or two percentages, which are the percentage of the block-level element's box width and height (respectively) at which the image (or repeated images) begins. If you supply only one percentage value, it applies to the horizontal measure, and the vertical measure is automatically set to 50%. Instead of percentages, you can specify length values (in the unit of measure that best suits the medium). You can also mix a percentage with a length. In lieu of the numerical values, you can create combinations of values with the two sets of constant values. Select one from each collection, as in `top left`, `top right`, or `bottom center`. Whenever you specify two values, they must be separated by a space.

Initial Value

`0% 0%`

Example

```
DIV.marked {background-image: url(watermark.jpg);
    background-position: center top}
```

Applies To

Block-level and replaced elements.

Object Model Reference

IE   [window.]document.all.*elementID*.style.backgroundPosition

background-repeat   NN *n/a*   IE *4*   CSS *1*

Inherited: No

Sets whether a background image (specified with the `background-image` attribute) should repeat and if so, along which axes. You can use repeating background images to create horizontal and vertical bands.

CSS Syntax

`background-repeat: no-repeat | repeat | repeat-x | repeat-y`

Value

With a setting of `no-repeat`, one instance of the image appears in the location within the element established by the `background-position` attribute (default is the top-left corner). Normal repeats are performed along both axes, but you can have the image repeat down a single column (`repeat-y`) or across a single row (`repeat-x`).

Initial Value

`repeat`

Example

`BODY {background-image: url(icon.gif); background-repeat: repeat-y}`

Applies To

All elements.

Object Model Reference

IE   [window.]document.all.*elementID*.style.backgroundRepeat

border

NN *n/a*   IE *4*   CSS *1*

A shorthand attribute for setting the width, style, and/or color of all four borders around an element in one assignment statement. Whichever attributes you don't explicitly set with this attribute assume their initial values. Numerous other attributes allow you to set the width, style, and color of individual edges or groups of edges, if you don't want all four edges to be the same.

Due to differences in the way browsers define their default behavior with regard to borders, every style sheet `border` rule should include the width and style settings. Failure to specify both attributes may result in the border not being seen in one browser or the other.

CSS Syntax

```
border: border-width || border-style || color
```

Value

For the *border-width* and *border-style* attribute values, see the respective attributes in this chapter. For details on the *color* value, see the section about colors at the beginning of this chapter.

Initial Value

None.

Example P {border: groove darkred 3px}

Applies To

All elements (CSS); block and replaced elements (IE).

Object Model Reference

IE   [window.]document.all.*elementID*.style.border

border-bottom, border-left, border-right, border-top

NN *n/a*   IE *4*   CSS *1*

All four attributes are shorthand attributes for setting the width, style, and/or color of a single border edge of an element in one assignment statement. Whichever attributes you don't explicitly set with this attribute assume their initial values.

CSS Syntax

```
border-bottom: border-bottom-width || border-bottom-style || color
border-left:   border-left-width || border-left-style || color
border-right:  border-right-width || border-right-style || color
border-top:    border-top-width || border-top-style || color
```

Value

For the width and style attribute values, see the `border-bottom-width` and `border-bottom-style` attributes in this chapter. For details on the *color* value, see the section about colors at the beginning of this chapter.

Initial Value

None.

Example

```
P {border-bottom: solid lightgreen 3px}
P {border-left: solid lightgreen 6px}
P {border-right: solid lightgreen 3px}
P {border-top: solid lightgreen 6px}
```

Applies To

All elements (CSS); block and replaced elements (IE).

Object Model Reference

IE   [window.]document.all.*elementID*.style.borderBottom
           [window.]document.all.*elementID*.style.borderLeft
           [window.]document.all.*elementID*.style.borderRight
           [window.]document.all.*elementID*.style.borderTop

border-bottom-color, border-left-color, border-right-color, border-top-color
NN *n/a*   IE *4*   CSS *2*

Inherited: No

Each attribute sets the color of a single border edge of an element. This power is easy to abuse by mixing colors that don't belong together. See also the `border-color` attribute for setting the color of multiple edges in one statement.

CSS Syntax

```
border-bottom-color: color
border-left-color: color
border-right-color: color
border-top-color: color
```

Value

For details on the *color* value, see the section about colors at the beginning of this chapter.

Initial Value

None.

Example

```
P {border-bottom-color: gray}
DIV {border-left-color: #33c088}
P.special {border-right-color: rgb(150, 75, 0)}
H3 {border-top-color: rgb(100%, 50%, 21%)}
```

Applies To

All elements (CSS); block and replaced elements (IE).

Object Model Reference

IE   [window.]document.all.*elementID*.style.borderBottomColor
           [window.]document.all.*elementID*.style.borderLeftColor
           [window.]document.all.*elementID*.style.borderRightColor
           [window.]document.all.*elementID*.style.borderTopColor

border-bottom-style, border-left-style, border-right-style, border-top-style

NN *n/a*   IE *4*   CSS *2*

Inherited: No

Each attribute sets the line style of a single border edge of an element. The edge-specific attributes let you override a style that has been applied to all four edges with the **border** or **border-style** attributes, but the edge-specific setting must come after the other one (in source code order) in the style sheet rule. See also the **border-style** attribute for setting the style of multiple edges in one statement.

CSS Syntax

```
border-bottom-style: style
border-left-style: style
border-right-style: style
border-top-style: style
```

Value

Style values are constants that are associated with specific ways of rendering border lines. Not all browsers recognize all of the values in the CSS recommendation. Style support is as follows:

Value	NN	IE	CSS
dashed	-	-*	1
dotted	-	-*	1
double	4	4	1
groove	4	4	1
hidden	-	-	2
inset	4	4	1
none	4	4	1
outset	4	4	1
ridge	4	4	1
solid	4	4	1

*Although not officially supported in Internet Explorer 4, the Mac version renders dashed and dotted borders accurately; the Windows version treats them as solid borders.

The precise manner in which browsers interpret the definitions of the style values is far from universal. Figure 10-1 shows a gallery of all styles as rendered by Windows and Macintosh versions of both Navigator 4 and Internet Explorer 4. Do not expect the exact same look in all browsers.

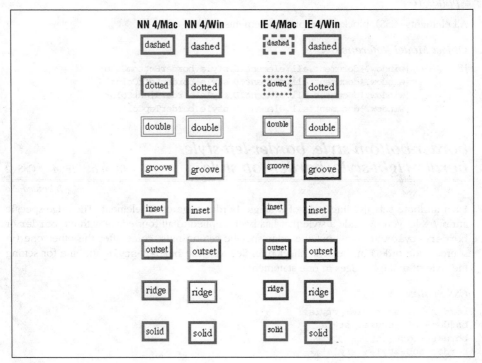

Figure 10-1. border-style gallery

Initial Value

Example

```
P {border-style: solid; border-bottom-style: none}
DIV {border-left-style: ridge}
```

Applies To

All elements.

Object Model Reference

IE   [window.]document.all.*elementID*.style.borderBottomStyle
        [window.]document.all.*elementID*.style.borderLeftStyle
        [window.]document.all.*elementID*.style.borderRightStyle
        [window.]document.all.*elementID*.style.borderTopStyle

border-bottom-width, border-left-width,
border-right-width, border-top-width   NN *4*   IE *4*   CSS *1*

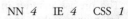

Inherited: No

Each attribute sets the width of a single border edge of an element. Note that Navigator's initial value is zero, which means that you must set the width for all border attribute settings if you expect to see the border in Navigator. See also the `border-width` attribute for setting the width of multiple edges in one statement.

CSS Syntax

```
border-bottom-width: thin | medium | thick | length
border-left-width: thin | medium | thick | length
border-right-width: thin | medium | thick | length
border-top-width: thin | medium | thick | length
```

JavaScript Equivalent

```
borderBottomWidth
borderLeftWidth
borderRightWidth
borderTopWidth
```

Value

Three constants—thin I medium I thick—allow the browser to define exactly how many pixels are used to show the border. For more precision, you can also assign a length value (see the discussion of length values at the beginning of this chapter).

Initial Value

medium (IE); 0 (NN).

Example

```
H2 {border-bottom-width: 2px}
DIV {border-left-width: thin}
P.special {border-right-width: 0.5em}
```

Applies To

All elements (CSS and NN); block and replaced elements (IE).

Object Model Reference

```
IE        [window.]document.all.elementID.style.borderBottomWidth
          [window.]document.all.elementID.style.borderLeftWidth
          [window.]document.all.elementID.style.borderRightWidth
          [window.]document.all.elementID.style.borderTopWidth
```

border-collapse

NN *n/a*   IE *n/a*   CSS *2*

Inherited: No

Sets whether borders of adjacent table elements (cells, row groups, column groups) are rendered separately or collapsed (merged) to ignore any padding or margins between adjacent borders.

CSS Syntax

```
border-collapse: collapse | separate
```

Value   Constant values: collapse I separate

Initial Value

separate

Applies To

Table elements.

border-color   NN *4*   IE *4*   CSS *1*

Inherited: No

A shortcut attribute that lets you set multiple border edges to the same or different colors. Navigator 4 allows only a single value, which applies to all four edges. For Internet Explorer (and the CSS specification), you may supply one to four space-delimited color values. The number of values determines which sides receive the assigned colors.

CSS Syntax

border-color: *color* {1,4}

JavaScript Equivalent

borderColor

Value

For Navigator, one color value only.

In Internet Explorer, this attribute accepts one, two, three, or four *color* values, depending on how many and which borders you want to set with specific colors. Value quantities and positions are interpreted as follows:

Number of Values	Effect
1	All four borders set to value
2	Top and bottom borders set to the first value, right and left borders set to the second value
3	Top border set to first value, right and left borders set to second value, bottom border set to third value
4	Top, right, bottom, and left borders set, respectively

Initial Value

The element's color property.

Example

H2 {border-color: red blue red}
DIV {border-color: red rgb(0,0,255) red}

Applies To

All elements (CSS and NN); block and replaced elements (IE).

Object Model Reference

IE   [window.]document.all.*elementID*.style.borderColor

border-style

NN *4*   IE *4*   CSS *1*

Inherited: No

A shortcut attribute that lets you set multiple border edges to the same or different style. Navigator 4 allows only a single value, which applies to all four edges. For Internet Explorer (and the CSS specification), you may supply one to four space-delimited border style values. The number of values determines which sides receive the assigned colors.

CSS Syntax

```
border-style: borderStyle {1,4}
```

JavaScript Equivalent

```
borderStyle
```

Value

Style values are constants that are associated with specific ways of rendering border lines. Not all browsers recognize all of the values in the CSS recommendation. Style support is as follows:

Value	NN	IE	CSS
dashed	-	-*	1
dotted	-	-*	1
double	4	4	1
groove	4	4	1
hidden	-	-	2
inset	4	4	1
none	4	4	1
outset	4	4	1
ridge	4	4	1
solid	4	4	1

*Although not officially supported in Internet Explorer 4, the Mac version renders dashed and dotted borders accurately; the Windows version treats them as solid borders.

The precise manner in which browsers interpret the definitions of the style values is far from universal. Figure 10-1 showed a gallery of all styles as rendered by Windows and Macintosh versions of both Navigator 4 and Internet Explorer 4. Do not expect the exact same look in all browsers.

For Navigator, you may apply one style value only.

In Internet Explorer, this attribute accepts one, two, three, or four *borderStyle* values, depending on how many and which borders you want to set with specific styles. Value quantities and positions are interpreted as follows:

Number of Values	Effect
1	All four borders set to value
2	Top and bottom borders set to the first value, right and left borders set to the second value
3	Top border set to first value, right and left borders set to second value, bottom border set to third value
4	Top, right, bottom, and left borders set, respectively

Initial Value

Example

```
H1 {border-style: ridge; border-width: 3px}
DIV {border-style: solid double; border-width: 4px}
```

Applies To

All elements (CSS and NN); block and replaced elements (IE).

Object Model Reference

IE   [window.]document.all.*elementID*.style.borderStyle

border-width   NN *4*   IE *4*   CSS *1*

Inherited: No

A shortcut attribute that lets you set multiple border edges to the same or different width. For both browsers, you may supply one to four space-delimited width length values. The number of values determines which sides receive the assigned widths.

CSS Syntax

```
border-width: thin | medium | thick | length {1,4}
```

JavaScript Equivalent

```
borderWidths()
```

Value

Three constants—thin | medium | thick—allow the browser to define exactly how many pixels are used to show the border. For more precision, you can also assign a length value (see the discussion of length values at the beginning of this chapter).

This attribute accepts one, two, three, or four *borderStyle* values, depending on how many and which borders you want to set with specific styles. Value quantities and positions are interpreted as follows:

Number of Values	Effect
1	All four borders set to value
2	Top and bottom borders set to the first value, right and left borders set to the second value
3	Top border set to first value, right and left borders set to second value, bottom border set to third value
4	Top, right, bottom, and left borders set, respectively

Initial Value

medium (IE); 0 (NN)

Example

```
H1 {border-style: ridge; border-width: 3px 5px 3px}
DIV {border-style: solid double; border-width: 4px}
```

Applies To

All elements (CSS and NN); block and replaced elements (IE).

Object Model Reference

IE   [window.]document.all.*elementID*.style.borderStyle

bottom   NN *n/a*   IE *n/a*   CSS *2*

Inherited: No

For positionable elements, defines the position of the bottom edge of an element content (exclusive of borders and margins) relative to the bottom edge of the next outermost block content container. When the element is absolute-positioned, the offset takes the place of a bottom margin setting for the element (although padding may still be set). When the element is relative-positioned, the offset is based on the bottom edge of the inline location of where the element would normally appear in the content.

CSS Syntax

bottom: *length* | *percentage* | auto

Value

See the discussion about length values at the beginning of this chapter. Negative lengths may be allowed in some contexts, but be sure to test the results on all browsers. You may also specify a percentage value, which is calculated based on the height of the next outermost container. The setting of auto lets the browser determine the bottom offset of the element box on its naturally flowing offset within the containing box.

Initial Value

auto

Applies To

All elements.

caption-side   NN *n/a*   IE *n/a*   CSS *2*

Inherited: Yes

Positions the CAPTION element above or below the tabular content of the enclosing TABLE element. This attribute supplants some deprecated ALIGN attribute settings of the CAPTION element.

CSS Syntax

caption-side: top | bottom

Value

Either of the two constant values: top | bottom.

Initial Value

top

Applies To

CAPTION elements.

cell-spacing

NN *n/a*   IE *n/a*   CSS *2*

Inherited: Yes

Determines the size of the space (if any) between cell borders in a table. This attribute requires that the display attribute be set to table. If you include only one length value, it applies to both the horizontal and vertical cell spacing; for two values, the first applies to the horizontal and the second to the vertical. See Figure 10-2 for a synopsis of a table's numerous dimension definitions.

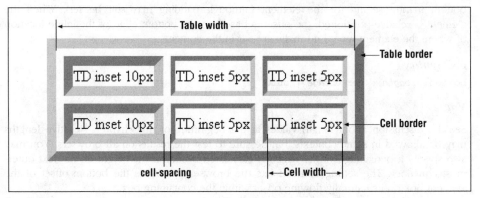

Figure 10-2. The geometry of a TABLE element

CSS Syntax

```
cell-spacing: length[length] | none
```

Value

See the discussion of length values at the beginning of this chapter. The none value applies to both vertical and horizontal cell spacing. If you want no spacing along one axis, set its value to zero.

Initial Value

None.

Applies To

All elements.

clear

NN *4*   IE *4*   CSS *1*

Inherited: No

Defines whether the element allows itself to be displayed in the same horizontal band as a floating element, such as an image. Typically, another element in the vicinity has its float style attribute set to left or right. To prevent the current element from being in the same band as the floating block, set the `clear` attribute to the same side (`left` or `right`). If you aren't sure where the potential overlap might occur, set the `clear` attribute to `both`. An element whose `clear` attribute is set to a value other than `none` is rendered at the beginning of the next available line below the floating element.

CSS Syntax

`clear: both | left | none | right`

JavaScript Equivalent

`clear`

Value   Any of the following constants: `both` | `left` | `none` | `right`

Initial Value

None.

Example

```
<IMG SRC="logo.gif" HEIGHT=40 WIDTH=60 STYLE="float: right">
<H1 STYLE="clear: right">Giantco Corporation</H1>
```

Applies To

All elements.

Object Model Reference

IE   `[window.]document.all.elementID.style.clear`

clip   NN 4   IE 4   CSS 2

Inherited: No

Defines a clipping region of a positionable element. The clipping region is the area of the element layer in which content is visible. For the best results in clipping content, wrap the content-holding element inside a DIV element whose `clip` attribute is set to the desired region. Clipping may not work properly in Internet Explorer 4 for the Macintosh. Also, when a clipped element is displayed at the very bottom of a page in Navigator 4, the browser window may not allow you to scroll to view the very bottom of the clipping region.

CSS Syntax

`clip: rect(lengthTop lengthRight lengthBottom lengthLeft) | auto`

JavaScript Equivalent

```
clip.bottom
clip.left
clip.right
clip.top
```

Value

Extending to CSS2, the only shape recognized for the clip attribute is `rect`. Other shapes may be admitted in the future.

When specifying lengths for each side of the clipping rectangle, observe the clockwise order of values: top, right, bottom, left. See the discussion about length values at the beginning of this chapter. A value of auto sets the clipping region to the block that contains the content. In Navigator, this block cinches up to the width and height of the available content; in Internet Explorer, the width may extend to the width of the next outermost container (such as the BODY element).

Initial Value

auto

Example

```
<SPAN STYLE="position: absolute; clip: rect(10px 110px 80px 10px)">
<IMG SRC="desk1.gif" HEIGHT=90 WIDTH=120>
</SPAN>
```

Applies To

Any element with a position:absolute attribute setting.

Object Model Reference

IE   [window.]document.all.*elementID*.style.clip

color

NN 4   IE 4   CSS 1

Inherited: Yes

Defines the foreground text color of the element. For some graphically oriented elements, such as form controls, the color attribute may also be applied to element edges or other features. Such extra-curricular behavior is browser-specific and may not be the same across browsers.

CSS Syntax

color: *color*

JavaScript Equivalent

color

Value   See the discussion of color attribute values at the beginning of this chapter.

Initial Value

black

Example   TH {color: darkred}

Applies To

All elements.

Object Model Reference

IE   [window.]document.all.*elementID*.style.color

column-span

Sets the number of columns to be spanned by a table cell, column, or column group. Analogous to the COLSPAN attribute of a TD or TH element and the SPAN attribute of a COL or COLGROUP element.

CSS Syntax

column-span: *integer*

Value   Any positive integer representing the number of columns.

Initial Value

1

Example   #divider {column-span: 5}

Applies To

TD, TH, COL, and COLGROUP elements and any other cell, column, or column group type of element.

content

Note that the details on this attribute are very preliminary. Defines the actual content or source of content to be displayed before and/or after the current element. This attribute is set only with the :before and :after pseudo-elements associated with a real element. For example, in the following style sheet rule:

```
BLOCKQUOTE:before, BLOCKQUOTE:after {
  content: "<HR STYLE=\"align: middle; width: 50%\">"}
```

a horizontal rule is drawn before and after every BLOCKQUOTE element. In this case, the content is a string of text that is rendered as HTML. If the situation warrants it, an external document can be assigned to the content attribute.

CSS Syntax

content: *string* | *uri* | *counter+*

Value

For a string value, any text inside a quoted pair. Internal quote marks should be escaped (\"). For a URI, any valid complete or relative URL. (Details of counter and anticipated future value types are not yet available.)

Initial Value

"" (empty string)

Example   BODY:before {content: header.htm}

Applies To

All elements plus a :before and/or :after pseudo-element.

cue

NN *n/a*   IE *n/a*   CSS *2*

Inherited: No

For aural style sheets only, provides a shorthand attribute for setting cue-before and cue-after attribute settings. A cue is a sound (also known as an auditory icon) that can be used to aurally delimit the reading of document content. Cue attributes are URIs to sound resources.

CSS Syntax

cue: *cue-before* || *cue-after*

Value

If there are two values, the first is applied to the cue-before attribute and the second to the cue-after attribute. If there is only one value, the same auditory icon is applied to both cue-before and cue-after.

Initial Value

None.

Applies To

All elements.

cue-after, cue-before

NN *n/a*   IE *n/a*   CSS *2*

Inherited: No

For aural style sheets only, a cue is a sound (also known as an auditory icon) that can be used to aurally delimit the reading of document content. The cue-before and cue-after attributes are URIs to sound files that are to be played before and after the content is rendered via text-to-speech or other aural medium.

CSS Syntax

cue-after: *uri* | none
cue-before: *uri* | none

Value

Any valid complete or relative URL to a sound file in a MIME type supported by the browser. You may apply the same values to both attributes for the same style selector if it makes aural sense for the listener.

Initial Value

Example LI {cue-before: url(ding.wav); cue-after(dong.wav)}

Applies To

All elements.

cursor

NN *n/a*   IE *4*   CSS *2*

Inherited: Yes

Sets the shape of the cursor when the screen pointer is on the element. The precise look of cursors depends on the operating system. Before deploying a modified cursor, be sure you understand the standard ways that the various types of cursors are used within the browser and operating system. Users expect a cursor design to mean the same thing across all applications. Figure 10-3 offers a gallery of Windows and Macintosh cursors for each of the cursor constant settings provided by Internet Explorer 4.

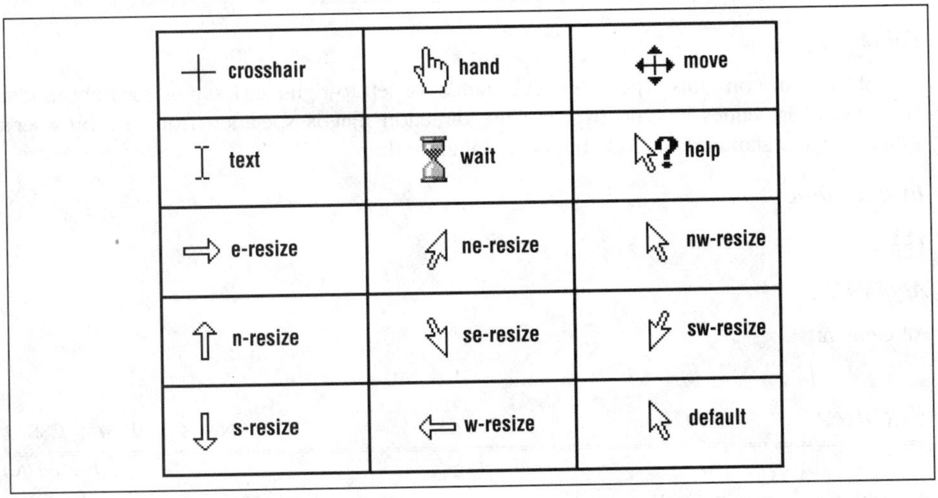

Figure 10-3. Internet Explorer cursor gallery

CSS Syntax

```
cursor: auto | crosshair | default | e-resize | help | move | n-resize |
ne-resize | nw-resize | pointer | s-resize | se-resize | sw-resize | text |
w-resize || wait || uri
```

Value

Any one cursor constant. Note that the CSS working draft specifies the `pointer` value for the cursor that points to a link value, whereas Internet Explorer 4 implements the value as `hand`. Although not supported in Internet Explorer 4, the URI value (specified in CSS2) indicates possible future support for a downloadable cursor. Presumably, browsers will allow a uniform file format across all operating systems.

Initial Value

`auto`

Example `A.helpLink {cursor: help}`

Applies To

All elements.

direction

Sets the direction of flow of inline portions of content (such as text) and the order in which table cells are filled along a row. Analogous to the DIR attribute of most elements, the direction style attribute lets you override the browser's default rendering direction for other languages or special content.

CSS Syntax

```
direction: ltr | rtl | ltr-override | rtl-override
```

Value

Any of the four constants. The value ltr stands for left-to-right; rtl stands for right-to-left. The override values let you override the direction that is specified from the browser's adherence to a standard Unicode bidirectional algorithm.

Initial Value

rtl

Applies To

All elements.

display

A multipurpose attribute that determines whether the element should be rendered in the document (and space reserved for it in the content). If the element is to be rendered, the attribute sets what type of element (block or inline) it is. The list of available values recognized by Navigator 4 and Internet Explorer 4 (and CSS1) is fairly short: block | inline | list-item | none, yet both browsers do not actually change the element type with values other than none. CSS2 expands the list significantly. When set to none, the element is hidden from view, and all surrounding content cinches up to occupy whatever space the element would normally occupy. This is different from the visibility attribute, which reserves space for the element while hiding it from view.

CSS Syntax

```
display: displayType
```

JavaScript Equivalent

```
display
```

Value

One of the constant values: `block` | `compact` | `inline` | `inline-table` | `list-item` | `none` | `run-in` | `table` | `table-caption` | `table-cell` | `table-column-group` | `table-footer-group` | `table-header-group` | `table-row` | `table-row-group`.

Initial Value

`inline`

Example `hidden {display: none}`

Applies To

All elements.

Object Model Reference

IE   `[window.]document.all.elementID.style.display`

elevation

NN *n/a*   IE *n/a*   CSS *2*

Inherited: Yes

Given a listener at the center of a three-dimensional sound space (like in a surround-sound-equipped theater), `elevation` sets the vertical angle of the source of the sound (for example, in a text-to-speech browser). See also the `azimuth` attribute.

CSS Syntax

`elevation: angle | angleConstant`

Value

Your choice of a specific angle (in degrees) or one of the five constant values. An angle value is any value in the range of -90 to +90 (inclusive) plus the letters "deg", as in `90deg`. The value `0deg` is at the same vertical level as the listener's ear. To set the angle above level, the value must be a positive value (`45deg`); below level requires a negative value (`-45deg`). Optionally, you can choose an `angleConstant` value from a library of descriptions that correspond to fixed points above and below level.

Value	Equals
`above`	`90deg` (directly overhead)
`below`	`-90deg` (directly beneath)
`higher`	+10 degrees from current
`level`	`0deg` (at listener's ear level)
`lower`	-10 degrees from current

In combination with the `azimuth` attribute, you can place a sound at any point around a spherical surround-sound stage.

Initial Value

`level`

Example

```
H1 {elevation: -45deg}
P.heavenly {elevation: above}
```

Applies To

All elements.

filter   NN *n/a*   IE *4*   CSS *n/a*

Inherited: No

Sets the visual, reveal, or blend filter used to display or change content of an element. A visual filter can be applied to an element to produce effects such as content flipping, glow, drop shadow, and many others. A reveal filter is applied to an element when its visibility changes. The value of the reveal filter determines what visual effect is to be applied to the transition from hidden to shown (or vice versa). This includes effects such as wipes, blinds, and barn doors. A blend filter sets the speed at which a transition between states occurs. As of this writing, the `filter` attribute is available only in Internet Explorer 4 but does not work in the Macintosh version.

CSS Syntax

```
filter: filterType1(paramName1=value1, paramName2=value2,...)
        filterType2(paramName1=value1,...) ...
```

Value

Each filter attribute may have more than one space-delimited filter type associated with it. Each filter type is followed by a pair of parentheses, which may convey parameters about the behavior of the filter for the current element. A parameter generally consists of a name/value pair, with assignment performed by the equals symbol. See the section "Notes", for details on *filterType* values and parameters.

Initial Value

None.

Example fastStuff {filter: blur(add=true, direction=225)}

Applies To

BODY, BUTTON, IMG, INPUT, MARQUEE, TABLE, TD, TEXTAREA, TFOOT, TH, THEAD, TR, and absolute-positioned DIV and SPAN elements.

Object Model Reference

IE   [window.]document.all.*elementID*.style.filter

Notes

Filters are divided into three broad categories: visual, reveal, and blend. Each category has its own parameter names. You can mix categories within a single filter attribute assignment and have quite a bit of fun experimenting with the combinations. Observe carefully the limitations about the elements to which you may assign filters.

The visual filters and their parameters are as follows:

alpha() Transparency level. The `opacity` and `finishopacity` parameters can be set from transparent (0) to opaque (100). The `style` parameter sets the opacity gradient shape: uniform (0), linear (1), radial (2), rectangular (3). `startX` and `startY` set the horizontal and vertical coordinates for opacity gradient start, whereas `finishX` and `finishY` set the horizontal and vertical coordinates for opacity gradient end.

blur() Gives the element impression of motion. The `add` parameter specifies whether to add the original image to the blurred image (1) or to omit it (0). `direction` sets the angle of the blurred image relative to the original image location: above (0); above-right (45); right (90); below-right (135); below (180); below-left (225); left (270); above-left (315). `strength` indicates the number of pixels for the blurred image to extend.

chroma() Sets a color transparent. The color parameter sets the hexadecimal triplet value of the color to be made transparent.

dropShadow()

Creates an offset shadow for apparent depth. The `color` parameter sets the hexadecimal triplet value of color for drop shadow. `offx` and `offy` specify the number of pixels between the element and the drop shadow along the x and y axes (positive values to the right/down; negative to the left/up). The `positive` parameter specifies whether only positive pixels generate drop shadows (1) or transparent pixels as well (0).

flipH() Creates a horizontally mirrored image.

flipV() Creates a vertically mirrored image.

glow() Adds radiance to outer edges. The color parameter sets the hexadecimal triplet value of the color for the radiance effect and strength sets the radiance intensity (1–255).

grayscale()

Removes colors but retains luminance.

invert() Reverses the hue, saturation, and brightness (HSV) levels.

light() Shines a light source on the element (numerous filter method calls are available to set specific types of light sources, locations, intensities, and colors).

mask() Creates a transparent mask. The `color` parameter sets the hexadecimal triplet value of the color applied to transparent regions.

shadow() Displays the element as a solid silhouette. The color parameter sets the hexadecimal triplet value of the color used for shadows and `direction` sets the angle of the shadow relative to the original image location: above (0); above-right (45); right (90); below-right (135); below (180); below-left (225); left (270); above-left (315).

wave() Renders the element with a sine wave distortion along the x-axis. The `add` parameter specifies whether to add the original image to waved image (1) or not (0). `freq` sets the number of waves to be applied to visual distortion, `light` sets the light strength (0–100), `phase` sets the percentage offset for the sine wave (0–100 corresponding to 0 to 360 degrees), and `strength` sets the wave effect intensity (0–255).

xRay() Renders only the edges.

The blend and reveal transition filters and parameters are as follows:

`blendTrans()`
> Fades the element in or out. The `duration` parameter sets the floating-point value (`seconds.milliseconds`) of how long the transition effect should take.

`revealTrans()`
> Sets a transition effect between hiding and showing of an element. The duration parameter sets the floating-point value (*seconds.milliseconds*) of how long the transition effect should take. `transitionshape` is a key integer that corresponds to one of the following transition types:

0	Box in	12	Random dissolve
1	Box out	13	Split vertical in
2	Circle in	14	Split vertical out
3	Circle out	15	Split horizontal in
4	Wipe up	16	Split horizontal out
5	Wipe down	17	Strips left down
6	Wipe right	18	Strips left up
7	Wipe left	19	Strips right down
8	Vertical blinds	20	Strips right up
9	Horizontal blinds	21	Random bars horizontal
10	Checkerboard across	22	Random bars vertical
11	Checkerboard down	23	Random

float

NN *4*   IE *4*   CSS *1*

Inherited: No

Determines on which side of the containing box the element aligns so that other content wraps around the element. When the attribute is set to none, the element appears in its source code sequence, and at most, one line of surrounding text content appears in the same horizontal band as the element.

There are some irreconcilable differences between browsers when deploying the `float` style attribute, especially for objects such as images. If you follow the CSS format and assign the `float` attribute to the `IMG` element, text tends to wrap as you'd expect in Internet Explorer (particularly when the setting is `float:left`). Navigator 4, however, requires that the `IMG` element be wrapped inside a `DIV` element, the latter receiving the `float` style attribute (and other style settings, such as margins). But IE 4 reacts poorly to this combination. The most reliable cross-browser workaround for now is to avoid style sheet rules for floating elements, and stick to the `ALIGN` attribute of the `IMG` element's tag.

Due to the prior usage of the `float` keyword in JavaScript, the JavaScript syntax equivalent of the `float` attribute is `align`. Assigned values are the same, however.

CSS Syntax
`float:` *alignmentSide* | none

JavaScript Equivalent
`align`

Value   An *alignmentSide* is one of the following constants: left | right | none.

Initial Value

Example `IMG.navButton {float: right}`

Applies To

All elements.

Object Model Reference

IE   `[window.]document.all.`*`elementID`*`.style.styleFloat`

font

Inherited: Yes

A shorthand attribute that lets you set one or more font-related attributes with one assignment statement. A space-delimited list of values (in any sequence) are applied to the specific font attribute for which the value is a valid type. In CSS2, some additional short-circuit constants apply named system fonts that have fixed values for each of the font-related attributes.

CSS Syntax

`font:` *`font-style`* `|| ` *`font-variant`* ` || ` *`font-weight`* ` || ` *`font-size`* ` || ` *`line-height`* ` ||`
`font-family` ` | ` *`CSS2FontConstant`*

Value

For syntax and examples of value types for font and line attributes, see the respective attribute listing. The CSS2 font constants are as follows: `caption` | `icon` | `menu` | `messagebox` | `smallcaption` | `statusbar`. These constants refer to browser and operating system fonts used by the client. Their precise appearance are therefore different on different operating systems but are consistent with the user's expectation for a particular type of font. In other words, these styles should be used when their function mirrors a system or browser function.

Initial Value

None.

Example

```
BODY {font: 12pt serif}
H2 {font: bolder small-caps 16pt}
.iconCaption {font: caption}
```

Applies To

All elements.

Object Model Reference

IE   `[window.]document.all.`*`elementID`*`.style.font`

font-family

Inherited: Yes

Sets a prioritized list of font families to be used to render the content. One or more font family names may be included in a space-delimited list of attribute values. If a font family name consists of multiple words, the family name must be inside quotes.

A font family may consist of multiple font definitions. For example, a Helvetica font family may also include a bold version and an italic version—genuinely distinct fonts rather than the approximated versions of bold and italic. When you specify a font family by name, the browser looks into the client's system to see if there is a font available by that name. If not, the browser looks to the next font family name in the list. Therefore, it is wise to include font family names in a sequence that goes from the most esoteric to the most generic. The final font family name should be the generic family (`serif`, `sans-serif`, `cursive`, `fantasy`, or `monospace`) that most closely resembles the desired font. Bear in mind that many fonts that are widely installed on one operating system may not be as popular on another operating system.

Browsers following the CSS2 specification should also be smart enough to recognize Unicode character codes and try to match them with named font families that cater to particular languages. Ideally, this will allow a browser to mix fonts from different languages and writing systems in the same element, provided each `font-family` is listed in the attribute value.

CSS Syntax
```
font-family: fontFamilyName || fontFamilyName || ...
```

JavaScript Equivalent
```
fontFamily
```

Value
Any number of font family names, space delimited. Multiword family names must be quoted. Recognized generic family names are: `serif` I `sans-serif` I `cursive` I `fantasy` I `monospace`.

Initial Value
Browser default.

Example `BODY {font-family: "Century Schoolbook" Times serif}`

Applies To
All elements.

Object Model Reference
IE   `[window.]document.all.elementID.style.fontFamily`

Notes
Navigator 4 and Internet Explorer 4 provide facilities for downloading font definition files for a browser that doesn't have a special font that the page designer wants for the page. The font definition files must be created by the author using browser-specific font conversion tools. Then, each browser has a different way of signalling the server to download the

font definition file. For Navigator, you can use a `@fontdef` directive in a `STYLE` element or a `LINK` element:

```
@fontdef url(http://www.giantco.com/fonts/neato.pfr)
<LINK REL=FONTDEF SRC="http://www.giantco.com/fonts/neato.pfr">
```

For Internet Explorer, use the `@font-face` directive in a `STYLE` element:

```
@font-face {font-family:Neato; src: url(http://www.giantco.com/fonts/
neato.eot}
```

See the previous section "At-Rules" for details on deploying this type of style rule. You then specify the font in regular `font-family` style attributes. If the font has yet to download, the browser displays the page in another font until the downloadable font has arrived. At that point, the page is reflowed with the downloaded font.

font-size

NN *4*   IE *4*   CSS *1*

Inherited: Yes

Determines the font size of the element. The font size can be set in several ways. A collection of constants (`xx-small`, `x-small`, `small`, `medium`, `large`, `x-large`, `xx-large`) defines what are known as absolute sizes. In truth, these are absolute as far as a single browser in a single operating system goes because the reference point for these sizes varies with browser and operating system (see Figure 10-4 and Figure 10-5 for size comparisons as viewed on the same video monitor). But they do let the author have confidence that one element set to `large` is rendered larger than another set to `medium.`

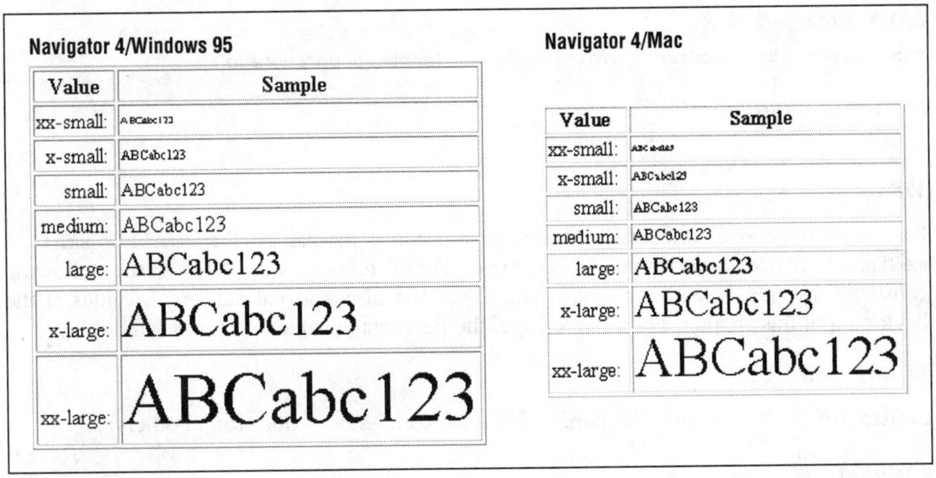

Figure 10-4. Font size constant values in Navigator on the Windows and Mac platforms

Another collection of constants (`larger`, `smaller`) are known as relative sizes. Because the `font-size` attribute is inherited from the parent element, these relative sizes are applied to the parent element to determine the font size of the current element. It is up to the browser to determine exactly how much larger or smaller the font size is, and a lot depends on how the parent element's font size is set. If it is set with one of the absolute sizes (`large`, for example), a child's font size of `larger` means that the font is rendered in the browser's

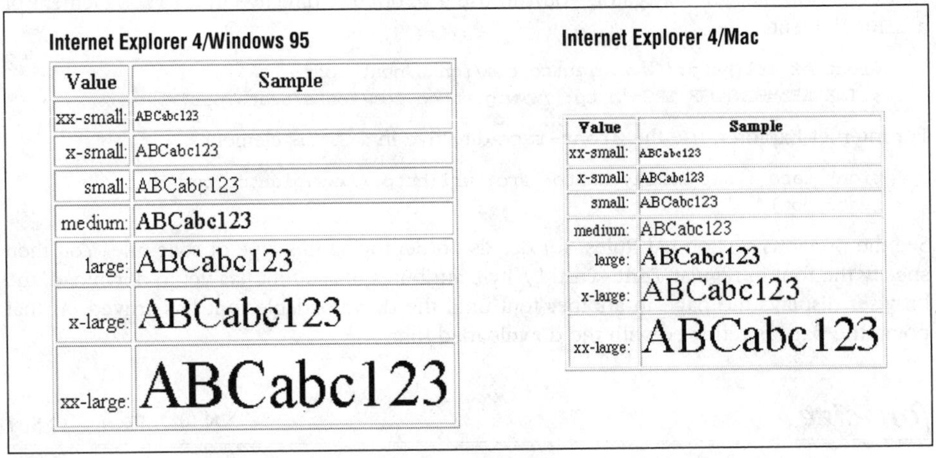

Internet Explorer 4/Windows 95	
Value	**Sample**
xx-small:	ABCabc123
x-small:	ABCabc123
small:	ABCabc123
medium:	ABCabc123
large:	ABCabc123
x-large:	ABCabc123
xx-large:	ABCabc123

Internet Explorer 4/Mac	
Value	**Sample**
xx-small:	ABCabc123
x-small:	ABCabc123
small:	ABCabc123
medium:	ABCabc123
large:	ABCabc123
x-large:	ABCabc123
xx-large:	ABCabc123

Figure 10-5. Font size constant values in IE on the Windows and Mac platforms

`x-large` size. The increments are not as clear cut when the parent font size is set with a length or percentage.

If you elect to use a length value for the `font-size` attribute, choose a unit that makes the most sense for fonts, such as points (`pt`) or ems (`em`). The latter bases its calculation on the size of the parent element's font size. Finally, you can set the `font-size` to a percentage, which is calculated based on the size of the parent element's font size.

CSS Syntax

```
font-size: absoluteSize | relativeSize | length | percentage
```

JavaScript Equivalent

```
fontSize
```

Value

For an absolute size, one of the following constants: `xx-small` | `x-small` | `small` | `medium` | `large` | `x-large` | `xx-large`. For a relative size, one of the following constants: `larger` | `smaller`. For a length, see the discussion about length values at the beginning of this chapter. For a percentage, the percentage value and the `%` symbol.

Initial Value

`medium` (for BODY element); the parent element's `font-size` value (for all others).

Example

```
BODY {font-size: 14pt}
P.teeny {font-size: x-small}
EM {font-size: larger}
SPAN.larger {font-size: 150%}
```

Applies To

All elements.

Object Model Reference

IE   `[window.]document.all.elementID.style.fontSize`

font-size-adjust
NN *n/a*   IE *n/a*   CSS *2*

Inherited: Yes

Allows an element to preserve the x-height (measured in exes) of a "first choice" font when substituting fonts. The z-factor is a ratio of the em- to x-heights of a font. Because different fonts set to the same font size can look larger or smaller than neighboring fonts on a page set to the same size, the z-factor can be used to calculate the ratio and apply it to other fonts. Even though the resulting font size may be larger or smaller than the "first choice" font setting, the perceived size is much more accurate. This also tends to equalize the horizontal metrics of fonts so that word-wrapped lines break at the same place with different font families.

CSS Syntax
`font-size-adjust: z`

Value   A choice from the following constant values: z | none.

Initial Value

Applies To

All elements.

font-style
NN *4*   IE *4*   CSS *1*

Inherited: Yes

Determines whether the element is rendered in a normal (Roman), italic, or oblique font style. If the `font-family` includes font faces labeled Italic and/or Oblique, the setting of the `font-style` attribute summons those particular font faces from the browser's system. But if the specialized font faces are not available in the system, the normal font face is usually algorithmically slanted to look italic. Output sent to a printer with such font settings rely on the quality of arbitration between the client computer and printer to render an electronically generated italic font style. Although personal computer software typically includes other kinds of font rendering under the heading of "Style," see `font-variant` and `font-weight` for other kinds of font "styles."

CSS Syntax
`font-style: fontStyle`

JavaScript Equivalent
`fontStyle`

Value

Navigator 4 recognizes: `normal | italic`. Internet Explorer 4 recognizes: `normal | italic | oblique` but treats both `italic` and `oblique` as italic.

Initial Value

None.

Example `H2 EM {font-style: italic}`

Applies To

All elements.

Object Model Reference

IE   `[window.]document.all.`*`elementID`*`.style.fontStyle`

font-variant   NN *n/a*   IE *4*   CSS *1*

Inherited: Yes

Determines whether the element should be rendered in all uppercase letters in such a way that lowercase letters of the source code are rendered in smaller uppercase letters. If a font family contains a small caps variant, the browser should use it automatically. More likely, however, the browser calculates a smaller size for the uppercase letters that take the place of source code lowercase letters. In practice, Internet Explorer 4 renders the entire source code content as uppercase letters of the same size as the parent element's font, regardless of the case of the source code.

CSS Syntax

`font-variant:` *`fontVariant`*

Value   Any of the following constant values: `normal | small-caps`.

Initial Value

`normal`

Example `EM {font-variant: small-caps}`

Applies To

All elements.

Object Model Reference

IE   `[window.]document.all.`*`elementID`*`.style.fontVariant`

font-weight   NN *4*   IE *4*   CSS *1*

Inherited: Yes

Sets the weight (boldness) of the element's font. CSS provides a weight rating scheme that is more granular than most browsers render on the screen, but the finely tuned weights may come into play when the content is sent to a printer. The scale is a numeric rating from 100 to 900 at 100-unit increments. Therefore, a `font-weight` of 100 is the least bold that can be displayed, whereas 900 is the boldest. A setting of `normal` (the default weight for any font) is equivalent to a `font-weight` value of 400; the standard bold setting is equivalent to 700. Other settings (`bolder` and `lighter`) let you specify a weight relative to the parent element's weight.

The CSS2 specification offers guidelines about how the weight values should correspond to font family names and internal characteristics of some font definition formats. For example, the OpenType font definition format provides slots for nine font weights. In this case, the numeric `font-weight` attribute values map directly to the weight definitions in that font. If the font family contains a face whose name contains the word Medium and one labeled Book, Regular, Roman, or Normal, the Medium face is equated with a weight value of 500 (whereas the other is at 400). All font face names including the word Bold are equated with a weight of 700. For font families that don't have all nine weights assigned, the browser should do its best to interpolate, but it is very likely that some weight values generate fonts of the same weight.

CSS Syntax

`font-weight:` *fontWeight*

JavaScript Equivalent

`fontWeight`

Value

Any of the following constant values: `bold` | `bolder` | `lighter` | `normal` | 100 | 200 | 300 | 400 | 500 | 600 | 700 | 800 | 900.

Initial Value

`normal`

Example `P EM {font-weight: bolder}`

Applies To

All elements.

Object Model Reference

IE   `[window.]document.all.`*elementID*`.style.fontWeight`

height   NN 4   IE 4   CSS 1

Inherited: No

Sets the height of a block-level element's content height (exclusive of borders, padding, and margins). Version 4 browsers apply the `height` attribute only to selected elements (IE 4) and absolute-positioned elements (which means DIV wrappers around other types of elements), but CSS2 recommends application to all replaceable elements as well.

For absolute-positioned elements, Navigator 4 and Internet Explorer 4 react differently to settings of the `height` style attribute. They agree on one thing: if the content requires more height than is specified for the attribute, the content requirements override the attribute value (use the clipping region to truncate the height of the viewport for the element if you need to). But if the `height` attribute value produces a box that is taller than the content requires, the browsers behave differently. Navigator cinches up the height of the box to accommodate the content (as if the `height` attribute is perennially set to `auto`), unless you also adjust the clipping rectangle; Internet Explorer retains the attribute height. This discrepancy can affect the look of borders around an absolute-positioned element generated via CSS syntax.

CSS Syntax

```
height: length | percentage | auto
```

JavaScript Equivalent

```
height
```

Value

See the discussion about length values at the beginning of this chapter. You may also specify a percentage value, which is calculated based on the height of the next outermost container. The setting of `auto` lets the browser determine the height of the element box based on the amount of space required to display the content.

Initial Value

```
auto
```

Example

```
DIV#announce {height: 240}
TEXTAREA {height: 90%}
```

Applies To

Navigator 4: all absolute-positioned elements.

Internet Explorer 4: APPLET, DIV, EMBED, FIELDSET, HR, IFRAME, IMG, INPUT, MARQUEE, OBJECT, SPAN, TABLE, and TEXTAREA elements.

CSS2: all elements except nonreplaced inline elements, table column elements, and column group elements.

Object Model Reference

IE   [window.]document.all.*elementID*.style.height

!important

Inherited: No

Increases the weight (importance) of an attribute setting with respect to cascading order. This keyword is a declaration rather than an attribute, but it can be attached to any attribute setting. The syntax requires an exclamation symbol between the attribute value and the `important` keyword. Extra whitespace around the exclamation symbol is acceptable. See Chapter 3.

CSS Syntax

```
!important
```

Value   No values assigned to this declaration.

Example P {font-size: 14pt ! important}

Applies To

All elements.

left

For positionable elements, defines the position of the left edge of an element's box (content plus left padding, border, and/or margin) relative to the left edge of the next outermost block content container. When the element is relative-positioned, the offset is based on the left edge of the inline location of where the element would normally appear in the content.

CSS Syntax

left: *length* | *percentage* | auto

JavaScript Equivalent

left

Value

See the discussion about length values at the beginning of this chapter. Negative lengths may be allowed in some contexts, but be sure to test the results on all browsers. You may also specify a percentage value, which is calculated based on the width of the next outermost container. The setting of auto lets the browser determine the left offset of the element box on its naturally flowing offset within the containing box. Navigator tends to push up against the left edge of the containing box, whereas Internet Explorer renders a bit of margin.

Initial Value

auto

Example

H1 {position: relative; left: 2em}
#logo {position: absolute; left: 80px; top: 30px}

Applies To

All elements.

Object Model Reference

IE   [window.]document.all.*elementID*.style.offsetLeft

letter-spacing

Defines the spacing between characters within an element. Browsers normally define the character spacing based on font definitions and operating system font rendering. To override those settings, assign a length value to the letter-spacing attribute. A negative value tightens up the spacing, but be sure to test the effect on the selected font for readability on different operating systems.

CSS Syntax

```
letter-spacing: normal | length | auto
```

Value

See the discussion at the beginning of this chapter about length values. The best results use units that are based on the rendered font size (**em** and **ex**). A setting of **normal** is how the browser sets the letters without any intervention. A setting of **auto** (CSS2) is intended for use with single-line elements (such as **H1** and the like) to space the letters such that the element content appears on a single line given the current width of the containing box.

Initial Value

```
normal
```

Example

```
.tight {letter-spacing: -0.03em}
BLOCKQUOTE {letter-spacing: 1.1em}
```

Applies To

All elements.

Object Model Reference

```
IE          [window.]document.all.elementID.style.letterSpacing
```

line-height   NN *4*   IE *4*   CSS *1*

Inherited: Yes

Sets the height of the inline box (the box holding one physical line of content). Under normal circumstances, the `line-height` of the tallest font in a line of text or the tallest object governs the line height for that content line. In theory, you should be able to set the `line-height` of a block element and have that value apply to all content lines, regardless of the font face or font size specified for inline content.

In practice, both Navigator 4 and Internet Explorer 4 can experience line space rendering problems when the `font-size` of inline text is larger than the size of surrounding text. Not all lines of the outer block adhere to the block's `line-height` setting as expected (especially lines after the larger text segment). Moreover, in Navigator 4, the `line-height` attribute does not traverse more than one generation if the second generation element becomes a block-level element (such as a positioned or floated element). Test these settings extensively to make sure you get the look you desire.

CSS Syntax

```
line-height: normal | number | length | percentage
```

JavaScript Equivalent

```
lineHeight
```

Value

A value of `normal` lets the browser calculate line spacing for the entire element, thus producing a computed value that can be inherited by nested elements. A *number* value (greater than zero) acts as a multiplier for the font-size of the current element. Therefore, if a nested element inherits the line-height multiplier from its parent, that multiplier is applied to the current element's `font-size` setting (the multiplier, not the computed value of the parent, is inherited). A *length* value assigns an actual value to the inline box height. And a *percentage* value is a multiplier applied to the font size of the current element. In this case, the computer value can be inherited by nested elements.

Initial Value

`normal`

Example

`P {line-height: normal}`	*Browser default; actual value is inheritable*
`P {line-height: 1.1}`	*Number value; the number value is inheritable*
`P {line-height: 1.1em}`	*Length value; the actual value is inheritable*
`P {line-height: 110%}`	*Percentage value; percentage times font size is inheritable*

Applies To

All elements.

Object Model Reference

IE   `[window.]document.all.elementID.style.lineHeight`

list-style
NN *n/a*   IE *4*   CSS *1*

Inherited: Yes

A shorthand attribute for setting up to three list-style attributes in one assignment statement. Whichever attributes you don't explicitly set with this attribute assume their initial values. These attributes define display characteristics for the markers automatically rendered for list items inside `OL` and `UL` elements.

CSS Syntax

`list-style:` *list-style-type* `||` *list-style-position* `||` *list-style-image*

Value

See the individual attribute entries for `list-style-type`, `list-style-position`, and `list-style-image` for details on acceptable values for each. You may include one, two, or all three values in the `list-style` attribute setting in any order you wish.

Initial Value

None.

Example   `UL {list-style: square outside none}`

Applies To

DD, DT, LI, OL, and UL elements and any other element assigned the display:list-item style attribute.

Object Model Reference

IE   [window.]document.all.*elementID*.style.listStyle

list-style-image   NN *n/a* IE *4* CSS *1*

Inherited: Yes

Provides the URL for an image that is to be used as the marker for a list item. Because this attribute can be inherited, a setting (including **none**) for an individual list item can override the same attribute setting in its parent.

CSS Syntax

list-style-image: none | *uri*

Value

Use **none** to override an image assigned to a parent element. For *uri*, supply any valid full or relative URL to an image file whose MIME type is readable by the browser.

Initial Value

Example

```
UL {list-style-image: url(images/folder.gif)}
LI {list-style-image: none}
```

Applies To

DD, DT, LI, OL, and UL elements and any other element assigned the display:list-item style attribute.

Object Model Reference

IE   [window.]document.all.*elementID*.style.listStyleImage

list-style-position   NN *n/a* IE *4* CSS *1*

Inherited: Yes

Determine whether the marker is inside or outside (outdented) from the box containing the list item's content. When the list-style-position is set to inside and the content is text, the marker appears to be part of the text block. In this case, the alignment (indent) of the list item is the same as normal, but without the outdented marker. Figure 10-6 demonstrates the effects of both settings on wrapped list item text. Note that in Internet Explorer 4 for Macintosh (not shown), wrapped text lines extend all the way to the left margin of the UL or OL element.

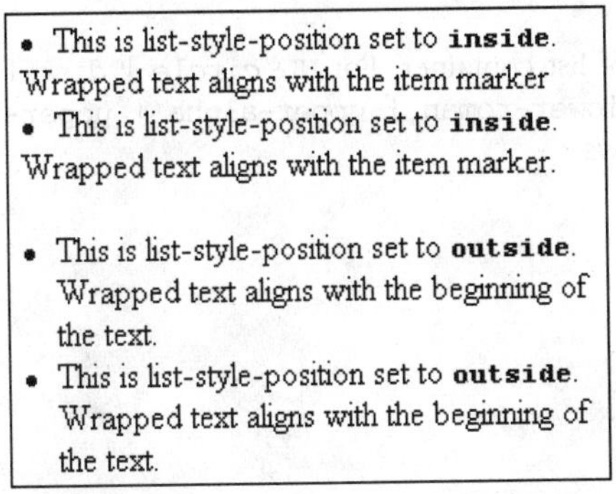

Figure 10-6. Results of list-style-position settings (Windows 95)

CSS Syntax

```
list-style-position: inside | outside
```

Value   Any of the constant values: inside | outside.

Initial Value

```
outside
```

Example UL {list-style-position: inside}

Applies To

DD, DT, LI, OL, and UL elements and any other element assigned the display:list-item style attribute.

Object Model Reference

IE   [window.]document.all.*elementID*.style.listStylePosition

list-style-type   NN *4*   IE *4*   CSS *1*

Inherited: Yes

Sets the kind of item marker to be displayed with each item. This attribute applies only if list-style-image is none (or not specified). The constant values available for this attribute are divided into two categories. One set is used with UL elements to present a filled disc, an empty circle, or a square (empty on the Macintosh, filled in Windows); the other set is for OL elements, whose list items can be marked in sequences of Arabic numerals, Roman numerals (uppercase or lowercase), or letters of the alphabet (uppercase or lowercase).

CSS Syntax

```
list-style-type: listStyleType
```

JavaScript Equivalent

```
listStyleType
```

Value

One constant value that is relevant to the type of list container. For UL: circle | disc | square. For OL: decimal | lower-alpha | lower-roman | upper-alpha | upper-roman. OL element sequences are treated as follows:

Type	Example
decimal	1, 2, 3, ...
lower-alpha	a, b, c, ...
lower-roman	i, ii, iii, ...
upper-alpha	A, B, C, ...
upper-roman	I, II, III, ...

Initial Value

disc (for UL); decimal (for OL).

Example

```
UL {list-style-type: circle}
LI {list-style-type: upper-roman}
```

Applies To

DD, DT, LI, OL, and UL elements and any other element assigned the display:list-item style attribute.

Object Model Reference

IE   [window.]document.all.*elementID*.style.listStyleType

margin   NN *4*   IE *4*   CSS *1*

Inherited: No

A shortcut attribute that can set the margin widths of up to four edges of an element with one statement. A margin is space that extends beyond the border of an element to provide extra empty space between adjacent or nested elements, especially those that have border attributes set. You may supply one to four space-delimited margin values. The number of values determines which sides receive the assigned margins.

CSS Syntax

margin: *marginThickness* | auto {1,4}

JavaScript Equivalent

margins()

Value

This attribute accepts one, two, three, or four values, depending on how many and which margins you want to set. Values for *marginThickness* can be *lengths*, percentages of the next outermost element size, or the auto constant. Value quantities and positions are interpreted as follows:

Number of Values	Effect
1	All four margin edges set to value
2	Top and bottom margins set to the first value, right and left margins set to the second value
3	Top margin set to first value, right and left margins set to second value, bottom margin set to third value
4	Top, right, bottom, and left margin set, respectively

Initial Value

0

Example P.highlight {margin: 10px 20px}

Applies To

All elements.

Object Model Reference

IE   [window.]document.all.*elementID*.style.margin

margin-bottom, margin-left, margin-right, margin-top

NN *4*   IE *4*   CSS *1*

Inherited: No

All four attributes set the width of a single margin edge of an element. A margin is space that extends beyond the element's border and is not calculated as part of the element's width or height.

CSS Syntax

```
margin-bottom: marginThickness | auto
margin-left: marginThickness | auto
margin-right: marginThickness | auto
margin-top: marginThickness | auto
```

JavaScript Equivalent

```
marginBottom
marginLeft
marginRight
marginTop
```

Value

Values for *marginThickness* can be *lengths*, percentages of the next outermost element size, or the auto constant.

Initial Value

0

Example
```
BLOCKQUOTE {margin-left: 20; margin-top: 10}
#narrowCol {margin-left: 30%; margin-right: 30%}
```

Applies To

All elements.

Object Model Reference

IE   `[window.]document.all.`*elementID*`.style.marginBottom`
            `[window.]document.all.`*elementID*`.style.marginLeft`
            `[window.]document.all.`*elementID*`.style.marginRight`
            `[window.]document.all.`*elementID*`.style.marginTop`

marks   NN *n/a*   IE *n/a*   CSS *2*

Inherited: n/a

A page context attribute that sets whether the page should be rendered with crop or registration marks outside of the page content area. This attribute must be set within an `@page` rule. See the previous section "At-Rules," for details on deploying this type of style rule.

CSS Syntax

marks: *markType* | none

Value

Available *markType* values are the following constant values: **crop** | **cross**. A **crop** mark shows where pages should be trimmed; a **cross** mark is used for alignment and registration.

Initial Value

Example @page {marks: crop}

Applies To

Page context.

max-height, min-height   NN *n/a*   IE *n/a*   CSS *2*

Inherited: No

These attributes let you establish a minimum and/or maximum height for an element. You can bracket the permissible height of an element regardless of the height caused by the natural flow of the content.

CSS Syntax
```
max-height: length | percentage
min-height: length | percentage
```

Value

See the discussion of length values at the beginning of the chapter. The value may also be a percentage that is calculated relative to the element's container.

Initial Value

0 (min-height); 100% (max-height).

Applies To

All elements.

max-width, min-width

NN *n/a*   IE *n/a*   CSS *2*

Inherited: No

These attributes let you establish a minimum and/or maximum width for an element. You can bracket the permissible width of an element regardless of the width caused by the natural flow of the content within a parent container.

CSS Syntax

```
max-width: length | percentage
min-width: length | percentage
```

Value

See the discussion of length values at the beginning of the chapter. The value may also be a percentage that is calculated relative to the element's container.

Initial Value

0 (min-width); 100% (max-width).

Applies To

All elements.

orphans

NN *n/a*   IE *n/a*   CSS *2*

Inherited: Yes

Sets the minimum number of lines of a paragraph that must be visible at the bottom of a page where a page break occurs. See the `widows` attribute for lines to be displayed at the top of a page after a page break.

CSS Syntax

```
orphans: lineCount
```

Value   An integer of the number of lines.

Initial Value

2

Applies To

Block-level elements.

overflow
NN *n/a*   IE *4*   CSS *2*

Inherited: No

For positioned elements, defines how the element treats content whose rendered dimensions exceed the height and/or width of the container. Except for some types of content that demand a fixed width (a PRE element, for instance), the default behavior of an element is to respect the width attribute setting and handle the issue of overflow in the height of the element.

A setting of visible causes the containing block to expand to allow the full width (if fixed) and height of the content to be displayed. If borders, margins, and padding are set for the element, they are preserved around the expanded content block.

A setting of hidden forces the block to observe the height and width settings, potentially causing the content to be clipped by the size of the block. Borders and padding are preserved, but margins may be lost along the edges that clip the content.

A setting of scroll should generate a set of horizontal and vertical scrollbars inside the rectangle of the content block. The bars become active only if the content actually requires scrolling in any direction. In practice, scrollbars are displayed for this setting in Internet Explorer 4 for Windows, but not on the Macintosh.

A setting of auto should generate scrollbars only if the content in the block requires it. Again, this works correctly in IE 4 Windows, but not in IE 4 Macintosh.

Note that Navigator 4 does not provide direct control over the overflow attribute. It is in a perennial state that sizes the height of a block element to the height of the content of the element. Therefore, it is not practical to create empty blocks (with borders, for instance) in Navigator 4, unless you artificially fill the block with padding (which then negatively affects the display in Internet Explorer).

CSS Syntax

```
overflow: overFlowType
```

Value   Any of the following constants: auto | hidden | scroll | visible.

Initial Value

visible

Example

```
DIV.aside {position: absolute; top: 200px; left: 10px; height: 100px;
width: 150px; overflow: scroll}
```

Applies To

All elements set to position:absolute.

Object Model Reference

IE   [window.]document.all.*elementID*.style.overflow

padding

A shortcut attribute that can set the padding widths of up to four edges of an element with one statement. Padding is space that extends around the content box of an element up to but not including any border that may be specified for the element. Padding picks up the background image or color of its element. As you add padding to an element, you increase the size of the visible rectangle of the element without affecting the content block size. You may supply one to four space-delimited padding values. The number of values determines which sides receive the assigned padding.

CSS Syntax

```
padding: paddingThickness {1,4}
```

JavaScript Equivalent

```
paddings()
```

Value

This attribute accepts one, two, three, or four values, depending on how many and which sides you want to assign padding to. Values for *paddingThickness* can be *lengths* or percentages of the next outermost element size. Value quantities and positions are interpreted as follows:

Number of Values	Effect
1	All four padding edges set to value
2	Top and bottom padding set to the first value, right and left padding set to the second value
3	Top padding set to first value, right and left padding set to second value, bottom padding set to third value
4	Top, right, bottom, and left padding set, respectively

Initial Value

0

Example

```
P.highlight {padding: 10px 20px}
```

Applies To

All elements (CSS and NN); BODY, CAPTION, DIV, IFRAME, MARQUEE, TABLE, TD, TEXTAREA, TR, and elements (IE).

Object Model Reference

IE   [window.]document.all.*elementID*.style.padding

Notes

Be aware that Navigator 4 adds its own three-pixel-wide transparent spacing around all four edges of an element. If the element has padding defined for it, the extra spacing is placed outside of the padding. An element's border then appears outside of the extra spacing. This means that the background image or color of a Navigator element cannot bleed all the way to the borders.

padding-bottom, padding-left, padding-right, padding-top

NN *4*   IE *4*   CSS *1*

Inherited: No

All four attributes set the padding width of a single side of an element. Padding is space that extends around the content box of an element up to but not including any border that may be specified for the element. Padding picks up the background image or color of its element. As you add padding to an element, you increase the size of the visible rectangle of the element without affecting the content block size.

CSS Syntax

```
padding-bottom: paddingThickness
padding-left: paddingThickness
padding-right: paddingThickness
padding-top: paddingThickness
```

JavaScript Equivalent

```
paddingBottom
paddingLeft
paddingRight
paddingTop
```

Value

Values for *paddingThickness* can be *lengths* or percentages of the next outermost container size.

Initial Value

0

Example

```
BLOCKQUOTE {padding-left: 20; padding-top: 10}
#narrowCol {padding-left: 30%; padding-right: 30%}
```

Applies To

All elements (CSS and NN); BODY, CAPTION, DIV, IFRAME, MARQUEE, TABLE, TD, TEXTAREA, TR, and elements (IE).

Object Model Reference

IE   [window.]document.all.*elementID*.style.paddingBottom
      [window.]document.all.*elementID*.style.paddingLeft
      [window.]document.all.*elementID*.style.paddingRight
      [window.]document.all.*elementID*.style.paddingTop

Notes

Be aware that Navigator 4 adds its own three-pixel-wide transparent spacing around all four edges of an element. If the element has padding defined for it, the extra spacing is placed outside of the padding. An element's border then appears outside of the extra spacing. This means that the background image or color of a Navigator element cannot run all the way to the borders.

page-break-after, page-break-before   NN *n/a*   IE 4   CSS 2

Inherited: No

Defines how content should treat a page break around an element when the document is sent to a printer. Page breaks are not rendered in the visual browser as they may be in word processing programs; on screen, long content flows in one continuous scroll.

Page breaks (and related attributes such as `widows` and `orphans`) are handled more fully in CSS2 than as deployed in Internet Explorer 4. Proper handling of pages for printers relies on the CSS2 concept of the *page box*, which is a rectangular region that ultimately reaches a printed page. Page break style attributes help the browser control the precise content of each page box. Without any assistance (or with the `auto` setting), the browser divides pages for printing much as it has in the past by doing a best-fit for the content to fill up as much of each page as there is space for it.

To force a page break above an element, associate a `page-break-before:always` style setting with the element. Similarly, to force a break after an element, use `page-break-after:always`. For example, if you want a special class of BR elements to break after them, you could set up a class selector style rule as follows:

```
<STYLE TYPE="text/css">
BR.pageEnd {page-break-after: always}
</STYLE>
```

Then, whenever you want to force a page break in the document, include the following tag:

```
<BR CLASS="pageEnd">
```

Attribute settings for `left` and `right` assume that the browser is equipped to detect left-facing from right-facing pages for double-sided printing (as specified in CSS2). Because you are likely to set different margins for each side of the gutter, indicating how pages break to start a new section requires forcing sufficient page breaks to plant new sections on the desired page. For example, if you want each H1 element to begin on a right-facing page, you would set a page break style for it as follows:

```
H1 {page-break-before: right}
```

This attribute forces the browser to at least one and at most two page breaks before the H1 element to make sure it starts on a right-facing page. When the browser generates a second page break for the left or right value, it means that the browser generates a blank page box for the second page break.

CSS Syntax

```
page-break-after: breakType
page-break-before: breakType
```

Value

Internet Explorer 4 recognizes four constant values: `always | auto | left | right`. CSS2 adds `avoid`, which urges the browser to avoid breaking the page in that element if at all possible.

Initial Value

`auto`

Example

`DIV.titlePage {page-break-before: always; page-break-after: always}`

Applies To

All elements except inline table elements `TD` and `TH`.

Object Model Reference

IE   `[window.]document.all.elementID.style.pageBreakAfter`
          `[window.]document.all.elementID.style.pageBreakBefore`

Notes

Values of `left` and `right` don't behave properly in Internet Explorer 4. The `always` setting may not always work in IE 4 for Windows but does the job in the Macintosh version.

pause   NN *n/a*   IE *n/a*   CSS *2*

Inherited: No

For aural style sheets, a shorthand attribute for setting both **pause-after** and **pause-before** attributes in one statement. You may supply one or two values for this attribute.

CSS Syntax

`pause:` *time* | *percentage* `{1,2}`

Value

This attribute accepts one or two values, depending on the values you want to assign to the **pause-before** and **pause-after** settings. A single value of the **pause** attribute is applied to both **pause-before** and **pause-after**. When two values are supplied, the first is assigned to **pause-before**; the second is assigned to **pause-after**.

Values for *time* are floating-point numbers followed by either the **ms** (milliseconds) or **s** (seconds) unit identifier. These settings are therefore absolute durations for pauses. Values for *percentage* are inversely proportional to the words-per-minute values of the **speech-rate** attribute setting. Because the **speech-rate** controls how long it takes for a single word (on average), a **pause** setting of **100%** means that a pause has the same duration as a single word; a setting of **50%** would be a pause of one-half the duration of speaking a single word.

Initial Value

Depends on the browser.

Applies To

All elements.

pause-after, pause-before

Inherited: No

For aural style sheets, sets the duration of a pause after or before the current element. You can assign both attributes to the same element to designate pauses before and after the element is spoken.

CSS Syntax

```
pause-after: time | percentage
pause-before: time | percentage
```

Value

Values for *time* are floating-point numbers followed by either the **ms** (milliseconds) or **s** (seconds) unit identifier. These settings are therefore absolute durations for pauses. Values for *percentage* are inversely proportional to the words-per-minute values of the **speech-rate** attribute setting. Because the **speech-rate** controls how long it takes for a single word (on average), a **pause** setting of **100%** means that a pause has the same duration as a single word; a setting of **50%** would be a pause of one-half the duration of speaking a single word.

Initial Value

Depends on the browser.

Applies To

All elements.

pitch

Inherited: No

For aural style sheets, sets the average pitch frequency of the voice used for text-to-speech output.

CSS Syntax

```
pitch: frequency | frequencyConstant
```

Value

A *frequency* value is any positive floating-point number followed by either the **Hz** (Hertz) or **kHz** (kiloHertz) units, as in **500Hz** or **5.5kHz**. Alternatively, you can use any of the following constant values: **x-low** | **low** | **medium** | **high** | **x-high**. As of the CSS2 working draft available for this book, no specific frequency values had yet been assigned to these constants.

Initial Value

```
medium
```

Applies To

All elements.

pitch-range
NN *n/a*   IE *n/a*   CSS *2*

Inherited: Yes

For aural style sheets, sets the range over which the average pitch frequency of a text-to-speech voice varies.

CSS Syntax

```
pitch-range: number
```

Value

Any positive number or zero. A value of 0 is a monotone voice; a value of 50 should offer a normal range; values above 50 might sound animated.

Initial Value

50

Applies To

All elements.

play-during
NN *n/a*   IE *n/a*   CSS *2*

Inherited: No

For aural style sheets, sets the sound mixing properties of a background sound with a text-to-speech rendering of the element's content.

CSS Syntax

```
play-during: uri [mix | repeat] | auto | none
```

Value

The uri value is a link to the sound file to be used as background sound (if desired). Optionally, you can specify that the background sound of the parent element's **play-during** attribute is started and mixed with the current element's background sound. If the background sound's length is shorter than it takes for the element's text to be spoken, the **repeat** constant tells the browser to repeat the sound until the spoken text has finished. A value of **auto** means that the parent element's sound continues to play without interruption. And a value of **none** means that no background sound (from the current or parent element) is heard for this element.

Initial Value

auto

Applies To

All elements.

position

Sets whether the element is positionable, and if so, what type of positionable element it is. The two primary types of positionable elements are set with values `relative` and `absolute`. See Chapter 4, *Adding Dynamic Positioning to Documents*, for details and examples.

CSS Syntax

```
position: positionConstant
```

Value

Browsers and the CSS standard recognize different sets of constant values for this attribute:

Value	NN 4	IE 4	CSS2
absolute	•	•	•
fixed	-	-	•
normal	-	-	•
relative	•	•	•
static	-	•	-

IE 4's `static` value is the same as CSS2's `normal` value: the element is rendered according to its regular inline behavior as an HTML element, generally meaning that any position-oriented attributes (such as `top` and `left`) are ignored by the browser.

Initial Value

`static` (IE 4); `normal` (CSS2); `none` (NN 4).

Applies To

You can apply the `absolute` value to: APPLET, DIV, EMBED, FIELDSET, HR, IFRAME, INPUT, MARQUEE, OBJECT, SPAN, TABLE, and TABLE elements.

You can apply the `relative` value to most other block-level elements.

Object Model Reference

IE   `[window.]document.all.elementID.style.position`

Notes

Navigator 4 treats elements that set the CSS syntax position attribute in the following ways: an absolute-positioned element is turned into the same kind of element as that created as a LAYER element; a relative-positioned element is turned into the same kind of element as that created as an ILAYER element.

richness

For aural style sheets, sets the brightness (stridency) of the voice used in text-to-speech rendering of the element.

CSS Syntax

```
richness: number
```

Value

A positive floating-point number to represent how strident the voice sounds. A value of 50 is normal. Lower values produce a softer, mellower voice; higher values produce a louder, more forceful voice.

Initial Value

50

Applies To

All elements.

right   NN *n/a*   IE *n/a*   CSS *2*

Inherited: No

For positionable elements, defines the position of the right edge of an element box (content plus padding, border, and/or margin) relative to the right edge of the next outermost block content container. When the element is relative-positioned, the offset is based on the right edge of the inline location of where the element would normally appear in the content.

CSS Syntax

```
right: length | percentage | auto
```

Value

See the discussion about length values at the beginning of this chapter. Negative lengths may be allowed in some contexts, but be sure to test the results on all browsers. You may also specify a percentage value, which is calculated based on the width of the next outermost container. The setting of auto lets the browser determine the right offset of the element box on its naturally flowing offset within the containing box.

Initial Value

auto

Applies To

All elements.

row-span   NN *n/a*   IE *n/a*   CSS *2*

Inherited: No

Sets the number of rows to be spanned by a table cell, row, or row group. Analogous to the ROWSPAN attribute of a TD or TH element.

CSS Syntax

```
row-span: integer
```

Value   Any positive integer representing the number of rows.

Initial Value

1

Example   #tallDrink {row-span: 3}

Applies To

TD and TH elements and any other cell type of element.

size
NN *n/a*   IE *n/a*   CSS *2*
Inherited: n/a

Sets the size and/or orientation of a page box. Intended primarily for printed page formatting, the settings may not affect how content is cropped or oriented on the video screen. This attribute is set within an @page declaration.

CSS Syntax

```
size: [length {1,2}] auto | portrait | landscape
```

Value

If you specify one or two *length* values, the page box becomes "absolute" regardless of the paper sheet size; without specific *length* values, the page box is sized relative to the selected paper sheet size. If you supply only one length value, it is applied to both the width and height of the page box; if two values, the first controls the page box width and the second controls the page box height. Bear in mind that printers frequently impose a minimum margin around the rendered page box. Even when the size attribute is set to auto, you can add more breathing space around the page box by adding a margin attribute to the @page declaration.

Initial Value

auto

Example   @page{size: landscape}

Applies To

Page context.

speak
NN *n/a*   IE *n/a*   CSS *2*
Inherited: Yes

For aural style sheets, specifies whether a browser equipped for text-to-speech should speak the element's content. If so, whether the speech should be as words or spelled out character-by-character.

CSS Syntax

```
speak: speechType
```

Value

Three possible constant values: none | normal | spell-out. A value of none means that speech is turned off. The browser does not delay over the duration of the speech and any specified pauses (see the volume:silent attribute value). A value of normal turns on speech and reads the text as words. A value of spell-out turns on speech and reads the content letter-by-letter (certainly applicable to ABBR and ACRONYM elements).

Initial Value

normal

Applies To

All elements.

speak-date   NN *n/a*   IE *n/a*   CSS *2*

Inherited: Yes

Note that the details on this attribute are very preliminary. For aural style sheets, specifies the sequence in which date components (month, day, and year) are spoken to account for regional preferences.

CSS Syntax

speak-date: *dateType*

Value

Three possible constant values: mdy | dmy | ymd. A value of mdy signifies a sequence of month-day-year. A value of dmy signifies a sequence of day-month-year. A value of ymd signifies a sequence of year-month-day.

Initial Value

Depends on browser localization.

Applies To

All elements.

speak-header   NN *n/a*   IE *n/a*   CSS *2*

Inherited: Yes

For text-to-speech-capable browsers, specifies whether the browser calls out the name of a table cell's header prior to the cell's value every time that value is read aloud or just one time for all adjacently read cells that share the same header (e.g., navigating downward through a table column).

CSS Syntax

speak-header: *headerFrequency*

Value   Two possible constant values: once | always.

Initial Value

once

Applies To

All elements.

Notes

The CSS2 working draft indicates that one or more additional attributes will provide greater control over designating more precisely which header cell is to be spoken.

speak-numeral

Inherited: Yes

Note that the details on this attribute are very preliminary. For aural style sheets, sets whether numbers are to be read as individual numerals ("One Four Two") or as full numbers (e.g., "One hundred forty two"). The language used for the spoken numbers is set with the element's LANG attribute.

CSS Syntax

```
speak-numeral: numeralType
```

Value   Three possible constant values: digits | continuous | none.

Initial Value

Applies To

All elements.

speak-punctuation

Inherited: Yes

Note that the details on this attribute are very preliminary. For aural style sheets, sets whether punctuation symbols should be read aloud ("period") or interpreted as the language's natural pauses for the various symbols.

CSS Syntax

```
speak-punctuation: punctuationType
```

Value

Two possible constant values: code | none. A value of code means that a symbol name is spoken when the symbol is encountered in element text.

Initial Value

Applies To

All elements.

speak-time

NN *n/a*   IE *n/a*   CSS *2*

Inherited: Yes

Note that the details on this attribute are very preliminary. For aural style sheets, sets whether time content is spoken in 12- or 24-hour time.

CSS Syntax

speak-time: *TimeType*

Value   Three possible constant values: 12 | 24 | none.

Initial Value

Applies To

All elements.

speech-rate

NN *n/a*   IE *n/a*   CSS *2*

Inherited: Yes

For aural style sheets, sets the number of words per minute of the text-to-speech output.

CSS Syntax

speech-rate: *wordsPerSecond* | *speedConstant*

Value

A *wordsPerSecond* value is any positive floating-point number with no unit appended. Alternatively, you can use any of the following constant values: x-slow | slow | medium | fast | x-fast | slower | faster. As of the CSS2 working draft available for this book, no specific speed values had yet been assigned to these constants, and no increment had been determined for slower and faster.

Initial Value

medium

Applies To

All elements.

stress

NN *n/a*   IE *n/a*   CSS *2*

Inherited: Yes

For aural style sheets, sets the amount of stress (inflection) in the spoken voice.

CSS Syntax

stress: *stressLevel*

Value

A *stressLevel* value is any positive floating-point number with no unit appended. A value of 50 is normal.

Initial Value

50

Applies To

All elements.

table-layout

NN *n/a*   IE *n/a*   CSS *2*

Inherited: No

Determines whether the browser uses computed heights and widths of the entire table's data to begin rendering the table or relies on the **TABLE** element's size attributes and uses the first row's cell widths to begin rendering table content. When the attribute is set to auto, the browser must load all of the table cells and their content before the first row of data can be rendered, causing a brief delay in drawing the table. Setting the value to fixed allows table rendering to begin sooner, which is helpful for large tables.

CSS Syntax

table-layout: *layoutType*

Value   Two possible constant values: auto | fixed.

Initial Value

auto

Applies To

TABLE elements.

text-align

NN *4*   IE *4*   CSS *1*

Inherited: Yes

Determines the horizontal alignment of text within an element. This attribute is inherited, so it can be set for a container to impact all nested elements, such as a P element within a DIV element. Values of center, left, and right are supported by Navigator 4 and Internet Explorer 4. The value of justify is not a CSS requirement, and implementation in Version 4 browsers is spotty (see Notes).

CSS Syntax

text-align: *alignment*

JavaScript Equivalent

textAlign

Value

One of the four constants: center | justify | left | right.

Initial Value

Depends on browser (left in both Navigator 4 and Internet Explorer 4, but this is not a CSS requirement).

Example

```
P.rightHand {text-align: right}
BLOCKQUOTE {text-align: center}
```

Applies To

Block-level elements.

Object Model Reference

IE   [window.]document.all.*elementID*.style.textAlign

Notes

If you assign the justify value, text is indeed justified in Navigator 4 for the Macintosh and Internet Explorer 4 for Windows. The value is treated as the left setting in Navigator 4 for Windows and IE 4 for Macintosh.

text-decoration

NN 4   IE 4   CSS 1

Inherited: No

Specifies additions to the text content of the element in the form of underlines, strikethroughs, overlines, and (in Navigator and CSS) blinking. You may specify more than one decoration style by supplying values in a space-delimited list. Although Internet Explorer 4 accepts the blink value, it does not blink the text. Navigator 4, on the other hand, does not recognize the overline decoration. Text decoration has an unusual parent-child relationship. Values are not inherited, but the effect of a decoration carries over to nested items. Therefore, unless otherwise overridden, an underlined P element underlines a nested B element within, for example.

CSS Syntax

text-decoration: *decorationStyle* | none

JavaScript Equivalent

textDecoration

Value

In addition to none, any of the following four constants: blink | line-through | overline | underline. Navigator 4 does not observe the overline value.

Initial Value

Example DIV.highlight {text-decoration: underline}

Applies To

All elements.

Object Model Reference

IE   [window.]document.all.*elementID*.style.textDecoration
        [window.]document.all.*elementID*.style.textDecorationBlink
        [window.]document.all.*elementID*.style.textDecorationLineThrough
        [window.]document.all.*elementID*.style.textDecorationNone
        [window.]document.all.*elementID*.style.textDecorationOverLine
        [window.]document.all.*elementID*.style.textDecorationUnderline

text-indent

NN *4*   IE *4*   CSS *1*

Inherited: Yes

Sets the size of indenting of the first line of a block of inline text (such as a P element). Only the first line is affected by this setting. A negative value can be used to outdent the first line, but be sure the text does not run beyond the left edge of the browser window or frame.

CSS Syntax

text-indent: *length* | *percentage*

JavaScript Equivalent

textIndent

Value

See the discussion about length values at the beginning of this chapter. Negative lengths may be allowed in some contexts, but be sure to test the results on all browsers. You may also specify a percentage value, which is calculated based on the width of the next outermost container.

Initial Value

0

Example

BODY {text-indent: 2em}
P.firstGraphs {text-indent: 0}

Applies To

Block-level elements.

Object Model Reference

IE   [window.]document.all.*elementID*.style.textIndent

Notes

Internet Explorer 4 for the Macintosh does not respond to the `text-indent` attribute properly.

text-shadow

Inherited: No

Sets shadow effects for the text of the current element. A text element can have more than one shadow, and each shadow can have its own color, vertical offset, horizontal offset, and blur radius. Each shadow exists in its own minilayer, stacked with the first shadow specification at the bottom of the heap. Even so, text shadows move with their text element as a unit when the `z-index` attribute of the element is set or modified. Values for each shadow are space-delimited, and multiple shadow value sets are comma-delimited.

CSS Syntax

```
text-shadow: [color] horizLength vertLength blurRadiusLength,
    [[color] horizLength vertLength blurRadiusLength] | none
```

Value

If you omit the *color* attribute value, the shadow uses the element's `color` property value (which may, itself, be inherited). The *color* attribute can be placed before or after whatever length values are set for a shadow. See the discussion of color values at the beginning of this chapter. Values for *horizLength* and *vertLength* are length values (see the beginning of this chapter), and their sign indicates the direction the shadow offset takes from the element text. For the *horizLength* value, a positive value places the shadow to the right of the element; a negative value to the left. For the *vertLength* value, a positive value places the shadow below the text; a negative value above. A blur radius is a length value (see the beginning of this chapter) that specifies the extent of the shadow from the edge of the text characters.

Initial Value

Applies To

All elements.

text-transform

Inherited: Yes

Controls the capitalization of the element's text. When a value other than **none** is assigned to this attribute, the cases of all letters in the source text are arranged by the style sheet, overriding the case of the source text characters.

CSS Syntax

```
text-transform: caseType | none
```

JavaScript Equivalent

`textTransform`

Value

A value of `none` allows the case of the source text to be rendered as-is. Other available constant values are: `capitalize | lowercase | uppercase`. A value of `capitalize` sets the first character of every word to uppercase. Values `lowercase` and `uppercase` render all characters of the element text in their respective cases.

Initial Value

Example

`H2 {text-transform: capitalize}`

Applies To

All elements.

Object Model Reference

IE   `[window.]document.all.elementID.style.textTransform`

top   NN 4   IE 4   CSS 2

Inherited: No

For positionable elements, defines the position of the top edge of an element box (content plus top padding, border, and/or margin) relative to the top edge of the next outermost block content container.

CSS Syntax

`top:` *length* `|` *percentage* `|` `auto`

JavaScript Equivalent

`top`

Value

See the discussion about length values at the beginning of this chapter. Negative lengths may be allowed in some contexts, but be sure to test the results on all browsers. You may also specify a percentage value, which is calculated based on the height of the next outermost container. The setting of `auto` lets the browser determine the top offset of the element box on its naturally flowing offset within the containing box.

Initial Value

auto

Example

```
H1 {position: relative; top: 2em}
#logo {position: absolute; left: 80px; top: 30px}
```

Applies To

All elements.

Object Model Reference

IE   [window.]document.all.*elementID*.style.offsetTop

vertical-align NN *n/a*   IE *4*   CSS *1*

Inherited: No

There are two sets of values for this attribute, and they affect different characteristics of the inline element to which they are applied. The major point of reference is that an inline element has its own line box that holds its content. Two values, top and bottom, affect how the text is rendered within the line box. The settings bring the text flush with the top or bottom of the box, respectively.

Application of this attribute is not limited to inline spans of text. Images and tables can use this style attribute. All other settings for vertical-align affect how the entire element box is vertically positioned relative to text content of the parent element. The default value, baseline, means that the line box is positioned such that the baselines of both the line box's text (or very bottom of an element such as an IMG) and the parent text are even. That's how an EM element can be its own line box element but still look as though it flows on the same baseline as its containing P element. The rest of the attribute constant values (and percentage or length) determine where the element's line box is set with respect to the parent line.

CSS Syntax

vertical-align: *vertAlignType* | *length* | *percentage*

Value

Two constant values apply to alignment of text within the element itself: bottom | top.

Six constant values apply to alignment of the element's line box relative to the surrounding text line (of the parent element): baseline | middle | sub | super | text-bottom | text-top. A value of baseline keeps the baseline of the element and parent element line even. A value of middle aligns the vertical midpoint of the element with the baseline plus one-half the x-height of the parent element's font. Values of sub and super shift the element into position for subscript and superscript but do not by themselves create a true subscript or superscript in that no adjustment to the font size is made with this attribute. A value of text-bottom aligns the bottom of the element with the bottom of the font line of the parent element text; a value of text-top does the same with the tops of the element and parent.

Initial Value

baseline

Example SPAN.sup {vertical-align: super; text-size: smaller}

Applies To

Inline elements only.

Object Model Reference

IE   [window.]document.all.*elementID*.style.verticalAlign

Notes

Internet Explorer 4 recognizes only the **sub** and **super** constant values.

visibility   NN 4   IE 4   CSS 2

For positioned elements, controls whether the element is rendered on the page. An element hidden via the `visibility` attribute preserves space in the document where the element normally appears. If you prefer surrounding content to cinch up the space left by a hidden element, see the `display` attribute.

The `visibility` attribute is inherited when its value is set to `inherit`. This setting means that if the parent is hidden, the child is also hidden. But, by setting the child's `visibility` attribute to `visible`, you can still keep the parent hidden while showing the child independently.

CSS Syntax

visibility: *visibilityType*

JavaScript Equivalent

visibility

Value

Navigator 4 features a set of constants that don't always match those of Internet Explorer 4 and CSS, but Navigator 4 does recognize the CSS standards:

Value	NN 4	IE 4	CSS2
hide	•	-	-
hidden	•	•	•
inherit	•	•	•
show	•	-	-
visible	•	•	•

Use the CSS attribute constants to maintain cross-browser compatibility. There have been reports of Navigator 4 not responding properly to the CSS values when scripting an element's visibility. For dynamically changing visibility of a positioned element, you might feel safer with some of the cross-browser API strategies detailed in Chapter 4.

Initial Value

inherit

Example #congrats {visibility: hidden}

Applies To

All elements whose **position** style attribute is set.

CSS Reference

Object Model Reference

IE   `[window.]document.all.`*`elementID`*`.style.visibility`

voice-family

Inherited: Yes

For aural style sheets, sets the voice family names the aural browser should try to use for speaking the content. Multiple, comma-delimited values are accepted. This feature is analogous to the `font-family` setting for visual browsers.

CSS Syntax

`voice-family:` *`voiceFamilyName`* `[,` *`voiceFamilyName`* `[, ...]]`

Value

A *voiceFamilyName* may be the identifier for a voice type provided by the aural browser or a generic voice name (yet to be determined by the W3C). As with `font-family` settings, you should specify multiple voice types, starting with the more specific and ending with the most generic for the type of speech you want for the element's content.

Initial Value

Depends on browser.

Applies To

All elements.

volume

Inherited: Yes

For aural style sheets, sets the dynamic range (softness/loudness) of the spoken element. Because normal speech has inflections that prevent an absolute volume to apply at all times, the volume attribute sets the median volume.

CSS Syntax

`volume:` *`number`* `|` *`percentage`* `|` *`volumeConstant`*

Value

A volume *number* value is any number. A value of zero should represent the minimum audible level for the equipment and ambient noise environment; a value of `100` should represent the maximum comfortable level under the same conditions. A *percentage* value is calculated relative to the parent element's volume attribute setting. Alternative settings include the following constants (and their representative values): `silent` (no sound) | `x-soft` (0) | `soft` (25) | `medium` (50) | `loud` (75) | `x-loud` (100).

Initial Value

`medium`

Applies To

All elements.

white-space   NN *4*   IE *n/a*   CSS *1*

Inherited: Yes

Sets how the browser should render whitespace (extra character spaces and carriage returns) that is part of the element's source code. Under normal circumstances, HTML ignores extra whitespace and thus collapses the rendered content around such space. For example, only single spaces are preserved between words and BR elements are required to force a line break within a paragraph. A whitespace attribute setting of pre treats whitespace as if you had surrounded the element in a PRE element. But although browsers have a tradition of rendering PRE elements in a monospace font, the look of an ordinary element set to white-space:pre preserves its font characteristics.

CSS Syntax

```
white-space: whiteSpaceType
```

JavaScript Equivalent

```
whiteSpace
```

Value

One of three constants: normal | nowrap | pre. A value of normal allows regular HTML treatment of whitespace to rule. A value of nowrap (not available in Navigator 4) tells the browser to ignore line breaks in the source text (in case the author breaks up lines for readability in the editor) and break them on the page only where there are explicit HTML line breaks (with a BR element, for example). A value of pre has the browser honor all whitespace entered by the author in the source content, without adjusting any font settings of the element.

Initial Value

```
normal
```

Example DIV.example {white-space: pre}

Applies To

Block-level elements.

widows   NN *n/a*   IE *n/a*   CSS *2*

Inherited: Yes

Sets the minimum number of lines of a paragraph that must be visible at the top of a page after a page break occurs. See the orphans attribute for lines to be displayed at the bottom of a page before a page break.

CSS Syntax

```
widows: lineCount
```

Value   An integer of the number of lines.

Initial Value

2

Applies To

Block-level elements.

width   NN *4*   IE *4*   CSS *1*

Inherited: No

Sets the width of a block-level or replaced element's content (exclusive of borders, padding, and margins). Internet Explorer 4 applies the width attribute only to selected elements and absolute-positioned elements (which means DIV wrappers around other types of elements), but CSS2 recommends application to all block-level and replaceable elements as well.

Navigator 4 and Internet Explorer 4 react differently to settings of the width style attribute. One thing they agree on is that if the content requires more width than is specified for the attribute (an IMG element's width, for instance), the content requirements override the attribute value (use the clipping region to truncate the width of the viewport for the element if you need to). But if the window is narrower than the specified width, Navigator tends to shrink the width of the element to fit the window width (to a point) so that the window doesn't need to scroll horizontally; IE 4, on the other hand, preserves the element's width setting regardless of the window width.

A number of other discrepancies between browsers (and between operating system versions of the same browser) plague the width attribute. For example, if you create a DIV element whose width is 300px and nest a P element inside whose width is set to 200px, Navigator 4 respects the narrower width of the P element, but Internet Explorer 4 causes the P element to fill the 300-pixel width of the DIV container. You may also encounter varying behavior of parent and child elements when both have borders set. In Internet Explorer 4 for the Macintosh, some edges of the parent border are obscured.

CSS Syntax

width: *length* | *percentage* | auto

JavaScript Equivalent

width

Value

See the discussion about length values at the beginning of this chapter. You may also specify a percentage value, which is calculated based on the width of the next outermost container. The setting of auto lets the browser determine the width of the element box based on the amount of space required to display the content within the current window width.

Initial Value

auto

Example

```
DIV#announce {position: relative; left: 30; width: 240}
TEXTAREA {width: 80%}
```

Applies To

Navigator 4: block-level and replaced elements.

Internet Explorer 4: APPLET, DIV, EMBED, FIELDSET, HR, IFRAME, IMG, INPUT, MARQUEE, OBJECT, SELECT, SPAN, TABLE, and TEXTAREA elements.

CSS2: all elements except nonreplaced inline elements, table rows, and row group elements.

Object Model Reference

IE   [window.]document.all.*elementID*.style.width

word-spacing

NN *n/a*   IE *n/a*   CSS *1*

Inherited: Yes

Sets the spacing between words when the text is not under external word spacing constraints (e.g., an align attribute set to justify).

CSS Syntax

```
word-spacing: length | normal
```

Value

A value of normal lets the browser handle word spacing according to its rendering calculations. See the discussion about length values at the beginning of this chapter.

Initial Value

normal

Applies To

All elements.

z-index

NN *4*   IE *4*   CSS *2*

Inherited: No

For a positioned element, sets the stacking order relative to other elements within the same parent container. See Chapter 4 for details on relationships of element layering amid multiple containers.

CSS Syntax

```
z-index: integer | auto
```

JavaScript Equivalent

zIndex

Value

Any integer value. A value of auto is the same as a value of zero. When all elements in the same parent container have the same z-index value, the stacking order is determined by element source code order.

Initial Value

auto

Example   DIV#instrux {position: absolute; left: 50;top: 70;z-index: 2}

Applies To

Any positioned element.

Object Model Reference

IE   [window.]document.all.*elementID*.style.zIndex

11

JavaScript Core Language Reference

The previous chapters in the reference part of the book have covered every aspect of Dynamic HTML authoring that affects elements, objects, and styles—the pieces that are often visible on the page. The one part yet to be covered is the scripting "glue" that makes it possible to dynamically access and control the items detailed up to this point. This chapter covers the core scripting language features that apply to cross-browser application development. This means that VBScript, ActiveX controls, and Java classes accessible through LiveConnect are intentionally omitted here in favor of the core language that has become an industry standard.

As described in Chapter 1, *The State of the Art*, the JavaScript language was a Netscape invention. Microsoft's version of the language is called JScript. But a browser-neutral version of the language has been given the nod as a common denominator standard for all JavaScript-derived languages: ECMAScript. There is a great deal of agreement in the implementation of the core elements of this scripting language among browser makers and the ECMA standards group. The biggest challenge for writing core language code (i.e., code that is independent of the scriptable document object model) is knowing what version of the language is supported by which versions of the browser. In the entries for this chapter, you can see at a glance which browser version first supported every core language object, property, method, function, operator, and control statement.

Internet Explorer JScript Versions

For the core scripting language in Internet Explorer, it is not enough to know which browser version introduced support for a particular object or property. Microsoft separates the core language functionality from the browser itself by implementing each language as a *.dll* file that can be updated and swapped in without a change in the browser version.

The first shipping versions of Internet Explorer 3 came with the first version of the *Jscript.dll* file. Later, while IE 3 was still the shipping product, Microsoft offered an upgrade of the *Jscript.dll* file to Version 2. This new version incorporated several new features to the core language. Internet Explorer 4 shipped with Version 3 of the *Jscript.dll* file. Unfortunately, you can't deduce from the most likely place you'd look—the `navigator.userAgent` property—which *Jscript.dll* file is installed in the browser. Internet Explorer does provide a pair of global functions (`ScriptEngineMajorVersion()` and `ScriptEngineMinorVersion()`) that you can use to determine what level of JScript is installed in the browser. This function, however, was not available in *Jscript.dll* Version 1 (currently running in many versions of IE 3), so this test is not foolproof either.

In the listings within this chapter, the versions listed for IE are shown as J1, J2, or J3, corresponding to Versions 1, 2, and 3 of the *Jscript.dll* file.

About Static Objects

Unlike the heavily object-oriented Java language, there is little of the traditional object-oriented vernacular in the object-based JavaScript language. As a result, scripters tend not to think in terms of static objects and object instantiation. But some of that does take place behind the scenes.

Some core language objects act as if they were true static objects. The **Math** object is a good example; it contains a number of properties and methods that scripts use without ever having to "peel off" an instance of that object to do some math.

In contrast, the **Date** object is a static object that generates an instance of itself each time someone creates a new date:

```
var now = new Date()
```

In this example, the `now` variable is an instance of the **Date** object—a snapshot of the object frozen in time. That instance provides access to many methods that let scripts get pieces of date and time, as well as set new values to those pieces. The methods actually "live" in the static object, but you access them through the instance that holds a value that can be influenced by those methods (yes, these methods are inherited, but JavaScript doesn't use this term much). Only on rare occasions do scripts ever need to look directly at the static **Date** object for other kinds of assistance (such as the `getTimezoneOffset()` method).

Most objects are either all static (**Math**) or completely suppress themselves from the scene once you create instances you work with (**String**, **Array**, **Number**). Only a few objects operate in both modes, depending on whether you need the data of an instance of the object or one of the static properties or methods. You've seen how the **Date** object performs double duty. The **RegExp** object and Navigator's **Event** object also perform this double duty; instances of these objects are created for you. At the same time, you can access static objects (such as **String** and **Array**) to modify their basic behavior by assigning new properties and methods to their prototype (via the **prototype** property).

Core Objects

Array   NN *3*   IE *J2*   ECMA *1*

An array is an ordered collection of one or more pieces of data. JavaScript array entries may be of any data type, including different data types in the same array. Each entry in an array has an index assigned to it. The default behavior is for the index to be a zero-based integer (the first entry has an index of zero). An index value may also be a string. Accessing an entry in an array requires the name of the array and the index in square brackets:

```
cars[0]
cars["Ford"]
```

The number of entries in a JavaScript array (its length) can vary over time. To add a new entry to an array, assign the value to the next higher array index value:

```
cars[cars.length] = "Bentley"
```

Internet Explorer first recognized the Array object in Version 2 of the *Jscript.dll* for Internet Explorer 3.

Creating an Array
```
var myArray = new Array()
var myArray = new Array(sizeInteger)
var myArray = new Array(element0, element1, ..., elementN)
```

Properties
length   prototype

Methods
concat()	push()	slice()
join()	reverse()	sort()
pop()	shift()	unshift()

length   NN *3*   IE *J2*   ECMA *1*
Read/Write

A count of the number of entries stored in the array. If the constructor function used to create the array specified a preliminary length, the length property reflects that amount, even if data does not occupy every slot.

Example
```
for (var i = 0; i < myArray.length; i++) {
    ...
}
```

Value   Integer.

prototype

NN *3*   IE *J2*   ECMA *1*

Read/Write

A property of the static **Array** object. Use the **prototype** property to assign new properties and methods to future instances of arrays created in the current document. For example, the following function creates a return-delimited list of elements in an array in reverse order:

```
function formatAsList() {
    var output = ""
    for (var i = this.length - 1; i >= 0; i--) {
        output += this[i] + "\n"
    }
    alert(output)
}
```

To give an array that power, assign this function reference to a prototype property whose name you want to use as the method to invoke this function:

```
Array.prototype.showReverseList = formatAsList
```

If a script creates an array at this point:

```
var stooges = new Array("Moe", "Larry", "Curly", "Shemp")
```

the new array has the **showReverseList()** method available to it. To invoke the method, the call is:

```
stooges.showReverseList()
```

You can add properties the same way. These allow you to attach information about the array (its creation time, for example) without disturbing the ordered sequence of array data. When a new document loads into the window or frame, the static **Array** object starts fresh again.

Example

```
Array.prototype.created = ""
```

Value   Any data, including function references.

concat()

NN *4*   IE *J3*   ECMA *n/a*

concat(*array2*)

Returns an array that combines the current array object with a second array object specified as the method parameter:

```
var combinedArray = myArray1.concat(myArray2)
```

Neither of the original arrays is altered in the process.

Returned Value

An **Array** object.

Parameters

`array2`   Any JavaScript array.

join()   NN *3*   IE *J2*   ECMA *1*

`join("delimiterString")`

Returns a string consisting of a list of items (as strings) contained by an array. The delimiter character(s) between items is set by the parameter to the method.

Returned Value

String.

Parameters

`delimiterString`

Any string of characters. Nonalphanumeric characters must use URL-encoded equivalents (`%0D` for carriage return).

pop()   NN *4*   IE *n/a*   ECMA *n/a*

Returns the value of the last item in an array and removes it from the array. The length of the array decreases by one.

Returned Value

Any JavaScript value.

Parameters

None.

push()   NN *4*   IE *n/a*   ECMA *n/a*

`push(value)`

Appends an item to the end of an array. The length of the array increases by one.

Returned Value

The value pushed into the array.

Parameters

`value`   Any JavaScript value.

reverse()   NN *3*   IE *J2*   ECMA *1*

Reverses the order of items in the array and returns a copy of the array in the new order. The original order of the array is changed after this method executes.

Returned Value

An `Array` object.

Parameters

None.

shift()   NN *4*   IE *n/a*   ECMA *n/a*

Returns the value of the first item in an array and removes it from the array. The length of the array decreases by one.

Returned Value

Any JavaScript value.

Parameters

None.

slice()   NN *4*   IE *J3*   ECMA *n/a*

```
slice(startIndex[, endIndex])
```

Returns an array that is a subset of contiguous items from the main array. Parameters determine where the selection begins and ends.

Returned Value

An **Array** object.

Parameters

startIndex

    A zero-based integer of the first item of the subset from the current array.

endIndex

    An optional zero-based integer of the last item of the subset from the current array. If omitted, the selection is made from the startIndex position to the end of the array.

sort()   NN *3*   IE *J3*   ECMA *1*

```
sort([compareFunction])
```

Sorts the values of the array either by the ASCII value of string versions of each array entry or according to a comparison function of your own design. The **sort()** method repeatedly invokes the comparison function, passing two values from the array. The comparison function should return an integer value, which is interpreted by the **sort()** function as follows:

Value	Meaning
<0	The second passed value should sort above the first value.
0	The sort order of the two values should not change.
>0	The first passed value should sort above the second.

The following comparison function sorts values of an array in numerical (instead of ASCII) order:

```
function doCompare(a, b) {
    return a - b
}
```

To sort an array by this function, the statement is:

```
myArray.sort(doCompare)
```

By the time the `sort()` method has completed its job, it has sent all values to the doCompare() function two values at a time and sorted the values on whether the first value is larger than the second.

Not only does the `sort()` method rearrange the values in the array, but it also returns a copy of the sorted array.

Returned Value

An `Array` object.

Parameters

`compareFunction`
> A reference to a function that receives two parameters and returns an integer result.

unshift()   NN *4*   IE *n/a*   ECMA *n/a*

`unshift(value)`

Inserts an item at the beginning of an array. The length of the array increases by one, and the method returns the new length of the array.

Returned Value

Integer.

Parameters

`value`   Any JavaScript value.

Boolean   NN *3*   IE *J2*   ECMA *1*

A `Boolean` object represents any value that evaluates to **true** or **false**. By and large, you don't have to worry about the `Boolean` object because the browsers automatically create such objects for you when you assign a **true** or **false** value to a variable.

Creating a Boolean Object

```
var myValue = new Boolean()
var myValue = new Boolean(BooleanValue)
var myValue = BooleanValue
```

Properties

`prototype`

Methods

`toString()`   `valueOf()`

prototype

A property of the static `Boolean` object. Use the `prototype` property to assign new properties and methods to future instances of a Boolean value created in the current document. See the `Array.prototype` property description for examples. There is little need to create new prototype properties or methods for the `Boolean` object.

Example `Boolean.prototype.author = "DG"`

Value   Any data, including function references.

toString()

Returns the object's value as a string data type. You don't need this method in practice, because the browsers automatically convert Boolean values to strings when they are needed for display in alert dialogs or in-document rendering.

Returned Value

`"true"` | `"false"`

Parameters

None.

valueOf()

Returns the object's value as a Boolean data type. You don't need this method when you create `Boolean` objects by simple value assignment.

Returned Value

Boolean value: `true` | `false`.

Parameters

None.

Date

The `Date` object is a static object that generates instances by way of several constructor functions. Each instance of a `Date` object is a snapshot of the date and time, measured in milliseconds relative to zero hours on January 1, 1970. Negative millisecond values represent time before that date; positive values represent time since that date.

The typical way to work with dates is to generate a new `Date` object instance, either for now or for a specific date and time (past or future, using the client local time). Then use the myriad of available date methods to get or set components of that time (e.g., minutes, hours, date, month). Browsers internally store a date as the millisecond value at Coordinated Universal Time (UTC, which is essentially the same as Greenwich Mean Time, or GMT). When you ask a browser for a component of that time, it automatically converts the value to the local time zone of the browser based on the client computer's control panel setting for the clock and time zone. If the control panel is set incorrectly, time and date calculations may go awry.

Early versions of scriptable browsers had numerous bugs when working with the Date object. One resource that explains the ins and outs of working with the Date object (and bugs) can be found at *http://developer.netscape.com/viewsource/goodman_dateobject.html.*

Creating a Date Object

```
var now = new Date()
var myDate = new Date("month dd, yyyy hh:mm:ss")
var myDate = new Date("month dd, yyyy")
var myDate = new Date(yy, mm, dd, hh, mm, ss)
var myDate = new Date(yy, mm, dd)
var myDate = new Date(milliseconds)
```

Properties

prototype

Methods

getDate()	getUTCMilliseconds()	setUTCDate()
getDay()	getUTCMinutes()	setUTCFullYear()
getFullYear()	getUTCMonth()	setUTCHours()
getHours()	getUTCSeconds()	setUTCMilliseconds()
getMilliseconds()	getYear()	setUTCMinutes()
getMinutes()	parse()	setUTCMonth()
getMonth()	setDate()	setUTCSeconds()
getSeconds()	setFullYear()	setYear()
getTime()	setHours()	toGMTString()
getTimezoneOffset()	setMilliseconds()	toLocaleString()
getUTCDate()	setMinutes()	toString()
getUTCDay()	setMonth()	toUTCString()
getUTCFullYear()	setSeconds()	UTC()
getUTCHours()	setTime()	valueOf()

prototype   NN *3*   IE *J2*   ECMA *1*

Read/Write

A property of the static Date object. Use the **prototype** property to assign new properties and methods to future instances of a Date value created in the current document. See the **Array.prototype** property description for examples.

Example   Date.prototype.author = "DG"

Value   Any data, including function references.

getDate()   NN *2*   IE *J1*   ECMA *1*

Returns the date within the month specified by the Date object.

Returned Value

Integer between 1 and 31.

Parameters

None.

getDay()   NN *2*   IE *J1*   ECMA *1*

Returns an integer corresponding to a day of the week for the date specified by the Date object.

Returned Value

Integer between 0 and 6. Sunday is 0, Monday is 1, and Saturday is 6.

Parameters

None.

getFullYear()   NN *4*   IE *J3*   ECMA *1*

Returns all digits of the year for the date specified by the Date object.

Returned Value

Integer. Navigator goes no lower than zero. Internet Explorer returns negative year values.

Parameters

None.

getHours()   NN *2*   IE *J1*   ECMA *1*

Returns a zero-based integer corresponding to the hours of the day for the date specified by the Date object. The 24-hour time system is used.

Returned Value

Integer between 0 and 23.

Parameters

None.

getMilliseconds()   NN *4*   IE *J3*   ECMA *1*

Returns a zero-based integer corresponding to the number of milliseconds past the seconds value of the date specified by the Date object.

Returned Value

Integer between 0 and 999.

Parameters

None.

getMinutes()

Returns a zero-based integer corresponding to the minute value for the hour and date specified by the Date object.

Returned Value

Integer between 0 and 59.

Parameters

None.

getMonth()

Returns a zero-based integer corresponding to the month value for the date specified by the Date object. That this method's values are zero-based frequently confuses scripters at first.

Returned Value

Integer between 0 and 11. January is 0, February is 1, and December is 11.

Parameters

None.

getSeconds()

Returns a zero-based integer corresponding to the seconds past the nearest full minute for the date specified by the Date object.

Returned Value

Integer between 0 and 59.

Parameters

None.

getTime()

Returns a zero-based integer corresponding to the number of milliseconds since January 1, 1970, to the date specified by the Date object.

Returned Value

Integer.

Parameters

None.

getTimezoneOffset()

Returns a zero-based integer corresponding to the number of minutes difference between GMT and the client computer's clock. Time zones to the west of GMT are positive values; time zones to the east are negative values. Numerous bugs plagued this method in earlier browsers, especially Macintosh versions.

Returned Value

Integer between -720 and 720.

Parameters

None.

getUTCDate()

Returns the date within the month specified by the Date object but in the UTC time stored internally by the browser.

Returned Value

Integer between 1 and 31.

Parameters

None.

getUTCDay()

Returns an integer corresponding to a day of the week for the date specified by the Date object but in the UTC time stored internally by the browser.

Returned Value

Integer between 0 and 6. Sunday is 0, Monday is 1, and Saturday is 6.

Parameters

None.

getUTCFullYear()

Returns all digits of the year for the date specified by the Date object but in the UTC time stored internally by the browser.

Returned Value

Integer. Navigator goes no lower than zero. Internet Explorer returns negative year values.

Parameters

None.

getUTCHours()   NN *4*   IE *J3*   ECMA *1*

Returns a zero-based integer corresponding to the hours of the day for the date specified by the Date object but in the UTC time stored internally by the browser. The 24-hour time system is used.

Returned Value

Integer between 0 and 23.

Parameters

None.

getUTCMilliseconds()   NN *4*   IE *J3*   ECMA *1*

Returns a zero-based integer corresponding to the number of milliseconds past the seconds value of the date specified by the Date object but in the UTC time stored internally by the browser.

Returned Value

Integer between 0 and 999.

Parameters

None.

getUTCMinutes()   NN *4*   IE *J3*   ECMA *1*

Returns a zero-based integer corresponding to the minute value for the hour and date specified by the Date object but in the UTC time stored internally by the browser.

Returned Value

Integer between 0 and 59.

Parameters

None.

getUTCMonth()   NN *4*   IE *J3*   ECMA *1*

Returns a zero-based integer corresponding to the month value for the date specified by the Date object but in the UTC time stored internally by the browser. That this method's values are zero-based frequently confuses scripters at first.

Returned Value

Integer between 0 and 11. January is 0, February is 1, and December is 11.

Parameters

None.

getUTCSeconds()   NN *4*   IE *J3*   ECMA *1*

Returns a zero-based integer corresponding to the seconds value past the nearest full minute of the date specified by the `Date` object but in the UTC time stored internally by the browser.

Returned Value

Integer between 0 and 59.

Parameters

None.

getYear()   NN *2*   IE *J1*   ECMA *1*

Returns a number corresponding to the year but exhibits irregular behavior. In theory, the method should return the number of years the date object represents since 1900. This would produce a one- or two-digit value for all years between 1900 and 1999. However when you reach 2000, the pattern fails. Instead of producing values starting with 100, the `getYear()` method starting with Navigator 3 and IE 4, returns the same four-digit value as `getFullYear()`. For this reason, it is best to use `getFullYear()` whenever possible (but observe the browser compatibility for that method).

Returned Value

Integer between 0 and 99 for the years 1900 to 1999; four-digit integer starting with 2000.

Parameters

None.

parse()   NN *2*   IE *J1*   ECMA *1*

parse(*dateString*)

Static method that returns the millisecond equivalent of the date specified as a string in the parameter.

Returned Value

Date in milliseconds.

Parameters

dateString

> Any valid string format equivalent to that derived from a `Date` object. See `toString()`, `toGMTString()`, and `toLocaleString()` methods for sample formats.

setDate()   NN *2*   IE *J1*   ECMA *1*

setDate(*dateInt*)

Sets the date within the month specified by the `Date` object. This method alters the value of the instance of the `Date` object.

Returned Value

New date in milliseconds.

Parameters

`dateInt`   Integer between 1 and 31.

setFullYear()

setFullYear(*yearInt*)

Assigns the year for the date specified by the **Date** object. This method alters the value of the instance of the **Date** object.

Returned Value

New date in milliseconds.

Parameters

`yearInt`   Integer. Navigator allows digits no lower than zero. Internet Explorer allows negative year values.

setHours()

setHours(*hourInt*)

Sets the hours of the day for the date specified by the **Date** object. The 24-hour time system is used. This method alters the value of the instance of the **Date** object.

Returned Value

New date in milliseconds.

Parameters

`hourInt`   Integer between 0 and 23.

setMilliseconds()

setMilliseconds(*msInt*)

Sets the number of milliseconds past the seconds value of the date specified by the **Date** object. This method alters the value of the instance of the **Date** object.

Returned Value

New date in milliseconds.

Parameters

`msInt`   Integer between 0 and 999.

setMinutes()

setMinutes(*minuteInt*)

Sets the minute value for the hour and date specified by the **Date** object. This method alters the value of the instance of the **Date** object.

Returned Value

New date in milliseconds.

Parameters

minuteInt   Integer between 0 and 59.

setMonth()   NN *2*   IE *J1*   ECMA *1*

`setMonth(monthInt)`

Sets the month value for the date specified by the **Date** object. That this method's values are zero-based frequently confuses scripters at first. This method alters the value of the instance of the **Date** object.

Returned Value

New date in milliseconds.

Parameters

monthInt Integer between 0 and 11. January is 0, February is 1, and December is 11.

setSeconds()   NN *2*   IE *J1*   ECMA *1*

`setSeconds(secInt)`

Sets the seconds value past the nearest full minute of the date specified by the **Date** object. This method alters the value of the instance of the **Date** object.

Returned Value

New date in milliseconds.

Parameters

secInt   Integer between 0 and 59.

setTime()   NN *2*   IE *J1*   ECMA *1*

`setTime(msInt)`

Sets the **Date** object to the number of milliseconds since January 1, 1970. This method alters the value of the instance of the **Date** object.

Returned Value

New date in milliseconds.

Parameters

msInt   Integer.

setUTCDate()   NN *4*   IE *J3*   ECMA *1*

`setUTCDate(dateInt)`

Sets the date within the month specified by the **Date** object but in the UTC time stored internally by the browser.

Returned Value

New UTC date in milliseconds.

Parameters

dateInt   Integer between 1 and 31.

setUTCFullYear()   NN *4*   IE *J3*   ECMA *1*

setUTCFullYear(*yearInt*)

Sets all digits of the year for the date specified by the Date object but in the UTC time stored internally by the browser. This method alters the value of the instance of the Date object.

Returned Value

New UTC date in milliseconds.

Parameters

yearInt   Integer. Navigator allows values no lower than zero. Internet Explorer allows
            negative year values.

setUTCHours()   NN *4*   IE *J3*   ECMA *1*

setUTCHours(*hourInt*)

Sets the hours of the day for the date specified by the Date object but in the UTC time stored internally by the browser. The 24-hour time system is used. This method alters the value of the instance of the Date object.

Returned Value

New UTC date in milliseconds.

Parameters

hourInt   Integer between 0 and 23.

setUTCMilliseconds()   NN *4*   IE *J3*   ECMA *1*

setUTCMilliseconds(*msInt*)

Sets the number of milliseconds past the seconds value of the date specified by the Date object but in the UTC time stored internally by the browser. This method alters the value of the instance of the Date object.

Returned Value

New UTC date in milliseconds.

Parameters

msInt   Integer between 0 and 999.

setUTCMinutes()   NN *4*   IE *J3*   ECMA *1*

setUTCMinutes(*minuteInt*)

Sets the minute value for the hour and date specified by the Date object but in the UTC time stored internally by the browser. This method alters the value of the instance of the Date object.

Returned Value

New UTC date in milliseconds.

Parameters

minuteInt   Integer between 0 and 59.

setUTCMonth()   NN *4*   IE *J3*   ECMA *1*

setUTCMonth(*monthInt*)

Sets the month value for the date specified by the Date object but in the UTC time stored internally by the browser. That this method's values are zero-based frequently confuses scripters at first. This method alters the value of the instance of the Date object.

Returned Value

New UTC date in milliseconds.

Parameters

monthInt Integer between 0 and 11. January is 0, February is 1, and December is 11.

setUTCSeconds()   NN *4*   IE *J3*   ECMA *1*

setUTCSeconds(*secInt*)

Sets the seconds value past the nearest full minute specified by the Date object but in the UTC time stored internally by the browser.

Returned Value

New UTC date in milliseconds.

Parameters

secInt   Integer between 0 and 59.

setYear()   NN *2*   IE *J1*   ECMA *1*

setYear(*yearInt*)

Sets the year of a Date object. Use setFullYear() if the browser versions you support allow it.

Returned Value

New date in milliseconds.

Parameters

yearInt   Integer between 0 and 99 for the years 1900 to 1999; four-digit integer starting
with 2000. Four-digit integers also accepted for years before 2000.

toGMTString()   NN *2*   IE *J1*   ECMA *1*

Returns a string version of the GMT value of a `Date` object instance in a standardized
format. This method does not alter the original `Date` object. For use in newer browsers, the
`toUTCString()` method is recommended in favor of `toGMTString()`.

Returned Value

String in the following format: *dayAbbrev, dd mmm yyyy hh:mm:ss* GMT. For example:

```
Wed 05 Aug 1998 02:33:22 GMT
```

Parameters

None.

toLocaleString()   NN *2*   IE *J1*   ECMA *1*

Returns a string version of the local time zone value of a `Date` object instance in a format
that may be localized for a particular country or an operating system's convention. This
method does not alter the original `Date` object.

Returned Value

String in a variety of possible formats. Examples of U.S. versions of browsers include:

Platform	String Value
Navigator 4/Win32	`03/31/98 11:22:44`
Navigator 4/MacPPC	`Mar 31 11:22:44 1998`
Internet Explorer 4/Win32	`03/31/98 11:22:44`
Internet Explorer 4/MacPPC	`Tuesday, 31 March, 1998 11:22:44 AM`

Parameters

None.

toString()   NN *2*   IE *J2*   ECMA *1*

A static method used mostly by the browser itself to convert `Date` objects to string values
when needed for display in dialog boxes or on-screen rendering. This method is inherited
by `Date` object instances, so you may use it to script string conversion if the other available
formats are not to your liking.

Returned Value

String in a variety of possible formats. Examples of U.S. versions of browsers include:

Platform	String Value
Navigator 4/Win32	`Tue Mar 31 11:22:04 Pacific Standard Time 1998`
Navigator 4/MacPPC	`Tue Mar 31 11:30:24 1998`

Platform	String Value
Internet Explorer 4/Win32	`Tue Mar 31 11:22:04 PST 1998`
Internet Explorer 4/MacPPC	`Tue Mar 31 11:30:24 PST 1998`

Parameters

None.

toUTCString()   NN *4*   IE *J3*   ECMA *1*

Returns a string version of the UTC value of a `Date` object instance in a standardized format. This method does not alter the original `Date` object. For use in newer browsers, the `toUTCString()` method is recommended in favor of `toGMTString()`.

Returned Value

String in the following format: *dayAbbrev, dd mmm yyyy hh:mm:ss* GMT. For example:

```
Wed 05 Aug 1998 02:33:22 GMT
```

Parameters

None.

UTC()   NN *2*   IE *J1*   ECMA *1*

`UTC(yyyy, mm, dd[, hh[, mm[, ss[, msecs]]]])`

A static method of the `Date` object that returns a numeric version of the date as stored internally by the browser for a `Date` object. Unlike parameters to the `Date` object constructor, the parameter values for the `UTC()` method must be in UTC time for the returned value to be accurate. This method does not generate a date object, as the `Date` object constructor does.

Returned Value

Integer of the UTC millisecond value of the date specified as parameters.

Parameters

yyyy	Four-digit year value.
mm	Two-digit month number (0-11).
dd	Two-digit date number (1-31).
hh	Optional two-digit hour number in 24-hour time (0-23).
mm	Optional two-digit minute number (0-59).
ss	Optional two-digit second number (0-59).
msec	Optional milliseconds past the last whole second (0-999).

valueOf()   NN *4*   IE *J3*   ECMA *1*

Returns the object's value.

Returned Value

Integer millisecond count.

Parameters

None.

Function   NN *2*   IE *J1*   ECMA *1*

A function is a group of one or more script statements that can be invoked at any time during or after the loading of a page. Invoking a function requires nothing more than including the function name with a trailing set of parentheses inside another script statement or as a value assigned to an event handler attribute in an HTML tag.

Since the first scriptable browsers, a function is created by the act of defining it inside a SCRIPT element:

```
function funcName() {...}
```

More recent browsers also allow the use of a constructor function, but this syntax is usually more complex than defining a function.

Functions may be built to receive zero or more parameters. Parameters are assigned to comma-delimited parameter variables defined in the parentheses pair following the function name:

```
function doSomething(param1, param2, ... paramN) {...}
```

A parameter value may be any JavaScript data type, including object references and arrays. There is no penalty for not supplying the same number of parameters to the function as are defined for the function. The function object receives all parameters into an array (called arguments), which script statements inside the function may examine to extract parameter data.

A function returns execution to the calling statement when the function's last statement has executed. A value may be returned to the calling statement via the return statement. Also, a return statement anywhere else in the function's statements aborts function statement execution at that point and returns control to the calling statement (optionally with a returned value). If one branch of a conditional construction in a function returns a value, each branch, including the main branch, must also return a value, even if that value is null.

Functions have ready access to all global variables that are defined outside of functions anywhere in the document. But variables defined inside a function (the var keyword is required) are accessible only to statements inside the function.

To reference a function object that is defined elsewhere in the document, use the function name without its parentheses. For example, to assign a function to an event handler property, the syntax is:

```
objReference.eventHandlerProperty = functionName
```

In Navigator 4, you may nest functions inside one another:

```
function myFuncA() {
    statements
    function myFuncB() {
        statements
    }
}
```

Nested functions (such as **myFuncB**) can be invoked only by statements in its next outermost function.

All functions belong to the window in which the function is defined. Therefore, if a script must access a function located in a sibling frame, the reference must include the frame and the function name:

```
parent.otherFrame.someFunction()
```

Creating a Function

```
function myFunction([param1[, param2[,...paramN]]]) {
    statement(s)
}
var myFunction = new Function([param1[,...paramN], "statement1[;
...statement2"])
obj.MethodName = function([param1[, param2[,...paramN]]]) {
    statement(s)
}
```

Properties

arguments	arity	caller	length	prototype

Methods

toString()	valueOf()

arguments   NN *3*   IE *J2*   ECMA *1*

Read-only

Returns an array of values passed as arguments to the function. The content of the array is independent of the parameter variables defined for the function. Therefore, if the function defines two parameter variables but the calling statement passes 10 parameters, the **arguments** array captures all 10 values in the order in which they were passed. Statements inside the function may then examine the length of the arguments array and extract values as needed. This allows one function to handle an indeterminate number of parameters if the need arises.

Example

```
function myFunc()
    for (var i = 0; i < myFunc.arguments.length; i++) {
        ...
    }
}
```

Value   Array of values of any JavaScript data type.

arity   NN *4*   IE *n/a*   ECMA *n/a*

Read-only

Returns an integer representing the number of parameters that are defined for the function. This property may be examined in a statement outside of the function, perhaps in preparation of parameters to be passed to the function.

Example `var paramCount = myFunction.arity`

Value Integer.

caller

NN *3* IE *J2* ECMA *n/a*

Read-only

Returns a reference to a function object that contained the statement invoking the current function.

Example

```
function myFunc()
    if (myFunc.caller == someFuncZ) {
        process for this function being called by someFuncZ
    }
}
```

Value `Function` object.

length

NN *4* IE *J3* ECMA *1*

Read-only

Returns an integer representing the number of parameters that are defined for the function. This property may be examined in a statement outside of the function, perhaps in preparation of parameters to be passed to the function. Navigator always returns a value of zero (see the `arity` property).

Example `var paramCount = myFunction.length`

Value Integer.

prototype

NN *3* IE *J2* ECMA *1*

Read/Write

A property of the static `Function` object. Use the `prototype` property to assign new properties and methods to future instances of functions created in the current document. See the `Array.prototype` property description for examples.

Example `Function.prototype.author = "DG"`

Value Any data, including function references.

toString()

NN *4* IE *J3* ECMA *1*

Returns the object's value (script statement listing and function wrapper) as a string data type. You don't need this method in practice because the browsers automatically convert values to strings when they are needed for display in alert dialogs or in-document rendering.

Returned Value

String.

Parameters

None.

valueOf()   NN *4*   IE *J3*   ECMA *1*

Returns the object's value.

Returned Value

A function object reference.

Parameters

None.

Math   NN *2*   IE *J1*   ECMA *1*

The `Math` object is used only in its static object form as a library of math constant values and (mostly trigonometric) operations. As a result, there is no constructor function. Invoking a `Math` object property or method adheres to the following syntax:

```
Math.propertyName
Math.method(param1[, param2])
```

Be sure to observe the uppercase "M" in the `Math` object in script statements. All expressions involving the `Math` object evaluate to or return a value.

Properties

E	LN10	LOG10E	SQRT1_2	SQRT2
LN2	LOG2E	PI		

Methods

abs()	atan2()	floor()	pow()	sin()
acos()	ceil()	log()	random()	sqrt()
asin()	cos()	max()	round()	tan()
atan()	exp()	min()		

E   NN *2*   IE *J1*   ECMA *1*

Read-only

Returns Euler's constant.

Example `var num = Math.E`

Value   2.718281828459045

LN2   NN *2*   IE *J1*   ECMA *1*

Read-only

Returns the natural logarithm of 2.

Example   var num = Math.LN2

Value   0.6931471805599453

LN10

Returns the natural logarithm of 10.

Example   var num = Math.LN10

Value   2.302585092994046

LOG2E

Returns the log base-2 of E.

Example   var num = Math.LOG2E

Value   1.4426950408889634

LOG10E

Returns the log base-10 of E.

Example   var num = Math.LOG10E

Value   0.4342944819032518

PI

Returns the value of π.

Example   var num = Math.PI

Value   3.141592653589793

SQRT1_2

Returns the square root of 0.5.

Example   var num = Math.SQRT1_2

Value   0.7071067811865476

SQRT2

Returns the square root of 2.

Example `var num = Math.SQRT2`

Value 1.4142135623730951

abs() NN *2*   IE *J1*   ECMA *1*

abs(*number*)

Returns the absolute value of the number passed as a parameter.

Returned Value

Positive number or zero.

Parameters

number   Any number.

acos() NN *2*   IE *J1*   ECMA *1*

acos(*number*)

Returns the arc cosine (in radians) of the number passed as a parameter.

Returned Value

Number.

Parameters

number   Any number from -1 to 1.

asin() NN *2*   IE *J1*   ECMA *1*

asin(*number*)

Returns the arc sine (in radians) of the number passed as a parameter.

Returned Value

Number.

Parameters

number   Any number from -1 to 1.

atan() NN *2*   IE *J1*   ECMA *1*

atan(*number*)

Returns the arc tangent (in radians) of the number passed as a parameter.

Returned Value

Number.

Parameters

number   Any number between negative infinity and infinity.

atan2()

`atan2(x, y)`

Returns the angle (in radians) of angle formed by a line to Cartesian point x, y.

Returned Value

Number between -π and π.

Parameters

x	Any number.
y	Any number.

ceil()

`ceil(number)`

Returns the next higher integer that is greater than or equal to the number passed as a parameter.

Returned Value

Integer.

Parameters

number	Any number.

cos()

`cos(number)`

Returns the cosine of the number passed as a parameter.

Returned Value

Number.

Parameters

number	Any number.

exp()

`exp(number)`

Returns the value of E to the power of the number passed as a parameter.

Returned Value

Number.

Parameters

number	Any number.

floor()   NN *2*   IE *J1*   ECMA *1*

```
floor(number)
```

Returns the next lower integer that is less than or equal to the number passed as a parameter.

Returned Value

Integer.

Parameters

number   Any number.

log()   NN *2*   IE *J1*   ECMA *1*

```
log(number)
```

Returns the natural logarithm (base e) of the number passed as a parameter.

Returned Value

Number.

Parameters

number   Any number.

max()   NN *2*   IE *J1*   ECMA *1*

```
max(number1, number2)
```

Returns the greater value of the two parameters.

Returned Value

Number.

Parameters

number1   Any number.
number2   Any number.

min()   NN *2*   IE *J1*   ECMA *1*

```
min(number1, number2)
```

Returns the lesser value of the two parameters.

Returned Value

Number.

Parameters

number1   Any number.
number2   Any number.

pow()

pow(*number1*, *number2*)

Returns the value of the first parameter raised to the power of the second parameter.

Returned Value

Number.

Parameters

number1   Any number.
number2   Any number.

random()

Returns a random number between 0 and 1. To calculate a random integer between zero and another maximum value, use the formula:

```
Math.round(Math.random() * n)
```

where *n* is the top integer of the acceptable range. To calculate a random integer between a range starting with a number other than zero, use the formula:

```
Math.round(Math.random() * n) + m
```

where *m* is the lowest integer of the acceptable range and *n+m* equals the maximum value of the range. Note that the `Math.random()` method does not work in the Windows and Macintosh versions of Navigator 2.

Returned Value

Number from 0 through 1.

Parameters

None.

round()

round(*number*)

Returns an integer that follows rounding rules. If the value of the passed parameter is greater than or equal to *x*.5, the returned value is *x* + 1; otherwise, the returned value is *x*.

Returned Value

Integer.

Parameters

number   Any number.

sin()

sin(*number*)

Returns the sine (in radians) of the number passed as a parameter.

Returned Value
Number.

Parameters
number   Any number.

sqrt()   NN *2*   IE *J1*   ECMA *1*

sqrt(*number*)

Returns the square root of the number passed as a parameter.

Returned Value
Number.

Parameters
number   Any number.

tan()   NN *2*   IE *J1*   ECMA *1*

tan(*number*)

Returns the tangent (in radians) of the number passed as a parameter.

Returned Value
Number.

Parameters
number   Any number between negative infinity and infinity.

Number   NN *3*   IE *J2*   ECMA *1*

A Number object represents any numerical value, whether it is an integer or floating-point number. By and large, you don't have to worry about the Number object because a numerical value automatically becomes a Number object instance whenever you use such a value or assign it to a variable. On the other hand, you might want access to the static properties that only a math major would love.

Creating a Number Object
```
var myValue = number
var myValue = new Number(number)
```

Properties
MAX_VALUE   NaN   NEGATIVE_INFINITY   POSITIVE_INFINITY   prototype
MIN_VALUE

Methods
toString()   valueOf()

MAX_VALUE

Read-only

Equal to the highest possible number that JavaScript can handle.

Example `var tiptop = Number.MAX_VALUE`

Value   1.7976931348623157e+308

MIN_VALUE

Read-only

Equal to the smallest possible number that JavaScript can handle.

Example `var itsybitsy = Number.MIN_VALUE`

Value   5e-324

NaN

Read-only

Equal to a value that is not-a-number. JavaScript returns this value when a numerical operation yields a non-numerical result because of a flaw in one of the operands. If you want to test whether a value is not a number, use the `isNaN()` global function rather than comparing to this property value.

Value   NaN

NEGATIVE_INFINITY, POSITIVE_INFINITY

Read-only

Values that are outside of the bounds of `Number.MIN_VALUE` and `Number.MAX_VALUE`, respectively.

Example `Number.NEGATIVE_INFINITY`

Value   -Infinity; Infinity

prototype

Read/Write

A property of the static `Number` object. Use the `prototype` property to assign new properties and methods to future instances of a `Number` value created in the current document. See the `Array.prototype` property description for examples. There is little need to create new prototype properties or methods for the `Number` object.

Example `Number.prototype.author = "DG"`

Value   Any data, including function references.

toString()   NN *4*   IE *J3*   ECMA *1*

Returns the object's value as a string data type. You don't need this method in practice because the browsers automatically convert **Number** values to strings when they are needed for display in alert dialogs or in-document rendering.

Returned Value

String.

Parameters

None.

valueOf()   NN *4*   IE *J3*   ECMA *1*

Returns the object's value.

Returned Value

A numeric value.

Parameters

None.

Object   NN *4*   IE *J3*   ECMA *1*

An Object represents a customizable object. Use the Object object to generate "things" in your scripts whose behaviors are defined by custom properties and/or methods. Most typically, you start by creating a blank object with the constructor and then assign values to new properties of that object.

Navigator 4 also lets you assign properties and values via a special literal syntax that also creates the Object instance in the process:

```
var myObject = {prop1Name:prop1Value[, prop2Name:prop2Value[,
...propNName:propNValue]]}
```

You can use objects as data structures for structured custom data in your scripts, much like creating an array with named index values.

Creating a Boolean Object

```
var myObject = new Object()
```

Properties
prototype

Methods
toString()   valueOf()

prototype

A property of the static `Object`. Use the `prototype` property to assign new properties and methods to future instances of an `Object` created in the current document. See the `Array.prototype` property description for examples.

Example `Object.prototype.author = "DG"`

Value   Any data, including function references.

toString()

Returns the object's value as a string data type.

Returned Value

String.

Parameters

None.

valueOf()

Returns the object's value.

Returned Value

An object reference.

Parameters

None.

RegExp

The `RegExp` object is a static object that both generates instances of a regular expression and monitors all regular expression in the current window or frame. Instances of the `RegExp` object are covered in the regular expressions object description that follows this section.

Regular expressions assist in locating text that matches patterns of characters or characteristics. For example, a regular expression can be used to find out very quickly if an entry in a text field is a five-digit number. Defining the pattern to match requires knowledge of a separate notation syntax that is beyond the scope of this book (but is covered in *Mastering Regular Expressions*, by Jeffrey E.F. Friedl, published by O'Reilly). A summary of the syntax can be found in the description of the regular expression object.

Properties of the `RegExp` object store information about the last operation of any regular expression in the document. Therefore, it is conceivable that each property could change after each regular expression operation. Such operations include not only the methods of a regular expression object instance (`exec()` and `test()`), but also the `String` object methods that accept regular expressions as parameters (`match()`, `replace()`, and `split()`). Some of these properties are passed to the regular expression object as well, in preparation for the next operation with the regular expression.

All properties have verbose names as well as shortcut names that begin with $.

Properties

input	leftContext	$1	$4	$7
lastMatch	multiline	$2	$5	$8
lastParen	rightContext	$3	$6	$9

input   NN *4*   IE *J3*   ECMA *n/a*

Read/Write

The main string against which a regular expression is compared. If the main string is handed to the regular expression operation as a parameter to a method, this value is `null`. The short version is `$_` (dollar sign, underscore).

Example `RegExp.input = "Four score and seven years ago..."`

Value   String.

lastMatch   NN *4*   IE *J3*   ECMA *n/a*

Read-only

Returns the string that matches the regular expression as a result of the most recent operation. The short version is `$&`.

Example `var matched = RegExp.lastMatch`

Value   String.

lastParen   NN *4*   IE *J3*   ECMA *n/a*

Read-only

Returns the string that matches the last parenthesized subcomponent of the regular expression as a result of the most recent operation. The short version is `$+`.

Example `var myValue = RegExp.lastParen`

Value   String.

leftContext, rightContext   NN *4*   IE *J3*   ECMA *n/a*

Read-only

The `leftContext` property returns the string starting with the beginning of the most recent searched text up to, but not including, the matching string. The `rightContext` property returns the string starting with the main string portion immediately following the matching string and extending to the end of the string. The short versions are `$`` and `$'`, respectively. Because the start of subsequent searches on the same main string move inexorably toward the end of the main string, the starting point of the `leftContext` value can shift with each operation.

Example
```
var wholeContext = RegExp.leftContext + RegExp.lastMatch +
RegExp.rightContext
```

Value   String.

multiline

NN 4   IE J3   ECMA n/a
Read/Write

If the search extends across multiple lines of text, the multiline property is set to `true`. A search through text in a **TEXTAREA** element, for example, is multiline. The short version is `$*`.

Example
```
if (RegExp.multiline) {
    ...
}
```

Value   Boolean.

$1, ..., $9

NN 4   IE J3   ECMA n/a
Read-only

Parenthesized subcomponents of a regular expression return results. These results are stored individually in properties labeled 1 through 9, preceded by the $ shortcut symbol. The order is based on the position of the left parenthesis of a subcomponent: the leftmost subcomponent result is placed into $1. These properties may be used directly within parameters to `String` methods that use regular expressions (see the `String.replace()` method).

Example   `RegExp.$2`

Value   String.

regular expression

NN 4   IE J3   ECMA n/a

A regular expression object is an instance of the **RegExp** object. Each regular expression object consists of a pattern that is used to locate matches within a string. Patterns for a regular expression can be simple strings or significantly more powerful expressions that use a notation that is essentially a language unto itself. The implementation of regular expressions in JavaScript 1.2 is very similar to the way they are implemented in Perl. You can read more about these concepts in books covering JavaScript 1.2.

To create a regular expression object, surround the pattern with forward slashes, and assign the whole expression to a variable. For example, the following statement creates a regular expression whose pattern is a simple word:

```
var re = /greet/
```

The `re` variable can then be used as a parameter is a variety of methods that search for the pattern within some string (you may also use an expression directly as a method parameter, rather than assigning it to a variable).

Regular expression notation also consists of a number of metacharacters that stand in for sometimes complex ideas, such as the boundary on either side of a word, any numeral, or one or more characters. For example, to search for the pattern of characters shown above but only when the pattern is a word (and not part of a word such as greetings), the regular expression notation uses the metacharacters to indicate that the pattern includes word boundaries on both sides of the pattern:

```
var re = /\bgreet\b/
```

Table 11-1 shows a summary of the regular expression notation used in JavaScript 1.2:

Table 11-1. Regular Expression Notation

Character	Matches	Example
\b	Word boundary	/\bto/ matches "tomorrow" /to\b/ matches "Soweto" /\bto\b/ matches "to"
\B	Word nonboundary	/\Bto/ matches "stool" and "Soweto" /to\B/ matches "stool" and "tomorrow" /\Bto\B/ matches "stool"
\d	Numeral 0 through 9	/\d\d/ matches "42"
\D	Nonnumeral	/\D\D/ matches "to"
\s	Single whitespace	/under\sdog/ matches "under dog"
\S	Single nonwhitespace	/under\Sdog/ matches "under-dog"
\w	Letter, numeral, or underscore	/1\w/ matches "1A"
\W	Not a letter, numeral, or underscore	/1\W/ matches "1%"
.	Any character except a newline	/../ matches "Z3"
[...]	Any one of the character set in brackets	/J[aeiou]y/ matches "Joy"
[^...]	Negated character set	/J[^eiou]y/ matches "Jay"
*	Zero or more times	/d*/ matches "", "5", or "444"
?	Zero or one time	/d?/ matches "" or "5"
+	One or more times	/d+/ matches "5" or "444"
{n}	Exactly n times	/d{2}/ matches "55"
{n,}	n or more times	/d{2,}/ matches "555"
{n,m}	At least n, at most m times	/d{2,4}/ matches "5555"
^	At beginning of a string or line	/^Sally/ matches "Sally says..."
$	At end of a string or line	/Sally.$/ matches "Hi, Sally."

When you create a regular expression, you may optionally wire the expression to work globally (as you probably do if the regular expression is doing a search-and-replace operation with a method) and to ignore case in its matches. The modifiers that turn on these switches are the letters g and i. They may be used by themselves or together as gi.

Once you have established a pattern with the regular expression notation, all the action takes place in the regular expression object methods and the String object methods that accept regular expression parameters.

Creating a regular expression Object

```
var regExpressionObj = /pattern/ [g | i | gi]
var regExpressionObj = new RegExp(["pattern", ["g" | "i" | "gi"]])
```

Properties

global   ignoreCase   lastIndex   source

Methods

compile()   exec()   test()

---

global, ignoreCase   NN *4*   IE *J3*   ECMA *n/a*

Read-only

Returns whether the object had the g or i modifiers set when it was created. If a regular expression object has both modifiers set (gi), you must still test for each property individually.

Example

```
if (myRE.global && myRE.ignoreCase) {
    ...
}
```

Value   Boolean.

---

lastIndex   NN *4*   IE *J3*   ECMA *n/a*

Read/Write

The zero-based index value of the character within the string where the next search for the pattern begins. In a new search, the value is zero. You can also set the value manually if you wish to start at a different location or skip some characters.

Example   myRE.lastIndex = 30

Value   Integer.

---

source   NN *4*   IE *J3*   ECMA *n/a*

Read-only

Returns a string version of the characters used to create the regular expression. The value does not include the forward slash delimiters that surround the expression.

Example   var myREasString = myRE.source

Value   String.

---

compile()   NN *4*   IE *J3*   ECMA *n/a*

```
compile(pattern[, g | i | gi])
```

Compiles a regular expression pattern into a genuine regular expression object. This method is used primarily to recompile a regular expression whose pattern may change during the execution of a script.

Returned Value

regular expression object reference.

Parameters

pattern Any regular expression pattern as a quoted string.

exec()   NN 4   IE J3   ECMA n/a

exec(*string*)

Performs a search through the string passed as a parameter for the current regular expression pattern. A typical sequence follows the format:

```
var myRE = /somePattern/
var resultArray = myRE.exec("someString")
```

Properties of both the static **RegExp** and regular expression (**myRE** in the example) objects are updated with information about the results of the search. In addition, the **exec()** method returns an array of data, much of it similar to **RegExp** object properties. The returned array includes the following properties:

index   Zero-based index of starting character in the string that matches the pattern
input   The original string being searched
[0]   String of the characters matching the pattern
[1]...[n] Strings of the results of the parenthesized component matches

You can stow away the results of the **exec()** method in a variable, whereas the **RegExp** property values change with the next regular expression operation. If the regular expression is set for global searching, a subsequent call to **myRE.exec("someString")** continues the search from the position of the previous match.

If no match is found for a given call to **exec()**, it returns **null**.

Returned Value

An array of match information if successful; **null** if there is no match.

Parameters

string The string to be searched.

test()   NN 4   IE J3   ECMA n/a

test(*string*)

Returns **true** if there is a match of the regular expression anywhere in the string passed as a parameter; **false** if not. No additional information is available about the results of the search. This is the fastest way to find out if a pattern matches within a string.

Returned Value

Boolean.

Parameters

string The string to be searched.

String

A `String` object represents any sequence of zero or more characters that are to be treated strictly as text (that is, no math operations are to be applied). A large library of methods are divided into two categories. One category surrounds a string with a pair of HTML tags for a variety of HTML character formatting. These methods are used primarily to assist statements that use `document.write()` to dynamically create content. The second method category is the more traditional set of string parsing and manipulation methods that facilitate character and substring extraction, case changes, and conversion from string lists to JavaScript arrays.

By and large, you don't have to worry about explicitly creating a string beyond a simple assignment of a quoted string value:

```
var myString = "howdy"
```

Occasionally, however, it is helpful to create a string object using the constructor of the static `String` object. Preparing string values for passage to Java applets often requires this type of string generation:

```
var myString = new String("howdy")
```

Other than the constructor, `prototype` property, and `fromCharCode()` method, all properties and methods are for use with instances of the `String` object, rather than the static `String` object.

Creating a String Object

```
var myValue = "someString"
var myValue = new String("someString")
```

Properties

length   prototype

Methods

anchor()	fromCharCode()	small()
big()	indexOf()	split()
blink()	italics()	strike()
bold()	lastIndexOf()	sub()
charAt()	link()	substr()
charCodeAt()	match()	substring()
concat()	replace()	sup()
fixed()	search()	toLowerCase()
fontcolor()	slice()	toUpperCase()
fontsize()		

length

Read-only

A count of the number of characters in the string. String values dynamically change their lengths if new values are assigned to them or if other strings are concatenated.

Example

```
for (var i = 0; i < myString.length; i++) {
    ...
}
```

Value   Integer.

prototype

NN *3*   IE *J2*   ECMA *1*

Read/Write

A property of the static `String` object. Use the `prototype` property to assign new properties and methods to future instances of a `String` value created in the current document. See the `Array.prototype` property description for examples. There is little need to create new prototype properties or methods for the `String` object.

Example `String.prototype.author = "DG"`

Value   Any data, including function references.

anchor()

NN *2*   IE *J1*   ECMA *n/a*

anchor(*anchorName*)

Returns a copy of the string embedded within an anchor (`<A>`) tag set. The value passed as a parameter is assigned to the `NAME` attribute of the tag.

Returned Value

A string within an `A` element.

Parameters

anchorName
        A string to use as the value of the NAME attribute.

big()

NN *2*   IE *J1*   ECMA *n/a*

Returns a copy of the string embedded within a `<BIG>` tag set.

Returned Value

A string within a `BIG` element.

Parameters

None.

blink()

NN *2*   IE *J1*   ECMA *n/a*

Returns a copy of the string embedded within a `<BLINK>` tag set.

Returned Value

A string within a `BLINK` element.

Parameters

None.

bold()   NN *2*   IE *J1*   ECMA *n/a*

Returns a copy of the string embedded within a <B> tag set.

Returned Value

A string within a B element.

Parameters

None.

charAt()   NN *2*   IE *J1*   ECMA *1*

charAt(*positionIndex*)

Returns a single character string of the character located at the zero-based index position passed as a parameter. Use this method instead of **substring**() when only one character from a known position is needed from a string.

Returned Value

A one-character string. In newer browser versions, an empty string is returned if the parameter value points to a character beyond the length of the string.

Parameters

positionIndex Zero-based integer.

charCodeAt()   NN *4*   IE *J3*   ECMA *1*

charCodeAt(*positionIndex*)

Returns a number of the decimal Unicode value for the character located at the zero-based index position passed as a parameter. For common alphanumeric characters, the Unicode values are the same as ASCII values.

Returned Value

A positive integer. Returns NaN if the parameter value points to a character beyond the length of the string.

Parameters

positionIndex Zero-based integer.

concat()   NN *4*   IE *J3*   ECMA *n/a*

concat(*string2*)

Returns a string that appends the parameter string to the current string object. The results of this method are the same as concatenating strings with the add (+) or add-by-value (+=) operators. Neither the method nor operators insert spaces between the two string components.

Returned Value

String.

Parameters

string2 Any string.

fixed( ) NN *2* IE *J1* ECMA *n/a*

Returns a copy of the string embedded within a <TT> tag set.

Returned Value

A string within a TT element.

Parameters

None.

fontcolor( ) NN *2* IE *J1* ECMA *n/a*

fontColor(*color*)

Returns a copy of the string embedded within a font (<FONT>) tag set. The value passed as a parameter is assigned to the COLOR attribute of the tag.

Returned Value

A string within a FONT element.

Parameters

color A string to use as the value of the COLOR attribute.

fontsize( ) NN *2* IE *J1* ECMA *n/a*

fontSize(*size*)

Returns a copy of the string embedded within a font (<FONT>) tag set. The value passed as a parameter is assigned to the SIZE attribute of the tag.

Returned Value

A string within a FONT element.

Parameters

size An integer to use as the value of the SIZE attribute.

fromCharCode( ) NN *4* IE *J3* ECMA *n/a*

fromCharCode(*num1*[, *num2*,[...*numN*]])

A static method that returns a string of one or more characters whose Unicode values are passed as a comma-delimited list of parameters. For example, the expression:

```
String.fromCharCode(120, 121, 122)
```

returns "xyz".

Returned Value

A string.

Parameters

num1...numN   One or more integer values in an unquoted, comma-delimited list.

indexOf()   NN *2*   IE *J1*   ECMA *1*

```
indexOf(searchString[, startPositionIndex])
```

Returns a zero-based integer of the position within the current string where the *searchString* parameter starts. Normally, the search starts with the first (index of zero) character, but you may have the search begin later in the string by specifying the optional second parameter, which is the index value of where the search should start. If there is no match, the returned value is -1. This is a backward-compatible quick way to find out if one string contains another: If the returned value is -1 then you know the *searchString* is not in the larger string. If the returned value is another number (the precise value doesn't matter), the *searchString* is in the larger string. For Version 4 browsers, the String object's search() method performs a similar function.

Returned Value

Integer.

Parameters

searchString
> A string to look for in the current string object

startPositionIndex
> A zero-based integer indicating the position within the current string object to begin the search of the first parameter

italics()   NN *2*   IE *J1*   ECMA *n/a*

Returns a copy of the string embedded within an <I> tag set.

Returned Value

A string within an I element.

Parameters

None.

lastIndexOf()   NN *2*   IE *J1*   ECMA *1*

```
lastIndexOf(searchString[, startPositionIndex])
```

Returns a zero-based integer of the position within the current string object where the *searchString* parameter starts. This method works like the indexOf() method but begins all searches from the end of the string or some index position. Even though searching starts from the end of the string, the *startPositionIndex* parameter is based on the start of the string, as is the returned value. If there is no match, the returned value is -1.

Returned Value

Integer.

Parameters

`searchString`
> A string to look for in the current string object.

`startPositionIndex`
> A zero-based integer indicating the position within the current string object to begin the search of the first parameter. Even though the search starts from the end of the string, this parameter value is relative to the front of the string.

link()   NN *2*   IE *J1*   ECMA *n/a*

`link(URL)`

Returns a copy of the string embedded within an anchor (`<A>`) tag set. The value passed as a parameter is assigned to the `HREF` attribute of the tag.

Returned Value

A string within an `A` element.

Parameters

`URL`   A string to use as the value of the `HREF` attribute.

match()   NN *4*   IE *J3*   ECMA *n/a*

`match(regexpression)`

Returns an array of strings within the current string that match the regular expression passed as a parameter. For example, if you pass a regular expression that specifies any five-digit number, the returned value of the `match()` method would be an array of all five-digit numbers (as strings) in the main string. Properties of the `RegExp` static object are influenced by this method's operation.

Returned Value

An array of strings.

Parameters

`regexpression`
> A regular expression object. See the regular expression object for the syntax to create a regular expression object.

replace()   NN *4*   IE *J3*   ECMA *n/a*

`replace(regexpression, replaceString)`

Returns the new string that results when all matches of the *regexpression* parameter are replaced by the *replaceString* parameter. The original string is unharmed in the process.

Returned Value

A string.

Parameters

`regexpression`
> A regular expression object. See the regular expression object for the syntax to create a regular expression object.

`replaceString`
> A string that is to take the place of all matches of *regexpression* in the current string.

search() NN *4*   IE *J3*   ECMA *n/a*

`search(regexpression)`

Returns the zero-based indexed value of the first character in the current string that matches the pattern of the *regexpression* parameter. This method is similar to the `indexOf()` method, but the search is performed with a regular expression rather than a straight string.

Returned Value

Integer.

Parameters

`regexpression`
> A regular expression object. See the regular expression object for the syntax to create a regular expression object.

slice() NN *4*   IE *J3*   ECMA *n/a*

`slice(startPositionIndex[, endPositionIndex])`

Returns a substring of the current string. The substring is copied from the main string starting at the zero-based index count value of the character in the main string. If no second parameter is provided, the substring extends to the end of the main string. The optional second parameter can be another zero-based index value of where the substring should end. This value may also be a negative value, which counts from the end of the string toward the front.

Returned Value

String.

Parameters

`startPositionIndex`
> A zero-based integer indicating the position within the current string object to start copying characters.

`endPositionIndex`
> A zero-based integer indicating the position within the current string object to end copying characters. Negative values count inward from the end of the string.

small()   NN *2*   IE *J1*   ECMA *n/a*

Returns a copy of the string embedded within a `<SMALL>` tag set.

Returned Value

A string within a SMALL element.

Parameters

None.

split()   NN *4*   IE *J3*   ECMA *1*

```
split(delimiter [, limitInteger])
```

Returns a new array object whose elements are segments of the current string. The current string is divided into array entries at each instance of the delimiter string specified as the first parameter of the method. The delimiter does not become part of the array. You do not have to declare the array prior to stuffing the results of the `split()` method. For example, if a string consists of a comma-delimited list of names, you can convert the list into an array as follows:

```
var listArray = stringList.split(",")
```

You may also use a regular expression as the parameter to divide the string by a pattern rather than a fixed character.

Returned Value

Array.

Parameters

`delimiter`
        A string or regular expression that defines where the main string is divided into elements of the resulting array.

`limitInteger`
        An optional integer that restricts the number of items converted into array elements. This parameter is recognized only by Navigator 4.

strike()   NN *2*   IE *J1*   ECMA *n/a*

Returns a copy of the string embedded within a `<STRIKE>` tag set.

Returned Value

A string within a STRIKE element.

Parameters

None.

sub()   NN *2*   IE *J1*   ECMA *n/a*

Returns a copy of the string embedded within a `<SUB>` tag set.

Returned Value

A string within a SUB element.

Parameters

None.

---

substr()

substr(*startPositionIndex* [, *length*])

Returns a copy of an extract from the current string. The extract begins at the zero-based index position of the current string as specified by the first parameter of the method. If no other parameter is provided, the extract continues to the end of the main string. The second parameter can specify an integer of the number of characters to be extracted from the main string. In contrast, the substring() method's parameters point to the start and end position index values of the main string.

Returned Value

A string.

Parameters

startPositionIndex

    A zero-based integer indicating the position within the current string object to start copying characters

length   An optional integer of the number of characters to extract, starting with the character indicated by the *startPositionIndex* parameter

---

substring()

substring(*startPositionIndex*, *endPositionIndex*)

Returns a copy of an extract from the current string. The extract begins at the zero-based index position of the current string as specified by the first parameter of the method and ends at the character whose index is specified by the second parameter. In contrast, the substr() method's parameters point to the start position of the main string and the number of characters (length) to extract.

Returned Value

A string.

Parameters

startPositionIndex

    A zero-based integer indicating the position within the current string object to start copying characters

endPositionIndex

    A zero-based integer indicating the position within the current string object to end copying characters

sup()   NN *2*   IE *J1*   ECMA *n/a*

Returns a copy of the string embedded within a <SUP> tag set.

Returned Value

A string within a SUP element.

Parameters

None.

toLowerCase(), toUpperCase()   NN *2*   IE *J1*   ECMA *1*

Returns a copy of the current string in all lowercase or uppercase letters. If you want to replace the current string with a case-adjusted version, assign the result of the method to the same string:

```
myString = myString.toUpperCase()
```

It is common to use either one of these methods to create a case-insensitive comparison of two strings. This is especially convenient if one of the strings being compared is entered by a user, who may submit a variety of case situations:

```
if (document.forms[0].entry.value.toLowerCase() == compareValue) {
    ...
}
```

Returned Value

String.

Parameters

None.

Operators

+   NN *2*   IE *J1*   ECMA *1*

The addition operator. This operator works with both numbers and strings, but its results vary with the data types of its operands. When both operands are numbers, the result is the sum of the two numbers; when both operands are strings, the result is a concatenation of the two strings (in the order of the operands); when one operand is a number and the other a string, the number data type is converted to a string, and the two strings are concatenated. To convert a string operand to a number, use the `parseInt()` or `parseFloat()` function.

Example

```
var mySum = number1 + number2
var newString = "string1" + "string2"
```

+=

The add-by-value operator. This class of operator combines a regular assignment operator (=) with one of the many other operators to carry out the assignment by performing the stated operation on the left operand with the value of the right operand. For example, if a variable named a has a string stored in it, you can append a string to a with the += operator:

```
a += " and some more."
```

Without the add-by-value operator, the operation had to be structured as follows:

```
a = a + " and some more"
```

Table 11-2 shows all the assignment operators that function this way:

Table 11-2. Assignment Operators

Operator	Example	Equivalent
+=	a += b	a = a + b
-=	a -= b	a = a - b
*=	a *= b	a = a * b
/=	a /= b	a = a / b
%=	a %= b	a = a % b
<<=	a <<= b	a = a << b
>>=	a >>= b	a = a >> b
>>>=	a >>>= b	a = a >>> b
&=	a &= b	a = a & b
|=	a |= b	a = a | b
^=	a ^= b	a = a ^ b

Example

```
output += "<H1>Section 2</H1>"
total *= .95
```

&&

The AND operator. This operator compares two Boolean expressions for equality. If both expressions evaluate to true, the result of the && operator also evaluates to true; if either or both expressions are false, the && operator evaluates to false.

A Boolean expression may consist of a comparison expression (using any of the many comparison operators) or a variety of other values. Here are the most common data types, values, and their Boolean value equivalent.:

Data Type	Boolean Equivalent
Number other than zero	true
Zero	false
Any nonempty string	true
Empty string	false
Any object	true

Data Type	Boolean Equivalent
null	false
undefined	false

Using this information, you can create compound conditions with the help of the && operator. For example, if you want to see if someone entered a value into a form field and it is a number greater than 100, the condition would look like the following:

```
var userEntry = document.forms[0].entry.value
if (userEntry && parseInt(userEntry) >= 100) {
    ...
}
```

If the user had not entered any value, the string is an empty string. In the compound condition, when the first operand evaluates to false, the && operator rules mean that the entire expression returns false (because both operands must be true for the operator to return true). Because evaluation of expressions such as the compound condition are evaluated from left to right, the false value of the first operand short-circuits the condition to return false, meaning that the second operand isn't evaluated.

Example

```
if (a <= b && b >= c) {
    ...
}
```

=   NN *2*   IE *J1*   ECMA *1*

The assignment operator. This operator assigns the evaluated value of the right-hand operand to the variable on the left. After the operation, the variable contains data of the same data type as the original value. Assignment operations can also be chained, with the evaluation of the entire statement starting from the right and working left. Therefore, after the expression:

```
a = b = c = 25
```

all three variables equal 25.

Example

```
var myName = "Theodore Roosevelt"
var now = new Date()
```

                                              NN *2*   IE *J1*   ECMA *1*

The bitwise AND operator. This operator performs binary math on two operands (their binary values). Each column of bits is subjected to the Boolean AND operation. If the value of a column in both operands is 1, the result for that column position is 1. All other combinations yield a zero. The resulting value of the operator is the decimal equivalent of the binary result. For example, the binary values of 3 and 6 are 0011 and 0110, respectively. After an AND operation on these two values, the binary result is 0010; the decimal equivalent is 3.

Example   var n = 3 & 6

<<

The bitwise left-shift operator. This operator shifts the bits of the first operand by the number of columns specified by the second operand. For example, if the binary value of 3 (0011) has its bits shifted to the left by 2, the binary result is 1100; the decimal equivalent is 12.

Example `var shifted = 3 << 2`

~

The bitwise NOT operator. This unary operator inverts the value of the binary digit in each column of a number. For example, the binary 6 is 0110 (with many more zeros off to the left). After the negation operation on each column's value, the binary result is 1001, plus all zeros to the left inverted to 1s. The decimal equivalent is a negative value (-5).

Example `var n = ~6`

|

The bitwise OR operator. This operator performs binary math on two operands (their binary values). Each column of bits is subjected to the Boolean OR operation. If the value of a column in both operands is 0, the result for that column position is 0. All other combinations yield a 1. The resulting value of the operator is the decimal equivalent of the binary result. For example, the binary values of 3 and 6 are 0011 and 0110, respectively. After an OR operation on these two values, the binary result is 0111; the decimal equivalent is 7.

Example `var n = 3 | 6`

>>

The bitwise right-shift operator. This operator shifts the bits of the first operand by the number of columns specified by the second operand. For example, if the binary value of 6 (0110) has its bits shifted to the right by 2, the binary result is 0001; the decimal equivalent is 1. Any digits that fall off the right end of the number are discarded.

Example `var shifted = 6 >> 2`

^

The bitwise exclusive OR (XOR) operator. This operator performs binary math on two operands (their binary values). Each column of bits is subjected to the Boolean XOR operation. If the value of a column in either operand (but not both operands) is 1, the result for that column position is 1. All other combinations yield a 0. The resulting value of the operator is the decimal equivalent of the binary result. For example, the binary values of 3 and 6 are 0011 and 0110, respectively. After an XOR operation on these two values, the binary result is 0101; the decimal equivalent is 5.

Example `var n = 3 ^ 6`

The bitwise zero-fill right-shift operator. This operator shifts (to the right) the bits of the first operand by the number of columns specified by the second operand. With the bitwise right-shift operator, new digits that fill in from the left end are 1s; with the zero-fill right-shift operator, the new digits at the left are zeros. Any digits that fall off the right end of the number are discarded. Microsoft also refers to this operator as the unsigned right-shift operator.

Example `var shifted = 6 >>> 2`

The comma operator. This operator can delimit expressions in the same line of script. It can be used in a number of ways. For example, to declare multiple variables, the syntax would be:

```
var varName1, varName2, ... varNameN
```

Multiple script statements may also be joined together on the same line. Therefore, the following script line:

```
alert("Howdy"),alert("Doody")
```

presents two alert dialog boxes in sequence (the second one appears after the first is dismissed by the user). Another application is in `for` loops when you wish to involve two (or more) variables in the loop:

```
for (var i = 0, var j = 2; i < 20; i++, j++) {
    ...
}
```

Example `var isNav, isIE`

The conditional operator. This operator provides a shortcut syntax to an `if/else` control structure. There are three components to the deployment of this operator: a condition and two statements. If the condition evaluates to true, the first of the statements is executed; if the condition evaluates to false, the second statement is evaluated. The syntax is as follows:

```
condition ? statement1 : statement2
```

This operator is a shortcut in appearance only. It invokes the same internal processing as an `if...else` construction.

Example `var newColor = (temp > 100) ? "red" : "blue"`

The decrement operator. This unary operator subtracts 1 from the current value of a variable expression. You can place the operator in front of or behind the variable for a different effect. When the operator is in front of the variable, the variable is decremented before it is evaluated in the current statement. For example, in the following sequence:

```
var a, b
a = 5
b = --a
```

one is subtracted from a before being assigned to b. Therefore, both b and a are 4 when these statements finish running. In contrast, in the following sequence:

```
var a, b
a = 5
b = a--
```

the subtraction occurs after a is assigned to b. When these statements complete, b is 5 and a is 4.

This behavior impacts the way for-loop-counting variables are defined and used. Typically, a loop counter that counts backwards from a maximum value decrements the counter after the statements in the loop have run. Thus most loop counters place the operator after the counter variable:

```
for (var i = 10; i >=0; i--) ...
```

Example

```
--n
n--
```

delete

NN 4   IE J3   ECMA 1

The delete operator. This operator removes a property from an object (e.g., a prototype property from an instance of an object to whose static object your script added the prototype earlier) or an element from a script-generated array. Internet Explorer and ECMA versions return a Boolean value based on the success of the deletion; Navigator 4 returns undefined.

Example delete myString.author

/

NN 2   IE J1   ECMA 1

The division operator. This operator divides the number to the left of the operator by the number to the right. Both operands must be numbers. An expression with this operator evaluates to a number.

Example var myQuotient = number1 / number2

==

NN 2   IE J1   ECMA 1

The equality operator. This operator compares two operand values and returns a Boolean result. The behavior of this operator differs with the version of JavaScript specified for the SCRIPT element. If the LANGUAGE attribute is set to JavaScript or JavaScript1.1, some operands are automatically converted as shown in the following table:

Left Operand	Right Operand	Description
Object reference	Object reference	Compare evaluation of object references.
Any data type	null	Convert left operand to its object type and compare against null .

JavaScript Reference

Left Operand	Right Operand	Description
Object reference	String	Convert object to string (via `toString()`) and compare strings.
String	Number	Convert string to a number and compare numeric values.

Version 1 of ECMAScript observes the same behavior.

The situation is a bit different in Navigator when the `SCRIPT` element is set to `LANGUAGE="JavaScript11.2"`. The browser is more literal about equality, meaning that no automatic data conversions are performed. Therefore, whereas the expression:

```
123 == "123"
```

evaluates to `true` in most situations due to automatic data type conversion, the expression evaluates to `false` in Navigator 4 but only in statements belonging to explicitly JavaScript 1.2 scripts. Internet Explorer 4's equivalent of unconverted equality comparison is the identity operator (`===`).

Regardless of version, if you wish to compare the values of objects (for example, strings explicitly generated with the `new String()` constructor), you need to convert the values beforehand with methods such as `toString()` or `valueOf()`.

Example

```
if (n == m) {
   ...
}
```

>   NN *2*   IE *J1*   ECMA *1*

The greater-than operator. This operator compares the values of operands on either side of the operator. If the numeric value of the left operand is larger than the right operand, the expression evaluates to `true`. Strings are converted to their Unicode values for comparison of those values.

Example

```
if (a > b) {
   ...
}
```

>=   NN *2*   IE *J1*   ECMA *1*

The greater-than-or-equal operator. This operator compares the values of operands on either side of the operator. If the numeric value of the left operand is larger than or equal to the right operand, the expression evaluates to `true`. Strings are converted to their Unicode values for comparison of those numeric values.

Example

```
if (a >= b) {
   ...
}
```

===

NN *n/a*   IE *J3*   ECMA *n/a*

The identity operator. This operator compares two operand values and returns a Boolean result. Both the value and data type of the two operands must be identical for this operator to return `true`. See the equality operator (==) for similar functionality in Navigator.

Example

```
if (n === m) {
    ...
}
```

++

NN *2*   IE *J1*   ECMA *1*

The increment operator. This unary operator adds 1 to the current value of a variable expression. You can place the operator in front of or behind the variable for a different effect. When the operator is in front of the variable, the variable is incremented before it is evaluated in the current statement. For example, in the following sequence:

```
var a, b
a = 5
b = ++a
```

1 is added to `a` before being assigned to `b`. Therefore, both `b` and `a` are 6 when these statements finish running. In contrast, in the following sequence:

```
var a, b
a = 5
b = a--
```

the addition occurs after `a` is assigned to `b`. When these statements complete, `b` is 5 and `a` is 6.

This behavior impacts the way `for`-loop-counting variables are defined and used. Typically, a loop counter that counts upward from a minimum value increments the counter after the statements in the loop have run. Thus most loop counters place the operator after the counter variable:

```
for (var i = 10; i >=0; i++) ...
```

Example

```
++n
n++
```

!=

NN *2*   IE *J1*   ECMA *1*

The inequality operator. This operator compares two operand values and returns a Boolean result. The behavior of this operator differs with the version of JavaScript specified for the SCRIPT element. If the LANGUAGE attribute is set to JavaScript or JavaScript1.1, some operands are automatically converted as for the equality (==) operator. Version 1 of ECMAScript observes the same behavior. The situation is a bit different in Navigator when the SCRIPT element is set to LANGUAGE="JavaScript1.2". The browser is more literal about inequality, meaning that no automatic data conversions are performed. Therefore, whereas the expression:

```
123 != "123"
```

evaluates to `false` in most situations due to automatic data type conversion, the expression evaluates to `true` in Navigator 4 but only in statements belonging to explicitly JavaScript 1.2 scripts. Internet Explorer 4's equivalent of unconverted equality comparison is the nonidentity operator (`!==`).

Regardless of version, if you wish to compare the values of objects (for example, strings explicitly generated with the `new String()` constructor), you need to convert the values beforehand with methods such as `toString()` or `valueOf()`.

Example

```
if (n != m) {
   ...
}
```

<   NN *2*   IE *J1*   ECMA *1*

The less-than operator. This operator compares the values of operands on either side of the operator. If the numeric value of the left operand is smaller than the right operand, the expression evaluates to `true`. Strings are converted to their Unicode values for comparison of those values.

Example

```
if (a < b) {
   ...
}
```

<=   NN *2*   IE *J1*   ECMA *1*

The less-than-or-equal operator. This operator compares the values of operands on either side of the operator. If the numeric value of the left operand is smaller than or equal to the right operand, the expression evaluates to `true`. Strings are converted to their Unicode values for comparison of those numeric values.

Example

```
if (a <= b) {
   ...
}
```

%   NN *2*   IE *J1*   ECMA *1*

The modulus operator. This operator divides the number to the left of the operator by the number to the right. If a remainder exists after the division, the expression evaluates to that remainder as an integer. If there is no remainder, the returned value is zero. Both operands must be numbers. An expression with this operator evaluates to a number. Even if you aren't interested in the remainder value, this operator is a quick way to find out if two values are evenly divisible.

Example

```
if ((dayCount % 7) > 0) {
   ...
}
```

---

*   NN *2*   IE *J1*   ECMA *1*

The multiplication operator. This operator multiplies the number to the left of the operator by the number to the right. Both operands must be numbers. An expression with this operator evaluates to a number.

Example `var myProduct = number1 * number2`

-   NN *2*   IE *J1*   ECMA *1*

The negation operator. This unary operator negates the value of the single operand. For example, in the following statements:

```
a = 5
b = -a
```

the value of b becomes -5. A negation operator applied to a negative value returns a positive value.

Example `var myOpposite = -me`

---

new   NN *2*   IE *J1*   ECMA *1*

The new operator. This operator creates instances of the following static objects:

* `Array`
* `Boolean`
* `Date`
* `Function`
* `Number`
* `Object`
* `RegExp`
* `String`

An expression with this operator evaluates to an instance of the object. Syntax rules allow naming the static object, the static object with empty parentheses, and the static object with parameters in parentheses:

```
var myArray = new Array
var myArray = new Array()
var myArray = new Array("Larry", "Moe", "Curly")
```

Only the last two examples are guaranteed to work in all scriptable browser versions. With the exception of the Date object, if you omit assigning parameters during the object creation, the newly minted instance has only the properties that are assigned to the prototype of the static object.

Example `var now = new Date()`

!==   NN *n/a*   IE *J3*   ECMA *n/a*

The nonidentity operator. This operator compares two operand values and returns a Boolean result. Both the value and data type of the two operands must be identical for this operator to return `false`. See the inequality operator (`!=`) for similar functionality in Navigator.

Example

```
if (n !== m) {
    ...
}
```

!   NN *2*   IE *J1*   ECMA *1*

The NOT operator. This unary operator evaluates to the negative value of a single Boolean operand. The NOT operator should be used with explicit Boolean values, such as the result of a comparison or a Boolean property setting.

Example

```
if (a == !b) {
    ...
}
```

|| NN *2*   IE *J1*   ECMA *1*

The OR operator. This operator compares two Boolean expressions for equality. If either or both expressions evaluate to `true`, the result of the || operator also evaluates to `true`; if both expressions are `false`, the || operator evaluates to `false`. A Boolean expression may consist of a comparison expression (using any of the many comparison operators) or a variety of other values. See the discussion of the AND operator for a summary of the most common data types, values, and their Boolean value equivalent.

You can create compound conditions with the help of the && operator. For example, if you want to see if either or both of two conditions are true, you would create a condition such as the following:

```
var userEntry1 = document.forms[0].entry1.value
var userEntry2 = document.forms[0].entry2.value
if (userEntry1 || userEntry2) {
    ...
}
```

In the compound condition, the || operator wants to know if either or both operands is `true` before it evaluates to `true`. If the user entered text into the first field, the condition short-circuits because a `true` value of either operand yields a `true` result. If text were entered only in the second field, the second operand is evaluated. Because it evaluates to `true` (a nonempty string), the condition evaluates to `true`. Only when both operands evaluate to `false` does the compound condition evaluate to `false`.

Example

```
if (a <= b || b >= c) {
    ...
}
```

NN *2*   IE *J1*   ECMA *1*

The subtraction operator. This operator subtracts the number to the right of the operator from the number on the left. Both operands must be numbers. An expression with this operator evaluates to a number.

Example `var myDifference = number1 - number2`

typeof

NN *3*   IE *J1*   ECMA *1*

The `typeof` operator. This unary operator returns one of six string descriptions of the data type of a value. Those returned types are:

- `boolean`
- `function`
- `number`
- `object`
- `string`
- `undefined`

The object type includes arrays, but the operator provides no further information about the type of object or array of the value.

Example

```
if (typeof someVar == "string") {
    ...
}
```

void

NN *3*   IE *J2*   ECMA *1*

The `void` operator. This unary operator evaluates the expression to its right but returns a value of undefined, even if the expression (such as a function call) evaluates to some value. This operator is commonly used with `javascript:` pseudo-URLs that invoke functions. If the function returns a value, that value is ignored by the calling expression.

Example `<A HREF="javascript: void getSound()">...</A>`

Control Statements

break

NN *2*   IE *J1*   ECMA *1*

Stops execution of the current loop and returns control to the next script statement following the end of the current loop. Note that without a label parameter, the scope of the `break` statement is its own loop. To break out of a nested loop, assign labels to each nested layer, and use the desired label as a parameter with the `break` statement. See the `label` statement (available only starting with Navigator 4 and Internet Explorer 4).

Syntax `break [label]`

Example See the `label` statement.

continue   NN *2*   IE *J1*   ECMA *1*

Stops execution of the current iteration through the loop and returns to the top of the loop for the next pass (executing the update expression if one is specified in a `for` loop). If you are using nested loop constructions, assign labels to each nested layer, and use the desired label as a parameter with the `continue` statement. See the `label` statement (available only starting with Navigator 4 and Internet Explorer 4).

Syntax   continue [*label*]

Example

```
outerLoop:
for (var i = 0; i <= maxValue1; i++) {
    for (var j = 0; j <= maxValue2; j++) {
        if (j*i == magic2) {
            continue outerLoop
        }
    }
}
```

do/while   NN *4*   IE *J3*   ECMA *n/a*

Executes statements in a loop while a condition is true. Because the condition is tested at the end of the loop, the statements inside it are always executed at least one time. It is imperative that the expression that makes up the condition have some aspect of its value potentially altered in the statements. Otherwise, an infinite loop occurs.

Syntax

```
do {
    statements
} while (condition)
```

Example

```
var i = 1
do {
    window.status = "Loop number " + i++
} while (i <= 10)
window.status = ""
```

for   NN *2*   IE *J1*   ECMA *1*

A construction that allows repeated execution of statements, usually for a controlled number of times.

Syntax

```
for ([initExpression]; [condition]; [updateExpression]) {
    statements
}
```

Example

```
var userEntry = document.forms[0].entry.value
var oneChar
for (var i = 0; i < userEntry.length; i++) {
    oneChar = userEntry.charAt(i)
    if (oneChar < "0" || oneChar > "9") {
        alert("The entry must be numerals only.")
    }
}
```

for/in   NN *2*   IE *J1*   ECMA *1*

A variation of the regular `for` loop that can extract the property names and values of an object.

Syntax

```
for (varName in objectRef) {
    statements
}
```

Example

```
function showProps() {
    objName = "image"
    obj = document.images[0]
    var msg = ""
    for (var i in obj) {
        msg += objName + "." + i + "=" + obj[i] + "\n"
    }
    alert(msg)
}
```

if   NN *2*   IE *J1*   ECMA *1*

A simple conditional statement that provides one alternate execution path.

Syntax

```
if (condition) {
    statement(s) if true
}
```

Example

```
if (myDateObj.getMonth() == 1) {
    calcMonthLength()
}
```

if/else   NN *2*   IE *J1*   ECMA *1*

A conditional statement that provides two execution paths depending on the result of the condition. You can nest another `if` or `if/else` statement inside either path of the `if/else` statement.

Syntax

```
if (condition) {
    statement(s) if true
} else {
    statement(s) if false
}
```

Example

```
var theMonth = myDateObj.getMonth()
if (theMonth == 1) {
    monLength = calcLeapMonthLength()
} else {
    monLength = calcMonthLength(theMonth)
}
```

label   NN *4*   IE *J3*   ECMA *n/a*

You can assign a label identifier to any block of executing statements, including control structures. The purpose of the label is to allow **break** and **continue** statements within deeply nested control structures to exit to a nested level that may be at levels beyond the scope of the normal **break** and **continue** statements.

Syntax   labelName:

Example

```
outerLoop:
for (var i = 0; i <= maxValue1; i++) {
    for (var j = 0; j <= maxValue2; j++) {
        if (i == magic1 && j == magic2) {
            break outerLoop
        }
    }
}
```

return   NN *2*   IE *J1*   ECMA *1*

Stops execution of the current function. A **return** statement can be located anywhere within the function, including inside control structures. You can optionally specify a value to be returned to the calling statement. This return value can be any JavaScript data type. If a **return** statement that returns a value is in a loop or other control structure, there must be a **return** statement for each branch of the execution tree, including a default **return** statement if execution should reach the main execution scope near or at the end of the function.

Syntax   return [value]

Example

```
function validateNumber(form) {
    var oneChar
    for (var i = 0; i < userEntry.length; i++) {
        oneChar = form.entry.value.charAt(i)
```

```
        if (oneChar < "0" || oneChar > "9") {
            return false
        }
    }
    return true
}
```

switch/case

Provides a shortcut to execution paths for numerous conditions of an expression.

Syntax

```
switch (expression) {
    case label1:
        statements
        [break]
    case label2:
        statements
        [break]
    ...
    [default:
        statements]
}
```

Example

```
var productList = document.forms[0].prodList
var chosenItem = productList.options[productList.selectedIndex].value
switch(chosenItem) {
    case "Small Widget":
        document.forms[0].price.value = "44.95"
        break
    case "Medium Widget":
        document.forms[0].price.value = "54.95"
        break
    case "Large Widget":
        document.forms[0].price.value = "64.95"
        break
    default:
        document.forms[0].price.value = "Nothing Selected"
}
```

while

Executes statements in a loop as long as a condition is true. Because the condition is tested at the beginning of the loop, it is conceivable that under the right conditions, the statements inside the loop do not execute. It is imperative that the expression that makes up the condition have some aspect of its value potentially altered in the statements. Otherwise an infinite loop occurs.

Syntax

```
while (condition) {
    statements
}
```

Example

```
var i = 0
while (!document.forms[0].radioGroup[i].checked) {
    i++
}
alert("You selected item number " + (i+1) + ".")
```

with   NN *2*   IE *J1*   ECMA *1*

The with statement adds an object to the scope of every statement nested within. This can shorten the code of some statement groups that rely on a particular object reference.

Syntax

```
with (objectRef) {
    statements
}
```

Example

```
with (document.forms[0]) {
    name1 = firstName.value
    name2 = lastName.value
    mail = eMail.value
}
```

Global Functions

escape()   NN *2*   IE *J1*   ECMA *1*

escape(*string*[, 1])

Returns a URL-encoded version of the string passed as a parameter to the function. URL encoding converts non-alphanumeric characters to hexadecimal values (such as %20 for the space character). URL-encoded strings do not normally encode the plus symbol because those symbols are used to separate components of search strings. If you must have the plus symbol encoded as well, Navigator 4 offers a second parameter (a numeral 1) to turn on that switch for the method.

Returned Value

A string.

Parameters

string   Any string value.

eval()   NN *2*   IE *J1*   ECMA *1*

eval(*string*)

Returns an object reference of the object described as a string in the parameter of the function. For example, if a form has a sequence of text fields named entry1, entry2, entry3, and so on, you can still use a `for` loop to cycle through all items by name if you let the `eval()` function convert the string representation of the names to object references:

```
for (var i = 1; i <=5; i++) {
    oneField = eval("document.forms[0].entry" + i)
    oneValue = oneField.value
    ...
}
```

Returned Value

Object reference.

Parameters

string   Any string representation of an object reference.

isFinite()   NN *4*   IE *J3*   ECMA *1*

`isFinite(expression)`

Returns a Boolean value of **true** if the number passed as a parameter is anything within the range of **Number.MIN_VALUE** and **Number.MAX_VALUE**, inclusive. String values passed as parameters cause the function to return **false**.

Returned Value

Boolean.

Parameters

expression   Any JavaScript expression.

isNaN()   NN *2*   IE *J1*   ECMA *1*

`isNaN(expression)`

Returns a Boolean value of **true** if the expression passed as a parameter does not evaluate to a numeric value.

Returned Value

Boolean.

Parameters

expression   Any JavaScript expression.

parseInt()   NN *2*   IE *J1*   ECMA *1*

`parseInt(string[, radix])`

Returns an integer value (as a number data type in base-10) of the numerals in the string passed as a parameter. The string value must at least begin with a numeral, or the result is NaN. If the string starts with numbers but changes to letters along the way, only the leading numbers are converted to the integer. Therefore, you can use the expression:

```
parseInt(navigator.appVersion)
```

to extract only the whole number of the version that leads the otherwise long string that is returned from that property.

The optional radix parameter lets you specify the base of the number being passed to the function. A number string that begins with zero is normally treated as an octal number, which gives you the wrong answer. It is a good idea to use the radix value of 10 on all `parseInt()` functions if all of your dealings are in base-10 numbers.

Returned Value

Integer of base-10.

Parameters

string   Any string that begins with one or more numerals.

radix   An integer of the number base of the number passed as the string parameter (e.g., 2, 10, 16).

parseFloat()   NN *2*   IE *J1*   ECMA *1*

```
parseFloat(string)
```

Returns a number value (either an integer or floating-point number) of the numerals in the string passed as a parameter. The string value must at least begin with a numeral, or the result is NaN. If the string starts with numbers but changes to letters along the way, only the leading numbers are converted to the integer. Therefore, you can use the expression:

```
parseFloat(navigator.appVersion)
```

to extract the complete version number (e.g., 4.03) that leads the otherwise long string that is returned from that property.

If the converted value does not have any nonzero values to the right of the decimal, the returned value is an integer. Floating-point values are returned only when the number calls for it.

Returned Value

Number.

Parameters

string   Any string that begins with one or more numerals.

ScriptEngine(), ScriptEngineBuildVersion(), ScriptEngineMajorVersion(), ScriptEngineMinorVersion()   NN *n/a*   IE *J2*   ECMA *n/a*

These Internet Explorer-only functions reveal information about the scripting engine (JScript, VBScript, or VBA) currently in force (executing the statement invoking the function) and which version of that engine is installed. For JScript, the version refers to the version of the *Jscript.dll* file installed among the browser's support files. The major version is the part of the version number to the left of the version decimal point; the minor version is the part to the right of the decimal point. More granular than that is the internal build number that Microsoft uses to keep track of release generations during development and through release.

Returned Value

ScriptEngine() returns a string of one of the following engine names: JScript | VBA | VBScript. All other functions return integer values.

Parameters

None.

toString()
NN *3*   IE *J3*   ECMA *n/a*

toString(*radix*)

Returns a string version of a number in the number base specified by the radix parameter. This variant of the toString() function lets you perform number base conversions. For example, the following sequence converts a base-10 number to a base-16 version as a string:

```
var a = 32
var b = a.toString(16)
```

After these statements execute, the value of b is "20".

Returned Value

A string.

Parameters

radix   An integer of the number base of the result (e.g., 2, 10, 16).

unescape()
NN *2*   IE *J1*   ECMA *1*

unescape(*string*)

Returns a decoded version of the URL-encoded string passed as a parameter to the function. URL encoding converts nonalphanumeric characters to hexadecimal values (such as %20 for the space character).

Returned Value

String.

Parameters

string   Any URL-encoded string value.

unwatch(), watch()
NN *4*   IE *n/a*   ECMA *n/a*

unwatch(*property*)
watch(*property, funcHandler*)

These Navigator-specific functions are used primarily by JavaScript debuggers. When a statement invokes the watch() function for an object, the parameters include the property whose value is to be watched and the reference to the function to be invoked whenever the value of the property is changed by an assignment statement. To turn off the watch operation, invoke the unwatch() function for the particular property engaged earlier.

Returned Value

Nothing.

Parameters

property   The name of the object's property to be watched.

funcHandler

> The name of the function (no parentheses) to be invoked whenever the watched property's value changes.

Statements

//, /*...*/   NN *2*   IE *J1*   ECMA *n/a*

Comment statements that let you enter nonexecuting text in a script. Any text following the // symbol anywhere in a statement line is ignored by the language interpreter. The next line of script, unless it begins with another // symbol, is interpreted by the browser.

For longer comment blocks, you can begin a block with the /* symbol. Comment blocks may run any number of lines. The block is closed with the */ symbol, after which the interpreter engages subsequent statements.

Example

```
// convert temp from C to F

/*
many lines
of
comments
*/
```

this   NN *2*   IE *J1*   ECMA *1*

A keyword that refers to the current object. For example, in a form element object event handler, you can pass the object as a parameter to the function:

```
<INPUT TYPE="text" NAME="ZIP" onChange="validate(this)">
```

Inside a custom object constructor, the keyword refers to the object itself, allowing you to assign values to its properties (even creating the properties at the same time):

```
function CD(label, num, artist) {
    this.label = label
    this.num = num
    this.artist = artist
}
```

Inside a function, the this keyword refers to the function object.

Example

```
<INPUT TYPE="text" NAME="phone" onChange="validate(this.value)">
```

var

A keyword that defines the creation of a new variable. Although the keyword is optional for global variables (those not declared or initialized inside a function), it is good form to use this keyword for each new variable. Using the **var** keyword inside a function makes the variable local to statements inside the function.

You may simply declare one or more variable names, in which case their initial values are null. Or you can also initialize a new variable with a value.

Example

```
var a, b, c

var myName = "Susan"
```

III

Cross References

This part of the book, Chapters 12 through 15, provides a different take on the information of Part II. If you have the name of an HTML attribute or an object property, method, or event handler, you can look it up in one of the indices here to find out which elements and/or objects support it.

- Chapter 12, *HTML Attribute Index*
- Chapter 13, *Document Object Properties Index*
- Chapter 14, *Document Object Methods Index*
- Chapter 15, *Document Object Event Handlers Index*

III

12

HTML Attribute Index

Entries in the following index are arranged alphabetically by HTML attribute. You can look up an attribute to find out which HTML elements support it. This listing is a union of attributes defined for elements in Navigator 4, Internet Explorer 4, and HTML 4.0. The same attribute name may mean different things for different elements. Be sure to look up the details of the attribute listing in Chapter 8, *HTML Reference*, to find out if the attribute is available for the browser(s) used by your intended audience and whether it does what you want.

ABBR   TD, TH

ABOVE   ILAYER, LAYER

ACCEPT   FORM, INPUT

ACCEPT-CHARSET   FORM

ACCESSKEY   A, AREA, BUTTON, INPUT, LABEL, LEGEND, OBJECT, SELECT, TEXTAREA

ACTION   FORM

ALIGN   APPLET, CAPTION, COL, COLGROUP, DIV, EMBED, FIELDSET, H1, H2, H3, H4, H5, H6, HR, IFRAME, IMG, INPUT, LEGEND, OBJECT, P, SELECT, SPACER, TABLE, TBODY, TD, TEXTAREA, TFOOT, TH, THEAD, TR

ALINK   BODY

ALT   APPLET, AREA, EMBED, IMG, INPUT

ARCHIVE   APPLET, OBJECT

AXIS   TD, TH

BACKGROUND   BODY, ILAYER, LAYER, TABLE, TD, TH

BALANCE   BGSOUND

BEHAVIOR   MARQUEE

BELOW   ILAYER, LAYER

BGCOLOR   BODY, ILAYER, LAYER, MARQUEE, TABLE, TBODY, TD, TFOOT, TH, THEAD, TR

BGPROPERTIES   BODY

BORDER   EMBED, FRAMESET, IFRAME, IMG, INPUT, OBJECT, TABLE

BORDERCOLOR   FRAME, FRAMESET, IFRAME, TABLE, TD, TH, TR

BORDERCOLORDARK   TABLE, TD, TH, TR

BORDERCOLORLIGHT   TABLE, TD, TH, TR

BOTTOMMARGIN   BODY

CELLPADDING   TABLE

CELLSPACING   TABLE

CHALLENGE   KEYGEN

CHAR   COL, COLGROUP, TBODY, TD, TFOOT, TH, THEAD, TR

CHAROFF   COL, COLGROUP, TBODY, TD, TFOOT, TH, THEAD, TR

CHARSET   A, DIV, LINK, SCRIPT, SPAN

CHECKED   INPUT

CITE   BLOCKQUOTE, DEL, INS, Q

CLASS   A, ABBR, ACRONYM, ADDRESS, APPLET, AREA, B, BASEFONT, BDO, BGSOUND,
    BIG, BLOCKQUOTE, BODY, BR, BUTTON, CAPTION, CENTER, CITE, CODE, COL,
    COLGROUP, DD, DEL, DFN, DIR, DIV, DL, DT, EM, EMBED, FIELDSET, FONT, FORM,
    FRAME, FRAMESET, H1, H2, H3, H4, H5, H6, HEAD, HR, I, IFRAME, IMG, INPUT, INS,
    ISINDEX, KBD, LABEL, LEGEND, LI, LINK, LISTING, MAP, MARQUEE, MENU, NOBR,
    NOFRAMES, NOSCRIPT, OBJECT, OL, OPTGROUP, OPTION, P, PLAINTEXT, PRE, Q,
    S, SAMP, SCRIPT, SELECT, SMALL, SPAN, STRIKE, STRONG, SUB, SUP, TABLE,
    TBODY, TD, TEXTAREA, TFOOT, TH, THEAD, TR, TT, U, UL, VAR, WBR, XMP

CLASSID   OBJECT

CLEAR   BR

CLIP   ILAYER, LAYER

CODE   APPLET, EMBED, OBJECT

CODEBASE   APPLET, EMBED, OBJECT

CODETYPE   OBJECT

COLOR   BASEFONT, FONT, HR

COLS   FRAMESET, MULTICOL, PRE, TABLE, TEXTAREA

COLSPAN   TD, TH

COMPACT   DIR, DL, MENU, OL, UL

CONTENT   META

COORDS   A, AREA

DATA   OBJECT

DATAFLD   A, APPLET, BUTTON, DIV, FRAME, IFRAME, IMG, INPUT, LABEL, MARQUEE,
    OBJECT, PARAM, SELECT, SPAN, TD, TEXTAREA, TH

DATAFORMATAS   BUTTON, DIV, LABEL, MARQUEE, PARAM, SPAN

DATAPAGESIZE   TABLE

DATASRC   A, APPLET, BUTTON, DIV, FRAME, IFRAME, IMG, INPUT, LABEL, MARQUEE,
    OBJECT, PARAM, SELECT, SPAN, TABLE, TEXTAREA

DATETIME DEL, INS

DECLARE OBJECT

DEFER SCRIPT

DIR A, ABBR, ACRONYM, ADDRESS, AREA, B, BASEFONT, BDO, BIG, BLOCKQUOTE, BODY, CAPTION, CITE, CODE, COL, COLGROUP, DD, DEL, DFN, DIR, DIV, DL, DT, EM, FIELDSET, FONT, FORM, H1, H2, H3, H4, H5, H6, HEAD, HTML, I, IMG, INPUT, INS, ISINDEX, KBD, LABEL, LEGEND, LI, LINK, MAP, MENU, META, NOFRAMES, NOSCRIPT, OBJECT, OL, OPTGROUP, OPTION, P, PRE, Q, S, SAMP, SMALL, SPAN, STRIKE, STRONG, STYLE, SUB, SUP, TABLE, TBODY, TD, TEXTAREA, TFOOT, TH, THEAD, TITLE, TR, TT, U, UL, VAR

DIRECTION MARQUEE,

DISABLED BUTTON, INPUT, LINK, OPTGROUP, OPTION, SELECT, STYLE, TEXTAREA

DYNSRC IMG

ENCTYPE FORM

EVENT SCRIPT

EXPORT OBJECT

FACE BASEFONT, FONT

FOR LABEL, SCRIPT

FRAME TABLE

FRAMEBORDER EMBED, FRAME, FRAMESET, IFRAME

FRAMESPACING FRAMESET, IFRAME

GUTTER MULTICOL

HEADERS TD, TH

HEIGHT APPLET, EMBED, FRAME, IFRAME, ILAYER, IMG, LAYER, MARQUEE, OBJECT, SPACER, TABLE, TD, TH

HIDDEN EMBED

HREF A, AREA, BASE, DIV, LINK, SPAN

HREFLANG A, DIV, LINK, SPAN

HSPACE APPLET, EMBED, IFRAME, IMG, MARQUEE, OBJECT

HTTP-EQUIV META

ID A, ABBR, ACRONYM, ADDRESS, APPLET, AREA, B, BASEFONT, BDO, BGSOUND, BIG, BLOCKQUOTE, BODY, BR, BUTTON, CAPTION, CENTER, CITE, CODE, COL, COLGROUP, DD, DEL, DFN, DIR, DIV, DL, DT, EM, EMBED, FIELDSET, FONT, FORM, FRAME, FRAMESET, H1, H2, H3, H4, H5, H6, HEAD, HR, I, IFRAME, ILAYER, IMG, INPUT, INS, ISINDEX, KBD, LABEL, LAYER, LEGEND, LI, LINK, LISTING, MAP, MAR-QUEE, MENU, NOBR, NOFRAMES, NOSCRIPT, OBJECT, OL, OPTGROUP, OPTION, P, PARAM, PLAINTEXT, PRE, Q, S, SAMP, SCRIPT, SELECT, SMALL, SPAN, STRIKE, STRONG, SUB, SUP, TABLE, TBODY, TD, TEXTAREA, TFOOT, TH, THEAD, TITLE, TR, TT, U, UL, VAR, WBR, XMP

ISMAP IMG

LABEL OPTGROUP, OPTION

LANG A, ABBR, ACRONYM, ADDRESS, AREA, B, BASEFONT, BDO, BGSOUND, BIG, BLOCKQUOTE, BODY, BUTTON, CAPTION, CENTER, CITE, CODE, COL, COL-GROUP, DD, DEL, DFN, DIR, DIV, DL, DT, EM, FIELDSET, FONT, FORM, FRAME, FRAMESET, H1, H2, H3, H4, H5, H6, HEAD, HR, HTML, I, IFRAME, IMG, INPUT, INS, ISINDEX, KBD, LABEL, LEGEND, LI, LINK, LISTING, MAP, MARQUEE, MENU, META, NOFRAMES, NOSCRIPT, OBJECT, OL, OPTGROUP, OPTION, P, PLAINTEXT, PRE, Q, S, SAMP, SELECT, SMALL, SPAN, STRIKE, STRONG, STYLE, SUB, SUP, TABLE, TBODY, TD, TEXTAREA, TFOOT, TH, THEAD, TITLE, TR, TT, U, UL, VAR, WBR, XMP

LANGUAGE A, ACRONYM, ADDRESS, AREA, B, BIG, BLOCKQUOTE, BODY, BR, BUT-TON, CAPTION, CENTER, CITE, CODE, DD, DEL, DFN, DIR, DIV, DL, DT, EM, FIELD-SET, FONT, FORM, FRAME, FRAMESET, H1, H2, H3, H4, H5, H6, HR, I, IFRAME, IMG, INPUT, INS, ISINDEX, KBD, LABEL, LEGEND, LI, LISTING, MAP, MARQUEE, MENU, OBJECT, OL, OPTGROUP, OPTION, P, PLAINTEXT, PRE, Q, S, SAMP, SCRIPT, SELECT, SMALL, SPAN, STRIKE, STRONG, SUB, SUP, TABLE, TBODY, TD, TEXTAREA, TFOOT, TH, THEAD, TR, TT, U, UL, VAR, XMP

LEFT ILAYER, LAYER

LEFTMARGIN BODY

LINK BODY

LONGDESC FRAME, IFRAME, IMG

LOOP BGSOUND, IMG, MARQUEE

LOWSRC IMG

MARGINHEIGHT FRAME, IFRAME

MARGINWIDTH FRAME, IFRAME

MAXLENGTH INPUT

MAYSCRIPT APPLET

MEDIA DIV, LINK, SPAN, STYLE

METHOD FORM

METHODS A

MULTIPLE SELECT

NAME A, APPLET, AREA, BASEFONT, BUTTON, EMBED, FORM, FRAME, IFRAME, IMG, INPUT, KEYGEN, MAP, META, OBJECT, PARAM, SELECT, TEXTAREA

NOHREF AREA

NORESIZE FRAME, IFRAME

NOSHADE HR

NOWRAP TD, TH

PAGEX LAYER

PAGEY LAYER

PALETTE EMBED

PLUGINSPAGE EMBED

PLUGINURL EMBED

POINT-SIZE FONT

PROFILE HEAD

PROMPT   ISINDEX

READONLY   INPUT, TEXTAREA

REL   A, DIV, LINK, SPAN

REPEAT   COL

REV   A, DIV, LINK, SPAN

RIGHTMARGIN   BODY

ROWS   FRAMESET, TEXTAREA

ROWSPAN   TD, TH

RULES   TABLE

SCHEME   META

SCOPE   TD, TH

SCROLL   BODY

SCROLLAMOUNT   MARQUEE

SCROLLDELAY   MARQUEE

SCROLLING   FRAME, IFRAME

SELECTED   OPTION

SHAPE   A, AREA

SHAPES   OBJECT

SIZE   BASEFONT, FONT, HR, INPUT, SELECT, SPACER

SPAN   COL, COLGROUP

SRC   APPLET, BGSOUND, EMBED, FRAME, IFRAME, ILAYER, IMG, INPUT, LAYER, LINK,
SCRIPT

STANDBY   OBJECT

START   IMG, OL

STYLE   A, ABBR, ACRONYM, ADDRESS, APPLET, AREA, B, BASEFONT, BDO, BIG,
BLOCKQUOTE, BODY, BR, BUTTON, CAPTION, CENTER, CITE, CODE, COL, COL-
GROUP, DD, DEL, DFN, DIR, DIV, DL, DT, EM, EMBED, FIELDSET, FONT, FORM,
FRAME, FRAMESET, H1, H2, H3, H4, H5, H6, HR, I, IFRAME, IMG, INPUT, INS, ISIN-
DEX, KBD, LABEL, LEGEND, LI, LINK, LISTING, MAP, MARQUEE, MENU, NOBR, NO-
FRAMES, NOSCRIPT, OBJECT, OL, OPTGROUP, OPTION, P, PLAINTEXT, PRE, Q, S,
SAMP, SELECT, SMALL, SPAN, STRIKE, STRONG, SUB, SUP, TABLE, TBODY, TD,
TEXTAREA, TFOOT, TH, THEAD, TR, TT, U, UL, VAR, WBR, XMP

SUMMARY   TABLE

TABINDEX   A, AREA, BUTTON, INPUT, LABEL, OBJECT, SELECT, TEXTAREA

TARGET   A, AREA, BASE, DIV, FORM, LINK, SPAN

TEXT   BODY, BR

TITLE   A, ABBR, ACRONYM, ADDRESS, APPLET, AREA, B, BASEFONT, BDO, BGSOUND,
BIG, BLOCKQUOTE, BODY, BR, BUTTON, CAPTION, CENTER, CITE, CODE, COL,
COLGROUP, DD, DEL, DFN, DIR, DIV, DL, DT, EM, EMBED, FIELDSET, FONT, FORM,
FRAME, FRAMESET, H1, H2, H3, H4, H5, H6, HEAD, HR, HTML, I, IFRAME, IMG,
INPUT, INS, ISINDEX, KBD, LABEL, LEGEND, LI, LINK, LISTING, MAP, MARQUEE,
MENU, META, NOBR, NOFRAMES, NOSCRIPT, OBJECT, OL, OPTGROUP, OPTION, P,

PLAINTEXT, PRE, Q, S, SAMP, SCRIPT, SMALL, SPAN, STRIKE, STRONG, STYLE, SUB, SUP, TABLE, TBODY, TD, TEXTAREA, TFOOT, TH, THEAD, TITLE, TR, TT, U, UL, VAR, WBR, XMP

TOP ILAYER, LAYER

TOPMARGIN BODY

TRUESPEED MARQUEE

TYPE A, BUTTON, DIV, EMBED, INPUT, LI, LINK, OBJECT, OL, PARAM, SCRIPT, SPACER, SPAN, STYLE, UL

UNITS EMBED

URN A

USEMAP IMG, INPUT, OBJECT

VALIGN CAPTION, COL, COLGROUP, FIELDSET, TBODY, TD, TFOOT, TH, THEAD, TR

VALUE BUTTON, INPUT, LI, OPTION, PARAM

VALUETYPE PARAM

VERSION HTML

VISIBILITY ILAYER, LAYER

VLINK BODY

VOLUME BGSOUND

VSPACE APPLET, EMBED, IFRAME, IMG, MARQUEE, OBJECT

WEIGHT FONT

WIDTH APPLET, COL, COLGROUP, EMBED, FRAME, HR, IFRAME, ILAYER, IMG, LAYER, MARQUEE, MULTICOL, OBJECT, PRE, SPACER, TABLE, TD, TH

WRAP PRE, TEXTAREA

Z-INDEX ILAYER, LAYER

13

Document Object Properties Index

Entries in the following index are arranged alphabetically by scriptable object properties. You can look up a property to find out which document objects support it. This listing is a union of properties defined for objects in Navigator 4, Internet Explorer 4, and a working draft of the DOM. The same property name may mean different things for different objects. Be sure to look up the details of the property listing in Chapter 9, *Document Object Reference*, to find if the property is available for the browser(s) used by your intended audience and whether it does what you want. Objects shown in all uppercase letters are objects that reflect HTML elements of the same name. The following objects reflect specific types of `INPUT` elements: `button`, `checkbox`, `fileUpload`, `password`, `radio`, `reset`, `submit`, and `text`.

ABORT Event

above layer

accessKey A, APPLET, BODY, BUTTON, button, checkbox, EMBED, FIELDSET, fileUpload, LABEL, LEGEND, MARQUEE, OBJECT, password, radio, reset, SELECT, submit, text, TEXTAREA

action FORM

activeElement document

align APPLET, CAPTION, COL, COLGROUP, DIV, FIELDSET, H1, H2, H3, H4, H5, H6, HR, IFRAME, IMG, LEGEND, OBJECT, P, TABLE, TBODY, TD, TFOOT, TH, THEAD, TR

alink BODY

alinkColor document

alt AREA, IMG

altHTML APPLET

altHtml OBJECT

altKey event

defaultChecked   checkbox, radio

defaultSelected   OPTION

defaultStatus   window

defaultValue   password, text, TEXTAREA

defer   SCRIPT

description   mimeType, plugin

dialogArguments   window

dialogHeight   window

dialogLeft   window

dialogTop   window

dialogWidth   window

dir   BDO, NOFRAMES, NOSCRIPT

direction   MARQUEE

disabled   BUTTON, button, checkbox, fileUpload, hidden, LINK, password, radio, reset, SELECT, STYLE, styleSheet, submit, text, TEXTAREA

display   style, tags

document   A, ACRONYM, ADDRESS, APPLET, AREA, B, BASE, BASEFONT, BGSOUND, BIG, BLOCKQUOTE, BODY, BR, BUTTON, button, CAPTION, CENTER, checkbox, CITE, CODE, COL, COLGROUP, COMMENT, DD, DEL, DFN, DIR, DIV, DL, DT, EM, EMBED, FIELDSET, fileUpload, FONT, FORM, FRAME, FRAMESET, H1, H2, H3, H4, H5, H6, HEAD, hidden, HR, HTML, I, IFRAME, IMG, INS, KBD, LABEL, layer, LEGEND, LI, LINK, LISTING, MAP, MARQUEE, MENU, META, OBJECT, OL, OPTION, P, password, PLAINTEXT, PRE, Q, radio, reset, S, SAMP, SCRIPT, SELECT, SMALL, SPAN, STRIKE, STRONG, STYLE, SUB, submit, SUP, TABLE, TBODY, TD, text, TEXTAREA, TFOOT, TH, THEAD, TITLE, TR, TT, U, UL, VAR, window, XMP

domain   document

DRAGDROP   Event

dynsrc   IMG

enabledPlugin   mimeType

encoding   FORM

ERROR   Event

event   SCRIPT, window

expando   document

face   BASEFONT, FONT

fgColor   document

filename   plugin

filter   style

FOCUS   Event

font   style

fontFamily   style, tags

fontSize   style, tags

EMBED, FIELDSET, FONT, FORM, H1, H2, H3, H4, H5, H6, I, INS, KBD, LABEL, LEGEND, LI, LISTING, MAP, MARQUEE, MENU, OL, P, PLAINTEXT, PRE, Q, S, SAMP, SCRIPT, SELECT, SMALL, SPAN, STRIKE, STRONG, SUB, SUP, TABLE, TBODY, TD, TFOOT, TH, THEAD, TR, TT, U, UL, VAR, XMP

innerWidth   window

isMap   IMG

isTextEdit   A, ACRONYM, ADDRESS, APPLET, AREA, B, BASE, BASEFONT, BGSOUND, BIG, BLOCKQUOTE, BODY, BR, BUTTON, button, CAPTION, CENTER, checkbox, CITE, CODE, COL, COLGROUP, COMMENT, DD, DEL, DFN, DIR, DIV, DL, DT, EM, EMBED, FIELDSET, fileUpload, FONT, FORM, FRAME, FRAMESET, H1, H2, H3, H4, H5, H6, HEAD, hidden, HR, HTML, I, IFRAME, IMG, INS, KBD, LABEL, LEGEND, LI, LISTING, MAP, MARQUEE, MENU, META, OBJECT, OL, OPTION, P, password, PLAINTEXT, PRE, Q, radio, reset, S, SAMP, SCRIPT, SELECT, SMALL, SPAN, STRIKE, STRONG, STYLE, SUB, submit, SUP, TABLE, TBODY, TD, text, TEXTAREA, TFOOT, TH, THEAD, TITLE, TR, TT, U, UL, VAR, XMP

keyCode   event

KEYDOWN   Event

KEYPRESS   Event

KEYUP   Event

lang   A, ACRONYM, ADDRESS, APPLET, AREA, B, BASE, BASEFONT, BDO, BIG, BLOCKQUOTE, BODY, BR, BUTTON, button, CAPTION, CENTER, checkbox, CITE, CODE, COL, COLGROUP, COMMENT, DD, DEL, DFN, DIR, DIV, DL, DT, EM, EMBED, FIELDSET, fileUpload, FONT, FORM, FRAME, FRAMESET, H1, H2, H3, H4, H5, H6, HR, I, IFRAME, IMG, INS, KBD, LABEL, LEGEND, LI, LISTING, MAP, MARQUEE, MENU, META, NOFRAMES, NOSCRIPT, OBJECT, OL, P, password, PLAINTEXT, PRE, Q, radio, reset, S, SAMP, SELECT, SMALL, SPAN, STRIKE, STRONG, STYLE, SUB, submit, SUP, TABLE, TBODY, TD, text, TEXTAREA, TFOOT, TH, THEAD, TITLE, TR, TT, U, UL, VAR, XMP

language   A, ACRONYM, ADDRESS, APPLET, AREA, B, BIG, BLOCKQUOTE, BODY, BR, BUTTON, button, CAPTION, CENTER, checkbox, CITE, CODE, COL, COLGROUP, COMMENT, DD, DEL, DFN, DIR, DIV, DL, DT, EM, EMBED, FIELDSET, fileUpload, FONT, FORM, FRAME, FRAMESET, H1, H2, H3, H4, H5, H6, hidden, HR, HTML, I, IFRAME, IMG, INS, KBD, LABEL, LEGEND, LI, LISTING, MAP, MARQUEE, MENU, META, navigator, OBJECT, OL, OPTION, P, password, PLAINTEXT, PRE, Q, radio, reset, S, SAMP, SCRIPT, SELECT, SMALL, SPAN, STRIKE, STRONG, STYLE, SUB, submit, SUP, TABLE, TBODY, TD, text, TEXTAREA, TFOOT, TH, THEAD, TITLE, TR, TT, U, UL, VAR, XMP

lastModified   document

layerX   event

layerY   event

left   layer, style, tags

leftMargin   BODY

length   all, anchors, applets, areas, cells, children, embeds, filters, FORM, forms, frames, history, images, links, options, plugin, plugins, rows, rules, scripts, SELECT, window

letterSpacing   style

name   A, APPLET, BUTTON, button, checkbox, EMBED, fileUpload, FORM, FRAME, hidden, IFRAME, IMG, layer, MAP, OBJECT, password, plugin, radio, reset, SELECT, submit, text, TEXTAREA, window

nameProp   A

navigator   window

next   history

noHref   AREA

noResize   FRAME, IFRAME

noShade   HR

noWrap   BODY, DD, DT, TD, TH

object   OBJECT

offscreenBuffering   window

offsetHeight   A, ACRONYM, ADDRESS, APPLET, AREA, B, BGSOUND, BIG, BLOCKQUOTE, BODY, BR, BUTTON, button, CAPTION, CENTER, checkbox, CITE, CODE, COL, COLGROUP, COMMENT, DD, DEL, DFN, DIR, DIV, DL, DT, EM, EMBED, FIELDSET, fileUpload, FONT, FORM, H1, H2, H3, H4, H5, H6, HR, I, IFRAME, IMG, INS, KBD, LABEL, LEGEND, LI, LISTING, MAP, MARQUEE, MENU, OBJECT, OL, OPTION, P, password, PLAINTEXT, PRE, Q, radio, reset, S, SAMP, SELECT, SMALL, SPAN, STRIKE, STRONG, SUB, submit, SUP, TABLE, TBODY, TD, text, TEXTAREA, TFOOT, TH, THEAD, TR, TT, U, UL, VAR, XMP

offsetLeft   A, ACRONYM, ADDRESS, APPLET, AREA, B, BGSOUND, BIG, BLOCKQUOTE, BODY, BR, BUTTON, button, CAPTION, CENTER, checkbox, CITE, CODE, COL, COLGROUP, COMMENT, DD, DEL, DFN, DIR, DIV, DL, DT, EM, EMBED, FIELDSET, fileUpload, FONT, FORM, H1, H2, H3, H4, H5, H6, HR, I, IFRAME, IMG, INS, KBD, LABEL, LEGEND, LI, LISTING, MAP, MARQUEE, MENU, OBJECT, OL, P, password, PLAINTEXT, PRE, Q, radio, reset, S, SAMP, SELECT, SMALL, SPAN, STRIKE, STRONG, SUB, submit, SUP, TABLE, TBODY, TD, text, TEXTAREA, TFOOT, TH, THEAD, TR, TT, U, UL, VAR, XMP

offsetParent   A, ACRONYM, ADDRESS, APPLET, AREA, B, BGSOUND, BIG, BLOCKQUOTE, BODY, BR, BUTTON, button, CAPTION, CENTER, checkbox, CITE, CODE, COL, COLGROUP, COMMENT, DD, DEL, DFN, DIR, DIV, DL, DT, EM, EMBED, FIELDSET, fileUpload, FONT, FORM, H1, H2, H3, H4, H5, H6, HR, I, IFRAME, IMG, INS, KBD, LABEL, LEGEND, LI, LISTING, MAP, MARQUEE, MENU, OBJECT, OL, OPTION, P, password, PLAINTEXT, PRE, Q, radio, reset, S, SAMP, SELECT, SMALL, SPAN, STRIKE, STRONG, SUB, submit, SUP, TABLE, TBODY, TD, text, TEXTAREA, TFOOT, TH, THEAD, TR, TT, U, UL, VAR, XMP

offsetTop   A, ACRONYM, ADDRESS, APPLET, AREA, B, BGSOUND, BIG, BLOCKQUOTE, BODY, BR, BUTTON, button, CAPTION, CENTER, checkbox, CITE, CODE, COL, COLGROUP, COMMENT, DD, DEL, DFN, DIR, DIV, DL, DT, EM, EMBED, FIELDSET, fileUpload, FONT, FORM, H1, H2, H3, H4, H5, H6, HR, I, IFRAME, IMG, INS, KBD, LABEL, LEGEND, LI, LISTING, MAP, MARQUEE, MENU, OBJECT, OL, P, password, PLAINTEXT, PRE, Q, radio, reset, S, SAMP, SELECT, SMALL, SPAN, STRIKE, STRONG, SUB, submit, SUP, TABLE, TBODY, TD, text, TEXTAREA, TFOOT, TH, THEAD, TR, TT, U, UL, VAR, XMP

offsetWidth A, ACRONYM, ADDRESS, APPLET, AREA, B, BGSOUND, BIG, BLOCK-
QUOTE, BODY, BR, BUTTON, button, CAPTION, CENTER, checkbox, CITE, CODE,
COL, COLGROUP, COMMENT, DD, DEL, DFN, DIR, DIV, DL, DT, EM, EMBED, FIELD-
SET, fileUpload, FONT, FORM, H1, H2, H3, H4, H5, H6, HR, I, IFRAME, IMG, INS,
KBD, LABEL, LEGEND, LI, LISTING, MAP, MARQUEE, MENU, OBJECT, OL, OPTION,
P, password, PLAINTEXT, PRE, Q, radio, reset, S, SAMP, SELECT, SMALL, SPAN,
STRIKE, STRONG, SUB, submit, SUP, TABLE, TBODY, TD, text, TEXTAREA, TFOOT,
TH, THEAD, TR, TT, U, UL, VAR, XMP

offsetX event

offsetY event

onLine navigator

opener window

outerHeight window

outerHTML A, ACRONYM, ADDRESS, APPLET, AREA, B, BASE, BASEFONT, BGSOUND,
BIG, BLOCKQUOTE, BODY, BR, BUTTON, button, CAPTION, CENTER, checkbox,
CITE, CODE, COL, COLGROUP, COMMENT, DD, DEL, DFN, DIR, DIV, DL, DT, EM,
EMBED, FIELDSET, fileUpload, FONT, FORM, H1, H2, H3, H4, H5, H6, HR, I, IFRAME,
IMG, INS, KBD, LABEL, LEGEND, LI, LISTING, MAP, MARQUEE, MENU, OBJECT, OL,
P, password, PLAINTEXT, PRE, Q, radio, reset, S, SAMP, SELECT, SMALL, SPAN,
STRIKE, STRONG, SUB, submit, SUP, TABLE, TBODY, TD, text, TEXTAREA, TFOOT,
TH, THEAD, TR, TT, U, UL, VAR, XMP

outerText A, ACRONYM, ADDRESS, APPLET, AREA, B, BASE, BASEFONT, BGSOUND,
BIG, BLOCKQUOTE, BODY, BR, BUTTON, button, CAPTION, CENTER, checkbox,
CITE, CODE, COL, COLGROUP, COMMENT, DD, DEL, DFN, DIR, DIV, DL, DT, EM,
EMBED, FIELDSET, fileUpload, FONT, FORM, H1, H2, H3, H4, H5, H6, HR, I, IFRAME,
IMG, INS, KBD, LABEL, LEGEND, LI, LISTING, MAP, MARQUEE, MENU, OBJECT, OL,
P, password, PLAINTEXT, PRE, Q, radio, reset, S, SAMP, SELECT, SMALL, SPAN,
STRIKE, STRONG, SUB, submit, SUP, TABLE, TBODY, TD, text, TEXTAREA, TFOOT,
TH, THEAD, TR, TT, U, UL, VAR, XMP

outerWidth window

overflow style

owningElement styleSheet

padding style

paddingBottom style, tags

paddingLeft style, tags

paddingRight style, tags

paddings tags

paddingTop style, tags

pageBreakAfter style

pageBreakBefore style

pageX event, layer

pageXOffset window

pageY event, layer

pageYOffset window

palette EMBED

parent window

parentElement A, ACRONYM, ADDRESS, APPLET, AREA, B, BASE, BASEFONT, BGSOUND, BIG, BLOCKQUOTE, BODY, BR, BUTTON, button, CAPTION, CENTER, checkbox, CITE, CODE, COL, COLGROUP, COMMENT, DD, DEL, DFN, DIR, DIV, DL, DT, EM, EMBED, FIELDSET, fileUpload, FONT, FORM, FRAME, FRAMESET, H1, H2, H3, H4, H5, H6, HEAD, hidden, HR, HTML, I, IFRAME, IMG, INS, KBD, LABEL, LEG-END, LI, LINK, LISTING, MAP, MARQUEE, MENU, META, OBJECT, OL, OPTION, P, password, PLAINTEXT, PRE, Q, radio, reset, S, SAMP, SCRIPT, SELECT, SMALL, SPAN, STRIKE, STRONG, STYLE, SUB, submit, SUP, TABLE, TBODY, TD, text, TEXTAREA, TFOOT, TH, THEAD, TITLE, TR, TT, U, UL, VAR, XMP

parentLayer layer

parentStyleSheet styleSheet

parentTextEdit A, ACRONYM, ADDRESS, APPLET, AREA, B, BASE, BASEFONT, BGSOUND, BIG, BLOCKQUOTE, BODY, BR, BUTTON, button, CAPTION, CENTER, checkbox, CITE, CODE, COL, COLGROUP, COMMENT, DD, DEL, DFN, DIR, DIV, DL, DT, EM, EMBED, FIELDSET, fileUpload, FONT, FORM, FRAME, FRAMESET, H1, H2, H3, H4, H5, H6, hidden, HR, HTML, I, IFRAME, IMG, INS, KBD, LABEL, LEGEND, LI, LINK, LISTING, MAP, MARQUEE, MENU, META, OBJECT, OL, OPTION, P, password, PLAINTEXT, PRE, Q, radio, reset, S, SAMP, SCRIPT, SELECT, SMALL, SPAN, STRIKE, STRONG, STYLE, SUB, submit, SUP, TABLE, TBODY, TD, text, TEXTAREA, TFOOT, TH, THEAD, TITLE, TR, TT, U, UL, VAR, XMP

parentWindow document

pathname A, AREA, location

personalbar window

pixelDepth screen

pixelHeight style

pixelLeft style

pixelTop style

pixelWidth style

platform navigator

pluginspage EMBED

port A, AREA, location

posHeight style

position style

posLeft style

posTop style

posWidth style

previous history

prompt ISINDEX

protocol A, AREA, location

useMap   IMG

userAgent   navigator

userLanguage   navigator

userProfile   navigator

vAlign   CAPTION, COL, COLGROUP, TBODY, TD, TFOOT, TH, THEAD, TR

value   BUTTON, button, checkbox, fileUpload, hidden, LI, OPTION, password, radio, reset, SELECT, submit, text, TEXTAREA

verticalAlign   style, tags

visibility   layer, style, tags

visible   locationbar, menubar, personalbar, scrollbars, statusbar, toolbar

vLink   BODY

vlinkColor   document

volume   BGSOUND

vspace   APPLET, IFRAME, IMG, MARQUEE, OBJECT

which   event

whiteSpace   tags

width   APPLET, COL, COLGROUP, HR, IMG, MARQUEE, OBJECT, screen, style, TABLE, TD, TH

wrap   TEXTAREA

x   event, IMG

XFER_DONE   Event

y   event, IMG

zIndex   layer, style, tags

14

Document Object Methods Index

Entries in the following index are arranged alphabetically by scriptable object methods. You can look up a method to find out which document objects support it. This listing is a union of methods defined for objects in Navigator 4, Internet Explorer 4, and a working draft of the DOM. The same method name may mean different things for different objects. Be sure to look up the details of the method listing in Chapter 9, *Document Object Reference*, to find if the method is available for the browser(s) used by your intended audience and whether it does what you want. Objects shown in all uppercase letters are objects that reflect HTML elements of the same name. The following objects reflect specific types of `INPUT` elements: `button`, `checkbox`, `fileUpload`, `password`, `radio`, `reset`, `submit`, and `text`.

add( ) options

addImport( ) styleSheet

addReadRequest( ) userProfile

addRule( ) styleSheet

alert( ) window

assign( ) location

back( ) history, window

blur( ) A, APPLET, AREA, BUTTON, button, CAPTION, checkbox, DIV, EMBED, FIELD-SET, fileUpload, IMG, LEGEND, MARQUEE, OBJECT, password, radio, reset, SELECT, SPAN, submit, TABLE, TD, text, TEXTAREA, TH, TR, window

captureEvents( ) document, layer, window

clear( ) document, selection

clearInterval( ) window

clearRequest( ) userProfile

clearTimeout( ) window

click( )   A, ACRONYM, ADDRESS, APPLET, AREA, B, BIG, BLOCKQUOTE, BODY, BR, BUTTON, button, CAPTION, CENTER, checkbox, CITE, CODE, DD, DEL, DFN, DIR, DIV, DL, DT, EM, EMBED, FIELDSET, fileUpload, FONT, FORM, H1, H2, H3, H4, H5, H6, HR, I, IMG, INS, KBD, LABEL, LEGEND, LI, LISTING, MAP, MARQUEE, MENU, OBJECT, OL, P, password, PLAINTEXT, PRE, Q, radio, reset, S, SAMP, SELECT, SMALL, SPAN, STRIKE, STRONG, STYLE, SUB, submit, SUP, TABLE, TBODY, TD, text, TEXT-AREA, TFOOT, TH, THEAD, TR, TT, U, UL, VAR, XMP

close( )   document, window

collapse( )   TextRange

compareEndPoints( )   TextRange

confirm( )   window

contains( )   A, ACRONYM, ADDRESS, APPLET, AREA, B, BASE, BASEFONT, BGSOUND, BIG, BLOCKQUOTE, BODY, BR, BUTTON, button, CAPTION, CENTER, checkbox, CITE, CODE, COL, COLGROUP, COMMENT, DD, DEL, DFN, DIR, DIV, DL, DT, EM, EMBED, FIELDSET, fileUpload, FONT, FORM, FRAME, FRAMESET, H1, H2, H3, H4, H5, H6, HEAD, hidden, HR, HTML, I, IFRAME, IMG, INS, KBD, LABEL, LEGEND, LI, LINK, LISTING, MAP, MARQUEE, MENU, META, OBJECT, OL, OPTION, P, password, PLAIN-TEXT, PRE, Q, radio, reset, S, SAMP, SCRIPT, SELECT, SMALL, SPAN, STRIKE, STRONG, STYLE, SUB, submit, SUP, TABLE, TBODY, TD, text, TEXTAREA, TFOOT, TH, THEAD, TITLE, TR, TT, U, UL, VAR, XMP

createElement( )   document

createRange( )   selection

createStyleSheet( )   document

createTextRange( )   BODY, BUTTON, text, TEXTAREA

disableExternalCapture( )   window

doReadRequest( )   userProfile

duplicate( )   TextRange

elementFromPoint( )   document

empty( )   selection

enableExternalCapture( )   window

execCommand( )   document, TextRange

execScript( )   window

expand( )   TextRange

find( )   window

findText( )   TextRange

focus( )   A, APPLET, AREA, BUTTON, button, CAPTION, checkbox, DIV, EMBED, FIELD-SET, fileUpload, IMG, LEGEND, MARQUEE, OBJECT, password, radio, reset, SELECT, SPAN, submit, TABLE, TD, text, TEXTAREA, TH, TR, window

forward( )   history, window

getAttribute( )   A, ACRONYM, ADDRESS, APPLET, AREA, B, BASE, BASEFONT, BGSOUND, BIG, BLOCKQUOTE, BODY, BR, BUTTON, button, CAPTION, CENTER, checkbox, CITE, CODE, COL, COLGROUP, COMMENT, DD, DEL, DFN, DIR, DIV, DL, DT, EM, EMBED, FIELDSET, fileUpload, FONT, FORM, FRAME, FRAMESET, H1, H2, H3, H4, H5,

H6, HEAD, hidden, HR, HTML, I, IFRAME, IMG, INS, KBD, LABEL, LEGEND, LI, LINK, LISTING, MAP, MARQUEE, MENU, META, OBJECT, OL, OPTION, P, password, PLAIN-TEXT, PRE, Q, radio, reset, S, SAMP, SCRIPT, SELECT, SMALL, SPAN, STRIKE, STRONG, style, STYLE, SUB, submit, SUP, TABLE, TBODY, TD, text, TEXTAREA, TFOOT, TH, THEAD, TITLE, TR, TT, U, UL, userProfile, VAR, XMP

getBookmark( )   TextRange

getSelection( )   document

go( )   history

handleEvent( )   button, checkbox, document, fileUpload, FORM, layer, password, radio, reset, submit, text, TEXTAREA, window

home( )   window

inRange( )   TextRange

insertAdjacentHTML( )   A, ACRONYM, ADDRESS, APPLET, AREA, B, BIG, BLOCKQUOTE, BODY, BR, BUTTON, button, CAPTION, CENTER, checkbox, CITE, CODE, DD, DEL, DFN, DIR, DIV, DL, DT, EM, EMBED, FIELDSET, fileUpload, FONT, FORM, H1, H2, H3, H4, H5, H6, HR, I, IFRAME, IMG, INS, KBD, LABEL, LEGEND, LI, LISTING, MARQUEE, MENU, OL, P, password, PLAINTEXT, PRE, Q, radio, reset, S, SAMP, SCRIPT, SELECT, SMALL, SPAN, STRIKE, STRONG, STYLE, SUB, submit, SUP, TABLE, TBODY, TD, text, TEXTAREA, TFOOT, TH, THEAD, TR, TT, U, UL, VAR, XMP

insertAdjacentText( )   A, ACRONYM, ADDRESS, APPLET, AREA, B, BIG, BLOCKQUOTE, BODY, BR, BUTTON, button, CAPTION, CENTER, checkbox, CITE, CODE, DD, DEL, DFN, DIR, DIV, DL, DT, EM, EMBED, FIELDSET, fileUpload, FONT, FORM, H1, H2, H3, H4, H5, H6, HR, I, IFRAME, IMG, INS, KBD, LABEL, LEGEND, LI, LISTING, MARQUEE, MENU, OL, P, password, PLAINTEXT, PRE, Q, radio, reset, S, SAMP, SCRIPT, SELECT, SMALL, SPAN, STRIKE, STRONG, STYLE, SUB, submit, SUP, TABLE, TBODY, TD, text, TEXTAREA, TFOOT, TH, THEAD, TR, TT, U, UL, VAR, XMP

isEqual( )   TextRange

item( )   all, filters, forms, frames, images, options, plugins, rows, scripts

javaEnabled( )   navigator

load( )   layer

move( )   TextRange

moveAbove( )   layer

moveBelow( )   layer

moveBy( )   layer

moveEnd( )   TextRange

moveStart( )   TextRange

moveTo( )   layer, window

moveToAbsolute( )   layer

moveToBookmark( )   TextRange

moveToElementText( )   TextRange

moveToPoint( )   TextRange

navigate( )   window

nextPage( ) TABLE

open( ) document, window

parentElement( ) TextRange

pasteHTML( ) TextRange

preference( ) navigator

previousPage( ) TABLE

print( ) window

prompt( ) window

queryCommandEnabled( ) document, TextRange

queryCommandIndeterm( ) TextRange

queryCommandState( ) document, TextRange

queryCommandSupported( ) document, TextRange

queryCommandText( ) document, TextRange

queryCommandValue( ) document, TextRange

refresh( ) plugin, TABLE

releaseEvents( ) document, layer, window

reload( ) location

remove( ) options

removeAttribute( ) A, ACRONYM, ADDRESS, APPLET, AREA, B, BASE, BASEFONT, BGSOUND, BIG, BLOCKQUOTE, BODY, BR, BUTTON, button, CAPTION, CENTER, checkbox, CITE, CODE, COL, COLGROUP, COMMENT, DD, DEL, DFN, DIR, DIV, DL, DT, EM, EMBED, FIELDSET, fileUpload, FONT, FORM, FRAME, FRAMESET, H1, H2, H3, H4, H5, H6, HEAD, hidden, HR, HTML, I, IFRAME, IMG, INS, KBD, LABEL, LEGEND, LI, LINK, LISTING, MAP, MARQUEE, MENU, META, OBJECT, OL, OPTION, P, password, PLAINTEXT, PRE, Q, radio, reset, S, SAMP, SCRIPT, SELECT, SMALL, SPAN, STRIKE, STRONG, style, STYLE, SUB, submit, SUP, TABLE, TBODY, TD, text, TEXTAREA, TFOOT, TH, THEAD, TITLE, TR, TT, U, UL, VAR, XMP

replace( ) location

reset( ) FORM

resizeBy( ) layer, window

resizeTo( ) layer, window

routeEvent( ) document, layer, window

scroll( ) window

scrollBy( ) window

scrollIntoView( ) A, ACRONYM, ADDRESS, APPLET, AREA, B, BIG, BLOCKQUOTE, BR, BUTTON, button, CAPTION, CENTER, checkbox, CITE, CODE, DD, DEL, DFN, DIR, DIV, DL, DT, EM, EMBED, FIELDSET, fileUpload, FONT, FORM, H1, H2, H3, H4, H5, H6, HR, I, IFRAME, IMG, INS, KBD, LABEL, LEGEND, LI, LISTING, MAP, MARQUEE, MENU, OBJECT, OL, OPTION, P, password, PLAINTEXT, PRE, Q, radio, reset, S, SAMP, SELECT, SMALL, SPAN, STRIKE, STRONG, STYLE, SUB, submit, SUP, TABLE, TBODY, TD, text, TEXTAREA, TextRange, TFOOT, TH, THEAD, TR, TT, U, UL, VAR, XMP

scrollTo( ) window

select( )   fileUpload, password, text, TEXTAREA, TextRange

setAttribute( )   A, ACRONYM, ADDRESS, APPLET, AREA, B, BASE, BASEFONT, BGSOUND, BIG, BLOCKQUOTE, BODY, BR, BUTTON, button, CAPTION, CENTER, checkbox, CITE, CODE, COL, COLGROUP, COMMENT, DD, DEL, DFN, DIR, DIV, DL, DT, EM, EMBED, FIELDSET, fileUpload, FONT, FORM, FRAME, FRAMESET, H1, H2, H3, H4, H5, H6, HEAD, hidden, HR, HTML, I, IFRAME, IMG, INS, KBD, LABEL, LEGEND, LI, LINK, LISTING, MAP, MARQUEE, MENU, META, OBJECT, OL, OPTION, P, password, PLAIN-TEXT, PRE, Q, radio, reset, S, SAMP, SCRIPT, SELECT, SMALL, SPAN, STRIKE, STRONG, style, STYLE, SUB, submit, SUP, TABLE, TBODY, TD, text, TEXTAREA, TFOOT, TH, THEAD, TITLE, TR, TT, U, UL, VAR, XMP

setEndPoint( )   TextRange

setInterval( )   window

setTimeout( )   window

showHelp( )   window

showModalDialog( )   window

start( )   MARQUEE

stop( )   MARQUEE

submit( )   FORM

tags( )   all, rows

taintEnabled( )   navigator

write( )   document

writeln( )   document

15

Document Object
Event Handlers Index

Entries in the following index are arranged alphabetically by scriptable object event handlers. You can look up an event handler to find out which document objects and HTML elements support it. This listing is a union of event handlers defined for objects in Navigator 4 and Internet Explorer 4. The same event handler name may mean different things for different objects. Be sure to look up the details of the event handler listing in Chapter 9, *Document Object Reference*, to find if the event handler is available for the browser(s) used by your intended audience and whether it does what you want. Objects shown in all uppercase letters are objects that reflect HTML elements of the same name. The following objects reflect specific types of `INPUT` elements: `button`, `checkbox`, `file-Upload`, `password`, `radio`, `reset`, `submit`, and `text`. All event handlers are listed here in all lowercase, as they are in Chapter 9. You may use any case combination you like when specifying the event handler as an HTML element attribute, but you must use the all-lowercase form in scripts for cross-browser compatibility.

onabort IMG

onafterupdate APPLET, AREA, BODY, BUTTON, button, CAPTION, checkbox, DIV, document, FIELDSET, IMG, MARQUEE, OBJECT, radio, SELECT, TABLE, TD, TEXTAREA, TH

onbeforeunload BODY, FRAMESET, TD, TEXTAREA, TH, window

onbeforeupdate APPLET, AREA, BODY, BUTTON, button, CAPTION, checkbox, DIV, document, FIELDSET, IMG, OBJECT, radio, SELECT, TABLE

onblur A, APPLET, AREA, BUTTON, button, CAPTION, checkbox, DIV, EMBED, FIELDSET, fileUpload, IMG, layer, LEGEND, MARQUEE, OBJECT, password, radio, reset, SELECT, SPAN, submit, TABLE, TD, text, TEXTAREA, TH, TR, window

onbounce MARQUEE

onchange BODY, button, CAPTION, checkbox, DIV, FIELDSET, fileUpload, IMG, LEGEND, password, radio, SELECT, text, TEXTAREA *onclick* A, ACRONYM, ADDRESS, APPLET, AREA, B, BIG, BLOCKQUOTE, BODY, BUT-TON, button, CAPTION, CENTER, checkbox, CITE, CODE, DD, DEL, DFN, DIR, DIV, DL, document, DT, EM, FIELDSET, fileUpload, FONT, FORM, H1, H2, H3, H4, H5, H6, HR, I, IMG, INS, KBD, LABEL, LEGEND, LI, LISTING, MAP, MARQUEE, MENU, OBJECT, OL, P, password, PLAINTEXT, PRE, Q, radio, reset, S, SAMP, SELECT, SMALL, SPAN, STRIKE, STRONG, SUB, submit, SUP, TABLE, TBODY, TD, text, TEXTAREA, TFOOT, TH, THEAD, TR, TT, U, UL, VAR, XMP

ondataavailable APPLET, AREA, BODY, IMG, OBJECT

ondatasetchanged APPLET, AREA, BODY, IMG, OBJECT

ondatasetcomplete APPLET, AREA, BODY, IMG, OBJECT

ondblclick A, ACRONYM, ADDRESS, APPLET, AREA, B, BIG, BLOCKQUOTE, BODY, BUTTON, button, CAPTION, CENTER, checkbox, CITE, CODE, DD, DEL, DFN, DIR, DIV, DL, document, DT, EM, FIELDSET, fileUpload, FONT, FORM, H1, H2, H3, H4, H5, H6, HR, I, IMG, INS, KBD, LABEL, LEGEND, LI, LISTING, MAP, MARQUEE, MENU, OBJECT, OL, P, password, PLAINTEXT, PRE, Q, radio, reset, S, SAMP, SELECT, SMALL, SPAN, STRIKE, STRONG, SUB, submit, SUP, TABLE, TBODY, TD, text, TEXTAREA, TFOOT, TH, THEAD, TR, TT, U, UL, VAR, XMP

ondragdrop window

ondragstart ACRONYM, ADDRESS, B, BIG, BLOCKQUOTE, BODY, BUTTON, CAPTION, CENTER, CITE, CODE, DD, DEL, DFN, DIR, DIV, DL, document, DT, EM, FIELDSET, FONT, FORM, H1, H2, H3, H4, H5, H6, HR, I, IMG, INS, KBD, LABEL, LEGEND, LI, LISTING, MARQUEE, MENU, OBJECT, OL, P, PLAINTEXT, PRE, Q, S, SAMP, SELECT, SMALL, SPAN, STRIKE, STRONG, SUB, SUP, TABLE, TBODY, TD, TEXTAREA, TFOOT, TH, THEAD, TR, TT, U, UL, VAR, XMP

onerror IMG, LINK, OBJECT, SCRIPT, STYLE, window

onerrorupdate APPLET, AREA, BODY, button, CAPTION, checkbox, document, FIELD-SET, OBJECT, radio, SELECT, TEXTAREA

onfilterchange ACRONYM, ADDRESS, B, BIG, BLOCKQUOTE, BODY, BUTTON, button, CAPTION, CENTER, checkbox, CITE, CODE, DD, DEL, DFN, DIR, DL, DT, EM, FIELD-SET, fileUpload, FONT, FORM, H1, H2, H3, H4, H5, H6, HR, I, IMG, INS, KBD, LABEL, LI, LISTING, MENU, OBJECT, OL, P, PLAINTEXT, PRE, Q, radio, reset, S, SAMP, SELECT, SMALL, SPAN, STRIKE, STRONG, SUB, submit, SUP, TBODY, TD, TEXTAREA, TFOOT, TH, THEAD, TR, TT, U, UL, VAR, XMP

onfinish MARQUEE

onfocus A, APPLET, AREA, BUTTON, button, CAPTION, checkbox, DIV, EMBED, FIELD-SET, fileUpload, IMG, layer, LEGEND, MARQUEE, OBJECT, password, radio, reset, submit, TABLE, text, TEXTAREA, window

onhelp A, ACRONYM, ADDRESS, APPLET, AREA, B, BIG, BLOCKQUOTE, BODY, BUT-TON, button, CAPTION, CENTER, checkbox, CITE, CODE, DD, DEL, DFN, DIR, DIV, DL, document, DT, EM, FIELDSET, fileUpload, FONT, FORM, H1, H2, H3, H4, H5, H6, HR, I, IMG, INS, KBD, LABEL, LEGEND, LI, LISTING, MAP, MARQUEE, MENU, OBJECT, OL, P, password, PLAINTEXT, PRE, Q, radio, reset, S, SAMP, SELECT, SMALL, SPAN, STRIKE, STRONG, SUB, submit, SUP, TABLE, TBODY, TD, text, TEXTAREA, TFOOT, TH, THEAD, TR, TT, U, UL, VAR, window, XMP

onkeydown A, ACRONYM, ADDRESS, APPLET, AREA, B, BIG, BLOCKQUOTE, BODY, BUTTON, button, CAPTION, CENTER, checkbox, CITE, CODE, DD, DEL, DFN, DIR,

DIV, DL, document, DT, EM, FIELDSET, fileUpload, FONT, FORM, H1, H2, H3, H4, H5, H6, HR, I, IMG, INS, KBD, LABEL, LEGEND, LI, LISTING, MAP, MARQUEE, MENU, OL, P, password, PLAINTEXT, PRE, Q, radio, reset, S, SAMP, SELECT, SMALL, SPAN, STRIKE, STRONG, SUB, submit, SUP, TABLE, TBODY, TD, text, TEXTAREA, TFOOT, TH, THEAD, TR, TT, U, UL, VAR, XMP

onkeypress   A, ACRONYM, ADDRESS, APPLET, AREA, B, BIG, BLOCKQUOTE, BODY, BUTTON, button, CAPTION, CENTER, checkbox, CITE, CODE, DD, DEL, DFN, DIR, DIV, DL, document, DT, EM, FIELDSET, fileUpload, FONT, FORM, H1, H2, H3, H4, H5, H6, HR, I, IMG, INS, KBD, LABEL, LEGEND, LI, LISTING, MAP, MARQUEE, MENU, OL, P, password, PLAINTEXT, PRE, Q, radio, reset, S, SAMP, SELECT, SMALL, SPAN, STRIKE, STRONG, SUB, submit, SUP, TABLE, TBODY, TD, text, TEXTAREA, TFOOT, TH, THEAD, TR, TT, U, UL, VAR, XMP

onkeyup   A, ACRONYM, ADDRESS, APPLET, AREA, B, BIG, BLOCKQUOTE, BODY, BUTTON, button, CAPTION, CENTER, checkbox, CITE, CODE, DD, DEL, DFN, DIR, DIV, DL, document, DT, EM, FIELDSET, fileUpload, FONT, FORM, H1, H2, H3, H4, H5, H6, HR, I, IMG, INS, KBD, LABEL, LEGEND, LI, LISTING, MAP, MARQUEE, MENU, OL, P, password, PLAINTEXT, PRE, Q, radio, reset, S, SAMP, SELECT, SMALL, SPAN, STRIKE, STRONG, SUB, submit, SUP, TABLE, TBODY, TD, text, TEXTAREA, TFOOT, TH, THEAD, TR, TT, U, UL, VAR, XMP

onload   APPLET, AREA, FRAMESET, IMG, layer, LINK, SCRIPT, STYLE, window

onmousedown   A, ACRONYM, ADDRESS, APPLET, AREA, B, BIG, BLOCKQUOTE, BODY, BUTTON, button, CAPTION, CENTER, checkbox, CITE, CODE, DD, DEL, DFN, DIR, DIV, DL, document, DT, EM, FIELDSET, fileUpload, FONT, FORM, H1, H2, H3, H4, H5, H6, HR, I, IMG, INS, KBD, LABEL, LEGEND, LI, LISTING, MAP, MARQUEE, MENU, OL, P, password, PLAINTEXT, PRE, Q, radio, reset, S, SAMP, SELECT, SMALL, SPAN, STRIKE, STRONG, SUB, submit, SUP, TABLE, TBODY, TD, text, TEXTAREA, TFOOT, TH, THEAD, TR, TT, U, UL, VAR, XMP

onmousemove   A, ACRONYM, ADDRESS, APPLET, AREA, B, BIG, BLOCKQUOTE, BODY, BUTTON, button, CAPTION, CENTER, checkbox, CITE, CODE, DD, DEL, DFN, DIR, DIV, DL, document, DT, EM, FIELDSET, fileUpload, FONT, FORM, H1, H2, H3, H4, H5, H6, HR, I, IMG, INS, KBD, LABEL, LEGEND, LI, LISTING, MAP, MARQUEE, MENU, OL, P, password, PLAINTEXT, PRE, Q, radio, reset, S, SAMP, SELECT, SMALL, SPAN, STRIKE, STRONG, SUB, submit, SUP, TABLE, TBODY, TD, text, TEXTAREA, TFOOT, TH, THEAD, TR, TT, U, UL, VAR, XMP

onmouseout   A, ACRONYM, ADDRESS, APPLET, AREA, B, BIG, BLOCKQUOTE, BODY, BUTTON, button, CAPTION, CENTER, checkbox, CITE, CODE, DD, DEL, DFN, DIR, DIV, DL, document, DT, EM, FIELDSET, fileUpload, FONT, FORM, H1, H2, H3, H4, H5, H6, HR, I, IMG, INS, KBD, LABEL, layer, LEGEND, LI, LISTING, MAP, MARQUEE, MENU, OL, P, password, PLAINTEXT, PRE, Q, radio, reset, S, SAMP, SELECT, SMALL, SPAN, STRIKE, STRONG, SUB, submit, SUP, TABLE, TBODY, TD, text, TEXTAREA, TFOOT, TH, THEAD, TR, TT, U, UL, VAR, XMP

onmouseover   A, ACRONYM, ADDRESS, APPLET, AREA, B, BIG, BLOCKQUOTE, BODY, BUTTON, button, CAPTION, CENTER, checkbox, CITE, CODE, DD, DEL, DFN, DIR, DIV, DL, document, DT, EM, FIELDSET, fileUpload, FONT, FORM, H1, H2, H3, H4, H5, H6, HR, I, IMG, INS, KBD, LABEL, layer, LEGEND, LI, LISTING, MAP, MARQUEE, MENU, OL, P, password, PLAINTEXT, PRE, Q, radio, reset, S, SAMP, SELECT, SMALL,

SPAN, STRIKE, STRONG, SUB, submit, SUP, TABLE, TBODY, TD, text, TEXTAREA, TFOOT, TH, THEAD, TR, TT, U, UL, VAR, XMP

onmouseup A, ACRONYM, ADDRESS, APPLET, AREA, B, BIG, BLOCKQUOTE, BODY, BUTTON, button, CAPTION, CENTER, checkbox, CITE, CODE, DD, DEL, DFN, DIR, DIV, DL, document, DT, EM, FIELDSET, fileUpload, FONT, FORM, H1, H2, H3, H4, H5, H6, HR, I, IMG, INS, KBD, LABEL, layer, LEGEND, LI, LISTING, MAP, MARQUEE, MENU, P, password, PLAINTEXT, PRE, Q, radio, reset, S, SAMP, SELECT, SMALL, SPAN, STRIKE, STRONG, SUB, submit, SUP, TABLE, TBODY, TD, text, TEXTAREA, TFOOT, TH, THEAD, TR, TT, U, VAR, XMP

onmove window

onreadystatechange APPLET, AREA, document, LINK, OBJECT, SCRIPT, STYLE

onreset FORM

onresize APPLET, AREA, BUTTON, DIV, FIELDSET, FRAMESET, IMG, MARQUEE, SELECT, TABLE, TD, TH, window

onrowenter APPLET, AREA, BODY, BUTTON, DIV, document, IMG, MARQUEE, OBJECT, SELECT, TABLE, TD, TEXTAREA, TH

onrowexit APPLET, AREA, BODY, BUTTON, DIV, document, IMG, MARQUEE, OBJECT, SELECT, TABLE, TD, TEXTAREA, TH

onscroll BODY, CAPTION, DIV, FIELDSET, IMG, LEGEND, MARQUEE, TABLE, TEXT-AREA, window

onselect button, CAPTION, checkbox, FIELDSET, fileUpload, password, radio, reset, submit, text, TEXTAREA

onselectstart A, ACRONYM, ADDRESS, B, BIG, BLOCKQUOTE, BODY, BUTTON, CAPTION, CENTER, CITE, CODE, DD, DEL, DFN, DIR, DIV, DL, document, DT, EM, FIELDSET, FONT, FORM, H1, H2, H3, H4, H5, H6, HR, I, IMG, INS, KBD, LABEL, LEGEND, LI, LISTING, MARQUEE, MENU, OBJECT, OL, P, PLAINTEXT, PRE, Q, S, SAMP, SELECT, SMALL, SPAN, STRIKE, STRONG, SUB, SUP, TABLE, TBODY, TD, TEXTAREA, TFOOT, TH, THEAD, TR, TT, U, UL, VAR, XMP

onstart MARQUEE

onsubmit FORM

onunload BODY, FRAMESET, window

IV

Appendixes

This part provides quick access to useful HTML authoring and scripting information. The glossary offers quick explanations of some of the new and potentially confusing terminology of DHTML.

- Appendix A, *Color Names and RGB Values*
- Appendix B, *HTML Character Entities*
- Appendix C, *Keyboard Event Character Values*
- Appendix D, *Internet Explorer Commands*
- Glossary

A

Color Names and
RGB Values

Netscape was the first to develop a library of color names that could be used as attribute and scripted object property color values in place of hexadecimal triplet values. Internet Explorer 4 also supports the use of these values. Color names in both tag attributes and scripts are case insensitive. Typically, if you set a color attribute or property to one of the named colors, the object property is reflected in scripts as the hexadecimal triplet value for that color. Also be aware that some colors in this collection require 16- or 24-bit color to achieve the proper hue.

Color Name	Red	Green	Blue
aliceblue	F0	F8	FF
antiquewhite	FA	EB	D7
aqua	00	FF	FF
aquamarine	7F	FF	D4
azure	F0	FF	FF
beige	F5	F5	DC
bisque	FF	E4	C4
black	00	00	00
blanchedalmond	FF	EB	CD
blue	00	00	FF
blueviolet	8A	2B	E2
brown	A5	2A	2A
burlywood	DE	B8	87
cadetblue	5F	9E	A0
chartreuse	7F	FF	00
chocolate	D2	69	1E
coral	FF	7F	50

Color Name	Red	Green	Blue
cornflowerblue	64	95	ED
cornsilk	FF	F8	DC
crimson	DC	14	3C
cyan	00	FF	FF
darkblue	00	00	8B
darkcyan	00	8B	8B
darkgoldenrod	B8	86	0B
darkgray	A9	A9	A9
darkgreen	00	64	00
darkkhaki	BD	B7	6B
darkmagenta	8B	00	8B
darkolivegreen	55	6B	2F
darkorange	FF	8C	00
darkorchid	99	32	CC
darkred	8B	00	00
darksalmon	E9	96	7A
darkseagreen	8F	BC	8F
darkslateblue	48	3D	8B
darkslategray	2F	4F	4F
darkturquoise	00	CE	D1
darkviolet	94	00	D3
deeppink	FF	14	93
deepskyblue	00	BF	FF
dimgray	69	69	69
dodgerblue	1E	90	FF
firebrick	B2	22	22
floralwhite	FF	FA	F0
forestgreen	22	8B	22
fuchsia	FF	00	FF
gainsboro	DC	DC	DC
ghostwhite	F8	F8	FF
gold	FF	D7	00
goldenrod	DA	A5	20
gray	80	80	80
green	00	80	00
greenyellow	AD	FF	2F
honeydew	F0	FF	F0

Color Name	Red	Green	Blue
hotpink	FF	69	B4
indianred	CD	5C	5C
indigo	4B	00	82
ivory	FF	FF	F0
khaki	F0	E6	8C
lavender	E6	E6	FA
lavenderblush	FF	F0	F5
lawngreen	7C	FC	00
lemonchiffon	FF	FA	CD
lightblue	AD	D8	E6
lightcoral	F0	80	80
lightcyan	E0	FF	FF
lightgoldenrodyellow	FA	FA	D2
lightgreen	90	EE	90
lightgrey	D3	D3	D3
lightpink	FF	B6	C1
lightsalmon	FF	A0	7A
lightseagreen	20	B2	AA
lightskyblue	87	CE	FA
lightslategray	77	88	99
lightsteelblue	B0	C4	DE
lightyellow	FF	FF	E0
lime	00	FF	00
limegreen	32	CD	32
linen	FA	F0	E6
magenta	FF	00	FF
maroon	80	00	00
mediumaquamarine	66	CD	AA
mediumblue	00	00	CD
mediumorchid	BA	55	D3
mediumpurple	93	70	DB
mediumseagreen	3C	B3	71
mediumslateblue	7B	68	EE
mediumspringgreen	00	FA	9A
mediumturquoise	48	D1	CC
mediumvioletred	C7	15	85
midnightblue	19	19	70

Color Name	Red	Green	Blue
mintcream	F5	FF	FA
mistyrose	FF	E4	E1
moccasin	FF	E4	B5
navajowhite	FF	DE	AD
navy	00	00	80
oldlace	FD	F5	E6
olive	80	80	00
olivedrab	6B	8E	23
orange	FF	A5	00
orangered	FF	45	00
orchid	DA	70	D6
palegoldenrod	EE	E8	AA
palegreen	98	FB	98
paleturquoise	AF	EE	EE
palevioletred	DB	70	93
papayawhip	FF	EF	D5
peachpuff	FF	DA	B9
peru	CD	85	3F
pink	FF	C0	CB
plum	DD	A0	DD
powderblue	B0	E0	E6
purple	80	00	80
red	FF	00	00
rosybrown	BC	8F	8F
royalblue	41	69	E1
saddlebrown	8B	45	13
salmon	FA	80	72
sandybrown	F4	A4	60
seagreen	2E	8B	57
seashell	FF	F5	EE
sienna	A0	52	2D
silver	C0	C0	C0
skyblue	87	CE	EB
slateblue	6A	5A	CD
slategray	70	80	90
snow	FF	FA	FA
springgreen	00	FF	7F

Color Name	Red	Green	Blue
steelblue	46	82	B4
tan	D2	B4	8C
teal	00	80	80
thistle	D8	BF	D8
tomato	FF	63	47
turquoise	40	E0	D0
violet	EE	82	EE
wheat	F5	DE	B3
white	FF	FF	FF
whitesmoke	F5	F5	F5
yellow	FF	FF	00
yellowgreen	9A	CD	32

B

HTML Character Entities

To display symbols and characters beyond the collection of common ASCII alphanumeric values (0-127), browsers recognize a special coding that lets you insert such characters into HTML document content. These *entity* characters start with an ampersand symbol (&) and end with a semicolon (;). Between those symbols goes a representation for the desired character. Each of these characters has a numeric value associated with it. You can insert the number of that value in the entity. For example, the numeric entity value for a copyright symbol is 169. An HTML statement using that symbol looks as follows:

```
<P STYLE="align: center">&#169;1998 MegaCorp, Inc. All Rights Reserved.</P>
```

Because the numbering system is not easy to remember, entities also have casesensitive word or abbreviation equivalents for their values. For the copyright symbol, for example, the entity is ©. This makes the code more readable, as in the following:

```
<P STYLE="align: center">&copy;1998 MegaCorp, Inc. All Rights Reserved.</P>
```

In this appendix, every entity defined in the HTML 4.0 specification is listed in alphabetical order. For each entity, the version of Navigator and Internet Explorer that first supported the entity is shown in the table. Browser support is indicated for the Win32 version of the browser as run under Windows 95. Some characters may not be available in all fonts or on all operating system platforms. A large number of entities in the table for math and technical symbols in Greek are not implemented in the Version 4 browsers at all, but support should improve with each new generation of browser.

Entity	Description	NN	IE
Á	Capital letter A with acute	2	3
á	Small letter a with acute	2	3

Entity	Description	NN	IE
&Acirc;	Capital letter A with circumflex	2	3
&acirc;	Small letter a with circumflex	2	3
&acute;	Acute accent	3	3
&AElig;	Capital letter AE	2	3
&aelig;	Small letter ae	2	3
&Agrave;	Capital letter A with grave	2	3
&agrave;	Small letter a with grave	2	3
&alefsym;	Alef symbol	-	-
&Alpha;	Capital letter alpha	-	-
&alpha;	Small letter alpha	-	-
&amp;	Ampersand	2	3
&and;	Logical and	-	-
&ang;	Angle	-	-
&Aring;	Capital letter A with ring above	2	3
&aring;	Small letter a with ring above	2	3
&asymp;	Almost equal to	-	-
&Atilde;	Capital letter A with tilde	2	3
&atilde;	Small letter a with tilde	2	3
&Auml;	Capital letter A with diaeresis	2	3
&auml;	Small letter a with diaeresis	2	3
&bdquo;	Double low-9 quotation mark	-	4
&Beta;	Capital letter beta	-	-
&beta;	Small letter beta	-	-
&brvbar;	Broken vertical bar	3	3
&bull;	Bullet	-	4
&cap;	Intersection	-	-
&Ccedil;	Capital letter C with cedilla	2	3
&ccedil;	Small letter c with cedilla	2	3
&cedil;	Cedilla	3	3
&cent;	Cent sign	3	3
&Chi;	Capital letter chi	-	-
&chi;	Small letter chi	-	-
&circ;	Modifier letter circumflex accent	-	4
&clubs;	Black club suit	-	-
&cong;	Approximately equal to	-	-
&copy;	Copyright sign	2	3
&crarr;	Downwards arrow with corner leftwards (carriage return)	-	-

Entity	Description	NN	IE
∪	Union	-	-
¤	Currency sign	3	3
†	Dagger	-	4
‡	Double dagger	-	4
↓	Downwards arrow	-	-
⇓	Downwards double arrow	-	-
°	Degree sign	3	3
Δ	Capital letter delta	-	-
δ	Small letter delta	-	-
♦	Black diamond suit	-	-
÷	Division sign	3	3
É	Capital letter E with acute	2	3
é	Small letter e with acute	2	3
Ê	Capital letter E with circumflex	2	3
ê	Small letter e with circumflex	2	3
È	Capital letter E with grave	2	3
è	Small letter e with grave	2	3
∅	Empty set/null set/diameter	-	-
	Em space	-	-
	En space	-	-
Ε	Capital letter epsilon	-	-
ε	Small letter epsilon	-	-
≡	Identical to	-	-
Η	Capital letter eta	-	-
η	Small letter eta	-	-
Ð	Capital letter ETH	2	3
ð	Small letter eth	2	3
Ë	Capital letter E with diaeresis	2	3
ë	Small letter e with diaeresis	2	3
€	Euro sign	-	-
∃	There exists	-	-
ƒ	Small f with hook	-	4
∀	For all	-	-
½	Fraction one-half	3	3
¼	Fraction one-quarter	3	3
¾	Fraction three-quarters	3	3
⁄	Fraction slash	-	-

Entity	Description	NN	IE
Γ	Capital letter gamma	-	-
γ	Small letter gamma	-	-
≥	Greater-than or equal to	-	-
>	Greater-than sign	2	3
↔	Left right arrow	-	-
⇔	Left right double arrow	-	-
♥	Black heart suit	-	-
…	Horizontal ellipsis	-	4
Í	Capital letter I with acute	2	3
í	Small letter i with acute	2	3
Î	Capital letter I with circumflex	2	3
î	Small letter i with circumflex	2	3
¡	Inverted exclamation mark	3	3
Ì	Capital letter I with grave	2	3
ì	Small letter i with grave	2	3
ℑ	Blackletter capital I	-	-
∞	Infinity	-	-
∫	Integral	-	-
Ι	Capital letter iota	-	-
ι	Small letter iota	-	-
¿	Inverted question mark	3	3
∈	Element of	-	-
Ï	Capital letter I with diaeresis	2	3
ï	Small letter i with diaeresis	2	3
Κ	Capital letter kappa	-	-
κ	Small letter kappa	-	-
Λ	Capital letter lambda	-	-
λ	Small letter lambda	-	-
⟨	Left-pointing angle bracket (bra)	-	-
«	Left-pointing double angle quotation mark (guillemet)	3	3
←	Leftwards arrow	-	-
⇐	Leftwards double arrow	-	-
⌈	Left ceiling	-	-
“	Left double quotation mark	-	4
≤	Less-than or equal to	-	-
⌊	Left floor	-	-
∗	Asterisk operator	-	-

Entity	Description	NN	IE
&loz;	Lozenge	-	-
&lrm;	Left-to-right mark	-	-
&lsaquo;	Single left-pointing angle quotation mark	-	4
&lsquo;	Left single quotation mark	-	4
&lt;	Less-than sign	2	3
&macr;	Macron (overline)	3	3
&mdash;	Em dash	-	4
&micro;	Micro sign	3	3
&middot;	Georgian comma	3	3
&minus;	Minus sign	-	-
&Mu;	Capital letter mu	-	-
&mu;	Small letter mu	-	-
&nabla;	Nabla	-	-
	Nonbreaking space	2	3
&ndash;	En dash	-	4
&ne;	Not equal to	-	-
&ni;	Contains as member	-	-
&not;	Not sign (discretionary hyphen)	3	3
&notin;	Not an element of	-	-
&nsub;	Not a subset of	-	-
&Ntilde;	Capital letter N with tilde	2	3
&ntilde;	Small letter n with tilde	2	3
&Nu;	Capital letter nu	-	-
&nu;	Small letter nu	-	-
&Oacute;	Capital letter O with acute	2	3
&oacute;	Small letter o with acute	2	3
&Ocirc;	Capital letter O with circumflex	2	3
&ocirc;	Small letter o with circumflex	2	3
&OElig;	Capital ligature OE	-	4
&oelig;	Small ligature oe	-	4
&Ograve;	Capital letter O with grave	2	3
&ograve;	Small letter o with grave	2	3
&oline;	Overline	-	-
&Omega;	Capital letter omega	-	-
&omega;	Small letter omega	-	-
&Omicron;	Capital letter omicron	-	-
&omicron;	Small letter omicron	-	-

Entity	Description	NN	IE
⊕	Circled plus	-	-
∨	Logical or	-	-
ª	Feminine ordinal indicator	3	3
º	Masculine ordinal indicator	3	3
Ø	Capital letter O with stroke	2	3
ø	Small letter o with stroke	2	3
Õ	Capital letter O with tilde	2	3
õ	Small letter o with tilde	2	3
⊗	Circled times	-	-
Ö	Capital letter O with diaeresis	2	3
ö	Small letter o with diaeresis	2	3
¶	Paragraph sign	3	3
∂	Partial differential	-	-
‰	Per mille sign	-	4
⊥	Up tack/orthogonal to/perpendicular	-	-
Φ	Capital letter phi	-	-
φ	Small letter phi	-	-
Π	Capital letter pi	-	-
π	Small letter pi	-	-
ϖ	π symbol	-	-
±	Plus-or-minus sign	3	3
£	Pound sign	3	3
′	Prime/minutes/feet	-	-
″	Double prime/seconds/inches	-	-
∏	N-ary product (product sign)	-	-
∝	Proportional to	-	-
Ψ	Capital letter psi	-	-
ψ	Small letter psi	-	-
"	Quotation mark	2	3
√	Square root	-	-
⟩	Right-pointing angle bracket (ket)	-	-
»	Right-pointing double angle quotation mark (guillemet)	3	3
→	Rightwards arrow	-	-
⇒	Rightwards double arrow	-	-
⌉	Right ceiling	-	-
”	Right double quotation mark	-	4
ℜ	Blackletter capital R	-	-

Entity	Description	NN	IE
®	Registered trademark sign	2	3
⌋	Right floor	-	-
Ρ	Capital letter rho	-	-
ρ	Small letter rho	-	-
‏	Right-to-left mark	-	-
›	Single right-pointing angle quotation mark	-	4
’	Right single quotation mark	-	4
‚	Single low-9 quotation mark	-	4
Š	Capital letter S with caron	-	4
š	Small letter s with caron	-	4
⋅	Dot operator	-	-
§	Section sign	3	3
­	Soft hyphen (discretionary hyphen)	3	3
Σ	Capital letter sigma	-	-
σ	Small letter sigma	-	-
ς	Small letter final sigma	-	-
∼	Tilde operator	-	-
♠	Black spade suit	-	-
⊂	Subset of	-	-
⊆	Subset of or equal to	-	-
∑	N-ary sumation	-	-
¹	Superscript digit one	3	3
²	Superscript digit two (squared)	3	3
³	Superscript digit three (cubed)	3	3
⊃	Superset of	-	-
⊇	Superset of or equal to	-	-
ß	Small letter sharp s (ess-zed)	2	3
Τ	Capital letter tau	-	-
τ	Small letter tau	-	-
∴	Therefore	-	-
Θ	Capital letter theta	-	-
θ	Small letter theta	-	-
ϑ	Small letter theta symbol	-	-
	Thin space	-	-
Þ	Capital letter thorn	2	3
þ	Small letter thorn	2	3
˜	Small tilde	-	4

Entity	Description	NN	IE
&times;	Multiplication sign	3	3
&trade;	Trademark sign	-	3
&Uacute;	Capital letter U with acute	2	3
&uacute;	Small letter u with acute	2	3
&uarr;	Upwards arrow	-	-
&uArr;	Upwards double arrow	-	-
&Ucirc;	Capital letter U with circumflex	2	3
&ucirc;	Small letter u with circumflex	2	3
&Ugrave;	Capital letter U with grave	2	3
&ugrave;	Small letter u with grave	2	3
&uml;	Diaeresis	3	3
&upsih;	Upsilon with hook symbol	-	-
&Upsilon;	Capital letter upsilon	-	-
&upsilon;	Small letter upsilon	-	-
&Uuml;	Capital letter U with diaeresis	2	3
&uuml;	Small letter u with diaeresis	2	3
&weierp;	Script capital P	-	-
&Xi;	Capital letter xi	-	-
&xi;	Small letter xi	-	-
&Yacute;	Capital letter Y with acute	2	3
&yacute;	Small letter y with acute	2	3
&yen;	Yen/yuan sign	3	3
&yuml;	Small letter y with diaeresis	2	3
&Yuml;	Capital letter Y with diaeresis	-	4
&Zeta;	Capital letter zeta	-	-
&zeta;	Small letter zeta	-	-
&zwj;	Zero width joiner	-	-
&zwnj;	Zero width nonjoiner	-	-

C

Keyboard Event Character Values

Version 4 browsers include event handlers for capturing keyboard action. Although Navigator and Internet Explorer expose the character information through different means (see Chapter 6, *Scripting Events*), the values associated with each character key are the same. Not all versions of all browsers pass through values for action keys such as the **Backspace** or **Delete** keys. For example, Navigator 4 passes these values with the event object when typing into a text INPUT element, but IE 4 does not. It is safest for cross-platform work to focus only on the keys that generate characters (letters, numbers, and punctuation). Function keys and navigation keys do not generate key values (except for navigation keys on Navigator 4 for the Macintosh). All of these values come from the ASCII and Unicode values for the first 128 characters. The characters and their values are listed here.

Key	Value	Key	Value
Backspace	8	(	40
Tab	9	)	41
Enter (Return on Mac)	13	*	42
		+	43
Space	32	,	44
!	33	-	45
"	34	.	46
#	35	/	47
$	36	0	48
%	37	1	49
&	38	2	50
'	39	3	51

Key	Value		Key	Value
4	52		Z	90
5	53		[	91
6	54		\	92
7	55		]	93
8	56		^	94
9	57		_	95
:	58		`	96
;	59		a	97
<	60		b	98
=	61		c	99
>	62		d	100
?	63		e	101
@	64		f	102
A	65		g	103
B	66		h	104
C	67		i	105
D	68		j	106
E	69		k	107
F	70		l	108
G	71		m	109
H	72		n	110
I	73		o	111
J	74		p	112
K	75		q	113
L	76		r	114
M	77		s	115
N	78		t	116
O	79		u	117
P	80		v	118
Q	81		w	119
R	82		x	120
S	83		y	121
T	84		z	122
U	85		{	123
V	86		|	124
W	87		}	125
X	88		~	126
Y	89		Delete	127

D

Internet Explorer Commands

Internet Explorer 4 includes a set of commands that work directly with the docu-ment and (Win32 only) TextRange objects. In many cases, these commands mimic the functionality available through setting properties or invoking methods of the objects. Even so, these commands exist outside of the primary document object model and are therefore treated separately in this appendix.

Access to these commands is through a set of document and TextRange object methods that are described in Chapter 9, *Document Object Reference*. These com-mands and syntax are:

```
execCommand("commandName"[, UIFlag[, value]])
queryCommandEnabled("commandName")
queryCommandIndeterm("commandName")
queryCommandState("commandName")
queryCommandSupported("commandName")
queryCommandText("commandName")
```

This appendix focuses on the commands and values that may be applied to the execCommand() method (the commands may also be applied to the other meth-ods).

Some commands work on the current selection in a document, which means that the selection must be made manually by the user or via a script and the Text-Range object. For example, the following function locates every instance of a string passed as a parameter and turns its text color to red:

```
function redden(txt) {
    var rng = document.body.createTextRange()
    for (var i = 0; rng.findText(txt) != false; i++) {
        rng.select()
```

```
            document.execCommand("ForeColor","false","red")
            rng.collapse(false)
            rng.select()
        }
    }
```

The process is iterative. After creating a text range for the entire document body, the function repeatedly looks for a match of the string. Whenever there is a match, the matched word is selected, and the **execCommand()** method invokes the **ForeColor** command, passing the value **red** as the color. To continue searching through the range, the range is collapsed after the previously found item, and the selection is removed (by selecting a range of zero length).

In general, I recommend using a regular object model method or property setting when one exists for the action you wish to take. Because these commands tend to work only with IE 4 on Win32 operating systems, you may be forced to avoid them if your audience has a wider browser base.

Command	Description	Parameter
BackColor	Sets background color of current selection	Color value (name or hex triplet)
Bold	Wraps a <B> tag around the range	None
Copy	Copies the range to the Clipboard	None
CreateBookmark	Wraps an <A Name=> tag around the range or modifies an existing <A> tag	A string of the anchor name; tag is removed if value is omitted
CreateLink	Wraps an <A HREF...> tag around the current selection	A string of a complete or relative URL
Cut	Copies the range to the Clipboard, then deletes range	None
Delete	Deletes the range	None
FontName	Sets the font face for current selection	A string of the FACE attribute
FontSize	Sets the font size of current selection	A string of the font size
ForeColor	Sets the foreground (text) color of current selection	Color value (name or hex triplet)
FormatBlock	Wraps a block tag around the current object	Unknown
Indent	Indents current selection	None
InsertButton	Inserts a <BUTTON> tag at current insertion point	A string for the element ID

Command	Description	Parameter
InsertFieldset	Inserts a `<FIELDSET>` tag at current insertion point	A string for the element ID
InsertHorizontalRule	Inserts `<HR>` at current insertion point	A string of the rule size (not working)
InsertIFrame	Inserts an `<IFRAME>` tag at current insertion point	A string of a URL for the `src` property
InsertInputButton	Inserts an `<INPUT TYPE="button">` tag at current insertion point	A string for the element ID
InsertInputCheckbox	Inserts an `<INPUT TYPE="checkbox">` tag at the current insertion point	A string for the element ID
InsertInputFileUpload	Inserts an `<INPUT TYPE="FileUpload">` tag at the current insertion point	A string for the element ID
InsertInputHidden	Inserts an `<INPUT TYPE="hidden">` tag at current insertion point	A string for the element ID
InsertInputImage	Inserts an `<INPUT TYPE="image">` tag at current insertion point	A string for the element ID
InsertInputPassword	Inserts an `<INPUT TYPE="password">` tag at current insertion point	A string for the element ID
InsertInputRadio	Inserts an `<INPUT TYPE="radio">` tag at current insertion point	A string for the element ID
InsertInputReset	Inserts an `<INPUT TYPE="reset">` tag at current insertion point	A string for the element ID
InsertInputSubmit	Inserts an `<INPUT TYPE="submit">` tag at current insertion point	A string for the element ID
InsertInputText	Inserts an `<INPUT TYPE="text">` tag at current insertion point	A string for the element ID
InsertMarquee	Inserts a `<MARQUEE>` tag at current insertion point	A string for the element ID
InsertOrderedList	Inserts an `<OL>` tag at current insertion point	A string for the element ID
InsertParagraph	Inserts a `<P>` tag at current insertion point	A string for the element ID
InsertSelectDropdown	Inserts a `<SELECT>` tag whose type is `select-one` at current insertion point	A string for the element ID

Command	Description	Parameter
InsertSelectListbox	Inserts a `<SELECT>` tag whose type is **select-multiple** at current insertion point	A string for the element ID
InsertTextArea	Inserts a `<TEXTAREA>` tag at current insertion point	A string for the element ID
InsertUnorderedList	Inserts a `<UL>` tag at current insertion point	A string for the element ID
Italic	Wraps an `<I>` tag around the range	None
JustifyCenter	Centers the current selection	None
JustifyFull	Full justifies the current selection	None
JustifyLeft	Left justifies the current selection	None
JustifyRight	Right justifies the current selection	None
Outdent	Outdents the current selection	None
OverWrite	Sets the input-typing mode to overwrite or insert	Boolean (**true** if mode is overwrite)
Paste	Pastes contents of the Clipboard at current insertion point or over the current selection	None
PlayImage	Starts playing dynamic images (if assigned to the **dynsrc** property) associated with an **IMG** element	None
Refresh	Reloads the current document	None
RemoveFormat	Removes formatting from current selection	None
SelectAll	Selects entire text of the document	None
StopImage	Stops playing a dynamic image	None
UnBookmark	Removes anchor tags from the selection or text range	
Underline	Wraps a `<U>` tag around the range	None

Command	Description	Parameter
Unlink	Removes a link from the selection or text range	None
Unselect	Clears a selection from the document	None

Glossary

absolute positioning

Setting the precise location of an element within the coordinate system of the next outermost container. An absolute-positioned element exists in its own transparent layer; it is removed from the flow of content that surrounds it in the HTML source code.

accessibility

The design concern for allowing users with physical disabilities to make as full a use of web content as possible. For example, aural style sheets provide increased web accessibility to users who have vision impairments.

API

Application Programming Interface, which is usually a collection of methods and properties that operate as a convenient layer between programmers and more complex internal computer activity. In Dynamic HTML, it is common to use or create a custom API to act as a buffer between the browser-specific implementations of element positioning and the programmer's desire to use a single coding scheme regardless of browser.

at-rule

A type of CSS command used inside a style sheet definition. Typical at-rule commands import external style sheets or download font specifications. An at-rule statement begins with the @ symbol.

attribute

A property of an HTML element or CSS style sheet. Attributes are usually assigned values by way of operators (the = symbol for HTML; the : symbol for CSS). In HTML, sometimes the presence of the attribute name is enough to turn on a feature associated with that attribute. HTML attribute names are case insensitive; CSS attribute names are case sensitive.

block-level element

> An HTML element that automatically forces a new line before and after the element, assuring that no other element appears in the same horizontal band of the page (unless another element is absolute-positioned on top of it). An example of a block-level element is the H1 element.

border

> In CSS, a region that exists outside of the content and padding area of a block-level element. The border is always present, even if its thickness is zero, and it can't be seen. A border is sandwiched between the *margin* and *padding*.

cascading rule

> One of the sequence of decisions that a CSS-equipped browser uses to determine which one of possibly several overlapping style sheet rules applies to a given element. Each cascading rule assigns a value to a specificity rating that helps determine which style sheet rule applies to the element.

class

> In CSS, a collection of one or more elements (of the same or different tag type) that are grouped together for the purpose of assigning the same style sheet rule throughout the document. Assigning a class identifier to elements via the CLASS attribute (and using that class selector in a style sheet rule) lets authors create element groupings that cannot be created only out of tag names or IDs.

collection

> Microsoft's terminology for an array of scriptable objects. To reference an item of a collection in a script statement in Internet Explorer 4, you may use either array notation (`collectionName[index]`) or collection notation (`collectionName(index)`).

container

> Any element that holds other elements of any type. Tags for contained elements appear between the container's start and end tags.

contextual selector

> In CSS, a way of specifying under what containment circumstances a particular type of element should have a style sheet rule applied to it. The containment hierarchy is denoted in the selector by a space-delimited list. Thus, the rule P EM {color: red} applies the red text color to all EM elements that are contained by P elements; an EM element inside an LI element is unaffected by this style sheet rule.

CSS

> Acronym for Cascading Style Sheets, a recommended standard created under the auspices of the World Wide Web Consortium (W3C). The acronym is commonly followed by a number designating the version number of the standard. Level 1 of CSS is known as CSS1.

CSS-P

Acronym for Cascading Style Sheets-Positioning. Initially undertaken as an effort separate from the CSS work, the two standards come together in CSS2.

data binding

A facility in Microsoft Internet Explorer 4 for Win32 platforms that allows web page content to be dynamically linked to a data source, such as a server database. For example, a MARQUEE element can grab the latest headlines from a database field as the page loads into the client and display those headlines as a scrolling tickertape.

declaration

In CSS, the combination of an attribute name, colon operator, and value assigned to the attribute. Multiple declarations in a single style sheet rule are separated by semicolons.

deprecated

In web standards, a feature (commonly an HTML element or attribute) that is still supported in a standards release version, but whose use is discouraged in documents that support the version. A term that is deprecated in one version release is usually removed in the following release. Browser support for deprecated items usually continues for many generations for backward compatibility with existing documents that use the element or attribute.

DHTML

Acronym for Dynamic Hypertext Markup Language. DHTML is an amalgam of several standards, including HTML, CSS, and DOM.

DOM

Acronym for the Document Object Model standards effort headed by the W3C. The term is commonly applied to a specific implementation of a document object model in a particular browser, but this is not entirely accurate.

dynamic content

Any HTML content that changes after the document has loaded. Content that does not require a reflow of the page can be accommodated in Navigator 3 and onward and Internet Explorer 4 and onward. The replaced IMG element is an example. IE 4 also allows body content to be changed after the document loads by automatically reflowing the page after the content changes.

ECMA

A Switzerland-based standards body formerly known as the European Computer Manufacturers Association.

ECMAScript

The common name for the JavaScript-based scripting language standard ECMA-262. The standard defines a core scripting language, without any specific references to web-based content. The functionality of ECMA-262 is roughly equivalent to JavaScript 1.1 as deployed in Navigator 3.

element

Refers to an HTML element, which is an item created by an HTML tag in a document. For example, the `<BODY>` tag creates a `BODY` element in the document.

event bubbling

The Internet Explorer 4 event model that propagates events from the target element upward through the HTML element hierarchy. After the event is processed (at the scripter's option) by the target element, event handlers further up the hierarchy may perform further processing on the event. Event propagation can be halted at any point via the `cancelBubble` property.

event handler

A script-oriented keyword that intercepts an event action (such as a mouse click) and initiates the execution of one or more script statements. An event handler can be specified as an attribute of an HTML element or assigned as a property of the scriptable object version of the element. Each element has its own set of events that it recognizes and corresponding event handlers (e.g., an `onKeyPress` event handler for the `keyPress` event) to bind to script statements.

event propagation

The process of event information coursing its way through the element or object hierarchy of a document. Navigator 4 events trickle down from the window level toward the target element; Internet Explorer 4 events bubble upward from the target element toward the `BODY` element. If event processing is to be handled by objects other than the target element (in which case the element's event handler is treated the same way in both browsers), different event scripting is required to accommodate both event propagation schemes within a single document.

filter

A rendering feature of Internet Explorer 4 (for the Win32 platform) that adds typographic effects to text content. A filter is assigned to an element by way of CSS syntax.

HTML

Acronym for Hypertext Markup Language, a simplified version of SGML tailored for content that is published across a network via the Hypertext Transfer Protocol (HTTP). Version 4.0 of the HTML standard (under the auspices of the W3C) extends the notion of separating content from form by letting HTML elements define the context of content, rather than its specific look.

ID

An identifier for an HTML element that should be unique among all elements within a single document. The ID of an element is assigned by the ID attribute supported by virtually every HTML 4.0 tag. An ID is used for many purposes but primarily for associating a CSS style sheet rule with a single element among all elements of a document. An element can belong to a *class* and have a unique ID at the same time.

identifier

A name assigned to an ID, CLASS, or NAME attribute of an element. An identifier is also used in script references, especially in Internet Explorer 4. The names can begin with any uppercase or lowercase letter of the English alphabet, but subsequent characters may include letters, numerals, or the underscore character.

inline element

An HTML element that is rendered as part of the same text line as its surrounding HTML content. An EM element that signifies an emphasized portion of a paragraph is an inline element because its content does not disturb the regular linear flow of the content. The opposite of an inline element is a block-level element.

intrinsic events

Event handlers defined by the HTML 4.0 standard as belonging to virtually every element that is rendered on the page. These events are primarily the common mouse and keyboard events.

JavaScript

A programming language devised by Brendan Eich at Netscape for simplified server and client programming. Originally developed under the name LiveScript, the name changed (under license from Sun Microsystems) before the first commercial release of a scriptable browser, Navigator 2. JavaScript became the basis for ECMAScript. Microsoft's name for its implementation of JavaScript is JScript.

JavaScript Style Sheets

A Navigator-only syntax for defining style sheet rules.

JScript

Microsoft's formal name for the JavaScript-based scripting language built into Internet Explorer 3 and later. JScript is compatible with ECMAScript and JavaScript.

layer

Navigator's model for a positionable element. A layer can be created via the <LAYER> tag or by associating a CSS-P position:absolute style sheet declaration with an element. Navigator scripts for accessing a positionable element (regardless of how the element is created) refer to the element as a layer object. Although Internet Explorer does not use the layer terminology, each absolute-positioned element exists in its own transparent layer above the main document body.

margin

In CSS, a region that extends outside of an element's *border*. Every element has a margin, even if its thickness is zero.

method

A scriptable object's action that can be initiated by any script statement. A reference to a JavaScript method is easily recognizable by the set of parentheses that follows the method name. Zero or more parameters may be included inside the parentheses. A method may return a value depending on what it has been programmed to do, but this is not a requirement.

modifier key

A keyboard key that is usually pressed in concert with a character key to initiate a special action. Modifier keys common to all operating system platforms include the **Shift**, **Control**, and **Alt** keys. Modern Microsoft keyboards also have the **Windows** key; Macintosh keyboards have the **Command** key. Keyboard events can be examined for which (if any) modifier keys were being held down at the time of the character key's event.

object

A representation of an HTML element or other programmable item in a scripting language, such as JavaScript. An object may have properties and methods that define the behavior and/or appearance of the object. Scripts typically read or modify object properties or invoke object methods to affect some change of value or appearance of the object. Objects in a browser's document object model reflect HTML elements defined by the document source code. For example, in recent browser versions, if a script assigns a new URL to the value of the *src* property of an image object, the new image replaces the old within the rectangular space occupied by the **IMG** element on the page. Other types of objects, such as dates and strings, do not appear on the screen directly but are used in script execution.

padding

In CSS, a region that extends between the element's content and the border. Padding provides some "breathing space" between the content and a border (if one is specified). Every element has padding, even if its thickness is zero. Navigator 4 automatically adds padding to all elements.

parent

For HTML elements, the next outermost element in source code order (the **P** element that surrounds an **EM** element, for example). For positioned elements, the element that is the next outermost container that determines the coordinate plane for the element's positioning. For scriptable window objects, the window or frame that contains a frameset document that defines the frame holding the current document.

platform

A software or hardware system that forms the basis for further product development. For web browsers, the term may apply to a browser brand (Netscape Navigator, Microsoft Internet Explorer, etc.) or the operating system on which a browser brand operates (Windows 95, Windows 3.1, Macintosh, Solaris, etc.). In this book, *platform* usually applies to the browser brand.

positioning

Specifying the precise location of an element on the page. An element may be absolute-positioned or relative-positioned.

property

A single characteristic of an object, such as its ID or value, which can be retrieved (and sometimes set) with the help of scripting. Style sheet attributes are also sometimes referred to as properties.

pseudo-class

A style sheet selector that points to a particular state or behavior of an HTML element, such as an `A` element set up as a link that has been visited recently by the user (`A:visited`).

pseudo-element

A style sheet selector that points to a very specific piece of an element, such as the first letter of a paragraph (`P:first-letter`).

relative positioning

Setting the precise location of an element within the coordinate system established by the location where the element would normally appear if it were not positioned. Documents preserve the space originally designated for a relative-positioned element so that surrounding content does not cinch up around the place left vacant by a positioned element.

replaced element

An inline or block-level element that can have its content replaced without requiring any adjustment of the document. An `IMG` element, for example, can have its content replaced by a script after the page has loaded.

rule

In CSS, a set of style declarations that are associated with one selector. A rule can also be embedded within an element as the value assigned to the `STYLE` attribute of the element's tag.

selector

In CSS, the name of the element(s), ID(s), class(es), or other permissible element groupings to which a style declaration is bound. The combination of a selector and declaration creates a style sheet rule.

Appendixes

style sheet

In CSS, one or more rules that defines how a particular segment of document content should be rendered by the browser. A style sheet may be defined in an external document, in the `STYLE` element, or assigned to an element via its `STYLE` attribute.

transition

In Internet Explorer 4, a visual effect for hiding and showing elements. Transitions are available only in the Win32 version of IE 4.

VBScript

A scripting language alternate to JScript in Internet Explorer 4. This language is not available in any version of Navigator.

Index

About the Author

Danny Goodman has been an active participant on the editorial side of the personal computer and consumer electronics revolutions since the late 1970s. His articles in the field have appeared in some of the most prestigious general-audience publications, and he has written dozens of feature articles for leading computer publications, such as *PC Magazine*, *PC World*, *Macworld*, and *MacUser*. He is currently a monthly columnist for Netscape Communication's online developer newsletter, *View Source*.

Danny is also the author of more than two dozen books on computing and information superhighway technologies. *The Complete HyperCard Handbook*, published by Bantam Books in 1987, claimed honors as the bestselling Macintosh book and fastest selling computer book in the history of the industry. That book is now in its fourth edition and has been translated into more than a half-dozen languages. His *HyperCard Handbook* and *HyperCard Developer's Guide* have both received Best Product-Specific Book awards from the Computer Press Association (1987 and 1988, respectively). *Danny Goodman's Macintosh Handbook* (1993), a radical departure from traditional computer books, won Danny's third CPA award.

To keep up to date on the needs of web developers for his recent books and Netscape articles, Danny is also a programming and design consultant to some of the industry's top intranet application development groups.

Danny, 47, was born in Chicago, Illinois. He earned a B.A. and M.A. in Classical Antiquity from the University of Wisconsin, Madison. He moved to California in 1983 and now lives in a small San Francisco area coastal community, where he alternates views between computer screens and the Pacific Ocean.

Colophon

The animal featured on the cover of *Dynamic HTML: The Definitive Reference* is a flamingo. Flamingos are easily identifiable by their long legs and neck, turned-down bill, and bright color, which ranges from white to pink to bright red. There are five living species of flamingo, encompassing the family Phoenicopteridae. Flamingos are found in Asia, Africa, Europe, South American, and the Caribbean islands. Although wild flamingos are sometimes seen in Florida, they do not naturally nest in the United States.

Flamingos feed on small crustaceans, algae, and other unicellular organisms. Their unusually shaped bills provide flamingos with a unique food-filtering system. A flamingo eats by placing its head upside down below the water surface and sucking in water and small food particles through the serrated edges of its bill. The flamingo then pushes its thick, fleshy tongue forward, forcing the water out but trapping the food particles on lamellae inside the beak.

As a result of this filtration system, flamingos can eat foods few other birds can, and thus can live in otherwise inhospitable salt lakes and brackish waters. The filtration technique varies in the different species of flamingo. As a result of this differentiation, several species can live in the same water source and not disturb each other.

Flamingos are very gregarious birds, and they nest in colonies that sometimes consist of thousands of birds. Males and females together build nests. The nests are composed of mud, stones, and shells, shaped in a cone formation. One, and occasionally two, eggs are laid in a shallow depression at the top of the cone. Both sexes incubate the eggs for 27 to 31 days.

In the wild, flamingos tend to live in remote, difficult-to-reach areas. In the suburbs, however, they stand guard over many a front lawn.

O'Reilly's production group put the finishing touches on this book. Mary Anne Weeks Mayo was the project manager and production editor. Deborah English and Kristine Simmons copyedited the book. Norma Emory and Lunaea Hougland served as proofreaders, and quality was assured by Sheryl Avruch. Seth Maislin created the index. Kathleen Wilson designed the back cover.

Edie Freedman designed the cover of this book, using a 19th-century engraving from the Dover Pictorial Archive. The cover layout was produced with Quark-XPress 3.32 using the ITC Garamond font. Whenever possible, our books use RepKover™, a durable and flexible lay-flat binding. If the page count exceeds RepKover's limit, perfect binding is used.

The inside layout was designed by Nancy Priest and formatted in FrameMaker 5.0 by Mike Sierra using the ITC Garamond Light and Garamond Book fonts. The screenshots that appear in the book were created in Adobe Photoshop 4 and the illustrations were created in Macromedia Freehand 7.0 by Robert Romano. This colophon was written by Clairemarie Fisher O'Leary.

More Titles from O'Reilly

Web Programming

CGI Programming on the World Wide Web

By Shishir Gundavaram
1st Edition March 1996
450 pages, ISBN 1-56592-168-2

This book offers a comprehensive explanation of CGI and related techniques for people who hold on to the dream of providing their own information servers on the Web. It starts at the beginning, explaining the value of CGI and how it works, then moves swiftly into the subtle details of programming.

Frontier: The Definitive Guide

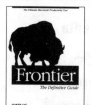

By Matt Neuburg
1st Edition February 1998
618 pages, 1-56592-383-9

This definitive guide is the first book devoted exclusively to teaching and documenting Userland Frontier, a powerful scripting environment for web site management and system level scripting. Packed with examples, advice, tricks, and tips, *Frontier: The Definitive Guide* teaches you Frontier from the ground up. Learn how to automate repetitive processes, control remote computers across a network, beef up your web site by generating hundreds of related web pages automatically, and more. Covers Frontier 4.2.3 for the Macintosh.

Web Client Programming with Perl

By Clinton Wong
1st Edition March 1997
228 pages, ISBN 1-56592-214-X

Web Client Programming with Perl shows you how to extend scripting skills to the Web. This book teaches you the basics of how browsers communicate with servers and how to write your own customized web clients to automate common tasks. It is intended for those who are motivated to develop software that offers a more flexible and dynamic response than a standard web browser.

JavaScript: The Definitive Guide, 3rd Edition

By David Flanagan & Dan Shafer
3rd Edition June 1998
800 pages, ISBN 1-56592-392-8

This third edition of the definitive reference to JavaScript covers the latest version of the language, JavaScript 1.2, as supported by Netscape Navigator 4.0. JavaScript, which is being standardized under the name ECMAScript, is a scripting language that can be embedded directly in HTML to give web pages programming-language capabilities.

Learning VBScript

By Paul Lomax
1st Edition July 1997
616 pages, includes CD-ROM
ISBN 1-56592-247-6

This definitive guide shows web developers how to take full advantage of client-side scripting with the VBScript language. In addition to basic language features, it covers the Internet Explorer object model and discusses techniques for client-side scripting, like adding ActiveX controls to a web page or validating data before sending to the server. Includes CD-ROM with over 170 code samples.

Web Authoring and Design

Web Navigation: Designing the User Experience

By Jennifer Fleming
1st Edition September 1998
288 pages, Includes CD-ROM
ISBN 1-56592-351-0

This book takes the first in-depth look at designing Web site navigation through design strategies to help you uncover solutions that work for your site and audience. It focuses on designing by purpose, with chapters on entertainment, shopping, identity, learning, information, and community sites. Comes with a CD-ROM that containing software demos and a "netography" of related Web resources.

O'REILLY®

TO ORDER: **800-998-9938** • *order@oreilly.com* • *http://www.oreilly.com/*
OUR PRODUCTS ARE AVAILABLE AT A BOOKSTORE OR SOFTWARE STORE NEAR YOU.
FOR INFORMATION: **800-998-9938** • **707-829-0515** • *info@oreilly.com*

Web Authoring and Design

Designing with JavaScript

By Nick Heinle
1st Edition September 1997
256 pages, Includes CD-ROM
ISBN 1-56592-300-6

Written by the author of the "JavaScript Tip of the Week" web site, this new Web Review Studio book focuses on the most useful and applicable scripts for making truly interactive, engaging web sites. You'll not only have quick access to the scripts you need, you'll finally understand why the scripts work, how to alter the scripts to get the effects you want, and, ultimately, how to write your own groundbreaking scripts from scratch.

Information Architecture for the World Wide Web

By Louis Rosenfeld & Peter Morville
1st Edition January 1998
226 pages, ISBN 1-56592-282-4

Learn how to merge aesthetics and mechanics to design web sites that "work." This book shows how to apply principles of architecture and library science to design cohesive web sites and intranets that are easy to use, manage, and expand. Covers building complex sites, hierarchy design and organization, and techniques to make your site easier to search. For webmasters, designers, and administrators.

HTML: The Definitive Guide, 3rd Edition

By Chuck Musciano & Bill Kennedy
3rd Edition August 1998
576 pages, ISBN 1-56592-492-4

This complete guide is chock full of examples, sample code, and practical, hands-on advice to help you create truly effective web pages and master advanced features. Learn how to insert images and other multimedia elements, create useful links and searchable documents, use Netscape extensions, design great forms, and lots more. The third edition covers HTML 4.0, Netscape 4.5, and Internet Explorer 4.0, plus all the common extensions.

Photoshop for the Web

By Mikkel Aaland
1st Edition April 1998
238 pages, ISBN 1-56592-350-2

Photoshop for the Web shows you how to use the world's most popular imaging software to create Web graphics and images that look great and download blazingly fast. The book is crammed full of step-by-step examples and real-world solutions from some of the country's hottest Web producers, including HotWired, cInet, Discovery Online, Second Story, SFGate, and more than 20 others.

Graphics/Multimedia

Encyclopedia of Graphics File Formats, 2nd Edition

By James D. Murray & William vanRyper
2nd Edition May 1996
1154 pages, Includes CD-ROM
ISBN 1-56592-161-5

The second edition of the Encyclopedia of Graphics File Formats provides the convenience of quick look-up on CD-ROM, up-to-date information through links to the World Wide Web, as well as a printed book—all in one package. Includes technical details on more than 100 file formats. The CD-ROM includes vendor file format specs, graphics test images, coding examples, and graphics conversion and manipulation software. An indispensable online resource for graphics programmers, service bureaus, and graphic artists.

O'REILLY®

TO ORDER: **800-998-9938** • *order@oreilly.com* • *http://www.oreilly.com/*
OUR PRODUCTS ARE AVAILABLE AT A BOOKSTORE OR SOFTWARE STORE NEAR YOU.
FOR INFORMATION: **800-998-9938** • **707-829-0515** • *info@oreilly.com*

Graphics/Multimedia

Photoshop in a Nutshell

By Donnie O'Quinn & Matt LeClair
1st Edition October 1997
610 pages, ISBN 1-56592-313-8

Photoshop 4's powerful features make it the software standard for desktop image design and production. But they also make it an extremely complex product. This detailed reference defines and describes every tool, command, palette, and sub-menu of Photoshop 4 to help users understand design options, make informed choices, and reduce time spent learning by trial-and-error.

Lingo in a Nutshell

By Bruce Epstein
1st Edition November 1998
634 pages, ISBN 1-56592-493-2

This companion book to *Director in a Nutshell* covers all aspects of Lingo, Director's powerful scripting language, and is the book for which both Director users and power Lingo programmers have been yearning. Detailed chapters describe messages, events, scripts, handlers, variables, lists, file I/O, Behaviors, child objects, Xtras, browser scripting, media control, performance optimization, and more.

Director in a Nutshell

By Bruce A. Epstein
1st Edition February 1999 (est.)
608 pages (est.), ISBN 1-56592-382-0

Director in a Nutshell is the most concise and complete guide available for Director®. The reader gets both the nitty-gritty details and the bigger context in which to use the multiple facets of Director. It is a high-end handbook, at a low-end price—an indispensable desktop reference for every Director user.

QuarkXPress in a Nutshell

By Donnie O'Quinn
1st Edition June 1998
546 pages, ISBN 1-56592-399-5

This quick reference describes every tool, command, palette, and sub-menu in QuarkXPress 4, providing users with a detailed understanding of the software so they can make informed choices and reduce time spent learning by trial-and-error.

O'REILLY®

TO ORDER: **800-998-9938** • *order@oreilly.com* • *http://www.oreilly.com/*
OUR PRODUCTS ARE AVAILABLE AT A BOOKSTORE OR SOFTWARE STORE NEAR YOU.
FOR INFORMATION: **800-998-9938** • **707-829-0515** • *info@oreilly.com*

How to stay in touch with O'Reilly

1. Visit Our Award-Winning Web Site

http://www.oreilly.com/

★ "Top 100 Sites on the Web" —*PC Magazine*
★ "Top 5% Web sites" —*Point Communications*
★ "3-Star site" —*The McKinley Group*

Our web site contains a library of comprehensive product information (including book excerpts and tables of contents), downloadable software, background articles, interviews with technology leaders, links to relevant sites, book cover art, and more. File us in your Bookmarks or Hotlist!

2. Join Our Email Mailing Lists

New Product Releases
To receive automatic email with brief descriptions of all new O'Reilly products as they are released, send email to:
listproc@online.oreilly.com
Put the following information in the first line of your message (*not* in the Subject field):
subscribe oreilly-news

O'Reilly Events
If you'd also like us to send information about trade show events, special promotions, and other O'Reilly events, send email to:
listproc@online.oreilly.com
Put the following information in the first line of your message (*not* in the Subject field):
subscribe oreilly-events

3. Get Examples from Our Books via FTP

There are two ways to access an archive of example files from our books:

Regular FTP
- ftp to:
  ftp.oreilly.com
  (login: anonymous
  password: your email address)
- Point your web browser to:
  ftp://ftp.oreilly.com/

FTPMAIL
- Send an email message to:
  ftpmail@online.oreilly.com
  (Write "help" in the message body)

4. Contact Us via Email

order@oreilly.com
To place a book or software order online. Good for North American and international customers.

subscriptions@oreilly.com
To place an order for any of our newsletters or periodicals.

books@oreilly.com
General questions about any of our books.

software@oreilly.com
For general questions and product information about our software. Check out O'Reilly Software Online at **http://software.oreilly.com/** for software and technical support information. Registered O'Reilly software users send your questions to: **website-support@oreilly.com**

cs@oreilly.com
For answers to problems regarding your order or our products.

booktech@oreilly.com
For book content technical questions or corrections.

proposals@oreilly.com
To submit new book or software proposals to our editors and product managers.

international@oreilly.com
For information about our international distributors or translation queries. For a list of our distributors outside of North America check out:
http://www.oreilly.com/www/order/country.html

O'Reilly & Associates, Inc.
101 Morris Street, Sebastopol, CA 95472 USA
TEL   707-829-0515 or 800-998-9938
       (6am to 5pm PST)
FAX   707-829-0104

O'REILLY®

Titles from O'Reilly

International Distributors

UK, EUROPE, MIDDLE EAST AND AFRICA (EXCEPT FRANCE, GERMANY, AUSTRIA, SWITZERLAND, LUXEMBOURG, LIECHTENSTEIN, AND EASTERN EUROPE)

INQUIRIES
O'Reilly UK Limited
4 Castle Street
Farnham
Surrey, GU9 7HS
United Kingdom
Telephone: 44-1252-711776
Fax: 44-1252-734211
Email: josette@oreilly.com

ORDERS
Wiley Distribution Services Ltd.
1 Oldlands Way
Bognor Regis
West Sussex PO22 9SA
United Kingdom
Telephone: 44-1243-779777
Fax: 44-1243-820250
Email: cs-books@wiley.co.uk

FRANCE

ORDERS
GEODIF
61, Bd Saint-Germain
75240 Paris Cedex 05, France
Tel: 33-1-44-41-46-16 (French books)
Tel: 33-1-44-41-11-87 (English books)
Fax: 33-1-44-41-11-44
Email: distribution@eyrolles.com

INQUIRIES
Éditions O'Reilly
18 rue Séguier
75006 Paris, France
Tel: 33-1-40-51-52-30
Fax: 33-1-40-51-52-31
Email: france@editions-oreilly.fr

GERMANY, SWITZERLAND, AUSTRIA, EASTERN EUROPE, LUXEMBOURG, AND LIECHTENSTEIN

INQUIRIES & ORDERS
O'Reilly Verlag
Balthasarstr. 81
D-50670 Köln
Germany
Telephone: 49-221-973160-91
Fax: 49-221-973160-8
Email: anfragen@oreilly.de (inquiries)
Email: order@oreilly.de (orders)

CANADA (FRENCH LANGUAGE BOOKS)
Les Éditions Flammarion ltée
375, Avenue Laurier Ouest
Montréal (Québec) H2V 2K3
Tel: 00-1-514-277-8807
Fax: 00-1-514-278-2085
Email: info@flammarion.qc.ca

HONG KONG
City Discount Subscription Service, Ltd.
Unit D, 3rd Floor, Yan's Tower
27 Wong Chuk Hang Road
Aberdeen, Hong Kong
Tel: 852-2580-3539
Fax: 852-2580-6463
Email: citydis@ppn.com.hk

KOREA
Hanbit Media, Inc.
Sonyoung Bldg. 202
Yeksam-dong 736-36
Kangnam-ku
Seoul, Korea
Tel: 822-554-9610
Fax: 822-556-0363
Email: hant93@chollian.dacom.co.kr

PHILIPPINES
Mutual Books, Inc.
429-D Shaw Boulevard
Mandaluyong City, Metro
Manila, Philippines
Tel: 632-725-7538
Fax: 632-721-3056
Email: mbikikog@mnl.sequel.net

TAIWAN
O'Reilly Taiwan
No. 3, Lane 131
Hang-Chow South Road
Section 1, Taipei, Taiwan
Tel: 886-2-23968990
Fax: 886-2-23968916
Email: benh@oreilly.com

CHINA
O'Reilly China
Room 2410
160, FuXingMenNeiDaJie
XiCheng District
Beijing
China PR 100031
Email: frederic@oreilly.com

INDIA
Computer Bookshop (India) Pvt. Ltd.
190 Dr. D.N. Road, Fort
Bombay 400 001 India
Tel: 91-22-207-0989
Fax: 91-22-262-3551
Email: cbsbom@giasbm01.vsnl.net.in

JAPAN
O'Reilly Japan, Inc.
Kiyoshige Building 2F
12-Bancho, Sanei-cho
Shinjuku-ku
Tokyo 160-0008 Japan
Tel: 81-3-3356-5227
Fax: 81-3-3356-5261
Email: japan@oreilly.com

ALL OTHER ASIAN COUNTRIES
O'Reilly & Associates, Inc.
101 Morris Street
Sebastopol, CA 95472 USA
Tel: 707-829-0515
Fax: 707-829-0104
Email: order@oreilly.com

AUSTRALIA
WoodsLane Pty., Ltd.
7/5 Vuko Place
Warriewood NSW 2102
Australia
Tel: 61-2-9970-5111
Fax: 61-2-9970-5002
Email: info@woodslane.com.au

NEW ZEALAND
Woodslane New Zealand, Ltd.
21 Cooks Street (P.O. Box 575)
Waganui, New Zealand
Tel: 64-6-347-6543
Fax: 64-6-345-4840
Email: info@woodslane.com.au

LATIN AMERICA
McGraw-Hill Interamericana
Editores, S.A. de C.V.
Cedro No. 512
Col. Atlampa
06450, Mexico, D.F.
Tel: 52-5-547-6777
Fax: 52-5-547-3336
Email: mcgraw-hill@infosel.net.mx

O'REILLY®

TO ORDER: **800-998-9938** • *order@oreilly.com* • *http://www.oreilly.com/*

OUR PRODUCTS ARE AVAILABLE AT A BOOKSTORE OR SOFTWARE STORE NEAR YOU.

FOR INFORMATION: **800-998-9938** • **707-829-0515** • *info@oreilly.com*